G000300462

THE DUBS

To Peter,

Best wishes and many thanks for
your support. Now for the
four-in-a-row.

Gerry Callan

Up The Dubs!

THE DUBS

The Complete Record
of Dublin Football

GERRY CALLAN

Ballpoint Press

Published in 2017 by Ballpoint Press
4 Wyndham Park, Bray,
Co Wicklow, Republic of Ireland.
Telephone: 00353 86 821 7631
Email: ballpointpress1@gmail.com
Web: www.ballpointpress.ie

ISBN 978–0–9954793–7–1

© Copyright Gerry Callan, 2017

All rights reserved. No part of this publication may be reproduced,
stored in a retrieval system, or in any form or by any means,
without the prior permission in writing of the publisher, nor be
otherwise circulated in any form of binding or cover other than that
in which it is published and without a similar condition including
this condition being imposed on the subsequent publisher.

While every effort has been made to ensure the accuracy of
all information contained in this book, neither the author
nor the publisher accepts liability for any errors or omissions made.

Book design and production by Joe Coyle Media&Design,
joecoyledesign@gmail.com

Cover photographs: © Sportsfile
Top: The Dublin team before the 1975 All-Ireland Final against Kerry in Croke Park.
Bottom: The Dublin players celebrate after beating Mayo in the 2017 All-Ireland Final.

Printed and bound by GraphyCems

Contents

Foreword
Pat Gilroy

FROM lockout to Rising to Civil War and War of Independence, the earliest casualties were mostly Dubliners. Students and workers, skilled and unskilled, city people bleeding together and dying together because they imagined something different. The brightest and bravest took to the grey streets and tilted at the second biggest empire the world had known.

Their moment was lost amidst the clamour of bigger turbulences. Empires slugging it out in trenches and muddy fields across Europe, Lenin taking the train home to revolution. Ireland was a footnote, opting for neither king nor kaiser. When the dust had settled and the blood had dried in Dublin city, people quietly set about scrubbing away the pain of the Rising and Civil War. They wanted a culture to suit their freedom.

All strands were tied together. In the new cultural landscape everything was possible. In Seville Place Edward Keegan was a founder member of the local Gaelic League and then of O'Tooles GAA club. He was a fine hurler and the club's first captain in 1901.

It was a time when the whole world was in 'a terrible state o' chassis'. The GAA became an anchor for Dublin people to find their feet again.

From 1921 to 1923, Dublin were the All Ireland football champions for three years in succession, those teams backboned by players from Seville Place and East Wall. A first edition of native heroes at the native games. Men like the Synotts, the McDonnells, Joe Norris and 'Stonewall' Jack Reilly, men who had survived Bloody Sunday now returning to the same field to cover themselves in glory. Their deeds spoke of a conscious embrace of an Irish working class culture and the freedom to express it.

By the early Thirties, war was over and a small club was formed in Marino with the aim of taming the wild young people pouring out of almost every house. Their massive energy would be channelled into the GAA, the most thriving example of a living Irish culture which the young state had. In those early days the membership of St. Vincent's reflected well the occupants of the Marino estate. St Vincent's led a new Dublin revolution which largely was reflected in many county titles but 1958 saw a national breakthrough.

The story since then is well known. The revolutionising of Gaelic Football after the colossal disappointment of the loss to the catch-and-kick traditionalists of Kerry in 1955. The glorious All Ireland of 1958, Dublin men winning for Dublin teams. The slow decline after 1963 until ten years later Kevin Heffernan had seen enough.

The fire Heffernan and his team lit when they won the All-Ireland final of 1974 would change the city and help to revive the GAA. The games were becoming rural curiosities whose finals were played out in Dublin every summer. Country people came to the city for the Spring Show, the All-Irelands and Christmas shopping on December 8th. Dubliners generally kept to themselves during those days. Again, as Dublin came, the economy lifted as if the team was the spirit of the city.

Dublin suddenly became part of the national culture again. Heroes had Dublin accents. From 1974 to 2017 Dublin would play in seventeen All Ireland finals and win ten of them. And as the houses of Marino once had, the culture imagined and dreamed of in St. Vincent's spread out like spokes from a radial across the city. Heroes didn't just have Dublin accents, they had southside Dublin accents. They played with other 'guys' instead of other 'lads'. The southside came to dominate hurling. The game was a real part of Dublin life again.

In the 1990s the team came again to coincide with the Celtic Tiger and then struggled for sixteen years but were always in the top four. Then some great seeds were planted in 2000, National Féile football titles were won by Kilmacud Crokes and St. Vincent's, 13-year-olds including Cian O'Sullivan and Diarmuid Connolly experienced national success. DCU won Sigerson Cups with lots of Dublin players, All-Ireland Club titles were to follow in 2008 and 2009 courtesy of St. Vincent's and Kilmacud Crokes.

Game on. Dublin has figured itself out once more. The first three-in-a-row since that backboned by the men of Seville Place has been achieved with a coalition of players representing the new Dublin. The new heroes of renown were young men from Coolock and Dalkey, from Raheny and Kilmacud, from Ballymun and Ballyboden and so on. Different accents, different backgrounds, one story.

Gerry's book represents a truly important factual account of this great story. I hope you enjoy it as much as I did.

A Message From The Dublin GAA County Board

John Costello

CUIREANN sé áthas orm an réamhrá seo a scríobh don leabhair seo. Beidh sé ina áis tábhachtach do leantóirí Cumann Lúthchleas Gael Átha Cliath.

Every sport, but particularly the GAA, depends on its past to define its future.

A team without the knowledge of its history, origin and culture is a bit like a tree without roots.

Which is why I am delighted to welcome *The Dubs — The Complete Record Of Dublin Football* into the canon of GAA literature and archives.

Gerry Callan has burnt the midnight oil trawling through a century and three decades of reports, fixtures and results to present us with a tome that every Dublin football fan will find fascinating.

It is in the first instance a publication of record, but also much more than that. The 400-plus pages are filled with a history of the various competitions which Dublin has competed in since the foundation of the GAA — and it highlights those names who have starred on the field of play down the generations.

Someone once said that history repeats itself because no one was listening the first time around. If that is the case, then the importance of this publication multiplies for followers in the capital as it documents the good times and bad, the scores and scorers, the winners and losers that have made Dublin GAA into what it is today.

On behalf of Dublin GAA, I am delighted to be associated with this book. It fills a vacuum and by bringing all big games up to date including this year's County Final, it provides the most comprehensive record of football ever undertaken in the county.

John Costello
Chief Executive of the Dublin County Board

Acknowledgements

BEING in one's sixty-ninth year can have its positives, especially for an undertaking such as this; for one thing, it means the 'old boy network' has had a chance to grow to a quite impressive membership level. In this regard, a quartet of colleagues and fellow travellers who helped both on and off the pitch are due special kudos, Martin Breheny (Irish Independent), Vincent Hogan (Irish Independent), Cian Murphy (formerly the Irish Daily Star but now Communications Executive with the G.A.A.) and Kevin Nolan (Evening Herald); the latter, indeed, is entitled to be acknowledged as Chief Sub Editor. Richie Hession, a friend for six decades, and Cathal Dervan (Irish Sun), a pal for three, also merit gratitude for services rendered.

As any historian cum statistician knows only too well, researching the basics is relatively straightforward, it is the plugging of the inevitable gaps that generates the real frustration. Here, an assortment of correspondents from various counties are due a sincere debt of gratitude; Alan Aherne (Wexford People), Tommy Callaghan (Leinster Leader), Kevin Carney (Freelance), Paddy Clarke (Mr. Louth Football), Charlie Keegan (Carlow Nationalist), Brian Lowry (Midland Tribune), Fergal Lynch (Meath Chronicle), Ger McNally (Kildare Nationalist) and Daragh Ó Conchúir (Freelance). The staff at the National Library and their equally helpful counterparts in Pearse Street Library must also be thanked, and sincere apologies if anyone has been inadvertently overlooked.

John Costello and his County Board colleagues are due a very special word of thanks for their extremely generous financial assistance and the same must surely be said of Pat Gilroy for his wonderfully scene-setting Foreword. The biggest thanks of all must surely go to my publisher, PJ Cunningham, his wife Rosemary and their team at Ballpoint Press. I especially want to acknowledge the design and creative work undertaken by Joe Coyle, the best in the business.

Gerry Callan
October 2017

Introduction

THIRTY-THREE thousand and nine hundred and fifty-eight days is one mighty long time for pretty well the entire native population of a capital city to have to wait for the realisation of a dream, but that ninety-three year plus spell is exactly how long it took Dublin's footballers to claim the county's fourth All-Ireland Football Final three-in-a-row. When, at a quarter past five on the afternoon of 17 September 2017, Cavan referee Joe McQuillan blew the final whistle on the 130th staging of the biggest football game on the GAA calendar, The Dubs had achieved something that had eluded them since they had beaten Kerry in the final of the Championship of 1923 (which, due to the Civil War, was not actually played until September 28 of the following year).

There can be little doubt that this particular Dublin hat-trick surpasses all other three-in-a-rows in the entire history of the Championship, those of their capital predecessors in 1897-1899, 1906-1908 and 1921-1923, Kerry in 1939-1941 and 1984-1986, and Galway in 1964-1966. The modern day game, after all, aside from — at the level at least — being professional in all but name, is much more competitive than in previous times and significantly more games have to be played to attain the ultimate prize; not only has the 'back door' system guaranteed that, but the introduction of quarter-finals alongside the second chance opportunity in 2001 ensures that, even if a team goes through the front door all the way, they still have to win half a dozen games — in Leinster and Ulster, at least — to lift the Sam Maguire Cup.

Indeed, a valid argument can be made that this current Dublin team is the greatest footballing unit ever to grace any field. With five All-Irelands in seven campaigns — and just two defeats in 42 games in the Championship — and four National League titles on the trot they have certainly well and truly surpassed the achievements of their legend-ary predecessors of the Heffo's Army era of the 1970s and, for the reasons cited above re the modern day Championship, a case can even be made that, given the changing game and the changing times, their three-in-a-row feat actually exceeds the four-in-a-rows achieved by Wexford in 1918 and Kerry in 1981. Wexford recorded 18 wins and one draw (with Dublin) in putting their run together while Kerry, thanks to a bye into the provincial decider in 1980, needed three fewer wins to complete their quartet of successes.

Quite apart from now obviously having their own four-in-a-row in their sights for 2018, Jim Gavin's crew have an interim target to aim at — if they extend their own current Leinster Championship winning record to an eighth year they will set an all time Gaelic Football record for the longest winning streak in Championship history. Wexford, who added two further victories in 1919 to make it a score of consecutive wins overall (discounting draws), are the current holders of that particular distinction; Dublin, again excluding stalemates, stand on 18 wins as of the end of the 2017 season so three more wins — in the provincial quarter-finals, semi-finals and final — would see them surpass anything ever previously achieved in the annals of Championship play.

Few dispute that Dublin — with more than a little help from arch rivals Kerry — rescued the GAA in the Seventies when it was on the verge of not just mediocrity but also bankruptcy; the current squad have brought it to a new level both on the field and in the receipts department. One not insignificant factor is the team's uncanny knack of pushing things to the very brink; all but one of their five final triumphs in recent years were gained by a single point — one following a replay — and the remaining one by three. Literally a kick of the ball in all five deciders. In the words of Eamonn Sweeney in the *Sunday Independent* following the 2016 final replay defeat of Mayo, 'No team in history has been as adept at finding that little bit extra when things are in the balance'.

The very term 'The Dubs' surely represents a phenomenon within Irish sport, a total merging of players and supporters into a cultural entity unique in the country. A 'them and us' siege mentality — the 31 counties against Dublin syndrome — may be a partial factor but other elements are in there too, such as the common character traits of the city natives, not least their humour, as evidenced by a banner that seemed to predict who would secure the county's 27th title triumph: 'Dean Rock strikes faster than Bus Éireann'. They have had several names over the years; when Michael Cusack founded his first club, a year prior to establishing the GAA itself, he called it Metropolitans and it quickly became the accepted nicknamed for the capital's county team and would remain so for well over three-quarters of a century. Liffeysiders — largely through journalist usage — came into vogue for a while in the Fifties and Sixties with the Boys in Blue being thrown in from time to time and The Jacks — as in the Jacks are Back- heralding in the Heffo's Army era only to be soon replaced by the term that is now so totally ingrained in GAA society and culture. The late Sean O'Ceallachain, who very probably knew more about Dublin GAA that any man who ever lived, always maintained that there was no such thing as a Dub until post 1974.

The motivation for this undertaking was simple, almost naively so. To a lifelong sports statistician cum anorak it always seemed decidedly odd, even incongruous, that by far the biggest unit — if not necessarily always the most successful one — within the GAA should remains sans any serious documentation of its records. The same charge could well be levelled at the GAA itself but that, perhaps, is a matter for another day. Cross channel soccer teams, virtually without exception, have full records of every league and cup game they have every played, going right back to the foundation of the Football Association in 1863, so why not GAA teams in general and the biggest one of them all in particular?

Some explanatory notes are in order. Every effort has been made to get the various records as accurate as absolutely possible but it cannot be denied that calculated guesses and even approximations have had to be resorted to in the early years, particularly as regards the first half a dozen or so. Newspapers of the time frequently produced conflicting reports and information and in such instances a go with the majority approach has been taken. Also, careful reading of early reports proved essential as mentions such as 'Joe Bloggs sent over for the victors' were commonplace; a point one would think but no, an 'over' in the journalistic vernacular of those times actually signified over the endline ... a wide.

The Championship

DUBLIN'S debut in the newly conceived All-Ireland Championship turned out to be a total non event; scheduled to meet Tipperary in what for its first year was an open draw competition at Mountrath on 30 July 1887, they conceded a walkover when county champions Erin's Hope were unable to field a team because to many of the teaching student players were on holidays. A year later, represented by Fiach McHughs — essentially Blackrock College — they finally made their Championship debut with a 1-6 to 0-1 win over Kildare at Benburb Park in Dublin only to then be ousted 0-4 to 0-3 by Wexford at Clonskeagh Park, also in Dublin.

The following year brought an emphatic 2-7 to 0-6 first round exit to Louth in Drogheda but in 1890 they beat Westmeath by 6-11 to 0-2 and Laois by 2-8 to 0-1 before, in their first appearance in a Leinster Final, losing out 1-3 to 1-2 to Wexford. John Joe Hoey from Isle of the Sea scored 2-4 in the first game, 1-3 in the second and a goal in the third; at the time a goal outweighed any number of points but two years later its value was set at five points before being reduced to three in 1896, so it could be argued that if Dublin's total against Laois was taken at the five point value then their total would come out at 41 points and their winning margin at 30 points — the former a record that would remain intact until 1960 and the latter a mark that, over a century and a quarter later, has still to be matched.

The progress was built on the following year. Dublin opened their programme with a 4-4 to no score defeat of Wicklow and then received a walkover in the final from Kildare; the latter had beaten Laois by five points to nil in a morning match at Clonturk Park on 15 November but then refused to play the previously scheduled decider that same afternoon. Dublin did not baulk at such a prospect — on the following February 28 they beat Cavan by 3-7 to 0-3 in the All-Ireland semi-final and then, four hours later, beat Cork by 2-1 to 1-1 despite the fact that, with no Connacht Championship that season, Cork had received a bye into the final. Dublin were All-Ireland champions for the very first time.

Schedules then began to fall seriously behind, a problem that would bedevil the GAA for over a decade and a half, largely due to transportation difficulties. It would be over a year and a fortnight after they won the 1891 title in February 1892 that Dublin would play their opening game in the latter year's Championship, beating Kildare by 3-5 to a single point in a provincial semi-final at Clonturk Park on March 12. There then arose another two games in one day argument; Louth had received a walkover from Laois in the other semi-final and Dublin refused to play the Wee County in the afternoon final unless they too had a match in between, against anybody. Fruitless efforts were made to find a Metropolitan club willing to meet the condition and Dublin eventually relented — but by then the Louth team had departed and, as it was still within the scheduled starting time for the decider, referee JP Cox awarded the game to Dublin. Roscommon were then beaten 1-9 to 1-1 in the All-Ireland semi-final before Dublin, with a 1-4 to 0-3 defeat of Kerry — thanks largely to a goal and a point by Johnny Geraghty from Young Irelands — set a record that can never be taken from them ... the first county ever to retain the All-Ireland title. From first game to last, Dublin's entire Championship programme had been compressed into exactly two weeks.

Dublin, after being drawn against Westmeath for their opening game, opted not to compete in the Championship for 1893 in a dispute over the Leinster Council's stance on the infamous Parnell Split but for the following year's campaign they were back in full swing. Given a bye into the provincial semi-final, they opened by chalking up 1-11 while keeping Wexford scoreless but then, in something of a foretaste of what would follow as far down the road as 1991, twice drew with Meath in the final — the second time at The Showgrounds in Navan — before winning 1-8 to 1-2 at the third attempt. With no Championships in either Ulster or Connacht, it was a straight final between Dublin and Cork at Clonturk Park in March 1895 and, with a goal then equaling five points and Dublin scoring six of the latter against a 1-1 tally for Cork, the result was another record; the first ever draw in an All-Ireland Final.

The replay, at the same venue four weeks later, was shrouded in controversy. The Freeman's Journal did its best to explain the chaos: 'By the time the game started something like 10,000 spectators had assembled on the sidelines. The order was very fair up till the last ten or fifteen minutes, when the crowd in their enthusiasm broke in, and as two of the Young Irelands players were assaulted by some Cork spectators, and the feeling of the crowd getting somewhat heated — disorder then reigning supreme — the Young Irelands refused to continue play, a few minutes then being required to complete the hour. The score at this point stood at a goal and two points for Cork against five points for the Young Irelands. The referee, Mr. Blake, refused to give a decision on the matter and the question consequently will be decided at the next meeting of the Central Council, which will be held at Thurles next Sunday.' That meeting ordered a replay but when Cork refused to play a third game the title was awarded to Dublin, making Jack Kirwan, at just ten weeks past his 17th birthday, the youngest ever All-Ireland medalist.

The following two campaigns, those of 1895 and 1896 (although both fell way behind schedule), brought serious disappointments. The first one saw a Leinster Final defeat to Meath by 0-6 to 0-2 and the second, even though the provincial crown was regained with victories over Laois, Kildare and Meath, ended in heartache as, again with no Championships in Ulster or Connacht, Limerick pipped them 1-5 to 0-7 in the first All-Ireland Final under the goal equals three points format. Happier days, however, were just around the corner.

DUBLIN, in mid-May 1898, began the previous year's campaign with an 0-14 to a lone point victory over Kilkenny in Carlow, followed it with a 2-15 to 0-2 trouncing of Kildare at Jones's Road but were then edged out 1-7 to 1-5 by Wexford in the provincial semi-final at the same venue. They then lodged an objection on the joint grounds that the winner's goal should have been disallowed and that Wexford had played an unregistered player and, in something akin to an early version of the 'back door' formula, were given a replay — which they subsequently won 0-10 to 0-9. After that there was no stopping them; Wicklow were brushed aside 1-9 to 0-3 in the Leinster Final and then Cork were thumped 2-6 to 0-2 in the All-Ireland Final, Bill Guiry from Kickhams scoring both goals and adding a point for good measure.

Due to begin their title defence against Kildare, Dublin offered to re-schedule their fixture when their opponents were unable to field a team for their provincial quarter-final at Jones's Road — in November 1899 — but the Lilywhites declined the offer and conceded a walkover, so the champions' first outing was a 1-16 to 0-5 victory over Kilkenny at the same venue. Wexford were then dismissed 2-6 to no score in the Leinster Final and then Waterford, in their one and only appearance in an All-Ireland Final, were cast aside 2-8 to 0-4, this time both goals coming from future soccer international Joe Ledwidge, who finished Dublin's three game campaign with a tally of 3-4.

Ledwidge, in the following season — 1899 but played in the second half of 1900 and the first quarter of 1901 — would do even better scorewise, hitting 3-11 in four games as Dublin raced past Laois, Kilkenny, Wexford and Cork — with keeper Jack Lane going unbeaten — to become the first team to complete an All-Ireland hat-trick. Wexford stunned them in their opening outing the following year but they bounced back in the 1901 campaign to reclaim their champions status with victories over Kilkenny, Louth, Wexford, Antrim, Cork and London.

The campaign for 1902 did not get underway until November of the following year when, after beating Wicklow and Louth, Dublin again faced Wexford in the provincial decider, at the Agricultural Grounds in Carlow. Thanks to goals from Jim Brennan and Tommy Errity, Dublin led by 2-5 to 0-2 when the game was abandoned due to the pitch being waterlogged; a replay was ordered but with the Championship already drastically behind schedule, the Leinster Council nominated Dublin to represent the province in the All-Ireland semi-final against Armagh. Dublin hammered the Ulster champions 4-13 to 1-6 at Shamrock Lodge in Drogheda and a week later outscored Wexford again — 1-5 to 0-5 — at the oddly named Asylum Lane in Kilkenny. Tipperary were edged out 0-6 to 0-5 in the All-Ireland 'home' decider and then, in September 1904 — a full two years behind schedule — Dublin beat London in the final 'proper', 2-8 to 0-4, thereby giving Tommy Errity the distinction of being the first player to win five All-Ireland medals.

One week after that victory but with only five of the same line-up (Jack Fahy, Jim McCann, Pat Daly, Jim Brennan and Paddy Weymes), Dublin were shocked 3-13 to 1-3 by Kildare at Geashill in Tullamore in a quarter-final of the 1903 campaign. It would be a year and a half — March 1906 — before Dublin would be in action again, scoring an 0-9 to 0-5 revenge win over the Lilywhites in their opener for the 1906 campaign before going on to beat Louth, Kilkenny and Mayo to set up an All-Ireland Final date with Kerry at the Athletic Grounds in Cork. Trailing by four points to two at halftime,

Dublin were beaten 0-5 to 0-2 by a Kerry side captained by Austin Stack and inspired by Dick Fitzgerald, Kingdom legends who subsequently would have the county grounds in Tralee and Killarney, respectively, named after them.

SIX weeks after their loss to Kerry, having again been nominated to represent Leinster in the All-Ireland series, Dublin beat London by 1-9 to 1-4 in a quarter-final at Jones's Road (where the goal and two of the visitors' points were scored by a certain Sam Maguire), but a week later they were again surprised — 0-6 to 0-2 — by Kildare at the Agricultural Grounds in Athy. The following season — played in 1907 — they beat Kilkenny and Louth and then, despite being 0-8 to 0-2 in arrears at halftime at St James's Park in Kilkenny, fought back to outscore Kildare by 1-9 to 0-8 courtesy of 1-1 from Mick Madigan to regain the provincial title. London, brought into the Championship at the semi-finals stage, were beaten 2-7 to 0-3 at Town Park in Wexford and, back in Athy (in October 1907), Dublin overcame an 0-3 to 0-2 halftime deficit to edge Cork 0-5 to 0-4 in the All-Ireland Final, the winning score coming from Tommy Walsh from Kickhams. The title had been reclaimed after a gap of seven years.

The following campaign, that of 1907, saw only Dublin's opening game, an 0-11 to 0-4 provincial quarter-final win over Kildare at Jones's Road in early December, played within the calendar year. Dublin followed this with victories over Louth and, in the Leinster Final in Athy, Offaly, before beating Monaghan by 1-5 to 0-3 in the All-Ireland semi-final. The final, in Tipperary Town, was a repeat of the previous season and this time Cork were ousted 0-6 to 0-2. For the sixth time in sixteen years, Dublin beat Cork in the All-Ireland Final and although the teams have clashed five times in semi-finals since then, they have yet to meet in another decider.

The next season was more of the same. Dublin marched through Leinster with wins over Meath, Laois and Kildare and then beat Antrim by 1-8 to 0-2. That latter victory, though, only got them into an All-Ireland 'home' decider, which they duly won with an 0-10 to 0-3 defeat of Kerry at the Sportsfield in Thurles. London, in the final 'proper', offered little opposition as Dublin won 1-10 to 0-4, the only goal of the game coming from Pat 'Cocker' Daly. In recording their second Championship hat-trick, Dublin won sixteen consecutive games without, remarkably, conceding a single goal. Jack Grace, considered by many one of the greatest footballers of all time, joined Tommy Errity as a five-time All-Ireland medal winner.

Dublin began the 1909 season — the schedule was finally back on track — by beating Wexford by 0-18 to 0-6 at Wexford Park but were then upset 1-11 to 1-7 by Louth at the Young Ireland Grounds in Dundalk. Louth's goal, scored by skipper Jack Carvin midway through the first half, was the first goal conceded by Dublin in almost nineteen hours of play, since Sam Maguire's for London in August 1906. It helped end a run of seventeen consecutive Championship wins, a record Dublin have since equalled but not broken. The defeat marked the start of a downward slide.

Dublin did contest — and even win — and All-Ireland quarter-final the following year, but that was as far as they went; wins over Wicklow, Wexford and Offaly (the latter in late September), they were nominated to represent Leinster in the All-Ireland series but, after a 3-5 to 1-2 defeat of Antrim, they were beaten by Louth in the delayed provincial final. The scoreline was three points to nil, the only time in their entire Championship history that Dublin failed to raise a single flag. An almost identical scenario arose two years later when Dublin recorded wins over Laois, Kilkenny (in a replay), Wicklow and, in the All-Ireland semi-final, Roscommon by 2-4 to 1-1, only to again be beaten by Louth in a delayed provincial final and then replaced in the final against Antrim by an ultimately successful Wee County side.

After semi-final losses in each of the two previous years, Dublin reached the provincial decider in 1915 but, after forcing a replay, were beaten by 1-5 to 1-3 by a Wexford side that would go on to capture the first of four successive All-Ireland titles. The following year came an embarrassing blunder when, after a number of their players had missed the train from what was then Kingsbridge Station, they were unable to fulfil their fixture with Wexford at Wexford; the home team sportingly offered to play the game at Town Park in New Ross the following Sunday but, when Dublin were unable to guarantee that they would be in a position to honour the fixture, the walkover was accepted.

A year later they did manage to fulfil a meeting with Wexford; it was in the provincial final and it resulted in a 1-3 to 1-1 defeat after wins over Kildare, Louth and Laois. Louth beat them 3-5 to 3-3 in a first round thriller at Shamrock Lodge in Drogheda in 1918 but in the following campaign, despite being pipped 1-3 to 1-2 by Kildare in the Leinster Final, they had the satisfaction of ending Wexford's four year reign as All-Ireland champions with an 0-11 to 1-1 victory in the provincial decider.

WITHOUT success at national or even provincial level in a dozen years but encouraged by recent improvements, Dublin began their 1920 campaign with a comfortable 3-5 to 0-3 victory at Maryborough — now O'Moore — Park in Portlaoise, Frank Burke scoring 2-1 and Toddy Pierce getting 1-3. Laois were then beaten 2-6 to 0-1 and, in a repeat of the previous year's decider, Dublin finally regained the Leinster crown with a 1-3 to 0-3 win over Kildare, the all important goal coming from sub Paddy Carey. Cavan, the Ulster champions for the third successive time, were overcome 3-6 to 0-3 in the All-Ireland semi-final at Navan in late September, but other events would mean the All-Ireland Final would not take place for over twenty-one months.

Dublin were to play the Munster champions in the decider but the problem was that the Championship in the southern province — which at the time was more involved in, and impacted on, by the on-going War of Independence than any other — had fallen way behind schedule. Then, on November 21, came an atrocity that resonates within the GAA to this day, Bloody Sunday, when British soldiers, in reprisal for the killing of fourteen of their spies and intelligence officers early that morning by squads directed by Michael Collins, opened fire at the start of a challenge game between Dublin and Tipperary at Croke Park and killed a like number of civilians (three of them dying over the following five day), including Tipperary right full back Michael Hogan, after whom the Hogan Stand — now in its third incarnation — has been named since 1925. When the final finally did take place, in June 1922, Dublin, thanks to another Burke goal, led by 1-2 to 0-3 at halftime but failed to raise a single flag in the second half while Tipperary added a goal and three points.

The scheduling difficulties of those chaotic times meant that even before Dublin played Tipperary in the above delayed decider, they had successfully completed the 1921 provincial campaign, beating Meath, Louth and, in a final replay, Kildare — and seven days after the Tipperary defeat they beat Monaghan by 2-8 to 2-2 in that year's All-Ireland semi-final at McGeough's Field in Dundalk. That game was played in June 1922 and with the Civil War having replaced the War of Independence as the major disruptive factor, Dublin had to wait one day short of a year to play the final against Mayo, runners-up to Wexford five years earlier. Dublin, four points to one up at half-time, ran out easy 1-9 to 0-2 winners with the goal — plus two points — coming from St. Mary's corner forward Bill Fitzsimons. Dublin had brought their All-Ireland tally to an even dozen with their first success since 1908 and, remarkably, goalkeeper Paddy Fallon, from the Geraldines club, was a survivor from the previous triumph. An anonymous report in the *Irish Independent* the following morning commented: 'The hero of the game was Joe Norris. He seems to have the strength of the bullock, the speed of the deer, and the agility of the cat. If ever there's a call for volunteers to run up against him, I won't answer the roll.'

O'Toole's keeper Johnny McDonnell, who had started the successful 1921 campaign but had then been replaced by Fallon (some suggested because of his intense political involvement), was back in favour for the following season and would remain unbeaten as Dublin — who only had to play two games to retain the provincial crown because of withdrawals due to travel difficulties — beat Kildare, Kilkenny, Monaghan and Galway without conceding a goal. At the other end of the field, McDonnell's brother Paddy finished top scorer with 2-8 from the four games.

The bid for another hat-trick went smoothly from the start; Dublin beat Laois, Meath — without conceding a single score — and Mayo to qualify for an All-Ireland Final showdown with Kerry. In their first final appearance in nine years, the Kingdom built up a 1-2 to 0-1 lead by halftime but a Paddy Kirwan goal just five minutes into the second half put Dublin on the road to a 1-5 to 1-3 triumph. The *Irish Independent* report on the game summed it up: 'There have been more brilliant finals, but few productive of such keen and vigorous play. Dublin fielded a strong team, whose experience told greatly in their favour as the Kerry players were, to a man, making their first appearance in a senior All-Ireland final.'

The target for 1924 was obvious; to equal Wexford's record four-in-a-row All-Irelands set half a dozen years earlier. Meath, Louth, Wexford (in a replay) were taken care of in the provincial series and when Cavan were edged out 0-6 to 1-1, the dream appeared within reach. Kerry, their victims from a year earlier, were the only obstacle remaining but the experience of the previous campaign stood them well as, with all but four of the same line-out, they edged into a three points to two halftime lead. Josie Synnott brought Dublin level ten minutes into the second half but a point from a Con Brosnan eight minutes from the end gave the Kingdom an 0-4 to 0-3 victory, matching Tipperary's defeat of Meath in 1895 as the lowest scoring All-Ireland Final ever.

WHAT still stands as the biggest Championship famine in Dublin's history was under-way. Wexford revived memories of their gold days of a decade or so earlier with a 2-4 to 1-6 defeat of Dublin in a quarter-final at St. James's Park in Kilkenny — they would go on to recapture the provincial crown — in 1925 and the following year, after Dublin had received a bye into the semi-finals, Kildare beat them in a replay in Portlaoise after an earlier draw in Tullamore. Kildare beat them again in 1927 by 0-5 to 0-3 and the following year did so for the third campaign in succession, edging home by 0-10 to 1-6 en route to retaining the All-Ireland title and becoming the first recipients of the Sam Maguire Cup.

Successive provincial semi-final defeats followed against Laois, Meath and West-meath followed and it was not until 1932 that, after wins over Meath in Newbridge and Westmeath in Portlaoise, Dublin again reached the provincial decider. Wexford, thanks to a 59th minute point from Nick Walsh, snatched a late draw but Dublin won the replay convincingly 4-6 to 1-5, with Paddy McDonnell getting one of the goals to bring his Championship tally to 16, a county record that would stand alone for exact-ly three decades until equalled by Kevin Heffernan and would remain unbeaten until surpassed by Jimmy Keaveney in 1979. Dublin's interest was ended by Kerry in the All-Ireland semi-final, 1-3 to 1-1; McDonnell scored the point in what was his 50th and final Championship appearance, earning him the distinction of being the first Dubliner to reach the half century mark.

Dublin's end result was very similar the following year; wins over Meath, Louth and Wexford brought a 20th provincial crown but was followed by another All-Ireland semi-final loss, this time to Galway by 0-8 to 1-4 at Cusack Park in Mullingar, where The Dubs dominated the second half, held their opponents scoreless through the period, but could only add two points to their halftime score.

The following year, 1934, would prove the most successful for a decade. Dublin began it with wins over Westmeath and Meath but then ran into a real gridlock with Louth in the Leinster Final, when the sides drew twice in Croke Park before, with a third stalemate looking likely, two points from frees by George Comerford gained Dublin a 2-9 to 1-10 victory. Kerry were beaten by a surprisingly easy 3-8 to 0-6 in the All-Ire-land semi-final at Austin Stack Park in Tralee to secure a place in the Silver Jubilee Final but Dublin, eight points down against Galway just three minutes into the second half, could not quite reel in all of the deficit and lost by two points, 3-5 to 1-9. George Comerford, from the Garda club, accounted for all but three points of Dublin's final total and finished the Championship with a record 3-21, a figure that would be equalled by Tommy Banks in 1941 and Ollie Freaney in 1955 but would remain unsurpassed until Freaney beat it by two points four years further on.

From if not the summit at least well up the mountain, Dublin would fall in calamitous fashion over the next five years. In fact, it had never in the past sunk so low and never would again; in an unprecedented four years in succession they would fall at the first hurdle — albeit on a replay on the second occasion — and it wasn't until 1940 that they managed to win a game. That was a 1-9 to 2-5 provincial quarter-final victory over Louth in Navan but it was quickly followed by another defeat, to Meath by 1-7 to 0-4 in Newbridge after only managing a single point in the second half. One of the losses in that sequence, to Kildare in a quarter-final in Portlaoise in May 1938, was keeper Johnny McDonnell's final game, thus ending what to this day remains the longest senior inter-county career in the Dublin colours at 18 years and 320 days, during which he made 52 appearances in the National League and 58 in the Championships thus breaking his brother Paddy's six year old record in the latter competition. His league appearances was also a record and would remain so until surpassed by Ollie Freaney in 1958.

THE first hint of improvement came at Gaelic Park in Drogheda on the first day of June 1941. Dublin, the previous month, had drawn with Louth at the same ground and then beaten the Wee County by 1-9 to 1-4 in a replay at Croke Park to set up a quarter-final clash with a Meath side that was chasing a hat-trick of provincial titles.

Thanks to six points from Tommy Banks, a goal from Paddy O'Connor and a starring role by keeper Charlie Kelly, Dublin pulled off a shock 1-8 to 1-6 win over the defending champions and the following month, showing equal grit, they qualified for a first Leinster Final in seven year with a 2-11 to 2-10 defeat of Kildare, with Banks again contributing half a dozen points and Matt Fletcher scoring both goals.

Dublin, however, would have to wait almost four months to play the final; their surprise opponents were decider debutants Carlow, but an outbreak of foot and mouth disease in the south Leinster area meant the game could not be played until the second Sunday in November, so Dublin were nominated to represent the province in the All-Ireland series and that meant a semi-final against defending champions Kerry. It took a last minute point from a free by Murt Kelly to earn the Kingdom a 0-4 each draw at Croke Park but in the replay in Tralee a week later Kerry had a dozen points to spare, winning 2-9 to 0-3 before going on to retain the Sam Maguire Cup.

When the provincial was finally played, Carlow — who, in a foretaste of Dublin and Meath half a century later, needed three replays to get past Wexford in the semi-final — were 3-3 to 0-4 behind at halftime, Dublin eventually winning 4-6 to 1-4 with future soccer legend Con Martin, who had been drafted in as a late replacement for the injured Paddy Holly, score a point in his one and only competitive appearance for Dublin. Corner forward Fletcher, from Peadar Mackens, finished the campaign with six goals, a county record that was equalled by Jimmy Keaveney in 1976, Barney Rock seven years later, and Ray Cosgrove in 2002 but has yet to be surpassed. Banks, from Sean McDermotts, finished with 0-30 to equal the overall scoring record set by George Comerford in 1934.

The following year began with a close shave against Longford at Cusack Park in Mullingar where it took a late free from Banks to earn Dublin an 0-7 each draw. The replay, in Croke Park, was more straightforward; Dublin won by 2-15 to 1-3 and then edged past Meath on a 3-5 to 1-10 scoreline thanks to goals from Pierce O'Connor, Mick Quigley and Sean McCarthy. That set up a provincial final repeat against Carlow that would be considerably tighter than their meeting a year earlier, the fulltime score being 0-8 to 0-6 for Dublin, thanks to points in the final five minutes by first Banks and then Jimmy Joy. Cavan, who the previous month had won the Ulster Championship for the 23rd time and the fifth in succession, were edged out 1-6 to 1-3 in the All-Ireland semi-final, the goal coming from Paddy 'Beefy' Kennedy, who five weeks later would find the net again when Dublin were beaten 2-14 to 3-4 in the All-Ireland hurling decider by a Cork team that was captained by future Taoiseach Jack Lynch and also included a 21-year-old Christy Ring.

Dublin trailed Galway in the final by 1-6 to 1-3 at halftime, the goal coming from Gerry Fitzgerald, but spearheaded by an all Kerry midfield pairing of Mick Falvey and skipper Joe Fitzgerald (no relation of Gerry), they restricted the Connacht champions to just two points in the second half while scoring seven themselves. Eight days short of eighteen years after they had last been crowned title holder (the 1923 final wasn't played until September 1924), Dublin were All-Ireland champion for the 14th time and had at last got their hands on the Sam Maguire Cup. Skerries born Dublin forward Bobby Beggs, who shared with Gerry Fitzgerald the distinction of being the only survivors from Dublin's previous final appearance eight years earlier, had won an All-Ireland with Galway in 1938 and been on the team beaten in the final three years later; a fisherman, he had moved west for work purposes but returned to Dublin just prior to the start of the Championship campaign. Centre back Peter O'Reilly, as team coach, was effectively player-manager and would train Dublin to their next All-Ireland success in 1958, Corner back Caleb Crone, a Dublin based Air Corps officer who was born in Killavullen near Mallow, later declared for his native county and was on the Cork side that beat Cavan in the All-Ireland Final three years later; he died at his home in Saggart on 8 January 1958 after a short illness, aged just 37.

Dublin's reign ended in their first Championship outing as title holders when, in a provincial quarter-final meeting with Louth in Drogheda in May 1943, they trailed 1-4 to 0-3 at halftime and couldn't quite pull the deficit back, going out 1-6 to 1-5 after having a goal disallowed for an infringement into the square. The following year they beat Meath, Louth (who had gone on to win the provincial title the previous year) and Longford to set up, for the third time in four years, a Leinster Final showdown with

Carlow. The game was played at Catherine Park in Athy and Dublin appeared to be on course for another title when leading 1-4 to 0-3 at halftime, but two goals within four minutes of the restart gave Carlow what remains their one and only provincial senior crown on a 2-6 to 1-6 scoreline.

A dismal ten years followed, only in the last of which Dublin made it to a provincial semi-final and that by only winning a single game after receiving a first round bye. Twice they were eliminated in the opening round and on seven occasions they were beaten at the quarter-final stage. Their overall record for the miserable run was four wins, one draw and ten defeats. Meath — with whom they had the lone draw — beat them four times, Louth and Offaly did so twice each, while the other losses were to Laois and Offaly. The third of the four wins, a 2-9 to 2-5 quarter-final victory over Longford at Cusack Park in Mullingar in early May 1949 would ultimately prove significant in that it marked the Championship debut of Kevin Heffernan, who launched his legendary career by scoring five points.

BUOYED by a second National League triumph in three seasons (in which they compiled a 19-2-2 record in the competition with one of their losses being at the semi-final stage in the middle season), Dublin began their bid for 1955 glory full of optimism, a feeling that was not dampened in any way when they opened with a 3-9 to 0-6 provincial quarter-final win over Carlow in Newbridge. Questions might have been asked when Offaly ran them to three points in Portlaoise — Dessie Ferguson scoring the decisive goal — but they were quickly forgotten when defending All-Ireland champions Meath — whom Dublin had beaten 2-12 to 1-3 in the league decider less than three months earlier — were blitzed 5-12 to 0-7 in the Leinster Final in front of a record crowd of 48,860. It was a record winning margin and would remain so until The Dubs beat Wexford by 3-23 to 0-9 in 2008; it was also — and still is — the biggest defeat ever handed out to reigning All-Ireland football champions. It was Dublin's first provincial crown since 1942 and Mick Dunne in the *Irish Independent* wrote of it: 'In all their striving up to now, this Dublin side has been stylish and often spectacular; but never were they so uniformly magnificent as yesterday. Unless the form explodes they must win the Sam Maguire Cup in September'.

There was still a long way to go, though. Connacht champions Mayo hung on for a draw — 1-4 for them and 0-7 for Dublin — in a classic All-Ireland semi-final thanks to a late wonder save by keeper Owen Roe O'Neill from a Kevin Heffernan rocket and the replay was every bit as close, Mayo rallying to cut a five point deficit to just one before time ran out on them, Dublin holding on for a 1-8 to 1-7 victory with Ollie Freaney accounting for 1-4 of their total.

The stage was set for what was surely the most eagerly awaited All-Ireland Final ever up to that time, Dublin v Kerry, urban v rural, modernised football v the traditional catch-and-kick. A mammoth attendance of 87,102 — the biggest crowd ever to witness any sporting event in Ireland, surpassing the 86,155 who watched Kerry's victory over Armagh in the decider two years previously — turned up and, apart from team loyalties as to the outcome, not a single one was disappointed as they were treated to an enthralling spectacle. Dublin, missing appendicitis victim Norman Allen and an injured Marcus Wilson through injury — but still with eleven St. Vincent's men in their starting line-up (another, Terry Jennings, would come on as a sub), trailed by 0-5 to 0-3 at halftime after a Cyril Freaney shot had rebounded off the crossbar with Kerry keeper Garry Mahony totally beaten and, after an Ollie Freaney goal from a 21-yard free, by 0-12 to 1-6 with just four minutes left. Dublin launched an all out final assault but the Kingdom rearguard held firm, John D. Hickey, in the *Irish Independent*, wrote of those closing moments: 'I have no doubt that long after many great combats of the past have lost their charm, even though they be embellished as the years roll on, the last four minutes of yesterday's encounter will be recalled with a quickening of the pulse'.

Heffernan, who had to have a painkilling injection for an ankle injury moments before the game, always acknowledged the loss as the biggest disappointment of his entire career in the game. As he said in an interview with the *Irish Times* nine years before his death in January 2013 at the age of 83: 'No defeat as a manager ever hit me like 1955. That was the first time there. It was Kerry. I had great hopes and so on and so on. That formed a large part of what I became as a person. That and the defeat by Louth two years later. I took some wrong options that day. Went for scores where I thought we needed to score a goal. I regret that very much still. If we had popped the points we might have got the goal. That's one thing I learned. In my memory that afternoon doesn't merge into other games but the hour compacts. I only remember small incidents. I remember putting a ball over the bar instead of giving it on to Johnny Boyle for instance, early on.'

The following year was a real anti-climax as, after a scrappy 0-11 to 0-5 defeat of Wicklow in a quarter-final clash at St Patrick's Park in Enniscorthy, a particularly wasteful Dublin crashed out to Wexford at Dr. Cullen Park in Carlow, 2-7 to 0-7. Then, in 1957, came Heffernan's second biggest disappointment. After emphatic wins over Longford and Wicklow (by 2-10 to 1-4 in Mullingar and 3-9 to 0-9 in Newbridge, respectively), they were back in Croke Park in pursuit of a 25th provincial crown, this time against Louth, the champions from four years previously.

Things did not go quite according to plan; leading by 1-6 to 1-2 four minutes into the second half, Dublin folded to a Wee County blitz that saw Kevin Beahan score three points in succession and then Jimmy McDonnell crack home his second goal, all in the space of six minutes. The final scoreline was 2-9 to 1-7 but with the benefit of hindsight it can hardly be classified as a complete sensation seeing as Louth went on to further victories over first Tyrone and then Cork to capture only their third All-Ireland crown and their first in four and a half decades.

HAVING claimed their third league title in six seasons with a 3-13 to 3-8 defeat of Kildare in mid May, Dublin began the following year's Championship campaign with a special target, a first ever National League and All-Ireland double. The bid, however, started in highly jittery fashion as Meath, in a quarter-final tie in Drogheda, cracked in two goals in the opening nine minutes and enjoyed a 2-4 to 0-4 halftime lead before being overhauled and edged out 1-12 to 2-7, Dublin's crucial goal coming from Lar Foley who, unusually, was lining out at midfield alongside Sean 'Yank' Murray. Carlow were then dismissed 3-9 to 2-7 in Portlaoise and the heartache of the previous year was at least partially atoned for when provincial and All-Ireland champions Louth were dethroned on a 1-11 to 1-6 scoreline, Ollie Freaney contributing half a dozen points and Heffernan providing the goal, plus a point.

The semi-final against Galway, the champions from just two years previously, proved to be the toughest test of all. Missing just two of their All-Ireland medallists, Galway held a one or two point advantage for most of the game but Dublin eventually drew level and in the dying seconds were awarded a free from around the half forward line. Just as Ollie Freaney was placing the ball for the kick Antrim referee Liam Friel informed him that it was literally the last kick of the game; Freaney sent the ball over the crossbar and Dublin had scraped home, 2-7 to 1-9, with both their goals coming from Johnny Joyce.

Derry, appearing in their first ever All-Ireland Final, were massive underdogs yet in the third quarter offered the possibility of a real shock. Trailing by 0-8 to 0-4 at the break but by the tenth minute of the second half had drawn level thanks to a Sean O'Connell point and then an Owen Gribben goal. Two minutes later disaster struck the Ulster champions when their left corner back Tommy Doherty slipped as he was going for a ball against Paddy Farnan and the latter, finding himself in possession and unchallenged, fired in a shot that keeper Patsy Gormley had no chance of stopping. That was the turning point, Johnny Joyce cracked home his fifth goal of the campaign shortly afterwards and Dublin were well and truly on the road to what in the end would be a 2-12 to 1-9 victory, a first All-Ireland since 1942 and their 16th in all. Ollie Freaney, with 0-29 from the five match campaign, repeated his 1955 feat of topping the Championship scoring table.

The provincial title was retained in 1959 but not easily. Carlow ran Dublin to four points in Portlaoise (1-11 to 2-4) in a game that saw the Championship debut of an 18-year-old Des Foley and then only a last second Freaney point from a free earned the champions a draw in Croke Park. The replay, at Páirc Tailteann in Navan, saw a marked improvement as goals from Johnny Joyce, Pádraig Haughey and Kevin Heffernan set Dublin on the road to a convincing 3-14 to 1-9 success. That form was continued in the Leinster Final in Tullamore as all six forwards plus midfielder Johnny Joyce and centre half back Cathal O'Leary scored from play in a 1-18 to 2-8 success that was all the more impressive given that Laois enjoyed a 2-6 to 0-7 lead at halftime.

Dublin's opponents in the semi-final were Kerry, the side that had ended their dream team's dream in the final four years earlier, and in many ways this meeting —

which attracted a semi-final record attendance of 70,148 — was an action replay of the previous one. Trailing by 1-5 to 0-4 at halftime and then by 1-9 to 0-4 with just ten minutes remaining on the clock, Dublin launched another of their famous rallies and goals by Haughey and Freaney followed by a point from the latter cut the margin to a single point, but a Kerry white flag from Tom Long ended the scoring. Dublin could claim an abundance of ill luck; keeper Paddy O'Flaherty had to retire injured six minutes before halftime — he was replaced by sub forward Cyril Meehan — in what proved to be his final game for The Dubs, and in a five minute spell in the first half Heffernan, Freaney, Mickey Whelan and Johnny Joyce all had shots come back off the uprights. Freaney, with 2-26 from another five match programme, topped the scoring chart for the third time but that was little consolation to the St. Vincent's star; in fact, he and clubmate Jim Lavin announced their retirement from the game two months after the final, each finishing his career with ten county titles.

Dublin began the following year's campaign with a game in which they would set three county records that remain unmatched to this day. In hammering Longford by 10-13 to 3-8 in a provincial quarter-final meeting at Cusack Park in Mullingar (they were 6-7 to 1-5 up at halftime), the team set new benchmarks for most goals and biggest winning margin and Johnny Joyce, at full forward, banged home five goals and three points — the first two within four minutes of the throw-in — and really should have been credited with a sixth green flag as another of his rockets, apparently goal bound anyway, was slightly deflected by, and attributed to, Longford corner back Billy Morgan.

There was a new power emerging in Leinster football, however, and from the high of a record shattering win Dublin slumped to a three goal defeat — 3-9 to 0-9 — to Offaly at O'Moore Park in Portlaoise after enjoying an 0-7 to 0-5 lead at halftime and having Kevin Heffernan blast a penalty over the bar two minutes after the restart. It was a similar story the next year, Dublin beat Wexford by 4-7 to 1-7 in Carlow and then Meath by 4-14 to 1-7 in Navan, but in the provincial decider again had to give way to Offaly, this time by 1-13 to 1-8.

AFTER two years of enforced isolation, Dublin finally got the better of Offaly in 1962. Louth pushed them to a single point in the provincial quarter-final and Laois ran them to two in the semi-final, but in a definite step up in performance in the decider, Offaly were dethroned on a 2-8 to 1-7 scoreline, the goals coming from Paddy Delaney and Bob McCrea. The form could not be sustained in the All-Ireland semi-final alas as a Mick O'Connell inspired Kerry raced into a 2-9 to 0-3 halftime lead en route to a 2-12 to 0-10 triumph in a game that was probably most notable for it being Heffernan's swansong in the county colours; his record of 115 competitive appearances would stand until surpassed by Paddy Cullen in 1979.

The following year it seemed Dublin's campaign would in reality be over inside the first half an hour; Dublin trailed Meath in a quarter-final tie at Croke Park by 2-5 to 1-1 at halftime but the switching of Lar Foley from left corner back to full forward proved to be an inspired move as he not only scored a pair of vital points but contributed significantly to goals from Mickey Whelan and John Timmons in a Dublin fightback that culminated in younger brother Des scoring the winning point in a 2-6 to 2-5 victory. A five point win over Kildare saw Dublin back in the provincial final and the title was retained with a 2-11 to 2-9 triumph over a Laois side that somewhat distorted the champions true superiority with a last-minute goal.

Down, in the All-Ireland semi-final, offered surprisingly little resistance; Dublin held a 1-5 to 0-4 halftime lead and went on to win 2-11 to 0-7 with Brian McDonald scoring both goals. Dublin, for the third time, would face Galway in the All-Ireland Final; each side had won once — Dublin in 1922 and Galway two decades later — and each time the margin was two points. And it would be again as a Galway halftime lead of 0-6 to 0-4 was transformed into a 1-9 to 0-10 victory for Dublin, the all-important goal coming from Gerry Davey nine minutes into the second half. Des Foley became the first man to captain Dublin to minor and senior All-Ireland titles, having skippered the teenage title winning squad five years earlier.

Dublin's title defence a year later began promisingly enough with a 1-14 to 1-5 defeat of Carlow in Newbridge but warning signs surfaced in the provincial semi-final in a hard earned 0-8 to 1-2 win over Laois in Tullamore and they proved justified in the Leinster Final when Meath, leading by just 1-6 to 1-5 at the break, outscored Dublin by 1-6 to just two points in the second half to capture their first provincial title in a decade. Dublin's bid for a first Leinster Championship hat-trick since 1934 had been stopped dead in its tracks.

A year later, in 1965, things looked a good deal better as, in turn, Wexford, Kildare and Longford were dismissed by an aggregate of 5-28 to 0-21, the Wexford game being noteworthy for a 1-3 contribution from a 20-year-old debutant named Jimmy Keaveney. Given that the All-Ireland semi-final opposition was Kerry, there was almost a sense of *déjà vu* about the meeting; Dublin, after all, had not beaten the Kingdom in a Championship clash since a semi-final victory in 1934 and since then had been beaten in three such showdowns as well as the still painful All-Ireland Final in 1955. And it would turn out to be the same old story as Dublin, ahead by 1-3 to 0-4 at the break, were overrun by 4-4 to 1-3 in the second half, two of the Kerry goals coming from sub Mick O'Dwyer.

Another slump was coming. It would be another nine years before Dublin would reach another provincial final and in 1970 and 1971 they would suffer the indignity of opening round defeats by Longford and Laois, respectively, and only in 1966, 1969 and 1972 did they even make it to the semi-finals stage. So low had Dublin's standing sunk that, in the draw for the Leinster Championship in 1974, defending champions Offaly, plus Kildare, Laois, Longford, Meath, Westmeath and Wicklow were all given byes into the quarter-finals while Dublin were lumped along with Carlow, Louth and Wexford in a sub group to determine the eighth and last place.

DUBLIN'S first game in the campaign, a 3-9 to 0-6 defeat of Wexford, was famously watched from Hill 16 by Jimmy Keaveney who, although retired from the inter-county scene for two years, was still playing with his St. Vincent's club. A week after the Wexford game, after some persuasion from new team boss Kevin Heffernan, he lined out at Páirc Tailteann in Navan and scored half a dozen points as Dublin beat Louth by 2-11 to 1-9 to make it into the last eight. Offaly, going for a fourth Leinster Championship in succession and given their vast experience, appeared to have victory within their grasp when they tied up the quarter-final at Pearse Park in Longford at 0-13 to 1-10 with three minutes left on the clock, but two minutes later Leslie Deegan — who had scored the only goal of the game in the 21st minute — slotted over the winning point.

With the champions — and All-Ireland winners in 1971 and 1972 — out of the way, the unthinkable began to be thought. Kildare were seen off 1-13 to 0-10 in the semi-final and then the provincial crown was regained with a 1-14 defeat of Meath, a mammoth 1-8 of Dublin's total coming from the boot of a by now totally rejuvenated Keaveney. Dublin, having been considered so sub standard that they were compelled to play an unprecedented five rounds just to get out of Leinster, were in the All-Ireland semi-finals for the first time since 1965.

Defending champions Cork stood between Dublin and a 24th appearance in the biggest game on the calendar, but the underdogs surprised them by carving out a three point lead at halftime, 0-7 to 0-4, and seven minutes after the restart — it was an 80 minute game — the Leesiders grip on the title was loosened further when Anton O'Toole fired an unstoppable shot past Cork keeper and skipper Billy Morgan. Eight minutes later came a controversial incident; Cork replaced Ned Kirby with Martin Doherty and the latter was barely on the field when he gathered a loose ball and, charging forward, was fouled in the penalty area — but the problem was Kirby had not left the field of play. Dublin protested vehemently about the extra man but Tyrone referee Patsy Devlin ignored their complaints and Jimmy Barry Murphy fired the penalty past Paddy Cullen to reduce the deficit to 1-8 to 1-5.

The bizarre ruling could well have swung the game Cork's way but if anything it gave Dublin extra motivation and in the 67th minute they had a penalty of their own, Brian Mullins making no mistake after Keaveney had been pulled down. Cork's fate was sealed and minutes after their 2-11 to 1-8 defeat, Brian Mullins confidently predicted: 'We'll win the All-Ireland now all right. Once we have Cork out of our system everything will be okay. I wonder will we be recognised as a good team now?' John D. Hickey in the *Irish Independent* wrote: 'The winners have progressed quite beyond recognition since I saw them defeat Wexford and Louth and now that they have scored a comprehensive triumph over a Cork side that looked all over a team of all the talents when beating Kerry in the Munster final, who is to say that they will not show even further improvement in the All-Ireland final?' before going on to note, somewhat prophetically: 'Every man in the victorious side has good reason to feel not only satisfied with, but proud of, the contribution he made to a triumph that is bound to prove of great benefit to the game in the capital.'

Galway, conquerors of Donegal in the other semi-final, had been beaten by Cork in the previous year's final and by Offaly in that of two years previously, and were considered strong favourites. That status appeared justified when they held a 1-4 to 0-5 halftime advantage, the goal coming from midfielder Michael Rooney just after the half hour. A dozen minutes into the second half Liam Sammon was brought down; the full forward took the spot kick himself but Paddy Cullen (who minutes earlier had pulled off a wonder save from goalscorer Rooney), diving to his left, brilliantly turned the ball around the post. Were it not for Cullen's heroics Galway would have opened up a 2-4 to 0-6 lead and the game might well have been over, but instead Dublin levelled and then went ahead through a pair of Keaveney points. They were never caught thereafter, eventually breaking the two point sequence in finals against Galway with an 0-4 to 1-6 victory.

Jimmy Keaveney, with eight points in the final, finished the campaign as top scorer with 1-36 in what was for him a six-game programme, thereby beating the record of 1-35 set by Offaly ace Tony McTague three years earlier and Cullen, in a post match interview, revealed a secret: 'Out in San Francisco earlier this year, I saw Liam practise penalty kicking, and I knew he placed them to his right, and slightly rising the ball off the ground. That's just what he did, and I went that way.'

A new era was born and Desmond Rushe, on the front page of the *Irish Independent* the following morning, described its birth: "The Westerners were outnumbered, outroared, outsung and outbragged by cocky camp followers of Heffo's Army, who brought a strange new image to Croke Park. The pre-match build-up had its effect, and if the game didn't produce much by way of good football, it gave Final Day a pop-age atmosphere in which the Artane Boys sounded like a bunch of old squares as they played Molly Malone.' Football in the capital would never be the same again and remarkably, the success of born again Dublin, to some extent at least, would be maintained for a further five years.

DUBLIN, playing a Championship game as Sam Maguire Cup holders for the first time since their Leinster Final loss to Meath in July 1964, beat Wexford in Carlow a lot more comfortably than the 4-17 to 3-10 scoreline might suggest; leading 3-9 to 1-6 at halftime in their initial game in the 70 minute era, they were 4-12 to 1-6 clear entering the final quarter before easing up and allowing Wexford two goals in the final five minutes. Jimmy Keaveney slotted over ten points and would top that with an outstanding 1-11 in a provincial semi-final defeat of Louth in Navan where Dublin, 2-12 to 1-5 in front when John McCarthy was red carded in the 53rd minute, had to survive a fierce fightback to win 3-14 to 4-7.

Kildare were accounted for by 3-13 to 0-8 in the Leinster Final but Derry provided sterner opposition in the All-Ireland semi-final and it was only in the final ten minutes that Dublin killed them off for a 3-13 to 3-8 ticket into a first All-Ireland Final showdown with Kerry in two decades. The throwing of stones and bottles and a post match invasion of the pitch by a minority of Dublin fans who charged straight at their Derry counterparts led to the installation of mesh fencing on Hill 16 and the Nally Stand areas in time for the final. The decider itself was a painful anti-climax for The Dubs; a Brian Mullins point in the second minute put them in front for the one and only time in the game but little over a minute later a soft John Egan goal — off an apparent misunderstanding between Paddy Cullen and Gay O'Driscoll set Mick O'Dwyer's eager youngsters — every one of them a bachelor — on the road to an emphatic 2-12 to 0-11 victory and a 23rd title. Jimmy Keaveney against topped the scoring chart with a record 1-38 from the five games (two points better than the previous year when he played one game more), while his return against Louth was the second highest ever by a Dubliner in a Championship game, beaten only by the 5-3 of Johnny Joyce against Longford in 1960.

Having won the National League for the first time since 1958 in May, it was a more confident Dublin that began their bid to regain the Championship in 1976. Longford were hammered 5-16 to 0-7 in Mullingar (Keaveney accounting for 3-4 and debutant Kevin Moran scoring three points), Laois were outscored 3-12 to 0-11 in Tullamore and only Meath, in the provincial decider, offered any real resistance, coming back from a 1-7 to 0-5 deficit to push Dublin to two points, 2-8 to 1-9. By completing their fifth Leinster Championship hat-trick and their first since 1934, Dublin set up a revenge final clash with Kerry by edging out Galway by 1-8 to 0-8 in a tough All-Ireland semi-final, the only goal of the game coming from Keaveney in the 51st minute.

Tradition, and the odds, were stacked against Dublin; they were without a Championship win against Kerry since a semi-final in 1934 and since then had been beaten six times including in two finals, and then there was the not inconsequential matter of the way they had been totally outclassed in the previous year's decider. Yet they not only beat both tradition and they odds, they did so in emphatic style, winning by 3-8 to 0-10 after leading by just a goal at the interval, 1-5 to 0-5. Paddy Downey in the *Irish Times* put the game and its backdrop in context: 'Dublin played with the fire and resolution that distinguished Kerry's success in last year's final. The roles were reversed and Kerry now felt the brunt of the onslaught that they delivered twelve months ago.'

The provincial three-in-a-row sequence was extended to four — a first since 1924 — in 1977 with victories over Kildare, Wexford and Meath, a feat that meant, for the first time ever, a Championship showdown with Kerry for a third year in succession. It would turn out to be an absolute classic that would swing back and forth with unwavering intensity; a Seanie Walsh goal in the 21st minute helped Kerry to a 1-6 to 0-6 half-time lead only for John McCarthy to level matters within a minute of the restart, Kerry went 1-9 to 1-7 in front within the following ten minutes but Dublin, with three points in a row from Anton O'Toole, David Hickey and Tony Hanahoe, were in the lead for the first time in the game by the 56 minute, 1-10 to 1-9.

The lead was shortlived, however, as Kerry equalised within a minute through Walsh and then, after first Bobby Doyle and then Paudie Lynch had exchanged points, the Kingdom again pulled two clear with just seven minutes left courtesy of Mikey

Sheehy and John Egan. Then came a stunning Dublin grand finale in the final six minutes when Hanahoe placed Hickey to rifle a shot past Kerry keeper Paudie O'Mahony and just over two minutes later Bernard Brogan finished a thirty yard solo run by firing the ball high into O'Mahony's net. Hanahoe scored the final point of a thrilling game a matter of seconds before Monaghan referee Seamus Murray blew the final whistle and Dublin, on a 3-12 to 1-13 scoreline, were into a fourth consecutive All-Ireland Final, a feat they had last achieved in the 1923 campaign. It was only the second time in history that Dublin had beaten their arch rivals in successive Championship meetings; the previous instance having covered over a decade and a half, the 'home' decider of 1908 (played in May 1909) and the actual final for 1923 (played in September 1924).

To say the following morning's papers were fulsome in their praise of the game — and both teams — was an understatement: Paddy Downey in the *Irish Times*: 'As the crowd left the stadium yesterday, groups of people, friends and strangers, stopped and talked in a hundred places — and the uppermost topic of conversation was almost universal: who could remember a greater semi-final, a greater game at any stage of the Championship?'; Pádraig Purcell in the *Irish Press*: 'If the first half was fast and furious, it was only a foretaste of the thrills to come. After the interval, two great teams gave us a contest of almost regal splendour with fortunes flaming and fading, and the only regret for the neutral spectator was that one team had to lose.'; Raymond Smith in the *Irish Independent*: 'I have seen nothing in my time to match the second half of this game. I do not write it lightly. I am not alone in describing it as an occasion that will go into the history books, providing as it did that sense of confrontation, that fierce intensity of endeavour and beauty of flowing movement that one is perhaps privileged to experience only once or twice in a lifetime when teams of the quality of Dublin and Kerry throw down the gauntlet to one another. We will talk by winter firesides of an afternoon touched by magic, when two teams got locked in a confrontation frightening in the intensity of its climax, something beyond a normal match. We dream of days like this but we seldom have them in Gaelic football today.'

The decider, against an Armagh side appearing in only their second All-Ireland Final (the previous one had been in 1953 when Kerry beat them by four points), was regarded as something of a foregone conclusion and, essentially, that assessment proved to be accurate. Ahead by 3-6 to 1-3 at halftime Dublin added 1-2 without reply in the first ten minutes of the second half and only two late goals from Joe Kernan made the final score a more respectable looking 5-12 to 3-6. Dublin, for the first time since the 1922 decider (played in October of the following year), had successfully defended the All-Ireland crown and Jimmy Keaveney scored 2-6 of Dublin's total, thereby surpassing the All-Ireland Final record of 2-5 set by Galway's legend Frank Stockwell in his side's 1956 victory over Cork. The game was played just five days after the death of Elvis Presley and Hill 16 displayed its topicality with a banner that read 'Elvis is gone but The Dubs live on!'

The highlight of Dublin's first step in their bid for a third consecutive All-Ireland crown, a provincial quarter-final hammering of Carlow by 6-15 to 2-9 at Croke Park, was a 3-7 contribution from John McCarthy, a return that saw him overtake Jimmy Keaveney as the second highest Dublin scorer in a single Championship game, behind only the aforementioned Johnny Joyce. Offaly, in the semi-final at O'Moore Park in Portlaoise, almost pulled off a stunning victory as they built up an 0-10 to 1-2 lead early in the second half only for the introduction of Kevin Moran — on summer leave from Manchester United — to inspire a Dublin revival that culminated in a McCarthy goal just two minutes from time and a narrow 2-9 to 0-12 victory. Kildare were overcome 1-17 to 1-6 in a record setting — for Dublin — fifth successive Leinster Final triumph and then a 1-16 to 0-8 defeat of Down in the All-Ireland semi-final set up yet another Championship shoot-out with Kerry.

Few matches in the entire history of the Championship have produced as dramatic a turnaround as the ninth meeting of the game's biggest rivals in an All-Ireland Final, including the 'home' decider of 1908. Dublin, going for another National League and Championship double, led by five points — 0-6 to 0-1 — with eleven minutes to go to halftime (and might well have been a further goal in front had not a Jimmy Keaveney ground shot gone inches wide), yet were outscored 5-10 to 0-3 in the remainder of the game. A fisted goal from John Egan stunned the Hill 16 faithful into total silence but there was worse, much worse, to come ... the most talked about goal in football final history.

It happened three minutes before the break, by which time Dublin's lead had been cut to a single point, 0-7 to 1-3. Kerry left half forward Ger Power appeared to back into Dublin keeper Paddy Cullen as he was about to clear a ball and Kildare referee Seamus Aldridge promptly blew his whistle but, to the surprise of just about everyone in the 71,503 crowd, awarded the free to Kerry from the 14-yard line, about ten yards to their right of the posts. Cullen went out to remonstrate with Aldridge and, getting no change out of the man in the middle, started back towards his goal; Mikey Sheehy, at the same time, was placing the ball and, with genius-like thinking and opportunism, floated the ball over the keeper and into the right top corner of the net as Cullen scampered backwards towards his goal. The score opened the floodgates; 2-3 to 0-7 in front at the interval, Kerry tagged on another 3-8 after the restart to just two points from Dublin with Eoin Liston, three weeks shy of his 21st birthday and playing in only his third Championship game, getting all the second half goals — between the 37th and 55th minutes — to become the first and so far only man to score a hat-trick in the All-Ireland Final.

What instantly became known as 'the Sheehy goal' was, of course, a subject of great controversy. Donal Carroll in the *Irish Independent* said of Cullen: 'He was adjudged — wrongly in my view — the transgressor when Power backed into him' and Pádraig Purcell in the *Irish Press* commented: 'Many spectators, and several in the press-box, myself included, felt the free might well have gone to Dublin'. Cullen himself, in a dressingroom interview, said: 'I had just parted with the ball when Ger Power crashed into me. I just could not understand why the free was given to Kerry instead of to Dublin. I suppose such is not the time to complain, I suppose you should just get on with the job you have to do — but I was so convinced I had been fouled that it was almost a spontaneous reaction that I seek a free.'

The immediate aftermath of the massacre saw much speculation that the 'old guard' of Cullen, Sean Doherty, Gay O'Driscoll, Tony Hanahoe and Jimmy Keaveney would hang up their boots but all returned the following year, 1979, although Doherty, skipper of the successful 1974 side, would lose his place in the course of a campaign that began with a 4-16 to 0-4 trouncing of Louth in Navan and was followed by a 3-13 to 2-7 defeat of Wicklow in Newbridge.

Offaly had given Dublin an almighty scare in the provincial semi-final the previous year and this time, in the final, they gave them an even bigger one; with Jimmy Keaveney sent off by Westmeath referee Paddy Collins for felling Offaly corner back Ollie Minnock in the 34th minute, Dublin, playing with the wind, trailed 0-5 to 0-3 at the break, by 0-7 to 0-5 by the 40th minute, and by a more worrying 0-9 to 0-5 with a dozen minutes to go. Points by Jim Ronayne, Bernard Brogan and Michael Hickey — the first and last of whom had come on as subs midway through the second half — cut the gap to a single point but Dublin still trailed inside the final minute; then, as Collins was checking his watch, Anton O'Toole passed to Brian Mullins who flicked the ball to Brogan — who cracked it past opposing keeper Martin Furlong for a sensational winning goal. Peadar O'Brien in the *Irish Press* summed up both the winners' performance and the match itself: 'Never since their rise to football eminence in 1974 was their wonderful spirit so necessary; never was the determination of this super team so called upon, and never did they show more grit and raw courage as that which helped Dublin to a record equalling sixth Leinster senior championship title in a row in this simply incredible final at Croke Park yesterday.' Keaveney subsequently received a two month ban that ruled him out of the rest of the Championship and, apart from a Ceannarus tournament semi-final against Monaghan in early October, never wore the Dublin colours again.

Keaveney's free taking duties were taken over by Michael Hickey in the All-Ireland semi-final against Roscommon and the brother of the better known David contributed nine points — all but one of them from placed balls — in a wafer-thin 0-14 to 1-10 victory for Dublin, who became the first county ever to win six successive All-Ireland semi-finals. Yet another Dublin and Kerry showdown had come to pass, the tenth in all and the fifth with the Sam Maguire Cup at stake. And it would be yet another humiliation as Kerry, 1-7 to 0-3 clear at halftime and 1-10 to 0-4 to the good when Páidí Ó Sé was sent off for a second bookable offence in the 52nd minute, still managed to outscore their rivals 2-3 to 0-4 while down a man. Paddy Cullen, Sean Doherty and Gay O'Driscoll retired after this defeat while Tony Hanahoe played in the opening league game of the new season — another loss to Kerry, by 1-16 to 0-10 at Austin Stack Park in Tralee — three weeks later and then hung up his boots.

There was one last gasp of breath from the dying beast the following year; wins over Laois and Meath saw them equal the feat of their own 1899 predecessors and Kildare in 1931 of reaching seven finals in succession but, almost inevitably after their last minute heartbreaks of the previous two campaigns, Offaly got the better of them in a game that marked the senior debut of goalkeeper John O'Leary — and this time it was the Midlanders who 'stole' the game, coming back from a 1-5 to 0-2 halftime deficit to capture a first provincial crown in seven years on a 1-10 to 1-8 scoreline. Two years later they would win a third successive Leinster title — beating Dublin by 1-16 to 1-7 in the final — en route to dramatically stopping Kerry's bid for a record breaking All-Ireland Final five-in-a-row.

HAVING gone since a provincial semi-final tie with Louth in 1959 without a draw, Dublin had two of them within the space of just over two months in 1983. The first, in a provincial quarter-final against Meath, was secured with the help of two goals in the final eleven minutes, the first from Barney Rock and the second turned in by Royal County corner back Phil Smith. Dublin, with Rock scoring 2-3, won the replay 3-9 to 0-16 and then dismissed Louth by 1-12 to 0-11 to return to the Leinster Final stage. Dublin, against reigning All-Ireland champions Offaly, trailed by 0-6 to 0-5 three minutes before the break but then a goal from Joe McNally and then another from John Caffrey on the stroke of it put them on the road to a 2-13 to 1-11 victory.

Next up was an All-Ireland semi-final with Cork and the second draw and once again it was secured with a late equaliser for Dublin; Cork led by 1-6 to 0-6 at halftime and by 2-11 to 1-9 with just nine minutes remaining, but while points by Rock and McNally gave The Dubs a glimmer of hope, they were still a goal behind entering the final minute — but then Rock, gathering a cross from Ray Hazley, blasted the ball past Cork keeper Michael Creedon. The replay, at Páirc Uí Chaoimh a week later (the first semi-final outside Croke Park since Kerry beat Dublin in another replay at Austin Stack Park in Tralee in 1941), was a totally different story as The Dubs, with all six forwards scoring from play and goals from Brian Mullins (penalty), Ciaran Duff, Rock and McNally ran out easy 4-15 to 2-10 winners.

The final against Galway, the fifth such meeting of the teams, gave Dublin their fourth win in the series and was the fourth of the games to be decided by a two point margin (the exception being The Dubs five point success in 1974), 1-10 to 1-8, with Barney Rock accounting for all but four points of Dublin's total — PJ Buckley, Jim Ronayne, Ciaran Duff and Joe McNally getting the others — as the county came of age by claiming the All-Ireland title for the 21st time. That takes care of the bare record book entry, now for the story behind surely the most contentious All-Ireland Final, one that, depending on one's loyalties, Dublin's match winning heroes will forever carry the tag of 'The Twelve Apostles' or 'The Dirty Dozen'.

Antrim referee John Gough sent off Brian Mullins in the 27th minute for felling midfielder Brian Talty, dismissed Ray Hazley and Tomas Tierney eight minutes later for some fisticuffs on the Hogan Stand sideline, and then red carded Ciaran Duff five minutes into the second half for apparently flooring wing back Pat O'Neill. Dublin, leading 1-5 to 0-2 at halftime (when there was a second clash between Mullins and Talty in the tunnel on the way to the dressingrooms), turned in a second half of unbelievable courage and determination. Galway got to within three points of them — 1-8 to 1-5 with a quarter of an hour remaining, but Rock points in the 56th and 63rd minutes gave them precious breathing space, sufficient to withstand further points for the Connacht champions from Seamus McHugh and Barry Brennan.

Dublin captain Tommy Drumm said in the dressingroom shortly after the presentation: 'Dublin have won many fine matches over the last eight years but I doubt if any could compare with this achievement. I doubt if you could ever get a greater example of will-to-win attitude', while Kevin Heffernan said of Galway criticism of Dublin's tactics: 'If they want to start complaining like that then they can go elsewhere. If we had 15 players we would have beaten them by ten points.'

Donal Carroll in the *Irish Independent*, wrote: 'Not since John Wayne rode the range in many a half-forgotten western have we seen such True Grit as that in evidence at Croke Park yesterday. There, it was mustered by twelve Dublin men, brave and bursting with dedication, who soaked up the best that fourteen Galwaymen could throw at them to gain a most deserving coming-of-age All-Ireland success. The latest crop of Dubs displayed coolness and character far beyond their years. More remarkable still, they achieved this feat though playing into the teeth of a gale force wind.' Paddy Downey in the *Irish Times* also turned to the Wild West for imagery: 'They battled on like giants in the face of gigantic odds and must have won the admiration of even the most partisan Galway supporters for the splendour of their spirit. In a sporting context, this was Custer's last stand — but with a happy ending.'

Mullins — despite his dismissal — and Anton O'Toole became the first Dubs since Jim Brennan in 1908 to win a quartet of All-Ireland medals and Joe McNally, goalkeeper on the previous year's minor title winning side, became the first — and, at the time of writing, only — player in football history to win minor and senior medals in successive years; the only one of his 87 competitive appearances for the county as keeper was the very first one, a drawn league tie with Armagh the previous March. Rock, whose 13th-minute goal had a touch of the Mikey Sheehy about it when he lobbed out of position keeper Padraic Coyne from some 30 yards, finished the campaign with 6-26 from the seven matches to break Jimmy Keaveney's county record of 1-38, although it should be pointed out that the latter played two games less when setting his mark in 1975.

The following year went along similar lines. Dublin retained the Leinster Championship with successive wins over Wexford, Offaly and Meath, beat Tyrone by 2-11 to 0-8 in the All-Ireland semi-final and then lost the Sam Maguire Cup decider to Kerry by five points, 0-14 to 1-6, with Tommy Conroy scoring a point for The Dubs and Barney Rock bagging everything else. More than one commentator noted that the great Dublin resurrection had finished on an exact reversal of the scoreline with which it had started in their All-Ireland Final victory over Galway a decade earlier but their obituaries were premature. In the words of Mark Twain. 'reports of my death were an exaggeration' — Heffo's Heroes had one last throw of the dice left in them for 1985.

Like in the previous campaign they opened with victories over first Wexford — against whom Barney Rock scored 2-4 for the second successive time — and then Offaly before completing another provincial title hat-trick, this time with an 0-10 to 0-4 defeat of Laois. A draw — 1-13 each — with Mayo in the All-Ireland semi-final followed after Dublin could only manage three points in the second half to a tally of 0-9 from their opponents but in the replay three weeks later The Dubs, thanks to two goals from Ciaran Duff, won by a comfortable 2-12 to 1-7 to qualify for yet another final showdown with Kerry.

This time Dublin, 1-8 to 0-4 in arrears at the break, fought back with two Joe McNally goals between the 52nd and 64th minutes and were just a point adrift with four minutes left on the clock, but successive white flags from Pat Spillane, Timmy Dowd and John Kennedy saw Kerry home 2-12 to 2-8. Kevin Heffernan stepped down for the second time a month later, departing with a record of just one win (1976) in five All-Ireland Finals against the Kingdom, Tony Hanahoe having been at the helm for the classic semi-final victory over their arch-rivals in 1977. The final — his eighth — also marked the 53rd and last Championship game of Brian Mullins' career, although he did make a single league appearance in each of the following two seasons. The bell had finally tolled.

DUBLIN, post 1985, would set an all-time Leinster Final record — as the first team to lose three deciders in a row... and what made it worse for The Dubs is that they were all to provincial arch rivals Meath. All three games were close, Meath's winning margins being two, four and two points, but another depressing point for Dublin was that they failed to score a single goal in the three and a half hours of play against the Royal County. The wastefulness even extending to a Charlie Redmond penalty in the third decider.

The miserable run finally ended in 1989 when, after beating both Kildare and Wicklow in Newbridge, Dublin stopped Meath's bid for a third successive All-Ireland crown with a somewhat surprise victory as, after leading 1-5 to 0-7 but trailing 1-10 to 1-9 with only eight minutes to go, a Vinnie Murphy goal inspired them to a 2-12 to 1-10 triumph. Not everyone was convinced, however: Vincent Hogan, in the *Irish Independent*, remarked, 'One suspects Billy Morgan will find the weeks ahead more bearable than normal. I, for one, believe Cork will now capture Sam Maguire'. And so it proved; Cork beat Dublin by 2-10 to 1-9 in the All-Ireland semi-final and then fulfilled the prophesy with an 0-17 to 1-11 defeat of Mayo. What was becoming normality was restored the following year when, in the first ever instance of the same two teams contesting the Leinster Final for a fifth consecutive year, Meath regained the title 1-14 to 0-14, the difference being a Colm O'Rourke goal after just half a minute that the Dublin camp felt should have been disallowed for a square infringement.

Only once previously in the entire history of the Leinster Championship had two teams needed a third replay to settle their difference, back in June and July of 1941 when Carlow eventually got the better of Wexford to qualify for the provincial final for the very first time. Exactly half a century later — to the very months — came an action replay, Dublin and old foes Meath providing an unforgettable summer of spectacular football jam-packed with atmosphere, tension and thrills in what was merely a first round clash. Each side could justifiably claim that they could, and even should, have shortened the marathon, but the vast majority of those who were in Croke Park for the games or watched them on television were surely thankful that that was not the case.

Dublin led 1-7 to 1-2 in the first game thanks to a goal from Mick Galvin but a late point by P.J. Gillic earned Meath a 1-12 each draw; second time round it was Dublin who had to produce a great escape act as Jack Sheedy punched a Barney Rock free to the net to tie things up for a second time at 1-11 apiece after extra time; The Dubs held an 0-10 to 0-5 lead with nine minutes to go in the third meeting only for a Bernard Flynn goal and two Brian Stafford points to again extend the saga to extra time, in which it took a Paul Curran point to earn his side another chance; the final instalment was surely the most dramatic of all as Dublin, two points up at the interval, were 0-15 to 1-8 in front with a mere six minutes left and still 0-15 to 1-9 to the good with two minutes remaining on the clock — only to then suffer the heartache of seeing first Kevin Foley grab an equalising goal and then David Beggy fire over a sensational winning point from thirty yards. After a mammoth 340 minutes of incredible action and drama, Meath had finally pipped Dublin by a single point, 6-44 to 3-52.

Fortunes were about to change the following year, however. Dublin, for the second campaign in succession, were called on to play a first round tie, and after an easy 2-17 to 1-9 defeat of Offaly in Tullamore, they chalked up further wins over Wexford and Louth before recapturing the provincial crown — their 40th — with a 1-13 to 0-10 victory over Kildare. The opposition in the All-Ireland semi-final was, to say the least, unusual; Clare had shocked Kerry by four points in the Munster Final to collect only their second ever provincial crown, their only other success being as far back as 1917. They got to the All-Ireland Final that year but lost by four points to a Wexford team that was winning the third of four consecutive Championships and they certainly did not disgrace themselves in their efforts to get to the decider again, eventually going down 3-14 to 2-12. Dublin, despite being odds on favourites, were outplayed 0-18 to 0-14 by Donegal in the final, so much so that it is doubtful if another penalty miss from Charlie Redmond was a real factor in their defeat.

Paddy Cullen stepped down as manager — a year prematurely — after that setback and was replaced by former team mate Pat O'Neill and the team, pulled out of the hat for a first round tie for the third year in a row, notched up wins over Wexford, Westmeath and Meath — by 1-10 to 0-12 — to advance to another provincial final clash with Kildare. This time Redmond was the saviour, contributing five crucial points to an 0-11 to 0-7 victory in a game that was badly marred by a fierce wind and driving rain; that wind, however, lost a lot of its lustre when Derry outpointed them 0-15 to 0-14 in the All-Ireland semi-final, a Johnny McGurk point deciding the issue after Dublin had held a five point lead at halftime, 0-9 to 0-4.

If luck had been against Dublin in that semi-final, it was certainly with them in their opening game of the following year's campaign as, in a quarter-final clash with Kildare, they squandered an 0-8 to 0-3 halftime lead and in the end had to rely on an injury-time point from Redmond to get away with a draw, 0-11 each. The replay went rather better as Dublin, nine points up at the interval, eventually won 1-14 to 1-9, Niall Buckley's goal for Kildare four minutes after the restart being the first time John O'Leary had been beaten in 534 minutes of Championship action, going back to Padraig Conway's second Clare goal in the All-Ireland semi-final of two years previously. Louth were ousted 1-15 to 1-8 in the provincial semi-final and then, in the final, Dublin survived a Meath rally that produced a goal and two points in the final five minutes to hang on for a 1-9 to 1-8 victory.

For the second time in three seasons Dublin faced unusual opposition in the All-Ireland semi-final, this time in the shape of Leitrim, whose only previous appearance at such an advanced stage of the Championship was back in 1927, when they were trained by none other than Michael O'Hehir's father, Jim. There would be no fairytale, though; Dublin marched to a 2-7 to 0-5 lead before running out comfortable 3-15 to 1-9 winners. The final, against Down, was one they might well have won despite the Mournemen's clear superiority for much of the game; the hapless Charlie Redmond again failed from the penalty spot, Down keeper Neil Collins saving superbly just eight minutes from time to help his side to a 1-12 to 0-13 victory.

♜ ♜ ♜

HAVING lost two All-Ireland Finals and a semi-final in the previous three years, Dublin were determined to go all out for the 1995 season and their efforts began optimistically with relatively clearcut wins over Louth, Laois and, in the Leinster Final, Meath by 1-18 to 1-8. Cork, thanks to seven points from Redmond and a goal from Jason Sherlock, were seen off 1-12 to 0-12 in the All-Ireland semi-final and, for the third time in four years, Dublin would face Ulster opposition in the Sam Maguire Cup decider. This time it was Peter Canavan inspired Tyrone, appearing in only their second All-Ireland Final, having been beaten by Kerry nine years earlier.

Not for the first time, Charlie Redmond would take centre stage in a finale drama. From the time Dessie Farrell edged Dublin into a three points to two lead on the quarter of an hour mark they were never headed, and after Redmond had scored the only goal of the game off a Jason Sherlock flick then minutes later to set The Dubs on the way to a 1-8 to 0-6 lead the outcome, it seemed, was becoming crystal clear. That was not the case, however; Canavan fired over three points in succession and then, in the tenth minute of the second half Tipperary referee Paddy Russell sent Redmond off for retaliation against Fergal Logan. Except that Charlie did not leave the scene of the crime; some two and a half minutes passed — during which Farrell tagged on another point — before Russell realised the red carded player was still and the field and personally escorted him off.

Despite being held scoreless for almost twenty-five minutes following Canavan's third second half point, Tyrone gradually turned their extra man advantage into scores and, three minutes into injury time, with the score at 1-10 to 0-12, what would have been an equalising point by Sean McLaughlin was disallowed by Russell on the grounds that Canavan — who got all but one of his side's scores, a points record for an All-Ireland Final — had handled the ball on the ground before flicking it to his wing back team mate. After a wait of a dozen years Dublin finally had their hands on Sam Maguire for the 22nd time. An interesting footnote to the game is that two future Dublin managers took part, with Jim Gavin playing throughout and Pat Gilroy coming on as a second half sub for Keith Galvin a quarter of an hour into the second half.

Redmond gave his version of the confusion surrounding his sending off: 'I'm disappointed the way it ended on a personal level; I thought it was a disgraceful decision. Basically, I was just guilty of reacting. The referee said I head-butted but, if I did, wouldn't you think the lad might have a cut or something to show for it? Anyway, the linesman seemed to be sticking up for me. I thought he told me that 1 wasn't being sent off. That's why I carried on. It's horrible for it to end this way. But, at the end of the day, I went out there to win an All-Ireland Final. We've done that and I've scored my first goal in a final along the way, so it's not all bad.'

Dublin's four most recent All-Ireland winning teams prior to this Pat O'Neill managed one — 1974, 1976, 1977 and 1983 — had all at least retained the provincial title the following year but, after victories over Westmeath and Louth, the history of 1964 repeated itself as Meath dethroned the All-Ireland champions 0-10 to 0-8 despite training 0-8 to 0-6 on the hour mark. Meath repeated the dose the following year but even more humiliatingly, by 1-13 to 1-10 in a provincial quarter-final and the next year Kildare ousted them at the same stage following a replay.

In the final year of the century, after wins over Louth and Laois (the latter following a replay), Dublin were again turned over by Meath, this time by 1-14 to 0-12, and the following year brought another provincial final loss, one of the most heartbreaking Dublin ever suffered. This time the opposition was provided by Kildare, and while it took a Colin Moran point three minutes from the end to secure a draw (0-14 each), the replay appeared destined to be a completely different story; Dublin held a comfortable 0-11 to 0-5 lead at halftime but goals from Tadhg Fennin and Dermot Earley inside the first minute and a half of the restart turned the game on its head. Totally shellshocked, Dublin could only muster a single point throughout the second half — and that, from Moran, not until the 61st minute — as Kildare finished with 2-11.

A year later, in 2001, came yet another Leinster Final loss to Meath but this time Dublin at least had the consolation of a second chance, courtesy of the 'back door' qualifiers. Sligo were hammered 3-17 to 0-12 and then, in an All-Ireland quarter-final at Semple Stadium in Thurles, it took a typically special point from Maurice Fitzgerald to earn Kerry a second chance. In the replay, at the same venue the following Saturday, Dublin rallied from nine points down at the end of the opening quarter but just could not pull all the deficit back as Kerry held on for a 2-12 to 1-12 victory.

The provincial title was finally regained a year later — for the first time since 1995 — with victories over Wexford, Meath and Kildare, in the course of which Ray Cosgrove scored 3-12, including 2-3 in the semi-final against the Royal County. The corner forward from Kilmacud Crokes netted twice more in the All-Ireland quarter-final against Donegal and while the second of them — in the 64th minute — opened up a three point lead for Dublin, a point from Paul McGonigle and two from Adrian Sweeney forced the tie to a second meeting. Dublin made no mistake in the replay, winning 1-14 to 0-7, but came up a point short in the semi-final against Ulster champions Armagh, going out 1-14 to 1-13 after a Cosgrove free in the second minute of injury time came back of an upright and was safely cleared. Cosgrove finished with a total of 6-23 from half a dozen games to jointly top the Championship scoring chart with Armagh star Oisin McConville, scorer of 1-38 from two games more.

The following two years, 2003 and 2004, saw Dublin relegated to the qualifiers after defeats to first Laois and then Westmeath. In the first season Dublin beat Derry but were then beaten by Armagh again — 0-15 to 0-11 — in round three of the qualifiers and in the second they beat London, Leitrim, Longford and Roscommon before Kerry put them out of the picture on a 1-15 to 1-8 scoreline in the All-Ireland quarter-final. Over the following thirteen years Dublin would play forty matches in the Leinster Championship, drawing one and suffering a single defeat and outscoring the opposition by 70-701 to 20-455.

THE first of five consecutive provincial titles was won in 2005, in a campaign that began with a 2-23 to 0-10 routing of Longford and was followed by victories over Meath and Wexford by, respectively, 1-12 to 1-10 and 1-17 to 2-10. The final, against Laois in front of a Leinster Final record crowd of 81,025, could hardly have been closer; Laois, managed by Mick O'Dwyer, led 0-13 to 0-11 with seven minutes remaining but Dublin stormed back with a point from Colin Moran and then two from frees by Tomas Quinn. The latter, better known as Mossy, did it again in the All-Ireland quarter-final against Tyrone when two late points — the second from an injury time free — earned The Dubs a second chance at 1-14 apiece. All to no avail, however; Dublin hit the same tally as in the draw but Tyrone, with Owen Mulligan hitting 1-7, scored 2-18, the most they had conceded in a Championship outing since Kerry fired 5-11 past them in the All-Ireland Final of 1978.

Dublin, a year later, marched through Leinster with wins over Longford, Laois and Offaly and then beat Westmeath — who had come through the qualifiers — in the All-Ireland quarter-final, all without conceding a goal while scoring 6-56 against 0-39. Dublin would leak just a single goal in their five match campaign but it, scored by Mayo sub Barry Moran in the 51st minute, cost them a place in the All-Ireland Final. Martin Breheny in the *Irish Independent* summed up Dublin's collective bewilderment: 'Dublin looked in through heaven's door, liked what they saw and were just about to step inside when Mayo's eviction squad arrived and ruthlessly ejected them from the premises. As the door slammed in their faces, Dublin were left outside in abject misery wondering how an All-Ireland semi-final that seemed comfortably secured when they led by seven points after 46 minutes was surrendered over the closing stretch.'

The story of the following year, 2007, was a similar one. Dublin needed a replay to see off Meath in the provincial quarter-final but then comfortably dismissed Offaly and, in the final, Laois, before claiming an 0-18 to 0-15 victory over Derry in the All-Ireland quarter-final. Kerry, in the semi-final, led 1-12 to 0-9 ten minutes into the second half with the goal coming from Declan O'Sullivan; Dublin outscored the Kingdom by 0-7 to 0-3 over the remainder of the game but it was not quite good enough.

Over the following two years Dublin were handed comprehensive All-Ireland quarter-final defeats, first by 3-14 to 1-8 by Tyrone and then by Kerry by 1-24 to 1-7, a margin that equalled that by which they were routed in the 1978 decider. Dublin began their 2010 campaign with a 2-16 to 0-15 defeat of Wexford before suffering that lone loss; but it was no ordinary beating, it was a savage mugging as Meath, with four second half goals, hammered them 5-9 to 0-13. Tipperary, Armagh and Louth were all overcome in the qualifiers and Tyrone in the All-Ireland quarter-finals but, in the semi-final against Cork, a 1-13 to 1-11 lead with only five minutes left was dramatically turned into a 1-15 to 1-14 defeat.

THE bridesmaid — surely that should be best man — tag was finally shelved a year later. In fact, Dublin were about to embark on their most successful era of some nine decades, surpassing even that of the 1970s.

It began with a 1-16 to 0-11 provincial quarter-final win over Laois, was followed by a 1-12 to 1-11 edging of Kildare — thanks to a last seconds free by Bernard Brogan — and then a 2-12 to 1-12 victory over Wexford in the Leinster Final for a 50th provincial title. Tyrone were eliminated 0-22 to 0-15 in the All-Ireland quarter-final and then a defensively obsessed Donegal were beaten 0-8 to 0-6 in what remains the lowest scoring All-Ireland semi-final of the 70 minute era; a messy game, yes, but Dublin were back in the All-Ireland Final for the first time since 1995. Diarmuid Connolly was red carded by Laois referee Maurice Deegan following a 58th minute incident with Donegal sub Marty Boyle but was subsequently cleared to play in the decider against Kerry.

The final provided a degree of drama in the final seven minutes that would be deemed unacceptably far-fetched in a Hollywood script. Kerry, who had trailed 0-6 to 1-2 at halftime, led 1-10 to 0-9 going into that final phase only for a Kevin McManamon goal then points from Kevin Nolan and Bernard Brogan to edge Dublin ahead entering the 70th minute. The drama, though was far from over as there were in fact two more twists to come; first, Kieran Donaghy levelled matters and then, in the second minute of injury time, keeper Stephen Cluxton came all the way up from his goal to send a 40-metre free unerringly between the Kingdom posts for a sensational match winning point.

Dublin's sheer resilience and determination to win had finally brought Sam back to the city. Vincent Hogan in the *Irish Independent* put it all in context: 'Just as we imagined Kerry to be applying a last coat of varnish, Dublin surged to the Hill with scarcely credible tidings. This was their field, their day. So they met the Kingdom's victory dance with a round of buckshot and everything we thought we knew about hierarchy and lineage suddenly felt counterfeit. For Dublin's total fidelity to a workers' constitution induced palpable despondency in Kerry. To win the closing seven minutes 1-3 to 0-1, the Dubs simply went to a place that maybe no old team could have access to. They reclaimed Sam with a game plan so rigid, so non-negotiable, Pat Gilroy might as well have presented it to them leather-bound and stamped with gold lettering. The team in blue was insatiable, playing as if defeat might curse them all the way to senility. And it felt less a team stretching for home in the end than a whole city reaching out to the glamours of its past.'

The jinx around Dublin retaining the Sam Maguire Cup surfaced again in 2012. Louth, Wexford and Meath were beaten in the provincial series and the qualifiers Laois were ousted 1-12 to 0-12 in the All-Ireland quarter-final, the crucial goal coming from Michael Darragh Macauley eight minutes before the interval. Mayo, who had beaten Down by a dozen points in the quarter-finals, raced into an 0-12 to 0-6 halftime lead and were 0-17 to 0-7 to the good a quarter of an hour into the second half before a Dublin rally cut the final deficit to three points, 0-19 to 0-16.

The provincial campaign the following year was a virtual stroll through Croke Park, at least for the first two games; Westmeath were dismissed 1-22 to 0-9 in the quarter-final, Kildare were handed a 4-16 to 1-9 hammering in the semi-final Stephen Cluxton — sending over four points — and while Meath, in the decider, put up dogged resistance for the first hour, they were eventually ground down 2-15 to 0-14. Cluxton, in the All-Ireland quarter-final, had to have set an all-time record for a goalkeeper by being the team's top scorer with half a dozen points in a 1-16 to 0-14 defeat of Cork. The semi-final with Kerry proved to not only be a classic but one with echoes of the sides' unforgettable 1977 showdown at the same stage of the Championship as Dublin, trailing 3-8 to 1-10 at the three-quarters of an hour mark, struck back with late goals from Kevin McManamon and Eoghan O'Gara for a dramatic 3-18 to 3-11 victory.

The final, against Mayo, represented only the second ever such meeting of the teams, the previous one being in June 1923 when Dublin triumphed 1-9 to 0-2 in what was actually the Championship decider for 1921. Mayo, who after their victory over Dublin the previous year had been beaten in the final by Donegal, were determined not to lose a second successive All-Ireland Final as they had done in 1997 but, after pulling back to level a quarter-of an hour into the second half, they were eventually undone by a pair of Bernard Brogan goals. Still, the margin at the end was just a single point, 2-12 to 1-14, and once again Cluxton had played a crucial role at both ends of the field, not least by putting two points on the scoreboard. Dublin had their first National League and Championship double since 1976.

The jinx struck again the following year, the 40th anniversary of the modern day breakthrough with Heffo's Army. Laois, Wexford, Meath and Monaghan were all brushed aside by an aggregate of 9-88 to 2-49 but in the All-Ireland semi-final Donegal, the side that had played so negatively at the same stage of the Championship three years previously, put on a staggeringly positive performance to tear the Dublin envisaged script to smithereens. Trailing by five points — 0-9 to 0-4 — with ten minutes to go in the first half, they outscored The Dubs by an amazing 3-10 to 0-8 over the remainder of the game. The stunning turnaround sent a message to all underdogs, one Donegal boss Jim McGuinness expressed shortly afterwards: 'Every single county in Ireland has fifteen good players and if they're all fully, fully focused and they've got the heart and there's a good game plan there, they're not going to be far away.'

Leinster was once again steamrolled the following year, Longford, Kildare and Westmeath being collectively outscored 11-56 to 0-30 and then Fermanagh, despite a late rally in the All-Ireland quarter-final, were beaten 2-23 to 2-15. In the semi-final, a repeat of the decider of two years earlier, Dublin led Mayo by a goal at the interval (1-7 to 0-7) and by 2-12 to 0-11 with just nine minutes left on the clock, but the Connacht champions hit back with an unanswered 1-4, the goal coming from a Cillian O'Connor penalty after Mayo wing back Colm Boyle had been pulled down. The replay, the following Saturday, had drama and controversy around it even before the throw-in; Diarmuid Connolly, sent off by Cavan referee Joe McQuillan in injury time in the draw, was cleared to play ... at half past two on the morning of the game.

The second match was essentially a reversal of the first as Dublin, four points down with a quarter of an hour to go, stormed back to outscore Mayo by 3-5 to 0-3 with goals from Bernard Brogan, Philly McMahon and Kevin McManamon giving them a 3-15 to 1-14 ticket into yet another decider against Kerry.

Played in incessant rain and in front of a modern day Croke Park record attendance of 82,300 (eleven more than witnessed Kerry's defeat of Mayo nine years earlier), the game — understandably given the conditions — was something short of a classic but nevertheless it produced an impressively disciplined and astute Dublin display as, 0-8 to 0-4 in front at halftime, held their nerve throughout a tight second half to become All-Ireland champions for the 25th time on an 0-12 to 0-9 scoreline, Kerry's lowest return in a Championship game since Cork beat them 1-11 to 0-7 in the Munster Final in 1974. Martin Breheny, in the *Irish Independent*, noted: 'It was the day this Dublin team came of age, showing a different side to their game as they calmly powered to victory in a game where the extent of their superiority wasn't reflected in the winning margin.' Malachy Clerkin in the *Irish Times*, said of Dublin's defence: 'They took Kerry's screen idols and turned them into cinema ushers.'

After marching through Leinster yet again in 2016 with decisive wins over Laois, Meath and Westmeath, the All-Ireland phase of the Championship took on a decidedly familiar look for Dublin; Donegal, Kerry and Mayo in that order. Donegal, in the quarter-final, pushed The Dubs all the way but a goal from sub Paul Mannion proved crucial in a 1-15 to 1-10 win and Kerry, in the semi-final, gave Dublin more than a few scares in a classic encounter that many compared favourably with the storied meeting of the teams at the same stage in 1977.

Dublin, seemingly cruising along nicely with an 0-9 to 0-4 lead with ten minutes to go to the halftime whistle, suddenly found themselves 2-8 to 0-9 down at the break after Stephen Cluxton, in what was surely the most miserable ten minutes of his otherwise glorious decade and a half career, made a pair of blunders that led directly to goals from Paul Geaney and Darran O'Sullivan. Dublin fought back to be level — 2-9 to 0-15 — after a quarter of an hour of the second half, but by the 62nd minute Kerry were back in front by three points, 2-13 to 0-16. Dublin, in the final fourteen minutes (there were six added) sensationally outscored the Kingdom six to one for a pulsating 0-22 to 2-14 triumph in a game of which legendary commentator Micheal O Muircheartaigh said: 'People have been talking about the '77 semi-final for years; from now on I think the semi-final of this year will be spoken of as well. It had everything from start to finish and Dublin were maybe slightly the better team in the end.'

The final, against old rivals Mayo, was bizarre in the extreme. Despite the fact that no Dublin player got on the scoresheet until Dean Rock pointed in the 31st minute, that score put The Dubs into a 2-1 to 0-4 lead thanks to own goals by Kevin McLoughlin and Colm Boyle in the ninth and 22nd minutes. Then, after leading by 2-4 to 0-5 at halftime and having James McCarthy controversially black carded, Dublin went another quarter of an hour without raising a flag, by which time Mayo had tagged on five points to draw level. The twists were far from over; Dublin pulled two points ahead, were again pulled back to parity, but were three points clear with two minutes of normal time and seven of additional time to come... yet Mayo clawed their way back to snatch a 2-9 to 0-15 draw, the match-levelling point coming from Cillian O'Connor in the 77th minute.

Martin Breheny in the *Irish Independent* summed up the game thus: 'How can a team concede two own goals and not lose and All-Ireland Final? And how does a team survive, despite their six starting forwards scoring only two points between them from open play? Cue yesterday's eccentric contest, which challenged just about every line of conventional wisdom known to sport. It spread through Dublin and Mayo like a contagion before eventually deciding that the best outcome was to invite them to a re-match on Saturday week. They will return with mindsets which has Mayo convinced their time is nigh and Dublin believing that they cannot possibly be as inefficient again.' Neither belief was very far off the mark.

The replay, the first in a final since Kerry beat Galway at the second attempt in 2000, was prefaced by a controversial dropping on each side just hours before the throw-in, Bernard Brogan being replaced at left corner forward by Paddy Andrews for Dublin and Mayo opting for Robbie Hennelly as goalkeeper instead of David Clarke (who had made two top drawer saves in the drawn game); both changes would be reversed in the course of the game but for vastly different reasons. Hennelly had a nightmare game, sending half a dozen of his kickouts to Dublin players and, six minutes into the second half, fumbling a Paul Flynn lob and fouling Paddy Andrews while attempting to retrieve the situation; that got him black carded and Clarke's first touch of the ball was when picking it out of the net from Diarmuid Connolly's penalty kick. Still, Mayo remained competitive to the end and two Dublin substitutions proved crucial in a 1-15 to 1-14 victory; Brogan for Andrews a dozen minutes into the second half and Cormac Costello for Kevin McManamon six minutes later, with the pair scoring one and three points from play, respectively.

Dublin, for the first time since 1977, had successfully defended the Sam Maguire

Cup and for the third time in half a dozen Championships had won it by a single point. As Eamonn Sweeney noted in the following day's *Sunday Independent*: 'In the last 55 years there have been just seven one-point finals. That three of them have come in the last five years and been won by Dublin can't be a coincidence. No team in history has been as adept at finding that little bit extra when things are in the balance.' Dublin also became the first team to record National League and Championship doubles in consecutive years since Kerry in 1932. Dean Rock, who scored a dozen points against Kerry and nine in the final replay, finished the Championship as top scorer with 1-58 in seven games; it was the third highest total ever, behind only Brian Stafford (4-62 for Meath in 1991) and Stephen O'Neill (5-49 for Tyrone in 2005), who both played ten matches.

The bid for a three-in-a-row opened comfortably enough with an 0-19 to 0-7 win over a defensively minded Carlow at O'Moore Park in Portlaoise where the chief talking point was a Diarmuid Connolly altercation with a linesman that subsequently earned the St. Vincent's star a three month suspension. That win was followed by a runaway 4-29 to 0-10 defeat of Westmeath, back on the more familiar ground of Croke Park, and then came a record breaking seventh successive provincial crown with a 2-23 to 1-17 victory over Kildare, a game in which, after Dean Rock had been black carded in the 24th minute, rookie Con O'Callaghan took over the place kicking duties and would finish the match with a dozen points, half of them from play. Monaghan were dismissed 1-19 to 0-12 in the All-Ireland quarter-final and then Tyrone by 2-17 to 0-11 in a semi-final that was marked by what amounted to a no-show by the Ulster champions and a late sub appearance by the back from suspension Connolly. For the second successive year, it would be a Dublin v Mayo decider.

It started as if it was going to be an easy afternoon for The Dubs, with Con O'Callaghan, after a brilliant run, sliding the ball past Mayo keeper David Clarke; it would be the one and only time in the game that the teams were separated by more than two points. By the 20th minute Mayo were in front and it took a Dean Rock free to leave Dublin just a point behind at the break, 1-5 to 0-9. A dozen minutes into the second half Dublin centre half back John Small and Mayo left half forward Donal Vaughan were red carded and after Dublin had edged ahead, lost the lead and regained it, Mayo were two points clear with just seven minutes of normal time left, 1-15 to 1-13. Points from Paul Mannion and James McCarthy drew Dublin level again at 1-16 apiece and Rock edged them in front only for Cillian O'Connor to tie things up again at 1-16 apiece as the game entered injury time. Then, with the clock reading 75:55, Rock, from 40 yards out and to the left of the Canal End goal, immaculately pointed a by no means easy free. Dublin played possession football after that and when Cavan referee Joe McQuillan finally blew the whistle to end an exhilarating game, Dublin had completed the three-in-a-row for the first time since the Championship of 1923. Comparing the latest Dublin hat-trick with the most recent previous one, Martin Breheny in the *Irish Independent* wrote: 'Since the game wasn't nearly as competitive back in the 1920s, yesterday's victory effectively elevates the squad to heights never previously reached by a team from the capital'.

Championship Results

1888

LEINSTER QUARTER-FINAL
June 3, Benburb Park, Dublin
DUBLIN 1–6   KILDARE 0–1
Dublin: G Dalton, T Keating, G McDermott, J Scully, P Halpin, T Connell, W Perry, T McNulty, T Brennan, T Roche, J Cullen, L Gibson, N McLoughlin, W Burke, JJ Walsh, P Fitzgerald, P Stapleton, P McNeill, P Carragher, J Byrne, G O'Neill.

LEINSTER SEMI-FINAL
Sep 2, Clonskeagh Park, Dublin
WEXFORD 0–4   DUBLIN 0–3
Dublin: G Dalton, T Keating, G McDermott, J Scully, P Halpin, T Connell, W Perry, T McNulty, T Brennan, T Roche, J Cullen, L Gibson, N McLoughlin, W Burke, JJ Walsh, J McMahon, P Fitzgerald, P Stapleton, P McNeill, P Carragher, T O'Connor.

1889

LEINSTER QUARTER-FINAL
Sep 1, Bryanstown, Drogheda
LOUTH 2-7   DUBLIN 0-6
Dublin: T Power, J Murphy, P O'Gorman, T O'Driscoll, T O'Brien, P Herbert, J Quane, N Madden, D Sheehan, T Doran, H Cummins, T Whelan, R Higgins, H McCarthy, D Ryan, P Ryan, J Hayes, T Byrne, J Egan, J Mulally, H Thornton.

1890

LEINSTER QUARTER-FINAL
Aug 17, Clonturk Park, Dublin
DUBLIN 6-11   WESTMEATH 0-2
Dublin: C Thompson, D Holland, T Dunne, F North 1-0, P North, B North 0-2, P Rourke, D Whelan, K Quinn 0-1, J Reid, K Fitzpatrick, W Connolly, P McGrath, R Byrne, P Hennessy, M Kearns, JJ Hoey 2-4, R Lalor, P Hore 1-1, G Kennedy 1-1, M Downes 1-2.

LEINSTER SEMI-FINAL
Oct 19, Clonturk Park, Dublin
DUBLIN 2-8   LAOIS 0-1
Dublin: C Thompson, D Holland, T Dunne, P Walsh, JJ Hoey 1-3, F North, D Whelan, P North, B North, P Rourke, K Quinn, K Fitzpatrick 1-1, W Connolly, P McGrath, R Byrne, P Hennessy, M Downes, M Kearns, P Hore 0-2, G Kennedy 0-2, R Lalor.

LEINSTER FINAL
Nov 2, Clonturk Park, Dublin
WEXFORD 1-3   DUBLIN 1-2
Dublin: C Thompson, P Walsh, D Holland, T Dunne, R Lalor, W Connolly, C Dunne, F North, B North, P North 0-1, G Stoker, M Kearns, K Fitzpatrick 0-1, K Quinn, JJ Hoey 1-0, P Rourke, G Kennedy, P Hore, D Whelan, P Hennessy, M Downes.

1891

LEINSTER SEMI-FINAL
Oct 25, Clonturk Park, Dublin
DUBLIN 4-4   WICKLOW 0-0
Dublin: G Charlemont, G Roche, J Roche, J Heslin, J Silke, M Cooney, P Kelly, J Scully, A O'Hagan 0-1, P O'Hagan, M O'Hagan, J Mahony 0-1, D Curtis 1-0, R Flood, S Flood 1-0, S Hughes, T Murphy 2-2, T Lyons, P Halpin, D Byrne, M Condon.

LEINSTER FINAL
Nov 15, Clonturk Park, Dublin
DUBLIN W/O   KILDARE SCR
* Kildare, having beaten Laois by five points to nil in a previously postponed semi-final that morning, refused to play a second match the same day and conceded a walkover.

ALL-IRELAND SEMI-FINAL
Feb 28, 1892, Clonturk Park, Dublin
DUBLIN 3-7   CAVAN 0-3
Dublin: G Charlemont, J Kennedy, G Roche, J Scully, T Lyons, J Roche, J Silke, J Mahony, J Heslin 0-1, A O'Hagan, P O'Hagan 1-1, D Curtis 1-0, S Flood 0-1, T Murphy 1-2, J Geraghty, P Halpin 0-1, M Cooney, P Kelly, R Flood 0-1, M Condon 0-1.

ALL-IRELAND FINAL
Feb 28, 1892, Clonturk Park, Dublin
DUBLIN 2-1   CORK 1-1
Dublin: George Charlemont, George Roche, John Scully, Tom Lyons, Jim Roche, John Silke, Jack Kennedy (capt), Pat Heslin, Jack Mahony, Owen O'Hagan, Paddy O'Hagan, Dick Curtis, Stphen Hughes, Sean Flood, Tommy Murphy 0-1, Johnny Geraghty, Paddy Halpin 1-0, Mick Cooney, Paddy Kelly 1-0, Dick Flood, Myles Condon.

1892

LEINSTER SEMI-FINAL
Mar 12, 1893, Clonturk Park, Dublin
DUBLIN 3-5   KILDARE 0-1
Dublin: G Charlemont, G Roche, J Roche, R Flood, J Kennedy, S Flood 0-1, S Hughes, F O'Malley, T Doran, L O'Kelly 1-0, P Kelly, J Heslin 0-2, J Geraghty 1-1, M Byrne, J Silke, T Errity 1-1, D Curtis.

LEINSTER FINAL
Mar 12, 1893, Clonturk Park, Dublin
DUBLIN W/O   LOUTH SCR
* Louth received a walkover from Laois in the morning semi-finals and Dublin, having had to beat Kildare, initially refused to play the final unless Louth had a match first; by the time Dublin relented Louth had departed and as it was still within the scheduled starting time, the referee, JP Cox, awarded the game to Dublin.

ALL-IRELAND SEMI-FINAL
Mar 19, 1893, Clonturk Park, Dublin
DUBLIN 1-9   ROSCOMMON 1-1
Dublin: G Charlemont, G Roche, J Roche, D Flood, J Kennedy, S Flood 0-1, S Hughes, F O'Malley, T Doran, L O'Kelly, P Kelly 0-2, J Heslin 0-1, J Geraghty 0-4, M Byrne 1-1, J Silke, T Errity, D Curtis.

ALL-IRELAND FINAL
Mar 26, 1893, Clonturk Park, Dublin
DUBLIN 1-4   KERRY 0-3
Dublin: George Charlemont, George Roche, Jim Roche, Dick Flood, Jack Kennedy (capt), Sean Flood 0-1, Sean Hughes, Frank O'Malley, Tom Doran, Luke O'Kelly, Paddy Kelly, Pat Heslin, Johnny Geraghty 1-1, Mick Byrne 0-1, John Silke, Tommy Errity 0-1, Dick Curtis.

1893

Dublin, drawn to play Westmeath, withdrew from the Championship in protest at the Leinster Council's stance on the Parnell Split.

1894

LEINSTER SEMI-FINAL
Sep 23, Clonturk Park, Dublin
DUBLIN 1-11   WEXFORD 0-0
Dublin: G Charlemont, G Roche, P Heslin, T Lyons, T Hughes, J Kennedy 0-1, T Mahony, M Condon, M Byrne 1-1, T Errity 0-2, P O'Toole 0-1, D Curtis 0-1, J Geraghty, L O'Kelly 0-2, P Kelly, J Kirwan 0-2, F O'Malley 0-1.

LEINSTER FINAL
Oct 14, Clonturk Park, Dublin
DUBLIN 0-4   MEATH 0-4
Dublin: G Charlemont, D Curtis, G Roche, P Heslin, T Lyons, L O'Kelly, P Kelly, T Hughes, J Kennedy, T Mahony, M Condon, M Byrne, J Geraghty 0-1, T Errity 0-2, P O'Toole, J Kirwan 0-1, F O'Malley.

LEINSTER FINAL REPLAY
Dec 16, Showgrounds, Navan
DUBLIN 0-2   MEATH 0-2
Dublin: G Charlemont, D Curtis, G Roche, P Heslin, T Lyons, T Hughes, J Kennedy, T Mahony, M Condon, M Byrne 0-1, T Errity, P O'Toole, J Geraghty 0-1, L O'Kelly, P Kelly, J Kirwan, F O'Malley.

LEINSTER FINAL SECOND REPLAY
Feb 24, 1895, Clonturk Park, Dublin
DUBLIN 1-8   MEATH 1-2
Dublin: G Charlemont, G Roche, J Roche, D Curtis, P Heslin, S Hughes, J Silke, J Kennedy 0-1, T Hughes, R Flood, P Kelly 0-2, L O'Kelly 0-3, M Condon, J Ryan, T Mahony, T Errity 1-1, M Byrne 0-1. Sub: T Gilligan for S Hughes.

ALL-IRELAND FINAL
Mar 24, 1895, Clonturk Park, Dublin
DUBLIN 0-6   CORK 1-1
Dublin: George Charlemont, Jack Kennedy, George Roche 0-1, Pat Heslin, Tom Lyons, Tom Hughes, Mick Byrne, Jack Heslin, Tommy Mahony, Myles Condon, Luke O'Kelly 0-1, Frank O'Malley, Paddy Kelly 0-1, Johnny Geraghty 0-1, Paddy O'Toole 0-1, Dick Curtis 0-1, Tommy Errity.
A goal equalled five points at the time.

ALL-IRELAND FINAL REPLAY
Apr 21, 1895, Sportsfield, Thurles
DUBLIN 0-5   CORK 1-2
Dublin: George Charlemont, Dick Curtis, George Roche, Pat Heslin, Tom Lyons, Tom Hughes, Jack Kennedy (capt), Tommy Mahony, Myles Condon, Johnny Geraghty 0-1, Luke O'Kelly, Paddy Kelly, Mick Byrne 0-1, Tommy Errity 0-2, Paddy O'Toole 0-1, Jack Kirwan, Frank O'Malley.
Dublin awarded title.

1895

LEINSTER SEMI-FINAL
Feb 16, 1896, Jones's Road, Dublin
DUBLIN 2-8   KILDARE 0-4
Dublin: T Dunne, B North, F Wall, S Cullen, M Ward, D Whelan, P North, J Matthews, D Adams, S Holland 0-1, M Byrne 1-2, T Knott, P Byrne, M O'Brien 1-2, A Murphy, MJ O'Brien, P Hore 0-2, MJ O'Brien 0-1.

LEINSTER FINAL
Mar 1, 1896, Jones's Road, Dublin
MEATH 0-6   DUBLIN 0-2
Dublin: Tom Dunne, S Cullen, Bartle North, M Ward, F Wall, D Whelan, P North, J Matthews, Pat Byrne, Denny Adams, Stephen Holland, Mick Byrne 0-1, Mick O'Brien 0-1, A Murphy, Tom Knott, MJ O'Brien, P Hore.

1896

LEINSTER QUARTER-FINAL
Nov 22, St James's Park, Kilkenny
DUBLIN 3-12   LAOIS 0-1
Dublin: R Flood, G Roche, T Hession, S Mooney, T Errity 0-2, J Westby, J Ledwidge, J Heslin 1-5, J Mahony, J Graham, D Curtis 0-1, M Byrne 1-1, T Downey, P O'Toole, J Kirwan 0-1, P Heslin 1-2, L O'Kelly.

LEINSTER SEMI-FINAL
May 30, 1897 Jones's Road, Dublin
DUBLIN 2-13   KILDARE 1-12
Dublin: D Scanlon, S Mooney, C Gannon, D Curtis, J Westby, G Roche, J Kirwan 0-1, B Conlan, T Hession, L O'Kelly 0-2, T Errity 1-1, J Heslin 0-5, M Byrne 0-1, J Brady, T Doran, P Heslin 0-1, M Hayes 0-2.

LEINSTER FINAL
Oct 24, 1897, Bryansford Park, Drogheda
DUBLIN 2-4   MEATH 1-5
Dublin: D Scanlon, A Graham, C Gannon, D Curtis, J Teeling, G Roche, J Kirwan, B Conlan, T Hession, L O'Kelly, T Errity 0-1, J Heslin 1-3, M Byrne 1-0, J Brady, T Doran, D Flood, M Hayes.

ALL-IRELAND FINAL:
Feb 6, 1898, Jones's Road, Dublin
LIMERICK 1-5   DUBLIN 0-7
Dublin: J Brady, A Graham, C Gannon, Dick Curtis, Tommy Errity, Jack Teeling, George Roche 0-1, Jack Kirwan, Luke O'Kelly, Jim Heslin 0-1, Jack Ledwidge 0-1, Mick Byrne, Paddy O'Toole, B Conlan 0-2, Tom Doran 0-1, Tom Hession 0-1, Sean Mooney. Sub: Jack Mahony for Conlan.

1897

LEINSTER FIRST ROUND
May 15, 1898, Carlow
DUBLIN 0-14   KILKENNY 0-1
Dublin: D Scanlon, A Graham, PJ Walsh, B Guiry 0-1, R O'Brien, C Gannon, J Fallon, J O'Brien, W Calnan, J Carvan, P Byrne 0-1, J Smith, M Byrne 0-5, M Chambers 0-2, D O'Donnell 0-2, P O'Donoghue 0-3, T Downey.

LEINSTER QUARTER-FINAL
July 17, 1898, Jones's Road
DUBLIN 2-15   KILDARE 0-2
Dublin: D Scanlon, A Graham, R O'Brien, C Gannon, J Fallon, PJ Walsh, B Guiry 0-1, J O'Brien, W Calnan, J Carvan, P Byrne, J Smith, M Chambers 0-1, M Byrne 0-6, T Downey 0-4, D O'Donnell 1-1, P O'Donoghue 1-2.

LEINSTER SEMI-FINAL
Sep 4, 1898, Jones's Road, Dublin
WEXFORD 1-7   DUBLIN 1-5
Dublin: D Scanlon, J Burke, A Graham, PJ Walsh, C Gannon, R O'Brien, B Guiry, P Byrne, W Calnan, V Skelly, P Comerford, J Carvan, P Redmond, D O'Donnell 0-1, M Byrne 1-2, P O'Donoghue 0-1, T Downey 0-1.
* Dublin lodged an objection and a replay was ordered.

LEINSTER SEMI-FINAL REPLAY
Oct 16, 1898, Jones's Road, Dublin
DUBLIN 0-10   WEXFORD 0-9
Dublin: D Scanlon, A Graham, PJ Walsh, C Gannon, R O'Brien, B Guiry, J Seeley, W Calnan, P Matthews, D Curtis, L O'Kelly 0-1, P Redmond 0-2, M Chambers 0-2, M Byrne 0-3, D O'Donnell, P O'Donoghue 0-1, T Downey 0-1.

LEINSTER FINAL
Dec 18, 1898, Jones's Road, Dublin
DUBLIN 1-9   WICKLOW 0-3
Dublin: D Scanlon, PJ Walsh, C Gannon, J O'Brien, T Downey, V Skelly, R O'Brien, B Guiry, W Calnan, L O'Kelly, M Chambers 0-1, P Redmond, J Matthews 0-2, D O'Donnell 0-2, M Byrne 0-1, D Curtis 0-2, P O'Donoghue 1-1.

ALL-IRELAND FINAL
Feb 5, 1899, Jones's Road, Dublin
DUBLIN 2-6   CORK 0-2
Dublin: Dick Scanlon, PJ Walsh (capt), C Gannon, R O'Brien, Ted Downey, V Skelly, J O'Brien, Bill Guiry 2-1, Luke O'Kelly 0-1, Matt Chambers 0-1, J Matthews 0-1, D O'Donnell 0-1, Dick Curtis 0-1, Paddy O'Donogue, Willie Calnan, Paddy Redmond, J Flynn. Sub: J Delaney for Downey.

1898

LEINSTER QUARTER-FINAL
Nov 19, 1899, Jones's Road
DUBLIN W/O   KILDARE SCR
* Kildare unable to field a team; Dublin offered to re-scheduled but were conceded the walkover.

LEINSTER SEMI-FINAL
Dec 17, 1899, Jones's Road, Dublin
DUBLIN 1-16   KILKENNY 0-5
Dublin: J Lane, JJ Keane, B Sherry, T Redmond, D O'Callaghan, P Levey, M Rea, C Sargent, P Redmond, P McCann 0-2, P Fitzsimmons 0-1, J Heslin 0-5, T Norton, T Errity 0-3, J Ryan 0-1, P Smith 0-1, J Ledwidge 1-2.

LEINSTER FINAL
Feb 4, 1900, Jones's Road, Dublin
DUBLIN 2-6   WEXFORD 0-0
Dublin: J Lane, JJ Keane, B Sherry, T Redmond, D O'Callaghan, P Leavy, M Rea, C Sargent, P Redmond, P McCann, J Heslin 1-2, T Norton, T Errity 1-1, P Fitzsimmons 0-2, J Ryan, J Ledwidge 0-1, P Smith.

ALL-IRELAND FINAL:
Apr 8, 1900, Tipperary Park, Tipperary
DUBLIN 2-8   WATERFORD 0-4
Dublin: Jack Lane, John Joe Keane, Tom 'Hoey' Redmond, Bill Sherry, Dan O'Callaghan, Paddy Leavy, Christy Sargent, Matt Rea (capt), Paddy Redmond, Pat Fitzsimmons 0-1, Jim Heslin 0-2, Peter McCann, Tommy Norton 0-1, Tommy Errity 0-2, Peadar Smith, John Ryan 0-1, Joe Ledwidge 2-1.

1899

LEINSTER QUARTER-FINAL
July 8, 1900, St James's Park, Kilkenny
DUBLIN 7-11   LAOIS 0-3
Dublin: J Lane, JJ Keane, P McCann, D Smith, W Sherry, T Errity 1-1, D Brady, J Ryan, M Rea 0-1, T Norton, J Farrelly, P Leavy, P Fitzsimmons 1-1, D O'Callaghan 2-2, J Heslin 1-2, J Ledwidge 2-3, T Redmond 0-1.

LEINSTER SEMI-FINAL
July 8, 1900, St James's Park, Kilkenny
DUBLIN 0-10   KILKENNY 0-2
Dublin: J Lane, JJ Keane, D Smith, W Sherry, D Brady, J Ryan, M Rea, T Errity, T Norton, P McCann 0-1, P Fitzsimmons 0-2, D O'Callaghan 0-2, J Heslin, J Ledwidge 0-4, T Redmond 0-1.
* Dublin were short two players and Kilkenny agreed to a 15-a-side match.

LEINSTER FINAL
Jan 13, 1901, Jones's Road, Dublin
DUBLIN 1-7   WEXFORD 0-3
Dublin: J Lane, JJ Keane, D Smith, T Redmond, B Sherry, D O'Callaghan, D Brady, P Leavy, M Rea 0-1, P McCann, J Farrelly, P Fitzsimons 1-0, T Errity 0-2, J Ryan 0-1, T Norton, J Heslin 0-2, J Ledwidge 0-1.

ALL-IRELAND FINAL
Feb 10, 1901, Jones's Road, Dublin
DUBLIN 1-10   CORK 0-6
Dublin: Jack Lane, John Joe Keane, Peter McCann, D Smith, Bill Sherry, Tommy Errity, Dave Brady, John Ryan, Matt Rea (capt) 0-1, Tommy Norton, Johnny Farrelly, Paddy Leavy, Pat Fitzsimmons 0-2, Dan O'Callaghan 0-1, Jim Heslin 0-3, Joe Ledwidge 1-3, Tom 'Hoey' Redmond.

1900

LEINSTER QUARTER-FINAL
May 26, 1901, St James's Park, Kilkenny
WEXFORD 1-7   DUBLIN 0-8
Dublin: D Scanlon, B Guiry, PJ Walsh, C. Sargent, P Redmond, P O'Donoghuoe, C Gannon, T Errity 0-2, T Murphy 0-1, P Cuddihy, P Gleeson, J Delaney, M Madigan 0-2, J O'Brien 0-1, M Chambers 0-3, J Butler.

1901

LEINSTER QUARTER-FINAL
Aug 10, 1902, Gaelic Park, Terenure
DUBLIN 3-13   KILKENNY 1-2
Dublin: J Gaffney, J Holland, M O'Brien, T Doyle, P O'Donoghue, M Madigan, P Redmond, D Holland, J Darcy, L O'Kelly 0-3, J Brennan 1-1, C Kelly, M Whelan 1-4, T Lawless 1-2, T Murphy 0-2, J O'Brien, J Fahy 0-1.

LEINSTER SEMI-FINAL
Feb 15, 1903, Jones's Road, Dublin
DUBLIN 1-6   LOUTH 1-2
Dublin: J Gaffney, J Holland, J Fahy, M O'Brien, P O'Donoghue, J Cullen, M Madigan 1-1, P Redmond, J Dooley, J Darcy 0-1, J Brennan, C Kelly, M Whelan 0-2, T Lawless 0-1, T Murphy, J O'Brien 0-1.

LEINSTER FINAL
Mar 22, 1903, St James's Park, Kilkenny
DUBLIN 1-9   WEXFORD 0-1
Dublin: J Gaffney, J Whelan 0-1, M Madigan, J Fitzpatrick, J Dooley, L O'Kelly, L Byrne, C Kelly, M Whelan 1-0, D Holland, M O'Brien 0-1, J O'Brien, J Darcy 0-2, V Harris 0-3, T Doyle, T Lawless 0-2, J Fahy. Sub: J Grace for Holland.

ALL-IRELAND SEMI-FINAL
Apr 12, 1903, Jones's Road, Dublin
DUBLIN 2-12   ANTRIM 0-2
Dublin: J Gaffney, J Whelan 0-1, M Madigan 1-0, G Fitzpatrick, J Dooley, J Gannon 0-1, L Byrne, C Kelly, M Whelan 1-1, J Holland, T Brien 0-1, J O'Brien 0-1, J Darcy 0-1, V Harris 0-1, T Doyle 0-1, T Lawless 0-1, J Fahy 0-3.

ALL-IRELAND 'HOME' FINAL

July 5, 1903, Tipperary Park, Tipperary

DUBLIN 1-2   CORK 0-4

Dublin: James McCullagh, Dave Brady, Peter McCann, Jack Grace, Jack O'Brien, Mick Madigan, Tom Doyle, Jack Darcy, Michael Whelan, Tom Lawless 1-0, Mick O'Brien, C Kelly, Jack Fahy, Val Harris 0-1, Jim McCann, Paddy Redmond, Pat Daly 0-1.

ALL-IRELAND FINAL

Aug 2, 1903, Jones's Road, Dublin

DUBLIN 0-14   LONDON 0-2

Dublin: James McCullagh, B Connor, Peter McCann, Jack Fahy, Jack O'Brien, Mick Madigan, Jack Grace, Jack Darcy (capt), Tom Doyle 0-2, Michael Whelan 0-3, Tom Lawless 0-2, Mick O'Brien, Luke O'Kelly 0-1, Val Harris 0-1, Paddy Redmond 0-2, Dan Holland, Pat Daly 0-3.

1902

LEINSTER QUARTER-FINAL

Nov 1, 1903, Jones's Road, Dublin

DUBLIN 1-16   WICKLOW 1-0

Dublin: J Byrne, J Dempsey, M Casey, M Leggat, M Hanley, J Dunne, T Black, J Devlin, T Doyle, T Doogan 0-1, S Mulvey 0-4, T Murphy 1-2, J O'Sullivan, M Flanagan 0-3, P Ashford 0-1, M Byrne 0-2, M Condron 0-3.

LEINSTER SEMI-FINAL

Dec 6, 1903, Showgrounds, Navan

DUBLIN 1-6   LOUTH 0-2

Dublin: J Lane, J Dempsey, D Brady, W Sherry, M Casey, J McCann 0-1, J Grace, E Brady, P McCann, S Mulvey 0-2, P Daly 1-1, T Murphy, J Brennan 0-1, A Wall, T Errity 0-1, PD Breen, J Fahy.

LEINSTER FINAL

May 1, 1904, Agricultural Grounds, Carlow

DUBLIN 2-5   WEXFORD 0-2

Dublin: JJ Keane, J Dempsey, D Brady, B Sherry, W Casey, J Dunne, J McCann, J Grace, P Brady, S Mulvey, T Murphy 0-1, P Daly 0-1, J Brennan 1-1, T Errity 1-1, P Weymes, PD Breen, J Fahy 0-1.

* Match abandoned after three-quarters of an hour due to a waterlogged pitch. A replay was ordered, but the Leinster Council, by six votes to two, decided Dublin would represent the province in the All-Ireland semi-final in the interim.

ALL-IRELAND SEMI-FINAL

June 5, 1904, Shamrock Lodge, Drogheda

DUBLIN 4-13   ARMAGH 1-6

Dublin: JJ Keane, D Brady, B Sherry, W Casey 0-1, J Dunne, J Dempsey 0-1, J McCann, J Grace, P Brady, S Mulvey 0-1, T Murphy, P Daly 1-2, J Brennan 1-3, T Errity 1-2, P Weymes, PD Breen, J Fahy 1-3.

LEINSTER FINAL REPLAY

June 12, 1904, Asylum Lane, Kilkenny

DUBLIN 1-5   WEXFORD 0-5

Dublin: JJ Keane, J Dempsey, S Mulvey, D Brady, B Sherry, W Casey, J Dunne, J McCann, J Grace, P Brady, T Murphy, P Daly 0-2, J Brennan 1-0, T Errity 0-1, P Weymes, PD Breen, J Fahy 0-2.

ALL-IRELAND 'HOME' FINAL

July 12, 1904, St James's Park, Kilkenny

DUBLIN 0-6   TIPPERARY 0-5

Dublin: John Joe Keane, Steve Mulvey, Dave Brady, Bill Sherry, Willie Casey 0-1, J Dunne, Jack Dempsey 0-1, Jim McCann 0-1, Jack Grace, Paddy Brady, Eddie Brady, Tommy Errity, Pat Daly 0-2, Jim Brennan 0-1, Paddy Weymes, PD Breen, Tadgh Murphy.

ALL-IRELAND FINAL

Sep 11, 1904, Athletic Grounds, Cork

DUBLIN 2-8   LONDON 0-4

Dublin: John Joe Keane, Steve Mulvey, Dave Brady, Willie Casey, Bill Sherry, Jim McCann 0-1, Jack Grace, Jack Dempsey (capt), Ned Brady, Pat Daly 0-2, Jim Brennan 0-2, Paddy Weymes, Tommy Errity 1-2, Amby Wall, Jack Fahy 1-1, PD Breen, Paddy Brady.

1903

LEINSTER QUARTER-FINAL

Sep 18, 1904, Geashill, Tullamore

KILDARE 3-13   DUBLIN 1-3

Dublin: JG Hearne, D Brady, JJ Byrne, J O'Hehir, J Fahy, J McCann, J Grace, P Cox, J Archdeacon, P McCann, J Crean, M Kelly 0-1, P Daly 0-1, T Murphy 1-0, P Wemyes, J Brennan 0-1, W Doherty.

1904

LEINSTER QUARTER-FINAL

Mar 19, 1906, Jones's Road, Dublin

DUBLIN 0-9   KILDARE 0-5

Dublin: M Quinn, J Lynch, D Brady, J Grace, M Barry, J Fahy, T Murphy 0-1, P O'Callaghan, P Casey, L Sheehan, J Ryan, M Madigan 0-1, J Brennan 0-2, P McCann, M Kelly 0-3, P Daly 0-2, J Cunningham.

LEINSTER SEMI-FINAL

Apr 1, 1906, Young Ireland Ground, Dundalk

DUBLIN 0-11   LOUTH 0-6

Dublin: M Quinn, J Dempsey, D Brady, J Cunningham, J Lynch, J Grace, J Fahy, M Barry, P Casey, P McCann, M Kelly 0-3, P Daly 0-2, T Murphy 0-1, L Sheehan 0-1, M Madigan 0-1, J Ryan, J Chadwick 0-1, J McDonneil, J Brennan 0-2.

LEINSTER FINAL
June 17, 1906, Wexford
DUBLIN 0-5   KILKENNY 0-1
Dublin: M Keane, J Dempsey, D Brady, J Grace, M Barry, P O'Callaghan, P Casey, T Murphy, P Daly, M Kelly, T McAuley, J Brennan 0-1, M Madigan, J Lynch 0-1, J Chadwick 0-2, L Sheehan, J Doyle.

ALL-IRELAND SEMI-FINAL
May 13, 1906, Jones's Road, Dublin
DUBLIN 0-8   MAYO 1-3
Dublin: M Quinn, J Lynch, J Grace, P O'Callaghan, T Murphy, M O'Dwyer, T Walsh, J English, M Madigan 0-1, P McCann 0-1, J Fahy, M Kelly 0-3, P Daly 0-2, M Griffin, J Dempsey, J Chadwick 0-1, P Casey.

ALL-IRELAND FINAL
July 1, 1906, Athletic Grounds, Cork
KERRY 0-5   DUBLIN 0-2
Dublin: Mick Keane, Dave Brady, Jack Dempsey, Jack Lynch 0-1, Jack Grace, Mick Barry, Pat O'Callaghan, Tom Murphy, Paddy Casey, Larry Sheehan, Jack Fahy, Mick Kelly 0-1, Peter McCann, Pat Daly 0-1, Jim Brennan 0-1, Tommy Walsh, Joe Chadwick.

1905

ALL-IRELAND QUARTER-FINAL
Aug 5, 1906, Jones's Road, Dublin
DUBLIN 1-9   LONDON 1-4
Dublin: M Quinn, D Brady, J Lynch, J Grace, J Fahy, M Curry, J Mulroney, P Matthews 0-1, P Casey 0-1, P McCann 0-1, J Murphy, M Kelly 0-3, T Quane 1-1, P Daly 0-2, T Walsh.
With the provincial championships well behind schedule, Dublin were nominated to represent Leinster in the All-Ireland series.

LEINSTER FIRST ROUND
Aug 18, 1906, Agricultural Grounds, Athy
KILDARE 0-6   DUBLIN 0-2
Dublin: M Quinn, D Brady, T Brady, D Kelleher, M Curry, J Mulroney, P Curley, P Matthews, T Kavanagh, M O'Dwyer, P O'Callaghan, M Kelly 0-1, T Murphy 0-1, T Quane, T Walsh, P Daly, J Chadwick.

1906

LEINSTER QUARTER-FINAL
Mar 3, 1907, Enniscorthy
DUBLIN 1-9   KILKENNY 0-5
Dublin: M Keane, D Brady, M Curry, J Lynch, J Grace, J Mulraney, J Dempsey, P Casey, M Kelly 0-2, J Brennan, P Cox 0-2, L Sheehan, P O'Callaghan, P Matthews 0-2, T Quane, H Hilliard 0-1, T Walsh 1-2.

LEINSTER SEMI-FINAL
May 5, 1907, Showgrounds, Navan
DUBLIN 0-8   LOUTH 0-6
Dublin: M Keane, J Lynch, J Grace, M Curry, J Brady, P Grace, J Dempsey, J Brennan, P Cox, P O'Callaghan, M Kelly 0-3, P Casey 0-1, H Hilliard 0-1, T Walsh 0-2, T Quane 0-1, J Ryan, J English.

LEINSTER FINAL
July 7, 1907, St James's Park, Kilkenny
DUBLIN 1-9   KILDARE 0-8
Dublin: M Keane, J Grace 0-1, J Lynch, M Barry, M Curry, P Grace, P O'Callaghan, P Casey 0-2, H Hilliard, T Walsh 0-3, M Madigan 1-1, T Quane 0-2, J Brennan, M Kelly, D Brady, J Dempsey, J McCann.

ALL-IRELAND SEMI-FINAL
Aug 4, 1907, Town Park, Wexford
DUBLIN 2-7   LONDON 0-3
Dublin: M Keane, T Brady, M Curry, J Grace, J Lynch, M Barry, P Grace, J Brennan 0-1, M Kelly 0-1, P O'Callaghan 0-1, P Casey, H Hilliard 1-0, T Quane, T Walsh 1-1, M Madigan 0-2, P Cox 0-1, J McCann.

ALL-IRELAND FINAL
Oct 20, 1907, Agricultural Grounds, Athy
DUBLIN 0-5   CORK 0-4
Dublin: Mick Keane, Mick Curry, Dave Brady, Jack Grace, Jack Dempsey, Dave Kelleher, Jim Brennan, Mick Kelly 0-1, Mick Barry, Pat O'Callaghan 0-1, Paddy Casey, Hugh Hilliard 0-1, Mick Madigan, Tom Quane, Tommy Walsh 0-2, Pierce Grace, Larry Sheehan.

1907

LEINSTER QUARTER-FINAL
Dec 8, Jones's Road, Dublin
DUBLIN 0-11   KILDARE 0-4
Dublin: M Keane, D Brady, D Kelleher, D Herlihy, J Grace, M Barry, P Grace, M Curry, E Sexton, P Casey 0-1, J Dempsey, P Cox, L Sheehan 0-2, T Walsh 0-3, M Madigan 0-1, M Kelly 0-2, J Brennan 0-1, H Hilliard 0-1, P O'Brien, J English.

LEINSTER SEMI-FINAL
Jan 26, 1908, Jones's Road, Dublin
DUBLIN 2-6   LOUTH 0-6
Dublin: M Keane, J Lynch, D Kelleher, J Grace, D Brady, M Curry, M Barry, P Casey 0-2, M Madigan 2-0, M Kelly 0-1, P O'Callaghan, H Hilliard 0-1, J Dempsey, P Cox 0-1, T Quane, T Walsh 0-1, L Sheehan.
Sub: P Grace for Curry.

LEINSTER FINAL
Apr 26, 1908, Agricultural Grounds, Athy
DUBLIN 1-11   OFFALY 0-4
Dublin: M Keane, J Grace, P Casey, J Lynch, D Kavanagh, D Kelleher, D Brady, E Herlihy, T Walsh 0-1, M Madigan 0-1, P Cox 1-3, J Dempsey, M Kelly 0-3, J Kelly, T Quane 0-2, L Sheehan.

ALL-IRELAND SEMI-FINAL
15 Mar, 1908, McGeough's Field, Dundalk
DUBLIN 1-5   MONAGHAN 0-2
Dublin: M Keane, J Grace, D Kelleher, J Lynch, D Kavanagh, J Brennan, E Herlihy, H Hilliard, P Cox, P Grace 0-1, T Walsh 1-0, J Dempsey, P O'Callaghan, M Kelly 0-2, J Kelly, T Quane 0-2, L Sheehan.

ALL-IRELAND FINAL
July 5, 1908, Tipperary Park, Tipperary
DUBLIN 0-6   CORK 0-2
Dublin: Dave Kelleher, Dave Brady, Jim Brennan, Jack Grace, Jack Lynch, Hugh Hilliard, Tom Quane, Jack Dempsey, Paddy Casey, Mick Curry, Mick Barry, Mick Madigan, Pierce Grace 0-3, Pat O'Callaghan, Tommy Walsh 0-1, Mick Kelly 0-1, Dan Kavanagh.

1908

LEINSTER QUARTER-FINAL
Sep 27, Jones's Road, Dublin
DUBLIN 1-9   MEATH 0-1
Dublin: P Fallon, J Lynch, D Kavanagh, J Grace, M Moore, D Kelleher, J Brennan, M Griffin, E Smyth 0-2, M Collins, T Quane 0-2, H Hilliard 1-2, W Halliden, J Shouldice 0-1, T Walsh 0-1, L Sheehan, P Daly 0-1.

LEINSTER SEMI-FINAL
Oct 18, Jones's Road, Dublin
DUBLIN 0-13   LAOIS 0-7
Dublin: P Fallon, J Lynch, D Kelleher, D Kavanagh, E Smyth, R Flood, M Moore, J Brennan, M Griffin, T Quane 0-3, P Whelan, P Daly 0-5, H Hilliard 0-3, W Halliden, L Sheehan, J Shouldice 0-1, M Collins 0-1.

LEINSTER FINAL
Dec 13, Africultural Ground, Athy
DUBLIN 1-7   KILDARE 0-3
Dublin: P Fallon, D Kelleher 0-2, E Herlihy, Jim Brennan, J Lynch, D Kavanagh, J Grace, H Hilliard, T Healy, M Collins, M Griffin, T Quane, Jem Brennan 0-1, T Walsh 0-1, J Shouldice 1-0, T McAuley, P Whelan 0-1, P Daly 0-2.

ALL-IRELAND SEMI-FINAL
Feb 21, 1909, Jones's Road, Dublin
DUBLIN 1-8   ANTRIM 0-2
Dublin: P Fallon, J Lynch, D Kavanagh, D Kelleher, Jim Brennan, E Herlihy 0-1, J Grace, M Griffin, T Quane 0-2, H Hilliard 0-3, M Collins, Jem Brennan, J Shouldice, T McAuley 1-1, P Whelan, P Daly, P Sheehan 0-1.

ALL-IRELAND 'HOME' FINAL
May 9, 1909, Sportsfield, Thurles
DUBLIN 0-10   KERRY 0-3
Dublin: Paddy Fallon, Jack Lynch, Dan Kavanagh, Dave Kelleher, Jim Brennan, Jack Grace, Mick Power 0-1, Fred Cooney, Tom Healy, Maurice Collins, Hugh Hilliard 0-3, Jem Brennan, Tommy Walsh 0-1, Jack Shouldice, Tom McAuley 0-4, Paddy Whelan, Pat Daly 0-1.

ALL-IRELAND FINAL
Aug 1, 1909, Jones's Road, Dublin
DUBLIN 1-10   LONDON 0-4
Dublin: Paddy Fallon, Dave Kelleher (capt), Jack Grace, Hugh Hilliard, Tommy Walsh 0-1, Jack Lynch, Dan Kavanagh, Jim Brennan, Tom Healy 0-1, Fred Cooney, Jem Brennan, Pat Daly 1-1, Tom McAuley 0-3, Paddy Whelan 0-1, Maurice Collins, Mick Power 0-2, Jack Shouldice 0-1.

1909

LEINSTER QUARTER-FINAL
June 13, Wexford Park, Wexford
DUBLIN 0-18   WEXFORD 0-6
Dublin: P Fallon, J Byrne, E Herlihy, P McManus, E Sexton, J Crean, F Cooney, M Collins, J Shouldice 0-1, T Healy 0-1, M Doherty, M Dempsey, H Hilliard 0-4, J Brennan 0-5, M Lynch, T Walsh 0-4, P Daly 0-3.

LEINSTER SEMI-FINAL
Sep 12, Young Ireland Grounds, Dundalk
LOUTH 1-11   DUBLIN 1-7
Dublin: P Fallon, J Grace, J Byrne, J Lynch, E Herlihy, E Sexton, P McManus, M Collins, J Shouldice, D Brady, T Walsh 1-1, M Dempsey, T Quane 0-4, J Brennan 0-1, F Cooney, T Healy, P Daly 0-1.

1910

LEINSTER FIRST ROUND
June 12, Jones's Road, Dublin
DUBLIN 1-11   WICKLOW 0-5
Dublin: P Fallon, D Kavanagh, D Flood, F Brady, E Letmon, J Brennan, T 0-1 Healy, J Brennan, H Hilliard 0-1, J Shouldice, P Daly 0-2, P Whelan 0-2, T Donnelly 0-4, M Collins, W Halliden, M Griffin, M Keane 1-1.

LEINSTER QUARTER-FINAL
Sep 4, Jones's Road, Dublin
DUBLIN 1-6   WEXFORD 0-1
Dublin: P Fallon, D Flood, J Brennan (Sandymount),

D Kavanagh, D Kelleher, J Brennan (Keatings), W Halliden, T Healy, M Collins, J Shouldice, J Collison 1-1, P Daly 0-1, T Donnelly 0-3, M Griffin, M Flaherty, J Sheehy, E Letmon 0-1.

LEINSTER SEMI-FINAL
Sept 25, Jones's Road, Dublin

DUBLIN 3-7   OFFALY 1-0

Dublin: P Fallon, D Flood, J Brennan (Sandymount), D Kavanagh, J Grace, J Brennan (Keatings), W Halliden, T Healy, J Shouldice, M Griffin, M Collins, P Whelan, P Daly 0-3, M Keane 1-2, H Hilliard, T Donnelly 2-0, E Letmon 0-2.

ALL-IRELAND QUARTER-FINAL
Oct 2, Jones's Road, Dublin

DUBLIN 3-5   ANTRIM 1-2

Dublin: P Fallon, D Flood, J Brennan (Sandymount), D Kelleher, T Walsh, J Brennan (Keatings), M Collins, W Hilliden 1-0, T Healy, J Shouldice 0-1, P Daly 0-1, P Whelan 0-1, M Griffin, H Hilliard 1-0, J Sheehy, T Donnelly 1-1, E Letmon 0-1.

LEINSTER FINAL
Oct 16, Showgrounds, Navan

LOUTH 0-3   DUBLIN 0-0

Dublin: P Fallon, D Flood, Jim Brennan (Sandymount), D Kavanagh, J Grace, Jem Brennan (Keatings), W Halliden, T Healy, J Shouldice, M Griffin, M Collins, P Whelan, P Daly, M Keane, H Hilliard, T Donnelly, E Letmon.

* As the Leinster Championship was behind schedule, Dublin were nominated to represent Leinster in the All-Ireland quarter-final; Louth subsequently beat Dublin in the provincial decider and took their place in the All-Ireland semi-finals.

1911

LEINSTER QUARTER-FINAL
29 July, Showgrounds, Navan

DUBLIN 3-2   LOUTH 1-4

Dublin: F Cooney, J Grace, J Lynch, D Kavanagh, T Walsh 1-0, M Dwyer, D Kelleher 0-1, M Collins, J Brennan (Sandymount), T McAuley, T Quane 1-0, T Healy, C Flynn, J Moran 1-1, T Clarke, M McCaffrey, E Herlihy.

LEINSTER SEMI-FINAL
Aug 20, Jones's Road, Dublin

MEATH 1-3   DUBLIN 0-2

Dublin: F Cooney, J Grace, J Lynch, D Kavanagh, M Dwyer, D Kelleher 0-2, J Ennis, J Brennan (Sandymount), T Healy, H Hilliard, M Collins, C Flynn, G Bailey, L Murray, T Clarke, M McCaffrey, E Herlihy.

1912

LEINSTER FIRST ROUND
June 16, Sportsfield, Portlaoise

DUBLIN 2-2   LAOIS 0-2

Dublin: F Cooney, R Downey, T Quane, J Grace, T Walsh, H Hilliard, R Fitzpatrick, M Kelly, J McDonnell, J Moran 1-0, T Healy, C Flynn, M Keane 1-1, M Collins, F Brady 0-1, D Manifold, M Byrne.

LEINSTER QUARTER-FINAL
July 14, Football Grounds, Athy

DUBLIN 2-3   KILKENNY 2-3

Dublin: F Cooney, R Downey, T Quane 0-1, J Grace, T Walsh, H Hilliard 1-1, R Fitzpatrick 0-1, M Kelly, J McDonnell, J Moran, T Healy, C Flynn, M Keane, M Collins, F Brady 1-0, R Manifold, M Byrne. Sub: T Doherty for Fitzpatrick.

LEINSTER QUARTER-FINAL REPLAY
Aug 11, Jones's Road, Dublin

DUBLIN 3-4   KILKENNY 0-1

Dublin: P Fallon, D Manifold, D Flood, J Grace, M Collins, J Shouldice, J Parker 1-0, W Halliden, T Quane 0-1, T Doherty 2-1, F Brady 0-1, T Healy, C Flynn 0-1, D Crampton, R Fitzpatrick, M Kelly, T Walsh.

LEINSTER SEMI-FINAL
Sep 22, Wexford Park, Wexford

DUBLIN 1-4   WICKLOW 0-4

Dublin: P Fallon, D Flood, D Manifold, J Grace, M Collins, J Shouldice, T Quane 1-0, J Parker, W Halliden, T Doherty 0-1, F Brady, C Flynn 0-3, F Brady, D Crampton, M Kelly, R Fitzpatrick, T Walsh.

ALL-IRELAND SEMI-FINAL
Sep 29, Jones's Road, Dublin

DUBLIN 2-4   ROSCOMMON 1-1

Dublin: P Fallon, D Manifold 1-0, D Flood, J Grace, D Kavanagh, J Brennan, M Collins 0-2, W Halliden, J Shouldice, J Parker, T Quane, F Brady 1-1, C Flynn, T Doherty, R Fitzpatrick, M Kelly 0-1, T Walsh. Sub: P Neville for Fitzpatrick.

LEINSTER FINAL
Oct 20, Showgrounds, Navan

LOUTH 1-2   DUBLIN 1-1

Dublin: P Fallon, D Manifold, D Flood, J Grace, D Kavanagh, R Downey, B Mullen, M Collins, R Franks, W Halliden, H Hilliard 0-1, C Flynn, J Parker, T Doherty 1-0, T Walsh, J English, M Kelly.

* By the time the semi-final was to be played, the Leinster championship was not finished, so Dublin were nominated to represent Leinster. When Louth beat Dublin in the Leinster final, they were given Dublin's place in the All-Ireland final.

1913

LEINSTER QUARTER-FINAL
July 6, Jones's Road, Dublin
DUBLIN 2-2   KILDARE 2-1
Dublin: P Fallon, T Walsh, E Letmon, R Downey, M McCaffrey, J O'Connor, E Caddell, P Neville, P Christie, W Halliden, M Collins, J Dowdall, M Manifold, P O'Connor, C Flynn 1-0. Sub: T Doherty 1-2 for O'Connor.

LEINSTER SEMI-FINAL
Aug 24, Wexford Park, Wexford
WEXFORD 2-3   DUBLIN 1-0
Dublin: P Fallon, T Walsh, R Downey, M McCaffrey, J O'Connor, E Caddell, P Christie, W Halliden, D Manifold, E Letmon, C Flynn 1-0, J Dowdall, M Manifold, J Finnerty, J Crystal.

1914

LEINSTER QUARTER-FINAL
June 7, Sportsfield, Portlaoise
DUBLIN 0-5   CARLOW 0-1
Dublin: P Fallon, R Flood, M Power 0-1, J Marren, A O'Connor, M Brazil, W Halliden, J Joyce, P Lynch, J Brennan, J Parker 0-1, C Flynn 0-2, M Donovan 0-1, W O'Flaherty, T Farrelly.

LEINSTER SEMI-FINAL
July 26, St James's Park, Kilkenny
WEXFORD 4-6   DUBLIN 1-1
Dublin: P Fallon, F Shouldice, M Power, J Marren, P Halligan, T Brady, T Donnelly, W Halliden 0-1, J Joyce, P Lynch, J Parker, M Donovan 1-0, J Shouldice, S Lawlor, T Farrelly.

1915

LEINSTER QUARTER-FINAL
June 6, O'Connor Park, Tullamore
DUBLIN 1-2   LAOIS 1-2
Dublin: P Fallon, F Shouldice, W Brady, R Flood, J Marren, T Farrelly, W Halliden, P Lynch, M Collins, J Doyle, M Manifold, S Synnott, J Kearney 0-1, J Parker, S Lawlor 1-1.

LEINSTER QUARTER-FINAL REPLAY
July 4, St Conleth's Park, Newbridge
DUBLIN 1-8   LAOIS 0-2
Dublin: P Fallon, F Shouldice, W Brady, T Farrelly, W Halliden, P Lynch, M Collins, J Doyle 0-2, M Manifold, S Synnott 1-1, J Parker 0-1, S Lawlor 0-4, P Hughes, J Shouldice, J Fitzpatrick.

LEINSTER SEMI-FINAL
Aug 8, Croke Park, Dublin
DUBLIN 1-2   KILDARE 0-1
Dublin: P Fallon, F Shouldice, R Fitzpatrick, P Hughes, W Brady, M Collins, W Halliden, M Manifold, T Farrelly, J Parker, S Lawlor 0-2, S Synnott, P Lynch 1-0, M Keane, G Doyle.

LEINSTER FINAL
Sep 12, Croke Park, Dublin
DUBLIN 2–2   WEXFORD 2-2
Dublin: Paddy Fallon, Frank Shouldice, R Fitzpatrick, Paddy Hughes, Willie Brady, Willie Halliden, Mick Manifold, Maurice Collins, Paddy Lynch, Tom Farrelly, Joe Parker 0-1, Stephen Synnott, J Kearney, Sean Lawlor 2-1, Willie Sole.

LEINSTER FINAL REPLAY
Oct 10, Croke Park, Dublin
WEXFORD 2–5   DUBLIN 1-3
Dublin: P Fallon, R Fitzpatrick, P Lynch, P Kerins, P Hughes 0-1, W Brady, M Manifold 1-0, F Shouldice, J Shouldice, M Collins, J Doyle, W Halliden, J Parker 0-1, S Lawlor 0-1, Tom Farrelly. Sub: L Kelly for Fallon.

1916

LEINSTER QUARTER-FINAL
Sep 3, Wexford Park, Wexford
WEXFORD W/O   DUBLIN SCR
* Dublin were unable to field a full side after several of their players missed the train; Wexford offered to re-fix the tie for a week later in New Ross but, when Dublin were unable to guarantee to play the game, the walkover was accepted.

1917

LEINSTER FIRST ROUND
July 8, St Conleth's Park, Newbridge
DUBLIN 1-6   KILDARE 2-1
Dublin: P Fallon, J Kelly, J O'Reilly, P Hughes, J Hayden, P Marville, B Considine 0-1, B McAllister 0-1, S O'Donovan, P McDonnell, S Lawlor 1-3, F Burke 0-1, M Collins, J Treacy, T Farrelly.

LEINSTER QUARTER-FINAL
Aug 5, Shamrock Lodge, Drogheda
DUBLIN 0-14   LOUTH 1-4
Dublin: P Fallon, J Kelly, D Flood, J O'Reilly, P Hughes, B Considine 0-2, T Farrelly, J Treacy, B McAllister 0-2, P McDonnell 0-2, S Lawlor 0-5, S O'Donovan, F Burke, P Kerins 0-3, A O'Connor.

LEINSTER SEMI-FINAL
Sep 23, Croke Park, Dublin
DUBLIN 0-5   **LAOIS 0-2**
Dublin: P Fallon, J Kelly, D Flood, J O'Reilly, P Hughes, B Considine, T Farrelly, A O'Connor, B McAllister 0-1, P McDonnell, S Lawlor 0-4, S O'Donovan, F Burke, P Kerins, M Collins.

LEINSTER FINAL
Oct 14, Croke Park, Dublin
WEXFORD 1-3   **DUBLIN 1-1**
Dublin: P Fallon, J Kelly, P Hughes, D Flood, T Farrelly, J O'Reilly, A O'Connor, P Kerins 0-1, P McDonnell, M Collins, F Burke, B Considine, S O'Donovan, B McAllister, S Lawlor 1-0.

1918

LEINSTER QUARTER-FINAL
Sep 8, Shamrock Lodge, Drogheda
LOUTH 3-5   **DUBLIN 3-3**
Dublin: P Fallon, P Carey, J Norris, T Farrelly, D Meade, J O'Reilly, P Cairns, S Synnott, P Lynch 0-1, P McDonnell 0-1, B Joyce, W Flaherty, S Lawlor 3-1, J O'Donovan, B McAllister.

1919

LEINSTER QUARTER-FINAL
July 13, Showgrounds, Navan
DUBLIN 0-7   **MEATH 0-2**
Dublin: J McDonnell, P Carey, P Hughes, J Joyce, J O'Reilly, J Norris, B Robbins 0-1, T Farrelly, Josie Synnott, John Synnott 0-1, B Joyce, B Considine 0-2, S Synnott, F Burke 0-2, P McDonnell 0-1.

LEINSTER SEMI-FINAL
Aug 31, Croke Park
DUBLIN 0-11   **WEXFORD 1-1**
Dublin: J McDonnell, P Carey, P Hughes, J Joyce, Josie Synnott, J O'Reilly, J Norris, B Considine 0-1, C Joyce 0-2, P McDonnell 0-4, B Joyce, B McAllister, John Synnott 0-2, J Dempsey 0-2, F Burke.

LEINSTER FINAL
Sep 7, Croke Park, Dublin
KILDARE 1-3   **DUBLIN 1-2**
Dublin: J McDonnell, P Carey, P Hughes, J Joyce, Josie Synnott, J O'Reilly, Joe Norris, P McDonnell 0-1, B Considine, B McAllister 0-1, C Joyce, B Joyce, John Synnott 1-0, J Dempsey, F Burke.

1920

LEINSTER QUARTER-FINAL
May 16, O'Moore Park, Portlaoise
DUBLIN 3-5   **OFFALY 0-3**
Dublin: J McDonnell, E Fleming, Joe Norris, J Joyce, P Hughes, W Reilly, J Murphy, P McDonnell, B McAllister, B Considine, John Synnott, Josie Synnott, T Pierce 1-3, F Burke 2-1, C Joyce 0-1.

LEINSTER SEMI-FINAL
June 27, Croke Park, Dublin
DUBLIN 2-6   **LAOIS 0-1**
Dublin: J McDonnell, B Robbins, J Joyce, P Hughes, Josie Synnott 0-1, Joe Norris, J O'Reilly, J Murphy, B Donovan, J McAuley 1-0, P McDonnell 0-4, John Synnott, S Synnott 0-1, C Joyce, F Burke 1-0.

LEINSTER FINAL
Aug 29, Croke Park, Dublin
DUBLIN 1-3   **KILDARE 0-3**
Dublin: J McDonnell, B Robbins 0-1, J Joyce, P Hughes, Josie Synnott, J Norris, J O'Reilly, J Murphy, B Donovan, J Carey, P McDonnell, C Joyce, John Synnott 0-1, S Synnott, F Burke 0-1. Sub: P Carey 1-0 for Murphy.

ALL-IRELAND SEMI-FINAL
Sep 26, Showgrounds, Navan
DUBLIN 3-6   **CAVAN 1-3**
Dublin: J McDonnell, W Robbins, J Joyce, Joe Norris, Josie Synnott, J O'Reilly, J Murphy, W Donovan 0-1, J Carey 0-1, P McDonnell 0-1, C Joyce, John Synnott 1-1, F O'Brien, S Synnott 2-1, F Burke 0-1.

ALL-IRELAND FINAL
June 11, 1922, Croke Park, Dublin
TIPPERARY 1-6   **DUBLIN 1-2**
Dublin: Johnny McDonnell, Billy Robbins, Joe Joyce, Paddy Carey, Josie Synnott, Joe Norris, Jack O'Reilly, Johnny Murphy, Bill Donovan, Jack Carey, Paddy McDonnell 0-1, Gerry Doyle, John Synnott, Stephen Synnott 0-1, Frank Burke 1-0.

1921

LEINSTER QUARTER-FINAL
May 1, Croke Park, Dublin
DUBLIN 3-6   **MEATH 0-0**
Dublin: J McDonnell, P Hughes, Joe Norris, J Sherlock, J Murphy 0-2, Josie Synnott 0-1, P O'Brien, T Pierce 1-0, P Sullivan, P McDonnell 1-1, John Synuott, J O'Reilly, J Malone, P Lenihan 1-2, B Donovan.

LEINSTER SEMI-FINAL
July 10, Croke Park, Dublin
DUBLIN 1-6   LOUTH 0-3
Dublin: P Fallon, Joe Norris, A Belmain, Josie Synnott 1-1, T Considine, C McDonnell, C O'Toole, M Shananan 0-1, P Considine 0-4, A Dixon, J O'Reilly, C McGuirk, B Donovan, J Malone, E Carroll.

LEINSTER FINAL
Aug 28, Croke Park, Dublin
DUBLIN 0-6   KILDARE 1-3
Dublin: P Fallon, A Belmain, E Carroll, P Carey, B Robbins, J Norris, J O'Reilly, J Murphy, B Donovan, C McGuirk, M Shanahan, P McDonnell 0-4, John Synnott, Josie Synnott, A Dixon 0-2.

LEINSTER FINAL REPLAY
Sep 18, Croke Park, Dublin
DUBLIN 3-3   KILDARE 1-2
Dublin: P Fallon, A Belmain, P Carey, E Carroll, B Robbins, J Norris, J O'Reilly, B Donovan, J Murphy, M Shanahan 0-1, P McDonnell 1-2, Josie Synnott 1-0, A Dixon, P Considine, John Synnott 1-0.

ALL-IRELAND SEMI-FINAL
June 18, 1922, McGeough's Field, Dundalk
DUBLIN 2-8   MONAGHAN 2-2
Dublin: P Fallon, E Carroll, A Belmain, M Shanahan 0-1, W Fitzsimons 1-1, M Bradshaw 0-1, J O'Grady, A Dixon 1-1, G Doyle 0-3, J Norris, J O'Reilly, T Murphy, B Donovan, J Kiely, T Pierce 0-1.

ALL-IRELAND FINAL
June 17, 1923, Croke Park, Dublin
DUBLIN 1-9   MAYO 0-2
Dublin: Paddy Fallon, Jack O'Reilly, Joe Norris, Paddy Carey, John Synnott 0-1, Paddy Kirwan 0-1, Bill Donovan 0-1, Eddie Carroll (capt), Johnny Murphy, Toddy Pierce 0-1, Frank Burke 0-3, Charlie McDonald, Alec Balmain, Jim O'Grady, Bill Fitzsimons 1-2.

1922

LEINSTER SEMI-FINAL
Oct 1, Croke Park, Dublin
DUBLIN 2-5   KILDARE 0-2
Dublin: J McDonnell, T Gibbons, B Robbins, Joe Norris, J O'Reilly, P Carey 0-1, Josie Synnott, John Synnott, J Joyce, P McDonnell 1-1, B Donovan, J Murphy, M Shanahan 0-2, F Burke, T Pierce 1-1, J Joyce.

LEINSTER FINAL
Nov 5, Croke Park, Dublin
DUBLIN 1-7   KILKENNY 0-2
Dublin: J McDonnell, J Norris, B Robbins 0-1, J O'Reilly, P Carey, Josie Synnott, John Synnott, P

McDonnell 1-5, F Burke, T Pierce, J Joyce, B Donovan 0-1, M Shanahan, C McDonald. Sub: T Gibbons for Joe Synnott.

ALL-IRELAND SEMI-FINAL
July 15, 1923, McGeough's Field, Dundalk
DUBLIN 2-5   MONAGHAN 0-0
Dublin: J McDonnell, T Gibbons, J O'Reilly, P Carey, T Fitzpatrick, B Robbins, J Norris, P McDonnell, Josie Synnott, John Synnott 2-1, B Rooney 0-1, F Burke, C McDonald 0-2, E Carroll, P Kirwan 0-1.

ALL-IRELAND FINAL
Oct 7, 1923, Croke Park, Dublin
DUBLIN 0-6   GALWAY 0-4
Dublin: Johnny McDonnell, Billy Robbins, Tony Gibbons, Josie Synnott 0-1, John Synnott, Paddy Carey (capt) 0-1, Joe Norris, Jack O'Reilly, Bill Rooney, Charlie McDonald, Bill Donovan, Paddy McDonnell 0-2, Paddy Kirwan, Frank Burke 0-1, Toddy Pierce 0-1.

1923

LEINSTER SEMI-FINAL
June 24, St James's Park, Kilkenny
DUBLIN 3-3   LAOIS 1-2
Dublin: J McDonnell, B Robbins, A Gibbons, Joe Norris, J O'Reilly, John Synnott 1-0, Josie Synnott, C McDonald, P McDonnell 1-0, P O'Beirne, W Donovan 1-1, J Murphy, P Kirwan 0-1, T Wheeler, J Henry 0-1.

LEINSTER FINAL
Aug 12, Croke Park, Dublin
DUBLIN 3-5   MEATH 0-0
Dublin: J McDonnell, B Robbins, T Gibbons, J Norris, J O'Reilly, John Synnott, P Carey, Josie Synnott 0-1, J Murphy, E Carroll, P McDonnell 0-2, P Kirwan 1-0, T Wheeler 1-1, B Donovan, F Burke.

ALL-IRELAND SEMI-FINAL
May 18, 1924, Croke Park, Dublin
DUBLIN 1-6   MAYO 1-2
Dublin: J McDonnell, P Carey 0-1, J Sherlock, J O'Reilly, John Synnott, Joe Norris, W Reilly, M Lennon, W Donovan, M Shanahan, P McDonnell 0-2, P Kirwan, Josie Synnott 0-1, J Stynes 0-1, F Burke 1-1.

ALL-IRELAND FINAL
Sep 28, 1924, Croke Park, Dublin
DUBLIN 1-5   KERRY 1-3
Dublin: Johnny McDonnell, Jack O'Reilly, Johnny Murphy 0-1, Joe Norris, John Synnott, Paddy Carey, Paddy Kirwan 1-0, Joe Stynes 0-2, Frank Burke, Josie Synnott 0-1, Martin Shanahan, Jack Sherlock, Paddy McDonnell (capt) 0-1, Paddy O'Beirne, Larry Stanley.

1924

LEINSTER QUARTER-FINAL
Apr 6, Showgrounds, Navan
DUBLIN 2-3   MEATH 1-4
Dublin: J McDonnell, B Robbins, T Gibbons, Joe Norris, J O'Reilly, Josie Synnott, John Synnott 1-0, W Rooney 0-2, C Grace, E Carroll, P McDonnell 0-1, B Donovan, P Kirwan, J Sherlock, J Stynes 1-0.

LEINSTER SEMI-FINAL
Sep 7, Showgrounds, Navan
DUBLIN 2-6   LOUTH 2-4
Dublin: J McDonnell, T Gibbons, Joe Norris, J O'Reilly, Josie Synnott, J Murphy, P Carey, J Sherlock, John Synnott, M Shanahan, P McDonnell 1-1, P Kirwan 1-1, P Synnott 0-2, J Stynes 0-1, F Burke 0-1.

LEINSTER FINAL
Oct 19, Croke Park, Dublin
DUBLIN 1-4   WEXFORD 1-4
Dublin: J McDonnell, P O'Beirne, P Carey, T Gibbons, J Sherlock, J Norris, J O'Reilly, J Murphy, Josie Synnott, P McDonnell, M Shanahan 0-3, John Synnott, P Kirwan, J Stynes 1-1, P Synnott.

LEINSTER FINAL REPLAY
Nov 30, Croke Park, Dublin
DUBLIN 3-5   WEXFORD 2-3
Dublin: J McDonnell, W Reilly, P O'Beirne, P Carey, J Norris, J O'Reilly 0-1, J Murphy, B Donovan, John Synnott 0-1, M O'Brien 1-0, P McDonnell 1-0, M Shanahan, F Burke 0-1, P Kirwan, J Stynes 1-2.

ALL-IRELAND SEMI-FINAL
Jan 18, 1925, Croke Park, Dublin
DUBLIN 0-6   CAVAN 1-1
Dublin: J McDonnell, W Reilly, P O'Beirne, P Carey, Joe Norris, J O'Reilly, J Murphy, Josie Synnott 0-2, P Synnott, M O'Brien 0-1, P McDonnell, M Shanahan 0-1, F Burke 0-2, G Doyle, P Kirwan.

ALL-IRELAND FINAL
Apr 26, 1925, Croke Park, Dublin
KERRY 0-4   DUBLIN 0-3
Dublin: Johnny McDonnell, Paddy Carey, Willie Reilly, Josie Synnott 0-1, Joe Norris, Jack O'Reilly, Peter Synnott 0-1, Mick O'Brien, Paddy O'Beirne, Johnny Murphy, Martin Shanahan, Frank Burke, Paddy McDonnell (capt) 0-1, Gerry Madigan, Paddy Kirwan.

1925

LEINSTER QUARTER-FINAL
July 5, St James's Park, Kilkenny
WEXFORD 2-4   DUBLIN 1-6
Dublin: J McDonnell, P Carey, Jim Norris, W Reilly, Joe Norris, Josie Synnott, P Synnott, J O'Reilly, John Synnott, M Lennon, P Stynes 0-2, P McDonnell 0-1, M Shanahan 0-1, F Burke 1-2, C McDonald.

1926

LEINSTER SEMI-FINAL
June 20, O'Connor Park, Tullamore
DUBLIN 1-3   KILDARE 0-6
Dublin: J McDonnell, P Carey, W Reilly, Jim Norris, Joe Norris, J O'Reilly, P Stynes 0-1, John Synnott, Josie Synnott, P McDonnell, M Lennon 0-1, M Durnin 1-1, J Sherlock, J Kirwan, W Corry.

LEINSTER SEMI-FINAL REPLAY
July 4, O'Moore Park, Portlaoise
KILDARE 2-5   DUBLIN 1-2
Dublin: J McDonnell, P Carey, W Reilly, Joe Norris, Josie Synnott, J O'Reilly, M Durnin, John Synnott, C Grace 0-1, W Corry, P McDonnell 1-1, J Sherlock, J Kirwan, JJ Scanlon, J Mohan.

1927

LEINSTER QUARTER-FINAL
June 19, Catherine Park, Athy
DUBLIN 2-5   LAOIS 0-3
Dublin: J McDonnell, P Flynn 0-1, Jim Kirwan, JJ Scanlan, J O'Toole, J Sherlock, J Lynam 0-1, P Russell 1-1, P McDonnell 0-1, Josie Synnott, M Durnin, P O'Beirne, R Mulcahy, John Kirwan 1-1, G Doyle.

LEINSTER SEMI-FINAL
July 10, St James's Park, Kilkenny
DUBLIN 0-11   WEXFORD 2-5
Dublin: J McDonnell, Jim Kirwan, P Flynn 0-1, J Lynam, J O'Toole, J Sherlock, Josie Synnott 0-1, Joe Norris, P McDonnell 0-3, M Durnin 0-1, P Russell 0-3, P O'Beirne, J Mohan 0-1, John Kirwan 0-1, R Mulcahy.

LEINSTER SEMI-FINAL REPLAY
July 31, St James's Park, Kilkenny
DUBLIN 0-8   WEXFORD 1-1
Dublin: J McDonnell, P Flynn, T Carty, Jim Kirwan 0-2, J Sherlock, J O'Toole, Joe Norris, John Kirwan 0-2, J O'Reilly, P Russell 0-1, P McDonnell 0-1, John Synnott 0-1, Josie Synnott, M Durnin, F Burke 0-1.

LEINSTER FINAL
Aug 14, Croke Park, Dublin
KILDARE 0-5   DUBLIN 0-3
Dublin: J McDonnell, JJ Scanlan, T Carty, Jim Kirwan, J Sherlock, J O'Toole, J Norris, John Kirwan, J O'Reilly, P Russell 0-2, P McDonnell 0-1, John Synnott, Josie Synnott, M Durnin, F Burke.

1928

LEINSTER QUARTER-FINAL
May 20, Pairc Tailteann, Navan
DUBLIN 0-5   LOUTH 0-3
Dublin: J McDonnell, W Reilly, Joe Norris, J O'Reilly, A Perkins 0-1, M Durnin 0-1, Josie Synnott, P McDonnell 0-2, P Stynes, P Synnott, M O'Brien, N McCann, J Quinn 0-1, J O'Shea, J O'Toole.

LEINSTER SEMI-FINAL
July 8, Croke Park, Dublin
DUBLIN 3-3   WEXFORD 0-4
Dublin: J McDonnell, Joe Norris, P Carey, P Synnott 1-0, W Reilly, J O'Reilly, P Stynes, M Durnin 1-1, John Synnott 0-1, P McDonnell 1-1, M O'Brien, A Perkins, J O'Toole, J Quinn, N McCann.

LEINSTER FINAL
July 22, Croke Park, Dublin
KILDARE 0-10   DUBLIN 1-6
Dublin: J McDonnell, W Reilly, P Carey, J O'Reilly 0-1, J Stynes 0-1, J Norris, A Perkins, Josie Synnott, John Synnott 0-3, P Synnott, P McDonnell, M Durnin 1-0, M O'Brien 0-1, J O'Toole, N McCann.

1929

LEINSTER QUARTER-FINAL
May 26, Cusack Park, Mullingar
DUBLIN 3-7   LONGFORD 1-6
Dublin: J McDonnell, M Byrne, J Sherlock, T O'Dowd, P Moore, John Kirwan, J O'Toole, M Langton, N McCann, M O'Brien 0-2, P McDonnell 1-1, G Magan 0-1, T Carroll 0-2, D Hearns 1-0, F Lynam 1-1)

LEINSTER SEMI-FINAL
June 30, Catherine Park, Athy
LAOIS 5-5   DUBLIN 3-10
Dublin: J McDonnell, J Sherlock, M Langton, J Doran, T O'Dowd, J O'Toole 0-1, John Kirwan, D Hearns, J Lynam, P McDonnell 2-2, M O'Brien 0-3, N McCann, W Higgins 0-1, P Moore 1-3, G Nolan.

1930

LEINSTER QUARTER FINAL
June 8, Cusack Park, Mullingar
DUBLIN 2-8   WESTMEATH 0-4
Dublin: J McDonnell, J Sherlock, M Langton, T O'Dowd, J Mohan, John Kirwan, John Synnott 1-1, J Lynam, M Wellington, P McDonnell, M O'Brien 1-4, N McCann, W Higgins, J Mulhall 0-3, G Nolan.

LEINSTER SEMI-FINAL
June 29, Athletic Grounds, Drogheda
MEATH 3-8   DUBLIN 1-4
Dublin: J McDonnell, J Sherlock, M Langton, T O'Dowd, John Kirwan, J Lynam, J Mohan 0-1, John Synnott, M Wellington 1-0, M O'Brien, P McDonnell 0-2, N McCann, J Mulhall 0-1, W Higgins, G Nolan.

1931

LEINSTER FIRST ROUND
June 14, Drogheda Park, Drogheda
DUBLIN 5-6   LOUTH 1-5
Dublin: D Smyth, T Ebbs, W Leonard, J Mohan, M O'Brien, P Synnott, M Durnin, M Kelly 2-1, P McDonnell, J Hickey, T O'Dowd 2-2, W Dowling 0-2, N McCann, T Tyrrell, S Lavan. Subs: J Monks 0-1 for Lavan, D Hearns 1-0 for Hickey.

LEINSTER QUARTER-FINAL
July 5, St Patrick's Park, Enniscorthy
DUBLIN 4-3   WEXFORD 1-3
Dublin: D Smyth, T Ebbs, W Leonard, J Mohan, M O'Brien 0-1, P Synnott, M Durnin, M Daly, P McDonnell 3-1, J Hickey, T O'Dowd, W Dowling 1-0, N McCann, T Tyrrell 0-1, S Lavan.

LEINSTER SEMI-FINAL
July 26, Ballyduff Park, Tullamore
WESTMEATH 2-4   DUBLIN 1-4
Dublin: D Smyth, T Ebbs, W Leonard, N McCann, M Daly, Joe Norris, P Hickey, M Kelly, P Synnott, M Durnin 1-0, J Mohan 0-1, P McDonnell 0-1, W Dowling 0-1, M O'Brien 0-1, A Perkins. Sub: G Fitzgerald for Perkins.

1932

LEINSTER QUARTER-FINAL
May 29, St Conleth's Park, Newbridge
DUBLIN 3-6   MEATH 0-4
Dublin: J McDonnell, P Synnott, M O'Brien, P Hickey, G McLoughlin, M Langton, T O'Dowd 0-1, W Dowling 2-2, A Dickson 0-1, M Kelly 0-1, G Fitzgerald 0-1, M Keating 1-0, D Brennan, J O'Shea, N McCann.

LEINSTER SEMI-FINAL:
July 17, O'Moore Park, Portlaoise
DUBLIN 3-7   WESTMEATH 2-5
Dublin: J McDonnell, W Leonard, A Perkins 1-0, M Durnin, T O'Dowd 0-1, W Dowling 1-1, P Hickey, J McLoughlin 0-1, P Moore, D Brennan, A Dickson, J O'Shea, N McCann 1-0, M Kelly 0-1, M Keating 0-1. Sub: P Synnott 0-2 for O'Shea.

LEINSTER FINAL
Aug 7, Croke Park, Dublin
DUBLIN 0-8   WEXFORD 1-5
Dublin: J McDonnell, M O'Brien 0-2, P Synnott, W Leonard, G McLoughlin, J O'Shea, D Brennan, N McCann, M Keating, P McDonnell, M Kelly 0-2, W Dowling 0-1, T O'Dowd 0-1, P Hickey, C Duffy 0-2.

LEINSTER FINAL REPLAY
Aug 14, Croke Park, Dublin
DUBLIN 4-6   WEXFORD 1-5
Dublin: J McDonnell, W Leonard, M O'Brien, P Synnott, G McLoughlin, J O'Shea, D Brennan, P Hickey, M Kelly 0-2, T O'Dowd 1-1, P McDonnell 1-0, W Dowling 0-1, M Keating, N McCann 0-1, C Duffy 0-1.

ALL-IRELAND SEMI-FINAL
Aug 21, Croke Park, Dublin
KERRY 1-3   DUBLIN 1-1
Dublin: Johnny McDonnell, Peter Synnott, Willie Leonard, Mick O'Brien, Jim O'Shea, Murt Kelly, Paddy Hickey, Gerry McLoughlin, Des Brennan, Paddy McDonnell 0-1, Tom O'Dowd 1-0, Willie Dowling, Charlie Duffy, Mick Keating, Ned McCann. Sub: Jim Kelly for O'Dowd.

1933

LEINSTER QUARTER-FINAL
June 11, Athletic Grounds, Drogheda
DUBLIN 1-8   MEATH 1-4
Dublin: J McDonnell, J O'Shea, G McLoughlin, D Brennan, P Hickey, G Fitzgerald, T O'Dowd, N McCann, G Powell 0-2, P Synnott 0-1, W Dowling 0-2, M Kelly 0-2, P Cavanagh, P Perry 1-1, M Keating.

LEINSTER SEMI-FINAL
June 25, Pairc Tailteann, Navan
DUBLIN 3-6   LOUTH 1-3
Dublin: J McDonnell, J O'Shea, G McLoughlin, D Brennan, P Hickey, G Fitzgerald 2-2, S Flood 1-0, N McCann, G Powell 0-1, P Synnott 0-1, W Dowling 0-1, M Kelly 0-1, P Perry, P Kavanagh, M Keating.

LEINSTER FINAL
July 30, Croke Park, Dublin
DUBLIN 0-9   WEXFORD 1-4
Dublin: J McDonnell, J O'Shea, G McLoughlin, D Brennan, P Hickey, N McCann, P Cavanagh, M Keating, M Kelly 0-3, W Dowling 0-1, G Fitzgerald 0-2, M O'Brien, P Synnott 0-2, S Flood, P Perry 0-1.

ALL-IRELAND SEMI-FINAL
Aug 20, Cusack Park, Mullingar
GALWAY 0-8   DUBLIN 1-4
Dublin: J McDonnell, J O'Shea, G McLoughlin, D Brennan, P Hickey, N McCann, P Cavanagh, M Keating, C Duffy, W Dowling, G Fitzgerald 1-0, M O'Brien 0-2, M Wellington, P Synnott 0-2, C Powell.

1934

LEINSTER QUARTER-FINAL
June 3, St Columbeille's Park, Kells
DUBLIN 2-10   WESTMEATH 1-4
Dublin: J McDonnell, J O'Shea, N McCann, P Hickey, P Cavanagh, F Cavanagh, M Keating 1-1, P Perry, M Kelly 0-1, M Casey, G Comerford 0-4, G Fitzgerald 1-3, P Synnott 0-1, W Dowling, B Beggs.

LEINSTER SEMI-FINAL
July 8, Drogheda Park, Drogheda
DUBLIN 2-8   MEATH 1-9
Dublin: J McDonnell, J O'Shea, M Casey, T O'Dowd, P Hickey, N McCann, F Cavanagh, B Beggs, M Kelly 1-3, M Wellington, G Fitzgerald 0-2, G Comerford 0-3, W Dowling, M Keating, P Cavanagh 1-0.

LEINSTER FINAL
July 29, Croke Park, Dublin
DUBLIN 1-2   LOUTH 0-5
Dublin: J McDonnell, J O'Shea, M Casey, T O'Dowd, P Hickey, N McCann, F Cavanagh, B Beggs, M Kelly 0-1, M Wellington, G Fitzgerald, G Comerford, W Dowling, P Colleran 1-1, P Cavanagh.

LEINSTER FINAL REPLAY
Aug 5, Croke Park, Dublin
DUBLIN 3-2   LOUTH 2-5
Dublin: J McDonnell, J O'Shea, M Casey, T O'Dowd, P Hickey, N McCann 0-1, F Cavanagh, B Beggs, M Kelly 1-1, M Wellington, G Fitzgerald 1-0, G Comerford, W Dowling, M Keating 1-0, P Cavanagh. Sub: D Brennan for F Cavanagh.

LEINSTER FINAL SECOND REPLAY
Aug 19, Drogheda Park, Drogheda
DUBLIN 2-9   LOUTH 1-10
Dublin: J McDonnell, J O'Shea, M Casey, D Brennan, P Hickey, N McCann, P Cavanagh, B Beggs 0-2, G Fitzgerald, G Comerford 1-5, W Dowling, M O'Brien, M Wellington 0-2, P Colleran 1-0, M Keating. Sub: M Kelly for Dowling.

ALL-IRELAND SEMI-FINAL
Sep 9, Austin Stack Park, Tralee
DUBLIN 3-8   KERRY 0-6
Dublin: J McDonnell, J O'Shea, P Hickey, W Dowling 0-1, M Casey, N McCann 0-1, M Kelly, E Beggs, M Wellington 1-1, G Comerford 1-3, J Colleran 1-2, F Cavanagh, P Cavanagh, M O'Brien, M Keating.

ALL-IRELAND FINAL
Sep 23, Croke Park, Dublin
GALWAY 3-5   DUBLIN 1-9
Dublin: Johnny McDonnell, Mick O'Brien, Des Brennan, Mick Casey, Frank Cavanagh, George Comerford 1-6, Paddy Cavanagh, Paddy Hickey, Willie Dowling 0-1, Bobby Beggs, Mick Wellington 0-1, Gerry Fitzgerald, Murt Kelly, Mick Keating (capt) 0-1, Ned McCann.

1935

LEINSTER QUARTER-FINAL
June 9, Pairc Tailteann, Navan
LOUTH 0-6   DUBLIN 0-3
Dublin: J McDonnell, D Brennan, M Casey, F Cavanagh, J O'Shea, P Whitty, P Cavanagh, M Kelly 0-1, T O'Sullivan, G Fitzgerald 0-1, M Keating, T O'Donnell 0-1, D Banville, P Synnott, J Brady.

1936

LEINSTER QUARTER-FINAL
May 24, Cusack Park, Mullingar
OFFALY 0-8   DUBLIN 1-3
Dublin: J McDonnell, D Brennan, G McLoughlin, F Cavanagh, J Rourke, J Houlihan, P Cavanagh, M Mahon, J Fanning 0-1, J O'Driscoll, G O'Reilly 0-2, P Bermingham, M Wellington, J O'Connor, J Lynam 1-0.

1937

LEINSTER QUARTER-FINAL
May 23, Showgrounds, Navan
DUBLIN 1-7   LOUTH 0-10
Dublin: J McDonnell, S Feeney, S O'Leary, F Cavanagh, P Lynch, P O'Reilly, J Green, J Houlihan, L McAuliffe, P Henry, P Mulhall 0-1, J Joy, P Bermingham 0-5, G Behan 1-1, F Henry.

LEINSTER QUARTER-FINAL REPLAY
June 20, Showgrounds, Navan
LOUTH 2-5   DUBLIN 1-4
Dublin: J McDonnell, S Feeney, S O'Leary, F Cavanagh, P Lynch, P O'Reilly 1-0, T Robinson, J Fanning, P Henry, L McAuliffe, J Joy, P Keaney, P Mulhall 0-3, J Brosnan 0-1, P Sherlock, F Henry. Sub: G Behan for Sherlock.

1938

LEINSTER QUARTER-FINAL
May 29, O'Moore Park, Portlaoise
KILDARE 4-7   DUBLIN 3-5
Dublin: J McDonnell, J Molloy, S O'Leary, W Malone, L McAuliffe, P Bermingham, C Rayfus, P Henry, J O'Dowd 0-1, G Hanway 0-1, P Mulhall 1-1, M Fanning, M McBride 1-0, S Sheehan 1-2, F Henry. Sub: M Higgins for Molloy.

1939

LEINSTER FIRST ROUND
May 28, Pairc Tailteann, Navan
LOUTH 3-4   DUBLIN 1-6
Dublin: R Pollard, J Murphy, S O'Leary, W Malone, L McAuliffe, J O'Connor, T Laffey, P Henry, J O'Dowd, M O'Malley 0-1, P Bermingham 1-1, M Quigley, J Brosnan 0-1, J Gibbons 0-3, J Kerr. Sub: P Mulhall for Henry.

1940

LEINSTER QUARTER-FINAL
May 19, Pairc Tailteann, Navan
DUBLIN 1-9   LOUTH 2-5
Dublin: P Dowling, H Donnelly 1-0, P Toolan, W Beggs, G Inghnm, P O'Reilly, B Quinn, M Richardson 0-1, G Fitzgerald, M Fletcher 0-4, P Bermingham, M McCann, M O'Reilly 0-4, P Mulhall, P Power. Sub: J Delaney for P O'Reilly.

LEINSTER SEMI-FINAL
July 7, St Conleth's Park, Newbridge
MEATH 1-7   DUBLIN 0-4
Dublin: P Dowling, P Toolan, G McLoughlin, I Levey, P O'Reilly, H Donnelly, B Quinn, G Fitzgerald, T Jenkinson 0-1, M Fletcher, P Birmingham, M Richardson 0-1, P Power, P Mulhall 0-2, M O'Reilly. Subs: F McLoughlin for Power, W Beggs for Levey.

1941

LEINSTER FIRST ROUND
May 18, Gaelic Park, Drogheda
DUBLIN 2-7   LOUTH 3-4
Dublin: C Kelly, M O'Shea, M Falvey, G McLoughlin, P O'Reilly, P Kennedy, B Quinn, P Holly, J O'Dowd, J Joy, P Fitzgerald 0-1, T Banks 0-4, M Fletcher 2-0, P O'Connor 0-1, J Buckley 0-1. Sub: P Henry for Joy.

LEINSTER FIRST ROUND REPLAY
May 25, Croke Park, Dublin
DUBLIN 1-9   LOUTH 1-4
Dublin: C Kelly, P O'Reilly, G O'Loughlin, J Moore, J Fitzgerald, P Kennedy 0-1, B Quinn, J O'Dowd, M Falvey, P Holly, P Bermingham 0-3, T Banks 0-5, M Fletcher 1-0, P O'Connor, J Buckley.

LEINSTER QUARTER-FINAL
June 1, Gaelic Park, Drogheda
DUBLIN 1-8   MEATH 1-6
Dublin: C Kelly, P O'Reilly, P Kennedy, J Fitzgerald, P Fitzgerald, M Falvey, B Quinn, P Holly, J O'Dowd 0-1, P Bermingham, T McCann, T Banks 0-6, M Fletcher 0-1, P O'Connor 1-0, M O'Reilly. Sub: M Richardson for Bermingham.

LEINSTER SEMI-FINAL
July 13, Croke Park, Dublin
DUBLIN 2-11   KILDARE 2-10
Dublin: C Kelly, P O'Reilly, P Kennedy, I Leavey, P Henry, M Falvey, B Quinn, P Holly, J O'Dowd, J Joy 0-2, G Fitzgerald 0-2, T Banks 0-6, J Counihan 0-1, P O'Connor, M Fletcher 2-0.

ALL-IRELAND SEMI-FINAL
Aug 10, Croke Park, Dublin
DUBLIN 0-4   KERRY 0-4
Dublin: C Kelly, P O'Reilly, P Kennedy, J Murphy, G Fitzgerald, M Falvey, B Quinn, P Holly, J O'Dowd, J Joy, P O'Connor 0-1, T Banks 0-3, J Counihan, J Gibbons, M Fletcher. Sub: S Prestage for O Dubhda.

ALL-IRELAND SEMI-FINAL REPLAY
Aug 17, Austin Stack Park, Tralee
KERRY 2-9   DUBLIN 0-3
Dublin: C Kelly, P O'Reilly, P Kennedy, J Murphy, G Fitzgerald, M Falvey, B Quinn, J Gibbons, P Holly, J Joy 0-1, P Bermingham, T Banks 0-2, J Counihan, P O'Connor, M Fletcher. Sub: T McCann for Counihan.

LEINSTER FINAL
Nov 9, Dr Cullen Park, Carlow
DUBLIN 4-6   CARLOW 1-4
Dublin: C Kelly, J Murphy, P Kennedy, C Crone, P O'Reilly, M Falvey, B Quinn, C Martin 0-1, J Fitzgerald, J Joy 0-1, G Fitzgerald 1-0, T Banks 0-4, M Fletcher 1-0, P O'Connor 1-0, T McCann 1-0.
* The provincial final was delayed due to an outbreak of foot and mouth disease in the Carlow area; Dublin were nominated by the Leinster Council to represent the province in the All-Ireland series.

1942

LEINSTER QUARTER-FINAL
May 10, Cusack Park, Mullingar
DUBLIN 0-7   LONGFORD 0-7
Dublin: C Kelly, J Murphy, P Kennedy, C Crone, P O'Reilly, B Beggs, B Quinn, J Fitzgerald, M Falvey, G Fitzgerald, J Ward, T Banks 0-4, M Fletcher 0-2, P O'Connor 0-1, M Quigley.

LEINSTER QUARTER-FINAL REPLAY
May 24, Croke Park, Dublin
DUBLIN 2-15   LONGFORD 1-3
Dublin: C Kelly, J Murphy, P Kennedy, C Crone, P Henry, B Beggs, B Quinn, J Fitzgerald, M Falvey, P O'Reilly, G Fitzgerald 1-4, T Banks 0-7, M Fletcher, P O'Connor 1-3, M Quigley. Sub: J Joy 0-1 for Quigley.

LEINSTER SEMI-FINAL
May 31, Athletic Grounds, Drogheda
DUBLIN 3-5   MEATH 1-10
Dublin: C Kelly, P O'Reilly, P Kennedy, C Crone, P Henry, B Beggs, B Quinn, M Falvey, J Fitzgerald, S McCarthy 1-1, G Fitzgerald, T Banks 0-4, M Fletcher, P O'Connor 1-0, M Quigley 1-0.

LEINSTER FINAL
July 19, Catherine Park, Athy
DUBLIN 0-8   CARLOW 0-6
Dublin: C Kelly, J Murphy, P Kennedy, C Crone, P Henry, P O'Reilly, J Fitzgerald, M Falvey, S McCarthy, J Joy 0-1, G Fitzgerald 0-1, B Quinn 0-1, P Bermingham, P O'Connor 0-1, T Banks 0-4.

ALL-IRELAND SEMI-FINAL
Aug 2, Croke Park, Dublin
DUBLIN 1-6   CAVAN 1-3
Dublin: C Kelly, J Murphy, P Kennedy 1-0, C Crone, P Henry, P O'Reilly, J Fitzgerald, M Falvey, G Fitzgerald 0-1, J Joy, P Bermingham, T Banks 0-4, S McCarthy 0-1, P O'Connor, B Quinn.

ALL-IRELAND FINAL
Sep 20, Croke Park, Dublin
DUBLIN 1-10   GALWAY 1-8
Dublin: Charlie Kelly, Bobby Beggs, Paddy Kennedy, Caleb Crone, Paddy Henry, Peter O'Reilly, Brendan Quinn, Joe Fitzgerald (capt), Mick Falvey 0-1, Jimmy Joy 0-2, Paddy Bermingham, Gerry Fitzgerald 1-0, Matt Fletcher 0-1, Piaddy O'Connor 0-1, Tommy Banks 0-5.

1943

LEINSTER QUARTER-FINAL
May 30, Athletic Grounds, Drogheda
LOUTH 1-6   DUBLIN 1-5
Dublin: F Ryan, S Healy, P Kennedy, C Crone, P Henry, P O'Reilly, B Quinn, J Fitzgerald, V Duffy, J Joy, M Falvey, P Bermingham 0-1, M Fletcher, P O'Connor 0-1, T Banks 1-2.

1944

LEINSTER FIRST ROUND
May 28, Athletic Grounds, Drogheda
DUBLIN 1-8   MEATH 1-6
Dublin: R Fagan, T Moore, P Kennedy, T Staunton, T

Lawlor, P McIntyre, D O'Sullivan, M Falvey, M Culhane 0-3, M Wall, P Bermingham 0-2, S McCarthy 0-1, B Devlin 0-1, P O'Connor 1-1, J Counihan. Sub: S O'Mahony for Wall.

LEINSTER QUARTER-FINAL:
June 18, Croke Park, Dublin
DUBLIN 2-10   LOUTH 3-6
Dublin: R Fagan, T Moore, P Kennedy, T Lawlor, S O'Mahony, P O'Reilly, T Lawlor, M Falvey 0-1, B Maguire 1-1, P Bermingham 0-1, S McCarthy, M Culhane 0-2, JJ Maher 0-5, P O'Connor 1-0, J Counihan.

LEINSTER SEMI-FINAL
July 9, Cusack Park, Mullingar
DUBLIN 2-2   LONGFORD 1-4
Dublin: R Fagan, P McIntyre, T Moore, T Staunton, S O'Mahony, P O'Reilly, T Lawlor, M Culhane 1-0, M Falvey 0-2, P Bermingham, S McCarthy, B Maguire, J Counihan, P O'Connor 1-0, JJ Maher.

LEINSTER FINAL
July 30, Catherine Park, Athy
CARLOW 2-6   DUBLIN 1-6
Dublin: R Fagan, P McIntyre, S McCarthy, D O'Sullivan, S O'Mahony, P O'Reilly, T Lawlor, M Falvey, M Culhane 0-2, P Berminingham 0-1, JJ Maher 0-1, G Fitzgerald, J Counihan 1-0, B Murphy, B Maguire 0-2.

1945

LEINSTER QUARTER-FINAL
June 10, Athletic Grounds, Drogheda
DUBLIN 4-3   MEATH 3-6
Dublin: G Ingham, P McIntyre, P Kennedy, M O'Reilly, J Lowry, P O'Reilly, S Healy, P Neville, B Quinn, M Falvey, M Culhane 2-0, P Bermingham 0-1, T Markey 1-0, J Gibbons 1-2, JJ Maher.

LEINSTER QUARTER-FINAL REPLAY
June 17, Croke Park, Dublin
MEATH 2-16   DUBLIN 1-10
Dublin: G Ingham, J Murphy, P Kennedy, P McIntyre, S O'Mahony, P O'Reilly, S Healy, M Falvey, P Neville, M Culhane 0-2, M Kelly 0-4, B Quinn, T Markey 0-2, J Gibbons 1-2, M Fletcher 0-1.

1946

LEINSTER FIRST ROUND
May 19, Catherine Park, Athy
LAOIS 1-3   DUBLIN 0-5
Dublin: G Ingham, J Kiely, P Toolin, S Healy, P O'Reilly, M Falvey, B Quinn, M Ryan 0-1, D O'Sullivan, G Fitzgerald, T Leahy, M Killeen 0-2, M Fletcher 0-1, M Kelly, M O'Reilly 0-1. Sub: T Markey for Kelly.

1947

LEINSTER FIRST ROUND
May 18, Cusack Park, Mullingar
DUBLIN 1-11   LONGFORD 0-5
Dublin: R Fagan, J Kiely, A Breslin, J McAuley, J Lowry, M Falvey, B Quinn, T Leahy 0-3, B McCarthy, C Manning 0-1, G Fitzgerald, N Dolan 1-1, D McEvoy, P Thornton 0-3, M O'Reilly 0-3.

LEINSTER QUARTER-FINAL
June 1, Pairc Tailteann, Navan
LOUTH 3-11   DUBLIN 1-9
Dublin: R Fagan, J Kiely, A Breslin, J Lowry, M Falvey, B Quinn, B McCarthy, T Leahy, C Manning, N Dolan 0-1, D Byrne 1-5, D McEvoy, M O'Reilly 0-2, P Thornton, S O'Callaghan 0-1. Sub: M Costelloe for Lowry.

1948

LEINSTER QUARTER-FINAL
June 13, Croke Park, Dublin
LOUTH 1-8   DUBLIN 0-6
Dublin: T O'Neill, D Mahony, A Breslin, S Healy, A Donnelly, J Leonard, P Cahalane, D McEvoy, M Byrne 0-1, C Manning, O Freaney 0-2, N Dolan 0-2, R Corcoran, C Smith 0-1, C Cooney.

1949

LEINSTER FIRST ROUND
May 1, Cusack Park, Mullingar
DUBLIN 2-9   LONGFORD 2-5
Dublin: V Russell, L Ledwidge, T Dunleavy, J Sullivan, J McArdle, D Mahony, L Synnott, J Tunney 0-1, D McEvoy 1-0, K Heffernan 0-5, E Carroll 1-1, C Manning 0-1, D Byrne, E Kenneally, P Walsh.

LEINSTER QUARTER-FINAL
June 5, O'Moore Park, Portlaoise
OFFALY 4-7   DUBLIN 3-7
Dublin: V Russell, L Ledwidge, M Falvey, R Dempsey, A Halpin, J Lavin, G McArdle, E Carroll 0-1, D McEvoy, K Heffernan 1-5, M Whelan, C Manning, J O'Connor 0-1, E Kenneally, P Walsh 2-0. Sub: D Mahony for Dempsey.

1950

LEINSTER FIRST ROUND
May 7, Cusack Park, Mullingar
KILDARE 2-11   DUBLIN 1-9
Dublin: V Russell, R Finnegan, J Lavin, N Fingleton, L Donnelly, R Healy, N Maher, M Whelan, R Bradley, S O'Callaghan 0-2, O Freaney 1-1, C Freaney, D Ferguson, E Kenneally 0-1, K Heffernan 0-5, J Tunney.

1951

LEINSTER FIRST ROUND
May 20, St Conleth's Park, Newbridge
DUBLIN 1-8   OFFALY 1-3
Dublin: V Russell, N Allen, J Lavin, M Scanlon, D Mahony, D O'Sullivan, F McCready, J Tunney 0-1, J Crowley 0-1, M Whelan 0-1, O Freaney, P Fitzgerald 1-0, L Collins 0-2, T Jennings, K Heffernan 0-2.
Sub: C O'Leary 0-1 for Tunney.

LEINSTER QUARTER-FINAL
June 3, Athletic Grounds, Drogheda
MEATH 0-11   DUBLIN 1-5
Dublin: V Russell, N Allen, J Lavin, D Mahony, D O'Sullivan, M Rickard, J Crowley, J Tunney, D Ferguson, O Freaney, M Whelan, L Collins, T Jennings 0-1, K Heffernan 1-4.
Subs: K Maher for Rickard, T Mahony for D Mahony.

1952

LEINSTER QUARTER-FINAL
May 25, Athletic Grounds, Drogheda
MEATH 2-7   DUBLIN 2-5
Dublin: G O'Toole, M Moylan, J Lavin, N Allen, S McGuinness, D O'Sullivan, F McCready, J Crowley 0-1, M Whelan, D Ferguson 1-1, C O'Leary, M Murphy, O Freaney 0-1, T Young, K Heffernan 1-2. Sub: D Mahony for McCready.

1953

LEINSTER QUARTER-FINAL
May 24, Pairc Tailteann, Navan
MEATH 2-6   DUBLIN 2-5
Dublin: T O'Grady, D Mahony, M Moylan, M Wilson, L Donnelly, N Allen, N Maher, M Whelan, J Crowley, D Ferguson 1-0, O Freaney 0-1, C O'Leary 1-1, B Atkins 0-1, T Young, K Heffernan 0-2.

1954

LEINSTER QUARTER-FINAL
May 23, Drogheda Park, Drogheda
DUBLIN 0-11   LOUTH 0-2
Dublin: M Mangan, D Mahony, J Lavin, M Moylan, N Allen, L Donnelly, N Maher, J Crowley 0-1, M Whelan 0-1, J Boyle 0-1, D Ferguson, C O'Leary 0-4, B Atkins, T Young 0-1, K Heffernan 0-1. Sub: O Freaney 0-2, for Atkins.

LEINSTER SEMI-FINAL
July 4, O'Moore Park, Portlaoise
OFFALY 2-5   DUBLIN 2-4
Dublin: M Mangan, D Mahony, J Lavin, M Wilson, S Scally, N Allen, N Maher, M Whelan, J Crowley, O Freaney 0-2, D Ferguson 1-0, C O'Leary, T Young, K Heffernan 1-2. Sub: M Moylan for Scally.

1955

LEINSTER QUARTER-FINAL
May 22, St Conleth's Park, Newbridge
DUBLIN 3-9   CARLOW 0-6
Dublin: P O'Flaherty, D Mahony, J Lavin, M Moylan, B Monks, N Allen, N Maher, J Crowley, M Whelan, D Ferguson 0-1, O Freaney 0-4, C O'Leary 1-1, P Haughey 0-1, K Heffernan 1-0, J Boyle 1-2.

LEINSTER SEMI-FINAL
July 10, O'Moore Park, Portlaoise
DUBLIN 1-9   OFFALY 2-3
Dublin: P O'Flaherty, D Mahony, J Lavin, M Moylan, B Monks, N Allen 0-1, N Maher, J Crowley, M Whelan, D Ferguson 1-0, O Freaney 0-5, C O'Leary 0-1, P Haughey, K Heffernan 0-1, J Boyle 0-1.

LEINSTER FINAL
July 24, Croke Park, Dublin
DUBLIN 5-12   MEATH 0-7
Dublin: P O'Flaherty, D Mahony, J Lavin, M Moylan, B Monks, N Allen, N Maher, J Crowley, S McGuinness, D Ferguson 1-1, O Freaney 0-5, C O'Leary 1-2, P Haughey 0-1, K Heffernan 2-0, J Boyle 1-3.

ALL-IRELAND SEMI-FINAL
Aug 21, Croke Park, Dublin
DUBLIN 0-7   MAYO 1-4
Dublin: P O'Flaherty, D Mahony, J Lavin, M Moylan, B Monks, M Wilson, N Maher 0-1, J Crowley, M Whelan, D Ferguson, O Freaney 0-4, C O'Leary 0-2, P Haughey, K Heffernan, J Boyle. Subs: C Freaney for O Freaney, S McGuinness for Monks.

ALL-IRELAND SEMI-FINAL REPLAY
Sep 11, Croke Park, Dublin
DUBLIN 1-8   MAYO 1-7
Dublin: P O'Flaherty, D Mahony, J Lavin, M Moylan, M Whelan 0-1, J Crowley, N Maher 0-1, S McGuinness, M Wilson, D Ferguson, O Freaney 1-4, C O'Leary, P Haughey, K Heffernan 0-2, J Boyle.

ALL-IRELAND FINAL
Sep 25, Croke Park, Dublin
KERRY 0-12   DUBLIN 1-6
Dublin: Paddy O'Flaherty, Denis Mahony (capt), Jim Lavin, Mick Moylan, Maurice Whelan, Jim Crowley, Nicky Maher, Seamus McGuinness, Cathal O'Leary,

Des Ferguson, Ollie Freaney 1-2, Johnny Boyle 0-3, Padraig Haughey, Kevin Heffernan 0-1, Cyril Freaney. Subs: Terry Jennings for McGuinness, Billy Monks for Jennings.

1956

LEINSTER QUARTER-FINAL
May 27, St Patrick's Park, Enniscorthy
DUBLIN 0-11   WICKLOW 0-5
Dublin: P O'Flaherty, D Mahony, J Lavin, M Moylan, M Wilson 0-1, N Allen 0-1, N Maher, J Crowley, M Whelan, J Boyle 0-4, O Freaney 0-3, C O'Leary, D Ferguson, K Heffernan 0-1, P Brennan 0-1.

LEINSTER SEMI-FINAL
June 24, Dr Cullen Park, Carlow
WEXFORD 2-7   DUBLIN 0-7
Dublin: P O'Flaherty, D Mahony, J Lavin, M Moylan, M Whelan, N Allen, N Maher, S McGuinness, C O'Leary, J Boyle 0-1, O Freaney 0-2, J Joyce, D Ferguson 0-3, M Cleary 0-1, P Brennan. Subs: S Manning for Mahony, D Carroll for Joyce.

1957

LEINSTER QUARTER-FINAL
June 2, Cusack Park, Mullingar
DUBLIN 2-10   LONGFORD 1-4
Dublin: P O'Flaherty, D Mahony, J Lavin, T Glllen, M Whelan, M Wilson, N Maher, J Crowley, P Downey, D Ferguson, O Freaney 0-7, C O'Leary 0-1, R Conroy, K Heffernan 1-2, J Boyle 1-0.

LEINSTER SEMI-FINAL
June 23, St Conleth's Park, Newbridge
DUBLIN 3-9   WICKLOW 0-9
Dublin: P O'Flaherty, D Mahony, J Lavin, T Gillen, M Whelan, M Wilson, N Maher, J Crowley, P Downey, D Ferguson 0-2, O Freaney 0-1, C O'Leary, R Conroy 1-1, K Heffernan 0-3, J Boyle 2-2.

LEINSTER FINAL
July 7, Croke Park, Dublin
LOUTH 2-9   DUBLIN 1-7
Dublin: P O'Flaherty, D Mahony, J Lavin, T Gillen, M Whelan, M Wilson, L Foley, J Crowley, P Downey 0-1, D Ferguson 1-1, O Freaney 0-4, C O'Leary 0-1, R Conroy, K Heffernan, J Boyle. Subs: N Maher for Foley, P Barrett for Conroy, P Heron for Freaney.

1958

LEINSTER QUARTER-FINAL
June 1, Drogheda Park, Drogheda
DUBLIN 1-12   MEATH 2-7
Dublin: P O'Flaherty, M Wilson, Joe Timmons, J Brennan, C O'Leary, J Crowley, J Boyle, S Murray, L Foley 1-0, P Haughey, O Freaney 0-6, D Ferguson 0-1, J Joyce 0-2, John Timmons, K Heffernan 0-2. Subs: B Leavey for Timmons, P Farnan 0-1 for Haughey.

LEINSTER SEMI-FINAL
June 22, O'Moore Park, Portlaoise
DUBLIN 3-9   CARLOW 2-7
Dublin: P O'Flaherty, M Wilson, Joe Timmons, J Brennan, C O'Leary, J Crowley, J Boyle, L Foley, S Murray, P Haughey, O Freaney 0-5, D Ferguson 0-1, P Farnon 0-1, J Joyce 2-1, K Heffernan 1-1.

LEINSTER FINAL
July 20, Croke Park, Dublin
DUBLIN 1-11   LOUTH 1-6
Dublin: P O'Flaherty, M Whelan, M Wilson, J Timmons, C O'Leary, J Crowley, J Boyle, S Murray, John Timmons 0-2, P Haughey, O Freaney 0-6, D Ferguson, P Farnan 0-2, J Joyce, K Heffernan 1-1. Sub: L Foley for O'Leary.

ALL-IRELAND SEMI-FINAL
Aug 17, Croke Park, Dublin
DUBLIN 2-7   GALWAY 1-9
Dublin: P O'Flaherty, L Foley, M Wilson, Joe Timmons, C O'Leary, J Crowley, J Brennan, John Timmons, S Murray, P Haughey 0-1, O Freaney 0-4, D Ferguson, P Farnan, J Joyce 2-2, K Heffernan. Sub: M Whelan for Brennan.

ALL-IRELAND FINAL
Sep 28, Croke Park, Dublin
DUBLIN 2-12   DERRY 1-9
Dublin: Paddy O'Flaherty, Lar Foley, Marcus Wilson, Joe Timmons, Cathal O'Leary, Jim Crowley, Johnny Boyle, John Timmons 0-1, Sean Murray, Padraig Haughey, Ollie Freaney 0-8, Dessie Ferguson, Paddy Farnan 1-1, Johnny Joyce 1-0, Kevin Heffernan (capt) 0-2. Subs: Maurice Whelan for Foley, Paddy Downey for Joe Timmons.

1959

LEINSTER QUARTER-FINAL
May 24, O'Moore Park, Portlaoise
DUBLIN 1-11   CARLOW 2-4
Dublin: P O'Flaherty L Foley, Joe Timmons, C O'Leary, J Crowiey, J Boyle, D Foley, John Timmons 0-1, P Haughey 0-2, O Freaney 0-6, D Ferguson, P Farnan 1-2, J Joyce, K Heffernan. Subs: J Brennan for Boyle, D Jones for Crowley.

LEINSTER SEMI-FINAL
July 5, Croke Park, Dublin
DUBLIN 1-8   LOUTH 0-11
Dublin: P O'Flaherty, M Wilson, L Foley, Joe Timmons, C O'Leary, J Crowley, J Brennan, D Foley, John Timmons, P Haughey, O Freaney 1-4, D Ferguson, P Farnan 0-2, J Joyce 0-1, K Heffernan 0-1. Sub: J Murray for John Timmons.

LEINSTER SEMI-FINAL REPLAY
July 26, Pairc Tailteann, Navan
DUBLIN 3-14   LOUTH 1-9
Dublin: P O'Flaherty, M Wilson, L Foley, Joe Timmons, C O'Leary, J Crowley, J Boyle, J Joyce 1-1, John Timmons, P Haughey 1-0, D Foley 0-1, D Ferguson, P Farnan 0-3, O Freaney 0-8, K Heffernan 1-1. Sub: J Brennan for Crowley.

LEINSTER FINAL
Aug 2, O'Connor Park, Tullamore
DUBLIN 1-18   LAOIS 2-8
Dublin: P O'Flaherty, J Crowley, L Foley, Joe Timmons, J Boyle, C O'Leary 0-1, J Brennan, D Ferguson, J Joyce 0-1, P Haughey 0-2, D Foley 0-3, M Whelan 1-3, P Farnan 0-1, O Freaney 0-5, K Heffernan 0-2.

ALL-IRELAND SEMI-FINAL
Aug 16, Croke Park, Dublin
KERRY 1-10   DUBLIN 2-5
Dublin: P O'Flaherty, J Crowley, L Foley, Joe Timmons, J Boyle, C O'Leary, J Brennan, J Joyce, D Foley, P Haughey 1-0, D Ferguson, M Whelan 0-1, P Farnan, O Freaney 1-3, K Heffernan 0-1. Subs: M Bohan for O'Leary, C Meehan for O'Flaherty, O'Leary for Bohan, N Fox for Ferguson, Ferguson for Fox.

1960

LEINSTER QUARTER-FINAL
May 29, Cusack Park, Mullingar
DUBLIN 10-13   LONGFORD 3-8
Dublin: P Flynn, M Wilson, L Foley, Joe Timmons, J Boyle, P Holden, J Brennan, L Quinn, D Foley, M Whelan 0-1, John Timmons 0-4, S Behan 0-1, D Ferguson 1-2, J Joyce 5-3, K Heffernan 2-1. Sub: P Farnan 1-1 for Heffernan. Own goal by W Morgan.

LEINSTER SEMI-FINAL
June 26, O'Moore Park, Portlaoise
OFFALY 3-9   DUBLIN 0-9
Dublin: P Plynn, P Holden, L Foley, Joe Timmons, D McKane, D Foley, C O'Leary, L Quinn, S Behan, D Ferguson, John Timmons 0-6, M Whelan, P Fernan, J Joyce 0-2, K Heffernan 0-1. Subs: M Wilson for McKane, J Boyle for Whelan.

1961

LEINSTER QUARTER-FINAL
June 4, Dr Cullen Park, Carlow
DUBLIN 4-7   WEXFORD 1-7
Dublin: P Flynn, C Kane, L Foley, Joe Timmons, C O'Leary, P Holden, M Whelan, D Foley, John Timmons 0-1, T Howard 1-0, B McCrea 0-2, S Behan 1-1, P Farnan, J Joyce 1-2, K Heffernan 1-1.

LEINSTER SEMI-FINAL
July 9, Pairc Tailteann, Navan
DUBLIN 4-14   MEATH 1-7
Dublin: P Flynn, C Kane, L Foley, Joe Timmons, P Holden, C O'Leary, N Fox, D Foley, M Whelan 0-3, T Howard, John Timmons 0-8, S Behan 1-0, P Farnan, K Heffernan 1-0, S Coen. Subs: J Joyce 1-1 for Howard, B McCrea 1-0 for Farnan.

LEINSTER FINAL
July 23, O'Moore Park, Portlaoise
OFFALY 1-13   DUBLIN 1-8
Dublin: P Flynn, C Kane, L Foley, Joe Timmons, P Holden, C O'Leary, N Fox, D Foley, M Whelan 1-1, S Behan, John Timmons 0-5, J Joyce, P Farnan 0-1, K Heffernan 0-1, S Coen. Subs: B McCrea for Coen, T Howard for Joyce, Joyce for John Timmons.

1962

LEINSTER QUARTER-FINAL
June 3, Pairc Tailteann, Navan
DUBLIN 1-8   LOUTH 0-10
Dublin: P Flynn, L Hickey, L Foley, B Casey, C Kane, P Holden, N Fox, C O'Leary 0-1, D McKane, M Whelan, P Farnan, T Donnelly, E Burgess, J Timmons 0-5, K Heffernan 1-1. Subs: J Joyce 0-1 for Donnelly, J Farrell for Casey.

LEINSTER SEMI-FINAL
June 17, Dr Cullen Park, Carlow
DUBLIN 0-13   LAOIS 1-8
Dublin: P Flynn, L Hickey, L Foley, C Kane, C O'Leary, P Holden, N Fox 0-1, J Timmons 0-3, D McKane, P Farnan 0-1, T Donnelly, M Whelan, P Delaney 0-4, J Joyce, K Heffernan 0-2. Subs: E Burgess 0-2 for Timmons, Timmons for Donnelly.

LEINSTER FINAL
July 15, Croke Park, Dublin
DUBLIN 2-8   OFFALY 1-7
Dublin: P Flynn, L Hickey, L Foley, C Kane, M Whelan, P Holden, N Fox, C O'Leary, D McKane, T Howard, John Timmons 0-3, E Burgess 0-1, P Delaney 1-2, B McCrea 1-1, K Heffernan. Subs: J Joyce 0-1 for Howard, P Farnan for McKane.

ALL-IRELAND SEMI-FINAL
Aug 5, Croke Park, Dublin
KERRY 2-12   DUBLIN 0-10
Dublin: P Flynn, L Hickey, L Foley, C Kane, M Whelan, P Holden, N Fox, C O'Leary 0-3, D McKane, J Joyce 0-2, D Foley, E Burgess 0-1, P Delaney 0-3, J Timmons 0-1, K Heffernan. Subs: B Casey for Hickey, P Farnan for McKane, B McCrea for Delaney.

1963

LEINSTER QUARTER-FINAL
June 2, Croke Park, Dublin
DUBLIN 2-6   MEATH 2-5
Dublin: F McPhillips, L Foley 0-2, B Casey, O Callaghan, J Rice, P Holden, M Kissane, D Foley 0-1, P Downey, E Breslin, M Whelan 1-0, S Behan, G Davey, J Timmons 1-3, J Joyce. Subs: T Howard for Breslin, L Hickey for Downey.

LEINSTER SEMI-FINAL
June 23, Croke Park, Dublin
DUBLIN 2-7   KILDARE 1-5
Dublin: F McPhillips, L Hickey, L Foley, B Casey, J Rice, P Downey, M Kissane, D Foley, J Timmons 0-1, E Breslin, M Whelan 0-3, G Davey, B McDonald 1-0, D Ferguson 1-2, S Behan 0-1. Subs: D McKane for Rice, S Lee for D Foley, J Joyce for Lee.

LEINSTER FINAL
July 14, Croke Park, Dublin
DUBLIN 2-11   LAOIS 2-9
Dublin: Pa Flynn, L Hickey, L Foley 0-2, B Casey, D McKane, P Holden, M Kissane, P Downey, John Timmons, E Breslin 0-1, M Whelan 0-6, G Davey 1-1, B McDonald 1-1, D Ferguson, S Behan. Sub: J Joyce for Breslin.

ALL-IRELAND SEMI-FINAL
Aug 18, Croke Park, Dublin
DUBLIN 2-11   DOWN 0-7
Dublin: P Flynn, L Hickey, L Foley, B Casey, D McKane, P Holden, M Kissane, J Timmons 0-3, D Foley 0-1, B McDonald 2-0, M Whelan 0-5, G Davey, N Fox, D Ferguson 0-1, S Behan 0-1.

ALL-IRELAND FINAL
Sep 22, Croke Park, Dublin
DUBLIN 1-9   GALWAY 0-10
Dublin: Pascal Flynn, Leo Hickey, Lar Foley, Bill Casey, Des McKane, Paddy Holden, Mick Kissane, Des Foley (capt), John Timmons 0-2, Brian McDonald 0-1, Mickey Whelan 0-5, Gerry Davey 1-0, Simon Behan, Dessie Ferguson 0-1, Noel Fox. Sub: Paddy Downey for Holden.

1964

LEINSTER QUARTER-FINAL
May 24, St Conleth's Park, Newbridge
DUBLIN 1-14   CARLOW 1-5
Dublin: P Flynn, L Hickey, L Foley, C Kane, D McKane, P Holden, N Fox, D Foley 0-1, J Timmons 1-5, B McDonald 0-1, B Casey, S Coen 0-4, D Ferguson 0-2, M Whelan, J Gilroy 0-1.

LEINSTER SEMI-FINAL
June 21, O'Connor Park, Tullamore
DUBLIN 0-8   LAOIS 1-2
Dublin: P Flynn, L Hickey, L Foley, C Kane, M Kissane, P Holden, N Fox, D Foley, B Casey, B McDonald 0-4, M Whelan 0-1, E Breslin, G Davey, J Timmons 0-3, D Ferguson.

LEINSTER FINAL
July 26, Croke Park, Dublin
MEATH 2-12   DUBLIN 1-7
Dublin: Paschal Flynn, Leo Hickey, Lar Foley, Christy Kane, Mick Kissane, Paddy Holden, Noel Fox, Des Foley, Simon Behan, Brian McDonald 1-2, Mickey Whelan, Sean Coen 0-3, Gerry Davey, Bill Casey 0-1, Des Ferguson 0-1. Subs: Eamonn Breslin for Casey, Des McKane for Coen, Ned Fahy for Fox.

1965

LEINSTER QUARTER-FINAL
May 30, Dr Cullen Park, Carlow
DUBLIN 2-11   WEXFORD 0-7
Dublin: P Flynn, C Kane, L Foley, B O'Shea, L Ferguson, P Holden, B Casey, D Foley, S Lee, T Donnelly 1-0, M Whelan 0-4, B McDonald 0-2, J Keaveney 1-3, D Mulligan 0-1, G Davey 0-1.

LEINSTER SEMI-FINAL
June 20, O'Connor Park, Tullamore
DUBLIN 1-11   KILDARE 0-5
Dublin: P Flynn, C Kane, B Casey, M Keane, M Kissane, P Holden, N Fox 0-1, D Foley, S Lee, B McDonald 1-0, J Timmons 0-7, T Donnelly, J Keaveney, D Mulligan 1-0, G Davey. Sub: C Leaney 0-2 for Davey.

LEINSTER FINAL
July 18, Croke Park, Dublin
DUBLIN 3-6   LONGFORD 0-9
Dublin: P Flynn, C Kane, B Casey, M Keane, M Kissane, P Holden, N Fox, D Foley 1-0, S Lee, B McDonald 1-0, M Whelan, T Donnelly, J Keaveney 1-1, J Timmons 0-3, G Davey 0-2. Sub: D Mulligan for Whelan 1-0.

ALL-IRELAND SEMI-FINAL
Aug 8, Croke Park, Dublin
KERRY 4-8   DUBLIN 2-6
Dublin: P Flynn, C Kane, L Foley, B Casey, M Kissane, P Holden, N Fox, D Foley, S Lee, T Donnelly, M Whelan 0-2, B McDonald, J Keaveney 1-0, J Timmons 1-4, G Davey.

1966

LEINSTER QUARTER-FINAL
June 12, Drogheda Park, Drogheda
DUBLIN 2-10   LOUTH 0-9
Dublin: A Griffin, L Hickey, L Foley, C Kane, M Kissane, B Casey, G O'Driscoll, T Donnelly 0-1, S Lee, D Bollard 0-1, J Keaveney 0-2, M Cranny, B McDonald, J Timmons 1-5, G Davey 1-1. Subs: P Holden for O'Driscoll.

LEINSTER SEMI-FINAL
July 10, Pairc Tailteann, Navan
KILDARE 3-9   DUBLIN 2-5
Dublin: A Griffin, L Hickey, L Foley, C Kane, M Kissane, P Holden, B Casey, T Donnelly 0-1, S Lee, D Bollard, M Whelan, M Cranny 1-0, B McDonald, J Timmons 1-4, G Davey. Subs: M Kelleher for Whelan, E Breslin for Davey.

1967

LEINSTER QUARTER-FINAL
June 11, O'Connor Park, Tullamore
WESTMEATH 1-6   DUBLIN 0-8
Dublin: P Cullen, B Casey, S Lee, E Mullen, M Kelleher, D Foley, G Davey, S O'Connor 0-1, T Donnelly 0-1, M Whelan, J Keaveney 0-6, M Cranny, J Evers, B McDonald, L Deegan. Subs: J Henry for Evers, C Kane for Henry.

1968

LEINSTER QUARTER-FINAL
June 2, O'Connor Park, Tullamore
LONGFORD 1-12   DUBLIN 0-12
Dublin: P Cullen, B Casey, L Foley, C Kane, P Markham, B O'Shea, G Davey 0-1, D Foley, S Lee, T Donnelly 0-1, M Whelan 0-4, J Keaveney, B McDonald 0-2, S O'Connor 0-2, P Delaney 0-2. Subs: M Keane for Keaveney, A Hempenstall for Lee.

1969

LEINSTER QUARTER-FINAL
May 4, Dr Cullen Park, Carlow
DUBLIN 3-7   LAOIS 1-5
Dublin: P Cullen, E Mullins, C Kane, M Kelleher, E Davey, P Markham, G Davey, B Casey, T Donnelly, S Foley 1-1, S O'Connor 0-1, D Bollard, L Deegan 1-0, D Foley 1-1, P Delaney.

LEINSTER SEMI-FINAL
June 15, Dr Cullen Park, Carlow
KILDARE 0-18   DUBLIN 0-7
Dublin: P Cullen, P Markham, C Kane, M Kelleher, E Davey, B Casey 0-1, G Davey, B O'Shea, S Donnelly, M Whelan 0-1, S O'Connor 0-2, D Bollard, L Deegan, D Foley 0-1, P Delaney 0-2. Subs: S Foley for Delaney, T Donnelly for O'Shea, J Keaveney for Whelan.

1970

LEINSTER FIRST ROUND
May 17, Cusack Park, Mullingar
LONGFORD 2-14   DUBLIN 3-8
Dublin: P Cullen, P Markham, S Doherty, C Maher, R Kelleher, S Donnelly, P O'Neill, S O'Connor 0-1, F Murray 0-1, D Hickey 2-1, T Hanahoe 0-1, J Reilly 0-1, J Keaveney 0-3, T O'Hanlon 1-0, P Leahy. Subs: S Roche for Maher, M Kelleher for Leahy, G O'Driscoll for Markham.

1971

LEINSTER QUARTER-FINAL
June 6, Dr Cullen Park, Carlow
LAOIS 3-8   DUBLIN 0-13
Dublin: P Cullen, G O'Driscoll, S Doherty, S Roche, P Markham, S Mullins, R Kelleher, F Murray 0-1, P O'Neill, J Keaveney 0-4, T Hanahoe, S Donnelly, D Hickey 0-1, T O'Hanlon 0-5, B Casey. Sub: J Reilly 0-2 for Keaveney.

1972

LEINSTER QUARTER-FINAL
June 11, Croke Park, Dublin
DUBLIN 2-8   WESTMEATH 0-8
Dublin: P Cullen, P O'Brien, S Doherty, G O'Driscoll, J Broe, R Kelleher, E Brady, F Murray 0-1, P O'Neill, G Wilson 0-1, T Hanahoe, M Whelan 2-4, B Casey, L Foley 0-2, J Reilly. Subs: A Larkin for O'Neill, J Keaveney for Reilly, P Wilson for Larkin.

LEINSTER SEMI-FINAL
July 2, Pairc Tailteann, Navan
KILDARE 0-16   DUBLIN 3-5
Dublin: P Cullen, P O'Brien, S Doherty, P Markham, P O'Neill, R Kelleher, E Brady, F Murray, L Sweeney, G Wilson, T Hanahoe, M Whelan 0-2, B Casey 1-1, L Foley 1-1, J Reilly 0-1. Subs: S Donnelly for Sweeney, J Keaveney 1-0 for Hanahoe, F Wilson for G Wilson.

1973

LEINSTER FIRST ROUND
May 20, Wexford Park, Wexford
DUBLIN 3-11   WEXFORD 0-5
Dublin: P Cullen, J O'Neill, S Doherty, P O'Brien, P Reilly, P O'Neill, R Kelleher, S Rooney 0-4, A Larkin 0-1, E Brady, F Murray 2-1, B Doyle 0-2, G Wilson 1-1, B Salmon, G Keavey 0-2. Sub: P Wilson for Larkin, D Redmond for Brady, G O'Driscoll for O'Brien.

LEINSTER SECOND ROUND
May 27, Pairc Tailteann, Navan
DUBLIN 2-6   LOUTH 1-9
Dublin: P Cullen, J O'Neill, S Doherty, G O'Driscoll, P Reilly, P O'Neill, R Kelleher, S Rooney 0-3, A Larkin, E Brady, F Murray 1-1, B Doyle 0-1, G Wilson, P O'Brien 1-1, G Keavey. Sub: P Wilson for Larkin, L McCabe for Brady

LEINSTER SECOND ROUND REPLAY
June 10, Pairc Tailteann, Navan
LOUTH 1-8   DUBLIN 0-9
Dublin: P Cullen, J O'Neill, S Doherty, G O'Driscoll, P Reilly, P O'Neill, R Kelleher, S Rooney 0-1, A Larkin, E Brady 0-1, F Murray 0-1, B Doyle 0-4, D Hickey 0-2, P Markham, G Wilson. Subs: J McCarthy for Markham, P O'Brien for Rooney.

1974

LEINSTER FIRST ROUND
May 26, Croke Park, Dublin
DUBLIN 3-9   WEXFORD 0-6
Dublin: P Cullen, D Billings, S Doherty, R Kelleher, P Reilly, A Larkin, G Wilson, B Mullins, S Rooney 0-3, B Doyle 2-1, T Hanahoe 1-1, D Hickey 0-2, A O'Toole 0-2, B Brogan, J McCarthy.

LEINSTER SECOND ROUND
June 2, Pairc Tailteann, Navan
DUBLIN 2-11   LOUTH 1-9
Dublin: P Cullen, D Billings, S Doherty, R Kelleher, P Reilly, A Larkin, G Wilson, S Rooney, B Mullins 1-0, B Doyle, T Hanahoe, D Hickey 1-2, A O'Toole 0-3, J Keaveney 0-6, J McCarthy. Sub: G O'Driscoll for Kelleher.

LEINSTER QUARTER-FINAL
June 16, Pearse Park, Longford
DUBLIN 1-11   OFFALY 0-13
Dublin: P Cullen, D Billings, S Doherty, R Kelleher, P Reilly, A Larkin, G Wilson, S Rooney 0-1, B Mullins 0-1, F Ryder, T Hanahoe 0-1, D Hickey 0-1, J McCarthy, J Keaveney 0-5, A O'Toole 0-1. Subs: L Deegan 1-1 for Ryder, G O'Driscoll for Billings, B Brogan for McCarthy.

LEINSTER SEMI-FINAL
July 14, Croke Park, Dublin
DUBLIN 1-13   KILDARE 0-10
Dublin: P Cullen, G. O'Driscoll S Doherty, R Kelleher, P Reilly, A Larkin, G Wilson 0-1, B Mullins 1-0, S Rooney, B Doyle 0-1, T Hanahoe, D Hickey 0-1, P Gogarty 0-3, J Keaveney 0-5, A O'Toole 0-2. Sub: J Rellly for Doyle.

LEINSTER FINAL
July 28, Croke Park, Dublin
DUBLIN 1-14   MEATH 1-9
Dublin: P Cullen, G O'Driscoll, S Doherty, R Kelleher, P Reilly, A Larkin, G Wilson, B Mullins, S Rooney 0-1, B Doyle, T Hanahoe, D Hickey 0-2, J McCarthy, J Keaveney 1-8, A O'Toole 0-3. Subs: P Gogarty for McCarthy, L Deegan for Gogarty.

ALL-IRELAND SEMI-FINAL
Aug 11, Croke Park, Dublin:
DUBLIN 2-11   CORK 1-8
Dublin: P Cullen, G O'Driscoll, S. Doherty, R Kelleher, P Reilly, A Larkin, G Wilson, B Mullins 1-1, S Rooney 0-1, B Doyle 0-2, T Hanahoe 0-1, D Hickey, J McCarthy 0-2, J Keaveney 0-4, A O'Toole 1-0. Subs: B Pocock for Wilson.

ALL-IRELAND FINAL
Sep 22, Croke Park, Dublin
DUBLIN 0-14   GALWAY 1-6
Dublin: Paddy Cullen, Gay O'Driscoll, Sean Doherty (capt), Robbie Kelliher, Paddy Reilly, Alan Larkin, George Wilson, Brian Mullins 0-2, Stephen Rooney, Bobby Doyle, Tony Hanahoe, David Hickey 0-2, John McCarthy 0-1, Jimmy Keaveney 0-8, Anton O'Toole 0-1.

1975

LEINSTER QUARTER-FINAL
June 8, Dr Cullen Park, Carlow
DUBLIN 4-17   WEXFORD 3-10
Dublin: P Cullen, G O'Driscoll, S Doherty, R Kelleher, P Reilly, A Larkin, G Wilson, B Mullins, B Brogan, B Doyle 0-2, T Hanahoe 1-1, D Hickey 1-1, J McCarthy 1-1, J Keaveney 0-10, A O'Toole 0-1. Subs: B Pocock for Wilson, M Noctor 1-1 for McCarthy, P O'Neill for Larkin.

LEINSTER SEMI-FINAL
July 6, Pairc Tailteann, Navan
DUBLIN 3-14   LOUTH 4-7
Dublin: P Cullen, G O'Driscoll, S Doherty, R Kelleher 0-1, P Reilly, A Larkin, G Wilson, B Mullins, B Brogan, B Doyle 1-0, T Hanahoe 1-0, D Hickey, M Noctor, J Keaveney 1-11, A O'Toole 0-2. Subs: J McCarthy for Noctor.

LEINSTER FINAL
July 27, Croke Park, Dublin
DUBLIN 3-13   KILDARE 0-8
Dublin: P Cullen, G O'Driscoll, S Doherty, R Kelleher, P Reilly, A Larkin, G Wilson, B Mullins 2-0, B Brogan 0-1, B Doyle 0-2, T Hanahoe 0-1, D Hickey 1-2, P Gogarty 0-4, J Keaveney 0-2, A O'Toole 0-1. Sub: P O'Neill for Larkin.

ALL-IRELAND SEMI-FINAL
Aug 24, Croke Park, Dublin
DUBLIN 3-13   DERRY 3-8
Dublin: P Cullen, G O'Driscoll, S O'Doherty, R Kelleher, P Reilly, A Larkin, G Wilson, B Mullins, B Brogan, B Doyle 0-1, T Hanahoe 1-0, D Hickey 0-2, A O'Toole 2-0, J Keaveney 0-9, P Gogarty 0-1. Sub: P O'Neill for Larkin.

ALL-IRELAND FINAL
Sep 28, Croke Park, Dublin
KERRY 2-12   DUBLIN 0-11
Dublin: Paddy Cullen, Gay O'Driscoll, Sean Doherty (capt), Robbie Kelleher, Paddy Reilly, Alan Larkin, George Wilson, Brian Mullins 0-1, Bernard Brogan, Anton O'Toole, Tony Hanahoe, David Hickey, John McCarthy, Jimmy Keaveney 0-6, Pat Gogarty 0-2. Subs: Bobby Doyle 0-1 for Brogan h/t, Pat O'Neill for McCarthy 47 Brendan Pocock 0-1 for Reilly 61 .

1976

LEINSTER QUARTER-FINAL
June 27, Cusack Park, Mullingar
DUBLIN 5-16   LONGFORD 0-7
Dublin: N Bernard, G O'Driscoll, S Doherty, R Keleher, P Reilly, A Larkin, K Synnott, B Mullins 0-1, B Brogan, A O'Toole 1-1, K Moran 0-3, D Hickey 0-3, B Doyle 0-1, J Keaveney 3-4, P Gogarty 1-3. Subs: P O'Neill for Reilly, J Corcoran for Mullins, T Drumm for Synnott.

LEINSTER SEMI-FINAL
July 11, O'Connor Park, Tullamore
DUBLIN 3-12   LAOIS 0-11
Dublin: P Cullen, G O'Driscoll, S Doherty, R Kelleher, P Reilly, K Moran, T Drumm, B Mullins 1-2, B Brogan, A O'Toole 0-3, T Hanahoe, D Hickey, B Doyle 0-2, J Keaveney 1-3, P Gogarty 1-2. Subs: F Ryder for Brogan, McCarthy for Doyle.

LEINSTER FINAL
July 25, Croke Park, Dublin
DUBLIN 2-8   MEATH 1-9
Dublin: P Cullen, G O'Driscoll, S Doherty, R Kelleher, P Reilly, K Moran, P O'Neill, B Mullins, F Ryder, A O'Toole 1-0, T Hanahoe 1-0, D Hickey 0-2, B Doyle 0-1, J Keaveney 0-4, P Gogarty 0-1. Subs: B Brogan for Reilly, J Brogan for Kelleher.

ALL-IRELAND SEMI-FINAL
Aug 29, Croke Park, Dublin
DUBLIN 1-8   GALWAY 0-8
Dublin: P Cullen, G O'Driscoll, S Doherty, R Kelleher, T Drumm, K Moran, P O'Neill, B Mullins, B Brogan, A O'Toole, T Hanahoe 0-2, D Hickey, B Doyle, J Keaveney 1-5, J McCarthy 0-1.

ALL-IRELAND FINAL
Sep 26, Croke Park, Dublin
DUBLIN 3-8   KERRY 0-10
Dublin: Paddy Cullen, Gay O'Driscoll, Sean Doherty, Robbie Kelleher, Tommy Drumm, Kevin Moran, Pat O'Neill, Brian Mullins 1-1, Bernard Brogan 0-1, Anton O'Toole 0-1, Tony Hanahoe (capt) 0-1, David Hickey 0-1, Bobby Doyle, Jimmy Keaveney 1-2, John McCarthy 1-1. Subs: Fran Ryder for Hanahoe, Pat Gogarty for Doyle.

1977

LEINSTER QUARTER-FINAL
May 29, Pairc Tailteann, Navan
DUBLIN 1-14   KILDARE 2-8
Dublin: P Cullen, G O'Driscoll, S Doherty, R Kelleher 0-1, P Reilly, K Moran, P O'Neill, B Mullins, A Larkin, A O'Toole, T Hanahoe 0-2, D Hickey 0-2, B Doyle 0-2, J Keaveney 0-6, B Brogan 1-1. Sub: F Ryder for O'Toole.

LEINSTER SEMI-FINAL
July 3, Dr Cullen Park, Carlow
DUBLIN 3-11   WEXFORD 0-6
Dublin: P Cullen, G O'Driscoll, S Doherty, R Kelleher 0-1, T Drumm, K Moran, P O'Neill, B Mullins, A Larkin, A O'Toole 0-2, T Hanahoe 1-1, D Hickey, B Doyle 1-0, J Keaveney 0-6, J McCarthy 1-1.

LEINSTER FINAL
July 31, Croke Park, Dublin
DUBLIN 1-9   MEATH 0-8
Dublin: P Cullen, G O'Driscoll, S Doherty, R Kelleher, T Drumm, K Moran, P O'Neill, B Mullins, A Larkin, A O'Toole 1-0, T Hanahoe, D Hickey, B Doyle 0-1, J Keaveney 0-6, J McCarthy 0-1. Sub: F Ryder 0-1 for Larkin.

ALL-IRELAND SEMI-FINAL
Aug 21, Croke Park, Dublin
DUBLIN 3-12   KERRY 1-13
Dublin: P Cullen, G O'Driscoll, S Doherty, R Kelleher, T Drumm, K Moran, P O'Neill, B Mullins, F Ryder, A O'Toole 0-4, T Hanahoe 0-3, D Hickey 1-1, B Doyle 0-1, J Keaveney 0-3, J McCarthy 1-0. Subs: B Brogan 1-0 for Ryder, P Gogarty for McCarthy.

ALL-IRELAND FINAL
Sep 25, Croke Park, Dublin
DUBLIN 5-12   ARMAGH 3-6
Dublin: Paddy Cullen, Gay O'Driscoll, Sean Doherty, Robbie Kelleher, Tommy Drumm, Kevin Moran, Pat O'Neill, Brian Mullins, Bernard Brogan, Anton O'Toole 0-1, Tony Hanahoe, David Hickey 0-1, Bobby Doyle 2-2, Jimmy Keaveney 2-6, John McCarthy 1-2. Subs: Paddy Reilly for O'Neill, Alan Larkin for B Brogan, Jim Brogan for Kelleher.

1978

LEINSTER QUARTER-FINAL
June 18, Croke Park, Dublin
DUBLIN 6-15   CARLOW 2-9
Dublin: P Cullen, G O'Driscoll, S Doherty, R Kelleher, T Drumm, J Brogan, P O'Neill, B Mullins, B Brogan, A O'Toole, T Hanahoe 1-4, D Hickey 1-0, B Doyle 1-0, J Keaveney 0-3, J McCarthy 3-7. Subs: P Hogan for Hickey, P Gogarty for Hanahoe, F Ryder 0-1 for Mullins.

LEINSTER SEMI-FINAL
July 9, O'Moore Park, Portlaoise
DUBLIN 2-9   OFFALY 0-12
Dublin: P Cullen, G O'Driscoll, S Doherty, R Kelleher, T Drumm, D Maher, P O'Neill, B Mullins, B Brogan, A O'Toole, T Hanahoe, D Hickey, B Doyle 0-1, J Keaveney 1-7, J McCarthy 1-1. Subs: K Moran for Maher.

LEINSTER FINAL
July 30, Croke Park, Dublin
DUBLIN 1-17   KILDARE 1-6
Dublin: P Cullen, G O'Driscoll, S Doherty, R Kelleher 0-1, T Drumm, K Moran, P O'Neill, B Mullins 0-1, B Brogan 0-1, A O'Toole 0-2, T Hanahoe 1-2, D Hickey, B Doyle, J Keaveney 0-7, J McCarthy 0-1. Subs: P Hogan 0-1 for Doyle, P Gogarty 0-1 for McCarthy.

ALL-IRELAND SEMI-FINAL
Aug 20, Croke Park, Dublin
DUBLIN 1-16   DOWN 0-8
Dublin: P Cullen, G O'Driscoll 0-1, S Doherty, R Kelleher, T Drumm, K Moran, P O'Neill 0-1, B Mullins, B Brogan 0-3, A O'Toole 0-1, T Hanahoe, D Hickey, B Doyle 0-2, J Keaveney 1-6, J McCarthy 0-2.

ALL-IRELAND FINAL
Sep 24, Croke Park, Dublin
KERRY 5-11   DUBLIN 0-9
Dublin: Paddy Cullen, Gay O'Driscoll, Sean Doherty, Robbie Kelleher, Tommy Drumm, Kevin Moran, Pat O'Neill, Brian Mullins, Bernard Brogan 0-1, Anton O'Toole, Tony Hanahoe (capt), David Hickey, Bobby Doyle, Jimmy Keaveney 0-8, John McCarthy.

1979

LEINSTER QUARTER-FINAL
June 3, Pairc Tailteann, Navan
DUBLIN 4-16   LOUTH 0-4
Dublin: P Cullen, D Foran, S Doherty, G O'Driscoll, P Reilly, T Drumm, P O'Neill, B Mullins, B Brogan 0-1, D Hickey 1-5, T Hanahoe 0-1, J McCarthy 0-2, B Doyle 1-0, J Keaveney 1-5, P Ellis 1-1. Subs: F Ryder for Brogan, M Hickey 0-1 for McCarthy.

LEINSTER SEMI-FINAL
July 1, St Conleth's Park, Newbridge
DUBLIN 3-13   WICKLOW 2-7
Dublin: P Cullen, D Foran, S Doherty, G O'Driscoll, T Drumm, F Ryder 0-1, P Reilly, B Mullins 1-0, B Brogan 0-1, D Hickey, T Hanahoe 1-2, S Kearns, P Ellis 0-2, J Keaveney 0-5, B Doyle. Sub: M Hickey 1-2 for Kearns.

LEINSTER FINAL
July 29, Croke Park, Dublin
DUBLIN 1-8   OFFALY 0-9
Dublin: P Cullen, G O'Driscoll, M Holden, D Foran, T Drumm, F Ryder, P O'Neill, B Mullins, B Brogan 1-1, D Hickey, T Hanahoe, J McCarthy, A O'Toole, J Keaveney 0-2, B Doyle 0-1. Subs: M Kennedy for O'Driscoll, J Ronayne 0-3 for McCarthy, M Hickey 0-1 for D Hickey.

ALL-IRELAND SEMI-FINAL
Aug 19, Croke Park, Dublin
DUBLIN 0-14   ROSCOMMON 1-10
Dublin: P Cullen, M Kennedy, M Holden, D Foran, T Drumm, F Ryder, P O'Neill, B Mullins, B Brogan, A O'Toole 0-2, T Hanahoe, D Hickey, M Hickey 0-9, B Doyle 0-2, J Roynane 0-1. Subs: J McCarthy for Roynane, B Pocook for McCarthy.

ALL-IRELAND FINAL
Sep 16, Croke Park, Dublin
KERRY 3-13   DUBLIN 1-8
Dublin: Paddy Cullen, Mick Kennedy, Mick Holden, David Foran, Tommy Drumm, Fran Ryder, Pat O'Neill, Brian Mullins, Bernard Brogan, Anton O'Toole 0-1, Tony Hanahoe 0-2, David Hickey 0-2, Michael Hickey, Bobby Doyle 0-3, John McCarthy. Subs: Jim Ronayne 1-0 for M Hickey, Gay O'Driscoll for McCarthy, Brendan Pocook for O'Toole.

1980

LEINSTER QUARTER-FINAL
June 8, O'Connor Park, Tullamore
DUBLIN 2–14   LAOIS 2–8
Dublin: M Kennedy, D Foran, M Holden, R Kelleher, T Drumm, F Ryder, PJ Buckley 0-1, B Mullins 1-0, B Brogan 0-1, A O'Toole 0-2, J Ronayne 0-1, D Hickey 1-0, A Roche 0-2, J Caffrey 0-2, C Duff 0-5. Sub: P Canavan for Foran.

LEINSTER SEMI-FINAL
July 6, Pairc Tailteann, Navan
DUBLIN 3–13   MEATH 2–7
Dublin: M Kennedy, D Foran, M Holden, R Kelleher, T Drumm, F Ryder, PJ Buckley 0-1, B Brogan 1-1, A Larkin, A O'Toole 0-2, J Ronayne 1-2, D Hickey, B Doyle 1-3, J Caffrey, C Duff 0-2. Subs: K Moran 0-1 for Larkin, B Rock 0-1 for Duff.

LEINSTER FINAL
July 27, Croke Park, Dublin
OFFALY 1–10   DUBLIN 1–8
Dublin: John O'Leary, Mick Kennedy, Mick Holden, Robbie Kelleher, Tommy Drumm 0-1, Fran Ryder, PJ Buckley, Bernard Brogan, Stephen Rooney, Anton O'Toole 0-1, Jim Ronayne, David Hickey 0-1, Bobby Doyle 1-1, John Caffrey 0-1, Ciaran Duff. Subs: B Rock 0-3 for Duff, P O'Neill for Rooney.

1981

LEINSTER QUARTER-FINAL
May 31, St Conleth's Park, Newbridge
DUBLIN 0-10   WICKLOW 0-8
Dublin: J O'Leary, J Brogan, M Holden, R Kelleher, D Foran, F Ryder, M Kennedy, G Sutton, J Kearns, A O'Toole, J Ronayne, K Duff 0-1, J McCarthy 0-5, J Thompson, A McCaul 0-3. Subs: B Brogan for Thompson, Thompson for Duff, PJ Buckley 0-1 for Sutton.

LEINSTER SEMI-FINAL
July 5, O'Connor Park, Tullamore
LAOIS 2-9   DUBLIN 0-11
Dublin: J O'Leary, D Foran, T Drumm, R Kelleher, M Kennedy, F Ryder, R Hazley, J Kearns, J Roynane 0-1, A O'Toole, D Hickey, J McCarthy, B Doyle, A McCaul 0-8, B Brogan. Subs: PJ Buckley for Kennedy, J Thompson 0-2 for Kearns, A Walsh for Hickey.

1982

LEINSTER QUARTER-FINAL
June 6, O'Connor Park, Tullamore
DUBLIN 1-15   LONGFORD 2-6
Dublin: J O'Leary, M Kennedy, J Brogan, R Hazley, P Canavan 0-1, M Holden, T Drumm, J Kearns 0-1, F Ryder, G O'Neill 0-1, M Hurley, B Rock 1-9, B Doyle, A McCaul, N Gaffney 0-2. Sub: C Duff 0-1 for O'Neill.

LEINSTER SEMI-FINAL
July 4, Pairc Tailteann, Navan
DUBLIN 1-13   KILDARE 0-12
Dublin: J O'Leary, M Kennedy, V Conroy, R Hazley, P Canavan, M Holden, T Drumm, F Ryder, B Kavanagh, M Hurley, B Mullins, B Rock 0-7, N Gaffney 0-2, A McCaul 0-2, C Duff 1-0. Subs: A Walsh 0-2 for Hurley, J Kearns for Kavanagh.

LEINSTER FINAL
Aug 1, Croke Park, Dublin
OFFALY 1-16   DUBLIN 1-7
Dublin: J O'Leary, M Kennedy, T Drumm, R Hazley, P Canavan, M Holden, S Wade, F Ryder, J Ronayne, A Walsh, B Mullins, B Rock 0-2, N Gaffney 1-1, A McCaul 0-1, C Duff 0-1. Subs: J Kearns 0-2 for Wade, B Kavanagh for Ronayne, M Loftus for Walsh.

1983

LEINSTER QUARTER-FINAL
June 12, Croke Park, Dublin
DUBLIN 2-8   MEATH 2-8
Dublin: J O'Leary, M Kennedy, G Hargan, R Hazley, T Drumm, F McGrath, PJ Buckley, J Kearns 0-3, B Mullins, B Rock 1-1, A O'Toole 0-2, C Duff 0-2, T Conroy, J McNally, A McCaul. Subs: B Jordan for McCaul, G O'Neill for Conroy. P Smith own goal.

LEINSTER QUARTER-FINAL REPLAY
July 3, Croke Park, Dublin
DUBLIN 3-9   MEATH 0-16
Dublin: J O'Leary, M Holden, G Hargan, R Hazley, P Canavan 0-1, T Drumm, PJ Buckley, J Kearns 0-1, B Mullins, B Rock 2-3, W Hughes, B Jordan 1-0, A McCaul, A O'Toole 0-1, C Duff 0-3. Subs: J Ronayne for Mullins, T Conroy for Hughes, Mullins for Kearns. Extra time: C Redmond for McCaul, G O'Neill for Jordan.

LEINSTER SEMI-FINAL
July 17, Croke Park, Dublin
DUBLIN 1-12   LOUTH 0-11
Dublin: J O'Leary, M Holden, G Hargan, R Hazley, M Kennedy, T Drumm, PJ Buckley, B Mullins, J Kearns, B Rock 0-4, W Hughes, B Jordan 0-1, A McCaul 0-2, A O'Toole 0-3, C Duff 1-0. Sub: T Conroy for Hughes, C Redmond 0-2 for Jordan, J Caffrey for Kearns.

LEINSTER FINAL
July 31, Croke Park, Dublin
DUBLIN 2-13   OFFALY 1-11
Dublin: J O'Leary, M Holden, G Hargan, R Hazley, P Canavan, T Drumm, PJ Buckley 0-1, J Ronayne, B Mullins, B Rock 0-5, T Conroy 0-2, C Duff 0-2, J Caffrey 1-0, A O'Toole, J McNally 1-2. Subs: J Kearns for Conroy, M Kennedy for Holden.

ALL-IRELAND SEMI-FINAL
Aug 21, Croke Park, Dublin
DUBLIN 2-11   CORK 2-11
Dublin: J O'Leary, M Holden, G Hargan, R Hazley, P

Canavan, T Drumm, PJ Buckley 0-1, J Roynane, B Mullins, B Rock 1-3, J Caffrey, C Duff 0-2, T Conroy 0-2, A O'Toole 1-1, J McNally 0-2. Subs: J Kearns for Roynane, A McCaul for Caffrey.

ALL-IRELAND SEMI-FINAL REPLAY
Aug 28, Pairc Ui Chaoimh, Cork
DUBLIN 4-15   CORK 2-10
Dublin: J O'Leary, M Holden, G Hargan, R Hazley, P Canavan, T Drumm, PJ Buckley, J Ronayne 0-1, B Mullins 1-0, J Caffrey 0-1, T Conroy 0-2, C Duff 1-3, B Rock 1-4, A O'Toole 0-1, J McNally 1-3. Sub: J Kearns for Caffrey.

ALL-IRELAND FINAL
Sep 18, Croke Park, Dublin
DUBLIN 1-10   GALWAY 1-8
Dublin: John O'Leary, Mick Holden, Gerry Hargan, Ray Hazley, Pat Canavan, Tommy Drumm (capt), PJ Buckley 0-1, Jim Ronayne 0-1, Brian Mullins, Barney Rock 1-6, Tommy Conroy, Ciaran Duff 0-1, John Caffrey, Anton O'Toole, Joe McNally 0-1. Subs: John Kearns for Conroy, Kieran Maher for Caffrey.

1984

LEINSTER QUARTER-FINAL
June 10, Croke Park, Dublin
DUBLIN 4-12   WEXFORD 0-9
Dublin: J O'Leary, M Holden, G Hargan, R Hazley, P Canavan, T Drumm, PJ Buckley, J Ronayne 0-1, B Mullins 0-1, B Rock 2-4, T Conroy 0-2, C Duff 1-2, J Caffrey 0-1, A O'Toole, J McNally 1-1. Sub: M Kennedy for Buckley, 36.

LEINSTER SEMI-FINAL
June 24, Croke Park, Dublin
DUBLIN 0-13   OFFALY 0-5
Dublin: J O'Leary, M Holden, G Hargan, V Conroy, P Canavan, T Drumm, PJ Buckley 0-1, J Ronayne 0-1, B Mullins 0-1, B Rock 0-4, T Conroy 0-1, C Duff 0-2, J Caffrey, A O'Toole 0-2, J McNally 0-1. Subs: J Kearns for Caffrey 12, M O'Callaghan for Rock 64.

LEINSTER FINAL
July 22, Croke Park, Dublin
DUBLIN 2-10   MEATH 1-9
Dublin: J O'Leary, M Holden, G Hargan, M Kennedy, P Canavan, T Drumm, PJ Buckley, J Ronayne, B Mullins, B Rock 1-4, T Conroy, C Duff 1-4, J Caffrey, A O'Toole 0-1, J McNally 0-1. Sub: C Sutton for Mullins.

ALL-IRELAND SEMI-FINAL
Aug 19, Croke Park, Dublin
DUBLIN 2-11   TYRONE 0-8
Dublin: J O'Leary, M Holden, G Hargan, M Kennedy, P Canavan, T Drumm, PJ Buckley, J Ronayne, B Mullins

0-1, B Rock 1-7, T Conroy 0-1, C Duff 0-1, J Caffrey, A O'TooJe, J McNally 1-0. Subs: C Sutton 0-1 for Caffrey, J McCarthy for McNally, T Cassin for Duff.

ALL-IRELAND FINAL
Sep 23, Croke Park, Dublin
KERRY 0-14   DUBLIN 1-6
Dublin: John O'Leary, Mick Holden, Gerry Hargan, Mick Kennedy, Pat Canavan, Tommy Drumm, PJ Buckley, Jim Ronayne, Brian Mullins, Barney Rock 1-5, Tommy Conroy 0-1, Ciaran Duff, John Kearns, Anton O'Toole, Joe McNally. Subs: Maurice O'Callaghan for McNally, Ciaran Sutton for Ronayne.

1985

LEINSTER QUARTER-FINAL
June 16, Wexford Park, Wexford
DUBLIN 4-13   WEXFORD 0-6
Dublin: J O'Leary, PJ Buckley, G Hargan, R Hazley, P Canavan 0-1, N McCaffrey, D Synnott, J Ronayne 0-1, B Mullins, B Rock 2-4, T Carr 1-3, C Duff 0-2, A McCaul 0-2, J Caffrey 1-0, J McNally. Subs: R Nevin for Synnott, P Dwane for Duff.

LEINSTER SEMI-FINAL
July 7, O'Connor Park, Tullamore
DUBLIN 2-13   OFFALY 0-10
Dublin: J O'Leary, M Holden, G Hargan, R Hazley, P Canavan, N McCaffrey, D Synnott, J Ronayne 0-1, B Mullins, B Rock 0-3, T Carr 0-3, C Duff 0-1, A McCaul 0-3, T Conroy 1-1, J McNally 1-1. Subs: M Kennedy for Holden, C Redmond for Duff, P Dwane for Carr.

LEINSTER FINAL
July 28, Croke Park, Dublin
DUBLIN 0-10   LAOIS 0-4
Dublin: J O'Leary, M Kennedy, G Hargan, R Hazley, P Canavan, N McCaffrey, D Synnott, J Ronayne 0-1, B Mullins, B Rock 0-6, T Carr 0-1, C Duff, A McCaul 0-2, J Caffrey, J McNally. Subs: C Redmond for Duff, P Dwane for Caffrey, M Holden for Kennedy.

ALL-IRELAND SEMI-FINAL
Aug 18, Croke Park, Dublin
DUBLIN 1-13   MAYO 1-13
Dublin: J O'Leary, M Holden, G Hargan, M Kennedy 0-1, P Canavan, N McCaffrey 0-1, D Synnott, J Ronayne, B Mullins, B Rock 1-7, T Carr, C Redmond 0-2, J Kearns 0-1, T Conroy 0-1, A McCaul. Subs: M O'Callaghan for Carr, J McNally for O'Callaghan.

ALL-IRELAND SEMI-FINAL REPLAY
Sep 8, Croke Park, Dublin
DUBLIN 2-12   MAYO 1-7
Dublin: J O'Leary, M Holden, G Hargan R Hazley, M Kennedy, N McCaffrey, D Synnott, J Ronayne 0-1, B

Mullins 0-1, B Rock 0-5, T Conroy 0-1, C Redmond, J Kearns 0-4, J McNally, C Duff 2-0. Sub: P Canavan for Kennedy, T Byrne for Ronayne.

ALL-IRELAND FINAL
Sep 22, Croke Park, Dublin
KERRY 2-12   **DUBLIN 2-8**
Dublin: John O'Leary, Mick Kennedy, Gerry Hargan, Ray Hazley, Pat Canavan, Noel McCaffrey, Dave Synnott, Jim Ronayne 0-2, Brian Mullins, Barney Rock 0-3, Tommy Conroy, Charlie Redmond, John Kearns 0-2, Joe McNally 2-0, Ciaran Duff. Subs: Tommy Carr 0-1 for Redmond, PJ Buckley for Mullins.

1986

LEINSTER QUARTER-FINAL
June 8, Croke Park, Dublin
DUBLIN 0-17   **WEXFORD 3-3**
Dublin: J O'Leary, S Fleming, G Hargan, M Kennedy, PJ Buckley, N McCaffrey, D Synnott 0-1, J Kearns, J Bissett, D Sheehan 0-1, J McNally 0-2, S Kearns 0-2, B Rock 0-6, T Carr 1-3, C Redmond 0-1. Subs: P Clarke for Kearns, C Duff 0-1 for Sheehan.

LEINSTER SEMI-FINAL
June 29, O'Moore Park, Portlaoise
DUBLIN 1-10   **OFFALY 0-7**
Dublin: J O'Leary, PJ Buckley, G Hargan, M Kennedy, P Canavan, N McCaffrey, D Synnott, J Ronayne, J Bissett, L Close 0-1, T Conroy 0-1, C Redmond 1-3, B Rock 0-3, T Carr 0-2, J McNally. Subs: C Duff for Close, F McGrath for Bissett.

LEINSTER FINAL
July 27, O'Moore Park, Portlaoise
MEATH 0-9   **DUBLIN 0-7**
Dublin: J O'Leary, PJ Buckley, G Hargan, M Kennedy, P Canavan, N McCaffrey, D Synnott, J Ronayne, J Bissett, L Close, C Duff 0-2, C Redmond 0-2, B Rock 0-3, T Carr, J McNally. Subs: T Conroy for Rock, P Clarke for Bissett, J Kearns for Close.

1987

LEINSTER QUARTER-FINAL
June 7, Croke Park, Dublin
DUBLIN 0-14   **WESTMEATH 0-7**
Dublin: J O'Leary, D Carroll, G Hargan, M Kennedy, D Synnott, E Heery, N McCaffrey, J Ronayne, D Bolger, C Redmond, J McNally 0-1, C Duff 0-2, B Rock 0-11, M Galvin, A McCaul. Sub: D Sheehan for Ronayne.

LEINSTER SEMI-FINAL
July 5, St Conleth's Park, Newbridge
DUBLIN 2-18   **WICKLOW 0-6**

Dublin: J O'Leary, D Carroll, G Hargan, M Kennedy, D Synnott 0-1, E Heery, N McCaffrey, D Bolger 0-2, J McNally, D DeLappe 1-2, C Redmond, C Crowley, B Rock 0-8, M Galvin 0-2, A McCaul 1-3. Subs: T Conroy for Crowley, L Close for Galvin.

LEINSTER FINAL
July 26, Croke Park, Dublin
MEATH 1-13   **DUBLIN 0-12**
Dublin: J O'Leary, D Carroll, G Hargan, M Kennedy, D Synnott, E Heery, N McCaffrey 0-2, J McNally 0-2, D Bolger 0-1, D DeLappe, C Redmond 0-1, C Duff, B Rock 0-4, M Galvin 0-1, A McCaul 0-1. Subs: J Ronayne for Bolger, T Carr for DeLappe.

1988

LEINSTER QUARTER-FINAL
June 6, Dr Cullen Park, Carlow
DUBLIN 1-14   **CARLOW 0-8**
Dublin: J O'Leary, B O'Hagan, G Hargan, M Kennedy, P Clarke, N McCaffrey, E Heery, J Ronayne, J Bissett 0-1, C Crowley 0-1, V Murphy 0-1, C Duff, D DeLappe 0-2, J McNally, M Galvin 1-2. Subs: C Redmond 0-5, for Duff, B Rock 0-2 for Redmond, D Carroll for Heery.

LEINSTER SEMI-FINAL
June 26, Cusack Park, Mullingar
DUBLIN 4-15   **LONGFORD 0-9**
Dublin: J O'Leary, D Synnott, G Hargan, M Kennedy, B O'Hagan, N McCaffrey, E Heery, J McNally 1-0, J Bissett 0-1, T Conroy 0-1, V Murphy 1-2, M Deegan, D Sheehan 1-4, M Galvin 1-1, B Rock 1-3. Sub: C Redmond 0-3 for Deegan.

LEINSTER FINAL
July 31, Croke Park, Dublin
MEATH 2-5   **DUBLIN 0-9**
Dublin: J O'Leary, D Synnott, G Hargan, M Kennedy, T Carr, N McCaffrey 0-1, E Heery, T Conroy, D Bolger, D Sheehan 0-3, V Murphy 0-2, C Redmond 0-1, J McNally, B Rock 0-1, M Galvin 0-1. Subs: B O'Hagan for Carr, J Bissett for Bolger.

1989

LEINSTER QUARTER-FINAL
June 5, St Conleth's Park, Newbridge
DUBLIN 1-13   **KILDARE 1-9**
Dublin: J O'Leary, P Curran, G Hargan, M Kennedy, E Heery, N McCaffrey, M Deegan, D Foran 0-1, P Clarke 0-1, V Murphy, T Carr 0-1, C Duff 1-2, B Rock 0-8, J McNally, A McCaul. Subs: G Walsh for Curran, C Redmond for Murphy, B Burke for McCaul.

LEINSTER SEMI-FINAL
June 25, St Conleth's Park, Newbridge
DUBLIN 1-12   WICKLOW 1-6
Dublin: J O'Leary, D Synnott, G Hargan, M Kennedy, K Barr, P Curran, E Heery, D Foran 0-1, P Clarke, V Murphy 0-2, T Carr 0-1, C Duff, B Rock 0-5, J McNally 1-0, M Galvin 0-3. Subs: T Conroy for Duff, G Walsh for Kennedy.

LEINSTER FINAL
July 30, Croke Park, Dublin
DUBLIN 2-12   MEATH 1-10
Dublin: J O'Leary, D Synnott, G Hargan, M Kennedy, K Barr, T Carr, E Heery, D Foran, P Clarke, V Murphy 1-2, C Duff 1-2, B Rock 0-5, P Curran 0-2, J McNally 0-1, M Galvin. Sub: M Deegan for Synnott.

ALL-IRELAND SEMI-FINAL
Aug 20, Croke Park, Dublin
CORK 2-10   DUBLIN 1-9
Dublin: J O'Leary, M Deegan, G Hargan, M Kennedy, K Barr, T Carr, E Heery D Foran, P Clarke 0-2, V Murphy 1-1, C Duff, B Rock 0-5, P Curran 0-1, J McNally, M Galvin. Subs: T Conroy for Galvin, A McCaul for Rock.

1990

LEINSTER QUARTER-FINAL
June 3, Drogheda Park, Drogheda
DUBLIN 1-13   LOUTH 1-8
Dublin: J O'Leary, M Deegan, G Hargan, M Kennedy, K Barr, T Carr, E Heery, D Bolger, D Foran 0-1, C Duff 0-5, C Redmond 0-1, V Murphy, N Clancy 0-3, M Galvin 0-3, J McNally 1-0. Sub: P Clarke for Foran, N McCaffrey for Carr.

LEINSTER SEMI-FINAL
June 24, St Conleth's Park, Newbridge
DUBLIN 2-14   WICKLOW 0-12
Dublin: J O'Leary, M Deegan, G Hargan, M Kennedy, N McCaffrey 0-1, K Barr, E Heery 0-3, P Clarke 0-1, D Bolger, C Duff 0-5, T Carr, N Gulden 0-1, N Clancy 0-2, M Galvin 0-1, J McNally 2-0. Subs: K Fagan for Kennedy, C Redmond for Guiden.

LEINSTER FINAL
July 29, Croke Park, Dublin
MEATH 1-14   DUBLIN 0-14
Dublin: J O'Leary, M Deegan, G Hargan, M Kennedy, K Barr 0-1, T Carr, E Heery, P Clarke 0-2, D Foran, V Murphy 0-1, C Duff, C Redmond 0-1, N Clancy, M Galvin, J McNally 0-1. Subs: B Rock 0-5 for Clancy, L Close 0-1 for Duff.

1991

LEINSTER FIRST ROUND
June 2, Croke Park, Dublin
DUBLIN 1-12   MEATH 1-12
Dublin: J O'Leary, M Deegan, C Walsh, M Kennedy, T Carr 0-1, K Barr, E Heery, P Clarke, P Curran 0-2, C Redmond 0-7, J Sheedy 0-1, N Guiden, V Murphy 0-1, D Foran, M Galvin 1-0. Subs: P Bealin for Foran, P Doherty for Galvin, C Duff for Guiden.

LEINSTER FIRST ROUND REPLAY
June 9, Croke Park, Dublin
DUBLIN 1-11   MEATH 1-11
Dublin: J O'Leary, M Deegan, C Walsh, M Kennedy, T Carr, K Barr, E Heery 0-1, D Foran, P Bealin, P Curran, B Rock 0-8, C Duff 0-1, J Sheedy 1-0, V Murphy, D McCarthy. Subs: P Clarke 0-1 for Curran, G Hargan for Kennedy. Extra time: Curran for Bealin, R Holland for Barr, P Doherty for Foran.

LEINSTER FIRST ROUND
SECOND REPLAY
June 23, Croke Park, Dublin
DUBLIN 1-14   MEATH 2-11
Dublin: J O'Leary, M Deegan, C Walsh, M Kennedy, T Carr, K Barr, E Heery, D Foran, P Bealin, P Clarke 1-1, J Sheedy 0-2, N Gulden 0-3, D Sheehan 0-1, V Murphy, B Rock 0-3. Subs: G Hargan for Walsh, J McNally 0-2 for Murphy, P Curran 0-1 for Guiden, R Holland for Kennedy, C Redmond for Foran. Extra time: Murphy for Redmond, Guiden for Carr, Kennedy for Barr.

LEINSTER FIRST ROUND
THIRD REPLAY
July 6, Croke Park, Dublin
MEATH 2-10   DUBLIN 0-15
Dublin: J O'Leary, M Deegan, G Hargan, M Kennedy, T Carr, K Barr, E Heery, J Sheedy, P Bealin, C Redmond 0-5, P Curran 0-2, N Gulden 0-3, D Sheehan 0-2, P Clarke, M Galvin 0-3. Subs: R Holland for Carr, J McNally for Clarke, V Murphy for Redmond.

1992

LEINSTER FIRST ROUND
May 31, O'Connor Park, Tullamore
DUBLIN 2-17   OFFALY 1-9
Dublin: J O'Leary, M Deegan, G Hargan, T Carr, P Curran, K Barr, E Heery, P Clarke 0-4, P Gilroy 0-2, C Redmond 1-2, J Sheedy 0-2, N Guiden 0-2, D Farrell 0-2, V Murphy 0-3, P Doherty 1-0. Subs: C Walsh for Barr, M Galvin for Doherty.

LEINSTER QUARTER-FINAL
June 28, O'Moore Park, Portlaoise
DUBLIN 1-18   WEXFORD 0-11
Dublin: J O'Leary, M Deegan, G Hargan, T Carr, P Curran, K Barr 0-1, E Heary, P Clarke 0-3, P Gilroy, C Redmond 0-7, J Sheedy 0-2, N Guiden 0-2, D Farrell 0-2, V Murphy 1-0, P Doherty. Sub: M Galvin 0-1 for Doherty.

LEINSTER SEMI-FINAL
July 12, O'Moore Park, Portlaoise
DUBLIN 0-15   LOUTH 1-9
Dublin: J O'Leary, M Deegan, G Hargan, T Carr, P Curran, K Barr, E Heery 0-1, P Clarke, P Gilroy, C Redmond 0-6, J Sheedy 0-2, N Guiden, D FarreJl 0-2, V Murphy 0-2, M Galvin 0-2. Sub: D Foran for Gilroy.

LEINSTER FINAL
July 26, Croke Park, Dublin
DUBLIN 1-13   KILDARE 0-10
Dublin: J O'Leary, M Deegan, G Hargan, T Carr, P Curran 0-1, K Barr 1-0. E Heery 0-1, P Clarke 0-1, D Foran, C Redmond 0-5, J Sheedy, N Guiden, D Farrell 0-1, V Murphy 0-3, M Galvin 0-1. Subs: P Gilroy for Sheedy, P Bealin for Foran.

ALL-IRELAND SEMI-FINAL
Aug 23, Croke Park, Dublin
DUBLIN 3-14   CLARE 2-12
Dublin: J O'Leary, M Deegan, G Hargan, T Carr, P Curran 0-1, K Barr, E Heery, P Clarke 0-2, D Foran, C Redmond 0-5, J Sheedy 0-2, N Guiden 0-1, D Farrell 0-1, V Murphy 2-1. M Galvin 1-1. Sub: P Bealin for Foran.

ALL-IRELAND FINAL
Sep 20, Croke Park, Dublin
DONEGAL 0-18   DUBLIN 0-14
Dublin: John O'Leary, Mick Deegan, Gerry Hargan, Tommy Carr, Paul Curran, Keith Barr, Eamonn Heery 0-1, Paul Clarke 0-2, David Foran, Charlie Redmond 0-3, Jack Sheedy 0-2, Niall Guiden 0-1, Dessie Farrell 0-1, Vinnie Murphy 0-2, Mick Galvin 0-2. Sub: Paul Bealin for Foran.

1993

LEINSTER FIRST ROUND
May 23, Wexford Park, Wexford
DUBLIN 0-11   WEXFORD 0-7
Dublin: J O'Leary, C Walsh, D Deasy, P Moran, E Heery, P Curran, M Deegan, P Bealin, J Sheedy 0-1, J Gavin, V Murphy 0-2, N Guiden 0-2, D Farrell 0-2, M Doran, P Clarke 0-4. Subs: P Gilroy for Bealin, P O'Donoghue for Gavin.

LEINSTER QUARTER-FINAL
June 7, O'Connor Park, Tullamore
DUBLIN 2-11   WESTMEATH 0-8
Dublin: J O'Leary, C Walsh, D Deasy, P Moran, E Heery, P Curran 0-1, M Deegan 0-1, P Gilroy, J Sheedy 0-1, P Clarke 0-3, K Barr 1-2, N Guiden, D Farrell 0-1, V Murphy 1-1, M Doran. Subs: J Gavin 0-1 for Clarke, C Redmond for Deegan, D Foran for Deegan.

LEINSTER SEMI-FINAL
July 4, Croke Park, Dublin
DUBLIN 1-10   MEATH 0-12
Dublin: J O'Leary, C Walsh, D Deasy, P Moran, E Heery, P Curran, D Harrington, P Gilroy, J Sheedy 0-1, J Gavin, K Barr, N Guiden 0-1, D Farrell, V Murphy 0-1, C Redmond l-7. Subs: P Bealin for Harrington, M Galvin for Gavin.

LEINSTER FINAL
July 25, Croke Park, Dublin
DUBLIN 0-11   KILDARE 0-7
Dublin: J O'Leary, C Walsh, D Deasy, P Moran, P Curran, K Barr, P O'Neill, J Sheedy, P Bealin 0-1, E Heery, D Farrell 0-1, P Gilroy 0-1, J Gavin, V Murphy 0-1, C Redmond 0-5. Subs: M Galvin 0-1 for Gavin, J Barr 0-1 for Galvin.

ALL-IRELAND SEMI-FINAL
Aug 22, Croke Park, Dublin
DERRY 0-15   DUBLIN 0-14
Dublin: J O'Leary, C Walsh, D Deasy, P Moran, P Curran 0-1, K Barr, P O'Neill, J Sheedy, P Bealin 0-1, E Heery 0-1, P Gilroy 0-2, P Clarke 0-1, D Farrell, V Murphy, C Redmond 0-7. Subs: M Deegan for Deasy, M Galvin for O'Neill, J Barr for Clarke.

1994

LEINSTER QUARTER-FINAL
June 18, Croke Park, Dublin
DUBLIN 0-11   KILDARE 0-11
Dublin: J O'Leary, C Walsh, D Deasy, P Moran, P Curran, K Barr, M Deegan, J Sheedy 0-1, P Bealin, P Gilroy, T Carr, V Murphy 0-1, N Gulden, D Farrell 0-1, C Redmond 0-8.

LEINSTER QUARTER-FINAL REPLAY
July 2, Croke Park, Dublin
DUBLIN 1-14   KILDARE 1-9
Dublin: J O'Leary, C Walsh, D Deasy, P Moran, P Curran, K Barr, M Deegan 0-2, B Stynes 0-1, P Bealin 0-1, P Gilroy, J Sheedy 0-2, N Guiden 0-1, D Farrell 0-1, M Galvin 0-1, C Redmond 1-4. Subs: P Clarke 0-1 for Galvin, V Murphy for Gilroy.

LEINSTER SEMI-FINAL
July 10, Croke Park, Dublin
DUBLIN 1-15   LOUTH 1-8
Dublin: J O'Leary, C Walsh, D Deasy, P Moran, P Curran, K Barr, M Deegan, B Stynes 0-1, S Cahill, P Gilroy 0-1, J Sheedy, N Gulden 0-2, D Farrell 0-2, M Galvin 0-5, C Redmond 1-4. Subs: J Barr for Sheedy, P O'Neill for Curran, G Regan for Walsh.

LEINSTER FINAL
July 31, Croke Park, Dublin
DUBLIN 1-9   MEATH 1-8
Dublin: J O'Leary, C Walsh, D Deasy, P Moran, P Curran, K Barr, M Deegan, B Stynes, P Bealin, P Gilroy, J Sheedy, N Guiden 0-1, D Farrell 0-1, M Galvin, C Redmond 1-4. Subs: P Clarke 0-1 for Bealin, V Murphy for Gilroy, G Regan for Deasy 0-2.

ALL-IRELAND SEMI-FINAL
Aug 21, Croke Park, Dublin
DUBLIN 3-15   LEITRIM 1-9
Dublin: J O'Leary, C Walsh, D Deasy, P Moran, P Clarke, K Barr, M Deegan, B Stynes 0-1, J Sheedy, P Gilroy, V Murphy 0-2, N Guiden 0-2, D Farrell 1-2, M Galvin 1-1, C Redmond 1-6. Subs: P Bealin 0-1 for Galvin, L Walsh for C Walsh, T Carr for Sheedy.

ALL-IRELAND FINAL
Sep 18, Croke Park, Dublin
DOWN 1-12   DUBLIN 0-13
Dublin: John O'Leary (capt), Paddy Moran, Dermot Deasy, Paul Curran 0-1, Paul Clarke 0-1, Keith Barr, Mick Deegan, Brian Stynes 0-1, Pat Gilroy, Jack Sheedy 0-2, Vinny Murphy 0-1, Niall Guiden 0-1, Dessie Farrell 0-1, Mick Galvin, Charlie Redmond 0-4. Subs: Paul Bealin for Gilroy, Sean Cahill 0-1 for Galvin, Johnny Barr for Guiden.

1995

LEINSTER QUARTER-FINAL
June 18, Pairc Tailteann, Navan
DUBLIN 0-19   LOUTH 2-5
Dublin: J O'Leary, K Galvin, D Deasy, P Moran, P Curran, K Barr, M Deegan, P Bealin, B Stynes 0-1, S Cahill, V Murphy 0-1, P Clarke, C Redmond 0-9, M Galvin 0-2, D Farrell 0-2. Subs: J Sherlock 0-1 for Cahill, J Gavin 0-1 for Murphy, E Sheehy for Redmond.

LEINSTER SEMI-FINAL
July 9, Pairc Tailteann, Navan
DUBLIN 1-13   LAOIS 0-9
Dublin: J O'Leary, P Moran, C Walsh, K Galvin, P Curran, K Barr, M Deegan 0-1, P Bealin, B Stynes, J Sherlock 1-0, D Farrell 0-1, S Cahill, P Clarke 0-3, M Galvin, C Redmond 0-7. Subs: J Gavin for Galvin, V Murphy 0-1 for Cahill, P Gilroy for Bealin.

LEINSTER FINAL
July 30, Croke Park, Dublin
DUBLIN 1-18   MEATH 1-8
Dublin: J O'Leary, K Galvin, D Deasy, P Moran, P Curran 0-2, K Barr, M Deegan, P Bealin, B Stynes, P Clarke 1-2, D Farrell 0-3, J Gavin 0-1, M Galvin 0-1, J Sherlock 0-2, C Redmond 0-7. Sub: V Murphy for M Galvin.

ALL-IRELAND SEMI-FINAL
Aug 20, Croke Park, Dublin
DUBLIN 1-12   CORK 0-12
Dublin: J O'Leary, P Moran, D Deasy, K Galvin, P Curran, K Barr, M Deegan, P Bealin, B Stynes, P Clarke 0-1, D Farrell, J Gavin, M Galvin 0-4, J Sherlock 1-0, C Redmond 0-7. Subs: P Gilroy for Bealin, C Walsh for K Galvin, V Murphy for Clarke.

ALL-IRELAND FINAL
Sep 17, Croke Park, Dublin
DUBLIN 1-10   TYRONE 0-12
Dublin: John O'Leary, Paddy Moran, Ciaran Walsh, Keith Galvin, Paul Curran 0-1, Keith Barr 0-1, Mick Deegan, Paul Bealin, Brian Stynes, Jim Gavin 0-1, Dessie Farrell 0-4, Paul Clarke 0-2, Mick Galvin, Jason Sherlock, Charlie Redmond 1-1. Subs: Pat Gilroy for K Galvin, Robbie Boyle for M Galvin, Vinnie Murphy for Farrell.

1996

LEINSTER QUARTER-FINAL
June 9, Pairc Tailteann, Navan
DUBLIN 1-18   WESTMEATH 0-11
Dublin: J O'Leary, M Deegan, D Martin, P Moran, P Curran 0-1, K Barr 1-0, E Heery 0-1, B Stynes 0-1, P Bealin 0-1, J Gavin 0-1, D Farrell 0-3, N Guiden 0-1, D O'Brien 0-1, J McNally 0-3, C Redmond 0-5. Sub: J Sherlock for Guiden, Robbie Boyle for O'Brien.

LEINSTER SEMI-FINAL
June 30, Pairc Tailteann, Navan
DUBLIN 1-9   LOUTH 0-8
Dublin: J O'Leary, P Moran, D Martin, M Deegan, P Curran, K Barr, E Heery, B Stynes, P Bealin 0-1, J Gavin 0-1, D Farrell, N Guiden 0-1, C Redmond 0-5, J McNally 1-1, D O'Brien.

LEINSTER FINAL
July 28, Croke Park, Dublin
MEATH 0-10   DUBLIN 0-8
Dublin: J O'Leary, P Moran, D Deasy, M Deegan, P Curran, K Barr, E Heery 0-1, B Stynes 0-1, P Bealin, C Whelan 0-2, P Gilroy, J Gavin, D Farrell, J Sherlock, C Redmond 0-4. Sub: D O'Brien for Gilroy, D Harrington for P Bealin, S Keogh for O'Brien.

1997

LEINSTER QUARTER-FINAL
June 15, Croke Park, Dublin
MEATH 1-13   DUBLIN 1-10
Dublin: J O'Leary, P Christie, I Robertson, C Walsh, P Curran 0-1, K Barr 1-0, E Heery 0-1, B Stynes 0-2, P Bealin, J Gavin 0-1, D Farrell, P Clarke, C Redmond 0-4, M Galvin, J Sherlock. Subs: M Deegan for P Clarke, P Ward 0-1 for Gavin, P Moran for Walsh.

1998

LEINSTER QUARTER-FINAL
June 7, Croke Park, Dublin
DUBLIN 0-10   KILDARE 0-10
Dublin: D Byrne, P Moran, P Christie, D Barnes, P Curran, K Barr, D Harrington 0-1, B Stynes 0-1, P Bealin, C Whelan, D Farrell, I Robertson, J Gavin 0-2, D Darcy 0-4, J Sherlock 0-1. Subs: M Deegan for Barnes 40, R Boyle for Whelan 49, E Heery for Bealin 60.

LEINSTER QUARTER-FINAL REPLAY
June 21, Croke Park, Dublin
KILDARE 0-12   DUBLIN 1-8
Dublin: D Byrne, E Heery, P Christie, P Moran, P Curran 0-1, K Barr, D Harrington, B Stynes 0-1, C Whelan, D Darcy 1-5, J Gavin 0-1, I Robertson, D Farrell, M Deegan, J Sherlock. Subs: P Bealin for Robertson 46, P Croft for Harrington 50, R Boyle for Sherlock 60.

1999

LEINSTER QUARTER-FINAL
June 6, Croke Park, Dublin
DUBLIN 2-15   LOUTH 0-14
Dublin: D Byrne, P Christie 0-1, P Moran, T Lynch, P Curran, S Ryan, K Galvin, C Whelan 0-4, B Stynes 0-2, E Sheehy, J Gavin, D Darcy 0-5, D Farrell, I Robertson 1-0, B O'Brien 0-3. Subs: M O'Keeffe 1-0 for Gavin h/t, D Homan for Sheehy 57, L Walsh for Ryan 65.

LEINSTER SEMI-FINAL
June 27, Croke Park, Dublin
DUBLIN 1-11   LAOIS 0-14
Dublin: D Byrne, P Moran, P Christie 0-1, T Lynch, P Croft, P Curran, K Galvin 0-1, C Whelan, B Stynes 0-1, E Sheehy, J Gavin 0-3, D Darcy 0-2, D Farrell 0-1, I Robertson 1-2, B O'Brien. Subs: J Sherlock for O'Brien h/t, D Homan for Stynes 46, S Ryan for Curran 48.

LEINSTER SEMI-FINAL REPLAY
July 18, Croke Park, Dublin
DUBLIN 0-16   LAOIS 1-11
Dublin: D Byrne, P Christie, P Moran, T Lynch, P Croft, J Magee, K Galvin, C Whelan 0-1, B Stynes 0-3, E Sheehy 0-1, D Farrell 0-1, D Darcy 0-5, J Gavin 0-1, I Robertson 0-4, J Sherlock. Subs: P Andrews for Lynch 21, D Homan for Sheehy 67.

LEINSTER FINAL
Aug 1, Croke Park, Dublin
MEATH 1-14   DUBLIN 0-12
Dublin: D Byrne, P Croft, P Christie, P Andrews, K Galvin, J Magee, P Moran, C Whelan 0-1, B Stynes, E Sheehy, D Farrell, D Darcy 0-6, J Gavin 0-5, I Robertson, J Sherlock. Subs: R Cosgrove for Farrell 16, D Homan for Cosgrove 49, P Ward for Sheehy 63.

2000

LEINSTER QUARTER-FINAL
June 11, Croke Park, Dublin
DUBLIN 2-20   WEXFORD 1-8
Dublin: D Byrne, S Ryan, P Christie, C Goggins, P Curran 1-1, J Magee 0-1, P Andrews, C Whelan 0-1, B Stynes 0-1, S Connell, E Sheehy 0-1, J Gavin 0-6, J Sherlock 0-3, V Murphy 1-3, D Darcy 0-2. Subs: C Moran for Darcy 50, D Homan 0-1 for Whelan 58, N O'Donoghue for Connell 65, T Lynch for Ryan 66, I Clarke for Curran 68.

LEINSTER SEMI-FINAL
July 2, Croke Park, Dublin
DUBLIN 1-14   WESTMEATH 0-11
Dublin: D Byrne, P Christie, S Ryan, C Goggins, P Curran 0-1, J Magee, P Andrews, B Stynes 0-2, E Sheehy, S Connell 0-3, C Moran, J Gavin 0-3, D Farrell 0-1, I Robertson 0-1, J Sherlock 1-2. Subs: V Murphy for Moran 60, D Homan 0-1 for Stynes 65.

LEINSTER FINAL
July 30, Croke Park, Dublin
DUBLIN 0-14   KILDARE 0-14
Dublin: D Byrne, S Ryan, P Christie, C Goggins, P Curran, J Magee 0-1, P Andrews, B Stynes 0-3, C Whelan 0-1, S Connell, D Farrell 0-1, J Gavin 0-1, C Moran 0-3, I Robertson, J Sherlock 0-3. Subs: V Murphy 0-1 for Robertson 17, E Sheehy for Connell 45, D Homan for Stynes 67.

LEINSTER FINAL REPLAY
Aug 12, Croke Park, Dublin
KILDARE 2-11   DUBLIN 0-12
Dublin: D Byrne, S Ryan, P Christie, C Goggins, P Curran, J Magee, P Andrews, C Whelan 0-2, B Stynes 0-1, S Connell, C Moran 0-3, J Gavin 0-1, D Farrell

0-2, J Sherlock 0-1, V Murphy 0-2. Subs: E Sheehy for Connell, D Homan for Gavin, T Lynch for Ryan, W McCarthy for Murphy.

2001

LEINSTER QUARTER-FINAL
May 27, Croke Park, Dublin
DUBLIN 2-19   LONGFORD 1-13
Dublin: S Cluxton, M Cahill, P Christie, C Goggins, T Lynch, P Curran 0-1, P Andrews, C Whelan 0-5, D Homan 0-1, S Connell 0-5, J Sherlock 0-2, E Sheehy 0-2, N O'Donoghue, D Farrell, W McCarthy 1-1. Subs: J Magee for Andrews 30, C Moran 1-0 for O'Donoghue h/t, V Murphy 0-1 for Sheehy 42, J Gavin for Farrell 55, S Ryan 0-1 for Curran 68.

LEINSTER SEMI-FINAL
June 17, Croke Park, Dublin
DUBLIN 1-12   OFFALY 0-13
Dublin: S Cluxton, M Cahill, P Christie, C Goggins, P Curran, J Magee, P Andrews, C Whelan, D Homan, C Moran, D Farrell 0-2, S Connell 0-2, J Sherlock 0-1, I Robertson 1-1, W McCarthy 0-4. Subs: K Darcy for Whelan 50, V Murphy 0-2 for Connell 58, N O'Donoghue for McCarthy 63, T Lynch for Cahill 66.

LEINSTER FINAL
July 15, Croke Park, Dublin
MEATH 2-11   DUBLIN 0-14
Dublin: D Byrne, M Cahill, P Christie, C Goggins, P Curran, P Andrews, J Magee, C Whelan 0-3, D Homan, S Connell, D Farrell 0-3, C Moran 0-4, W McCarthy 0-3, I Robertson, J Sherlock 0-1. Subs: S Ryan for Cahill 11, E Sheehy for Robertson 48, V Murphy for Connell 53.

ALL-IRELAND QUALIFIER, ROUND FOUR
July 22, Croke Park, Dublin
DUBLIN 3-17   SLIGO 0-12
Dublin: D Byrne, S Ryan, P Christie, C Goggins 0-1, P Curran 0-1, J Magee, P Andrews, C Whelan 1-2, D Homan, E Sheehy 1-0, I Robertson, C Moran, J Sherlock, D Farrell 1-4, D Darcy 0-5. Subs: S Connell 0-2 for Homan 25, V Murphy for Robertson 39, T Lynch for Goggins 46, W McCarthy 0-1 for Moran 51, K Darcy 0-1 for Darcy 64.

ALL-IRELAND QUARTER-FINAL
Aug 4, Semple Stadium, Thurles
DUBLIN 2-11   KERRY 1-14
Dublin: D Byrne, S Ryan, P Christie, C Goggins, P Curran, J Magee, P Andrews, C Whelan 0-1, D Homan 1-1, E Sheehy, D Farrell 0-1, C Moran, D Darcy 0-6, I Robertson, J Sherlock 0-1. Subs: K Darcy for Robertson 43, S Connell for Sheehy 49, V Murphy 1-0 for Moran 57, W McCarthy 0-1 for Darcy 60,

ALL-IRELAND QUARTER-FINAL REPLAY
Aug 11, Semple Stadium, Thurles
KERRY 2-12   DUBLIN 1-12
Dublin: D Byrne, S Ryan, P Christie, C Goggins, P Curran 0-1, J Magee, P Andrews, C Whelan 0-1, D Homan 1-0, E Sheehy, K Darcy, C Moran 0-1, D Darcy 0-4, D Farrell 0-1, J Sherlock 0-1. Subs: S Connell 0-1 for K Darcy h/t, V Murphy for Sheehy 44, W McCarthy 0-2 for D Darcy 54, N O'Donoghue for Moran 65.

2002

LEINSTER QUARTER-FINAL
June 1, Dr Cullen Park, Carlow
DUBLIN 0-15   WEXFORD 1-10
Dublin: S Cluxton, B Cahill, P Christie, C Goggins, P Casey, J Magee, P Andrews, D Homan, C Whelan 0-2, S Connell 0-1, S Ryan, C Moran 0-2, A Brogan 0-1, D Farrell 0-1, R Cosgrove 0-5. Subs: P Curran 0-1 for Goggins 27, D Magee for Curran 40, T Mulligan for Moran 55, J Sherlock 0-2 for Brogan 60, J Connell for Gavin 69.

LEINSTER SEMI-FINAL
June 23, Croke Park, Dublin
DUBLIN 2-11   MEATH 0-10
Dublin: S Cluxton, B Cahill, P Christie, C Goggins, P Casey, J Magee, P Andrews, C Whelan, D Homan 0-1, C Moran 0-4, S Ryan, S Connell, A Brogan 0-3, R Cosgrove 2-3, J McNally. Subs: D Magee for Homan 54, D Farrell for McNally 58, D Henry for Andrews 59, J Sherlock for Moran 67.

LEINSTER FINAL
July 14, Croke Park, Dublin
DUBLIN 2-13   KILDARE 2-11
Dublin: S Cluxton, B Cahill, P Christie 0-1, C Goggins, P Casey, P Andrews, P Curran, C Whelan 0-1, D Homan, C Moran, S Ryan, S Connell 0-2, A Brogan 1-2, R Cosgrove 1-4, J McNally 0-3. Subs: D Magee for Curran 41, J Sherlock for Connell 55, D Farrell for McNally 58, D Henry for Homan 60.

ALL-IRELAND QUARTER-FINAL
Aug 5, Croke Park, Dublin
DUBLIN 2-8   DONEGAL 0-14
Dublin: S Cluxton, J Magee, P Christie, C Goggins, P Andrews, P Casey, B Cahill, C Whelan 0-1, D Homan, C Moran, S Ryan 0-1, S Connell 0-1, A Brogan 0-1, R Cosgrove 2-2, J McNally 0-1. Subs: D Magee 0-1 for Casey 10, D Farrell for Connell 48, J Sherlock for Moran 50, S Connell for Ryan 65, K Darcy for Homan 69.

ALL-IRELAND QUARTER-FINAL REPLAY
Aug 17, Croke Park, Dublin
DUBLIN 1-14   DONEGAL 0-7
Dublin: S Cluxton, B Cahill, P Christie 0-1, P Andrews, P Casey, J Magee 0-1, C Goggins, C Whelan 0-4, D Magee, S Connell 0-2, J McNally 0-1, C Moran, A Brogan 0-2, R Cosgrove 1-3, D Farrell. Subs: J Sherlock for Farrell 42, S Ryan for Moran 51, P Curran for McNally 64, D Homan for D Magee 66.

ALL-IRELAND SEMI-FINAL
Sep 1, Croke Park, Dublin
ARMAGH 1-14   DUBLIN 1-13
Dublin: S Cluxton, B Cahill, P Christie, C Goggins, P Casey, J Magee, P Andrews, C Whelan 1-1, D Magee 0-1, S Connell 0-2, D Farrell, S Ryan, A Brogan 0-2, J McNally, R Cosgrove 0-6. Subs: C Moran 0-1 for Ryan h/t, D Homan for D Magee 45, J Sherlock for McNally 62, D Darcy for Moran 70.

2003

LEINSTER QUARTER-FINAL
June 1, Croke Park, Dublin
DUBLIN 1-19   LOUTH 0-9
Dublin: S Cluxton, B Cahill, P Christie, P Griffin, D Henry 0-1, J Magee, C Moran, C Whelan 0-3, D Magee 0-1, B Cullen 0-3, S Ryan, S Connell 0-1, A Brogan 1-0, R Cosgrove 0-3, J McNally. Subs: T Quinn 0-3 for Brogan 43, T Mulligan 0-1 for Ryan 43, L Og O hEineachain for Connell 52, D O'Callaghan 0-2 for McNally 53, C Goggins 0-1 for Moran 64.

LEINSTER SEMI-FINAL
June 15, Croke Park, Dublin
LAOIS 0-16   DUBLIN 0-14
Dublin: S Cluxton, P Griffin, P Christie, B Cahill, C Moran 0-1, J Magee, P Casey, C Whelan, D Magee, T Mulligan 0-3, S Ryan 0-1, B Cullen, A Brogan 0-3, R Cosgrove 0-2, L Og O Eineachain. Subs: T Quinn 0-3 for O hEineachain h/t, S Connell 0-1 for Cullen 42, C Goggins for Casey 55, D Homan for Ryan 59, D O'Callaghan for Cosgrove 68.

ALL-IRELAND QUALIFIERS, ROUND TWO
June 28, St Tiernach's Park, Clones
DUBLIN 3-9   DERRY 1-9
Dublin: S Cluxton, D Henry, P Christie, P Griffin, S Ryan, J Magee, C Moran, C Whelan 0-1, D Homan 0-1, S Connell 1-1, D Farrell 1-1, J McNally, A Brogan, T Mulligan, R Cosgrove 0-2. Subs: D Magee for Mulligan h/t, J Sherlock 1-3 for McNally 42, C Goggins for Henry 51, T Quinn for Cosgrove 63, B Cullen for Farrell 68.

ALL-IRELAND QUALIFIERS, ROUND THREE
July 5, Croke Park, Dublin
ARMAGH 0-15   DUBLIN 0-11
Dublin: S Cluxton, P Griffin, P Christie, C Moran, S Ryan, J Magee, D Henry, C Whelan, D Homan 0-1, S Connell 0-1, B Cullen, A Brogan, D Farrell 0-2, R Cosgrove 0-5, J Sherlock 0-2. Subs: D Magee for Homan 42, B Murphy for J Magee 44, D O'Callaghan for Brogan 56, T Mulligan for Connell 65.

2004

LEINSTER QUARTER-FINAL
June 6, Croke Park, Dublin
WESTMEATH 0-14 DUBLIN 0-12
Dublin: B Murphy, B Cahill, P Christie, P Griffin, S Ryan, D Magee, P Andrews, C Whelan, D Homan, C Keaney, B Cullen 0-1, C Moran 0-1, A Brogan 0-4, J Sherlock 0-4, S Connell 0-2. Subs: R Cosgrove for Keaney 48, C Goggins for Homan 52, D Lally for Cullen 61, T Quinn for Moran 75.

ALL-IRELAND QUALIFIERS, ROUND ONE
June 12, Parnell Park, Dublin
DUBLIN 3-24   LONDON 0-6
Dublin: S Cluxton, B Cahill, P Christie, P Griffin, S Ryan, D Magee 0-1, P Andrews, C Whelan, D O'Mahony 0-1, C Moran 0-2, T Quinn 1-5, S Connell 0-7, A Brogan 2-4, J Sherlock 0-1, J McNally. Subs: P Casey for Ryan h/t, D Henry for Griffin 42, C Goggins for Andrews 44, D Lally for McNally 48, R Cosgrove 0-3 for Moran 55.

ALL-IRELAND QUALIFIERS, ROUND TWO
July 3, McDermott Park, Carr-on-Shannon
DUBLIN 0-13   LEITRIM 1-4
Dublin: S Cluxton, B Cahill, P Christie, C Goggins, P Casey 0-1, B Cullen, P Griffin, J Magee, D Magee, S Connell 1-2, C Whelan, D Lally, A Brogan 0-3, J Sherlock 0-2, T Quinn 0-3. Subs: I Robertson for Lally 15, D Farrell 0-1 for Quinn 53, R Cosgrove for Sherlock 63, D O'Mahony for D Magee 68, S Ryan for J Magee 69.

ALL-IRELAND QUALIFIERS, ROUND THREE
July 10, O'Moore Park, Portlaoise
DUBLIN 1-17   LONGFORD 0-11
Dublin: S Cluxton, B Cahill, P Christie, C Goggins, P Casey, B Cullen, P Griffin, D Homan, D Magee, J Sherlock 0-2, C Whelan 0-3, S Connell, A Brogan 0-4, I Robertson 1-1, T Quinn 0-5. Subs: S Ryan 0-1 for Casey 39, D Farrell 0-1 for Brogan 58, J Magee for Homan 59, R Boyle for Robertson 65, R Cosgrove for Connell 66.

ALL-IRELAND QUALIFIERS, ROUND FOUR
Aug 1, Croke Park, Dublin
DUBLIN 1-14   ROSCOMMON 0-13
Dublin: S Cluxton, B Cahill, P Christie, C Goggins, P Casey, B Cullen 0-2, P Griffin, D Homan 0-1, D Magee, C Keaney 0-1, C Whelan 0-2, S Connell 0-1, A Brogan 0-3, I Robertson, J Sherlock 1-4. Subs: J Magee for Homan 44, S Ryan for Goggins 48, D Farrell for Keaney 55, T Quinn for Farrell 61.

ALL-IRELAND QUARTER-FINAL
Aug 14, Croke Park, Dublin
KERRY 1-15   DUBLIN 1-8
Dublin: S Cluxton, B Cahill, P Christie, P Griffin, P Casey, B Cullen, S Ryan, D Homan 0-2, D Magee, C Keaney 0-1, C Whelan, S Connell 0-5, A Brogan, I Robertson, J Sherlock 1-0. Subs: T Quinn for Keaney 53, R Cosgrove for Robertson 58, D O'Mahony for Homan 63.

2005

LEINSTER FIRST ROUND
May 15, Croke Park, Dublin
DUBLIN 2-23   LONGFORD 0-10
Dublin: S Cluxton, P Griffin, P Christie, S O'Shaughnessy, P Casey, B Cahill, C Goggins 0-1, C Whelan 0-1, S Ryan 0-2, C Moran 0-1, A Brogan 1-3, B Cullen 0-2, J Sherlock 0-1, C Keaney 1-4, T Quinn 0-5. Subs: M Vaughan 0-2 for Moran 50, D O'Mahony for Whelan 59, D O'Callaghan 0-1 for Quinn 60, D Homan for Keaney 64, S Connell for Brogan 68.

LEINSTER QUARTER-FINAL
June 5, Croke Park, Dublin
DUBLIN 1-12   MEATH 1-10
Dublin: S Cluxton, P Griffin, P Christie, S O'Shaughnessy, P Casey, B Cahill 0-1, C Goggins, C Whelan, S Ryan, C Moran, A Brogan 1-3, B Cullen 0-1, J Sherlock, C Keaney 0-3, T Quinn 0-1. Subs: S Connell 0-1 for Moran h/t, M Vaughan 0-2 for Sherlock h/t, D Homan for Quinn 60, J Sherlock for Homan 64 (blood sub), P Andrews for Casey 66.

LEINSTER SEMI-FINAL
June 19, Croke Park, Dublin
DUBLIN 1-17   WEXFORD 2-10
Dublin: S Cluxton, P Griffin, P Christie, S O'Shaughnessy, P Casey, B Cahill, C Goggins, C Whelan 0-2, S Ryan, C Moran 0-2, A Brogan 0-1, B Cullen 0-1, M Vaughan, C Keaney 0-1, T Quinn 0-10. Subs: P Andrews for O'Shaughnessy 32, J Sherlock 1-0 for Vaughan h/t, S Connell for Moran 51, D Homan for Ryan 67.

LEINSTER FINAL
July 17, Croke Park, Dublin
DUBLIN 0-14   LAOIS 0-13
Dublin: S Cluxton, P Griffin, P Christie, S O'Shaughnessy 0-1, C Goggins, B Cahill, P Casey, C Whelan 0-1, S Ryan, C Moran 0-1, A Brogan 0-1, B Cullen 0-3, J Sherlock 0-2, C Keaney 0-1, T Quinn 0-4. Subs: P Andrews for Christie 18, S Connell for Goggins h/t, D Homan for Ryan 60.

ALL-IRELAND QUARTER-FINAL
Aug 13, Croke Park, Dublin
DUBLIN 1-14   TYRONE 1-14
Dublin: S Cluxton, P Griffin, P Christie, S O'Shaughnessy, P Casey, B Cahill, C Goggins, C Whelan, S Ryan, C Moran, A Brogan 0-2, B Cullen, J Sherlock 0-2, C Keaney 0-3, T Quinn 1-7. Subs: P Andrews for Griffin 54, D Homan for Cahill 65, S Connell for Ryan 61, D Farrell for Moran 72.

ALL-IRELAND QUARTER-FINAL REPLAY
Aug 27, Croke Park, Dublin
TYRONE 2-18   DUBLIN 1-14
Dublin: S Cluxton, P Andrews, P Griffin, S O'Shaughnessy, P Casey, B Cahill, S Ryan 0-1, C Whelan, D Magee, C Moran 0-1, C Keaney 0-5, B Cullen 0-1, J Sherlock 0-1, A Brogan 0-2, T Quinn 0-2. Subs: S Connell for Brogan 25, D Lally for Magee h/t, M Vaughan for Quinn 57, D O'Callaghan for Lally 59, D Farrell 1-0 for Keaney 67.

2006

LEINSTER QUARTER-FINAL
June 4, Pearse Park, Longford
DUBLIN 1-12   LONGFORD 0-13
Dublin: S Cluxton, D Henry, B Cahill, N O'Shea, P Casey, C Goggins, P Griffin, C Whelan, S Ryan, M Vaughan 1-0, A Brogan 0-1, B Cullen 0-1, K Bonner 0-1, C Keaney 0-8, T Quinn. Subs: P Andrews for Cahill, J Sherlock for Quinn 44, D Lally 0-1 for Ryan 60, R Cosgrove for Bonner 66.

LEINSTER SEMI-FINAL
June 25, Croke Park, Dublin
DUBLIN 3-17   LAOIS 0-12
Dublin: S Cluxton, D Henry, B Cahill, P Griffin, P Casey 0-1, B Cullen, C Goggins, C Whelan, S Ryan, K Bonner, J Sherlock, R Cosgrove 1-3, A Brogan 0-2, C Keaney 0-6, T Quinn 2-3. Subs: D Lally for Bonner 53, D O'Callaghan 0-2 for Sherlock 62, S Connell for Cosgrove 65, M Vaughan for Goggins 67, D O'Mahony for Ryan 70.

LEINSTER FINAL

July 16, Croke Park, Dublin

DUBLIN 1-15   OFFALY 0-9

Dublin: S Cluxton, P Griffin, B Cahill, D Henry, P Casey, B Cullen, C Goggins, C Whelan, S Ryan, D Lally, J Sherlock 1-1, R Cosgrove, A Brogan 0-4, C Keaney 0-3, T Quinn 0-7. Subs: S Connell for Cosgrove 57, D O'Callaghan for Lally 62, D Magee for Quinn 68, C Moran for Goggins 70, S O'Shaughnessy for Griffin 71.

ALL-IRELAND QUARTER-FINAL

Aug 12, Croke Park, Dublin

DUBLIN 1-12   WESTMEATH 0-5

Dublin: S Cluxton, D Henry, B Cahill, P Griffin, P Casey, B Cullen, C Goggins, C Whelan, S Ryan 0-1, K Bonner, J Sherlock 0-1, R Cosgrove 0-1, A Brogan 0-4, C Keaney 0-2, T Quinn 1-2. Subs: D Lally for Bonner 48, D O'Callaghan for Cosgrove 56, M Vaughan for Quinn 60, D Magee 0-1 for Whelan 61, C Moran for Sherlock 67.

ALL-IRELAND SEMI-FINAL

Aug 27, Croke Park, Dublin

MAYO 1-16   DUBLIN 2-12

Dublin: S Cluxton, D Henry, B Cahill, P Griffin, P Casey, B Cullen, C Goggins, C Whelan, S Ryan, K Bonner 0-1, J Sherlock 1-0, R Cosgrove 0-2, A Brogan 0-4, C Keaney 1-3, T Quinn 0-2. Subs: D Magee for Cahill h/t, S Connell for Cosgrove 50, D Lally for Ryan 61, M Vaughan for Quinn 65, C Moran for Bonner 67.

2007

LEINSTER QUARTER-FINAL

June 3, Croke Park, Dublin

DUBLIN 0-14   MEATH 0-14

Dublin: S Cluxton, D Henry, R McConnell, P Griffin, P Casey, B Cullen, B Cahill, C Whelan, D Magee, C Moran 0-1, S Ryan 0-1, D Connolly, C Keaney 0-5, A Brogan 1-1, T Quinn 0-3. Sub: R Cosgrove for Connolly 53.

LEINSTER QUARTER-FINAL REPLAY

June 17, Croke Park, Dublin

DUBLIN 0-16   MEATH 0-12

Dublin: S Cluxton, D Henry 0-1, R McConnell, P Griffin, P Casey, B Cullen, B Cahill, C Whelan 0-1, S Ryan, D Connolly, T Quinn, C Moran 0-1, A Brogan 0-1, C Keaney 0-4, M Vaughan 0-8. Subs: R Cosgrove for Connolly h/t, J Sherlock for Quinn 53, D Magee for Ryan 63, B Brogan for Moran 71.

LEINSTER SEMI-FINAL

June 24, Croke Park, Dublin

DUBLIN 1-12   OFFALY 0-10

Dublin: S Cluxton, D Henry, R McConnell, P Griffin,

P Casey, B Cullen, B Cahill, C Whelan 0-1, S Ryan, B Brogan, T Quinn 0-1, C Moran 0-1, C Keaney 0-3, A Brogan 0-2, M Vaughan 0-3. Subs: J Sherlock 0-1 for B Brogan 43, R Cosgrove for Quinn 53, C Goggins for Casey 60, D Magee for Whelan 65, D Lally for Moran 67. M Quinn own goal.

LEINSTER FINAL

July 15, Croke Park, Dublin

DUBLIN 3-14   LAOIS 1-14

Dublin: S Cluxton, D Henry, R McConnell, P Griffin, P Casey, B Cullen, B Cahill, C Whelan 0-2, S Ryan, C Moran, J Sherlock, B Brogan 1-1, C Keaney 0-2, A Brogan 1-1, M Vaughan 0-8. Subs: T Quinn 0-1 for Sherlock 63, K Bonner for Vaughan 66, G Brennan 0-1 for Casey 68, D Connolly for B Brogan 69, J Magee for Whelan 71.

ALL-IRELAND QUARTER-FINAL

Aug 11, Croke Park, Dublin

DUBLIN 0-18   DERRY 0-15

Dublin: S Cluxton, D Henry, R McConnell, P Griffin, P Casey, B Cullen, B Cahill, C Whelan, S Ryan, C Moran 0-1, J Sherlock 0-2, B Brogan 0-3, A Brogan 0-3, C Keaney 0-3, M Vaughan 0-6. Subs: K Bonner for B Brogan 62, D Magee for Whelan 65, J Magee for Moran 69.

ALL-IRELAND SEMI-FINAL

Aug 26, Croke Park, Dublin

KERRY 1-15   DUBLIN 0-16

Dublin: S Cluxton, D Henry, R McConnell, P Griffin, P Casey, B Cullen 0-2, B Cahill 0-1, C Whelan, S Ryan, B Brogan 0-1, J Sherlock, C Moran, C Keaney 0-4, A Brogan 0-3, M Vaughan 0-5. Subs: R Cosgrove for Sherlock 41, D Magee for B Brogan 54, T Quinn for Vaughan 69.

2008

LEINSTER QUARTER FINAL

June 8, Croke Park, Dublin

DUBLIN 1-22   LOUTH 0-12

Dublin: S Cluxton, D Henry, R McConnell, S O'Shaughnessy, P Casey, B Cullen, B Cahill, E Fennell, S Ryan, C Moran 0-2, J Sherlock 0-2, P Andrews 0-1, A Brogan 1-7, C Keaney 0-3, T Quinn 0-6. Subs: M Vaughan 0-1 for Andrews 54, B McManamon for Sherlock 60, K Nolan for 66, P McMahon for Cahill 68, D Magee for Fennell 68.

LEINSTER SEMI-FINAL

June 29, Croke Park, Dublin

DUBLIN 0-13   WESTMEATH 1-8

Dublin: S Cluxton, D Henry 0-1, R McConnell, S O'Shaughnessy, B Cahill 0-1, B Cullen, C Moran 0-1,

E Fennell, S Ryan, P Flynn, J Sherlock 0-1, B Brogan, A Brogan 0-1, C Keaney 0-2, T Quinn 0-3. Subs: D Connolly 0-2 for B Brogan 16, M Vaughan for P Flynn h/t, P Casey for McConnell h/t, C Whelan 0-1 for Fennell 55, B McManamon for Quinn 65.

LEINSTER FINAL
July 20, Croke Park, Dublin
DUBLIN 3-23   WEXFORD 0-9
Dublin: S Cluxton, D Henry, C Moran 0-1, P Griffin, K Nolan, B Cullen, B Cahill 0-1, C Whelan, S Ryan 0-1, C Keaney 0-6, J Sherlock 0-3, K Bonner, A Brogan 1-4, D Connolly 1-3, T Quinn 0-4. Subs: P Casey for Nolan 24, P Flynn for Bonner 56, M Vaughan 1-0 for Connolly 58, R McConnell for Moran 62, D Murray for Sherlock 65.

ALL-IRELAND QUARTER-FINAL
Aug 16, Croke Park, Dublin
TYRONE 3-14   DUBLIN 1-8
Dublin: S Cluxton, D Henry, R McConnell, P Griffin, C Moran, B Cullen, B Cahill 0-1, C Whelan, S Ryan, D Connolly, J Sherlock, D Bonner, A Brogan, C Keaney 1-1, T Quinn 0-2. Subs: B Brogan 0-3 for A Brogan 14, P Casey for Connolly 48, M Vaughan 0-1 for Sherlock 52, B McMenamin for Quinn 53, E Fennell for McConnell 62.

2009

LEINSTER QUARTER-FINAL
June 7, Croke Park, Dublin
DUBLIN 0-14   MEATH 0-12
Dublin: S Cluxton, D Henry, D Bastick, A Hubbard, B Cahill, P Griffin, G Brennan 0-1, R McConnell, D Magee, P Flynn, P Andrews 0-1, B Brogan 0-2, C Keaney 0-5, M Davoren 0-2, A Brogan 0-3. Subs: C Whelan for McConnell 50, J Sherlock for B Brogan 50, P Burke for Davoren 55, D Connolly for Andrews 60, B Kelly for Flynn 70.

LEINSTER SEMI-FINAL
June 28, Croke Park, Dublin
DUBLIN 4-26   WESTMEATH 0-11
Dublin: S Cluxton, D Henry, D Bastick, R O'Carroll, P Griffin, G Brennan, B Cahill 0-1, R McConnell 0-1, D Magee 1-0, P Flynn 0-1, A Brogan 0-4, D Connolly 0-1, C Keaney 0-3, B Brogan 2-8, J Sherlock 0-6. Subs: P Burke for A Brogan 51, T Quinn 1-1 for Keaney 54, B Cullen for Brennan 58, C Whelan for Magee 61, S Ryan for B Brogan 61.

LEINSTER FINAL
July 12, Croke Park, Dublin
DUBLIN 2-15   KILDARE 0-18
Dublin: S Cluxton, D Henry, D Bastick, P Andrews,

P Griffin, G Brennan, B Cahill 1-1, R McConnell, D Magee, P Flynn, A Brogan 0-2, D Connolly, C Keaney 0-3, B Brogan 0-7, J Sherlock 1-1. Subs: B Cullen for Connolly 24, C Whelan 0-1 for Magee h/t, T Quinn for Sherlock 51, S Ryan for McConnell 56, P Burke for Flynn 65.

ALL-IRELAND QUARTER-FINAL
Aug 3, Croke Park, Dublin
KERRY 1-24   DUBLIN 1-7
Dublin: S Cluxton, D Henry, D Bastick, P Andrews, P Griffin, B Cullen, B Cahill 0-1, R McConnell, D Magee, P Flynn, D Connolly, B Brogan 0-3, A Brogan 0-3, C Keaney 1-0, J Sherlock. Subs: C Whelan for Magee 15, P Burke for Sherlock 24, C O'Sullivan for Cullen 28, A Hubbard for Henry 40, S Ryan for Connolly 63.

2010

LEINSTER QUARTER-FINAL
June 13, Croke Park, Dublin
DUBLIN 2-16   WEXFORD 0-15
Dublin: S Cluxton, M Fitzsimons, R O'Carroll, P McMahon, D Bastick, C O'Sullivan, B Cahill, E Fennell, R McConnell, P Flynn 0-1, D Henry, N Corkery, C Keaney 0-3, B Brogan 2-4, K McManamon. Subs: G Brennan for O'Sullivan 4, MD Macauley for Henry 43, A Brogan 0-2 for Fennell 20, E O'Gara for McManamon h/t, Fennell for Corkery 75, K Nolan 0-1 for Flynn 79, P Andrews for B Brogan 90. Bastick and Brennan red carded in the 57th and 71st minutes; replaced by B Cullen 0-1 and T Quinn 0-4 for extra time.

LEINSTER SEMI-FINAL
June 27, Croke Park, Dublin
MEATH 5-9   DUBLIN 0-13
Dublin: S Cluxton, M Fitzsimons, R O'Carroll, P McMahon, G Brennan, B Cullen 0-1, B Cahill, E Fennell, R McConnell, N Corkery, A Brogan, P Flynn, C Keaney 0-1, B Brogan 0-3, T Quinn 0-7. Subs: E O'Gara for Keaney 44, M Macauley for McConnell 49, K Nolan for McMahon 55, K McManamon 0-1 for Quinn 59, D Henry for Corkery 61.

ALL-IRELAND QUALIFIER, ROUND TWO
July 10, Croke Park, Dublin
DUBLIN 1-21   TIPPERARY 1-13
Dublin: S Cluxton 0-1, M Fitzsimons, R O'Carroll, P McMahon, K Nolan, G Brennan, D Henry, MD Macauley 1-1, R McConnell 0-2, N Corkery, A Brogan 0-4, P Flynn, B Brogan 0-7, E O'Gara 0-1, K McManamon 0-1. Subs: E Fennell 0-1 for Flynn h/t, C Keaney 0-3 for K McManamon 43, B Cullen for Corkery 55, P Casey for Nolan 68.

ALL-IRELAND QUALIFIER, ROUND THREE
July 17, Croke Park, Dublin
DUBLIN 0-14   ARMAGH 0-11
Dublin: S Cluxton 0-1, M Fitzsimons, R O'Carroll, P McMahon 0-1, K Nolan, G Brennan, B Cahill, MD Macauley, R McConnell, B Cullen, D Henry, N Corkery, B Brogan 0-9, E O'Gara, A Brogan. Subs: K McManamon 0-1 for O'Gara h/t, E Fennell 0-1 for Corkery 45, P Flynn 0-1 for Henry 55, D Magee for McConnell 58, P Andrews for Cullen 64.

ALL-IRELAND QUALIFIER, ROUND FOUR
July 24, Croke Park, Dublin
DUBLIN 2-14   LOUTH 0-13
Dublin: S Cluxton 0-2, M Fitzsimons, R O'Carroll, P McMahon, K Nolan, G Brennan 0-1, B Cahill, MD Macauley, R McConnell 0-1, B Cullen 0-3, A Brogan 0-1, N Corkery, D Henry, E O'Gara 2-1, B Brogan 0-3. Subs: P Flynn 0-1 for Corkery 41, C Keaney for Henry 42, E Fennell for McConnell 50, D Magee for Macauley 54, T Quinn 0-1 for A Brogan 59.

ALL-IRELAND QUARTER-FINAL
July 31, Croke Park, Dublin
DUBLIN 1-15   TYRONE 0-13
Dublin: S Cluxton 0-1, M Fizsimons, R O'Carroll, P McMahon 0-1, K Nolan, G Brennan, B Cahill, M Macauley 0-1, R McConnell, N Corkery, A Brogan 0-1, B Cullen 0-1, D Henry, E O'Gara 1-0, B Brogan 0-9. Subs: C O'Sullivan for Cahill h/t, P Flynn for Henry h/t, E Fennell for Corkery 43, C Keaney 0-1 for A Brogan 50, A Brogan for Cullen 67.

ALL-IRELAND SEMI-FINAL
Aug 22, Croke Park, Dublin
CORK 1-15   DUBLIN 1-14
Dublin: S Cluxton, M Fitzsimons, R O'Carroll, P McMahon 0-1, K Nolan, G Brennan, C O'Sullivan, MD Macauley 0-1, R McConnell 0-1, B Cullen 0-1, A Brogan 0-2, N Corkery, D Henry, E O'Gara, B Brogan 1-7. Subs: B Cahill for O'Sullivan 33, P Flynn for Henry 46, E Fennell for Corkery 57, C Keaney 0-1 for O'Gara 63, D Bastick for O'Carroll 68.

2011

LEINSTER QUARTER-FINAL
June 5, Croke Park, Dublin
DUBLIN 1-16   LAOIS 0-11
Dublin: S Cluxton 0-3, P McMahon, R O'Carroll, M Fitzsimons, J McCarthy, G Brennan, K Nolan, MD Macauley, B Cahill, P Flynn, K McManamon, B Cullen 0-1, A Brogan 0-3, D Connolly 1-3, B Brogan 0-5. Subs: D Bastick for Cahill 43, E O'Gara for

McManamon 47, T Quinn 0-1 for B Brogan 63, R McConnell for Macauley 65, D Lally for Cullen 68.

LEINSTER SEMI-FINAL
June 26, Croke Park, Dublin
DUBLIN 1-12   KILDARE 1-11
Dublin: S Cluxton 0-2, P Conlon, R O'Carroll, M Fitzsimons, J McCarthy, G Brennan, K Nolan, D Bastick, MD Macauley, P Flynn 1-1, A Brogan 0-2, B Cullen 0-1, D Connolly, E O'Gara, B Brogan 0-6. Subs: E Fennell for Macauley h/t, K McManamon for Connolly 54, D Lally for Flynn 61, R McConnell for Bastick 66, B Cahill for Cullen 68.

LEINSTER FINAL
July 10, Croke Park, Dublin
DUBLIN 2-12   WEXFORD 1-12
Dublin: S Cluxton 0-1, P Conlon, R O'Carroll, M Fitzsimons, J McCarthy 1-0, G Brennan, K Nolan, D Bastick 0-1, E Fennell, P Flynn 0-1, A Brogan 0-3, B Cullen 0-1, D Connolly, B Brogan 0-3, E O'Gara. Subs: T Quinn for Connolly 31, K McManamon 0-1 for O'Gara h/t, B Cahill for Fennell 51, D Henry for B Brogan 61, R McConnell 0-1 for Quinn 68. Own goal by G Molloy.

ALL-IRELAND QUARTER-FINAL
Aug 6, Croke Park, Dublin
DUBLIN 0-22   TYRONE 0-15
Dublin: S Cluxton 0-2, M Fitzsimons, R O'Carroll, C O'Sullivan, J McCarthy, G Brennan, K Nolan, D Bastick 0-1, MD Macauley, P Flynn 0-2, B Cahill 0-1, B Cullen 0-1, A Brogan 0-3, D Connolly 0-7, B Brogan 0-5. Subs: R McConnell for Macauley 58, K McManamon for Flynn 65, E Fennell for Bastick 68, P McMahon for Nolan 70.

ALL-IRELAND SEMI-FINAL
Aug 28, Croke Park, Dublin
DUBLIN 0-8   DONEGAL 0-6
Dublin: S Cluxton 0-2, C O'Sullivan, R O'Carroll, M Fitzsimons, J McCarthy, G Brennan, K Nolan, D Bastick, MD Macauley, P Flynn, B Cahill, B Cullen 0-1, A Brogan, D Connolly, B Brogan 0-4. Subs: P McMahon for O'Carroll 26, K McManamon 0-1 for Cahill h/t, E O'Gara for McCarthy 61, E Fennell for Bastick 65, R McConnell for Flynn 67.

ALL-IRELAND FINAL
Sep 18, Croke Park, Dublin
DUBLIN 1-12   KERRY 1-11
Dublin: Stephen Cluxton 0-2, Michael Fitzsimons, Rory O'Carroll, Cian O'Sullivan, James McCarthy, Ger Brennan, Kevin Nolan 0-1, Denis Bastick 0-1, Michael Darragh Macauley, Paul Flynn, Barry Cahill, Bryan Cullen (capt), Alan Brogan 0-2, Diarmuid Connolly, Bernard Brogan 0-6. Subs: Philly McMahon for McCarthy 46, Kevin McManamon 1-0 for Flynn 51, Eoghan O'Gara for Cahill 57, Eamonn Fennell for Bastick 63.

2012

LEINSTER QUARTER-FINAL
June 3, Croke Park, Dublin
DUBLIN 2-22   LOUTH 0-12
Dublin: S Cluxton 0-2, P McMahon, R O'Carroll, M Fitzsimons, J McCarthy, G Brennan, K Nolan, E Fennell, D Bastick 0-1, P Flynn 0-2, K McManamon 0-3, B Cullen 0-2, D Connolly 0-3, A Brogan 0-2, B Brogan 2-5. Subs: C Dias 0-2 for Cullen h/t, E O'Gara for Flynn 50, R McConnell for Fennell 57, J Cooper for McMahon 57, P Casey for Brennan 65.

LEINSTER SEMI-FINAL
July 1, Croke Park, Dublin
DUBLIN 2-11   WEXFORD 1-10
Dublin: S Cluxton 0-1, P McMahon, R O'Carroll, M Fitzsimons, J McCarthy, G Brennan, K Nolan 0-2, E Fennell, D Bastick, P Flynn, A Brogan 0-1, B Cullen 0-2, D Connolly 1-1, K McManamon 1-3, B Brogan 0-1. Subs: C O'Sullivan for Brennan 31, MD Macauley for Fennell h/t, E O'Gara for B Brogan 62, C Kilkenny for McManamon 68, R McConnell for Bastick 69.

LEINSTER FINAL
July 22, Croke Park, Dublin
DUBLIN 2-13   MEATH 1-13
Dublin: S Cluxton, M Fitzsimons, R O'Carroll, P McMahon, J McCarthy 0-1, K Nolan, C O'Sullivan, E Fennell, D Bastick 1-0, P Flynn, A Brogan 0-2, B Cullen, B Brogan 1-7, MD Macauley, K McManamon 0-1. Subs: E O'Gara 0-2 for A Brogan 29, P Andrews for McManamon 48, B Cahill for Fennell 57, C Dias for Flynn 60, P Brogan for Cullen 65.

ALL-IRELAND QUARTER-FINAL
Aug 4, Croke Park, Dublin
DUBLIN 1-12   LAOIS 0-12
Dublin: S Cluxton 0-3, M Fitzsimons, R O'Carroll, P McMahon, J McCarthy, K Nolan 0-1, C O'Sullivan, E Fennell, D Bastick 0-1, P Flynn 0-2, MD Macauley 1-0, B Cullen, B Brogan 0-4, D Connolly, E O'Gara 0-1. Subs: C Kilkenny for Connolly 42, K McManamon for Bastick 52, G Brennan for McMahon 53, T Quinn for Brogan 62, J McCaffrey for O'Gara 71.

ALL-IRELAND SEMI-FINAL
Sep 2, Croke Park, Dublin
MAYO 0-19   DUBLIN 0-16
Dublin: S Cluxton 0-3, M Fitzsimons, R O'Carroll, C O'Sullivan, J McCarthy, G Brennan, K Nolan, E Fennell, D Bastick, P Flynn 0-2, MD Macauley, B Cullen, C Kilkenny 0-3, D Connolly 0-2, B Brogan 0-6. Subs: A Brogan for Cullen h/t, P McMahon for Fitzsimons h/t, E O'Gara for Bastick 49, K McManamon for A Brogan 53, C Dias for Fennell 72.

2013

LEINSTER QUARTER-FINAL
June 2, Croke Park, Dublin
DUBLIN 1-22   WESTMEATH 0-9
Dublin: S Cluxton, D Daly, R O'Carroll, J Cooper, J McCarthy, G Brennan, J McCaffrey 0-1, MD Macauley, C O'Sullivan 0-1, P Flynn 0-3, C Kilkenny 0-1, D Connolly 0-3, P Mannion 0-1, P Andrews 1-3, B Brogan 0-7. Subs: K O'Brien for Daly 43, N Devereux for McCarthy 48, D Rock 0-2 for Mannion 54, D Bastick for MacAuley 55, C Costello for Brogan 61.

LEINSTER SEMI-FINAL
June 30, Croke Park, Dublin
DUBLIN 4-16   KILDARE 1-9
Dublin: S Cluxton 0-4, D Daly, R O'Carroll, J Cooper, J McCarthy, G Brennan 0-1, J McCaffrey, MD Macauley, C O'Sullivan, P Flynn, C Kilkenny 0-4, D Connolly 1-0, P Mannion 1-1, P Andrews 0-1, B Brogan 1-1. Subs: E O'Gara 1-2 for Andrews h/t, K McManamon for Brogan 48, N Devereux for O'Sullivan 60, D Rock 0-2 for Connolly 60, K O'Brien 6 for Daly 60.

LEINSTER FINAL
July 14, Croke Park, Dublin
DUBLIN 2-15   MEATH 0-14
Dublin: S Cluxton 0-3, K O'Brien, R O'Carroll, J Cooper, J McCarthy, G Brennan, J McCaffrey, MD Macauley, C O'Sullivan, P Flynn 1-1, C Kilkenny 0-3, D Connolly 0-1, P Mannion 1-4, E O'Gara, B Brogan 0-1. Subs: D Bastick for O'Sullivan 46, K McManamon for O'Gara 46, D Daly for Brennan 57, D Rock 0-2 for Brogan 60, B Cullen for Connolly 66.

ALL-IRELAND QUARTER-FINAL
Aug 3, Croke Park, Dublin
DUBLIN 1-16   CORK 0-14
Dublin: S Cluxton 0-6, J Cooper, R O'Carroll, K O'Brien, J McCarthy, G Brennan, J McCaffrey 1-0, MD Macauley 0-1, C O'Sullivan, P Flynn 0-2, C Kilkenny 0-2, D Connolly, P Mannion, B Cullen, B Brogan 0-1. Subs: D Rock 0-2 for Cullen 41, P McMahon for Cooper 51, K McManamon 0-1 for Mannion 54, D Bastick 0-1 for Macauley 60, E O'Gara for Kilkenny 65.

ALL-IRELAND SEMI-FINAL
Sep 1, Croke Park, Dublin
DUBLIN 3-18   KERRY 3-11
Dublin: S Cluxton 0-1, K O'Brien, R O'Carroll, J Cooper, J McCarthy, G Brennan, J McCaffrey, MD Macauley 0-1, C O'Sullivan 0-1, P Flynn, C Kilkenny 0-1, D Connolly 0-4, P Mannion 1-0, P Andrews 0-1, B Brogan 0-6. Subs: P McMahon 0-1 for O'Brien 17, D Bastick for Brennan h/t, D Rock 0-2 for Kilkenny 43, E O'Gara 1-0 for Mannion 60, K McManamon 1-0 for Brogan 65.

ALL-IRELAND FINAL
Sep 22, Croke Park, Dublin
DUBLIN 2-12   MAYO 1-14
Dublin: Stephen Cluxton 0-2, Philly McMahon,
Rory O'Carroll, Jonny Cooper, James McCarthy,
Ger Brennan 0-1, Jack McCaffrey, Michael Darragh
Macauley, Cian O'Sullivan 0-1, Paul Flynn 0-1, Ciaran
Kilkenny, Diarmuid Connolly 0-1, Paul Mannion 0-1,
Paddy Andrews, Bernard Brogan 2-3. Subs: Eoghan
O'Gara 0-2 for Mannion 15, Darren Daly for McCaffrey
h/t, Dean Rock for Kilkenny 42, Kevin McManamon
for Andrews 49, Denis Bastick for Cooper 53.

2014

LEINSTER QUARTER-FINAL
June 8, Croke Park, Dublin
DUBLIN 2-21   LAOIS 0-16
Dublin: S Cluxton 0-2, P McMahon, R O'Carroll,
J Cooper, J McCarthy 0-1, N Deveraux, D Daly,
MD Macauley 1-0, C O'Sullivan 0-1, P Flynn 0-3, P
Andrews 0-1, D Connolly 1-1, A Brogan 0-1, E O'Gara
0-1, B Brogan 0-1. Subs: K McManamon 0-2 for B
Brogan 24, J McCaffrey for Daly 29, B Cullen 0-1 for
O'Gara 44, C Costello 0-3 for A Brogan 41, D Rock 0-3
for O'Sullivan 59, P Mannion for Andrews 67.

LEINSTER SEMI-FINAL
June 29, Croke Park, Dublin
DUBLIN 2-25   WEXFORD 1-12
Dublin: S Cluxton 0-1, P McMahon 0-1, R O'Carroll, J
Cooper, J McCarthy, P Flynn 1-2, K Nolan, A Brogan
0-1, N Devereux 0-1, D Connolly 0-2, MD Macauley
0-1, P Mannion 0-3, C O'Sullivan, D Rock 0-4, K
McManamon. Subs: C Costello 1-5 for Rock h/t,
E O'Gara 0-2 for Brogan 47, J McCaffrey for Nolan
50, T Brady 0-2 for O'Sullivan 59, M Fitzsimons for
Devereux 63, B Cullen for Macauley 67.

LEINSTER FINAL
July 20, Croke Park, Dublin
DUBLIN 3-20   MEATH 1-10
Dublin: S Cluxton 0-1, P McMahon, R O'Carroll, M
Fitzsimons, J McCarthy, N Devereux, J McCaffrey
0-1, MD Macauley, C O'Sullivan 0-1, P Flynn 0-1, K
McManamon 1-5, D Connolly 0-1, A Brogan 0-1, P
Mannion, B Brogan 1-6. Subs: C Costello 0-1 for
Mannion h/t, D Rock 0-1 for Connolly 42, E O'Gara 1-1
for A Brogan 49, D Bastick for Macauley 59, D Daly
for Deveraux 59, T Brady for O'Sullivan 69.

ALL-IRELAND QUARTER-FINAL
Aug 9, Croke Park, Dublin
DUBLIN 2-22   MONAGHAN 0-11
Dublin: S Cluxton 0-1, M Fitzsimons, R O'Carroll, P

McMahon, J McCarthy, J Cooper 0-1, N Devereux,
MD Macauley, C O'Sullivan, D Connolly 1-2, K
McManamon 0-1, P Flynn 0-2, A Brogan 0-3, E
O'Gara 0-2, B Brogan 1-6. Subs: C Costello 0-1 for
McManamon 43, D Rock 0-2 for O'Sullivan 47, J
McCaffrey for Cooper 52, P Andrews for O'Gara 54, D
Daly for McMahon 58, P Mannion for A Brogan 65.

ALL-IRELAND SEMI-FINAL
Aug 31, Croke Park
DONEGAL 3-14   DUBLIN 0-17
Dublin: S Cluxton, M Fitzsimons, R O'Carroll, P
McMahon 0-1, J McCaffrey, J Cooper, J McCarthy, MD
Macauley, C O'Sullivan, P Flynn 0-4, A Brogan 0-2,
D Connolly 0-5, C Costello, E O'Gara, B Brogan 0-3.
Subs: N Devereux for McCaffrey h/t, K McManamon
for Costello 40, D Rock for O'Gara 48, P Andrews 0-2
for A Brogan 53, D Daly for Cooper 62, P Mannion for
O'Sullivan 68.

2015

LEINSTER QUARTER-FINAL
May 31, Croke Park, Dublin
DUBLIN 4-25   LONGFORD 0-10
Dublin: S Cluxton, P McMahon 0-1, D Byrne (St
Olaf's), J Cooper, D Daly, J Small, J McCaffrey, B
Fenton 0-1, D Bastick, P Flynn 1-3, C Kilkenny 0-3,
D Connolly 1-0, D Rock 1-6, K McManamon 0-2,
B Brogan 1-6, Subs: T Brady 0-1 for Connolly h/t,
M Fitzsimons for McMahon h/t, MD Macauley for
Bastick 45, P Andrews 0-1 for Flynn 52, E Lowndes
0-1 for Cooper 55, A Brogan for B Brogan 60.

LEINSTER SEMI-FINAL
June 28, Croke Park, Dublin
DUBLIN 5-18   KILDARE 0-14
Dublin: S Cluxton, J Cooper, R O'Carroll, P McMahon
0-1, C O'Sullivan, J Small, J McCaffrey, B Fenton, MD
Macauley, P Flynn, K McManamon, C Kilkenny 0-4, D
Rock 1-4, D Connolly 2-3, B Brogan 2-3. Subs: J McCarthy
for Small 46, A Brogan 0-3 for McManamon 48, M
Fitzsimons for O'Carroll 58, P Andrews for Flynn 58, E
O'Conghaile for Fenton 63, D Daly for O'Sullivan 64.

LEINSTER FINAL
July 12, Croke Park, Dublin
DUBLIN 2-13   WESTMEATH 0-6
Dublin: S Cluxton, J Cooper, R O'Carroll, P McMahon
0-1, J McCarthy 0-1, C O'Sullivan, J McCaffrey 1-0, B
Fenton, MD Macauley 0-1, P Flynn, C Kilkenny 0-3, D
Connolly 0-3, D Rock 0-2, K McManamon, B Brogan
1-1. Subs: M Fitzsimons for Cooper h/t, P Andrews for
McManamon 47, D Bastick for Macauley 50, A Brogan
0-1 for Rock 55, J Small for McMahon 61.

ALL-IRELAND QUARTER-FINAL
Aug 2, Croke Park, Dublin
DUBLIN 2-23   FERMANAGH 2-15
Dublin: S Cluxton, J Cooper, R O'Carroll, P McMahon, J McCarthy, C O'Sullivan, J McCaffrey, B Fenton 0-1, D Bastick, P Flynn 1-1, C Kilkenny 0-3, D Connolly 0-2, D Rock 0-7, P Andrews 0-3, B Brogan 1-6. Subs: MD Macauley for Bastick h/t, K McManamon for Kilkenny h/t, A Brogan for Connolly 48, M Fitzsimons for Cooper 50, J Small for McCarthy 55, C Costello for Andrews 66.

ALL-IRELAND SEMI-FINAL
Aug 30, Croke Park, Dublin
DUBLIN 2-12   MAYO 1-15
Dublin: S Cluxton, J Cooper, R O'Carroll, P McMahon, J McCarthy, C O'Sullivan, J McCaffrey 0-1, B Fenton, MD Macauley, P Flynn, C Kilkenny 0-3, D Connolly 1-2, D Rock, P Andrews 0-2, B Brogan 0-2. Subs: M Fitzsimons for O'Carroll 3, K McManamon 1-1 for Rock h/t, J Small for Cooper 43, D Bastick for Macauley 50, A Brogan 0-1 for Andrews 54, T Brady for Fenton 58.

ALL-IRELAND SEMI-FINAL REPLAY
Sep 5, Croke Park, Dublin
DUBLIN 3-15   MAYO 1-14
Dublin: S Cluxton, J Cooper, R O'Carroll, P McMahon 1-2, J McCarthy 0-1, C O'Sullivan, J McCaffrey, B Fenton 0-1, D Bastick, P Flynn, P Andrews 0-5, C Kilkenny 0-2, D Rock 0-2, D Connolly, B Brogan 1-1. Subs: M Fitzsimons for Cooper 43, MD Macauley for Bastick 43, A Brogan for Flynn 50, K McManamon 1-1 for D Rock 51, E Lownes for D Connolly 68, J Small for B Brogan 70.

ALL-IRELAND FINAL
Sep 20, Croke Park, Dublin
DUBLIN 0-12   KERRY 0-9
Dublin: Stephen Cluxton (capt) 0-1, Johnny Cooper, Rory O'Carroll, Philly McMahon 0-1, James McCarthy, Cian O'Sullivan, Jack McCaffrey 0-1, Brian Fenton 0-1, Denis Bastick, Paul Flynn 0-2, Diarmuid Connolly, Ciaran Kilkenny, Paddy Andrews 0-1, Dean Rock 0-2, Bernard Brogan 0-2. Subs: Kevin McManamon for Rock h/t, Michael Darragh Macauley for Bastick 40, Michael Fitzsimons for Cooper 49, John Small for McCaffrey 53, Darren Daly for O'Sullivan 61, Alan Brogan 0-1 for Fenton 67.

2016

LEINSTER QUARTER-FINAL
June 4, Nowlan Park, Kilkenny
DUBLIN 2-21   LAOIS 2-10
Dublin: S Cluxton, D Byrne 0-1, J Cooper, P

McMahon, J McCarthy, C O'Sullivan, J Small, B Fenton, MD Macauley, C Kilkenny 0-4, K McManamon 0-1, D Connolly 1-4, P Mannion, D Rock 1-10, B Brogan. Subs: D Bastick for Macauley 28, Macauley for Bastick 45, C Costello for Brogan 51, C O'Callaghan 0-1 for Mannion 57, D Daly for O'Sullivan 59, E Lowndes for Cooper 63, E O'Gara for Rock 63.

LEINSTER SEMI-FINAL
June 26, Croke Park, Dublin
DUBLIN 0-21   MEATH 0-11
Dublin: S Cluxton, David Byrne, J Cooper, P McMahon, J Small, C O'Sullivan, J McCarthy, B Fenton 0-1, D Bastick, P Flynn 0-2, C Kilkenny, D Connolly 0-4, K McManamon, D Rock 0-10, B Brogan 0-3. Subs: MD Macauley for Bastick h/t, P Mannion 0-1 for Brogan 53, P Andrews for McManamon 58, E Lowndes for Small 60, M Fitzsimons for O'Sullivan 64, C O'Callaghan for Flynn 67.

LEINSTER FINAL
July 17, Croke Park, Dublin
DUBLIN 2-19   WESTMEATH 0-10
Dublin: S Cluxton, J Cooper, P McMahon, D Byrne, J Small 0-1, C O'Sullivan, E Lowndes, B Fenton, MD Macauley, P Flynn 0-1, C Kilkenny, D Connolly 0-1, K McManamon 1-2, D Rock 0-8, B Brogan 1-4. Subs: P Andrews 0-2 for Lowndes h/t, C O'Callaghan for Macauley 48, D Bastick for Connolly 52, D Daly for Small 56, M Fitzsimons for O'Sullivan 60, P Mannion for Rock 63.

ALL-IRELAND QUARTER-FINAL
Aug 6, Croke Park, Dublin
DUBLIN 1-15   DONEGAL 1-10
Dublin: S Cluxton, P McMahon 0-1, J Cooper 0-1, D Byrne, C Kilkenny 0-1, C O'Sullivan, J Small, B Fenton, MD Macauley, P Flynn, K McManamon 0-3, P Andrews 0-1, D Rock 0-5, D Connolly 0-2, B Brogan. Subs: D Daly for Brogan 48, D Bastick for Macauley 53, P Mannion 1-1 for Andrews 56, E O'Gara for McManamon 67, E Lowndes for Rock 72.

ALL-IRELAND SEMI-FINAL
Aug 28, Croke Park, Dublin
DUBLIN 0-22   KERRY 2-14
Dublin: S Cluxton, P McMahon 0-1, J Cooper, D Byrne, J McCarthy, C O'Sullivan, J Small, B Fenton 0-1, MD Macauley, P Flynn, K McManamon 0-2, C Kilkenny, D Rock 0-12, D Connolly 0-3, B Brogan 0-2. Subs: P Andrews for Flynn 46, P Mannion for Small 50, E O'Gara 0-1 for Macauley 60, M Fitzsimons for Cooper 67, C Costello for Brogan 71.

ALL-IRELAND FINAL
Sep 18, Croke Park, Dublin
DUBLIN 2-9   MAYO 0-15
Dublin: Stephen Cluxton, Philly McMahon, Johnny Cooper, David Byrne, James McCarthy, Cian O'Sullivan, John Small 0-1, Brian Fenton 0-1, Michael Darragh MacAuley, Paul Flynn, Kevin McManamon, Ciaran Kilkenny, Dean Rock 0-4, Diarmuid Connolly 0-1, Bernard Brogan. Subs: Paddy Andrews 0-2 for McCarthy 24, Paul Mannion for McManamon 46, Michael Fitzsimons for Macauley, Eoghan O'Gara for Brogan 61, Darren Daly for Byrne 66, Denis Bastick for Flynn 69.

ALL-IRELAND FINAL REPLAY
Oct 1, Croke Park, Dublin
DUBLIN 1-15   MAYO 1-14
Dublin: Stephen Cluxton (capt), Michael Fitzsimons, Philly McMahon, Jonny Cooper, James McCarthy, Cian O'Sullivan, John Small, Brian Fenton, Paul Flynn, Ciaran Kilkenny, Kevin McManamon 0-1, Diarmuid Connolly 1-1, Paul Mannion, Dean Rock 0-9, Paddy Andrews. Subs: Davy Byrne for Cooper 21, Bernard Brogan 0-1 for Andrews 47, Michael Darragh Macauley for Mannion 52, Cormac Costello 0-3 for McManamon 56, Eric Lowndes for Small 60, Darren Daly for O'Sullivan 72.

2017

LEINSTER QUARTER-FINAL
June 3, O'Moore Park, Portlaoise
DUBLIN 0-19   CARLOW 0-7
Dublin: S Cluxton, E Lowndes, J Cooper, M Fitzsimons, J McCaffrey 0-2, C O'Sullivan, J McCarthy, B Fenton, C Kilkenny 0-3, N Scully 0-1, C O'Callaghan 0-2, D Connolly 0-1, P Mannion 0-1, D Rock 0-6, K McManamon. Subs: B Brogan 0-2 for McManamon 45, S Carthy for McCaffrey 53, M Schutte for Scully 59, C McHugh 0-1 for Rock 59, D Byrne for O'Sullivan 63, D Bastick for Fenton 67.

LEINSTER SEMI-FINAL
June 25, Croke Park
DUBLIN 4-29   WESTMEATH 0-10
Dublin: S Cluxton, M Fitzsimons, J Cooper, E Lowndes, D Daly, C O'Sullivan, J McCaffrey 0-1, B Fenton 0-2, J McCarthy, C Kilkenny 1-3, C O'Callaghan 0-3, N Scully, D Rock 1-5, P Andrews 0-2, P Mannion 0-8. Subs: E O'Gara 1-0 for

Andrews h/t, S Carthy 0-2 for Cooper 43, D Byrne for Fitzsimons 43, B Brogan 0-2 for Rock 47, K McManamon 1-1 for Scully 47, B Howard for O'Callaghan 60.

LEINSTER FINAL
July 16, Croke Park
DUBLIN 2-23   KILDARE 1-17
Dublin: S Cluxton, P McMahon, C O'Sullivan, M Fitzsimons, E Lowndes, J Small, J McCaffrey, B Fenton, J McCarthy 1-0, N Scully, C Kilkenny 0-2, P Mannion 0-1, C O'Callaghan 0-12, P Andrews 0-1, P Mannion 0-1, D Rock 1-0. Subs; B Brogan 0-5 for Rock (black card) 25, S Carthy 0-1 for Scully 47, D Daly for McMahon 48, K McManamon for Andrews 51, D Byrne for O'Sullivan 58, B Howard 0-1 for Fenton 66.

ALL-IRELAND QUARTER-FINAL
Aug 5, Croke Park, Dublin
DUBLIN 1-19   MONAGHAN 0-12
Dublin: S Cluxton; J Cooper, M Fitzsimons, P McMahon, J Small, C O'Sullivan, J McCaffrey 0-1, B Fenton, J McCarthy 0-1, E Lowndes, C O'Callaghan 0-1, C Kilkenny, P Mannion 0-1, P Andrews 0-1, D Rock 1-8. Subs: B Brogan for Lowndes 42, D Daly for Small 51, P Flynn 0-1 for McCarthy 51, E O'Gara 0-1 for Andrews 54, MD Macauley for Kilkenny 58, D Byrne for Cooper 61.

ALL-IRELAND SEMI-FINAL
Aug 27, Croke Park, Dublin
DUBLIN 2-17   TYRONE 0-11
Dublin: S Cluxton, P McMahon, C O'Sullivan, M Fitzsimons, J Cooper, J Small, J McCaffrey 0-1, B Fenton 0-1, J McCarthy, C Kilkenny 0-1, C O'Callaghan 1-2, N Scully, P Mannion 0-1, P Andrews 0-2, D Rock 0-5. Subs: P Flynn 0-3 for Scully 45, K McManamon for Andrews 45, D Daly for Small 52, E O'Gara 1-1 for D Rock 63, E Lowndes for Mannion 66, D Connolly for O'Callaghan 71.

ALL-IRELAND FINAL
Sep 17, Croke Park, Dublin
DUBLIN 1-17   MAYO 1-16
Dublin: S Cluxton, J Cooper, P McMahon, M Fitzsimons, J Small 0-1, C O'Sullivan, J McCaffrey, B Fenton 0-1, J McCarthy 0-2, D Rock 0-7, C O'Callaghan 1-0, C Kilkenny, P Mannion 0-3, E O'Gara 0-1, P Andrews. Subs: P Flynn for McCaffrey 7, D Connolly 0-1 for Andrews h/t, K McManamon 0-1 for O'Gara h/t, B Brogan for Flynn 65, N Scully for O'Callaghan 68, C Costello for Mannion 70+4.

THE COMPLETE RECORD

County	P	W	D	L	For	Agt
Antrim	3	3	0	0	6-25	1-6
Armagh	5	3	0	2	10-63	5-52
Carlow	11	10	0	1	10-116	10-63
Cavan	4	4	0	0	7-25	3-10
Clare	1	1	0	0	3-14	2-12
Cork	15	11	2	2	6-39	4-32
Derry	5	4	0	1	8-66	5-56
Donegal	6	3	1	2	4-76	4-69
Down	3	2	0	1	3-40	1-27
Fermanagh	1	1	0	0	2-23	2-15
Galway	9	7	0	2	40-320	36-294
Kerry	29	10	2	17	30-247	36-292
Kildare	54	36	5	13	65-483	41-391
Kilkenny	8	7	1	0	6-16	0-4
Laois	33	26	2	5	51-363	25-236
Leitrim	2	2	0	0	3-28	2-13
Limerick	1	0	0	1	0-7	1-5
London	6	6	0	0	9-72	1-23
Longford	18	15	1	2	39-162	14-129
Louth	55	36	6	13	72-478	52-376
Mayo	15	9	4	2	19-171	12-162
Meath	62	35	8	19	80-589	61-519
Monaghan	5	5	0	0	8-59	2-27
Offaly	24	17	0	7	34-227	19-196
Roscommon	4	4	0	0	4-41	3-25
Sligo	1	1	0	0	3-17	0-12
Tipperary	3	2	0	1	2-29	2-24
Tyrone	8	5	1	2	9-111	6-105
Waterford	1	1	0	0	2-8	0-4
Westmeath	19	16	0	3	34-259	7-143
Wexford	49	33	4	12	73-429	42-268
Wicklow	12	12	0	0	19-131	5-65
TOTALS	472	327	37	108	661-4,734	404-3,665

LEINSTER CHAMPIONSHIP ROLL OF HONOUR

Dublin (56): 1891, 1892, 1894, 1896, 1897, 1898, 1899, 1901, 1902, 1904, 1906, 1907, 1908, 1920, 1921, 1922, 1923, 1924, 1932, 1933, 1934, 1941, 1942, 1955, 1958, 1959, 1962, 1963, 1965, 1974, 1975, 1976, 1977, 1978, 1979, 1983, 1984, 1985, 1989, 1992, 1993, 1994, 1995, 2002, 2005, 2006, 2007, 2008, 2009, 2011, 2012, 2013, 2014, 2015, 2016, 2017.

Meath (21): 1895, 1939, 1940, 1947, 1949, 1951, 1952, 1954, 1964, 1966, 1967, 1970, 1986, 1987, 1988, 1990, 1991, 1996, 1999, 2001, 2010.

Kildare (13): 1903, 1905, 1919, 1926, 1927, 1928, 1929, 1930, 1931, 1935, 1956, 1998, 2000.

Wexford (10): 1890, 1893, 1913, 1914, 1915, 1916, 1917, 1918, 1925, 1945.

Offaly (10): 1960, 1961, 1969, 1971, 1972, 1973, 1980, 1981, 1982, 1997.

Louth (8): 1909, 1910, 1912, 1943, 1948, 1950, 1953, 1957.

Laois (6): 1889, 1936, 1937, 1938, 1946, 2003.

Kilkenny (3): 1888, 1900, 1911.

Carlow (1): 1944.

Longford (1): 1968.

Westmeath (1): 2004.

ALL-IRELAND CHAMPIONSHIP ROLL OF HONOUR

Kerry (37): 1903, 1904, 1909, 1913, 1914, 1924, 1926, 1929, 1930, 1931, 1932, 1937, 1939, 1940, 1941, 1946, 1953, 1955, 1959, 1962, 1969, 1970, 1975, 1978, 1979, 1980, 1981, 1984, 1985, 1986, 1997, 2000, 2004, 2006, 2007, 2009, 2014.

Dublin (27): 1891, 1892, 1894, 1897, 1898, 1899, 1901, 1902, 1906, 1907, 1908, 1921, 1922, 1923, 1942, 1958, 1963, 1974, 1976, 1977, 1983, 1995, 2011, 2013, 2015, 2016, 2017.

Galway (9): 1925, 1934, 1938, 1956, 1964, 1965, 1966, 1998, 2001.

Meath (7): 1949, 1954, 1967, 1987, 1988, 1996, 1999.

Cork (7): 1890, 1911, 1945, 1973, 1989, 1990, 2010.

Wexford (5): 1893, 1915, 1916, 1917, 1918.

Cavan (5): 1933, 1935, 1947, 1948, 1952.

Down (5): 1960, 1961, 1968, 1991, 1994.

Tipperary (4): 1889, 1895, 1900, 1920.

Kildare (4): 1905, 1919, 1927, 1928.

Mayo (3): 1936, 1950, 1951.

Louth (3): 1910, 1912, 1957.

Offaly (3): 1971, 1972, 1982.

Tyrone (3): 2003, 2005, 2008.

Limerick (2): 1887, 1896.

Roscommon (2): 1943, 1944.

Donegal (2): 1992, 2012.

Derry (1): 1993.

Armagh (1): 2002.

National League

JOE SYNNOTT, better known as Josie, holds a record than can never be taken from him; he scored Dublin's first ever goal in the National League. It came after just five minutes of the county's initial outing in the inaugural 'secondary' competition, against Louth at St. Brigid's Park in Dundalk on 11 October 1925 and was in fact an equaliser, Jack Byrne having found the net for the home side three minutes earlier. Dublin eventually won the tie by 3-3 to 1-5 and it was a real family affair for the famous O'Tooles clan — Josie added a point and his siblings John and Peter provided the other two goals.

That first staging of the league was organised on a regional basis to reduce travel in what, after all, was largely an experiment. Apart from Louth, Dublin were also grouped with Meath and Kildare, both of whom they subsequently beat at Croke Park, by 0-9 to 1-2 and by 2-5 to 1-3, respectively, to qualify for a semi-final meeting with Antrim back at the same ground on which they had beaten Louth. A fourth win on the trot, by 0-8 to 0-5 set up a final showdown with Laois — who had beaten Sligo in the other semi-final — at Barrett's Park in New Ross where, in a low scoring game, Dublin were beaten by 2-1 to 1-0, the goal coming from Peter Stynes just four minutes from the end.

The competition was sidelined in the 1926/27 and 1929/30 seasons and there was little to shout about for The Dubs in the two campaigns in between. They managed just one win (over Armagh) and one draw (with Cavan) in half a dozen games in the first and although they claimed two wins and a draw from four games the following season, a 2-6 to 0-3 defeat by Kildare at Croke Park ruled them out of the knockout stages. Three more fruitless campaigns followed in which, chronologically, they won three out of four games but were beaten by Kerry, lost all three, and won just one of three.

A breakout finally came in the 1933/34 season when, after drawing with Laois in their opening game, successive victories over Kildare, Wexford and Kerry put them into a straight final against Mayo at MacHale Park in Castlebar. Ahead by 1-5 to 1-2 at halftime, they were overhauled and trailed by a point as Mayo added a goal and a point without reply, but a last minute point by Mickey Wellington earned them a second chance at Croke Park, where not even a Gearoid Fitzgerald goal could save Dublin from a 2-4 to 1-5 defeat as Mayo won the first of what would be a remarkable six successive league titles.

Six more barren seasons followed — although they did finish joint second with Cork in the 1935/36 campaign, the only one ever staged on a purely league basis — and it wasn't until the 1940/41 competition that they again made the knockout stages. Wins over Westmeath, Longford and Meath were offset by a 3-5 to 0-8 defeat by Louth that left the two counties jointly topping the section. Dublin won a playoff at Croke Park by 3-4 to 1-4 and then a 2-7 to 1-4 victory over Kerry at the same venue put them into their third league decider. Once again Mayo provided the opposition and once again defeat was Dublin's lot; after leading by 0-5 to 1-0 at halftime they could add just two points in the second half while Mayo tagged on 2-5. The league, as a national competition, was suspended for the remainder of World War II chiefly due to petrol rationing and replaced by a series of regional tournaments; Dublin won a North Leinster event involving home and away games with Meath and Louth in 1942 — when corner forward Mick Quigley from Civil Service scored all four goals in a 4-8 to 5-5 draw in the first meeting with the Royal County — but otherwise drew a blank.

THE resumption of the league on a national level in November 1945 began promisingly for Dublin as wins over Laois, Kildare and Wicklow and a draw with Offaly in Tullamore saw them top their section but then, in a semi-final showdown with Wexford at St Patrick's Park in Enniscorthy they were hit with a 3-2 blitz in the final ten minutes and lost 5-6 to 1-2. Three seasons later they again topped their section — they only had to play two games to do so — but, in the Divisional Final against All-Ireland champions Cavan at Croke Park they suffered another humiliating defeat as, just three points adrift at halftime, 2-5 to 2-2, they suffered another second half collapse and in the end were beaten 3-17 to 2-4.

The county's entire programme for the 1948/49 league campaign, oddly, consisted of just a single game; grouped with Louth and Longford, they lost to the former but after their scheduled meeting with the latter was cancelled due to snow, Louth's subsequent victory over Longford settled the qualification issue and the postponed game was never played.

Three seasons later, by now backboned by up to ten members of already three-time county champions St. Vincent's, Dublin had their most successful league campaign in over a decade. Victories over Louth, Westmeath, Wicklow, Kildare and Meath by aggregate scores of 15-41 for and just 3-18 against saw them win their section with full points. Then, in the semi-final of the 'Home' leg of the competition (New York had come in two years previously), Dublin produced a real routing of Laois at O'Moore Park in Portlaoise, powering into a 5-2 to 1-2 halftime lead and easing up in the second half but still winning by six clear goals, 7-5 to 1-5.

The decider, against Cork at Croke Park, finished in controversy. With the Leesiders leading 2-3 to 1-5 and time almost up, Dublin were awarded a free from just over 40 yards out; Kevin Heffernan's kick struck an upright and, just as Ollie Freaney gathered the rebound and appeared to have been fouled, Kerry referee Dan Ryan blew the final whistle. Dublin fans streamed onto the pitch to vent their anger at a second free not being awarded and Ryan had to be given a Garda escort off the field. It later transpired that Ryan had informed Heffernan that time was up and he would have to score direct from the free if Dublin were to get a second chance. Cork later trounced New York in the 'proper' decider by 1-12 to 0-3 so for The Dubs it was definitely a missed opportunity.

The following campaign, 1952/1953, began nicely for Dublin with victories over Louth and Westmeath but suffered a hiccup when Meath beat them 1-10 to 2-3 in Navan.

Two more wins, over Wicklow and Kildare, meant they shared the top spot in the section with their lone conquerors and they made no mistake in the play-off at Croke Park, leading by 1-8 to 1-3 at halftime before winning by 3-13 to 2-3 with Jim Crowley and Mossy Whelan giving outstanding performances at midfield. The semi-final against Tipperary at Croke Park was a surprisingly tough affair, but an 0-9 to 0-3 victory saw Dublin into the National League Final for the fourth time, excluding the previous year's 'Home' decider.

If the old maxim that 'you have to lose one before you win one' is true, Dublin, after three final disappointments, gave it a new dimension in the final against reigning All-Ireland champions Cavan. Lining out with Air Corps goalkeeper Tony O'Grady as the lone exception to an all St. Vincent's selection (and wearing the county champion's colours), they hit Cavan with a blitzkrieg start that yielded three goals and a point in the opening ten minutes, were 3-2 to 0-4 to the good at the interval, and eventually won 4-6 to 0-9. Mick Dunne in the *Irish Press*, began his report with gushing appreciation of a quite stunning performance: 'Magnificent, dazzling, superb, spectacular ... and I'm not handing out film publicity. I'm talking of Dublin's forwards — Des Ferguson, Ollie and Cyril Freaney, Bernie Atkins, Tony Young and Kevin Heffernan — who yesterday drove the All-Ireland champions, Cavan, dizzy and so brought the National Football League title, to the Capital for the first time.' John D. Hickey in the *Irish Independent* expressed similar sentiments: 'Dublin's forwards were as covetous of every chance as if utter ignominy attached to wasting it, and the manner in which they gave the opposing defence the run-about as they swapped positions when on the move was the most effective operation that Croke Park has seen in many a day.'

The defence of the title started somewhat nervously with a draw with Galway in Croke Park (secured by a late point from Heffernan), but thereafter Dublin reeled off successive wins over Laois, Offaly, Wicklow, Roscommon and Louth — Heffernan hitting 2-4 in a 3-10 to 2-3 defeat of the latter — to again top their section. Old rivals — and league specialists — Mayo provided the opposition in the semi-final and their decision to fly Padraig Carney back from New York was fully justified as the Swinford born doctor contributed seven points as his side advanced to yet another final on an 0-11 to 0-7 scoreline in front of what was a then semi-final record crowd of 37,424. Carney, incidentally, flew back to America just hours after the final whistle but returned for the final against Carlow a fortnight later and, in the very last game of a distinguished career that included a pair of All-Irelands, scored four points as Mayo captured their ninth National League title.

FOR the second league campaign in succession, Dublin opened their programme by drawing with Galway — this time at St Jarleth's Park in Tuam — and then ran up five consecutive victories over the same counties (and in the same order) they had beaten the previous season. Once again they topped their section and then progressed to another final with an 0-12 to 0-9 defeat of a Cork side that included, at midfield, Paddy Harrington, father of future golf champion Padraig. Once more they faced the reigning All-Ireland champions in the final, Meath on this occasion, and once more — with 'only' a dozen St. Vincent's players on board — they ran out convincing winners, 2-12 to 1-3 after leading by 2-4 to 1-1 at halftime.

A second successive league crown seemed a distinct possibility as Dublin went through the section games undefeated with successive wins over Laois, Wicklow, Roscommon, Galway, Offaly and Louth to set up a semi-final with Cork for the second season in a row. Dublin had to travel to what was then the Athletic Grounds where, despite a goal from Johnny Boyle in the 45th minute, they needed a last minute point from Mossy Whelan to secure a 1-4 to 0-7 draw. The replay at Croke Park a fortnight later was a major disappointment. Dublin, minus Mick Moylan and Marcus Wilson in defence, trailed by 1-9 to 1-6 at the break and could only add three points to Cork's seven in the second half. The defeat ended a fifteen match (two draws) unbeaten run in the competition for Dublin while Cork, with Harrington still on board, would go on to edge out Meath by 0-8 to 0-7 in the final.

After topping their section five seasons in a row and winning two titles in three campaigns, the 1956/57 league bordered on a disaster. Dublin opened with wins over Laois, Wicklow and Roscommon before suffering a 2-8 to 2-6 setback against Galway at Tuam. They rebounded with a comfortable 3-9 to 1-4 defeat of Offaly and could still force a play-off with the Tribesmen for a semi-final place if they could beat Louth at the Athletic Grounds in Drogheda. Things looked good when they led 1-8 to 2-1 with a mere three minutes left but Louth — captained by Dermot O'Brien who would lift the Sam Maguire Cup for the Wee County six months later — struck with a goal and a point to draw the game and deprive Dublin of a play-off chance.

The next campaign, that of 1957/58, was in some ways a mirrored opposite. Dublin, after wins over Laois, Offaly, Roscommon and Wicklow, again slipped up against Galway — by 2-4 to 0-7 at the Dunlo Grounds in Ballinasloe — and thus found themselves in the exact same position as a year previously, having to beat Louth to secure a play-off against their conquerors. This time they did it, by 0-12 to 1-4 at Croke Park and three weeks later, at the same venue, earned a semi-final place with a 3-5 to 1-7 defeat of Galway. The semi-final opposition was provided by Mayo, a side they had never beaten in three previous clashes in the knockout stages of the league, but the hoodoo was broken with an 0-10 to 0-7 victory at Croke Park. The final, against Kildare, was an action packed and high scoring thriller but Dublin, with Ollie Freaney contributing nine points and Johnny Joyce finding the net twice, took their third league crown on a 3-13 to 3-8 scoreline. Jim Crowley, Des Ferguson and Kevin Heffernan all shared a county record by appearing on three National League winning teams and just over four months later Dublin would become only the fourth county — after Kerry (three times), Mayo and Cavan — to complete the National League and All-Ireland double in the same season by beating Derry by 2-12 to 1-9 in the Sam Maguire decider.

The defence of their title brought them back to familiar ground; a draw with Offaly was sandwiched in between wins over Laois and Roscommon and further victories over Wicklow and Galway — Johnny Joyce scored 3-1 in the latter triumph — left then needing to beat Louth in their final game to earn a play-off with Offaly for a semi-finals spot ... but yet again the Wee County sent them packing with a 2-10 to 1-10 success at Drogheda. The following campaign, that of 1959/60, they won their six divisional games by an average of almost seven points but in the semi-final at Páirc Tailteann in Navan, after a 38th minute fisted goal from Paddy Farnan was ruled out for a square infringement by Offaly referee John Dowling, Cavan scored an upset 2-8 to 1-8 victory.

Louth, fast becoming Dublin's bogey team as far as the league was concerned, beat them 2-11 to 3-3 in St. Brigid's Park in Dundalk in the opening game of the next campaign but successive wins over Laois, Wicklow, Roscommon, Galway — Joyce finding the back of the Tribesmens' net four times on this occasion — and Offaly put them into the semi-finals. Meath were duly beaten 0-15 to 1-8 at Croke Park but in the final at the same venue in front of a record league final crowd of 56,515, double All-Ireland champions Down, thanks to a Sean O'Neill goal from a penalty just two minutes from the final whistle, sneaked a 2-5 to 1-7 victory, one that John D. Hickey in the *Irish Independent* called 'a fantastic act of football larceny.'

Dublin, in March 1963, suffered heavy losses to Galway and Offaly — by 2-12 to 0-7 and 3-7 to 0-3, respectively — and certainly did not look like a team that would lift the Sam Maguire Cup just six months later but in the following league campaign, imbued with the confidence of champions, they won five out of six divisional ties, the exception being a two point loss to a Galway side that later that year would win the first of three successive All-Ireland titles. Kerry were pipped 0-10 to 0-9 in front of a record semi-final crowd of 53,088 but with New York back in the league fold, all the win secured for Dublin was a place in the 'home' final against Down.

Eight months previously Dublin had beaten the Mournemen by 2-11 to 0-7 in the All-Ireland semi-final and this time the score was almost exactly replicated, 2-9 to 0-7, with Brian McDonald hitting 1-4. That game was in early May and Dublin's interest in the Championship ended with a Leinster Final defeat to Meath in late July, but the league decider 'proper' didn't take place in Gaelic Park in New York until mid October, a fact that may have militated against The Dubs; either way, in a game played in 27 degrees Celsius, Dublin fought back from six points down entering the final quarter to cut the game to the minimum but a miss from a close range free by John Timmons and then a final New York point from Kildare native Pat Cummins meant a 2-12 to 1-13 defeat for the visitors. For the following three years the league final proper would be played on a two legged basis; had that been the case for the 1963/64 competition Dublin would have emerged easy winners as a week later again at Gaelic Park, they beat New York by 3-10 to 1-6 in a game for which the ball was thrown in by then U.S. Attorney General Robert Kennedy.

Just two days after their return to the Big Apple, Dublin opened their 1964/65 league campaign with a 1-11 to 0-10 defeat of Laois at Croke Park in a game that will be forever remembered for its only goal: scored by right corner forward Eamonn Breslin in the 20th minute and headed into Laois keeper Tom Miller's net. Dublin chalked up another four successive wins — over Wicklow, Offaly, Louth (in which John Timmons scored 3-3) and Roscommon — but their final game, against Galway at Tuam Stadium, turned out to be the decider for a semi-final place and a 2-11 to 1-7 defeat ended Dublin's interest in the competition.

Two years later Dublin beat Laois, Kildare and Cork in a four-team group and then beat Carlow in the section semi-final and Wexford in the final. That run secured a place in the league semi-final which resulted in a 1-15 to 1-7 victory over Meath but in the 'home' final, against Galway, the All-Ireland champions for the last three years, Dublin went down 0-12 to 1-7. The following season Dublin got out of a four-team group despite a loss to Westmeath but were then beaten by Down by 3-7 to 2-4 in a section semi-final, and in 1968/69 they got to the divisional final — which doubled as a league quarter-final — but lost out 1-8 to 1-3 to Westmeath. The defeat was all the more galling for Dublin as they had already twice beaten the same opposition in the campaign, by 0-10 to 0-7 in their sectional meeting and then by 0-7 to 0-3 in a play-off to determine the winners of the section.

The nearest Dublin came to success as the Sixties turned into the Seventies was in the 1970/71 season when, despite losing to Kerry and once again having to settle for a draw with Galway, they beat Offaly, Kildare, Roscommon, Cork and Longford to jointly top Division 1B with Kerry. Both qualified for the semi-finals but as a play-off was required to decide the pecking order; Kerry triumphed once again — by 0-15 to 1-8 — and three weeks later went down to Mayo in the semi-final, 1-9 to 0-8. Then came an indifferent campaign consisting of three wins and two draw in seven outings and the season after that came the ultimate humiliation, relegation for the first time ever after they could only manage a single win in seven matches. The final game of that 1972/73 campaign, against Roscommon at O'Rourke Park in Castlerea, was postponed until September and, as scoring difference would determine the finishing order, Dublin spent the summer knowing they would have to win by eight points if they were to avoid the drop and send their opponents down along with Kildare. They lost by five, 3-7 to 0-11.

THAT game, however, would turn out to be perhaps the most significant watershed in the entire history of Dublin football ... it was the county's first ever game under the then radical concept of a lone manager as distinct from a five-man selection committee assisted by a trainer. The lone manager's name was Kevin Heffernan, and the times were about to be a changing.

The changes were slow and subtle, at least on the field. An obvious consequence of relegation was not only a lower level of opposition but also unique opposition. In addition to recording wins over Wexford, Kildare, Carlow and Waterford, Dublin beat Limerick in only the second competitive meeting of the counties — the previous one was in February 1898 when the Shannonsiders had won 1-5 to 0-7 in the All-Ireland

Final of 1896 — and also had a 6-16 to 0-4 routing of Kilkenny in the first meeting of the sides since the 1922 provincial decider. John McCarthy found the net four times in that latter game but he was held scoreless in Dublin's final divisional tie, a surprise 4-9 to 2-9 loss to Clare at Croke Park in the first ever meeting of the counties in either the National League or the Championship. Antrim were then beaten 1-13 to 1-8 in the Division II semi-final to guarantee immediate promotion but Kildare — whom they had pipped 1-10 to 1-9 in Athy earlier in the campaign — beat them 3-13 to 2-9 in the decider at Croke Park in early May. Few in the sparse crown of 4,049 could have predicted that Dublin captain Sean Doherty would be lifting the Sam Maguire Cup exactly 140 days later.

Promoted back to Division IA, Dublin suffered a 1-8 to 0-10 defeat to Cork in their first game as All-Ireland champions and could only manage an 0-8 apiece draw in their second, against Kerry at Fitzgerald Stadium in Killarney, but then reeled off wins over Kildare, Offaly and Roscommon to qualify for the semi-finals. Tyrone were comprehensively dismissed 3-12 to 1-7, but in the final Meath, 1-8 to 0-5 adrift when Bobby Doyle netted a minute into the second half, fought back for a deserved 0-16 to 1-9 victory.

The hiccups against Cork and Kerry in 1974/75 were more than made up for the following season with 1-12 to 0-4 and 2-11 to 0-13 victories at The Mardyke and Croke Park, respectively, and followed by equally clearcut wins over Kildare and Offaly. Only in their final group game, when they travelled to Dr. Hyde Park in Roscommon minus Pat Gogarty, Brian Mullins, Tony Hanahoe and Jimmy Keaveney did they slip up, 2-8 to 1-6. Galway were beaten 1-11 to 0-12 in the semi-final — Tony Hanahoe getting the goal and a teenage debutant by name of Kevin Moran adding a crucial point — but the final against Derry proved to be unexpectedly close; a 44th minute goal from Keaveney proving decisive in a 2-10 to 0-15 triumph for Heffernan's foot soldiers. Still, all that mattered was that Dublin had won the National League for the fourth time and the first since 1958. Five months later Dublin would complete their second National League and Championship double after waiting for the same period of time.

They went desperately close to a successful defence the following season. Despite a loss to Kerry and a draw with Meath, they qualified for a quarter-final clash with Cavan at Pearse Park in Longford and, with a 2-12 to 1-7 victory, set up a semi-final with league nemesis Mayo. Playing with the benefit of a near gale force wind, Dublin built up a halftime lead of 0-8 to 0-2 but few in the 22,235 attendance could have been confident they would retain their advantage when playing into such a strong wind — yet playing what Pádraig Purcell in the *Irish Press* called "vintage Dublin football", they outscored their rivals by 2-4 to 0-3 and such was their dominance that Mayo's only point from play throughout the game was their last, scored by Willie Nally eight minutes from the end. Dublin, for the first time ever, were in the final of the National League for a third successive time but the decider, against Kerry, was a real letdown; missing Brian Mullins due to 'flu, The Dubs trailed 1-6 to 0-4 at halftime and lost Alan Larkin through injury shortly after the restart yet fought back ferociously only to fall heartbreakingly short and finish on the wrong end of a 1-8 to 1-6 scoreline.

The following campaign, that of 1977/78, was one of triumph all the way. Kerry, Kildare, Cork, Offaly and Galway were beaten in that order in a table topping run that earned a semi-final clash with Laois, a game that, despite having to line out minus an injured Jimmy Keaveney, Dublin overcame strong resistance to win 0-12 to 0-7. Mayo, their opponents in the final, had beaten Dublin in the deciders of 1933/34 and 1940/41 but there was to be no hat-trick for the men from the west as The Dubs sprinted into a 1-7 to 0-1 lead by the 17th minute and, despite a strong rally by the Connacht side, still held a 1-10 to 1-5 advantage at the break. Both sides scored 1-8 in the second half and Dublin were National League champions for the fifth time and the second in three campaigns.

NOBODY was to know it at the time, but that success was the last at national level for Heffo's Heroes; having won three All-Irelands and two National Leagues in just over three and a half years, that Dublin squad of the Seventies would draw a complete blank in both competitions, failing to reach another league decider and suffering crushing All-Ireland Final defeats against Kerry in both 1978 and 1979. Heffernan would guide the county to another Sam Maguire triumph in 1983 but with an almost totally new squad — only Tommy Drumm, Brian Mullins and Anton O'Toole bridged the gap between April '78 and September '83.

Dublin, with just one win and a draw per season, could only finish fifth of six teams in each of the next two league campaigns and failed to score a goal in half a dozen of their ten games in that spell. Only in the 1980/81 competition — when the league was restructured into a single top flight of eight teams — was there even a hint of promise when four wins and a draw against two losses (to Kerry and Roscommon) earned them a play-off for a quarter-finals place. Dublin had beaten the Orchard County by 2-8 to 2-3 at Croke Park in their final divisional game to secure the play-off and a fortnight later at the same venue did it again, this time by 1-7 to 1-5. The quarter-final, against Mayo at Dr. Hyde Park in Roscommon, was lost 1-11 to 1-10, when Dublin's cause was certainly not helped by the fact that their opponents had 1-3 without reply on the scoreboard inside a dozen minutes.

After two more fruitless campaigns the ultimate league humiliation followed in the 1983/84 campaign when — despite being reigning All-Ireland champions — Dublin were relegated for only the second time when they could only muster a single win and two draws from seven outings. Unlike the previous occasion eleven years earlier, there was to be no immediate return to the top flight; Dublin beat Monaghan, Offaly, Donegal and Louth, but losses to Roscommon, Mayo and Wexford ensured another season in Division Two. Despite losses to Longford and Mayo, they did make it back to the top division the following season as runners-up to the latter and even edged a 2-8 to 1-10 quarter-final win over Meath but then suffered an 0-12 to 1-7 semi-final defeat to eventual champions Laois, the same county that had conquered them in the final of the inaugural league six decades previously.

The following season, 1986/87, began disastrously with successive defeats against Meath, Monaghan and Kerry but Dublin would rebound with victories over Armagh, Mayo, Down and Roscommon to, a little miraculously, finish fourth in the division and earn a place in the quarter-finals. Cork provided the opposition and a contribution of 1-4 from Barney Rock was a major factor in a 1-10 to 1-7 triumph, a win that was followed by a 1-8 to 0-8 semi-final defeat of Galway at O'Moore Park in Portlaoise. Kerry, who had beaten Dublin 0-10 to 0-8 in their divisional meeting at Austin Stack Park in Tralee five months previously, were outscored 1-11 to 0-11 in the decider, the match winner this time being Ciaran Duff with 1-3. Dublin, under manager Gerry McCaul, had won their first National League title in nine seasons.

Once again it would be a brave defence; Dublin, in fact, went closer than ever to retaining the National League. Draws with Meath and Cork in their first and last divisional games, separated by victories over Monaghan, Kerry, Armagh, Mayo and Derry saw them top the table undefeated and they followed up with an 0-10 to 0-4 defeat of Longford in the quarter-finals and an emphatic 4-12 to 1-8 triumph over Monaghan in the semi-finals, thereby setting up a final shoot-out with neighbours Meath — who just happened to be the reigning All-Ireland champions. A late fisted goal from Mick Galvin and an injury time point from Joe McNally earned Dublin — who were minus injured Ballymun Kickhams team mates Barney Rock and Anto McCaul — a 1-8 to 0-11 draw but there was to be no such Houdini act in the replay; Meath, despite having Kevin Foley red carded after a dozen minutes, were 1-6 to 0-6 to the good at halftime and eventually won by eight points, 2-13 to 0-11.

The next two seasons, those of 1988/89 and 1989/90, would see The Dubs emerge from the divisional phase but then fall short. In the first, they jointly topped the table with Kerry — both teams having five wins and two losses — and after further wins over Wexford in the quarter-final and Cavan in the semi-final, lost out to Cork by 0-15 to 0-12 in what, to date at least, would be the last 'home' decider. McNally scored all the goals in a 4-18 to 1-9 victory over Derry in the opening game of the following campaign but things filtered out after that; defeats by Cork, Donegal and Armagh left them needing to beat the latter in a play-off to make the quarter-finals. This they did, by 1-14 to 1-9 in Drogheda, but Division Two champions Roscommon rolled them over in extra time in the semi-final in Portlaoise by 2-22 to 3-13, outscoring The Dubs by 2-8 to 2-2 in the additional play.

♜ ♜ ♜

DUBLIN'S prospects for the 1990/91 campaign looked far from bright when Derry handed then a 2-11 to 1-9 beating in their opening game, at MacCumhail Park in Ballybofey, but they bounced back with successive wins over Armagh, Cork, Roscommon, Down and Kerry — by 3-11 to 0-7, their biggest ever win over the Kingdom in National League or Championship action — before topping the table by drawing their final divisional tie, against Meath at Croke Park. Wicklow were beaten 2-10 to 0-11 in the quarter-final, Roscommon were outscored 1-18 to 0-11 in the semi-final, and Dublin captured their seventh league crown when a Vinnie Murphy goal proved crucial in a 1-9 to 0-10 final victory over Kildare. John O'Leary kept seven clean sheets in the ten games and another All-Star goalkeeper, Paddy Cullen, who had won National Leagues in 1976 and 1978, now had another as manager.

The league was restructured once more for the following season, with Division One divided into A and B sections with half a dozen teams in each. Dublin beat Galway, Armagh and Mayo and lost to Tyrone — by 4-11 to 0-11 — and Cork to finish joint second, but made it through to the quarter-finals by beating Galway for a second time, 2-8 to 0-8 in a play-off. Donegal were edged out 3-6 to 1-10 in the quarter-final but, in the semi-final, Dublin were beaten by Tyrone for the second time in five months, on this occasion by 0-13 to 1-9 after regular freetaker Charlie Redmond had been controversially taken off with eight minutes remaining.

As had been the case two seasons previously, Derry upset Dublin on the opening day of the league (by 0-11 to 0-9 in Croke Park), but, as had also been the case in the previous instance, that would be the one and only setback of an otherwise perfect campaign. Sligo, Louth, Antrim, Wexford Galway and Limerick were all beaten with varying comfort and wins over Kildare by 1-13 to 0-8 in the quarter-final and Kerry by 1-10 to 0-11 in the semi-final saw Dublin into the league decider for the 18th time.

Donegal, their quarter-final victims by just two points a year earlier and their 0-18 to 0-14 conquerors in the All-Ireland Final the previous September, provided the opposition and it took two late points from first Manus Boyle and then Noel Hegarty to secure the Ulster side an 0-9 to 0-9 draw after Wexford referee Brian White — who gave 35 frees to Donegal and just a dozen to Dublin — had sent off Charlie Redmond and Keith Barr. In the replay just a week later White again red carded a Dub, (this time Tommy Carr just short of the five minute mark), but Dublin responded by firing over eight points without reply before Donegal got off the mark in the second minute of first half injury time. The final outcome was an 0-10 to 0-6 victory for the by now Pat O'Neill managed Dublin and an eighth league title, and once again John O'Leary's contribution to the success stood out with a remarkable nine clean sheets in the eleven games, including in the last five in succession. He also made history by becoming the first Dub to win three National League titles.

The following season, despite a loss to Donegal — 0-11 to 0-7 in Ballybofey — and draws with Kildare and Down, Dublin advanced to the quarter-finals but their interest ended there with a 2-13 to 1-9 defeat by Armagh at Breffni Park in Cavan. Then came relegation to Division Two, where they would spend four seasons before returning to the top flight, not as a result of direct promotion as such but due to the realigning of the competition. Then, in the 1999/00 season, they finished joint second behind Kerry — whom they had beaten 1-8 to 0-9 at Parnell Park — but lost out on a semi-final place to Roscommon on scoring difference. After that came a decade of virtually zero success; in 2007 (the league having switched to a calendar year schedule five years previously), despite finishing joint fifth in an eight team division, they were relegated in yet another realignment of the competition. The following year they topped the table and won promotion but were beaten 0-15 to 0-10 in the Division decider at Pairc Tailteann in Navan by Westmeath, a side they had beaten 1-7 to 1-5 in their opening divisional game.

AFTER two uneventful campaigns back in the top flight with a combined record of seven wins, two draws and five losses, the tide began to turn in 2011. Successive wins over Armagh, Cork, Kerry, Monaghan, Mayo — with Diarmuid Connolly hitting 3-3 in a 4-15 to 3-13 win at Croke Park — and Down were followed by a draw with Galway at Pearse Stadium in Salthill, a run that saw Dublin top the table by three points and go straight into a final clash with runners-up Cork. Just over two months earlier the Leesiders, the defending title holders as well as reigning All-Ireland champions, had been beaten 3-13 to 0-16 at Croke Park but the competition decider, at the same venue, would be something short of an action replay. Dublin, 1-10 to 0-10 ahead at the break, scored 1-2 without replay in the opening five minutes of the second half — but could only add two further points thereafter while Cork rifled over eleven to sneak a single point victory, 0-21 to 2-14.

The following year was a mediocre one for Dublin — by then the All-Ireland champions — with just three wins and four defeats but it did have one notable footnote; nine days short of a year after he had scored 3-3 against Mayo at Croke Park, Connolly exactly duplicated his feat in a 4-17 to 1-10 trouncing of Armagh, again at Headquarters. There may have been overall disappointment, but Dublin's greatest ever days in the National League were just around the corner.

It began just as the previous campaign had ended; with a clash with Cork at Croke Park. This one was won 1-18 to 2-9 and was followed by a 1-11 to 0-4 defeat of Kerry in Killarney and further victories over Mayo (Bernard Brogan scoring 1-10) and Kildare. Dublin, without the injured Brogan (who had scored 3-28 in the previous four games and would also miss the final two divisional games), were then pipped 0-18 to 1-14 by Tyrone but rallied to top the table by first beating Down and then drawing with All-Ireland champions Donegal in Ballybofey. In the semi-final against Mayo, Dublin were held scoreless for the first dozen minutes yet by halftime were 2-9 to 0-8 to the good and eventually won 2-16 to 0-16.

The final was against Tyrone, the only team to beat Dublin in the run-up to the decider, Tyrone. It turned out to be only marginally short of a classic, of which Martin Breheny in the *Irish Independent* said: 'If the sign-off game from NFL 2013 holds any indication of what the championship has in store, then it is going to be a wonderful summer,' Tyrone led on six separate occasions in the second half but two massive late points from Dean Rock — who had come on as a sub for Brogan — and a third from Jack McCaffrey edged The Dubs home 0-18 to 0-17.

Dublin were league champions for the ninth time but the first in two decades. Team manager Jim Gavin, in his first season at the helm, had been left half forward on that successful 1993 side and no fewer than four members of his final line-out were sons of previous National League winners with Dublin; Brogan (Bernard, 1976 and 1978), James McCarthy (John, 1978), McCaffrey (Noel, 1987) and Rock (Barney, 1987). Keeper and skipper John O'Leary equalled the 1958 record of Jim Crowley, Des Ferguson and Kevin Heffernan by winning a third league title. Five months later Dublin would complete their third National League and Championship double and the first since 1976.

The defence of the crown in 2014 was somewhat stuttery in the beginning; wins over Kerry, Westmeath, Tyrone and Kildare — all but the last by just a single point margin — and a draw with Mayo were interspersed with defeats against Cork and Derry, but a finishing place of fourth in the table was enough to secure a semi-final date with Cork. In a game that turned out to be a total opposite of the final meeting between the sides three years previously, Cork held a remarkable 2-11 to 0-7 lead by the 40th minute mark but could only raise two more white flags while Dublin struck for 2-13 to eventually win by seven points, 2-20 to 2-13.

Dublin's opposition in the final was provided by the other side to beat them in the divisional phase of the competition, Derry, who had won out at Celtic Park by 1-16 to 0-13 just six weeks earlier. This time it was pretty much no contest; indeed, had it been a boxing bout the referee would surely have stopped it on the grounds that Derry were unable to defend themselves as Dublin raced into an 0-13 to 1-3 halftime lead and eventually romped home by 3-19 to 1-10 to retain the National League for the first time ever. Vincent Hogan in the *Irish Independent* noted: 'This isn't a team Jim Gavin is building. It's a movement.'

The bid, in 2015, for a first ever league hat-trick began with something short of intimidation of the opposition; two point losses to both Cork and Kerry, with a 2-10 to 0-11 victory over Donegal sandwiched in between. The Kerry defeat in Killarney, however, would be the last Dublin would suffer in National League or Championship action for over two years and wins over Tyrone, Mayo, Derry and Monaghan earned them a semi-final showdown with the latter just a week later. Dublin had won the first meeting in Clones by 1-22 to 1-11 but the second one was much closer, as close as it could get, in fact, 0-17 to 0-16.

For the second time in five seasons the league final was a Dublin v Cork shoot-out but this meeting had none of the drama of the first one. A goal from a Diarmuid Connolly penalty set Dublin up for a 1-9 to 0-5 lead at halftime and half a dozen unanswered points in just over the first ten minutes of the second half killed off the game. The final score was 1-21 to 2-7; Dublin had completed the first National League three in a row since Kerry had accomplished the feat in 1973 before winning again the following year.

The following campaign, in 2016, was one of success all the way. Kerry, Mayo, Monaghan, Cork, Down, Donegal and Roscommon were all beaten in turn as The Dubs topped the table by a clear four points ahead of the men from the Kingdom and Donegal, beaten 1-10 to 0-7 in their divisional meeting just three weeks earlier, were ousted 1-20 to 0-13 in the semi-final. Considering they shared a rivalry that had begun all of 123 years previously and had embraced the entire nine decades of the National League, Dublin now faced Kerry in the decider of the secondary competition for only the third time.

Kerry had won the first such meeting 1-8 to 1-6 in 1977 and Dublin had balanced the books with a 1-11 to 0-11 triumph a decade later, but the 'rubber' was nowhere near as close. Dublin's lead at the break might have been just two points, 0-10 to 0-8, but the second half was a totally different story as, aided by goals from Paul Flynn and sub Eric Lowndes, they romped to a 2-18 to 0-13 victory. Dublin had achieved their first ever league four in a row and eight players — Stephen Cluxton, Philly McMahon, Jonny Cooper, James McCarthy, Cian O'Sullivan, Diarmuid Connolly, Kevin McManamon and Bernard Brogan — had featured in all four final successes. Cluxton missed three of the divisional ties but played in the remaining four and the semi-final and final and in his half a dozen games was beaten just once — and by himself at that, when he spilled a high ball from Down full forward Donal O'Hare into his net at Pairc Esler in Newry. Five months later Dublin would become only the second team to complete the National League and Championship double in successive seasons, the first being Kerry in 1932.

Semi-finals were dispensed with for the 2017 campaign so if Dublin were to have a chance of winning a fifth successive crown — a feat that had only ever been achieved once before, by Mayo in 1938 (they won again the next year) — they had to finish in the top two in the divisional phase. An opening victory over Cavan at Breffni Park was followed by successive draws against Tyrone and Donegal and, after a comprehensive 1-16 to 0-7 defeat of Mayo, another stalemate with Kerry in Tralee, when injury time points by Dean Rock and Paul Mannion enabled The Dubs to equal the Kingdom's record of 34 competitive games unbeaten, set in 1932. In their next game, at Croke Park a week later, Dublin racked up 2-29 against Roscommon (0-14), thereby beating by three their previous white flag record set when beating Westmeath in a provincial semi-final eight years previously; three months later Dublin would equal their new record when again beating Westmeath in an identical Championship fixture, 4-29 to 0-10.

A single goal victory over Monaghan — 2-15 to 1-15 — at St. Tiernach's Park in Clones in their seventh and last divisional game gave Dublin a unique piece of National League history as the first team ever to qualify for five successive finals, the third of Mayo's six consecutive titles, in 1935/36, having been won on the one and only occasion that the competition was run on a totally league basis with no knockout stages. Old foes Kerry qualified for the final through what might be called an unofficial back door; sixth of the eight teams going into the final round of divisional ties the previous weekend, they not only needed to beat Tyrone but also had to rely on fifth placed Mayo beating second placed Donegal to get through on scoring difference.

Kerry had been the last side to hand Dublin a competitive defeat with an 0-15 to 1-10 success in a league clash at Fitzgerald Stadium in Killarney two years and six weeks earlier and they did it again when, after The Dubs had narrowed the gap to the minimum after being five points down entering the final quarter, a last second Dean Rock free into the Hill 16 goal struck the right upright to give the Kingdom an 0-20 to 1-16 victory. Dublin's record breaking run of 36 games (six draws) in the National League and the Championship had finally ended.

National League Results

1925/26

DUBLIN 3-3   LOUTH 1-5
Oct 11, St Brigid's Park, Dundalk
Dublin: H Stynes, J O'Reilly, Joe Norris, Jim Norris, C Grace, John Synnott 1-0, Josie Synnott 1-1, P Synnott 1-0, N Lennon 0-1, P McDonnell 0-1, P Carey, M Shanahan, C McDonald, J Hunt, J O'Toole.

DUBLIN 0-9   MEATH 1-2
Oct 18, Croke Park, Dublin
Dublin: J McDonnell, Jim Norris, T Fitzgerald, Joe Norris, Josie Synnott, John Synnott 0-1, P Synnott 0-2, P Stynes 0-4, C Grace 0-1, M O'Brien 0-1, J O'Reilly, M Shanahan, C McDonald, J Hunt, J O'Toole.

DUBLIN 2-5   KILDARE 1-3
Nov 8, Croke Park, Dublin
Dublin: J McDonnell, Joe Norris, Jim Norris, W Reilly, John Synnott 1-0, Josie Synnott, P Synnott 0-1, P Stynes 0-1, C Grace 0-1, P McDonnell 0-1, M O'Brien 1-0, C McDonald, M Shanahan 0-1, J Hunt, J O'Toole.

GROUP C	P	W	D	L	Pts
DUBLIN	3	3	0	0	6
KILDARE	3	2	0	1	4
LOUTH	3	1	0	1	2
MEATH	3	0	0	3	0

SEMI-FINAL
Apr 25, St Brigid's Park, Dundalk
DUBLIN 0-8   ANTRIM 0-5
Dublin: J McDonnell, W Reilly, P Carey, T Fitzgerald, Josie Synnott 0-2, Joe Norris, John Synnott, C Grace 0-1, M Durnin, P McDonnell 0-1, M O'Brien, M Shanahan 0-2, J Hunt, J O'Toole 0-2, W Corry 0-1.

FINAL
Sep 19, Barrett's Park, New Ross
LAOIS 2-1   DUBLIN 1-0
Dublin: Johnny McDonnell, Josie Synnott, John Synnott, Jack O'Reilly, Paddy Kirwan, Morgan Durnin, Jim Molloy, Jim Norris, Paddy Carey, Mick Lennon, Paddy McDonnell, Jim Mohan, Joe Norris, Charlie McDonald, Peter Stynes 1-0.

1926/27

No competition

1927/28

KILDARE 1-3   DUBLIN 0-2
Feb 27, St Conleth's Park, Newbridge
Dublin: J McDonnell, Joe Norris, Jim Norris, T Fitzgerald, P Molloy, J O'Reilly, P Carey, M Durnin, Josie Synnott, P Moore, P Mohan, W Manifold, P McDonnell 0-2, John Kirwan, R Mulcahy.

DUBLIN 1-7   CAVAN 3-1
Mar 20, Croke Park, Dublin
Dublin: J McDonnell, W Reilly, Jim Norris, Joe Norris, Josie Synnott 0-1, John Synnott, P Moore 0-1, R Mulcahy, J Doyle 0-1, P Molloy, J Flynn 0-1, J Mohan 0-1, M Devine, W Manifold 1-0, C Grace 0-2.

MEATH 1-3   DUBLIN 1-2
Apr 24, Showgrounds, Navan
Dublin: J McDonnell, J Smith, P Kennedy, J Duffy, J O'Toole, M Allen, P Synnott, J Kavanagh 0-1, M O'Brien, J Sherlock, C Grace, P Stynes 1-1, W Manifold, P Flynn, J Lynam.

DOWN 2-7   DUBLIN 2-6
Oct 30, Croke Park, Dublin
Dublin: J McDonnell, P Flynn, Jim Kirwan, John Kirwan 1-1, J Mullen, J Lynam 0-2, J O'Reilly, J Rice, P McDonnell 0-2, P Carey, Josie Synnott 1-1, P Synnott, M O'Brien, M Durnin, Joe Norris.

LOUTH 4-4   DUBLIN 0-2
Nov 13, Athletic Grounds, Drogheda
Dublin: J McDonnell, P Flynn, J Sherlock, John Kirwan, Jim Kirwan, J O'Toole, J O'Reilly, J Lynam 0-1, M Egan, M O'Brien, J Kealy, P McDonnell 0-1, M Durnin, Josie Synnott, P Molloy.

DUBLIN 3-5   ARMAGH 0-8
Nov 27, Croke Park, Dublin
Dublin: J McDonnell, John Kirwan, P Flynn, M Reidy, J O'Reilly 0-1, J Sherlock, J Lynam, J O'Toole, Jim Kirwan 3-2, P McDonnell, P Synnott, J Mohan 0-1, P O'Beirne, M Durnin, P Lynam 0-1.

NORTHERN SECTION	P	W	D	L	Pts
KILDARE	8	7	1	0	15
LOUTH	8	6	0	2	12
ARMAGH	8	5	1	2	11
DOWN	8	4	0	4	8
CAVAN	7	3	1	3	7
MEATH	7	3	0	4	4
MONAGHAN	6	1	1	4	3
DUBLIN	6	1	1	4	3
TYRONE	6	0	1	5	1

* Full programme not completed as Kildare had

already won the section and qualified for the semi-finals. Meath beat Down but forfeited the points for being late onto the field.

1928/29

KILDARE 2-6   DUBLIN 0-3
Oct 14, Croke Park, Dublin
Dublin: J McDonnell, W Reilly, J Quinn 0-1, Josie Synnott, P Stynes, J O'Toole, John Synnott, N McCann 0-1, J Stack, J Farrell, P Synnott, M Durnin, P McDonnell 0-1, A Perkins, M O'Brien.

DUBLIN 4-1   MEATH 0-2
Nov 18, Showgrounds, Navan
Dublin: J McDonnell, W Reilly, J Quinn 0-1, Josie Synnott, P Stynes, J O'Toole, John Synnott 1-0, N McCann 1-0, J Stack, J Farrell, P Synnott 1-0, M Durnin, P McDonnell 1-1, A Perkins, M O'Brien.

DUBLIN 1-4   LAOIS 1-4
Mar 24, O'Moore Park, Portlaoise
Dublin: J McDonnell, J Stack, J O'Shea, J O'Reilly, Joe Norris, M O'Brien 0-1, M Durnin, W Leonard 0-1, P Synnott 1-1, John Synnott, J O'Toole, N McCann, C Grace 0-1, T Dowd, T Carroll.

DUBLIN 2-3   WEXFORD 0-5
Apr 28, Croke Park, Dublin
Dublin: J McDonnell, M O'Brien, J O'Reilly, J Ebbs 0-1, M Durnin 1-0, W Leonard 1-0, J Stack, J O'Shea, P Daly, J Sherlock 0-1, J O'Toole, N McCann, P McDonnell 0-1, T Dowd, T Carroll.

SOUTH-EASTERN SECTION	P	W	D	L	Pts
KILDARE	4	3	0	1	6
DUBLIN	4	2	1	1	5
LAOIS	4	1	2	1	4
WEXFORD	4	2	0	2	4
MEATH	4	0	1	3	1

1929/30

No competition

1930/31

DUBLIN 2-3   KILDARE 1-1
Mar 23, St Conleth's Park, Newbridge
Dublin: J McDonnell, M Langton, J Mohan, J Quinn, John Synnott, P Synnott 1-2, P Moore, W Leonard, P McDonnell, C Duffy, M O'Brien 1-0, T Dowd, W Dowling 0-1, N McCann, J Daly.

DUBLIN 4-5   WEXFORD 2-2
Apr 6, Croke Park, Dublin
Dublin: J McDonnell, J Mohan, J Quinn, M Langton,

Joe Norris, P Moore, John Synnott, P Synnott 1-0, M O'Brien 2-1, M Durnin, W Leonard, P McDonnell 0-2, J Lawlor 0-1, N McCann, W Dowling 1-1.

DUBLIN 2-4   LAOIS 2-3
Aug 31, O'Moore Park, Portlaoise
Dublin: John Mulhall, P Moore, Jim Mulhall, M Curley, T Newman, M O'Brien 1-0, P Synnott, W Leonard, P McDonnell 1-4, M Langton, T Dowd, W Dowling, N McCann, M Brennan, T Tyrrell.

KERRY 0-8   DUBLIN 0-3
Dec 7, Croke Park, Dublin
Dublin: John Mulhall, J O'Shea, P Moore, P Hickey, J Mohan, M Brennan, M Langton, P Synnott, Jim Mulhall, C Duffy, P McDonnell 0-2, T Dowd 0-1, W Dowling, T Tyrrell, S Lavan. Sub: T Newman for Synnott.

SECTION A	P	W	D	L	Pts
KERRY	4	3	1	1	7
DUBLIN	4	3	0	1	6
KILDARE	4	2	1	1	5
LAOIS	4	1	0	3	2
WEXFORD	4	0	0	4	0

1931/32

Mar 8, Croke Park, Dublin
KILDARE 2-10   DUBLIN 2-4
Dublin: John Mulhall, P Moore, J Kelly, M Curley, J Byrne, J Quinn, J O'Shea, P Cavanagh, Jim Mulhall 1-0, M Wellington 0-1, W Leonard, J Mohan, M O'Brien 0-2, P Synnott 1-1, C Collier.

May 24, Croke Park, Dublin
LAOIS 2-2   DUBLIN 0-6
Dublin: J O'Reilly, P Moore, R Creagh, J O'Shea, M Curley, J Byrne, P Hickey, P Cavanagh, T O'Dowd, M Wellington 0-1, W Leonard, J Mohan, W Dowling 0-2, M O'Brien 0-2, P Synnott 0-1, S Lavan.

Nov 15, Frank Sheehy Park, Listowel
KERRY 1-10   DUBLIN 3-2
Dublin: J McDonnell, J O'Shea, D Brennan, P Cavanagh, M O'Brien, P Synnott, N McCann, P Hickey, P Tyrell, P McDonnell 1-1, J O'Rourke 0-1, W Dowling 2-0, P Kearney, P Rogers, F Williams.

SECTION A	P	W	D	L	Pts
KERRY	3	3	0	0	6
LAOIS	3	2	0	1	4
KILDARE	3	1	0	2	2
DUBLIN	3	0	0	3	0

1932/33

KERRY 0-9   DUBLIN 0-7
Nov 13, Austin Stack Park, Tralee

Dublin: J McDonnell, P Rogers, G McLoughlin, D Brennan, P Hickey, N McCann 0-2, W Leonard, M Keating, C Duffy 0-1, T O'Dowd 0-1, W Dowling, M Kelly 0-2, P Synott 0-1, P McDonnell, M O'Brien.

MEATH 1-4   DUBLIN 0-2
Nov 27, Showgrounds, Navan
Dublin: J McDonnell, M O'Brien, W Leonard, P Synnott, A Dickson, G McLonghlin, D Brennan, N McCann, W Dowling, P Hickey, M Keating, C Duffy, P Mulhall, P Rogers, P O'Neill 0-2. Sub: J O'Rourke for Mulhall.

DUBLIN 2-8   LAOIS 0-6
Mar 5, Croke Park, Dublin
Dublin: J McDonnell, J O'Shea, D Brennan, G McLoughlin, N McCann, P Hickey, P Synnott, J Brown 0-1, T O'Dowd, B Beggs, B Quinn 0-1, M Kelly 1-2, A Dickson 0-1, F McCann 0-2, M Keating 1-1.

SECTION A	P	W	D	L	Pts
MEATH	3	3	0	0	6
KERRY	3	2	0	1	4
DUBLIN	3	1	0	2	2
LAOIS	3	0	0	3	0

1933/34

DUBLIN 2-3   LAOIS 1-6
Nov 5, O'Moore Park, Portlaoise
Dublin: J McDonnell, D Brennan, J O'Shea, F Cavanagh, P Hickey, N McCann, P Cavanagh, P Hickey 1-0, B Beggs, M Kelly, M O'Brien, G Fitzgerald, M Keating 1-1, G Powell 0-1, T Markham 0-1.

DUBLIN 1-5   KILDARE 0-6
Nov 19, Croke Park, Dublin
Dublin: J McDonnell, D Brennan, J O'Shea, F Cavanagh, P Hickey, N McCann 0-1, P Cavanagh, B Beggs 0-1, M Kelly, M O'Brien, G Fitzgerald 0-1, M Keating 0-2, W Dowling, P Synnott 1-0, T Markham.

DUBLIN 1-9   WEXFORD 2-3
Dec 3, Wexford Park, Wexford
Dublin: J McDonnell, J O'Shea, D Brennan, F Cavanagh, P O'Brien, N McCann, P Hickey, P Synnott, W Dowling, B Quinn 0-1, B Beggs 1-0, M Kelly 0-5, G Fitzgerald 0-2, M Keating, T Markham 0-1.

DUBLIN 2-6   KERRY 1-7
Apr 8, Croke Park, Dublin
Dublin: J McDonnell, J O'Shea, D Brennan, F Cavanagh, P O'Brien, N McCann, P Cavanagh, M Kelly 0-1, B Beggs 0-1, W Dowling 0-2, G Fitzgerald, M O'Brien, M Wellington 0-2, M Keating 2-0, T Markham.

GROUP II	P	W	D	L	Pts
DUBLIN	4	3	1	0	7
KILDARE	4	3	0	1	6
KERRY	4	2	0	2	4
LAOIS	4	1	1	2	3
WEXFORD	4	0	0	4	4

FINAL
May 13, MacHale Park, Castlebar
MAYO   2-3   DUBLIN 1-6
Dublin: Johnny McDonnell, Des Brennan, Ned McCann, Frank Cavanagh, Jim O'Shea, Paddy Hickey, Paddy Cavanagh, Charlie McMahon 0-1, Bobby Beggs 0-1, Willie Dowling 1-0, Gerry Fitzgerald, Mick O'Brien, Mickey Wellington 0-4, Mick Keating, Paddy Perry.

FINAL REPLAY
Oct 21, Croke Park, Dublin
MAYO 2-4   DUBLIN 1-5
Dublin: Johnny McDonnell, Des Brennan, Peter Lambe, Frank Cavanagh, Paddy Hickey, Ned McCann, Paddy Cavanagh, Bobby Beggs, Murt Kelly, Willie Dowling, Gearoid Fitzgerald 1-1, Mick Keating 0-1 Mick O'Brien 0-1, Mickey Wellington 0-1, Harry Farnan 0-1.

1934/35

MAYO 2-5   DUBLIN 1-7
Oct 28, GAA Grounds, Ballina
Dublin: J McDonnell, D Brennan, P Lambe, F Cavanagh, M O'Brien, N McCann, P Cavanagh 0-1, B Beggs 0-1, M Kelly 0-3, G Comerford 0-1, M Keating 0-1, D Banville, M Wellington, H Farnan, J Brady 1-0.

DUBLIN 3-3   LAOIS 1-3
Nov 11, Croke Park, Dublin
Dublin: J McDonnell, D Brennan, P Lambe, F Cavanagh, D Banville 1-0, N McCann, P Cavanagh, M Kelly, M O'Brien, P Synnott, B Beggs, G Comerford 1-0, M Wellington 1-0, A Dixon 0-1, J Brady 0-2.

DUBLIN 3-6   LOUTH 2-5
Jan 13, Croke Park, Dublin
Dublin: J McDonnell, P Lambe, D Brennan, S Feeney, P Hickey, B Beggs, P Cavanagh, M Keating, G O'Reilly, M Kelly 0-1, G Comerford 0-4, D Banville 1-0, M Wellington 2-1, J Brady, A Dixon.

GALWAY 2-4   DUBLIN 1-5
Mar 3, Duggan Park, Ballinasloe
Dublin: J McDonnell, D Brennan, J Martin, F Cavanagh, J Hannon, M Casey, P Cavanagh, B Beggs 0-1, G Comerford 0-1, D Banville 1-1, G O'Reilly 0-2, M O'Brien, M Wellington, A Dixon, W Dowling.

DUBLIN 0-8   MEATH 1-4
Mar 31, Croke Park, Dublin
Dublin: J McDonnell, D Brennan, M Casey, F Cavanagh, P Hickey, B Beggs 0-1, P Cavanagh, M Kelly, G Comerford 0-1, D Banville 0-1, G Fitzgerald 0-1, M O'Brien, M Wellington 0-2, J Colleran 0-2, J Brady. Sub: E Heron for Hickey.

KILDARE 0-10   DUBLIN 0-1
Apr 14, Sallins Road, Naas
Dublin: J McDonnell, D Brennan, M Casey, F Cavanagh, J O'Shea, B Beggs, W Malone, G Comerford, M Kelly 0-1, W Dowling, G Fitzgerald, M O'Brien, M Wellington, J Colleran, M Keating. Sub: E Heron for Colleran.

SECTION A	P	W	D	L	Pts
MAYO	6	5	0	1	10
LOUTH	6	4	0	2	8
DUBLIN	6	3	3	0	6
KILDARE	6	3	0	3	6
LAOIS	6	3	0	3	6
MEATH	6	2	0	4	4
GALWAY	6	1	0	5	2

1935/36

DUBLIN 2-4   LOUTH 1-6
Oct 13, St Brigid's Park, Dundalk
Dublin: J McDonnell, D Brennan, G McLoughlin, F Cavanagh, J O'Shea, P Whitty, P Cavanagh 0-1, M Kelly 0-2, W McMahon, T O'Donnell 0-1, M Keating, G Fitzgerald, P Russell 2-0, C Boland, J Stack.

DUBLIN 2-5   MAYO 0-6
Oct 27, Croke Park, Dublin
Dublin: J McDonnell, D Brennan, G McLoughlin, F Cavanagh, J O'Shea, P Whitty, P Cavanagh, M Kelly 1-1, C Boland, T O'Donnell, M Keating, G Fitzgerald 0-2, W Dowling, P Russell 1-2, P Bermingham.

LAOIS 2-5   DUBLIN 1-7
Nov 10, McCann Park, Portarlington
Dublin: J McDonnell, D Brennan, G McLoughlin, F Cavanagh, J O'Shea, P Whitty, P Cavanagh, J Fanning, M Kelly 1-2, T O'Donnell 0-1, M Keating 0-1, G Fitzgerald 0-1, M Wellington, J Lockhart 0-2, P Lyons.

DUBLIN 3-3   GALWAY 1-2
Nov 24, Croke Park, Dublin
Dublin: J McDonnell, D Brennan, G McLoughlin, F Cavanagh, J O'Shea, P Whitty, P Cavanagh 0-1, M Kelly 0-1, J Fanning 0-1, T O'Donnell, C Duffy, G Fitzgerald, M Wellington 1-0, J Mulhall, M Keating 2-0.

CAVAN 1-5   DUBLIN 0-6
Dec 8, Breffni Park, Cavan
Dublin: J McDonnell, D Brennan, G McLoughlin, F Cavanagh, J O'Shea, P Whitty, P Cavanagh 0-1, M Kelly 0-1, C McMahon, T O'Donnell, J Fanning 0-3, G Fitzgerald, M Wellington, J Mulhall, M Keating.

DUBLIN 2-8   TIPPERARY 1-4
Feb 23, Croke Park, Dublin
Dublin: J McDonnell, D Brennan, G McLoughlin, F Cavanagh, J O'Shea, P Whitty 0-1, P Cavanagh, M Kelly, A Dixon 2-0, G Fitzgerald 0-1, W Dowling, J Fanning 0-3, P Bermingham 0-2, M Wellington, J Lynam 0-1.

DUBLIN 1-5   MEATH 0-5
Mar 8, Showgrounds, Navan
Dublin: J McDonnell, D Brennan, G McLoughlin, F Cavanagh, P Gargan, D Darcy, J O'Toole, P Cavanagh 0-1, M Mahon, M Kelly, P Bermingham, J Fanning 0-3, G Fitzgerald, M Wellington, T Lawless 0-1, J Lynam 1-0.

KILDARE 0-12   DUBLIN 1-6
Mar 29, St Conleth's Park, Newbridge
Dublin: J McDonnell, D Brennan, G McLoughlin, F Cavanagh, P Gargan, D Darcy, P Whitty, P Cavanagh, M Kelly 0-1, C Boland 1-0, M Wellington 0-3, W Dowling 0-1, P Bermingham, G Fitzgerald 0-1, J Lynam.

DIVISION 1	P	W	D	L	Pts
MAYO	8	6	0	2	12
DUBLIN	8	5	0	3	10
CAVAN	8	5	0	3	10
MEATH	8	4	1	3	9
GALWAY	8	4	1	3	9
LOUTH	8	4	1	3	9
LAOIS	8	3	0	5	6
KILDARE	8	2	1	5	5
TIPPERARY	8	1	0	7	2

* This was the only time the competition was run on a purely league basis with no knockout element.

1936/37

CAVAN 0-8   DUBLIN 0-5
Oct 11, Breffni Park, Cavan
Dublin: J McDonnell, D Brennan, S Feeney, F Murtagh, G McLoughlin, F Cavanagh, M Mahon, P O'Reilly 0-1, P Cavanagh 0-1, L McAuliffe, P Bermingham 0-2, M Wellington, J Lynam, J Fanning 0-2, S Lockhart. Sub: J Green for Lockhart.

KILDARE 0-7   DUBLIN 0-5
Oct 25, Croke Park, Dublin
Dublin: J McDonnell, P O'Reilly, S Feeney, D Brennan, P Cavanagh 0-1, J Green, P Houlihan, L McAuliffe, J Fanning, F Murtagh, J McClean 0-1, M Wellington, P Bermingham 0-2, C Boland 0-1, J O'Dowd.

MEATH 2-4   DUBLIN 1-4
Nov 8, St Colmbeille's Park, Kells
Dublin: J McDonnell, D Brennan, S Feeney, F
Cavanagh, P Houlihan 0-1, M Walsh, P Cavanagh, J
Fanning 1-0, F Murtagh 0-1, L McAuliffe 0-1, P O'Reilly
0-1, M Smith, M Wellington, J O'Dowd, P O'Connor.

DUBLIN 3-2   MONAGHAN 1-7
Nov 22, Croke Park, Dublin
Dublin: J McDonnell, F Cavanagh, D Brennan, S
Feeney, P Houlihan, J Barnes, P Cavanagh, J Fanning,
F Murtagh 0-1, P O'Reilly, P Berminghnm 1-1, L
McAuliffe 1-0, P O'Connor, J Sherlock 1-0, J O'Dowd.

DUBLIN 2-6   WEXFORD 1-2
Dec 6, Wexford Park, Wexford
Dublin: J McDonnell, D Brennan, S Feeney, F
Cavanagh, P Houlihan, P Cavanagh, P O'Reilly,
J Fanning 0-1, P Berminghnm, P Mulhall 2-3, M
Wellington, L McAuliffe 0-1, P O'Connor, J Sherlock
0-1, J O'Dowd.

LOUTH 2-6   DUBLIN 2-5
Feb 14, Athletic Grounds, Drogheda
Dublin: J McDonnell, J Barnes, D Brennan, F
Cavanagh, P Houlhan, J Brady, W Malone, F Murtagh,
J Fanning, L McAuliffe 0-2, P Bermingham 1-3, P
O'Reilly 0-1, P O'Connor, J Sherlock, P Barnes.

DIVISION 1A	P	W	D	L	Pts
MEATH	6	5	0	1	10
CAVAN	6	4	0	2	8
KILDARE	6	4	0	2	8
DUBLIN	6	2	0	4	4
LOUTH	6	2	0	4	4
WEXFORD	6	2	0	4	4
MONAGHAN	6	2	0	4	4

1937/38

DUBLIN 0-7   MONAGHAN 0-7
Oct 10, Emmet Park, Carrickmacross
Dublin: J McDonnell, S Feeney, G O'Leary, F
Cavanagh, P Houlihan, P O'Reilly, W Malone, J
O'Dowd, P Henry, P Bermingham 0-3, P Mulhall 0-2,
L McAuliffe, J Brosnan 0-2, G Hanway, G Behan.

KILDARE 3-5   DUBLIN 2-4
Oct 31, Sallins Road, Naas
Dublin: J McDonnell, S Feeney, G O'Leary, F Cavanagh,
J Farrell, P Houlihan, W Malone, T Robinson, J O'Dowd,
L McAuliffe 1-0, P Mulhall 0-1, P Bermingham 0-1,
J Brosnan 0-1, C Hanway 0-1, G Behan 1-0. Subs: P
Robinson for Farrell, M Wellington for Hanway.

DUBLIN 2-3   MEATH 1-5
Nov 14, Croke Park, Dublin
Dublin: J McDonnell, P O'Neill, S Feeney, F Cavanagh,

P Robinson 0-1, P Houlihan 1-0, W Malone, P Robbins,
J O'Dowd, P O'Reilly, P Birmingham, L McAuliffe, J
Brosnan, P Mulhall 1-1, M Wellington 0-1.

WEXFORD 1-7   DUBLIN 0-6
Nov 28, Wexford Park, Wexford
Dublin: J McDonnell, S Feeney, P O'Neill, F Cavanagh,
G O'Leary, P O'Reilly, W Malone, L McAuliffe, J
O'Dowd 0-1, P Houlihan, P Mulhall 0-1, C Hanway, M
Wellington 0-2, P Bermingham 0-2, J Brosnan.

DUBLIN 1-6   CAVAN 1-6
Feb 27, Croke Park, Dublin
Dublin: J McDonnell, G O'Leary, S Feeney, C Rayfus,
P Lynch, P Houlihan, P Darcy, C Hatch, J O'Dowd,
L McAuliffe 0-1, P Bermingham 0-2, J Jones, M
McBride 0-2, P Mulhall 0-1, F Henry 0-1.

LOUTH 1-7   DUBLIN 1-6
Mar 27, Athletic Grounds, Drogheda
Dublin: J McDonnell, W Higgins, S Feeney, P O'Neill,
M Daly, P Houlihan 0-1, C Rayfus, J O'Dowd 0-1, T
Gorman 0-1, J Brosnan, P Mulhall, L McAuliffe 1-0, M
McBride 0-2, C O'Brien, F Henry 0-1.

GROUP C	P	W	D	L	Pts
WEXFORD	6	5	0	1	10
LOUTH	6	5	0	1	10
KILDARE	6	4	0	2	8
DUBLIN	6	1	2	3	4
CAVAN	6	1	2	3	4
MEATH	6	2	0	4	4
MONAGHAN	6	0	2	4	2

1938/39

ARMAGH 5-5   DUBLIN 2-6
Nov 13, Athletic Grounds, Armagh
Dublin: C Kelly, J Collins, J Murphy 1-0, W Malone, M
Higgins, M Fanning, J Brosnan, E Boland, P Houlihan
0-1, L McAuliffe, J O'Dowd, P Berminghma 0-3, M
McBride 0-1, P Mulhall, F Henry 1-0.

DUBLIN 2-5   MONAGHAN 1-0
Nov 27, Bremore Park, Balbriggan
Dublin: C Kelly, J McMahon, F Cavanagh, L McAuliffe,
J Collins, G Fitzgerald, J O'Dowd, T Gibbons, J
Brosnan, P Bermingham 0-2, E Boland 0-2, M
McBride, P Mulhall 1-1, F Henry 1-0, P Cavanagh.

DUBLIN 0-5   CAVAN 0-5
Dec 11, Breffni Park, Cavan
Dublin: C Kelly, J Collins, J Murphy, W Malone, L
McAuliffe, M Falvey, M Fanning, J O'Dowd, P Kennedy,
E Boland 0-2, P Bermingham 0-2, P Mulhall, J
Brosnan 0-1, P Power, F Henry.

LOUTH 0-5   DUBLIN 0-2
Feb 5, Bremore Park, Balbriggan

Dublin: C Kelly, J Collins, G O'Leary, W Malone, L McAuliffe, P Kennedy, P Henry, J O'Dowd, M Fanning, G Fitzgerald, R Smith, P Mulhall 0-1, A Allen, J Sheehan, F Henry 0-1. Sub: E Boland for Smith.

MEATH 3-5   DUBLIN 1-2

Mar 5, Showgrounds, Navan

Dublin: C Kelly, J Murphy, G O'Leary, W Malone, M Higgins, P Kennedy, J Greene, J O'Dowd, L McAuliffe, C Hanway, P Bermingham 0-2, P Mulhall, M Fletcher, P O'Connor, F Henry 1-0.

DUBLIN 0-18   DOWN 0-10

Mar 26, St Patrick's Park, Newcastle

Dublin: C Kelly, P Kennedy, G O'Leary, M Higgins, J Greene, P Henry, J Cunningham, L McAuliffe 0-1, J O'Dowd 0-1, P Bermingham 0-5, P Mulhall 0-5, M Fletcher 0-1, E Boland 0-2, P O'Connor 0-1, F Henry 0-2.

GROUP C	P	W	D	L	Pts
MEATH	6	4	2	0	10
LOUTH	6	4	2	0	10
CAVAN	6	3	3	0	9
DUBLIN	6	2	1	3	5
MONAGHAN	6	2	0	4	4
ARMAGH	6	1	0	5	2
DOWN	6	1	0	5	2

1939/40

DUBLIN 3-16   MONAGHAN 0-3

Oct 29, Bremore Park, Balbriggan

Dublin: P Dowling, P Toolan, G O'Leary, W Malone, B Murphy, H Donnelly, B Quinn, R Smith 0-1, P Kennedy, M O'Malley 1-2, P Bermingham 1-2, T Banks 0-5, T Markey 1-1, J Gibbons 0-4, M O'Reilly 0-1.

DUBLIN 3-1   MEATH 0-8

Nov 12, Pairc Tailteann, Navan

Dublin: P Dowling, B Murphy, G O'Leary, W Malone, T Laffey, H Donnelly, B Quinn, R Smith, J O'Dowd, M O'Malley 0-1, P Bermingham 1-0, T Banks, T Markey 1-0, J Gibbons 1-0, M O'Reilly.

LOUTH 2-5   DUBLIN 1-7

Nov 26, Croke Park, Dublin

Dublin: P Dowling, B Murphy, G O'Leary, W Malone, T Laffey, H Donnelly, B Quinn, J O'Dowd, J Richardson, M O'Malley, P Bermingham 0-2, T Banks 0-5, T Markey 1-0, J Gibbons, M O'Reilly. Subs: P Toolan for Murphy, R Smith for Richardson.

GROUP C	P	W	D	L	Pts
DUBLIN	3	2	0	1	4
LOUTH	3	2	0	1	4
MEATH	3	2	0	1	4
MONAGHAN	3	0	0	3	0

PLAY-OFF

Feb 4, Athletic Grounds, Drogheda

LOUTH 4-5   DUBLIN 1-5

Dublin: P Dowling, B Murphy, J Murphy, T Laffey, H Donnelly, J Greene, B Quinn, J O'Dowd, J Gibbons, P O'Connor, P Bermingham 1-1, T Banks 0-3, P Power, P Kennedy, M O'Reilly 0-1.

1940/41

DUBLIN 4-7   WESTMEATH 0-1

Oct 6, Croke Park, Dublin

Dublin: J Pollard, B Murphy, G McLaughlin, W Beggs, P O'Reilly, P Kennedy, P Henry, J O'Dowd, B Quinn, G Fitzgerald 0-1, P Birmingham 0-2, T Banks 0-3, M Richardson 2-0, J Counihan 0-1, A Breslin 2-0.

LOUTH 3-5   DUBLIN 0-8

Oct 13, St Brigid's Park, Dundalk

Dublin: C Kelly, B Murphy, G McLoughlin, W Rayburn, P Henry, P Kennedy, B Quinn, J O'Dowd, M Kilkenny, G Fitzgerald 0-1, P Bermingham 0-1, T Banks 0-4, T Markey, A Breslin 0-1, M O'Reilly 0-1.

DUBLIN 3-3   LONGFORD 1-4

Nov 24, Pearse Park, Longford

Dublin: C Kelly, P O'Reilly, G McLoughlin, J Gartland, P Henry, M Falvey, B Quinn, J O'Dowd 0-1, P Holly, G Fitzgerald 1-1, P Bermingham, T Banks 1-0, M Richardson 1-0, P Kennedy, M O'Reilly. Sub: M Fletcher 0-1 for Gartland.

DUBLIN 1-5   MEATH 0-7

Dec 8, Croke Park, Dublin

Dublin: C Kelly, J Manning, G McLoughlin, W Reyburn, P O'Reilly, M Falvey, B Quinn, P Holly, J O'Leary, G Fitzgerald 0-2, P Kennedy, T Banks 0-2, M Fletcher 1-0, A Breslin 0-1, M Quigley.

GROUP C	P	W	D	L	Pts
DUBLIN	4	3	0	1	6
LOUTH	4	3	0	1	6
MEATH	4	2	0	2	4
LONGFORD	4	2	0	2	4
WESTMEATH	4	0	0	4	0

PLAY-OFF

Feb 23, Croke Park, Dublin

DUBLIN 3-4   LOUTH 1-5

Dublin: C Kelly, B Murphy, G McLoughlin, W Rayburn, P O'Reilly, M Falvey, B Quinn, P Holly, J Joy, G Fitzgerald, P Birmingham 0-1, T Banks 0-2, M Fletcher 1-0, P Kennedy, J Buckley 2-1.

SEMI-FINAL
Mar 9, Croke Park, Dublin
DUBLIN 2-7   KERRY 1-4
Dublin: C Kelly, T Moore, G McLoughlin 1-0, B Murphy, P O'Reilly, M Falvey, B Quinn, P Holly, J O'Dowd, J Joy 1-1, G Fitzgerald 0-1, T Banks 0-4, M Fletcher 0-1, J Gibbons, J Buckley.

FINAL
Apr 27, Croke Park, Dublin
MAYO   3-5   DUBLIN 0-7
Dublin: Charlie Kelly, Tim Moore, Gerry McLoughlin, Bertie Murphy, Peter O'Reilly 0-2, Mick Falvey, Brendan Quinn, Paddy Holly, James O'Dowd, Jimmy Joy, Gerry Fitzgerald 0-2, Tommy Banks 0-3, Matt Fletcher, Paddy Bermingham, Jimmy Buckley.

1942

NORTH LEINSTER LEAGUE
DUBLIN 4-8   MEATH 5-5
Mar 22, Showgrounds, Navan
Dublin: J Thornton, J Murphy, C Crone, B Quinn, G Fitzgerald, P O'Reilly 0-1, M Keating, M Falvey 0-1, J Fitzgerald, J Kennedy 0-1, T McCann 0-5, A Tansey, J McGovern, P O'Connor, M Quigley 4-0.

DUBLIN 4-8   LOUTH 0-10
Mar 29, Croke Park, Dublin
Dublin: C Kelly, C Crone, B Quinn, P O'Reilly, P Kennedy, G Fitzgerald 0-1, B Beggs, J Fitzgerald 0-1, M Falvey, A Tansey, T Banks 0-3, P O'Connor 2-1, M Quigley 2-0, T McCann 0-1, M Fletcher 0-1.

DUBLIN 1-5   LOUTH 1-4
Apr 25, St Brigid's Park, Dundalk
Dublin: C Kelly, C Crone, B Quinn, P O'Reilly 0-1, P Kennedy, G Fitzgerald, B Beggs, M Falvey, S Healy, J O'Dowd 0-1, J Fitzgerald, P O'Connor 1-0, M Quigley 0-2, T McCann, M Fletcher 0-1.

DUBLIN 2-8   MEATH 0-8
Oct 18, Croke Park, Dublin
Dublin: F Ryan, B Beggs, P Kennedy, C Crone, P Henry, P O'Reilly 0-1, B Quinn, J Fitzgerald, M Falvey, J Joy 0-1, P Bermingham, G Fitzgerald 0-2, M Fletcher 1-0, P O'Connor 1-4, M Richardson.

N LEINSTER	P	W	D	L	Pts
DUBLIN	4	3	1	0	7
MEATH	4	2	1	1	5
LOUTH	4	0	0	4	0

1943

LEINSTER LEAGUE
LOUTH 0-8   DUBLIN 1-4

Nov 14, Athletic Grounds, Drogheda
Dublin: R Fagan, L Murray, P Kennedy, I Leavey, P O'Reilly, D O'Sullivan, V Duffy, M Culhane, M Falvey, M Richardson, M Fletcher 0-1, B Quinn 0-1, G Fitzgerald, P O'Connor 1-0, P Fitzgerald 0-2.

MEATH 0-7   DUBLIN 0-6
Nov 28, Croke Park, Dublin
Dublin: R Fagan, D O'Sullivan, P McIntyre, C Crone, P O'Reilly, M Falvey, S O'Shea, M Culhane 0-1, T Jenkinson, G Fitzgerald 0-1, P Bermingham 0-2, P Byrne, P Fitzgerald, P O'Connor 0-2, M Richardson.

LEINSTER (GROUP 4)	P	W	D	L	Pts
MEATH	2	2	0	0	4
DUBLIN	2	0	0	2	0
LOUTH	2	0	0	2	0

1944/45

LEINSTER LEAGUE
DUBLIN 0-8   KILDARE 1-3
Oct 15, St Conleth's Park, Newbridge
Dublin: R Fagan, S O'Shea, P Kennedy, D O'Sullivan, S O'Mahony, P O'Reilly, S Healy 0-1, T Jenkinson 0-3, P Bermingham, T O'Neill, B Maguire 0-1, C Bellew 0-2, J Counihan, S Dalton 0-1, JJ Maher.

DUBLIN 2-10   WICKLOW 1-7
Oct 29, Bramble Glade, Ashford
Dublin: R Fagan, S O'Shea, P Kennedy, D O'Sullivan, P O'Reilly, S McCarthy, S Healy, T Jenkinson 0-1, T Lalor 1-0, C Bellew 0-2, T O'Neill 0-4, M Fenton 1-2, J Counihan, M Culhane 0-1, P Fagan.

LEINSTER (GROUP 4)	P	W	D	L	Pts
DUBLIN	2	2	0	0	4
KILDARE	2	1	0	1	2
WICKLOW	2	0	0	2	0

SEMI-FINAL
July 29, Sallins Road, Naas
CARLOW 2-9   DUBLIN 1-7
Dublin: G Ingham, J Murphy P Ring, S Healy, S O'Mahony, P O'Reilly, B Quinn, P McIntyre 0-1, P Neville 0-1, P Bermingham, M Culhane 0-2, T O'Neill, T Markey 1-0, J Gibbons, B Maguire 0-3.

1945/46

DUBLIN 2-4   LAOIS 1-4
Nov 4, O'Moore Park, Portlaoise
Dublin: G Ingham, J Kiely, P Toolan, J Darling, J Doran, P O'Reilly, B Quinn, P Neville, M Falvey, M Culhane 0-1, P Bermingham 1-0, D O'Sullivan, T Markey 0-3, J Gibbons, M O'Reilly 1-0.

DUBLIN 4-5   KILDARE 2-4

Nov 18, Croke Park, Dublin

Dublin: G Ingham, J Kiely, P Toolan, S Healy, N Dolan, P O'Reilly, B Quinn, P Neville 1-0, M Falvey 0-1, M Culhane 0-1, P Bermingham, D O'Sullivan, T Markey 2-1, J Gibbons 1-1, M O'Reilly 0-1. Subs: J Darling for Healy.

DUBLIN 0-6   OFFALY 1-3

Feb 17, O'Connor Park, Tullamore

Dublin: G Ingham, J Kiely, P Toolan, J Coghlan, N Dolan, P O'Reilly, B Quinn, G Fitzgerald, M. Culhane 0-2, K Matthews, D O'Sullivan, J Fitzgerald 0-2, L Roche 0-2, P O'Connor, M O'Reilly.

DUBLIN 1-9   WICKLOW 0-3

Mar 3, Croke Park, Dublin

Dublin: J Lowry, J Kiely, P Toolan, D O'Sullivan, J Doran, P O'Reilly, B Quinn, M Hodgins, T Leahy, J Fitzgerald 1-1, G Fitzgerald 0-2, K Cooney 0-1, P Fitzgerald 0-1, J Gibbons 0-2, M O'Reilly 0-2.

GROUP VI	P	W	D	L	Pts
DUBLIN	4	3	1	0	7
WICKLOW	4	2	0	2	4
KILDARE	4	2	0	2	4
OFFALY	4	1	1	2	3
LAOIS	4	1	0	3	2

SEMI-FINAL

Apr 14, St Patrick's Park, Enniscorthy

WEXFORD 5-6   DUBLIN 1-2

Dublin: G Ingham, J Kiely, P Toolan, M Fenton, J Doran, P O'Reilly, B Quinn, H Wall, D O'Sullivan, K Stritch, P Bermingham, K Cooney, M Culhane 1-0, J Gibbons 0-2, M O'Reilly. Sub: G Fitzgerald for Fenton, J Collins for P O'Reilly.

1946/47

KILDARE 0-8   DUBLIN 0-2

Nov 3, St Conleth's Park, Newbridge

Dublin: R Fagan, J Kiely, S Sharry, G Harden, D O'Sullivan, J Healy, L Synnott, T Leahy, D Healy, L Roche, P Seville, M O'Reilly, K Matthews, P Bermingham 0-1, P Rogers 0-1. Sub: M Killeen for O'Reilly.

LAOIS 2-7   DUBLIN 0-10

Nov 24, Croke Park, Dublin

Dublin: R Fagan, J Kiely, S Sharry, T O'Neill, J Lowry, J Healy, B Quinn, S Synnott 0-1, D Cantwell, K Cooney 0-1, D Healy, M O'Reilly 0-3, P McMahon 0-1, J Gibbons 0-3, S O'Callaghan 0-1.

* The Central Council of the GAA decided at a meeting on March 15 to abandon the competition after weather conditions had prevented any play for over two months.

1947/48

DUBLIN 3-5   LONGFORD 1-6

Nov 23, Pearse Park, Longford

Dublin: J McEvoy, J Kiely, A Breslin, F Lynch, M Hannigan, G Leonard, P Rogers, B McCarthy, N Fingleton, C Manning, T Leahy, M Caslin, K Cooney 1-2, P Bermingham 2-2, M O'Reilly 0-1.

DUBLIN 2-9   LOUTH 4-3

Dec 7, Croke Park, Dublin

Dublin: D Acton, J O'Brien, J McAuley, F Lynch, C Smith 0-4, J Leonard, P Rogers, B McCarthy, N Singleton, C Manning 0-1, T Leahy 2-0, M Caslin 0-1, K Cooney 0-1, O Freaney 0-1, M O'Reilly 0-1.

GROUP VI (A)	P	W	D	L	Pts
DUBLIN	2	2	0	0	4
LOUTH	2	1	0	1	2
LONGFORD	2	0	0	2	0

DIVISIONAL FINAL

Mar 21, Croke Park, Dublin

CAVAN 3-17   DUBLIN 2-4

Dublin: D Acton, F Lynch, A Breslin, N Fingleton, P O'Reilly, J Leonard, P Rogers, B McCarthy 0-1, S Scally, V Browne 1-1, T Leahy, K Cooney, P Bermingham, C Smith 1-0, P Fitzgerald 0-2.

1948/49

LOUTH 2-10   DUBLIN 2-5

Nov 14, Athletic Grounds, Drogheda

Dublin: V Russell, L Ledwedge, A Breslin, M McCaffrey, A Halpin, J Leonard, P Cahalane, J Tunney, M Byrne, C Manning, D Byrne 0-3, L Synnott, L McDonnell, B Kenneally, K Heffernan 1-2. Sub: G O'Donoghue 1-0 for McDonnell.

GROUP VI (A)	P	W	D	L	Pts
LOUTH	2	2	0	0	4
DUBLIN	1	0	0	1	2
LONGFORD	1	0	0	1	2

Dublin v Longford, postponed from December 12, not rearranged as Louth subsequently beat Longford to secure the qualifying place.

1949/50

LOUTH 2-6   DUBLIN 1-6

Oct 16, St Brigid's Park, Dundalk:

Dublin: V Russell, D Mahony, J Lavin, N Maher, O Wardle, D Healy, C Sullivan, S Synnott, M Whelan, S O'Callaghan 0-1, O Freaney 0-1, C Freeney 1-1, J O'Toole, P Bridgette 0-2, K Heffernan 0-1. Sub: A Halpin for Sullivan.

WESTMEATH 2-8   DUBLIN 1-6
Oct 30, Cusack Park, Mullingar
Dublin: V Russell, A Halpin, J Lavin, N Maher, G McArdle, G O'Donoghue, P Irwin, R Healy, M Whelan, S O'Callaghan, O Freaney 1-0, C Freaney, J Copeland, P Bridgette, K Heffernan 0-6.

MEATH 1-6   DUBLIN 0-5
Nov 27, Croke Park, Dublin
Dublin: V Russell, D Mahony J Lavin, N Maher, A Halpln, D Healy, T Nolan, M Whelan, G McArdle, S O'Callaghan, O Freaney 0-1, C Freaney, J Copeland 0-1, E Kenneally, K Heffernan 0-3.

DUBLIN 1-6   WICKLOW 1-1
Feb 5, County Ground, Aughrim
Dublin: V Russell, D Mahony, J Lavin, N Maher, A Halpin, D Healy, P Irwin, M Whelan, G McArdle 0-1, S O'Callaghan 1-0, O Freaney 0-2, C Freaney 0-3, C Sullivan, E Kenneally, G Guidon.

DUBLIN 2-11   KILDARE 3-3
Mar 5, Croke Park, Dublin
Dublin: V Russell, D Mahony, J Lavin, N Maher, A Halpin, R Healy, P Irwin, M Whelan 0-1, G McArdle 0-2, S O'Callaghan, O Freaney 0-2, C Freaney 0-1, D Ferguson 2-0, E Kenneally 0-1, K Heffernan 0-4.

SECTION IV	P	W	D	L	Pts
MEATH*	5	4	0	1	8
LOUTH	5	3	1	1	7
DUBLIN*	5	3	0	2	6
KILDARE	5	2	1	2	5
WESTMEATH	5	2	0	3	4
WICKLOW	5	0	0	5	0

* Dublin awarded points v Meath on appeal, when Meath corner back Mick O'Brien refused to leave the field having been ordered to do so by Louth referee Joe McArdle.

1950/51

DUBLIN 1-4   LOUTH 1-4
Oct 8, Croke Park, Dublin
Dublin: V Russell, D Mahony, J Lavin, T O'Mahony, L Donnelly, D Healy, N Allen, J Crowley 0-1, M Whelan, S O'Callaghan, O Freaney 1-1, C Freaney, C Manning, N Fingleton, K Heffernan 0-2.

DUBLIN 5-10   WESTMEATH 1-3
Oct 29, Croke Park, Dublin
Dublin: V Russell, D Mahony, J Lavin, T O'Mahony, L Donnelly, D Healy, N Allen 0-1, J Crowley, M Whelan 1-0, S O'Callaghan, T Jennings 0-1, C Freaney 1-3, S Collins 1-0, N Fingleton, K Heffernan 2-5.

MEATH 3-6   DUBLIN 2-3
Nov 12, Pairc Tailteann, Navan

Dublin: M Mangan, R Finnegan, J Lavin, T Mahony, D Mahony, L Donnelly, N Maher, J Tunney, J Crowley, N Allen, M Whelan, O Freaney, S Collins 1-0, T Jennings 0-1, K Heffernan 1-2.

DUBLIN 1-7   KILDARE 1-5
Mar 11, St Bridget's Park, Kildare
Dublin: V Russell, R Finnegan, J Lavin, T Mahony, J Scally, P McCreedy, D Sullivan, J Tunney, J Crowley, W Monks 0-1, M Whelan 0-2, C Freaney, L Collins, O Freeney 1-4, B Atkins).

SECTION IV	P	W	D	L	Pts
MEATH	5	5	0	0	10
LOUTH	5	3	1	1	7
DUBLIN	4	2	1	1	5
KILDARE	5	2	0	3	4
WESTMEATH	5	1	0	4	2
WICKLOW	4	0	0	4	0

* Dublin v Wicklow, postponed by snow, was not played as the qualification issue was decided.

1951/52

DUBLIN 3-5   LOUTH 1-7
Oct 7, Croke Park, Dublin
Dublin: G O'Toole, N Allen, J Lavin, D Mahony, S Scally, D O'Sullivan, P McCready, M Whelan, J Crowley 0-1, D Ferguson, C O'Leary 2-1, P Murphy 0-1, L Collins, O Freaney, K Heffernan 1-2.

DUBLIN 4-11   WESTMEATH 1-2
Oct 21, Cusack Park, Mullingar
Dublin: G O'Toole, N Allen, J Lavin, D Mahony, S Scally, D O'Sullivan, P McCready, M Whelan, J Crowley 0-1, D Ferguson 0-1, O Freaney 1-2, P Murphy 1-1, L Collins 2-3, C O'Leary 0-1, K Heffernan 0-2.

DUBLIN 4-7   WICKLOW 0-3
Nov 18, Croke Park, Dublin
Dublin: G O'Toole, M Moylan, J Lavin, D Mahony S Scally, D O'Sullivan, P McCready, J Crowley 1-1, M Whelan, C O'Leary 1-0, N Allen 0-1, C Freaney 0-1, D Ferguson 1-1, T Young, K Heffernan 1-2. Sub: P Murphy 0-1 for Freaney.

DUBLIN 3-9   KILDARE 1-4
Feb 3, Croke Park, Dublin
Dublin: G O'Toole, M Moylan, J Lavin, N Allen, S Scally, D O'Sullivan, P McCready, J Crowley, M Wheian 0-1, C O'Leary, C Freaney 0-2, P Murphy 1-2, D Ferguson 0-1, T Young 1-0, K Heffernan 1-3.

DUBLIN 1-9   MEATH 0-2
Feb 17, Croke Park, Dublin
Dublin: G O'Toole, M Moylan, J Lavin, N Allen, J Scally, D O'Sullivan, P McCready, M Whelan, J Crowley, C O'Leary 0-1, O Freaney 0-3, M Murphy 0-1, D

Ferguson 0-1, T Young 0-1, K Heffernan 1-2.

SECTION IV	P	W	D	L	Pts
DUBLIN	5	5	0	0	10
MEATH	5	4	0	1	8
KILDARE	5	2	0	3	4
LOUTH	5	2	0	3	4
WESTMEATH	4	1	0	3	2
WICKLOW	4	0	0	3	0

* Westmeath v Wicklow not played as the qualification issue was decided.

SEMI-FINAL
Mar 30, O'Moore Park, Portlaoise
DUBLIN 7-5   LAOIS 1-5
Dublin: G O'Toole, M Moylan, J Lavin, N Allen 0-2, S Scally, D O'Sullivan, P McCready, J Crowley, M Whelan, C O'Leary 1-0, O Freaney, P Murphy 1-0, D Ferguson 2-1, T Young 2-0, K Heffernan 1-2. Sub: D Mahony for Whelan.

'HOME' FINAL
Apr 27, Croke Park, Dublin
CORK 2-3   DUBLIN 1-5
Dublin: Gerry O'Toole, Mick Moylan, Jim Lavin, Norman Allen, Sean Scally, Denis O'Sullivan, Frank McCready, Jim Crowley, Maurice Whelan, Cathal O'Leary 1-1, Ollie Freaney 0-1, Michael Murphy, Des Ferguson, Tony Young, Kevin Heffernan 0-3. Sub: Denis Mahony for McCready.

1952/53

DUBLIN 1-7   LOUTH 1-4
Oct 19, St Brigid's Park, Dundalk
Dublin: G O'Toole, J Crosier, M Moylan, N Allen, S Scally, S Farrell, C Sullivan, M Whelan, S McGuinness, D Ferguson, O Freaney 0-1, M O'Regan 0-1, L Collins, C O'Leary, K Heffernan 1-5.

DUBLIN 2-9   WESTMEATH 0-4
Nov 2, Croke Park, Dublin
Dublin: T O'Grady, J Fitzgerald, M Moylan, N Allen, S Scally, S Farrell, C Sullivan, M Whelan 1-1, S McGuinness, M Wilson 0-1, O Freaney 1-2, M O'Regan 0-1, C O'Leary 0-1, T Young, K Heffernan 0-3.

MEATH 1-10   DUBLIN 2-3
Nov 16, Pairc Tailteann, Navan
Dublin: T O'Grady, N Allen, M Moylan, J Fitzgerald, S Scally, S Farrell, C Sullivan, M Whelan, S McGuinness, D Ferguson, C O'Leary 0-2, C Freaney 1-0, M O'Regan 1-0, T Young, K Heffernan 0-1.

DUBLIN 3-8   WICKLOW 1-5
Feb 1, Pearses' Park, Arklow
Dublin: T O'Grady, D Mahony, M Moylan, J Timmons,

J Lavin, S Scally, N Maher, M Whelan, J Crowley, C O'Leary, O Freaney 0-1, C Freaney 1-2, B Atkins 1-1, T Young, K Heffernan 0-4.

DUBLIN 1-4   KILDARE 1-3
Mar 15, St Bridget's Park, Kildare
Dublin: T O'Grady, D Mahony, M Moylan, T Mahony, D Ferguson, S Scally, N Maher, J Crowley, M Whelan, C O'Leary, O Freaney 1-0, C Freaney, B Atkins, T Young, K Heffernan 0-4.

SECTION IV	P	W	D	L	Pts
DUBLIN	5	4	0	1	8
MEATH	5	4	0	1	8
LOUTH	5	3	0	2	6
KILDARE	5	3	0	2	6
WICKLOW	5	1	0	4	2
WESTMEATH	5	0	0	5	2

PLAY-OFF
Mar 22, Croke Park, Dublin
DUBLIN 3-13   MEATH 2-3
Dublin: T O'Grady, D Mahony, M Moylan, T Mahony, N Allen, S Scally, N Maher, J Crowley, M Whelan, D Ferguson 2-1, O Freaney, C Freaney 0-2, B Atkins 0-2, T Young 0-1, K Heffernan 0-6. Sub: M Wilson for Maher.

SEMI-FINAL:
Mar 29, Croke Park, Dublin
DUBLIN 0-9   TIPPERARY 0-3
Dublin: T O'Grady, D Mahony, M Moylan, T Mahony, N Allen, S Scally, N Maher, J Crowley, M Whelan 0-1, D Ferguson, O Freaney 0-1, C Freaney 0-2, B Atkins, T Young, K Heffernan 0-5.

FINAL
Apr 26, Croke Park, Dublin
DUBLIN 4-6   CAVAN 0-9
Dublin: Tony O'Grady, Denis Mahony, Mick Moylan, Marcus Wilson, Jim Lavin, Norman Allen, Nicky Maher, Maurice Whelan (capt), Jim Crowley 0-1, Des Ferguson 0-1, Ollie Freaney 1-1, Cyril Freaney 0-1, Bernie Atkins 1-0, Tony Young, Kevin Heffernan 2-2.

1953/54

DUBLIN 0-8   GALWAY 2-2
Oct 11, Croke Park, Dublin
Dublin: S Lombard, D Mahony, M Moylan, J Monaghan, J Lavin, S Scally, N Maher, M Whelan, J Crowley, D Ferguson, O Freaney 0-1, C Freeny 0-1, J Boyle 0-1, M Wilson, K Heffernan 0-5.

DUBLIN 3-7   LAOIS 1-6
Nov 8, O'Moore Park, Portlaoise
Dublin: S Lombard, D Mahony, P King, J Monaghan, T

Jennings, N Allen, N Maher, M Whelan 1-0, J Crowley, J Boyle 0-3, O Freaney 1-0, C O'Leary 0-3, D Ferguson 1-1, M Moylan, K Heffernan. Sub: C Freaney for O Freaney.

DUBLIN 2-8   OFFALY 0-4
Nov 22, Croke Park, Dublin
Dublin: S Lombard, D Mahony, M Moylan, J Monaghan, S Scally, N Allen 0-1, N Maher, J Crowley, M Whelan, J Boyle, C Freaney 1-2, D Ferguson, C O'Leary 0-1, M Wilson 0-1, K Heffernan 1-3.

DUBLIN 1-10   WICKLOW 1-4
Feb 7, Croke Park, Dublin
Dublin: S Lombard, D Mahony, J Lavin, J Monaghan, L Donnelly, N Allen, N Maher, M Wilson 0-2, M Whelan, J Boyle 1-4, C O'Leary 0-1, O Freaney 0-1, D Ferguson, T Jennings, C Freaney 0-2. Subs: T Mahony for Monaghan, L Healy for Jennings.

DUBLIN 1-12   ROSCOMMON 0-1
Feb 28, Croke Park, Dublin
Dublin: S Lombard, D Mahony, J Lavln, M Moylan, L Donnelly, N Allen, N Maher, M Whelan 0-1, J Crowley, C O'Leary 0-3, O Freaney 1-0, J Boyle 0-2, D Ferguson, M Wilson 0-2, K Heffernan 0-4.

DUBLIN 3-10   LOUTH 2-3
Mar 28, Athletic Grounds, Drogheda
Dublin: S Lombard, D Mahony, J Lavin, M Moylan, P Bates, L Donnelly 0-1, N Maher, J Crowley 0-1, M Whelan, D Ferguson, C O'Leary, J Boyle 1-1, O Freaney 0-1, M Wilson, K Heffernan 2-4.

SECTION III	P	W	D	L	Pts
DUBLIN	6	5	1	0	11
GALWAY	6	4	1	1	9
LOUTH	6	4	0	2	8
WICKLOW	6	2	0	4	4
OFFALY	6	2	0	4	4
ROSCOMMON	5	2	0	3	4
LAOIS	5	0	0	5	0

* Laois v Roscommon not played as the semi-final qualification issue was decided.

SEMI-FINAL
Apr 25, Croke Park, Dublin

MAYO 0-11   DUBLIN 0-7
Dublin: T O'Grady, D Mahony, J Lavin, M Moylan, L Donnelly, N Allen, N Maher, M Whelan 0-1, J Crowley 0-1, O Freaney 0-2, C O'Leary, J Boyle 0-1, D Ferguson, M Wilson, K Heffernan 0-1. Sub: T Young 0-1 for Wilson.

1954/55

DUBLIN 1-6   GALWAY 1-6
Oct 10, St Jarleth's Park, Tuam
Dublin: P O'Flaherty, D Mahony, J Lavin, M Moylan,

B Monks, N Allen, N Maher, C O'Leary, P Bates, J Crowley, D Ferguson, O Freaney 1-0, J Boyle 0-2, T Jennings, K Heffernan 0-2.

DUBLIN 2-9   LAOIS 1-8
Nov 7, Croke Park, Dublin
Dublin: P O'Flaherty, J Fitzgerald, V Bell, B Monks, H Boylan, D Mahony, N Maher, C O'Leary 0-1, J McGuinness, D Ferguson 0-1, O Freaney 1-3, J Boyle 0-1, R Thompson, J Crowley 1-2, J Brophy 0-1. Sub: T Jennings for Boylan.

DUBLIN 1-10   OFFALY 1-4
Nov 28, O'Connor Park, Tullamore
Dublin: P O'Flaherty, D Mahony, J Lavin, M Moylan, B Monks, N Allen 0-2, N Maher, C O'Leary 0-1, J McGuinness, D Ferguson 0-1, O Freaney 0-3, J Boyle 1-1, J Brophy 0-1, J Crowley 0-1, T Jennings. Sub: C Freaney for O Freaney.

DUBLIN 1-6   WICKLOW 1-3
Dec 5, Croke Park, Dublin
Dublin: P O'Flaherty, P Bell, J Lavin, M Moylan, B Monks, D Mahony, N Maher, N Allen 0-1, J McGuinness, D Ferguson, O Freaney 0-2, C Freaney, J Brophy, J Crowley 1-0, J Boyle 0-3. Subs: V Bell for Brophy, D Osborne for Monks.

DUBLIN 3-7   ROSCOMMON 2-3
Feb 6, Sportsfield, Knockcroghery
Dublin: P O'Flaherty, G O'Brien, J Lavin, M Moylan, B Monks, M Whelan, N Maher, N Allen, J McGuinness, D Ferguson, O Freaney 1-3, J Boyle, P Haughey 0-2, J Crowley, K Heffernan 2-2. Sub: B Houlihan for O'Brien.

DUBLIN 0-8   LOUTH 1-2
Mar 13, Croke Park, Dublin
Dublin: P O'Flaherty, B Monks, J Lavin, M Moylan, M Whelan, D Mahony, N Maher, N Allen, J McGuinness, D Ferguson, O Freaney, J Boyle 0-1, P Haughey 0-1, L Murray, K. Heffernan 0-5. Sub: C O'Leary 0-1 for Murray.

SECTION III	P	W	D	L	Pts
DUBLIN	6	5	1	0	11
WICKLOW	6	5	1	0	10
LOUTH	6	4	2	0	8
GALWAY	6	3	2	1	7
OFFALY	6	2	4	0	4
LAOIS	5	0	5	0	0
ROSCOMMON	5	0	5	0	0

* Laois v Roscommon not played as the semi-final qualification issue was decided

SEMI-FINAL
Apr 17, Croke Park, Dublin

DUBLIN 0-12   CORK 0-9
Dublin: P O'Flaherty, D Mahony, J Lavin, M Moylan, B Monks, N Allen, N Maher, J McGuinness, C O'Leary

0-1, D Ferguson 0-1, O Freaney 0-5, J Boyle 0-1, P Haughey 0-2, J Crowley, K Heffernan 0-2.

FINAL
May 8, Croke Park, Dublin
DUBLIN 2-12   MEATH 1-3
Dublin: Paddy O'Flaherty, Denis Mahony (capt), Jim Lavin, Mick Moylan, Billy Monks, Norman Allen, Nicky Maher, Jim Crowley, Seamus McGuinness, Des Ferguson 0-2, Ollie Freaney 1-4, Cathal O'Leary 0-2, Padraig Haughey 0-2, Kevin Heffernan 1-2, Johnny Boyle. Sub: Maurice Whelan for McGuinness.

1955/56

DUBLIN 1-7   LAOIS 1-3
Oct 23, O'Moore Park, Portlaoise
Dublin: P O'Flaherty, S Manning, M Moylan, A Gillen, M Whelan, N Maher, PJ Considine, J McGuinness, J Crowley, M Brennan 0-1, J Boyle 0-2, J Brennan, P Haughey 1-2, P Brennan 0-1, J Gray 0-1. Subs: T Ryan for J Brennan.

DUBLIN 2-2   WICKLOW 1-2
Nov 6, Croke Park, Dublin
Dublin: P O'Flaherty, S Manning, M Moylan, PJ Considine, M Whelan, A Gillen, N Maher, J McGuinness, J Crowley J Boyle, O Freaney 1-1, J Gray, M Brennan, P Brennan 1-1, W Monks.

DUBLIN 1-9   ROSCOMMON 1-4
Nov 20, Croke Park, Dublin
Dublin: P O'Flaherty, N Allen, J Lavin, M Moylan, M Whelan, A Gillen, N Maher 0-1, J Crowley, T Ryan, J Boyle 0-1, D Ferguson 0-1, K Heffernan 0-4, M Brennan 0-1, P Brennan, J Gray 1-1.

DUBLIN 1-6   GALWAY 1-5
Dec 4, St Jarleth's Park, Tuam
Dublin: P O'Flaherty, N Allen, M Moylan, D Osborne, J Boyle 1-0, A Gillen, N Maher, M Whelan, J Crowley, M Brennan, D Ferguson, K Heffernan 0-5, O Freaney, P Brennan, J Gray. Subs: C O'Leary 0-1 for Gray, J McGuinness for P Brennan.

DUBLIN 3-10   OFFALY 2-4
Feb 5, O'Connor Park, Tullamore
Dublin: P O'Flaherty, S Manning, J Lavin, M Moylan, D Mahony, A Gillen, N Maher, M Whelan 0-1, M Wilson, J Boyle 0-1, O Freaney 0-3, C O'Leary, D Ferguson 2-0, K Heffernan 0-3, P Brennan 1-2.

DUBLIN 0-13   LOUTH 0-7
Feb 26, Croke Park, Dublin
Dublin: P O'Flaherty, D Mahony, J Lavin, M Moylan, M Whelan, A Gillen, N Maher, J Crowley, M Wilson, J Boyle 0-2, O Freaney 0-6, C O'Leary 0-1, D Ferguson 0-1, K Heffernan 0-1, P Brennan 0-2.

SECTION III	P	W	D	L	Pts
DUBLIN	6	6	0	0	12
GALWAY	6	4	0	2	8
LOUTH	6	4	0	2	8
OFFALY	6	2	1	3	5
ROSCOMMON	5	2	0	3	4
WICKLOW	5	1	0	4	2
LAOIS	6	0	1	5	1

* Roscommon v Wicklow was not played as the semi-final qualification issue was decided

SEMI-FINAL
Apr 15, Athletic Grounds, Cork
DUBLIN 1-4   CORK 0-7
Dublin: P O'Flaherty, D Mahony, J Lavin, M Moylan, M Whelan, N Allen, N Maher, J Crowley, M Wilson, J Boyle 1-0, O Freaney, C O'Leary, D Ferguson 0-2, P Brennan 0-2, K Heffernan.

SEMI-FINAL REPLAY
Apr 29, Croke Park, Dublin
CORK 1-16   DUBLIN 1-9
Dublin: P O'Flaherty, D Mahony, J Lavin, S Manning, A Gillen, N Allen, N Maher, J Crowley, C O'Leary, J Boyle 0-5, O Freaney, K Heffernan, D Ferguson 0-2, P Brennan 1-1, S Daly. Subs: P Joyce for Freaney, M Whelan for Mahony, J Gray for Daly, D Osborne for Gillen.

1956/57

DUBLIN 2-9   LAOIS 1-8
Nov 4, Croke Park, Dublin
Dublin: P O'Flaherty, D Mahony, J Lavin, M Moylan, N Allen, T Gillen, N Maher, J Joyce 0-1, C O'Leary, M Brennan 0-1, O Freaney 0-2, J Boyle, D Ferguson 1-1, D Carroll 0-4, K Heffernan 1-0. Sub: M Tallon for Joyce.

DUBLIN 2-6   WICKLOW 1-4
Nov 18, County Ground, Aughrim
Dublin: P O'Flaherty, D Mahony, J Lavin, M Moylan, T Gillen, N Allen, N Maher, P Downey, C O'Leary 0-1, M Brennan, O Freaney 0-3, J Boyle, D Ferguson 1-0, D Carroll, K Heffernan 1-1. Subs: S Murray for Gillen, C Kelly 0-1 for Murray.

DUBLIN 1-9   ROSCOMMON 0-4
Nov 25, Croke Park, Dublin
Dublin: P O'Flaherty, D Mahony, J Lavin, M Moylan, C Kelly, N Allen, N Maher, P Downey, C O'Leary 0-2, M Brennan, O Freaney 0-2, J Joyce, D Ferguson 0-1, J Crowley 1-2, K Heffernan 0-2.

GALWAY 2-8   DUBLIN 2-6
Feb 3, St Jarleth's Park, Tuam
Dublin: P O'Flaherty, D Mahony, J Lavin, M Moylan,

M Whelan, M Wilson, N Maher, C Kelly, C O'Leary, M Brennan, O Freaney 1-4, J Boyle 0-1, D Ferguson, J Crowley, K Heffernan 1-0. Subs: P Downey for Moylan, J Joyce 0-1 for Kelly.

DUBLIN 3-9   OFFALY 1-4
Mar 3, Parnell Park, Dublin
Dublin: P O'Flaherty, D Mahony, J Lavin, N Allen, M Whelan, M Wilson 0-1, N Maher, J Crowley, P Downey, D Ferguson, O Freaney 2-1, C O'Leary 0-2, M Brennan 0-3, K Heffernan 1-1, J Boyle 0-1.

DUBLIN 1-8   LOUTH 3-2
Mar 24, Athletic Grounds, Drogheda
Dublin: P O'Flaherty, D Mahony, J Lavin, T Gillen, P Heron, M Wilson, N Maher, J Crowley 0-1, P Downey, D Ferguson, O Freaney 0-3, J Boyle 1-0, M Brennan 0-1, K Heffernan 0-2, P Feeney. Sub: N Allen 0-1 for Heron.

SECTION III	P	W	D	L	Pts
GALWAY	6	6	0	0	12
DUBLIN	6	4	1	1	9
LOUTH	6	3	2	1	8
OFFALY	6	2	0	4	4
WICKLOW	6	2	0	4	4
LAOIS	6	1	1	4	3
ROSCOMMON	6	1	0	5	2

1957/58

DUBLIN 2-6   LAOIS 1-6
Oct 6, O'Moore Park, Portlaoise
Dublin: P O'Flaherty, S Clarkin, J Lavin, J Timmons, M Whelan, J Crowley, L Foley, P Downey, S Murray, J Joyce 1-1, O Freaney 0-3, J Boyle 0-1, R Conroy, C Meehan 1-1, S Murphy. Sub: P Gilton for Joyce.

DUBLIN 4-7   OFFALY 2-11
Nov 3, Croke Park, Dublin
Dublin: P O'Flaherty, J Timmons, J Lavin, B Linehan, P Heron, J Crowley, L Foley, P Downey, S Murray, D Ferguson, O Freaney 0-6, B Murphy, F Gilton 3-0, J Joyce 0-1, K Heffernan 1-0.

DUBLIN 4-6   ROSCOMMON 0-4
Nov 17, Croke Park, Dublin
Dublin: P O'Flaherty, J Crowley, J Lavin, J Timmons, P Heron, M Wilson, J Boyle, P Downey, L Foley, E Murphy 0-1, O Freaney 0-3, C O'Leary 0-1, F Gilton 0-1, J Joyce 2-0, B Morris 2-0. Sub: J Brennan for Murphy.

DUBLIN 1-11   WICKLOW 0-8
Feb 2, O'Toole Park, Dublin
Dublin: P O'Flaherty, J Crowley, J Lavin, J Timmons, M Wilson, P Downey, J Brennan, C O'Leary 0-1, J Murray, M Brennan, O Freaney 0-5, J Boyle, B Morris 0-1, J Joyce 1-2, K Heffernan 0-2.

GALWAY 2-4   DUBLIN 0-7
Mar 9, Dunlo Grounds, Ballinasloe
Dublin: P O'Flaherty, M Wilson, J Lavin, J Timmons, C O'Leary, J Crowley, J Brennan, S Murray, P Downey, D Ferguson, O Freaney 0-4, J Boyle, B Morris, J Joyce, K Heffernan 0-3. Subs: P Haughey for Boyle, M Whelan for Murray.

DUBLIN 0-12   LOUTH 1-4
Mar 23, Croke Park, Dublin
Dublin: P O'Flaherty, M Wilson, J Timmons, J Brennan, C O'Leary, J Crowley, J Boyle, S Murray, P Downey, P Haughey 0-1, O Freaney 0-6, D Ferguson 0-1, P Farnan, J Joyce 0-2, K Heffernan 0-2.

SECTION III	P	W	D	L	Pts
DUBLIN	6	5	0	1	10
GALWAY	6	5	0	1	10
LOUTH	6	4	0	2	8
LAOIS	6	3	0	3	6
OFFALY	6	3	0	3	6
ROSCOMMON	6	1	0	5	2
WICKLOW	6	0	0	6	0

PLAY-OFF
Apr 13, Croke Park, Dublin
DUBLIN 3-5   GALWAY 1-7
Dublin: P O'Flaherty, M Whelan, J Timmons, J Brennan, C O'Leary, J Crowley, J Boyle, S Murray, P Downey, P Haughey, O Freaney 0-3, D Ferguson 0-1, P Farnan 1-1, J Joyce 1-0, K Heffernan 1-0. Sub: G Guidon for O'Leary.

SEMI-FINAL
Apr 20, Croke Park, Dublin
DUBLIN 0-10   MAYO 0-7
Dublin: P O'Flaherty, M Wilson, J Timmons, J Brennan, M Whelan, C O'Leary, J Boyle, S Murray, P Downey, P Haughey, O Freaney 0-4, D Ferguson 0-2, P Farnan, J Joyce 0-2, K Heffernan 0-2. Subs: B Morris for Heffernan, Heffernan for Morris, Morris for Freaney.

FINAL
May 18, Croke Park, Dublin
DUBLIN 3-13   KILDARE 3-8
Dublin: Paddy O'Flaherty, Marcus Wilson, Joe Timmons, Joe Brennan, Cathal O'Leary, Jim Crowley, Sean O'Boyle, Sean Murray, Paddy Downey, Padraig Haughey 0-1, Ollie Freaney 0-9, Des Ferguson 0-1, Paddy Farnan, Johnny Joyce 2-0, Kevin Heffernan (capt) 1-2.
Subs: Lar Foley for Downey, Christy Leaney for Ferguson.

1958/59

DUBLIN 0-11   LAOIS 1-6
Oct 19, O'Toole Park, Dublin
Dublin: P Flynn, T Gillen, J Crowley, Joe Timmons, C O'Leary, M Wilson, J Boyle, John Timmons, L Foley, P Haughey, O Freaney 0-5, D Ferguson 0-3, P Farnan 0-2, J Joyce, K Heffernan 0-1.

DUBLIN 1-5   OFFALY 1-5
Nov 16, O'Connor Park, Tullamore
Dublin: P Flynn, L Foley, J Crowley, Joe Timmons, D Jones, C O'Leary, J Boyle, D Foley, S Murray, P Haughey, O Freaney 0-1, D Ferguson, P Farnan, J Joyce 1-1, K Heffernan 0-2. Sub: John Timmons 0-1 for Joyce.

DUBLIN 3-6   ROSCOMMON 0-4
Nov 30, O'Toole Park, Dublin
Dublin: P Flynn, L Foley, M Wilson, Joe Timmons, D Jones, J Crowley, J Boyle, John Timmons, D Foley 0-1, P Haughey, K Heffernan 0-2, D Ferguson 0-1, P Farnan 1-1, J Joyce 2-1, C Leaney.

DUBLIN 3-4   WICKLOW 2-4
Feb 1, Burgage Park, Blessington
Dublin: P O'Flaherty, L Foley, M Wilson, Joe Timmons, D Jones, J Crowley, J Boyle, D Foley, John Timmons, P Haughey 1-1, O Freaney 1-1, D Ferguson 0-1, P Farnan, J Joyce 1-1, K Heffernan. Sub: P Downey for D Foley.

DUBLIN 3-10   GALWAY 3-6
Mar 1, Croke Park, Dublin
Dublin: P O'Flanerty, L Foley, M Wilson, Joe Timmons, C O'Leary, J Crowley, J Boyle, D Foley, John Timmons 0-1, P Haughey, O Freaney 0-6, D Ferguson, P Farnan, J Joyce 3-1, K Heffernan 0-2.

LOUTH 2-10   DUBLIN 1-10
Mar 22, Athletic Grounds, Drogheda
Dublin: P Flynn, M Wilson, J Crowley, Joe Timmons D Jones, C O'Leary, J Boyle, S Murray, John Timmons 0-1, P Haughey, O Freaney 1-6, D Ferguson, P Farnon 0-1, J Joyce 0-1, K Heffernan 0-1. Subs: A Gillen for Murray, J Brennan for Joyce, Joyce for Heffernan.

SECTION III	P	W	D	L	Pts
OFFALY	6	5	1	0	11
DUBLIN	6	4	1	1	9
GALWAY	6	4	1	2	7
ROSCOMMON	6	3	0	3	6
LOUTH	6	3	0	3	6
WICKLOW	6	1	1	4	3
LAOIS	6	0	0	6	0

1959/60

DUBLIN 0-12   OFFALY 0-6
Nov 1, O'Connor Park, Tullamore
Dublin: P Flynn, E Grainger, L Foley, Joe Timmons, M Wilson, D Foley, D Ferguson, P Downey, L Quinn, P Haughey 0-2, J Joyce, M Whelan 0-2, P Farnan, John Timmons 0-4, K Heffernan 0-4. Sub: P Holden for D Foley.

DUBLIN 3-8   ROSCOMMON 2-8
Nov 15, Croke Park, Dublin
Dublin: P Flynn, E Grainger, L Foley, Joe Timmons, M Wilson, D Foley, D Ferguson, P Downey, L Quinn, P Haughey 0-2, J Joyce, M Whelan 1-2, B McDonald 1-2, John Timmons 0-2, K Heffernan 1-0. Sub: P Holden for Downey.

DUBLIN 1-10   LOUTH 1-5
Nov 29, Athletic Grounds, Drogheda
Dublin: P Flynn, M Wilson, L Foley, Joe Timmons, P Holden, D Foley, D Ferguson, L Quinn, J Joyce 0-1, P Haughey, John Timmons 0-3, M Whelan 0-1, B McDonald 0-1, K Heffernan 1-4, J Boyle.

DUBLIN 1-13   GALWAY 1-5
Feb 7, Croke Park, Dublin
Dublin: P Flynn, P Holden 0-1, L Foley, M Wilson, J Boyle, C O'Leary, D Ferguson, D Foley 0-1, P Haughey, John Timmins 0-7, M Whelan 0-1, P Farnan, J Joyce 1-2, K Heffernan 0-1. Sub: J Brennan for Ferguson.

DUBLIN 6-6   LAOIS 1-8
Mar 6, O'Moore Park, Portlaoise
Dublin: P Flynn, M Wilson, L Foley, Joe Timmons, P Holden, C O'Leary, D Ferguson 0-1, J Joyce 0-1, L Quinn, P Haughey, John Timmons, M Whelan 0-1, P Farnan 1-2, K Heffernan 2-1, B McDonald 3-0.

DUBLIN 3-10   WICKLOW 1-12
Mar 27, Croke Park, Dublin
Dublin: P Flynn, J Brennan, M Wilson, Joe Timmons, J Boyle, P Holden 0-1, D Ferguson, D Foley, L Quinn, M Whelan 1-0, John Timmons 0-4, J Joyce 0-4, P Farnan, K Heffernan 1-0, B McDonald 1-1. Subs: P Delaney for Boyle, S Coen for Heffernan.

SECTION III	P	W	D	L	Pts
DUBLIN	6	6	0	0	12
OFFALY	6	5	0	1	10
GALWAY	6	4	0	2	8
ROSCOMMON	6	2	1	3	5
LOUTH	6	2	1	3	5
LAOIS	6	1	0	5	2
WICKLOW	6	0	0	6	0

SEMI-FINAL
Apr 24, Pairc Tailteann, Navan
CAVAN 2-8   DUBLIN 1-8
Dublin: P Flynn, M Wilson, L Foley, Joe Timmons, P Holden, C O'Leary, D Ferguson, D Foley, L Quinn, P Haughey, John Timmons 0-5, M Whelan, P Farnan 0-1, J Joyce 0-1, K Heffernan 1-1.

1960/61

OFFALY 5-10   DUBLIN 4-7
Oct 30, Croke Park, Dublin
Dublin: M Leonard, D McKane, L Foley, Joe Timmons, C Kane, P Holden, A Whelan, S Behan, John Timmons 0-4, P Haughey, B McCrea 2-1, M Whelan, C Leaney 1-1, J Joyce 1-0, K Heffernan.

DUBLIN 1-10   ROSCOMMON 1-10
Nov 13, Sportsfield, Knockcroghery
Dublin: M Leonard, S Clinton, J Farrell, Joe Timmins, C Kane, P Holden, M Whelan, John Timmons 0-4, D Foley, P Delaney 1-1, B McCrea 0-1, C Leaney, P Farnan, J Joyce 0-1, K Heffernan 0-3. Sub: O Callaghan for Foley.

DUBLIN 1-8   GALWAY 0-3
Feb 5, Duggan Park, Ballinasloe
Dublin: P Flynn, C Kane, L Foley, Joe Timmons, M Whelan, P Holden, O Callaghan, John Timmons 0-2, D McKane, P Delaney 0-3, B McCrea, P Farnan 0-1, C Leaney 0-1, J Joyce, K Heffernan 1-1.

DUBLIN 3-9   LOUTH 2-3
Feb 12, O'Toole Park, Dublin
Dublin: P Flynn, C Kane, L Foley, Joe Timmons, M Whelan, P Holden, O Callaghan, John Timmons, D McKane, P Delaney 2-2, B McCrea 0-2, T Howard 1-0, P Farnan 0-1, J Joyce 0-3, K Heffernan 0-1.

DUBLIN 2-10   LAOIS 0-15
Mar 5, Croke Park, Dublin
Dublin: P Flynn, C Kane, L Foley, Joe Timmons, M Whelan, P Holden, O Callaghan, D McKane, D Foley, C Leaney, B McCrea 0-5, N Fox, P Farnan, J Joyce 0-1, K Heffernan 2-4. Sub: L Quinn for D McKane.

DUBLIN 4-7   WICKLOW 0-7
Mar 26, County Ground, Aughrim
Dublin: P Flynn, C Kane, J Farrell, Joe Timmons, S Clinton, P Holden, O Callaghan, D Foley 0-1, D McKane, P Farnan 0-1, B McCrea 0-4, N Fox 0-1, P Delaney 1-0, J Joyce 2-0, K Heffernan 1-0.

SECTION III	P	W	D	L	Pts
ROSCOMMON	6	5	1	0	11
OFFALY	6	5	0	1	10
DUBLIN	6	4	1	1	9
LAOIS	6	3	0	3	6
GALWAY	6	2	0	4	4
LOUTH	6	1	0	5	2
WICKLOW	6	0	0	6	0

1961/62

LOUTH 2-11   DUBLIN 3-3
Nov 5, St Brigid's Park, Dundalk
Dublin: P Flynn, C Kane, L Hickey, Joe Timmons,
D McKane, P Holden, N Fox, John Timmons 0-2, L Quinn, P Harrington, M Whelan, B McCrea 1-1, P Farnan 1-0, J Joyce, E Burgess 1-0. Subs: S Behan for Harrington, P Donnelly for Farnan, B Casey for Fox.

DUBLIN 3-14   LAOIS 3-3
Nov 12, Croke Park, Dublin
Dublin: P Flynn, C Kane, L Hickey, B Casey, C O'Leary 0-1, M Whelan 0-1, N Fox, P Holden, John Timmons 1-8, E Burgess 0-2, P Harrington, A Donnelly, P Delaney, B McCrea 1-2, T Howard 1-0. Sub: D Keenan for Harrington.

DUBLIN 4-8   WICKLOW 2-4
Nov 19, Croke Park, Dublin
Dublin: P Flynn, L Foley, L Hickey, B Casey, M Whelan, C Kane, N Fox, P Holden, D Foley 0-3, E Burgess, B Ennis, T Howard 1-1, P Delaney 0-2, J Joyce 2-1, S Behan 1-1.

DUBLIN 3-10   ROSCOMMON 2-4
Feb 4, Croke Park, Roscommon
Dublin: P Flynn, L Hickey, L Foley, C Kane, C O'Leary, P Holden, B Casey, John Timmons 0-2, D Foley, E Burgess 1-0, B McCrea 0-1, P Delaney 0-2, P Farnan 0-1, J Joyce 1-1, K Heffernan 0-3. Subs: A Donnelly for Burgess, Burgess for Donnelly.

DUBLIN 6-7   GALWAY 1-4
Mar 4, Pearse Stadium, Salthill
Dublin: P Flynn, L Hickey, L Foley, C Kane, C O'Leary, P Holden, B Casey, D Foley 0-1, John Timmons 0-3, A Donnelly, M Whelan 0-1, B McCrea 2-1, P Farnan, J Joyce 4-0, K Heffernan 0-1.

DUBLIN 2-9   OFFALY 1-5
Mar 25, Croke Park, Dublin
Dublin: P Flynn, B Casey, L Foley, C Kane, C O'Leary 0-1, P Holden, D McKane, D Foley, John Timmons 0-3, A Donnelly, B McCrea, M Whelan 0-1, P Farnon, J Joyce 1-2, K Heffernan 1-2.

SECTION III	P	W	D	L	Pts
DUBLIN	6	5	0	1	10
OFFALY	6	4	1	1	9
LOUTH	6	4	0	2	8
GALWAY	6	3	1	2	7
LAOIS	6	3	0	3	6
ROSCOMMON	6	1	0	5	2
WICKLOW	6	0	0	6	0

SEMI-FINAL
Apr 29, Croke Park, Dublin
DUBLIN 0-15   MEATH 1-8
Dublin: P Flynn, L Hickey, L Foley, B Casey, C Kane, P Holden, D McKane, John Timmons 0-9, C O'Leary, T Howard, B McCrea 0-1, M Whelan, P Farnan, J Joyce, K Heffernan 0-5. Subs: A Donnelly for Howard, N Fox for Holden.

FINAL

May 13, Croke Park, Dublin

DOWN 2-5   DUBLIN 1-7

Dublin: Pascal Flynn, Leo Hickey, Lar Foley, Bill Casey, Cathal O'Leary, Paddy Holden, Christy Kane, John Timmons 0-2, Des McKane, Maurice Whelan 1-2, Paddy Farnan 0-1, Aidan Donnelly, Eamonn Burgess 0-2, Johnny Joyce, Kevin Heffernan. Subs: Noel Fox for Timmons, Timmons for Farnan.

1962/63

DUBLIN 1-11   LOUTH 1-3

Nov 18, Croke Park, Dublin

Dublin: P Flynn, J Farrell, L Foley, B Casey, M Foley, P Holden, C Kane, M Kissane, D McKane, T Donnelly 0-1, M Whelan 1-4, N Fox 0-1, B McDonald 0-1, J Timmons 0-3, J Gilroy. Subs: S Coen for Gilroy, E Burgess 0-1 for McDonald.

LAOIS 2-7   DUBLIN 0-6

Nov 25, O'Moore Park, Portlaoise

Dublin: P Flynn, M Foley, J Farrell, F Gilton, J Rice, P Holden, M Kissane, J Timmons 0-1, D McKane, E Burgess, T Donnelly, N Fox, B McDonald 0-3, D Foley 0-2, S Coen. Subs: P Delaney for Burgess, F Kavanagh for M Foley.

DUBLIN 3-14   WICKLOW 1-3

Dec 2, Croke Park, Dublin

Dublin: P Flynn, J Farrell, M Foley, B Casey, D McKane, P Holden, D Dempsey, M Kissane, D Foley 0-2, T Donnelly 1-2, B McDonald 0-3, N Fox 0-2, G Davey 1-1, J Timmons 0-1, S Coen 1-3.

GALWAY 2-12   DUBLIN 0-7

Mar 3, Croke Park, Dublin

Dublin: P Flynn, C Kane, L Foley, B Casey, D McKane, M Kissane, N Fox, M Whelan, D Foley 0-1, T Donnelly, B McCrea, B McDonald 0-1, G Davey, J Joyce 0-2, S Coen. Sub: P Holden for McDonald, J Timmons 0-3 for Donnelly, D Callaghan for Fox.

DUBLIN 2-6   ROSCOMMON 1-1

Mar 24, GAA Grounds, Athleague

Dublin: M Leonard, M Foley, L Hickey, C Kane, D Gahan, J Rice, T Howard, S Clinton 1-0, S Murray 1-0, R Sugrue 0-1, B Ennis, J Houlihan 0-3, P Lawless 0-1, N Daly 0-1, J Levins.

OFFALY 3-7   DUBLIN 0-3

Mar 31, O'Connor Park, Tullamore

Dublin: M Leonard, M Foley, L Hickey, C Kane, J Rice, P Doherty, S Clinton, S Murray, J Lee, T Howard 0-1, B Ennis, R Sugrue, B Beggs, N Daly, M Breslin 0-2.

SECTION III	P	W	D	L	Pts
GALWAY	6	5	1	0	11
OFFALY	6	4	0	2	8
LAOIS	6	4	0	2	8
DUBLIN	6	3	0	3	6
LOUTH	6	2	1	3	5
ROSCOMMON	6	1	0	5	2
WICKLOW	6	1	0	5	2

1963/64

DUBLIN 4-11   WICKLOW 1-7

Oct 6, Croke Park, Dublin

Dublin: P Flynn, L Hickey, L Foley, B Casey, D McKane, P Downey, M Kissane, D Foley, J Timmons 0-2, B McDonald 0-1, M Whelan 0-5, G Davey 2-1, S Behan 1-4, T Donnelly 0-1, N Fox 1-0.

DUBLIN 2-11   OFFALY 1-5

Dec 1, O'Connor Park, Tullamore

Dublin: P Flynn, C Kane, L Hickey, B Casey, D McKane, P Holden, M Kissane, D Foley 0-1, J TImmons 0-2, B McDonald, M Whelan 1-5, T Donnelly, G Davey 0-1, D Ferguson 1-1, E Breslin 0-1. Sub: P Downey for Holden.

DUBLIN 3-9   LOUTH 0-7

Feb 9, Croke Park, Dublin

Dublin: P Flynn, L Hickey, P Downey, C Kane, B Casey, P Holden, M Kissane, D Foley 1-0, J Timmons, B McDonald 0-2, M Whelan 0-3, G Davey 0-1, E Breslin 1-0, D Ferguson 0-1, J Gilroy 1-2.

DUBLIN 4-7   LAOIS 1-8

Feb 16, O'Moore Park, Portlaoise

Dublin: P Flynn, L Hickey, P Downey, C Kane, B Casey, P Holden, M Kissane, D Foley 0-1, T Donnelly, B McDonald, M Whelan 1-3, N Fox 0-1, E Breslin 1-0, D Ferguson 1-1, J Gilroy 1-1.

GALWAY 2-7   DUBLIN 1-8

Mar 1, Croke Park, Dublin

Dublin: P Flynn, L Hickey, L Foley, C Kane, B Casey, P Holden, M Kissane, D Foley 0-1, J Timmons, B McDonald 0-3, M Whelan 0-2, G Davey, E Breslin 0-1, D Ferguson, J Gilroy 1-1. Sub: N Fox for Davey.

DUBLIN 1-7   ROSCOMMON 0-7

Mar 8, St Coman's Park, Roscommon

Dublin: P Flynn, L Hickey, P Downey, C Kane, D McKane, P Holden, M Kissane, D Foley 0-2, T Donnelly, B McDonald 0-2, M Whelan 0-3, E Breslin, P Nally, J Gilroy, G Davey 1-0. Sub: B Beggs for Nally.

SECTION III	P	W	D	L	Pts
DUBLIN	6	5	0	1	10
GALWAY	6	4	1	1	9
ROSCOMMON	6	3	0	3	6
OFFALY	6	3	0	3	6
WICKLOW	6	2	1	3	5
LOUTH	6	2	1	3	5
LAOIS	6	0	1	5	1

SEMI-FINAL
Apr 12, Croke Park, Dublin
DUBLIN 0-10   KERRY 0-9
Dublin: P Flynn, L Hickey, L Foley, C Kane, D McKane, P Holden, M Kissane, D Foley 0-1, J Timmons 0-5, B McDonald 0-1, B Casey 0-1, E Breslin 0-1, G Davey, D Ferguson 0-1, J Gilroy. Sub: S Behan for Gilroy.

'HOME' FINAL
May 3, Croke Park, Dublin
DUBLIN 2-9   DOWN 0-7
Dublin: Pascal Flynn, Leo Hickey, Lar Foley, Christy Kane, Bill Casey, Paddy Holden, Mick Kissane, John Timmons 0-2, Des Foley, Brian McDonald 1-4, Mickey Whelan 0-2, Eamonn Breslin, Gerry Davey 1-1, Des Ferguson, Jackie Gilroy.

FINAL
Oct 18, Gaelic Park, New York
NEW YORK 2-12   DUBLIN 1-13
Dublin: Pascal Flynn, Leo Hickey, Lar Foley, Christy Kane, Des McKane, Paddy Holden, Mick Kissane, John Timmons 0-1, Des Foley, Brian McDonald 0-5, Mickey Whelan 1-3, Noel Fox 0-1, Gerry Davey 0-1, Bill Casey 0-1, Des Ferguson 0-1. Sub: Matt Keane for Hickey.

1964/65

DUBLIN 1-11   LAOIS 0-10
Nov 1, Croke Park, Dublin
Dublin: P Flynn, L Hickey, L Foley, P Downey, T Hanahoe, P Holden, M Kissane, D Foley, D Mulligan, B McDonald 0-1, E Breslin 1-2, J Levins, G Davey 0-1, J Timmons 0-7, J Gilroy.

DUBLIN 0-16   WICKLOW 0-4
Nov 22, Croke Park, Dublin
Dublin: P Flynn, L Hickey, L Foley, C Kane, E Fahy, P Holden, M Kissane, D Foley 0-2, D Mulligan, B McDonald 0-6, M Whelan 0-5, G Davey 0-1, J Keaveney, D Ferguson 0-2, E Breslin. Sub: J Connolly for Holden.

DUBLIN 1-8   OFFALY 0-10
Feb 14, Croke Park, Dublin
Dublin: P Flynn, L Hickey, L Foley, B Casey, M Keane,

P Holden, M, Kissane, D Foley 0-1, D Mulligan, B McDonald 0-1, M Whelan, T Hanahoe, G Davey 0-1, J Timmons 1-4, E Breslin 0-1. Sub: S Lee for Mulligan.

DUBLIN 5-11   LOUTH 0-3
Mar 7, St Brigid's Park, Dundalk
Dublin: P Flynn, L Hickey, L Foley, M Keane, B Casey, P Holden, M Kissane, D Foley 0-1, S Lee 0-2, J Keaveney 1-1, M Whelan 0-2, B McDonald 0-1, G Davey, J Timmons 3-3, J Gilroy 1-1.

DUBLIN 1-17   ROSCOMMON 1-1
Mar 21, Croke Park, Dublin
Dublin: P Flynn, L Hickey, L Foley, C Kane, B Casey, P Holden, M Kissane, D Foley 0-2, S Lee, J Keaveney 0-2, M Whelan 0-1, B McDonald 0-3, G Davey 0-3, J Timmons 0-5, J Gilroy 1-1.

GALWAY 2-11   DUBLIN 1-7
Mar 28, Tuam Stadium, Tuam
Dublin: P Flynn, L Hickey, L Foley, C Kane, M Kissane, P Holden, B Casey, D Foley, S Lee, J Keaveney, M Whelan, B MacDonald 1-3, G Davey, J Timmons 0-4, J Gilroy. Sub: M Keane for Gilroy.

SECTION III	P	W	D	L	Pts
GALWAY	6	6	0	0	12
DUBLIN	6	5	0	1	10
LOUTH	6	4	0	2	8
OFFALY	6	3	0	3	6
ROSCOMMON	6	2	0	4	4
WICKLOW	6	1	0	5	2
LAOIS	6	0	0	6	0

1965/66

DUBLIN 1-15   KILDARE 1-9
Oct 17, St Conleth's Park, Newbridge
Dublin: A Griffin, J Connolly, L Foley, C Kane, M Kissane, P Holden, G Davey, D Mulligan 0-2, S Lee, T Donnelly 0-3, M Whelan 0-2, D Bollard 1-1, L Deegan, J Timmons 0-6, B McDonald 0-1.

DUBLIN 1-12   LAOIS 0-6
Oct 31, Croke Park, Dublin
Dublin: A Griffin, L Hickey, B Casey, C Kane, M Kissane, P Holden, G Freyne 0-1, S Lee 0-2, T Donnelly, E Mullins 0-2, M Whelan, M Canny 0-2, L Deegan 1-1, J Timmons 0-3, G Davey 0-1. Subs: D Bollard for Timmons.

CORK 2-10   DUBLIN 0-9
Nov 28, Croke Park, Dublin
Dublin: A Griffin, L Hickey, C Kane, B Casey, P Holden, M Keane, S Lee, T Donnelly 0-1, D Bollard 0-2, D Foley 0-1, M Whelan 0-4, E Breslin, L Deegan 0-1, J Keaveney, G Davey. Subs: S Connolly for Keane, G O'Driscoll for Casey.

SECTION III (A)	P	W	D	L	Pts
Dublin	3	2	0	1	4
Kildare	2	1	0	1	2
Cork	2	1	0	1	2
Laois	3	1	0	2	2

* Postponed game between Kildare and Cork not played as qualification had been decided.

SECTION SEMI-FINAL

Mar 6, Croke Park, Dublin

DUBLIN 1-16   WATERFORD 1-2

Dublin: A Griffin, M Kissane, L Hickey, C Kane, E Breslin, P Holden, G Davey, T Donnelly, S Lee 0-2, D Bollard 0-3, B McDonald 0-6, M Cranny 0-1, J Keaveney 0-2, S O'Connor 1-1, L Deegan 0-1. Sub: E Mullins for Holden.

SECTION FINAL

Mar 13, Pairc Tailteann, Navan

KILDARE 0-10   DUBLIN 0-7

Dublin: A Griffin, L Hickey, B Casey, C Kane, M Kissane, P Holden, E Breslin, D Foley 0-1, S Lee, D Bollard 0-2, B McDonald 0-1, T Donnelly 0-1, J Keaveney, S O'Connor 0-2, G Davey. Subs: L Ferguson for Holden, E Mullins for O'Connor.

1966/67

DUBLIN 2-10   LAOIS 1-6

Oct 16, McCann Park, Portarlington

Dublin: A Griffin, L Ferguson, L Hickey, C Kane, S Mullins, P Holden, G Davey, B Casey, S Lee, M Whelan 0-1, J Keaveney 1-7, M Cranny 0-1, D Donovan, J Evers, L Deegan 1-1. Subs: T Donnelly for Hickey, D Bollard for Donovan.

DUBLIN 2-10   KILDARE 3-6

Oct 30, Croke Park, Dublin

Dublin: A Griffin, L Ferguson, B Casey, C Kane, S Mullins, M Kelleher, G Davey, T Donnelly, P Murphy, M Whelan 1-1, J Keaveney 0-3, M Cranny 0-3, D Bollard, J Timmons 0-3, L Deegan 1-0. Subs: P Holden for Kelleher, J Evers for Murphy, B McDonald for Timmons.

DUBLIN 2-8   CORK 2-5

Jan 22, Athletic Grounds, Cork

Dublin: M McCann, B Casey, L Hickey, C Kane, M Kissane, M Kelleher, G Davey, T Donnelly 0-1, S O'Connor, M Whelan, J Keaveney 1-2, M Cranny 0-2, D Bollard 0-1, J Evers 0-1, B McDonald 1-1. Sub: S Donovan for Cranny.

SECTION III (A)	P	W	D	L	Pts
Dublin	3	3	0	0	6
Kildare	3	2	0	1	4
Cork	3	1	0	2	2
Laois	3	0	0	3	0

SECTION SEMI-FINAL

Feb 19, Croke Park, Dublin

DUBLIN 3-9   CARLOW 1-6

Dublin: M McCann, B Casey, L Hickey, C Kane, M Kissane, M Kelleher, G Davey, T Donnelly, S O'Connor 1-0, J Evers 1-2, J Keaveney 0-4, M Cranny, D Bollard 1-1, B McDonald 0-2, L Deegan. Sub: J Wallace for McDonald.

SECTION FINAL

Mar 5, Croke Park, Dublin

DUBLIN 4-12   WEXFORD 0-6

Dublin: M McCann, B Casey, L Hickey, C Kane, M Kissane, M Kelleher, G Davey, T Donnelly, S O'Connor, M Whelan, J Keaveney 1-7, M Cranny 0-1, D Bollard, J Evers 1-1, L Deegan 2-3. Sub: B Dowling for Whelan.

SEMI-FINAL

Apr 9, Croke Park, Dublin

DUBLIN 1-15   MEATH 1-7

Dublin: P Cullen, B Casey, L Hickey, C Kane, M Kissane, M Kelleher 0-1, G Davey, T Donnelly 0-1, S O'Connor 0-1, M Whelan 0-2, J Keaveney 0-5, M Cranny 0-2, B McDonald 0-1, J Evers 0-2, L Deegan 1-0. Sub: S Lee for Evers.

FINAL

Apr 30, Croke Park, Dublin

GALWAY 0-12   DUBLIN 1-7

Dublin: Paddy Cullen, Bill Casey, Leo Hickey, Christy Kane, Mick Kissane, Michael Kelleher, Gerry Davey, Shay O'Connor, Aidan Donnelly, Mickey Whelan 0-1, Jimmy Keaveney 0-1, Mick Cranny, Brian Dowllng 0-1, Jim Evers 0-4, Leslie Deegan 1-0. Subs: Sean Lee for Cranny, Donal Bollard for Dowllng, Des Foley for Kissane.

1967/68

DUBLIN 1-10   MONAGHAN 3-3

Oct 15, Emmet Park, Carrickmacross

Dublin: P Cullen, B Dowling, L Hickey, C Kane, S Mullins, B Casey, G Davey 0-1, T Donnelly 0-1, D Foley 0-1, E Davey, M Whelan 0-1, M Cranny 0-1, L Deegan 0-1, J Evers 0-3, B McDonald 1-1.

WESTMEATH 1-5   DUBLIN 0-7

Oct 22, Pairc Ciaran, Athlone

Dublin: P Cullen, B Casey, L Hickey, C Kane, S Mulllns, M Kelleher, G Davey, T Donnelly 0-1, S Lee, J Keaveney 0-2, E Mullen 0-1, M Cranny, L Deegan, J Evers 0-2, B MacDonald 0-1. Sub: B Dowllng for Lee.

DUBLIN 1-9   ARMAGH 1-6

Nov 12, Croke Park, Dublin

Dublin: P Cullen, B Casey, L Hickey, C Kane, E Davey, O Callaghan, G Davey, T Donnelly 0-1, D Foley, S Lee,

M Whelan, M Cranny 1-1, B McDonald 0-1, J Keaveney 0-6, S Rooney. Sub: J Evers for Lee.

DIVISION 1B	P	W	D	L	Pts
WESTMEATH	3	3	0	0	6
DUBLIN	3	2	0	1	4
ARMAGH	3	1	0	2	2
MONAGHAN	3	0	0	3	0

SECTION SEMI-FINAL
Feb 12, Croke Park, Dublin

DOWN 3-7   DUBLIN 2-4
Dublin: P Cullen, B Casey, L Hickey, C Kane, E Davey, M Whelan, G Davey, T Donnelly 0-2, S O'Connor, J Keaveney 0-1, D Foley, M Cranny, B McDonald, L Foley 2-0, S Rooney. Subs: G O'Driscoll for Hickey, F Murphy 0-1 for O'Connor, S Lee for Keaveney.

1968/69

DUBLIN 0-10   WESTMEATH 0-7
Oct 13, Croke Park, Dublin
Dublin: P Cullen, L Hickey, B O'Donoghue, C Kane, B Casey, T Donnelly, G Davey, T Donnelly, M Kelleher, S Foley 0-2, J Keaveney 0-2, D Bollard 0-1, P Delaney 0-4, S Wright, J Henry 0-1, Subs: T Hempenstall for T Donnelly, P Markham for Kelleher.

DUBLIN 1-10   ARMAGH 0-7
Oct 20, Athletic Grounds, Armagh
Dublin: P Cullen, L Hickey, B O'Donoghue, P Markham, B Casey, T Donnelly, G Davey, T Donnelly, M Kelleher, S Foley 0-2, J Keaveney 1-1, D Bollard 0-1, P Delaney 0-6, J Wright, J Henry.

MONAGHAN 3-7   DUBLIN 2-6
Nov 11, Croke Park, Dublin
Dublin: P Cullen, B Casey, L Hickey, P Markham, E Davey, M Whelan 0-1, G Davey, S Donnelly, B O'Shea, S Foley 0-1, J Keaveney, D Bollard 0-1, P Delaney 0-3, S Wright 2-0, J Henry. Subs: T Hempenstail for Henry, T Donnelly for O'Shea.

DIVISION 1B	P	W	D	L	Pts
DUBLIN	3	2	0	1	4
WESTMEATH	3	2	0	1	4
MONAGHAN	3	1	1	1	3
ARMAGH	3	0	1	2	1

PLAY-OFF
Mar 9, The Oval, Dublin

DUBLIN 0-7   WESTMEATH 0-3
Dublin: P Cullen, L Hickey, C Kane, M Kelleher, B Casey, T Donnelly, G Davey, B O'Shea, S Donnelly, S Yates, M Whelan, D Bollard, S Foley 0-1, J Wright, P Delaney 0-5, Sub: J Keaveney for Yates.

DIVISIONAL SEMI-FINAL
Mar 16, Athletic Grounds, Drogheda

DUBLIN 1-10   MEATH 0-9
Dublin: P Cullen, P Markham, C Kane, M Kelleher, B Casey 0-1, T Donnelly, G Davey, B O'Shea, S Donnelly, E Davey, M Whelan, D Bollard 0-1, S Foley, J Wright, P Delaney 1-8. Sub: D Foley for Wright.

DIVISIONAL FINAL
(LEAGUE QUARTER-FINAL)
Mar 30, Pairc Tailteann, Navan

WESTMEATH 1-8   DUBLIN 1-6
Dublin: P Cullen, P Markham, C Kane, M Kelleher, B Casey, T Donnelly, G Davey, B O'Shea, S Donnelly, T Hempenstall 0-1, M Whelan, D Bollard 1-0, S Foley, J Wright, P Delaney 0-5. Sub: D Foley for S Donnelly, T Donnelly for Whelan.

1969/70

DUBLIN 1-14   MONAGHAN 0-5
Oct 19, Emmet Park, Carrickmacross
Dublin: P Cullen, P Markham, S Doherty, M Kelleher, R Kelleher, S Donnelly, P O'Neill, F Murray, S O'Connor 0-2, D Hickey 0-1, J Keaveney 0-6, P Leahy 0-1, S Foley 0-1, T O'Hanlon, K Hegarty 1-2. Sub: J Featherson 0-1 for Foley.

DUBLIN 2-11   ARMAGH 0-7
Nov 16, Croke Park, Dublin
Dublin: P Cullen, P Markham, S Doherty, M Kelleher, R Kelleher, S Donnelly, P O'Neill, S O'Connor, F Murray 0-1, D Hickey 1-2, J Keaveney 0-3, P Leahy 0-1, L Deegan 1-0, T O'Hanlon 0-2, K Hegarty 0-2. Sub: P Gogarty for Leahy.

DUBLIN 2-6   WESTMEATH 2-3
Nov 30, Cusack Park, Mullingar
Dublin: P Cullen, P Markham, S Doherty, M Kelleher, R Kelleher, S Donnelly, J Hackett, P O'Neill, F Murray, D Hickey, P Gogarty 0-2, P Leahy 1-3, K Hegarty 1-1, T O'Hanlon, B Lee.

DIVISION 1B	P	W	D	L	Pts
DUBLIN	3	3	0	0	6
WESTMEATH	3	2	0	1	4
ARMAGH	3	1	0	2	2
MONAGHAN	3	0	0	3	0

DIVISIONAL SEMI-FINAL
Mar 8, Croke Park, Dublin

DUBLIN 1-12   LOUTH 1-12
Dublin: P Cullen, S Roche, S Doherty, C Maher, R Kelleher, S Donnelly, P O'Neill, F Murray 0-1, S O'Connor, D Hickey 0-2, J Keaveney 0-8, P Leahy, T O'Hanlon, M Kelleher 1-0, K Hegarty 0-1. Sub: S Foley for Maher.

DIVISIONAL SEMI-FINAL REPLAY
Mar 22, Pairc Tailteann, Navan

LOUTH 0-10   DUBLIN 0-8
Dublin: P Cullen, S Roche, S Doherty, P Markham, J Broe, S Donnelly, P O'Neill, F Murray, S O'Connor, P Gogarty 0-1, J Keaveney 0-6, P Leahy 0-1, S Foley, M Kelleher, D Hickey. Sub: C Maher for O'Neill.

1970/71

KERRY 0-16   DUBLIN 2-4
Oct 18, Austin Stack Park, Tralee
Dublin: P Cullen, P Markham, B Casey, M Kelleher, R Kelleher, S Mullins, M Kissane, S Donnelly 1-0, F Murray, D Hickey 0-2, T Hanahoe, J Keaveney 0-2, L Deegan, S O'Connor 1-0, T O'Hanlon. Sub: S Doherty for Mullins.

DUBLIN 2-12   OFFALY 1-10
Nov 1, Croke Park, Dublin
Dublin: P Cullen, S Roche, S Doherty, M Kelleher, P Markham, S Mullins, J Broe, P O'Neill, F Murray 0-1, D Hickey 0-1, J Keaveney 0-4, J Reilly, L Deegan 1-2, T O'Hanlon 0-3, B Casey 1-1. Sub: T Hanahoe for O'Neill.

DUBLIN 0-14   KILDARE 0-10
Nov 15, Sallins Road, Naas
Dublin: P Cullen, S Roche, S Doherty, M Kelleher, P Markham, S Mullins, J Broe, F Murray 0-1, P O'Neill, D Hickey 0-2, T Hanahoe 0-2, J Reilly, S O'Connor 0-7, T O'Hanlon, B Casey. Subs: R Kelleher for Broe, S Donnelly 0-2 for Reilly.

DUBLIN 3-5   GALWAY 1-11
Nov 29, Croke Park, Dublin
Dublin: P Cullen, S Roche, S Doherty, M Kelleher, P Markham, S Mullins, R Kelleher 1-0, F Murray, P O'Neill, S O'Connor 0-2, T Hanahoe, S Donnelly, D Hickey 0-2, T O'Hanlon 1-1, B Casey. Subs: L Deegan 1-0 for O'Connor, G O'Driscoll for Roche, P Hallinan for Murray.

DUBLIN 3-8   ROSCOMMON 1-8
Feb 14, Orchard Park, Elphin
Dublin: P Cullen, G O'Driscoll, S Doherty, M Kelleher, P Markham, S Mullins 0-1, R Kelleher, F Murray 1-1, P O'Neill, S O'Connor 0-3, T Hanahoe 0-1, J Keaveney, D Hickey 2-1, T O'Hanlon 0-1, B Casey. Sub: B Lee for Hanahoe.

DUBLIN 1-8   CORK 1-7
Mar 14, Croke Park, Dublin
Dublin: P Cullen, G O'Driscoll, S Doherty, M Kelleher, P Markham, S Mullins, R Kelleher, S O'Connor 0-4, F Murray 1-1, D Hickey, T Hanahoe, S Donnelly, L Deegan, T O'Hanlon 0-2, B. Casey 0-1. Subs: P O'Neill for M Kelleher, S Foley for Hickey.

DUBLIN 2-9   LONGFORD 0-8
Apr 25, Pearse Park, Longford
Dublin: P Cullen, G O'Driscoll, S Doherty, M Kelleher, P Markham, B Casey, R Kelleher, P O'Neill, F Murray 0-1, D Hickey 0-1, T Hanahoe, J Keaveney 0-6, L Deegan, T O'Hanlon 1-1, S Donnelly 1-0. Sub: S O'Connor for Hickey.

DIVISION 1B	P	W	D	L	Pts
KERRY	7	5	1	1	11
DUBLIN	7	5	1	1	11
OFFALY	7	4	2	1	10
CORK	7	4	0	3	8
KILDARE	7	3	1	3	7
GALWAY	7	3	1	3	7
LONGFORD	7	1	0	2	2
ROSCOMMON	7	0	0	7	0

PLAY-OFF
May 2, Croke Park, Dublin

KERRY 0-15   DUBLIN 1-8
Dublin: P Cullen, G O'Driscoll, S Doherty, S Roche, P Markham, S O'Connor, R Kelleher, F Murray 0-1, P O'Neill 0-1, J Keaveney 0-5, S Donnelly 1-0, D Hickey, L Deegan, T O'Hanlon, T Hanahoe 0-1. Sub: M Kelleher for Hanahoe.

SEMI-FINAL
May 23, Croke Park, Dublin

MAYO 1-9   DUBLIN 0-8
Dublin: P Cullen, G O'Driscoll, S Doherty, B Casey, P Markham, S Mullins, R Kelleher, F Murray, P O'Neill, S O'Connor, T Hanahoe 0-1, D Hickey, L Deegan, J Keaveney 0-5, S Donnelly 0-1. Subs: J Reilly 0-1 for Hickey, M Kelleher for O'Neill.

1971/72

OFFALY 0-16   DUBLIN 2-3
Oct 31, O'Connor Park, Tullamore
Dublin: P Cullen, P O'Brien, S Doherty, G O'Driscoll, P Markham, B Casey, R Kelleher, F Murray 1-0, L Sweeney, J Reilly, T O'Hanlon 1-0, T Hanahoe 0-1, M Matthews, S Foley 0-1, S Rooney 0-1. Subs: P O'Neill for Markham, N Kelly for Rooney, N Wilde for Matthews.

DUBLIN 3-8   KILDARE 1-10
Nov 14, Croke Park, Dublin
Dublin: P Cullen, P O'Brien, S Doherty, P O'Neill, P Markham, B Casey, G Wilson, R Kelleher, F Murray 0-1, L Sweeney, J Reilly 0-3, T O'Hanlon 1-1, T Hanahoe 2-1, C Hanley 0-1, N Kelly 0-1.

DUBLIN 0-8   GALWAY 0-8
Nov 28, Pearse Stadium, Salthill
Dublin: P Cullen, P O'Brien, S Doherty, P Markham, P O'Neill, B Casey, R Kelleher, F Murray, L Sweeney, G Wilson, T Hanahoe 0-1, C Hanley, J Reilly 0-6, T O'Hanlon 0-1, N Kelly. Subs: S Foley for Kelly, P Wilson for Foley.

TIPPERARY 0-12   DUBLIN 1-4
Dec 12, Croke Park, Dublin
Dublin: P Cullen, P O'Brien, S Doherty, P Markham, P O'Neill, B Casey, R Kelleher, F Murray 1-0, L Sweeney, G Wilson, T Hanahoe, C Hanley, J Reilly 0-1, S Foley, E Brady 0-3. Subs: P Wilson for Casey, T O'Hanlon for Foley.

DUBLIN 3-9   KERRY 0-11
Dec 19, Croke Park, Dublin
Dublin: P Cullen, P O'Brien, S Doherty, P Markham, P O'Neill, R Kelleher, E Brady, F Murray 0-1, L Sweeney 1-1, S O'Connor 0-1, T Hanahoe 0-1, G Wilson 0-1, B Casey 0-1, T O'Hanlon 1-1, J Reilly 0-2. Sub: C Hanley 1-0 for O'Connor.

DUBLIN 3-6   WATERFORD 0-6
Feb 27, Croke Park, Dublin
Dublin: P Cullen, P O'Brien, S Doherty, P Markham, P O'Neill, R Kelleher, E Brady, F Murray, L Sweeney 0-3, G Wilson 1-0, T Hanahoe 1-0, C Hanley, B Casey 1-0, T O'Hanlon 0-2, J Reilly 0-1. Subs: S O'Connor for Hanley, D Hickey for Casey, G O'Driscoll for Markham.

DUBLIN 2-4   CORK 1-7
Apr 30, Athletic Grounds, Cork
Dublin: P Cullen, A Larkin, S Doherty, G O'Driscoll, J Broe, R Kelleher, E Brady, P Wilson, L Sweeney, A Kearney, T Hanahoe 1-0, A O'Toole 0-3, B Casey 0-1, C Hanley, J Keaveney. Sub: B Doyle 1-0 for Kearney.

DIVISION 1A	P	W	D	L	Pts
OFFALY	7	7	0	0	14
KERRY	7	5	0	2	10
DUBLIN	7	3	2	2	8
CORK	7	3	1	3	7
GALWAY	7	2	2	3	6
KILDARE	7	2	1	4	5
WATERFORD	7	1	2	4	4
TIPPERARY	7	1	0	6	2

1972/73

OFFALY 2-15   DUBLIN 1-5
Oct 29, Croke Park, Dublin
Dublin: P Cullen, G O'Driscoll, S Doherty, A Larkin, E Brady, P O'Neill, R Kelleher 0-1, F Murray, T Hanahoe, G Wilson 0-1, J Reilly 0-2, D Hickey, F Hutchinson 0-1, D Clarke, B Doyle 1-0. Subs: M Noonan for Brady, T Flanagan for Murray.

GALWAY 2-7   DUBLIN 1-4
Nov 26, Croke Park, Dublin
Dublin: P Cullen, G O'Driscoll, S Doherty, A Larkin, P Reilly, P O'Neill, R Kelleher, M Noonan, F Murray 0-1, G Wilson 0-1, S O'Connor, J Reilly 0-1, F Hutchinson, D Clarke 0-1, B Doyle. Subs: P O'Brien for Larkin, S Foley 1-0 for Hutchinson.

LONGFORD 4-4   DUBLIN 0-3
Dec 10, Pearse Park, Longford
Dublin: P Cullen, P O'Brien, S Doherty, A Larkin, P Reilly, M Noonan, R Kelleher, S Rooney, F Murray, G Wilson, A O'Toole 0-1, S O'Connor, D Clarke, S Foley, J Reilly 0-2. Subs: P O'Neill for Rooney, J Jones for Foley, F Hutchinson for J Reilly.

CORK 3-11   DUBLIN 1-10
Feb 3, Croke Park, Dublin
Dublin: P Cullen, S Doherty, P O'Neill, A Larkin, P Reilly, P O'Neill, R Kelleher, F Murray 0-1, S Rooney 0-4, P Duggan 0-1, D Clarke 0-1, A O'Toole, B Salmon 0-2, J Jones, S McShane 1-1. Subs: M Noonan for Jones, M McMenamin for Reilly.

DUBLIN 2-11   KILDARE 1-8
Feb 11, Catherine Park, Athy
Dublin: T Milner, J O'Neill, S Doherty, A Larkin, P Reilly 0-1, P O'Neill, R Kelleher, F Murray, S Rooney 0-6, G Wilson 0-1, B Salmon 1-1, D Clarke 0-1, A O'Toole, P Duggan 0-1 S McShane. Sub: J Reilly 1-0 for Salmon.

KERRY 1-10   DUBLIN 1-6
Mar 11, Austin Stack Park, Tralee
Dublin: P Cullen, J O'Neill, S Doherty, P O'Brien, P Reilly, P O'Neill, R Kelleher, S Rooney, A Larkin 0-2, G Wilson 0-2, A O'Toole, D Clarke 1-1, P Duggan 0-1, F Murray, S McShane. Subs: J Reilly for Murray, B Doyle for McShane.

ROSCOMMON 3-7 DUBLIN 0-11
Sep 16, O'Rourke Park, Castlerea
Dublin: P Cullen, J O'Neill, M Conway, S Doherty, P Reilly, A Larkin, G Wilson, S Rooney 0-1, P O'Neill 0-1, B Doyle 0-7, B Donovan, A O'Toole 0-1, T Hanahoe 0-1, D Hickey, F Murray. Subs: J Reilly for O'Toole, M Ryan for Donovan, J Jones for Hickey.

DIVISION 1A	P	W	D	L	Pts
OFFALY	7	6	0	1	12
KERRY	7	5	0	2	10
GALWAY	7	5	0	2	10
LONGFORD	7	4	0	3	8
CORK	7	3	0	4	6
ROSCOMMON	7	3	0	4	4
DUBLIN	7	1	0	6	2
KILDARE	7	1	0	6	2

1973/74

DUBLIN 3-6   WEXFORD 1-8
Oct 14, Croke Park, Dublin
Dublin: P Cullen, M Corcoran, S Doherty, J O'Neill, P Reilly, S Furlong, G Wilson, P O'Neill, S Rooney 0-2, B Doyle 1-0, F Murray 0-1, A O'Toole 0-2, J McCarthy 1-0, P Gogarty 1-1, J Reilly.

DUBLIN 1-10   KILDARE 1-9
Oct 28, Catherine Park, Athy
Dublin: P Cullen, M Hannick, S Doherty, J O'Neill, R Kelleher, P O'Neill, G Wilson 0-1, S Rooney, J Furlong 0-1, B Doyle, F Murray 1-1, J McCarthy 0-1, A O'Toole 0-2, P Gogarty, T Hanahoe 0-2. Subs: J Reilly 0-2 for McCarthy, A Larkin for J O'Neill, B Pocock for Wilson.

DUBLIN 1-8   LIMERICK 0-6
Nov 11, Croke Park, Dublin
Dublin: P Cullen, G O'Driscoll, S Doherty, M Hannick, R Kelleher, P O'Neill, G Wilson, S Rooney 0-2, J Furlong, B Doyle 1-4, F Murray, J McCarthy, A O'Toole, P Gogarty, T Hanahoe. Subs: J Reilly 0-2 for McCarthy, B Pocock for O'Toole.

DUBLIN 1-9   CARLOW 0-4
Nov 25, Dr Cullen Park, Carlow
Dublin: P Cullen, A Larkin, G O'Driscoll, M Hannick, R Kelleher, P O'Neill, G Wilson, J O'Neill, S Rooney, B Doyle 1-1, A O'Toole 0-1, J Reilly 0-2, T Hanahoe 0-2, P Gogarty 0-1, F Murray 0-1. Sub: J Furlong 0-1 for Rooney.

DUBLIN 6-16   KILKENNY 0-4
Dec 9, Nowlan Park, Kilkenny
Dublin: P Cullen, A Larkin, S Doherty, M Canny, G Wilson, P O'Neill, R Kelleher, J Furlong 0-2, J O'Neill, B Doyle 1-2, J McCarthy 4-0, J Reilly 0-5, A O'Toole 0-4, P Gogarty 1-1, F Murray 0-1. Subs: J Jones for O'Neill, S McCarthy 0-1 for Murray, B Brogan for Furlong.

DUBLIN 2-15   WATERFORD 0-5
Feb 3, Croke Park, Dublin
Dublin: P Cullen, G O'Driscoll, S Doherty, M Hannick, R Kelleher, A Larkin, G Wilson, J Furlong 0-1, S Rooney 0-3, B Doyle 1-0, T Hanahoe 0-1, S McCarthy, J Reilly 0-6, P Gogarty, J McCarthy 0-3. Subs: PJ Reid 1-0 for S McCarthy, B Donovan 0-1 for Gogarty.

CLARE 4-9   DUBLIN 2-9
Feb 17, Croke Park, Dublin
Dublin: P Cullen, G O'Driscoll, S Doherty, S Falvey, P Reilly, A Larkin, B Pocock, PJ Reid, S Rooney 0-1, S McCarthy 0-3, T Hanahoe 0-1, B Donovan 0-2, J McCarthy, T McNally 2-0, P Gogarty. Subs: M Hannick for Falvey h/t, B Doyle 0-2 for Reid h/t, D Billings for O'Driscoll 52.

DIVISION 2A	P	W	D	L	Pts
DUBLIN	7	6	0	1	12
KILDARE	7	5	1	1	11
WATERFORD	7	5	0	2	10
CLARE	7	4	1	2	9
WEXFORD	7	3	0	4	6
LIMERICK	7	2	0	5	6
CARLOW	7	2	0	5	4
KILKENNY	7	0	0	7	0

DIVISION 2 SEMI-FINAL
Apr 21, Croke Park, Dublin
DUBLIN 1-13   ANTRIM 1-8
Dublin: P Cullen, G O'Driscoll, S Doherty, R Kelleher, P Reilly, A Larkin, G Wilson, J Furlong 0-2, S Rooney 0-2, B Doyle 0-2, T Hanahoe 1-5, J Reilly 0-2, J McCarthy, B Mullins, A O'Toole. Subs: F Murray for O'Toole, B Brogan for J Reilly.

DIVISION 2 FINAL:
May 5, Croke Park, Dublin
KILDARE 3-13   DUBLIN 2-9
Dublin: Paddy Cullen, Gay O'Driscoll, Sean Doherty, Robbie Kelleher, Paddy Reilly, Alan Larkin, George Wilson, Stephen Rooney 0-5, Brian Mullins 0-1, Bobby Doyle 1-0, Tony Hanahoe, Frank Murray, Anton O'Toole, Johnny Furlong 1-1, Joe Reilly 0-2. Subs: Brendan Pocock for P Reilly, Bernard Brogan for O'Toole.

1974/75

CORK 1-8   DUBLIN 0-10
Oct 20, Croke Park, Dublin
Dublin: P Cullen, G O'Driscoll, S Doherty, R Kelleher, P Reilly, A Larkin, G Wilson, B Mullins, S Rooney 0-1, B Doyle, T Hanahoe, A O'Toole 0-1, J McCarthy, J Keaveney 0-7, P Gogarty 0-1. Subs: D Hickey for Gogarty, B Donovan for McCarthy.

DUBLIN 0-8   KERRY 0-8
Nov 10, Fitzgerald Stadium, Killarney
Dublin: P Cullen, G O'Driscoll, S Doherty, R Kelleher, P Reilly, A Larkin, G Wilson, B Mullins, B Donovan, A O'Toole, T Hanahoe, B Doyle 0-1 J McCarthy, J Keaveney 0-7, P Gogarty. Sub: J Brogan for Donovan.

DUBLIN 3-13   KILDARE 1-4
Jan 19, Croke Park, Dublin
Dublin: P Cullen, G O'Driscoll, S Doherty, R Kelleher, P Reilly 0-1, A Larkin, G Wilson, B Mullins 1-0, S Rooney, B Doyle 0-1, T Hanahoe 1-1, D Hickey, J McCarthy 1-1, J Keaveney 0-5, A O'Toole 0-2. Subs: F Ryder for Rooney, P Gogarty 0-2 for McCarthy.

DUBLIN 0-10   OFFALY 1-5
Feb 2, O'Connor Park, Tullamore
Dublin: P Cullen, G O'Driscoll, S Doherty, R Kelleher, P Reilly 0-1, A Larkin, G Wilson, B Mullins, S Rooney, B Doyle 0-1, T Hanahoe 0-2, D Hickey, P Gogarty 0-2, J Keaveney 0-3, A O'Toole 0-1. Sub: B Pocock for Wilson.

DUBLIN 1-13   ROSCOMMON 1-4
Mar 2, Croke Park, Dublin
Dublin: P Cullen, G O'Driscoll, S Doherty, R Kelleher, P Reilly, A Larkin, G Wilson, B Mullins 1-0, S Rooney, B Doyle, T Hanahoe 0-1, D Hickey 0-1, J McCarthy 0-2, J Keaveney 0-7, A O'Toole 0-2. Sub: B Brogan for Mullins.

DIVISION 1A	P	W	D	L	Pts
DUBLIN	5	3	1	1	7
KERRY	5	3	1	1	7
CORK	5	3	0	2	6
ROSCOMMON	5	3	0	2	6
OFFALY	5	1	0	4	2
KILDARE	5	1	0	4	2

SEMI-FINAL
May 4, Croke Park, Dublin
DUBLIN 3-12   TYRONE 1-7
Dublin: P Cullen, G O'Driscoll, S Doherty, R Kelleher, P Reilly, A Larkin, G Wilson, B Mullins 1-0, P O'Neill 0-1, B Doyle 0-1, T Hanahoe 0-1, D Hickey 0-1 J McCarthy 0-1, J Keaveney 1-3, A O'Toole 1-2.

FINAL
May 18, Croke Park, Dublin
MEATH 0-16   DUBLIN 1-9
Dublin: Paddy Cullen, Gay O'Driscoll, Sean Doherty, Robbie Kelleher, Paddy Reilly, Alan Larkin, George Wilson, Brian Mullins, Stephen Rooney, Bobby Doyle 1-1, Tony Hanahoe, David Hickey, John McCarthy 0-1, Jimmy Keaveney 0-6, Anton O'Toole 0-1. Sub: Pat Gogarty for Hickey.

1975/76

DUBLIN 1-12   CORK 0-4
Oct 26, The Mardyke, Cork
Dublin: P Cullen, K Synnott, S Doherty, R Kelleher, P Reilly, P O'Neill, B Pocock, B Mullins 0-2, B Brogan 0-1, A O'Toole 0-1, T Hanahoe 0-1, D Hickey 0-3, J McCarthy, J Keaveney 1-2, P Gogarty 0-2. Sub: S Rooney for Brogan.

DUBLIN 2-11   KERRY 0-13
Nov 9, Croke Park, Dublin
Dublin: P Cullen, G O'Driscoll, S Doherty, R Kelleher, P Reilly, P O'Neill, B Pocock, B Mullins 1-0, L Egan, A O'Toole 1-0, T Hanahoe 0-2, D Hickey, B Doyle, J Keaveney 0-6, P Gogarty 0-2. Subs: B Brogan 0-1 for Egan h/t, K Synnott for O'Reilly h/t.

DUBLIN 1-14   KILDARE 0-7
Nov 23, Geraldine Park, Athy
Dublin: P Cullen, G O'Driscoll, S Doherty, R Kelleher, K Synnott, P O'Neill, B Pocock, S Rooney, B Brogan, A O'Toole 1-0, T Hanahoe 0-4, D Hickey 0-2, B Doyle 0-1, J Keaveney 0-2, P Gogarty 0-5.

DUBLIN 5-8   OFFALY 1-8
Dec 7, Croke Park, Dublin
Dublin: P Cullen, J Brogan, S Doherty, R. Kelleher, K Synnott, P O'Neill, B Pocock, B Mullins 0-2, S Rooney, A O'Toole 0-1, T Hanahoe 1-2, D Hickey 1-0, B Doyle 1-1, J Keaveney 1-1, P Gogarty 1-1. Sub: B Brogan for Mullins.

ROSCOMMON 2-8   DUBLIN 1-6
Feb 1, Dr Hyde Park, Roscommon
Dublin: P Cullen, G O'Driscoll, S Doherty, R Kelleher, B Pocock, L Egan, G Wilson, S Rooney, P O'Neill, B Doyle 0-1, B Brogan, D Hickey, M Noctor 1-5, J McCarthy, P Gogarty. Subs: J Brogan for Wilson, A O'Toole for B Brogan.

DIVISION 1A (SOUTH)	P	W	D	L	Pts
DUBLIN	5	4	0	1	8
CORK	5	3	1	1	7
KERRY	5	3	1	1	7
ROSCOMMON	5	3	0	2	6
KILDARE	5	1	0	4	2
OFFALY	5	0	0	5	0

SEMI-FINAL
DUBLIN 1-11   GALWAY 0-12
Apr 4, Croke Park, Dublin
Dublin: P Cullen, G O'Driscoll, S Doherty, R Kelleher, P Reilly, P O'Neill, B Pocock, B Mullins, K Moran 0-1, A O'Toole, T Hanahoe 1-1, D Hickey, B Doyle 0-3, J Keaveney 0-4, P Gogarty 0-1. Subs: K Synnott 0-1 for Pocock, B Brogan for Hickey.

FINAL
May 2, Croke Park, Dublin
DUBLIN 2-10   DERRY 0-15
Dublin: Paddy Cullen, Gay O'Driscoll, Sean Doherty, Robbie Kelleher, Brendan Pocock 0-1, Pat O'Neill, Kevin Synnott, Brian Mullins, Kevin Moran 0-2, Anton O'Toole, Tony Hanahoe (capt), David Hickey 0-2, Bobby Doyle 0-1, Jimmy Keaveney 1-4, Pat Gogarty 1-0. Sub: Bernard Brogan for Pat O'Neill.

1976/77

DUBLIN 1-13   CORK 2-9
Oct 10, Croke Park, Dublin
Dublin: P Cullen, G O'Driscoll, S Doherty, J Brogan, P Reilly, K Moran, P O'Neill, F Ryder, B Brogan 0-1, P Gogarty, B Mullins 1-3, D Hickey, M Hickey 0-2, J

Keaveney 0-6, J McCarthy 0-1. Sub: A O'Toole for Gogarty.

KERRY 0-12   DUBLIN 0-7
Oct 24, Austin Stack Park, Tralee
Dublin: N Bernard, G O'Driscoll, S Doherty, R Kelleher, T Drumm, K Moran, P O'Neill, B Mullins, B Brogan, A O'Toole, T Hanahoe 0-1, D Hickey, B Doyle, J Keaveney 0-5, J McCarthy. Subs: J Corcoran 0-1 for Doyle, F Ryder for Brogan.

DUBLIN 3-13   KILDARE 1-10
Nov 7, Croke Park, Dublin
Dublin: P Cullen, G O'Driscoll, S Doherty, R Kelleher, T Drumm, K Moran, P O'Neill, B Mullins, B Brogan, A O'Toole 0-2, T Hanahoe 2-1, D Hickey 0-1, B Doyle 1-2, J Keaveney 0-5, J McCarthy 0-1. Subs: M Hickey 0-1 for D Hickey, P Gogarty for McCarthy.

DUBLIN 3-3   MEATH 1-9
Nov 21, Pairc Tailteann, Navan
Dublin: P Cullen, G O'Driscoll, S Doherty, R Kelleher, T Drumm, K Moran, P O'Neill, B Mullins, B Brogan, A O'Toole, T Hanahoe 1-0, J McCarthy, B Doyle 2-1, J Keaveney 0-2, P Gogarty. Subs: P Reilly for Moran, D Hickey for Gogarty.

DUBLIN 0-11   GALWAY 0-7
Dec 5, Croke Park, Dublin
Dublin: P Cullen, G O'Driscoll, S Doherty, R Kelleher, P Reilly, T Drumm, P O'Neill, L Egan 0-3, B Brogan, A O'Toole, T Hanahoe, M Hickey 0-6, B Doyle 0-1, J Brogan, J McCarthy 0-1. Subs: F Ryder for Egan, G Wilson for O'Neill.

DIVISION 1A (SOUTH)	P	W	D	L	Pts
KERRY	5	4	1	0	9
DUBLIN	5	3	1	1	7
CORK	5	2	2	1	6
KILDARE	5	2	0	3	4
GALWAY	5	0	2	3	2
MEATH	5	0	2	3	2

QUARTER-FINAL
Mar 13, Pearse Park, Longford
DUBLIN 2-12   CAVAN 1-7
Dublin: P Cullen, G O'Driscoll, S Doherty, R Kelleher, T Drumm, K Moran, P O'Neill, B Mullins, A Larkin, A O'Toole 1-1, T Hanahoe 0-1, D Hickey 1-0, B Doyle, J Keaveney 0-9, J McCarthy 0-1.

SEMI-FINAL
Mar 27, Croke Park, Dublin
DUBLIN 2-12   MAYO 0-5
Dublin: P Cullen, G O'Driscoll, S Doherty, R Kelleher, T Drumm, K Moran, P O'Neill, B Mullins 1-0, A Larkin, A O'Toole 0-1, T Hanahoe 1-1, D Hickey 0-1, B Doyle 0-1, J Keaveney 0-7, J McCarthy 0-1. Subs: B Brogan for Keaveney.

FINAL
Apr 17, Croke Park, Dublin
KERRY 1-8   DUBLIN 1-6
Dublin: Paddy Cullen, Gay O'Driscoll, Sean Doherty, Robbie Kelleher, Tommy Drumm, Kevin Moran, Pat O'Neill, Bernard Brogan, Alan Larkin, Anton O'Toole, Tony Hanahoe, David Hickey, Bobby Doyle, Jimmy Keaveney 1-4, John McCarthy 0-2. Subs: Michael Hickey for Brogan, Fran Ryder for Larkin.

1977/78

DUBLIN 2-11   KERRY 2-7
Oct 23, Croke Park, Dublin
Dublin: P Cullen, G O'Driscoll, S Doherty, R Kelleher, T Drumm, K Moran, P O'Neill, B Brogan, A Larkin, A O'Toole 0-1, T Hanahoe 0-1, D Hickey, B Doyle 0-1, J Keaveney 0-7, J McCarthy 2-1. Subs: P Gogarty for Hanahoe, J Brogan for Kelleher.

DUBLIN 2-9   KILDARE 1-8
Nov 6, St Conleth's Park, Newbridge
Dublin: P Cullen, G O'Driscoll, S Doherty, R Kelleher, T Drumm, K Moran, P O'Neill, A Larkin, B Brogan 1-0, A O'Toole 0-1, T Hanahoe, D Hickey 0-2, B Doyle, J Keaveney 1-3, J McCarthy 0-3. Sub: P Reilly for O'Neill.

DUBLIN 0-8   CORK 0-5
Nov 13, Pairc Ui Chaoimh, Cork
Dublin: P Cullen, G O'Driscoll, S Doherty, R Kelleher, T Drumm, K Moran, P O'Neill, A Larkin, B Brogan 0-1, A O'Toole 0-2, T Hanahoe, F Ryder 0-2, B Doyle, J Keaveney 0-3, J McCarthy. Sub: L Egan for Larkin.

DUBLIN 4-7   OFFALY 0-3
Nov 20, Croke Park, Dublin
Dublin: P Cullen, J Brogan, S Doherty, R Kelleher, T Drumm, K Moran, P Reilly, B Mullins 2-0, A Larkin, A O'Toole 0-1, B Brogan 0-1, F Ryder 1-1, M Hickey 0-3, J Keaveney 1-0, P Gogarty 0-1.

DUBLIN 1-6   GALWAY 0-8
Dec 4, Tuam Stadium, Tuam
Dublin: P Cullen, G O'Driscoll, S Doherty, L Egan, B Pocock, K Moran, P O'Neill, B Mullins, A Larkin, A O'Toole, T Hanahoe 1-2, D Hickey, B Doyle, J Keaveney 0-4, J McCarthy. Subs: B Brogan for Larkin, R Kelleher for O'Driscoll, J Brogan for Egan.

DIVISION 1A (SOUTH)	P	W	D	L	Pts
DUBLIN	5	5	0	0	10
KILDARE	5	3	1	1	7
CORK	5	2	0	3	4
GALWAY	5	2	0	3	4
KERRY	5	1	1	3	3
OFFALY	5	1	0	4	2

SEMI-FINAL
Apr 2, Croke Park, Dublin

DUBLIN 0-12   LAOIS 0-7

Dublin: P Cullen, G O'Driscoll, S Doherty, R Kelleher, T Drumm 0-1, A Roche, P O'Neill 0-1, B Mullins 0-2, B Brogan 0-1, A O'Toole 0-2, T Hanahoe, D Hickey 0-1, B Doyle 0-3, F Ryder 0-1, J McCarthy. Sub: D Maher for Roche.

FINAL:
Apr 23, Croke Park, Dublin

DUBLIN 2-18   MAYO 2-13

Dublin: Paddy Cullen, Gay O'Driscoll, Sean Doherty, Robbie Kelleher, Fran Ryder, Jim Brogan, Pat O'Neill, Brian Mullins 0-1, Bernard Brogan 1-2, Anton O'Toole 0-3, Tony Hanahoe (capt) 0-1, David Hickey 1-1, Bobby Doyle 0-2, Jimmy Keaveney 0-7, John McCarthy 0-1.

1978/79

KERRY 2-9   DUBLIN 0-8

Oct 8, Croke Park, Dublin

Dublin: P Cullen, G O'Driscoll, S Doherty, R Kelleher, T Drumm, D Maher, P O'Neill, B Mullins 0-3, B Brogan, A O'Toole, T Hanahoe, D Hickey, B Doyle, J Keaveney 0-4, J McCarthy. Subs: P Hogan 0-1 for McCarthy, P Gogarty for Keaveney, J Brogan for Maher.

DUBLIN 3-15   LAOIS 0-11

Nov 5, Croke Park, Dublin

Dublin: P Cullen, R Kelleher, J Brogan, S Doherty, T Drumm, P O'Neill, P Reilly, B Mullins, B Brogan, B Doyle 1-2, T Hanahoe 1-4, A Roche 0-1, P Hogan 0-1, J Keaveney 1-5, P Gogarty 0-2.

KILDARE 2-11   DUBLIN 0-6

Nov 19, Croke Park, Dublin

Dublin: P Cullen, G O'Driscoll, S Doherty, R Kelleher, D Hickey 0-1, P O'Neill, P Reilly, B Mullins, B Brogan, B Doyle, T Hanahoe 0-1, A Roche 0-2, P Hogan, J Keaveney 0-2, P Gogarty. Sub: F Ryder for Doyle.

DUBLIN 0-5   GALWAY 0-5

Dec 3, Tuam Stadium, Tuam

Dublin: N Bernard, R Kelleher, J Brogan, S Doherty, P Reilly, T Drumm, B Pocock, F Ryder, B Brogan, A Roche 0-1, B Mullins 0-1, D Hickey, J McCarthy, J Keaveney 0-1, P Gogarty 0-1. Subs: A O'Toole 0-1 for Ryder, E Butler for Gogarty.

CORK 2-10   DUBLIN 0-5

Dec 10, Pairc Ui Chaoimh, Cork

Dublin: N Bernard, R Kelleher, J Brogan, S Doherty, P Reilly, T Drumm, P O'Neill, B Mullins 0-1, B Brogan, A Roche, D Hickey, A O'Toole 0-1, J McCarthy, J Keaveney 0-3, P Gogarty. Subs: E Butler for Roche, P Hogan for Gogarty.

DIVISION 1 (SOUTH)	P	W	D	L	Pts
CORK	5	4	1	0	9
KERRY	5	4	0	1	8
KILDARE	5	3	0	2	6
GALWAY	5	1	2	2	5
DUBLIN	5	1	1	3	3
LAOIS	5	0	0	5	0

1979/80

KERRY 1-16   DUBLIN 0-10

Oct 7, Austin Stack Park, Tralee

Dublin: M Kennedy, D Foran, M Holden, R Kelleher, T Drumm, F Ryder, J Brogan, J Roynane, B Brogan, P Canavan, B Mullins 0-2, P Ellis 0-1, A O'Toole 0-3, A Larkin 0-2, T Hanahoe. Subs: M Hickey 0-2 for J Brogan, B Rock for Ellis, S Doherty for Ryder.

DUBLIN 3-4   CORK 2-7

Nov 11, Croke Park, Dublin

Dublin: T Fayne, M Kennedy, R Kelleher, D Foran, T Drumm, F Ryder, P Canavan, B Mullins 0-1, J Ronayne, A O'Toole 1-0, B Brogan 0-1, B Doyle 0-1, C Duff, A Larkin 1-0, B Rock 1-1. Subs: P O'Neill for Foran, B Pocock for Duff.

OFFALY 0-12   DUBLIN 1-4

Nov 25, O'Connor Park, Tullamore

Dublin: T Fayne, M Kennedy, D Foran, R Kelleher, T Drumm, F Ryder, P Canavan, B Brogan, J Ronayne, A O'Toole, B Mullins 1-1, B Doyle, P Norton, A Larkin, B Rock 0-3. Sub: PJ Buckley for Larkin.

DUBLIN 2-7   KILDARE 0-12

Dec 9, Catherine Park, Athy

Dublin: T Fayne, M Kennedy, D Foran, R Kelleher, P O'Neill, F Ryder, P Canavan, B Mullins, A Larkin 0-1, A O'Toole 0-1, J Roynane 0-2, PJ Buckley, B Rock 1-3, B Brogan 1-0, C Duff. Sub: T Drumm for Larkin.

GALWAY 1-6   DUBLIN 0-8

Feb 3, Croke Park, Dublin

Dublin: T Fayne, M Kennedy, D Foran, R Kelleher, T Drumm, F Ryder, P O'Neill, J Ronayne, B Mullins, A O'Toole, B Brogan 0-2, PJ Buckley, B Doyle, D Hickey, B Rock 0-6. Sub: P Canavan for Kelleher.

DIVISION 1A (SOUTH)	P	W	D	L	Pts
GALWAY	5	4	1	0	8
KERRY	5	3	1	1	7
CORK	5	2	1	2	5
KILDARE	5	2	0	3	4
DUBLIN	5	1	1	3	3
OFFALY	5	1	0	4	2

1980/81

DUBLIN 0-11   OFFALY 2-5
Nov 2, O'Connor Park, Tullamore
Dublin: J O'Leary, D Foran, T Drumm, R Kelleher, M Kennedy, M Holden, J Thompson, J Ronayne, C Sutton, B Rock 0-1, B Brogan 0-1, J Kearns 0-2, A O'Toole 0-2, V Holden 0-2, M Hickey 0-2. Subs: J Caffrey for Hickey, A Roche for Rock.

DUBLIN 3-9   KILDARE 0-11
Nov 16, Croke Park, Dublin
Dublin: J O'Leary, J Brogan, T Drumm, R Kelleher, M Kennedy, M Holden, PJ Buckley, C Sutton, B Brogan, A O'Toole 1-1, J Caffrey 0-1, J Kearns, C Duff 1-4, V Holden 0-1, J McCarthy 0-1. Sub: B Rock 1-1 for Kearns.

KERRY 2-11   DUBLIN 2-7
Nov 30, Fitzgerald Stadium, Killarney
Dublin: J O'Leary, J Brogan, T Drumm, R Kelleher, M Kennedy 0-1, M Holden, PJ Buckley, B Brogan, C Sutton, J Ronayne 0-1, A O'Toole, C Duff 0-4, J Caffrey 2-0, V Holden, J McCarthy. Subs: B Rock for Sutton, J Thompson 0-1 for McCarthy.

DUBLIN 1-11   CORK 1-9
Dec 14, Croke Park, Dublin
Dublin: J O'Leary, J Brogan, T Drumm, R Kelleher, G McCabe, M Holden, PJ Buckley 0-1, J Ronayne, C Sutton, A O'Toole 0-3, B Brogan 0-2, J Caffrey 0-1, B Rock 0-2, V Holden, J Thompson 0-3. Subs: M Hickey for Caffrey, C Duff 1-0 for V Holden, D Foran for J Brogan.

ROSCOMMON 0-11 DUBLIN 1-5
Feb 1, Dr Hyde Park, Roscommon
Dublin: J O'Leary, J Brogan, T Drumm, R Kelleher, M Kennedy, M Holden, PJ Buckley, C Sutton, J Kearns, A O'Toole, B Brogan, P O'Toole 0-1, B Rock 1-3, C Duff, J Thompson. Subs: J Roynane 0-1 for Kearns, J Caffrey for P O'Toole.

DUBLIN 2-8   DOWN 0-9
Feb 22, Croke Park, Dublin
Dublin: J O'Leary, J Brogan, T Drumm, R Kelleher, G McCabe, M Holden, M Kennedy, B Brogan, J Ronayne, A O'Toole 0-1, B Doyle 0-1, C Duff 1-2, J McCarthy, J Thompson 0-3, A McCaul 1-1.

DUBLIN 2-8   ARMAGH 2-3
Mar 1, Croke Park, Dublin
Dublin: J O'Leary J Brogan, T Drumm, R Kelleher, G McCabe, M Holden, M Kennedy, B Brogan, J Ronayne, A O'Toole 0-1, B Rock 1-2, C Duff 0-3, J McCarthy, J Thompson 1-1, A McCaul 0-1. Subs: PJ Buckley for McCabe, V Holden for McCarthy.

DIVISION 1	P	W	D	L	Pts
KERRY	7	5	1	1	11
ROSCOMMON	7	4	2	1	10
ARMAGH	7	4	1	2	9
DUBLIN	7	4	1	2	9
CORK	7	3	2	2	8
OFFALY	7	2	2	3	6
DOWN	7	1	1	5	3
KILDARE	7	0	0	7	0

PLAY-OFF
Mar 15, Croke Park, Dublin
DUBLIN 1-7   ARMAGH 1-5
Dublin: J O'Leary, J Brogan, T Drumm, R Kelleher, PJ Buckley 0-1, M Holden, M Kennedy, B Brogan, J Ronayne, A O'Toole, B Rock 0-2, C Duff 1-3, J Thompson 0-1, V Holden, A McCaul. Subs: J McCarthy for V Holden, J Kearns for Duff.

QUARTER-FINAL:
Apr 5, Dr Hyde Park, Roscommon
MAYO 1-11   DUBLIN 1-10
Dublin: J O'Leary, J Brogan, T Drumm, R Kelleher, PJ Buckley, M Holden, G McCabe, B Brogan 0-2, J Ronayne, A O'Toole, B Rock 0-1, C Duff 0-4, J Thompson 0-1, A Roche 1-1, A McCaul 0-1. Subs: D Foran for McCabe, M Hickey for McCaul, D Deasy for Rock.

1981/82

DUBLIN 1-12   MAYO 1-4
Oct 4, Flanagan Park, Ballinrobe
Dublin: J O'Leary, M Kennedy, V Conroy, P Heffernan, T Drumm, M Holden, PJ Buckley, J Ronayne, J Kearns 0-3, B Jordan, P Ellis 0-1, C Duff 0-3, B Doyle, A McCaul 0-5, J McCarthy 1-0. Sub: C Sutton for Ronayne.

OFFALY 1-11   DUBLIN 0-12
Oct 18, Croke Park, Dublin
Dublin: J O'Leary, M Kennedy, V Conroy, P Heffernan, T Drumm, M Holden, PJ Buckley, J Ronayne, J Kearns 0-2, B Jordan, P Ellis, C Duff, J Thompson 0-4, A McCaul 0-5, J McCarthy. Sub: C Sutton 0-1 for Ellis.

DUBLIN 0-9   GALWAY 0-9
Nov 1, Dunlo Grounds, Ballinasloe
Dublin: J O'Leary, M Kennedy, V Conroy, P Heffernan, S Wade, M Holden, PJ Buckley, J Kearns, J Ronayne, B Doyle, B Jordan 0-2, C Duff 0-3, J Thompson 0-1, A McCaul 0-3, J McCarthy. Subs: D Foran for Heffernan, C Sutton for Kearns, Kearns for McCarthy.

KERRY 1-7   DUBLIN 1-7
Nov 15, Croke Park, Dublin
Dublin: J O'Leary, M Kennedy, V Conroy, D Foran, R Hazley, M Holden, PJ Buckley, T Drumm 0-1, J Ronayne, D Carr, B Jordan, C Duff 0-3, J Thompson 0-1, A McCaul 0-2, M Loftus. Subs: J McCarthy for Carr, J Brogan for Kennedy, B Kavanagh for Loftus.

DUBLIN 1-5   CORK 0-6
Nov 29, Pairc Ui Chaoimh, Cork
Dublin: J O'Leary, M Kennedy, V Conroy, D Foran, R Hazley, M Holden, PJ Buckley, T Drumm 0-1, B Kavanagh, D Carr, B Jordan 1-0, A Walsh 0-1, J Thompson 0-1, A McCaul 0-2, M Loftus. Subs: S Wade for Hazley, B Doyle for Carr.

DUBLIN 4-13   ROSCOMMON 1-8
Jan 31, Croke Park, Dublin
Dublin: J O'Leary, M Kennedy, V Conroy, D Foran, S Wade, M Holden, PJ Buckley, T Drumm 0-1, B Kavanagh, M Loftus 1-1, B Jordan 0-2, A Walsh, J Thompson 0-2, A McCaul 2-2, C Duff 1-4. Sub: J Kearns 0-1 for Walsh.

ARMAGH 0-8   DUBLIN 0-5
Feb 21, Athletic Grounds, Armagh
Dublin: J O'Leary, M Kennedy, P Canavan, D Foran, S Wade, M Holden, R Hazley, B Kavanagh 0-1, T Drumm, M Loftus, B Jordan, A Walsh 0-2, J Thompson, A McCaul 0-1, C Duff 0-1. Subs: C Sutton for Foran, J Kearns for Thompson.

DIVISION 1	P	W	D	L	Pts
ARMAGH	7	4	2	1	10
CORK	7	4	0	3	8
KERRY	7	4	0	3	8
OFFALY	7	4	0	3	8
DUBLIN	7	3	1	3	7
MAYO	7	3	1	3	7
GALWAY	7	2	1	4	5
ROSCOMMON	7	1	1	5	3

1982/83

DUBLIN 3-7   MAYO 0-6
Oct 10, Croke Park, Dublin
Dublin: J O'Leary, M Kennedy, R Hazley, V Conroy, P Canavan, T Drumm, S Wade, G O'Neill 0-1, P Ryan, B Rock 0-1, B Jordan 1-0, C Duff 0-2, N Gaffney, A McCaul 1-1, B Murray. Subs: C Redmond 1-2 for Gaffney, B Mullins for Jordan, D Deasy for O'Neill.

OFFALY 4-9   DUBLIN 3-1
Oct 24, O'Connor Park, Tullamore
Dublin: J O'Leary, M Kennedy, V Conroy, R Hazley, P Canavan, T Drumm, S Wade, G O'Neill, P Ryan, B Rock 1-0, B Jordan, C Duff 0-1, C Redmond 1-0, A

McCaul 1-0, B Murray. Subs: J Caffrey for Canavan, K Barry for Jordan, M Holden for O'Neill.

DOWN 1-6   DUBLIN 0-8
Nov 7, Croke Park, Dublin
Dublin: J O'Leary, M Kennedy, V Conroy, R Hazley, T Drumm, M Holden, S Wade, P Ryan, J Caffrey, B Rock 0-4, G O'Neill, PJ Buckley, C Redmond, A McCaul 0-4, B Murray. Subs: M Loftus for Redmond, D Foran for Kennedy, A White for Murray.

DUBLIN 0-8   KERRY 0-7
Nov 21, Austin Stack Park, Tralee
Dublin: J O'Leary, D Foran, G Hargan, R Hazley, T Drumm, P Ryan, S Wade, J Kearns 0-1, J Caffrey, B Rock 0-1, W Hughes 0-2, C Duff 0-3, C Redmond, M Kennedy, A McCaul 0-1.

DUBLIN 1-8   CORK 1-7
Feb 13, Croke Park, Dublin
Dublin: J O'Leary, D Foran, G Hargan, R Hazley, T Drumm, P Ryan, PJ Buckley, D Deasy, J Kearns 0-1, B Rock 1-2, W Hughes 0-1, C Duff 0-3, C Redmond, M Kennedy, A McCaul 0-1. Subs: J Ronayne for Deasy, D McGrath for Ryan.

DERRY 1-11   DUBLIN 1-10
Feb 27, Wolfe Tone Park, Bellaghy
Dublin: J O'Leary, D Foran, G Hargan, R Hazley T Drumm, M Kennedy, PJ Buckley, J Kearns 0-1, T Conroy 0-1, B Rock 0-1, W Hughes, C Duff 0-3, C Redmond 1-1, D McGrath 0-1, A McCaul 0-2. Sub: D Deasy for Conroy.

DUBLIN 1-8   ARMAGH 0-11
Mar 13, Croke Park, Dublin
Dublin: J McNally, M Kennedy, G Hargan, R Hazley, T Drumm, P Ryan, PJ Buckley, J Kearns 1-1, T Conroy, B Rock, W Hughes, C Duff 0-4, C Redmond 0-1, D McGrath, A McCaul 0-2. Subs: R Crean for Redmond, J Ronayne for Conroy.

DIVISION 1	P	W	D	L	Pts
ARMAGH	7	5	2	0	12
DOWN	7	4	3	0	11
CORK	7	4	1	2	7
DUBLIN	7	3	1	3	7
KERRY	7	3	1	3	7
OFFALY	7	3	0	4	6
DERRY	7	2	0	5	4
MAYO	7	0	0	7	0

1983/84

DUBLIN 1-6   MEATH 1-6
Oct 9, Pairc Tailteann, Navan
Dublin: J O'Leary, M Holden, G Hargan, M Kennedy, P Canavan, T Drumm, PJ Buckley, J Ronayne, C

Maher, B Rock 0-3, T Conroy, C Redmond, J Caffrey 0-1, A McCaul 0-1, J McNally 1-0. Subs: J Kearns for Redmond, R Crean 0-1 for McCaul.

OFFALY 1-4   DUBLIN 0-3
Oct 23, Croke Park, Dublin
Dublin: J O'Leary, M Holden, G Hargan, M Kennedy, P Canavan, T Drumm, PJ Buckley, J Ronayne, C Maher, B Rock 0-3, J Kearns, R Crean, J Caffrey, C Redmond, J McNally. Subs: A McCaul for Crean, V Conroy for Maher.

DOWN 1-6   DUBLIN 0-7
Nov 6, Pairc Esler, Newry
Dublin: J O'Leary, M Holden, G Hargan, M Kennedy, P Canavan, T Drumm, PJ Buckley 0-2, J Ronayne 0-1, C Maher, B Rock 0-2, J McNally, J Kearns 0-1, J Caffrey, A McCaul, C Redmond 0-1. Subs: V Conroy for McCaul, R Crean for Redmond.

DUBLIN 2-9   KERRY 2-9
Nov 20, Croke Park, Dublin
Dublin: J O'Leary, M Holden, G Hargan, M Kennedy, P Canavan, T Drumm, PJ Buckley, D Sheehan, J Kearns 0-4, B Rock 1-1, J Caffrey, B Jordan, D O'Brien 0-3, B Brogan, J McNally 0-1. Sub: M O'Callaghan 1-0 for Jordan.

CORK 1-9 DUBLIN 1-3
Dec 4, Pairc Ui Chaoimh
Dublin: J O'Leary, M Holden, G Hargan, M Kennedy, P Canavan, T Drumm, PJ Buckley, J Kearns, D Sheehan, B Rock 0-1, J Caffrey, M O'Callaghan, D O'Brien, A McCaul 1-2, J McNally. Subs: J Ronayne for O'Brien, E Jordan for O'Callaghan.

DUBLIN 1-9   KILDARE 1-2
Feb 5, Croke Park, Dublin
Dublin: J O'Leary, M Holden, G Hargan, M Kennedy, P Canavan, T Drumm, PJ Buckley, B Mullins, J Ronayne 0-1, B Rock 1-4, T Conroy, M O'CalJaghan, J Caffrey 0-1, B Brogan 0-1, J McNally 0-2. Subs: D Sheehan for O'Callaghan, R Hazley for Kennedy, J Kearns for Brogan.

ARMAGH 0-7   DUBLIN 0-5
Feb 19, Davitt Park, Lurgan
Dublin: J O'Leary, M Holden, G Hargan, M Kennedy, R Hazley, T Drumm, PJ Buckley 0-1, B Mullins, J Ronayne 0-1, B Rock 0-1, T Conroy 0-2, J Kearns, D Sheehan, B Brogan, J McNally. Sub: A McCaul for Sheehan.

DIVISION 1	P	W	D	L	Pts
KERRY	7	3	4	0	10
DOWN	7	3	2	2	8
MEATH	7	3	2	2	8
CORK	7	3	1	3	7
ARMAGH	7	3	1	3	7
OFFALY	7	3	0	4	6
KILDARE	7	2	2	3	6
DUBLIN	7	1	2	4	4

1984/85

DUBLIN 1-8   MONAGHAN 0-5
Oct 14, St Mary's Park, Castleblaney
Dublin: L Lillis, M Holden, G Hargan, M Kennedy, J McCarthy, T Byrne, PJ Buckley, J Ronayne 0-1, J Kearns 0-1, B Rock 0-5, T Conroy, C Duff, M Egan 0-1, M O'Callaghan 1-0, J McNally. Subs: T Cassin for Egan, C Sutton for Ronayne.

ROSCOMMON 0-8   DUBLIN 0-6
Nov 11, Croke Park, Dublin
Dublin: J O'Leary, D McGrath, G Hargan, M Kennedy, P Canavan, T Byrne, PJ Buckley, J Kearns, J Bissett, M Egan 0-1, M O'Callaghan, C Duff 0-5, T Conroy, P Dwane, J McNally. Subs: B Mullins for Kearns, J Ronayne for Egan.

MAYO 1-8 DUBLIN 1-5
Nov 18, James Stephens Park, Ballina
Dublin: J O'Leary, D McGrath, G Hargan, M Kennedy, P Canavan, T Byrne, D Synnott 0-1, J Ronayne, C Sutton, T Cassin 0-3, J McNally 1-1, M O'Callaghan, T Conroy, B Mullins, C Duff. Subs: F McGrath for Kennedy, J McCarthy for Duff, J Bissett for Sutton.

DUBLIN 1-16   OFFALY 0-7
Nov 25, Croke Park, Dublin
Dublin: J O'Leary, D McGrath, F McGrath, PJ Buckley, P Canavan, T Byrne, D Synnott 0-1, T Conroy 0-3, B Mullins, G O'Neill, J McNally 0-3, M O'Callaghan 0-1, A McCaul 0-1, C Duff 1-5, J McCarthy 0-2.

DUBLIN 1-6   DONEGAL 1-4
Dec 2, MacCumhail Park, Ballybofey
Dublin: J O'Leary, D McCarthy, P McCarthy, PJ Buckley, P Canavan, T Byrne, D Synnott, T Conroy, B Mullins, A McCaul, J McNally, M O'Callaghan, G O'Neill, C Duff 0-2, J McCarthy. Subs: B Rock 1-3 O'Neill, T Cassin for O'Callaghan 0-1.

WEXFORD 1-5   DUBLIN 0-7
Feb 3, Croke Park, Dublin
Dublin: J O'Leary, M Holden, D McGrath, P Canavan 0-1, T Byrne, D Synnott, T Conroy, B Mullins, B Rock 0-2, J McNally, PJ Buckley, T Cassin 0-1, C Duff 0-1, M O'Callaghan 0-2, Sub: J Ronayne for Buckley.

DUBLIN 2-8   LOUTH 0-4
Feb 10, St Mary's Park, Ardee
Dublin: J O'Leary, M Holden, F McGrath, D McGrath, M Johnson, P Canavan, D Synnott, J Ronayne, B Mullins, B Rock 1-2, T Conroy 0-1, C Duff 0-1, T Cassin 0-2, S Reilly, M O'Callaghan 1-2.

DIVISION 2	P	W	D	L	Pts
MONAGHAN	7	4	2	1	10
WEXFORD	7	4	1	2	9
ROSCOMMON	7	4	1	2	9
DUBLIN	7	4	0	3	8
MAYO	7	2	2	3	6
LOUTH	7	2	1	4	5
DONEGAL	7	2	1	4	5
OFFALY	7	1	2	4	4

1985/86

DUBLIN 0-13   CORK 0-8
Oct 13, Pairc Ui Chaoimh, Cork
Dublin: J O'Leary, M Kennedy G Hargan, D McGrath, P Canavan, N McCaffrey, D Synnott, J Ronayne, J Kearns 0-2, P Dwane 0-2, T Conroy 0-1, T Carr 0-1, A McCaul 0-1, J McNally, C Duff 0-5.

LONGFORD 3-8   DUBLIN 1-11
Oct 27, Croke Park, Dublin
Dublin: J O'Leary, M Holden, G Hargan, R Hazley, M Deegan, N McCaffrey, D Synnott 0-1, J Kearns 0-1, J Ronayne 1-0, P Dwane, T Conroy 0-1, T Carr, C Duff, B Rock 0-6, J McNally 0-2. Subs: J Caffrey for Duff, A McCaul for Dwane.

DUBLIN 2-7   WEXFORD 0-6
Nov 10, Belfield Park, Enniscorthy
Dublin: J O'Leary, M Holden, G Hargan, T Byrne, M Kennedy, N McCaffrey, D Synnott, J Ronayne, J Kearns 0-1, M Deegan, T Conroy, T Carr 1-1, B Rock 1-3, J Caffrey, J McNally 0-1. Subs: R Cooke for Deegan, C Duff 0-1 for Rock.

DUBLIN 0-15   DONEGAL 0-8
Nov 24, Croke Park, Dublin
Dublin: J O'Leary, M Holden, G Hargan, M Kennedy, M Deegan, N McCaffrey, D Synnott, J Kearns 0-2, J Ronayne, B Rock 0-5, P Clarke 0-1, T Carr 0-2, J Pearse 0-1, T Conroy 0-3, J McNally. Subs: P Cavanan for Deegan, C Duff for Clarke, M O'Callaghan 0-1 for Pearse.

MAYO 2-5   DUBLIN 0-4
Dec 1, MacHale Park, Castlebar
Dublin: J O'Leary, M Holden, G Hargan, M Kennedy, P Canavan, N McCaffrey, D Synott, J Ronayne, J Kearns 0-1, B Rock 0-1, B Mullins 0-1, M O'Callaghan, J Pearse, T Conroy, J McNally 0-1. Subs: C Duff for Pearse, P Dwane for O'Callaghan, D McGrath for Kennedy.

DUBLIN 0-12   GALWAY 0-10
Feb 2, Duggan Park, Ballinasloe
Dublin: J O'Leary, P Canavan, G Hargan, M Kennedy, PJ Buckley, N McCaffrey, D Synnott, J Caffrey, J

Ronayne, C Redmond 0-3, T Carr 0-2, C Duff, B Rock 0-5, T Conroy, J McNally 0-1. Subs: S Fleming 0-1 for Buckley, B Cooke for Caffrey.

DUBLIN 3-6   CAVAN 0-9
Mar 2, Croke Park, Dublin:
Dublin: J O'Leary, PJ Buckley, G Hargan, M Kennedy, P Clarke, N McCaffrey, D Synnott, J Ronayne, J Bissett, C Redmond, T Carr 0-1, C Duff 0-1, B Rock 2-4, J Caffrey, J McNally 1-0. Subs: D Sheehan for Caffrey, T Cassin for Duff.

DIVISION 2	P	W	D	L	Pts
MAYO	7	5	1	1	11
DUBLIN	7	5	0	2	10
DONEGAL	7	4	1	2	9
CORK	7	4	1	2	9
CAVAN	7	3	1	3	7
LONGFORD	7	3	0	4	6
GALWAY	7	2	0	5	4
WEXFORD	7	0	0	7	0

QUARTER-FINAL
Mar 30, Croke Park, Dublin
DUBLIN 2-8   MEATH 1-10
Dublin: J O'Leary, P Canavan, G Hargan, M Kennedy, P Clarke, N McCaffrey, D Synnott, J Kearns 0-1, J Bissett, C Redmond, T Carr 1-1, C Duff, B Rock 1-5, T Conroy 0-1, J McNally. Subs: D Sheehan for Duff, F O'Brien for McNally, J Caffrey for Bissett.

SEMI-FINAL
Apr 20, Croke Park, Dublin
LAOIS 0-12   DUBLIN 1-7
Dublin: J O'Leary, P Canavan, G Hargan, M Kennedy, P Clarke, N McCaffrey, D Synnott, J Ronayne, J Kearns 0-1, C Redmond, T Conroy, D Sheehan 1-0, B Rock 0-4, T Carr 0-1, J McNally 0-1. Subs: T Cassin for Redmond, J Bissett for Cassin.

1986/87

MEATH 2-13   DUBLIN 0-9
Nov 2, Croke Park, Dublin
Dublin: P Smith, V Conroy, G Hargan, M Kennedy, B Hickey, G O'Neill, D Synnott, J Bissett, T Carr, L Close, B Mullins, C Duff 0-3, C Redmond, D Deasy 0-2, J McNally 0-2. Subs: P Clarke 0-1 for Bissett, P Caffrey for Hickey, D DeLappe 0-1 for Close.

MONAGHAN 2-10   DUBLIN 2-8
Nov 16, Croke Park, Dublin
Dublin: C McMahon, V Conroy, G Hargan, M Kennedy 1-0, P Caffrey, D Carroll 0-1, D Synnott, J McNally, P Clarke, D Sheehan 1-1, J Kearns, C Redmond 0-3, D DeLappe, C Duff 0-3, L Close. Sub: E Heery for Kearns.

KERRY 0-10   DUBLIN 0-8
Nov 30, Austin Stack Park, Tralee
Dublin: C McMahon, V Conroy, G Hargan, M Kennedy, P Caffrey, E Heery, D Synnott, P Clarke, J McNally, D Sheehan, T Carr, C Redmond 0-2, D DeLappe 0-2, D McCarthy, C Duff 0-4. Subs: D Deasy for Clarke, J Bissett for Duff.

DUBLIN 0-11   ARMAGH 1-6
Dec 14, Croke Park, Dublin
Dublin: C McMahon, V Conroy, G Hargan, M Kennedy, D Synnott, E Heery, P Caffrey, J McNally, B Kavanagh, D Sheehan 0-1, C Duff 0-4, C Redmond 0-2, D DeLappe 0-2, D McCarthy, A McCaul 0-2. Sub: M Galvin for Kavanagh.

DUBLIN 0-8   MAYO 0-6
Feb 8, Croke Park, Dublin
Dublin: J O'Leary, G O'Neill, V Conroy, M Kennedy, P Caffrey, D Carrol, T O'Driscoll 0-1, M Galvin, D Bolger 0-1, D Sheehan 0-1, J McNally 0-1, C Duff 0-4, C Redmond, B Rock, D McCarthy. Sub: E Heery for Caffrey.

DUBLIN 2-12   DOWN 2-8
Feb 22, St Patrick's Park, Newcastle
Dublin: J O'Leary, S Fleming, V Conroy, M Kennedy, E Heery, D Carroll, T O'Driscoll, J McNally, M Galvin 0-2, D McCarthy 0-1, C Redmond 1-0, C Duff 0-1, D DeLappe 0-3, B Rock 0-4, A McCaul 1-1. Sub: N McCaffrey for Fleming.

DUBLIN 1-11   ROSCOMMON 0-8
Mar 8, Croke Park, Dublin
Dublin: J O'Leary, D Carroll, V Conroy, M Kennedy, E Heery, N McCaffrey, T O'Driscoll, M Galvin 0-2, D Bolger, B Rock 0-3, C Redmond 1-0, C Duff 0-3, D DeLappe 0-1, J McNally, A McCaul 0-2.

DIVISION 1	P	W	D	L	Pts
KERRY	7	5	0	2	10
MEATH	7	4	1	2	9
MONAGHAN	7	4	1	2	9
DUBLIN	7	4	0	3	8
MAYO	7	3	0	4	6
ROSCOMMON	7	2	1	4	5
ARMAGH	7	2	1	4	5
DOWN	7	2	0	5	4

QUARTER-FINAL
Apr 5, Croke Park, Dublin
DUBLIN 1-10   CORK 1-7
Dublin: J O'Leary, G O'Neill, G Hargan, M Kennedy, D Synnott, N McCaffrey, P Caffrey, J Ronayne, D Bolger, D Sheehan 0-1, B Rock 1-4, C Duff, D DeLappe 0-2, J McNally, A McCaul 0-3. Sub: T O'Driscoll for McCaffrey.

SEMI-FINAL
Apr 19, O'Moore Park, Portlaoise
DUBLIN 1-8   GALWAY 0-8
Dublin: J O'Leary, D Carroll, G Hargan, M Kennedy, D Synnott, G O'Neill 1-0, T O'Driscoll, J Ronayne, D Bolger, B Rock 0-4, M Galvin, C Duff 0-1, D DeLappe 0-1, J McNally, A McCaul 0-2. Subs: N McCaffrey for O'Driscoll, C Redmond for Bolger, P Caffrey for O'Neill.

FINAL
Apr 26, Croke Park, Dublin
DUBLIN 1-11   KERRY 0-11
Dublin: John O'Leary, Dave Carroll, Gerry Hargan, Mick Kennedy, Dave Synnott, Glen O'Neill, Noel McCaffrey, Jim Roynane 0-2, Declan Bolger 0-1, Barney Rock 0-3, Joe McNally, Ciaran Duff 1-3, David DeLappe, Mick Galvin 0-1, Anto McCaul. Sub: Declan Sheehan 0-1 for DeLappe.

1987/88

DUBLIN 2-5   MEATH 0-11
Nov 8, Croke Park, Dublin
Dublin: J O'Leary, D Carroll, G Hargan, D Synnott, P Clarke 0-1, N McCaffrey, E Heery, J Bissett, D Bolger, C Redmond, J McNally, C Duff 1-2, D DeLappe 0-1, J Prendergast 1-0, M O'Hanlon. Sub: T Conroy 0-1 for O'Hanlon.

DUBLIN 1-13   MONAGHAN 0-5
Nov 22, St Mary's Park, Castleblaney
Dublin: J O'Leary, D Carroll, G Hargan, D Synnott, P Clarke 0-1, N McCaffrey, E Heery 0-1, J Bissett, D Bolger, T Conroy, C Redmond, C Duff 1-6, D DeLappe 0-4, J Prendergast 0-1, A McCaul. Subs: J McNally for Bissett, C Crowley for Redmond, J Kearns for Prendergast.

DUBLIN 1-9   KERRY 2-5
Dec 6, Croke Park, Dublin
Dublin: J O'Leary, D Carroll, G Hargan, D Synnott, P Clarke, N McCaffrey, E Heery 0-1, J Bissett, D Bolger, T Conroy, C Redmond, C Duff 0-5, D DeLappe 0-2, J McNally, A McCaul 1-1. Sub: J Prendergast for Bissett.

DUBLIN 0-9   ARMAGH 1-3
Dec 13, Davitt Park, Lurgan
Dublin: J O'Leary, M Kennedy, G Hargan, D Synnott, P Clarke, N McCaffrey, E Heery, J Bissett, D Bolger 0-1, D DeLappe 0-1, J McNally, C Duff 0-2, C Redmond 0-1, J Prendergast 0-1, A McCaul 0-3. Subs: J Kearns Ior Bissett, T Conroy for Prendergast.

DUBLIN 1-7   MAYO 1-4
Feb 7, MacHale Park, Castlebar
Dublin: J O'Leary, D Carroll, G Hargan, M Kennedy, D

Synnott, N McCaffrey, E Heery, J Kearns, D Bolger, V Murphy, J McNally, C Duff 0-1, C Redmond 0-3, M Galvin, A McCaul 0-2. Subs: T Conroy for Kearns, D DeLappe for Duff, P Clarke 1-1 for Galvin.

DUBLIN 1-9   DERRY 0-5
Feb 14, Parnell Park, Dublin
Dublin: J O'Leary, D Carroll, G Hargan, M Kennedy, D Synnott, N McCaffrey, E Heery, T Conroy, D Bolger, P Clarke 0-1, J Prendergast 1-0, V Murphy 0-2, D DeLappe, J McNally, A McCaul. Subs: B O'Hagan for Synnott.

DUBLIN 1-10   CORK 1-10
Feb 28, Pairc Ui Chaoimh, Cork
Dublin: J O'Leary, D Carroll, G Hargan, M Kennedy, D Synnott, E Heery 0-1, P Clarke, T Conroy, J Bissett, V Murphy, J Prendergast, M O'Hanlon 0-3, D DeLappe 0-2, J McNally 1-0, A McCaul 0-4. Subs: T O'Driscoll for Synnott, J Kearns for Bissett.

DIVISION 1	P	W	D	L	Pts
Dublin	7	5	2	0	12
Meath	7	4	2	1	10
Monaghan	7	4	1	2	9
Derry	7	3	0	4	6
Armagh	7	2	1	1	5
Kerry	7	2	1	4	5
Mayo	7	2	1	4	5
Cork	7	1	2	4	4

QUARTER-FINAL
Mar 27, Croke Park, Dublin
DUBLIN 0-10   LONGFORD 0-4
Dublin: J O'Leary, D Carroll, G Hargan, M Kennedy, D Synnott, N McCaffrey, E Heery, T Conroy, D Bolger, V Murphy 0-1, J Prendergast, M O'Hanlon 0-1, D DeLappe 0-3, J McNally, A McCaul 0-1. Subs: C Redmond 0-1 for Conroy, C Duff 0-2 for Prendergast, P Clarke 0-1 for Murphy.

SEMI-FINAL
Apr 3, Croke Park, Dublin
DUBLIN 4-12   MONAGHAN 1-8
Dublin: J O'Leary, D Carroll, G Hargan, M Kennedy, D Synnott, N McCaffrey, E Heery, J Bissett 0-1, D Bolger, V Murphy 0-1, C Redmond 0-1, C Duff 1-5, D DeLappe 0-3, J McNally 2-0, A McCaul. Sub: M Galvin 1-1 for McCaul.

FINAL
Apr 17, Croke Park, Dublin
DUBLIN 1-8   MEATH 0-11
Dublin: John O'Leary, Dave Carroll, Gerry Hargan, Mick Kennedy, David Synnott, Noel McCaffrey, Eamonn Heery, Jim Bissett, Declan Bolger, Tommy Conroy 0-1, Vinnie Murphy 0-1, Ciaran Duff 0-3, David DeLappe 0-2, Joe McNally 0-1, Mick Galvin 1-0. Sub: Paul Clarke for Bolger.

FINAL REPLAY
May 22, Croke Park, Dublin
MEATH 2-13   DUBLIN 0-11
Dublin: John O'Leary, Dave Carroll, Gerry Hargan, Mick Kennedy, David Synnott, Noel McCaffrey, Paul Clarke, Jim Bissett, Declan Bolger, Vinnie Murphy 0-2, Charlie Redmond, Ciaran Duff 0-1, David DeLappe, Joe McNally 0-1, Barney Rock 0-7. Subs: Tim O'Driscoll for Synnott, Brian O'Hagan for Carroll, John Prendergast for O'Driscoll.

1988/89

DERRY 1-7   DUBLIN 0-6
Oct 23, Wolfe Tone Park, Bellaghy
Dublin: J O'Leary, B O'Hagan, G Hargan, M Kennedy, G Walsh, T Carr, D Synnott 0-1, P Bealin, D Bolger, M Bissett, V Murphy, C Duff 0-2, C Redmond, M Galvin 0-3, J McNally. Subs: M Deegan for O'Hagan, A McNally for Bealin, B Rock for Bolger.

DUBLIN 1-16   DOWN 0-4
Nov 6, Croke Park, Dublin
Dublin: J O'Leary, G Walsh, G Hargan, M Kennedy, D Synnott 0-1, T Carr, M Deegan, T Conroy, D Bolger, V Murphy 0-2, C Redmond 0-3, C Duff 1-4, D DeLappe 0-1, M Galvin 0-2, A McNally 0-2. Subs: B Rock 0-1 for Redmond, K Walsh for Synnott, P Bealin for Duff.

DUBLIN 2-12   MONAGHAN 1-8
Nov 20, Croke Park, Dublin
Dublin: J O'Leary, C Walsh, G Hargan, M Kennedy, D Synnott 0-1, T Carr, M Deegan, P Bealin, D Bolger 0-2, V Murphy 0-1, C Redmond 0-4, C Duff 1-1, D DeLappe 0-2, M Galvin 1-1, A McNally. Subs: B Rock for Redmond, P Nugent for Duff.

DUBLIN 1-12   MEATH 0-4
Dec 4, Pairc Tailteann, Navan
Dublin: J O'Leary, E Heery, C Walsh, M Kennedy, D Synnott, T Carr, M Deegan 0-1, P Bealin 0-1, D Bolger, V Murphy 0-3, C Redmond, C Duff 1-3, D DeLappe 0-3, M Galvin 0-1, A McNally.

DUBLIN 1-12   ARMAGH 0-7
Feb 5, Croke Park, Dublin
Dublin: J O'Leary, C Walsh, G Hargan, M Kennedy, N McCaffrey, T Carr, M Deegan, P Bealin, D Bolger, B Rock 0-4, C Redmond 0-4, C Duff 0-1, P Nugent 1-1, M Galvin 0-1, A McNally. Subs: E Heery 0-1 for Duff, M Bissett for Bolger, D Carroll for Hargan.

KERRY 1-10   DUBLIN 0-11
Feb 12, Austin Stack Park, Tralee
Dublin: J O'Leary, C Walsh, G Hargan, M Kennedy, N McCaffrey, T Carr, M Deegan, P Bealin, D Bolger 0-1, V Murphy, C Redmond 0-1, B Rock 0-8, P Nugent

0-1, M Galvin, A McNally. Subs: D Carroll for Walsh, E Heery for Bolger.

DUBLIN 1-10   DONEGAL 0-9
Feb 26, Croke Park, Dublin
Dublin: J O'Leary, D Carroll, G Hargan, M Kennedy, G Walsh, T Carr, M Deegan 0-1, P Bealin, J Ronayne, V Murphy 0-1, C Redmond 0-1, B Rock 0-5, M O'Callaghan, M Galvin 1-1, A McNally 0-1. Subs: E Heery for Bealin, M Bissett for O'Callaghan.

DIVISION 1	P	W	D	L	Pts
DUBLIN	7	5	0	2	10
KERRY	7	5	0	2	10
DERRY	7	4	1	2	9
ARMAGH	7	4	0	3	8
DOWN	7	3	1	3	7
DONEGAL	7	3	0	4	6
MONAGHAN	7	2	0	5	4
MEATH	7	1	0	6	2

QUARTER-FINAL
Mar 26, O'Moore Park, Portlaoise
DUBLIN 1-11   WEXFORD 0-7
Dublin: J O'Leary, D Carroll, G Hargan, M Kennedy, E Heery, T Carr 0-1, M Deegan 0-1, J Roynane, D Bolger, V Murphy, C Redmond 0-1, C Duff 0-1, P Nugent, B Rock 0-7, A McNally. Sub: A McCaul 1-0 for Bolger.

SEMI-FINAL
Apr 9, Croke Park, Dublin
DUBLIN 1-10   CAVAN 1-9
Dublin: J O'Leary, D Carroll, G Hargan, M Kennedy, E Heery, T Carr, M Deegan, J Ronayne, V Murphy, P Nugent, C Redmond 0-3, C Duff, B Rock 0-6, M Galvin 1-1, A McCaul. Subs: N McCaffrey for Nugent, A McNally for McCaul.

'HOME' FINAL
Apr 23, Croke Park, Dublin
CORK 0-15   DUBLIN 0-12
Dublin: John O'Leary, Eamonn Heery 0-1, Gerry Hargan, Mick Kennedy, Noel McCaffrey 0-1, Tommy Carr 0-1, Mick Deegan, Jim Ronayne, Paul Bealin, Vinnie Murphy, Charlie Redmond 0-1, Ciaran Duff 0-2, Barney Rock 0-5, Mick Galvin, Alan McNally 0-1. Sub: Dave Carroll for Bealin.

1989/90

DUBLIN 4-18   DERRY 1-9
Oct 22, Croke Park, Dublin
Dublin: J O'Leary, M O'Neill, G Hargan, E Heery 0-1, K Barr, T Carr 0-2, P Curran 0-3, D Foran 0-2, P Clarke, P Nugent, V Murphy 0-5, M Galvin 0-1, C Duff 0-2, J McNally 4-0, A McNally 0-1. Subs: D Keegan 0-1 for A McNally, R Collier for Heery.

DUBLIN 1-17   DOWN 2-11
Nov 5, Pairc Esler, Newry
Dublin: J O'Leary, R Collier, D Foran, E Heery, K Barr, T Carr, P Curran 0-1, P Nugent, P Clarke 0-1, V Murphy 0-2, T Conroy, C Duff 0-7, B Rock 1-5, J McNally 0-1, D Keegan. Subs: M O'Neill for Collier, M Galvin for Keegan, J Pierce for Nugent.

CORK 3-13   DUBLIN 1-16
Nov 19, Pairc Ui Chaoimh, Cork
Dublin: J O'Leary, P O'Donoghue, G Hargan, M Kennedy, K Barr, T Carr, P Curran 0-2, D Foran, P Clarke 0-2, T Conroy 1-0, V Murphy 0-2, J Madden 0-1, B Rock 0-6, J McNally 0-2, M Galvin 0-1. Subs: C Duff for Madden, P Nugent for Murphy.

DUBLIN 2-12   CAVAN 3-7
Dec 3, Croke Park, Dublin
Dublin: J O'Leary, E Heery, G Hargan, M Kennedy, K Barr, T Carr 0-1, P Curran 0-2, P Bealin 0-1, P Clarke 0-1, J Madden 1-0, T Conroy, C Duff 0-4, B Rock 0-3, J McNally 1-0, V Murphy. Subs: M Galvin for Madden, D Foran for Bealin.

ARMAGH 1-11   DUBLIN 0-10
Feb 4, Athletic Grounds, Armagh
Dublin: D O'Farrell, M Deegan, G Hargan, M Kennedy, K Barr, T Carr 0-1, E Heery, D Foran, P Curran, J Hayes 0-1, N McCaffrey 0-1, C Duff 0-1, B Rock 0-4, V Murphy 0-1, A McNally 0-1. Subs: D Bolger for Foran, D Farrell for Hayes.

DUBLIN 1-15   KERRY 3-7
Feb 11, Croke Park, Dublin
Dublin: D O'Farrell, M Deegan 0-1, G Hargan, M Kennedy, K Barr 0-1, T Carr, E Heery 0-2, D Foran, P Curran 0-3, J Hayes, C Duff, N McCaffrey 0-2, D DeLappe 0-1, B Rock 0-3, V Murphy 1-2, Sub: T Conroy for DeLappe.

DONEGAL 1-10   DUBLIN 0-9
Mar 4, MacCumhail Park, Ballybofey
Dublin: J O'Leary, M Deegan, G Hargan, M Kennedy, K Barr, T Carr, E Heery 0-1, D Foran, P Curran, V Murphy, C Duff 0-1, N McCaffrey 0-2, N Clancy 0-1, J McNally 0-1, B Rock 0-2. Subs: R Holland 0-1 for Rock, D DeLappe for Murphy.

DIVISION 1	P	W	D	L	Pts
CORK	7	5	1	1	11
DONEGAL	7	5	0	2	10
DOWN	7	5	0	2	10
ARMAGH	7	3	2	2	8
DUBLIN	7	4	0	3	8
KERRY	7	2	0	5	4
CAVAN	7	1	1	5	3
DERRY	7	1	0	6	2

PLAY-OFF
Mar 11, Drogheda Park, Drogheda

DUBLIN 1-14   ARMAGH 1-9

Dublin: J O'Leary, M Deegan, G Hargan, M Kennedy, N McCaffrey, T Carr, E Heery, D Foran 0-1, P Clarke 0-2, P Curran 0-1, T Conroy, C Duff 0-3, N Clancy 1-2, J McNally 0-1, B Rock 0-4. Sub: V Murphy for Rock.

QUARTER-FINAL
Apr 1, O'Moore Park, Portlaoise

ROSCOMMON 2-22 DUBLIN 3-13

Dublin: J O'Leary, N McCaffrey, G Morgan, M Kennedy, P Curran 0-1, T Carr 0-1, E Heery, D Foran, P Clarke, R Holland, B Rock 1-3, C Duff 0-4, N Clancy 1-1, M Galvin, V Murphy 0-1. Subs: J McNally 1-1 for Rock. Extra time: K Barr 0-1 for Foran, J Hayes for Duff, A McNally for Murphy.

1990/91

DONEGAL 2-11   DUBLIN 1-9

Oct 7, MacCumhail Park, Ballybofey

Dublin: J O'Leary, M Deegan, K Fagan, C Henry, K Barr, T Carr, N McCaffrey, D Foran, P Clarke 1-1, D Sheehan, P Curran 0-1, C Duff 0-1, C Redmond, J McNally, B Rock 0-6. Subs: D O'Reilly for Barr, C Walsh for Fagan, P Foley for McCaffrey.

DUBLIN 0-12   ARMAGH 0-9

Oct 21, Croke Park, Dublin

Dublin: J O'Leary, M Deegan, K Fagan, M Kennedy, K Barr 0-1, T Carr, E Heery, D Foran, P Clarke, P Curran 0-3, V Murphy 0-4, N Guiden 0-1, D Sheehan 0-1, P Dwane, B Rock 0-2. Subs: D Bolger for Clarke, G Kilmartin for Barr.

DUBLIN 0-10   CORK 0-6

Nov 25, Croke Park, Dublin

Dublin: J O'Leary, M Deegan, P Moran, M Kennedy, D Carroll, K Barr, E Heery, P Clarke 0-2, D Foran, P Curran, J Sheedy 0-I, N Guiden 0-2, D Sheehan, V Murphy, D McCarthy 0-1. Sub: C Redmond 0-1 for Murphy.

DUBLIN 2-14   ROSCOMMON 0-6

Dec 2, Croke Park, Dublin

Dublin: J O'Leary, M Deegan, P Moran, M Kennedy T Carr, K Barr, E Heery, D Foran, P Clarke 0-1, D Sheehan 0-2, J Sheedy, N Guiden 0-2, P Curran 0-4, V Murphy 1-4, D McCarthy 0-1. Subs: C Walsh for Moran, C Redmond 1-0 for McCarthy, L Close for Sheehan.

DUBLIN 2-10   DOWN 1-7

Feb 17, St Patrick's Park, Newcastle

Dublin: J O'Leary, M Deegan, C Walsh, M Kennedy, T Carr, K Barr, E Heery, D Foran, P Clarke, P Curran, J Sheedy 1-1, N Guiden, C Redmond 0-7, V Murphy 0-2, D McCarthy 1-0. Subs: N McCaffrey for Guiden, D Bolger for Sheedy.

DUBLIN 3-11   KERRY 0-7

Feb 24, Croke Park, Dublin

Dublin: J O'Leary, M Deegan, C Walsh, M Kennedy, T Carr 0-1, K Barr, E Heery, D Foran, P Clarke, P Curran 0-2, J Sheedy I-0, N Guiden 0-1, C Redmond 0-1, V Murphy 1-4, D McCarthy 1-2. Subs: D Synnott for Kennedy, P Dwane for Murphy.

DUBLIN 0-11   MEATH 1-8

Mar 10, Croke Park, Dublin

Dublin: J O'Leary, M Deegan, C Walsh, D Synnott 0-1, T Carr, K Barr 0-1, E Heery, D Bolger, P Clarke, D Sheehan, J Sheedy, N Guiden 0-4, C Duff, B Rock 0-3, D McCarthy 0-1. Subs: C Redmond 0-1 for Sheehan, N McCaffrey for Bolger.

DIVISION 1	P	W	D	L	Pts
DUBLIN	7	5	1	1	11
DONEGAL	7	4	1	2	9
KERRY	7	4	0	3	8
ROSCOMMON	7	4	0	3	8
ARMAGH	7	3	1	3	7
MEATH	7	2	2	3	6
DOWN	7	1	2	4	4
CORK	7	1	1	5	3

QUARTER-FINAL
Apr 14, Croke Park, Dublin

DUBLIN 2-10   WICKLOW 0-11

Dublin: J O'Leary, M Deegan, C Walsh, M Kennedy, T Carr 0-1, K Barr, E Heery, D Foran, P Clarke 0-I, P Curran 0-I, J Sheedy 1-4, N Guiden, C Redmond 0-1, V Murphy I-0, D McCarthy 0-2. Subs: M Galvin for Foran, C Duff for Murphy.

SEMI-FINAL
Apr 21, Croke Park, Dublin

DUBLIN 1-18   ROSCOMMON 0-11

Dublin: J O'Leary, M Deegan, C Walsh, M Kennedy, T Carr, K Barr 0-2, E Heery, D Foran, P Clarke 0-2, C Redmond, J Sheedy 0-4, N Guiden, P Curran 0-2, V Murphy 1-4, D McCarthy 0-1. Subs: C Duff 0-2 for Guiden, M Galvin 0-1 for McCarthy.

FINAL
May 5, Croke Park, Dublin

DUBLIN 1-9   KILDARE 0-10

Dublin: John O'Leary, Mick Deegan, Ciaran Walsh, Mick Kennedy, Tommy Carr (capt), Keith Barr, Eamon Heery, David Foran, Paul Clarke 0-2, Charlie Redmond 0-1, Paul Curran, Niall Guiden, Jack Sheedy 0-4, Vinnie Murphy 1-1, Donal McCarthy. Subs: Mick Galvin for McCarthy, Ciaran Duff for Guiden.

1991/92

DUBLIN 1-5   GALWAY 0-7
Oct 27, Pearse Stadium, Salthill
Dublin: J O'Leary, E Heery, G Hargan, M Kennedy, T Carr, P Curran, M Deegan, P Bealin, D Foran, J Sheedy, C Redmond 0-2, N Guiden, C Duff 0-3, P Clarke, M Galvin. Subs: L Callan for Foran, K Barr 1-0 for Clarke, J Madden for Curran.

TYRONE 4-11   DUBLIN 0-11
Nov 10, Croke Park, Dublin
Dublin: J O'Leary, M Deegan, G Hargan, G Kilmartin, T Carr, K Barr, E Heery, P Bealin 0-1, L Callan, J Madden, P Curran, N Guiden 0-2, C Duff 0-6, J Sheedy, M Galvin 0-1. Subs: M Kennedy for Kilmartin, P Nugent 0-1 for Madden, V Murphy for Guiden.

DUBLIN 2-10   ARMAGH 1-8
Nov 24, Croke Park, Dublin
Dublin: M Pender, M Deegan, G Hargan, M Kennedy, K Barr 1-2, P Curran, E Heery, P Clarke, P Bealin 0-1, J Sheedy 0-1, T Carr 0-1, N Guiden 0-1, C Duff 0-3, M Galvin 1-1, P Nugent.

DUBLIN 1-9   MAYO 0-10
Feb 23, MacHale Park, Castlebar
Dublin: M Pender, M Deegan, G Hargan, M Kennedy, K Barr, P Curran, E Heery, D Foran, J Sheedy, P Clarke 0-2, C Redmond 0-4, N Guiden 0-3, D Farrell 1-0, M Galvin, P Nugent. Subs: P Bealin for Sheedy, T Carr for Farrell.

CORK 2-8   DUBLIN 1-10
Mar 8, Croke Park, Dublin
Dublin: M Pender, M Deegan, G Hargan, M Kennedy, K Barr, P Curran 0-2, E Heery, D Foran, J Sheedy, C Redmond 0-6, T Carr 0-1, P Nugent 0-1, D Farrell 1-0, M Galvin, V Murphy. Sub: P Bealin for Sheedy.

DIVISION 1A	P	W	D	L	Pts
TYRONE	5	4	0	1	8
DUBLIN	5	3	0	2	6
GALWAY	5	3	0	2	6
CORK	5	2	1	2	5
ARMAGH	5	1	1	3	3
MAYO	5	1	0	4	2

PLAY-OFF
Mar 22, Croke Park, Dublin
DUBLIN 2-8   GALWAY 0-8
Dublin: J O'Leary, M Deegan 0-1, G Hargan, E Heery, K Barr, P Curran, T Carr 0-1, P Bealin 1-0, D Foran, J Sheedy 1-0, D Farrell 0-1, N Guiden 0-2, C Redmond 0-2, M Galvin, P Nugent 0-1. Subs: V Murphy for Galvin, M Kennedy for Heery.

QUARTER-FINAL
Apr 5, Breffni Park, Cavan
DUBLIN 3-6   DONEGAL 1-10
Dublin: J O'Leary, M Deegan, G Hargan, E Heery, K Barr, P Curran, T Carr, P Bealin, D Foran 0-1, J Sheedy 0-1, D Farrell 0-2, N Guiden, C Redmond 1-2, M Galvin, P Nugent. Subs: P Clarke 1-0 for Nugent, V Murphy 1-0 for Galvin, L Callan for Bealin.

SEMI-FINAL
Apr 19, Croke Park, Dublin
TYRONE 0-13   DUBLIN 1-9
Dublin: J O'Leary, M Deegan, G Hargan, M Kennedy, K Barr, P Curran 0-1, T Carr, D Foran, P Bealin 1-0, P Clarke, J Sheedy 0-3, N Guiden, D Farrell, V Murphy 0-1, C Redmond 0-4. Sub: P Doherty for Redmond.

1992/93

DERRY 0-11   DUBLIN 0-9
Oct 18, Croke Park, Dublin
Dublin: J O'Leary, M Deegan, D Deasy, C Walsh, P Curran 0-1, K Barr, E Heery, D Foran, P Bealin 0-1, J Sheedy 0-4, T Carr 0-1, N Guiden, J Barr 0-1, V Murphy 0-1, P Nugent. Subs: P Clarke for Nugent, P Gilroy for Bealin, L Callan for Guiden.

DUBLIN 0-18   SLIGO 0-8
Nov 1, Markievicz Park, Sligo
Dublin: J O'Leary, M Deegan, G Hargan, C Walsh, C McCormack, K Barr, E Heery, P Bealin 0-1, P Gilroy 0-4, J Barr, C Redmond 0-7, P Clarke 0-2, T Carr, V Murphy 0-3, M Doran 0-1. Sub: N Guiden for J Barr.

DUBLIN 1-8   LOUTH 0-9
Nov 15, Croke Park, Dublin
Dublin: J O'Leary, C McCormack, G Hargan, C Walsh, P Curran, K Barr 0-3, E Heery, P Bealin, P Gilroy, J Sheedy 1-0, T Carr, M Deegan 0-2, J Gavin 0-1, V Murphy 0-1, M Doran 0-1. Subs: D Foran for Gilroy, G Regan for Gavin.

DUBLIN 1-7   ANTRIM 0-5
Nov 29, Casement Park, Belfast
Dublin: J O'Leary, C McCormack, D Deasy, C Walsh, P Curran, K Barr 0-1, M Deegan, P Bealin, L Callan, C Redmond 1-1, T Carr 0-3, J Sheedy, J Gavin 0-2, V Murphy, M Doran. Subs: G Regan for Curran, P Ward for Doran, D Foran for Callan.

DUBLIN 0-11   WEXFORD 1-7
Feb 14, Wexford Park, Wexford
Dublin: J O'Leary, C Walsh, D Deasy, J Calvert, P Curran, K Barr, M Deegan, P Bealin, D Bolger, J Sheedy 0-1, T Carr, C Redmond 0-4, J Gavin 0-2, V Murphy 0-4, M Doran. Subs: P O'Donoghue for Doran, D Foran for Bolger.

DUBLIN 0-13   GALWAY 1-6
Feb 28, Croke Park, Dublin
Dublin: J O'Leary, C Walsh, D Deasy, J Calvert, P Curran 0-1, K Barr 0-3, M Deegan, P Bealin, P Gilroy 0-1, D Farrell, T Carr 0-3, J Sheedy, J Gavin 0-2, V Murphy 0-1, C Redmond. Sub: Clarke 0-2 for Redmond.

DUBLIN 0-15   LIMERICK 0-9
Mar 14, Gaelic Grounds, Askeaton
Dublin: J O'Leary, C Walsh, D Deasy, J Calvert, P Curran, K Barr, M Deegan, P Gilroy 0-1, J Sheedy 0-1, D Farrell 0-1, T Carr 0-2. P Clarke 0-2, J Gavin, V Murphy 0-3, C Redmond 0-5. Subs: M Galvin for Gavin, P Moran for Barr, N Guiden for Carr.

SECTION A	P	W	D	L	Pts
DUBLIN	7	6	0	1	12
DERRY	7	6	0	1	12
GALWAY	7	5	1	1	11
LOUTH	7	3	1	3	7
WEXFORD	7	3	0	4	6
ANTRIM	7	3	0	4	6
SLIGO	7	1	0	6	2
LIMERICK	7	0	0	7	0

QUARTER-FINAL
Apr 11, Croke Park, Dublin
DUBLIN 1-13   KILDARE 0-8
Dublin: J O'Leary, C Walsh, D Deasy, J Calvert, P Curran, K Barr 0-3, M Deegan, P Bealin, J Sheedy, E Heery 0-2, T Carr 0-1, N Guiden 0-1, M Doran 1-1, V Murphy 0-3, P O'Donoghue. Subs: C Redmond 0-2 for O'Donoghue, M Galvin for Doran.

SEMI-FINAL
Apr 18, Croke Park, Dublin
DUBLIN 1-10   KERRY 0-11
Dublin: J O'Leary, C Walsh, D Deasy, J Calvert, P Curran 0-1, K Barr, M Deegan, P Bealin, J Sheedy 0-3, P Gilroy, T Carr 0-1, N Guiden 1-0, M Doran 0-1, V Murphy 0-1, P O'Donoghue 0-1. Subs: C Redmond 0-2 for O'Donoghue, M Galvin for Doran.

FINAL
May 2, Croke Park, Dublin
DUBLIN 0-9   DONEGAL 0-9
Dublin: John O'Leary (capt), Ciaran Walsh, Dermot Deasy, Paddy Moran, Eamon Heery, Paul Curran, Mick Deegan, Jack Sheedy, Paul Bealin 0-1, John Calvert, Tommy Carr, Niall Guiden 0-1, Charlie Redmond 0-3, Vinnie Murphy 0-4, Martin Doran. Subs: Keith Barr for Calvert, Mick Galvin for Doran.

REPLAY
May 9, Croke Park, Dublin
DUBLIN 0-10   DONEGAL 0-6
Dublin: John O'Leary (capt), Ciaran Walsh, Dermot

Deasy, Paddy Moran, Eamon Heery, Paul Curran, Mick Deegan, Jack Sheedy, Paul Bealin, Jim Gavin 0-1, Tommy Carr, Niall Guiden 0-2, Paul Clarke 0-5, Vinnie Murphy 0-2, Martin Doran.

1993/94

DUBLIN 0-8   CLARE 0-6
Oct 10, Cusack Park, Ennis
Dublin: J O'Leary, G Regan, D Deasy, P Moran, S Carslake, P Curran, P O'Neill, P Gilroy 0-2, P Bealin, J Sheedy 0-1, T Carr 0-2, N Guiden, D O'Brien 0-1, V Murphy 0-1, M Doran. Sub: J Gavin for Doran.

DUBLIN 2-12   KERRY 1-13
Oct 24, Croke Park, Dublin
Dublin: J O'Leary, C Walsh, D Deasy, P Moran, G Regan 0-1, K Barr I-O, P O'Neill, P Gilroy 0-1, P Bealin, N Clancy, T Carr 0-1, M Deegan 0-I, D Farrell 0-2, V Murphy, M Galvin 0-4. Subs: C Redmond 1-2 for Clancy, J Barr for Gilroy.

DONEGAL 0-11   DUBLIN 0-7
Nov 7, MacCumhail Park, Ballybofey
Dublin: J O'Leary, C Walsh, D Deasy, P Moran, G Regan 0-1, K Barr, M Deegan, P Bealin, J Barr 0-1, V Murphy, T Carr, N Guiden, D Farrell, C Redmond 0-4, M Galvin 0-1. Subs: J Sheedy for Murphy, S Carslake for Walsh, J Gavin for Galvin.

DUBLIN 1-19   MAYO 0-8
Nov 21, Croke Park, Dublin
Dublin: J O'Leary, G Regan, D Deasy P Moran, M Deegan 0-1, K Barr, P Curran 0-1, J Sheedy 0-3, P Bealin 0-2, D Boyle 0-1, T Carr 0-2, J Barr 0-1, D Farrell 0-1, D O'Brien 0-1, C Redmond 1-5. Subs: S Carslake 0-1 for K Barr, M Galvin for Carr, J Calvert for Deasy.

DUBLIN 0-7   KILDARE 1-4
Feb 6, St Conleth's Park, Newbridge
Dublin: J O'Leary, C Walsh, D Deasy, G Regan, P Curran 0-I, K Barr, M Deegan, P Bealin 0-1, J Sheedy 0-2, D O'Boyle, N Guiden, T Carr 0-1, D Farrell, C Redmond 0-2, J Barr. Subs: B Stynes for J Barr, E Heery for O'Boyle, M Galvin for Farrell.

DUBLIN 1-7   DOWN 1-7
Feb 20, Croke Park, Dublin
Dublin: J O'Leary, C Walsh, D Deasy, P Moran, P Curran, K Barr, M Deegan, J Sheedy, P Bealin, D O'Boyle, T Carr, P Clarke, D Farrell, V Murphy 0-2, C Redmond 0-5. Subs: S Carslake for Deegan, J Barr 1-0 for Moran.

DUBLIN 0-15   DERRY 2-6
Mar 13, Wolfe Tone Park, Bellaghy
Dublin: J O'Leary, C Walsh, D Deasy, J Calvert, P

Curran, K Barr 0-1, P Clarke, J Sheedy 0-1, P Bealin, B Stynes, T Carr 0-1, P Gilroy 0-1, M Galvin, V Murphy 0-2, C Redmond 0-7. Subs: E Heery for Calvert, J Barr 0-1 for Stynes, D Farrell 0-1 for Galvin.

DIVISION 1	P	W	D	L	Pts
DERRY	7	6	0	1	12
DUBLIN	7	4	2	1	10
DONEGAL	7	4	0	3	8
KERRY	7	4	0	3	8
DOWN	7	3	2	2	8
KILDARE	7	2	1	4	5
CLARE	7	1	1	5	3
MAYO	7	1	0	6	2

QUARTER-FINAL
Apr 3, Breffni Park, Cavan
ARMAGH 2-13   DUBLIN 1-9
Dublin: J O'Leary, C Walsh, P Clarke 1-0, J Calvert, E Heery 0-1, P Curran, M Deegan, P Bealin 0-1, P Gilroy 0-2, B Stynes, T Carr 0-1, N Guiden, M Galvin, V Murphy 0-1, C Redmond 0-2. Subs: J Sheedy 0-1 for Stynes, D Farrell for Galvin, D Harrington for Guiden.

1994/95

MEATH 1-8   DUBLIN 0-7
Oct 16, Croke Park, Dublin
Dublin: J O'Leary, B Lambe, L Walsh, J Calvert, P Curran 0-1, P Moran, P O Neill, P Bealin, S Cahill, P Gilroy, T Carr, J Sheedy, J Gavin 0-1, D Farrell 0-5, M Galvin. Subs: B Stynes for Carr, V Murphy for Galvin.

KERRY 1-12   DUBLIN 1-11
Oct 30, Fitzgerald Stadium, Killarney
Dublin: M Pender, P Moran, J Calvert, R Leahy, I Robertson, B Stynes 0-1, L Walsh, P Bealin, J Sheedy 0-2, S Keogh 0-1, P Curran 0-1, S Cahill 0-3, D Farrell 0-2, L Callan, J Sherlock 1-0. Subs: A Stack 0-1 for Walsh, M Doran for Callan.

DONEGAL 0-12   DUBLIN 1-8
Nov 13, Croke Park, Dublin
Dublin: M Pender, P Moran, L Walsh, R Leahy, P Curran 0-1, K Barr, I Robertson, P Bealin 0-1, J Sheedy, S Keogh 0-1, B Stynes, S Cahill, D Farrell 0-3, C Redmond 0-1, J Sherlock 1-1.

DUBLIN 0-15   LAOIS 1-8
Nov 27, O'Moore Park, Portlaoise
Dublin: M Pender, P Moran, K Barr, K Spratt, P Curran 0-I, B Stynes 0-1, L Walsh, P Bealin, J Sheedy, I Robertson, S Cahill 0-3, E Sheehy 0-2, C Redmond 0-3, M Doran 0-4, J Sherlock 0-1.

KILDARE 0-10   DUBLIN 0-8
Feb 19, St Conleth's Park, Newbridge
Dublin: J O'Leary, C Walsh, D Deasy, P Moran, P Curran, P Clarke, M Deegan, P Bealin, J Sheedy 0-1, B Stynes, S Cahill, E Sheehy 0-1, I Robertson, D Farrell, C Redmond 0-5. Subs: V Murphy for Robertson, K Barr for Stynes, M Galvin 0-1 for Clarke.

DUBLIN 1-7   DOWN 0-1
Mar 5, Pairc Esler, Newry
Dublin: J O'Leary, C Walsh, D Deasy, P Moran, P Curran, B Barnes, M Deegan, B Stynes 1-0, P Clarke 0-3, S Cahill 0-I, J Sheedy, E Sheehy, C Redmond 0-1, M Galvin 0-2, D Farrell. Sub: V Murphy for Farrell.

DUBLIN 1-9   DERRY 1-9
Mar 19, Croke Park, Dublin
Dublin: J O'Leary, C Walsh, D Deasy, P Moran, W Daly, P Curran, M Deegan, B Stynes, P Clarke, S Cahill, J Sheedy 0-1, E Sheehy 0-1, C Redmond 0-5, M Galvin, D Farrell 1-2. Subs: J O Callaghan for Daly, S Keogh for Sheehy, J Sherlock for Moran.

DIVISION 1	P	W	D	L	Pts
LAOIS	7	5	0	2	10
DERRY	7	4	1	2	9
DONEGAL	7	4	0	1	8
KERRY	7	4	0	3	8
KILDARE	7	4	0	3	8
MEATH	7	3	0	4	6
DUBLIN	7	2	1	4	5
DOWN	7	1	0	6	2

1995/96

DUBLIN 1-13   LEITRIM 1-10
Oct 15, Croke Park, Dublin
Dublin: J O'Leary, K Galvin, C Walsh, P Moran, B Whelan, B Barnes, P Clifford, P Bealin 0-1, P Gilroy 0-2, P Clarke 0-2, D Farrell 1-2, J Gavin 0-1, S Cahill 0-2, E Sheehy 0-1, I Robertson 0-1. Subs: P Christie for Walsh, V Murphy 0-1 for Clifford, S Keogh for Galvin.

ARMAGH 0-8   DUBLIN 0-6
Oct 29, Athletic Grounds, Armagh
Dublin: J O'Leary, K Spratt, P Moran, G Regan, B Whelan, B Barnes, K Galvin, P Bealin, K Murray, P Clarke 0-3, D Farrell, J Gavin 0-2, S Cahill, E Sheehy, I Robertson. Subs: V Murphy 0-1 for Cahill, S Keogh for Murray, L O'Hare for Robertson.

CORK 2-9   DUBLIN 0-8
Nov 12, Croke Park, Dublin
Dublin: J O'Leary, P Moran, C Walsh, K Galvin, B Barnes, K Barr, G Regan, P Bealin, K Murray, P Gilroy 0-1, D Farrell, J Gavin 0-2, P Clarke 0-1, L Callan 0-3, V

Murphy. Subs: E Sheehy for Murray, I Robertson 0-1 for Clarke, E Heery for Moran.

DUBLIN 0-13   WESTMEATH 0-7
Nov 26, Pairc Chiarain, Athlone
Dublin: J O'Leary, P Moran, C Walsh, K Galvin, P Curran, K Barr, E Heery, P Bealin, P Gilroy, P Clarke 0-7, D Farrell, I Robertson 0-1, V Murphy 0-2, L Callan 0-1, R Boyle. Subs: C O'Hare 0-2 for Boyle, G Regan for Gilroy, K Murray for Robertson.

LOUTH 0-9   DUBLIN 1-5
Feb 4, St Brigid's Park, Dundalk
Dublin: J O'Leary, P Christie, D Martin, P Moran, P Curran, K Barr, E Heery 0-2, B Stynes 0-2, S Moylan, D O'Brien, M Doran, K Lawlor, D Farrell, J McNally 1-0, V Murphy 0-1. Subs: P Gilroy for Moylan, G Reagan for Moran.

DUBLIN 2-9   CAVAN 2-7
Feb 11, Parnell Park, Dublin
Dublin: J O'Leary, P Christie, D Martin, C Walsh, G Regan 0-1, D Harrington, E Heery, B Stynes 0-1, P Bealin 0-1, D O'Brien 1-1, D Farrell, N Guiden 1-0, C Redmond 0-1, J McNally 0-2, M Galvin 0-1. Subs: P Moran for Martin, J Sherlock 0-1 for O'Brien, K Galvin for Walsh.

DUBLIN 0-15   DOWN 1-5
Feb 25, St Patrick's Park, Newcastle
Dublin: J O'Leary, P Christie, D Martin, C Walsh, P Curran 0-1, D Harrington 0-1, E Heery, B Stynes 0-3, P Bealin, D O'Brien 0-1, D Farrell 0-1, N Guiden 0-1, C Redmond 0-6, J McNally 0-1, J Gavin. Sub: G Regan for Walsh.

DIVISION 2	P	W	D	L	Pts
CORK	7	6	0	1	12
CAVAN	7	5	0	2	10
ARMAGH	7	4	0	3	8
DUBLIN	7	4	0	3	8
LELTRLM	7	4	0	3	8
LOUTH	7	3	0	4	6
DOWN	7	1	0	6	2
WESTMEATH	7	1	0	6	2

1996/97

LEITRIM 1-10   DUBLIN 0-10
Oct 13, McDermott Park, Carrick-on-Shannon
Dublin: J O'Leary, P Moran, D Homan, G Regan, P Curran, K Barr 0-1, E Heery 0-1, B Stynes 0-2, P Bealin, C Whelan 0-1, D Farrell, E Sheehy, R Cosgrove 0-2, D Harrington, S Keogh 0-2. Subs: W Daly for Regan, P Clarke 0-1 for Sheehy.

DUBLIN 1-7   ARMAGH 0-10
Oct 27, Parnell Park, Dublin
Dublin: D Byrne, P Moran, D Homan, C Walsh, J O'Callaghan, K Barr, E Heery, D Harrington 0-1, B Stynes, I Robertson, C Whelan 0-1, P Clarke 0-3, D O'Brien 0-1, D Farrell, R Cosgrove 1-1. Subs: M Doran for Cosgrove, E Horgan for Harrington.

DUBLIN 0-10   MAYO 0-10
Nov 10, MacHale Park, Castlebar
Dublin: J O'Leary, P Moran, C Walsh, W Daly, D Harrington, K Barr, E Heery, P Bealin, B Stynes, R Cosgrove, C Whelan 0-2, P Clarke, M Doran 0-1, D Farrell 0-3, C Redmond 0-3. Subs: P Christie for Daly, J McNally 0-1, for Bealin, I Robertson for Doran.

DUBLIN 0-11   CLARE 0-8
Nov 24, Parnell Park, Dublin
Dublin: D Byrne, P Moran, C Walsh, P Christie, D Harrington, K Barr, P Curran, B Stynes 0-2, C Whelan 0-3, B Gogarty 0-1, D Farrell 0-2, E Sheehy, C Redmond, J McNally 0-1, M Doran 0-2. Subs: D O'Brien for Gogarty, W Daly for O'Brien.

LOUTH 1-7   DUBLIN 0-8
Feb 2, Parnell Park, Dublin
Dublin: D Byrne, P Christie, C Walsh, E Heery, D Harrington, K Barr, P Curran, B Stynes 0-1, D Homan, C Whelan, D Farrell 0-1, P Clarke 0-1, C Redmond 0-5, M Doran, R Cosgrove. Subs: D Ducie for Homan, K Rowe for R Cosgrove.

DUBLIN 2-7   MONAGHAN 1-7
Feb 16, St Tiernach's Park, Clones
Dublin: D Byrne, P Christie, P Moran, C Walsh, P Curran, K Barr, E Heery, B Stynes 1-0, D Homan, C Whelan, D Farrell, P Clarke, C Redmond 0-3, M Doran 1-2, J Sherlock 0-1. Subs: P Ward for Homan, M Deegan 0-1 for Walsh.

DUBLIN 0-15   LAOIS 0-4
Mar 2, Parnell Park, Dublin
Dublin: J O'Leary, P Moran, P Christie, C Walsh, P Curran 0-1, K Barr, E Heery 0-1, P Bealin 0-1, D Homan, C Whelan 0-2, D Farrell 0-2, B Stynes 0-2, R Cosgrove 0-3, M Doran, C Redmond 0-3. Subs: N Guiden for Doran, M Deegan for Walsh.

DIVISION 2	P	W	D	L	Pts
LAOIS	7	5	0	2	10
LOUTH	7	5	0	2	10
DUBLIN	7	3	2	2	8
ARMAGH	7	2	3	2	7
LEITRIM	7	3	1	3	7
CLARE	7	3	0	4	6
MAYO	7	2	2	3	6
MONAGHAN	7	1	0	6	2

1997/98

SLIGO 2-7   DUBLIN 0-12
Oct 19, Markievicz Park, Sligo
Dublin: D Byrne, P Moran, I Robertson, P Christie
J Magee, K Barr, E Heery, P Bealin 0-2, D Homan, P
Ward 0-1, D Darcy 0-7, C Whelan, M Barnes 0-1, R
Boyle 0-1, M Doran. Subs: M Deegan for Barnes, A
Lyons for Boyle.

OFFALY 1-11   DUBLIN 1-8
Nov 2, Parnell Park, Dublin
Dublin: D Byrne, P Moran, I Robertson, P Christie, J
Magee, K Barr, E Heery, P Bealin 1-1, D Homan 0-1,
C Whelan, P Curran, E Sheehy, J Gavin 0-2, D Darcy
0-4, M Doran. Subs: D Harrington for Moran, M
Deegan for Dolan, R Boyle for Curran.

DUBLIN 1-9   WEXFORD 0-4
Nov 16, Belfied Park, Enniscorthy
Dublin: D Byrne, I Robertson, K Barr, P Christie, P
Curran, D Harrington, E Heery, P Bealin, B Stynes
0-2, D Madden, D Homan, C Whelan 0-3, C O'Hare
1-1, D Darcy 0-2, J Gavin 0-1. Subs: J Magee for
Homan, M Deegan for Madden, E Sheehy for
Stynes.

DUBLIN 2-14   CAVAN 0-8
Nov 30, Parnell Park, Dublin
Dublin: D Byrne, I Robertson, K Barr, P Christie, P
Curran, D Harrington, E Heery 0-1, B Stynes 0-2, P
Bealin 0-1, D Homan, C Whelan 0-2, E Sheehy 1-0, J
Gavin 0-4, D Darcy 0-3, M Barnes 0-1. Subs: P Ward
for D Homan, P Gilroy 1-0 for Bealin, J Magee for
Barr.

MONAGHAN 2-12   DUBLIN 0-12
Feb 15, Parnell Park, Dublin
Dublin: D Byrne, P Christie, D Harrington, J Magee,
K Barr, I Robertson 0-1, E Heery, C Whelan 0-2, D
Homan, P Ward, D Farrell 0-1, D Darcy 0-4, C O'Hare
0-2, J Gavin 0-2, D O'Brien. Subs: B Stynes for
Ward, E Sheehy for O'Brien, M Deegan for O'Hare.

DUBLIN 1-7   TYRONE 1-2
Mar 1, O'Neill Park, Dungannon
Dublin: D Byrne, P Christie, D Harrington, P Moran,
P Curran, K Barr, K Galvin, C Whelan, P Bealin 0-1,
I Robertson, D Farrell 1-1, B Stynes, J Gavin 0-3, D
Darcy 0-2, M Deegan.

DUBLIN 0-18   KERRY 1-3
Mar 15, Parnell Park, Dublin
Dublin: D Byrne, P Moran, D Martin, P Christie, E
Heery 0-2, D Harrington, K Galvin 0-1, P Bealin
0-1, C Whelan 0-2, I Robertson 0-1, D Farrell 0-1, B
Stynes 0-2, J Gavin 0-3, D Darcy 0-2, J Sherlock
0-3. Subs: E Sheehy for Darcy, J Magee for
Harrington, P Ward for Farrell.

DIVISION 2	P	W	D	L	Pts
OFFALY	7	6	0	1	13
MONAGHAN	7	4	2	1	10
DUBLIN	7	4	0	3	8
TYRONE	7	4	0	3	8
SLIGO	7	3	2	2	8
KERRY	7	3	0	4	6
CAVAN	7	2	0	5	4
WEXFORD	7	0	0	7	0

1998/99

DUBLIN 1-15   TYRONE 1-9
Nov 1, Parnell Park, Dublin
Dublin: D Byrne, S Ryan, P Christie, K Galvin, T Lynch,
I Robertson, P Croft, C Whelan 1-2, E Sheehy, J Gavin
0-1, D Darcy 0-5, B Stynes, R Cosgrave 0-3, D Farrell
0-2, M O'Keeffe 0-2. Subs: S Cowap for Darcy, C
Moran for Galvin, B Irwin for O'Keeffe.

DUBLIN 0-14   ARMAGH 1-11
Nov 15, Athletic Grounds, Armagh
Dublin: D Byrne, S Ryan, P Christie, K Galvin, T Lynch,
I Robertson 0-1, P Croft, C Whelan 0-1, E Sheehy, J
Gavin 0-5, S Cowap, B Stynes 0-3, R Cosgrove 0-2, D
Farrell, M O'Keeffe 0-1. Subs: P Curran for Cowap, D
Darcy 0-1 for O'Keeffe.

DUBLIN 2-11   OFFALY 0-13
Nov 29, O'Connor Park, Tullamore
Dublin: D Byrne, S Ryan, P Christie, K Galvin, P
Curran, I Robertson, T Lynch, C Whelan 1-0, E Sheehy
0-1, J Gavin 0-2, D Darcy 0-1, B Stynes 0-1, S Connell
0-2, D Farrell 1-3, D O'Brien 0-1. Sub: R Cosgrove for
O'Brien.

DUBLIN 1-19   LEITRIM 0-6
Feb 14, Parnell Park, Dublin
Dublin: D Byrne, L Walsh, S Ryan, T Lynch, P Croft, P
Curran 0-1, K Galvin, E Sheehy, C Whelan 0-3, J Gavin
0-3, D Darcy 0-2, B Stynes 0-6, N O'Donoghue 0-1,
D Farrell 1-2, S Connell. Subs: J Magee for Walsh, R
Cosgrove for Connell, E Crennan 0-1 for Sheehy.

DONEGAL 1-8   DUBLIN 0-9
Feb 28, Fr Tierney Park, Ballyshannon
Dublin: D Byrne, L Walsh, S Ryan, T Lynch, P Croft, P
Curran, K Galvin 0-1, E Sheehy, C Whelan, S Connell,
D Darcy 0-2, B Stynes 0-2, R Cosgrove, D Farrell 0-3,
N O'Donoghue 0-1. Subs: I Robertson for Connell,
J Sherlock for O'Donoghue, M O'Keeffe 0-1 for
Cosgrove.

DUBLIN 0-15   GALWAY 1-12
Mar 14, Parnell Park, Dublin
Dublin: D Byrne, S Ryan, P Christie, T Lynch, P Curran
0-1, I Robertson, P Croft 0-1, E Sheehy, C Whelan 0-1,

S Connell, D Darcy 0-8, B Stynes 0-1, B Irwin, D Farrell 0-1, N O'Donoghue 0-2. Sub: M O'Keefe for Irwin.

CORK 0-10　　　DUBLIN 0-7
Mar 28, Pairc Ui Rinn, Cork
Dublin: D Byrne, P Moran, S Ryan, P Christie, T Lynch, I Robertson, P Croft, C Whelan 0-2, E Sheehy, P Ward, D Darcy 0-3, B Stynes, N O'Donoghue 0-1, D Farrell 0-1, M O'Keeffe. Sub: J Sherlock for O'Keeffe, B O'Brien for Ward.

DIVISION 1A	P	W	D	L	Pts
ARMAGH	7	5	1	1	11
CORK	7	4	1	2	9
DUBLIN	7	3	2	2	8
TYRONE	7	3	2	2	8
GALWAY	7	3	1	3	7
DONEGAL	7	3	0	4	6
OFFALY	7	2	2	3	6
LEITRIM	7	0	1	6	1

QUARTER-FINAL
Apr 11, Croke Park, Dublin
DUBLIN 1-17　　　KILDARE 2-8
Dublin: D Byrne, P Moran, S Ryan, P Christie, P Curran 0-1, I Robertson, K Galvin 0-1, C Whelan 0-1, E Sheehy, J Gavin 0-3, D Darcy 0-7, B Stynes 0-2, R Cosgrove 0-1, D Farrell 1-1, N O'Donoghue. Subs: J Sherlock for N O'Donoghue, C Moran for Gavin, D O'Brien for Farrell.

SEMI-FINAL
Apr 25, Croke Park, Dublin
DUBLIN 0-11　　　ARMAGH 0-11
Dublin: D Byrne, P Moran, S Ryan, P Christie, T Lynch, P Curran 0-1, K Galvin, C Whelan 0-1, E Sheehy 0-2, J Gavin 0-4, D Darcy, B Stynes, R Cosgrove, D Farrell 0-3, N O'Donoghue. Subs: J Sherlock for R Cosgrove, D Homan for N O'Donoghue.

SEMI-FINAL REPLAY
May 2, Croke Park, Dublin
DUBLIN 1-14　　　ARMAGH 0-12
Dublin: D Byrne, P Christie, S Ryan, P Moran, T Lynch, P Curran, K Galvin, C Whelan 1-3, B Stynes 0-2, J Gavin 0-2, D Darcy 0-2, E Sheehy, N O'Donoghue, D Farrell 0-3, B O'Brien 0-2. Subs: M O'Keeffe for O'Donoghue, D Homan for Sheehy, L Walsh for Moran.

FINAL
May 9, Pairc Ui Chaoimh, Cork
CORK 1-12　　　DUBLIN 0-7
Dublin: David Byrne, Paddy Moran, Paddy Christie, Shane Ryan, Tom Lynch, Paul Curran, Keith Galvin, Ciaran Whelan 0-1, Enda Sheehy, Jim Gavin, Declan Darcy 0-5, Brian Stynes, Brendan O'Brien, Dessie Farrell 0-1, Niall O'Donoghue. Subs: Darren Homan 1-0 for O'Donoghue, Jason Sherlock for O'Brien.

1999/00

TYRONE 1-13　　　DUBLIN 0-9
Oct 31, Healy Park, Omagh
Dublin: D Byrne, D Conlon, P Christie, S Ryan, I Clarke, J Magee, P Andrews, E Sheehy, C Whelan, J Sherlock 0-1, C Moran, S Connell 0-1, J Gavin 0-2, D Farrell, M O'Keeffe 0-4. Subs: E Crennan 0-1 for Conlon, P Croft for Ryan, D Herlihy for Connell, T Lynch for Christie, D Stynes for Sheehy.

DUBLIN 0-14　　　ARMAGH 0-6
Nov 14, Parnell Park, Dublin
Dublin: D Byrne, D Conlon, P Christie, M Cahill, P Curran, P Andrews, S Ryan 0-1, C Whelan 0-2, J Magee 0-3, J Gavin, C Moran 0-2, E Crennan, D Darcy 0-4, E Sheehy 0-1, M O'Keeffe. Subs: P Croft 0-1 for Crennan 32, B O'Brien for O'Keeffe 45, M Casey for Curran 51, S Cowap for Gavin 64, D Homan for Whelan 69.

DUBLIN 1-8　　　KERRY 0-9
Nov 28, Parnell Park, Dublin
Dublin: D Byrne, D Conlon, P Christie, M Cahill, P Curran, P Andrews, S Ryan, C Whelan, J Magee, J Gavin 0-3, C Moran 1-1, P Croft 0-1, D Darcy 0-3, E Sheehy, M O'Keeffe. Subs: E Morgan for Moran, D Moore for O'Keeffe.

ROSCOMMON 1-10　　DUBLIN 0-6
Feb 13, Dr Hyde Park, Roscommon
Dublin: D Byrne, M Cahill, P Christie, D Conlon, P Curran, P Andrews, S Ryan, B Stynes 0-3, J Magee, J Gavin 0-1, C Moran, P Croft, M O'Keeffe, E Sheehy, D Darcy 0-2. Subs: I Robertson for O'Keeffe 28, C Whelan for Gavin 41, J Ward for Sheehy 87, M Casey for Croft 64.

DUBLIN 1-11　　　DONEGAL 0-11
Mar 5, Parnell Park, Dublin
Dublin: D Byrne, D Conlon 0-1, P Christie, K Galvin, P Curran, S Ryan, P Andrews, C Whelan 0-2, J Magee, J Gavin 0-4, B Stynes, C Moran 1-0, J Ward, I Robertson, D Darcy 0-4. Subs: P Croft for Moran 56, E Sheehy for Conlon 58, B O'Brien for Magee 66.

DUBLIN 2-15　　　GALWAY 0-20
Mar 19, Tuam Stadium, Tuam
Dublin: D Byrne, I Clarke, P Christie, K Galvin, P Curran 0-2, S Ryan, P Andrews, J Ward, J Magee, E Sheehy, C Whelan 1-1, C Moran 1-2, J Gavin 0-3, I Robertson, D Darcy 0-7. Subs: D Farrell for Sheehy 14, S Connell for Ward 68.

DUBLIN 2-10　　　CORK 1-11
Apr 9, Parnell Park, Dublin
Dublin: D Byrne, I Clarke, P Christie, S Ryan, P Curran, J Magee, P Andrews, C Whelan 1-3, J Ward, C Moran 0-1, D Farrell, S Connell, J Gavin 0-2, I Robertson 1-4,

B O'Brien. Subs: P Croft for Farrell 3, D Homan for Cornell 46, J Sherlock for O'Brien 46, T Lynch for Ward 53, M Casey for Curran 66.

DIVISION 1A	P	W	D	L	Pts
KERRY	7	5	0	2	10
ROSCOMMON	7	5	0	2	10
DUBLIN	7	5	0	2	10
GALWAY	7	4	1	2	9
DONEGAL	7	2	1	4	5
TYRONE	7	2	1	4	5
ARMAGH	7	1	2	4	4
CORK	7	1	1	5	3

2000/01

TYRONE 0-19   DUBLIN 2-10
Oct 29, Parnell Park, Dublin
Dublin: D Byrne, I Clarke, P Christie, C Goggins, S Ryan, J Magee 0-1, P Andrews, D Homan 1-0, E Sheehy 0-1, N O'Donoghue 1-2, C Whelan, K Galvin, M O'Keeffe 0-1, V Murphy 0-3, W McCarthy 0-2. Subs: M Casey for Homan 50, P Croft for Galvin 50, A Brogan for O'Donoghue 65, R McDonald for Clarke 66.

OFFALY 1-10   DUBLIN 0-9
Nov 12, O'Connor Park, Tullamore
Dublin: D Byrne, M Cahill, P Christie, M Casey, S Ryan, I Clarke, P Andrews, D Homan, C Whelan, J Magee, J Ward, N O'Donoghue 0-3, B O'Brien, V Murphy, W McCarthy 0-4. Subs: P Curran 0-1 for Ward 23, I Robertson 0-1 for O'Brien h/t, K Kelly for Magee 57, K Galvin for Clarke 70.

ROSCOMMON 0-12 DUBLIN 0-10
Feb 10, Parnell Park, Dublin
Dublin: D Byrne, M Cahill, P Christie, P Andrews, S Ryan, J Magee, C Goggins, C Whelan, D Homan, S Connell, C Moran 0-1, E Sheehy 0-1, D Farrell 0-4, V Murphy 0-2, J Sherlock. Subs: I Robertson 0-1 for Murphy 50, W McCarthy 0-1 for Moran 58, N O'Donoghue for Connell 70.

DUBLIN 0-11   DONEGAL 0-8
Feb 25, Fr Tierney Park, Ballyshannon
Dublin: D Byrne, M Cahill, P Christie, C Goggins, S Ryan, J Magee, P Andrews, D Homan, E Sheehy, S Connell 0-2, I Robertson 0-1, C Moran 0-2, D Farrell 0-3, V Murphy 0-1, W McCarthy 0-2.

KERRY 2-9   DUBLIN 0-10
Apr 1, Fitzgerald Stadium, Killarney
Dublin: D Byrne, M Cahill, P Christie, C Goggins, S Ryan, J Magee 0-1, P Andrews, C Whelan 0-1, E Sheehy, C Moran 0-2, N O'Donoghue, S Connell 0-1, D Farrell 0-2, V Murphy 0-1, W McCarthy 0-1. Subs: T Lynch for Cahill 34, D Homan for Moran 46, K Darcy

for O'Donoghue 51, M Casey for Ryan 61, D Darcy 0-1 for McCarthy 66.

DUBLIN 1-10   GALWAY 1-8
Apr 8, Parnell Park, Dublin
Dublin: C O'Boyle, C Coggins, P Christie, M Cahill, M Casey, J Magee, P Andrews, C Whelan 0-3, D Homan, S Connell, E Sheehy 0-1, K Darcy, D Farrell, V Murphy 1-2, N O'Donoghue 0-2. Subs: T Lynch for Magee 36, K Donnelly for Darcy 42, W McCarthy 0-1 for Murphy 63, D Darcy 0-1 for O'Donoghue 65.

DIVISION 1A	P	W	D	L	Pts
GALWAY	7	5	1	1	11
ROSCOMMON	7	4	1	2	9
TYRONE	7	4	0	3	8
OFFALY	7	3	2	2	8
DUBLIN	7	3	0	4	6
DONEGAL	7	2	1	4	5
KERRY	7	2	0	5	4
LOUTH	7	1	1	5	3

* Dublin awarded walkover v Louth due to outbreak of foot and mouth disease

2002

DUBLIN 2-10   DONEGAL 0-14
Feb 10, Parnell Park, Dublin
Dublin: S Cluxton, D Henry, P Andrews, C Goggins 0-1, P Casey, B Cahill, D Darcy, D Homan, D Magee, J O'Connor, C Whelan 0-1, E Bennis, A Brogan 1-3, J McNally 0-2, R Cosgrave 0-3. Subs: S Ryan for O'Connor h/t, J Magee 1-0 for McNally 45, C Murphy for D Magee 69, J Gavin for Cosgrave 71.

TYRONE 0-18   DUBLIN 2-10
Feb 17, O'Neill Park: Dungannon
Dublin: S Cluxton, D Henry, P Andrews, C Goggins, P Casey, D Darcy, B Cahill 0-1, D Homan, D Magee 0-1, C Whelan, S Ryan, E Bennis, A Brogan 1-3, J McNally 0-2, R Cosgrave 1-3. Subs: C Moran for Homan 39, J Gavin for Moran 46, P Curran for Darcy 56.

DUBLIN 0-10   OFFALY 1-7
Feb 23, O'Connor Park, Tullamore
Dublin: B Murphy, D Henry, P Andrews, C Goggins, P Casey, J Magee, P Curran, K Darcy 0-1, D Magee, C Whelan, D Darcy, E Bennis, A Brogan 0-3, J McNally 0-3, R Cosgrave 0-3. Sub: S Connell for Bennis 30, M Casey for P Casey 69, J Gavin for Cosgrave 73.

DUBLIN 3-13   WESTMEATH 1-16
Mar 3, Parnell Park, Dublin
Dublin: S Cluxton, D Henry, P Andrews, C Goggins, P Casey, D Darcy, P Curran, D Homan, K Darcy 0-1, C Whelan, S Ryan 2-1, E Bennis, A Brogan 0-3, J

McNally 1-3, R Cosgrove 0-5. Subs: D Magee for K Darcy 43, B Cahill for Casey 47, S Connell 0-1 for Bennis 51, J Sherlock for Whelan 71.

CORK 1-13   DUBLIN 0-10
Mar 10, Pairc Ui Chaoimh, Cork
Dublin: B Murphy, P Christie, P Andrews, C Goggins, B Cahill, D Darcy, P Curran, D Homan, D Magee, C Whelan 0-4, S Ryan 0-1, P Casey, A Brogan 0-1, J McNally 0-1, R Cosgrove 0-2. Subs: J Magee for McNally h/t, S Connell for Christie h/t, K Darcy for D Magee 48, E Bennis for Homan 55, E Crennan 0-1 for Darcy 63.

ROSCOMMON 2-12   DUBLIN 0-16
Mar 24, Parnell Park, Dublin
Dublin: S Cluxton, D Henry, P Christie, C Goggins, P Andrews, J Magee, P Curran, D Homan, C Whelan, E Crennan 0-1, D Darcy, E Bennis, A Brogan 0-3, S Ryan, R Cosgrove 0-8. Subs D Magee 0-1 for J Magee, S Keogh 0-3 for Darcy, S Connell for Bennis, J Sherlock for Crennan.

DUBLIN 1-12   GALWAY 1-12
Mar 31, Tuam Stadium, Tuam
Dublin: S Cluxton, D Henry, P Christie, C Goggins, P Andrews, D Magee, P Curran, D Homan, C Whelan 0-2, E Crennan, S Ryan, S Connell 0-3, A Brogan, J Sherlock, R Cosgrove 1-4. Subs: J Magee for Curran h/t, S Keogh for Sherlock h/t, P Casey 0-1 for Homan 56, J Gavin for Ryan 62.

DIVISION 1A	P	W	D	L	Pts
ROSCOMMON	7	5	1	1	11
TYRONE	7	5	0	2	10
DONEGAL	7	4	0	2	8
GALWAY	7	3	2	2	8
CORK	7	3	0	4	6
DUBLIN	7	2	2	3	6
OFFALY	7	2	1	4	5
WESTMEATH	7	1	0	6	2

2003

ARMAGH 1-15   DUBLIN 0-7
Feb 2, Croke Park, Dublin
Dublin: S Cluxton, B Cahill, P Christie, D Henry, C Goggins, S Ryan, P Andrews, C Whelan, D Magee, C Moran 0-1, B Cullen 0-1, S Connell, E Bennis, J McNally 0-2, T Quinn 0-3. Subs: D O'Mahony for Bennis h/t, D Homan for Connell 40, P Casey for Andrews 46, J Sherlock for Moran 51, P Griffin for Goggins 55.

DUBLIN 1-10   DONEGAL 0-9
Feb 9, Fr Tierney Park, Ballyshannon
Dublin: B Murphy, B Cahill, P Christie, D Henry,

P Casey, J Magee, S Ryan, C Whelan, D Magee 0-1, E Crennan, B Cullen 0-2, S Connell 0-2, A Brogan, J McNally, T Quinn 1-5. Subs: C Moran for E Crennan 57, D Homan for Connell 63.

DUBLIN 0-12   TYRONE 0-11
Feb 16, Parnell Park, Dublin
Dublin: S Cluxton, D Henry, P Christie, P Griffin, C Goggins 0-1, J Magee, P Casey, C Whelan 0-1, D Magee 0-1, J McNally, C Moran 0-2, S Connell, A Brogan 0-2, B Cullen 0-2, T Quinn 0-1. Subs: S Ryan for Moran 42, L Og O hEineachain 0-1 for D Magee 49, D O'Mahony 0-1 for Quinn 55, E Crennan for McNally 56.

KERRY 2-11   DUBLIN 0-14
Mar 2, Fitzgerald Stadium, Killarney
Dublin: S Cluxton, B Cahill, P Christie, P Griffin, P Casey, S Ryan, C Goggins, C Whelan, D Magee, C Moran 0-2, B Cullen 0-1, L Og O hEineachain 0-2, A Brogan 0-4, R Cosgrove 0-2, T Quinn 0-3. Subs: S Connell for Moran 52, J Sherlock for Quinn 56, P Andrews for Casey 58, J McNally for Cullen 59, D O'Mahony for Cosgrove 67.

CORK 0-16   DUBLIN 0-8
Mar 9, Parnell Park, Dublin
Dublin: B Murphy, D Henry, P Christie, P Andrews, P Casey, B Cahill, C Goggins, C Whelan 0-2, J Magee 0-1, S Connell 0-1, B Cullen, C Moran, J Sherlock 0-2, R Cosgrove 0-1, J McNally. Subs: P Griffin for Andrews 60, D O'Mahony for Cahill h/t, A Brogan for McNally h/t, D Magee for Moran 54, E Crennan for Connell 65.

DUBLIN 0-17   ROSCOMMON 0-14
Mar 23, Dr Hyde Park, Roscommon
Dublin: S Cluxton, D Henry, P Christie, P Griffin, P Casey, J Magee 0-1, C Goggins 0-1, C Whelan 0-3, D Magee 0-1, B Cullen 0-2, S Ryan, S Connell 0-5, T Mulligan 0-1, R Cosgrove 0-1, T Quinn 0-2. Subs: C Moran for Casey 8, J Sherlock for Quinn 43, J McNally for Mulligan 51, D Homan for D Magee 58, E Crennan for Goggins 73.

DUBLIN 0-12   GALWAY 1-9
Apr 6, Parnell Park, Dublin
Dublin: S Cluxton, D Henry, P Christie, P Griffin, C Moran, J Magee, C Goggins 0-1, C Whelan, D Magee, B Cullen 0-1, S Ryan 0-1, S Connell, A Brogan 0-6, R Cosgrove, J McNally 0-3. Subs: D Homan for Connell 51, T Quinn for Cosgrove 59, L Og O'hEineachain for Ryan 66, J Sherlock for D Magee 66.

DIVISION 1A	P	W	D	L	Pts
TYRONE	7	5	0	2	10
ARMAGH	7	4	0	3	8
CORK	7	4	0	3	8
KERRY	7	4	0	3	8
GALWAY	7	3	1	3	7
DUBLIN	7	3	1	3	7
ROSCOMMON	7	3	0	4	6
DONEGAL	7	1	0	6	2

2004

DUBLIN 0-9   TYRONE 0-8
Feb 1, Parnell Park, Dublin
Dublin: S Cluxton, D Henry, P Christie, P Griffin, S Ryan, D Magee, C Moran, C Whelan 0-1, D Homan, C Keaney 0-2, B Cullen, S Connell, T Quinn 0-1, R Cosgrove 0-3, J Sherlock 0-2. Subs: D Lally for Connell 3, T Mulligan for Homan 52, J McNally for Lally 63.

MAYO 1-10   DUBLIN 0-3
Feb 8, MacHale Park, Castlebar
Dublin: S Cluxton, D Henry, P Christie, P Griffin, S Ryan, D Magee, C Moran, C Whelan, D Homan 0-1, C Keaney 0-1, B Cullen, J McNally, J Sherlock, R Cosgrove, T Quinn 0-1. Subs: D Lally for McNally h/t, C Goggins for Whelan h/t, B Kennedy for Cosgrove 45, T Mulligan for Cullen 49.

KERRY 1-12   DUBLIN 0-12
Feb 15, Parnell Park, Dublin
Dublin: S Cluxton, D Henry, P Christie, P Griffin, S Ryan, D Magee, C Moran, C Whelan 0-1, D Homan 0-1, C Keaney 0-5, B Cullen, S Connell, T Quinn 0-4, R Cosgrove, J Sherlock 0-1. Subs: J Coughlan for Homan 42, L Og O hEanachain for G Cullen 59, J McNally for Cosgrove 59.

DUBLIN 0-15   WESTMEATH 0-10
Mar 7, Cusack Park, Mullingar
Dublin: S Cluxton, D Henry, P Christie, P Griffin, C Moran, D Magee, S Ryan, C Whelan 0-3, D O'Mahony, C Keaney 0-1, B Cullen 0-2, S Connell 0-4, T Quinn 0-4, J Sherlock 0-1, D Lally. Subs: C Goggins for Christie h/t, D Homan for Lally 46, P Andrews for Griffin 56, K Golden for Sherlock 68.

DUBLIN 0-12   FERMANAGH 0-12
Mar 14, Bewster Park, Enniskillen
Dublin: B Murphy, D Henry, S Ryan, P Griffin, C Goggins 0-1, D Magee, C Moran, C Whelan, D O'Mahony, S Connell 0-2, B Cullen, D Lally 0-3, T Quinn 0-3, R Cosgrove 0-2, J Sheriock 0-1. Subs: D Homan for O'Mahony 50, K Golden for Lally 62.

DUBLIN 0-9   CORK 0-9
Mar 21, Parnell Park, Dublin
Dublin: S Cluxton, D Henry, P Christie, P Griffin, P Andrews, D Magee, C Moran 0-1, C Whelan, S Ryan, J Sherlock, B Cullen, D Lally 0-1, R Cosgrove, K Golden 0-1, S Connell 0-5. Subs: L Og O hEineachain 0-1 for Golden h/t, J McNally for Cosgrove 55, D Homan for Magee 65.

DUBLIN 2-12   LONGFORD 2-9
Apr 4, Parnell Park, Dublin
Dublin: B Murphy, S O'Shaughnessy, P Christie, C Goggins, S Ryan, P Casey, P Andrews, C Whelan 0-1, D Magee, C Keaney 0-1, T Quinn 0-4, D Lally 0-1, S Connell 0-4, J McNally 1-0, A Brogan 0-1. Subs: J Sherlock 1-0 for Brogan 44, C Moran for O'Shaughnessy 53, R Cosgrove for McNally 59, D Homan for Magee 54, L Og O hEineachain for Lally 65.

DIVISION 1A	P	W	D	L	Pts
TYRONE	7	5	1	1	11
KERRY	7	5	0	2	10
CORK	7	3	3	1	9
DUBLIN	7	3	2	2	8
MAYO	7	3	0	4	6
WESTMEATH	7	1	2	4	4
FERMANAGH	7	1	2	4	4
LONGFORD	7	2	0	5	4

2005

Feb 6, Parnell Park, Dublin
DUBLIN 2-13   MAYO 0-15
Dublin: S Cluxton, P Griffin, P Christie, S O'Shaughnessy, P Casey, B Cullen 0-1, P Andrews 0-1, C Whelan 0-2, S Ryan 0-1, D Henry 0-1, J Sherlock, S Connell 0-2, D O'Callaghan 0-1, R Boyle 0-1, T Quinn 2-2. Subs: B Murphy for Cluxton 20, A Brogan 0-1 for Boyle 43, R Cosgrove for Brogan 56, D Lally for Henry 66.

TYRONE 1-10   DUBLIN 0-9
Feb 13, Healy Park, Omagh
Dublin: S Cluxton, P Griffin, P Christie, S O'Shaughnessy, P Casey, B Cullen, P Andrews, C Whelan 0-3, S Ryan, C Keaney, J Sherlock, D Henry, D O'Callaghan 0-1, S Connell, T Quinn 0-4. Subs: C Goggins for O'Shaughnessy 29, R Boyle 0-1 for Henry h/t, R Cosgrove for Keaney 52, D Homan for Ryan 52, J Magee for Whelan 53, L Og O hEineachain for Sherlock 69.

KERRY 2-13   DUBLIN 2-11
Mar 6, Austin Stack Park, Tralee
Dublin: S Cluxton, P Griffin, P Christie, S

O'Shaughnessy, P Casey, B Cullen, P Andrews, C Whelan 1-2, S Ryan 0-1, D Lally 1-1, L Óg Ó hEineachain, S Connell 0-1, D O'Callaghan, C Keaney 0-2, T Quinn 0-1. Subs: M Vaughan 0-2 for O'Callaghan h/t, C Moran for Casey h/t, C Goggins for Andrews 42, J Sherlock for O hEineachain 54, B Cahill for O'Shaughnessy 64, D Homan for Quinn 64.

DUBLIN 0-11   WESTMEATH 0-9
Mar 12, Parnell Park, Dublin
Dublin: S Cluxton, P Griffin, P Christie, S O'Shaughnessy, P Casey, B Cullen, P Andrews, C Whelan, S Ryan, D Lally 0-1, L Og O hEineachain, C Moran, M Vaughan, C Keaney 0-1, T Quinn 0-7. Subs: D Homan for Whelan 36, S Connell 0-1 for O hEineachain h/t, C Goggins for O'Shaughnessy 43, J Sherlock 0-1 for Vaughan 47.

Mar 20, Parnell Park, Dublin

DUBLIN 1-11   DONEGAL 0-13
Dublin: S Cluxton, P Griffin, P Christie, S O'Shaughnessy, P Casey, B Cullen 0-1, P Andrews, C Whelan 0-3, D Homan 0-1, C Moran, S Ryan, D Lally, M Vaughan 0-1, C Keaney 0-1, T Quinn 1-4. Subs: S Connell for Ryan 26), J Sherlock for Vaughan h/t, C Goggins for Griffin 53, R Cosgrove for Keaney 68.

CORK 0-18   DUBLIN 1-6
Mar 26, Pairc Ui Rinn, Cork
Dublin: S Cluxton, P Griffin, P Christie, S O'Shaughnessy, P Casey, B Cullen, P Andrews, C Whelan, S Ryan, C Moran, J Sherlock 1-0, D Lally, M Vaughan 0-1, C Keaney, T Quinn 0-3. Subs: D Homan 0-1 for Ryan 20, C Goggins for Andrews h/t, S Connell 0-1 for Vaughan h/t, A Brogan for Lally 49, D O'Callaghan for Moran 61, Ryan for Homan 61.

DUBLIN 1-13   OFFALY 2-6
Apr 3, O'Connor Park, Tullamore
Dublin: S Cluxton, P Griffin, P Christie, S O'Shaughnessy, P Casey, B Cahill 0-1, C Goggins, C Whelan, D Homan 0-1, D Lally, A Brogan 0-2, C Moran 0-1, J Sherlock 0-1, C Keaney 0-3, T Quinn 1-2. Subs: S Ryan for Whelan 34, D Bastic for Homan 42, S Connell 0-2 for Lally 46, P Andrews for Goggins 63, L Og O hEineachain for Andrews 68, D O'Callaghan for Moran 71.

DIVISION 1A	P	W	D	L	Pts
TYRONE	7	5	0	2	10
MAYO	7	5	0	2	10
KERRY	7	5	0	2	10
DUBLIN	7	4	0	7	8
CORK	7	2	2	3	6
OFFALY	7	2	1	4	5
DONEGAL	7	2	0	5	4
WESTMEATH	7	1	1	5	3

2006

DUBLIN 1-9   TYRONE 1-6
Feb 5, Healy Park, Omagh
Dublin: P Copeland, N O'Shea, B Cahill, D Henry 0-1, P Casey, C Goggins, P Andrews, C Whelan, D Bastick, D Murray, T Quinn 1-7, B Cullen 0-1, D O'Callaghan, K Bonner, A Brogan. Subs: D Lally for O'Callaghan 51, J Sherlock for Bonner 55, S Ryan for Murray 65.

MONAGHAN 1-11   DUBLIN 0-7
Feb 12, Parnell Park
Dublin: S Cluxton, N O'Shea, B Cahill, D Henry, P Casey, C Goggins, P Andrews, C Whelan, D Bastick, D Murray, K Bonner 0-1, B Cullen, A Brogan 0-2, D O'Callaghan, T Quinn 0-4. Subs: D Lally for O'Callaghan h/t, J Sherlock for Murray 46, B Brogan for Bonner 56, M Fitzpatrick for O'Shea 65, S Ryan for Cullen 68.

DUBLIN 1-10   OFFALY 3-2
Mar 4, Parnell Park, Dublin
Dublin: S Cluxton, P Griffin, B Cahill, D Henry, P Casey, C Goggins, P Andrews, D Bastick, D Magee 0-1, C Keaney 1-3, J Sherlock, D Lally 0-1, D O'Callaghan 0-3, S Ryan, T Quinn 0-2. Subs: M Vaughan for Quinn 52, G O'Meara for Keaney 61, R McConnell for Bastick 62, D Murray for Goggins 64.

CORK 1-11   DUBLIN 1-10
Mar 11, Pairc Ui Rinn, Cork
Dublin: S Cluxton, P Griffin, B Cahill, D Henry, P Casey, C Goggins, P Andrews, D Bastick, D Magee, C Keaney 0-1, B Cullen 0-3, D Lally 1-0, D O'Callaghan 0-2, S Ryan, T Quinn 0-2. Subs: C Whelan 0-1 for Magee 34, A Brogan 0-1 for Ryan h/t, K Bonner for Keaney 49, M Vaughan for O'Callaghan 67.

FERMANAGH 0-9   DUBLIN 0-8
Mar 19, Brewster Park, Enniskillen
Dublin: S Cluxton, P Griffin, B Cahill, D Henry, P Casey, C Goggins, P Andrews, D Magee, C Whelan, B Cullen, T Quinn 0-5, D Lally, A Brogan 0-1, C Keaney 0-1, K Bonner. Subs: P Burke for Bonner 33, S Ryan for Keaney 62, D Marshall for Brogan 68.

DUBLIN 4-10   MAYO 1-10
Mar 25, Parnell Park, Dublin
Dublin: S Cluxton, P Casey, B Cahill, D Henry, P Griffin, C Goggins, P Andrews, D Magee 0-1, C Whelan, D Lally, T Quinn 2-2, B Cullen 0-1, M Vaughan, C Keaney 1-2, A Brogan 1-2. Subs: S Ryan for Whelan 11, P Burke for Lally 65, D Bastick for Andrews 70.

DUBLIN 0-13   KERRY 0-13
Apr 9, Fitzgerald Stadium, Killarney
Dublin: S Cluxton, N O'Shea, B Cahill, D Henry, P Casey, C Goggins, P Grifin, S Ryan 0-1, D Magee,

D Lally, J Sherlock 0-1, B Cullen, A Brogan 0-2, C Keaney 0-4, M Vaughan 0-5. Subs: R Cosgrove for Lally 60, D O'Callaghan for Sherlock 64, B Brogan for Vaughan 72.

DIVISION 1A	P	W	D	L	Pts
MAYO	7	5	1	1	11
KERRY	7	4	1	2	9
TYRONE	7	4	1	2	9
DUBLIN	7	3	1	3	7
CORK	7	3	0	4	6
FERMANAGH	7	3	0	4	6
OFFALY	7	2	1	4	5
MONAGHAN	7	1	0	6	2

2007

TYRONE 0-11   DUBLIN 0-10
Feb 3, Croke Park, Dublin
Dublin: S Cluxton, D Henry 0-1, N O'Shea, P Griffin, P Casey, C Moran, G Brennan, D O'Mahony, D Magee 0-1, D Murray, A Brogan 0-1, D Connolly 0-3, D O'Callaghan 0-2, K Bonner 0-1, C Keaney 0-1. Subs: S Ryan for Magee 48, B Cullen for O'Mahony 53, B Brogan for O'Callaghan 61, C Goggins for Murray 65.

DUBLIN 0-14   LIMERICK 1-10
Feb 10, Gaelic Grounds, Limerick
Dublin: S Cluxton, P Griffin, D Henry, N O'Shea, P Casey, B Cullen, G Brennan, D Magee 0-2, R McConnell, D Murray, A Brogan 0-1, D Connolly 0-1, D O'Callaghan 0-3, K Bonner, C Keaney 0-3. Subs: T Quinn 0-4 for Connolly 37, B Brogan for Murray h/t, D Lally for Bonner 62, C Goggins for O'Shea 63, C Moran for Keaney 69.

DONEGAL 0-9   DUBLIN 0-5
Feb 25, Fr Tierney Park, Ballyshannon
Dublin: S Cluxton, D Henry, N O'Shea, P Griffin, B Cahill, B Cullen, G Brennan, D Magee 0-1, R McConnell, C Keaney 0-1, T Quinn, D Murray, D O'Callaghan 0-1, K Bonner 0-2, A Brogan. Subs: C Moran for Murray 23, P Casey for O'Shea h/t, D Connolly for Quinn 45, B Brogan for Keaney 48, C Whelan for McConnell 55.

DUBLIN 1-13   CORK 0-7
Mar 10, Parnell Park, Dublin
Dublin: S Cluxton, D Henry 0-1, R McConnell, P Griffin, B Cahill, B Cullen, G Brennan, D Magee, C Whelan, C Moran 0-1, J Sherlock 0-1, B Brogan, C Keaney 1-4, K Bonner, T Quinn 0-5. Subs: D Connolly 0-1 for Sherlock 23, S Ryan for Brogan 58, P Casey for Brennan 63, J Magee for Bonner 67, C Goggins for Cahill 69.

DUBLIN 3-15   FERMANAGH 0-7
Mar 24, Parnell Park, Dublin
Dublin: S Cluxton, D Henry, R McConnell, P Griffin, B Cahill, B Cullen, G Brennan, S Ryan, D Magee, C Moran 0-3, J Sherlock 0-1, C Keaney 0-5, B Brogan 0-1, K Bonner 1-1, T Quinn 1-1. Subs: P Casey for Brennan 45, D Connolly 1-1 for Quinn 50, M Vaughan 0-1 for Brogan 55, D O'Callaghan 0-1 for Sherlock 60, J Magee for D Magee 63.

MAYO 0-10   DUBLIN 0-9
Apr 1, MacHale Park, Castlebar
Dublin: S Cluxton, D Henry, R McConnell, P Griffin, B Cahill 0-1, B Cullen, G Brennan, D Magee, C Whelan, C Moran 0-1, J Sherlock, B Brogan 0-1, C Keaney 0-3, K Bonner 0-2, T Quinn 0-1. Subs: D Connolly for Quinn 58, S Ryan for Whelan 58, P Casey for Bonner 60, R Cosgrove for Brogan 67, C Goggins for Brennan 69.

KERRY 1-12   DUBLIN 2-7
Apr 8, Parnell Park, Dublin
Dublin: S Cluxton, D Henry, R McConnell, P Griffin, B Cahill, B Cullen, G Brennan, C Whelan, D Magee, C Moran, J Sherlock 1-2, B Brogan, C Keaney 0-1, K Bonner, M Vaughan 0-3. Subs: A Brogan 0-1 for B Brogan h/t, P Casey 1-0 for Brennan 50, T Quinn for Bonner 56, S Ryan for Whelan 56.

DIVISION 1A	P	W	D	L	Pts
DONEGAL	7	6	1	0	13
MAYO	7	6	0	1	12
KERRY	7	4	1	2	9
TYRONE	7	3	1	3	7
DUBLIN	7	3	0	4	6
CORK	7	3	0	4	6
LIMERICK	7	1	0	6	2
FERMANAGH	7	0	0	7	0

2008

DUBLIN 1-7   WESTMEATH 1-5
Feb 2, Parnell Park, Dublin
Dublin: S Cluxton, D Henry, N O'Shea, S O'Shaughnessy, P McMahon, P Casey, C Moran, E Fennell, S Ryan, B Cullen 0-1, J O'Brien, P Flynn 1-0, J Sherlock, C Keaney 0-1, M Vaughan 0-5. Subs: B McManamon for O'Brien 43, D Murray for Flynn 65, K Bonner for Keaney 68, D Lally for Cullen 71.

DUBLIN 1-9   CAVAN 0-7
Mar 2, Breffni Park, Cavan
Dublin: S Cluxton, D Henry, R McConnell, S O'Shaughnessy, P McMahon, P Casey, C Moran, E Fennell, S Ryan, B Cullen, A Brogan, M Vaughan 0-4, J Sherlock, B Brogan 1-1, B McManamon 0-2. Subs: C

Keaney 0-2 for McManamon 46, C Whelan for Fennell 57, P Flynn for A Brogan 65, D O'Mahony for Ryan 67, D Lally for McMahon 69.

DUBLIN 1-10   MONAGHAN 0-13
Mar 24, Parnell Park, Dublin
Dublin: S Cluxton, D Murray, R McConnell, D Henry 0-1, P Casey, B Cullen, C Moran, E Fennell, S Ryan, P Flynn 1-0, B Brogan 0-2, M Vaughan 0-2, C Keaney 0-4, K Bonner, J Sherlock 0-1. Subs: C Whelan for Bonner 60, B McManamon for Flynn 66, D Magee for Brogan 72.

DUBLIN 3-20   ROSCOMMON 0-7
Apr 5, Parnell Park, Dublin
Dublin: M Savage, D Murray, R McConnell, S O'Shaughnessy, B Cahill, G Brennan, P Andrews, C Whelan 0-1, S Ryan, B Brogan 0-3, A Brogan 0-1, B McManamon 0-3, D Connolly 1-3, C Keaney 1-5, T Quinn 1-3. Subs: P Flynn for Ryan 29, D Magee for Whelan 49, T Diamond for A Brogan 54, K Nolan for McConnell 59, E O'Gara 0-1 for B Brogan 65.

ARMAGH 3-13   DUBLIN 1-10
Apr 13, Oliver Plunkett Park, Crossmaglen
Dublin: S Cluxton, D Henry, R McConnell, D Murray, P Casey, B Cullen, G Brennan, E Fennell 0-1, P Flynn, C Moran, B Brogan 1-3, M Vaughan, J Sherlock 0-2, C Keaney 0-4, K Bonner. Subs: B Cahill for Brennan 20, P Andrews for Murray 24, C Whelan for Flynn h/t, D Connolly for Vaughan 45, A Brogan for Bonner 52 mins, S Ryan for Whelan 62.

DUBLIN 0-13   MEATH 2-6
Apr 20, Parnell Park, Dublin
Dublin: S Cluxton, D Henry, R McConnell, P Andrews, C Moran 0-1, B Cullen, G Brennan, C Whelan, E Fennell, B McManamon 0-1, J Sherlock 0-1, P Flynn, T Quinn 0-6, D Connolly 0-3, B Brogan. Subs: S Ryan for McManamon 48, P Casey for Fennell 58, B Cahill for Brennan 61, M Vaughan 0-1 for Quinn 68.

DIVISION 1A	P	W	D	L	Pts
DUBLIN	7	5	1	1	11
WESTMEATH	7	5	0	2	10
MONAGHAN	7	4	1	2	9
ARMAGH	7	3	1	3	7
CORK	7	3	1	3	7
MEATH	7	3	1	3	7
ROSCOMMON	7	1	1	5	3
CAVAN	7	1	0	6	2

* Cork forfeited the points for their scheduled meeting with Dublin.

FINAL
Apr 27, Pairc Tailteann, Navan
WESTMEATH 0-15   DUBLIN 0-10
Dublin: Stephen Cluxton, David Henry, Barry Cahill,

Paul Casey, Colin Moran, Bryan Cullen 0-1, Ger Brennan, Darren Magee, Shane Ryan, Kevin Bonner 0-1, Mark Vaughan 0-2, Brendan McManamon 0-1, Jason Sherlock 0-2, Conal Keaney 0-1, John O'Brien 0-2. Subs: Ray Cosgrove for Sherlock 31, Tony Diamond for Cosgrove 53, Eoghan O'Gara for McManamon 56, Derek Murray for Bonner 65.

2009

TYRONE 1-18   DUBLIN 1-16
Jan 31, Croke Park, Dublin
Dublin: S Cluxton, P Andrews, D Bastick, A Hubbard, B Cullen, G Brennan 0-1, B Cahill, R McConnell, C Whelan 0-1, J Brogan, D Henry 0-1, T Diamond, C Keaney 0-5, J Sherlock 0-2, B Brogan 1-5. Subs: S Ryan for McConnell 20, P Flynn 0-1 for Ryan 46, K Bonner for Diamond 52, B McManamon for J Brogan 65.

GALWAY 3-12   DUBLIN 0-13
Feb 15, Pearse Stadium, Salthill
Dublin: S Cluxton, P Andrews, D Bastick, A Hubbard, B Cullen, G Brennan, B Cahill 0-1, C Whelan 0-3, P Flynn, D Henry 0-1, T Diamond, J Brogan, C Keaney 0-2, J Sherlock, B Brogan 0-6. Subs: D Murray for Hubbard 30, R McConnell for Flynn 35, K Bonner for Diamond 35, D Connolly for Sherlock 35, B Kelly for Cullen 49, S Ryan for Cahill 52.

DUBLIN 0-13   DONEGAL 1-8
Mar 8, Fr Tierney Park, Ballyshannon
Dublin: S Cluxton, P Andrews, D Bastick, A Hubbard, J Brogan, G Brennan 0-1, B Cahill, C Whelan, R McConnell 0-3, D Connolly, C Keaney 0-4, D Henry 0-1, B Kelly, K Bonner 0-1, B Brogan. Subs: J Sherlock for Connolly 20, B Cullen for Bonner 35, D Lally for J Brogan 37, Connolly for Kelly 54, A Brogan for Henry 55)

DERRY 0-20   DUBLIN 1-12
Mar 14, Parnell Park, Dublin
Dublin: S Cluxton, P Andrews, D Bastick, A Hubbard, J Brogan, G Brennan 1-0, B Cahill, C Whelan, R McConnell, D Connolly 0-1, C Keaney 0-3, D Henry, B Kelly 0-2, K Bonner, B Brogan 0-5. Subs: A Brogan 0-1 for Bonner 31, S Ryan for McConnell 43, B Cullen for Connolly 46, D Lally for J Brogan 50, P Conlon for Hubbard 59.

DUBLIN 0-9   MAYO 0-9
Mar 22, James Stephens Park, Ballina
Dublin: M Savage, D Henry, D Bastick, A Hubbard, B Cullen, G Brennan, B Cahill, C Whelan, R McConnell, D Connolly 0-5, K Bonner, D Lally, B Kelly 0-1, C Keaney 0-1, B Brogan 0-2. Subs: A Brogan for B Brogan 47, D Daly for Brennan 49, S Ryan for Bonner

62, T Quinn for Kelly 65, J O'Connor for McConnell
68, B Brogan for D Lally 69.

DUBLIN 1-15   KERRY 1-15
Mar 29, Parnell Park, Dublin
Dublin: S Cluxton, D Henry 0-1, D Bastick, A Hubbard,
B Cullen, P Griffin, G Brennan, D Magee, R McConnell
0-2, P Flynn, K Bonner, D Connolly 0-4, C Keaney
0-2, M Davoren 1-3, P Andrews 0-2. Subs: P Burke
0-1 for Bonner 12, A Brogan for McConnell 57, S Ryan
for Flynn 61, D Lally for Connolly 65, R O'Carroll for
Henry 68.

DUBLIN 5-22   WESTMEATH 0-10
Apr 12, Parnell Park, Dublin
Dublin: S Cluxton, D Henry, D Bastick, A Hubbard, P
Griffin, G Brennan 0-1, B Cahill 0-2, C Whelan 1-0, D
Magee 1-0, A Brogan 0-4, K Bonner, P Flynn 1-0, C
Keaney 1-7, M Davoren 0-2, B Kelly 0-6. Subs: P Burke
1-0 for Bonner 3, B Cullen for Griffin h/t, R McConnell
for Davoren 48, T Quinn for Kelly 54, M Vaughan for
Keaney 55.

DIVISION 1	P	W	D	L	Pts
KERRY	7	6	1	0	13
DERRY	7	4	1	2	9
GALWAY	7	4	1	2	9
MAYO	7	2	3	1	7
TYRONE	7	3	1	3	7
DUBLIN	7	2	2	3	6
DONEGAL	7	2	1	4	5
WESTMEATH	7	0	0	7	0

2010

DUBLIN 1-12   KERRY 1-10
Feb 7, Fitzgerald Stadium, Killarney
Dublin: S Cluxton, P Conlon, R O'Carroll, P McMahon,
P Griffin, C O'Sullivan, J McCarthy, E Fennell 0-3, R
McConnell, A Hubbard 0-1, MD Macauley 0-1, P Flynn
1-2, D Henry, B Kelly 0-2, K McManamon 0-2. Subs:
B Brogan 0-1 for Kelly 49, D Kelly for Hubbard 62, T
Diamond for McManamon 69.

DUBLIN 1-11   DERRY 0-7
Feb 14, Parnell Park, Dublin
Dublin: M Savage, P Conlon, R O'Carroll, M Fitzsimons,
P Griffin, C O'Sullivan, J Brogan, E Fennell 0-2, R
McConnell 0-1, A Hubbard, MD Macauley, K Bonner,
T Diamond, B Kelly 0-1, K McManamon 1-1. Subs: D
Nelson 0-1 for J Brogan h/t, B McManamon 0-1 for
Diamond h/t, D Kelly 0-1 for Hubbard 49, B Brogan 0-3
for B Kelly 51, P Casey for K McManamon 58.

DUBLIN 1-9   MAYO 0-8
Mar 7, MacHale Park, Castlebar
Dublin: S Cluxton, P Conlon, M Fitzsimons, P

McMahon, H Gill, C O'Sullivan, G Brennan, E
Fennell 0-1, R McConnell 0-2, A Hubbard 0-1, P
Flynn 0-1, K Bonner 0-1 D Henry, MD Macauley
0-1, K McManamon 0-1. Subs: K Nolan for Conlon
35, B Brogan 1-0 for K McManamon 47, D Magee
for Fennell 50, C Keaney 0-1 for Henry 50, B
McManamon for Hubbard 57.

DUBLIN 2-11   MONAGHAN 1-9
Mar 14, Parnell Park, Dublin
Dublin: S Cluxton, M Fitzsimons, R O'Carroll, P
McMahon, J McCarthy, C O'Sullivan, G Brennan,
E Fennell 0-1, R McConnell 0-1, A Hubbard 0-1,
MD Macauley, P Flynn, D Henry, B Brogan 1-6, K
McManamon 1-0. Subs: P Griffin for McCarthy h/t,
B McMenamon 0-1 for Henry 47, D Magee 0-1 for
Fennell 48, H Gill for Griffin 49, K Bonner for Flynn 65.

CORK 2-13   DUBLIN 2-6
Mar 20, Pairc Ui Rinn, Cork
Dublin: M Savage, P Conlon, M Fitzsimons, P
McMahon, H Gill, C O'Sullivan, G Brennan, E Fennell
0-1, R McConnell, A Hubbard 0-1, MD Macauley, P
Flynn, D Henry, B Brogan 1-2, K McManamon 1-1.
Subs: K Nolan for Brennan 30, D Kelly for Macauley
h/t, D Magee for McConnell 43, C Keaney 0-1 for
Flynn 48, Macauley for Fennell 63.

GALWAY 1-14   DUBLIN 0-14
Mar 27, Parnell Park, Dublin
Dublin: S Cluxton, P Conlon, R O'Carroll, P McMahon,
B Cahill, C O'Sullivan 0-1, H Gill, E Fennell, R
McConnell, A Hubbard, P Flynn, K Bonner 0-1, D
Henry, B Brogan 0-11, K McManamon. Subs: M
Macauley for Fennell h/t, B McManamon for Bonner
h/t, C Keaney 0-1 for Henry 45, B Kelly for Hubbard
66.

DUBLIN 2-14   TYRONE 0-11
Apr 11, Healy Park, Omagh
Dublin: M Savage, P Conlon, R O'Carroll, P McMahon,
P Casey, C O'Sullivan, D Bastick, E Fennell 0-1, R
McConnell, D Henry 0-1, N Corkery 1-0, P Flynn, A
Hubbard, K McManamon 0-2, B Brogan 0-8. Subs:
MD Macauley 0-1 for McConnell 25, A Brogan 1-1 for
Hubbard 29, B Cahill for Bastick 35, D Connolly for
Flynn 49, E O'Gara for Macauley 63.

DIVISION 1	P	W	D	L	Pts
MAYO	7	6	0	1	12
CORK	7	5	0	2	10
DUBLIN	7	5	0	2	10
KERRY	7	3	0	4	6
GALWAY	7	3	0	4	6
MONAGHAN	7	2	0	5	4
DERRY	7	2	0	5	4
TYRONE	7	2	0	5	4

2011

DUBLIN 2-12   ARMAGH 1-11
Feb 6, Athletic Grounds, Armagh
Dublin: S Cluxton, A Hubbard, S Murray, M Fitzsimons, D Lally 0-1, J McCarthy, P Casey, D Bastick, MD Macauley 0-1, B Cullen, K McManamon 0-2, D Connolly 1-1, B Brogan 1-3, E O'Gara 0-1, T Quinn 0-2. Subs: P Flynn 0-1 for Quinn 47, B Cahill for Bastick 51, A Brogan for Connolly 59, P Andrews for O'Gara 64.

DUBLIN 3-13   CORK 0-16
Feb 19, Croke Park, Dublin
Dublin: S Cluxton, M Fitzsimons, S Murray, A Hubbard, P Casey, J McCarthy 0-1, D Lally 0-2, D Bastick 0-1, B Cahill 1-0, P Flynn, K McManamon 1-0, D Connolly 0-1, B Brogan 0-6, E O'Gara, T Quinn 1-1. Subs: D Nelson for D Lally 43, B Cullen 0-1 for Connolly 47, A Brogan for O'Gara 55, P Andrews for Quinn 61, C Murphy for Flynn 65.

DUBLIN 3-10   KERRY 1-15
Feb 26, Croke Park, Dublin
Dublin: S Cluxton, A Hubbard, S Murray, M Fitzsimons, D Lally 0-1, J McCarthy, P Casey, D Bastick, B Cahill, P Flynn 0-1, K McManamon 1-1, D Connolly, B Brogan 0-4, E O'Gara 0-1, T Quinn 1-0. Subs: MD Macauley 1-1 for Bastick h/t, B Cullen for Connolly 40, A Brogan 0-1 for Quinn 49, G Brennan for McCarthy 52, P Andrews for Flynn 64.

DUBLIN 0-13   MONAGHAN 1-9
Mar 13, St Tiernach's Park, Clones
Dublin: S Cluxton, D Daly, S Murray, R O'Carroll, P Casey, G Brennan, D Lally 0-1, D Bastick, B Cahill, P Flynn, K McManamon 0-1, MD Macauley, T Quinn 0-1, D Connolly 0-3, B Brogan 0-4. Subs: D Nelson 0-1 for Lally 29, B Cullen for Flynn h/t, A Brogan 0-1 for Quinn h/t, P Andrews 0-1 for Macauley 43, P Brogan for O'Carroll 54.

DUBLIN 4-15   MAYO 3-13
Mar 20, Croke Park, Dublin
Dublin: M Savage, D Daly, S Murray, P Brogan, P Casey, G Brennan, D Nelson 0-1, D Bastick, M Macauley 0-1, P Flynn, K McManamon 0-2, B Cahill, T Quinn 1-7, D Connolly 3-3, A Brogan 0-1. Subs: P McMahon for Daly h/t, B Cullen for Macauley 42, K Nolan for Casey 47, P Andrews for Flynn 60, P Burke for A Brogan 69.

DUBLIN 2-10   DOWN 0-13
Apr 2, Croke Park, Dublin
Dublin: S Cluxton, P McMahon, P Brogan, N Devereux, K Nolan, G Brennan, D Nelson, D Bastick, B Cahill 0-1, P Flynn 1-1, K McManamon, B Cullen 0-1, A Brogan 1-1, D Connolly 0-1, T Quinn 0-4. Subs: B Brogan 0-1 for McManamon 42, MD Macauley for Bastick 43, P Andrews for Cullen 58, P Burke for Quinn 67, D Kelly for Flynn 70.

DUBLIN 2-9   GALWAY 0-15
Apr 10, Pearse Stadium, Salthill
Dublin: M Savage, P McMahon, P Brogan, N Devereux, K Nolan, G Brennan, P Casey, D Bastick 0-1, S Murray 0-1, P Flynn 0-1, P Burke 1-0, B Cullen, B Brogan 0-5, D Connolly, A Brogan 1-0. Subs: M Fitzsimons for Devereux h/t, D Kelly 0-1 for Burke 54, D Lally for Connolly 60, P Andrews for Cullen 67, D Nelson for Kelly 70.

DIVISION 1	P	W	D	L	Pts
DUBLIN	7	6	1	0	13
CORK	7	5	0	2	10
KERRY	7	5	0	2	10
DOWN	7	3	1	3	7
MAYO	7	2	1	5	5
ARMAGH	7	2	0	5	4
MONAGHAN	7	2	0	5	4
GALWAY	7	1	1	3	3

FINAL
Apr 24, Croke Park, Dublin
CORK 0-21   DUBLIN 2-14
Dublin: Stephen Cluxton, Michael Fitzsimons, Paul Brogan, Philly McMahon, Barry Cahill 0-1, Ger Brennan, Kevin Nolan 0-1, Denis Bastick, Michael Darragh Macauley, Bryan Cullen, Kevin McManamon 0-5, Paul Flynn, Bernard Brogan 1-3, Diarmuid Connolly 0-2, Tomas Quinn 1-2. Subs: Darren Daly for Cullen 47, Pat Burke for Bernard Brogan 50, Dean Kelly for Connolly 54, Paddy Andrews for Daly 62, Declan Lally for Cahill 72.

2012

KERRY 1-14   DUBLIN 0-11
Feb 4, Croke Park, Dublin
Dublin: S Cluxton 0-2, M Fitzsimons, R O'Carroll, P McMahon, J McCarthy, G Brennan, C Dias, R McConnell, MD Macauley, P Brogan, K McManamon 0-3, B Cullen 0-1, D Connolly 0-1, E O'Gara, T Quinn 0-4. Subs: P Flynn for Brogan 44, K Nolan for Fitzsimons 50, E Fennell for McConnell 51, D Kelly for O'Gara 63, S Murray for Macauley 64.

DUBLIN 0-8   MAYO 0-5
Feb 11, MacHale Park, Castlebar
Dublin: S Cluxton 0-1, K Nolan, R O'Carroll, P McMahon, J McCarthy, G Brennan, C Dias, R McConnell, MD Macauley, P Brogan 0-1, K McManamon 0-1, B Cullen, D Connolly 0-3, E O'Gara, T Quinn 0-2.
* Match abandoned at halftime due to fog — not included in players' scoring or appearances records.

DUBLIN 1-14   LAOIS 0-9
Mar 3, O'Moore Park, Portlaoise
Dublin: M Savage, D Daly, R O'Carroll, P McMahon, D Byrne, G Brennan, C Dias, R McConnell, E Fennell, P Brogan, K McManamon, P Flynn 0-1, D Connolly 0-5, E O'Gara 1-5, T Quinn 0-2. Subs: B Cullen for P Brogan 32, MD Macauley for McConnell 54, A Brogan 0-1 for McManamon 54, P Andrews for Quinn 61.

DUBLIN 4-17   ARMAGH 1-10
Mar 11, Croke Park, Dublin
Dublin: M Savage, D Daly, R O'Carroll, P McMahon, J McCarthy 0-1, G Brennan, C Dias, MD Macauley 0-1, E Fennell 0-1, P Flynn 0-2, A Brogan 0-1, P Brogan, D Connolly 3-3, E O'Gara 0-3, T Quinn 1-3. Subs: P Andrews for A Brogan 49, D Byrne for P Brogan 56, S Murray for Macauley 60, J Cooper 0-2 for McCarthy 61, C Murphy for Fennell 65.

DOWN 0-15   DUBLIN 1-10
Mar 18, Pairc Esler, Newry
Dublin: S Cluxton 0-1, D Daly, R O'Carroll, J Cooper, J McCarthy, G Brennan, C Dias, E Fennell 0-1, MD Macauley 0-2, P Brogan, K McManamon 1-1, P Flynn, D Connolly 0-3, B Cullen, A Brogan 0-2. Subs: P McMahon for Dias h/t, B Cahill for Flynn 47, T Quinn for Brogan 58, R McConnell for Fennell 66, K Nolan for McCarthy 70.

DUBLIN 2-16   DONEGAL 0-13
Mar 24, Croke Park, Dublin
Dublin: S Cluxton 0-1, C O'Sullivan, R O'Carroll, P McMahon, J Cooper 0-1, G Brennan, K Nolan, MD Macauley 0-1, E Fennell 0-1, P Flynn 0-1, A Brogan 0-1, B Cullen 1-1, T Quinn 0-1, D Connolly 1-3, K McManamon 0-3. Subs: S Murray for Brennan 24, D Rock 0-1 for Brogan 30, D Kelly 0-1 for Quinn h/t, C Dias for Cooper 59.

MAYO 0-20   DUBLIN 0-8
April 1, MacHale Park, Castlebar
Dublin: S Cluxton, D Daly, R O'Carroll, C O'Sullivan, J McCarthy, G Brennan 0-1, K Nolan, R McConnell, MD Macauley, P Brogan, P Andrews 0-1, B Cullen 0-2, T Quinn 0-2, D Connolly 0-1, K McManamon. Subs: P Flynn for Brogan 26, E Fennell for McConnell h/t, C Dias for McCarthy h/t, D Kelly for Quinn 45, D Rock 0-1 for Andrews 49.

CORK 1-12   DUBLIN 0-12
Apr 8, Pairc Ui Chaoimh, Cork
Dublin: M Savage, R O'Carroll, C O'Sullivan, P McMahon, J Cooper, J McCarthy, K Nolan, S Murray, E Fennell 0-1, D Byrne, MD Macauley 0-2, B Cullen 0-2, C Dias, D Connolly 0-5, K McManamon 0-2. Subs: D Bastick for Murray 31, B Cahill for Byrne h/t, P Brogan for Nolan 61, D Kelly for Dias 62, R McConnell for Fennell 66.

DIVISION 1	P	W	D	L	Pts
KERRY	7	5	1	1	11
CORK	7	4	1	2	9
DOWN	7	4	0	3	8
MAYO	7	3	1	3	7
DUBLIN	7	3	0	4	6
DONEGAL	7	3	0	4	6
ARMAGH	7	2	1	4	5
LAOIS	7	2	0	5	4

2013

DUBLIN 1-18   CORK 2-9
Feb 2, Croke Park, Dublin
Dublin: S Cluxton, J Cooper, R O'Carroll, K O'Brien, D Daly, G Brennan, J McCaffrey 0-2, MD Macauley 0-1, P Mannion, P Flynn, P Andrews 0-5, P Quinn, K McManamon, D Connolly 1-2, B Brogan 0-6. Subs: C Costello 0-1 for Mannion 28, E Ó'Conghaile for McManamon 28, C O'Sullivan 0-1 for Macauley 46, C Reddin for Quinn 54, D Nelson for Daly 63, S Carthy for O'Conghaile 63.

DUBLIN 1-11   KERRY 0-4
Feb 10, Fitzgerald Stadium, Killarney
Dublin: S Cluxton, J Cooper, R O'Carroll, K O'Brien, J McCaffrey, G Brennan, D Daly, MD Macauley, C O'Sullivan, P Flynn, T Brady, C Reddin, P Andrews 0-3, D Connolly, B Brogan 0-7. Subs: P Ryan 0-1 for Connolly 28, C Dias 1-0 for Reddin h/t, D Nelson for Daly 47, D O'Mahony for Ryan 62, P Quinn for Flynn 67.

DUBLIN 2-14   MAYO 0-16
Mar 2, Croke Park, Dublin
Dublin: S Cluxton, K O'Brien, R O'Carroll, J Cooper, J McCaffrey, G Brennan, D Daly, D O'Mahony, C O'Sullivan 0-1, P Flynn, T Brady, C Reddin, P Andrews 0-2, B Brogan 1-10, C Kilkenny. Subs: K McManamon 1-1 for Brady 20, D Nelson for O'Carroll h/t, B Cullen for Reddin 51, P Quinn for Kilkenny 60, N Deveraux for McCaffrey 65.

DUBLIN 2-20   KILDARE 2-7
Mar 10, Croke Park, Dublin
Dublin: S Supple, K O'Brien, R O'Carroll, J Cooper, J McCaffrey 1-1, C O'Sullivan, D Daly 0-1, MD Macauley, D O'Mahony, P Flynn 0-1, C Kilkenny 0-4, D Connolly 0-2, P Andrews 0-3, B Brogan 1-5, C Reddin. Subs: D Bastick for Macauley h/t, K McManamon 0-2 for Reddin h/t, B Cullen for Kilkenny 52, C Guckian for Daly 56, P Ryan 0-1 for O'Mahony 60.

TYRONE 0-18   DUBLIN 1-14
Mar 16, Croke Park, Dublin
Dublin: S Supple, D Nelson, G Brennan, K O'Brien, J McCaffrey, C O'Sullivan, D Daly, D O'Mahony, D Bastick, P Flynn 0-2, D Connolly 0-6, C Kilkenny, P

Ryan 1-0, P Andrews 0-2, K McManamon 0-2. Subs: C Dias 0-1 for Kilkenny 6, MD Macauley 0-1 for O'Mahony h/t, P Mannion for Ryan 52, N Devereux for Nelson 61.

DUBLIN 1-15   DOWN 0-9
Mar 23, Croke Park, Dublin
Dublin: S Cluxton 0-1, D Daly, J Cooper, K O'Brien, J McCaffrey, G Brennan, N Devereux 0-1, C O'Sullivan 0-1, D Bastick, C Dias, P Andrews 0-2, B Cullen 0-1, K McManamon 1-0, D Connolly 0-4, P Mannion 0-5. Subs: MD Macauley for Bastick 23, S Carthy for Dias 47, P Ryan for Connolly 61, K Nolan for McCaffrey 65.

DUBLIN 0-13   DONEGAL 1-10
Apr 7, MacCumhaill Park, Ballybofey
Dublin: S Cluxton 0-1, K O'Brien, J Cooper, P McMahon, J McCaffrey 0-1, D Daly, G Brennan, MD Macauley, C O'Sullivan 0-1, P Flynn, T Brady, D Connolly 0-1, P Mannion 0-6, P Andrews 0-3, K McManamon. Subs: J Whelan for Flynn h/t, B Cullen for Brady h/t, D Bastick for Macauley 55, D Rock for Connolly 57, M Fitzsimons for Brennan 63.

DIVISION 1	P	W	D	L	Pts
DUBLIN	7	5	1	1	11
TYRONE	7	5	0	2	10
KILDARE	7	4	0	3	8
MAYO	7	3	0	4	6
CORK	7	3	0	4	6
KERRY	7	3	0	4	6
DONEGAL	7	2	1	4	5
DOWN	7	2	0	5	4

SEMI-FINAL
Apr 14, Croke Park, Dublin
DUBLIN 2-16   MAYO 0-16
Dublin: S Cluxton 0-1, K O'Brien, J Cooper, P McMahon, J McCaffrey 0-1, G Brennan, D Daly 0-1, MD Macauley, C O'Sullivan, J Whelan 1-1, D Connolly 0-3, P Flynn, P Mannion 1-4, P Andrews, B Brogan 0-5. Subs: N Devereux for Daly 47, D Bastick for O'Sullivan 50, B Cullen for Flynn 54, K McManamon for Connolly 55, M Fitzsimons for Cooper 65.

FINAL
Apr 28, Croke Park, Dublin
DUBLIN 0-18   TYRONE 0-17
Dublin: Stephen Cluxton 0-1, Kevin O'Brien, Johnny Cooper, Darren Daly, James McCarthy, Ger Brennan, Jack McCaffrey 0-1, Michael Darragh Macauley, Cian O'Sullivan, Jason Whelan, Diarmuid Connolly 0-2, Bryan Cullen 0-1, Paul Mannion 0-4, Paddy Andrews 0-1, Bernard Brogan 0-5, Subs: Shane Carthy for Whelan h/t, Kevin McMenamon for Cullen 45, Denis Bastick for O'Sullivan 46, Philly McMahon 0-1 for Macauley 51, Dean Rock 0-2 for Brogan 58.

2014

DUBLIN 2-8   KERRY 1-10
Feb 2, Croke Park, Dublin
Dublin: S Cluxton, S George, M Fitzsimons, P McMahon, E Lowndes, C O'Sullivan, J Cooper, D O'Mahony, S Carthy 0-2, C Kilkenny, A Brogan, C Reddin, K McManamon 1-1, E O'Gara 1-0, C Costello 0-2. Subs: MD Macauley for O'Mahony 46, J McCaffrey 0-1 for Reddin 50, P Mannion 0-2 for McManamon 54, D Byrne for O'Gara 57), K Nolan for Carthy 64, D Nelson for Cooper 68.

DUBLIN 0-14   WESTMEATH 2-7
Feb 9, Cusack Park, Mullingar
Dublin: S Cluxton 0-3, M Fitzsimons, P McMahon, D Nelson, J Cooper, C O'Sullivan, E Lowndes, MD Macauley, S Carthy, P Flynn, C Kilkenny 0-3, C Reddin 0-2, P Mannion, K McManamon 0-1, E O'Gara. Subs: K O'Brien for Nelson 51, P Hudson 0-3 for McManamon 51, D Byrne 0-1 for O'Gara 58, J McCaffrey for Macauley 60, D Watson for Mannion 62, K Nolan for Cooper 66.

CORK 1-17   DUBLIN 0-18
Mar 1, Croke Park, Dublin
Dublin: S Cluxton 0-3, P McMahon, S George, M Fitzsimons, E Lowndes, J McCarthy 0-1, J Cooper, C O'Sullivan, MD Macauley, D Byrne, C Kilkenny 0-3, B Cullen, K McManamon 0-3, C Reddin 0-2, C Costello 0-4. Subs: J McCaffrey for George 23, D Nelson for Lowndes h/t, E O'Gara for Byrne 47, P Hudson 0-1 for Costello 52, S Carty 0-1 for Reddin 63.

DUBLIN 1-22   KILDARE 1-12
Mar 9, Croke Park, Dublin
Dublin: S Cluxton 0-2, S George, P McMahon, M Fitzsimons, J McCaffrey, J McCarthy, J Cooper 0-2, C O'Sullivan 0-2, MD Macauley, P Andrews 1-2, C Kilkenny, B Cullen 0-1, K McManamon 0-8, C Reddin, E O'Gara 0-2. Subs: D Byrne 0-1 for Kilkenny 3, A Brogan for Reddin h/t, D Nelson 0-1 for Fitzsimons h/t S Carthy for Cullen 44, D Daly for Cooper 51, T Brady 0-1 for O'Sullivan 59.

DERRY 1-16   DUBLIN 0-13
Mar 16, Celtic Park, Derry
Dublin: S Cluxton, S George, P McMahon 0-1, M Fitzsimons, D Nelson, J Cooper, D Daly, C O'Sullivan, MD Macauley 0-1, D Byrne, A Brogan 0-6, B Cullen, P Hudson 0-2, E O'Gara, P Andrews 0-2. Subs: K Nolan for George h/t, T Brady for Cullen h/t, J Whelan 0-1 for Hudson h/t, N Devereux for Nelson 45, C Reddin for Byrne 52, D O'Mahony for O'Sullivan 66.

DUBLIN 3-14   MAYO 2-17

Mar 30, Croke Park, Dublin

Dublin: S Cluxton 0-1, J Cooper, R O'Carroll, D Daly, J McCarthy, C O'Sullivan, K Nolan, MD Macauley, T Brady, P Flynn 0-1, A Brogan 0-2, D Connolly 0-2, K McManamon 1-2, C Costello 0-4, P Andrews 0-1. Subs: J Whelan 0-1 for Flynn 27, S Currie for Brady 30, N Devereux for Andrews h/t, J McCaffrey for O'Sullivan h/t, D Nelson for Daly 51, E O'Gara 2-0 for Costello 56.

DUBLIN 3-10   TYRONE 1-15

Apr 6, Healy Park, Omagh

Dublin: S Currie, J Cooper, R O'Carroll, P McMahon 0-1, J McCarthy 1-0, K Nolan, J McCaffrey, MD Macauley 1-0, T Brady, J Whelan 1-1, D Connolly 0-5, B Cullen 0-1, A Brogan 0-1, E O'Gara, K McManamon 0-1. Subs: P Andrews for Cullen 44, D Byrne for Brady 44, N Devereux for McCaffrey 54, C Costello for Brogan 56.

DIVISION 1	P	W	D	L	Pts
CORK	7	5	1	1	11
DERRY	7	4	1	2	9
MAYO	7	4	1	2	9
DUBLIN	7	4	1	2	9
TYRONE	7	3	2	2	8
KERRY	7	3	0	4	6
KILDARE	7	2	0	5	4
WESTMEATH	7	0	0	7	0

SEMI-FINAL

Apr 13, Croke Park, Dublin

DUBLIN 2-20   CORK 2-13

Dublin: S Cluxton, J Cooper 0-1, R O'Carroll, P McMahon, N Devereux, K Nolan, J McCarthy, MD Macauley 1-1, D O'Mahony, P Flynn 0-1, D Connolly 1-2, J Whelan, K McManamon 0-1, P Andrews 0-3, A Brogan 0-1. Subs: E O'Gara 0-3 for Whelan 26, D Byrne 0-1 for O'Mahony h/t, B Brogan 0-5 for McManamon 44, D Nelson for Nolan 56, C Reddin 0-1 for Andrews 66, T Brady for O'Gara 71.

FINAL

Apr 27, Croke Park, Dublin

DUBLIN 3-19   DERRY 1-10

Dublin: Stephen Cluxton 0-1, Philly McMahon, Rory O'Carroll, Johnny Cooper 0-1, James McCarthy, Niall Devereux, Kevin Nolan, Michael Darragh Macauley, Cian O'Sullivan, Paul Flynn 0-3, Paddy Andrews, Diarmuid Connolly 1-2, Alan Brogan 0-2, Eoghan O'Gara 0-2, Bernard Brogan 1-6. Subs: Kevin McManamon 1-0 for Andrews 29, David Byrne for Nolan 45, M Fitzsimons for O'Carroll 60, Ciaran Reddin 0-1 for O'Gara 61, Darragh Nelson 0-1 for O'Sullivan 63, Tomas Brady for A Brogan 67.

2015

CORK 1-15   DUBLIN 0-16

Feb 1, Pairc Ui Rinn, Cork

Dublin: S Currie, E Culligan, R O'Carroll, D Daly, J McCaffrey, J Small, J Cooper, D Bastick, S Carthy 0-1, T Brady 0-1, D Rock 0-8, E O'Conghaile, K McManamon 0-2, E O'Gara 0-2, C Costello 0-1. Subs: D Byrne for O'Conghaile h/t, B Fenton for Bastick 46, C Reddin for Carthy 54, E Lowndes for Cooper 57, C McHugh for Costello 57, M Deegan 0-1 for O'Gara 68.

DUBLIN 2-10   DONEGAL 0-11

Feb 8, Croke Park, Dublin

Dublin: S Currie, M Fitzsimons, E Culligan, D Daly, J Cooper, J Small, E Lowndes, D Bastick, E O'Conghaile 0-1, T Brady, D Rock 0-5, D Byrne (Ballymun) 0-1, K McManamon, E O'Gara 0-1, C Costello 1-0. Subs: D Byrne (St Olaf's) for Culligan 18, C Kilkenny 0-1 for Brady 19, J McCaffrey 1-1 for Lowndes 48, P McMahon for Cooper 60, B Brogan for Costello 64, C Reddin for Byrne (St Olaf's) 70.

KERRY 0-15   DUBLIN 1-10

Mar 1, Fitzgerald Stadium, Killarney

Dublin: S Currie, M Fitzsimons, R O'Carroll, D Daly, J McCaffrey 0-2, P McMahon, J Cooper, D Bastick, S Carthy 0-1, T Brady 0-1, D Rock 0-1, C Kilkenny 0-1, K McManamon 0-1, E O'Gara 0-1, C Costello. Subs: C O'Sullivan for Bastick 14, B Brogan 1-2 for Costello h/t, P Andrews for Rock 45, N Devereux for McMahon 53, B Fenton for Brady 57, E Lowndes for Cooper 63.

DUBLIN 1-9   TYRONE 0-12

Mar 8, Croke Park, Dublin

Dublin: S Cluxton, E Culligan, R O'Carroll, J Cooper, N Devereaux, P McMahon, J McCaffrey, D Bastick, E O'Conghaile 0-1, T Brady, D Rock 1-6, C Kilkenny, K McManamon, P Andrews, B Brogan 0-1. Subs: C O'Sullivan for Bastick 29, E O'Gara for Andrews h/t, P Flynn 0-1 for Kilkenny h/t, J McCarthy for McMahon 59, S Carthy for O'Conghaile 64, C Costello for Brady 67.

DUBLIN 2-18   MAYO 0-10

Mar 14, MacHale Park, Castlebar

Dublin: S Cluxton, E Culligan, R O'Carroll, J Cooper 0-1, P McMahon, C O'Sullivan, J McCaffrey 0-1, D Bastick 1-0, T Brady 0-2, P Flynn 0-1, D Connolly 0-1, C Kilkenny 0-5, B Brogan 1-1, D Rock 0-6, K McManamon. Subs: M Fitzsimons for O'Carroll h/t, J Small for Culligan 50, B Fenton for Bastick 59, E O'Gara for Brogan 59, J McCarthy for Brady 61, P Ryan 0-1 for McManamon 64.

DUBLIN 0-8   DERRY 0-4

Mar 28, Croke Park, Dublin

Dublin: S Cluxton, P McMahon, R O'Carroll, E

Culligan, J Cooper, J Small, J McCaffrey, MD
Macauley 0-1, T Brady, P Flynn, D Connolly 0-2, C
Kilkenny, K McManamon, D Rock 0-3, B Brogan.
Subs: C Costello 0-1 for McManamon h/t, J
McCarthy for Brady 41, D Byrne (St Olaf's) for
Culligan 41, P Andrews 0-1 for Kilkenny 51, B Fenton
for Macauley 70, D Byrne (Ballymun) for Brogan 70.

DUBLIN 1-22   MONAGHAN 1-11
Apr 5, St Tiernach's Park, Clones
Dublin: S Cluxton, J Cooper 0-1, R O'Carroll, E
Culligan, J McCarthy, J Small, J McCaffrey, MD
Macauley, D Bastick, P Flynn 0-2, D Connolly 0-2,
B Fenton 1-1, K McManamon 0-2, D Rock 0-6, B
Brogan 0-2. Subs: P McMahon 0-2 for Culligan
21, E O'Conghaile 0-1 for Macauley 42, C Kilkenny
for McManamon 49, T Brady 0-2 for Bastick 52,
D Byrne 0-1 for O'Conghaile 56, N Devereux for
Cooper 56.

DIVISION 1	P	W	D	L	Pts
CORK	7	5	0	2	10
DUBLIN	7	4	1	2	9
MONAGHAN	7	4	0	3	8
DONEGAL	7	3	1	3	7
MAYO	7	3	1	3	7
KERRY	7	3	1	3	7
TYRONE	7	1	3	3	5
DERRY	7	1	1	5	3

SEMI-FINAL
Apr 12, Croke Park, Dublin
DUBLIN 0-17   MONAGHAN 0-16
Dublin: S Cluxton, J Cooper, D Byrne (St Olaf's), P
McMahon 0-2, J McCarthy, J Small, J McCaffrey 0-1,
D Bastick 0-1, C O'Sullivan, P Flynn 0-1, D Connolly,
B Fenton 0-2, C Kilkenny, D Rock 0-7, K McManamon
0-2. Subs: MD Macauley for O'Sullivan 44, P
Andrews for McManamon 49, D Daly for Byrne 52, E
O'Conghaile 0-1 for Bastick 52, C Costello for Fenton
60, T Brady for Flynn 68.

FINAL
Apr 26, Croke Park, Dublin
DUBLIN 1-21   CORK 2-7
Dublin: Stephen Cluxton, Philly McMahon 0-1,
Rory O'Carroll, Johnny Cooper, James McCarthy,
Cian O'Sullivan, Jack McCaffrey 0-1, Denis Bastick,
Brian Fenton, Tomas Brady 0-1, Ciaran Kilkenny
0-3, Diarmuid Connolly 1-0, Dean Rock 0-10, Kevin
McManamon 0-1, Bernard Brogan 0-2. Subs: Michael
Fitzsimons for O'Carroll 26, Paddy Andrews 0-2
for Brady 46, Emmet O'Conghaile for Bastick 54,
Cormac Costello for Connolly 58, John Small for
McMahon 52, Darren Daly for Fenton 64.

2016

DUBLIN 2-14   KERRY 0-14
Jan 30, Croke Park, Dublin
Dublin: S Cluxton, J Cooper, M Fitzsimons, D Byrne
(St Olaf's), D Byrne (Ballymun), C O'Sullivan, J Small,
J McCarthy, D Bastick, T Brady 0-1, D Connolly 1-0,
C Kilkenny 0-1, P Mannion, D Rock 0-7, P Andrews
1-4. Subs: J McCaffrey for Byrne (Ballymun) 41, E
O'Conghaile for Bastick 50, C Costello 0-1 for Brady
53, C Reddin for Kilkenny 57, D Daly for O'Sullivan 61,
C O'Callaghan for Mannion 67.

DUBLIN 0-9   MAYO 0-7
Feb 6, MacHale Park, Castlebar
Dublin: S Cluxton, M Fitzsimons, J Cooper, D Byrne
(St Olaf's), E O'Conghaile 0-1, P McMahon, J Small, J
McCarthy 0-1, D Bastick 0-1, T Brady, D Connolly 0-1,
C Kilkenny, P Andrews, D Rock 0-4, P Mannion. Subs:
J McCaffrey for McMahon 2, S Carthy for Bastick h/t,
C Reddin for Brady 45, C Costello 0-1 for Mannion 53,
P Ryan for Andrews 64, D Daly for Cooper 70.

DUBLIN 1-14   MONAGHAN 0-16
Feb 27, Croke Park, Dublin
Dublin: S Cluxton, P McMahon 0-2, M Fitzsimons, D
Byrne (St Olaf's), J McCarthy, C O'Sullivan, J Small,
D Bastick, E O'Conghaile 0-1, P Flynn 0-1, D Connolly
1-0, T Brady, D Rock 0-7, P Andrews, C Costello
0-2. Subs: S Carthy for Bastick h/t, J Cooper for
Fitzsimons 53, B Brogan 0-1 for Brady 56, P Ryan for
Rock 58, B Fenton for E O'Conghaile 62, SB Carthy
for Connolly 66, D Byrne (Ballymun) for Costello 73.

DUBLIN 2-14   CORK 2-10
Mar 6, Croke Park, Dublin
Dublin: M Savage, J Cooper, P McMahon, D Byrne
(St Olaf's), J McCarthy 1-0, C O'Sullivan, E Lowndes,
B Fenton, E O'Conghaile, P Flynn, D Connolly 1-3, C
Kilkenny, C Costello 0-9, P Andrews 0-2, B Brogan.
Subs: J Small for Lowndes h/t, M Fitzsimons for
Fenton h/t, S Carthy for E O'Conghaile 48, D Rock
for Brogan 49, K McManamon for Andrews 65, SB
Carthy for Flynn 71.

DUBLIN 1-15   DOWN 1-7
Mar 12, Pairc Esler, Newry
Dublin: S Cluxton, D Byrne (St Olaf's), M Fitzsimons, J
Small, J McCarthy, P McMahon, J Cooper 0-1, B Fenton,
S Carthy, P Flynn 0-2, D Connolly, C Kilkenny 0-2, C
Costello 1-4, D Rock 0-3, K McManamon 0-2. Subs:
SB Carthy for Flynn 44, E Lowndes for S Carthy 46, P
Andrews 0-1 for McManamon 46, D Bastick for Fenton
50, T Brady for Costello 55, D Daly for Cooper 65.

DUBLIN 1-10   DONEGAL 0-7
Mar 26, Croke Park, Dublin
Dublin: M Savage, P McMahon 1-0, J Cooper,

D Byrne, J McCarthy, E Lowndes, J Small, B Fenton 0-1, D Bastick, P Flynn, K McManamon 0-3, C Kilkenny 0-1, C Costello 0-3, P Andrews 0-1, B Brogan. Subs: D Rock 0-1 for Brogan 41, E O'Conghaile for Bastick 45, SB Carthy for Lowndes 53, M Fitzsimons for Small 53, T Brady for Costello 59, D Daly for McManamon 70.

DUBLIN 1-13   ROSCOMMON 1-12
Apr 3, Pairc Diarmuda, Carrick-on-Shannon
Dublin: M Savage, K O'Brien, M Fitzsimons, D Daly, E Lowndes, C O'Sullivan, D Byrne, B Fenton, E O'Conghaile, T Brady, D Rock 1-8, SB Carthy 0-2, P Mannion, K McManamon 0-1, C McHugh 0-1. Subs: R McDaid for O'Sullivan h/t, P Flynn for Brady 44, E O'Gara for McManamon 49, J Small 0-1 for Daly 51, C Costello for Mannion 57, C Kilkenny for Lowndes 64.

DIVISION 1	P	W	D	L	Pts
DUBLIN	7	7	0	0	14
KERRY	7	5	0	2	10
ROSCOMMON	7	4	0	3	8
DONEGAL	7	3	0	4	6
MAYO	7	3	0	4	6
MONAGHAN	7	3	0	4	6
CORK	7	3	0	4	6
DOWN	7	0	0	7	0

SEMI-FINAL
Apr 10, Croke Park, Dublin
DUBLIN 1-20   DONEGAL 0-13
Dublin: S Cluxton, P McMahon 0-1, J Cooper 0-1, D Byrne, J McCarthy 0-1, C O'Sullivan, J Small 0-1, B Fenton, D Bastick, P Flynn, D Rock 0-5, C Kilkenny 0-3, P Mannion 0-2, P Andrews 0-2, B Brogan 1-2. Subs: C Costello 0-1 for Andrews 45, E Lowndes 0-1 for Bastick 48, M Fitzsimons for McMahon 52, SB Carthy for Flynn 61, K O'Brien for Cooper 61, S Carthy for O'Sullivan 66.

FINAL
Apr 24, Croke Park, Dublin
DUBLIN 2-18   KERRY 0-13
Dublin: Stephen Cluxton, Philly McMahon, Johnny Cooper 0-1, David Byrne, James McCarthy, Cian O'Sullivan, John Small, Brian Fenton 0-1, Denis Bastick, Paul Flynn 1-0, Dean Rock 0-5, Ciaran Kilkenny 0-2, Paul Mannion 0-1, Diarmuid Connolly 0-1, Bernard Brogan 0-4. Subs: Michael Darragh Macauley for Bastick 48, Kevin McManamon 0-2 for Connolly 54, Cormac Costello 0-1 for Rock 60, Michael Fitzsimons for McMahon 68, Eric Lowndes 1-0 for Mannion 68, Darren Daly for Small 69.

2017

DUBLIN 0-18   CAVAN 0-11
Feb 5, Breffni Park, Cavan
Dublin: S Cluxton, M Fitzsimons, P McMahon, E Lowndes, J McCarthy 0-2, J Small, J McCaffrey 0-1, B Fenton 0-1, MD Macauley 0-1, J Whelan 0-1, C Kilkenny 0-1, N Scully 0-2, P Mannion, D Rock 0-7, K McManamon 0-1. Subs: C Costello 0-1 for McManamon 42, C Basquel for Whelan 46, E O'Gara for Mannion 55, D Byrne for Fitzsimons 58, C Reddin for Macauley 62, C McHugh for Rock 69.
Feb 11, Croke Park, Dublin

DUBLIN 0-10   TYRONE 1-7
Dublin: S Cluxton, P McMahon 0-1, M Fitzsimons, J Cooper 0-1, J McCarthy, J Small, J McCaffrey, B Fenton 0-1, MD Macauley, N Scully, P Mannion, C Kilkenny 0-1, C Basquel, E O'Gara, D Rock 0-6. Subs: E Lowndes for Basquel h/t, K McManamon for Macauley 44, C Reddin for Mannion 50, D Byrne for McCaffrey 51, J Whelan for Small 57, D Daly for Cooper 59.

DUBLIN 1-8   DONEGAL 2-5
Feb 26, MacCumhaill Park, Ballybofey
Dublin: S Cluxton, P McMahon, M Fitzsimons, D Daly, E Lowndes, J McCaffrey, J Small, B Fenton, C Reddin, S Carthy (St Vincent's) 0-1, C Kilkenny 0-1, N Scully 1-1, C McHugh 0-1, E O'Gara, D Rock 0-3. Subs: MD Macauley for Reddin 41, P Flynn for Carthy 41, K McManamon for O'Gara 44, D Byrne 0-1 for McCaffrey 56, J Whelan for McHugh 62, E O Conghaile for Daly 69.

DUBLIN 1-16   MAYO 0-7
Mar 4, Croke Park, Dublin
Dublin: S Cluxton, P McMahon 0-2, M Fitzsimons, D Byrne, D Daly, J Small, E Lowndes 0-2, B Fenton, MD Macauley, N Scully, C Kilkenny, SB Carthy, D Rock 0-8, E O'Gara, C McHugh 1-3. Subs: P Andrews for O'Gara 48, P Flynn 0-1 for Carthy 51, K McManamon for McHugh 55, C Reddin for Byrne 65, E O Conghaile for Fenton 70, C Mullally for Small 72.

DUBLIN 0-13   KERRY 0-13
Mar 18, Austin Stack Park, Tralee
Dublin: S Cluxton, D Daly, P McMahon, M Fitzsimons, J Small, D Byrne, E Lowndes, B Fenton, MD Macauley, N Scully, C Kilkenny, SB Carthy, D Rock 0-9, P Andrews, C McHugh 0-2. Subs: C O'Sullivan for Byrne h/t, P Flynn for Scully 41, K McManamon for Macauley 44, E O'Gara 0-1 for Andrews 46, P Mannion 0-1 for Small 48, B Brogan for McHugh 69.

DUBLIN 2-29   ROSCOMMON 0-14
Mar 25, Croke Park, Dublin
Dublin: S Cluxton, P McMahon, M Fitzsimons, D Daly,

D Byrne, C O'Sullivan, E Lowndes 0-1, B Fenton 0-2, C Reddin 0-2, P Flynn 1-6, K McManamon 1-1, N Scully 0-2, D Rock 0-3, P Andrews 0-3, B Brogan 0-3. Subs: SB Carthy 0-1 for Byrne 30mins, J McCaffrey 0-1 for Daly 40, C McHugh 0-3 for Rock 40, D Connolly 0-1 for Fenton 44, MD Macauley for Reddin 47, P Mannion for O'Sullivan 50.

DUBLIN 2-15   MONAGHAN 1-15
Apr 2, St. Tiernach's Park, Clones
Dublin: S Cluxton, M Fitzsimons, D Byrne, P McMahon 0-1, J McCarthy 0-2, C Reddin 0-2, E Lowndes, B Fenton 0-1, C Kilkenny 0-1, P Flynn, N Scully, K McManamon, D Rock 0-5, P Andrews 0-2, C McHugh. Subs: B Brogan 1-1 for McHugh 35, D Connolly for Scully h/t, J McCaffrey 1-0 for Reddin 41, P Mannion for McManamon 47, C O'Sullivan for Connolly 50 (black card), MD Macauley for Flynn 65.

DIVISION 1	P	W	D	L	Pts
DUBLIN	7	4	3	0	11
KERRY	7	3	2	2	8
DONEGAL	7	3	2	2	8
MONAGHAN	7	3	2	2	8
MAYO	7	4	0	3	8
TYRONE	7	3	1	3	7
CAVAN	7	1	2	4	4
ROSCOMMON	7	1	0	6	2

FINAL
Apr 9, Croke Park, Dublin
KERRY 0-20   DUBLIN 1-16
Dublin: S Cluxton, D Daly, M Fitzsimons, P McMahon 0-1, E Lowndes, C O'Sullivan, J McCarthy 0-1, C Kilkenny 0-2, B Fenton, P Flynn 0-1, C Reddin 0-2, D Rock 0-6, P Andrews, D Connolly 0-1, B Brogan. Subs: N Scully for Connolly 30 (black card), P Mannion 1-2 for Andrews 42, MD Macauley for Reddin 49, K McMenamin for O'Sullivan 49, D Byrne for Lowndes 61, E O'Gara for Flynn 68.

ROLL OF HONOUR
Kerry (20): 1928, 1929, 1931, 1932, 1959, 1961, 1963, 1969, 1971, 1972, 1973, 1974, 1977, 1982, 1984, 1997, 2004, 2006, 2009, 2017.
Dublin (13): 1953, 1955, 1958, 1964, 1976, 1978, 1987, 1991, 1993, 2013, 2014, 2015, 2016.
Mayo (11): 1934, 1935, 1936, 1937, 1938, 1939, 1941, 1949, 1954, 1970, 2001.
Cork (8): 1952, 1956, 1980, 1989, 1999, 2010, 2011, 2012.
Meath (7): 1933, 1946, 1951, 1975, 1988, 1990, 1994.
Derry (6): 1947, 1992, 1995, 1996, 2000, 2008.
Galway (4): 1957, 1965, 1967, 1981.

Down (4): 1960, 1962, 1968, 1983.
Cavan (2): 1948, 1950.
Laois (2): 1926, 1986.
Tyrone (2): 2002, 2003.
Longford (1): 1966.
Roscommon (1): 1979.
Monaghan (1): 1985.
Offaly (1): 1998.
Armagh (1): 2005.
Donegal (1): 2007.

THE COMPLETE RECORD

County	P	W	D	L	For	Agt
Antrim	3	3	0	0	2-28	1-18
Armagh	28	15	4	9	25-274	20-247
Carlow	3	2	0	1	6-25	3-19
Cavan	16	9	3	4	22-133	17-124
Clare	3	2	0	1	2-28	4-23
Cork	45	19	4	22	8-91	5-64
Derry	13	7	1	5	14-149	8-130
Donegal	24	15	3	6	19-246	10-229
Down	19	12	1	6	22-201	17-144
Fermanagh	3	2	0	1	3-35	0-28
Galway	37	16	10	11	8-91	5-64
Kerry	48	20	6	22	52-472	37-496
Kildare	38	27	1	10	56-341	43-277
Kilkenny	1	1	0	0	10-65	3-17
Laois	31	23	2	6	55-257	30-197
Leitrim	3	2	0	1	2-42	2-26
Limerick	3	3	0	0	1-37	1-25
Longford	6	5	0	1	11-50	7-39
Louth	38	19	4	15	58-268	50-225
Mayo	34	19	4	11	38-339	25-308
Meath	34	16	6	12	42-246	36-233
Monaghan	22	16	2	4	31-241	20-187
New York	1	0	0	1	1-13	2-12
Offaly	30	17	4	9	48-247	37-207
Roscommon	29	19	2	8	46-314	24-232
Sligo	2	2	0	0	0-30	2-15
Tipperary	3	2	0	1	321	1-19
Tyrone	20	9	2	9	19-223	13-236
Waterford	3	3	0	0	6-37	1-13
Westmeath	17	13	0	4	26-175	12-119
Wexford	13	10	0	3	21-94	14-68
Wicklow	18	18	0	0	41-155	14-92
TOTALS	588	346	59	183	698-4,968	464-4,133

Dublin Against The Rest

WHY not start this section with a question: What is the only team Dublin have never beaten in competitive action; that is, Championship or National League? The answer will surprise many — our American cousins ... New York.

The sides, it is true, clashed several times in the long defunct St. Brendan's Cup — a glorified exhibition — but only ever had one competitive showdown, at Gaelic Park in the Big Apple in October 1964. That was back in the days when the National League had two finals, a 'home' or domestic one and then a 'proper' one, in which the exiles played the winners of the first decider. Dublin, in early May, claimed the domestic portion of the title with a 2-9 to 0-7 defeat of Down at Croke Park and just over five months later faced New York, whose only previous success in the competition was a 2-8 to 0-12 triumph over Cavan in 1950. Missing only Simon Behan from the side that started the previous year's All-Ireland Final triumph over Galway, Dublin built up a 1-7 to 1-4 by halftime but an unfortunate deflection by Lar Foley six minutes into the second half turned the tide and New York — who would reclaim the title three years later at the expense of Galway — edged home on a 2-12 to 1-13 scoreline.

The only other team to have a better record against Dublin than The Dubs have against them is hardly surprising in the least — arch rivals Kerry. In a combined total of 77 meetings, the Kingdom hold a 39-30 lead with eight draws and 17-10 and two draws in Championship action; had Dublin not failed in their bid for a fifth league title on the trot in April 2017, the National League score would be deadlocked at 21-21 and half a dozen draws.

The first ever meeting of the now fierce rivals was at Clonturk Park on 26 March 1893 when Dublin scored a 1-4 to 0-3 victory in the All-Ireland Final for the previous year and Johnny Geraghty from Young Irelands earned the distinction of scoring Dublin's first ever goal against the Kingdom. Four more Championship deciders, split two each, were played out between then and 1925 and the first league meeting of the teams was at Croke Park in December 1930 when Kerry won 0-8 to 0-3 and, by and large, the Kingdom held the upper hand over the next half a century or so.

Going into the All-Ireland Final in 1976, Dublin's last Championship win over Kerry had been in a semi-final at Austin Stack Park in Tralee — their first ever win on Kerry soil — in 1934 and subsequent to that, after drawing another semi-final in 1941, they not only lost the replay but suffered five further defeats in 1955, 1959, 1962, 1965 and 1975, the first and last in the sequence being in All-Ireland Finals. The losing streak was finally ended with a 3-8 to 0-10 victory for a 19th title for Dublin and the following year came a 3-12 to 1-13 semi-final win in a game many consider to be the greatest ever played, although a serious rival to it emerged in more recent times when, in an August 2016 semi-final showdown, Dublin, 2-8 to 0-9 adrift at halftime (after being 0-9 to 0-4 ahead nine minutes earlier until Stephen Cluxton took an uncustomary attack of the wobbles), stormed back for an 0-22 to 2-14 win. That was Dublin's fourth consecutive

Championship win over Kerry, something they had never previously achieved in the long and storied rivalry.

One of the most famous clashes of the counties was in the All-Ireland Final in 1978, the game of the Mike Sheehy goal fame; Kerry's victory on a 5-11 to 0-9 scoreline was their biggest ever over The Dubs but it seems to have gone relatively unnoticed that they equalled that winning margin over two decades later with a 1-124 to 1-7 victory in an All-Ireland quarter-final in August 2009. Dublin's biggest ever win in the rivalry was a 3-11 to 0-7 triumph in a league clash at Croke Park in February 1991 while their most convincing triumph in the Championship was a 3-8 to 0-6 success in the aforementioned All-Ireland semi-final in Tralee in September 1934.

AT the other end of the results spectrum, there are five teams that have never beaten Dublin; Antrim, Kilkenny, London, Waterford and Wicklow.

Antrim have drawn a blank in half a dozen meeting, half of them in the Championship and the remainder in the National League. The first three were all in All-Ireland semi-final, for 1901, 1908 and 1910, while the most recent meeting of the side was a quarter of a century ago, Dublin scoring a 1-7 to 0-5 win in a league clash at Casement Park in November 1992. Kilkenny, alone among the quintet, actually managed to hold The Dubs to a draw on one occasion; a 2-3 each stalemate in a provincial quarter-final tie at Athy in July 1912, a result that was not quite the shock that it would be nowadays given that Kilkenny were the reigning champions, having beaten Meath by 2-4 to 1-1 in the previous year's decider. Dublin won the replay 3-4 to 0-1 at the then Jones's Road and, in the Noresiders last appearance in a provincial senior football final, scored a 1-7 to 0-2 success in the by now Croke Park in November 1922. Dublin's eight victory in nine meetings with Kilkenny was by 6-16 to 0-4 in a Division II league game at Nowlan Park in December 1973, when John McCarthy became the first Dubliner to score four goals in a competitive game since Johnny Joyce in a league win over Galway at Pearse Stadium in Salthill.

London were beaten by Dublin in the All-Ireland Finals of 1901, 1902 and 1908, as well as in a semi-final of the 1906 campaign; the 1908 decider was played in August of the following year and the only other clash of the teams was all of nine and a half decades later when Dublin scored a runaway 3-24 to 0-6 victory in an All-Ireland qualifier at Parnell Park in June 2004, a scoreline that meant London failed to score a single goal in five meetings with The Dublin while totalling a mere 19 points. Waterford, for their part, fared little better, managing just a single goal in four meetings, a 1-16 to 1-2 victory for Dublin in a league sectional semi-final at Croke Park in March 1966. The one and only Championship clash of the counties was in the All-Ireland Final of 1998 — Waterford's lone provincial success — when Dublin scored a convincing 2-8 to 0-4 win at Tipperary Park and the most recent meeting of the teams was when Dublin won 2-15 to 0-5 in a Division II league game at Croke Park in February 1974.

Spare a though for Wicklow; not only is the Garden County last in the list of opponents alphabetically but it is also last statistically — not as much as even a single draw in 30 — yes, 30 — competitive clashes with their neighbours to the north. The first ever meeting of the teams, in a provincial semi-final at Clonturk Park in October 1891, was indicative of what was to follow: Dublin scored 4-4 while their opponents failed to raise even a single flag. The closest Wicklow ever got was an 0-10 to 0-8 defeat in a provincial quarter-final at St. Conleth's Park in Newbridge in May 1981 while Dublin's most emphatic success was, ironically, in the very next meeting, a 2-18 to 0-6 win for Dublin in a semi-final at the same venue in July 1987.

THE three teams with which Dublin have had the most enduring rivalries — and they only ones they have faced more often than Kerry — are hardly surprising given that they are all fellow travellers along the same provincial road; Meath, Louth and Kildare with, respectively, 96, 93 and 92 meetings over the years.

Dublin's familiarity with Meath began in 1894 with a glimpse into the future close to a century down the road; they needed three meetings to decide the provincial title after drawing 0-4 each at Clonturk Park and 0-2 each at the Showgrounds in Navan before, in February 1895, they returned to Clonturk Park where Dublin scored a relatively comfortable 1-8 to 1-2 victory. (It tends to be forgotten that Dublin and Meath actually played four consecutive draws at Croke Park in 1991 — the sides finished all square (Dublin 0-11, Meath 1-8) in a league meeting in March, exactly a dozen weeks before they began their classic four match Championship series.)

Those two stalemates in 1894 were but the first of many, eight in the Championship and another half a dozen in the National League. The games, generally, went nip and tuck until in the first half of the 1940s when Dublin, with seven wins in eight meetings, gradually opened up a bit of a gap only for Meath to claw things back until, in the space of eleven weeks in 1955, Dublin handed their neighbours not one but two crushing defeats at Croke Park, by 2-12 to 1-3 in the National League decider and then by a whopping 5-12 to 0-7 in the provincial final which Meath went into as not only the defending champions but also the reigning All-Ireland title holders.

Those two emphatic successes heralded almost three decades of Dublin dominance as Meath could only manage two wins — significant ones, though, in the provincial final in 1964 and the league decider in 1975 — and three draws. Then the pendulum swung decidedly in Meath's favour when, from 1986 onwards and for what remains the only time in history, the same two counties contested the Leinster Final for five consecutive years ... and Dublin won just one of them, in 1989. That was the lead in to the history making 1991 series which attracted a staggering total of 236,383 fans to what, after all, was a provincial first round tie. (The attendances, in chronological order, were 51,144, 60,960, 62,736 and 61,543.)

The rivalry with Louth is also highlighted by a marathon type series when three games were needed to decide the provincial title in 1934, Dublin finally winning out in Drogheda by 2-9 to 1-10 thanks to goals by Paddy Colleran and George Comerford, who also contributed five points. The first meeting of the sides had been in a Leinster quarter-final tie at Shamrock Lodge in Drogheda in September 1889 when Louth won 2-7 to 0-6 but would then suffer half a dozen defeats on the trot and, on average over the following three decades, only one of every three meetings with The Dubs although their rare victories included the provincial finals in 1910 and 1912 when they went on to win the All-Ireland on each occasion, although the first instance was via a walkover against Kerry. Louth famously beat Dublin in the 1957 final en route to capturing their third and most recent All-Ireland title but since then their lone Championship victory over The Dubs was in 1973.

Dublin's rivalry with Kildare is their oldest of all, beginning as it did with the Liffey-siders' debut in the Championship when they scored a 1-6 to 0-1 victory in a quarter-final match-up at Benburb Park in June 1888. Three years later Dublin won the Leinster Final on a walkover and since then have beaten the Lilywhites in ten other deciders while Kildare, for their part, have conquered The Dubs in four such clashes, in 1919, 1927, 1928 — when Bill Gannon became the first captain to be presented with the Sam Maguire Cup — and 2000. That latter success was a real turnaround as Dublin, ahead 0-11 to 0-5 at the interval, were stunned by goals from Dermot Earley and Tadhg Fennin within a minute and a half of the resumption and, shellshocked, could only add a single point in the entire second half as Kildare totalled 2-11.

Dublin Results Against The Rest

ANTRIM

ALL-IRELAND SEMI-FINAL, 1901
Apr 12, 1903, Jones's Road, Dublin
DUBLIN 2-12   ANTRIM 0-2

ALL-IRELAND SEMI-FINAL, 1908
Feb 21, 1909, Jones's Road, Dublin
DUBLIN 1-8   ANTRIM 0-2

ALL-IRELAND SEMI-FINAL
Oct 2, 1910, Jones's Road, Dublin
DUBLIN 3-5   ANTRIM 1-2

NATIONAL LEAGUE SEMI-FINAL
Apr 25, 1926, St Brigid's Park, Dundalk
DUBLIN 0-8   ANTRIM 0-5

**NATIONAL LEAGUE,
DIVISION 2 SEMI-FINAL**
Apr 21, 1974, Croke Park, Dublin
DUBLIN 1-13   ANTRIM 1-8

NATIONAL LEAGUE SECTION A
Nov 29, 1992, Casement Park, Belfast
DUBLIN 1-7   ANTRIM 0-5

	P	W	D	L	For	Agt
Championship	3	3	0	0	6-25	1-6
National League	3	3	0	0	2-28	1-18
TOTAL	6	6	0	0	8-53	2-24

ARMAGH

ALL-IRELAND SEMI-FINAL, 1902
June 5, 1904, Shamrock Lodge, Drogheda
DUBLIN 4-13   ARMAGH 1-6

NATIONAL LEAGUE, NORTHERN SECTION
Nov 27, 1927, Croke Park, Dublin
DUBLIN   3-5   ARMAGH 0-8

NATIONAL LEAGUE, SECTION C
Nov 13, 1938, Athletic Grounds, Armagh
ARMAGH 5-5   DUBLIN 2-6

NATIONAL LEAGUE, SECTION III
Nov 12, 1967, Croke Park, Dublin
DUBLIN 1-9   ARMAGH 1-6

NATIONAL LEAGUE, DIVISION 1B
Oct 20, 1968, Athletic Grounds, Armagh
DUBLIN 1-10   ARMAGH 0-7

NATIONAL LEAGUE, DIVISION 1B
Nov 16, 1969, Croke Park, Dublin
DUBLIN 2-11   ARMAGH 0-7

ALL-IRELAND FINAL
Sep 25, 1977, Croke Park, Dublin
DUBLIN   5-12   ARMAGH 3-6

NATIONAL LEAGUE, DIVISION ONE
Mar 1, 1981, Croke Park, Dublin
DUBLIN 2-8   ARMAGH 2-3

**NATIONAL LEAGUE, DIVISION ONE
PLAY-OFF**
Mar 15, 1981, Croke Park, Dublin
DUBLIN 1-7   ARMAGH 1-5

NATIONAL LEAGUE, DIVISION ONE
Feb 21, 1982, Athletic Grounds, Armagh
ARMAGH 0-8   DUBLIN 0-5

NATIONAL LEAGUE, DIVISION ONE
Mar 13, 1983, Croke Park, Dublin
DUBLIN 1-8   ARMAGH 0-11

NATIONAL LEAGUE, DIVISION ONE
Feb 19, 1984, Davitt Park, Lurgan
ARMAGH 0-7   DUBLIN 0-5

NATIONAL LEAGUE, DIVISION ONE
Dec 14, 1986, Croke Park, Dublin
DUBLIN 0-11   ARMAGH 1-6

NATIONAL LEAGUE, DIVISION ONE
Dec 13, 1987, Davitt Park, Lurgan
DUBLIN 0-9   ARMAGH 1-3

NATIONAL LEAGUE, DIVISION ONE
Feb 5, 1989, Croke Park, Dublin
DUBLIN 1-12   ARMAGH 0-7

NATIONAL LEAGUE, DIVISION ONE
Feb 4, 1990, Athletic Grounds, Armagh
ARMAGH 1-11   DUBLIN 0-10

**NATIONAL LEAGUE,
DIVISION ONE PLAY-OFF**
Mar 11, 1990, Drogheda Park, Drogheda
DUBLIN 1-14   ARMAGH 1-9

NATIONAL LEAGUE, DIVISION ONE
Oct 21, 1990, Croke Park, Dublin
DUBLIN 0-12   ARMAGH 0-9

NATIONAL LEAGUE, DIVISION IA
Nov 24, 1991, Croke Park, Dublin
DUBLIN 2-10   ARMAGH 1-8

NATIONAL LEAGUE QUARTER-FINAL
Apr 3, 1994, Breffni Park, Cavan
ARMAGH 2-13   DUBLIN 1-9

NATIONAL LEAGUE, DIVISION TWO
Oct 29, 1995, Athletic Grounds, Armagh
ARMAGH 0-8   DUBLIN 0-6

NATIONAL LEAGUE, DIVISION TWO
Oct 27, 1996, Parnell Park, Dublin
DUBLIN 1-7   ARMAGH 0-10

NATIONAL LEAGUE, DIVISION 1A
Nov 15, 1998, Athletic Grounds, Armagh
DUBLIN 0-14   ARMAGH 1-11

NATIONAL LEAGUE SEMI-FINAL
Apr 25, 1999, Croke Park, Dublin
DUBLIN 0-11   ARMAGH 0-11

NATIONAL LEAGUE SEMI-FINAL REPLAY
May 2, 1999, Croke Park, Dublin
DUBLIN 1-14   ARMAGH 0-12

NATIONAL LEAGUE, DIVISION 1A
Nov 14, 1999, Parnell Park, Dublin
DUBLIN 0-14   ARMAGH 0-6

ALL-IRELAND SEMI-FINAL
Sep 1, 2002, Croke Park, Dublin
ARMAGH 1-14   DUBLIN 1-13

NATIONAL LEAGUE, DIVISION 1A
Feb 2, 2003, Croke Park, Dublin
ARMAGH 1-15   DUBLIN 0-7

ALL-IRELAND QUALIFIER, ROUND THREE
July 5, 2003, Croke Park, Dublin
ARMAGH 0-15   DUBLIN 0-11

NATIONAL LEAGUE, DIVISION TWO
Apr 13, 2008, Plunkett Park, Crossmaglen
ARMAGH 3-13   DUBLIN 1-10

ALL-IRELAND QUALIFIER, ROUND THREE
July 17, 2010, Croke Park, Dublin
DUBLIN 0-14   ARMAGH 0-11

NATIONAL LEAGUE, DIVISION ONE
Feb 6, 2011, Athletic Grounds, Armagh
DUBLIN 2-12   ARMAGH 1-11

NATIONAL LEAGUE, DIVISION ONE
Mar 11, 2012, Croke Park, Dublin
DUBLIN 4-17   ARMAGH 1-10

	P	W	D	L	For	Agt
Championship	5	3	0	2	10-63	5-52
National League	28	15	4	9	25-274	20-247
TOTAL	33	20	4	11	35-337	25-299

CARLOW

LEINSTER QUARTER-FINAL
June 7, 1914, Sportsfield, Portlaoise
DUBLIN 0-5   CARLOW 0-1

LEINSTER FINAL
Nov 9, 1941, Dr Cullen Park, Carlow
DUBLIN 4-6   CARLOW 1-4

LEINSTER FINAL
July 19, 1942, Catherine Park, Athy
DUBLIN 0-8   CARLOW 0-6

LEINSTER FINAL
July 30, 1944, Catherine Park, Athy
CARLOW 2-6   DUBLIN 1-6

LEINSTER LEAGUE SEMI-FINAL
July 29, 1945, Sallins Road, Naas
CARLOW 2-9   DUBLIN 1-7

LEINSTER QUARTER-FINAL
May 22, 1955, St Conleth's Park, Newbridge
DUBLIN 3-9   CARLOW 0-6

LEINSTER SEMI-FINAL
June 22, 1958, O'Moore Park, Portlaoise
DUBLIN 3-9   CARLOW 2-7

LEINSTER QUARTER-FINAL
May 24, 1959, O'Moore Park, Portlaoise
DUBLIN 1-11   CARLOW 2-4

LEINSTER QUARTER-FINAL
May 24, 1964, St Conleth's Park, Newbridge
DUBLIN 1-14   CARLOW 1-5

NATIONAL LEAGUE, SECTION III SEMI-FINAL
Feb 19, 1967, Croke Park, Dublin
DUBLIN 3-9   CARLOW 1-6

NATIONAL LEAGUE, DIVISION IIA
Nov 25, 1973, Dr Cullen Park, Carlow
DUBLIN 1-9   CARLOW 0-4

LEINSTER QUARTER-FINAL
June 18, 1978, Croke Park, Dublin
DUBLIN 6-15   CARLOW 2-9

LEINSTER QUARTER-FINAL
June 6, 1988, Dr Cullen Park, Carlow
DUBLIN 1-14   CARLOW 0-8

LEINSTER QUARTER-FINAL
June 3, 2017, O'Moore Park, Portlaoise
DUBLIN 0-19   CARLOW 0-7

	P	W	D	L	For	Agt
Championship	11	10	0	1	10-116	10-63
National League	3	2	0	1	6-25	3-19
TOTAL	14	12	0	2	16-141	13-82

CAVAN

ALL-IRELAND SEMI-FINAL, 1891
Feb 28, 1892, Clonturk Park, Dublin
DUBLIN 3-7   CAVAN 0-3

ALL-IRELAND SEMI-FINAL
Sep 26, 1920, Showgrounds, Navan
DUBLIN 3-6   CAVAN 1-3

ALL-IRELAND SEMI-FINAL, 1925
Jan 18, 1925, Croke Park, Dublin
DUBLIN 0-6   CAVAN 1-1

**NATIONAL LEAGUE,
NORTHERN SECTION**
Mar 20, 1927, Croke Park, Dublin
DUBLIN 1-7   CAVAN 3-1

NATIONAL LEAGUE, DIVISION ONE
Dec 8, 1935, Breffni Park, Cavan
CAVAN 1-5   DUBLIN 0-6

NATIONAL LEAGUE, DIVISION 1A
Oct 11, 1936, Breffni Park, Cavan
CAVAN 0-8   DUBLIN 0-5

NATIONAL LEAGUE,SECTION C
Feb 27, 1938, Croke Park, Dublin
DUBLIN 1-6   CAVAN 1-6

NATIONAL LEAGUE,SECTION C
Dec 11, 1938, Breffni Park, Cavan
DUBLIN 0-5   CAVAN 0-5

ALL-IRELAND SEMI-FINAL
Aug 2, 1942, Croke Park, Dublin
DUBLIN   1-6   CAVAN 1-3

**NATIONAL LEAGUE,GROUP VI,
DIVISIONAL FINAL**
Mar 21, 1948, Croke Park, Dublin
CAVAN 3-17   DUBLIN 2-4

NATIONAL LEAGUE FINAL
Apr 26, 1953, Croke Park, Dublin
DUBLIN 4-6   CAVAN 0-9

NATIONAL LEAGUE SEMI-FINAL
Apr 24, 1960, Pairc Tailteann, Navan
CAVAN 2-8   DUBLIN 1-8

**NATIONAL LEAGUE
QUARTER-FINAL**
Mar 13, 1977, Pearse Park, Longford
DUBLIN 2-12   CAVAN 1-7

**NATIONAL LEAGUE,
DIVISION TWO**
Mar 2, 1986, Croke Park, Dublin
DUBLIN 3-6   CAVAN 0-9

NATIONAL LEAGUE SEMI-FINAL
Apr 9, 1989, Croke Park, Dublin
DUBLIN 1-10   CAVAN 1-9

NATIONAL LEAGUE, DIVISION ONE
Dec 3, 1989, Croke Park, Dublin
DUBLIN 2-12   CAVAN 3-7

NATIONAL LEAGUE, DIVISION TWO
Feb 11, 1996, Parnell Park, Dublin
DUBLIN 2-9   CAVAN 2-7

NATIONAL LEAGUE, DIVISION TWO
Nov 30, 1997, Parnell Park, Dublin
DUBLIN 2-14   CAVAN 0-8

NATIONAL LEAGUE, DIVISION TWO
Mar 2, 2008, Breffni Park, Cavan
DUBLIN 1-9   CAVAN 0-7

NATIONAL LEAGUE, DIVISION ONE
Feb 5, 2017, Breffni Park, Cavan
DUBLIN 0-18   CAVAN 0-11

	P	W	D	L	For	Agt
Championship	4	4	0	0	7-25	3-10
National League	16	9	3	4	22-133	17-124
TOTAL	20	13	3	4	29-158	20-134

CLARE

NATIONAL LEAGUE, DIVISION IIA
Feb 17, 1974, Croke Park, Dublin
CLARE 4-9   DUBLIN 2-9

ALL-IRELAND SEMI-FINAL
Aug 23, 1992, Croke Park, Dublin
DUBLIN 3-14   CLARE 2-12

NATIONAL LEAGUE, DIVISION ONE
Oct 10, 1993, Cusack Park, Ennis
DUBLIN 0-8   CLARE 0-6

NATIONAL LEAGUE, DIVISION TWO
Nov 24, 1996, Parnell Park, Dublin
DUBLIN 0-11   CLARE 0-8

	P	W	D	L	For	Agt
Championship	1	1	0	0	3-14	2-12
National League	3	2	0	1	2-28	4-23
TOTAL	4	3	0	1	5-42	6-35

CORK

ALL-IRELAND FINAL, 1891
Feb 28, 1892, Clonturk Park, Dublin
DUBLIN 2-1   CORK 1-1

ALL-IRELAND FINAL, 1894
Mar 24, 1895, Clonturk Park, Dublin
DUBLIN 0-6   CORK 1-1

ALL-IRELAND FINAL REPLAY, 1894
Apr 21, 1895, Clonturk Park, Dublin
DUBLIN 0-5   CORK 1-2
*Dublin won when Cork refused to play
on following a dispute*

ALL-IRELAND FINAL, 1897
Feb 5, 1899, Jones's Road, Dublin
DUBLIN 2-6   CORK 0-2

ALL-IRELAND FINAL, 1899
Feb 10, 1901, Jones's Road, Dublin
DUBLIN 1-10   CORK 0-6

**ALL-IRELAND 'HOME'
FINAL, 1901**
July 5, 1903, Tipperary Park, Tipperary
DUBLIN 1-2   CORK 0-4

ALL-IRELAND FINAL, 1905
Oct 20, 1907, Agricultural Grounds, Athy
DUBLIN 0-5   CORK 0-4

ALL-IRELAND FINAL, 1907
July 5, 1908, Tipperary Park, Tipperary
DUBLIN 0-6   CORK 0-2

NATIONAL LEAGUE 'HOME' FINAL
Apr 27,1952, Croke Park, Dublin
CORK 2-3   DUBLIN 1-5

NATIONAL LEAGUE SEMI-FINAL
Apr 17, 1955, Croke Park, Dublin
DUBLIN 0-12   CORK 0-9

NATIONAL LEAGUE SEMI-FINAL
Apr 15, 1956, Athletic Grounds, Cork
DUBLIN 1-4   CORK 0-7

**NATIONAL LEAGUE
SEMI-FINAL REPLAY**
Apr 29, 1956, Croke Park, Dublin
CORK 1-16   DUBLIN 1-9

NATIONAL LEAGUE, SECTION III
Nov 28, 1965, Croke Park, Dublin
CORK 2-10   DUBLIN 0-9

NATIONAL LEAGUE, SECTION III
Jan 22, 1967, Athletic Grounds, Cork
DUBLIN 2-8   CORK 2-5

NATIONAL LEAGUE, DIVISION IB
Mar 14, 1971, Croke Park, Dublin
DUBLIN 1-8   CORK 1-7

NATIONAL LEAGUE, DIVISION IA
Apr 30, 1972, Athletic Grounds, Cork
DUBLIN 2-4   CORK 1-7

NATIONAL LEAGUE, DIVISION IB
Feb 3, 1973, Croke Park, Dublin
CORK 3-11   DUBLIN 1-10

ALL-IRELAND SEMI-FINAL
Aug 11, 1974, Croke Park, Dublin
DUBLIN 2-11   CORK 1-8

NATIONAL LEAGUE, DIVISION IA
Oct 20, 1974, Croke Park, Dublin
CORK 1-8   DUBLIN 0-10

NATIONAL LEAGUE, DIVISION IA
Oct 26, 1975, The Mardyke, Cork
DUBLIN 1-12   CORK 0-4

NATIONAL LEAGUE, DIVISION IA
Oct 10, 1976, Croke Park, Dublin
DUBLIN 1-13   CORK 2-9

NATIONAL LEAGUE, DIVISION IA
Nov 13, 1977, Pairc Ui Chaoimh, Cork
DUBLIN 0-8   CORK 0-5

NATIONAL LEAGUE, DIVISION IA
Dec 10, 1978, Pairc Ui Chaoimh, Cork
CORK 2-10   DUBLIN 0-5

NATIONAL LEAGUE, DIVISION IA
Nov 11, 1979, Croke Park, Dublin
DUBLIN 3-4   CORK 2-7

NATIONAL LEAGUE, DIVISION ONE
Dec 14, 1980, Croke Park, Dublin
DUBLIN 1-11   CORK 1-9

NATIONAL LEAGUE, DIVISION ONE
Nov 29, 1981, Pairc Ui Chaoimh, Cork
DUBLIN 1-5   CORK 0-6

NATIONAL LEAGUE, DIVISION ONE
Feb 13, 1983, Croke Park, Dublin
DUBLIN 1-8   CORK 1-7

ALL-IRELAND SEMI-FINAL
Aug 21, 1983, Croke Park, Dublin
DUBLIN 2-11   CORK 2-11

ALL-IRELAND SEMI-FINAL REPLAY
Aug 28, 1983, Pairc Ui Chaoimh, Cork
DUBLIN 4-15   CORK 2-10

NATIONAL LEAGUE, DIVISION ONE
Dec 4, 1983, Pairc Ui Chaoimh
CORK 1-9   DUBLIN 1-3

NATIONAL LEAGUE, DIVISION TWO
Oct 13, 1985, Pairc Ui Chaoimh, Cork
DUBLIN 0-13   CORK 0-8

**NATIONAL LEAGUE
QUARTER-FINAL**
Apr 5, 1987, Croke Park, Dublin
DUBLIN 1-10   CORK 1-7

NATIONAL LEAGUE, DIVISION TWO
Feb 28, 1988, Pairc Ui Chaoimh, Cork
DUBLIN 1-10   CORK 1-10

NATIONAL LEAGUE 'HOME' FINAL
Apr 23, 1989, Croke Park, Dublin
CORK 0-15   DUBLIN 0-12

ALL-IRELAND SEMI-FINAL
Aug 20, 1989, Croke Park, Dublin
CORK   2-10   DUBLIN 1-9

NATIONAL LEAGUE, DIVISION ONE
Nov 19, 1989, Pairc Ui Chaoimh, Cork
CORK 3-13   DUBLIN 1-16

NATIONAL LEAGUE, DIVISION ONE
Nov 25, 1990, Croke Park, Dublin
DUBLIN 0-10   CORK 0-6

NATIONAL LEAGUE, DIVISION IA
Mar 8, 1992, Croke Park, Dublin
CORK 2-8   DUBLIN 1-10

ALL-IRELAND SEMI-FINAL
Aug 20, 1995, Croke Park, Dublin
DUBLIN   1-12   CORK 0-12

NATIONAL LEAGUE, DIVISION ONE
Nov 12, 1995, Croke Park, Dublin
CORK 2-9   DUBLIN 0-8

NATIONAL LEAGUE, DIVISION IA
Mar 28,1999, Pairc Ui Rinn, Cork
CORK 0-10   DUBLIN 0-7

NATIONAL LEAGUE FINAL
May 9, 1999, Pairc Ui Chaoimh, Cork
CORK 1-12   DUBLIN 0-7

NATIONAL LEAGUE, DIVISION IA
Apr 9, 2000, Parnell Park, Dublin
DUBLIN 2-10   CORK 1-11

NATIONAL LEAGUE, DIVISION IA
Mar 10, 2002, Pairc Ui Chaoimh, Cork
CORK 1-13   DUBLIN 0-10

NATIONAL LEAGUE, DIVISION IA
Mar 9, 2003, Parnell Park, Dublin
CORK 0-16   DUBLIN 0-8

NATIONAL LEAGUE, DIVISION IA
Mar 21, 2004, Parnell Park, Dublin
DUBLIN 0-9   CORK 0-9

NATIONAL LEAGUE, DIVISION IA
Mar 26, 2005, Pairc Ui Rinn, Cork
CORK 0-18   DUBLIN 1-6

NATIONAL LEAGUE, DIVISION IA
Mar 11, 2006, Pairc Ui Rinn, Cork
CORK 1-11   DUBLIN 1-10

NATIONAL LEAGUE, DIVISION IA
Mar 10, 2007, Parnell Park, Dublin
DUBLIN 1-13   CORK 0-7

NATIONAL LEAGUE, DIVISION ONE
Mar 20, 2010, Pairc Ui Rinn, Cork
CORK 2-13   DUBLIN 2-6

ALL-IRELAND SEMI-FINAL
Aug 22, 2010, Croke Park, Dublin
CORK 1-15   DUBLIN 1-14

NATIONAL LEAGUE, DIVISION ONE
Feb 19, 2011, Croke Park, Dublin
DUBLIN 3-13   CORK 0-16

NATIONAL LEAGUE FINAL
Apr 24, 2011, Croke Park, Dublin
CORK 0-21   DUBLIN 2-14

NATIONAL LEAGUE, DIVISION ONE
Apr 8, 2012, Pairc Ui Chaoimh, Cork
CORK 1-12   DUBLIN 0-12

**ALL-IRELAND
QUARTER-FINAL**
Aug 3, 2013, Croke Park, Dublin
DUBLIN 1-16   CORK 0-14

NATIONAL LEAGUE, DIVISION ONE
Feb 2, 2013, Croke Park, Dublin
DUBLIN 1-18   CORK 2-9

NATIONAL LEAGUE, DIVISION ONE
Mar 1, 2014, Croke Park, Dublin
CORK 1-17   DUBLIN 0-18

NATIONAL LEAGUE SEMI-FINAL
Apr 13, 2014, Croke Park, Dublin
DUBLIN 2-20   CORK 2-13

NATIONAL LEAGUE, DIVISION ONE
Feb 1, 2015, Pairc Ui Rinn, Cork
CORK 1-15   DUBLIN 0-16

NATIONAL LEAGUE FINAL
Apr 26, 2015, Croke Park, Dublin
DUBLIN 1-21   CORK 2-7

NATIONAL LEAGUE, DIVISION ONE
Mar 6, 2016, Croke Park, Dublin
DUBLIN 2-14   CORK 2-10

	P	W	D	L	For	Agt
Championship	15	12	1	2	18-129	11-102
National League	46	19	5	22	40-469	48-465
TOTALS	61	31	6	24	58-598	59-567

DERRY

ALL-IRELAND FINAL
Sep 28, 1958, Croke Park, Dublin
DUBLIN   2-12   DERRY 1-9

ALL-IRELAND SEMI-FINAL
Aug 24, 1975, Croke Park, Dublin
DUBLIN   3-13   DERRY 3-8

NATIONAL LEAGUE FINAL
May 2, 1976, Croke Park, Dublin
DUBLIN 2-10   DERRY 0-15

NATIONAL LEAGUE, DIVISION ONE
Feb 27, 1982, Wolfe Tone Park, Bellaghy
DERRY 1-11   DUBLIN 1-10

NATIONAL LEAGUE, DIVISION ONE
Feb 14, 1988, Parnell Park, Dublin
DUBLIN 1-9   DERRY 0-5

NATIONAL LEAGUE, DIVISION ONE
Oct 23, 1988, Wolfe Tone Park, Bellaghy
DERRY 1-7 DUBLIN 0-6

NATIONAL LEAGUE, DIVISION ONE
Oct 22, 1989, Croke Park, Dublin
DUBLIN 4-18   DERRY 1-9

NATIONAL LEAGUE, SECTION A
Oct 18, 1992, Croke Park, Dublin
DERRY 0-11   DUBLIN 0-9

ALL-IRELAND SEMI-FINAL
Aug 22, 1993, Croke Park, Dublin
DERRY   0-15   DUBLIN   0-14

NATIONAL LEAGUE, DIVISION ONE
Mar 13, 1994, Wolfe Tone Park, Bellaghy
DUBLIN 0-15   DERRY 2-6

NATIONAL LEAGUE, DIVISION ONE
Mar 19, 1995, Croke Park, Dublin
DUBLIN 1-9   DERRY 1-9

ALL-IRELAND QUALIFIERS, ROUND TWO
June 28 , 2003, St Tiernach's Park, Clones
DUBLIN   3-9   DERRY 1-9

ALL-IRELAND QUARTER-FINAL
Aug 11, 2008, Croke Park, Dublin
DUBLIN   0-18   DERRY 0-15

NATIONAL LEAGUE, DIVISION ONE
Mar 14, 2009, Parnell Park, Dublin
DERRY 0-20   DUBLIN 1-12

NATIONAL LEAGUE, DIVISION ONE
Feb 14, 2010, Parnell Park, Dublin
DUBLIN 1-11   DERRY 0-7

NATIONAL LEAGUE, DIVISION ONE
Mar 16, 2014, Celtic Park, Derry
DERRY 1-16   DUBLIN 0-13

NATIONAL LEAGUE FINAL
Apr 27, 2014, Croke Park, Dublin
DUBLIN 3-19   DERRY 1-10

NATIONAL LEAGUE, DIVISION ONE
Mar 28, 2015, Croke Park, Dublin
DUBLIN 0-8   DERRY 0-4

	P	W	D	L	For	Agt
Championship	5	4	0	1	8-66	5-56
National League	13	7	1	5	14-149	8-130
TOTAL	18	11	1	6	22-215	13-186

DONEGAL

National League, Division Two
Dec 2, 1984, MacCumhail Park, Ballybofey
DUBLIN 1-6   DONEGAL 1-4

NATIONAL LEAGUE, DIVISION TWO
Nov 24, 1985, Croke Park, Dublin
DUBLIN 0-15   DONEGAL 0-8

NATIONAL LEAGUE, DIVISION ONE
Feb 26, 1989, Croke Park, Dublin
DUBLIN 1-10   DONEGAL 0-9

NATIONAL LEAGUE, DIVISION ONE
Mar 4, 1990, MacCumhail Park, Ballybofey
DONEGAL 1-10   DUBLIN 0-9

NATIONAL LEAGUE, DIVISION ONE
Oct 7, 1990, MacCumhail Park, Ballybofey
DONEGAL 2-11   DUBLIN 1-9

NATIONAL LEAGUE QUARTER-FINAL
Apr 5, 1992, Breffni Park, Cavan
DUBLIN 3-6   DONEGAL 1-10

ALL-IRELAND FINAL
Sep 20, 1992, Croke Park, Dublin
DONEGAL 0-18   DUBLIN 0-14

NATIONAL LEAGUE FINAL
May 2, 1993, Croke Park, Dublin
DUBLIN 0-9   DONEGAL 0-9

NATIONAL LEAGUE FINAL REPLAY
May 9, 1993, Croke Park, Dublin
DUBLIN 0-10   DONEGAL 0-6

NATIONAL LEAGUE, DIVISION ONE
Nov 7, 1993, MacCumhail Park, Ballybofey
DONEGAL 0-11   DUBLIN 0-7

NATIONAL LEAGUE, DIVISION ONE
Nov 13, 1994, Croke Park, Dublin
DONEGAL 0-12   DUBLIN 1-8

NATIONAL LEAGUE, DIVISION IA
Feb 28, 1999, Fr Tierney Park, Ballyshannon
DONEGAL 1-8   DUBLIN 0-9

NATIONAL LEAGUE, DIVISION IA
Mar 5, 2000, Parnell Park, Dublin
DUBLIN 1-11   DONEGAL 0-11

NATIONAL LEAGUE, DIVISION IA
Feb 25, 2001, Fr Tierney Park, Ballyshannon
DUBLIN 0-11   DONEGAL 0-8

NATIONAL LEAGUE, DIVISION IA
Feb 10, 2002, Parnell Park, Dublin
DUBLIN 2-10   DONEGAL 0-14

ALL-IRELAND QUARTER-FINAL
Aug 5, 2002, Croke Park, Dublin
DUBLIN   2-8   DONEGAL 0-14

ALL-IRELAND QUARTER-FINAL REPLAY
Aug 17, 2002, Croke Park, Dublin
DUBLIN   1-14   DONEGAL 0-7

NATIONAL LEAGUE, DIVISION IA
Feb 9, 2003, Fr Tierney Park, Ballyshannon
DUBLIN 1-10   DONEGAL 0-9

NATIONAL LEAGUE, DIVISION IA
Mar 20, 2005, Parnell Park, Dublin
DUBLIN 1-11   DONEGAL 0-13

NATIONAL LEAGUE, DIVISION IA
Feb 25, 2007, Fr Tierney Park, Ballyshannon
DONEGAL 0-9   DUBLIN 0-5

NATIONAL LEAGUE, DIVISION ONE
Mar 8, 2009, Fr Tierney Park, Ballyshannon
DUBLIN 0-13   DONEGAL 1-8

ALL-IRELAND SEMI-FINAL
Aug 28, 2011, Croke Park, Dublin
DUBLIN 0-8   DONEGAL 0-6

NATIONAL LEAGUE, DIVISION ONE
Mar 24, 2012, Croke Park, Dublin
DUBLIN 2-16   DONEGAL 0-13

NATIONAL LEAGUE, DIVISION ONE
Apr 7, 2013, MacCumhaill Park, Ballybofey
DUBLIN 0-13   DONEGAL 1-10

ALL-IRELAND SEMI-FINAL
Aug 31, 2014, Croke Park, Dublin
DONEGAL 3-14   DUBLIN 0-17

NATIONAL LEAGUE, DIVISION ONE
Feb 8, 2015, Croke Park, Dublin
DUBLIN 2-10   DONEGAL 0-11

NATIONAL LEAGUE, DIVISION ONE
Mar 26, 2016, Croke Park, Dublin
DUBLIN 1-10   DONEGAL 0-7

NATIONAL LEAGUE SEMI-FINAL
Apr 10, 2016, Croke Park, Dublin
DUBLIN 1-20   DONEGAL 0-13

ALL-IRELAND QUARTER-FINAL
Aug 6, 2016, Croke Park, Dublin
DUBLIN 1-15   DONEGAL 1-10

NATIONAL LEAGUE, DIVISION ONE
Feb 26, 2017, MacCumhaill Park, Ballybofey
DUBLIN 1-8   DONEGAL 2-5

	P	W	D	L	For	Agt
Championship	6	3	1	2	4-76	4-69
National League	24	15	3	6	19-246	10-229
TOTAL	30	18	4	8	23-322	14-298

DOWN

NATIONAL LEAGUE, NORTHERN SECTION
Oct 30, 1927, Croke Park, Dublin
DOWN 2-7   DUBLIN 2-6

NATIONAL LEAGUE, SECTION C
Mar 26, 1939, St Patrick's Park, Newcastle
DUBLIN 0-18   DOWN 0-10

NATIONAL LEAGUE FINAL
May 13, 1962, Croke Park, Dublin
DOWN 2-5   DUBLIN 1-7

ALL-IRELAND SEMI-FINAL
Aug 18, 1963, Croke Park, Dublin
DUBLIN 2-11   DOWN 0-7

NATIONAL LEAGUE 'HOME' FINAL
May 3, 1964, Croke Park, Dublin
DUBLIN 2-9   DOWN 0-7

NATIONAL LEAGUE, SECTION III FINAL
Feb 12, 1968, Croke Park, Dublin
DOWN 3-7   DUBLIN 2-4

ALL-IRELAND SEMI-FINAL
Aug 20, 1978, Croke Park, Dublin
DUBLIN 1-16   DOWN 0-8

NATIONAL LEAGUE, DIVISION ONE
Feb 22, 1981, Croke Park, Dublin
DUBLIN 2-8   DOWN 0-9

NATIONAL LEAGUE, DIVISION ONE
Nov 7, 1982, Croke Park, Dublin
DOWN 1-6   DUBLIN 0-8

NATIONAL LEAGUE, DIVISION ONE
Nov 6, 1983, Pairc Esler, Newry
DOWN 1-6   DUBLIN 0-7

NATIONAL LEAGUE, DIVISION ONE
Feb 22, 1987, St Patrick's Park, Newcastle
DUBLIN 2-12   DOWN 2-8

NATIONAL LEAGUE, DIVISION ONE
Nov 6, 1988, Croke Park, Dublin
DUBLIN 1-16   DOWN 0-4

NATIONAL LEAGUE, DIVISION ONE
Nov 5, 1989, Pairc Esler, Newry
DUBLIN 1-17   DOWN 2-11

NATIONAL LEAGUE, DIVISION ONE
Feb 17, 1991, St Patrick's Park, Newcastle
DUBLIN 2-10   DOWN 1-7

NATIONAL LEAGUE, DIVISION ONE
Feb 20, 1994, Croke Park, Dublin
DUBLIN 1-7   DOWN 1-7

ALL-IRELAND FINAL
Sep 18, 1994, Croke Park, Dublin
DOWN 1-12   DUBLIN 0-13

NATIONAL LEAGUE, DIVISION ONE
Mar 5, 1995, Pairc Esler, Newry
DUBLIN 1-7   DOWN 0-1

NATIONAL LEAGUE, DIVISION TWO
Feb 25, 1996, St Patrick's Park, Newcastle
DUBLIN 0-15   DOWN 1-5

NATIONAL LEAGUE, DIVISION ONE
Apr 2, 2011, Croke Park, Dublin
DUBLIN 2-10   DOWN 0-13

NATIONAL LEAGUE, DIVISION ONE
Mar 18, 2012, Pairc Esler, Newry
DOWN 0-15   DUBLIN 1-10

NATIONAL LEAGUE, DIVISION ONE
Mar 23, 2013, Croke Park, Dublin
DUBLIN 1-15   DOWN 0-9

NATIONAL LEAGUE, DIVISION ONE
Mar 12, 2016, Pairc Esler, Newry
DUBLIN 1-15   DOWN 1-7

	P	W	D	L	For	Agt
Championship	3	2	0	1	3-40	1-27
National League	19	12	1	6	22-201	17-144
TOTAL	22	14	1	7	25-241	18-171

FERMANAGH

NATIONAL LEAGUE, DIVISION IA
Mar 14, 2004, Bewster Park, Enniskillen
DUBLIN 0-12   FERMANAGH 0-12

NATIONAL LEAGUE, DIVISION IA
Mar 19, 2006, Brewster Park, Enniskillen
FERMANAGH 0-9   DUBLIN 0-8

NATIONAL LEAGUE, DIVISION IA
Mar 24, 2007, Parnell Park, Dublin
DUBLIN 3-15   FERMANAGH 0-7

ALL-IRELAND QUARTER-FINAL
Aug 2, 2015, Croke Park, Dublin
DUBLIN 2-23   FERMANAGH 2-15

	P	W	D	L	For	Agt
Championship	1	1	0	0	2-23	2-15
National League	3	2	0	1	3-35	0-28
TOTAL	4	3	0	1	5-58	2-43

GALWAY

ALL-IRELAND FINAL, 1922
Oct 7, 1923, Croke Park, Dublin
DUBLIN 0-6   GALWAY 0-4

ALL-IRELAND SEMI-FINAL
Aug 20, 1933, Cusack Park, Mullingar
GALWAY 0-8   DUBLIN 1-4

ALL-IRELAND FINAL
Sep 23, 1934, Croke Park, Dublin
GALWAY 3-5   DUBLIN 1-9

NATIONAL LEAGUE, SECTION A
Mar 3, 1935, Duggan Park, Ballinasloe
GALWAY 2-4   DUBLIN 1-5

NATIONAL LEAGUE, DIVISION ONE
Nov 24, 1935, Croke Park, Dublin
DUBLIN 3-3   GALWAY 1-2

ALL-IRELAND FINAL
Sep 20, 1942, Croke Park, Dublin
DUBLIN 1-10   GALWAY 1-8

NATIONAL LEAGUE, SECTION III
Oct 11, 1953, Croke Park, Dublin
DUBLIN 0-8   GALWAY 2-2

NATIONAL LEAGUE, SECTION III
Oct 10, 1954, St Jarleth's Park, Tuam
DUBLIN 1-6   GALWAY 1-6

NATIONAL LEAGUE, SECTION III
Dec 4, 1955, St Jarleth's Park, Tuam
DUBLIN 1-6   GALWAY 1-5

NATIONAL LEAGUE, SECTION III
Feb 3,1957, St Jarleth's Park, Tuam
GALWAY 2-8   DUBLIN 2-6

NATIONAL LEAGUE, SECTION III
Mar 9, 1958, Dunlo Grounds, Ballinasloe
GALWAY 2-4   DUBLIN 0-7

NATIONAL LEAGUE, SECTION III PLAY-OFF
Apr 13, 1958, Croke Park, Dublin
DUBLIN 3-5   GALWAY 1-7

ALL-IRELAND SEMI-FINAL
Aug 17,1958, Croke Park, Dublin
DUBLIN 2-7   GALWAY 1-9

NATIONAL LEAGUE, SECTION III
Mar 1, 1959, Croke Park, Dublin
DUBLIN 3-10   GALWAY 3-6

NATIONAL LEAGUE, SECTION III
Feb 7, 1960, Croke Park, Dublin
DUBLIN 1-13   GALWAY 1-5

NATIONAL LEAGUE, SECTION III
Feb 5, 1961, Duggan Park, Ballinasloe
DUBLIN 1-8   GALWAY 0-3

NATIONAL LEAGUE, SECTION III
Mar 4, 1962, Pearse Stadium, Salthill
DUBLIN 6-7   GALWAY 1-4

NATIONAL LEAGUE, SECTION III
Mar 3, 1963, Croke Park, Dublin
GALWAY 2-12   DUBLIN 0-7

ALL-IRELAND FINAL
Sep 22, 1963, Croke Park, Dublin
DUBLIN 1-9   GALWAY 0-10

NATIONAL LEAGUE, SECTION III
Mar 1, 1964, Croke Park, Dublin
GALWAY 2-7   DUBLIN 1-8

NATIONAL LEAGUE, SECTION III
Mar 28, 1965, Tuam Stadium, Tuam
GALWAY 2-11   DUBLIN 1-7

NATIONAL LEAGUE FINAL
Apr 30, 1967, Croke Park, Dublin
GALWAY 0-12   DUBLIN 1-7

NATIONAL LEAGUE, DIVISION IB
Nov 29, 1970, Croke Park, Dublin
DUBLIN 3-5   GALWAY 1-11

NATIONAL LEAGUE, DIVISION IA
Nov 28, 1971, Pearse Stadium, Salthill
DUBLIN 0-8   GALWAY 0-8

NATIONAL LEAGUE, DIVISION IA
Nov 26, 1972, Croke Park, Dublin
GALWAY 2-7   DUBLIN 1-4

ALL-IRELAND FINAL
Sep 22, 1974, Croke Park, Dublin
DUBLIN 0-14   GALWAY 1-6

NATIONAL LEAGUE SEMI-FINAL
Apr 4, 1976, Croke Park, Dublin
DUBLIN 1-11   GALWAY 0-12

ALL-IRELAND SEMI-FINAL
Aug 29, 1976, Croke Park, Dublin
DUBLIN 1-8   GALWAY 0-8

NATIONAL LEAGUE, DIVISION IA
Dec 5, 1976, Croke Park, Dublin
DUBLIN 0-11   GALWAY 0-7

NATIONAL LEAGUE, DIVISION IA
Dec 3, 1978, Tuam Stadium, Tuam
DUBLIN 0-5   GALWAY 0-5

NATIONAL LEAGUE, DIVISION IA
Feb 3, 1980, Croke Park, Dublin
GALWAY 1-6   DUBLIN 0-8

NATIONAL LEAGUE, DIVISION ONE
Nov 1, 1981, Dunlo Grounds, Ballinasloe
DUBLIN 0-9   GALWAY 0-9

ALL-IRELAND FINAL
Sep 18, 1983, Croke Park, Dublin
DUBLIN   1-10   GALWAY 1-8

NATIONAL LEAGUE, DIVISION TWO
Feb 2, 1986, Duggan Park, Ballinasloe
DUBLIN 0-12   GALWAY 0-10

NATIONAL LEAGUE SEMI-FINAL
Apr 19, 1987, O'Moore Park, Portlaoise
DUBLIN 1-8   GALWAY 0-8

NATIONAL LEAGUE, DIVISION IA
Oct 27, 1991, Pearse Stadium, Salthill
DUBLIN 1-5   GALWAY 0-7

**NATIONAL LEAGUE,
DIVISION IA PLAY-OFF**
Mar 22, 1992, Croke Park, Dublin
DUBLIN 2-8   GALWAY 0-8

NATIONAL LEAGUE, SECTION A
Feb 28, 1993, Croke Park, Dublin
DUBLIN 0-13   GALWAY 1-6

NATIONAL LEAGUE, DIVISION IA
Mar 14, 1999, Parnell Park, Dublin
DUBLIN 0-15   GALWAY 1-12

NATIONAL LEAGUE, DIVISION IA
Mar 19, 2000, Tuam Stadium, Tuam
DUBLIN 2-15   GALWAY 0-20

NATIONAL LEAGUE, DIVISION IA
Apr 8, 2001, Parnell Park, Dublin
DUBLIN 1-10   GALWAY 1-8

NATIONAL LEAGUE, DIVISION IA
Mar 31, 2002, Tuam Stadium, Tuam
DUBLIN 1-12   GALWAY 1-12

NATIONAL LEAGUE, DIVISION IA
Apr 6, 2003, Parnell Park, Dublin
DUBLIN 0-12   GALWAY 1-9

NATIONAL LEAGUE, DIVISION ONE
Feb 15, 2009, Pearse Stadium, Salthill
GALWAY 3-12   DUBLIN 0-13

NATIONAL LEAGUE, DIVISION ONE
Mar 27, 2010, Parnell Park, Dublin
GALWAY 1-14   DUBLIN 0-14

NATIONAL LEAGUE, DIVISION ONE
Apr 10, 2011, Pearse Stadium, Salthill
DUBLIN 2-9   GALWAY 0-15

	P	W	D	L	For	Agt
Championship	9	7	0	2	40-320	36-294
National League	37	16	10	11	8-91	5-64
TOTAL	46	23	10	13	48-411	41-358

KERRY

ALL-IRELAND FINAL, 1892
Mar 26, 1893, Clonturk Park, Dublin
DUBLIN 1-4   KERRY 0-3

ALL-IRELAND FINAL, 1904
July 1, 1906, Athletic Grounds, Cork
KERRY 0-5   DUBLIN 0-2

ALL-IRELAND 'HOME' FINAL, 1908
May 9, 1909, Sportsfield, Thurles
DUBLIN 0-10   KERRY 0-3

ALL-IRELAND FINAL, 1923
Sep 28, 1924, Croke Park, Dublin
DUBLIN 1-5   KERRY 1-3

ALL-IRELAND FINAL, 1924
Apr 26, 1925, Croke Park, Dublin
KERRY 0-4   DUBLIN 0-3

NATIONAL LEAGUE, SECTION A
Dec 7, 1930, Croke Park, Dublin
KERRY 0-8   DUBLIN 0-3

NATIONAL LEAGUE, SECTION A
Nov 15, 1931, Frank Sheehy Park, Listowel
KERRY 1-10   DUBLIN 3-2

ALL-IRELAND SEMI-FINAL
Aug 21, 1932, Croke Park, Dublin
KERRY 1-3 DUBLIN 1-1

NATIONAL LEAGUE, SECTION A
Nov 13, 1932, Austin Stack Park, Tralee
KERRY 0-9   DUBLIN 0-7

NATIONAL LEAGUE, GROUP II
Apr 8, 1934, Croke Park, Dublin
DUBLIN 2-6   KERRY 1-7

ALL-IRELAND SEMI-FINAL
Sep 9, 1934, Austin Stack Park, Tralee
DUBLIN 3-8   KERRY 0-6

NATIONAL LEAGUE, SEMI-FINAL
Mar 9, 1941, Croke Park, Dublin
DUBLIN 2-7   KERRY 1-4

ALL-IRELAND SEMI-FINAL
Aug 10, 1941, Croke Park, Dublin
DUBLIN 0-4   KERRY 0-4

ALL-IRELAND SEMI-FINAL REPLAY
Aug 17, 1941, Austin Stack Park, Tralee
KERRY 2-9   DUBLIN 0-3

ALL-IRELAND FINAL
Sep 25, 1955, Croke Park, Dublin
KERRY 0-12   DUBLIN 1-6

ALL-IRELAND SEMI-FINAL
Aug 16, 1959, Croke Park, Dublin
KERRY 1-10   DUBLIN 2-5

ALL-IRELAND SEMI-FINAL
Aug 5, 1962, Croke Park, Dublin
KERRY 2-12   DUBLIN 0-10

NATIONAL LEAGUE, SEMI-FINAL
Apr 12,1964, Croke Park, Dublin
DUBLIN 0-10   KERRY 0-9

ALL-IRELAND SEMI-FINAL
Aug 8, 1965, Croke Park, Dublin
KERRY 4-8   DUBLIN 2-6

NATIONAL LEAGUE, DIVISION 1B
Oct 18, 1970, Austin Stack Park, Tralee
KERRY 0-16   DUBLIN 2-4

NATIONAL LEAGUE, DIVISION 1B PLAY-OFF
May 2, 1971, Croke Park, Dublin
KERRY 0-15   DUBLIN 1-8

NATIONAL LEAGUE, DIVISION 1B
Dec 19, 1971, Croke Park, Dublin
DUBLIN 3-9   KERRY 0-11

NATIONAL LEAGUE, DIVISION 1B
Mar 11, 1972, Austin Stack Park, Tralee
KERRY 1-10   DUBLIN 1-6

NATIONAL LEAGUE, DIVISION IA
Nov 10, 1974, Fitzgerald Stadium, Killarney
DUBLIN 0-8   KERRY 0-8

ALL-IRELAND FINAL
Sep 28, 1975, Croke Park, Dublin
KERRY 2-12   DUBLIN 0-11

NATIONAL LEAGUE, DIVISION IA
Nov 9, 1975, Croke Park, Dublin
DUBLIN 2-11   KERRY 0-13

ALL-IRELAND FINAL
Sep 26, 1976, Croke Park, Dublin
DUBLIN 3-8   KERRY 0-10

NATIONAL LEAGUE, DIVISION IA
Oct 24, 1976, Austin Stack Park, Tralee
KERRY 0-12   DUBLIN 0-7

NATIONAL LEAGUE FINAL
Apr 17, 1977, Croke Park, Dublin
KERRY 1-8   DUBLIN 1-6

ALL-IRELAND SEMI-FINAL
Aug 21, 1977, Croke Park, Dublin
DUBLIN 3-12   KERRY 1-13

NATIONAL LEAGUE, DIVISION IA
Oct 23, 1977, Croke Park, Dublin
DUBLIN 2-11   KERRY 2-7

ALL-IRELAND FINAL
Sep 24, 1978, Croke Park, Dublin
KERRY 5-11   DUBLIN 0-9

NATIONAL LEAGUE, DIVISION IA
Oct 8, 1978, Croke Park, Dublin
KERRY 2-9   DUBLIN 0-8

ALL-IRELAND FINAL
Sep 16, 1979, Croke Park, Dublin
KERRY 3-13   DUBLIN 1-8

NATIONAL LEAGUE, DIVISION IA
Oct 7, 1979, Austin Stack Park, Tralee
KERRY 1-16   DUBLIN 0-10

NATIONAL LEAGUE, DIVISION ONE
Nov 30,1980, Fitzgerald Stadium, Killarney
KERRY 2-11   DUBLIN 2-7

NATIONAL LEAGUE, DIVISION ONE
Nov 15, 1981, Croke Park, Dublin
DUBLIN 1-7   KERRY 1-7

NATIONAL LEAGUE, DIVISION ONE
Nov 21, 1982, Austin Stack Park, Tralee
DUBLIN 0-8   KERRY 0-7

NATIONAL LEAGUE, DIVISION ONE
Nov 20, 1983, Croke Park, Dublin
DUBLIN 2-9   KERRY 2-9

ALL-IRELAND FINAL
Sep 23, 1984, Croke Park, Dublin
KERRY 0-14   DUBLIN 1-6

ALL-IRELAND FINAL
Sep 22, 1985, Croke Park, Dublin
KERRY 2-12   DUBLIN 2-8

NATIONAL LEAGUE, DIVISION ONE
Nov 30, 1986, Austin Stack Park, Tralee
KERRY 0-10   DUBLIN 0-8

NATIONAL LEAGUE, DIVISION ONE
Dec 6, 1987, Croke Park, Dublin
DUBLIN 1-9   KERRY 2-5

NATIONAL LEAGUE, DIVISION ONE
Feb 12, 1989, Austin Stack Park, Tralee
KERRY 1-10   DUBLIN 0-11

NATIONAL LEAGUE, DIVISION ONE
Feb 11, 1990, Croke Park, Dublin
DUBLIN 1-15   KERRY 3-7

NATIONAL LEAGUE, DIVISION ONE
Feb 24, 1991, Croke Park, Dublin
DUBLIN 3-11   KERRY 0-7

NATIONAL LEAGUE SEMI-FINAL
Apr 18, 1993, Croke Park, Dublin
DUBLIN 1-10   KERRY 0-11

NATIONAL LEAGUE, DIVISION ONE
Oct 24, 1993, Croke Park, Dublin
DUBLIN 2-12   KERRY 1-13

NATIONAL LEAGUE, DIVISION ONE
Oct 30, 1994, Fitzgerald Stadium, Killarney
KERRY 1-12   DUBLIN 1-11

NATIONAL LEAGUE, DIVISION TWO
Mar 15, 1998, Parnell Park, Dublin
DUBLIN 0-18   KERRY 1-3

NATIONAL LEAGUE, DIVISION IA
Nov 28, 1999, Parnell Park, Dublin
DUBLIN 1-8   KERRY 0-9

NATIONAL LEAGUE, DIVISION IA
Apr 1, 2001, Fitzgerald Stadium, Killarney
KERRY 2-9   DUBLIN 0-10

ALL-IRELAND QUARTER-FINAL
Aug 4, 2001, Semple Stadium, Thurles
DUBLIN 2-11   KERRY 1-14

ALL-IRELAND QUARTER-FINAL REPLAY
Aug 11, 2001, Semple Stadium, Thurles
KERRY 2-12   DUBLIN 1-12

NATIONAL LEAGUE, DIVISION IA
Mar 2, 2003, Fitzgerald Stadium, Killarney
KERRY 2-11   DUBLIN 0-14

NATIONAL LEAGUE, DIVISION IA
Feb 15, 2004, Parnell Park, Dublin
KERRY 1-12   DUBLIN 0-12

ALL-IRELAND QUARTER-FINAL
Aug 14, 2004, Croke Park, Dublin
KERRY 1-15   DUBLIN 1-8

NATIONAL LEAGUE, DIVISION IA
Mar 6, 2005, Austin Stack Park, Tralee
KERRY 2-13   DUBLIN 2-11

NATIONAL LEAGUE, DIVISION IA
Apr 9, 2006, Fitzgerald Stadium, Killarney
DUBLIN 0-13   KERRY 0-13

NATIONAL LEAGUE, DIVISION IA
Apr 8, 2007, Parnell Park, Dublin
KERRY 1-12   DUBLIN 2-7

ALL-IRELAND SEMI-FINAL
Aug 26, 2007, Croke Park, Dublin
KERRY 1-15   DUBLIN 0-16

NATIONAL LEAGUE, DIVISION ONE
Mar 29, 2009, Parnell Park, Dublin
DUBLIN 1-15   KERRY 1-15

ALL-IRELAND QUARTER-FINAL
Aug 3, 2009, Croke Park, Dublin
KERRY 1-24   DUBLIN 1-7

NATIONAL LEAGUE, DIVISION ONE
Feb 7, 2010, Fitzgerald Stadium, Killarney
DUBLIN 1-12   KERRY 1-10

NATIONAL LEAGUE, DIVISION ONE
Feb 26, 2011, Croke Park, Dublin
DUBLIN 3-10   KERRY 1-15

ALL-IRELAND FINAL
Sep 18, 2011, Croke Park, Dublin
DUBLIN 1-12   KERRY 1-11

NATIONAL LEAGUE, DIVISION ONE
Feb 4, 2012, Croke Park, Dublin
KERRY 1-14   DUBLIN 0-11

NATIONAL LEAGUE, DIVISION ONE
Feb 10, 2013, Fitzgerald Stadium, Killarney
DUBLIN 1-11   KERRY 0-4

ALL-IRELAND SEMI-FINAL
Sep 1, 2013, Croke Park, Dublin
DUBLIN 3-18   KERRY 3-11

NATIONAL LEAGUE, DIVISION ONE
Feb 2, 2014, Croke Park, Dublin
DUBLIN 2-8   KERRY 1-10

NATIONAL LEAGUE, DIVISION ONE
Mar 1, 2015, Fitzgerald Stadium, Killarney
KERRY 0-15   DUBLIN 1-10

ALL-IRELAND FINAL
Sep 20, 2015, Croke Park, Dublin
DUBLIN 0-12   KERRY 0-9

NATIONAL LEAGUE, DIVISION ONE
Jan 30, 2016, Croke Park, Dublin
DUBLIN 2-14   KERRY 0-14

NATIONAL LEAGUE FINAL
Apr 24, 2016, Croke Park, Dublin
DUBLIN 2-18   KERRY 0-13

ALL-IRELAND SEMI-FINAL
Aug 28, 2016, Croke Park, Dublin
DUBLIN 0-22   KERRY 2-14

NATIONAL LEAGUE, DIVISION ONE
Mar 18, 2017, Austin Stack Park, Tralee
DUBLIN 0-13   KERRY 0-13

NATIONAL LEAGUE FINAL
Apr 9, 2017, Croke Park, Dublin
KERRY 0-20   DUBLIN 1-16

	P	W	D	L	For	Agt
Championship	29	10	2	17	30-247	36-292
National League	48	20	6	22	52-472	37-496
TOTAL	77	30	8	39	82-719	73-788

KILDARE

LEINSTER QUARTER-FINAL
June 3, 1888, Benburb Park, Dublin
DUBLIN   1–6   KILDARE 0–1

LEINSTER FINAL
Nov 15, 1891, Clonturk Park, Dublin
DUBLIN W/O   KILDARE SCR

LEINSTER SEMI-FINAL, 1892
Mar 12, 1893, Clonturk Park, Dublin
DUBLIN 3-5   KILDARE 0-1

LEINSTER SEMI-FINAL, 1895
Feb 16, 1896, Jones's Road, Dublin
DUBLIN 2-8   KILDARE 0-4

LEINSTER SEMI-FINAL, 1896
May 30, 1897 Jones's Road, Dublin
DUBLIN 2-13   KILDARE 1-12

LEINSTER QUARTER-FINAL, 1897
July 17, 1898, Jones's Road, Dublin
DUBLIN 2-15   KILDARE 0-2

LEINSTER QUARTER-FINAL, 1898
Nov 19, 1899, Jones's Road, Dublin
DUBLIN W/O   KILDARE SCR

LEINSTER QUARTER-FINAL, 1903
Sep 18, 1904, Geashill, Offaly
KILDARE 3-13   DUBLIN 1-3

LEINSTER QUARTER-FINAL, 1904
Mar 19, 1906, Jones's Road, Dublin
DUBLIN 0-9   KILDARE 0-5

LEINSTER FIRST ROUND, 1905
Aug 18, 1906, Agricultural Grounds, Athy
KILDARE 0-6   DUBLIN 0-2

LEINSTER FINAL, 1906
July 7, 1907, St James's Park, Kilkenny
DUBLIN 1-9   KILDARE 0-8

LEINSTER QUARTER-FINAL
Dec 8, 1907, Jones's Road, Dublin
DUBLIN 0-11   KILDARE 0-4

LEINSTER FINAL
Dec 13, 1908, Africultural Ground, Athy
DUBLIN 1-7   KILDARE 0-3

LEINSTER QUARTER-FINAL
July 6, 1913, Jones's Road, Dublin
DUBLIN 2-2   KILDARE 2-1

LEINSTER SEMI-FINAL
Aug 8, 1914, Croke Park, Dublin
DUBLIN 1-2   KILDARE 0-1

LEINSTER FIRST ROUND
July 8, 1917, St Conleth's Park, Newbridge
DUBLIN 1-6   KILDARE 2-1

LEINSTER FINAL
Sep 7, 1919, Croke Park, Dublin
KILDARE 1-3   DUBLIN 1-2

LEINSTER FINAL
Aug 29, 1920, Croke Park, Dublin
DUBLIN 1-3   KILDARE 0-3

LEINSTER FINAL
Aug 28, 1921, Croke Park, Dublin
DUBLIN 0-6   KILDARE 1-3

LEINSTER FINAL REPLAY
Sep 18, 1921, Croke Park, Dublin
DUBLIN 3-3   KILDARE 1-2

LEINSTER SEMI-FINAL
Oct 1, 1922, Croke Park, Dublin
DUBLIN 2-5   KILDARE 0-2

NATIONAL LEAGUE, GROUP C
Nov 8, 1925, Croke Park, Dublin
DUBLIN 2-5   KILDARE 1-3

LEINSTER SEMI-FINAL
June 20, 1926, O'Connor Park, Tullamore
DUBLIN 1-3   KILDARE 0-6

LEINSTER SEMI-FINAL REPLAY
July 4, 1926, O'Moore Park, Portlaoise
KILDARE 2-5   DUBLIN 1-2

NATIONAL LEAGUE, NORTHERN SECTION
Feb 27, 1927, St Conleth's Park, Newbridge
KILDARE 1-3   DUBLIN 0-2

LEINSTER FINAL
Aug 14, 1927, Croke Park, Dublin
KILDARE 0-5   DUBLIN 0-3

LEINSTER FINAL
July 22, 1928, Croke Park, Dublin
KILDARE 0-10   DUBLIN 1-6

NATIONAL LEAGUE, SOUTH EASTERN SECTION
Oct 14, 1928, Croke Park, Dublin
KILDARE 2-6   DUBLIN 0-3

NATIONAL LEAGUE, SECTION A
Mar 23, 1930, St Conleth's Park, Newbridge
DUBLIN 2-3   KILDARE 1-1

NATIONAL LEAGUE, SECTION A
Mar 8, 1931, Croke Park, Dublin
KILDARE 2-10   DUBLIN 2-4

NATIONAL LEAGUE, GROUP II
Nov 19, 1933, Croke Park, Dublin
DUBLIN 1-5   KILDARE 0-6

NATIONAL LEAGUE, DIVISION ONE
Mar 29, 1936, St Conleth's Park, Newbridge
KILDARE 0-12   DUBLIN 1-6

NATIONAL LEAGUE, DIVISION IA
Oct 25, 1936, Croke Park, Dublin
KILDARE 0-7   DUBLIN 0-5

NATIONAL LEAGUE, GROUP C
Oct 31,1937, Sallins Road, Naas
KILDARE 3-5   DUBLIN 2-4

LEINSTER QUARTER-FINAL
May 29, 1938, O'Moore Park, Portlaoise
KILDARE 4-7   DUBLIN 3-5

LEINSTER SEMI-FINAL
July 13, 1941, Croke Park, Dublin
DUBLIN 2-11   KILDARE 2-10

LEINSTER LEAGUE
Oct 15, 1944, St Conleth's Park, Newbridge
DUBLIN 0-8   KILDARE 1-3

NATIONAL LEAGUE, GROUP VI
Nov 18, 1945, Croke Park, Dublin
DUBLIN 4-5   KILDARE 2-4

NATIONAL LEAGUE, GROUP VI
Nov 3, 1946, St Conleth's Park, Newbridge
KILDARE 0-8   DUBLIN 0-2

NATIONAL LEAGUE, SECTION IV
Mar 5, 1950, Croke Park, Dublin
DUBLIN 2-11   KILDARE 3-3

LEINSTER FIRST ROUND
May 7, 1950, Cusack Park, Mullingar
KILDARE 2-11   DUBLIN 1-9

NATIONAL LEAGUE, SECTION IV
Mar 11, 1951, St Bridget's Park, Kildare
DUBLIN 1-7   KILDARE 1-5

NATIONAL LEAGUE, SECTION IV
Feb 3, 1952, Croke Park, Dublin
DUBLIN 3-9   KILDARE 1-4

NATIONAL LEAGUE, SECTION IV
Mar 15, 1953, St Bridget's Park, Kildare
DUBLIN 1-4   KILDARE 1-3

NATIONAL LEAGUE FINAL
May 18, 1958, Croke Park, Dublin
DUBLIN 3-13   KILDARE 3-8

LEINSTER SEMI-FINAL
June 23, 1963, Croke Park, Dublin
DUBLIN 2-7   KILDARE 1-5

LEINSTER SEMI-FINAL
June 20, 1965, O'Connor Park, Tullamore
DUBLIN 1-11   KILDARE 0-5

NATIONAL LEAGUE, SECTION III
Oct 17, 1965, St Conleth's Park, Newbridge
DUBLIN 1-15   KILDARE 1-9

LEINSTER SEMI-FINAL
July 10, 1966, Pairc Tailteann, Navan
KILDARE 3-9   DUBLIN 2-5

NATIONAL LEAGUE, SECTION III
Oct 30, 1966, Croke Park, Dublin
DUBLIN 2-10   KILDARE 3-6

LEINSTER SEMI-FINAL
June 15, 1969, Dr Cullen Park, Carlow
KILDARE 0-18   DUBLIN 0-7

NATIONAL LEAGUE, DIVISION IB
Nov 15, 1970, Sallins Road, Naas
DUBLIN 0-14   KILDARE 0-10

NATIONAL LEAGUE, DIVISION IA
Nov 14, 1971, Croke Park, Dublin
DUBLIN 3-8   KILDARE 1-10

LEINSTER SEMI-FINAL
July 2, 1972, Pairc Tailteann, Navan
KILDARE 0-16   DUBLIN 3-5

**NATIONAL LEAGUE,
DIVISION IA**
Feb 11, 1973, Catherine Park, Athy
DUBLIN 2-11   KILDARE 1-8

NATIONAL LEAGUE, DIVISION IIA
Oct 28, 1973, Catherine Park, Athy
DUBLIN 1-10   KILDARE 1-9

**NATIONAL LEAGUE,
DIVISION II FINAL**
May 5, 1974, Croke Park, Dublin
KILDARE 3-13   DUBLIN 2-9

LEINSTER SEMI-FINAL
July 14, 1974, Croke Park, Dublin
DUBLIN 1-13   KILDARE 0-10

NATIONAL LEAGUE, DIVISION IA
Jan 19, 1975, Croke Park, Dublin
DUBLIN 3-13   KILDARE 1-4

LEINSTER FINAL
July 27, 1975, Croke Park, Dublin
DUBLIN 3-13   KILDARE 0-8

NATIONAL LEAGUE, DIVISION IA
Nov 23, 1975, Geraldine Park, Athy
DUBLIN 1-14   KILDARE 0-7

NATIONAL LEAGUE, DIVISION IA
Nov 7, 1976, Croke Park, Dublin
DUBLIN 3-13   KILDARE 1-10

LEINSTER QUARTER-FINAL
May 29, 1977, Pairc Tailteann, Navan
DUBLIN 1-14   KILDARE 2-8

NATIONAL LEAGUE, DIVISION IA
Nov 6, 1977, St Conleth's Park, Newbridge
DUBLIN 2-9   KILDARE 1-8

LEINSTER FINAL
July 30, 1978, Croke Park, Dublin
DUBLIN 1-17   KILDARE 1-6

NATIONAL LEAGUE, DIVISION IA
Nov 19, 1978, Croke Park, Dublin
KILDARE 2-11   DUBLIN 0-6

NATIONAL LEAGUE, DIVISION IA
Dec 9, 1979, Catherine Park, Athy
DUBLIN 2-7   KILDARE 0-12

NATIONAL LEAGUE, DIVISION ONE
Nov 16, 1980, Croke Park, Dublin
DUBLIN 3-9   KILDARE 0-11

LEINSTER SEMI-FINAL
July 4, 1982, Pairc Tailteann, Navan
DUBLIN 1-13   KILDARE 0-12

NATIONAL LEAGUE, DIVISION ONE
Feb 5, 1984, Croke Park, Dublin
DUBLIN 1-9   KILDARE 1-2

LEINSTER QUARTER-FINAL
June 5, 1989, St Conleth's Park, Newbridge
DUBLIN 1-13   KILDARE 1-9

NATIONAL LEAGUE FINAL
May 5, 1991, Croke Park, Dublin
DUBLIN 1-9   KILDARE 0-10

LEINSTER FINAL
July 26, 1992, Croke Park, Dublin
DUBLIN 1-13   KILDARE 0-10

NATIONAL LEAGUE
QUARTER-FINAL
Apr 11, 1993, Croke Park, Dublin
DUBLIN 1-13   KILDARE 0-8

LEINSTER FINAL
July 25, 1993, Croke Park, Dublin
DUBLIN 0-11   KILDARE 0-7

NATIONAL LEAGUE, DIVISION ONE
Feb 6, 1994, St Conleth's Park, Newbridge
DUBLIN 0-7   KILDARE 1-4

LEINSTER QUARTER-FINAL
June 18, 1994, Croke Park, Dublin
DUBLIN 0-11   KILDARE 0-11

LEINSTER QUARTER-FINAL
REPLAY
July 2, 1994, Croke Park, Dublin
DUBLIN 1-14   KILDARE 1-9

NATIONAL LEAGUE, DIVISION ONE
Feb 19, 1995, St Conleth's Park, Newbridge
KILDARE 0-10   DUBLIN 0-8

LEINSTER QUARTER-FINAL
June 7, 1998, Croke Park, Dublin
DUBLIN 0-10   KILDARE 0-10

LEINSTER QUARTER-FINAL
REPLAY
June 21, 1998, Croke Park, Dublin
KILDARE 0-12   DUBLIN 1-8

NATIONAL LEAGUE
QUARTER-FINAL
Apr 11, 1999, Croke Park, Dublin
DUBLIN 1-17   KILDARE 2-8

LEINSTER FINAL
July 30, 2000, Croke Park, Dublin
DUBLIN 0-14   KILDARE 0-14

LEINSTER FINAL REPLAY
Aug 12, 2000, Croke Park, Dublin
KILDARE 2-11   DUBLIN 0-12

LEINSTER FINAL
July 14, 2002, Croke Park, Dublin
DUBLIN 2-13   KILDARE 2-11

LEINSTER FINAL
July 12, 2009, Croke Park, Dublin
DUBLIN 2-15   KILDARE 0-18

LEINSTER SEMI-FINAL
June 26, 2011, Croke Park, Dublin
DUBLIN 1-12   KILDARE 1-11

NATIONAL LEAGUE, DIVISION ONE
Mar 10, 2013, Croke Park, Dublin
DUBLIN 2-20   KILDARE 2-7

LEINSTER SEMI-FINAL
June 30, 2013, Croke Park, Dublin
DUBLIN 4-16   KILDARE 1-9

NATIONAL LEAGUE, DIVISION ONE
Mar 9, 2014, Croke Park, Dublin
DUBLIN 1-22   KILDARE 1-12

LEINSTER SEMI-FINAL
June 28, 2015, Croke Park, Dublin
DUBLIN 5-18   KILDARE 0-14

LEINSTER FINAL
July 16, 2017, Croke Park, Dublin
DUBLIN 2-23   KILDARE 1-17

	P	W	D	L	For	Agt
Championship	54	36	5	13	65-483	41-391
National League	38	27	1	10	56-341	43-277
TOTAL	92	63	6	23	121-824	84-668

KILKENNY

LEINSTER FIRST ROUND, 1897
May 15, 1898, Agricultural Grounds, Carlow
DUBLIN 0-14   KILKENNY 0-1

LEINSTER SEMI-FINAL, 1899
July 8, 1900, St James's Park, Kilkenny
DUBLIN 0-10   KILKENNY 0-2

LEINSTER QUARTER-FINAL, 1901
Aug 10, 1902, Gaelic Park, Terenure
DUBLIN 3-13   KILKENNY 1-2

LEINSTER FINAL, 1904
June 17, 1906, Wexford
DUBLIN 0-5   KILKENNY 0-1

LEINSTER QUARTER-FINAL, 1906
Mar 3, 1907, Enniscorthy
DUBLIN 1-9   KILKENNY 0-5

LEINSTER QUARTER-FINAL
July 14, 1912, Football Grounds, Athy
DUBLIN 2-3   KILKENNY 2-3

LEINSTER QUARTER-FINAL REPLAY
Aug 11, 1912, Jones's Road, Dublin
DUBLIN 3-4   KILKENNY 0-1

LEINSTER FINAL
Nov 5, 1922, Croke Park, Dublin
DUBLIN 1-7   KILKENNY 0-2

NATIONAL LEAGUE, DIVISION IIA
Dec 9, 1973, Nowlan Park, Kilkenny
DUBLIN 6-16   KILKENNY 0-4

	P	W	D	L	For	Agt
Championship	1	1	0	0	6-16	0-4
National League	8	7	1	0	10-65	3-17
TOTAL	9	8	1	0	16-81	3-21

LAOIS

LEINSTER SEMI-FINAL
Oct 19, 1890, Clonturk Park, Dublin
DUBLIN 2-8   LAOIS 0-1

LEINSTER QUARTER-FINAL
Nov 22, 1896, St James's Park, Kilkenny
DUBLIN 3-12   LAOIS 0-1

LEINSTER SEMI-FINAL, 1899
July 8, 1900, Jones's Road, Dublin
DUBLIN 7-11   LAOIS 0-3

LEINSTER SEMI-FINAL
Oct 18, 1908, Jones's Road, Dublin
DUBLIN 0-13   LAOIS 0-7

LEINSTER FIRST ROUND
June 16, 1912, Sportsfield, Portlaoise
DUBLIN 2-2   LAOIS 0-2

LEINSTER QUARTER-FINAL
June 6, 1915, O'Connor Park, Tullamore
DUBLIN 1-2   LAOIS 1-2

LEINSTER QUARTER-FINAL REPLAY
July 4, 1915, St Conleth's Park, Newbridge
DUBLIN 1-8   LAOIS 0-2

LEINSTER SEMI-FINAL
Sep 23, 1917, Croke Park, Dublin
DUBLIN 0-5   LAOIS 0-2

LEINSTER SEMI-FINAL
June 27, 1920, Croke Park, Dublin
DUBLIN 2-6   LAOIS 0-1

LEINSTER SEMI-FINAL
June 24, 1923, St James's Park, Kilkenny
DUBLIN 3-3   LAOIS 1-2

NATIONAL LEAGUE FINAL
Sep 19, 1926, Barrett's Park, New Ross
LAOIS 2-1   DUBLIN 1-0

LEINSTER QUARTER-FINAL
June 19, 1927, Catherine Park, Athy
DUBLIN 2-5   LAOIS 0-3

NATIONAL LEAGUE, SOUTH-EASTERN SECTION
Mar 24, 1929, O'Moore Park, Portlaoise
DUBLIN 1-4   LAOIS 1-4

LEINSTER SEMI-FINAL
June 30, 1929, Catherine Park, Athy
LAOIS 5-5 DUBLIN 3-10

NATIONAL LEAGUE, SECTION A
Aug 31, 1930, O'Moore Park, Portlaoise
DUBLIN 2-4   LAOIS 2-3

NATIONAL LEAGUE, SECTION A
May 24, 1931, Croke Park, Dublin
LAOIS 2-2   DUBLIN 0-6

NATIONAL LEAGUE, SECTION A
Mar 5, 1933, Croke Park, Dublin
DUBLIN 2-8   LAOIS 0-6

NATIONAL LEAGUE GROUP II
Nov 5, 1933, O'Moore Park, Portlaoise
DUBLIN 2-3   LAOIS 1-6

NATIONAL LEAGUE, SECTION A
Nov 11, 1934, Croke Park, Dublin
DUBLIN 3-3   LAOIS 1-3

NATIONAL LEAGUE, DIVISION ONE
Nov 10, 1935, McCann Park, Portarlington
LAOIS 2-5   DUBLIN 1-7

NATIONAL LEAGUE, GROUP VI
Nov 4, 1945, O'Moore Park, Portlaoise
DUBLIN 2-4   LAOIS 1-4

LEINSTER FIRST ROUND
May 19, 1946, Catherine Park, Athy
LAOIS 1-3   DUBLIN 0-5

NATIONAL LEAGUE, GROUP VI
Nov 24, 1946, Croke Park, Dublin
LAOIS 2-7   DUBLIN 0-10

NATIONAL LEAGUE SEMI-FINAL
Mar 31,1952, O'Moore Park, Portlaoise
DUBLIN 7-5   LAOIS 1-5

NATIONAL LEAGUE, SECTION III
Nov 8, 1953, O'Moore Park, Portlaoise
DUBLIN 3-7   LAOIS 1-6

NATIONAL LEAGUE, SECTION III
Nov 7, 1954, Croke Park, Dublin
DUBLIN 2-9   LAOIS 1-8

NATIONAL LEAGUE, SECTION III
Oct 23, 1955, O'Moore Park, Portlaoise
DUBLIN 1-7   LAOIS 1-3

NATIONAL LEAGUE, SECTION III
Nov 4, 1956, Croke Park, Dublin
DUBLIN 2-9   LAOIS 1-8

NATIONAL LEAGUE, SECTION III
Oct 6, 1957, O'Moore Park, Portlaoise
DUBLIN 2-6   LAOIS 1-6

NATIONAL LEAGUE, SECTION III
Oct 19, 1958, O'Toole Park, Dublin
DUBLIN 0-11   LAOIS 1-6

LEINSTER FINAL
Aug 2, 1959, O'Connor Park, Tullamore
DUBLIN 1-18   LAOIS 2-8

NATIONAL LEAGUE, SECTION III
Mar 6, 1960, O'Moore Park, Portlaoise
DUBLIN 6-6   LAOIS 1-8

NATIONAL LEAGUE, SECTION III
Mar 5, 1961, Croke Park, Dublin
DUBLIN 2-10   LAOIS 0-15

NATIONAL LEAGUE, SECTION III
Nov 12, 1961, Croke Park, Dublin
DUBLIN 3-14   LAOIS 3-3

NATIONAL LEAGUE, SECTION III
Nov 25, 1962, O'Moore Park, Portlaoise
LAOIS 2-7   DUBLIN 0-6

LEINSTER FINAL
July 14, 1963, Croke Park, Dublin
DUBLIN 2-11   LAOIS 2-9

NATIONAL LEAGUE, SECTION III
Feb 16, 1964, O'Moore Park, Portlaoise
DUBLIN 4-7   LAOIS 1-8

LEINSTER SEMI-FINAL
June 21, 1964, O'Connor Park, Tullamore
DUBLIN 0-8   LAOIS 1-2

NATIONAL LEAGUE, SECTION III
Nov 1, 1964, Croke Park, Dublin
DUBLIN 1-11   LAOIS 0-10

NATIONAL LEAGUE, SECTION III
Oct 31, 1965, Croke Park, Dublin
DUBLIN 1-12   LAOIS 0-6

NATIONAL LEAGUE, SECTION III
Oct 16, 1966, McCann Park, Portarlington
DUBLIN 2-10   LAOIS 1-6

LEINSTER QUARTER-FINAL
May 4, 1969, Dr Cullen Park, Carlow
DUBLIN 3-7   LAOIS 1-5

LEINSTER QUARTER-FINAL
June 6, 1971, Dr Cullen Park, Carlow
LAOIS 3-8 DUBLIN 0-13

LEINSTER SEMI-FINAL
July 11, 1976, O'Connor Park, Tullamore
DUBLIN 3-12   LAOIS 0-11

NATIONAL LEAGUE SEMI-FINAL
Apr 2, 1978, Croke Park, Dublin
DUBLIN 0-12   LAOIS 0-7

NATIONAL LEAGUE, DIVISION IA
Nov 5, 1978, Croke Park, Dublin
DUBLIN 3-15   LAOIS 0-11

LEINSTER QUARTER-FINAL
June 8, 1980, O'Connor Park, Tullamore
DUBLIN 2–14   LAOIS 2–8

LEINSTER SEMI-FINAL
July 5, 1981, O'Connor Park, Tullamore
LAOIS 2-9   DUBLIN 0-11

LEINSTER FINAL
July 28, 1985, Croke Park, Dublin
DUBLIN 0-10   LAOIS 0-4

NATIONAL LEAGUE SEMI-FINAL
Apr 20, 1986, Croke Park, Dublin
LAOIS 0-12   DUBLIN 1-7

NATIONAL LEAGUE, DIVISION ONE
Nov 27, 1994, O'Moore Park, Portlaoise
DUBLIN 0-15   LAOIS 1-8

LEINSTER SEMI-FINAL
July 9, 1995, Pairc Tailteann, Navan
DUBLIN 1-13   LAOIS 0-9

NATIONAL LEAGUE, DIVISION TWO
Mar 2, 1997, Parnell Park, Dublin
DUBLIN 0-15   LAOIS 0-4

LEINSTER SEMI-FINAL
June 27, 1999, Croke Park, Dublin
DUBLIN 1-11   LAOIS 0-14

LEINSTER SEMI-FINAL REPLAY
July 18, 1999, Croke Park, Dublin
DUBLIN 0-16   LAOIS 1-11

LEINSTER SEMI-FINAL
June 15, 2003, Croke Park, Dublin
LAOIS 0-16   DUBLIN 0-14

LEINSTER FINAL
July 17, 2005, Croke Park, Dublin
DUBLIN 0-14   LAOIS 0-13

LEINSTER SEMI-FINAL
June 25, 2006, Croke Park, Dublin
DUBLIN 3-17   LAOIS 0-12

LEINSTER FINAL
July 15, 2007, Croke Park, Dublin
DUBLIN 3-14   LAOIS 1-14

LEINSTER QUARTER-FINAL
June 5, 2011, Croke Park, Dublin
DUBLIN 1-16   LAOIS 0-11

NATIONAL LEAGUE, DIVISION ONE
Mar 3, 2012, O'Moore Park, Portlaoise
DUBLIN 1-14   LAOIS 0-9

ALL-IRELAND QUARTER-FINAL
Aug 4, 2012, Croke Park, Dublin
DUBLIN 1-12   LAOIS 0-12

LEINSTER QUARTER-FINAL
June 8, 2014, Croke Park, Dublin
DUBLIN 2-21   LAOIS 0-16

LEINSTER QUARTER-FINAL
June 4, 2016, Nowlan Park, Kilkenny
DUBLIN 2-21   LAOIS 2-10

	P	W	D	L	For	Agt
Championship	33	26	2	5	51-363	25-236
National League	31	23	2	6	55-257	30-197
TOTAL	64	48	4	11	106-620	55-433

LEITRIM

ALL-IRELAND SEMI-FINAL
Aug 21, 1994, Croke Park, Dublin
DUBLIN 3-15   LEITRIM 1-9

ALL-IRELAND QUALIFIERS, ROUND TWO
July 3, 2004, McDermott Park, Carrick-on-Shannon
DUBLIN 0-13   LEITRIM 1-4

NATIONAL LEAGUE, DIVISION TWO
Oct 15, 1995, Croke Park, Dublin
DUBLIN 1-13   LEITRIM 1-10

NATIONAL LEAGUE, DIVISION TWO
Oct 13, 1996, McDermott Park, Carrick-on-Shannon
LEITRIM 1-10   DUBLIN 0-10

NATIONAL LEAGUE, DIVISION IA
Feb 14, 1999, Parnell Park, Dublin
DUBLIN 1-19   LEITRIM 0-6

	P	W	D	L	For	Agt
Championship	2	2	0	0	3-28	2-13
National League	3	2	0	1	2-42	2-26
TOTAL	5	0	0	1	5-70	4-39

LIMERICK

ALL-IRELAND FINAL, 1896
Feb 6, 1898, Jones's Road, Dublin
LIMERICK 1-5   DUBLIN 0-7

NATIONAL LEAGUE, DIVISION IIA
Nov 11, 1973, Croke Park, Dublin
DUBLIN 1-8   LIMERICK 0-6

NATIONAL LEAGUE, SECTION A
Mar 14, 1993, Gaelic Grounds, Askeaton
DUBLIN 0-15   LIMERICK 0-9

NATIONAL LEAGUE, DIVISION IA
Feb 10, 2007, Gaelic Grounds, Limerick
DUBLIN 0-14   LIMERICK 1-10

	P	W	D	L	For	Agt
Championship	1	0	0	1	0-7	1-5
National League	3	3	0	0	1-37	1-25
TOTAL	4	3	0	4	1-44	2-30

LONDON

ALL-IRELAND FINAL, 1901
Aug 2, 1903, Jones's Road, Dublin
DUBLIN 0-14   LONDON 0-2

ALL-IRELAND FINAL, 1902
Sep 11, 1904, Athletic Grounds, Cork
DUBLIN 2-8   LONDON 0-4

ALL-IRELAND QUARTER-FINAL, 1905
Aug 5, 1906, Jones's Road, Dublin
DUBLIN 1-9   LONDON 1-4

ALL-IRELAND SEMI-FINAL, 1906
Aug 4, 1907, Town Park, Wexford
DUBLIN 2-7   LONDON 0-3

ALL-IRELAND FINAL, 1908
Aug 1, 1909, Jones's Road, Dublin
DUBLIN 1-10   LONDON 0-4

ALL-IRELAND QUALIFIERS, ROUND ONE
June 12, 2004, Parnell Park, Dublin
DUBLIN 3-24   LONDON 0-6

	P	W	D	L	For	Agt
Championship	6	6	0	0	9-72	1-23
TOTAL	6	6	0	0	9-72	1-23

LONGFORD

LEINSTER QUARTER-FINAL
May 26, 1929, Cusack Park, Mullingar
DUBLIN 3-7   LONGFORD 1-6

NATIONAL LEAGUE, GROUP C
Nov 24, 1940, Pearse Park, Longford
DUBLIN 3-3   LONGFORD 1-4

LEINSTER QUARTER-FINAL
May 10, 1942, Cusack Park, Mullingar
DUBLIN 0-7   LONGFORD 0-7

LEINSTER QUARTER-FINAL REPLAY
May 24, 1942, Croke Park, Dublin
DUBLIN 2-15   LONGFORD 1-3

LEINSTER SEMI-FINAL
July 9, 1944, Cusack Park, Mullingar
DUBLIN 2-2   LONGFORD 1-4

LEINSTER FIRST ROUND
May 18, 1947, Cusack Park, Mullingar
DUBLIN 1-11   LONGFORD 0-5

NATIONAL LEAGUE, GROUP VI
Nov 23, 1947, Pearse Park, Longford
DUBLIN 3-5   LONGFORD 1-6

LEINSTER FIRST ROUND
May 1, 1949, Cusack Park, Mullingar
DUBLIN 2-9   LONGFORD 2-5

LEINSTER QUARTER-FINAL
May 29, 1960, Cusack Park, Mullingar
DUBLIN 10-13   LONGFORD 3-8

LEINSTER FINAL
July 18, 1965, Croke Park, Dublin
DUBLIN 3-6   LONGFORD 0-9

LEINSTER QUARTER-FINAL
June 2, 1968, O'Connor Park, Tullamore
LONGFORD 1-12   DUBLIN 0-12

LEINSTER QUARTER-FINAL
May 17, 1970, Cusack Park, Mullingar
LONGFORD 2-14   DUBLIN 3-8

NATIONAL LEAGUE, DIVISION IB
Apr 25, 1971, Pearse Park, Longford
DUBLIN 2-9   LONGFORD 0-8

LEINSTER QUARTER-FINAL
June 27,1976, Cusack Park, Mullingar
DUBLIN 5-16   LONGFORD 0-7

LEINSTER QUARTER-FINAL
June 6, 1982, O'Connor Park, Tullamore
DUBLIN 1-15   LONGFORD 2-6

NATIONAL LEAGUE, DIVISION TWO
Oct 27, 1985, Croke Park, Dublin
LONGFORD 3-8   DUBLIN 1-11

**NATIONAL LEAGUE
QUARTER-FINAL**
Mar 27, 1988, Croke Park, Dublin
DUBLIN 0-10   LONGFORD 0-4

LEINSTER SEMI-FINAL
June 26, 1988, Cusack Park, Mullingar
DUBLIN 4-15   LONGFORD 0-9

LEINSTER QUARTER-FINAL
May 27, 2001, Croke Park, Dublin
DUBLIN 2-19   LONGFORD 1-13

NATIONAL LEAGUE, DIVISION IA
Apr 4, 2004, Parnell Park, Dublin
DUBLIN 2-12   LONGFORD 2-9

**ALL-IRELAND QUALIFIERS,
ROUND THREE**
July 10, 2004, O'Moore Park, Portlaoise
DUBLIN 1-17   LONGFORD 0-11

LEINSTER FIRST ROUND
May 15, 2005, Croke Park, Dublin
DUBLIN 2-23   LONGFORD 0-10

LEINSTER QUARTER-FINAL
June 4, 2006, Pearse Park, Longford
DUBLIN 1-12   LONGFORD 0-13

LEINSTER QUARTER-FINAL
May 31, 2015, Croke Park, Dublin
DUBLIN 4-25   LONGFORD 0-10

	P	W	D	L	For	Agt
Championship	18	15	1	2	39-162	14-129
National League	6	5	0	1	11-50	7-39
TOTAL	24	20	1	3	50-212	21-168

LOUTH

LEINSTER QUARTER-FINAL
Sep 1, 1889, Shamrock Lodge, Drogheda
LOUTH 2-7   DUBLIN 0-6

LEINSTER FINAL, 1892
Mar 12, 1893, Clonturk Park, Dublin
DUBLIN W/O   LOUTH SCR

LEINSTER SEMI-FINAL, 1901
Feb 15, 1903, Jones's Road, Dublin
DUBLIN 1-6   LOUTH 1-2

LEINSTER SEMI-FINAL, 1902
Dec 6, 1903, Showgrounds, Navan
DUBLIN 1-6   LOUTH 0-2

LEINSTER SEMI-FINAL, 1904
Apr 1, 1906, Young Ireland Ground, Dundalk
DUBLIN 0-11   LOUTH 0-6

LEINSTER SEMI-FINAL, 1906
May 5, 1907, Showgrounds, Navan
DUBLIN 0-8   LOUTH 0-6

LEINSTER SEMI-FINAL, 1907
Jan 26, 1908, Jones's Road, Dublin
DUBLIN 2-6   LOUTH 0-6

LEINSTER SEMI-FINAL
Sep 12, 1909, Y Ireland Grounds, Dundalk
LOUTH 1-11   DUBLIN 1-7

LEINSTER FINAL
Oct 16, 1910, Showgrounds, Navan
LOUTH 0-3   DUBLIN 0-0

LEINSTER QUARTER-FINAL
29 July, 1911, Showgrounds, Navan
DUBLIN 3-2   LOUTH 1-4

LEINSTER FINAL
Oct 20, 1912, Showgrounds, Navan
LOUTH 1-2   DUBLIN 1-1

LEINSTER QUARTER-FINAL
Aug 5, 1917, Shamrock Lodge, Drogheda
DUBLIN 0-14   LOUTH 1-4

LEINSTER QUARTER-FINAL
Sep 8, 1918, Shamrock Lodge, Drogheda
LOUTH 3-5   DUBLIN 3-3

LEINSTER SEMI-FINAL
July 10, 1921, Croke Park, Dublin
DUBLIN 1-6   LOUTH 0-3

LEINSTER SEMI-FINAL
Sep 7, 1924, Showgrounds, Navan:
DUBLIN 2-6   LOUTH 2-4

NATIONAL LEAGUE, GROUP C
Oct 11, 1925, St Brigid's Park, Dundalk
DUBLIN 3-3   LOUTH 1-5

**NATIONAL LEAGUE,
NORTHERN SECTION**
Nov 13, 1927, Athletic Grounds, Drogheda
LOUTH 4-4   DUBLIN 0-2

LEINSTER QUARTER-FINAL
May 20, 1928, Pairc Tailteann, Navan
DUBLIN 0-5   LOUTH 0-3

LEINSTER FIRST ROUND
June 14, 1931, Drogheda Park, Drogheda
DUBLIN 5-6   LOUTH 1-5

LEINSTER SEMI-FINAL
June 25, 1933, Pairc Tailteann, Navan
DUBLIN 3-6   LOUTH 1-3

LEINSTER FINAL
July 29, 1934, Croke Park, Dublin
DUBLIN 1-2   LOUTH 0-5

LEINSTER FINAL REPLAY
Aug 5, 1934, Croke Park, Dublin
DUBLIN 3-2   LOUTH 2-5

LEINSTER FINAL SECOND REPLAY
Aug 19, 1934, Drogheda Park, Drogheda
DUBLIN 2-9   LOUTH 1-10

NATIONAL LEAGUE, SECTION A
Jan 13, 1935, Croke Park, Dublin
DUBLIN 3-6   LOUTH 2-5

LEINSTER QUARTER-FINAL
June 9, 1935, Pairc Tailteann, Navan
LOUTH 0-6   DUBLIN 0-3

NATIONAL LEAGUE, DIVISION ONE
Oct 13, 1935, St Brigid's Park, Dundalk
DUBLIN 2-4   LOUTH 1-6

NATIONAL LEAGUE, DIVISION IA
Feb 14, 1937, Athletic Grounds, Drogheda
LOUTH 2-6   DUBLIN 2-5

LEINSTER QUARTER-FINAL
May 23, 1937, Pairc Tailteann, Navan
DUBLIN 1-7   LOUTH 0-10

LEINSTER QUARTER-FINAL REPLAY
June 20, 1937, Pairc Tailteann, Navan
LOUTH 2-5   DUBLIN 1-4

NATIONAL LEAGUE, GROUP C
Mar 27, 1938, Athletic Grounds, Drogheda
LOUTH 1-7   DUBLIN 1-6

NATIONAL LEAGUE, GROUP C
Feb 5, 1939, Bremore Park, Balbriggan
LOUTH 0-5   DUBLIN 0-2

LEINSTER FIRST ROUND
May 28, 1939, Pairc Tailteann, Navan
LOUTH 3-4   DUBLIN 1-6

NATIONAL LEAGUE, GROUP C
Nov 26, 1939, Croke Park, Dublin
LOUTH 2-5   DUBLIN 1-7

**NATIONAL LEAGUE,
GROUP C PLAY-OFF**
Feb 4, 1940, Athletic Grounds, Drogheda
LOUTH 4-5   DUBLIN 1-5

LEINSTER QUARTER-FINAL
May 19, 1940, Pairc Tailteann, Navan
DUBLIN 1-9   LOUTH 2-5

NATIONAL LEAGUE, GROUP C
Oct 13, 1940, St Brigid's Park, Dundalk
LOUTH 3-5   DUBLIN 0-8

NATIONAL LEAGUE, GROUP C PLAY-OFF
Feb 23, 1941, Croke Park, Dublin
DUBLIN 3-4   LOUTH 1-5

LEINSTER FIRST ROUND
May 18, 1941, Drogheda Park, Drogheda
DUBLIN 2-7   LOUTH 3-4

**LEINSTER FIRST ROUND
REPLAY**
May 25, 1941, Croke Park, Dublin
DUBLIN 1-9   LOUTH 1-4

NORTH LEINSTER LEAGUE
Mar 29, 1942, Croke Park, Dublin
DUBLIN 4-8   LOUTH 0-10

NORTH LEINSTER LEAGUE
Apr 25, 1942, St Brigid's Park, Dundalk
DUBLIN 1-5   LOUTH 1-4

LEINSTER QUARTER-FINAL
May 30, 1943, Athletic Grounds, Drogheda
LOUTH 1-6   DUBLIN 1-5

LEINSTER LEAGUE
Nov 14, 1943, Athletic Grounds, Drogheda
LOUTH 0-8   DUBLIN 1-4

LEINSTER QUARTER-FINAL
June 18, 1944, Croke Park, Dublin
DUBLIN 2-10   LOUTH 3-6

LEINSTER QUARTER-FINAL
June 1, 1947, Pairc Tailteann, Navan
LOUTH 3-11   DUBLIN 1-9

NATIONAL LEAGUE, GROUP VI
Dec 7, 1947, Croke Park, Dublin
DUBLIN 2-9   LOUTH 4-3

LEINSTER QUARTER-FINAL
June 13, 1948, Croke Park, Dublin
LOUTH 1-8   DUBLIN 0-6

NATIONAL LEAGUE, GROUP VI
Nov 14, 1948, Athletic Grounds, Drogheda
LOUTH 2-10   DUBLIN 2-5

NATIONAL LEAGUE, SECTION IV
Oct 16, 1949, St Brigid's Park, Dundalk
LOUTH 2-6   DUBLIN 1-6

NATIONAL LEAGUE, SECTION IV
Oct 8, 1950, Croke Park, Dublin
DUBLIN 1-4   LOUTH 1-4

NATIONAL LEAGUE, SECTION IV
Oct 7, 1951, Croke Park, Dublin
DUBLIN 3-5   LOUTH 1-7

NATIONAL LEAGUE, SECTION IV
Oct 19, 1952, St Brigid's Park, Dundalk
DUBLIN 1-7   LOUTH 1-4

NATIONAL LEAGUE, SECTION III
Mar 28, 1954, Athletic Grounds, Drogheda
DUBLIN 3-10   LOUTH 2-3

LEINSTER QUARTER-FINAL
May 23, 1954, Drogheda Park, Drogheda
DUBLIN 0-11   LOUTH 0-2

NATIONAL LEAGUE, SECTION III
Mar 13, 1955, Croke Park, Dublin
DUBLIN 0-8   LOUTH 1-2

NATIONAL LEAGUE, SECTION III
Feb 26, 1956, Croke Park, Dublin
DUBLIN 0-13   LOUTH 0-7

NATIONAL LEAGUE, SECTION III
Mar 24, 1957, Athletic Grounds, Drogheda
DUBLIN 1-8   LOUTH 3-2

LEINSTER FINAL
July 7, 1957, Croke Park, Dublin
LOUTH   2-9   DUBLIN 1-7

NATIONAL LEAGUE, SECTION III
Mar 23, 1958, Croke Park, Dublin
DUBLIN 0-12   LOUTH 1-4

LEINSTER FINAL
July 20, 1958, Croke Park, Dublin
DUBLIN   1-11   LOUTH 1-6

NATIONAL LEAGUE, SECTION III
Mar 22, 1959, Athletic Grounds, Drogheda
LOUTH 2-10   DUBLIN 1-10

LEINSTER SEMI-FINAL
July 5, 1959, Croke Park, Dublin
DUBLIN 1-8   LOUTH 0-11

**LEINSTER SEMI-FINAL
REPLAY**
July 26, 1959, Pairc Tailteann, Navan
DUBLIN 3-14   LOUTH 1-9

NATIONAL LEAGUE, SECTION III
Nov 29, 1959, Athletic Grounds, Drogheda
DUBLIN 1-10   LOUTH 1-5

NATIONAL LEAGUE, SECTION III
Feb 12, 1961, O'Toole Park, Dublin
DUBLIN 3-9   LOUTH 2-3

NATIONAL LEAGUE, SECTION III
Nov 5, 1961, St Brigid's Park, Dundalk
LOUTH 2-11   DUBLIN 3-3

LEINSTER QUARTER-FINAL
June 3, 1962, Pairc Tailteann, Navan
DUBLIN 1-8   LOUTH 0-10

NATIONAL LEAGUE, SECTION III
Nov 18, 1962, Croke Park, Dublin
DUBLIN 1-11   LOUTH 1-3

NATIONAL LEAGUE, SECTION III
Feb 9, 1964, Croke Park, Dublin
DUBLIN 3-9   LOUTH 0-7

NATIONAL LEAGUE, SECTION III
Mar 7, 1965, St Brigid's Park, Dundalk
DUBLIN 5-11   LOUTH 0-3

LEINSTER QUARTER-FINAL
June 12, 1966, Drogheda Park, Drogheda
DUBLIN 2-10   LOUTH 0-9

**NATIONAL LEAGUE, DIVISION I
SEMI-FINAL**
Mar 8, 1970, Croke Park, Dublin
DUBLIN 1-12   LOUTH 1-12

**NATIONAL LEAGUE, DIVISION I
SEMI-FINAL REPLAY**
Mar 22, 1970, Pairc Tailteann, Navan
LOUTH 0-10   DUBLIN 0-8

LEINSTER SECOND ROUND
May 27, 1973, Pairc Tailteann, Navan
DUBLIN 2-6   LOUTH   1-9

**LEINSTER SECOND ROUND
REPLAY**
June 10, 1973, Pairc Tailteann, Navan
LOUTH 1-8   DUBLIN 0-9

LEINSTER SECOND ROUND
June 2, 1974, Pairc Tailteann, Navan
DUBLIN 2-11   LOUTH 1-9

LEINSTER SEMI-FINAL
July 6, 1975, Pairc Tailteann, Navan
DUBLIN 3-14   LOUTH 4-7

LEINSTER QUARTER-FINAL
June 3, 1979, Pairc Tailteann, Navan
DUBLIN 4-16   LOUTH 0-4

LEINSTER SEMI-FINAL
July 17, 1983, Croke Park, Dublin
DUBLIN 1-12   LOUTH 0-11

NATIONAL LEAGUE, DIVISION TWO
Feb 10, 1985, St Mary's Park, Ardee
DUBLIN 2-8   LOUTH 0-4

LEINSTER QUARTER-FINAL
June 3, 1990, Drogheda Park, Drogheda
DUBLIN 1-13   LOUTH   1-8

LEINSTER SEMI-FINAL
July 12, 1992, O'Moore Park, Portlaoise
DUBLIN 0-15   LOUTH 1-9

NATIONAL LEAGUE, SECTION A
Nov 15, 1992, Croke Park, Dublin
DUBLIN 1-8   LOUTH 0-9

LEINSTER SEMI-FINAL
July 10, 1994, Croke Park, Dublin
DUBLIN 1-15   LOUTH 1-8

LEINSTER QUARTER-FINAL
June 18, 1995, Pairc Tailteann, Navan
DUBLIN 0-19   LOUTH 2-5

**NATIONAL LEAGUE,
DIVISION TWO**
Feb 4, 1996, St Brigid's Park, Dundalk
LOUTH 0-9   DUBLIN 1-5

LEINSTER SEMI-FINAL
June 30, 1996, Pairc Tailteann, Navan
DUBLIN 1-9   LOUTH 0-8

NATIONAL LEAGUE, DIVISION TWO
Feb 2, 1997, Parnell Park, Dublin
LOUTH 1-7   DUBLIN 0-8

LEINSTER QUARTER-FINAL
June 6, 1999, Croke Park, Dublin
DUBLIN   2-15   LOUTH 0-14

LEINSTER QUARTER-FINAL
June 1, 2003, Croke Park, Dublin
DUBLIN   1-19   LOUTH 0-9

LEINSTER QUARTER-FINAL
June 8, 2008, Croke Park, Dublin
DUBLIN 1-22   LOUTH 0-12

ALL-IRELAND QUALIFIERS, ROUND FOUR
July 24, 2010, Croke Park, Dublin
DUBLIN 2-14   LOUTH   0-13

LEINSTER QUARTER-FINAL
June 3, 2012, Croke Park, Dublin
DUBLIN 2-22   LOUTH 0-12

	P	W	D	L	For	Agt
Championship	55	36	6	13	72-478	52-376
National League	38	19	4	15	58-268	50-225
TOTAL	93	55	10	28	130-746	102-601

MAYO

ALL-IRELAND SEMI-FINAL, 1904
May 13, 1906, Jones's Road, Dublin
DUBLIN 0-8   MAYO 1-3

ALL-IRELAND FINAL, 1921
June 17, 1923, Croke Park, Dublin
DUBLIN 1-9   MAYO 0-2

ALL-IRELAND SEMI-FINAL, 1923
May 18, 1924, Croke Park, Dublin
DUBLIN 1-6   MAYO 1-2

NATIONAL LEAGUE FINAL
May 13, 1934, MacHale Park, Castlebar
MAYO 2-3   DUBLIN 1-6

NATIONAL LEAGUE FINAL REPLAY
Oct 21, 1934, Croke Park, Dublin
MAYO 2-4   DUBLIN 1-5

NATIONAL LEAGUE, SECTION A
Oct 28, 1934, GAA Grounds, Ballina
MAYO 2-5 DUBLIN 1-7

NATIONAL LEAGUE, DIVISION ONE
Oct 27, 1935, Croke Park, Dublin
DUBLIN 2-5   MAYO 0-6

NATIONAL LEAGUE FINAL
Apr 27, 1941, Croke Park, Dublin
MAYO 3-5   DUBLIN 0-7

NATIONAL LEAGUE SEMI-FINAL
Apr 25, 1954, Croke Park, Dublin
MAYO 0-11   DUBLIN 0-7

ALL-IRELAND SEMI-FINAL
Aug 21, 1955, Croke Park, Dublin
DUBLIN 0-7   MAYO 1-4

ALL-IRELAND SEMI-FINAL REPLAY
Sep 11, 1955, Croke Park, Dublin
DUBLIN 1-8   MAYO 1-7

NATIONAL LEAGUE SEMI-FINAL
Apr 20, 1958, Croke Park, Dublin
DUBLIN 0-10   MAYO 0-7

NATIONAL LEAGUE SEMI-FINAL
May 23, 1971, Croke Park, Dublin
MAYO 1-9   DUBLIN 0-8

NATIONAL LEAGUE SEMI-FINAL
Mar 27, 1977, Croke Park, Dublin
DUBLIN 2-12   MAYO 0-5

NATIONAL LEAGUE FINAL
Apr 23, 1978, Croke Park, Dublin
DUBLIN 2-18   MAYO 2-13

NATIONAL LEAGUE QUARTER-FINAL
Apr 5, 1981, Dr Hyde Park, Roscommon
MAYO 1-11   DUBLIN 1-10

NATIONAL LEAGUE, DIVISION ONE
Oct 4, 1981, Flanagan Park, Ballinrobe
DUBLIN 1-12   MAYO 1-4

NATIONAL LEAGUE, DIVISION ONE
Oct 10, 1982, Croke Park, Dublin
DUBLIN 3-7   MAYO 0-6

NATIONAL LEAGUE, DIVISION TWO
Nov 18, 1984, James Stephens Park, Ballina
MAYO 1-8   DUBLIN 1-5

ALL-IRELAND SEMI-FINAL
Aug 18, 1985, Croke Park, Dublin
DUBLIN 1-13   MAYO 1-13

ALL-IRELAND SEMI-FINAL REPLAY
Sep 8, 1985, Croke Park, Dublin
DUBLIN 2-12   MAYO 1-7

NATIONAL LEAGUE, DIVISION TWO
Dec 1, 1985, MacHale Park, Castlebar
MAYO 2-5   DUBLIN 0-4

NATIONAL LEAGUE, DIVISION ONE
Feb 8, 1987, Croke Park, Dublin
DUBLIN 0-8   MAYO 0-6

NATIONAL LEAGUE, DIVISION ONE
Feb 7, 1988, MacHale Park, Castlebar
DUBLIN 1-7   MAYO 1-4

NATIONAL LEAGUE, DIVISION ONE B
Feb 23, 1992, MacHale Park, Castlebar
DUBLIN 1-9   MAYO 0-10

NATIONAL LEAGUE, DIVISION ONE
Nov 21, 1993, Croke Park, Dublin
DUBLIN 0-19   MAYO 0-8

NATIONAL LEAGUE, DIVISION TWO
Nov 10, 1996, MacHale Park, Castlebar
DUBLIN 0-10   MAYO 0-10

NATIONAL LEAGUE, DIVISION IA
Feb 8, 2004, MacHale Park, Castlebar
MAYO 1-10   DUBLIN 0-3

NATIONAL LEAGUE, DIVISION IA
Feb 6, 2005, Parnell Park, Dublin
DUBLIN 2-13   MAYO 0-15

NATIONAL LEAGUE, DIVISION IA
Mar 25, 2006, Parnell Park, Dublin
DUBLIN 4-10   MAYO 1-10

ALL-IRELAND SEMI-FINAL
Aug 27, 2006, Croke Park, Dublin
MAYO 1-16 DUBLIN 2-12

NATIONAL LEAGUE, DIVISION IA
Apr 1, 2007, MacHale Park, Castlebar
MAYO 0-10   DUBLIN 0-9

NATIONAL LEAGUE, DIVISION ONE
Mar 22, 2009, James Stephens Park, Ballina
DUBLIN 0-9   MAYO 0-9

NATIONAL LEAGUE, DIVISION ONE
Mar 7, 2010, MacHale Park, Castlebar
DUBLIN 1-9   MAYO 0-8

NATIONAL LEAGUE, DIVISION ONE
Mar 20, 2011, Croke Park, Dublin
DUBLIN 4-15   MAYO 3-13

NATIONAL LEAGUE, DIVISION ONE
April 1, 2012, MacHale Park, Castlebar
MAYO 0-20   DUBLIN 0-8

ALL-IRELAND SEMI-FINAL
Sep 2, 2012, Croke Park, Dublin
MAYO 0-19   DUBLIN 0-16

NATIONAL LEAGUE, DIVISION ONE
Mar 2, 2013, Croke Park, Dublin
DUBLIN 2-14   MAYO 0-16

**NATIONAL LEAGUE
SEMI-FINAL**
Apr 14, 2013, Croke Park, Dublin
DUBLIN 2-16   MAYO 0-16

ALL-IRELAND FINAL
Sep 22, 2013, Croke Park, Dublin
DUBLIN   2-12   MAYO 1-14

NATIONAL LEAGUE, DIVISION ONE
Mar 30, 2014, Croke Park, Dublin
DUBLIN 3-14   MAYO 2-17

NATIONAL LEAGUE, DIVISION ONE
Mar 14, 2015, MacHale Park, Castlebar
DUBLIN 2-18   MAYO 0-10

ALL-IRELAND SEMI-FINAL
Aug 30, 2015, Croke Park, Dublin
DUBLIN 2-12   MAYO 1-15

ALL-IRELAND SEMI-FINAL REPLAY
Sep 5, 2015, Croke Park, Dublin
DUBLIN 3-15   MAYO 1-14

NATIONAL LEAGUE, DIVISION ONE
Feb 6, 2016, MacHale Park, Castlebar
DUBLIN 0-9   MAYO 0-7

ALL-IRELAND FINAL
Sep 18, 2016, Croke Park, Dublin
DUBLIN 2-9   MAYO 0-15

ALL-IRELAND FINAL REPLAY
Oct 1, 2016, Croke Park, Dublin
DUBLIN 1-15   MAYO 1-14

NATIONAL LEAGUE, DIVISION ONE
Mar 4, 2017, Croke Park, Dublin
DUBLIN 1-16   MAYO 0-7

ALL-IRELAND FINAL
Sep 17, 2017, Croke Park
DUBLIN 1-17   MAYO 1-16

	P	W	D	L	For	Agt
Championship	15	9	4	2	19-171	12-162
National League	34	19	4	11	38-339	25-308
TOTAL	49	28	8	13	57-510	37-470

MEATH

LEINSTER FINAL
Oct 14, 1894, Clonturk Park, Dublin
DUBLIN 0-4   MEATH 0-4

LEINSTER FINAL REPLAY
Dec 15, 1894, Showgrounds, Navan
DUBLIN 0-2   MEATH 0-2

LEINSTER FINAL 1894, SECOND REPLAY
Feb 24, 1895, Clonturk Park, Dublin
DUBLIN 1-8   MEATH 1-2

LEINSTER FINAL, 1895
Mar 1, 1896, Jones's Road, Dublin
MEATH 0-6   DUBLIN 0-2

LEINSTER FINAL, 1896
Oct 24, 1897, Bryansford Park, Drogheda
DUBLIN 2-4   MEATH 1-5

LEINSTER QUARTER-FINAL
Sep 27, 1908, Jones's Road, Dublin
DUBLIN 1-9   MEATH 0-1

LEINSTER SEMI-FINAL
Aug 20, 1911, Jones's Road, Dublin
MEATH 1-3   DUBLIN 0-2

LEINSTER QUARTER-FINAL
July 13, 1919, Showgrounds, Navan
DUBLIN 0-7   MEATH 0-2

LEINSTER QUARTER-FINAL
May 1, 1921, Croke Park, Dublin
DUBLIN 3-6   MEATH 0-0

LEINSTER FINAL
Aug 12, 1923, Croke Park, Dublin
DUBLIN   3-5   MEATH 0-0

LEINSTER QUARTER-FINAL
Apr 6, 1924, Showgrounds, Navan
DUBLIN 2-3   MEATH 1-4

NATIONAL LEAGUE, GROUP C
Oct 18, 1925, Croke Park, Dublin
DUBLIN 0-9   MEATH 1-2

NATIONAL LEAGUE, NORTHERN SECTION
Apr 24, 1927, Showgrounds, Navan
MEATH 1-3   DUBLIN 1-2

**NATIONAL LEAGUE,
SOUTH-EASTERN SECTION**
Nov 18, 1928, Showgrounds, Navan
DUBLIN 4-1   MEATH 0-2

LEINSTER SEMI-FINAL
June 29, 1930, Athletic Grounds, Drogheda
MEATH 3-8   DUBLIN 1-4

LEINSTER QUARTER-FINAL
May 29, 1932, St Conleth's Park, Newbridge
DUBLIN 3-6   MEATH 0-4

NATIONAL LEAGUE, SECTION A
Nov 27, 1932, Showgrounds, Navan
MEATH 1-4   DUBLIN 0-2

LEINSTER QUARTER-FINAL
June 11, 1933, Athletic Grounds, Drogheda
DUBLIN 1-8   MEATH 1-4

LEINSTER SEMI-FINAL
July 8, 1934, Drogheda Park, Drogheda
DUBLIN 2-8   MEATH 1-9

NATIONAL LEAGUE, SECTION A
Mar 31, 1935, Croke Park, Dublin
DUBLIN 0-8   MEATH 1-4

NATIONAL LEAGUE, DIVISION IA
Nov 8, 1936, St Colmbeille's Park, Kells
MEATH 2-4   DUBLIN 1-4

NATIONAL LEAGUE, GROUP C
Nov 14, 1937, Croke Park, Dublin
DUBLIN 2-3   MEATH 1-5

NATIONAL LEAGUE, GROUP C
Mar 5, 1939, Showgrounds, Navan
MEATH 3-5   DUBLIN 1-2

NATIONAL LEAGUE, GROUP C
Nov 12, 1939, Pairc Tailteann, Navan
DUBLIN 3-1   MEATH 0-8

LEINSTER SEMI-FINAL
July 7, 1940, St Conleth's Park, Newbridge
MEATH 1-7   DUBLIN 0-4

NATIONAL LEAGUE, GROUP C
Dec 8, 1940, Croke Park, Dublin
DUBLIN 1-5   MEATH 0-7

LEINSTER QUARTER-FINAL
June 1, 1941, Athletic Grounds, Drogheda
DUBLIN 1-8   MEATH 1-6

NORTH LEINSTER LEAGUE
Mar 22, 1942, Showgrounds, Navan
DUBLIN 4-8   MEATH 5-5

LEINSTER SEMI-FINAL
May 31 , 1942, Athletic Grounds, Drogheda
DUBLIN 3-5   MEATH 1-10

NORTH LEINSTER LEAGUE
Oct 18, 1942, Croke Park, Dublin
DUBLIN 2-8   MEATH 0-8

LEINSTER LEAGUE
Nov 28, 1943, Croke Park, Dublin
MEATH 0-7   DUBLIN 0-6

LEINSTER FIRST ROUND
May 28, 1944, Athletic Grounds, Drogheda
DUBLIN 1-8   MEATH 1-6

LEINSTER QUARTER-FINAL
June 10, 1945, Athletic Grounds, Drogheda
DUBLIN 4-3   MEATH 3-6

LEINSTER QUARTER-FINAL REPLAY
June 17, 1945, Croke Park, Dublin
MEATH 2-16   DUBLIN 1-10

NATIONAL LEAGUE, SECTION IV
Nov 27, 1949, Croke Park, Dublin
MEATH 1-6   DUBLIN 0-5

NATIONAL LEAGUE, SECTION IV
Nov 12, 1950, Pairc Tailteann, Navan
MEATH 3-6   DUBLIN 2-3

LEINSTER QUARTER-FINAL
June 3, 1951, Athletic Grounds, Drogheda
MEATH 0-11   DUBLIN 1-5

NATIONAL LEAGUE, SECTION IV
Feb 17, 1952, Croke Park, Dublin
DUBLIN 1-9   MEATH 0-2

LEINSTER QUARTER-FINAL
May 25, 1952, Athletic Grounds, Drogheda
MEATH 2-7   DUBLIN 2-5

NATIONAL LEAGUE, SECTION IV
Nov 16, 1952, Pairc Tailteann, Navan
MEATH 1-10   DUBLIN 2-3

**NATIONAL LEAGUE,
SECTION IV PLAY-OFF**
Mar 22, 1953, Croke Park, Dublin
DUBLIN 3-13   MEATH 2-3

LEINSTER QUARTER-FINAL
May 24, 1953, Pairc Tailteann, Navan
MEATH 2-6   DUBLIN 2-5

NATIONAL LEAGUE FINAL
May 8, 1955, Croke Park, Dublin
DUBLIN 2-12   MEATH 1-3

LEINSTER FINAL
July 24, 1955, Croke Park, Dublin
DUBLIN 5-12   MEATH 0-7

LEINSTER QUARTER-FINAL
June 1, 1958, Drogheda Park, Drogheda
DUBLIN 1-12   MEATH 2-7

LEINSTER SEMI-FINAL
July 9, 1961, Pairc Tailteann, Navan
DUBLIN 4-14   MEATH 1-7

NATIONAL LEAGUE SEMI-FINAL
Apr 29, 1962, Croke Park, Dublin
DUBLIN 0-15   MEATH 1-8

LEINSTER QUARTER-FINAL
June 2, 1963, Croke Park, Dublin
DUBLIN 2-6   MEATH 2-5

LEINSTER FINAL
July 26, 1964, Croke Park, Dublin
MEATH 2-12   DUBLIN 1-7

NATIONAL LEAGUE SEMI-FINAL
Apr 9, 1967, Croke Park, Dublin
DUBLIN 1-15   MEATH 1-7

**NATIONAL LEAGUE,
DIVISION IB SEMI-FINAL**
Mar 16, 1968, Athletic Grounds, Drogheda
DUBLIN 1-10   MEATH 0-9

LEINSTER FINAL
July 28, 1974, Croke Park, Dublin
DUBLIN 1-14   MEATH 1-9

NATIONAL LEAGUE FINAL
May 19, 1975, Croke Park, Dublin
MEATH 0-16   DUBLIN 1-9

LEINSTER FINAL
July 25, 1976, Croke Park, Dublin
DUBLIN 2-8   MEATH 1-9

NATIONAL LEAGUE, DIVISION IA
Nov 21, 1976, Pairc Tailteann, Navan
DUBLIN 3-3   MEATH 1-9

LEINSTER FINAL
July 31, 1977, Croke Park, Dublin
DUBLIN 1-9   MEATH 0-8

LEINSTER SEMI-FINAL
July 6, 1980, Pairc Tailteann, Navan
DUBLIN 3–13   MEATH 2–7

LEINSTER QUARTER-FINAL
June 12, 1983, Croke Park, Dublin
DUBLIN 2-8   MEATH 2-8

LEINSTER QUARTER-FINAL REPLAY
July 3, 1983, Croke Park, Dublin
DUBLIN 3-9   MEATH 0-16

NATIONAL LEAGUE, DIVISION ONE
Oct 9, 1983, Pairc Tailteann, Navan
DUBLIN 1-6   MEATH 1-6

LEINSTER FINAL
July 22, 1984, Croke Park, Dublin
DUBLIN 2-10   MEATH 1-9

NATIONAL LEAGUE QUARTER-FINAL
Mar 30, 1986, Croke Park, Dublin
DUBLIN 2-8   MEATH 1-10

LEINSTER FINAL
July 27, 1986, O'Moore Park, Portlaoise
MEATH 0-9   DUBLIN 0-7

NATIONAL LEAGUE, DIVISION ONE
Nov 2, 1986, Croke Park, Dublin
MEATH 2-13   DUBLIN 0-9

LEINSTER FINAL
July 26, 1987, Croke Park, Dublin
MEATH 1-13   DUBLIN 0-12

NATIONAL LEAGUE, DIVISION ONE
Nov 8, 1987, Croke Park, Dublin
DUBLIN 2-5   MEATH 0-11

NATIONAL LEAGUE FINAL
Apr 17, 1988, Croke Park, Dublin
DUBLIN 1-8   MEATH 0-11

NATIONAL LEAGUE FINAL REPLAY
May 22, 1988, Croke Park, Dublin
MEATH 2-13   DUBLIN 0-11

LEINSTER FINAL
July 31,1988, Croke Park, Dublin
MEATH 2-5   DUBLIN 0-9

NATIONAL LEAGUE, DIVISION ONE
Dec 4, 1988, Pairc Tailteann, Navan
DUBLIN 1-12   MEATH 0-4

LEINSTER FINAL
July 30, 1989, Croke Park, Dublin
DUBLIN 2-12   MEATH 1-10

LEINSTER FINAL
July 29, 1990, Croke Park, Dublin
MEATH 1-14   DUBLIN 0-14

NATIONAL LEAGUE, DIVISION ONE
Mar 10, 1991, Croke Park, Dublin
DUBLIN 0-11   MEATH 1-8

LEINSTER FIRST ROUND
June 2, 1991, Croke Park, Dublin
DUBLIN 1-12   MEATH 1-12

LEINSTER FIRST ROUND REPLAY
June 9, 1991, Croke Park, Dublin
DUBLIN 1-11   MEATH 1-11

**LEINSTER FIRST ROUND
SECOND REPLAY**
June 23, 1991, Croke Park, Dublin
DUBLIN 1-14   MEATH 2-11

LEINSTER FIRST ROUND THIRD REPLAY
July 6, 1991, Croke Park, Dublin
MEATH 2-10   DUBLIN 0-15

LEINSTER SEMI-FINAL
July 4, 1993, Croke Park, Dublin
DUBLIN 1-10   MEATH   0-12

LEINSTER FINAL
July 31, 1994, Croke Park, Dublin
DUBLIN 1-9   MEATH 1-8

**NATIONAL LEAGUE,
DIVISION ONE**
Oct 16, 1994, Croke Park, Dublin
MEATH 1-8   DUBLIN 0-7

LEINSTER FINAL
July 30, 1995, Croke Park, Dublin
DUBLIN 1-18   MEATH 1-8

LEINSTER FINAL
July 28, 1996, Croke Park, Dublin
MEATH 0-10   DUBLIN 0-8

LEINSTER QUARTER-FINAL
June 15, 1997, Croke Park, Dublin
MEATH 1-13   DUBLIN 1-10

LEINSTER FINAL
Aug 1, 1999, Croke Park, Dublin
MEATH 1-14   DUBLIN 0-12

LEINSTER FINAL
July 15, 2001, Croke Park, Dublin
MEATH 2-11   DUBLIN 0-14

LEINSTER SEMI-FINAL
June 23, 2002, Croke Park, Dublin
DUBLIN 2-11   MEATH 0-10

LEINSTER QUARTER-FINAL
June 5, 2005, Croke Park, Dublin
DUBLIN 1-12   MEATH 1-10

LEINSTER QUARTER-FINAL
June 3, 2007, Croke Park, Dublin
DUBLIN 0-14   MEATH 0-14

**LEINSTER QUARTER-FINAL
REPLAY**
June 17, 2007, Croke Park, Dublin
DUBLIN 0-16   MEATH 0-12

**NATIONAL LEAGUE,
DIVISION TWO**
Apr 20, 2008, Parnell Park, Dublin
DUBLIN 0-13   MEATH 2-6

LEINSTER QUARTER-FINAL
June 7, 2009, Croke Park, Dublin
DUBLIN 0-14   MEATH 0-12

LEINSTER SEMI-FINAL
June 27, 2010, Croke Park, Dublin
MEATH 5-9   DUBLIN 0-13

LEINSTER FINAL
July 22, 2012, Croke Park, Dublin
DUBLIN 2-13   MEATH 1-13

LEINSTER FINAL
July 14, 2013, Croke Park, Dublin
DUBLIN 2-15   MEATH 0-14

LEINSTER FINAL
July 20, 2014, Croke Park, Dublin
DUBLIN   3-20   MEATH 1-10

LEINSTER SEMI-FINAL
June 26, 2016, Croke Park, Dublin
DUBLIN 0-21   MEATH 0-11

	P	W	D	L	For	Agt
Championship	62	35	8	19	80-589	61-519
National League	34	16	6	12	42-246	36-233
TOTAL	96	50	14	32	122-835	97-746

MONAGHAN

ALL-IRELAND SEMI-FINAL, 1907
15 Mar, 1908, McGeough's Field, Dundalk
DUBLIN 1-5   MONAGHAN 0-2

ALL-IRELAND SEMI-FINAL, 1921
June 18, 1922, McGeough's Field, Dundalk
DUBLIN   2-8   MONAGHAN 2-2

ALL-IRELAND SEMI-FINAL, 1922
July 15, 1923, McGeough's Field, Dundalk
DUBLIN   2-5   MONAGHAN 0-0

NATIONAL LEAGUE, GROUP C
Nov 22, 1936, Croke Park, Dublin
DUBLIN 3-2   MONAGHAN 1-7

NATIONAL LEAGUE, GROUP C
Oct 10, 1937, Emmet Park, Carrickmacross
DUBLIN 0-7   MONAGHAN 0-7

NATIONAL LEAGUE, GROUP C
Oct 29, 1939, Bremore Park, Balbriggan
DUBLIN 3-16   MONAGHAN 0-3

NATIONAL LEAGUE, GROUP C
Nov 27, 1938, Bremore Park, Balbriggan
DUBLIN 2-5   MONAGHAN 1-0

NATIONAL LEAGUE, SECTION III
Oct 15, 1967, Emmet Park, Carrickmacross
DUBLIN 1-10   MONAGHAN 3-3

NATIONAL LEAGUE, DIVISION IB
Nov 11, 1968, Croke Park, Dublin
MONAGHAN 3-7   DUBLIN 2-6

NATIONAL LEAGUE, DIVISION IB
Oct 19, 1969, Emmet Park, Carrickmacross
DUBLIN 1-14   MONAGHAN 0-5

NATIONAL LEAGUE, DIVISION TWO
Oct 14, 1984, St Marys Park, Castleblaney
DUBLIN 1-8   MONAGHAN 0-5

NATIONAL LEAGUE, DIVISION ONE
Nov 16, 1986, Croke Park, Dublin
MONAGHAN 2-10   DUBLIN 2-8

NATIONAL LEAGUE, DIVISION ONE
Nov 22, 1987, St Mary's Park, Castleblaney
DUBLIN 1-13   MONAGHAN 0-5

NATIONAL LEAGUE SEMI-FINAL
Apr 3, 1988, Croke Park, Dublin
DUBLIN 4-12   MONAGHAN 1-8

NATIONAL LEAGUE, DIVISION ONE
Nov 20, 1988, Croke Park, Dublin
DUBLIN 2-12   MONAGHAN 1-8

NATIONAL LEAGUE, DIVISION TWO
Feb 16, 1997, St Tiernach's Park, Clones
DUBLIN 2-7   MONAGHAN 1-7

NATIONAL LEAGUE, DIVISION TWO
Feb 15, 1998, Parnell Park, Dublin
MONAGHAN 2-12   DUBLIN 0-12

NATIONAL LEAGUE, DIVISION IA
Feb 12, 2006, Parnell Park
MONAGHAN 1-11   DUBLIN 0-7

NATIONAL LEAGUE, DIVISION TWO
Mar 24, 2008, Parnell Park, Dublin
DUBLIN 1-10   MONAGHAN 0-13

NATIONAL LEAGUE, DIVISION ONE
Mar 14, 2010, Parnell Park, Dublin
DUBLIN 2-11   MONAGHAN 1-9

NATIONAL LEAGUE, DIVISION ONE
Mar 13, 2011, St Tiernach's Park, Clones
DUBLIN 0-13   MONAGHAN 1-9

ALL-IRELAND QUARTER-FINAL
Aug 9, 2014, Croke Park, Dublin
DUBLIN 2-22   MONAGHAN 0-11

NATIONAL LEAGUE, DIVISION ONE
Apr 5, 2015, St Tiernach's Park, Clones
DUBLIN 1-22   MONAGHAN 1-11

NATIONAL LEAGUE SEMI-FINAL
Apr 12, 2015, Croke Park, Dublin
DUBLIN 0-17   MONAGHAN 0-16

NATIONAL LEAGUE, DIVISION ONE
Feb 27, 2016, Croke Park, Dublin
DUBLIN 1-14   MONAGHAN 0-16

NATIONAL LEAGUE, DIVISION ONE
Apr 2, 2017, St. Tiernach's Park, Clones
DUBLIN 2-15   MONAGHAN 1-15

ALL-IRELAND QUARTER-FINAL
Aug 5, 2017, Croke Park, Dublin
DUBLIN 1-19   MONAGHAN 0-12

	P	W	D	L	For	Agt
Championship	5	5	0	0	8-59	2-27
National League	22	16	2	4	31-241	20-187
TOTAL	27	21	2	4	39-300	22-214

NEW YORK

NATIONAL LEAGUE FINAL
Oct 18, 1964, Gaelic Park, New York
NEW YORK 2-12   DUBLIN 1-13

	P	W	D	L	For	Agt
National League	1	0	0	1	1-13	2-12
TOTAL	1	0	0	1	1-13	2-12

OFFALY

LEINSTER FINAL, 1907
Apr 26, 1908, Agricultural Grounds, Athy
DUBLIN   1-11   OFFALY 0-4

LEINSTER SEMI-FINAL
Sept 25, 1910, Jones's Road, Dublin
DUBLIN 3-7   OFFALY   1-0

LEINSTER QUARTER-FINAL
May 16, 1920, O'Moore Park, Portlaoise
DUBLIN   3-5   OFFALY 0-3

LEINSTER QUARTER-FINAL
May 24, 1936, Cusack Park, Mullingar
OFFALY 0-8   DUBLIN 1-3

NATIONAL LEAGUE, GROUP VI
Feb 17 ,1946, O'Connor Park, Tullamore
DUBLIN 0-6   OFFALY 1-3

LEINSTER QUARTER-FINAL
June 5, 1949, O'Moore Park, Portlaoise
OFFALY   4-7   DUBLIN 3-7

LEINSTER FIRST ROUND
May 20, 1951, St Conleth's Park, Newbridge
DUBLIN   1-8   OFFALY 1-3

NATIONAL LEAGUE, SECTION III
Nov 22, 1953, Croke Park, Dublin
DUBLIN 2-8   OFFALY 0-4

LEINSTER SEMI-FINAL
July 4, 1954, O'Moore Park, Portlaoise
OFFALY 2-5   DUBLIN   2-4

NATIONAL LEAGUE, SECTION III
Nov 28, 1954, O'Connor Park, Tullamore
DUBLIN 1-10   OFFALY 1-4

LEINSTER SEMI-FINAL
July 10, 1955, O'Moore Park, Portlaoise
DUBLIN   1-9   OFFALY 2-3

NATIONAL LEAGUE, SECTION III
Feb 5, 1956, O'Connor Park, Tullamore
DUBLIN 3-10   OFFALY 2-4

NATIONAL LEAGUE, SECTION III
Mar 3, 1957, Parnell Park, Dublin
DUBLIN 3-9   OFFALY 1-4

NATIONAL LEAGUE, SECTION III
Nov 3, 1957, Croke Park, Dublin
DUBLIN 4-7   OFFALY 2-11

NATIONAL LEAGUE, SECTION III
Nov 16, 1958, O'Connor Park, Tullamore
DUBLIN 1-5   OFFALY 1-5

NATIONAL LEAGUE, SECTION III
Nov 1, 1959, O'Connor Park, Tullamore
DUBLIN 0-12   OFFALY 0-6

LEINSTER SEMI-FINAL
June 26, 1960, O'Moore Park, Portlaoise
OFFALY 3-9   DUBLIN 0-9

NATIONAL LEAGUE, SECTION III
Oct 30, 1960, Croke Park, Dublin
OFFALY 5-10   DUBLIN 4-7

LEINSTER FINAL
July 23, 1961, O'Moore Park, Portlaoise
OFFALY 1-13   DUBLIN 1-8

NATIONAL LEAGUE, SECTION III
Mar 25, 1962, Croke Park, Dublin
DUBLIN 2-9   OFFALY 1-5

LEINSTER FINAL
July 15, 1962, Croke Park, Dublin
DUBLIN 2-8   OFFALY 1-7

NATIONAL LEAGUE, SECTION III
Mar 31, 1963, O'Connor Park, Tullamore
OFFALY 3-7   DUBLIN 0-3

NATIONAL LEAGUE, SECTION III
Dec 1, 1963, O'Connor Park, Tullamore
DUBLIN 2-11   OFFALY 1-5

NATIONAL LEAGUE, SECTION III
Feb 14, 1965, Croke Park, Dublin
DUBLIN 1-8   OFFALY 0-10

NATIONAL LEAGUE, DIVISION IB
Nov 1, 1970, Croke Park, Dublin
DUBLIN 2-12   OFFALY 1-10

NATIONAL LEAGUE, DIVISION IA
Oct 31, 1971, O'Connor Park, Tullamore
OFFALY 0-16   DUBLIN 2-3

LEINSTER QUARTER-FINAL
June 16, 1974, Pearse Park, Longford
DUBLIN 1-11   OFFALY 0-13

NATIONAL LEAGUE, DIVISION IA
Feb 2, 1975, O'Connor Park, Tullamore
DUBLIN 0-10   OFFALY 1-5

NATIONAL LEAGUE, DIVISION IA
Dec 7, 1975, Croke Park, Dublin
DUBLIN 5-8   OFFALY 1-8

NATIONAL LEAGUE, DIVISION IA
Nov 20, 1977, Croke Park, Dublin
DUBLIN 4-7   OFFALY 0-3

LEINSTER SEMI-FINAL
July 9, 1978, O'Moore Park, Portlaoise
DUBLIN 2-9   OFFALY 0-12

LEINSTER FINAL
July 29, 1979, Croke Park, Dublin
DUBLIN 1-8   OFFALY 0-9

NATIONAL LEAGUE, DIVISION IA SOUTH
Nov 25, 1979, O'Connor Park, Tullamore
OFFALY 0-12   DUBLIN 1-4

LEINSTER FINAL
July 27, 1980, Croke Park, Dublin
OFFALY 1–10   DUBLIN 1–8

NATIONAL LEAGUE, DIVISION ONE
Nov 2, 1980, O'Connor Park, Tullamore
DUBLIN 0-11   OFFALY 2-5

NATIONAL LEAGUE, DIVISION ONE
Oct 18, 1981, Croke Park, Dublin
OFFALY 1-11   DUBLIN 0-12

LEINSTER FINAL
Aug 1, 1982, Croke Park, Dublin
OFFALY 1-16   DUBLIN 1-7

NATIONAL LEAGUE, DIVISION ONE
Oct 24, 1982, O'Connor Park, Tullamore
OFFALY 4-9   DUBLIN 3-1

LEINSTER FINAL
July 31, 1983, Croke Park, Dublin
DUBLIN 2-13   OFFALY 1-11

NATIONAL LEAGUE, DIVISION ONE
Oct 23, 1983, Croke Park, Dublin
OFFALY 1-4   DUBLIN 0-3

LEINSTER SEMI-FINAL
June 24, 1984, Croke Park, Dublin
DUBLIN 0-13   OFFALY 0-5

NATIONAL LEAGUE, DIVISION TWO
Nov 25, 1984, Croke Park, Dublin
DUBLIN 1-16   OFFALY 0-7

LEINSTER SEMI-FINAL
July 7, 1985, O'Connor Park, Tullamore
DUBLIN 2-13   OFFALY 0-10

LEINSTER SEMI-FINAL
June 29, 1986, O'Moore Park, Portlaoise
DUBLIN 1-10   OFFALY 0-7

LEINSTER FIRST ROUND
May 31, 1992, O'Connor Park, Tullamore
DUBLIN 2-17   OFFALY 1-9

NATIONAL LEAGUE, DIVISION TWO
Nov 2, 1997, Parnell Park, Dublin
OFFALY 1-11   DUBLIN 1-8

NATIONAL LEAGUE, DIVISION IA
Nov 29, 1998, O'Connor Park, Tullamore
DUBLIN 2-11   OFFALY 0-13

NATIONAL LEAGUE, DIVISION IA
Nov 12, 2000, O'Connor Park, Tullamore
OFFALY 1-10   DUBLIN 0-9

LEINSTER SEMI-FINAL
June 17, 2001, Croke Park, Dublin
DUBLIN   1-12   OFFALY 0-13

NATIONAL LEAGUE, DIVISION IA
Feb 23, 2002, O'Connor Park, Tullamore
DUBLIN 0-10   OFFALY 1-7

NATIONAL LEAGUE, DIVISION IA
Apr 3, 2005, O'Connor Park, Tullamore
DUBLIN 1-13   OFFALY 2-6

NATIONAL LEAGUE, DIVISION IA
Mar 4, 2006, Parnell Park, Dublin
DUBLIN 1-10   OFFALY 3-2

LEINSTER FINAL
July 16, 2006, Croke Park, Dublin
DUBLIN   1-15   OFFALY 0-9

LEINSTER SEMI-FINAL
June 24, 2007, Croke Park, Dublin
DUBLIN   1-12   OFFALY 0-10

	P	W	D	L	For	Agt
Championship	24	17	0	7	34-227	19-196
National League	30	17	4	9	48-247	37-207
TOTAL	54	34	4	16	82-474	56-403

ROSCOMMON

ALL-IRELAND SEMI-FINAL, 1892
Mar 19, 1893, Clonturk Park, Dublin
DUBLIN 1-9   ROSCOMMON 1-1

ALL-IRELAND SEMI-FINAL
Sep 29, 1912, Jones's Road, Dublin
DUBLIN 2-4   ROSCOMMON 1-1

NATIONAL LEAGUE, SECTION III
Feb 6, 1955, Sportsfield, Knockcroghery
DUBLIN 3-7   ROSCOMMON 2-3

NATIONAL LEAGUE, SECTION III
Nov 20, 1955, Croke Park, Dublin
DUBLIN 1-9   ROSCOMMON 1-4

NATIONAL LEAGUE, SECTION III
Nov 25, 1956, Croke Park, Dublin
DUBLIN 1-9   ROSCOMMON 0-4

NATIONAL LEAGUE, SECTION III
Nov 17, 1957, Croke Park, Dublin
DUBLIN 4-6   ROSCOMMON 0-4

NATIONAL LEAGUE, SECTION III
Nov 30, 1958, O'Toole Park, Dublin
DUBLIN 3-6   ROSCOMMON 0-4

NATIONAL LEAGUE, SECTION III
Nov 15, 1959, Croke Park, Dublin
DUBLIN 3-8   ROSCOMMON 2-8

NATIONAL LEAGUE, SECTION III
Nov 13, 1960, Sportsfield, Knockcroghery
DUBLIN 1-10   ROSCOMMON 1-10

NATIONAL LEAGUE, SECTION III
Feb 4, 1962, Croke Park, Roscommon
DUBLIN 3-10   ROSCOMMON 2-4

NATIONAL LEAGUE, SECTION III
Mar 24, 1963, GAA Grounds, Athleague
DUBLIN 2-6   ROSCOMMON 1-1

NATIONAL LEAGUE, SECTION III
Mar 8, 1964, St Coman's Park, Roscommon
DUBLIN 1-7   ROSCOMMON 1-7

NATIONAL LEAGUE, SECTION III
Mar 21, 1965, Croke Park, Dublin
DUBLIN 1-17   ROSCOMMON 1-1

NATIONAL LEAGUE, DIVISION IB
Feb 14, 1971, Orchard Park, Elphin
DUBLIN 3-8   ROSCOMMON 1-8

NATIONAL LEAGUE, DIVISION IA
Sep 16, 1973, O'Rourke Park, Castlerea
ROSCOMMON 3-7   DUBLIN 0-11

NATIONAL LEAGUE, DIVISION IA
Mar 2, 1975, Croke Park, Dublin
DUBLIN 1-13   ROSCOMMON 1-4

NATIONAL LEAGUE, DIVISION IA
Feb 1, 1976, Dr Hyde Park, Roscommon
ROSCOMMON 2-8   DUBLIN 1-6

ALL-IRELAND SEMI-FINAL
Aug 19, 1979, Croke Park, Dublin
DUBLIN   0-14   ROSCOMMON 1-10

NATIONAL LEAGUE, DIVISION ONE
Feb 1, 1981, Dr Hyde Park, Roscommon
ROSCOMMON 0-11   DUBLIN 1-5

NATIONAL LEAGUE, DIVISION ONE
Jan 31, 1982, Croke Park, Dublin
DUBLIN 4-13   ROSCOMMON 1-8

NATIONAL LEAGUE, DIVISION TWO
Nov 11, 1984, Croke Park, Dublin
ROSCOMMON 0-8   DUBLIN 0-6

NATIONAL LEAGUE, DIVISION ONE
Mar 8, 1987, Croke Park, Dublin
DUBLIN 1-11   ROSCOMMON 0-8

NATIONAL LEAGUE QUARTER-FINAL
Apr 1, 1990, O'Moore Park, Portlaoise
ROSCOMMON 2-22   DUBLIN 3-13

NATIONAL LEAGUE, DIVISION ONE
Dec 2, 1990, Croke Park, Dublin
DUBLIN 2-14   ROSCOMMON 0-6

NATIONAL LEAGUE SEMI-FINAL
Apr 21, 1991, Croke Park, Dublin
DUBLIN 1-18   ROSCOMMON 0-11

NATIONAL LEAGUE, DIVISION IA
Feb 13, 2000, Dr Hyde Park, Roscommon
ROSCOMMON 1-10   DUBLIN 0-6

NATIONAL LEAGUE, DIVISION IA
Feb 10, 2001, Parnell Park, Dublin
ROSCOMMON 0-12   DUBLIN 0-10

NATIONAL LEAGUE, DIVISION IA
Mar 24, 2002, Parnell Park, Dublin
ROSCOMMON 2-12   DUBLIN 0-16

NATIONAL LEAGUE, DIVISION IA
Mar 23, 2003, Dr Hyde Park, Roscommon
DUBLIN 0-17   ROSCOMMON 0-14

ALL-IRELAND QUALIFIERS, ROUND FOUR
Aug 1, 2004, Croke Park, Dublin
DUBLIN 1-14   ROSCOMMON 0-13

NATIONAL LEAGUE, DIVISION TWO
Apr 5, 2008, Parnell Park, Dublin
DUBLIN 3-20   ROSCOMMON 0-7

NATIONAL LEAGUE, DIVISION ONE
Apr 3, 2016, Pairc Diarmuda, C-on-Shannon
DUBLIN 1-13   ROSCOMMON 1-12

NATIONAL LEAGUE, DIVISION ONE
Mar 25, 2017, Croke Park, Dublin
DUBLIN 2-29   ROSCOMMON 0-14

	P	W	D	L	For	Agt
Championship	4	4	0	0	4-41	3-25
National League	29	19	2	8	46-314	24-232
TOTAL	33	23	2	8	48-355	27-257

SLIGO

NATIONAL LEAGUE, SECTION A
Nov 1, 1992, Markievicz Park, Sligo
DUBLIN 0-18   SLIGO 0-8

NATIONAL LEAGUE, DIVISION TWO
Oct 19, 1997, Markievicz Park, Sligo
SLIGO 2-7 DUBLIN 0-12

ALL-IRELAND QUALIFIERS, ROUND FOUR
July 22, 2001, Croke Park, Dublin
DUBLIN 3-17   SLIGO 0-12

	P	W	D	L	For	Agt
Championship	1	1	0	0	3-17	0-12
National League	2	2	0	0	0-30	2-15
TOTAL	3	2	0	1	3-47	2-27

TIPPERARY

ALL-IRELAND 'HOME' FINAL, 1902
July 12, 1904, St James's Park, Kilkenny
DUBLIN 0-6   TIPPERARY 0-5

ALL-IRELAND FINAL, 1920
June 11, 1922, Croke Park, Dublin
TIPPERARY 1-6   DUBLIN 1-2

NATIONAL LEAGUE, DIVISION ONE
Feb 23, 1936, Croke Park, Dublin
DUBLIN 2-8   TIPPERARY 1-4

NATIONAL LEAGUE SEMI-FINAL
Mar 29, 1953, Croke Park, Dublin
DUBLIN 0-9   TIPPERARY 0-3

NATIONAL LEAGUE, DIVISION IA
Dec 12, 1971, Croke Park, Dublin
TIPPERARY 0-12   DUBLIN 1-4

ALL-IRELAND QUALIFIERS, ROUND TWO
July 10, 2010, Croke Park, Dublin
DUBLIN   1-21   TIPPERARY 1-13

	P	W	D	L	For	Agt
Championship	3	2	0	1	2-29	2-24
National League	3	2	0	1	3-21	1-19
TOTAL	6	4	0	2	5-50	3-43

TYRONE

NATIONAL LEAGUE SEMI-FINAL
May 4, 1975, Croke Park, Dublin
DUBLIN 3-12   TYRONE 1-7

ALL-IRELAND SEMI-FINAL
Aug 19, 1984, Croke Park, Dublin
DUBLIN   2-11   TYRONE 0-8

NATIONAL LEAGUE, DIVISION IA
Nov 10, 1991, Croke Park, Dublin
TYRONE 4-11   DUBLIN 0-11

NATIONAL LEAGUE SEMI-FINAL
Apr 19, 1992, Croke Park, Dublin
TYRONE 0-13   DUBLIN 1-9

ALL-IRELAND FINAL
Sep 17, 1995, Croke Park, Dublin
DUBLIN   1-10   TYRONE 0-12

NATIONAL LEAGUE, DIVISION TWO
Mar 1, 1998, O'Neill Park, Dungannon
DUBLIN 1-7   TYRONE 1-2

NATIONAL LEAGUE, DIVISION IA
Nov 1, 1998, Parnell Park, Dublin
DUBLIN 1-15   TYRONE 1-9

NATIONAL LEAGUE, DIVISION IA
Oct 31, 1999, Healy Park, Omagh
TYRONE 1-13   DUBLIN 0-9

NATIONAL LEAGUE, DIVISION IA
Oct 29, 2000, Parnell Park, Dublin
TYRONE 0-19   DUBLIN 2-10

NATIONAL LEAGUE, DIVISION IA
Feb 17, 2002, O'Neill Park. Dungannon
TYRONE 0-18   DUBLIN 2-10

NATIONAL LEAGUE, DIVISION IA
Feb 16, 2003, Parnell Park, Dublin
DUBLIN 0-12   TYRONE 0-11

NATIONAL LEAGUE, DIVISION IA
Feb 1, 2004, Parnell Park, Dublin
DUBLIN 0-9   TYRONE 0-8

NATIONAL LEAGUE, DIVISION IA
Feb 13, 2005, Healy Park, Omagh
TYRONE 1-10   DUBLIN 0-9

ALL-IRELAND QUARTER-FINAL
Aug 13, 2005, Croke Park, Dublin
DUBLIN 1-14   TYRONE   1-14

**ALL-IRELAND QUARTER-FINAL
REPLAY**
Aug 27, 2005, Croke Park, Dublin
TYRONE   2-18   DUBLIN 1-14

NATIONAL LEAGUE, DIVISION IA
Feb 5, 2006, Healy Park, Omagh
DUBLIN 1-9   TYRONE 1-6

NATIONAL LEAGUE, DIVISION IA
Feb 3, 2007, Croke Park, Dublin
TYRONE 0-11   DUBLIN 0-10

ALL-IRELAND QUARTER-FINAL
Aug 16, 2008, Croke Park, Dublin
TYRONE 3-14   DUBLIN 1-8

NATIONAL LEAGUE, DIVISION IA
Jan 31, 2009, Croke Park, Dublin
TYRONE 1-18   DUBLIN 1-16

NATIONAL LEAGUE, DIVISION ONE
Apr 11, 2010, Healy Park, Omagh
DUBLIN 2-14   TYRONE 0-11

ALL-IRELAND QUARTER-FINAL
July 31, 2010, Croke Park, Dublin
DUBLIN 1-15   TYRONE 0-13

ALL-IRELAND QUARTER-FINAL
Aug 6, 2011, Croke Park, Dublin
DUBLIN   0-22   TYRONE 0-15

NATIONAL LEAGUE, DIVISION ONE
Mar 16, 2013, Croke Park, Dublin
TYRONE 0-18   DUBLIN 1-14

NATIONAL LEAGUE FINAL
Apr 28, 2013, Croke Park, Dublin
DUBLIN 0-18   TYRONE 0-17

NATIONAL LEAGUE, DIVISION ONE
Apr 6, 2014, Healy Park, Omagh
DUBLIN 3-10   TYRONE 1-15

NATIONAL LEAGUE, DIVISION ONE
Mar 8, 2015, Croke Park, Dublin
DUBLIN 1-9   TYRONE 0-12

NATIONAL LEAGUE, DIVISION ONE
Feb 11, 2017, Croke Park, Dublin
DUBLIN 0-10   TYRONE 1-7

ALL-IRELAND SEMI-FINAL
Aug 27, 2017, Croke Park, Dublin
DUBLIN 2-17   TYRONE 0-11

	P	W	D	L	For	Agt
Championship	8	5	1	2	9-111	6-105
National League	20	9	2	9	19-223	13-236
TOTAL	28	14	3	11	28-334	19-341

WATERFORD

ALL-IRELAND FINAL, 1898
Apr 8, 1900, Tipperary Park, Tipperary
DUBLIN   2-8   WATERFORD 0-4

**NATIONAL LEAGUE,
SECTION III SEMI-FINAL**
Mar 6, 1966, Croke Park, Dublin
DUBLIN 1-16   WATERFORD 1-2

NATIONAL LEAGUE, DIVISION IA
Feb 27, 1971, Croke Park, Dublin
DUBLIN 3-6   WATERFORD 0-6

NATIONAL LEAGUE, DIVISION IIA
Feb 3 , 1974, Croke Park, Dublin
DUBLIN 2-15   WATERFORD 0-5

	P	W	D	L	For	Agt
Championship	1	1	0	0	2-8	0-4
National League	3	3	0	0	6-37	1-13
TOTAL	4	4	0	0	8-45	1-17

WESTMEATH

LEINSTER QUARTER-FINAL
Aug 17, 1890, Clonturk Park, Dublin
DUBLIN 6-11   WESTMEATH 0-2

LEINSTER QUARTER-FINAL
June 8, 1930, Cusack Park, Mullingar
DUBLIN 2-8   WESTMEATH 0-4

LEINSTER SEMI-FINAL
July 26, 1931, Ballyduff Park, Tullamore
WESTMEATH 2-4   DUBLIN 1-4

LEINSTER SEMI-FINAL
July 17, 1932, O'Moore Park, Portlaoise
DUBLIN 3-7   WESTMEATH 2-5

LEINSTER QUARTER-FINAL
June 3, 1934, St Columbeille's Park, Kells
DUBLIN 2-10   WESTMEATH 1-4

NATIONAL LEAGUE, GROUP C
Oct 6, 1940, Croke Park, Dublin
DUBLIN 4-7   WESTMEATH 0-1

NATIONAL LEAGUE, SECTION IV
Oct 30, 1949, Cusack Park, Mullingar
WESTMEATH 2-8   DUBLIN 1-6

NATIONAL LEAGUE, SECTION IV
Oct 29, 1950, Croke Park, Dublin
DUBLIN 5-10   WESTMEATH 1-3

NATIONAL LEAGUE, SECTION IV
Oct 21, 1951, Cusack Park, Mullingar
DUBLIN 4-11   WESTMEATH 1-2

LEINSTER QUARTER-FINAL
June 11, 1967, O'Connor Park, Tullamore
WESTMEATH 1-6   DUBLIN 0-8

NATIONAL LEAGUE, SECTION III
Oct 22, 1967, Pairc Ciaran, Athlone
WESTMEATH 1-5   DUBLIN 0-7

NATIONAL LEAGUE, DIVISION IB
Oct 13, 1968, Croke Park, Dublin
DUBLIN 0-10   WESTMEATH 0-7

NATIONAL LEAGUE,
DIVISION IB PLAY-OFF
Mar 9, 1969, The Oval, Dublin
DUBLIN 0-7   WESTMEATH 0-3

NATIONAL LEAGUE, DIVISION I FINAL,
LEAGUE QUARTER-FINAL
Mar 30, 1969, Pairc Tailteann, Navan
WESTMEATH 1-8   DUBLIN 1-6

NATIONAL LEAGUE, DIVISION IB
Nov 30, 1969, Cusack Park, Mullingar
DUBLIN 2-6   WESTMEATH 2-3

LEINSTER QUARTER-FINAL
June 11, 1972, Croke Park, Dublin
DUBLIN 2-8   WESTMEATH 0-8

LEINSTER QUARTER-FINAL
June 7, 1987, Croke Park, Dublin
DUBLIN 0-14   WESTMEATH 0-7

LEINSTER QUARTER-FINAL
June 7, 1993, O'Connor Park, Tullamore
DUBLIN 2-11   WESTMEATH   0-8

NATIONAL LEAGUE, DIVISION TWO
Nov 26, 1995, Pairc Chiarain, Athlone
DUBLIN 0-13   WESTMEATH 0-7

LEINSTER QUARTER-FINAL
June 9, 1996, Pairc Tailteann, Navan
DUBLIN 1-18   WESTMEATH 0-11

LEINSTER SEMI-FINAL
July 2, 2000, Croke Park, Dublin
DUBLIN 1-14   WESTMEATH 0-11

NATIONAL LEAGUE, DIVISION TWO
Mar 3, 2002, Parnell Park, Dublin
DUBLIN 3-13   WESTMEATH 1-16

NATIONAL LEAGUE, DIVISION IA
Mar 7, 2004, Cusack Park, Mullingar
DUBLIN 0-15   WESTMEATH 0-10

LEINSTER QUARTER-FINAL
June 6, 2004, Croke Park, Dublin
WESTMEATH 0-14   DUBLIN 0-12

NATIONAL LEAGUE, DIVISION IA
Mar 12, 2005, Parnell Park, Dublin
DUBLIN 0-11   WESTMEATH 0-9

ALL-IRELAND QUARTER-FINAL
Aug 12, 2006, Croke Park, Dublin
DUBLIN   1-12   WESTMEATH 0-5

NATIONAL LEAGUE, DIVISION TWO
Feb 2, 2008, Parnell Park, Dublin
DUBLIN 1-7   WESTMEATH 1-5

NATIONAL LEAGUE, DIVISION TWO
FINAL
Apr 27, 2008, Pairc Tailteann, Navan
WESTMEATH 0-15   DUBLIN 0-10

LEINSTER SEMI-FINAL
June 29, 2008, Croke Park, Dublin
DUBLIN 0-13   WESTMEATH 1-8

NATIONAL LEAGUE, DIVISION ONE
Apr 12, 2009, Parnell Park, Dublin
DUBLIN 5-22   WESTMEATH 0-10

LEINSTER SEMI-FINAL
June 28, 2009, Croke Park, Dublin
DUBLIN 4-26   WESTMEATH 0-11

LEINSTER QUARTER-FINAL
June 2, 2013, Croke Park, Dublin
DUBLIN 1-22   WESTMEATH 0-9

NATIONAL LEAGUE, DIVISION ONE
Feb 9, 2014, Cusack Park, Mullingar
DUBLIN 0-14   WESTMEATH 2-7

LEINSTER FINAL
July 12, 2015, Croke Park, Dublin
DUBLIN 2-13   WESTMEATH 0-6

LEINSTER FINAL
July 17, 2016, Croke Park, Dublin
DUBLIN 2-19   WESTMEATH 0-10

	P	W	D	L	For	Agt
Championship	18	15	0	3	30-230	7-133
National Leagu:e	17	13	0	4	26-175	12-119
TOTAL	35	28	0	7	56-405	19-252

WEXFORD

LEINSTER SEMI-FINAL
Sep 2, 1888, Clonskeagh Park, Dublin
WEXFORD 0–4   DUBLIN 0–3

LEINSTER FINAL
Nov 2, 1890, Clonturk Park, Dublin
WEXFORD 1-3   DUBLIN 1-2

LEINSTER SEMI-FINAL
Sep 23, 1894, Clonturk Park, Dublin
DUBLIN 1-11   WEXFORD 0-0

LEINSTER SEMI-FINAL, 1897
Sep 4, 1898, Jones's Road, Dublin
WEXFORD 1-7   DUBLIN 1-5
Dublin lodged an objection and
a replay was ordered.

LEINSTER SEMI-FINAL, 1987, REPLAY
Oct 16, 1898, Jones's Road, Dublin
DUBLIN 0-10   WEXFORD 0-9

LEINSTER FINAL, 1898
Feb 4, 1900, Jones's Road, Dublin
DUBLIN   2-6   WEXFORD 0-0

LEINSTER FINAL, 1899
Jan 13, 1901, Jones's Road, Dublin
DUBLIN   1-7   WEXFORD 0-3

LEINSTER QUARTER-FINAL, 1900
May 26, 1901, St James's Park, Kilkenny
WEXFORD 1-7   DUBLIN 0-8

LEINSTER FINAL, 1901
Mar 22, 1903, St James's Park, Kilkenny
DUBLIN   1-9   WEXFORD 0-1

LEINSTER FINAL, 1902
May 1, 1904, Agricultural Grounds, Carlow
DUBLIN   2-5   WEXFORD 0-2
Match abandoned after three-quarters of an hour due
to waterlogged pitch, replay ordered

LEINSTER FINAL, 1902, REPLAY
June 12, 1904, Asylum Lane, Kilkenny
DUBLIN   1-5   WEXFORD 0-5

LEINSTER QUARTER-FINAL
June 13, 1909, Wexford Park, Wexford
DUBLIN 0-18   WEXFORD 0-6

LEINSTER QUARTER-FINAL
Sep 4, 1910, Jones's Road, Dublin
DUBLIN 1-6   WEXFORD 0-1

LEINSTER SEMI-FINAL
Aug 24, 1913, Wexford Park, Wexford
WEXFORD 2-3   DUBLIN 1-0

LEINSTER SEMI-FINAL
July 26, 1914, St James's Park, Kilkenny
WEXFORD 4-6   DUBLIN 1-1

LEINSTER FINAL
Sep 12, 1915, Croke Park, Dublin
DUBLIN 2–2   WEXFORD 2-2

LEINSTER FINAL REPLAY
Oct 10, 1915, Croke Park, Dublin
WEXFORD 2–5   DUBLIN 1-3

LEINSTER QUARTER-FINAL
Sep 3, 1916, Wexford Park, Wexford
WEXFORD W/O   DUBLIN SCR
Dublin were unable to field a full side after
several of their players missed the train

LEINSTER FINAL
Oct 14, 1917, Croke Park, Dublin
WEXFORD 1-3   DUBLIN 1-1

LEINSTER SEMI-FINAL
Aug 31, 1919, Croke Park, Dublin
DUBLIN 0-11   WEXFORD 1-1

LEINSTER FINAL
Oct 19, 1924, Croke Park, Dublin
DUBLIN   1-4   WEXFORD 1-4

LEINSTER FINAL REPLAY
Nov 30, 1924, Croke Park, Dublin
DUBLIN   3-5   WEXFORD 2-3

LEINSTER QUARTER-FINAL
July 5, 1925, St James's Park, Kilkenny
WEXFORD 2-4   DUBLIN 1-6

LEINSTER SEMI-FINAL
July 10, 1927, St James's Park, Kilkenny
DUBLIN 0-11   WEXFORD 2-5

LEINSTER SEMI-FINAL REPLAY
July 31, 1927, St James's Park, Kilkenny
DUBLIN 0-8   WEXFORD 1-1

LEINSTER SEMI-FINAL
July 8, 1928, Croke Park, Dublin
DUBLIN 3-3   WEXFORD 0-4

NATIONAL LEAGUE, SOUTH-EASTERN SECTION
Apr 28, 1929, Croke Park, Dublin
DUBLIN 2-3   WEXFORD 0-5

NATIONAL LEAGUE, SECTION A
Apr 6, 1930, Croke Park, Dublin
DUBLIN 4-5   WEXFORD 2-2

LEINSTER QUARTER-FINAL
July 5, 1931, St Patrick's Park, Enniscorthy
DUBLIN 4-3   WEXFORD 1-3

LEINSTER FINAL
Aug 7, 1932, Croke Park, Dublin
DUBLIN   0-8   WEXFORD 1-5

LEINSTER FINAL REPLAY
Aug 14, 1932, Croke Park, Dublin
DUBLIN   4-6   WEXFORD 1-5

LEINSTER FINAL
July 30, 1933, Croke Park, Dublin
DUBLIN   0-9   WEXFORD 1-4

NATIONAL LEAGUE, GROUP II
Dec 3, 1933, Wexford Park, Wexford
DUBLIN 1-9   WEXFORD 2-3

NATIONAL LEAGUE, DIVISION IA
Dec 6, 1936, Wexford Park, Wexford
DUBLIN 2-6   WEXFORD 1-2

NATIONAL LEAGUE, GROUP C
Nov 28, 1937, Wexford Park, Wexford
WEXFORD 1-7   DUBLIN 0-6

NATIONAL LEAGUE SEMI-FINAL
Apr 14, 1946, St Patrick's Park, Enniscorthy
WEXFORD 5-6   DUBLIN 1-2

LEINSTER SEMI-FINAL
June 24, 1956, Dr Cullen Park, Carlow
WEXFORD 2-7   DUBLIN 0-7

LEINSTER QUARTER-FINAL
June 4, 1961, Dr Cullen Park, Carlow
DUBLIN 4-7   WEXFORD 1-7

LEINSTER QUARTER-FINAL
May 30, 1965, Dr Cullen Park, Carlow
DUBLIN 2-11   WEXFORD 0-7

**NATIONAL LEAGUE,
SECTION III FINAL**
Mar 5, 1967, Croke Park, Dublin
DUBLIN 4-12   WEXFORD 0-6

LEINSTER FIRST ROUND
May 20, 1973, Wexford Park, Wexford
DUBLIN   3-11   WEXFORD 0-5

NATIONAL LEAGUE, DIVISION IIA
Oct 14, 1973, Croke Park, Dublin
DUBLIN 3-6   WEXFORD 1-8

LEINSTER FIRST ROUND
May 26, 1974, Croke Park, Dublin
DUBLIN 3-9   WEXFORD 0-6

LEINSTER QUARTER-FINAL
June 8, 1975, Dr Cullen Park, Carlow
DUBLIN   4-17   WEXFORD 3-10

LEINSTER SEMI-FINAL
July 3, 1977, Dr Cullen Park, Carlow
DUBLIN 3-11   WEXFORD 0-6

LEINSTER QUARTER-FINAL
June 10, 1984, Croke Park, Dublin
DUBLIN 4-12   WEXFORD 0-9

NATIONAL LEAGUE, DIVISION TWO
Feb 3, 1985, Croke Park, Dublin
WEXFORD 1-5   DUBLIN 0-7

LEINSTER QUARTER-FINAL
June 16, 1985, Wexford Park, Wexford
DUBLIN 4-13   WEXFORD 0-6

NATIONAL LEAGUE, DIVISION TWO
Nov 10, 1985, Belfield Park, Enniscorthy
DUBLIN 2-7   WEXFORD 0-6

LEINSTER QUARTER-FINAL
June 8, 1986, Croke Park, Dublin
DUBLIN 0-17   WEXFORD 3-3

NATIONAL LEAGUE QUARTER-FINAL
Mar 26, 1989, O'Moore Park, Portlaoise
DUBLIN 1-11   WEXFORD 0-7

LEINSTER QUARTER-FINAL
June 28, 1992, O'Moore Park, Portlaoise
DUBLIN 1-18   WEXFORD 0-11

NATIONAL LEAGUE, SECTION A
Feb 14, 1993, Wexford Park, Wexford
DUBLIN 0-11   WEXFORD 1-7

LEINSTER FIRST ROUND
May 23, 1993, Wexford Park, Wexford
DUBLIN   0-11   WEXFORD 0-7

NATIONAL LEAGUE, DIVISION TWO
Nov 16, 1997, Belfied Park, Enniscorthy
DUBLIN 1-9   WEXFORD 0-4

LEINSTER QUARTER-FINAL
June 1, 2002, Dr Cullen Park, Carlow
DUBLIN   0-15   WEXFORD 1-10

LEINSTER SEMI-FINAL
June 19, 2005, Croke Park, Dublin
DUBLIN   1-17   WEXFORD 2-10

LEINSTER FINAL
July 20, 2008, Croke Park, Dublin
DUBLIN 3-23   WEXFORD 0-9

LEINSTER QUARTER-FINAL
June 13, 2010, Croke Park, Dublin
DUBLIN 2-16   WEXFORD 0-15

LEINSTER FINAL
July 10, 2011, Croke Park, Dublin
DUBLIN 2-12   WEXFORD 1-12

LEINSTER SEMI-FINAL
July 1, 2012, Croke Park, Dublin
DUBLIN 2-11   WEXFORD 1-10

LEINSTER SEMI-FINAL
June 29, 2014, Croke Park, Dublin
DUBLIN 2-25   WEXFORD 1-12

	P	W	D	L	For	Agt
Championship	49	33	4	12	73-429	42-268
National League	13	10	0	3	21-94	14-68
TOTAL	62	43	6	13	93-523	56-336

WICKLOW

LEINSTER SEMI-FINAL
Oct 25, 1891, Clonturk Park, Dublin
DUBLIN 4-4   WICKLOW 0-0

LEINSTER SEMI-FINAL, 1897
Dec 18, 1898, Jones's Road, Dublin
DUBLIN   1-9   WICKLOW 0-3

LEINSTER QUARTER-FINAL, 1902
Nov 1, 1903, Jones's Road, Dublin
DUBLIN 1-16   WICKLOW 1-0

LEINSTER FIRST ROUND
June 12,1910, Jones's Road, Dublin
DUBLIN 1-11   WICKLOW 0-5

LEINSTER SEMI-FINAL
Sep 22, 1912, Wexford Park, Wexford
DUBLIN 1-4   WICKLOW 0-4

LEINSTER LEAGUE
Oct 29, 1944, Bramble Glade, Ashford
DUBLIN 2-10   WICKLOW 1-7

NATIONAL LEAGUE, GROUP VI
Mar 3, 1946, Croke Park, Dublin
DUBLIN 1-9   WICKLOW 0-3

NATIONAL LEAGUE, SECTION IV
Feb 5, 1950, County Ground, Aughrim
DUBLIN 1-6   WICKLOW 1-1

NATIONAL LEAGUE, SECTION IV
Nov 18, 1951, Croke Park, Dublin
DUBLIN 4-7   WICKLOW 0-3

NATIONAL LEAGUE, SECTION IV
Feb 1, 1953, Pearses' Park, Arklow
DUBLIN 3-8   WICKLOW 1-5

NATIONAL LEAGUE, SECTION III
Feb 7, 1954, Croke Park, Dublin
DUBLIN 1-10   WICKLOW 1-4

NATIONAL LEAGUE, SECTION III
Dec 5, 1954, Croke Park, Dublin
DUBLIN 1-6   WICKLOW 1-3

NATIONAL LEAGUE, SECTION III
Nov 6, 1955, Croke Park, Dublin
DUBLIN 2-2   WICKLOW 1-2

LEINSTER QUARTER-FINAL
May 27, 1956, St Patrick's Park, Enniscorthy
DUBLIN 0-11   WICKLOW 0-5

NATIONAL LEAGUE, SECTION III
Nov 18, 1956, County Ground, Aughrim
DUBLIN 2-6   WICKLOW 1-4

LEINSTER SEMI-FINAL
June 23, 1957, St Conleth's Park, Newbridge
DUBLIN 3-9   WICKLOW 0-9

NATIONAL LEAGUE, SECTION III
Feb 2, 1958, O'Toole Park, Dublin
DUBLIN 1-11   WICKLOW 0-8

NATIONAL LEAGUE, SECTION III
Feb 1, 1959, Burgage Park, Blessington
DUBLIN 3-4   WICKLOW 2-4

NATIONAL LEAGUE, SECTION III
Mar 27, 1960, Croke Park, Dublin
DUBLIN 3-10   WICKLOW 1-12

NATIONAL LEAGUE, SECTION III
Mar 26, 1961, County Ground, Aughrim
DUBLIN 4-7   WICKLOW 0-7

NATIONAL LEAGUE, SECTION III
Nov 19, 1961, Croke Park, Dublin
DUBLIN 4-8   WICKLOW 2-4

NATIONAL LEAGUE, SECTION III
Dec 2, 1962, Croke Park, Dublin
DUBLIN 3-14   WICKLOW 1-3

NATIONAL LEAGUE, SECTION III
Oct 6, 1963, Croke Park, Dublin
DUBLIN 4-11   WICKLOW 1-7

NATIONAL LEAGUE, SECTION III
Nov 22, 1964, Croke Park, Dublin
DUBLIN 0-16   WICKLOW 0-4

LEINSTER SEMI-FINAL
July 1, 1979, St Conleth's Park, Newbridge
DUBLIN 3-13   WICKLOW 2-7

LEINSTER QUARTER-FINAL
May 31, 1981, St Conleth's Park, Newbridge
DUBLIN 0-10   WICKLOW 0-8

LEINSTER SEMI-FINAL
July 5, 1987, St Conleth's Park, Newbridge
DUBLIN 2-18   WICKLOW 0-6

LEINSTER SEMI-FINAL
June 25, 1989, St Conleth's Park, Newbridge
DUBLIN 1-12   WICKLOW 1-6

LEINSTER SEMI-FINAL
June 24, 1990, St Conleth's Park, Newbridge
DUBLIN 2-14   WICKLOW 0-12

NATIONAL LEAGUE QUARTER-FINAL
Apr 14, 1991, Croke Park, Dublin
DUBLIN 2-10   WICKLOW 0-11

	P	W	D	L	For	Agt
Championship	12	12	0	0	19-131	5-65
National League	18	18	0	0	41-155	14-92
TOTAL	30	30	0	0	60-286	19-157

Managers' Records

Kevin Heffernan

The first ever official manager was appointed on 30 July 1973; prior to that all team affairs had been under the aegis of a five man Selection Committee. Also named by the County Board were two co-selectors to assist Heffernan, Donal Colfer and Lorcan Redmond, the latter being the lone member of the previous regime to be retained.

NATIONAL LEAGUE 1972/73
Sep 16, 1973, O'Rourke Park, Castlerea
ROSCOMMON 3-7   DUBLIN 0-11
Delayed tie; result relegated Dublin to Division IIA

NATIONAL LEAGUE, DIVISION IIA
Oct 14, 1973, Croke Park, Dublin
DUBLIN 3-6   WEXFORD 1-8

NATIONAL LEAGUE, DIVISION IIA
Oct 28, 1973, Catherine Park, Athy
DUBLIN 1-10   KILDARE 1-9

NATIONAL LEAGUE, DIVISION IIA
Nov 11, 1973, Croke Park, Dublin
DUBLIN 1-8   LIMERICK 0-6

NATIONAL LEAGUE, DIVISION IIA
Nov 25, 1973, Dr Cullen Park, Carlow
DUBLIN 1-9   CARLOW 0-4

NATIONAL LEAGUE, DIVISION IIA
Dec 9, 1973, Nowlan Park, Kilkenny
DUBLIN 6-16   KILKENNY 0-4

NATIONAL LEAGUE, DIVISION IIA
Feb 3, 1974, Croke Park, Dublin
DUBLIN 2-15   WATERFORD 0-5

NATIONAL LEAGUE, DIVISION IIA
Feb 17, 1974, Croke Park, Dublin
CLARE 4-9   DUBLIN 2-9

NATIONAL LEAGUE, DIVISION II SEMI-FINAL
Apr 21, 1974, Croke Park, Dublin
DUBLIN 1-13   ANTRIM 1-8

NATIONAL LEAGUE, DIVISION II FINAL
May 5, 1974, Croke Park, Dublin
KILDARE 3-13   DUBLIN 2-9

LEINSTER FIRST ROUND
May 26, 1974, Croke Park, Dublin
DUBLIN 3-9   WEXFORD 0-6

LEINSTER SECOND ROUND
June 2, 1974, Pairc Tailteann, Navan
DUBLIN 2-11   LOUTH 1-9

LEINSTER QUARTER-FINAL
June 16, 1974, Pearse Park, Longford
DUBLIN 1-11   OFFALY 0-13

LEINSTER SEMI-FINAL
July 14, 1974, Croke Park, Dublin
DUBLIN 1-13   KILDARE 0-10

LEINSTER FINAL
July 28, 1974, Croke Park, Dublin
DUBLIN 1-14   MEATH 1-9

ALL-IRELAND SEMI-FINAL
Aug 11, 1974, Croke Park, Dublin
DUBLIN 2-11   CORK 1-8

ALL-IRELAND FINAL
Sep 22, 1974, Croke Park, Dublin
DUBLIN 0-14   GALWAY 1-6

NATIONAL LEAGUE, DIVISION IA
Oct 20, 1974, Croke Park, Dublin
CORK 1-8   DUBLIN 0-10

NATIONAL LEAGUE, DIVISION IA
Nov 10, 1974, Fitzgerald Stadium, Killarney
DUBLIN 0-8   KERRY 0-8

NATIONAL LEAGUE, DIVISION IA
Jan 19, 1975, Croke Park, Dublin
DUBLIN 3-13   KILDARE 1-4

NATIONAL LEAGUE, DIVISION IA
Feb 2, 1975, O'Connor Park, Tullamore
DUBLIN 0-10   OFFALY 1-5

NATIONAL LEAGUE, DIVISION IA
Mar 2, 1975, Croke Park, Dublin
DUBLIN 1-13   ROSCOMMON 1-4

NATIONAL LEAGUE, SEMI-FINAL
May 4, 1975 Croke Park, Dublin
DUBLIN 3-12   TYRONE 1-7

NATIONAL LEAGUE, FINAL
May 18, 1975, Croke Park, Dublin
MEATH 0-16   DUBLIN 1-9

LEINSTER QUARTER-FINAL
June 8, 1975, Dr Cullen Park, Carlow
DUBLIN 4-17   WEXFORD 3-1

LEINSTER SEMI-FINAL
July 6, 1975, Pairc Tailteann, Navan
DUBLIN 3-14   LOUTH 4-7

LEINSTER FINAL
July 27, 1975, Croke Park, Dublin
DUBLIN 3-13   KILDARE 0-8

ALL-IRELAND SEMI-FINAL
Aug 24, 1975, Croke Park, Dublin
DUBLIN 3-13   DERRY 3-8

ALL-IRELAND FINAL
Sep 28, 1975, Croke Park, Dublin
KERRY 2-12   DUBLIN 0-11

NATIONAL LEAGUE, DIVISION IA
Oct 26, 1975, The Mardyke, Cork
DUBLIN 1-12   CORK 0-4

NATIONAL LEAGUE, DIVISION IA
Nov 9, 1975, Croke Park, Dublin
DUBLIN 2-11   KERRY 0-13

NATIONAL LEAGUE, DIVISION IA
Nov 23, 1975, Geraldine Park, Athy
DUBLIN 1-14   KILDARE 0-7

NATIONAL LEAGUE, DIVISION IA
Dec 7, 1975, Croke Park, Dublin
DUBLIN 5-8   OFFALY 1-8

NATIONAL LEAGUE, DIVISION IA
Feb 1, 1976, Dr Hyde Park, Roscommon
ROSCOMMON 2-8   DUBLIN 1-6

NATIONAL LEAGUE, SEMI-FINAL
Apr 4, 1976, Croke Park, Dublin
DUBLIN 1-11   GALWAY 0-12

NATIONAL LEAGUE, FINAL
May 2, 1976, Croke Park, Dublin
DUBLIN 2-10   DERRY 0-15

LEINSTER QUARTER-FINAL
June 27, 1976, Cusack Park, Mullingar
DUBLIN 5-16   LONGFORD 0-7

LEINSTER SEMI-FINAL
July 11, 1976, O'Connor Park, Tullamore
DUBLIN 3-12   LAOIS 0-11

LEINSTER FINAL
July 25, 1976, Croke Park, Dublin
DUBLIN 2-8   MEATH 1- 9

ALL-IRELAND SEMI-FINAL
Aug 29, 1976, Croke Park, Dublin
DUBLIN 1-8   GALWAY 0-8

ALL-IRELAND FINAL
Sep 26, 1976, Croke Park, Dublin
DUBLIN 3-8   KERRY 0-10

NATIONAL LEAGUE, DIVISION IA
Oct 10, 1976, Croke Park, Dublin
DUBLIN 1-13   CORK 2-9

	P	W	D	L	For	Agt
Championship	17	16	0	1	37-203	17-151
National League	25	18	1	6	41-266	23-201
TOTAL	42	34	1	7	78-469	40-352

Tony Hanahoe

Kevin Heffernan announced he was stepping down at a meeting of players and County Board officials on October 19; team captain Tony Hanahoe was appointed player-manager at the same meeting.

NATIONAL LEAGUE, DIVISION IA
Oct 24, 1976, Austin Stack Park, Tralee
KERRY 0-12   DUBLIN 0-7

NATIONAL LEAGUE, DIVISION IA
Nov 7, 1976, Croke Park, Dublin
DUBLIN 3-13   KILDARE 1-10

NATIONAL LEAGUE, DIVISION IA
Nov 21, 1976, Pairc Tailteann, Navan
DUBLIN 3-3   MEATH 1-9

NATIONAL LEAGUE, DIVISION IA
Dec 5, 1976, Croke Park, Dublin
DUBLIN 0-11   GALWAY 0-7

NATIONAL LEAGUE, QUARTER-FINAL
Mar 13, 1977, Pearse Park, Longford
DUBLIN 2-12   CAVAN 1-7

NATIONAL LEAGUE, SEMI-FINAL
Mar 27, 1977, Croke Park, Dublin
DUBLIN 2-12   MAYO 0-5

NATIONAL LEAGUE FINAL
Apr 17, 1977, Croke Park, Dublin
KERRY 1-8   DUBLIN 1-6

LEINSTER QUARTER-FINAL
May 29, 1977, Pairc Tailteann, Navan
DUBLIN 1-14   KILDARE 2-8

LEINSTER SEMI-FINAL
July 3, 1977, Dr Cullen Park, Carlow
DUBLIN 3-11   WEXFORD 0-6

LEINSTER FINAL
July 31, 1977, Croke Park, Dublin
DUBLIN 1-9   MEATH 0-8

ALL-IRELAND SEMI-FINAL
Aug 21, 1977, Croke Park, Dublin
DUBLIN 3-12   KERRY 1-13

ALL-IRELAND FINAL
Sep 25, 1977, Croke Park, Dublin
DUBLIN 5-12   ARMAGH 3-6

NATIONAL LEAGUE, DIVISION IA
Oct 23, 1977, Croke Park, Dublin
DUBLIN 2-11   KERRY 2-7

NATIONAL LEAGUE, DIVISION IA
Nov 6, 1977, St Conleth's Park, Newbridge
DUBLIN 2-9   KILDARE 1-8

NATIONAL LEAGUE, DIVISION IA
Nov 13, 1977, Pairc Ui Chaoimh, Cork
DUBLIN 0-8   CORK 0-5

NATIONAL LEAGUE, DIVISION IA
Nov 20, 1977, Croke Park, Dublin
DUBLIN 4-7 **OFFALY 0-3**

NATIONAL LEAGUE, DIVISION IA
Dec 4, 1977, Tuam Stadium, Tuam
DUBLIN 1-6 **GALWAY 0-8**

NATIONAL LEAGUE SEMI-FINAL
Apr 2, 1978, Croke Park, Dublin
DUBLIN 0-12 **LAOIS 0-7**

NATIONAL LEAGUE FINAL
Apr 23, 1978, Croke Park, Dublin
DUBLIN 2-18 **MAYO 2-13**

LEINSTER QUARTER-FINAL
June 18, 1978, Croke Park, Dublin
DUBLIN 6-15 **CARLOW 2-9**

LEINSTER SEMI-FINAL
July 9, 1978, O'Moore Park, Portlaoise
DUBLIN 2-9 **OFFALY 0-12**

LEINSTER FINAL
July 30, 1978, Croke Park, Dublin
DUBLIN 1-17 **KILDARE 1-6**

ALL-IRELAND SEMI-FINAL
Aug 20, 1978, Croke Park, Dublin
DUBLIN 1-16 **DOWN 0-8**

ALL-IRELAND FINAL
Sep 24, 1978, Croke Park, Dublin
KERRY 5-11 **DUBLIN 0-9**

	P	W	D	L	For	Agt
Championship	10	9	0	1	23-124	14- 87
National League	14	11	1	2	22-135	9-109
TOTAL	24	20	1	3	45-259	23-196

Kevin Heffernan

* Kevin Heffernan returned to "assist" with squad training in mid-June and was appointed "team advisor" on October 1; he was never formally or officially appointed manager for his second term at the helm. In the words of Tommy Drumm in a 2015 interview with Balls,ie, "He kind of just moseyed back in and we all just accepted it because he was such a vital part of the organisation up to a year before."

NATIONAL LEAGUE, DIVISION I SOUTH
Oct 8, 1978, Croke Park, Dublin
KERRY 2-9 **DUBLIN 0-8**

NATIONAL LEAGUE, DIVISION I SOUTH
Nov 5, 1978, Croke Park, Dublin
DUBLIN 3-15 **LAOIS 0-11**

NATIONAL LEAGUE, DIVISION I SOUTH
Nov 19, 1978, Croke Park, Dublin
KILDARE 2-11 **DUBLIN 0-6**

NATIONAL LEAGUE, DIVISION I SOUTH
Dec 3, 1978, Tuam Stadium, Tuam
DUBLIN 0-5 **GALWAY 0-5**

NATIONAL LEAGUE, DIVISION I SOUTH
Dec 10, 1978, Pairc Ui Chaoimh, Cork
CORK 2-10 **DUBLIN 0-5**

LEINSTER QUARTER-FINAL
June 3, 1979, Pairc Tailteann, Navan
DUBLIN 4-16 **LOUTH 0-4**

LEINSTER SEMI-FINAL
July 1, 1979, St Conleth's Park, Newbridge
DUBLIN 3-13 **WICKLOW 2-7**

LEINSTER FINAL
July 29, 1979, Croke Park, Dublin
DUBLIN 1-8 **OFFALY 0-9**

ALL-IRELAND SEMI-FINAL
Aug 19, 1979, Croke Park, Dublin
DUBLIN 0-14 **ROSCOMMON 1-10**

ALL-IRELAND FINAL
Sep 16, 1979, Croke Park, Dublin
KERRY 3-13 **DUBLIN 1-8**

NATIONAL LEAGUE, DIVISION I SOUTH
Oct 7, 1979, Austin Stack Park, Tralee
KERRY 1-16 **DUBLIN 0-10**

NATIONAL LEAGUE, DIVISION I SOUTH
Nov 11, 1979, Croke Park, Dublin
DUBLIN 3-4 **CORK 2-7**

NATIONAL LEAGUE, DIVISION I SOUTH
Nov 25, 1979, O'Connor Park, Tullamore
OFFALY 0-12 **DUBLIN 1-4**

NATIONAL LEAGUE, DIVISION I SOUTH
Dec 9, 1979, Catherine Park, Athy
DUBLIN 2-7 **KILDARE 0-12**

NATIONAL LEAGUE, DIVISION I SOUTH
Feb 3, 1980, Croke Park, Dublin
GALWAY 1-6 **DUBLIN 0-8**

LEINSTER QUARTER-FINAL
June 8, 1980, O'Connor Park, Tullamore
DUBLIN 2–14 **LAOIS 2–8**

LEINSTER SEMI-FINAL
July 6, 1980, Pairc Tailteann, Navan
DUBLIN 3–13 **MEATH 2–7**

LEINSTER FINAL
July 27, 1980, Croke Park, Dublin
OFFALY 1–10 **DUBLIN 1–8**

NATIONAL LEAGUE, DIVISION ONE
Nov 2, 1980, O'Connor Park, Tullamore
DUBLIN 0-11 **OFFALY 2-5**

NATIONAL LEAGUE, DIVISION ONE
Nov 16, 1980, Croke Park, Dublin
DUBLIN 3-9   KILDARE 0-11

NATIONAL LEAGUE, DIVISION ONE
Nov 30, 1980, Fitzgerald Stadium, Killarney
KERRY 2-11   DUBLIN 2-7

NATIONAL LEAGUE, DIVISION ONE
Dec 14, 1980, Croke Park, Dublin
DUBLIN 1-11   CORK 1-9

NATIONAL LEAGUE, DIVISION ONE
Feb 1, 1981, Dr Hyde Park, Roscommon
ROSCOMMON 0-11 DUBLIN 1-5

NATIONAL LEAGUE, DIVISION ONE
Feb 22, 1981, Croke Park, Dublin
DUBLIN 2-8   DOWN 0-9

NATIONAL LEAGUE, DIVISION ONE
Mar 1, 1981, Croke Park, Dublin
DUBLIN 2-8   ARMAGH 2-3

NATIONAL LEAGUE, PLAY-OFF
Mar 15, 1981, Croke Park, Dublin
DUBLIN 1-7   ARMAGH 1-5

**NATIONAL LEAGUE,
QUARTER-FINAL**
Apr 5, 1981, Dr Hyde Park, Roscommon
MAYO 1-11   DUBLIN 1-10

LEINSTER QUARTER-FINAL
May 31, 1981, St Conleth's Park, Newbridge
DUBLIN 0-10   WICKLOW 0-8

LEINSTER SEMI-FINAL
July 5, 1981, O'Connor Park, Tullamore
LAOIS 2-9   DUBLIN 0-11

NATIONAL LEAGUE, DIVISION ONE
Oct 4, 1981, Flanagan Park, Ballinrobe
DUBLIN 1-12   MAYO 1-4

NATIONAL LEAGUE, DIVISION ONE
Oct 18, 1981, Croke Park, Dublin
OFFALY 1-11   DUBLIN 0-12

NATIONAL LEAGUE, DIVISION ONE
Nov 1, 1981, Dunlo Grounds, Ballinasloe
DUBLIN 0-9   GALWAY 0-9

NATIONAL LEAGUE, DIVISION ONE
Nov 15, 1981, Croke Park, Dublin
KERRY 1-7   DUBLIN 1-7

NATIONAL LEAGUE, DIVISION ONE
Nov 29, 1981, Pairc Ui Chaoimh, Cork
DUBLIN 1-5   CORK 0-6

NATIONAL LEAGUE, DIVISION ONE
Jan 31, 1982, Croke Park, Dublin
DUBLIN 4-13   ROSCOMMON 1-8

NATIONAL LEAGUE, DIVISION ONE
Feb 21, 1982, Athletic Grounds, Armagh
ARMAGH 0-8   DUBLIN 0-5

LEINSTER QUARTER-FINAL
June 6, 1982, O'Connor Park, Tullamore
DUBLIN 1-15   LONGFORD 2-6

LEINSTER SEMI-FINAL
July 4, 1982, Pairc Tailteann, Navan
DUBLIN 1-13   KILDARE 0-12

LEINSTER FINAL
Aug 1, 1982, Croke Park, Dublin
OFFALY 1-16   DUBLIN 1-7

NATIONAL LEAGUE, DIVISION ONE
Oct 10, 1982, Croke Park, Dublin
DUBLIN 3-7   MAYO 0-6

NATIONAL LEAGUE, DIVISION ONE
Oct 24, 1982, O'Connor Park, Tullamore
OFFALY 4-9   DUBLIN 3-1

NATIONAL LEAGUE, DIVISION ONE
Nov 7, 1982, Croke Park, Dublin
DOWN 1-6   DUBLIN 0-8

NATIONAL LEAGUE, DIVISION ONE
Nov 21, 1982, Austin Stack Park, Tralee
DUBLIN 0-8   KERRY 0-7

NATIONAL LEAGUE, DIVISION ONE
Feb 13, 1983, Croke Park, Dublin
DUBLIN 1-8   CORK 1-7

NATIONAL LEAGUE, DIVISION ONE
Feb 27, 1983, Wolfe Tone Park, Bellaghy
DERRY 1-11   DUBLIN 1-10

NATIONAL LEAGUE, DIVISION ONE
Mar 13, 1983, Croke Park, Dublin
DUBLIN 1-8   ARMAGH 0-11

LEINSTER QUARTER-FINAL
June 12, 1983, Croke Park, Dublin
DUBLIN 2-8   MEATH 2-8

**LEINSTER QUARTER-FINAL
REPLAY**
July 3, 1983, Croke Park, Dublin
DUBLIN 3-9   MEATH 0-16

LEINSTER SEMI-FINAL
July 17, 1983, Croke Park, Dublin
DUBLIN 1-12   LOUTH 0-11

LEINSTER FINAL
July 31, 1983, Croke Park, Dublin
DUBLIN 2-13   OFFALY 1-11

ALL-IRELAND SEMI-FINAL
Aug 21, 1983, Croke Park, Dublin
DUBLIN 2-11   CORK 2-11

ALL-IRELAND SEMI-FINAL REPLAY
Aug 28, 1983, Pairc Ui Chaoimh, Cork
DUBLIN 4-15   CORK 2-10

ALL-IRELAND FINAL
Sep 18, 1983, Croke Park, Dublin
DUBLIN 1-10   GALWAY 1-8

NATIONAL LEAGUE, DIVISION ONE
Oct 9, 1983, Pairc Tailteann, Navan
DUBLIN 1-6   MEATH 1-6

NATIONAL LEAGUE, DIVISION ONE
Oct 23, 1983, Croke Park, Dublin
OFFALY 1-4   DUBLIN 0-3

NATIONAL LEAGUE, DIVISION ONE
Nov 6, 1983, Pairc Esler, Newry
DOWN 1-6   DUBLIN 0-7

NATIONAL LEAGUE, DIVISION ONE
Nov 20, 1983, Croke Park, Dublin
DUBLIN 2-9   KERRY 2-9

NATIONAL LEAGUE, DIVISION ONE
Dec 4, 1983, Pairc Ui Chaoimh
CORK 1-9 DUBLIN 1-3

NATIONAL LEAGUE, DIVISION ONE
Feb 5, 1984, Croke Park, Dublin
DUBLIN 1-9   KILDARE 1-2

NATIONAL LEAGUE, DIVISION ONE
Feb 19, 1984, Davitt Park, Lurgan
ARMAGH 0-7   DUBLIN 0-5

LEINSTER QUARTER-FINAL
June 10, 1984, Croke Park, Dublin
DUBLIN 4-12   WEXFORD 0-9

LEINSTER SEMI-FINAL
June 24, 1984, Croke Park, Dublin
DUBLIN 0-13   OFFALY 0-5

LEINSTER FINAL
July 22, 1984, Croke Park, Dublin
DUBLIN 2-10   MEATH 1-9

ALL-IRELAND SEMI-FINAL
Aug 19, 1984, Croke Park, Dublin
DUBLIN 2-11   TYRONE 0-8

ALL-IRELAND FINAL
Sep 23, 1984, Croke Park, Dublin
KERRY 0-14   DUBLIN 1-6

NATIONAL LEAGUE, DIVISION TWO
Oct 14, 1984, St Mary's Park, Castleblaney
DUBLIN 1-8   MONAGHAN 0-5

NATIONAL LEAGUE, DIVISION TWO
Nov 11, 1984, Croke Park, Dublin
ROSCOMMON 0-8 DUBLIN 0-6

NATIONAL LEAGUE, DIVISION TWO
Nov 18, 1984, James Stephens Park, Ballina
MAYO 1-8   DUBLIN 1-5

NATIONAL LEAGUE, DIVISION TWO
Nov 25, 1984, Croke Park, Dublin
DUBLIN 1-16   OFFALY 0-7

NATIONAL LEAGUE, DIVISION TWO
Dec 2, 1984, MacCumhail Park, Ballybofey
DUBLIN 1-6   DONEGAL 1-4

NATIONAL LEAGUE, DIVISION TWO
Feb 3, 1985, Croke Park, Dublin
WEXFORD 1-5   DUBLIN 0-7

NATIONAL LEAGUE, DIVISION TWO
Feb 10, 1985, St Mary's Park, Ardee
DUBLIN 2-8   LOUTH 0-4

LEINSTER QUARTER-FINAL
June 16, 1985, Wexford Park, Wexford
DUBLIN 4-13   WEXFORD 0-6

LEINSTER SEMI-FINAL
July 7, 1985, O'Connor Park, Tullamore
DUBLIN 2-13   OFFALY 0-10

LEINSTER FINAL
July 28, 1985, Croke Park, Dublin
DUBLIN 0-10   LAOIS 0-4

ALL-IRELAND SEMI-FINAL
Aug 18, 1985, Croke Park, Dublin
DUBLIN 1-13   MAYO 1-13

ALL-IRELAND SEMI-FINAL REPLAY
Sep 8, 1985, Croke Park, Dublin
DUBLIN 2-12   MAYO 1-7

ALL-IRELAND FINAL
Sep 22, 1985, Croke Park, Dublin
KERRY 2-12   DUBLIN 2-8

NATIONAL LEAGUE, DIVISION TWO
Oct 13, 1985, Pairc Ui Chaoimh, Cork
DUBLIN 0-13   CORK 0-8

NATIONAL LEAGUE, DIVISION TWO
Oct 27, 1985, Croke Park, Dublin
LONGFORD 3-8   DUBLIN 1-11

NATIONAL LEAGUE, DIVISION TWO
Nov 10, 1985, Belfield Park, Enniscorthy
DUBLIN 2-7   WEXFORD 0-6

NATIONAL LEAGUE, DIVISION TWO
Nov 24, 1985, Croke Park, Dublin
DUBLIN 0-15   DONEGAL 0-8

NATIONAL LEAGUE, DIVISION TWO
Dec 1, 1985, MacHale Park, Castlebar
MAYO 2-5   DUBLIN 0-4

	P	W	D	L	For	Agt
Championship	31	22	3	6	53-349	29-301
National League	52	21	8	23	52-411	45-401
TOTAL	83	43	11	29	105-760	74-702

**KEVIN HEFFERNAN'S OVERALL
FIGURES (BOTH TERMS)**

	P	W	D	L	For	Agt
Championship	48	38	3	7	90-552	46-452
National League	77	39	9	29	93-677	68-602
TOTAL	125	77	12	36	183-1,229	109-1,054

Brian Mullins, Robbie Kelleher and Sean Doherty

Kevin Heffernan – along with his fellow selectors, Tony Hanahoe, Lorcan Redmond and Donal Colfer – resigned via a letter sent to new County Board chairman Phil Markey on 13 January 1986, one day after the latter's election at the annual convention. Ten days later the County Board appointed Brian Mullins, Robbie Kelleher and Sean Doherty as selectors the trio were empowered to nominate one of their number as manager but opted instead to operate as a team.

NATIONAL LEAGUE, DIVISION TWO
Feb 2, 1986, Duggan Park, Ballinasloe
DUBLIN 0-12   GALWAY 0-10

NATIONAL LEAGUE, DIVISION TWO
Mar 2, 1986, Croke Park, Dublin
DUBLIN 3-6   CAVAN 0-9

NATIONAL LEAGUE, QUARTER-FINAL
Mar 30, 1986, Croke Park, Dublin
DUBLIN 2-8   MEATH 1-10

NATIONAL LEAGUE, SEMI-FINAL
Apr 20, 1986, Croke Park, Dublin
LAOIS 0-12   DUBLIN 1-7

LEINSTER QUARTER-FINAL
June 8, 1986, Croke Park, Dublin
DUBLIN 0-17   WEXFORD 3-3

LEINSTER SEMI-FINAL
June 29, 1986, O'Moore Park, Portlaoise
DUBLIN 1-10   OFFALY 0-7

LEINSTER FINAL
July 27, 1986, O'Moore Park, Portlaoise
MEATH 0-9   DUBLIN 0-7

	P	W	D	L	For	Agt
Championship	3	2	0	1	1-34	3-19
National League	4	3	0	1	6-33	1-41
TOTAL	7	5	0	2	7-67	4-60

Gerry McCaul

Brian Mullins and Robbie Kelleher withdrew their names from reselection and on October 18 the County Board named Gerry McCaul as manager, with Sean Doherty and Tony Hempenstall as his co-selectors.

NATIONAL LEAGUE, DIVISION ONE
Nov 2, 1986, Croke Park, Dublin
MEATH 2-13   DUBLIN 0-9

NATIONAL LEAGUE, DIVISION ONE
Nov 16, 1986, Croke Park, Dublin
MONAGHAN 2-10   DUBLIN 2-8

NATIONAL LEAGUE, DIVISION ONE
Nov 30, 1986, Austin Stack Park, Tralee
KERRY 0-10   DUBLIN 0-8

NATIONAL LEAGUE, DIVISION ONE
Dec 14, 1986, Croke Park, Dublin
DUBLIN 0-11   ARMAGH 1-6

NATIONAL LEAGUE, DIVISION ONE
Feb 8, 1987, Croke Park, Dublin
DUBLIN 0-8   MAYO 0-6

NATIONAL LEAGUE, DIVISION ONE
Feb 22, 1987, St Patrick's Park, Newcastle
DUBLIN 2-12   DOWN 2-8

NATIONAL LEAGUE, DIVISION ONE
Mar 8, 1987, Croke Park, Dublin
DUBLIN 1-11   ROSCOMMON 0-8

NATIONAL LEAGUE, QUARTER-FINAL
Apr 5, 1987, Croke Park, Dublin
DUBLIN 1-10   CORK 1-7

NATIONAL LEAGUE, SEMI-FINAL
Apr 19, 1987, O'Moore Park, Portlaoise
DUBLIN 1-8   GALWAY 0-8

NATIONAL LEAGUE FINAL
Apr 26, 1987, Croke Park, Dublin
DUBLIN 1-11   KERRY 0-11

LEINSTER QUARTER-FINAL
June 7, 1987, Croke Park, Dublin
DUBLIN 0-14   WESTMEATH 0-7

LEINSTER SEMI-FINAL
July 5, 1987, St Conleth's Park, Newbridge
DUBLIN 2-18   WICKLOW 0-6

LEINSTER FINAL
July 26, 1987, Croke Park, Dublin
MEATH 1-13   DUBLIN 0-12

NATIONAL LEAGUE, DIVISION ONE
Nov 8, 1987, Croke Park, Dublin
DUBLIN 2-5   MEATH 0-11

NATIONAL LEAGUE, DIVISION ONE
Nov 22, 1987, St Mary's Park, Castleblaney
DUBLIN 1-13   MONAGHAN 0-5

NATIONAL LEAGUE, DIVISION ONE
Dec 6, 1987, Croke Park, Dublin
DUBLIN 1-9   KERRY 2-5

NATIONAL LEAGUE, DIVISION ONE
Dec 13, 1987, Davitt Park, Lurgan
DUBLIN 0-9   ARMAGH 1-3

NATIONAL LEAGUE, DIVISION ONE
Feb 7, 1988, MacHale Park, Castlebar
DUBLIN 1-7   MAYO 1-4

NATIONAL LEAGUE, DIVISION ONE
Feb 14, 1988, Parnell Park, Dublin
DUBLIN 1-9   DERRY 0-5

NATIONAL LEAGUE, DIVISION ONE
Feb 28, 1988, Pairc Ui Chaoimh, Cork
DUBLIN 1-10   CORK 1-10

NATIONAL LEAGUE, QUARTER-FINAL
Mar 27, 1988, Croke Park, Dublin
DUBLIN 0-10   LONGFORD 0-4

NATIONAL LEAGUE, SEMI-FINAL
Apr 3, 1988, Croke Park, Dublin
DUBLIN 4-12   MONAGHAN 1-8

NATIONAL LEAGUE, FINAL
Apr 17, 1988, Croke Park, Dublin
DUBLIN 1-8   MEATH 0-11

NATIONAL LEAGUE, FINAL REPLAY
May 22, 1988, Croke Park, Dublin
MEATH 2-13   DUBLIN 0-11

LEINSTER QUARTER-FINAL
June 6, 1988, Dr Cullen Park, Carlow
DUBLIN 1-14   CARLOW 0-8

LEINSTER SEMI-FINAL
June 26, 1988, Cusack Park, Mullingar
DUBLIN 4-15   LONGFORD 0-9

LEINSTER FINAL
July 31, 1988, Croke Park, Dublin
MEATH 2-5   DUBLIN 0-9

NATIONAL LEAGUE, DIVISION ONE
Oct 23, 1988, Wolfe Tone Park, Bellaghy
DERRY 1-7   DUBLIN 0-6

NATIONAL LEAGUE, DIVISION ONE
Nov 6, 1988, Croke Park, Dublin
DUBLIN 1-16   DOWN 0-4

NATIONAL LEAGUE, DIVISION ONE
Nov 20, 1988, Croke Park, Dublin
DUBLIN 2-12   MONAGHAN 1-8

NATIONAL LEAGUE, DIVISION ONE
Dec 4, 1988, Pairc Tailteann, Navan
DUBLIN 1-12   MEATH 0-4

NATIONAL LEAGUE, DIVISION ONE
Feb 5, 1989, Croke Park, Dublin
DUBLIN 1-12   ARMAGH 0-7

NATIONAL LEAGUE, DIVISION ONE
Feb 12, 1989, Austin Stack Park, Tralee
KERRY 1-10   DUBLIN 0-11

NATIONAL LEAGUE, DIVISION ONE
Feb 26, 1989, Croke Park, Dublin
DUBLIN 1-10   DONEGAL 0-9

NATIONAL LEAGUE, QUARTER-FINAL
Mar 26, 1989, O'Moore Park, Portlaoise
DUBLIN 1-11   WEXFORD 0-7

NATIONAL LEAGUE, SEMI-FINAL
Apr 9, 1989, Croke Park, Dublin
DUBLIN 1-10   CAVAN 1-9

NATIONAL LEAGUE 'HOME' FINAL
Apr 23, 1989, Croke Park, Dublin
CORK 0-15   DUBLIN 0-12

LEINSTER QUARTER-FINAL
June 5, 1989, St Conleth's Park, Newbridge
DUBLIN 1-13   KILDARE 1-9

LEINSTER SEMI-FINAL
June 25, 1989, St Conleth's Park, Newbridge
DUBLIN 1-12   WICKLOW 1-6

LEINSTER FINAL
July 30, 1989, Croke Park, Dublin
DUBLIN 2-12   MEATH 1-10

ALL-IRELAND SEMI-FINAL
Aug 20, 1989, Croke Park, Dublin
CORK 2-10   DUBLIN 1-9

NATIONAL LEAGUE, DIVISION ONE
Oct 22, 1989, Croke Park, Dublin
DUBLIN 4-18   DERRY 1-9

NATIONAL LEAGUE, DIVISION ONE
Nov 5, 1989, Pairc Esler, Newry
DUBLIN 1-17   DOWN 2-11

NATIONAL LEAGUE, DIVISION ONE
Nov 19, 1989, Pairc Ui Chaoimh, Cork
CORK 3-13   DUBLIN 1-16

NATIONAL LEAGUE, DIVISION ONE
Dec 3, 1989, Croke Park, Dublin
DUBLIN 2-12   CAVAN 3-7

NATIONAL LEAGUE, DIVISION ONE
Feb 4, 1990, Athletic Grounds, Armagh
ARMAGH 1-11   DUBLIN 0-10

NATIONAL LEAGUE, DIVISION ONE
Feb 11, 1990, Croke Park, Dublin
DUBLIN 1-15   KERRY 3-7

NATIONAL LEAGUE, DIVISION ONE
Mar 4, 1990, MacCumhail Park, Ballybofey
DONEGAL 1-10   DUBLIN 0-9

NATIONAL LEAGUE, PLAY-OFF
Mar 11, 1990, Drogheda Park, Drogheda
DUBLIN 1-14   ARMAGH 1-9

NATIONAL LEAGUE, QUARTER-FINAL
Apr 1, 1990, O'Moore Park, Portlaoise
ROSCOMMON 2-22 DUBLIN 3-13

LEINSTER QUARTER-FINAL
June 3, 1990, Drogheda Park, Drogheda
DUBLIN 1-13   LOUTH 1-8

LEINSTER SEMI-FINAL
June 24, 1990, St Conleth's Park, Newbridge
DUBLIN 2-14   WICKLOW 0-12

LEINSTER FINAL
July 29, 1990, Croke Park, Dublin
MEATH 1-14   DUBLIN 0-14

	P	W	D	L	For	Agt
Championship	13	9	0	4	15-164	10-122
National League	40	26	3	11	41-435	37-345
TOTAL	53	35	3	15	56-599	47-467

Paddy Cullen

Paddy Cullen – with Pat O'Neill and Jim Brogan as his co-selectors – was appointed manager on October 1, six days before Dublin's opening National League game against Donegal in Ballybofey.

NATIONAL LEAGUE, DIVISION ONE
Oct 7, 1990, MacCumhail Park, Ballybofey
DONEGAL 2-11   DUBLIN 1-9

NATIONAL LEAGUE, DIVISION ONE
Oct 21, 1990, Croke Park, Dublin
DUBLIN 0-12   ARMAGH 0-9

NATIONAL LEAGUE, DIVISION ONE
Nov 25, 1990, Croke Park, Dublin
DUBLIN 0-10   CORK 0-6

NATIONAL LEAGUE, DIVISION ONE
Dec 2, 1990, Croke Park, Dublin
DUBLIN 2-14   ROSCOMMON 0-6

NATIONAL LEAGUE, DIVISION ONE
Feb 17, 1991, St Patrick's Park, Newcastle
DUBLIN 2-10   DOWN 1-7

NATIONAL LEAGUE, DIVISION ONE
Feb 24, 1991, Croke Park, Dublin
DUBLIN 3-11   KERRY 0-7

NATIONAL LEAGUE, DIVISION ONE
Mar 10, 1991, Croke Park, Dublin
DUBLIN 0-11   MEATH 1-8

NATIONAL LEAGUE QUARTER-FINAL
Apr 14, 1991, Croke Park, Dublin
DUBLIN 2-10   WICKLOW 0-11

NATIONAL LEAGUE SEMI-FINAL
Apr 21, 1991, Croke Park, Dublin
DUBLIN 1-18   ROSCOMMON 0-11

NATIONAL LEAGUE FINAL
May 5, 1991, Croke Park, Dublin
DUBLIN 1-9   KILDARE 0-10

LEINSTER FIRST ROUND
June 2, 1991, Croke Park, Dublin
DUBLIN 1-12   MEATH 1-12

LEINSTER FIRST ROUND, REPLAY
June 9, 1991, Croke Park, Dublin
DUBLIN 1-11   MEATH 1-11

LEINSTER FIRST ROUND, SECOND REPLAY
June 23, 1991, Croke Park, Dublin
DUBLIN 1-14   MEATH 2-11

LEINSTER FIRST ROUND, THIRD REPLAY
July 6, 1991, Croke Park, Dublin
MEATH 2-10   DUBLIN 0-15

NATIONAL LEAGUE, DIVISION ONE
Oct 27, 1991, Pearse Stadium, Salthill
DUBLIN 1-5   GALWAY 0-7

NATIONAL LEAGUE, DIVISION ONE
Nov 10, 1991, Croke Park, Dublin
TYRONE 4-11   DUBLIN 0-11

NATIONAL LEAGUE, DIVISION ONE
Nov 24, 1991, Croke Park, Dublin
DUBLIN 2-10   ARMAGH 1-8

NATIONAL LEAGUE, DIVISION ONE
Feb 23, 1992, MacHale Park, Castlebar
DUBLIN 1-9   MAYO 0-10

NATIONAL LEAGUE, DIVISION ONE
Mar 8, 1992, Croke Park, Dublin
CORK 2-8   DUBLIN 1-10

NATIONAL LEAGUE PLAY-OFF
Mar 22, 1992, Croke Park, Dublin
DUBLIN 2-8   GALWAY 0-8

NATIONAL LEAGUE QUARTER-FINAL
Apr 5, 1992, Breffni Park, Cavan
DUBLIN 3-6   DONEGAL 1-10

NATIONAL LEAGUE SEMI-FINAL
Apr 19, 1992, Croke Park, Dublin
TYRONE 0-13   DUBLIN 1-9

LEINSTER FIRST ROUND
May 31, 1992, O'Connor Park, Tullamore
DUBLIN 2-17   OFFALY 1-9

LEINSTER QUARTER-FINAL
June 28, 1992, O'Moore Park, Portlaoise
DUBLIN 1-18   WEXFORD 0-11

LEINSTER SEMI-FINAL
July 12, 1992, O'Moore Park, Portlaoise
DUBLIN 0-15   LOUTH 1-9

LEINSTER FINAL
July 26, 1992, Croke Park, Dublin
DUBLIN 1-13   KILDARE 0-10

ALL-IRELAND SEMI-FINAL
Aug 23, 1992, Croke Park, Dublin
DUBLIN 3-14   CLARE 2-12

ALL-IRELAND FINAL
Sep 20, 1992, Croke Park, Dublin

DONEGAL 0-18   DUBLIN 0-14

	P	W	D	L	For	Agt
Championship	10	5	3	2	10-143	10-113
National League	18	13	1	4	23-182	12-161
TOTAL	28	18	4	6	33-325	22-274

Pat O'Neill

Although he still had another season to go, Paddy Cullen announced his resignation on October 13. His co-selectors, Pat O'Neill and Jim Brogan, took charge of the team for the opening National League game against Derry but two days after that match they too resigned. A week later, on October 22, O'Neill was appointed manager with Brogan and Fran Ryder as his co-selectors and shortly afterwards Bobby Doyle was added to the team.

NATIONAL LEAGUE DIVISION ONE
Oct 18, 1992, Croke Park, Dublin
DERRY 0-11   DUBLIN 0-9

NATIONAL LEAGUE DIVISION ONE
Nov 1, 1992, Markievicz Park, Sligo
DUBLIN 0-18   SLIGO 0-8

NATIONAL LEAGUE DIVISION ONE
Nov 15, 1992, Croke Park, Dublin
DUBLIN 1-8   LOUTH 0-9

NATIONAL LEAGUE DIVISION ONE
Nov 29, 1992, Casement Park, Belfast
DUBLIN 1-7   ANTRIM 0-5

NATIONAL LEAGUE DIVISION ONE
Feb 14, 1993, Wexford Park, Wexford
DUBLIN 0-11   WEXFORD 1-7

NATIONAL LEAGUE DIVISION ONE
Feb 28, 1993, Croke Park, Dublin
DUBLIN 0-13   GALWAY 1-6

NATIONAL LEAGUE DIVISION ONE
Mar 14, 1993, Gaelic Grounds, Askeaton
DUBLIN 0-15   LIMERICK 0-9

NATIONAL LEAGUE QUARTER-FINAL
Apr 11, 1993, Croke Park, Dublin
DUBLIN 1-13   KILDARE 0-8

NATIONAL LEAGUE SEMI-FINAL
Apr 18, 1993, Croke Park, Dublin
DUBLIN 1-10   KERRY 0-11

NATIONAL LEAGUE FINAL
May 2, 1993, Croke Park, Dublin
DUBLIN 0-9   DONEGAL 0-9

NATIONAL LEAGUE FINAL REPLAY
May 9, 1993, Croke Park, Dublin
DUBLIN 0-10   DONEGAL 0-6

LEINSTER FIRST ROUND
May 23, 1993, Wexford Park, Wexford
DUBLIN 0-11   WEXFORD 0-7

LEINSTER QUARTER-FINAL
June 7, 1993, O'Connor Park, Tullamore
DUBLIN 2-11   WESTMEATH 0-8

LEINSTER SEMI-FINAL
July 4, 1993, Croke Park, Dublin
DUBLIN 1-10   MEATH 0-12

LEINSTER FINAL
July 25, 1993, Croke Park, Dublin
DUBLIN 0-11   KILDARE 0-7

ALL-IRELAND SEMI-FINAL
Aug 22, 1993, Croke Park, Dublin
DERRY 0-15   DUBLIN 0-14

NATIONAL LEAGUE DIVISION ONE
Oct 10, 1993, Cusack Park, Ennis
DUBLIN 0-8   CLARE 0-6

NATIONAL LEAGUE DIVISION ONE
Oct 24, 1993, Croke Park, Dublin
DUBLIN 2-12   KERRY 1-13

NATIONAL LEAGUE DIVISION ONE
Nov 7, 1993, MacCumhail Park, Ballybofey
DONEGAL 0-11   DUBLIN 0-7

NATIONAL LEAGUE DIVISION ONE
Nov 21, 1993, Croke Park, Dublin
DUBLIN 1-19   MAYO 0-8

NATIONAL LEAGUE DIVISION ONE
Feb 6, 1994, St Conleth's Park, Newbridge
DUBLIN 0-7   KILDARE 1-4

NATIONAL LEAGUE DIVISION ONE
Feb 20, 1994, Croke Park, Dublin
DUBLIN 1-7   DOWN 1-7

NATIONAL LEAGUE DIVISION ONE
Mar 13, 1994, Wolfe Tone Park, Bellaghy
DUBLIN 0-15   DERRY 2-6

NATIONAL LEAGUE QUARTER-FINAL
Apr 3, 1994, Breffni Park, Cavan
ARMAGH 2-13   DUBLIN 1-9

LEINSTER QUARTER-FINAL
June 18, 1994, Croke Park, Dublin
DUBLIN 0-11   KILDARE 0-11

LEINSTER QUARTER-FINAL REPLAY
July 2, 1994, Croke Park, Dublin
DUBLIN 1-14   KILDARE 1-9

LEINSTER SEMI-FINAL
July 10, 1994, Croke Park, Dublin
DUBLIN 1-15   LOUTH 1-8

LEINSTER FINAL
July 31, 1994, Croke Park, Dublin
DUBLIN 1-9   **MEATH 1-8**

ALL-IRELAND SEMI-FINAL
Aug 21, 1994, Croke Park, Dublin
DUBLIN 3-15   **LEITRIM 1-9**

ALL-IRELAND FINAL
Sep 18, 1994, Croke Park, Dublin
DOWN 1-12   **DUBLIN 0-13**

NATIONAL LEAGUE DIVISION ONE
Oct 16, 1994, Croke Park, Dublin
MEATH 1-8   **DUBLIN 0-7**

NATIONAL LEAGUE DIVISION ONE
Oct 30, 1994, Fitzgerald Stadium, Killarney
KERRY 1-12   **DUBLIN 1-11**

NATIONAL LEAGUE DIVISION ONE
Nov 13, 1994, Croke Park, Dublin
DONEGAL 0-12   **DUBLIN 1-8**

NATIONAL LEAGUE DIVISION ONE
Nov 27, 1994, O'Moore Park, Portlaoise
DUBLIN 0-15   **LAOIS 1-8**

NATIONAL LEAGUE DIVISION ONE
Feb 19, 1995, St Conleth's Park, Newbridge
KILDARE 0-10   **DUBLIN 0-8**

NATIONAL LEAGUE DIVISION ONE
Mar 5, 1995, Pairc Esler, Newry
DUBLIN 1-7   **DOWN 0-1**

NATIONAL LEAGUE DIVISION ONE
Mar 19, 1995, Croke Park, Dublin
DUBLIN 1-9   **DERRY 1-9**

LEINSTER QUARTER-FINAL
June 18, 1995, Pairc Tailteann, Navan
DUBLIN 0-19   **LOUTH 2-5**

LEINSTER SEMI-FINAL
July 9, 1995, Pairc Tailteann, Navan
DUBLIN 1-13   **LAOIS 0-9**

LEINSTER FINAL
July 30, 1995, Croke Park, Dublin
DUBLIN 1-18   **MEATH 1-8**

ALL-IRELAND SEMI-FINAL
Aug 20, 1995, Croke Park, Dublin
DUBLIN 1-12   **CORK 0-12**

ALL-IRELAND FINAL
Sep 17, 1995, Croke Park, Dublin
DUBLIN 1-10   **TYRONE 0-12**

	P	W	D	L	For	Agt
Championship	16	13	1	2	13-206	7-152
National League	26	15	4	7	13-272	13-215
TOTAL	28	18	4	6	26-478	20-367

Mickey Whelan

* Pat O'Neill and his fellow selectors Jim Brogan, Fran Ryder and Bobby Doyle announced their intention to step down on October 10 but agreed to oversee the team for the opening National League game against Leitrim. For the second match, against Armagh, County Board secretary John Costello and vice-chairman Paddy Delaney took charge. The new team of manager Mickey Whelan and co-selectors Lorcan Redmond and Christy Kane was in place for the third game, against Cork. The first two matches are noted here for reference purposes but are not included in Whelan's managerial record.

NATIONAL LEAGUE DIVISION TWO
Oct 15, 1995, Croke Park, Dublin
DUBLIN 1-13   **LEITRIM 1-10**

NATIONAL LEAGUE DIVISION TWO
Oct 29, 1995, Athletic Grounds, Armagh
ARMAGH 0-8   **DUBLIN 0-6**

NATIONAL LEAGUE DIVISION TWO
Nov 12, 1995, Croke Park, Dublin
CORK 2-9 DUBLIN 0-8

NATIONAL LEAGUE DIVISION TWO
Nov 26, 1995, Pairc Chiarain, Athlone
DUBLIN 0-13   **WESTMEATH 0-7**

NATIONAL LEAGUE DIVISION TWO
Feb 4, 1996, St Brigid's Park, Dundalk
LOUTH 0-9   **DUBLIN 1-5**

NATIONAL LEAGUE DIVISION TWO
Feb 11, 1996, Parnell Park, Dublin
DUBLIN 2-9   **CAVAN 2-7**

NATIONAL LEAGUE DIVISION TWO
Feb 25, 1996, St Patrick's Park, Newcastle
DUBLIN 0-15   **DOWN 1-5**

LEINSTER QUARTER-FINAL
June 9, 1996, Pairc Tailteann, Navan
DUBLIN 1-18   **WESTMEATH 0-11**

LEINSTER SEMI-FINAL
June 30, 1996, Pairc Tailteann, Navan
DUBLIN 1-9   **LOUTH 0-8**

LEINSTER FINAL
July 28, 1996, Croke Park, Dublin
MEATH 0-10   **DUBLIN 0-8**

NATIONAL LEAGUE DIVISION TWO
Oct 13, 1996, Pairc macDuirmada, Carrick-on-Shannon
LEITRIM 1-10   **DUBLIN 0-10**

NATIONAL LEAGUE DIVISION TWO
Oct 27, 1996, Parnell Park, Dublin
DUBLIN 1-7   **ARMAGH 0-10**

NATIONAL LEAGUE DIVISION TWO
Nov 10, 1996, MacHale Park, Castlebar
DUBLIN 0-10   MAYO 0-10

NATIONAL LEAGUE DIVISION TWO
Nov 24, 1996, Parnell Park, Dublin
DUBLIN 0-11   CLARE 0-8

NATIONAL LEAGUE DIVISION TWO
Feb 2, 1997, Parnell Park, Dublin
LOUTH 1-7   DUBLIN 0-8

NATIONAL LEAGUE DIVISION TWO
Feb 16, 1997, St Tiernach's Park, Clones
DUBLIN 2-7   MONAGHAN 1-7

NATIONAL LEAGUE DIVISION TWO
Mar 2, 1997, Parnell Park, Dublin
DUBLIN 0-15   LAOIS 0-4

LEINSTER QUARTER-FINAL
June 15, 1997, Croke Park, Dublin
MEATH 1-13   DUBLIN 1-10

NATIONAL LEAGUE DIVISION TWO
Oct 19, 1997, Markievicz Park, Sligo
SLIGO 2-7   DUBLIN 0-12

NATIONAL LEAGUE DIVISION TWO
Nov 2, 1997, Parnell Park, Dublin
OFFALY 1-11   DUBLIN 1-8

	P	W	D	L	For	Agt
Championship	4	2	0	2	3-45	1-42
National League	14	6	2	6	7-138	11-111
TOTAL	18	8	2	8	10-183	12-153

Tommy Carr

Mickey Whelan resigned after the National League defeat to Offaly on November 2. His fellow selectors, Lorcan Redmond and Christy Kane, along with Liam Moggan, took charge of the team for the next two games against Wexford and Cavan. Tommy Carr was appointed manager on December 1 and shortly afterwards John O'Leary, Richie Crean and Dom Toomey were named as his co-selectors. The games against Wexford and Cavan are shown here for reference only and are not included in Carr's managerial record.

NATIONAL LEAGUE DIVISION TWO
Nov 16, 1997, Belfied Park, Enniscorthy
DUBLIN 1-9   WEXFORD 0-4

NATIONAL LEAGUE DIVISION TWO
Nov 30, 1997, Parnell Park, Dublin
DUBLIN 2-14   CAVAN 0-8

NATIONAL LEAGUE DIVISION TWO
Feb 15, 1998, Parnell Park, Dublin
MONAGHAN 2-12   DUBLIN 0-12

NATIONAL LEAGUE DIVISION TWO
Mar 1, 1998, O'Neill Park, Dungannon
DUBLIN 1-7   TYRONE 1-2

NATIONAL LEAGUE DIVISION TWO
Mar 15, 1998, Parnell Park, Dublin
DUBLIN 0-18   KERRY 1-3

LEINSTER QUARTER-FINAL
June 7, 1998, Croke Park, Dublin
DUBLIN 0-10   KILDARE 0-10

LEINSTER QUARTER-FINAL REPLAY
June 21, 1998, Croke Park, Dublin
KILDARE 0-12   DUBLIN 1-8

NATIONAL LEAGUE, DIVISION IA
Nov 1, 1998, Parnell Park, Dublin
DUBLIN 1-15   TYRONE 1-9

NATIONAL LEAGUE, DIVISION IA
Nov 15, 1998, Athletic Grounds, Armagh
DUBLIN 0-14   ARMAGH 1-11

NATIONAL LEAGUE, DIVISION IA
Nov 29, 1998, O'Connor Park, Tullamore
DUBLIN 2-11   OFFALY 0-13

NATIONAL LEAGUE, DIVISION IA
Feb 14, 1999, Parnell Park, Dublin
DUBLIN 1-19   LEITRIM 0-6

NATIONAL LEAGUE, DIVISION IA
Feb 28, 1999, Fr Tierney Park, Ballyshannon
DONEGAL 1-8   DUBLIN 0-9

NATIONAL LEAGUE, DIVISION IA
Mar 14, 1999, Parnell Park, Dublin
DUBLIN 0-15   GALWAY 1-12

NATIONAL LEAGUE, DIVISION IA
Mar 28, 1999, Pairc Ui Rinn, Cork
CORK 0-10   DUBLIN 0-7

NATIONAL LEAGUE QUARTER-FINAL
Apr 11, 1999, Croke Park, Dublin
DUBLIN 1-17   KILDARE 2-8

NATIONAL LEAGUE SEMI-FINAL
Apr 25, 1999, Croke Park, Dublin
DUBLIN 0-11   ARMAGH 0-11

**NATIONAL LEAGUE
SEMI-FINAL REPLAY**
May 2, 1999, Croke Park, Dublin
DUBLIN 1-14   ARMAGH 0-12

NATIONAL LEAGUE FINAL
May 9, 1999, Pairc Ui Chaoimh, Cork
CORK 1-12   DUBLIN 0-7

LEINSTER QUARTER-FINAL
June 6, 1999, Croke Park, Dublin
DUBLIN 2-15   LOUTH 0-14

LEINSTER SEMI-FINAL
June 27, 1999, Croke Park, Dublin
DUBLIN 1-11   LAOIS 0-14

LEINSTER SEMI-FINAL
REPLAY
July 18, 1999, Croke Park, Dublin
DUBLIN 0-16   LAOIS 1-11

LEINSTER FINAL
Aug 1, 1999, Croke Park, Dublin
MEATH 1-14   DUBLIN 0-12

NATIONAL LEAGUE, DIVISION IA
Oct 31, 1999, Healy Park, Omagh
TYRONE 1-13   DUBLIN 0-9

NATIONAL LEAGUE, DIVISION IA
Nov 14, 1999, Parnell Park, Dublin
DUBLIN 0-14   ARMAGH 0-6

NATIONAL LEAGUE, DIVISION IA
Nov 28, 1999, Parnell Park, Dublin
DUBLIN 1-8   KERRY 0-9

NATIONAL LEAGUE, DIVISION IA
Feb 13, 2000, Dr Hyde Park, Roscommon
ROSCOMMON 1-10 DUBLIN 0-6

NATIONAL LEAGUE, DIVISION IA
Mar 5, 2000, Parnell Park, Dublin
DUBLIN 1-11   DONEGAL 0-11

NATIONAL LEAGUE, DIVISION IA
Mar 19, 2000, Tuam Stadium, Tuam
DUBLIN 2-15   GALWAY 0-20

NATIONAL LEAGUE, DIVISION IA
Apr 9, 2000, Parnell Park, Dublin
DUBLIN 2-10   CORK 1-11

LEINSTER QUARTER-FINAL
June 11, 2000, Croke Park, Dublin
DUBLIN 2-20   WEXFORD 1-8

LEINSTER SEMI-FINAL
July 2, 2000, Croke Park, Dublin
DUBLIN 1-14   WESTMEATH 0-11

LEINSTER FINAL
July 30, 2000, Croke Park, Dublin
DUBLIN 0-14   KILDARE 0-14

LEINSTER FINAL REPLAY
Aug 12, 2000, Croke Park, Dublin
KILDARE 2-11   DUBLIN 0-12

NATIONAL LEAGUE, DIVISION IA
Oct 29, 2000, Parnell Park, Dublin
TYRONE 0-19   DUBLIN 2-10

NATIONAL LEAGUE, DIVISION IA
Nov 12, 2000, O'Connor Park, Tullamore
OFFALY 1-10   DUBLIN 0-9

NATIONAL LEAGUE, DIVISION IA
Feb 10, 2001, Parnell Park, Dublin
ROSCOMMON 0-12 DUBLIN 0-10

NATIONAL LEAGUE, DIVISION IA
Feb 25, 2001, Fr Tierney Park, Ballyshannon
DUBLIN 0-11   DONEGAL 0-8

NATIONAL LEAGUE, DIVISION IA
Apr 1, 2001, Fitzgerald Stadium, Killarney
KERRY 2-9   DUBLIN 0-10

NATIONAL LEAGUE, DIVISION IA
Apr 8, 2001, Parnell Park, Dublin
DUBLIN 1-10   GALWAY 1-8

Dublin were awarded a walkover v Louth when the match couldn't be played due to an outbreak of foot and mouth disease. Not included in managerial record.

LEINSTER QUARTER-FINAL
May 27, 2001, Croke Park, Dublin
DUBLIN 2-19   LONGFORD 1-13

LEINSTER SEMI-FINAL
June 17, 2001, Croke Park, Dublin
DUBLIN 1-12   OFFALY 0-13

LEINSTER FINAL
July 15, 2001, Croke Park, Dublin
MEATH 2-11   DUBLIN 0-14

ALL-IRELAND QUALIFIER, ROUND FOUR
July 22, 2001, Croke Park, Dublin
DUBLIN 3-17   SLIGO 0-12

ALL-IRELAND QUARTER-FINAL
Aug 4, 2001, Semple Stadium, Thurles
DUBLIN 2-11   KERRY 1-14

ALL-IRELAND QUARTER-FINAL REPLAY
Aug 11, 2001, Semple Stadium, Thurles
KERRY 2-12   DUBLIN 1-12

	P	W	D	L	For	Agt
Championship	16	7	4	5	16-217	11-194
National League	27	14	3	10	16-309	17-275
TOTAL	43	21	7	15	32-526	28-469

Tommy Lyons

Tommy Carr, initially appointed for a three-year term and then for a further two years and therefore still with a season to go, was controversially dismissed on 1 October 2001 when, after County Board delegates deadlock 46-46 on a Management Committee sponsored motion of no confidence in him, chairman John Bailey used his casting vote against Carr. Four weeks later, on 7 November, Tommy Lyons — who in a three-year stint as Offaly manager had guided the Faithful County to a first Leinster title in a decade and a half in 1997 and a first ever National League crown the following year — was appointed manager for a three-year term, with Paul Caffrey, Dave Billings and Paddy Canning as his co-selectors. Lyons, born in Mayo but living in Dublin since the age of nine, thus became the county's first ever non native manager.

NATIONAL LEAGUE, DIVISION IA
Feb 10, 2002, Parnell Park, Dublin
DUBLIN 2-10   DONEGAL 0-14

NATIONAL LEAGUE, DIVISION IA
Feb 17, 2002, O'Neill Park, Dungannon
TYRONE 0-18   DUBLIN 2-10

NATIONAL LEAGUE, DIVISION IA
Feb 23, 2002, O'Connor Park, Tullamore
DUBLIN 0-10   OFFALY 1-7

NATIONAL LEAGUE, DIVISION IA
Mar 3, 2002, Parnell Park, Dublin
DUBLIN 3-13   WESTMEATH 1-16

NATIONAL LEAGUE, DIVISION IA
Mar 10, 2002, Pairc Ui Chaoimh, Cork
CORK 1-13   DUBLIN 0-10

NATIONAL LEAGUE, DIVISION IA
Mar 24, 2002, Parnell Park, Dublin
ROSCOMMON 2-12 DUBLIN 0-16

NATIONAL LEAGUE, DIVISION IA
Mar 31, 2002, Tuam Stadium, Tuam
DUBLIN 1-12   GALWAY 1-12

LEINSTER QUARTER-FINAL
June 1, 2002, Dr Cullen Park, Carlow
DUBLIN 0-15   WEXFORD 1-10

LEINSTER SEMI-FINAL
June 23, 2002, Croke Park, Dublin
DUBLIN 2-11   MEATH 0-10

LEINSTER FINAL
July 14, 2002, Croke Park, Dublin
DUBLIN 2-13   KILDARE 2-11

ALL-IRELAND QUARTER-FINAL
Aug 5, 2002, Croke Park, Dublin
DUBLIN 2-8   DONEGAL 0-14

ALL-IRELAND QUARTER-FINAL REPLAY
Aug 17, 2002, Croke Park, Dublin
DUBLIN 1-14   DONEGAL 0-7

ALL-IRELAND SEMI-FINAL
Sep 1, 2002, Croke Park, Dublin
ARMAGH 1-14   DUBLIN 1-13

NATIONAL LEAGUE, DIVISION IA
Feb 2, 2003, Croke Park, Dublin
ARMAGH 1-15   DUBLIN 0-7

NATIONAL LEAGUE, DIVISION IA
Feb 9, 2003, Fr Tierney Park, Ballyshannon
DUBLIN 1-10   DONEGAL 0-9

NATIONAL LEAGUE, DIVISION IA
Feb 16, 2003, Parnell Park, Dublin
DUBLIN 0-12   TYRONE 0-11

NATIONAL LEAGUE, DIVISION IA
Mar 2, 2003, Fitzgerald Stadium, Killarney
KERRY 2-11   DUBLIN 0-14

NATIONAL LEAGUE, DIVISION IA
Mar 9, 2003, Parnell Park, Dublin
CORK 0-16   DUBLIN 0-8

NATIONAL LEAGUE, DIVISION IA
Mar 23, 2003, Dr Hyde Park, Roscommon
DUBLIN 0-17   ROSCOMMON 0-14

NATIONAL LEAGUE, DIVISION IA
Apr 6, 2003, Parnell Park, Dublin
DUBLIN 0-12   GALWAY 1-9

LEINSTER QUARTER-FINAL
June 1, 2003, Croke Park, Dublin
DUBLIN 1-19   LOUTH 0-9

LEINSTER SEMI-FINAL
June 15, 2003, Croke Park, Dublin
LAOIS 0-16   DUBLIN 0-14

ALL-IRELAND QUALIFIERS, ROUND TWO
June 28, 2003, St Tiernach's Park, Clones
DUBLIN 3-9   DERRY 1-9

ALL-IRELAND QUALIFIERS, ROUND THREE
July 5, 2003, Croke Park, Dublin
ARMAGH 0-15   DUBLIN 0-11

	P	W	D	L	For	Agt
Championship	10	6	1	3	12-217	5-115
National League	14	5	3	6	9-161	10-177
TOTAL	24	11	4	9	21-378	15-292

Paul Caffrey

Tommy Lyons announced his decision not to seek a renewal of his tenure on September 6, yet it took almost three months and a considerable degree of controversy before the position was filled. After reported approaches to Kerry legend Mick O'Dwyer and former Down boss Pete McGrath, Brian Mullins was offered the job in the first week in November but, after considering the offer for a fortnight, declined turned it down on November 20 when informed that the Management Committee had rejected several of his structural proposals – including the right to choose his own co-selectors and the introduction of a sports science programme – at a meeting the previous night. Five days after the withdrawal of Mullins, Paul Caffrey was named manager with Brian Talty, Dave Billings and Paul Clarke as his fellow selectors.

NATIONAL LEAGUE, DIVISION IA
Feb 1, 2004, Parnell Park, Dublin
DUBLIN 0-9   TYRONE 0-8

NATIONAL LEAGUE, DIVISION IA
Feb 8, 2004, MacHale Park, Castlebar
MAYO 1-10   DUBLIN 0-3

NATIONAL LEAGUE, DIVISION IA
Feb 15, 2004, Parnell Park, Dublin
KERRY 1-12   DUBLIN 0-12

NATIONAL LEAGUE, DIVISION IA
Mar 7, 2004, Cusack Park, Mullingar
DUBLIN 0-15   WESTMEATH 0-10

NATIONAL LEAGUE, DIVISION IA
Mar 14, 2004, Bewster Park, Enniskillen
DUBLIN 0-12   FERMANAGH 0-12

NATIONAL LEAGUE, DIVISION IA
Mar 21, 2004, Parnell Park, Dublin
DUBLIN 0-9   CORK 0-9

NATIONAL LEAGUE, DIVISION IA
Apr 4, 2004, Parnell Park, Dublin
DUBLIN 2-12   LONGFORD 2-9

LEINSTER QUARTER-FINAL
June 6, 2004, Croke Park, Dublin
WESTMEATH 0-14   DUBLIN 0-12

ALL-IRELAND QUALIFIERS, ROUND ONE
June 12, 2004, Parnell Park, Dublin
DUBLIN 3-24   LONDON 0-6

ALL-IRELAND QUALIFIERS, ROUND TWO
July 3, 2004, McDermott Park, Carrick-on-Shannon
DUBLIN 0-13   LEITRIM 1-4

**ALL-IRELAND QUALIFIERS,
ROUND THREE**
July 10, 2004, O'Moore Park, Portlaoise
DUBLIN 1-17   LONGFORD 0-11

ALL-IRELAND QUALIFIERS, ROUND FOUR
Aug 1, 2004, Croke Park, Dublin
DUBLIN 1-14   ROSCOMMON 0-13

ALL-IRELAND QUARTER-FINAL
Aug 14, 2004, Croke Park, Dublin
KERRY 1-15   DUBLIN 1-8

NATIONAL LEAGUE, DIVISION IA
Feb 6, 2005, Parnell Park, Dublin
DUBLIN 2-13   MAYO 0-15

NATIONAL LEAGUE, DIVISION IA
Feb 13, 2005, Healy Park, Omagh
TYRONE 1-10   DUBLIN 0-9

NATIONAL LEAGUE, DIVISION IA
Mar 6, 2005, Austin Stack Park, Tralee
KERRY 2-13   DUBLIN 2-11

NATIONAL LEAGUE, DIVISION IA
Mar 12, 2005, Parnell Park, Dublin
DUBLIN 0-11   WESTMEATH 0-9

NATIONAL LEAGUE, DIVISION IA
Mar 20, 2005, Parnell Park, Dublin
DUBLIN 1-11   DONEGAL 0-13

NATIONAL LEAGUE, DIVISION IA
Mar 26, 2005, Pairc Ui Rinn, Cork
CORK 0-18   DUBLIN 1-6

NATIONAL LEAGUE, DIVISION IA
Apr 3, 2005, O'Connor Park, Tullamore
DUBLIN 1-13   OFFALY 2-6

LEINSTER FIRST ROUND
May 15, 2005, Croke Park, Dublin
DUBLIN 2-23   LONGFORD 0-10

LEINSTER QUARTER-FINAL
June 5, 2005, Croke Park, Dublin
DUBLIN 1-12   MEATH 1-10

LEINSTER SEMI-FINAL
June 19, 2005, Croke Park, Dublin
DUBLIN 1-17   WEXFORD 2-10

LEINSTER FINAL
July 17, 2005, Croke Park, Dublin
DUBLIN 0-14   LAOIS 0-13

ALL-IRELAND QUARTER-FINAL
Aug 13, 2005, Croke Park, Dublin
DUBLIN 1-14   TYRONE 1-14

**ALL-IRELAND QUARTER-FINAL
REPLAY**
Aug 27, 2005, Croke Park, Dublin
TYRONE 2-18   DUBLIN 1-14

NATIONAL LEAGUE, DIVISION IA
Feb 5, 2006, Healy Park, Omagh
DUBLIN 1-9   TYRONE 1-6

NATIONAL LEAGUE, DIVISION IA
Feb 12, 2006, Parnell Park
MONAGHAN 1-11   DUBLIN 0-7

NATIONAL LEAGUE, DIVISION IA
Mar 4, 2006, Parnell Park, Dublin
DUBLIN 1-10   OFFALY 3-2

NATIONAL LEAGUE, DIVISION IA
Mar 11, 2006, Pairc Ui Rinn, Cork
CORK 1-11   DUBLIN 1-10

NATIONAL LEAGUE, DIVISION IA
Mar 19, 2006, Brewster Park, Enniskillen
FERMANAGH 0-9   DUBLIN 0-8

NATIONAL LEAGUE, DIVISION IA
Mar 25, 2006, Parnell Park, Dublin
DUBLIN 4-10   MAYO 1-10

NATIONAL LEAGUE, DIVISION IA
Apr 9, 2006, Fitzgerald Stadium, Killarney
DUBLIN 0-13   KERRY 0-13

LEINSTER QUARTER-FINAL
June 4, 2006, Pearse Park, Longford
DUBLIN 1-12   LONGFORD 0-13

LEINSTER SEMI-FINAL
June 25, 2006, Croke Park, Dublin
DUBLIN 3-17   LAOIS 0-12

LEINSTER FINAL
July 16, 2006, Croke Park, Dublin
DUBLIN 1-15   OFFALY 0-9

ALL-IRELAND QUARTER-FINAL
Aug 12, 2006, Croke Park, Dublin
DUBLIN 1-12   WESTMEATH 0-5

ALL-IRELAND SEMI-FINAL
Aug 27, 2006, Croke Park, Dublin
MAYO 1-16   DUBLIN 2-12

NATIONAL LEAGUE, DIVISION IA
Feb 3, 2007, Croke Park, Dublin
TYRONE 0-11   DUBLIN 0-10

NATIONAL LEAGUE, DIVISION IA
Feb 10, 2007, Gaelic Grounds, Limerick
DUBLIN 0-14   LIMERICK 1-10

NATIONAL LEAGUE, DIVISION IA
Feb 25, 2007, Fr Tierney Park, Ballyshannon
DONEGAL 0-9   DUBLIN 0-5

NATIONAL LEAGUE, DIVISION IA
Mar 10, 2007, Parnell Park, Dublin
DUBLIN 1-13   CORK 0-7

NATIONAL LEAGUE, DIVISION IA
Mar 24, 2007, Parnell Park, Dublin
DUBLIN 3-15   FERMANAGH 0-7

NATIONAL LEAGUE, DIVISION IA
Apr 1, 2007, MacHale Park, Castlebar
MAYO 0-10   DUBLIN 0-9

NATIONAL LEAGUE, DIVISION IA
Apr 8, 2007, Parnell Park, Dublin
KERRY 1-12   DUBLIN 2-7

LEINSTER QUARTER-FINAL
June 3, 2007, Croke Park, Dublin
DUBLIN 0-14   MEATH 0-14

LEINSTER QUARTER-FINAL REPLAY
June 17, 2007, Croke Park, Dublin
DUBLIN 0-16   MEATH 0-12

LEINSTER SEMI-FINAL
June 24, 2007, Croke Park, Dublin
DUBLIN 1-12   OFFALY 0-10

LEINSTER FINAL
July 15, 2007, Croke Park, Dublin
DUBLIN 3-14   LAOIS 1-14

ALL-IRELAND QUARTER-FINAL
Aug 11, 2007, Croke Park, Dublin
DUBLIN 0-18   DERRY 0-15

ALL-IRELAND SEMI-FINAL
Aug 26, 2007, Croke Park, Dublin
KERRY 1-15   DUBLIN 0-16

NATIONAL LEAGUE, DIVISION TWO
Feb 2, 2008, Parnell Park, Dublin
DUBLIN 1-7   WESTMEATH 1-5

NATIONAL LEAGUE, DIVISION TWO
Mar 2, 2008, Breffni Park, Cavan
DUBLIN 1-9   CAVAN 0-7

NATIONAL LEAGUE, DIVISION TWO
Mar 24, 2008, Parnell Park, Dublin
DUBLIN 1-10   MONAGHAN 0-13

NATIONAL LEAGUE, DIVISION TWO
Apr 5, 2008, Parnell Park, Dublin
DUBLIN 3-20   ROSCOMMON 0-7

NATIONAL LEAGUE, DIVISION TWO
Apr 13, 2008, Plunkett Park, Crossmaglen
ARMAGH 3-13   DUBLIN 1-10

NATIONAL LEAGUE, DIVISION TWO
Apr 20, 2008, Parnell Park, Dublin
DUBLIN 0-13   MEATH 2-6

* Dublin received a walkover from Cork.
Not included in managerial record.

NATIONAL LEAGUE DIVISION TWO FINAL
Apr 27, 2008, Pairc Tailteann, Navan
WESTMEATH 0-15 DUBLIN 0-10

LEINSTER QUARTER-FINAL
June 8, 2008, Croke Park, Dublin
DUBLIN 1-22   LOUTH 0-12

LEINSTER SEMI-FINAL
June 29, 2008, Croke Park, Dublin
DUBLIN 0-13   WESTMEATH 1-8

LEINSTER FINAL
July 20, 2008, Croke Park, Dublin
DUBLIN 3-23   WEXFORD 0-9

ALL-IRELAND QUARTER-FINAL
Aug 16, 2008, Croke Park, Dublin
TYRONE 3-14   DUBLIN 1-8

	P	W	D	L	For	Agt
Championship	27	19	2	6	29-406	15-316
National League	35	17	4	14	29-365	24-348
TOTAL	62	36	6	20	58-771	39-664

Pat Gilroy

Paul Caffrey, having been given an extension to his three-year term, stepped down minutes after Dublin's dozen point All-Ireland quarter-final hammering — 3-14 to 1-0 — by Tyrone on August 16. Two months later, on October 10, Pat Gilroy, still three weeks short of his 37th birthday, only recently retired as a player and with no managerial experience, was a surprise appointee. Mickey Whelan, Paddy O'Donoghue and Paul Nugent were named as his co-selectors; the latter stepped down a year later for business reasons and was replaced by David Hickey and Ian Robertson came in for Whelan in 2012.

NATIONAL LEAGUE, DIVISION ONE
Jan 31, 2009, Croke Park, Dublin
TYRONE 1-18   DUBLIN 1-16

NATIONAL LEAGUE, DIVISION ONE
Feb 15, 2009, Pearse Stadium, Salthill
GALWAY 3-12   DUBLIN 0-13

NATIONAL LEAGUE, DIVISION ONE
Mar 8, 2009, Fr Tierney Park, Ballyshannon
DUBLIN 0-13   DONEGAL 1-8

NATIONAL LEAGUE, DIVISION ONE
Mar 14, 2009, Parnell Park, Dublin
DERRY 0-20   DUBLIN 1-12

NATIONAL LEAGUE, DIVISION ONE
Mar 22, 2009, James Stephens Park, Ballina
DUBLIN 0-9   MAYO 0-9

NATIONAL LEAGUE, DIVISION ONE
Mar 29, 2009, Parnell Park, Dublin
DUBLIN 1-15   KERRY 1-15

NATIONAL LEAGUE, DIVISION ONE
Apr 12, 2009, Parnell Park, Dublin
DUBLIN 5-22   WESTMEATH 0-10

LEINSTER QUARTER-FINAL
June 7, 2009, Croke Park, Dublin
DUBLIN 0-14   MEATH 0-12

LEINSTER SEMI-FINAL
June 28, 2009, Croke Park, Dublin
DUBLIN 4-26   WESTMEATH 0-11

LEINSTER FINAL
July 12, 2009, Croke Park, Dublin
DUBLIN 2-15   KILDARE 0-18

ALL-IRELAND QUARTER-FINAL
Aug 3, 2009, Croke Park, Dublin
KERRY 1-24   DUBLIN 1-7

NATIONAL LEAGUE, DIVISION ONE
Feb 7, 2010, Fitzgerald Stadium, Killarney
DUBLIN 1-12   KERRY 1-10

NATIONAL LEAGUE, DIVISION ONE
Feb 14, 2010, Parnell Park, Dublin
DUBLIN 1-11   DERRY 0-7

NATIONAL LEAGUE, DIVISION ONE
Mar 7, 2010, MacHale Park, Castlebar
DUBLIN 1-9   MAYO 0-8

NATIONAL LEAGUE, DIVISION ONE
Mar 14, 2010, Parnell Park, Dublin
DUBLIN 2-11   MONAGHAN 1-9

NATIONAL LEAGUE, DIVISION ONE
Mar 20, 2010, Pairc Ui Rinn, Cork
CORK 2-13   DUBLIN 2-6

NATIONAL LEAGUE, DIVISION ONE
Mar 27, 2010, Parnell Park, Dublin
GALWAY 1-14   DUBLIN 0-14

NATIONAL LEAGUE, DIVISION ONE
Apr 11, 2010, Healy Park, Omagh
DUBLIN 2-14   TYRONE 0-11

LEINSTER QUARTER-FINAL
June 13, 2010, Croke Park, Dublin
DUBLIN 2-16   WEXFORD 0-15

LEINSTER SEMI-FINAL
June 27, 2010, Croke Park, Dublin
MEATH 5-9   DUBLIN 0-13

ALL-IRELAND QUALIFIER, ROUND TWO
July 10, 2010, Croke Park, Dublin
DUBLIN 1-21   TIPPERARY 1-13

ALL-IRELAND QUALIFIER, ROUND THREE
July 17, 2010, Croke Park, Dublin
DUBLIN 0-14   ARMAGH 0-11

ALL-IRELAND QUALIFIER, ROUND FOUR
July 24, 2010, Croke Park, Dublin
DUBLIN 2-14   LOUTH 0-13

ALL-IRELAND QUARTER-FINAL
July 31, 2010, Croke Park, Dublin
DUBLIN 1-15   TYRONE 0-13

ALL-IRELAND SEMI-FINAL
Aug 22, 2010, Croke Park, Dublin
CORK 1-15   DUBLIN 1-14

NATIONAL LEAGUE, DIVISION ONE
Feb 6, 2011, Athletic Grounds, Armagh
DUBLIN 2-12   ARMAGH 1-11

NATIONAL LEAGUE, DIVISION ONE
Feb 19, 2011, Croke Park, Dublin
DUBLIN 3-13   CORK 0-16

NATIONAL LEAGUE, DIVISION ONE
Feb 26, 2011, Croke Park, Dublin
DUBLIN 3-10   KERRY 1-15

NATIONAL LEAGUE, DIVISION ONE
Mar 13, 2011, St Tiernach's Park, Clones
DUBLIN 0-13   MONAGHAN 1-9

NATIONAL LEAGUE, DIVISION ONE
Mar 20, 2011, Croke Park, Dublin
DUBLIN 4-15   MAYO 3-13

NATIONAL LEAGUE, DIVISION ONE
Apr 2, 2011, Croke Park, Dublin
DUBLIN 2-10   DOWN 0-13

NATIONAL LEAGUE, DIVISION ONE
Apr 10, 2011, Pearse Stadium, Salthill
DUBLIN 2-9   GALWAY 0-15

NATIONAL LEAGUE FINAL
Apr 24, 2011, Croke Park, Dublin
CORK 0-21   DUBLIN 2-14

LEINSTER QUARTER-FINAL
June 5, 2011, Croke Park, Dublin
DUBLIN 1-16   LAOIS 0-11

LEINSTER SEMI- FINAL
June 26, 2011, Croke Park, Dublin
DUBLIN 1-12   **KILDARE 1-11**

LEINSTER FINAL
July 10, 2011, Croke Park, Dublin
DUBLIN 2-12   **WEXFORD 1-12**

ALL-IRELAND QUARTER-FINAL
Aug 6, 2011, Croke Park, Dublin
DUBLIN 0-22   **TYRONE 0-15**

ALL-IRELAND SEMI-FINAL
Aug 28, 2011, Croke Park, Dublin
DUBLIN 0-8   **DONEGAL 0-6**

ALL-IRELAND FINAL
Sep 18, 2011, Croke Park, Dublin
DUBLIN 1-12   **KERRY 1-11**

NATIONAL LEAGUE, DIVISION ONE
Feb 4, 2012, Croke Park, Dublin
KERRY 1-14   **DUBLIN 0-11**

NATIONAL LEAGUE, DIVISION ONE
Mar 3, 2012, O'Moore Park, Portlaoise
DUBLIN 1-14   **LAOIS 0-9**

NATIONAL LEAGUE, DIVISION ONE
Mar 11, 2012, Croke Park, Dublin
DUBLIN 4-17   **ARMAGH 1-10**

NATIONAL LEAGUE, DIVISION ONE
Mar 18, 2012, Pairc Esler, Newry
DOWN 0-15   **DUBLIN 1-10**

NATIONAL LEAGUE, DIVISION ONE
Mar 24, 2012, Croke Park, Dublin
DUBLIN 2-16   **DONEGAL 0-13**

NATIONAL LEAGUE, DIVISION ONE
April 1, 2012, MacHale Park, Castlebar
MAYO 0-20   **DUBLIN 0-8**

NATIONAL LEAGUE, DIVISION ONE
Apr 8, 2012, Pairc Ui Chaoimh, Cork
CORK 1-12   **DUBLIN 0-12**

LEINSTER QUARTER-FINAL
June 3, 2012, Croke Park, Dublin
DUBLIN 2-22   **LOUTH 0-12**

LEINSTER SEMI-FINAL
July 1, 2012, Croke Park, Dublin
DUBLIN 2-11   **WEXFORD 1-10**

LEINSTER FINAL
July 22, 2012, Croke Park, Dublin
DUBLIN 2-13   **MEATH 1-13**

ALL-IRELAND QUARTER-FINAL
Aug 4, 2012, Croke Park, Dublin
DUBLIN 1-12   **LAOIS 0-12**

ALL-IRELAND SEMI-FINAL
Sep 2, 2012, Croke Park, Dublin
MAYO 0-19   **DUBLIN 0-16**

	P	W	D	L	For	Agt
Championship	22	18	0	4	26-325	13-286
National League	29	16	3	10	43-361	20-370
TOTAL	51	34	3	14	69-686	33-656

Jim Gavin

Having ended an All-Ireland famine that had lasted all of 16 years, Gilroy was offered a two year extension but, as the father of four young children and a highly successful businessman, felt unable to commit to more than one and stepped down in September 2012 just three days after Dublin's three point All-Ireland semi-final loss to Mayo. Jim Gavin, who five months earlier had for the second time in three years guided the county to All-Ireland Under-21 success, was appointed manager on October 1 and four days later Declan Darcy, Mick Deegan and Shane O'Hanlon were named as his co-selectors. In early May 2017, with Dublin yet to kick a ball in the Championship, Gavin agreed a two year extension that would carry him through to at least the end of the 2019 season

NATIONAL LEAGUE, DIVISION ONE
Feb 2, 2013, Croke Park, Dublin
DUBLIN 1-18   **CORK 2-9**

NATIONAL LEAGUE, DIVISION ONE
Feb 10, 2013, Fitzgerald Stadium, Killarney
DUBLIN 1-11   **KERRY 0-4**

NATIONAL LEAGUE, DIVISION ONE
Mar 2, 2013, Croke Park, Dublin
DUBLIN 2-14   **MAYO 0-16**

NATIONAL LEAGUE, DIVISION ONE
Mar 10, 2013, Croke Park, Dublin
DUBLIN 2-20   **KILDARE 2-7**

NATIONAL LEAGUE, DIVISION ONE
Mar 16, 2013, Croke Park, Dublin
TYRONE 0-18   **DUBLIN 1-14**

NATIONAL LEAGUE, DIVISION ONE
Mar 23, 2013, Croke Park, Dublin
DUBLIN 1-15   **DOWN 0-9**

NATIONAL LEAGUE, DIVISION ONE
Apr 7, 2013, MacCumhaill Park, Ballybofey
DUBLIN 0-13   **DONEGAL 1-10**

NATIONAL LEAGUE SEMI-FINAL
Apr 14, 2013, Croke Park, Dublin
DUBLIN 2-16   **MAYO 0-16**

NATIONAL LEAGUE FINAL
Apr 28, 2013, Croke Park, Dublin
DUBLIN 0-18   **TYRONE 0-17**

LEINSTER QUARTER-FINAL
June 2, 2013, Croke Park, Dublin
DUBLIN 1-22   WESTMEATH 0-9

LEINSTER SEMI-FINAL
June 30, 2013, Croke Park, Dublin
DUBLIN 4-16   KILDARE 1-9

LEINSTER FINAL
July 14, 2013, Croke Park, Dublin
DUBLIN 2-15   MEATH 0-14

ALL-IRELAND QUARTER-FINAL
Aug 3, 2013, Croke Park, Dublin
DUBLIN 1-16   CORK 0-14

ALL-IRELAND SEMI-FINAL
Sep 1, 2013, Croke Park, Dublin
DUBLIN 3-18   KERRY 3-11

ALL-IRELAND FINAL
Sep 22, 2013, Croke Park, Dublin
DUBLIN 2-12   MAYO 1-14

NATIONAL LEAGUE, DIVISION ONE
Feb 2, 2014, Croke Park, Dublin
DUBLIN 2-8   KERRY 1-10

NATIONAL LEAGUE, DIVISION ONE
Feb 9, 2014, Cusack Park, Mullingar
DUBLIN 0-14   WESTMEATH 2-7

NATIONAL LEAGUE, DIVISION ONE
Mar 1, 2014, Croke Park, Dublin
CORK 1-17   DUBLIN 0-18

NATIONAL LEAGUE, DIVISION ONE
Mar 9, 2014, Croke Park, Dublin
DUBLIN 1-22   KILDARE 1-12

NATIONAL LEAGUE, DIVISION ONE
Mar 16, 2014, Celtic Park, Derry
DERRY 1-16   DUBLIN 0-13

NATIONAL LEAGUE, DIVISION ONE
Mar 30, 2014, Croke Park, Dublin
DUBLIN 3-14   MAYO 2-17

NATIONAL LEAGUE, DIVISION ONE
Apr 6, 2014, Healy Park, Omagh
DUBLIN 3-10   TYRONE 1-15

NATIONAL LEAGUE SEMI-FINAL
Apr 13, 2014, Croke Park, Dublin
DUBLIN 2-20   CORK 2-13

NATIONAL LEAGUE FINAL
Apr 27, 2014, Croke Park, Dublin
DUBLIN 3-19   DERRY 1-10

LEINSTER QUARTER-FINAL
June 8, 2014, Croke Park, Dublin
DUBLIN 2-21   LAOIS 0-16

LEINSTER SEMI-FINAL
June 29, 2014, Croke Park, Dublin
DUBLIN 2-25   WEXFORD 1-12

LEINSTER FINAL
July 20, 2014, Croke Park, Dublin
DUBLIN 3-20   MEATH 1-10

ALL-IRELAND QUARTER-FINAL
Aug 9, 2014, Croke Park, Dublin
DUBLIN 2-22   MONAGHAN 0-11

ALL-IRELAND SEMI-FINAL
Aug 31, 2014, Croke Park, Dublin
DONEGAL 3-14   DUBLIN 0-17

NATIONAL LEAGUE, DIVISION ONE
Feb 1, 2015, Pairc Ui Rinn, Cork
CORK 1-15   DUBLIN 0-16

NATIONAL LEAGUE, DIVISION ONE
Feb 8, 2015, Croke Park, Dublin
DUBLIN 2-10   DONEGAL 0-11

NATIONAL LEAGUE, DIVISION ONE
Mar 1, 2015, Fitzgerald Stadium, Killarney
KERRY 0-15   DUBLIN 1-10

NATIONAL LEAGUE, DIVISION ONE
Mar 8, 2015, Croke Park, Dublin
DUBLIN 1-9   TYRONE 0-12

NATIONAL LEAGUE, DIVISION ONE
Mar 14, 2015, MacHale Park, Castlebar
DUBLIN 2-18   MAYO 0-10

NATIONAL LEAGUE, DIVISION ONE
Mar 28, 2015, Croke Park, Dublin
DUBLIN 0-8   DERRY 0-4

NATIONAL LEAGUE, DIVISION ONE
Apr 5, 2015, St Tiernach's Park, Clones
DUBLIN 1-22   MONAGHAN 1-11

NATIONAL LEAGUE SEMI-FINAL
Apr 12, 2015, Croke Park, Dublin
DUBLIN 0-17   MONAGHAN 0-16

NATIONAL LEAGUE FINAL
Apr 26, 2015, Croke Park, Dublin
DUBLIN 1-21   CORK 2-7

LEINSTER QUARTER-FINAL
May 31, 2015, Croke Park, Dublin
DUBLIN 4-25   LONGFORD 0-10

LEINSTER SEMI-FINAL
June 28, 2015, Croke Park, Dublin
DUBLIN 5-18   KILDARE 0-14

LEINSTER FINAL
July 12, 2015, Croke Park, Dublin
DUBLIN 2-13   WESTMEATH 0-6

ALL-IRELAND QUARTER-FINAL
Aug 2, 2015, Croke Park, Dublin
DUBLIN 2-23   FERMANAGH 2-15

ALL-IRELAND SEMI-FINAL
Aug 30, 2015, Croke Park, Dublin
DUBLIN 2-12   MAYO 1-15

ALL-IRELAND SEMI-FINAL REPLAY
Sep 5, 2015, Croke Park, Dublin
DUBLIN 3-15   MAYO 1-14

ALL-IRELAND FINAL
Sep 20, 2015, Croke Park, Dublin
DUBLIN 0-12   KERRY 0-9

NATIONAL LEAGUE, DIVISION ONE
Jan 30, 2016, Croke Park, Dublin
DUBLIN 2-14   KERRY 0-14

NATIONAL LEAGUE, DIVISION ONE
Feb 6, 2016, MacHale Park, Castlebar
DUBLIN 0-9   MAYO 0-7

NATIONAL LEAGUE, DIVISION ONE
Feb 27, 2016, Croke Park, Dublin
DUBLIN 1-14   MONAGHAN 0-16

NATIONAL LEAGUE, DIVISION ONE
Mar 6, 2016, Croke Park, Dublin
DUBLIN 2-14   CORK 2-10

NATIONAL LEAGUE, DIVISION ONE
Mar 12, 2016, Pairc Esler, Newry
DUBLIN 1-15   DOWN 1-7

NATIONAL LEAGUE, DIVISION ONE
Mar 26, 2016, Croke Park, Dublin
DUBLIN 1-10   DONEGAL 0-7

NATIONAL LEAGUE, DIVISION ONE
Apr 3, 2016, Pairc Diarmuda, C-on-Shannon
DUBLIN 1-13   ROSCOMMON 1-12

NATIONAL LEAGUE SEMI-FINAL
Apr 10, 2016, Croke Park, Dublin
DUBLIN 1-20   DONEGAL 0-13

NATIONAL LEAGUE FINAL
Apr 24, 2016, Croke Park, Dublin
DUBLIN 2-18   KERRY 0-13

LEINSTER QUARTER-FINAL
June 4, 2016, Nowlan Park, Kilkenny
DUBLIN 2-21   LAOIS 2-10

LEINSTER SEMI-FINAL
June 26, 2016, Croke Park, Dublin
DUBLIN 0-21   MEATH 0-11

LEINSTER FINAL
July 17, 2016, Croke Park, Dublin
DUBLIN 2-19   WESTMEATH 0-10

ALL-IRELAND QUARTER-FINAL
Aug 6, 2016, Croke Park, Dublin
DUBLIN 1-15   DONEGAL 1-10

ALL-IRELAND SEMI-FINAL
Aug 28, 2016, Croke Park, Dublin
DUBLIN 0-22   KERRY 2-14

ALL-IRELAND FINAL
Sep 18, 2016, Croke Park, Dublin
DUBLIN 2-9   MAYO 0-15

ALL-IRELAND FINAL REPLAY
Oct 1, 2016, Croke Park, Dublin
DUBLIN 1-15   MAYO 1-14

NATIONAL LEAGUE, DIVISION ONE
Feb 5, 2017, Breffni Park, Cavan
DUBLIN 0-18   CAVAN 0-11

NATIONAL LEAGUE, DIVISION ONE
Feb 11, 2017, Croke Park, Dublin
DUBLIN 0-10   TYRONE 1-7

NATIONAL LEAGUE, DIVISION ONE
Feb 26, 2017, MacCumhaill Park, Ballybofey
DUBLIN 1-8   DONEGAL 2-5

NATIONAL LEAGUE, DIVISION ONE
Mar 4, 2017, Croke Park, Dublin
DUBLIN 1-16   MAYO 0-7

NATIONAL LEAGUE, DIVISION ONE
Mar 18, 2017, Austin Stack Park, Tralee
DUBLIN 0-13   KERRY 0-13

NATIONAL LEAGUE, DIVISION ONE
Mar 25, 2017, Croke Park, Dublin
DUBLIN 2-29   ROSCOMMON 0-14

NATIONAL LEAGUE, DIVISION ONE
Apr 2, 2017, St. Tiernach's Park, Clones
DUBLIN 2-15   MONAGHAN 1-15

NATIONAL LEAGUE FINAL
Apr 9, 2017, Croke Park, Dublin
KERRY 0-20   DUBLIN 1-16

LEINSTER QUARTER-FINAL
June 3, 2017, O'Moore Park, Portlaoise
DUBLIN 0-19   CARLOW 0-7

LEINSTER SEMI-FINAL
June 25, 2017, Croke Park, Dublin
DUBLIN 4-29   WESTMEATH 0-10

LEINSTER FINAL
July 16, 2017, Croke Park, Dublin
DUBLIN 2-23   KILDARE 1-17

ALL-IRELAND QUARTER-FINAL
Aug 5, 2017, Croke Park, Dublin
DUBLIN 1-19   MONAGHAN 0-12

ALL-IRELAND SEMI-FINAL
Aug 27, 2017, Croke Park, Dublin
DUBLIN 2-17   TYRONE 0-11

ALL-IRELAND FINAL
Sep 17, 2017, Croke Park, Dublin
DUBLIN 1-17   MAYO 1-16

	P	W	D	L	For	Agt
Championship	31	28	2	1	58-568	22-374
National League	44	33	6	5	51-663	28-512
TOTAL	75	61	8	6	109-1,131	50-886

Player Pen Pics

ALLEN, NORMAN (St. Vincent's): Defender. His first appearance in the county colours at senior level came in a league draw with Louth in Croke Park in October 1950 and his Championship debut followed the following May in a provincial first round win over Offaly at St Conleth's Park in Newbridge. He won National League titles in 1953 and 1955 and a Leinster medal in the latter year but an attack of appendicitis the night before ruled him out of the All-Ireland Final that latter year, when Dublin were upset 0-12 to 1-6 by Kerry. He won seven successive county titles from 1949 and was a stalwart of St. Vincent's remarkable eight year unbeaten streak from 1948 to 1956; indeed, in his entire club career he was only ever on the losing side on three occasion in over 100 matches. A dual star, he captained the Dublin team beaten by Cork in the All-Ireland Final in 1952 and county hurling titles in 1953, 1954 and 1955 and, after a seven year stint in New York, 1964 and 1967. He starred in a trio of famous New York hurling victories in 1958, over All-Ireland champions Kilkenny in games at the Polo Grounds and Gaelic Park in June and over National League champions Wexford in Croke Park in September when he scored three points as the exiles won the St. Brendan's Cup for the first time on a 3-8 to 3-7 scoreline. His son Damien captained St. Vincent's to their most recent county hurling title in 1993.

ANDREWS, PADDY (St. Brigid's): Forward, born 18 July 1988. Won a provincial Under-21 medal in 2009 (when Dublin were edged out 1-10 to 1-9 by Cork in the All-Ireland semi-final) but had made his senior debut the previous year; in a league win over Roscommon at Parnell Park in April and, in the Championship, in a Leinster quarter-final victory over Louth at Croke Park. He would go on to win All-Ireland medals in 2011 (as a panellist), 2013, 2015, 2016 and 2017 and was a key member of the side that won the National League four years in a row from 2013. He won a county medal in 2011 but St. Brigid's were subsequently edged out 1-8 to 0-10 by Westmeath champions Garrycastle in the provincial final.

ANDREWS, PEADAR (St Brigid's): Defender, born 1977, older brother of Paddy. A minor in 1996 and an Under-21 in 1998 and 1999 when Dublin were beaten by Laois in all three years (the first and last instances being in provincial finals), he made his senior debut when coming on as a sub in a Leinster quarter-final relay victory in July 1999... against Laois. An older brother of Paddy, he won provincial medals in 2002, 2005 and 2006 (as an unused sub) and played in five county finals (1999, 2001, 2003, 2007, 2010), being on the winning side in the middle one and going on to earn a Leinster medal before St. Brigid's lost out to Kerry and Munster champions An Ghaeltacht in the All-Ireland semi-final. He made his 65th and last senior appearance as a sub in a provincial quarter-final victory over Longford at Pearse Park in June 2006 and, unable to secure a permanent place in then manager Paul Caffrey's starting line-up, announced his retirement from inter-county action the following December.

BANKS, TOMMY (Sean McDermotts): Forward. Scored 2-19 in six games as Dublin won the All-Ireland Junior 'Home' Final in 1939 but then missed the victory over London in the decider proper in early October 1939 through injury, but made his senior debut in a league win over Monaghan at Bremore Park in Balbriggan just three weeks later. In a brief inter-county career of 26 games in three and a half years, he scored 2-94, was on the teams beaten by Mayo in the National League Final in 1941 and by Kerry in the All-Ireland Final later that year, won Leinster and All-Ireland medals the following year, and made his final appearance in a shock provincial quarter-final loss to Louth in Drogheda in May 1943.

BARR, KEITH (Erin's Isle): Defender, born 26 January 1968. The winner of a provincial minor medal in 1985 when Dublin were beaten by Cork in the All-Ireland semi-final, he made his senior debut in a Leinster semi-final defeat of Wicklow at St. Conleth's Park in Newbridge in June 1989. After being on the side that lost All-Ireland Finals to Donegal in 1992 and Down two years later, he finally collected a winner's medal in 1995 against Tyrone. During his nine year career he made 98 appearances, won five Leinster titles (1989, 1992, 1993, 1994, 1995), two National Leagues (1991, 1993), two All-Star awards (1991, 1995) and had his final game in the county colours in a provincial quarter-final replay loss to Kildare at Croke Park in June 1998. He played in five consecutive county finals from 1993, winning the first and last but losing the middle three (the first of them following a replay) and was on the side that won the Leinster title in December 1997 but was beaten in the All-Ireland Final three months later by Galway and Connacht champions Corofin.

BASTICK, DENIS (Templeogue Synge Street): Defender, born 8 May 1981. Made his senior debut when coming on as a sub in a league win over Offaly at O'Connor Park in Tullamore in April 2005 and made five more appearances the next year before a cruciate knee injury sidelined him for the entire 2007 season. The following year he was an ever present as Dublin won the All-Ireland Junior Championship for the sixth time but the first since 1960. He returned to the senior ranks in 2009 and played every minute of all seven league games and all four Championship ties as Dublin won a fifth successive Leinster title but fell to Kerry in the All-Ireland quarter-final, his debut in the showcase event coming in a provincial quarter-final win over arch rivals Meath in early June. Thereafter he remained an intrinsic member of the squad, being part of a quintet of All-Ireland success (2011, 2013, 2015, 2016 and 2017) and a quartet of National League triumphs (2013, 2014, 2015, 2016).

BEALIN, PAUL (Ballyboden St Enda's): Midfielder. A junior in 1988 (when Dublin got to the provincial final but were beaten by Meath), he made his senior debut in a league defeat to Derry at Wolfe Tone Park in Bellaghy in October of that year and got his first Championship outing when coming on as a sub in the first game of the famous four match series with Meath in June 1991. He kept his place for the next seven years, won four provincial medals in succession from 1992 and played in three All-Ireland Finals, losing to Donegal in 1992 and to Down two years later before winning a Celtic Cross at the third attempt as part of the team that pipped Tyrone in 1995. That same year, as player-manager, he steered Ballyboden to their first ever county title. He missed the successful 1990/91 league campaign through injury but collected a National League medal two seasons later and made his 82nd and last appearance in a provincial quarter-final replay loss to Kildare at Croke Park in June 1998. He later had spells as the manager of the Carlow, Wexford and Westmeath teams.

BEHAN, SIMON (St Vincent's): Forward. Won successive Leinster and All-Ireland minor medals in 1958 and 1959 and earlier in the latter year scored 2-1 as St. Joseph's (Fairview), captained by Des Foley, beat St. Nathy's from Ballaghaderreen by 3-9 to 2-8 to become the first ever Dublin winners of the All-Ireland colleges title. He made his senior debut in a provincial quarter-final win over Longford at Cusack Park in Mullingar in May 1960 and was an ever present on the side that won the Leinster and All-Ireland crowns, again captained by Foley. He scored 4-8 in 15 games for Dublin, the last of which was when he came on as a sub in a single point league semi-final win over Kerry at Croke Park in April 1964, although he remained a member of the county panel for a further three years. He won five county titles (1960, 1961, 1964, 1966, 1967) and, as company PRO, administered the Texaco Awards for some four decades. He died on 26 January 2009, aged 67.

BERMINGHAM, PADDY (St Mary's): Forward. After winning provincial medals at minor level in 1933 and 1934, he was selected for the juniors in the latter year and again in 1935 before making his senior debut in a league victory over Tipperary at Croke Park in February 1936. Six and a half years later he manned the centre half forward position when Dublin won a first All-Ireland since 1923 with a 1-10 to 1-0 victory over Galway. The winner of three Railway Cups (1939, 1940, 1944), he scored 9-61 in 55 senior games, the last being a league divisional final loss to Cavan in Croke Park in March 1948.

BOYLE, JOHNNY (Clanna Gael): Forward. Born in Dublin but raised in Suncroft in Kildare, he captained his local club to the county minor title in 1949 and Kildare to the Leinster Minor Final, in which he scored three points in a 3-10 to 1-5 trouncing... against Dublin. His senior Championship debut came in May 1952 when Kildare suffered an almost identical beating (3-8 to 0-5) against Longford in a provincial first round tie at Cusack Park in Mullingar, but the following year, having joined the Air Corp and stationed in Baldonnel, he declared for his native county and made his Sky Blue debut in a league clash with Galway at Croke Park in October, scoring a crucial point as Dublin, the defending champions, opened their campaign with a draw. He had his first Championship outing in the Dublin colours in a provincial quarter-final win over Louth at Drogheda in May 1954, and the following season scored 3-18 as Dublin regained the National League crown but were shocked by Kerry in the All-Ireland

Final. Three years later, in 1958, another National League success was followed by a comprehensive victory over Derry in the All-Ireland Final and even though Dublin were out-hussled by Kerry in the All-Ireland semi-final the following year, Boyle did win a third provincial medal and a Railway Cup before making his final appearance as a sub in a Leinster semi-final loss to Offaly at O'Moore Park in Portlaoise in June 1960. Despite being pulled back to the half back line for his final three seasons and two dozen games, he scored a total of 11-51 in his 65 appearances with Dublin. Also a basketball international, he emigrated to New Zealand in 1972, worked for Air New Zealand for over two decades and, following his retirement, settled on the Gold Coast in Australia. He died on 25 February 2017.

BOYLE, ROBBIE (Erin's Isle): Forward. Was on the losing side in three successive provincial finals, minor in 1991 and then two at Under-21, and made his senior debut when coming on for Mick Galvin after 61 minutes of the All-Ireland Final victory over Tyrone in 1995. The only one of his four senior outings that he started was the second — a league win at Pairc Chiarain in Athlone two months after the All-Ireland Final — and in that he had to come off injured at half-time; he was called on as a sub in his other two outings, a provincial quarter-final draw with and replay loss to Kildare at Croke Park in June 1998, and his entire senior career lasted approximately an hour and a quarter. He won a county championship medal in 1997, scoring 1-1 in a 2-10 to 1-11 victory over St. Sylvester's and going on to add a Leinster medal before Erin's Isle lost out 0-15 to 0-10 to Galway and Connacht champions Corofin in the All-Ireland Final.

BRENNAN, GER (St Vincent's): Defender. Won a Leinster minor medal and was on the side beaten by Laois in an All-Ireland Final replay in 2003 and spent the next three years with the Under-21s before making his senior debut in a league loss to Tyrone at Croke Park in February 2007. His first Championship appearance came five months later when called in as a sub in a Leinster Final victory over Laois. He won three more provincial medals in 2009, 2011 and 2013, being on the All-Ireland winnings sides in the latter two years and completing a National League and Championship double in the final one. That second Sam Maguire victory, over Mayo, was his 67th and last senior outing in the county colours but he continued to compete at the highest club level, winning a quartet of county titles (2007, 2013, 2014, 2016) and going on to play his part in All-Ireland triumphs in the first two campaigns.

BRENNAN, JIM (Keatings): Midfielder, born near Ballyragget in Kilkenny on 21 January 1881. Made his debut in the Championship for 1902 in a provincial semi-final victory over Louth in Navan — played in December 1902 — and went on to win four All-Ireland medals, in the campaigns for 1902, 1906, 1907 and 1908, as well as an additional provincial medal in 1904 and county titles in 1903 and 1909. A civil servant — under his Irish name of Séamus Ó Braonáin — with the Department of Education for almost four decades, he served as Director General of Raidió Éireann for seven years until his retirement in 1947. An all-round sportsman, he drafted the original rules for camogie, played rugby with St. Mary's College, was a keen cricketer and a founder member — and later captain — of Donabate golf club. He died on 2 May 1970, aged 89.

BRESLIN, EAMONN (Ballyfermot Gaels): Forward. On the junior side beaten by Westmeath in a provincial quarter-final at Cusack Park in Mullingar in April 1963, he made the first of only 18 senior appearances in another Leinster quarter-final just eight weeks later, a 2-6 to 2-5 edging out of Meath at Croke Park. Held his position for the semi-final and final defeats of first Kildare and then Laois but lost his place thereafter, although he did get an All-Ireland medal as an unused sub in the final victory over Galway. His brief career ended with a league victory over Waterford at Croke Park in March 1966 but he will forever be remembered for a goal he scored in another league win at the same venue in November 1964 ... when he head a chipped cross from Jackie Gilroy — father of future All-Ireland winner as both player and manager, Pat — past keeper Tommy Miller into the Laois net for the only goal of a game Dublin won by 1-11 to 0-10. The match referee pondered the rules briefly before allowing the goal to stand (it was, after all, still the era of "The Ban"); almost 14 years later the same referee, Seamus Aldridge from Kildare, would allow another contentious goal to stand at the same Canal End when Mikey Sheehy outwitted Paddy Cullen in the All-Ireland Final.

BROGAN, ALAN (St Oliver Plunkett's): Forward, born 11 January 1982. After winning a provincial medal at minor level — but losing out to Down in the All-Ireland semi-final — in 1999, he made his senior debut in a league win over Donegal at Parnell Park in February 2002, scoring 1-3. The following year he won an All-Ireland medal at Under-21 level and also captured the first of ten Leinster medals (the others being 2005, 2006, 2007, 2008, 2009, 2011, 2012, 2014, 2015). He won All-Ireland medals in 2011 and 2015 — he missed the 2013 campaign through a groin injury — and collected a National League medal in 2014. The winner of All-Star awards in 2006, 2007 and 2011, he announced his retirement three months after his second All-Ireland success and finished his career of over a dozen years with 15-193 in 118 appearances.

BROGAN, BERNARD Jnr (St. Oliver Plunkett's): Forward, born 3 April 1984. On the Under-21 side beaten by Down in the All-Ireland semi-final in 2005, his first senior outing came in February of the following year as a sub in a league loss to Monaghan in Parnell Park, but his Championship debut didn't come until June 2007 — again as a sub — in a provincial quarter-final replay victory over Meath at Croke Park. In 2010, despite the fact that Dublin were beaten by Meath in the Leinster semi-final and, having come through the 'back door' qualifiers, by Cork at the same stage of the All-Ireland series, he scored a county record 6-73 in 14 matches, won the first of four All-Star awards (the others coming in 2013, 2015 and 2016) and succeeded his brother Alan as Footballer of the Year. A provincial medal winner every year from 2007 to 2017 except for 2010, he featured strongly in the All-Ireland triumphs of 2011, 2013, 2015, 2016 and 2017 —

scoring 10-88 in the course of the five campaigns — as well as four successive National League wins from 2013.

BROGAN, BERNARD Snr (St Oliver Plunkett's): Forward, born 24 September 1953, father of Bernard Jnr and Alan, brother of Jim. The first of 70 appearances in the county colours was when he came on as a sub in a league win over Kilkenny at Nowlan Park in December 1973, and the last was in a four point loss to Laois in a Leinster semi-final at O'Connor Park in Tullamore. In between those two milestones he won every honour it was possible to win at inter-county level; two All-Irelands (1976, 1977), two National Leagues (1976, 1978), four provincial titles (1975, 1976, 1977, 1978, 1979, the middle one as an unused sub) and an All-Star in 1979. During his career he scored 7-29, including a memorable goal when coming on as a sub in the classic All-Ireland semi-final defeat of Kerry in 1977.

BROGAN, JIM (St Oliver Plunkett's): Defender. Brother of Bernard Snr and uncle of Alan and Bernard Jnr, he lined out with the juniors in 1972 and four years later, in February, he made his first senior appearance when coming on as a sub in a league defeat to Roscommon at Dr. Hyde Park. Five months later came his Championship debut, again as a sub, in the Leinster Final victory over Meath; with just one league outing in between, his second Championship appearance was in the following year's All-Ireland Final win over Armagh, when he yet again came off the bench. Only in the 1980/81 season was he a starting regular, playing in all but two of Dublin's eleven competitive games, and he made his 21st and final appearance in a provincial quarter-final win over Longford at O'Connor Park in Tullamore in June 1982.

BUCKLEY, PJ (Erin's Isle): Defender. Made his senior debut in a league victory over Kildare at Catherine Park in Athy in December 1979 and four years later won the first of two consecutive Leinster medals, capping the year with a Celtic Cross following Dublin's defeat of Galway. Also figured on the team beaten by Kerry in the All-Ireland Final of 1984 (when he won an All-Star award), and although he lost his place the following year, he was brought on as a sub in what was a second successive Sam Maguire decider defeat by the Kingdom. He made 53 appearance in all, the last being a provincial final loss to Meath in July 1986. His only county football final appearance ended in a replay loss to Erin's Hope in 1979 but he did win a hurling title four years later when Erin's Isle defeated Ballyboden St Enda's.

BURKE, FRANK (Collegians): Forward. Born in Carbury in Kildare in 1895, he became a boarder at Padraig Pearse's famous St Enda's School — first in Ranelagh and then in Rathfarnham — at the age of 14 and quickly became a protégé of the academy's founder, serving with him in the GPO during the Easter Rising and subsequently being interned, first in Stafford Detention Barracks and then in Frongoch Internment Camp in Wales, where one of his fellow detainees was Michael Collins. Released just before

Christmas 1916, he resumed his playing career and soon added that year's All-Ireland junior title — not decided until November 1917 — to the one he had won in 1914. He had made his senior debut in a provincial first round win over his native Kildare in Newbridge four months earlier (but retained his junior status until the end of that campaign) and was on the pitch in Croke Park on Bloody Sunday when his immediate marker Michael Hogan was shot dead. On the teams beaten by Tipperary in the delayed All-Ireland Final of 1920 and that pipped by a point by Kerry in the decider of 1924, he was one of the stars of the Championship hat-trick in between; he missed the 1921 provincial final but was a member of the successful teams of 1920, 1922, 1923 and 1924 and made his 26th and final appearance for the county in the Leinster Final loss to Kildare in Croke Park in August 1927. The foremost dual star of his era, he remains the only man to wear the Dublin colours in nine senior All-Ireland Finals, adding to his five football deciders with another four in hurling, winning in 1917 against Tipperary and 1920 against Cork and losing to the latter in 1919 and to Limerick in 1921. Because of delays and the fixture congestion brought about by the Civil War, he actually played in five All-Ireland Finals — three football and two hurling — between May 1922 and October of the following year. He never won a county football title — Collegians were beaten by O'Tooles in the 1918 decider — but he did win three hurling in a row from 1917. A teacher at St Enda's from the start of 1917 following his graduation from UCD, he subsequently became principal and remained in that position until the closure of the school in 1935. He died on 28 December 1987, aged 92, and is buried in Cruagh Cemetery in Rathfarnham.

CAFFREY, JOHN (Na Fianna): Forward. Made his senior debut in a league loss to Down at Croke Park in November 1982, had his first Championship outing when coming on as a sub in a provincial semi-final win over Louth the following July, and two months later played his part in defeating Galway in the All-Ireland Final. A brother of Paul, the Dublin manager for four years from 2004, his inter-county career was relatively short, his 24th and last appearance being as a sub in a league quarter-final win over Meath at Croke Park in March 1986. He won a county championship medal in 1979.

CAHILL, BARRY (St Brigid's): Defender, born 10 May 1981. Made his debut in a league win over Donegal at Parnell Park in February 2002 and got his first Championship outing in a Leinster quarter-final victory over Wexford at Dr Cullen Park in Carlow four months later. Won the first of half a dozen consecutive provincial medals later that summer and would add another in 2011 en route to helping Dublin to a first All-Ireland success since 1985. An All-Star award winner in 2007, he won an eighth Leinster medal when coming on as a sub in the win over Meath in 2012, his 92nd and last appearance in the county colours. He missed his club's first ever county championship win in October 2003 through injury but was back for the All-Ireland Final setback against Kerry champions An Ghaeltacht the following March, and finally got his medal in 2011, six weeks after collecting his All-Ireland one.

CANAVAN, PAT (St Vincent's): Defender, born 4 September 1960. On the minor team in both 1977 and 1978 (he won a provincial medal in the latter year but lost out to Cork in the All-Ireland Final), he was on the Under-21 side in 1979 and made his senior debut in October of that year in a league loss to Kerry at Austin Stack Park in Tralee. His first Championship outing was when he came on as a sub in a Leinster quarter-final win over Laois at O'Connor Park in Tullamore in June 1980 and won a hat-trick of provincial medals from 1983 and played in the All-Ireland Finals in those same years, beating Galway in the first but losing out to Kerry in the other two. He won an All-Star award in 1983 and county championship medals in 1981 and 1984, winning a Leinster medal in the latter year only to be beaten in the All-Ireland Final the following spring by Kerry and Munster champions Castleisland. His last appearance in the county colours — his 48th at senior level — was in the Leinster Final defeat to Meath in July 1986.

CAREY, PADDY (O'Toole's): Defender. Made his debut in a provincial quarter-final loss to Louth at Shamrock Lodge in Drogheda in September 1918, was on the team on Bloody Sunday in November 1920 as well as the side beaten by Tipperary in the All-Ireland Final of the same year, a game that was not actually played until June of two years later. One of the backbones of the three-in-a-row side that won the Championships of 1921, 1922 — when he was captain — and 1923, he tasted defeat again when on the losing side to Kerry in the delayed final of 1924. Apart from five consecutive provincial medals from 1920, he won nine county titles (1918, 1919, 1920, 1922, 1923, 1924, 1925, 1926, 1928) and played his 31st and final game in the Leinster Final loss to Kildare in July 1928.

CARR, TOMMY (Lucan Sarsfields): Defender, born 2 May 1961. Raised partly in Holycross, he played with Tipperary in the Centenary Championship in 1984 but declared for his native Dublin the following year. Originally a half forward, he scored 1-3 on his debut in a provincial quarter-final defeat of Wexford at Wexford Park in June 1985 but inside two years was converted to the right half back position by then Dublin boss Gerry McCaul, although he would retain an attacking style throughout his career and would end up with a 4-56 scoring tally. He was on the teams that won the National League in 1991 and 1993 (he was captain for the latter success) and those beaten by Kerry and Donegal in the All-Ireland Finals of 1985 and 1992, respectively, but he did win a Celtic Cross as a panellist in 1995. An All-Star award winner in 1991, he managed Dublin between 1999 and 2001 when they were beaten in the Leinster Final each year, the first and last time by Meath and the second by Kildare following a replay and subsequently had spells as manager of the Roscommon and Cavan teams. His brother Declan won All-Ireland hurling medals with Tipperary in 1989 and 1991, captaining the side on the latter occasion.

CASEY, BILL (Na Fianna): Defender. Won a provincial minor medal in 1961 — when Dublin were beaten 1-10 to 2-6 by Mayo in the All-Ireland semi-final in August — and made his senior debut that November when coming on as a sub in a league loss to Louth at St. Brigid's Park in Dundalk. He missed the following year's provincial decider through injury but in 1963 won both Leinster and All-Ireland medals and added a second Leinster title two years later. His 76th and final appearance was in a provincial semi-final loss to Kildare at Pairc Tailteann in Navan in July 1972, when he scored 1-1. An international basketballer, he also represented Dublin at handball.

CASEY, PAUL (Lucan Sarsfields): Defender, born 14 October 1981. Won a provincial medal — as captain — at minor in 1999 (when the All-Ireland semi-final was lost to Down following a replay) and repeated the achievement at Under-21 level three years later (when losing out to Galway in the All-Ireland decider). He made his senior debut a month before that latter campaign started, in a league victory over Donegal at Parnell Park in February, and got his first Championship outing in a Leinster quarter-final defeat of Wexford at Cullen Park in Carlow on the first day of June. Six weeks later he won the first of four provincials medals on the field of play (2006, 2007 and 2008 being the others) to go with three won from the dugout (2005, 2009 and 2011). His 79th and final appearance was in a league draw with Galway at Salthill in April 2011.

CHARLEMONT, GEORGE (Young Irelands): Goalkeeper, born Enniskerry 16 September 1873. Made his debut in a provincial semi-final win over Kildare in October 1891 and would remain in position as Dublin won the delayed All-Irelands of 1891, 1892 and 1894 while opting out of the 1893 competition. He won county medals with Young Irelands in 1891, 1892, 1894 and 1896 and died from tuberculosis on 13 August 1907, five weeks before his 34th birthday.

CHRISTIE, PADDY (Ballymun Kickhams): Defender. Made his senior debut in a league defeat to Louth in Dundalk in February 1996 and was on the losing side again in his first Championship outing, against Meath in a Leinster quarter-final clash at Croke Park in June of the following year. He also suffered defeats in three successive provincial finals from 1999 but finally collected a medal — as well as an All-Star award — in 2002 and then won a second three years later. He made 97 appearances in all, the last one being in an All-Ireland semi-final draw with Tyrone in August 2005 (Dublin losing the replay).

CLARKE, PAUL (Whitehall Colmcille): Midfielder, born 1966. Captained the team that won the All-Ireland Minor Championships in 1984 — scoring 0-22 in the five games of the campaign — and made the first of 91 senior appearances in a league win over Donegal at Croke Park in November of the following year. Won a quartet of provincial medals (1989, 1992, 1994, 1995), an All-Ireland and an All-Star in the latter year, and a pair of National Leagues in 1991 and 1993. His last outing was in a losing provincial quarter-final against Meath in Croke Park in June 1997 and he finished his career with a scoring contribution of 6-90.

CLUXTON, STEPHEN (Parnells): Goalkeeper, born 17 December 1981. Won a provincial minor medal in 1999 — when Dublin lost out to Down in the All-Ireland semi-final after a replay — and three years later was on the side beaten by Galway in the All-Ireland Under-21 Final, having made his senior debut in a Leinster quarter-final defeat of Longford at Croke Park in May of the previous year. Won the first of a remarkable baker's dozen provincial medals in 2002, (2005, 2006, 2007, 2008, 2009, 2011, 2012, 2013, 2014, 2015, 2016 and 2017 being the others), five All-Irelands (2011, 2013, 2015, 2016 and 2017), four National Leagues (in succession from 2013) and five All-Stars (2002, 2006, 2007, 2011, 2013) as well as being nominated on four other occasions. In mid 2010 he began taking long range frees and famously scored the winning point from a last gasp 40 metre free when Dublin edged Kerry 1-12 to 1-11 in the All-Ireland Final in 2011; as of the conclusion of the 2017 he had scored 0-66, including six points in a 1-16 to 0-14 win over Cork in an All-Ireland quarter-final in 2013. In September 2016 he became the first man to lift the Sam Maguire Cup for a third time and a year later he uniquely captained an All-Ireland football title winning team for the fourth time, extending the record he had previously shared with Jack Kennedy from Dublin (1891, 1892, 1894) and Sean O'Kennedy from Wexford (1915, 1916, 1917).

CONNOLLY, DIARMUID (St. Vincent's): Forward, born 7 July 1987. A minor in both 2004 and 2005 — when he scored 2-10 in four games — and on Under-21 teams that fell at the first hurdle in 2006 and again in 2007, he made his senior debut in a one point league loss to Tyrone at Croke Park in February 2007 and had his first Championship outing in a provincial quarter-final win over Meath at the same venue four months later. He would go on to win five All-Irelands (2011, 2013, 2015, 2016 and 2017) and the four National Leagues, all in succession from 2013. A prolific scorer (he hit 3-3 in league games against Mayo in March 2011 and against Armagh a year almost to the very day later, he won All-Star awards in 2014 and 2016. The winner of five county medals (2007, 2013, 2014, 2016, 2017) as well as provincial titles in the same years, he won All-Ireland Club Championships in both 2008 and 2014, memorably scoring 2-5 from play on the latter occasion when St. Vincent's were 4-12 to 2-11 winners over Mayo and Connacht champions Castlebar Mitchels. He also won a Leinster Under-21 hurling title in 2007, when Dublin were beaten by Cork in the All-Ireland Final.

CONROY, TOMMY (St Vincent's): Forward, born 1963. Won a Leinster minor medal in 1981; Dublin were beaten by Derry in the All-Ireland semi-final and in February 1983 he was again on the losing side against the same opposition on his senior debut, in a league clash at Wolfe Tone Park in Bellaghy. Seven months and eight games later he was the possessor of Leinster and All-Ireland medals at the age of 20. The following year he won both a second provincial title and his one and only county medal (St. Vincent's would go on to lose the All-Ireland Final to Kerry and Munster champions Catleisland by a point and in 1985, although Dublin were beaten in the All-Ireland decider by Kerry for a second year in a row, he had the consolation of picking up an All-Star award. His 55th and final outing came in a league victory over Kerry at Croke Park in February 1990 and he subsequently went on to manage St. Vincent's, guiding them to an All-Ireland success in 2014.

COOPER, JONNY (Na Fianna): Defender, born 4 November 1989. The winner of an All-Ireland medal at junior level in 2008, he added an Under-21 one two years later and made his senior debut when coming on as a late sub and scoring two points in nine minutes in a league win over Armagh at Croke Park in March 2012. His debut in the Championship came three months later in a Leinster quarter-final win over Louth — again as a sub — but he played no further part in that particular campaign. By the following year, though, he was an automatic first choice and played all but 46 minutes of 15 games as Dublin completed a National League and Championship double. Over the next three years Cooper — the recipient of an All-Star award in 2016 — figured in all but two of the 46 matches Dublin played in winning another league title in 2014 and completing further National League and Championship doubles in 2015 and 2016. A fourth senior All-Ireland in 2017 brought his total in all grades to six, a Dublin record he shares with Denis Bastick, Michael Fitzsimons, Eoghan O'Gara, James McCarthy, Cormac Costello.

COSGROVE, RAY (Kilmacud Crokes): Forward. Made his senior debut in a league win over Armagh at Parnell Park in November 1998 and ten months later had his first outing in the Championship when coming on as a sub in the provincial final loss to Meath but had to wait two full seasons for any further recognition. By then the National League had been moved into the calendar year and that one, 2002, was a glory one for Cosgrove; he scored 2-28 in the league and 6-23 in the Championship as Dublin made it as far as the All-Ireland semi-final before bowing out to Armagh and finished the season with an All-Star award. He won a second provincial title in 2006, a trio of county medals (1998, 2004, 2005) and a Leinster Club Championship in 2006. His final outing was as a sub in the All-Ireland semi-final loss to Kerry in August 2007, ending his career with a scoring haul of 9-87 from 55 appearances.

COSTELLO, CORMAC (Whitehall Colmcille): Forward, born 18 July 1994. Uniquely completed a hat-trick of All-Ireland medals in different grades while still in his teens; winning at minor in 2012 (when he scored 3-4 in the provincial final against Meath and 5-26 in the seven match campaign), as a senior panellist the following year (when he had one appearance as a sub) and, on 3 May 2014, as one of the stars of a 1-21 to 3-6 defeat of Roscommon in the Under-21 decider. Other senior medals followed in 2015, 2016 and 2017, and he also was part of the squad that won four successive National League titles from 2013, scoring 1-22 in the course of the 2016 campaign.

CROWLEY, JIM (St Vincent's): Defender, born in New York. He began his inter-county career as a member of the team beaten by Mayo in an All-Ireland Junior Championship semi-final in August 1950, made his senior debut in a drawn league game against

Louth at Croke Park just two months later, had his Championship outing in a Leinster first round win over Offaly at St Conleth's Park in Newbridge the following May, and collected his first medal when coming on as a sub in the Railway Cup Final in March 1952. More medals followed: an All-Ireland in 1958, three National Leagues (1953, 1955, 1958), a similar number of provincial titles (1955, 1958, 1959) and ten county medals (1950, 1951, 1952, 1953, 1954, 1955, 1957, 1958, 1959, 1960). Despite operating at corner or half back — with a few appearances at midfield — throughout his career, he managed to put 4-16 on the scoreboard in 77 outings, the last of which was in the All-Ireland semi-final defeat by Kerry in 1959.

CULLEN, BRYAN (Skerries Harps): Defender, born 7 April 1984. Won a provincial minor medal and reached the All-Ireland Minor Final in 2001 before losing to Tyrone and was still five weeks short of his 18th birthday when he made his Under-21 debut the following year, duplicating his minor feat of winning a Leinster medal and being on the losing side in the All-Ireland Final, this time to Galway. The next year, 2003, he not only won another provincial medal but collected an All-Ireland one as well when Dublin beat Tyrone by 1-12 to 0-7 at Pairc Tailteann in Navan in October, eight months after his senior debut in a league loss to Armagh and four months after his initial Championship outing in a Leinster quarter-final win over Louth at Croke Park. He would win a third provincial Under-21 crown in 2005 (when Down got the better of Dublin in the All-Ireland semi-final) and that same year would win the first of eight Leinster senior medals (the others coming in 2006, 2007, 2008, 2009, 2011, 2012 and 2013). He captained Dublin to All-Ireland victory against Kerry in 2011, won a second Celtic Cross — as a panellist — with the victory over Mayo two years later, and also collected National League medals in 2013 and 2014. He played his 122nd and last senior game for Dublin when coming on as a sub in a provincial quarter-final win over Laois in June 2014.

CULLEN, PADDY (Scoil Ui Conaill): Goalkeeper, born 18 October 1944. Began his inter-county career by captaining Dublin when the beat Kildare by 2-12 to 1-7 in their first ever match — a Leinster quarter-final at St. Conleth's Park in Newbridge — in the inaugural Under-21 Championship in April 1964 ... as centre back. He made his senior debut in a National League semi-final win over Meath at Croke Park almost exactly three years later and then two months further on had his first Championship outing in a 1-6 to 0-8 provincial quarter-final loss to Westmeath at O'Connor Park in Tullamore. He famously, a minute into the second half at a point where Dublin were trailing 1-4 to 0-5, saved a penalty from Liam Sammon as Dublin captured a first All-Ireland in eleven years with an 0-14 to 1-6 victory over Galway in the 1974 final, and four years later would acquire equal notoriety for his part in Mikey Sheehy's exquisitely cheeky goal in Kerry's near record 5-11 to 0-9 hammering of The Dubs in the fourth All-Ireland Final meeting of the arch rivals in five campaigns. In between, he won further All-Irelands in 1976 and 1977, two National Leagues (1976, 1978) and a sixth successive provincial title in 1979. He also won a quartet of All-Star awards (1974, 1976, 1977, 1979) and made his 121st and final appearance in another All-Ireland Final loss to Kerry, in 1979. During his career — which lasted over a dozen years — he kept 49 clean sheets.

CURRAN, PAUL (Thomas Davis): Defender, although he played at midfield and among the forwards on occasions. On the team beaten by Kildare in the provincial minor final in 1987, he made his senior debut in a Leinster quarter-final victory over the same opposition two years later, going on to win the first of half a dozen provincial titles (1992, 1993, 1994, 1995 and 2002 being the others). Won two National Leagues (1991, 1993) and an All-Ireland in 1995, after defeats against Donegal in 1992 and Down in 1994. The winner of a hat-trick of county medals from 1989, provincial club titles in 1990 and 1991, and was on the team beaten by Kerry champions Dr Crokes in the finals of the All-Ireland Club Championship in 1992. He won All-Star awards in 1992, 1995 — when he was also named Footballer of the Year — and 1996 and the last of his 132 appearances (the eighth highest of all-time) was when coming on as a sub in an All-Ireland quarter-final win over Donegal at Croke Park in August 2002. A decade later he managed the Ballymun Kickhams side that won the county title and reached the All-Ireland Final the following year before going down by 2-11 to 2-10 to St. Brigid's from Roscommon. His father, Noel, was full forward on the Meath team which was beaten in the All-Ireland Final by Galway in 1966 but came back to overcome Cork in the decider a year later.

DALY, DARREN (Fingal Ravens): Defender, born 1 March 1987. Won an All-Ireland Junior title in 2008 but had to wait almost five years for his senior debut in a league win over Cork at Croke Park in February 2013 and made his first Championship appearance in a provincial quarter-final win over Westmeath at the same venue four months later. Went on to win All-Ireland medals when coming on as a sub in the finals of 2013, 2015 and 2016 and won a fourth medal as a panellist in 2017. He also won four successive National League titles from 2013.

DAVEY, GERRY (Clanna Gael): Forward. Made his debut in a league victory over Wicklow at Croke Park in December 1962 — scoring 1-1 — and got his first Championship outing in a provincial quarter-final win over Meath at the same venue the following June, going on to score the decisive goal when Dublin beat Galway by 1-9 to 0-10 in the All-Ireland Final three months later. He made 52 senior appearance in all, the last of them when part of a team beaten by Kildare in a Leinster semi-final, again at Croke Park. After final disappointments in 1962 and the following year, he finally won a county medal in 1968.

DEEGAN, MICK (Erin's Isle): Defender. After winning Leinster and All-Ireland medals at minor level in 1982, he made his senior debut in a league loss to Longford at Croke Park in October 1985. He had two more outings before Christmas but then had to wait more than two and a half years for his next call-up, a Championship debut in a provincial semi-final win at Cusack Park in Mullingar in June 1988, again against Longford. In a career that lasted over a dozen years and totalled 96 appearances, he won an All-Ireland medal in 1995 after being on the losing side in 1992 and 1994, two National Leagues (1991, 1993) and Leinster medals in 1989, 1992, 1994 and 1995 after missing the provincial semi-final and final in 1994 through injury. Winner of an All-Star award in 1991, he won county titles in 1993 and 1997 while being on the losing side in each of the three years in between.

DEMPSEY, JACK (Bray Emmets): Defender, born Wexford in 1878. Made his debut at the start of the 1902 campaign — played the following year — and went on to captain the team to All-Ireland success. He was also on the teams that won the Championships of 1906 and 1907 and won his only county title with Bray Emmets — who were then playing in the Dublin Championship in 1901. He died from tuberculosis on 10 December 1913, aged 35.

DOHERTY, SEAN (Ballyboden St Enda's): A native of Wicklow, he made his debut in a league win over Monaghan at Emmet Park in Carrickmacross in October 1969 and his 105th and final appearance in a Leinster semi-final victory over Wicklow at St Conleth's Park in Newbridge in July 1979, In the decade in between he won a trio of All-Irelands (1974, 1976, 1977, the first as captain), two National Leagues (1976, 1978), five consecutive provincial crowns from 1974 and an All-Star in 1974.

DOWNEY, PADDY (St Brigid's): Midfielder. Made just 29 senior appearances in an eight year senior career, yet finished with two All-Ireland medals and a National League one. His first outing was in a league win over Wicklow at the County Ground in Aughrim in November 1956 and his Championship debut came the following June in a provincial quarter-final win over Longford at Cusack Park in Mullingar. The next year, 1958, he won a National League medal in April when Dublin beat Mayo and an All-Ireland one five months later against Derry. Five years later he won a second All-Ireland when Galway were the beaten finalists; the unique thing about his two Celtic Crosses is that they were both won when he came on as a substitute, for Joe Timmons in the first instance and for Paddy Holden in the second. In fact, he only ever played seven Championship games throughout his career (two as a sub), and his final appearance was in a league win over Laois at Croke Park in November 1964.

DOYLE, BOBBY (St Vincent's): Forward, born 7 October 1949. Made hut in a league defeat to Offaly at Croke Park in October 1972 and almost immediately became a permanent fixture on the team for the next seven seasons. He won every possible honour in the game at both county and club level; three All-Irelands (1974, 1976, 1977), two National Leagues (1976, 1978), six provincial titles in succession (1974, 1975, 1976, 1977, 1978, 1979), two All-Stars (1976, 1977), half a dozen county medals (1972, 1975, 1976, 1977, 1981, 1984) and an All-Ireland Club Championship in 1976. His final appearance for the county was in a Leinster quarter-final win over Longford at O'Connor Park in

Tullamore in June 1982 and in 87 games he scored 24-85 (including 2-2 in the All-Ireland Final victory over Armagh in 1977), making him jointly the county's eighth most prolific goalscorer ever.

DRUMM, TOMMY (Whitehall Colmcille): Defender, born 22 March 1955. Made his debut in a provincial semi-final win over Laois at O'Connor Park in Tullamore in July 1976, and although relegated to the dugout for the decider, he was recalled for both the All-Ireland semi-final and final wins over, respectively, Galway and Kerry. He won further All-Irelands in 1977 and 1983 (as captain), but missed the triumphant National League decider in 1978 through injury. Apart from five Leinster medals (1976, 1977, 1978, 1979, 1983), he won four All-Star awards (1977, 1978, 1979, 1983) and, because of business commitments, retired fron inter-county football following the All-Ireland Final defeat by Kerry in 1984, his 82nd senior appearance.

DUFF, CIARAN (Fingallians): Forward, born 14 February 1961. On the teams that lost the All-Ireland Minor Final to Mayo in 1978 and beat Kerry in the following year's decider, he made his senior debut in a league win over Cork at Croke Park just two months after that latter success. Scored in all seven matches — 2-13 in total — in the successful Championship campaign in 1983 (when he was one of three Dublin players sent off in the final against Galway), but tasted defeat against Kerry in the following two deciders, after having also been on the side beaten by Cork in the Under-21 Final in 1980. Aside from 1983, he won three further provincial medals (1984, 1985, 1988), two National Leagues (1987, 1991), four successive Railway Cups from 1985, and All-Star awards in 1987 and again the following year. In a career that lasted over a dozen years, he scored a total of 22-227 in 118 games, the last of which was a league tie against Armagh at Croke Park in November 1981, when he bowed out with three points in a 2-10 to 1-8 victory.

FALLON, PADDY (Geraldines): Goalkeeper. Made his debut in a Leinster quarter-final win over Meath at Jones's Road in September 1908 and the following August collected an All-Ireland medal when Dublin beat London in a delayed final: Fallon kept a clean sheet throughout the six match campaign in which Dublin conceded and aggregate of just 20 points, a record average of just three and a third per game. He won three provincial titles (1908, 1915, 1921) and five county ones (1908, 1910, 1914, 1915, 1917) and capped his near decade and a half long career with, in his 36th and last appearance, keeping his 18th clean sheet in the All-Ireland Final of 1921. That game wasn't played until 17 June 1923, which meant Fallon went 13 years and 320 days between his All-Ireland wins. His son Willie scored the decisive goal when Dublin beat Mayo by 1-3 to 0-5 in the All-Ireland Minor Final in 1930.

FARNAN, PADDY (St Vincent's): Forward. Won an All-Ireland Minor Championship medal in 1954 (scoring the second goal in a 3-3 to 1-8 defeat of Kerry), made his senior debut in a league win over Louth at Croke Park in March 1958, and three games and two months later had himself a National League medal. Within just over another five months he had added first Leinster and then All-Ireland honours and the following year won a second provincial title and a Railway Cup. His last game for Dublin was in an All-Ireland semi-final loss to Kerry in August 1962 — finishing his inter-county career with 7-28 from 42 games — and won a fifth consecutive county title three months later.

FARRELL, DESSIE (Na Fianna): Forward. As a minor in 1988 he scored 8-7 in four games — including four goals in a quarter-final against New York — as Dublin won the Leinster title before going down to Kerry in the All-Ireland Final. He scored the only goal of the game on his debut when Dublin beat Mayo by 1-9 to 0-10 at MacHale Park in Castlebar in February 1992 and three months later had his first Championship outing in a provincial first round win over O'Connor Park in Tullamore. He won a National League as a squad member in 1993 and an All-Ireland one two years later, scoring four points in a 1-10 to 0-12 defeat of Tyrone, a performance that clinched an All-Star award for him. In his 103 senior games he scored 12-117 and won three successive county medals from 1999, reaching the All-Ireland Final in that first campaign. A founder member of the GPA (Gaelic Players Association) in 1999, he served as its CEO from 2003 until stepping down in late 2016. He managed Dublin to an All-Ireland Minor Championship in 2012 and to Under-21 triumphs in 2014 and 2017. A keen hockey player throughout his active career, he represented Ireland at Under-21 level and is a first cousin and Everton and Ireland soccer star Seamus Coleman.

FENTON, BRIAN (Raheny): Midfielder, born 2 March 1993. Won an Under-21 medal in 2014 and had his first senior outing when coming on as a sub in a league loss to Kerry at Fitzgerald Stadium in Killarney in March 2015, his Championship debut coming the following June in a provincial quarter-final win over Longford at Croke Park. He played a central role in Dublin's successive National League and Championship doubles in 2015 and 2016, winning an All-Star award each year, and missed just three games in Dublin's record 36 match unbeaten run between March 2015 and their league final defeat by Kerry in April 2017. Won a third senior All-Ireland in 2017, by the end of which campaign he had played 40 senior competitive games for Dublin and had been on the losing side just twice; on his debut and in the league final of 2017, also against the Kingdom.

FERGUSON, DES (St Vincent's): Forward, born in Newcastle, Co. Down but brought to Dublin as a three-year-old child. Found the net in each of Dublin's five matches when runners-up to a Tyrone team that included one Barney Eastwood in the All-Ireland Minor Championship in 1948, made his first senior appearance in the Leinster first round loss to Kildare in Cusack Park in Mullingar in May 1950, and his 101st and last almost a decade and a half later in a league games against Wicklow in November 1964. In between, he won two All-Irelands (1958, 1963), three National Leagues (1953, 1955, 1958), a quartet of provincial titles (1955, 1958, 1969, 1963), and put 20-58 on the scoreboard. Living in Meath by the time of Dublin's defeat by Offaly in the Leinster semi-final in June 1960, he retired from the inter-county scene shortly afterwards but exactly three years later he was persuaded to return by Kevin Heffernan — a selector at the time — on the eve of the provincial semi-final against Kildare and scored 1-2... and just 91 days later collected his second All-Ireland medal. Heffernan, of course, would use his persuasive powers again over a decade later when successfully luring Jimmy Keaveney out of retirement. Known throughout the game as 'Snitchy', Ferguson actually beats Heffernan 22-21 in county medals with 13 in football (1949, 1950, 1951, 1952, 1953, 1954, 1955, 1957, 1958, 1959, 1960, 1962, 1964), seven in hurling (1953, 1954, 1955, 1957, 1960, 1962, 1964) and then, after moving first to Oldcastle and then to Kells to take up teaching positions, he added a pair of Meath medals with Gaeil Colmcille in 1966 and 1968 — and all that despite missing the successful 1961 decider through injury! One of the top dual stars of his era, he was a member of the Dublin hurling teams that won Leinster titles in 1952 and 1961 but lost the All-Ireland deciders to Cork and Tipperary, respectively. He and his Dublin born son Terry share a record entirely unique in the annals of the GAA: not only did they win All-Ireland medals with different counties but, with Terry being on the successful Meath sides of 1987 and 1988, neither won their medals with the county in which they were born.

FITZGERALD, JOE (Geraldines): Midfielder, born in Ventry. Had one of the more sporadic careers with the county, playing just 16 games spread over half a dozen seasons. Made his debut in a provincial first round replay win over Louth at Croke Park in May 1941. He held his place for the semi-final and final wins over Kildare and Carlow, respectively, but was dropped for the All-Ireland semi-finals — a draw and subsequent loss — against Kerry. Recalled for the 1941/42 league campaign, he captained the team to Leinster and All-Ireland Final wins over first Carlow and then Galway. The winner of county titles in 1941 and 1942, his final appearance for Dublin was in a league win over Wicklow at Croke Park in March 1946.

FITZSIMONS, MICHAEL (Cuala): Defender, born 9 April 1989. An All-Ireland winner at junior in 2010, he had his first senior outing in a league win over Derry at Parnell Park in February of that year and made his Championship debut at senior level in a provincial quarter final win over Wexford four months later. The winner of six successive Leinster titles from 2010, he won All-Ireland medals in 2011, 2013 (as a panellist), 2015, 2016 and 2017 and a quartet of consecutive National Leagues from 2013.

FLYNN, PASCAL (St Mary's): Goalkeeper. He started his inter-county career in a league win over Laois at O'Toole Park in October 1958, made his Championship debut in a Leinster quarter-final defeat of Longford at Cusack Park in Mullingar in May 1960, and was on the All-Ireland winning team three years later. He won a trio of provincial medals (1962, 1963, 1965, played his last game for the county in the All-Ireland semi-final loss to Kerry in 1965, and kept 20 clean sheets in 61 appearances.

FLYNN, PAUL (Fingallians): Forward, born 8 July 1986. His first senior appearance was a league tie against Westmeath at Parnell Park in February 2008 when he scored the crucial goal in a 1-7 to 1-5 win and four months later he made his Championship debut in a provincial semi-final victory over the same opposition at Croke Park. He won nine Leinster medals (2008, 2009, 2011, 2012, 2013, 2014, 2015, 2016, 2017), five All-Irelands (2011, 2013, 2015, 2016, 2017), four National Leagues (2013, 2014, 2015, 2016) and made history by being the first Dublin footballer to win four successive All-Star awards (2011, 2012, 2013, 2014), the first player from any county to do so since the late Páidí Ó Sé in 1984. As of the end of the 2017 season, he made 111 appearances and scored 12-81.

FOLEY, DES (St Vincent's): Midfielder, born 12 September 1940. After winning All-Ireland minor medals in 1956 — just 25 days past his 16th birthday — and 1958 (as captain), he made his senior debut in a National League game against Offaly in November of the latter year, 65 days after he turned 18. He captained the All-Ireland winning team of 1963 and two years later won a second provincial medal when scoring the only goal of his 62 game inter-county career in the Leinster Final win over Long-ford, and in 1963 and again in 1965 he won a Cu Chulainn award, the forerunner of the All-Stars. A dual player, he famously played in and won the Railway Cup final in both codes on St Patrick's Day 1962, won a quartet of county hurling titles (1960, 1962, 1964, 1967), and was on the Dublin team that in 1961 won the Leinster crown and was pipped (0-16 to 1-12) by Tipperary in the All-Ireland Final. Despite missing the 1962, 966 and 1970 finals through injury, he won seven football county titles (1959, 1960, 1961, 1962, 1964, 1967, 1971, 1972), the first of them coming just five months after he captained St Joseph's (Fairview) to the distinction of being the first Dublin winners of the All-Ireland Senior Colleges Championship. He made his final appearance for Dublin in their Leinster semi-final loss to Kildare at Dr Cullen Park in Carlow in June 1969, but continued to play with St Vincents for a further four years. He subsequently served as a Fianna Fail TD for Dublin North County and died on 5 February 1995, aged 54.

FOLEY, LAR (St Vincent's): Defender, born 23 November 1938. Began his inter-county career by winning successive All-Ireland minor titles in 1955 and 1956, partnering his brother Des at midfield in the second decider and also captaining the team. Made his senior debut in the 1957 provincial final loss to eventual All-Ireland champions Louth but, by now converted to a defender, won both a National League and an All-Ireland the following year and won a second Celtic Cross in 1963 (when he was named Texaco Footballer of the Year). In his 70 senior appearance with The Dubs, he also won a quartet of provincial titles (1958, 1959, 1962, 1963) and, at club level, eleven county medals (1957, 1958, 1959, 1960, 1961, 1962, 1964, 1966, 1967, 1971, 1972). A noted dual player, he won a quartet of county hurling titles (1957, 1960, 1962, 1964) and was one of the stars of the Dublin team that, after conceding two late frees, lost the All-Ireland Final of 1961 to Tipperary by a single point, 0-16 to 1-12. His last inter-county appearance was in a provincial football quarter-final loss to Longford in O'Connor Park in Tullamore in June 1968. He died on 4 May 2003, aged 64.

FORAN, DAVID (Thomas Davis): Defender. Made his debut in a Leinster quarter-final win over Louth at Pairc Tailteann in Navan in June 1979 and was a regular for the next three seasons before falling out of favour. His role in leading Thomas Davis to a hat-trick of county titles from 1989 led to a separate second inter-county career, being recalled after an absence of more than half a dozen years; indeed, his Championship return was even more remarkable — his tenth appearance coming just a month short of eight years after his ninth. Apart from 1979, he won further provincial titles in 1989 and 1992 and a National League in 1991 and made his 66th and last appearance when coming on as a sub in a Leinster quarter-final defeat of Westmeath at Tullamore in June 1993, three days and 14 years after his debut.

FOX, NOEL (St. Vincent's): Forward. A minor for three years from 1958 and on the winning All-Ireland teams in his first and third seasons (he scored 2-19 in a dozen games in the grade), his senior debut came when he came on as a sub in the All-Ireland semi-final loss to Kerry in August 1959. On the team that beat Galway in the All-Ireland Final in 1963, he ended his career as he began it, with an All-Ireland semi-final defeat to Kerry in July of the following year. He won half a dozen county medals (1959, 1960, 1961, 1962, 1964, 1966).

FREANEY, OLLIE (St Vincent's): Forward, born 16 November 1928. Won an All-Ireland minor medal in 1945 and made his senior debut in a league win over Louth at Croke Park in December 1947, his first outing in the Championship coming in a provincial quarter-final loss to the same opposition at the same venue six months later. In the course of scoring 23-242 in 90 competitive games for the county, he won an All-Ireland in 1958 (scoring eight points in the final win over Derry), three National Leagues (1953, 1955, 1958), three Leinster titles (1955, 1958, 1959), five Railway Cups (1952, 1953, 1954, 1955, 1959) and ten county medals (1949, 1950, 1951, 1952, 1953, 1954, 1955, 1957, 1958, 1959). The scorer of a remarkable goal from a 14 yard free — despite the fact that the goalmouth was lined with half a dozen defenders — in the upset defeat by Kerry in the All-Ireland Final in 1955, he played is final game for Dublin in another loss to the Kingdom in the All-Ireland semi-final four years later and announced his complete retirement immediately after the county final eight weeks later. He died suddenly at the age of 62 while on a family holiday in Donegal on 27 September 1991.

GALVIN, KEITH (St. Sylvester's): Defender, born 3 April 1975. A minor in 1993 and an Under-21 in both 1995 and 1996, he made his senior debut in between those latter two call-ups, in a provincial quarter-final win over Louth at Pairc Tailteann in Navan in June 1995. He retained his place throughout successful Leinster and All-Ireland campaigns and the following year helped his club to their first ever county title. His 25th and last appearance was in a provincial final defeat by Meath at Croke Park in August 1999.

GALVIN, MICK (Na Fianna): Forward. Made his debut when coming on as a sub in a league win over Armagh at Croke Park in December 1986 and had his first Championship outing in a Leinster quarter-final defeat of Westmeath at the same venue seven months later. After being on the losing side in two All-Ireland Finals, against Donegal in 1992 and Down two years later, he finally won a Celtic Cross when part of the victorious Dublin team against Tyrone in 1995. In his decade long career he won three National Leagues (1987, 1991, 1993, the latter as an unused sub) and five provincial medals (1989, 1992, 1993, 1994, 1995) and made his 75th and last appearance in a Leinster quarter-final loss to Meath at Croke Park in June 1997. He began his club career with St. Oliver Plunkett's but later transferred to Na Fianna with whom he won a hat-trick of county titles from 1999, the first two as a player and the last as manager.

GAVIN, JIM (Round Towers): Forward, born 1 July 1971. A minor in 1989 when Dublin fell 0-8 to 0-7 to Kildare at the first hurdle, he made his senior debut in a league win over Louth at Croke Park in November 1992 and had his first Championship outing in a provincial first round victory over Wexford at Wexford Park the following May. He won an All-Ireland medal in 1995 (scoring a point in a 1-10 to 0-12 win over Tyrone, a National League in 1993, and three successive provincial medals in a row from the same year. Within a year of his own retirement as a player he guided Dublin to Leinster and All-Ireland Under-21 Championships at trainer, a feat he would repeat as manager in both 2010 and 2012. At the end of that latter year he succeeded Pat Gilroy as manager of the senior squad and, with four All-Irelands and a similar number of National Leagues since then, has proved himself the county's most successful manager ever in terms of major trophies won.

GILROY, PAT (St. Vincent's): Forward, born 3 November 1971. Made his senior debut in a provincial first round win over Offaly at O'Connor Park in Tullamore in May 1992 and two months later won the first of four consecutive Leinster medals. He won a National League medal the following year, was on the losing side in the All-Ireland Final against Down in 1994 but fared better the next year, coming on as a sub in the victory over Tyrone. His final game was in November 1997 when he found the net in a league victory over Cavan at Parnell Park. He won county and provincial club medal in late 2007 and was full forward on the St. Vincent's team that beat Cork and Munster champions Nemo Rangers by 1-11 to 0-13 in the All-Ireland Final the following St. Patrick's Day. His father Jackie, who died in 2007, won county medals with St. Vincent's in 1962 and 1964 and in a dozen appearances for Dublin between November 1962 and March 1965 scored 5-7, was a member of the All-Ireland winning squad in 1963 and won a National League 'home' medal the following year.

GOGARTY, PAT (Raheny): Forward. Won a Leinster minor medal in 1968 and was on the Under-21 side for the following two years; he made his senior debut when coming on as a sub in a league win over Armagh at Croke Park in November 1969 and had two further outings in that campaign but then had to wait over two and a half years for his next appearance, scoring 1-1 in a 3-6 to 1-8 league win over Wexford at Croke Park in October 1973. He won Leinster and All-Ireland medals as a panellist in 1974 (coming on as a sub in the provincial final win over Meath), was on the National League winning side in 1976 and later that year the sides that again completed the Leinster and All-Ireland double. He won a second National League medal — as a sub — in 1978 and made his final appearance was in a league win over Cork at Pairc Ui Chaoimh in December of that year. He scored 6-43 in his 42 senior appearances and his only county final was in 1970 when Raheny were beaten by 1-11 to 1-8 by St. Vincent's.

GOGGINS, COMAN (Ballinteer St. John's): Defender. A member of the junior squad in 1998 and the following year, he made the first of 74 senior appearances in a Leinster quarter-final victory over Wexford at Croke Park in June 2000. He won a quartet of provincial medals (2002, 2005, 2006 and 2007, the latter as a panellist with just one appearance as a sub) and an All-Star award in 2001, despite the fact that Dublin could only finish fifth in the league, lost the provincial final to Meath and were ousted from the All-Ireland series by Kerry at the quarter-final stage. His 74th and last senior appearance was when coming on as a sub in a Leinster quarter-final win over Offaly at Croke Park in June 2007 and he announced his retirement the following January.

GRACE, JACK (Kickhams): Born in Tullaroan, 8 February 1884. Was just five months past his 19th birthday when he made his debut in the semi-final of the delayed Championship for 1901 in July 1903. He went on to All-Ireland success in that campaign and also in those for 1902, 1906, 1907 — being captain in the last two seasons — and in 1909, thereby becoming the first man in history to win five All-Ireland medals. Dublin also triumphed in the Championship for 1908 but, having played up to the semi-final, he missed the final victory over London through injury and also suffered All-Ireland disappointment in hurling, being on the Dublin sides that lost the finals of 1902, 1906 and 1908. He won four successive county titles with Kickhams from 1904 and a fifth in 1912. He died of pneumonia in Jervis St. hospital on 9 March 1915, aged 31, and is buried in Ballinamara Cemetery in Kilkenny.

GRACE, PIERCE (Kickhams): Forward, born in Tullaroan, born 9 September 1885. A brother of Jack, he made his debut in the Leinster Final of 1906 — played a year later — and won All-Ireland medals for that campaign and the next, both of which were captained by his sibling. He won a county medal with Kickhams in 1907 but early the following year returned to Kilkenny with whom he won All-Ireland hurling medals in 1911, 1912, and 1913, making him still the only player to win more than one All-Ireland medal in both football and hurling (he was also on the Dublin side beaten by Tipperary in a replay of the 1908 hurling final). He died at his Kilkenny home on 4 October 1966, aged 71, and is buried in St Kieran's Cemetery. A third brother, Dick, won All-Ireland hurling medals with Kilkenny in 1909, 1911, 1912, 1913 and 1922 — the first when coming on as a

19-year-old sub — and was also on the losing sides in 1916 and again a decade later when he was past his 36thbirthday.

GUIRY, BILL (Kickhams): Midfielder. Born in Limerick, he won two county medals there with Commercials and was on the Limerick team that beat Dublin by 1-5 to 0-7 in the All-Ireland Final of 1896, played on 6 February 1898. Shortly afterwards he moved to Dublin and on 5 February 1899 won a second All-Ireland medal when scoring two goals and a point for Dublin in their 2-6 to 0-2 victory over Cork in the final of the Championship for 1897. He won a county medal with Kickhams for that same year and was in the sides beaten in the following four finals.

HANAHOE, TONY (St Vincent's): Forward, born 29 April 1945. On the side beaten by Westmeath in the provincial minor final at O'Connor Park in Tullamore in 1963, he made his senior debut in a league win over Offaly at Croke Park in February 1965 but his career in the top grade really did not begin until he was selected for an ultimately losing Leinster first round tie against Longford at Cusack Park in Mullingar in May 1970. Thereafter he would win every honour in the game; three All-Irelands 1974, 1976, 1977), two National Leagues (1976, 1978), six successive provincial medals from 1974 and an All-Star in 1976. He captained Dublin in 1976 and again the following year when he was in fact player-manager — making him the county's first back-to-back All-Ireland winning skipper since Jack Grace in 1907 — and played his final game in a league defeat by Kerry at Austin Stack Park in Tralee in October 1979. In an inter-county career that lasted almost a decade and a half (but included a more than five year gap as he concentrated on his legal studies), he scored 21-74 in 90 games, while in a club career that spanned over two decades he won ten county titles (1964, 1966, 1967, 1970, 1971, 1972, 1975, 1977, 1981, 1984, missing the 1976 final through injury) and three provincial medals, culminating in victory in the All-Ireland Club Championship in 1976 when, as captain, he scored two goals in the final win over Roscommon Gaels.

HARGAN, GERRY (Ballymun Kickhams): Defender. The first of his 111 senior appearances came in a league win over Kerry at Austin Stack Park in Tralee in November 1982, and his Championship debut followed in a provincial quarter-final draw with Meath at Croke Park the following June; Dublin won the replay and within ten months of his debut Hargan had won Leinster and All-Ireland meals. Four more provincial titles followed (1984, 1985, 1989, 1992), a National League medal in 1987, and All-Star awards in 1985 and 1989. At club level, he won county championship medals in 1982 and 1985.

HARRIS, VAL (Isles of the Sea): Forward, born 13 June 1884. Played just four games with the county, scoring in each one; he made his debut in the Leinster Final of 1901 with three points against Wexford and then added one in each of the three remaining marches of the All-Ireland winning campaign, against Antrim in the semi-final, Cork in the 'home' final, and London in the decider proper. All his appearances were actually in

1903 and immediately after the victory over London he switched to soccer, signing with Shelbourne, and in 1906 added an Irish Cup medal to his All-Ireland one when Shelbourne scored a 2-0 win over Belfast Celtic at Dalymount Park. From the summer of 1908 he spent half a dozen seasons with Everton — making 190 appearances — before returning to Shelbourne, winning a second Irish Cup medal in 1921 and a League of Ireland title five years later. He won 20 international caps, 13 of them with Shelbourne — still a club record.

HAUGHEY, PADRAIG (St Vincent's): Forward, born 10 October 1932. Universally known as Jock and a brother of three-time Taoiseach, Charlie (who came on as a sub for Parnells in their county final victory over Civil Service in 1945), he won a provincial medal at junior level in 1954 and made his senior debut in a league win over Roscommon at the Sportsfield in Knockcroghery in February of the following year, going on to earn a winner's medal in the competition and then being a member of the side shocked by Kerry in the All-Ireland Final. Three years later, in 1958, he was part of a National League double. The winner of half a dozen county titles (1954, 1955, 1958, 1959, 1960, 1961), the last of his three dozen appearances was in a league loss to Offaly at Croke Park in October 1960. He died on his 71st birthday in 2003.

HAZLEY, RAY (St Vincent's): Defender. Made his debut in a Leinster semi-final loss to Laois at O'Connor Park in Tullamore in July 1981 and two years later was an ever present on the side that beat Offaly in the provincial decider and then Galway in the All-Ireland Final. He broke his right leg in a training session at Parnell Park the Wednesday before the following year's Leinster decider win over Meath and missed the rest of the campaign — including the All-Ireland Final defeat to Kerry — but was back in 1985 for another provincial triumph and another Sam Maguire loss to the Kingdom. His final appearance — his 29th — was in an upset league defeat against Longford at Croke Park in October 1985. He won county championships in 1981 and 1984, following up the latter success with a Leinster title but losing out in the All-Ireland decider to Kerry and Munster champions Castleisland.

HEERY, EAMONN (St. Vincent's): Defender, born 1964. Won an All-Ireland minor medal in 1982 and two years later picked up another provincial medal at Under-21 level as Dublin reached the All-Ireland semi-final only to be beaten by Mayo. Came on as a sub for his senior debut in a league loss to Monaghan at Croke Park in November 1986 — Dublin would go on to win the competition and Heery collected a medal as a squad member — and his first Championship outing came the following June in a provincial quarter-final win over Westmeath. He won further National League honours in 1991 and 1993 (when he was named Man of the Match) and was on the side that lost to Donegal in the All-Ireland Finals of 1992, when he won an All-Star award. A disagreement with management led to him opting out of the county panel for the Championship campaigns of 1994 and 1995 — thereby missing two All-Ireland Finals including a victory over Tyrone in the second — and he only returned when Mickey Whelan had succeeded Pat O'Neill as manager. An attacking left half back, he played exactly 100 games for Dublin, the last being a league victory over Kerry at Parnell Park in March 1998. His only county medal came in 1984 when St. Vincent's went on to capture the provincial title also but were then beaten in the All-Ireland Final by Kerry and Munster champions Castleisland Desmonds.

HEFFERNAN, KEVIN (St Vincent's): Forward, born 20 August 1929. Scored 5-10 in five matches as Dublin to the All-Ireland Minor Final in 1946 before losing to Kerry, bagged 6-3 — including two goals in the final — as London were beaten in the junior final in October 1948, and made his senior debut in a league loss to Louth in Drogheda the following month less than three months after his 19th birthday, contributing 1-2. His senior Championship debut came in a provincial first round win over Longford at Cusack Park in Mullingar in May 1949 and four years later he contributed 3-30 in eight games as Dublin captured the National League for the first time ever with a 4-6 to 0-9 final victory over Cavan. He won another league title in May 1955 but the following September suffered what he always acknowledged as the biggest disappointment of his entire career when hot favourites Dublin were upset by Kerry on an 0-12 to 1-6 scoreline in the All-Ireland Final. Three years later, as captain, he guided The Dubs to a National League and Championship double, beating Kildare in the first final and Derry in the second. He won four provincial titles (1955, 1958, 1959, 1962) and seven Railway Cups (1952, 1953, 1954, 1955, 1959, 1961, 1962) and made his 115th and final senior inter-county appearance in the All-Ireland semi-final loss to Kerry in August 1962 (although he was recalled as an unused sub for the victorious All-Ireland Final against Galway the following year), finishing his career with 52-226 and remains the county's all-time goalscorer as well as its leading scorer in the National League. He was named on both the Team of the Century for the GAA's anniversary in 1984 and the Team of the Millennium a decade and a half later. At club level, Heffernan had one of the most remarkable in the history of the game; after winning 13 titles in 14 years (1949, 1950, 1951, 1952, 1953, 1954, 1955, 1957, 1958, 1959, 1960, 1961, 1962), he announced his retirement but, after turning out in just a quartet of tournament games over the next two and a half years (and also becoming club chairman in the interim), he came on as a second half substitute in the club's 1-12 to 1-5 defeat by U.C.D. in the 1965 final and went on to bring his County Championship medals total to 15 with further successes over the following two years. He also won half a dozen hurling titles (1953, 1954, 1955, 1957, 1959 and 1962) but it was at football that he compiled an unequalled record; in a career total of 79 matches in the county competition — not including an abandoned game in 1954 — he scored a total of 35 goals and 187 points and was only ever on the losing side on three occasions and was part of just five draws. Eight years after his final retirement he embarked on a managerial career that would see him become the county's most famous mentor ever, guiding the team to All-Ireland success in 1974 and then a National League and Championship double two years later before suddenly stepping down and handing the reins over to Tony Hanahoe as player-manager, the first Dublin occupant of that dual role since Paddy McDonnell almost half a century earlier. After just one season away he returned to guide the squad to another National League and Championship double in 1978 and a further All-Ireland in 1983, but before he retired for the second and final time in January 1986 the side had suffered a quartet of All-Ireland Final losses to arch rival Kerry (1978, 1979, 1984, 1985). Conferred with the freedom of Dublin on 17 May 2004, he died on 25 January 2013, aged 83.

HICKEY, DAVID (Raheny): Forward. A minor in 1968 when Dublin won the provincial titles but were beaten by Cork in the All-Ireland semi-final, he was on the Under-21 team for three years — when Dublin won just a single game — from 1970. His senior debut came in a league win against Monaghan at Emmet Park in Carrickmacross in October 1969 — when Sean Doherty and Robbie Kelleher also had their first senior outings — and his first Championship outing was a provincial first round loss to Longford at Cusack Park in Mullingar the following May, when Doherty and Kelleher were again in tow. Hickey scored 2-1 in that latter game and would go on to contribute a total of 15-66 in 83 appearances, winning three All-Ireland (1974, 1976, 1977), two National Leagues (1976, 1978, six consecutive Leinster titles from 1974 and two All-Star awards (1974, 1976). His last game for Dublin was a Leinster semi-final loss to Laois at O'Connor Park in Tullamore in July 1981 and his only ever appearance in a county final was in 1970, when Raheny were beaten by St. Vincent's.

HICKEY, LEO (Ballyboughal): Defender. He made his senior debut in a league defeat by Louth at St Brigid's Park in Dundalk in November 1961, won a Leinster title seven months later and in 1963 a second provincial medal was followed by an All-Ireland one as Dublin beat Galway by 1-9 to 0-10. His 56th and final senior appearance was in a league play-off win over Westmeath at The Oval (the then home of St Vincents) in March 1969, but two years later he was on the Dublin junior team that beat Cork in the All-Ireland 'Home' Final but was then lost to London by a goal in the final 'proper'.

HOLDEN, MICK (Cuala): Defender, born 3 October 1954. A provincial medallist at minor in 1971 and again at Under-21 four years later (when Dublin lost to Kerry in the All-Ireland Final), he made his senior debut when getting a surprise call-up for the Leinster Final win over Offaly in July 1979. He won three further provincial medals in succession from 1983 (when he also featured in the All-Ireland Final triumph over Galway), was on the side that lost the Sam Maguire decider to Kerry in 1984, and was an used sub for the defeat to the same opposition the following year. His final senior appearance — his 56th — was in a league loss to Mayo at MacHale Park in Castlebar in December 1985. A dual performer, he won a Railway Cup hurling medal in 1979, added a football one six years later and won county hurling titles in 1989, 1991 and 1994, the latter six weeks after his 40th birthday. He died suddenly on 26 September 2007, aged 52.

HOLDEN, PADDY (Clanna Gael): Defender. Won provincial and All-Ireland minor medals in 1958 and another Leinster one at junior level the following year when Dublin were beaten in the national semi-final by Fermanagh after a replay. Seven weeks later, in early November, he made his senior debut when coming on as a sub in a league win over Offaly at O'Connor Park in Tullamore and the following May he had his first Championship outing in a provincial quarter-final defeat of Longford at Cusack Park in Mullingar. He won Leinster medals in 1962, 1963 and 1965 and on the middle occasion won an All-Ireland medal although injury forced him to retire after just 19 minutes of the final against Galway. He never won a National League — he was a member of the teams beaten in the final by Down in 1962 and by New York two years later — but he did win a hat-trick of Cu Chulainn awards (the forerunner of the All-Stars) from 1963. The last of his 68 appearances was as a sub in a league victory over Kildare at Croke Park in October 1966. After successive defeats to St. Vincents in 1963 and UCD the following year, he won his only county medal in 1968.

HOMAN, DARREN (Ballyboden & Round Towers): Midfielder, born 31 December 1974. Made his senior debut in a league loss to Louth at Parnell Park in early February 1997 but had to wait almost two and a half years for his first Championship appearance when coming on as a sub in a provincial quarter-final win over the same opposition at Croke Park. He won his only Leinster medal in 2002 and the last of his 71 senior appearances came when he went in as a sub in an All-Ireland quarter-final draw with Tyrone at Croke Park in August 2005, A back injury suffered in training the following month forced him to retire from inter-county play but three years later, having been given medical clearance, he returned to action and won an All-Ireland junior medal when Dublin beat Roscommon by 0-13 to 0-7. .

JOYCE, JOHNNY (St Vincent's): Forward. The county's second highest goalscorer and the number one in terms of average per game, 39 in 61 matches, including a record 12 in 14 games in the 1957/58 season. He made his debut in a Leinster semi-final loss to Wexford at Dr Cullen Park in Carlow in June 1956, scored 5-5 in the five games en route to the All-Ireland triumph of two years later, and two years after that, in a provincial quarter-final route of Longford at Cusack Park in Mullingar, he scored 5-3 and had another goal controversially disallowed. He scored 2-1 in the successful All-Ireland Minor Final in 1955, 7-9 when Dublin won the National League three years later, and four goals in a league win over Galway at Salthill in March 1962. He won four provincial medals (1958, 1959, 1962, 1963), eight county titles (1955, 1957, 1958, 1959, 1960, 1961, 1962, 1964), two Railway Cups (1959, 1961) and last played for Dublin in the Leinster Final win over Laois in July 1963.

KEANE, JJ (Geraldines): Defender, born John James Keane in Anglesboro on the Limerick side of the border with Cork on 14 April 1871. Made his debut in a provincial semi-final win over Kilkenny in the Championship for 1898 — played in November of the following year — and won an All-Ireland medal for that campaign in April 1900, then won two more for the Championships of 1899 and 1902, as well as county titles with Geraldines in 1897 and 1898. A noted athlete, he served as chairman of the Athletic Council for two decades when the sport was under the umbrella of the GAA and in 1922 became founding president of the organisation that succeeded it, the NACA (National Athletics and Cycling Association). In June 1922, in Paris, he was elected to the International Olympic Committee after being proposed by the movement's founder and president, Baron Pierre de Coubertin, and early the following year he founded the Olympic Council of Ireland, then known as the Irish Olympic Council. He served as the body's first president until stepping down in 1931 to concentrate on his IOC duties, which he continued to fulfill until retiring in 1951 due to ill health, being succeeded by Lord Killanin. Also a delegate to the IAAF (International Amateur Athletics Federation) for over a decade, he was instrumental in getting both the IOC and the IAAF to accept the OCI and the NACA as all Ireland entities. He died on 1 April 1956 (Easter Sunday), just short of his 85th birthday.

KEARNS, JOHN (Ballymun Kickhams): Midfielder, born 17 January 1959. On the side beaten by Cork in the All-Ireland Under-21 Final in 1980, he made his senior debut in November of that year in a drawn league tie with Offaly in Tullamore and got his first Championship start in a Leinster quarter-final win over Wicklow in Newbridge the following May. He played a part in all seven games in the All-Ireland winning campaign of 1983, starting four matches and coming on as a sub in both the provincial and national deciders. The following two years brought further Leinster success, mostly as a sub but he did play in the second of two successive All-Ireland Final defeats by Kerry in 1985. He won county championship medals in 1981 and 1985 and ended his inter-county career as he began it with an appearance as a sub in a league draw, against Cork at Pairc Ui Chaoimh in February 1988, his 52nd senior outing in the Dublin colours. He won county titles in 1982 and 1985.

KEAVENEY, JIMMY (St Vincent's): Forward, born 12 February 1945. Dublin's all-time top scorer in senior competitive action with 30-402 (492) from 104 matches for a record average of 4.731, although he is only joint second and second, respectively, in the Championship and National League tables. Made his senior debut in a League tie against Wicklow in November 1964; he drew a blank in that one but scored 1-3 in his first Championship appearance against Wexford the following May. He retired from inter-county play at the age of 27 after Dublin's loss to Kildare in a Leinster semi-final in 1972 but two years later, having watched the Dubs' first round victory over Wexford from Hill 16, he was famously lured out of his retirement by Kevin Heffernan and proceeded to score 1-32 in his six games as Dublin went on to claim a first All-Ireland crown in eleven years. He won two more All-Irelands in 1976 and 1978, two National Leagues in the same years, seven Leinster titles (1965, 1974, 1975, 1976, 1977, 1978, 1979) and three All-Star awards (1974, 1977, 1978). The only Dub to top the Championship scoring chart on four occasions (1974, 1975, 1977, 1979, the penultimate one being shared with Dermot Earley), he was sent off in the Leinster semi-final win over Offaly in July 1979 and, apart from one tournament game four months later, never played inter-county again. At club level, he won ten county titles (1964, 1966, 1967, 1970, 1971, 1972, 1975, 1976, 1977, 1981), two provincial ones (1973 and 1975) and an All-Ireland in 1976. He scored 2-76 in the 1974/75 season to set a county record that would stand for three and a half decades until finally bettered by Bernard Brogan and subsequently further improved on by Dean Rock another six years later.

KELLEHER, DAVE (Geraldines): Defender, born in Charleville, Co. Cork 24 May 1887. Made his debut in a provincial first round loss to Kildare in Athy in August 1906 — in the previous year's Championship — and went on to win three successive All-Irelands, those of 1906, 1907 and 1908. A dual player, he was on the Dublin team beaten by Tipperary in the All-Ireland Final of 1908 following a replay.

KELLEHER, ROBBIE (Scoil Uí Conaill): Defender, born 1950. Made his debut in a league win over Monaghan at Emmet Park in Carrickmacross in October 1969 and was virtually an ever present for almost a dozen years, playing his 114th and last appearance in a Leinster semi-final defeat by Laois at O'Connor Park in Tullamore in July 1981. In between he won three All-Irelands (1974, 1976, 1977), two National Leagues (1976, 1978), five Leinster titles (1974, 1975, 1976, 1977, 1978), four All-Star awards (1974, 1975, 1977, 1978) and a county medal in 1983.

KENNEDY, JACK (Young Irelands): Defender. Made his debut in the All-Ireland semi-final of the 1891 campaign — played in 1892 — and went on to captain the Championship winning sides of that season and those for 1892 and 1894, Dublin declining to compete in the campaign in between. The winner of county medals in the same three years, he was never on a losing side with Dublin.

KENNEDY, MICK (St Margaret's): Defender. A minor in 1975 and 1976 (when he won a provincial medal with a side beaten by Galway by a point in the All-Ireland semi-final, he spent the following three years with the Under-21s and made his senior debut when coming on as a sub in a Leinster quarter-final win over Offaly at Croke Park in July 1979, holding his place through to an All-Ireland Final loss to Kerry. Four years later he was on the team that won a first All-Ireland since 1977 by beating Galway, as well as the sides beaten by Kerry in the following two Sam Maguire deciders. In a career that lasted over a dozen years, he won National League titles in 1987 and 1991, five provincial medals (1979, 1983, 1984, 1985, 1989), an All-Star award in 1988, and made his 135th and final senior appearance in a league semi-final loss to Tyrone at Croke Park in April 1992.

KILKENNY, CIARAN (Castleknock): Forward, born 7 July 1993. After winning provincial medals in both football and hurling but then being on the losing side in both

All-Ireland finals in 2011, he won an Under-21 medal in May of the following year — scoring 2-30 in six games — and three months later made his senior debut when coming on as a sub in the All-Ireland quarter-final win over Laois. In mid November he joined Australian Rules side Hawthorn in Melbourne but just two months later, home in Dublin for the Christmas and New Year holidays, he opted to remain in Ireland, saying in a statement on social media, "Achieving success and realising my potential as a hurler and footballer with my club and county will always be more important to me than any of the benefits to be obtained from professional sport. Sport has always been something I did for enjoyment and I have found that it's not something I can do merely because it's my job. The passion I feel for hurling and football is not transferable to any other sport and seeing my neighbours and team-mates happy when we do well is reward enough." He won All-Ireland medals in 2013, 2015, 2016 and 2017 and three successive National League titles from 2014, as well as All-Star awards in 2015 and 2016.

KIRWAN, JACK (Young Irelands): Forward, born 9 February 1878, was just 16 years and 226 days old when he made his debut — and scored two points — in the Leinster semi-final win over Wexford in September 1894 and was a mere 71 days past his 17th birthday when he was on the All-Ireland winning side in a delayed and replayed final the following April. His entire career with Dublin comprised only eight games and included a defeat by Limerick in the 1896 decider, played in February 1898. Thereafter he switched to soccer and spent the 1898/99 season with Everton, where one of his team mates was Val Harris, who himself was on the Dublin side that won the All-Ireland of 1901 although the final wasn't played until two years later. He then moved on for a six season stint with Tottenham Hotspur and in 1901 helped them became the first and still only non-league team to win the FA Cup with a 3-1 victory over Sheffield United in a replay at Burnden Park in Bolton after a 2-2 draw in front of a crowd of 110,820 at Crystal Palace in London; Kirwan, who played on the left wing, thus became the first man to win All-Ireland and FA Cup medals, beating Kevin Moran to the distinction by 82 years. He won 17 international caps in the decade from 1900, then spent three seasons with Chelsea — helping them win promotion to the First Division in 1907 — before finishing his career with a season each at first Clyde and then Leyton. He then, from 1910 to 1915, became the first professional manager of Dutch side Ajax, guiding them to the Second Division title in his second season and later managed Italian side Livorno for the 1923/24 season. He died in London on 9 January 1959, a month short of his 81st birthday.

KIRWAN, PADDY (Garda): Forward, born in Cavan, 13 November 1899. Made his debut in the All-Ireland Final for 1921 and inside less than four months had a second medal for the Championship of 1922; both final were played in 1923, in July and October, respectively. Less than a year after that double — in September 1923 — he won a third medal, scoring the decisive goal as Dublin scored a 1-5 to 1-3 victory over Kerry in the decider of the Championship for 1923. He was also on the team beaten by Kerry in the following season's final, as well as the Garda side that lost out to O'Tooles in the 1923 county decider. He died on 1 February 1963, aged 63.

KISSANE, MICK (St Vincent's): Defender. Winner of Leinster and All-Ireland minor medals in 1958 and again the following year, he repeated that success at junior level in 1960, although only an unused sub for the national decider. Made his senior debut in a league victory over Louth at Croke Park in November 1962 and his Championship one in a provincial quarter-final defeat of Meath at the same venue the following June. Less than four months later he and team mates Brian McDonald and Sean Coen (the latter as an unused sub) shared the distinction of being the first Dublin players to win All-Ireland medals in three separate grades — Johnny Cooper joined them exactly half a century later — won a 17th senior title with a 1-9 to 0-10 defeat of Galway. He won five county medals (1962, 1964, 1966, 1967, 1970) and his 39th and last senior outing for Dublin was as a member of the side beaten 0-12 to 1-7 by Galway in the National League Final in April 1967.

LARKIN, ALAN (Raheny): Defender. Made his debut when brought on as a sub in a Leinster quarter-final win over Westmeath at Croke Park in June 1972 and two years later won provincial and All-Ireland medals as Dublin captured Sam Maguire for the first time since 1963. He held his place in 1975 as Dublin went down to Kerry in the All-Ireland Final, fell out of favour the following year but regained his place for another Leinster and All-Ireland double in 1977. He was on the losing side in three National League Finals, to Kildare (Division II) in 1974, to Meath after a replay the following year, and to Kerry in 1977. His 49th and final appearance was in a league victory over Galway at Tuam Stadium in December 1977.

LAVIN, JIM (St Vincent's): Defender. Won a medal as an unused sub in the All-Ireland Minor Final in 1946 after starting two of the earlier games in the campaign, made his senior debut in a league defeat to Louth at St Brigid's Park in Dundalk in October 1949, and had his first Championship outing in another loss the following May, to Kildare in a provincial first round tie at Cusack Park in Mullingar. Was on the National League winning side in 1953 and again two years, and in that latter season won a Leinster title in 1955 but tasted defeat to Kerry in the All-Ireland Final. He played his 62nd and final game for Dublin against Galway in a league tie in Ballinasloe in March 1958 and, at club level, won seven consecutive county titles from 1949 and another three from 1957.

LEDWIDGE, JOE (Young Ireland & Geraldines): Forward, born 8 June 1877. A county medal winner with Young Irelands in 1896 and with Geraldines three years later, the only time he was ever on the losing side in his brief seven match inter-county career was on his debut ... in the All-Ireland Final of 1896 when Dublin were edged out by Limerick on a 1-5 to 0-7 scoreline. He was on the winning sides in 1898 and the following year and scored 4-13 in his brief career. He switched to soccer thereafter, won an Irish Cup medal with Shelbourne in 1906 when he won international caps against Scotland and Wales. He also won runners-up medals in 1905, 1907 and 1908 and played cricket for Clontarf. He died on 19 January 1953, aged 75, and is buried in Mount Jerome Cemetery.

LOWNDES, ERIC (St. Peregrine's): Defender, born 9 June 1994. On the team pipped 3-9 to 1-14 by Tipperary for the All-Ireland minor title in 2011, he went one better the following year when Meath were comfortably accounted for in the decider and added an Under-21 medal in May 2014, three months after making his senior debut in a league defeat of Kerry at Croke Park. His debut in the Championship came in May of the following year when he came on as a second half sub in a Leinster quarter-final win over Longford. Was part of the squads that won All-Irelands in 2015, 2016 — coming on as a sub in the second decider — and 2017 as well as National League titles in 2014, 2015 and 2016. A dual player, he won Leinster minor hurling medals in 2011 and 2012, but Dublin were beaten by Galway in the first All-Ireland Final and by Tipperary in the second after a replay.

MACAULEY, MICHAEL DARRAGH (Ballyboden St. Enda's): Midfielder, born 21 August 1986. He made his senior debut when coming on as a sub in a 1-12 to 1-10 win over Kerry in a league tie at Fitzgerald Stadium in Killarney in February 2010, was an ever present for the rest of the campaign and had his first Championship outing in a provincial quarter-final win over Wexford that June. He collected the first of five All-Ireland medals the following year — the others came in 2013, 2015, 2016 and 2017 — and won a quartet of National League titles in succession from 2013, although injury curtailed his involvement in 2016. Named as the Footballer of the Year in 2013, he won county and provincial club titles in 2009 and 2015, going on to capture an All-Ireland medal after the latter success.

MAGEE, DARREN (Kilmacud Crokes): Midfielder. Won a provincial minor medal and was an unused sub in the squad beaten by Down in the All-Ireland semi-final in 1999 and made the Under-21 team in 2001 and 2002 and in the latter year was an ever present as Dublin beat Wicklow in the Leinster Final and got to the All-Ireland decider before losing out to Galway. Made the first of 70 senior appearances in a league victory over Donegal at Parnell Park in February 2002 and got his first Championship outing when coming on as a sub in a provincial quarter-final win over Wexford at Dr. Cullen Park in Carlow four months later. He won three Leinster medals (2002, 2006, 2009), was on the team beaten by Westmeath in the National League Division II Final in 2008 and made his final senior appearance as a sub in an All-Ireland Qualifier victory over Louth in July 2010. He won county medals in 2004 and 2005, and although he missed the 2008 triumph through injury, he was back for the All-Ireland Final victory over Armagh and Ulster champions Crossmaglen Rangers the following St. Patrick's Day.

MAGEE, JOHNNY (Kilmacud Crokes): Defender, born 30 May 1978, older brother of Darren. A minor in 1995 and 1996 and an Under-21 selection for the following three years, he made his senior debut when still in his teens in a league win over Sligo at

Markievicz Park in October 1997 but had to wait more than a further year and a half for his first Championship appearance, in a provincial quarter-final victory over Wexford at Croke Park. He won Leinster medals in 2002 (as an unused sub) and 2007 (when he came on just two minutes from the end), but had rather more success at club level, winning a quartet of county titles (1998, 2004, 2005, 2008), a trio of provincial medals (1998, 2005, 2008) and an All-Ireland in 2009 when Kilmacud Crokes upset three-time winners Crossmaglen Rangers from Armagh on a 1-9 to 0-7 scoreline. In addition, he was on the losing side in a trio of county deciders (2000, 2003, 2004) and made his final inter-county appearance — his 56th — when he came on as a sub in an All-Ireland quarter-final defeat of Derry at Croke Park in August 2007. Seven years later, after controversial Australian snooker star Quinten Hann had criticised GAA footballers as "soft" and "pansies" and Graham Geraghty from Meath and Oisin McConville from Armagh had declined a public call from him for a boxing bout, Magee took up the challenge and, following intensive coaching from Olympic gold medallist — and Dublin football fanatic — Michael Carruth, beat Hann (and broke his nose) in a three round fight at the National Stadium in September, the proceeds of the event going to the Irish Society for Autism. Magee subsequently had a spell as manager of the Wicklow football team.

MAHONY, DENIS (St Vincent's): Defender, born in Cork. Won an All-Ireland minor medal in 1945 and made his senior debut in a Leinster quarter-final loss to Louth in Croke Park three years later. He was on the National League winning sides of 1953 and 1955 and in the latter year also won a provincial medal and was on the team beaten by Kerry in the All-Ireland Final. His retired from inter-county football after Dublin's loss to eventual All-Ireland champion Louth in the Leinster Final — his 58th appearance — in mid July and from the club scene ten days later after winning his eighth county title in nine years (1949, 1950, 1951, 1952, 1953, 1954, 1955, 1957). He died on 3 April 2017, aged 88.

MANNION, PAUL (Kilmacud Crokes): Forward, born 25 May 1993. A member of the minor team beaten by Tipperary in the All-Ireland Final in 2011, he was a key figure in the Under-21 final wins over Roscommon in 2012 and 2014, scoring 1-4 in the first decider and 0-9 in the second. Made his senior debut in between, in a league win over Cork at Croke Park in February 2013 and went on to be part of a National League and Championship double that year. Opted out of the 2015 season to spend the year in Beijing and Wuhan as part of his studies in Chinese and International Commerce at UCD but returned in 2016 for another double success and won a third All-Ireland in 2017.

MARTIN, CON (St Maur's & St. Mary's): Midfielder, born 20 March 1923. One of Ireland's most famous soccer players ever, he played one single game for Dublin yet won a Leinster Championship medal; he was called in as a late replacement for the 1941 decider against Carlow and contributed a point as the county won a first provincial title in seven years with a 4-6 to 1-4 victory. He was playing soccer with Drumcondra at the time — he would win an FAI Cup with them in 1946 — and when this was discovered his medal was withheld until the lifting of the notorious Ban three decades later. He went on to play for Glentoran, Leeds United and Aston Villa and won 30 international caps. He died on 24 February 2013, just 24 days before his 90th birthday. His son Mick played for, amongst others, Manchester United, West Bromwich Albion and Newcastle United and won 51 caps for Ireland.

McCAFFREY, JACK (Clontarf): Defender, born 19 October 1993. He was on the team beaten by Tipperary in the All-Ireland Minor Final in 2010, won Under-21 medals in 2012 and 2014, made his senior debut in a league win over Cork at Croke Park in February 2013 and had his first Championship outing four months later in a Leinster quarter-final victory over Westmeath at the same venue. He completed National League and Championship doubles in both 2013 and 2015 — and won All-Star and Footballer of the Year honours in the latter season — as well as winning another league medal in between. After playing in the first two league games of 2016, he took the rest of the season off to do volunteer work in Ethiopia, Kenya, Zambia, Malawi and Tanzania as part of his medical studies but rejoined the county squad in January 2017 and won a third senior All-Ireland the following September.

McCAFFREY, NOEL (Clontarf): Defender. Father of Jack, he made his debut in a provincial quarter-final defeat of Wexford at Wexford Park in June 1985, collected his lone Leinster medal six weeks later and that September was on the side beaten by Kerry in the All-Ireland Final. Won two National League medals, in 1987 and 1991, although he was just a panellist for the closing stages of the latter success. The winner of an All-Star award in 1988 despite the fact that Dublin lost both the National League and Leinster deciders to arch rivals Meath, his 51st and final appearance was when coming on as a sub in a league draw with the Royal County at Croke Park in March 1991.

McCARTHY, JAMES (Ballymun Kickhams): Defender, born 1 March 1990. He made his senior debut in a league win over Kerry in Killarney in February 2010 and three months later was on the side that beat Donegal by 1-10 to 1-8 in the All-Ireland Under-21 Final. He had to wait until June of the following year for his first Championship appearance in a Leinster quarter-final win over Laois but has been a regular ever since and has won five All-Irelands (2011, 2013, 2015, 2016, 2017) and four National League titles in succession from 2013, as well as an All-Star award in 2014. He won a county medal in late 2012 and was on the side beaten by Roscommon and Connacht champions St. Brigid's in the All-Ireland Club Final the following St. Patrick's Day.

McCARTHY, JOHN (Garda): Forward, born 1955: Father of James, he won provincial medals at minor in 1971 and Under-21 three years later, and in between made his senior debut in a Leinster second round replay loss to Louth at Pairc Tailteann in Navan. Usually operating from the corner, he scored 14-50 in his 67 outings, won three All-Irelands (1974, 1976, 1977), a National League in 1978, half a dozen successive provincial titles from 1974, and made his final appearance in a league loss to Kerry at Croke Park in November 1981. Later in his career he changed clubs, playing for both Ballymun Kickhams and Na Fianna.

McDONALD, BRIAN (Synge Street): Forward. Won a trio of All-Ireland medals in successive years, minor 1958 and 1959 and junior in 1960, before making his senior debut in a league win over Louth at Croke Park in November 1962. The following year he won a senior All-Ireland when, after collecting a provincial medal against Laois and finding the net twice in a semi-final win over Down, he scored a crucial point in a 1-9 to 0-10 victory over Galway in the final. He won a second provincial medal in 1965 and made his 45th and last appearance in June 1968, scoring two points — to bring his career total to 11-69 — in a Leinster quarter-final loss to Longford at O'Connor Park in Tullamore. Shortly afterwards he moved to Castlebar and subsequently won a Connacht junior title with Mayo and two county medals with Castlebar Mitchels.

McDONNELL, JOHNNY (O'Toole's): Goalkeeper. Lasting all of 18 years and 320 days from his first senior appearance until his 110th and last, he began the longest senior career in the entire history of Dublin football in a provincial quarter-final win over Meath at the Showgrounds in Navan in July 1919 and ended it with another Leinster quarter-final, this time a loss to Kildare at O'Moore Park in Portlaoise in May 1938. Between those two milestones he kept three dozen clean sheets, including all four in the successful Leinster and All-Ireland campaigns of 1922, and won a second All-Ireland the following year. In addition, although he played in first game of the Championship for 1921 but lost his place to Paddy Fallon from Geraldines for the rest of the provincial and All-Ireland winning campaign, he won half a dozen Leinster medals (1920, 1922, 1923, 1924, 1932, 1934), five Railway Cups (1929, 1930, 1932, 1933, 1935) and ten county titles (1918, 1919, 1920, 1922, 1923, 1924, 1925, 1926, 1928, 1931). He not only played in the Bloody Sunday game in Croke Park in November 1920 but was implicated, at least as a driver and storer of guns, if not an actual participant in two of the killings of 14 secret service agents in and around Mount Street that morning, an action that led to the afternoon reprisals at the match by the British forces.

McDONNELL, PADDY (O'Toole's): Forward, born 1895. On the teams that beat Mayo and Limerick in the All-Ireland Junior Finals of 1914 and 1916, respectively, he made his senior debut in a Leinster first round win over Kildare at Newbridge in July 1917. Surprisingly dropped — after scoring 2-7 in the provincial campaign — to the substitutes bench for the successful All-Ireland Final for 1921 (played two years later), he was a central part of the side that went on to win the next two All-Irelands and was captain for the third success. He won half a dozen Leinster titles (1920, 1921, 1922, 1923, 1924, 1932), three consecutive Railway Cups from 1928, and ten county titles (1918, 1919, 1920, 1922, 1923, 1924, 1925, 1926, 1928, 1931). The last two games of his decade and a half long senior career both resulted in two point losses to Kerry in 1932, by 0-9 to 0-7 in the All-Ireland semi-final at Croke Park in late August and by 1-3 to 1-1 in a league tie at Austin Stack Park in Tralee in mid November. Famous for scoring points with overhead kicks, he chalked up 19-77 in 67 games and remains unchallenged as the top football scorer in the first seven decades of the GAA. Like his younger brother, Johnny, he was implicated in the executions on Bloody Sunday morning, but perhaps less directly than his sibling. He died in 1977.

McKANE, DES (St. Vincent's): Defender. His debut in a relatively short 28 game senior career came in a provincial semi-final loss to Offaly in Portlaoise in June 1963 and he enjoyed his greatest moment when, along with half back colleagues Paddy Holden and Mick Kissane, playing a starring role when Dublin beat Galway by 1-9 to 0-10 in the All-Ireland Final in 1963. His final game appearance was as a sub in a provincial final loss to Meath in July of the following year. He won five county medals (1959, 1960, 1961, 1962, 1964).

McMAHON, PHILLY (Ballymun Kickhams): Defender, born 5 September 1987. Made his senior debut in a league win over Westmeath at Parnell Park in February 2008 and had his first Championship outing when coming on as a sub in a provincial quarter-final defeat of Louth at Croke Park four months later. A regular from the start of the 2010 season onwards, he won five All-Ireland medals (2011, 2013, 2015, 2016, 2017) and, from 2013, four successive National League medals. The winner of All-Star awards in 2015 and 2016, he won county and provincial club championship medals in late 2010 but suffered disappointment in the All-Ireland Final on St. Patrick's Day of the following year when Ballymun Kickhams were edged out 2-11 to 2-10 by Armagh and Ulster champions Crossmaglen Rangers. A successful businessman (he owns the Fit Food home delivery company and two BeDo7.ie fitness clubs), he founded the Half Time Talk charity to support high risk youths and drug addicts following the heroin induced death of his brother John in September 2012.

McMANAMON, KEVIN (St. Jude's): Forward, born 9 December 1986. Made his debut in a league win over Kerry at Fitzgerald Stadium in Killarney in February 2010 — James McCarthy, Michael Darragh Macauley and Cian O'Sullivan all also debuted in the same game — and his first Championship outing came four months later in a Leinster quarter-final victory over Wexford at Croke Park. Won four consecutive National League titles from 2013 — scoring 3-17 in eight games in the 2014 campaign — and a quintet of All-Ireland medals (2011, 2013, 2015, 2016, 2017), scoring a critical 1-1 in the All-Ireland semi-finals against Mayo in 2015, draw and replay.

McNALLY, JOE (St Anne's): Forward. The goalkeeper on the side that won the All-Ireland Minor Championship with a 1-11 to 1-5 defeat of Kerry in 1982, he made his senior debut the following March, keeping a clean sheet in a draw with Armagh in Dublin's final game of that season's National League in Croke Park — and never played in goal again in 86 further games for the county! His next appearance in the county colours was at full forward in a drawn provincial first round tie with Meath, and although he lost his place for the replay and the subsequent semi-final win over Laois, he was back for the Leinster Final and scored a decisive 1-2 in a 2-13 to 1-11 victory over Offaly. He scored a further 1-6 in the remaining three matches of the campaign, a drawn and replayed semi-final against Cork and a 1-10 to 1-8 win over Galway in the All-Ireland Final, thus making history by becoming the first — and still only — football to win minor and senior Championship medals in successive years — and then capped a remarkable debut season by winning an All-Star award after just six competitive games. He won three further provincial titles (1984, 1985, 1988), both a National League and Railway Cup in 1987, and made his final appearance in the last game of the legendary four match series with Meath in 1991. He scored all four goals in a 4-18 to 1-9 win over Derry in a league game in October 1989 and finished that season with a career best haul of 9-7 in just ten matches.

MORAN, COLIN (Ballyboden St Enda's): Defender, born 6 June 1980. The centre back on the Dublin team beaten by Laois in the Leinster Minor Championship Final in early August 1998, he made his senior debut just three months later when coming on as a sub in a league win over Tyrone at Parnell Park — at the age of 18 years and 148 days — and was also caled on from the dugout for his first Championship appearance, a provincial quarter-final defeat of Wexford at Croke Park two years later. Popularly known as 'Collie' and often placed on the half forward line, he scored 5-59 in 85 appearances, won five Leinster titles (2002, 2005, 2006, 2007, 2008) but never made it to an All-Ireland Final and was on the side beaten by Westmeath in the Division Two league final in April 2008. His senior career ended four months later with an All-Ireland quarter-final defeat by the same opposition against whom it started, Tyrone.

MORAN, KEVIN (Good Counsel): Defender, born 29 April 1956. If we are talking about achievements within the confines of an extremely brief career, then Moran has to be one of the most successful Dublin footballers of all time. His senior career with the county lasted less than two and a half years — two years and 173 days to be precise — and encompassed a mere 28 games, yet in that time he appeared in three All-Ireland Finals (winning the first two), a pair of National League deciders in 1976 and 1978 (winning the first), claimed a hat-trick of provincial titles and won an All-Star award in his very first season. He made his senior debut in a league semi-final win over Galway in April 1976 — 25 days before his 20th birthday — and four weeks later scored two points as Dublin won the National League for the fourth time and the first since 1958 with a 2-10 to 0-15 victory over Derry. All the while he was also playing soccer with, in turn, Bohemians, UCD and Pegasus and, after All-Ireland success later that year and again in 1977, soccer fame came calling in February 1978 in the form of then Manchester United manager Dave Sexton. The move across the Irish Sea instantly ended his involvement in the National League — which Dublin went on to win — but he was, uniquely, given permission to return for the Championship and that September, with Sexton watching from the Hogan Stand, he played his final game for Dublin as the legendary Mikey Shee-hy goal contributed to a record 5-11 to 0-9 defeat by Kerry. Moran went on to make over 230 appearances for Manchester United — in one of which, in 1985, he became the first player to be sent off in an FA Cup Final — and a further 180 for first Sporting Gijon and then Blackburn Rovers, as well as winning 71 caps for the Republic of Ireland.

MORAN, PADDY (Whitehall Colmcille): Defender, born 28 May 1967. He made his debut when coming on as a sub in a defeat of Limerick in the final National League divi-sional game in Askeaton in March 1993 but was returned to the bench for the quarter-fi-nal and semi-final victories over, respectively, Kildare and Derry. He was similarly listed for the final against Donegal — who had shocked Dublin in the All-Ireland Final little more than seven months earlier — but was dramatically drafted into the starting line-up just an hour before the throw-in when Keith Barr was demoted, apparently as a con-sequence of a disagreement with management; the game was drawn, Moran retained his place for the replay and, in mid May, collected a National League medal after less than two and a half games. His first Championship appearance came a fortnight later against Wexford and by late July he had the first of three successive provincial medals, the final one being capped with an All-Ireland Final victory over Tyrone. The last of his 62 appearances was in the Leinster Final loss to Meath in 1999.

MULLINS, BRIAN (St Vincent's): Midfielder, born 27 September 1954. On the team beaten by Meath in the provincial minor final in 1972, he made his senior debut in the National League Division II semi-final win over Antrim at Croke Park in April 1974, a week after scoring 2-1 against Wicklow at Blessington in the first round of an ultimately successful Leinster Under-21 Championship campaign that ended with defeat by Mayo in the All-Ireland semi-final. His full Championship debut came the following month in a first round defeat of Wexford and he remained an ever present thereafter, collecting an All-Ireland medal in only his eighth senior outing as Dublin claimed a first title since 1963 with an 0-14 to 1-6 victory over Galway in the decider. He won three more All-Ire-lands (1976, 1977, 1983), nine Leinster titles (1974, 1975, 1976, 1977, 1978, 1979, 1983, 1984, 1985), two National Leagues (1976, 1978), two All-Stars (1976, 1977) and a Railway Cup in 1985. Mullins, who scored 17-35 and made his 97th and last senior appearance in a league game against Meath in November 1986, won nine county medals (1974, 1975, 1976, 1977, 1978, 1979, 1983, 1984, 1985) and an All-Ireland Club Championship in 1976 as well as runner-up medals in 1973 and 1985. His uncle, Bill Casey, a centre back, won three successive All-Irelands with Kerry from 1939 and a fourth in 1946. Mullins took over the managerial role at St Vincent's in early 2017 and led the team to their record 28th county championship after victory over Ballymun Kickhams in October.

MULVEY, STEVE (Bray Emmets): Defender, born in Bray, 3 March 1878. Won a coun-ty medal with Bray Emmets — who were then playing the Dublin Championship — in the 1901 competition, the final of which wasn't played until April 1903. His entire inter-county career consisted of seven games in 1904 and culminated in an All-Ireland medal for the Championship of 1902. A member of the Irish Volunteers who he took part in the Easter Rising, he died on 19 October 1954, aged 76.

MURPHY, VINNIE (Trinity Gaels): Forward. A minor in 1987 when he scored a goal as Dublin went down 0-13 to 2-5 to Kildare in the provincial final in late July, he made his senior debut the following February in a league win over Mayo at MacHale Park in Castlebar; that was Dublin's fifth game in the campaign and, despite his youth, he held his place right through another five as Dublin reached the final only to lose to Meath after a replay in late May. His first Championship appearance was just a fortnight later in a provincial quarter-final win over Carlow at their Dr Cullen Park, and the following year he won the first of five Leinster medals (1989, 1992, 1993, 1994, 1995). That latter year also brought All-Ireland success to go with National League wins in 1991 and 1993, in between which he won an All-Star. In early 1996 he moved to Tralee for work purposes and while there he played with the Kerins O'Rahillys club, with whom he won a county league medal in 1999. He returned to Dublin after four years and regained his place in the squad although usually as a sub; in his final campaign in 2001, for instance, he came off the bench in all six of Dublin's games in the Championship, his 108th appearance — in which he scored 17-126 — being in an All-Ireland semi-final loss to Kerry.

NOLAN, KEVIN (Kilmacud Crokes): Defender. A minor in both 2005 and 2006, he won a provincial medal at Under-21 in 2009 — when Dublin were beaten by Cork in the All-Ireland semi-final — and in between made his senior debut when coming on as a sub in a league defeat of Roscommon at Parnell Park in April 2008. Two months later he again came off the bench for a Championship debut in a provincial quarter-final win over Louth at Croke Park but it was to be the best part of another two years before he was able to command a regular starting place. He scored a crucial point as Dublin ended a 16 year long All-Ireland famine by edging Kerry in the 2011 decider — and won an All-Star award shortly afterwards — but thereafter his career was plagued by illness; diagnosed as both a celiac and a diabetic, he drifted out of favour and the last of his 40 senior appearances was in a provincial semi-final win over Wexford in June 2014.

NORRIS, JOE (O'Toole's): Defender. Made his debut in a provincial quarter-final loss to Louth at Shamrock Lodge in Drogheda in September 1919 and his 47th and last in a league draw with Laois at O'Moore Park in Portlaoise in March 1929. In between, he won three successive All-Irelands (1921, 1922, 1923), five Leinster titles in a row (1920, 1921, 1922, 1923, 1924), three Railway Cups (1929, 1930, 1932), ten county medals (1918, 1919, 1920, 1922, 1923, 1924, 1925, 1926, 1928, 1931) and played in the infamous Bloody Sunday game at Croke Park in November 1920. His grandnephew, PJ Gillic, won two All-Irelands (1987, 1988) and two National Leagues (1988, 1990) with Meath.

O'CALLAGHAN, CON (Cuala): Forward, born April 1996. Made his debut when coming on as a late sub in a league win over Kerry at Croke Park in January 2016. The following June he had his first Championship appearance when again coming off the bench in a Leinster quarter-final defeat of Laois at Nowlan Park in Kilkenny and he was again called on as a sub in the provincial semi-final and final victories over, respectively, Meath and Westmeath. Was an ever present throughout the successful 2017 campaign, scoring 2-20 in the six games including 0-12 in the Leinster Final against Kildare when he took over the place kicking duties after Dean Rock had been blacked carded and a crucial goal after less than a minute and a half of the All-Ireland Final against Mayo. That latter victory gave him a remarkable third All-Ireland medal in the space of just 184 days, as he had been on the victorious Cuala side that won the club hurling title on St. Patrick's Day as well as the Dublin team that won the Under-21 crown six weeks later.

O'CARROLL, RORY (Kilmacud Crokes): Defender, born 30 November 1989. Won provincial Under-21 medals in 2009 and 2010, going on to All-Ireland success in the second year and making his senior debut in the first when coming on as a sub in a league draw with Kerry at Parnell Park in March. His debut in the Championship came three months later in a Leinster semi-final defeat of Westmeath at Croke Park, a campaign in which he would go on to win the first of six provincial medals (2009, 2011, 2012, 2013, 2014, 2015). He was a member of the teams the won the All-Ireland in 2011, 2013 and 2015 and the National League in 2013, 2014 and 2015 and was awarded an All-Star in 2013 and 2015. At club level he won county and provincial club titles in 2008 and 2010, going on to All-Ireland glory in the first campaign. He also won a county hurling medal in 2012 and was on the Dublin teams that won provincial titles at minor in 2007 and Under-21 three years later. In late December 2015 he informed Dublin manager Jim Gavin that he was taking time out to travel and work in New Zealand.

O'DRISCOLL, GAY (St Vincent's): Defender, born 20 March 1946. Made first of 82 senior appearances when coming on as a sub in a league loss to Cork at Croke Park in November 1965, got his first Championship start in a Leinster quarter-final win over Louth in Drogheda eight months later, but then managed just a single outing over the next four seasons. From the start of the 1970/71 season, however, he became a more or less automatic choice and played a vital role in the great revival under Kevin Heffernan, winning three All-Irelands (1974, 1976, 1977), two National Leagues (1976, 1978), half a dozen provincial titles in succession from 1974, and All-Star awards in 1975 and 1977. A winner of eight county medals (1966, 1967, 1970, 1971, 1972, 1975, 1976, 1977), he won an All-Ireland Club Championship in 1976, having been on the losing side in the final three years earlier. His last inter-county outing was as a sub in the All-Ireland Final loss to Kerry in 1979.

O'FLAHERTY, PADDY (Ben Edar): Goalkeeper. Won a Leinster Junior Championship in 1954 and, having been beaten by Kerry in the All-Ireland semi-final in the interim, made his senior debut in a league draw with Galway at St. Jarleth's Park in Tuam that October. Was on the side that, in the space of just over four months in 1958, won the National League, Leinster and All-Ireland titles. He won a second provincial title the following year, but in the subsequent All-Ireland semi-final loss to Kerry he suffered a serious shoulder injury six minutes before half time — he was replaced by sub full forward Cyril Meehan from St. Vincents — and, after 54 games, never played again.

O'GARA, EOGHAN (Templeogue Synge Street): Forward, born 24 September 1985. Was on the team that captured the All-Ireland Junior Championship in 2008 and had a pair of league appearances that year but had to wait until June 2010 for his senior Championship debut, coming on as a halftime sub in a provincial quarter-final win over Wexford at Croke Park. Won All-Ireland medals in 2011, 2013 — when he came off the bench to score two crucial points in a 2-12 to 1-14 victory over Mayo — 2016 and 2017 but missed the successful 2015 campaign after suffering a torn cruciate ligament in a club game. The injury also ruled him out of the bulk of the following year's successful National League programme but he did pick up a medal as a squad member, to add to his three in succession from 2013.

O'LEARY, CATHAL (St Vincent's): Defender. A provincial minor medal winner in 1949 (when he scored 1-2 in the final win over Kildare before Dublin were beaten by Kerry in the All-Ireland semi-final), he made his senior debut when coming on as a sub in a Leinster first round defeat of Offaly at St. Conleth's Park in Newbridge. Originally a forward (he scored 5-3 in the National League in 1952/53 when Dublin reached the 'Home' decider before losing to Cork), he switched to first midfield and then the half back line. An unused sub for the National League Final victory over Cavan in 1953 (when the entire outfield was made up of his St. Vincent's team mates), he quickly regained his place and two years later won a league medal and was on the team shocked by Kerry in the All-Ireland Final. Three years later, in 1958, he was part of a National League and All-Ireland double, won a third provincial medal the following year, and made his 88th and last appearance in an All-Ireland semi-final loss to Kerry in August 1962. He won nine county titles with St. Vincent's (1950, 1951, 1952, 1953, 1954, 1957, 1958, 1959, 1961) and, missing the surprise 1956 final loss to Erin's Hope through injury, was never on the losing side in 49 county championship matches (one draw).

O'LEARY, JOHN (O'Dwyer's): Goalkeeper. Holds the all-time appearance record with 197 games (127 in the League and a then record 70 consecutive in the Championship), keeping a record 96 clean sheets including a remarkable 11 in succession; from when Fergal O'Neill found the net for Galway in the 44th minute of a league match at Croke Park on 28/2/1993, O'Leary went unbeaten for 875 minutes until Sean McElligott netted for Kerry in the final minute of another league game at the same venue the following October 24. A member of the All-Ireland Minor Championship winning team in 1979, he made his senior debut when given a surprise call up for the following summer's Leinster Final against Offaly. Dublin lost that one, but O'Leary would go on to enjoy All-Ireland success in 1983 and 1995 (as captain), win eight Leinster titles (1983,

1984, 1985, 1989, 1992, 1993, 1994, 1995), three Nationals Leagues (1987, 1991, 1993), three Railway Cups (1985, 1986, 1987) and five All-Star awards (1984, 1985, 1993, 1994, 1995) as well as winning a remarkable seven further nominations. His final match was a Leinster quarter-final loss to Meath in June 1997 and his inter-county career span of 16 years and 323 days is the second longest ever; Stephen Cluxton, although only three behind in terms of clean sheets as of the end of the 2016 season, will have to play two dozen more games to overtake him in appearances and will have to play until 16 April 2018 to surpass him as second only to Johnny McDonnell in longevity.

O'NEILL, PAT (Civil Service & UCD): Defender, born 22 October 1950. A provincial minor medal winner in 1968 when Dublin were ousted by Cork in the All-Ireland semi-final, he made the Under-21 team in 1970 and again the following year but had to wait until May 1975 for his senior debut in a league semi-final win over Tyrone. His first outing in the Championship came the following month when he was brought off the bench in a Leinster quarter-final defeat of Wexford at Dr. Cullen Park in Carlow and he would go on to be part of a National League and Championship double the following year and another All-Ireland success in 1977, when he also picked up an All-Star award. He won a second league medal in 1978 and the last of his 51 appearances was in a provincial final loss to Offaly in July 1980, again as a sub. He later managed Dublin to a National League title in 1993 and an All-Ireland Final triumph over Tyrone two years later.

O'REILLY, JACK (O'Toole's): Defender, born 1897. Known as 'Stonewall' and from Mayor Street in East Wall, he made the first of 49 appearances in a Leinster first round win over Kildare in Newbridge in July 1917 and four months later was on the team that won the delayed All-Ireland Junior Championship for the previous year, temporarily not forfeiting his junior status as he had played in the earlier rounds of the campaign, in accordance with the rules at the time. Was on the field on Bloody Sunday and on the side beaten by Tipperary in the All-Ireland Final of 1920 — which wasn't actually played until June 1922 — and was an automatic choice on the team that won the following three Championships with victories over, respectively, Mayo, Galway and Kerry. He was also on the team beaten by Laois in the inaugural National League final in September 1926 and made his 49th and last appearance in a win over Wexford in the same competition at Croke Park in April 1929. Won five successive provincial titles from 1920 and seven county medals (1918, 1919, 1920, 1922, 1924, 1925, 1926) after missing the 1923 and 1928 finals through injury. He died in 1942. His name is often erroneously recorded as Reilly rather than O'Reilly.

O'REILLY, PETER (St Mary's): Born in 1916, he started and ended his 52 match senior inter-county with league losses to his native county, at Breffni Park in October 1936 and at Croke Park in March of a dozen years later. In between he was on the team beaten by Mayo in the National League Final in 1941, won an All-Ireland in 1942 (when he was effectively play-manager), a second successive provincial title in the same year, and Railway Cups in

1944 and 1945. He trained the Dublin team that won the National League and reached the All-Ireland in 1955 and then the side that lifted Sam Maguire in 1958. Two years later, after Dublin had retained the provincial title in the interim and O'Reilly had had a falling out with the County Board, he trained Offaly to dethrone the treble seeking champions in the Leinster semi-final at O'Moore Park in Portlaoise. He died on 14 April 1994, aged 77.

O'SULLIVAN, CIAN (Kilmacud Crokes): Defender, born 27 March 1988. Won a provincial Under-21 medal in 2009 — when Dublin were pipped 1-10 to 1-9 by Cork in the All-Ireland semi-final at Semple Stadium in Thurles — and made his first senior appearance in a league win over Kerry at Fitzgerald Stadium in Killarney in February of the following year. His debut in the Championship came just four months later in a provincial quarter-final win over Wexford and he went on to figure in five successful All-Ireland campaigns (2011, 2013, 2015, 2016, 2017) as well as a quartet of consecutive National League triumphs from 2013. The winner of All-Star awards in 2013 and 2015, he won county and provincial club titles in 2008 and 2010, going on to win the All-Ireland crown in the first instance but losing out to Armagh champions — and eventual winners — Crossmaglen Rangers in the semi-final by 2-11 to 1-12 in the second.

O'TOOLE, ANTON (Synge Street): Forward, born 18 February 1951. After two years with the juniors and winning a Leinster title and reaching the All-Ireland Final in 1971 only to be beaten by London, he made his senior debut in a league game against Longford in December of the following year and made his first Championship appearance in the opening game of the successful 1974 campaign, scoring two points against Wexford. That initial All-Ireland success was followed by three others, in 1976, 1977 and 1983 and National League crowns in 1976 and 1978, while his first Leinster Championships triumph in 1974 was repeated in each of the next five years and again in 1983 and 1984. The winner of three successive All-Star awards from 1975, he made his 106th and final appearance in the All-Ireland Final loss to Kerry in 1984, finishing a senior inter-county career that lasted almost a dozen years with a scoring contribution of 13-104.

PIERSE, TODDY (University College): Forward, born Thomas Edward Pierse in Wexford, 21 July 1898. He won an All-Ireland medal when Wexford completed their historic four-in-a-row in 1918 and three years later moved to Dublin to pursue his medical studies. He made his debut for Dublin in the semi-final of the All-Ireland for 1921 (played in June 1922), scoring a point and repeating the feat in the final victory over Mayo, which wasn't played until exactly a year later. He won a second medal in the following Championship, the final of which was played less than four months after the previous one. He died on 11 October 1968, aged 70.

QUINN, BRENDAN (Parnells): Defender. Started with St Vincent's as a minor but moved up the road to Coolock and Parnells and helped his new club to a county title in July 1939, making his senior debut in a league routing of Monaghan at Bremore Park in Balbriggan three months later. Was on the National League Final losing side against Mayo in 1941, but won provincial titles that year and the next, scoring the only point of his career in the latter decider before going on to play a prominent role in the 1-10 to 1-8 defeat of Galway in that year's All-Ireland Final. He won a second county title in 1945 and made his 41st and final inter-county appearance in a league defeat by Laois at Croke Park in November of the following year.

QUINN, TOMAS (St Vincent's): Forward. The county's eighth highest scorer of all time despite the fact that his near decade long career coincided with something of a famine during which Dublin failed to win with an All-Ireland or a National League. In his 81 senior appearances he scored 21-213, scored ten points in a provincial semi-final win over Wexford in 2005 and twice hit 1-7 against Tyrone in the space of less than six months, in the All-Ireland semi-final in August 2005 and in a league game at Healy Park in omagh the following February. He won half a dozen Leinster titles (five in a row from 2005 and then another in 2011) and enjoyed greater success at club level, winning a quartet of county medals (2007, 2013, 2014, 2016), a similar number of provincials medals in the same years, and All-Ireland Championships in 2008 and 2014.

REA, MATT (Geraldines): Defender, born 10 April 1873 in Limerick. Made his debut in a provincial semi-final win over Kilkenny in December 1899 — in the Championship for two years previously — and went on to captain Dublin to victory in that campaign and the following one. One of the founders of the Geraldines club, he won county titles with them in 1898 and 1899 and died from mouth cancer on 10 November 1942, aged 69. His grandnephew, Ned Rea, was full forward on the Limerick team that won the All-Ireland hurling title, scoring two points in his side's 1-21 to 1-14 victory over Kilkenny.

REDMOND, CHARLIE (Erin's Isle): Forward. Made his debut when coming on as a sub in the Leinster semi-final against Offaly at O'Connor Park in Tullamore in July 1985 and was on the teams beaten by Kerry in the All-Ireland Final less than three months later. After further All-Ireland Final disappointments in 1992 and 1994 he finally won a Celtic Cross in 1995, scoring a goal and a point in a 1-10 to 0-12 win over Tyrone — and then being sent off by Tipperary referee Paddy Russell in the 46th minute for an alleged head butt on Peter Canavan but playing on for a further two minutes before being again ordered off by Russell. In all, Redmond won two National Leagues (1991, 1993), five Leinster medals (1985, 1992, 1993, 1994, 1995) and three All-Star awards (1993, 1994, 1995). He also won county titles in 1993 and 1997; Erin's Isle were beaten in the three deciders in between but Redmond missed the middle one through injury. He was the county's top scorer for seven consecutive seasons — a feat unmatched by other multiple number ones such as Jimmy Keaveney, Kevin Heffernan and Barney Rock — and despite missing penalties in two All-Ireland Final defeats (to Donegal in 1992 and Down two years later, as well as the 1988 provincial final loss to Meath), he finished his 116 game career after a Leinster quarter-final loss to Meath in June 1997 with 15-306 for fifth place in the all-time Dublin scoring list.

REILLY, PADDY (St Margaret's): Defender. A member of the unsuccessful Under-21 team in 1971, he made his senior debut in a league defeat against Galway at Croke Park in November of the following year. Played a central role in Dublin's march to Leinster and All-Ireland glory in 1974 (when he capped the year with an All-Star award), but thereafter was largely relegated to the dugout. Nevertheless, he did win a second Celtic Cross when coming on for Pat O'Neill in the All-Ireland Final win over Armagh in 1977, won five provincial medals (1974, 1975, 1976, 1977, 1979) and was twice on the losing side in National League deciders, against Kildare (Division II) in 1974 and against Meath a year later. Out of the picture altogether throughout the entire 1977/78 season, he made his 48th and last appearance in a provincial semi-final win over Wicklow at St Conleth's Park in Newbridge in July 1979.

ROBERTSON, IAN (Ballymun Kickhams): Forward. Made his senior debut in a single point league loss to Kerry at Fitzgerald Stadium in Killarney in November 1994, just over two months after being on the Dublin side beaten by Galway in the All-Ireland Minor Final. He had to wait almost three years for his first Championship outing, however, a provincial quarter-final loss to Meath at Croke Park in June 1977 but, frequent injuries aside, would remain a regular for the next four years. A doctor by profession, it was his ironic fate to be increasingly plagued by injuries and, after two years on the sidelines, he returned for the 2004 campaign but bowed out after an All-Ireland quarter-final loss to Kerry in August, his 46th senior appearance in the county colours.

ROCK, BARNEY (Ballymun Kickhams): Forward, born 10 January 1961. Topped only by Jimmy Keaveney as the county's all-time leading scorer with 30-360 from 99 appearance, he won an All-Ireland Minor Championship medal in 1979 after being on the side beaten by Mayo in the previous year's final and scoring 7-35 in the two campaigns. He made his senior debut when coming on as a sub in the Leinster semi-final win over Meath at Pairc Tailteann in Navan in July 1980 and made his 99th and final appearance in the third game of the famous four match saga with the same opposition in June 1991. He added a senior All-Ireland to his minor one in 1983, won a National League four years later, four provincial titles (1983, 1984, 1985, 1988), a Railway Cup in 1986, county medals in 1982 and 1985 and a trio of successive All-Stars in 1983, 1984 and 1985, topping the Championship scoring charts in the latter three years, the only such hat-trick ever achieved by a Dubliner. He was foiled of a hat-trick of medals when Dublin were beaten by Cork in the Under-21 decider in 1980 and in April 1997, almost six years after his final senior appearance, he scored 1-4 in a provincial junior quarter-final loss to Louth at Parnell Park; if his scoring hauls in all grades are taken into account, he overtakes Keaveney — who scored just 0-14 in other grades — to be the highest scoring Dublin footballer of all time with a total of 41-423 in 116 games, a career average of 4.707. A junior champion-ship appearance at the age of 36 enabled him to overtake — initially by less than a month — Johnny McDonnell's all grades record for longevity in the Dublin colours, a record that had stood for almost six decades. He subsequently kicked the record out of sight by being recalled for the provincial junior final in 2000 when within six months of his big Four-0.

ROCK, DEAN (Ballymun Kickhams): Forward, born 26 February 1990. Like his father, Barney, he is one of only a handful of players to represent the county in all four grades. A minor in 2008 and a junior the following year, he had three years in the Under-21 ranks, winning an All-Ireland — and scoring 2-20 in five games — in 2010. He made his senior debut when coming on as a sub in a league victory over Donegal in March 2012 and the following year made his first Championship appearance, again as a sub, in a provincial quarter-final defeat of Westmeath in Croke Park; indeed, he would come off the bench — and score 0-10 — in all six games as Dublin capped a successful All-Ireland campaign with a 2-12 to 1-14 victory over May in the decider. He won further All-Ire-lands in 2015, 2016 — when he scored 1-58 in seven games — 2017, and four consecu-tive National Leagues from 2013. In 2016 he beat Bernard Brogan's six year old season record by being the first man to break the 100 point barrier with 2-98 in 16 games and collecting an All-Star award in the process. He won county and provincial titles in 2012 but Ballymun Kickhams were beaten 2-11 to 2-10 by Roscommon and Connacht champi-ons St. Brigid's in the All-Ireland Final.

RONAYNE, JIM (Clontarf): Midfielder, born 28 February 1959. A member of the team beaten by Meath by a point in the provincial minor final in 1977, he won a Leinster medal at Under-21 level three years later but was on the losing side in the All-Ireland Final against Cork. He had already made his senior debut by that time, coming on as a sub to score three crucial points in a 1-8 to 0-9 victory over Offaly in the provincial decider in July 1979; he retained his place for the All-Ireland semi-final win over Roscommon but was again a sub for the Sam Maguire showdown, coming on to score Dublin's lone goal in a comprehensive 3-13 to 1-8 loss to Kerry. Four years later he earned his All-Ireland medal in the defeat of Galway but over the next two years again lost finals to the King-dom. He won a National League medal in 1987 and a quartet of Leinster titles (1979, 1983, 1984, 1985), and the last of his 74 senior appearances was in the National League 'Home' Final loss to Cork in April 1989.

ROONEY, STEPHEN (O'Dwyers): Midfielder. His relatively brief career — it lasted just a little over four years — began in a league loss to Offaly at O'Connor Park in Tulla-more in October 1971 and his Championship debut came in May of 1973 when he scored four points in a 3-11 to 0-5 win over Wexford in a Leinster first round tie at Wexford Park. Was an ever present when Dublin stormed to surprise Leinster and All-Ireland triumphs in 1974 but lost his place to Bernard Brogan the following year. Won a National

League medal in 1976 as a panellist when he made four appearances in the divisional stage, the last — his 33nd overall — being in a 2-8 to 1-6 loss to Roscommon at Dr. Hyde Park in February 1976.

RYAN, SHANE (Naomh Mearnog): Defender, born 5 October 1978. Made his senior debut in the opening game of the 1998/99 league — a win over Tyrone at Parnell Park at the start of November — and was an ever present as Dublin went all the way to the final before going down to Cork by 1-12 to 0-7. His first Championship outing came in a provincial quarter-final defeat of Louth at Croke Park that June and although he won half a dozen Leinster titles (2002, 2005, 2006, 2007, 2008, 2009), the Dublin team of his era never made it past the semi-finals in the All-Ireland series and he was also on the losing side in a pair of National League Finals, against Cork in 1999 and against Westmeath in the Division II decider nine years later. The winner of an All-Star award in 2008, he made his final appearance — his 119th — when coming on as a sub in the All-Ireland quarter-final loss to Kerry at Croke Park in August 2009. A dual star, he concentrated exclusively on hurling thereafter and played a major role in Dublin's defeat of Kilkenny in the National League Final at Croke Park in May 2011, the county's first triumph in the competition in 72 years. Both his grandfathers held high positions within the GAA; his mother's father, Sean O Siochain from Cork, was the Association's first Director General and held the office for a decade and a half from 1964, while his father's father, Seamus O'Riain from Tipperary, was the organisation's President from 1967 to 1970. As if that wasn't sufficient depth of heritage, both his parents were All-Ireland winners; his late mother, Orla, completed a hat-trick of camogie titles with Dublin in 1966 (and was on the team beaten by Antrim in a replay the following year), and his father, Jack, won a National Hurling League with Tipperary in 1968 and an All-Ireland medal as an unused sub three years later.

RYDER, FRAN (St Vincent's): Defender. Won provincial Under-21 medals in 1974 and the following year and was on the side beaten by Kerry in the All-Ireland Final in the latter campaign. He made his senior debut when coming on as a sub in a Leinster semi-final win over Laois at O'Connor Park in Tullamore in July 1976, played in the provincial final success later that same month and then again was called on in the All-Ireland Final victory over Kerry two months later. He won the second of four successive Leinster medals the following year and also another Celtic Cross as a panelist, won a National League medal in 1978 and was on the sides beaten by Kerry in the All-Ireland Finals of that year and the next. He won four county titles (1975, 1976, 1977, 1981), a Leinster club title for 1975 — played in January 1976 — and an All-Ireland Club medal in the same campaign. His 38th and last senior inter-county appearance was in the provincial final loss to Offaly in August 1982.

SHEEDY, JACK (Lucan Sarsfields): Midfielder. A provincial medallist and All-Ireland runner-up — to Cork — at junior level in 1987, he made his senior debut in a league defeat of Cork at Croke Park in November 1990, going on to score 3-14 in eight games as Dublin regained the National League after a gap of four years. His introduction to Championship action came that summer when he played every minute of the classic four match series with Meath and the following year, 1992, he won the first of three successive Leinster medals. He was on the teams beaten in the All-Ireland Final by Donegal in 1992 and again by Down two years later, but won a second National League medal in between. The winner of an All-Star award in 1994, he suffered a cruciate ligament injury in a league draw with Derry in March of the following year — a result that relegated Dublin — that effectively ended an inter-county career in which he scored 6-57 in 61 games. He later managed Moorefield to a Kildare county title in 2010 and subsequently had a spell as Longford manager.

SHERLOCK, JASON (Na Fianna & St. Oliver Plunketts): Forward, born 10 January 1976. Won a provincial minor medal in 1994; Dublin were beaten by Galway in the All-Ireland semi-final in late August and ten weeks later, 72 days before his 19th birthday, he made his senior debut and scored the Dublin goal in a 2-12 to 1-10 loss to Kerry in a league tie at Fitzgerald Stadium in Killarney. The following summer, still a teenager, he was one of the side's stars as Dublin won a first All-Ireland in a dozen years, Sherlock scoring the decisive goal in a 1-12 to 0-12 semi-final victory over Cork. In the course of a senior career that lasted just under a decade and a half, he scored 14-91 in 111 appearances. He won three successive county titles from 1999, Na Fianna going on to win the provincial title in the first campaign but losing out to Armagh and Ulster — and defending — champions Crossmaglen Rangers. He was also on the losing side in four finals, with Na Fianna in 1998 and 2005 and, after he transferred to St. Oliver Plunkett's in the interim, in 2008 and 2011. A noted soccer player, he lined out for four seasons with UCD and one with Shamrock Rovers and in June 1995 he was called on as a sub in the Republic of Ireland's 3-0 win over Austria in a European Under-21 Championship qualifier at Richmond Park.

SHOULDICE, JACK (Geraldines): Forward, born in Ballaghaderreen, 12 March 1882. Emigrated to London in 1899 and joined the Hibernians club there, winning four consecutive county championships with them from 1901 and playing for London in three successive losing All-Ireland Finals from 1901, the first two against Dublin and the third against Kerry. He left London in 1906 to join the Civil Service as a Department of Agriculture official and joined the Geraldines club, with whom he won four more county titles, in 1908, 1910, 1914 and 1915. He made his debut for Dublin in a provincial quarter-final win over Meath in September 1908 and won an All-Ireland medal with them in that campaign — the final wasn't played until August of the following year — against his old London team mates. Having joined both the Irish Republican Brotherhood and the Gaelic League while in London, he took an active part in both the Easter Rising — he was among those compelled to surrender in the Four Courts — and the War of Independence and subsequently served as secretary of the Leinster Council for ten years. He died on 15 February 1965, aged 82..

SMALL, JOHN (Ballymun Kickhams): Defender, born 10 January 1993. A member of the minor team edged out by Tipperary by a single point in the All-Ireland Final in 2011, he was an ever present in the successful Under-21 side of three years later. His senior debut came in a league loss to Cork at Pairc Ui Rinn in February 2015 and by the end of that season he had completed a National League and Championship double, a feat he would repeat in 2016 before adding a third All-Ireland medal in 2017. While still a teenager he won a county championship medal in October 2012 and played on the side beaten by Crossmaglen Rangers in the All-Ireland semi-final the following February.

STYNES, BRIAN (Ballyboden St Enda's): Midfielder, born 29 September 1971. Scored 1-11 in five games as Dublin won the Leinster minor title and reached the All-Ireland Final before going down to Kerry in 1988 and three years later followed his brother Jim into Australian Rules Football with the same Melbourne club. His career Down Under never managed to match that of his older sibling and he returned to Ireland in late 1993, rejoining Ballyboden and making his senior inter-county debut in a league win over Derry at Wolfe Tone Park in Bellaghy in March of the following year. His first taste of Championship action came in a Leinster quarter-final replay win over Kildare at Croke Park in July 1994 en route to winning the first of two successive provincial titles before he and his team mates suffered the disappointment of a 1-12 to 0-13 defeat by Down in the All-Ireland Final. He and Dublin had success all the way a year later, culminating in an even closer 1-10 to 0-12 defeat of Tyrone in the Sam Maguire decider and collecting an All-Star award for his performances during the campaign. He won his only county title that same year but lasted another five seasons with the county side, his senior career ending as it started in a Championship replay against Kildare — this time a final loss — in August 2000. He scored 2-62 in 58 senior outings for Dublin.

STYNES, JOE (McCrackens & O'Toole's): Forward, born 15 January 1903. An IRA activist who was sworn in by future Taoiseach Sean Lemass in 1920, he scored the last two points in the county's 1-5 to 1-3 over Kerry in the All-Ireland Final of 1923, which was actually played in September 1924. He missed the deciders immediately before and after for differing but equally controversial reasons; the first because he was interned in the Curragh Camp for his political views and the second because he was banned by the GAA after being found to have played soccer with Bohemians. He emigrated to New York in 1926 but regularly returned to Ireland largely for political meetings and in 1928, while also representing America at the Tailteann Games, he lined out for Dublin in a Leinster Final against Kildare, scoring a point in an 0-10 to 1-6 loss to Kildare. He died in the New York suburb of Queens on 29 January 1991, a fortnight after his 88th birthday. His grandson Chris Stynes played major league base-ball for half a dozen teams between 1995 and 2004; Kansas City Royals (1995–1996), Cincinnati Reds (1997–2000), Boston Red Sox (2001), Chicago Cubs (2002), Colorado Rockies (2003) and Pittsburgh Pirates (2004). Joe's brother Peter was Dublin's only scorer when they lost to Laois in the first ever National League Final at Barrett's

Park in New Ross in September 1926 and won county medals with O'Toole's in 1925, 1926 and 1928; Peter's grandsons — cousins of Chris — included Australian Rules star Jim Stynes and his above mentioned brother Brian, a member of Dublin's triumphant All-Ireland winning team in 1995.

SYNNOTT, JOE (O'Toole's): Midfielder, born 22 September 1893. More commonly known as Josie, he made his debut in a Leinster quarter-final win over Meath at the Showgrounds in Navan in July 1919 and was on the side that won the Championship of 1922 (played in October 1923), the middle one of the three-in-a-row. The winner of nine county titles (1918, 1919, 1920, 1922, 1923, 1924, 1925, 1926, 1928), he scored Dublin's first ever goal in the National League, his brothers John and Peter scoring the other two in a 3-3 to 1-5 win over Louth at St Brigid's Park in Dundalk in October 1925. He died on 14 August 1952, aged 58.

SYNNOTT, JOHN (O'Toole's): Forward, born 10 October 1895. Made his debut in the same game as his brother and, after being on the losing side to Tipperary in the All-Ireland Final in 1921, would be on the sides that won the next three Championships. He scored 10-10 in 42 games for Dublin, the last of them being a league win over Wexford at Croke Park in April 1931, two months before he won his tenth county medal (1918, 1919, 1920, 1922, 1923, 1924, 1925, 1926, 1928, 1931).

TIMMONS, JOE (St Mary's): Defender, born 16 August 1933. Actually had two careers with Dublin, four and a half years apart; he played at left corner back on the team that beat Wicklow by 3-8 to 1-5 in a league game at Pearses' Park in Arklow in February 1953 but, living in and playing his club football with Annacurra, he then declared for Wicklow and made his debut for the Garden County in a provincial first round win over Longford at O'Connor Park in Tullamore just two months later. He was an ever present for the next four years — during which he had a quartet of league outings against Dublin — but then, having moved to Clondalkin and taken up employment with Roadstone, he redeclared for Dublin and made his second 'debut' for the county in a league defeat of Laois at O'Moore Park in Portlaoise in October 1957. Two years later he won National League, Leinster and All-Ireland honours and, the following year, a second provincial title and a Railway Cup. His 44th and final game for Dublin was in a league defeat to Louth at St Brigid's Park in Dundalk in November 1961. He died on 30 January 2009, aged 75.

TIMMONS, JOHN (St Mary's): Forward. Born in Dublin but, as he and his brother Joe spent several years living with their grandparents in Annacurra, he began his senior inter-county career with Wicklow and in 1957 scored 4-16 in three games as the Garden County reached the provincial semi-final before being ousted by Dublin at St Conleth's Park in Newbridge. Early the following year, having returned to live in Dublin and joined the St Mary's club, he followed Joe by declaring for the capital county, made his debut in the provincial quarter-final win over Meath in Drogheda and, in only his fourth appearance — he missed the Leinster semi-final because of injury — won an All-Ireland medal as Dublin beat Derry by 2-12 to 1-9. Two years later, following the retirement of Ollie Freaney, he took over the place-kicking duties and by the end of his career — which included a second All-Ireland success in 1963 — he had scored 9-204 in 70 games. A winner of five provincial titles (1958, 1959, 1962, 1963, 1965) and a Railway Cup in 1962, he made his final appearance for Dublin came in a league victory over Kildare at Croke Park in October 1966.

TUNNEY, JIM (Erin's Isle): Midfielder, born 25 December 1923. A member of the team that beat London by 2-11 to 1-5 in the All-Ireland Junior Championship decider in October 1948, he made his senior debut in a league loss to Louth at the Athletic Grounds in Drogheda the following month. His first Championship outing came in a provincial first round win over Longford at Cusack Park in Mullingar in May 1949 but his career was short lived and his seventh and final competitive appearance was in a Leinster quarter-final defeat to Meath two years later. He later went into politics and was a TD for the Dublin North-West and Dublin Finglas constituencies from 1969 to 1992, was chairman of the Fianna Fail Parliamentary Party fron a decade from 1982, and was Lord Mayor of Dublin in 1985/86. He died on 16 January 2002, aged 78.

WALSH, CIARAN (St Anne's): Defender. A member of the team that won the Leinster and All-Ireland Minor Championships in 1984 but had to wait more than four years for his senior debut, in a league win over Monaghan at Croke Park in November 1988. Even then it was a false dawn; that was the first of four successive appearances but then came another two years in the wilderness until he was recalled for a league loss to Donegal at MacCumhail Park in Ballybofey The wait would prove worthwhile as he tasted All-Ireland glory in 1995 and also won National Leagues in 1991 and 1993, as well as a quartet of provincial titles (1992, 1993, 1994, 1995). He played 61 games for the county, the last being a Leinster quarter-final defeat against Meath in June 1997.

WHELAN, CIARAN (Raheny): Midfielder, born 28 August 1976. The county's third most experienced representative with 137 appearances in a career that lasted a baker's dozen of years plus six days and yielded 9-131, making him Dublin's highest scoring midfielder ever. Probably one of the finest Dublin footballers never to win an All-Ireland medal (his lengthy career spanned almost the entirety of the 'famine' from 1985 to 2011), he made his debut in the Leinster Final loss to Meath in 1996 and had his final outing in the All-Ireland quarter-final loss to Kerry in 2009. In between, he won seven provincial medals (2000, 2002, 2005, 2006, 2007, 2008, 2009), a Railway Cup in 1997 and All-Star awards in 1999 and 2007.

WHELAN, MAURICE (St Vincent's): Midfielder. Known as Mossy, he made his debut in a Leinster quarter-final loss to Offaly at O'Moore Park in Portlaoise in June 1949 and just under four years later captained the side that captured Dublin's first ever National

League with a 4-6 to 0-9 victory over Cavan, the famous occasion when Air Corp goal-keeper Tony O'Grady was the lone non St Vincent's player in the line-up. Two years later he won a second National League medal but had to settle for second best in the All-Ireland Final against Kerry. He finally won Leinster and All-Ireland medals in 1958 (coming on as a sub in the latter decider for his 68th and final appearance), and won nine county medals in ten years (1949, 1950, 1951, 1952, 1953, 1954, 1955, 1957, 1958).

WHELAN, MICKEY (Clanna Gael & St Vincent's): Forward. Made his debut in the 1959 provincial final win over Laois at O'Connor Park in Tullamore, scoring 1-3 in a 1-18 to 2-8 victory and contributed 1-19 in five games when, four years later, Dublin captured their first All-Ireland since 1942. He won a trio of provincial titles (1962, 1963, 1965) and a Railway Cup in 1962 but never won a National League medal, being a member of the teams that lost the finals of 1962, 1964 and 1967 to Down, New York and Galway, respectively. Whelan, who scored 11-102 in 76 inter-count outings, is one of only a handful of players to win county medals with two different clubs, Clanna Gael in 1968 and St Vincent's in 1975 and 1976, winning provincial and All-Ireland Club titles in the latter year. After his retirement — his final game for Dublin was a Leinster semi-final loss to Kildare at Dr Cullen Park in Carlow in June 1969 — he managed the county squad for three years from the 1995/96 season but without success; he had better fortune with St Vincents, guiding them to county, provincial and All-Ireland glory in the 2007/2008 season.

WILSON, GEORGE (O'Dwyer's): Defender. A member of the Under-21 side in 1968 and 1969, he made his senior debut in a league victory over Kildare at Croke Park in November 1971 and had his first Championship outing the following June in a provincial quarter-final win over Westmeath at Croke Park. An ever present throughout the 1973/74 and 1974/75 seasons (when he won two provincial medals and was on the teams that beat Galway in the All-Ireland Final in 1974 but lost to Kerry in the decider the following year), he lost his place thereafter and made just two further league appearances, the final one — his 44th in all — being when coming on as a sub in an 0-11 to 0-7 win over Galway at Croke Park in December 1977.

WILSON, MARCUS (St. Vincent's): Defender, born 1932. As a minor he scored 0-18 in four games when Dublin reached the provincial before bowing to Wexford in 1949, His first senior appearance was in a league victory over Westmeath in Croke Park in November 1952 and his Championship debut came in a single point loss — 2-6 to 2-5 — in a Leinster quarter-final against Meath at Pairc Tailteann in Navan the following May. Won a league title in 1953 and a Championship and National League double in 1958, but injury impacted on much of his career, particularly in 1955 when he missed another league triumph and the All-Ireland Final defeat to Kerry. He won county medals in 1952, 1953, 1954, 1955, 1958, 1959 and 1960, injury again ruling him out of the 1957 success.

Junior Championship

DUBLIN won a score of provincial titles at junior level yet on two of those occasions were unable to challenge for All-Ireland honours. How come? Well, having sat out the first three stagings of the competition, the county won out in Leinster at the first attempt in 1908 but the All-Ireland series would not commence for another four years. Something similar happened almost a decade and a half later when the championships were suspended for five years throughout all four provinces due to the travel and other difficulties presented by the on-going political unrest; Leinster resumed action in 1922 and although Dublin won a final that was played in January 1923, the other provinces did not return to the field of play until the following summer.

What was actually won in that debut campaign was officially known as the Leinster Second Division Championship, the 'Junior' designation only came in when the series went national in 1912. Dublin's very first foray in the grade came at Mill Road in Greystones when Wicklow were beaten on a 1-8 to 1-2 scoreline; captained by Dick Manifold and with his Parnells team mate Tommy Donnelly contributing 2-11 in the three games, the provincial crown was secured with further victories over Carlow (1-6 to 1-3 in Newbridge) and Meath (1-8 to 0-3 in Drogheda).

Five barren years followed, in the first of which Dublin were ousted by Kildare in a provincial quarter-final replay at Maryborough Park in Portlaoise and in the second, after a comfortable win over Offaly at the same venue, Louth pulled off an 0-11 to 0-6 win at St. Brigid's Park in Dundalk.

The campaign of 1911 was an odd one, to say the least. Dublin conceded just 3-1 in three games yet failed to come out of Leinster; Wicklow and Offaly were both held scoreless while having, respectively, 3-5 and 2-4 chalked up against them, but in the decider against a Wexford team that included three players — Gus O'Kennedy, Tom Murphy and Aiden Doyle — who four years later would win the first of four successive senior All-Irelands, Dublin themselves could only muster a miserable two points at Wexford Park. They fared even worse in their one and only game the following year, managing just a single point against 1-3 for Carlow who, after Dublin had beaten Kilkenny by 2-2 to 0-2 in a first round tie a year later, repeated the dose with a 2-2 to 1-0 triumph in a quarter-final meeting at the Showgrounds in Athy before going on to a first provincial success and then an 0-7 to 1-2 loss to Kerry in the All-Ireland Final.

WHAT would prove to be Dublin's most successful spell ever in the grade began on 17 May 1914 in Croke Park when goals from Stephen Synnott and Mick Nolan put them on the road to a 2-9 to 0-1 victory over Wicklow in a provincial quarter-final. Meath, their semi-final opponents, could also muster just a single white flag as Dublin hit 1-7 —

Nolan getting 1-4 this time — and in the final, Kilkenny — who wouldn't reach another decider until 1953 — actually gave Dublin their closest call of the campaign before going down 2-2 to 0-3.

Captained by Paddy Carey (who would be one of the stars of the senior three-in-a-row in the next decade and skippered the side in the 1922 campaign), Dublin simply overwhelmed Cavan in the All-Ireland semi-final at Croke Park (played in January 1915), holding their opponents scoreless and registering 3-8 themselves. Mayo, in the final at the same venue four months later, raced into a 1-6 to 0-2 halftime lead but couldn't raise a single flag after the restart as Dublin banged in 5-2 without replay; Nolan, predictably, got one of the goals and finished the programme with 6-7 from the five games. Paddy McDonnell, who would go on to become one of the true all-time legends of Dublin football, first wore the county colours in the provincial final while Frank Burke, who would end his career with seven All-Ireland medals (three football and two hurling at senior level plus a pair of junior honours at the big ball game), made his debut against Mayo.

Dublin selected very much a second string side for the first defence of their titles and paid the price when Louth sprang a 1-4 to 0-4 surprise, again at St. Brigid's Park in Dundalk. Normal service was resumed for the 1916 competition, however; McDonnell and Burke were back in the fold and were joined by another future senior star in Jack O'Reilly. Still, Louth fell short at Croke Park by just a point — 2-3 to 2-2 — in the provincial quarter final, but Kildare and Wexford were accounted for rather more comfortably in the semi-final and final, by 4-1 to 2-2 and 2-7 to 0-2, respectively.

With no competition in Connacht that season, Dublin received a bye into the final against Limerick, a game that wasn't played until September 1917. In it the Munster champions very nearly pulled off a real shock; ahead by 1-1 to 0-1 at halftime, they were still 1-2 to 0-2 to the good with just three minutes remaining when captain James Maguire found the net to earn the Dubs a second chance. They made no mistake in the replay two months later, two goals from Burke helping them into a 5-2 to 0-1 lead at the break and Felix McCann raising a second half green flag en route to an emphatic 6-4 to 0-3 victory.

Not only would it be more than two decades before Dublin would win another All-Ireland in the grade, but that very first success would quickly be tinged by a tragic aftermath. Cork born Jack Cromien, who scored one of the five second half goals in the 1914 decider against Mayo and was a member of the 1st Battalion of the Irish Republican Brotherhood, was shot dead by a sniper on Prussia Street on 26 April 1916, the third day of the Easter Rising.

THE deteriorating political situation in the wake of the Easter Rising, with first the War of Independence and then the Civil War, meant that action at junior level was suspended for five full years in Leinster and six in the rest of the country. Dublin won the revived Leinster Championship in 1922 and despite the fact that they couldn't play anyone outside the province, still managed to get in half a dozen games, one more than in either of their All-Ireland winning years. That was because not only did they have to play a provincial first round tie against Kilkenny before a quarter-final clash against Wexford and then a semi-final and final against Westmeath and Wicklow, respectively, but each of the latter forced them to a replay.

More than a decade and a half of only modest success followed the resumption of action on a nationwide basis in 1923. Dublin did reach the provincial decider that year with wins over Laois in Portlaoise and Kildare in Athy but Carlow, whose only previous Leinster success in the grade was at the expense of The Dubs a decade earlier, did the trick again with a 2-5 to 1-1 triumph at Croke Park. Longford dumped them at the first hurdler the following year — when one of Dublin's midfielders was Mick Gill, who would win an All-Ireland senior hurling medal with his native Galway the following year and later two more with Dublin — and in 1925, after opening with a win over Laois they were beaten by Kildare but were given a reprieve when the Lilywhites were kicked out of the competition for playing an unregistered player in their quarter-final meeting at St. James's Park in Kilkenny. The second chance helped Dublin at least in the short term as they accounted for Meath on a 4-6 to 1-2 scoreline in the provincial semi-final but, not for the first time, Louth edged them 1-3 to 0-4 in the decider at the Showgrounds in Navan.

The provincial crown was reclaimed in the following campaign when after a walkover against Longford in the quarter-final, Kilkenny were hammered 6-2 to 0-1 and then, in the final, Kildare were pipped 0-4 to 0-3 thanks to a late point from full forward Martin Langton. Kerry, courtesy of goals from Tom Kavanagh and Archie Doyle, were dismissed 2-5 to 1-4 in the All-Ireland Final at Walsh Park in Waterford in July 1927 but the decider — played a month later — was a definite anti-climax as Armagh, 1-4 to 0-2 in front at halftime, romped home 4-11 to 0-4.

A fortnight after that victory over Kerry in the All-Ireland semi-final, Dublin, who had earlier beaten Wicklow by 3-5 to 2-2 thanks largely to a 3-1 haul from Willie Dowling, were out of the 1927 campaign, beaten 1-5 to 0-2 by Kildare in a quarter-final clash at Croke Park. The following year promised mush with wins over Wicklow, Westmeath and Wexford but once again, this time at the Gaelic Grounds in Drogheda, Louth pipped them 1-5 to 1-4 in the provincial decider and a year later beat them on a more comfortable 3-1 to 0-6 scoreline, this time in a first round tie at St. Brigid's Park in Dundalk.

After three losses to Louth in the previous five campaigns, Dublin finally got the better of the Wee County with a 4-5 to 1-7 first round win at Drogheda in April 1930 and further victories over Westmeath, Kildare and Carlow secured a sixth provincial title. Donegal put the brakes on them with a draw (0-7 each) in the All-Ireland semi-final at Corrigan Park in Belfast but the replay at Emmett Park in Carrickmacross ended in a convincing 3-6 to 1-2 victory for the Leinster champions. Dublin could be considered decidedly unfortunate not to beat Kerry in the All-Ireland Final (which was played at the University Grounds in Cork; wasteful finishing by their own forwards and a Tom

Landers goal ten minutes from the finish combined to give the Kingdom a wafer thin 2-2 to 1-4 victory. Three of the Dublin team in that decider, Paddy Hickey and the Cavanagh brother, Paddy and Frank (plus Willie Dowling from the 1927 campaign), would go on to feature on the senior team that went down to a two point defeat to Galway in the All-Ireland Final four years later.

Eight more years would go by without another provincial title success and only two deciders were reached in that period; Kildare winning 1-6 to 1-4 in 1931 and Offaly coming out on top by 2-3 to 0-2 at St Brendan's Park in Birr four years later after a 1-6 each draw in Croke Park. Otherwise it was a blank all the way although 1938 did produce a piece of history when Jack Canning from the long defunct Pioneers club became the first Dubliner — in any grade — to score a hat-trick in successive championships games, hitting three goals in a first round win over Longford at Pearse Park, three more plus a point in a quarter-final victory over Carlow at Geraldine Park in Athy, and throwing in a further 1-2 in a 1-6 to 1-4 semi-final loss to Kildare at Dr. Cullen Park in Carlow.

♜ ♜ ♜

THE long famine for a third All-Ireland success and a first since the 1916 campaign was finally ended in 1939, but there were a couple of closes escapes along the way. Wicklow were accounted for easily enough at Novara Road in Bray on a 2-10 to 0-2 scoreline in a provincial quarter-final, but only a last minute goal from Tommy Banks snatched a 2-7 to 3-3 victory over Louth in the semi-final at the Gaelic Grounds in Drogheda. The provincial decider in Newbridge provided the closest shave of all as Meath, with five minutes to go, were 1-7 to 1-3 to the good, only for Dublin to grab a second chance with first a point from Banks and then, three minutes later, a goal from Paddy Kennedy.

The replay, at Sallins Road in Naas, wasn't anywhere near as competitive as Dublin scored 1-6 in each half while Meath claimed five points in the first period but could only add two more in the second as a seventh provincial title was wrapped up with, in the end, some ease. Donegal, who had taken Dublin to a second game in the All-Ireland semi-final nine years previously, were swamped 5-10 to 1-2 at Breffni Park in Cavan this time round and Roscommon, with a quartet of players — including future GAA president Donal Keenan — who would help the county to its first senior All-Ireland four years later, were beaten 2-9 to 1-9 in the 'Home' decider at Croke Park in early September. The final 'Proper' at the same venue four weeks later was a totally one-sided affair as London came out on the wrong end of a 2-12 to 0-4 scoreline. Banks, from Sean McDermotts, scored 2-19 en route to the final but then missed the big day through injury; he would earn some serious consolation three years later, however, scoring 0-28 in six games — including a crucial five points in the 1-10 to 1-8 final defeat of Galway — as Dublin won a first senior All-Ireland crown in a dismal and still record 19 attempts since the 1923 decider, which wasn't played until September of the following year.

Once again there would be a fruitless eight years although half of them — 1942 to 1945 when petrol rationing was largely responsible for the suspension of the entire championship — saw no action at all. Meath were edged out 1-3 to 1-2 in a provincial first round tie at Pairc Colmcille in Kells in April 1940 but a month later, at Croke Park, Westmeath — en route to their fourth and to date last provincial title at the grade, scored a 2-5 to 2-2 win. The following year was an even bigger disappointment as Kildare came out 1-8 to 2-3 winners in a first round clash, Tommy Banks scoring 1-2 to no avail in his final game at junior level.

The opening two campaigns on the resumption of activity in 1946 were by no means overly successful. The first, after a two point victory over Offaly at Barnes Field in Edenderry, ended in a four point loss to Kildare at the same ground and the second, despite reasonably emphatic successes against Offaly, Laois and Wicklow, ended in disappointment when Meath sneaked home 2-3 to 1-4 in the provincial decider at Croke Park.

THE following year, 1948, would not only bring a fifth All-Ireland title and introduce the most significant name in the history of Dublin football but would also see the side play no fewer than ten championship games (a county record for any grade), including three replays.

The marathon season began with a relatively easy 4-8 to 0-4 defeat of Louth in a first round tie at the Iveagh Grounds in Crumlin and was followed by a tight 2-8 to 2-7 victory over Meath at St. Loman's Park in Trim, where future politician Jim Tunney wore the Dublin colours for the first time. Then came a semi-final draw with Kildare in Naas thanks to late points from Sean Farrell and Pearse Walsh, followed by a 2-10 to 0-7 replay win at Croke Park, where Walsh accounted for 1-7 of Dublin's total.

Next up was a second draw when, in the Leinster decider at the County Ground in Aughrim where Dublin, a massive 4-2 to 0-5 behind at halftime, rallied to score 2-4 to Wexford's lone point in the second half to force a replay at the same venue a week later. One of Dublin's points was scored by a former minor who was making his debut at right half forward and who was just under three weeks short of his 19th birthday … his name was Kevin Heffernan.

The second game, as is often the case, was nowhere near as competitive as the first; Dublin, 2-1 to 0-2 in front at the break, romped home on a 6-3 to 2-4 scoreline with Heffernan among the six different goalscorers. Waterford were dismissed 5-11 to 1-3 in the All-Ireland semi-final at their own Walsh Park and then came the 'Home' decider against Armagh at St. Brigid's Park in Dundalk; Dublin, with goals from Heffernan and Ned Kenneally, were leading by 2-6 to 2-3 when a crowd invasion of the pitch encroachment compelled Meath referee Paul Russell to abandon the game with five minutes left on the clock and a replay was subsequently ordered. It took place at Croke Park three weeks later and Dublin made no mistake this time round, winning by 3-8 to 2-6.

The final 'Proper', against London at Croke Park in mid October, was a pretty straightforward affair with Dublin, thanks to a Heffernan goal just after the ten minute mark, leading 1-4 to 0-5 at halftime before going on to win 2-11 to 1-5. Heffernan added the second goal from a penalty and finished the campaign with a tally of 6-3 from five games while Walsh established a still standing record for the grade of 4-35 from nine outings — and neither total included the duo's scores from the aborted tie with Armagh, a goal for Heffernan and four points for team captain Walsh.

LOUTH delivered a reality check by bringing down the champions at the first fence with a 1-3 to 1-2 win in Drogheda in April 1949 but The Dubs were about to enter a decade that would bring success and frustration in equal measure; a period in which the provincial title was won five times yet not a single All-Ireland Final was reached.

Dublin, with a team that included future senior stars Jim Crowley, Seamus McGuinness and Johnny Boyle, came through Leinster in 1950 without being particularly impressive and the shortcomings were exposed in a 4-9 to 0-5 hammering by Mayo in the All-Ireland semi-final. The provincial title was retained the following year — the first time Dublin ever achieved the feat — but yet again Mayo proved the stumbling block, grabbing a draw at Croke Park with two late frees and then winning 3-8 to 2-7 in the replay at Pearse Park in Longford.

Louth again provided first round knockouts in 1952 and 1953 but then, after wins over Wicklow and Kildare, Dublin turned the tables on the Wee County in the Leinster decider, albeit in a replay at Pairc Tailteann in Navan after a draw at the same venue — and then the national semi-final jinx struck again when Kerry scored a 2-7 to 0-9 victory at Fitzgerald Stadium in Killarney. Pretty much the same thing happened again in 1955; the provincial crown was again retained after a replay — this time against Meath — before an All-Ireland semi-final exit to the Munster champions, Cork in this instance.

The next three years all brought elimination by Meath, in the opening round on the first two occasions and in the Leinster Final at Pairc Colmcille in Kells on the third, 1-5 to 1-3. Then the decade ended as it had begun; provincial success against, in order, Louth, Wexford and Longford, and then a fifth All-Ireland semi-final disappointment in ten seasons when, after a 2-8 each draw at O'Toole Park in Dublin, Fermanagh — who would go on to capture what remains their one and only All-Ireland football title in any grade — scored a convincing 4-14 to 3-8 victory in the replay at St Molaise's Park in Irvinestown.

IF the Fifties were frustrating in the extreme, the Sixties very definitely represented a massive false dawn; the decade began with Leinster and All-Ireland glory but that was it, full stop. Not another title of any kind was won, indeed, only one other provincial decider was even reached and that was in 1961.

The campaign which would culminate in a fifth All-Ireland crown began in impressive fashion at St. Conleth's Park in Newbridge in early April when Kildare were routed

5-10 to 2-7 in a provincial quarter-final in which Brian McDonald — who would be on the Sam Maguire winning side three years later — contributed 2-2. Carlow were then beaten 3-9 to 0-6 at Nowlan Park in Kilkenny and, in the final, Meath were overcome 2-9 to 0-5 at Cusack Park in Mullingar, McDonald again finding the net on each occasion. Trailing 1-6 to 0-3 in the final minute of the first half of the All-Ireland semi-final against Kerry at Austin Stack Park in Tralee, Dublin cut the arrears in half with a goal from Sean 'Blackie' Coen before snatching a 1-9 to 1-8 victory thanks to a 59th minute point from full forward Kevin Russell — who was making his lone appearance of the six man campaign. Things were relatively clearcut after that; Galway were accounted for on a 1-12 to 0-9 scoreline in the All-Ireland 'Home' Final at Croke Park in mid September that then London were conquered 2-5 to 0-5 in the decider 'Proper' at the same venue three weeks later.

Aside from McDonald (who finished the campaign with 5-7), the triumphant Dublin side included a number of other notable names, such as Skerries midfielder Sean Murray from the senior All-Ireland winning side of two years previously, defenders Christy Kane and Donal Mulligan who would join McDonald on the provincial senior title winning side in 1965, and Vincent Murphy, father of future superstar Vinny. Mick Kissane and Simon Behan, who would be team mates of McDonald in the Sam Maguire triumph in 1963, both played in the first two games of the campaign but were relegated to the bench thereafter.

Dublin, with 1963 senior All-Ireland winner Leo Hickey at full back, stumbled through to another provincial final the following year with wins over Kildare and Wicklow — the latter at the second attempt — but came unstuck against Louth at Pairc Tailteann in Navan when wasteful shooting played a major part in a 2-4 to 0-8 defeat. It got even worse from then on; Dublin would win only four games in the remaining eight years of the decade and, after one of those victories, found themselves compelled to pull of the competition!

Westmeath were beaten 2-7 to 1-5 in a first round meeting at Croke Park in April 1962 but Dublin would then suffer four defeats in succession, to Wexford and Westmeath and then twice to Kildare. With a certain Paddy Cullen lining out at right corner back, they did manage a 1-9 to 0-6 defeat of Laois at Dr. Cullen Park in Carlow in April 1966 but then, when ordered to play their quarter-final against Louth at Gaelic Grounds in Drogheda in conjunction with the senior championship meeting of the same counties, withdrew in protest. Quarter-final wins over Meath and Louth were recorded in 1967 and 1968 but those successful openings were quickly cancelled out by Offaly and Westmeath, respectively, and the decade ended with a 2-5 to 1-6 loss to Meath, despite the fact that the full back berth was filled by the man who would skipper the county to Sam Maguire success five years later, Sean Doherty.

Another future Celtic Cross winner — a four-timer, in fact — was on the junior team in 1970 when, after wins over Meath and Offaly, Dublin blew a 1-9 to 1-3 halftime lead to Kildare in Navan, conceding 2-10 after the restart while only adding two points themselves. Anton O'Toole was there again the following year when a first provincial title since 1960 was captured with wins over Louth, Meath, Longford and Kilkenny and followed by victories over Down (0-15 to 1-6) in the All-Ireland semi-final at Croke Park and, in the 'Home' decider, Cork (1-14 to 2-5) at Clonmel before London ended the run with a 1-9 to 0-9 triumph in the final 'Proper' at New Eltham. Right corner forward Fred Hutchinson, a clubmate of O'Toole with Synge Street, scored 1-34 in the course of the seven match campaign and another ever present, at right full back, was Leo Hickey, a decade after his debut in the grade and eight year's after being on the senior All-Ireland winning side.

The following two years, 1972 and 1973, yielded little, a quarter-final win over Louth being followed by a loss to Offaly in the first campaign and a 2-10 to 0-11 loss to Meath in the second. The entire championships, provincial and national, were suspended from 1974 to 1982 inclusive and, on their return to the calendar, Dublin had but limited success.

THE initial resumption of action was promising as Dublin, with wins over Kildare, Wexford and Meath secured a 16th provincial title and then a 2-14 routing of Tyrone in the All-Ireland semi-final at Park Road in Rush set up a decider against Kerry at McDonagh Park in Nenagh. By halftime it appeared to be all over as the Kingdom opened up a massive 1-8 to 0-3 lead only for Dublin to put in a magnificent rally and, thanks to a goal from Anthony White and three points in the final four minutes from Tom Cashin, snatched a 1-9 to 1-9 draw. The replay at Cusack Park in Ennis a fortnight later, however, was a major letdown; Kerry again forged a substantial interval lead of 1-7 to 0-4 but his time there was no Dublin fightback and the title went to the Kingdon on a 1-9 to 0-5 scoreline.

The following four campaigns brought two more provincial crowns in 1985 and 1987 but again the ultimate prize proved unobtainable. White was there for both campaigns as was Jack Sheedy, but Galway scored a narrow 1-13 to 2-8 victory in the All-Ireland semi-final at Parnell Park in the first instance and then two years later, when both Connacht and Ulster had suspended their championships, Cork came out on top by 2-7 to 0-8 in the All-Ireland decider at Semple Stadium.

Three provincial deciders were lost to Meath over the next four campaigns (1988, 1990 and 1991, the latter following a replay), first round defeats against Longford and Carlow followed, and it wasn't until 1994 that a 19th provincial crown was captured. Successive wins over Meath (1-13 to 0-12), Laois (1-16 to 0-2) and Louth (0-9 to 0-5) set up a national decider against Kerry; goalkeeper Alan Durnan remained unbeaten through the campaign but Kerry notched up 0-13 to 1-7 for the Dubs and yet another All-Ireland title was lost.

Almost a decade and a half would pass without further success of any kind; first round exits were suffered on five occasions, against Meath in 1996, Louth the following year (when Barney Rock reappeared to score 1-4 to no avail), Offaly in 2001, Wicklow a year later, and Kildare in 2005, and the nearest Dublin got to winning anything was a quartet of provincial final defeats, to Meath in 1999, Wexford in 2000 (when Rock again resurfaced to score 1-2 over 22 years after he had first pulled on a county jersey), Kildare in 2004 and Wexford again in 2007.

WHEN the long awaited sixth All-Ireland title finally came in 2008, it did so in pretty straightforward fashion. Cavan — competing in Leinster because Ulster had abandoned the grade — were beaten 1-12 to 0-11 in the provincial quarter-final, Kildare then fell 0-11 to 1-6 in the semi-final, and Meath were beaten 1-13 to 1-9 in the decider. The All-Ireland semi-final offered unusual opposition at an unusual venue but little in the way of a test, as Gloucestershire were hammered 5-24 to 0-9 at Gaelic Field in Cardiff and only Roscommon at O'Moore Park in Portlaoise stood between Dublin and a first junior championship in just two years short of half a century.

The crown was duly lifted on an 0-13 to 0-7 scoreline with a side that included five players — Darren Daly, Michael Fitzsimons, Denis Bastick, Eoghan O'Gara, Jonny Cooper — who would play prominent roles in the subsequent senior success under first Pat Gilroy and then Jim Gavin, plus another senior star in Darren Homan who, having been forced to retire through injury three years earlier, made a one season comeback and was brought on from the bench for the final two games. Warren Finnegan, from St. Brigid's, finished the five match programme with 2-24, the fourth best ever by a Dub in the grade.

That was as good as it was to get. Dublin edged Kildare by 0-13 to 0-12 in the provincial quarter-final the following year — when Dean Rock scored all but four points of the side's total — but were then ousted 1-13 to 0-11 by Louth at McGeough Park in Haggardstown, Kildare sent them packing at the first hurdle in 2010 and beat them again a year later at Parnell Park after Dublin had overcome Wicklow at the same venue a fortnight earlier. Dublin opted out of the competition for 2012 and have remained outside the fold since.

Junior Championship Results

1905–07

Dublin did not enter the first three stagings of the Championship. Although the Leinster Championship was inaugurated in 1905, the All-Ireland series would not begin for another seven years. Prior to the commencement of the latter, the competition within the province was known as the Leinster Second Division Championship.

1908

LEINSTER QUARTER-FINAL
Aug 30, Mill Road, Greystones
DUBLIN 1-8   WICKLOW 1-2
Dublin: J Duffy, P Callaghan, R Downey, P Connor, T Lonergan, D Manifold, P Kenny, W Moore, P Christie, T Geraghty, C Carberry, J Beggs, T Donnelly 1-3, F Brady 0-1, P Reilly 0-1, J Cooney, F Sharkey.

LEINSTER SEMI-FINAL
Dec 6, St Conleth's Park, Newbridge
DUBLIN 1-6   CARLOW 1-3
Dublin: J Duffy, R Downey, T Geraghty, M Callaghan, D Manifold, W Moore, J Beggs, F Brady, P Connor, J Nathan, T Donnelly 1-4, W Murphy, C Carberry 0-1, E Letmon, T Lonergan 0-1, P Reilly, F Sharkey.

LEINSTER FINAL
May 2, 1909, Shamrock Lodge, Drogheda
DUBLIN 1-8   MEATH 0-3
Dublin: J Duffy, R Downey, Pat Connor, T Lonergan, Chris Carberry, M Toby, D Manifold, W Moore, P Christie, W Murphy 0-1, E Letmon 0-1, T Geraghty, T Bedford 0-1, M Callaghan, T Donnelly 0-4, J Nathan, J Beggs, F Brady 1-0, P Reilly 0-1, P Brady, F Sharkey.

1909

LEINSTER QUARTER-FINAL
July 18, Jones's Road, Dublin
DUBLIN 0-8   KILDARE 0-8
Dublin: J Dunne, J Quinn, E Bailey, T Byrne, D Mehigan, M Kennedy 0-2, J O'Toole, P Sheridan, F Dowling, P Finlay, M Kinsella, M Lonergan, R Wall, J Lecky 0-4, J Nugent 0-1, P Galligan 0-1, J Halligan.

LEINSTER QUARTER-FINAL REPLAY
Aug 8, Maryborough Park, Portlaoise
KILDARE 2-13   DUBLIN 0-7
Dublin: J Dunne, J Quinn, E Bailey, T Byrne, W

McGrane, M Kennedy 0-1, O'Toole, P Sheridan, F Dowling, P Finlay, M Kinsella, J Power, F Adrill, J Lecky 0-3, J Nugent 0-1, P Galligan 0-1, J Halligan 0-1.

1910

LEINSTER QUARTER-FINAL:
July 17, Maryborough Park, Portlaoise
DUBLIN 2-16   OFFALY 1-1
Dublin: J Duffy, L Hanney, A O'Connor, P White, J McGovern, C Hanney, D Reilly 0-2, M Hanney, M Kinsella, P Finlay, J Cooke, P Kearns 0-1, J Nugent 0-2, P Smith 1-5, M Doran 1-3, F O'Brien 0-2, P Galligan 0-1.

LEINSTER SEMI-FINAL
Aug 8, Maryborough Park, Portlaoise
LOUTH 0-11   DUBLIN 0-6
Dublin: J Duffy, A O'Connor, P White, J McGovern, C Hanney, D Reilly, M Hanney, M Kinsella, P Finlay, P Kearns, J Cooke, J Dowling 0-1, J Cooke, F O'Brien 0-1, P Smith 0-3, M Doran 0-1, P Galligan.

1911

LEINSTER QUARTER-FINAL
June 11, Jones's Road, Dublin
DUBLIN 3-5   WICKLOW 0-0
Dublin: J Duffy, P Kearns, P Kelly, M O'Callaghan, J Guilfoyle, P Bailey, A Byrne, W Crowley 0-1, D Mehigan, J Rice, R Mooney, E Norton 0-1, P Rice, J Murray, J Cooke 1-1, J Joyce 1-1, W Redmond 0-1.

LEINSTER SEMI-FINAL
July 9, Jones's Road, Dublin
DUBLIN 2-4   OFFALY 0-0
Dublin: J Duffy, P Kelly, P Kearns, J Guilfoyle, P Bailey, A Byrne, M O'Callaghan, D Mehigan, W Crowley 1-0, J Rice, R Mooney, D Kiely, J Murray, J Cooke 0-2, J Joyce 1-1, M Carroll 0-1, E Hannigan.

LEINSTER FINAL
Jan 21, 1912, Wexford Park, Wexford
WEXFORD 3-1   DUBLIN 0-2
Dublin: L Kelly, P Kearns, J Duffy, M O'Callaghan, J Guilfoyle, P Bailey, L Byrne, J O'Connor, R Mooney, J Rice, J Cooke, W Crowley, J Murray, P Rice, J Joyce 0-1, M Carroll, J Cooney, W Redmond 0-1, P Forde, E Norton, J Hughes.

1912

LEINSTER FIRST ROUND
May 19, Graigue Park, Carlow
CARLOW 1-3   DUBLIN 0-1
Dublin: J Duffy, R Mooney, J Rice, A Byrne, B Kelly, J Sweeney, M Coogan, P Kelly, P Carey, J Guilfoyle, J Halligan, W Blockburne, S Synnott, J Joyce, P Kearns, J Cooke 0-1, W Redmond.

1913

LEINSTER FIRST ROUND
June 8, Maryborough Park, Portlaoise
DUBLIN 2-2   KILKENNY 0-2
Dublin: M Nolan, J Brennan, J Cullen, J Treacy, P Carey, J Manifold, J McDonnell, S Synnott, P Blackburn, M Nolan, J Taaffe, T Dunbar, E Ryan, J Halligan, J Lecky 1-1, P Kearns 1-0, J Cooke 0-1.

LEINSTER QUARTER-FINAL
Aug 10, Showgrounds, Athy
CARLOW 2-2   DUBLIN 1-0
Dublin: J Deegan, J McDonnell, M Norton, G Kinder, J Deegan, J Treacy, S Synnott, P Carey, T Cooke, M Flynn, J Halligan, J Cooke, J Sweeney, G Hackett, G Sweeney, J Lecky 1-0, J Brennan, P Martin.

1914

LEINSTER QUARTER-FINAL
May 17, Croke Park, Dublin
DUBLIN 2-9   WICKLOW 0-1
Dublin: L Kelly, J Whelan, M Timmins, T McAdams, P Carey 0-1, M Brennan, D Kiely, S Synnott 1-0, P Kerins, M Nolan 1-2, J Minehan, J Treacy, M Norton, F McCann 0-2, S Lawlor 0-4.

LEINSTER SEMI-FINAL
July 5, Croke Park, Dublin
DUBLIN 1-7   MEATH 0-1
Dublin: L Kelly, P Smith, T Corr, T McAdams, P Kerins, S Synnott, D Kiely, P Carey 0-1, P Whelan, M Norton 0-1, P McDonnell, J Cromien 0-1, J Halligan, S Lawlor, M Nolan 1-4.

LEINSTER FINAL
Sep 27, Showgrounds, Athy
DUBLIN 2-2   KILKENNY 0-3
Dublin: L Kelly, P Carey, T Corr, P Smith, D Kelly, P Kerins, P Whelan, M Morton, S Synnott 0-1, T McAdams, P McDonnell, F McCann 1-0, J Cromien 0-1, J Halligan, M Nolan 1-0. Sub: Josie Synnott for Halligan.

ALL-IRELAND SEMI-FINAL
Jan 17, 1915, Croke Park, Dublin
DUBLIN 3-8   CAVAN 0-0
Dublin: L Kelly, P Smith, P Whelan, D Kiely 0-1, T Corr, T McAdams, P Kerins, C McAuley, J Synnott 0-1, P McDonnell, F McCann 1-2, P Carey, J Cromien 0-2, M Nolan 2-1, S Synnott 0-1.

ALL-IRELAND FINAL
Apr 25, 1915, Croke Park, Dublin
DUBLIN 5-4   MAYO 1-6
Dublin: Leo Kelly, Paddy Carey, Tom Corr, Peadar Smith, Diarmuid Kelly 0-1, Paddy Kerins, Stephen Synnott 1-0, Frank Burke, Felix McCann 1-0, Jack Cromien 1-0, Paddy McDonnell 1-1, Mick Nolan 1-0, Jack Coogan, Tommy McAdams 0-2, Pat Whelan.

1915

LEINSTER QUARTER-FINAL
May 23, St Brigid's Park, Dundalk
LOUTH 1-4   DUBLIN 0-4
Dublin: J Neville, J Treacy, C Hannery, M McGarry, P Lawless, R Davey, M Reynolds, J Minehan, M Gibbons, J Fox 0-2, P White 0-1, J McGrath 0-1, J O'Reilly 0-1, J O'Connell, J McGrath.

1916

LEINSTER QUARTER-FINAL
July 23, Croke Park, Dublin
DUBLIN 2-3   LOUTH 2-2
Dublin: W Tynan, W Grealy, H O'Neill, J Byrne, W Brien, P Clarke, M Kenneally, R Davey, J Quinn, T Byrne, F Cooney 0-1, J O'Reilly, J Hayden, J Hickey 1-0, J McKittrick 0-1.

LEINSTER SEMI-FINAL
Oct 29, Sportsfield, Newbridge
DUBLIN 4-1   KILDARE 2-2
Dublin: W Tynan, P White, W Grealy, H O'Neill, P Clarke, J Treacy, R Davey, J Byrne 1-1, J O'Reilly, J Quinn, T Byrne, J Hayden, P Norton 1-0, T Ennis 2-0, J Fox.

LEINSTER FINAL
June 24, 1917, Croke Park
DUBLIN 2-7   WEXFORD 0-2
Dublin: J Molloy, H O'Neill, M Sheridan, J Maguire, J Treacy 0-1, J Byrne, P White, J Fox 1-0, J Mulvihill, J Donovan, B Joyce, F Burke 1-1, F McCann 0-2, P McCarvill 0-3, J O'Reilly.

ALL-IRELAND FINAL
Sep 16, 1917, Croke Park, Dublin
DUBLIN 1-2   LIMERICK 1-2
Dublin: J Molloy, Hugh O'Neill, J Maguire 1-0, Michael Sheridan, J Donovan, Paddy McDonnell, J Fox, Frank Burke 0-1, Brian Joyce, J Treacy, J Hayden, J Byrne,

Felix McCann 0-1, Jack O'Reilly, J Mulvihill.
* Dublin received a bye into the final as there was no Championship in Connacht.
ALL-IRELAND FINAL REPLAY
Nov 18, 1917, Croke Park, Dublin
DUBLIN 6-4   LIMERICK 0-3
Dublin: J Molloy, Hugh O'Neill, J Maguire (capt), Michael Sheridan, Jack O'Reilly, Paddy McDonnell 0-2, P White, J Donovan 1-1, Felix McCann 1-0, Pat McCarvill 1-0, Frank Burke 2-0, Brian Joyce, J Hayden, J Treacy 1-1, J Byrne.

1917-21

* Championship suspended.

1922

LEINSTER FIRST ROUND
May 21, Croke Park, Dublin
DUBLIN 2-0   KILKENNY 0-4
Dublin: P Higgins, J Nolan, F Mahony, R Fox, G Manley, M Quinn, W Ellard, T Brady, J Wilson, P Duffy, P Cullen, J Cleary 1-0, D Meade, A Hunston 1-0, S O'Connor.

LEINSTER QUARTER-FINAL
Oct 1, Croke Park, Dublin
DUBLIN 2-4   WEXFORD 0-3
Dublin: P Higgins, P Dillon, J O'Connor, P Killane, T Cowley, D Meade, A Hunston 1-1, P Duffy, J Teeling 1-2, T Mahony, T Kavanagh, M Gill, S Quinn, M Nolan, J Wilson 0-1.

LEINSTER SEMI-FINAL
Oct 22, Croke Park, Dublin
DUBLIN 2-1   WESTMEATH 1-4
Dublin: P Higgins, S Quinn, J O'Connor, J Cleary, M Keogh, P Cullen, J Wilson, P Killane, P Duffy, B Higgins, T Mahony, D Meade, A Hunston 1-1, J Rogers, T Kavanagh 1-0.

LEINSTER SEMI-FINAL REPLAY
Nov 5, Croke Park, Dublin
DUBLIN 1-3   WESTMEATH 0-2
Dublin: P Higgins, J O'Connor, J Cleary, M Keogh, P Cullen, J Wilson, P Killane, P Duffy, T Mahony, D Meade, A Hunston 1-3, J Rogers, J Teeling, T Kavanagh, P Geraghty.

LEINSTER FINAL
Nov 26, Croke Park, Dublin
DUBLIN 0-3   WICKLOW 0-3
Dublin: P Higgins, D Meade, J Rogers, A Hunston 0-1, J Wilson, M Keogh, P Killane, P Duffy, P Cullen, T Mahony 0-1, B Higgins, T Kavanagh, P Geraghty, J Cleary, P Hopkins. Sub: J Teeling 0-1 for B Higgins.

LEINSTER FINAL REPLAY
Jan 21, 1923, Croke Park, Dublin
DUBLIN 2-2   WICKLOW 0-3
Dublin: Pat Higgins, Dan Meade, J Rogers, M Keogh, Sean O'Connor, J Wilson (capt), P Killane, Tom Mahony, Jimmy Teeling 0-2, J Russell 2-0, T Kavanagh, P Geraghty, P Hopkins, P Cullen, Joe Cleary.
* There was no All-Ireland series as the Championship had yet to resume in the other provinces.

1923

LEINSTER QUARTER-FINAL
Apr 15, Maryborough Park, Portlaoise
DUBLIN 3-2   LAOIS 1-1
Dublin: P Smullen, J Kelly, C McGuinness, J Norris, J Casserly, J Molloy, J Doyle, W Finlay 0-1, J Kennedy, J Lynam, J Hayden, M Roe 1-1, M Gill 2-0, V Barry, P Byrne.

LEINSTER SEMI-FINAL
June 10, Showgrounds, Athy
DUBLIN 2-1   KILDARE 1-2
Dublin: P Smullen, C McGuinness, J Molloy, J Norris, J Kelly, J Casserly, W Finlay 1-0, P Byrne, A Hunston 0-1 J Doyle, P Barry, M Roe, M Gill 1-0, J Moore, J Lynham.

LEINSTER FINAL
Nov 18, Croke Park, Dublin
CARLOW 2-5   DUBLIN 1-1
Dublin: P Smullen, J Molloy, J Norris, P Synnott 0-1, C McGuinness, A Hunston, P Byrne, J Doyle, W Finlay, M Gill, M Roe, P Reilly, J Moore, J Casserley 1-0, W Corcoran. Sub: J Kelly for Moore.

1924

LEINSTER QUARTER-FINAL
July 20, Pearse Park, Longford
LONGFORD 1-6   DUBLIN 1-3
Dublin: W Sheeran, J Kelly, P Byrne, J Brady, C McGuinness, M Walsh, P Stynes, J Hayden, M Gill 0-2, M Butler, M Roe 1-0, P Barry, R Butler 0-1, J McHugh, P Gill.

1925

LEINSTER FIRST ROUND
May 17, Showgrounds, Athy
DUBLIN 2-4   LAOIS 2-2
Dublin: W Collins, M Cullen, G Knight, W Corcoran, M Murray, Pat Byrne, C Bissett, B Hudson, L Shaw 2-1, S Nolan, A Dixon 0-2, J O'Toole, J Doran, M Durnin 0-1, Paddy Byrne.

LEINSTER QUARTER-FINAL
July 5, St James's Park, Kilkenny
KILDARE 2-4   DUBLIN 0-4
Dublin: W Collins, P Lawless, C Bisset, M Cullen, W Corcoran, G Knight 0-2, Pat Byrne, B Hudson, G Canavan, J Doran, Paddy Byrne, T Banehan, S Banehan, A Dixon 0-2, M Durnan.
* Dublin reinstated after Kildare were removed from the Championship for fielding an unregistered player.

LEINSTER SEMI-FINAL
Sep 20, St Brigid's Park, Dundalk
DUBLIN 4-6   MEATH 1-2
Dublin: W Collins, M Cullen, C Bissett, G Canavan, J Brady, Paddy Byrne, G Knight 1-0, Pat Byrne, F Patten 2-1, J Doran, B Higgins 0-1, S Baneham 0-1, A Dixon 1-2, M Durnin 0-1, S Nolan.

LEINSTER FINAL
Nov 1, Showgrounds, Navan
LOUTH 1-3   DUBLIN 0-4
Dublin: W Collins, M Cullen, J Moore 0-1, G Knight, Paddy Byrne, G Canavan, F Patten 0-1, Pat Byrne, J Brady, C Bissett, S Baneham, A Dixon, S Nolan, J Doran 0-1, M Durnin 0-1. Sub: B Higgins for Bissett.

1926

LEINSTER SEMI-FINAL
Oct 10, Showgrounds, Athy
DUBLIN 6-2   KILKENNY 0-1
Dublin: P Connolly, E Rice, G Nolan, J Rogers, W Finlay, T Kavanagh, D Murphy, T Keogh 0-2, J Doran, G McDermott, G Devine 1-0, J Sherlock, A Doyle 2-0, E Whelan 2-0, S Baneham 1-0.
* Dublin received a walkover from Longford in the quarter-final.

LEINSTER FINAL
Nov 7, Croke Park, Dublin
DUBLIN 0-4   KILDARE 0-3
Dublin: P Connolly, E Rice 0-1, J Rogers, G Nolan, D Murphy, S Baneham 0-1, E Whelan 0-1, J Rogers, G Devine, T Kavanagh, W Finlay, A Doyle, S Nolan, M Langton 0-1, J Sherlock,

ALL-IRELAND SEMI-FINAL
July 10, 1927, Walsh Park, Waterford
DUBLIN 2-5   KERRY 1-4
Dublin: P Connolly, E Rice, G Nolan, J Sherlock, D Murphy, J Rogers, S Nolan, M Langton, J Doran, J Kinsella, J Corcoran, S Baneham, T Kavanagh 1-1, W Finlay 0-2, A Doyle 1-2.

ALL-IRELAND FINAL
Aug 14, 1927, Croke Park, Dublin
ARMAGH 4-11   DUBLIN 0-4
Dublin: H Kelly, Eddie Rice, George Nolan, Jim Rogers, Martin Langton, Joe Corcoran, Tom Kavanagh 0-1, Willie Finlay 0-2, Sam Baneham, Denis Murphy, Archie Doyle 0-1, Joe Sherlock, Stephen Nolan, Sean Doran, Mick Gill.

1927

LEINSTER FIRST ROUND
May 15, Croke Park, Dublin
DUBLIN 3-5   WICKLOW 2-2
Dublin: J Mooney, R Matthews, T Byrne, M Byrne, G McDermott, W McEvoy, E McEvoy, W Maguire, N McCann 0-1, R Whittaker, W Dowling 3-1, M Coates 0-2, W McCann, F Cavanagh 0-1, P Nugent.

LEINSTER QUARTER-FINAL
July 24, Croke Park, Dublin
KILDARE 1-5   DUBLIN 0-2
Dublin: J Mooney, R Matthews, T Byrne, M Byrne, J Brady, G McDermott, W McEvoy, E McEvoy, W Maguire, N McCann, R Whittaker, W Dowling, M Coates, F Cavanagh, P Nugent 0-2.

1928

LEINSTER FIRST ROUND
Apr 15, County Ground, Aughrim
DUBLIN 3-4   WICKLOW 2-3
Dublin: J Mulhall, C Rochfort, Johnny Macken, Joe Macken, C Duffy, S Whiston 0-1, W Barry, M Curley, T Newman 1-2, W Dowling 0-1, P Hickey, J O'Toole, M O'Brien 2-0, A Perkins, T McConnon.

LEINSTER QUARTER-FINAL
July 1, Cusack Park, Mullingar
DUBLIN 4-5   WESTMEATH 3-1
Dublin: J Mulhall, C Rochfort, S Whiston, Joe Macken, C Duffy 1-0, P Moore, W Moore, Johnny Macken, W Barry, T Newman 2-3, T McKane, P Hickey, M Curley 1-0, W Dowling 0-1, P Rogers 0-1.

LEINSTER SEMI-FINAL
July 8, Croke Park, Dublin
DUBLIN 3-5   WEXFORD 3-1
Dublin: J Mulhall, C Rochfort, Joe Macken, C Duffy, P Moore, P Hickey, W Dowling, T McConnon, J O'Rourke, Johnny Macken 0-2, S Whiston 1-2, J McCann, F Cavanagh, T Newman 1-1, P Kearney. Own goal by R Freeman.

LEINSTER FINAL
July 29, Gaelic Grounds, Drogheda
LOUTH 1-5   DUBLIN 1-4
Dublin: J Mulhall, C Rochfort, C Duffy, P Moone, W
Dowling, P Hickey, S Whiston, J Macken, J O'Rourke, T
Newman 1-2, F Cavanagh, P Rogers 0-1, T McConnon,
J McCann 0-1, P Kearney.

1929

LEINSTER FIRST ROUND
Apr 21, St Brigid's Park, Dundalk
LOUTH 3-1   DUBLIN 0-6
Dublin: J Mulhall, C Rochfort, P McManus, F Kellett,
P Rogers, Joe O'Rourke, T McConnon, F Cavanagh, M
Wellington, S Whiston 0-2, M Curley, T Newman 0-2,
W Dowling, G Monks, John O'Rourke 0-1.

1930

LEINSTER FIRST ROUND
Apr 27, Gaelic Grounds, Drogheda
DUBLIN 4-5   LOUTH 1-7
Dublin: J Begley, H Kelly, P Byrne, P Rogers, P Dingle
0-1, E Lee 0-1, T Coates, P Cavanagh, P Hickey, W
Dowling, G O'Reilly 0-3, T Dunne, J Dowling 0-1, C
Duffy 1-0, J Dormer 2-0.

LEINSTER QUARTER-FINAL
July 13, Cusack Park, Mullingar
DUBLIN 2-3   WESTMEATH 1-4
Dublin: J Begley, H Kelly, P Byrne, P Rogers, P Dingle,
E Lee, F Cavanagh, P Hickey, P Cavanagh, S Lavin,
G O'Reilly 0-1, T Dunne, A Dixon 0-1, C Duffy 1-1, J
Dormer 1-0.

LEINSTER SEMI-FINAL
Aug 17, O'Moore Park, Portlaoise
DUBLIN 3-5   KILDARE 1-2
Dublin: J Begley, H Kelly, P Rogers, F Cavanagh, P
Cavanagh, P Byrne, E Hunston, G O'Reilly, T Dunne,
John O'Rourke, S Lavin 1-0, Duffy 0-1, A Dixon, J
Coffey 1-1, J Dormer.

LEINSTER FINAL
Aug 31, Showground, Athy
DUBLIN 3-3   CARLOW 0-2
Dublin: J Begley, F McCann, H Kelly, P Hickey, F
Cavanagh, J O'Rourke, P Byrne, G O'Reilly, S Lavin, J
Coffey 1-1, P Cavanagh, J Dormer 1-0, A Dixon 0-2, C
Duffy 1-0, T Dunne.

ALL-IRELAND SEMI-FINAL
Sep 21, Corrigan Park, Belfast
DUBLIN 0-7   DONEGAL 0-7
Dublin: J Begley, H Kelly, E Hunston, F Cavanagh, P

Hickey, J O'Rourke, P Cavanagh, P Byrne, C Duffy
0-3, J Dormer 0-1, G O'Reilly 0-2, S Lavin, A Boylan, A
Dixon 0-1, J Coffey.

ALL-IRELAND SEMI-FINAL REPLAY
Oct 26, Emmett Park, Carrickmacross
DUBLIN 3-6   DONEGAL 1-2
Dublin: J Begley, H Kelly, F Cavanagh, P Rogers,
P Cavanagh, P Byrne, P Hickey, G O'Reilly 1-0, E
Hunston 0-2, J O'Rourke, A Dixon 0-1, S Lavan 1-1, E
Lee, M Brennan 1-0, C Duffy 0-2.

ALL-IRELAND FINAL
Nov 23, University Grounds, Cork
KERRY 2-2   DUBLIN 1-4
Dublin: Joe Begley, Hugh Kelly, Pat Rogers, Frank
Cavanagh, Paddy Hickey, John O'Rourke, Pat Byrne,
Paddy Cavanagh, Sean Lavin 0-1, Eddie Hunston,
Chris Duffy 0-2, Michael Brennan 1-0, Eddie Lee,
Gerry O'Reilly, Arthur Dixon 0-1.

1931

LEINSTER QUARTER-FINAL
Apr 19, Pearses' Park, Arklow
DUBLIN 1-3   WICKLOW 0-4
Dublin: P Higgins, J Moore, I Doyle, P Kane 0-1, P
O'Brien, P Lyons, J Molloy, D Rickard, L Hanway, T
McConnon, J Delaney, C Collier, J O'Rourke 1-0, M
Brennan 0-1, J Carroll 1-0.

LEINSTER SEMI-FINAL
June 14, McGrath Park, Bagenalstown
DUBLIN 2-3   WEXFORD 1-3
Dublin: P Higgins, J Moore, I Doyle, P Kane, P
O'Brien, P Lyons, J Molloy 1-0, D Rickard, L Hanway,
T McConnon, J Delaney 0-1, C Collier, J Dolan 0-1, M
Brennan, J Murray 1-0.

LEINSTER FINAL
Aug 23, Croke Park, Dublin
KILDARE 1-6   DUBLIN 1-4
Dublin: P Higgins, J Dolan, P Cullen, J Murray,
J Delaney, T Doyle, J O'Rourke, J O'Hare 0-1, T
McConnon 0-2, F Williams 0-1, C Collier 1-0, J Molloy,
L Hanley, P Kane, J Lyons. Sub: J Moore for Murray.

1932

LEINSTER QUARTER-FINAL
May 1, Novara Road, Bray
DUBLIN 2-7   WICKLOW 0-3
Dublin: G Nolan, T Ronan, J O'Neill, J Dolan, M
Browne, W Doyle, J Teeling, M Donnelly, T McConnon
0-2, C Gaughran 1-1, P Moran, J O'Neill 1-1, J Crosby
0-3, E Timmons, B Beggs.

LEINSTER SEMI-FINAL
May 15, St Brigid's Park, Dundalk
LOUTH 2-6   DUBLIN 1-4
Dublin: G Nolan, T Ronan, W Doyle, J O'Neill 1-0, J Dolan, M Browne 0-1, P Moran, P O'Neill, M Donnelly 0-1, T McConnon 0-1, C Gaughran, J Teeling, G Stewart, B Beggs, E Timmons. Sub: J Crosby 0-1 for O'Neill.

1933

LEINSTER FIRST ROUND
Apr 30, Showgrounds, Navan
DUBLIN 5-4   MEATH 3-6
Dublin: C Clarke, P O'Toole, P Walsh, H Kelly, M Donnelly, M Gargan, J Jones, J O'Hare, J McDermott, P O'Neill, P Mulhall 0-2, T Rock 1-1, G Stewart, C Gaughran 3-0, W Redmond 1-1.

LEINSTER QUARTER-FINAL
June 4, St Conleth's Park, Newbridge
DUBLIN 2-6   KILDARE 2-3
Dublin: C Clarke, P O'Toole, J Nolan, H Kelly, M Donnelly, B Beggs, J Butler, M Gargan, J O'Hare, P O'Neill, S Lawless, G Stewart 1-0, W Redmond 1-3, C Gaughran, T Rock 0-1.

LEINSTER SEMI-FINAL
July 16, Geraldine Park, Athy
DUBLIN 0-8   CARLOW 0-8
Dublin: C Clarke, P O'Toole, D O'Brien, H Kelly, M Donnelly, B Beggs, J Butler, C Gaughran, J O'Hare, P O'Neill, M Wellington 0-3, T Rock 0-1, G Stewart, W Redmond 0-3, W Brady.

LEINSTER SEMI-FINAL REPLAY
Aug 6, O'Moore Park, Portlaoise
CARLOW 2-9   DUBLIN 1-2
Dublin: C Clarke, P O'Toole, D O'Brien, W Brady, M Donnelly, B Beggs, J Butler, C Gaughran, J O'Hare, P O'Neill, M Wellington 0-1, T Rock 1-0, G Stewart 0-1, W Redmond 0-3, J Brady.

1934

LEINSTER FIRST ROUND
Apr 15, Croke Park, Dublin
DUBLIN 3-3   MEATH 1-7
Dublin: P Dowling, P Walsh, G Griffin, M Kenny, P Cluskey, J O'Hara, M Smith, T Robinson, P McMahon, P Bermingham 1-0, J O'Hare, N Dunne 0-3, J Curran, C McGinty 1-0, C White 1-0.

LEINSTER QUARTER-FINAL
June 24, County Ground, Aughrim
WICKLOW 2-5   DUBLIN 2-1
Dublin: P Dowling, P Cluskey, T Robinson, M Smith, P McMahon, N Dunne, D Banville, J O'Hare, M McEvoy, P Bermingham, J Colleran 2-0, T Rock, J Curran 0-1, A Allen, J Richardson.

1935

LEINSTER QUARTER-FINAL
Apr 7, St Brigid's Park, Dundalk
DUBLIN 1-0   LOUTH 0-3
Dublin: R Earls, P Treacy, P Baxter, J Martin, J Delaney, J Murphy, P Bermingham, P Murray, H Murphy, J Jones, T Rock 1-0, N Boland, S Byrne, D Doyle, T Griffin.

LEINSTER QUARTER-FINAL REPLAY
Apr 28, Gaelic Grounds, Drogheda
DUBLIN 5-7   LOUTH 0-4
Dublin: P Dowling, P Baxter, J Martin, P Treacy, B O'Donnell, G McLoughlin, M Smith, N Boland 0-1, H Murphy, P Murray 1-1, J Delaney, T Rock 0-3, P Bermingham 1-2, P O'Connor 1-0, J Jones 1-0. Own goal by M Byrne.

LEINSTER SEMI-FINAL
June 2, Cusack Park, Mullingar
DUBLIN 3-9   WESTMEATH 5-1
Dublin: P Dowling, P Baxter, J Martin, P Treacy, B O'Donnell, J Murphy, M Smith, M Mohan, H Murphy, P Murray 0-1, N Boland 0-2, T Rock 1-1, P Bermingham 1-3, P O'Connor 1-1, J Jones 0-1.

LEINSTER FINAL
June 30, Croke Park, Dublin
DUBLIN 1-6   OFFALY 1-6
Dublin: A Dowling, D Doyle, J Martin, H Kelly, B O'Donnell, J Murphy, M Smith, H Murphy, E Boland, P Murray 0-5, K Cahill, T Rock, P Bermingham 1-1, P O'Connor, J Jones.

LEINSTER FINAL REPLAY
July 14, St Brendan's Park, Birr
OFFALY 2-3   DUBLIN 0-2
Dublin: R Earls, J Greene, J Martin, H Kelly, B O'Donnell, Dinny Doyle, J Walsh, K Cahill, E Boland, M Williams, Paddy Bermingham, P Murray 0-2, J Williams, P O'Connor, J Jones.

1936

LEINSTER FIRST ROUND
Apr 19, Parnell Park, Dublin
DUBLIN 0-7   LOUTH 1-3
Dublin: P Rock, John Jones, G Nolan, P O'Reilly, J O'Neill, P Howe, P Dempsey, J Barnes, T Rock 0-1, M Fletcher 0-1, J O'Toole, M Smith, W Bradshaw, J O'Brien, Joe Jones 0-5.

LEINSTER QUARTER-FINAL
May 17, Cusack Park, Mullingar
DUBLIN 1-6   LONGFORD 0-8
Dublin: P Rock, John Jones, J Mulhall, P O'Reilly,
P Dempsey, J O'Neill, P Howe, J Barnes, T Rock
0-1, M Fletcher, J Canning 0-2, P Mulhall 0-2, W
Bradshaw, J O'Brien, Joe Jones 1-1. Sub: P Dempsey
for Barnes.

LEINSTER SEMI-FINAL
June 28, County Ground, Aughrim
WICKLOW 4-3   DUBLIN 1-5
Dublin: P Rock, J Barnes, J Mulhall, P O'Reilly, P
Agnew, J Delaney, M Smith, M Halligan, T Rock, M
Dunne, M Fletcher, J Canning, H Hanaway, P Mulhall
1-1, J Jones 0-4.

1937

LEINSTER FIRST ROUND
Apr 18, Croke Park, Dublin
LONGFORD 4-5   DUBLIN 1-4
Dublin: T McManus, Jack Barnes, Jim Barnes,
H Kelly, T Tighe, J Brady, J Hanley, F Murtagh, J
O'Connor, M Fletcher 1-0, R Smyth 0-2, M Hannon, J
Curley 0-1, W Griffin, N Savage. Subs: J Delaney for
Jim Barnes, M O'Brien for Hanley, P French 0-1 for
Hannon.

1938

LEINSTER FIRST ROUND
Apr 24, Pearse Park, Longford
DUBLIN 3-4   LONGFORD 2-5
Dublin: B Bruen, Jack Barnes, Jim Barnes, H Kelly, P
Harford, H O'Donnell, M Falvey, D Smyth, S Moriarty
0-2, J Joyce, P Caul, J Canning 3-0, T Driver, M
Fletcher 0-2, P Kennedy. Sub: M Richardson for
Joyce, T Griffin for Caul.

LEINSTER QUARTER-FINAL
May 15, Geraldine Park, Athy
DUBLIN 7-5   CARLOW 3-3
Dublin: B Bruen, Jack Barnes, Jim Barnes, H Kelly,
P Harford, H O'Donnell, D Smyth, S Moriarty 1-0, J
Joyce, M Falvey 1-1, T Griffin, J Canning 3-1, D Byrne
0-1, M Fletcher 2-2, P Kennedy.

LEINSTER SEMI-FINAL
June 12, Dr Cullen Park, Carlow
KILDARE 1-6   DUBLIN 1-4
Dublin: B Bruen, P Barnes, D Smyth, P Langan,
S Farrell, M Collins, H Kelly, J Barnes, M Falvey, M
Richardson, P Podge 0-1, S Moriarty 0-1, M Fletcher, J
Canning 1-2, D Byrne.

1939

LEINSTER QUARTER-FINAL
Apr 23, Novara Road, Bray
DUBLIN 2-10   WICKLOW 0-2
Dublin: P Dowling, H O'Donnell, J Collins, L Clifford,
M Tobin, P Kennedy 0-2, D Smyth 0-1, P Langan, R
Smyth 0-1, M Byrne 0-1, S Farrell 0-1, T Banks 0-1, J
Kennedy, C Donnellan 2-2, T Markey 0-1.

LEINSTER SEMI-FINAL
May 21, Gaelic Grounds, Drogheda
DUBLIN 2-7   LOUTH 3-3
Dublin: P Dowling, H O'Donnell, J Collins, L Clifford,
M Tobin, P Kennedy 0-1, D Smyth, R Smyth 0-1, P
Langan 1-1, J Shanahan, S Farrell 0-1, T Banks 1-2, T
Markey, C Donnellan 0-1, J Kennedy. Sub: J Dignam
for Clifford.

LEINSTER FINAL
July 23, St Conleth's Park, Newbridge
DUBLIN 2-4   MEATH 1-7
Dublin: P Dowling, B Murphy, J Collins, J Sweeney, H
Donnelly, J Farrell, D Smyth, R Smyth, P Langan, M
Richardson, P Kennedy 1-1, T Banks 0-3, T Markey, C
Donnellan 1-0, J Kennedy.

LEINSTER FINAL REPLAY
Aug 6, Sallins Road, Naas
DUBLIN 2-12   MEATH 0-7
Dublin: Paddy Dowling, Bertie Murphy, Charlie
Donnellan, W Rayburn, H Delap, Harry Donnelly,
Des Smyth, Ronnie Smyth 0-2, P Langan 0-1, Tom
Dowling, Mickey Richardson 1-0, Tommy Banks 0-6,
Tom Markey 1-0, Paddy Kennedy, Mick O'Reilly 0-3.

ALL-IRELAND SEMI-FINAL
Aug 27, Breffni Park, Cavan
DUBLIN 5-10   DONEGAL 1-2
Dublin: P Dowling, B Murphy, F Harford, W Reyburn,
M Browne, H Donnelly, D Smyth, R Smyth, P Langan,
T Dowling, M Richardson, T Banks 1-6, T Markey 0-2,
P Kennedy 3-1, M O'Reilly 1-1.

ALL-IRELAND 'HOME' FINAL
Sep 10, Croke Park, Dublin
DUBLIN 2-9   ROSCOMMON 1-9
Dublin: Paddy Dowling, Mick Browne, Frank Harford,
Willie Reyburn, John Farrell, Harry Donnelly, Des
Smyth, Ronnie Smyth 1-2, Paddy Langan 0-1, Tom
Dowling, Mickey Richardson, Tommy Banks 0-1, Tom
Markey 1-3, Paddy Kennedy 0-1, Mick O'Reilly 0-1.

ALL-IRELAND FINAL
Oct 8, Croke Park, Dublin
DUBLIN 2-12   LONDON 0-4
Dublin: Paddy Dowling, Bertie Murphy, Charlie
Donnellan, Willie Rayburn, Frank Harford, Harry

Donnelly, Des Smyth, Ronnie Smyth 0-4, John Farrell, Tom Dowling, Mickey Richardson 1-1, Mick Meehan 0-1, Tom Markey 0-2, Johnny Sweeney, Mick O'Reilly 0-4. Sub: Paddy Kennedy 1-0 for Sweeney.

1940

LEINSTER FIRST ROUND
Apr 21, Pairc Colmcille, Kells
DUBLIN 1-3   MEATH 1-2
Dublin: P Dunne, J O'Keeffe, A Breslin, C O'Dwyer, C Hatch, P Ellis, T Tighe, P O'Gorman, T O'Sullivan 0-1, C Heenan, P Fitzgerald 1-2, J Maguire, B Maguire, M Higgins, C O'Hara.

LEINSTER QUARTER-FINAL
May 26, Croke Park, Dublin
WESTMEATH 2-5   DUBLIN 2-2
Dublin: P Dunne, J O'Keeffe, A Breslln, C Crone, C Hatch, P Ellis, J Callaghan, T Hogan 1-0, J Skelly, P Fitzgerald 0-1, M Higgins, T O'Sullivan 0-1, E Smith, H Donnelly 1-0, J Maguire.

1941

LEINSTER FIRST ROUND
May 4, Croke Park, Dublin
KILDARE 1-8   DUBLIN 2-3
Dublin: P Ryan, J Manning, G Donnellan, J O'Connor, J Macken, W Doherty, T Walsh, J Skelly, B O'Gorman, P Somerville 0-1, W Cannon, T Banks 1-2, B Markey 1-0, C Heenan, K O'Rourke.

1942–45

Championship suspended.

1946

LEINSTER FIRST ROUND:
Mar 31, Barnes Field, Edenderry
DUBLIN 1-5   OFFALY 0-6
Dublin: P Slattery, A Coakley, T Prendergast, M Scanlan, H Condron, M O'Rourke 0-1, W Stacy, N O'Reilly, C O'Donoghue 0-1, J McLoughlin, J Armstrong, S O'Neill, P Browne 1-0, M Killeen 0-3, M Healy.

LEINSTER QUARTER-FINAL
Apr 14, Barnes Field, Edenderry
KILDARE 2-3   DUBLIN 1-2
Dublin: P Slattery, A Coakley, T Prendergast, M Scanlan, H Condron, M O'Rourke 0-1, W Stacy, N O'Reilly, C O'Donoghue, J McLoughlin, J Armstrong,

S O'Neill, P Browne, M Killeen 1-1, M Healy. Sub: P Bridgette for O'Reilly.

1947

LEINSTER FIRST ROUND
May 25, Barnes Field, Edenderry
DUBLIN 3-5   OFFALY 0-6
Dublin: P Corr, J Smyth, F Lynch, M Wall, J Keogh, T Prendergast, S Farrell, P Browne, R Smyth, J Martin 0-4, H Condron, E Kyne 1-1, F O'Donnell, P Mulhall 0-1, M Duke 0-1.

LEINSTER QUARTER-FINAL
June 15, Geraldine Park, Athy
DUBLIN 2-11   LAOIS 1-3
Dublin: P Corr, J Smyth, F Lynch, M Wall, J Keogh, T Prendergast, S Farrell 0-2, P Browne, R Smyth 1-1, M Scanlon 0-2, J Martin 0-5, E Kyne 0-1, F O'Donnell, J McDonnell, J Rochford 1-0. Sub: P Mulhall for O'Donnell.

LEINSTER SEMI-FINAL
July 13, County Ground, Aughrim
DUBLIN 2-8   WICKLOW 3-1
Dublin: P Mulhall, J Smyth, F Lynch, J Keogh, M Wall, T Prendergast, S Farrell 0-1, P Browne 0-1, R Smyth, J Martin 0-2, E Kyne 1-0, F O'Donnell 0-1, H Condron 0-1, J McDonnell 1-2, J Rochford.

LEINSTER FINAL
July 27, Croke Park, Dublin
MEATH 2-3   DUBLIN 1-4
Dublin: P Corr, J Smyth, T Prendergast, F Lynch, M Wall, J Keogh 0-1, M Scanlon, J Martin 0-1, S Farrell, P Browne, R Smyth 0-2, H Condron, E Kyne, J O'Donnell, J Rochford. Sub: J O'Neill 1-0 for Condron.

1948

LEINSTER FIRST ROUND
Apr 4, Iveagh Grounds, Dublin
DUBLIN 4-8   LOUTH 0-4
Dublin: V Russell, L Ledwidge, G O'Donoghue, N Lyons, S Farrell, N Fingleton, M Richardson, M Scanlon 0-1, J Tunney, V Trotman 1-0, N Maher, J McDonnell 1-0, P Walsh 1-4, J O'Toole 1-0, C Smith 0-3.

LEINSTER QUARTER-FINAL
Apr 18, St Loman's Park, Trim
DUBLIN 2-8   MEATH 2-7
Dublin: V Russell, L Ledwidge, G O'Donoghue, J O'Brien, S Farrell, N Fingleton, M Richardson, M Scanlon, J Tunney, V Trotman, W O'Shea 0-2, J McDonnell, P Walsh 1-5, C Smith 1-1, J O'Toole.

LEINSTER SEMI-FINAL
May 30, Sallins Road, Naas
DUBLIN 1-9   KILDARE 3-3
Dublin: V Russell, L Ledwidge, G O'Donoghue, N Fingleton, S Farrell 0-1, M Richardson, M Scanlon, J Tunney, J McDonnell, W O'Shea 0-2, P Walsh 0-4, C O'Sullivan, N Kenneally 1-0, J O'Toole 0-1, C Smith 0-1.

LEINSTER SEMI-FINAL REPLAY
July 4, Croke Park, Dublin
DUBLIN 2-10   KILDARE 0-7
Dublin: E Cunningham, J Maguire, N Lyons, P Lynch, L Ledwidge, M Scanlon, N Fingleton, S Farrell, L Lawlor 1-0, C O'Sullivan, J Tunney 0-1, J McDonnell, P Walsh 1-7, N Kenneally 0-1, J O'Toole 0-1.

LEINSTER FINAL
Aug 1, County Ground, Aughrim
DUBLIN 2-9   WEXFORD 4-3
Dublin: V Russell, L Ledwidge, G O'Donoghue, N Fingleton, M Richardson, N Lyons, M Scanlon, S Farrell, J Tunney, K Heffernan 0-1, N Maher 1-0, J McDonnell 0-1, P Walsh 0-6, N Kenneally 0-1, J O'Toole 1-0.

LEINSTER FINAL REPLAY
Aug 8, County Ground, Aughrim
DUBLIN 6-3   WEXFORD 2-4
Dublin: V Russell, L Ledwidge G O'Donoghue, N Fingleton, M Richardson, N Lyons, M Scanlon, S Farrell, J Tunney, K Heffernan 1-0, N Maher 1-0, J McDonnell 1-0, P Walsh 1-0, N Kenneally 1-1, J O'Toole 1-2.

ALL-IRELAND SEMI-FINAL
Aug 22, Walsh Park, Waterford
DUBLIN 5-11   WATERFORD 1-3
Dublin: V Russell, J Ledwidge, J O'Donoghue, N Fingleton, M Richardson, N Lyons 0-1, M Scanlon, S Farrell, J Tunney, P Walsh 0-3, J O'Toole 0-4, J McDonnell 1-1, J Copeland 1-2, N Kenneally 1-0, K Heffernan 2-0.

ALL-IRELAND 'HOME' FINAL
Sep 19, St Brigid's Park, Dundalk
DUBLIN 2-6   ARMAGH 2-3
Dublin: Vinny Russell, Larry Ledwidge, Gerry O'Donoghue, Nicky Fingleton, Mickey Richardson, Ned Lyons, Mick Scanlon, Sean Farrell, Jim Tunney, Pearse Walsh 0-4, Jimmy O'Toole, Joe McDonnell, Jackie Copeland, Ned Kenneally 1-1, Kevin Heffernan 1-0.
* Match abandoned five minutes before full-time due to a pitch invasion by spectators; replay ordered.

ALL-IRELAND 'HOME' FINAL REPLAY
Oct 3, Croke Park, Dublin
DUBLIN 3-8   ARMAGH 2-6
Dublin: Vinny Russell, Larry Ledwidge, Gerry O'Donoghue, Nicky Fingleton, Mickey Richardson, Ned Lyons, Mick Scanlon, Sean Farrell, Jim Tunney, Pearse Walsh 2-0, Joe McDonnell 0-3, Jackie Copeland 0-2, Ned Kenneally 0-1, Kevin Heffernan 1-2.

ALL-IRELAND FINAL
Oct 17, Croke Park, Dublin
DUBLIN 2-11   LONDON 1-5
Dublin: Vinny Russell, Larry Ledwidge, Gerry O'Donoghue, Nicky Fingleton, Mickey Richardson, Ned Lyons, Mick Scanlon, Sean Farrell, Jim Tunney 0-1, Pearse Walsh (capt) 0-6, Jimmy O'Toole 0-2, Joe McDonnell, Jackie Copeland, Ned Kenneally 0-2, Kevin Heffernan 2-0.

1949

LEINSTER FIRST ROUND
Apr 3, Gaelic Grounds, Drogheda
LOUTH 1-3   DUBLIN 1-2
Dublin: B Bruen, J Maguire, P Kennedy, B Halpin, K McGovern, L Delaney, A Boggins, P Mooney, B O'Rourke, P O'Dea 1-0, P Halassy 0-1, P McCormack, C Dignam 0-1, L West, L Darcy.

1950

LEINSTER FIRST ROUND
Apr 2, Parnell Park, Dublin
DUBLIN 0-9   LAOIS 0-3
Dublin: D Gray, J Maguire, J Crowley, T Bell, M McLoughlin, M O'Reilly, A Boggins, D Forde 0-2, M Jenkinson, T Faulkner 0-1, T O'Brien 0-1, J Guidon 0-1, B Atkins, J Bell 0-1, T Tallon 0-3.

LEINSTER QUARTER-FINAL
Apr 16, St Conleth's Park, Newbridge
DUBLIN 1-7   KILDARE 1-4
Dublin: D Gray, M McLoughlin, J Crowley, J Sheridan, S McGuinness, A Boggins, T Bell, M Jenkinson, W Dunbar, T Faulkner, D Forde, J Bell 1-0, B Atkins 0-2, J Bell 1-0, T Tallon 0-5.

LEINSTER SEMI-FINAL
May 7, Cusack Park, Mullingar
DUBLIN 0-5   LONGFORD 0-4
Dublin: D Gray, M McLoughlin, J Crowley, J Sheridan, S McGuinness, A Boggins, T Bell, M Jenkinson, W Dunbar, T Faulkner 0-1, D Forde, J Bell, B Atkins, A Monks 0-1, T Tallon 0-3.

LEINSTER FINAL
June 25, Dr Cullen Park, Carlow
DUBLIN 1-15   WEXFORD 2-8
Dublin: D Gray, M McLoughlin, J Crowley, J

Sheridan, R Collier, W Dunbar, T Bell 1-4, D Forde,
S McGuinness, T Faulkner 0-3, A Monks 0-1,
J Boyle 0-2, B Atkins 0-1, M Jenkinson 0-1,
P O'Leary 0-3.

ALL-IRELAND SEMI-FINAL
Aug 20, James Stephens Park, Ballina
MAYO 4-9   DUBLIN 0-5
Dublin: Dinny Gray, M McLoughlin, J Crowley, J
Sheridan, R Collier, W Dunbar, T Bell, D Forde, S
McGuinness, T Faulkner, A Monks, J Boyle 0-1, B
Atkins 0-2, M Jenkinson 0-2, J Bellston.

1951

LEINSTER QUARTER-FINAL
Apr 1, O'Moore Park, Portlaoise
DUBLIN 3-4   LAOIS 0-3
Dublin: G O'Toole, A Caffrey, J Brophy, D Stanley, M
O'Sullivan, J Farrell, P Duggan, A Connolly, M Dennis,
J Moore, R Cannon 0-1, M Cowley 1-1, J Nugent 2-0, J
Holland 0-1, P Broderick 0-1.

LEINSTER SEMI-FINAL
Apr 15, St Conleth's Park, Newbridge
DUBLIN 3-4   KILDARE 1-2
Dublin: G O'Toole, A Caffrey, J Brophy, D Stanley, M
O'Sullivan, J Farrell, P Duggan, A Connolly, M Dennis,
J Moore, R Cannon 0-1, M Cowley 1-3, J Nugent 2-0, J
Reid, J Holland.

LEINSTER FINAL
June 24, Geraldine Park, Athy
DUBLIN 5-7   CARLOW 0-7
Dublin: G O'Toole, A Caffrey, S Murphy, D Stanley, M
O'Sullivan, S Farrell, P Duggan, A Connolly, M Dennis,
J Moore 1-1, R Cannon 1-0, M Crowley 1-5, J Reid 1-1, S
Holland, J Nugent 1-0.

ALL-IRELAND SEMI-FINAL
Aug 5, Croke Park, Dublin
DUBLIN 1-4   MAYO 0-7
Dublin: G O'Toole, A Caffrey, J Brophy, D Stanley,
M O'Sullivan, J Farrell, P Duggan, A Connolly, M
Dennis, J Moore 0-1, R Cannon 0-1, M Crowley 0-1,
J Reid 1-1, J Holland, J Nugent. Sub: J Maguire for
Connolly.

ALL-IRELAND SEMI-FINAL REPLAY
Aug 26, Pearse Park, Longford
MAYO 3-8   DUBLIN 2-7
Dublin: G O'Toole, A Caffrey, J Brophy, D Stanley,
M O'Sullivan, J Farrell, P Duggan, A Connolly, A
Monks, J Moore 0-1, R Cannon 1-2, M Lynch 0-1, J
Maguire 0-1, J Reid 0-1, S Nugent. Subs: J Nugent
1-1 for Brophy, T Quinlan for Nugent, M Dennis for
O'Sullivan.

1952

LEINSTER FIRST ROUND
Apr 6, St Brigid's Park, Dundalk
LOUTH 1-5   DUBLIN 1-3
Dublin: T O'Grady, M McLoughlin, G O'Donoghue,
M McGuinness, J Bell, P Redmond, M Hayes, J
McGuinness, M Armstrong 0-1, M Jenkinson, M Rice,
E O'Connor 0-1, D Osborn, N Butterly 1-0, P Bissett.

1953

LEINSTER FIRST ROUND
Apr 12, Bremore Park, Balbriggan
LOUTH 1-9   DUBLIN 1-6
Dublin: P O'Flaherty, N Bransfield, T Moloney, J
Monahan, J Bell, D Healy, D Doherty, J Keenan 0-1, J
Tunney 0-1, J Maguire 0-1, M Jenkinson, K O'Reilly, I
Ward, E O'Connor 0-1, K Drennan 1-2.

1954

LEINSTER FIRST ROUND
Apr 4, County Ground, Aughrim
DUBLIN 3-7   WICKLOW 0-4
Dublin: P O'Flaherty, N Bransfield, P Bell, R Dolan, T
Scannell, B Houlihan, M Fogarty, S McGuinness 0-1,
L Healy, P O'Sulllvan 0-2, B Morris, S O'Connell, J
Brophy 2-4, P Downey, S Daly. Sub: E O'Connor 1-0
for Morris.

LEINSTER QUARTER-FINAL
Apr 25, Croke Park, Dublin
DUBLIN 1-9   KILDARE 1-8
Dublin: P O'Flaherty, N Bransfield, J Bell, P Bell, R
Dolan, B Houlihan, H Boylan, T Ryan, C Cawley 0-1,
M Lynch 0-1, L Healy, P Haughey, D O'Carroll 0-2, J
Brophy 1-4, E Kennedy 0-1.

LEINSTER SEMI-FINAL
July 11, Belfield Park, Enniscorthy
DUBLIN 2-10   WEXFORD 1-5
Dublin: P O'Flaherty, J Bell, P Bell, R Dolan, T Egan
0-1, B Houlihan, P O'Brien, D Carroll 0-2, M Lynch 0-1,
E Kennedy 2-2, C Cawley, B Morris 0-1, J Brophy 0-2,
P Downey 0-1, S Daly.

LEINSTER FINAL
Aug 8, Pairc Tailteann, Navan
DUBLIN 0-10   LOUTH 0-10
Dublin: P O'Flaherty, J Bell, P Bell, T Ryan, H Boylan,
B Houlilan, D Osborne, C Cawley, M Lynch 0-2, P
Haughey 0-2, L Healy 0-1, E Kennedy 0-2, S Daly
0-2, P Downey 0-1, J Brophy. Sub: P O'Brien for
Lynch.

LEINSTER FINAL REPLAY
Aug 15, Pairc Tailteann, Navan
DUBLIN 2-11   LOUTH 2-4
Dublin: P O'Flaherty, J Bell, P Bell, T Ryan, H Boylan, B Houlihan, D Osborne, J Young 0-1, P O'Brien, P Haughey 0-2, C Cawley 0-1, E Kennedy 1-1, J Brophy 0-5, P O'Sulllvan 1-0, L Healy 0-1. Sub: P Downey for Cawley.

ALL-IRELAND SEMI-FINAL
Aug 22, Fitzgerald Stadium, Killarney
KERRY 2-7   DUBLIN 0-9
Dublin: P O'Flaherty, J Bell, P Bell, T Ryan, H Boylan, B Houlihan, D Osborne, P O'Brien, J Young, P Haughey 0-1, C Cawley E Kennedy 0-3, J Brophy 0-5, P O'Sullivan, J Nugent. Subs: P Bates for Cawley, L Healy for Nugent, P Downey for O'Brien.

1955

LEINSTER QUARTER-FINAL
Apr 3, Croke Park, Dublin
DUBLIN 1-10   WICKLOW 0-3
Dublin: R Brady, B O'Boyle, L McCarthy, T Gillen, J McDonnell, PJ Considine, J Brennan, S McGuinness, S Cahill, S Murray, V Bell 1-6, P Barrett, A Kavanagh 0-3, B Lyons, M Power 0-1.

LEINSTER SEMI-FINAL
May 1, O'Connor Park, Tullamore
DUBLIN 2-7   KILDARE 0-4
Dublin: R Brady, B O'Boyle, L McCarthy, T Gillen, J McDonnell, PJ Considine, J Brennan, S McGuinness, S Cahill, V Bell 1-3, P Barrett, A Kavanagh, B Lyons 0-3, S Murray, M Power 1-0. Sub: D Carroll 0-1 for Barrett.

LEINSTER FINAL
July 31, Gaelic Grounds, Drogheda
DUBLIN 1-12   MEATH 4-3
Dublin: R Brady, S Clerkin, L McCarthy, T Gillen, P McDonnell, P Considine, J Brennan, S Cahill 0-1, J Walsh, B Lyons 0-1, D O'Carroll 1-3, A Kavanagh 0-2, J O'Riordan, S Murray 0-3, M Power 0-2.

LEINSTER FINAL REPLAY
Aug 7, Gaelic Grounds, Drogheda
DUBLIN 1-8   MEATH 0-5
Dublin: R Brady, B O'Boyle, L McCarthy, PJ Considine, P McDonnell, T Gillan, J Brennan, S Cahill, J Walsh, M Power, S Murray, A Kavanagh 0-2, J O'Riordan 1-2, D O'Carroll 0-1, C Waters 0-1. Sub: J Cullen 0-2 for Walsh.

ALL-IRELAND SEMI-FINAL
Aug 28, Croke Park, Dublin
CORK 2-5   DUBLIN 0-6
Dublin: R Brady, B O'Boyle, L McCarthy, PJ Considine,

T Gillen, H Boylan, J Brennan, S Cahill 0-1, J Walsh 0-1, V Bell 0-1, S Murray 0-1, D Carroll, J Cullen, P Downey, A Kavanagh. Subs: J O'Riordan for Boylan, M Power 0-2 for Cullen.

1956

LEINSTER FIRST ROUND
Apr 8, Pairc Tailteann, Navan
MEATH 1-5   DUBLIN 0-3
Dublin: T Nynam, J Bourke, D Sweeney, J Brophy, J Clinton, N Doyle, J Dunne, J Connolly, J Sheridan, H Hughes 0-1, P Barrett, R Conroy 0-1, M Coffey 0-1, P Feeney, A Thompson. Subs: C McSweeney for Thompson, M Rice for Connolly, O Reynolds for Conroy.

1957

LEINSTER FIRST ROUND
Apr 7, Parnell Park, Dublin
MEATH 2-4   DUBLIN 0-9
Dublin: P Nolan, J Dignam, P Bell, J Dunne, R Doherty, J Fitzgerald, F Kavanagh, N Clerkin, C Jones 0-2, T Howard 0-1, A Thompson 0-1, S O'Rourke 0-1, F Black 0-1, P Whelan 0-2, B Fahy 0-1.

1958

LEINSTER QUARTER-FINAL
Mar 30, Drogheda Park, Drogheda
DUBLIN 0-11   LOUTH 0-10
Dublin: M Leonard, C Kenny, A Carroll, A Browne, P Rogers, E Meenan, R Doherty, P Barrett, C Jones, T Howard 0-2, J Brophy 0-5, P Farnan 0-3, S Hall, J Stuart, C McSweeney 0-1.

LEINSTER SEMI-FINAL
Apr 27, Pearse's Park, Arklow
DUBLIN 4-9   WICKLOW 1-3
Dublin: M Leonard, D McNulty, A Browne, C Kenny, E Meenan, P Rogers, R Doherty, P Barrett, C Jones 0-1, T Howard 1-1, P Farnan 1-2, C McSweeney 0-1, J Brophy 2-4, P Moran, J Tormey.

LEINSTER FINAL
July 27, Pirc Colmcille, Kells
MEATH 1-5   DUBLIN 1-3
Dublin: M Leonard, D McNulty, A Browne, C Kenny, P Rogers, E Meenan, R Doherty, P Barrett, C Jones, T Howard, J Brophy 0-1, W Mongey, S Hall 0-1, S Hughes, C McSweeney. Subs: J Stuart 1-0 for Hughes, S McAllister 0-1 for Doherty.

1959

LEINSTER QUARTER-FINAL
Apr 5, O'Toole Park, Dublin
DUBLIN 1-14   LOUTH 2-6
Dublin: M Leonard, S McAllister, A Browne, L Barber, C Browne, T Whelan, M Ronan, P Barrett, M Bohan, A Fitzsimons, T Culhane, P Murray 0-5, J Brophy 1-8, J Sergeant 0-1, L Whittaker.

LEINSTER SEMI-FINAL
Apr 19, Gorey
DUBLIN 6-9   WEXFORD 4-3
Dublin: M Leonard, S McAllister, A Browne, L Barber, C Browne, T Whelan, M Ronan, P Barrett, M Bohan, D Jones 2-2, T Culhane, P Murray 0-3, J Brophy 2-1, K Russell 2-0, A Fitzsimons 0-3.

LEINSTER FINAL
July 26, Pairc Tailteann, Navan
DUBLIN 2-16   LONGFORD 0-5
Dublin: M Leonard, P Holden, A Browne, L McCarthy, L Keevan, M Bohan, D Phelan, P Barrett, T Culhane, A Fitzsimons 0-5, M Clancy 1-3, P Murray 0-5, J Brophy 1-2, K Russell, R Smith 0-1. Sub: V McAllister for Barrett.

ALL-IRELAND SEMI-FINAL
Aug 30, O'Toole Park, Dublin
DUBLIN 2-8   FERMANAGH 2-8
Dublin: M Leonard, P Holden, A Browne, L McCarthy, P Rogers, P Brennan 0-1, T Whelan, P Barrett, T Culhane, A Fitzsimons, N Clerkin 1-1, P Murray 0-1, J Brophy 1-4, T Ryan, K Russell 0-1. Sub: P Reynolds for Holden, R Smith for Ryan.

ALL-IRELAND SEMI-FINAL REPLAY
Sep 13, St Molaise's Park, Irvinestown
FERMANAGH 4-14 DUBLIN 3-8
Dublin: M Leonard, P Holden, A Browne, L McCarthy, T Whelan, N Clerkin, P Rogers, P Brennan 1-2, K Russell 1-2, A Fitzsimons 0-1, T Culhane, P Murray 0-1, R Smith, P Barrett, J Brophy 0-2. Subs: M Clancy 1-0 for Rogers, T Ryan for Barrett.

1960

LEINSTER QUARTER-FINAL
Apr 3, St Conleth's Park, Newbridge
DUBLIN 5-10   KILDARE 2-7
Dublin: F McPhillips, T Stanley, J Farrell, F McHugh, C Carroll, S Gormley, M Kissane, S Behan, P Hallinan, P Delaney, V Murphy 0-1, S Coen 0-5, B McDonald 2-2, J Kirwan 2-1, L Doyle 1-1.

LEINSTER SEMI-FINAL
May 1, Nowlan Park, Kilkenny
DUBLIN 3-9   CARLOW 0-6
Dublin: F McPhillips, T Stanley, J Farrell, F McHugh,

J McCormack, S Gormley, M Kissane, S Behan, P Hallinan, P Delaney, V Murphy 0-3, S Coen 0-3, B McDonald 1-0, J Kirwan 1-0, L Doyle 1-0.

LEINSTER FINAL
Aug 7, Cusack Park, Mullingar
DUBLIN 2-9   MEATH 0-5
Dublin: F McPhillips, T Stanley, J Farrell, F McHugh, F Black, S Gormley, C Carroll, P Hallinan, D Mulligan, P Delaney 0-2, V Murphy 0-2, S Coen 0-4, B McDonald 1-1, B Walsh, F McCourt 1-0.

ALL-IRELAND SEMI-FINAL
Aug 28, Austin Stack Park, Tralee
DUBLIN 1-9   KERRY 1-8
Dublin: F McPhillips, T Stanley, J Farrell, F McHugh, C Carroll 0-1, S Gormley, O Callaghan, S Murray, P Hallinan, P Delaney 0-5, V Murphy 0-1, S Coen 1-0, B McDonald 0-1, K Russell 0-1, F McCourt. Subs: F Black for McCourt, D Mulligan for Gormley.

ALL-IRELAND 'HOME' FINAL
Sep 11, Croke Park, Dublin
DUBLIN 1-12   GALWAY 0-9
Dublin: Frank McPhillips, Christy Kane, J Farrell, Fred McHugh, C Carroll, Donal Mulligan, Ollie Callaghan, Sean Murray, Pat Hallinan 0-1, Paddy Delaney 0-5, Vincent Murphy 0-2, Sean Coen 0-1, Brian McDonald 1-3, Jim Kirwan, Fergus McCourt.

ALL-IRELAND FINAL
Oct 2, Croke Park, Dublin
DUBLIN 2-5   LONDON 0-5
Dublin: Frank McPhillips, Christy Kane, Joe Farrell, Fred McHugh, C Carroll, Donal Mulligan, Ollie Callaghan, Sean Murray, Pat Hallinan, Paddy Delaney 1-2, Vincent Murphy 0-1, Sean Coen 0-1, Brian McDonald, Jim Kirwan, Fergus McCourt 1-1.

1961

LEINSTER QUARTER-FINAL
Apr 2, Croke Park, Dublin
DUBLIN 2-5   KILDARE 1-1
Dublin: M Leonard, P Sylvester, L Hickey, C Fox, P Fox, M Bohan, M Ronan, F Sheehan, F McKearney, D Dempsey, P Barrett, G Griffin, P Maguire 1-1, T Burke, P Somers 1-3. Subs: E Burgess for Dempsey, B Ennis 0-1 for Maguire.

LEINSTER SEMI-FINAL
May 7, County Ground, Aughrim
DUBLIN 1-6   WICKLOW 1-6
Dublin: M Leonard, P Archibald, L Hickey, B Cooney, P Fox, M Bohan, D Dempsey, C Fox, F McKearney, E Burgess 0-2, P Barrett, P Somers 0-1, S Murphy, T Burke 0-2, B Ennis 1-1.

LEINSTER SEMI-FINAL REPLAY
June 4, Dr Cullen Park, Carlow
DUBLIN 2-9   WICKLOW 0-3
Dublin: M Leonard, P Archibald, L Hickey, B Cooney, P Fox, L O'Hagan, D Dempsey, C Fox, F McKearney, A Dunne 2-1, P Barrett 0-2, S Kinsella 0-3, S Finnegan, T Burke, B. Ennis 0-2. Sub: N Dempsey for Finnegan.

LEINSTER FINAL
Aug 6, Pairc Tailteann, Navan
LOUTH 2-4   DUBLIN 0-8
Dublin: M Leonard, P Archibald 0-2, L Hickey, B Cooney 0-1, P Fox, L O'Hagan, D Dempsey, C Fox 0-1, F McKearney, P Barrett 0-2, B Ennis 0-1, S Kinsella, N Dempsey, A Burke, P Somers 0-1. Subs: P Nally for Burke.

1962

LEINSTER FIRST ROUND
Apr 1, Croke Park, Dublin
DUBLIN 2-7   WESTMEATH 1-5
Dublin: J Browne, P Murphy, L Hickey, J Houlihan, A Halpin, S O'Reilly, D Dempsey, P Hallinan, B Stynes 1-0, P Norton, V Murphy 0-2, A Donnelly 0-1, E Burgess 0-2, D Langan 0-2, B Ennis 1-0.

LEINSTER SEMI-FINAL
June 17, Dr Cullen Park, Carlow
WEXFORD 1-6   DUBLIN 0-7
Dublin: J Browne, P Archibald, P Murphy, A Halpin, P Fox, S O'Reilly, D Dempsey, P Hallinan, R O'Siochru, S Lee 0-1, P Barrett 0-1, L Doyle 0-3, V Murphy 0-1, D Langan 0-1, P Somers. Sub: B Stynes for Hallinan.

1963

LEINSTER QUARTER-FINAL
Apr 7, Cusack Park, Mullingar
WESTMEATH 1-8   DUBLIN 1-7
Dublin: J Hannon, B Groves, C Brady, J Connolly, F Fitzgerald, C Browne, J Kennedy 0-1, L Carr, S Lee, E Breslin, B McKeown 0-3, C Reilly 0-1, F Murphy 0-1, C Lee, J Levins 1-1.

1964

LEINSTER QUARTER-FINAL
Apr 19, St Conleth's Park, Newbridge
KILDARE 1-9   DUBLIN 2-3
Dublin: M McCann, S Reilly, L Carr, P Murphy, J Dennis, M Bohan 1-0, A Byrne, A Hempenstall, C Browne, J Levin, B McKeown 0-2, P Murray 1-0, C Dowling, C Lee, L Keenan 0-1. Subs: P Doherty for Reilly, W Sherry for Hempenstall.

1965

LEINSTER QUARTER-FINAL
Apr 25, Moyglare Road, Maynooth
KILDARE 0-4   DUBLIN 0-3
Dublin: J Hannon, P Foley, O O'Callaghan, S O'Shea, F Kavanagh, P Doherty, A Byrne, A Donnelly, S Lee, J Scahill, C Dowling 0-3, P Byrne, C Delaney, B Leonard, M Howard.

1966

LEINSTER FIRST ROUND
Apr 3, Dr Cullen Park, Carlow
DUBLIN 1-9   LAOIS 0-6
Dublin: J Hannon, P Cullen, B Cooney, P Foley, B Keenan, B Ennis, D Dempsey, P Wilson, T O'Neill, E Breslin 0-3, J Wright 0-1, S Ryan 0-2, N Noonan 0-1, N Scahill, J Mulvaney 1-2. Sub: R Leonard for Ennis.
* Dublin withdrew in protest after being ordered to play their quarter-final against Louth in Drogheda on June 12 in conjunction with the senior championship meeting of the same counties.

1967

LEINSTER QUARTER-FINAL
Apr 16, Croke Park, Dublin
DUBLIN 5-6   MEATH 2-6
Dublin: C McDermott, S O'Connor, P Foley, B Keenan, D Smith, S Moyles, James Mulvaney, P Murphy, T O'Neill, R Grey 0-2, N Scahill 0-1, C O'Reilly 1-0, J Wallace 1-1, M Howard, Joe Mulvaney 2-2. Own goal by K Sheerin.

LEINSTER SEMI-FINAL
June 4, O'Moore Park, Portlaoise
OFFALY 2-11   DUBLIN 2-7
Dublin: C McDermott, S O'Connor, P Foley, A Whelan, M McShane, S Moyles, James Mulvaney, T O'Neill, P Murphy 0-1, B Grey 0-3, N Scahill 0-1, C Reilly, B Keenan 1-0, M Howard 1-0, Joe Mulvaney. S O'Hale 0-2 for Joe Mulvaney.

1968

LEINSTER QUARTER-FINAL
May 5, Drogheda Park, Drogheda
DUBLIN 1-8   LOUTH 1-6
Dublin: C Noone, F Barry, L Hickey, P Markham, J Turner, P Doherty, S O'Haire, P Wilson, P Murphy, E Breslin, N Scahill, C Reilly, S. Foley 0-4, M Howard 1-3, R Bray. Sub: R Gibney 0-1 for Scahill.

LEINSTER SEMI-FINAL
June 2, O'Connor Park, Tullamore
WESTMEATH 1-6   DUBLIN 1-3
Dublin: C Noone, F Berry, L Hickey, P Foley, S O'Hare, S Doherty, T Wright, P Wilson, T O'Neill, N Scahill 0-1, E Breslin 1-0, C Reilly 0-1, S Foley, B Keenan 0-1, R Grey. Subs: P Muiphy for P Foley, P Farnan for O'Neill.

1969

LEINSTER FIRST ROUND
Apr 13, Pairc Tailteann, Navan
MEATH 2-5   DUBLIN 1-6
Dublin: G McLaughlin, T O'Neill, S Doherty, J Grimes, D Donovan, S O'Haire, P Farnan, P Wilson 0-2, D Smith, J Greer, M Howard, S McShane 0-1, B Keenan, J Wright 0-1, P Leahy 0-2. Subs: E Doyle 1-0 for Smith.

1970

LEINSTER QUARTER-FINAL
Apr 26, Park Road, Rush
DUBLIN 1-8   MEATH 0-8
Dublin: T Morgan, J Colgan, S Doherty, S O'Haire, D Donovan, P Foley, P Farren, P Wilson, T O'Neill, M Nocter 1-0, A Desmond, A O'Toole, E Doyle, F Farren 0-2, V Daly 0-3. Subs: T Wright 0-1 for Doyle, S Fitzgibbon 0-1 for Desmond.

LEINSTER SEMI-FINAL
June 21, St Conleth's Park, Newbridge
DUBLIN 0-10   OFFALY 0-4
Dublin: T Morgan, J Grimes, P Foley, S O'Haire, D Donovan, F McCarthy, P Farren, P Wilson 0-2, D Douglas, S Fitzgibbon, J Kelly, A O'Toole 0-1, V Daly 0-1, F Farren 0-1, B Keenan 0-5.

LEINSTER FINAL
July 12, Pairc Tailteann, Navan
KILDARE 3-13   DUBLIN 1-11
Dublin: T Morgan, J Grimes, P Grimes, P Foley, S O'Haire, D Donovan, F McCarthy, P Farren, P Wilson 0-1, D Douglas, E Flynn 0-4, J Kelly 0-1, A O'Toole, V Daly 1-4, F Farren 0-1, S Fitzgibbon.

1971

LEINSTER FIRST ROUND
Apr 11, The Grove, Castlebellingham
DUBLIN 3-10   LOUTH 1-11
Dublin: T Milner, B O'Sullivan, L Hickey, T Morgan, D Donovan, F Kavanagh, M McMenamon, P Wilson 0-1, C Reilly 0-1, F Farren 0-1, D Lynch 2-0, A O'Toole 0-1, F Hutchinson 0-2, B Keenan 1-1, V Daly 0-3.

LEINSTER QUARTER-FINAL
Apr 25, Whyte Park, Stamullen
DUBLIN 4-8   MEATH 0-10
Dublin: T Milner, B O'Sullivan, L Hickey, T Morgan, D Donovan, F Kavanagh, M McMenamon, P Wilson, F Farren, J Clarke 1-0, W McCabe, A O'Toole 1-1, F Hutchinson 0-3, B Keenan 1-1, V Daly 1-3.

LEINSTER SEMI-FINAL
June 13, Cusack Park, Mullingar
DUBLIN 1-13   LONGFORD 2-4
Dublin: T Milner, B O'Sullivan, L Hickey, T Morgan, D Donovan, F Kavanayh, M McMenamon, P Wilson 0-1, F Farren, J Clarke, W McCabe 0-2, A O'Toole 0-1, F Hutchinson 0-6, B Keenan 0-2, V Daly 1-1. Sub: J O'Neill for Donovan.

LEINSTER FINAL
July 18, Dr Cullen Park, Carlow
DUBLIN 2-9   KILKENNY 0-5
Dublin: T Milner, L Hickey, J O'Neill, T Morgan, D Donovan, F Kavanagh, P Farren, P Wilson 0-2, F Farren, J Clarke 1-0, W McCabe 0-1, A O'Toole, F Hutchinson 1-3, B Keenan 0-2, V Daly 0-1.

ALL-IRELAND SEMI-FINAL
Aug 1, Croke Park, Dublin
DUBLIN 0-15   DOWN 1-6
Dublin: T Milner, L Hickey, J O'Neill, T Morgan, D Donovan, F Kavanagh, P Farren, P Wilson 0-1, F Farren, C Hanley, D Lynch 0-1, A O'Toole 0-1, F Hutchinson 0-8, B Keenan 0-3, J Clarke. Sub: V Daly 0-1 for Clarke.

ALL-IRELAND 'HOME' FINAL
Oct 24, GAA Grounds, Clonmel
DUBLIN 1-14   CORK 2-5
Dublin: Tommy Milner, Leo Hickey, Joe O'Neill, Tony Morgan, Denis Donovan, Fred Kavanagh, Packie Farren, Pat Wilson, Finbarr Farren, Christy Hanley 0-1, Anton O'Toole 0-2, Willie McCabe 0-3, Fred Hutchinson 0-6, Brendan Keenan 1-2, P Pierce.

ALL-IRELAND FINAL
Nov 7, New Eltham, London
LONDON 1-9   DUBLIN 0-9
Dublin: Tommy Milner, Leo Hickey, Joe O'Neill, Seamus O'Haire, Denis Donovan, Fred Kavanagh, Packie Farren, Pat Wilson, Finbarr Farren, Christy Hanley, Anton O'Toole 0-1, Willie McCabe 0-1, Fred Hutchinson 0-6, Brendan Keenan 0-1, Jimmy Clarke. Subs: Mick McMenamon for O'Neill, Joe Kelly for Clarke.

1972

LEINSTER QUARTER-FINAL
Apr 30, St Brigid's Park, Dundalk
DUBLIN 1-6   LOUTH 2-2

Dublin: S McCann, P O'Brien, C Clerkin, S Ryan, S Farrelly, J Mansfield, P Kinsella, M Reilly 0-1, J Brogan, Sean Foley, Sarsfield Foley 0-3, G Wilson 1-0, D Bollard 0-1, S Fitzgibbon 0-1, R Grey.

LEINSTER SEMI-FINAL
May 21, St Conleth's Park, Newbridge
OFFALY 1-12   DUBLIN 0-10
Dublin: S McCann, P O'Brien, C Clerkin, S Ryan, S Farrelly, J Mansfield, P Kinsella, R Flanagan, J Brogan, Sean Foley 0-2, Sarsfield Foley 0-2, G Wilson 0-2, D Bollard 0-2, S Fitzgibbon, R Grey 0-1. Sub: A Larkin 0-1 for Flanagan.

1973

LEINSTER QUARTER-FINAL
May 6, Bremore Park, Balbriggan
MEATH 2-10   DUBLIN 0-11
Dublin: T Milner, B Finn, S Roche, D Lynch 0-1, S Farrelly, K Synnott, P Farren, M McMenamon 0-1, S Yeates, W McCabe 0-4, M Ryan 0-1, B Keenan 0-2, T Dunne 0-1, J Wright, J Lee 0-1.

1974–1982

Championship not staged.

1983

LEINSTER QUARTER-FINAL
June 29, Parnell Park, Dublin
DUBLIN 0-12   KILDARE 1-7
Dublin: B Campbell, P Ellis, S Foran, M Doherty, C Griffin, M Cooke, T Fallon, A White, R Crean 0-3, P Heffernan, K Barry, T Tormley 0-1, T Cashin 0-4, P Dwane 0-1, M O'Hanlon 0-3.

LEINSTER SEMI-FINAL
July 13, Dr Cullen Park, Carlow
DUBLIN 1-12   WEXFORD 0-12
Dublin: B Campbell, P Ashton, S Foran, M Doherty, K Griffin, P Ellis, D Carroll, A White 0-1, R Crean 0-2, A Tormey 0-2, P Heffernan 0-2, M O'Hanlon, T Cashin 0-2, P Dwane 1-1, K Barry.

LEINSTER FINAL
Aug 17, Drogheda Park, Drogheda
DUBLIN 2-8   MEATH 0-5
Dublin: B Campbell, P Ellis, S Foran, M Doherty, C Griffin, M Cooke, T Fallon, A White, R Crean 0-1, P Heffernan, K Barry, T Tormley 0-3, T Cashin 1-1, P Dwane 1-0, M O'Hanlon 0-3. Subs: C Sheridan for Griffin, J Daly for Barry.

ALL-IRELAND SEMI-FINAL
Aug 29, Park Road, Rush
DUBLIN 2-14   TYRONE 0-7
Dublin: B Campbell, P Ellis, S Foran, D Carroll, T Fallon, M Cooke, C Sheridan, A White, R Crean 0-5, J Daly, P Heffernan 0-1, A Tormey 0-2, T Cashin 1-2, P Dwane 0-1, M O'Hanlon 1-3. Subs: L Norton for Sheridan, J White for Heffernan.

ALL-IRELAND FINAL
Sep 11, MacDonagh Park, Nenagh
DUBLIN 1-9   KERRY 0-9
Dublin: Brian Campbell, Pat Ellis, Sean Foran, Martin Doherty, Ciaran Griffin, Martin Cooke 0-1, Tadgh Fallon, Anthony White 1-0, Richie Crean 0-1, Pat Heffernan, Jim Daly 0-1, Tony Tormey, Tom Cashin 0-4, Pat Dwane 0-1, Mark O'Hanlon 0-1. Subs: Dave Carroll for Fallon, C Moynihan for Heffernan.

ALL-IRELAND FINAL REPLAY
Sep 25, Cusack Park, Ennis
KERRY 1-9   DUBLIN 0-5
Dublin: Brian Campbell, Pat Ellis, Sean Foran, Martin Doherty, Dave Carroll, Martin Cooke, Ciaran Griffin, Anthony White, Richie Crean 0-2, Con Moynihan, Pat Heffernan, Tony Tormey, Tom Cashin 0-1, Pat Dwane 0-1, Mark O'Hanlon 0-1. Subs: Tadgh Fallon for Cooke, Kevin Barry for O'Hanlon, John White for Moynihan.

1984

LEINSTER QUARTER-FINAL
Apr 28, Parnell Park, Dublin
DUBLIN 0-11   WICKLOW 0-8
Dublin: N Whelan, F Somerville, C Horan, R Callanan, B McGee, B Field, G Heaslip, P Lamb, D McCarthy, J Bissett 0-1, A Costello, T Cassidy 0-2, G O'Connor 0-3, J Sheedy 0-2, R Holland 0-1. Sub: G Callery 0-1 for Costello.

LEINSTER SEMI-FINAL
May 19, Drogheda Park, Drogheda
LOUTH 1-8   DUBLIN 1-6
Dublin: N Whelan, F Somerville, C Horan, R Callanan, B McGee, B Field, G Heaslip, P Lamb, D McCarthy, J Bissett, A Costello, P Nolan, G O'Connor 0-3, J Sheedy, R Holland 0-2. Subs: A Lyons 1-1 for Costello.

1985

LEINSTER QUARTER-FINAL
May 15, Parnell Park, Dublin
DUBLIN 3-8   KILDARE 0-4
Dublin: B Campbell, T Mannion, M Cooke, C Walsh, C Griffin, T O'Brien, D McCarthy, A White 0-1, A Costello,

D DeLappe, N McHugh 1-6, J Sheedy, J Watson 0-1, J White 1-0, C Richardson 1-0.

LEINSTER SEMI-FINAL
June 5, Cusack Park, Mullingar
DUBLIN 1-17   WESTMEATH 2-3
Dublin: B Campbell, T Mannion, M Cooke, C Walsh, C Griffin, T O'Brien, D McCarthy, A White 0-1, A Costello 0-1, D DeLappe 0-1, N McHugh 0-1, J Sheedy 0-2, J Watson 0-2, R Crean 0-5, C Richardson 1-4.

LEINSTER FINAL
June 12, Pairc Tailteann, Navan
DUBLIN 3-16   LOUTH 2-4
Dublin: B Campbell, T Mannion, M Cooke 0-1, C Walsh, C Griffin 0-1, T O'Brien, D McCarthy 0-1, A White, A Costelloe 0-1, D DeLappe 1-4, N McHugh 0-2, J Sheedy 0-2, J Watson 0-1, R Crean, C Richardson 2-2. Sub: G O'Connor for Watson.

ALL-IRELAND SEMI-FINAL
July 6, Parnell Park, Dublin
GALWAY 1-13   DUBLIN 2-8
Dublin: B Campbell, T Mannion, M Cooke, C Walsh, C Griffin, T O'Brien, C McCarthy, A White, A Costelloe, D DeLappe, N McHugh 1-3, J Sheedy 1-3, J Watson, R Crean 0-1, C Richardson. Sub: G O'Connor 0-1 for Watson.

1986

LEINSTER FIRST ROUND
May 21, Castletown-Geoghegan
WESTMEATH 1-7   DUBLIN 0-6
Dublin: A McAllister, H Hayes, D Carroll, B Newcomen, G Heaslip, P Boylan, C McCormack, D Hetherington, B Cooke, B Heaslip 0-4, S Barry, M Kerins, P McCarthy, T O'Driscoll, J White 0-1. Subs: D O'Brien for P McCarthy 35, D Fairbrother 0-1 for J White 38.

1987

LEINSTER QUARTER-FINAL
May 10, Parnell Park, Dublin
DUBLIN 1-9   KILKENNY 1-7
Dublin: B Campbell, L Harford, D Price, P Cahill, C McCormack, S Barry, J Sheedy 1-0, D Hetherington, B O'Reilly, P Nugent, D O'Brien 0-1, N McHugh 0-3, P McCarthy 0-1, D Whelan 0-2, S O'Brien 0-1. Sub: C Crowley 0-1 for Nugent.

LEINSTER SEMI-FINAL
May 27, Parnell Park, Dublin
DUBLIN 2-12   WEXFORD 0-9
Dublin: B Campbell, S Barry, D Price, P Cahill, C McCormack, S Barry, J Sheedy, D Hetherington, P

Nugent, C Crowley 1-2, W Hughes 0-3, S O'Brien 0-1, P McCarthy, B O'Reilly 1-0, D Whelan 0-5.

LEINSTER FINAL
June 14, O'Moore Park, Portlaoise
DUBLIN 1-8   MEATH 0-4
Dublin: B Campbell, P Cahill, D Price, S Barry, C McCormack, M Price, J Sheedy, D Hetherington, P Nugent, C Crowley 0-1, W Hughes 0-1, S O'Brien, P McCarthy 1-0, B O'Reilly 0-2, D Whelan 0-4. Subs: D O'Brien for Crowley, P Flynn for Nugent.
* No championships in Ulster and Connacht, therefore no All-Ireland semi-finals.

ALL-IRELAND FINAL
July 25, Semple Stadium, Thurles
CORK 2-7   DUBLIN 0-8
Dublin: Brian Campbell, Sean Sammon, Phil Cahill, Sean Barry, Mick Price, Anthony White, Jack Sheedy 0-2, Declan Hetherington, Bobby O'Reilly, Paul Nugent, Willie Hughes 0-2, Paul Flynn, Pat McCarthy, Eddie Kirk, David Whelan 0-3. Subs: Ronan Brennan 0-1 for Kirk, Ciaran Richardson for McCarthy.

1988

LEINSTER QUARTER-FINAL
May 1, Drogheda Park, Drogheda
DUBLIN 2-7   LOUTH 2-7
Dublin: M Pender, R McGovern, C Monk, J Goode, P Curran, N Thompson, A Moore, P Bealin 0-2, T Carroll 1-0, M Barnes, M Walsh 0-1, B Cooke, B Redmond 0-3, B Holland 1-1, A Kelly. Subs: P Boylan for McGovern, P Ward for Kelly.

LEINSTER QUARTER-FINAL REPLAY
May 11, Parnell Park, Dublin
DUBLIN 1-13   LOUTH 2-6
Dublin: M Pender, P Boylan, S Barry, J Goode, S Salmon, N Thompson, A Moore, T Carroll, P Bealin 0-5, B Cooke 0-1, B Holland, M Walsh 0-1, M Cooke 1-2, P Curran 0-1, R Nally 0-3.

LEINSTER SEMI-FINAL
May 18, Nowlan Park, Kilkenny
DUBLIN 1-14   KILKENNY 0-4
Dublin: B Campbell, S Salmon, S Barry, J Goode, P Curran, P Boylan, N Thompson, B Cooke 0-1, P Bealin 0-5, D O'Brien 0-1, B Holland 1-4, M Barnes 0-3, S Gibbons, M Cooke, B Redmond. Subs: D Bollard for Redmond, A Kelly for M Cooke T Dunbarr for Curran.

LEINSTER FINAL
June 5, Drogheda Park, Drogheda
MEATH 0-10   DUBLIN 1-4
Dublin: B Campbell, S Sammon, S Barry, J Goode, P Curran, A White 1-0, A Moore, P Bealin 0-2, B Cooke

0-1, D O'Brien, B Holland, M Barnes, B Redmond, M Cooke 0-1, S Gibbons. Subs: M Walsh for Redmond, D Bollard for Gibbons, P Boylan for B Cooke.

1989

LEINSTER QUARTER-FINAL
May 3, Drogheda Park, Drogheda
LOUTH 0-10   DUBLIN 0-5
Dublin: B Campbell, T O'Brien, D Griffin, D O'Mahony, D Bollard, N Thompson, C Feely, S Barry, D Whelan, T Nealon, D McCarthy, M Barnes 0-4, B Holland 0-1, A Costello, E Flaherty.

1990

LEINSTER QUARTER-FINAL
May 5, O'Toole Park, Dublin
DUBLIN 1-12   KILKENNY 1-2
Dublin: A Doyle, P Wilde, D Hetherton, S Salmon, T Behan, S Barry, A Moore, B Cooke 0-1, K Rowe 0-1, J Madden 0-4, S Murray, P O'Hara 0-2, N Heffernan, S Callery 1-1, C O'Hara 0-2. Sub: M Barnes 0-1 for A Moore.

LEINSTER SEMI-FINAL
May 16, Parnell Park, Dublin
DUBLIN 1-12   WEXFORD 0-7
Dublin: A Doyle, P Wilde, D Hetherton, S Salmon, T Behan, S Barry, A Moore, B Cooke 0-1, K Rowe, J Madden 0-3, S Murray 0-1, P O'Hara 0-3, N Heffernan, S Callery 1-1, P Hegarty. Subs: M Barnes 0-2 for Heffernan, N Lally 0-1 for Hegarty.

LEINSTER FINAL
June 3, Drogheda Park, Drogheda
MEATH 0-15   DUBLIN 0-11
Dublin: A Doyle, T O'Brien, D Hetherington, C Feely, A Moore, S Barry 0-1, T Behan, B Cooke 0-1, P Bealin, P O'Hara, N Lally 0-1, J Madden 0-3, C O'Hara 0-2, S Callery 0-1, P Hegarty 0-1. Subs: M Barnes 0-1 for Lally, N Carter for O'Hara.

1991

LEINSTER QUARTER-FINAL
Apr 30, O'Toole Park, Dublin
DUBLIN 4-13   KILKENNY 0-4
Dublin: A McAllister, T Behan, S Barry, R Caverley, S Herbert 0-2, D Dowling, A Moore, D Hetherton 0-1 Murray 0-4, P O'Hara 0-2, G Murphy 0-2, C O'Reilly, I Mullett 1-0, K Rowe 2-0, J Watson 1-3.

LEINSTER SEMI-FINAL
May 15, Parnell Park, Dublin
DUBLIN 2-11   LAOIS 0-11

Dublin: A McAllister, T Behan, S Barry, R Caverley, S Herbert 0-1, D Dowling, A Moore, P Feehan, S Murray 0-2, P O'Hara 1-2, G Murphy, C O'Reilly 0-2, I Mullet 0-1t, K Rowe 1-1, J Watson 0-1.

LEINSTER FINAL
June 2, Croke Park, Dublin
DUBLIN 1-10   MEATH 1-10
Dublin: A McAllister, T Behan, R Caverley, S Barry, S Herbert, D Dowling, A Moore, D Hetherington, P Tiernan, P O'Hara 0-5, S Murray, C O'Reilly 0-1, K Rowe 0-2, I Mullett 0-1, J Watson 0-1. Subs: P Feehan for Dowling, G Maher 1-0 for Mullett.

LEINSTER FINAL REPLAY
June 9, Croke Park, Dublin
MEATH 1-14   DUBLIN 2-2
Dublin: A McAllister, T Behan, S Barry, R Caverley, S Herbert 0-1, D Dowling, A Moore, P Feehan, J Ward, P O'Hara 1-0, P Tiernan, C O'Reilly, G Maher, K Rowe 0-1, J Watson. Subs: G Troy for Caverley 15, S Murray 1-0 for Ward 39, B Barnes for Watson 45.

1992

LEINSTER FIRST ROUND
Apr 25, Parnell Park, Dublin
LONGFORD 0-11   DUBLIN 0-7
Dublin: R Lyons, C Daly, K Curtin, S Barry, D Dowling, T Behan, A Moore, D Bolger, P Brennan, K Craven 0-1, J Ward, G Anderson, D May 0-1, V Conroy 0-3, J Doran 0-2. Subs: S Cronin for Daly, C Whelan for Brennan.

1993

LEINSTER QUARTER-FINAL
May 5, Dr Cullen Park, Carlow
CARLOW 4-11   DUBLIN 1-7
Dublin: A Durnan, P Delaney, J Foran, J Jameson 1-5, R Quinn, K Rowe 0-1, P Jameson 0-1, J McGuinness, K Craven, T Behan, S Barry, D Murray, E Clarke, J Campbell, S Cronin. Subs: E Fitzsimons for Craven, K Donovan for Quinn.

1994

LEINSTER QUARTER-FINAL
May 2, Parnell Park, Dublin
DUBLIN 1-13   MEATH 0-12
Dublin: A Durnan, D North, B Molloy, K Donovan, J Campbell, F McNulty, W Daly, J McGuinness 1-0, A Costello, P Feehan 0-2, D O'Brien 0-1, A White 0-1, A Falvey 0-1, C Foran 0-1, B Heaslip 0-7.

LEINSTER SEMI-FINAL
May 18, Parnell Park, Dublin
DUBLIN 1-16   LAOIS 0-2
Dublin: A Durnan, D North, B Molloy, K Donovan, D Dowling, F McNulty, W Daly 0-l, J McGuinness, A Costello, P Feehan, K Rowe 0-1, B Rowe 0-3, J Jameson 0-2, C Foran 1-1, B Heaslip 0-8. Subs: R Davis for Costello, J Campbell for North, C Kelly for McNulty.

LEINSTER FINAL
June 12, Pairc Tailteann, Navan
DUBLIN 0-9   LOUTH 0-5
Dublin: A Durnan, D North, B Molloy, K Donovan, J Campbell, F McNulty, W Daly, A Costello, J McGuinness 0-2, P Feehan, D O'Brien 0-3, B Rowe, K Rowe 0-1, C Foran, B Heaslip 0-2. Subs: R Davis 0-1 for McGuinness, A White for Foran, C Kelly for Campbell.

ALL-IRELAND SEMI-FINAL
July 16, Croke Park, Dublin
KERRY 0-13   DUBLIN 1-7
Dublin: A Durnan, D North, B Molloy, K Donovan, J Campbell, F McNulty, W Daly, J McGuinness, A Costello, P Feehan 0-1, J Benton, D O'Brien 0-2, K Rowe, C Foran, B Heaslip 1-4. Subs: A White for McGuinness, B Rowe for Foran.

1995

LEINSTER QUARTER-FINAL
May 17, Nowlan Park, Kilkenny
DUBLIN 1-14   KILKENNY 0-10
Dublin: A Durnan, M O'Shea, S Walsh, A Carroll, T Behan, F McNulty, C Kelly, D Harrington 0-2, J McGuinness, N Carter, A McNally 0-2, P Jameson 0-1, C Kielty 0-3, A Toft 1-1, P Doherty 0-5. Subs: J Jameson for McGuinness, B McMahon for P Jameson.

LEINSTER SEMI-FINAL
May 28, Pairc Tailteann, Navan
OFFALY 1-12   DUBLIN 1-9
Dublin: A Durnan, J Mills, S Walsh, P Giles, P Walsh, F McNulty, C Kelly, D Harrington, C Whelan, P Jameson, A McNally 0-1, P Joyce, C Kielty 0-3, A Toft 0-1, P Doherty 1-4. Subs: C Breslin for P Jameson, J Jameson for Joyce.

1996

LEINSTER QUARTER-FINAL
May 22, Parnell Park, Dublin
MEATH 0-11   DUBLIN 0-7
Dublin: J Leonard, D Ryan, C Reilly, D O'Reilly, D Cahill, W Daly, T Behan, D Harrington, C Whelan 0-1, F McNulty 0-1, T Carr 0-1, D Madden, C Wilson, D O'Brien, P Doherty 0-4.

1997

LEINSTER QUARTER-FINAL
June 4, Parnell Park, Dublin
LOUTH 2-12   DUBLIN 1-8
Dublin: A Durnan, F Walsh 0-1, L O'Grady, M Green, J Grogan, P Cullen, T White, J Reddy, A Costello, K Russell, D Breen 0-1, J Kettle, B Rock 1-4, J Walsh 0-2, G Murphy. Subs: C MacCriostal for Costello, T Behan for Kettle, M Kavanagh for Murphy.

1998

LEINSTER QUARTER-FINAL
May 27, O'Toole Park, Dublin
DUBLIN 3-4   LOUTH 1-9
Dublin: W Linnie, A Darcy, M Devoy, J Grogan, B Gaughran, C Goggins, J Dillon, C Breslin, P Cullen, R Hainsfort 1-0, S Cowap 0-2, J McNally, L Eviston 0-1, L O'Dwyer 1-0, M Duncan 1-1. Subs: D O'Brien for O'Dwyer, T Rodgers for Eviston.

LEINSTER SEMI-FINAL
June 21, Croke Park, Dublin
KILDARE 3-12   DUBLIN 2-12
Dublin: W Linnie, B Gaughran, M Devoy, A Darcy, D Fulham, P Cullen, J Dillon, C Breslin 0-1, D Farrelly, R Hainsfort 0-1, S Cowap 0-1, M Duncan 1-0, L Eviston 0-6, L O'Dwyer 1-2, D Bolger 0-1. Subs: S Healy for Gaughran, D O'Brien for Bolger.

1999

LEINSTER QUARTER-FINAL
May 30, Nowlan Park, Kilkenny
DUBLIN 1-11   WEXFORD 1-5
Dublin: R Doolan, P Carey, B OToole, G Farrelly, A Farrell, K Kehilly, C Goggins 1-2, P Bohan 0-1, G Devine 0-3, T Connolly, J Nolan 0-1, J McNally 0-1, M Doran 0-1, L Driver, P Jameson 0-1. Subs: G Gavin for Connolly 38, A O'Brien for Driver 54.

LEINSTER SEMI-FINAL
June 16, O'Moore Park, Portlaoise
DUBLIN 1-12   LAOIS 0-10
Dublin: R Doolan, P Carey, W O'Toole, G Farrelly, A Farrell 0-1, K Kehilly 0-1, C Goggins 0-2, P Bohan 0-1, T White, G Dolan 0-1, J Nolan, J McNally 0-6, C Brady 1-0, M Doran, L Driver. Subs: J Oiwer for Driver, T Connolly for Doran.

LEINSTER FINAL
July 18, Croke Park, Dublin
MEATH 1-9   DUBLIN 1-6
Dublin: R Doolan, P Carey, B O'Toole, G Farrelly, A Farrell, K Kehilly, C Goggins, J Nolan, G Devine, C Brady, S Cafferty 0-1, J McNally, M Doran 1-2, P Behan, P Jameson 0-3. Subs: J Oliver for Brady, A O'Brien for Bohan.

2000

LEINSTER FIRST ROUND
May 18, Dr Cullen Park, Carlow
DUBLIN 3-14   CARLOW 0-1
Dublin: N Peacock, P Carey, P Grey, C O'Sullivan, T O'Gorman, T White, P Gilford 0-1, J O'Connor, D Noonan   A Farrell 0-2, D Byrne 0-1, A Lalor, A Briody 2-7, R Mullins 0-2, Morgan Doran 0-1. Subs: Myles Doran for Mullins, C McGuinness 1-0 for Farrell, P Condron for O'Gorman, S Richardson for Carey, N McGrath for Briody.

LEINSTER QUARTER-FINAL
May 24, O'Toole Park, Dublin
DUBLIN 2-7   KILKENNY 0-1
Dublin: A Durnan, P Condron, P Casey, C O'Sullivan, S Cunningham, T White, T O'Gorman, D Noonan, M Doran, N McGrath 0-1, D Byrne 0-1, C McGuinness 1-1, A Briody 1-1, R Mullins, P Clifford 0-2. Subs: M Doran 0-1 for Briody, A Lawlor for McGrath, A Holly for Byrne, D McGll for Gorman, S White for Mullins.

LEINSTER SEMI-FINAL
June 4, Croke Park, Dublin
DUBLIN 1-7   LOUTH 1-6
Dublin: A Durnan, P Carey, P Grey, C O'Sullivan, P Condron 0-1, T White, S Cunningham, J O'Connor 0-1, D Noonan, C McGuiness 0-1, Myles Doran, D Byrne, A Briody 0-4, D Madden, P Clifford 1-0. Subs: T Gorman for Cunningham h/t, Morgan Doran for Byrne 44, N McGrath for Myles Doran 52.

LEINSTER FINAL
July 12, Dr Cullen Park, Carlow
WEXFORD 1-9   DUBLIN 1-5
Dublin: N Peacock, JJ O'Keeffe, T White, C O'Sullivan, P Clifford, S Cunningham, T O'Gorman, J O'Connor, D Noonan, D Madden, N McGrath 0-1, A Farrell 0-2, P Carey, B Rock 1-2, A Briody. Subs: M Doran for Noonan h/t, D Byrne for Clifford 41, A Lawlor for Briody 52, J O'Leary for Madden 52.

2001

LEINSTER FIRST ROUND
May 23, O'Connor Park, Tullamore
OFFALY 0-12   DUBLIN 0-9
Dublin: A Durnan, K Spratt, K McGrath, C O'Sullivan, K Flynn 0-1, C Farrelly, A Holly, R McDonald 0-1, K McDermott, P Keane 0-3, M Doran, C McGuinness 0-2, I McDonnell, G Coughlan, D Meehan 0-1. Subs: K Russell for Holly, L Ryan 0-1 for Farrelly, D McGill for Coughlan, L Prout for Meehan.

2002

LEINSTER QUARTER-FINAL
May 29, County Ground, Aughrim
WICKLOW 1-12   DUBLIN 2-8
Dublin: A Durnan, M Fitzpatrick, S Halpin, G Farley, P Keogh, K McGrath, C Prenderville, D Noonan, D Byrne, S Cowap, P Grey 0-1, M Whelan 0-1, C Farrelly 1-2, T Mulligan 0-3, C McGuinness 1-1. Sub: D Burke for Farrelly.

2003

LEINSTER FIRST ROUND
May 14, Nowlan Park, Kilkenny
DUBLIN 1-15   KILKENNY 1-7
Dublin: A Durnan, L Browne, B Byrne, F Condron, G Daly, K Kavanagh, C Prenderville, D Noonan, M Whelan 0-1, G Smith 0-5, G Cullen, C McGuinness 0-4, P Murtagh 1-3, B McEvoy, N Crossan 0-2. Subs: L Prout for Crossan, G Brennan for Cullen, J Donnelly for McGuinness, D Bastick for Noonan, R McBride for Byrne.

LEINSTER QUARTER-FINAL
May 28, Parnell Park, Dublin
DUBLIN 0-20   OFFALY 0-5
Dublin: A Durnan, L Browne 0-1, M Fitzpatrick, F Condron, B Byrne, K Kavanagh, C Prenderville, D Noonan, D Bastick, G Smith 0-6, M Whelan 0-1, C McGuinness 0-3, P Murtagh 0-1, B McEvoy 0-1, N Crossan 0-4. Subs: D O'Callaghan 0-2 for P Murtagh 36, S O'Sullivan 0-1 for McGuinness 42, D O'Reilly for Kavanagh 45, G Dillon for Whelan 56, L Prout for McEvoy 60.

LEINSTER SEMI-FINAL
June 14, Dr Cullen Park, Carlow
WEXFORD 3-9   DUBLIN 0-13
Dublin: A Durnan, L Brown, M Fitzpatrick, F Condron, B Byrne, K Kavanagh, C Prenderville 0-1, D Noonan, G Cullen, G Smith 0-4, M Whelan 0-3, C McGuinness

0-1, P Murtagh, B McEvoy, N Crossan 0-2. Subs: B Brogan 0-2 for Murtagh, K McGrath for Condron, S Sullivan for McEvoy, D Flanagan for Crossan.

2004

LEINSTER SEMI-FINAL
June 27, Croke Park, Dublin
DUBLIN 2-12   WEXFORD 1-10
Dublin: P Copeland, M Fitzpatrick, C Cleere, B Byrne 0-1, G Lewis, K McGrath, C Prenderville 0-1, D Bastick, P Gray 0-1, K Kavanagh, G Cullen 1-2, P Keogh 0-2, J Donnelly 0-1, S Mills 1-2, A Brennan. Subs: N McGrath 0-1 for Brennan 28, B McEvoy for Lewis h/t, D Flanagan for Bastick 58, N McCaffrey for Byrne 59, B Kelly for Keogh 63.

LEINSTER FINAL
July 8, St Conleth's Park, Newbridge
KILDARE 0-9   DUBLIN 0-8
Dublin: P Copeland, M Fitzpatrick, C Cleere, B Byrne, N McGrath, K McGrath, C Prenderville, D Bastick, P Gray 0-1, K Kavanagh, G Cullen 0-2, P Keogh 0-1, J Donnelly, S Mills 0-3, B McEvoy. Subs: B Kelly 0-1 for McEvoy, D McConn for McGrath, A Brennan for Keogh.

2005

LEINSTER QUARTER-FINAL
June 1, Richardstown, Newbridge
KILDARE 1-9   DUBLIN 1-7
Dublin: P Copeland, M White, K McGrath, L Browne, A Daly, K Kavanagh, C Prenderville, D Bastick, P Brennan 0-2, D Flanagan, G Cullen 1-0, P Keogh, L Eviston 0-2, C McGuinness 0-1, N McGrath. Subs: D Reilly for Flanagan, C Reilly for McGrath, B Byrne for White, S Mills 0-2 for Keogh.

2006

LEINSTER QUARTER-FINAL
May 31, Parnell Park, Dublin
DUBLIN 2-12   WEXFORD 2-7
Dublin: K Gorman, C McCormack, D Daly, C Reilly, F Kennedy, A Daly 0-1, C Prenderville, D Bastick 0-1, M Moffatt, P Whelan 0-2, K Kavanagh, D Reilly, G Cullen 1-1, E Kinsella 1-1, P Lawless 0-4.

LEINSTER SEMI-FINAL
June 14, Parnell Park, Dublin
LOUTH 1-11   DUBLIN 0-9
Dublin: K Gorman, A Daly, C McCormack, D Daly, C Reilly, F Kennedy, C Prenderville, D Bastick, M Moffatt 0-2, E O'Gara, K Kavanagh 0-1, D Reilly, E Kinsella 0-1,

G Cullen, P Lawless 0-4. Subs: C Smith for Kennedy 45, P Brennan for O'Gara 47, C Donoghue 0-1 for D Reilly 55, S Keogh for Donoghue 55, C Doyle for Kinsella 57.

2007

LEINSTER QUARTER-FINAL
May 30, Parnell Park, Dublin
DUBLIN 1-11   LOUTH 0-12
Dublin: K Walsh, I Kavanagh, F Kennedy, C Prenderville, D Daly, D Reilly, C Guckian, G Brennan, K Devine 0-1, E O'Gara, K Kavanagh, D Kelly, K Leahy 0-9, G Cullen, J Green 1-0. Subs: C McGuinness 0-1 for Green 34, P Brennan for Kavanagh 44.

LEINSTER SEMI-FINAL
June 13, Parnell Park, Dublin
DUBLIN 0-16   WICKLOW 1-7
Dublin: K Walsh, I Kavanagh, F Kennedy, C Prenderville, D Daly 0-1, D Reilly, D Fox, G Brennan, K Devine 0-1, E O'Gara, K Kavanagh 0-2, D Kelly 0-1, K Leahy 0-8, G Cullen, C McGuinness 0-1. Subs: P Brennan for O'Gara 36, C Farrelly for Devine 44, D Kelly for Green 49, P Kelly for McGuinness 56.

LEINSTER FINAL
June 27, Wexford Park, Wexford
WEXFORD 1-10   DUBLIN 1-8
Dublin: K Walsh, I Kavanagh, F Kennedy, C Prenderville, D Daly, D Reilly, D Fox, K Devine, P Brennan, M Forde 0-1, K Kavanagh 0-1, D Kelly 0-1, K Leahy 0-4, G Cullen 1-0, C McGuinness. Subs: E O'Meara for Forde, B O'Hanlon 0-1 for Fox, P Kelly for McGuinness, D Bastick for D Kelly.

2008

LEINSTER QUARTER-FINAL
May 28, Parnell Park, Dublin
DUBLIN 1-12   CAVAN 0-11
Dublin: C Clarke, C Prenderville, M Fitzsimons, C Durney, M White, A Dennis 0-1, N Brogan, D Bastick, G Brennan 0-2, R Joyce 0-1, E O'Gara 1-0, D Daly, K Connolly 0-3, W Finnegan 0-4, A Darcy 0-1. Subs: K Galvin for Prenderville, D Herlihy for O'Gara.

LEINSTER SEMI-FINAL
June 8, Croke Park, Dublin
DUBLIN 0-11   KILDARE 1-6
Dublin: C Clarke, M Fitzsimons, D Daly, C Prenderville, M White, A Dennis, N Brogan, D Bastick, C Daly, R Joyce 0-1, K Connolly, G Brennan, W Finnegan 0-5, E O'Gara 0-1, A Darcy 0-4. Subs: B Sexton for Joyce 48, C Norton for Darcy 58.

LEINSTER FINAL
June 29, Croke Park, Dublin
DUBLIN 1-13   MEATH 1-9
Dublin: C Clarke, C Prenderville 0-1, M Fitzsimons, D Daly, N Brogan, A Dennis, M White, C Daly, D Bastick, R Joyce, K Connolly 0-2, B Sexton, W Finnegan 1-7, E O'Gara 0-1, A Darcy 0-1. Subs: D Homan for Darcy, J Cooper 0-1 for Brogan, N Tormey for Connolly.

ALL-IRELAND SEMI-FINAL
July 12, Gaelic Field, Cardiff
DUBLIN 5-24   GLOUCESTERSHIRE 0-9
Dublin: C Clarke, C Prendeville, M Fitzsimons, D Daly, N Brogan, A Dennis, M White, C Daly, D Bastick, R Joyce 1-1, K Connolly 0-4, B Sexton 1-1, W Finnegan 1-6, E O'Gara 0-3, C Norton 1-3. Subs: N Tormey 1-4 for Bastick, D Homan for Joyce, J Cooper for C Daly, K Kavanagh 0-1 for M White, S Green 0-1 for C Norton.

ALL-IRELAND FINAL
July 26, O'Moore Park, Portlaoise
DUBLIN 0-13   ROSCOMMON 0-7
Dublin: Colin Clarke, Darren Daly, Michael Fitzsimons, Colin Prenderville, Michael White, Austin Dennis, Niall Brogan, Denis Bastick 0-1, Colin Daly, Ronan Joyce, Karl Connolly 0-3, Jonny Cooper 0-2, Warren Finnegan 0-2, Eoghan O'Gara 0-1, Adrian Darcy 0-3. Subs: Darren Homan 0-1 for Joyce, Ciaran Norton for Finnegan, N Tormey for Connolly.

2009

LEINSTER QUARTER-FINAL
May 27, Lawless Memorial Park, Swords
DUBLIN 0-13   KILDARE 0-12
Dublin: D Mitchell, D Hennessy, B Kirby, D Maher, D Gallagher, D Reilly, J Whelan 0-1, P Brennan, C Dunleavy 0-1, J Collins 0-1, D Rock 0-9, P Kelly, D Quinn 0-1, P Callaghan, N Collins. Subs: M Ferguson for Mitchell 7, R Corcoran for Kelly 40, M Coughlan for Maher 45, A O'Neill for Quinn 56.

LEINSTER SEMI-FINAL
June 10, McGeough Park, Haggardstown
LOUTH 1-13   DUBLIN 0-11
Dublin: D Mitchell, D Hennessy, Brendan Kirby 0-1, D Maher, D Gallagher, Donnacha Reilly, J Whelan 0-1, P Brennan, James McCarthy, J Collins, P Callaghan 0-1, K Fitzgerald 0-1, R Corcoran, Dean Rock 0-5, N Collins 0-2. Subs: F Aughney for Corcoran 30, G Bedford for Mitchell h/t, L Prout for J Collins 43, Philip Kelly for Callaghan 71, E Culligan for Maher 72, C Dolan for Fitzgerald 79.

2010

LEINSTER QUARTER-FINAL
May 26, St Conleth's Park, Newbridge
KILDARE 1-12   DUBLIN 1-5
Dublin: J Mooney, C Freeman, M Fitzsimons, L Redden, C Ó Scannaill, D Reilly, J Sheenan, J McGuirk, R Downey, C Dias 0-1, G Seaver 0-1, K Kilmurray, D O'Connor, C Daly 1-0, M McCarthy 0-3. Subs: B White for Reilly 12, A Casey for O'Connor 39, R Cleere for Casey 51.

2011

LEINSTER QUARTER-FINAL
May 25, Parnell Park, Dublin
DUBLIN 2-13   WICKLOW 1-9
Dublin: D Downey, R Pocock, B Hehir, E O'Connor, S Dunne, C O'Brien 0-1, G Dungan, S O'Connor, C Coady, R Croft 0-2, D Dineen, H Dawson 0-5, G Seavers 0-4, O McCann 1-0, E Kinsella 1-0. Subs: M O'Driscoll for Dineen 45, S Whyte for Dungan 51, M Moffat for Croft 53, J Noonan 0-1 for Kinsella 59, G O'Reilly for O'Connor 60.

LEINSTER SEMI-FINAL
June 8, Parnell Park, Dublin
KILDARE 1-9   DUBLIN 0-5
Dublin: D Downey, R Pocock, B Hehir, J Sheanon, S Dunne, C O'Brien, G Dungan, S O'Connor, C Coady, R Croft, O McCann 0-1, G Seaver 0-3 H Dawson 0-1, M O'Driscoll, E Kinsella. Subs: S Whyte for Dungan 24, J Noonan for Kinsella 41, P Turner for Croft 41, C McLoughlin for Dawson 47, G O'Reilly for O'Driscoll 51.

2012–Present

Dublin have not contested the championship.

LEINSTER CHAMPIONSHIP ROLL OF HONOUR
Dublin (20): 1908, 1914, 1916, 1922, 1926, 1930, 1939, 1948, 1950, 1951, 1954, 1955, 1959, 1960, 1971, 1983, 1985, 1987, 1994, 2008.
Meath (16): 1947, 1952, 1958, 1962, 1964, 1986, 1988, 1990, 1991, 1995, 1996, 1997, 1999, 2003, 2005, 2006.
Louth (12): 1910, 1912, 1925, 1928, 1932, 1934, 1946, 1957, 1961, 1966, 2009, 2010.
Kildare (11): 1927, 1931, 1938, 1956, 1965, 1967, 1970, 1989, 2004, 2011, 2013.
Wexford (8): 1911, 1963, 1984, 1992, 2000, 2007,

2015, 2016.
Wicklow (6): 1906, 1909, 1936, 1949, 1969, 2002.
Laois (5): 1907, 1941, 1968, 1973, 1993.
Westmeath (4): 1905, 1915, 1929, 1940
Offaly (4): 1935, 1972, 1998, 2001.
Carlow (3): 1913, 1923, 1933
Longford (3): 1924, 1937, 1953.
Cavan (2): 2012, 2014.

ALL-IRELAND CHAMPIONSHIP ROLL OF HONOUR

Cork (17): 1951, 1953, 1955, 1964, 1972, 1984, 1987, 1989, 1990, 1993, 1996, 2001, 2005, 2007, 2009, 2011, 2013.
Kerry (17): 1913, 1915, 1924, 1928, 1930, 1941, 1949, 1954, 1963, 1967, 1983, 1991, 1994, 2006, 2012, 2015, 2016.
London (6): 1938, 1966, 1969, 1970, 1971, 1986.
Dublin (6): 1914, 1916, 1939, 1948, 1960, 2008.
Mayo (5): 1933, 1950, 1957, 1995, 1997.
Meath (5): 1947, 1952, 1962, 1988, 2003.
Louth (4): 1925, 1932, 1934, 1961.
Galway (4): 1931, 1958, 1965, 1985.
Tipperary (3): 1912, 1923, 1998.
Roscommon (2): 1940, 2000.
Wicklow (2): 1936, 2002
Waterford (2): 1999, 2004.
Sligo (2): 1935, 2010.
Cavan (2): 1927, 2014.
Armagh (1): 1926.
Westmeath (1): 1929.
Longford (1): 1937.
Down (1): 1946.
Monaghan (1): 1956.
Fermanagh (1): 1959.
Tyrone (1): 1968.
Laois (1): 1973.
Wexford (1): 1992.

Under-21 Championship

GIVEN that they won four of the last eight stagings of the competition, Dublin's relationship with the newest of the four grades — and the first to be dispensed with — was always something of a love/hate one, with the more positive emotion taking quite some time to develop; almost four decades, in fact. Not only did the county delegates decline to support a successful Kerry motion at the Annual Congress at the Gresham Hotel on Easter Sunday 1963 calling for the introduction of the Championships from the following year, but the lack of enthusiasm for the grade within the capital prompted the County Board to opted out of the competition in 1973 and again for six years from 1985. (Another interesting and significant motion passed at the Gresham Hotel gathering was a Wexford one decreeing that goalkeepers should "wear a distinctive jersey from all other players".)

The most noteworthy thing about Dublin's initial foray in the competition was that the team that outscored Kildare by 2-12 to 1-7 in a provincial quarter-final at St. Conleth's Park in Newbridge on 26 April 1964 included a trio of significant names; Gerry Davey, the goalscoring hero of the county's 1-9 to 0-10 victory over Galway in the (senior) All-Ireland Final seven months earlier and two teenagers who had yet to make their senior debuts, Jimmy Keaveney and Paddy Cullen, the latter actually captaining the side from the centre back position he regularly filled with his club, Scoil Ui Chonaill. Dublin would fall to heavily Offaly at the second hurdle on a 1-8 to 0-2 scoreline at O'Connor Park in Tullamore and, over the following eight campaigns would win just six games and fail to reach a single provincial decider. On the positive side, however, those barren years saw the emergence in the grade of players such as Tony Hanahoe, Robbie Kelleher, David Hickey, Paddy Reilly, Stephen Rooney and Anton O'Toole, all of whom would play key roles in the upcoming glory days under Kevin Heffernan.

Having failed to make any serious impression at the level, Dublin — as noted above — sat out the 1973 campaign and then, somewhat ironically, returned to claim their first provincial title with victories over Wicklow, Westmeath, Longford and, by 1-10 to 0-8, Wexford in the decider. That was as good as it got, however, as a team that included Fran Ryder, Brian Mullins and John McCarthy suffered a heartbreaking 1-11 to 2-7 loss to Mayo in the All-Ireland semi-final at Croke Park, the decisive score coming from a 40 yard solo by JP Kean a mere ten seconds before Cork referee Frank Halbert blew the final whistle.

Still, the provincial duck had been broken and the Dubs would go one stage further a year later, retaining the Leinster title with, in sequence, wins over Westmeath, Wexford, Wicklow and Laois and then turning the tables on Mayo with a 1-12 to 1-10 at MacHale Park in Castlebar to set up an All-Ireland Final showdown with Kerry.

Dublin's team for the final included Ryder and Mullins again plus Gerry McCaul, Mick Holden and PJ Buckley but Kerry's line-out contained Páidí Ó Sé, Tim Kennelly, Pat Spillane and Ger O'Driscoll, all of whom had featured in the Kingdom's seven point victory over the Dubs in the senior final just a fortnight previously; the end result was a clearcut 1-15 to 0-10 triumph for the Kingdom at Sean Treacy Park in Tipperary, Mikey Sheehy beating keeper and captain Tony Fayne after just 20 seconds.

THERE then followed a barren spell that, with just two exceptions, lasted over a quarter of a century. Five provincial finals were lost, in 1976 v Kildare, 1992 v Kildare, 1993 v Meath, 1998 v Laois and 2001 v Meath, and the humiliation of a first round exit was suffered half a dozen times, in 1977 v Laois, 1979 v Longford, 1982 v Laois, 1991 v Longford, 1996 v Louth and 2000 v Meath. The honourable exceptions came in 1980 and 1984 when a third and fourth provincial titles were won but each campaign fell short of the ultimate prize.

The team in 1980 was backboned by eight of the successful minor squad from the previous year, John O'Leary, Vincent Conroy, Stephen Wade, Colm Eustace, Pat Boylan, Mick Loftus, Ciaran Duff and Barney Rock — O'Leary and the last two would also feature in the 'Twelve Apostles' success in 1983 — and was hotly fancied from the outset. Louth and Carlow were beaten with relative ease but an injury time point earned Kildare a replay in the provincial final; Dublin won 0-10 to 0-8 at the second attempt and then, thanks largely to a sixth minute goal from Duff, Mayo were edged out 1-13 to 2-8 in the All-Ireland semi-final at Pearse Park in Longford.

The final, against Cork at MacDonagh Park in Nenagh, was a definite anti-climax for the Dubs. Rock, who had scored 3-20 in the five games en route to the decider, was held to a single point, a double strike from Finbarr O'Mahoney helped the Leesiders to a 2-4 to 0-5 lead at halftime and, but for the brilliance of O'Leary between the posts, Cork's winning margin would have been considerably more than the 2-8 to 1-5 it turned out to be.

Four years later, with a squad that included Eamonn Heery, Joe McNally — already an All-Ireland winner at both minor and senior — and Shane Dalton, big things were expected but again the promise was to go unfulfilled. The provincial crown was regained with successive wins over Westmeath, Kildare, Wexford and Carlow (the latter by just 0-9 to 1-5 in the final at St. Conleth's Park in Newbridge), but defending champions Mayo, thanks to two points in the last minute and a half, ended the title dream with an 0-9 to 0-7 win in yet another All-Ireland semi-final meeting of the teams, again at Pearse Park in Longford. Defensively the team was sound, conceding just 1-36 in five matches, but the forwards were clearly lacking any real firepower — Dublin's lone goal in the entire campaign was their very first score in same, from Paul O'Carroll in the fifth minute of the opening tie at Parnell Park, and they added a mere 42 points thereafter. Martin Coffey, for instance, top scored for the campaign with an average of two points per game.

PERHAPS surprisingly having gone so close, Dublin opted out of the next six campaigns and achieved little for a dozen years on their return and it wasn't until 2002 that the provincial crowned was regained after an absence of 18 years with a team that included Stephen Cluxton, Barry Cahill, Bryan Cullen, Alan Brogan and Conal Keaney. Carlow were hammered by 29 points (5-16 to 0-2) in the opening game and then came further wins over Longford, Kildare and, in the final, Wicklow as Tomas Quinn hit 1-7 in a 1-17 to 2-4 win in Newbridge.

Tyrone, bidding for a hat-trick and a fifth title in the grade in a dozen years, provided the opposition in the All-Ireland semi-final at Breffni Park in Cavan with a side that included four players who almost exactly a year later would figure in the county's first ever Sam Maguire triumph, John Devine, Enda McGinley, Sean Cavanagh and Eoin Mulligan. Yet it was Dublin, with Darren Magee outstanding at midfield, who dominated from the start; a fifth minute goal from Declan Lally setting them on the road to a 1-13 to 0-8 lead with just eight minutes remaining. The grip was relaxed thereafter and Tyrone added a point from Mark Donnelly and then a goal from Cavanagh but a first All-Ireland Final appearance since 1980 had been comfortably secured.

Yet again the performance in the decider did not match expectations. Captain and senior representative Barry Cahill was forced to withdraw just an hour before the throw-in with a neck injury but that misfortune alone failed to explain a decidedly dismal Dublin performance as they could only muster a single point from Brogan in their entire first half, a period in which Galway put eight points on the board. Wholesale second half changes by manager Tommy Lyons — he swapped three forwards and a midfielder — brought a bit of a revival in the third quarter but Galway reasserted themselves to claim only their second title in the grade — three decades after the first — on an 0-15 to 0-7 scoreline.

A year later, at the 33rd attempt (given their seven opt-outs), Dublin could finally call themselves All-Ireland Under-21 champions and it was a feat achieved with some style. The provincial title was retained for only the second time — and the first since 1975 — when Louth, Westmeath and Longford by an aggregate margin of 26 points and then Waterford, who had shocked Kerry to capture a first ever Munster title, were hammered 3-10 to 1-7 in the All-Ireland semi-final at Semple Stadium.

Once again Tyrone, now looking for a third national crown in the space of four campaigns, were the opposition, this time for a Saturday showdown at Pairc Tailteann in Navan. Only the previous Sunday the O'Neill County had lifted Sam Maguire for the very first time with an 0-12 to 0-9 defeat of neighbours Armagh in the first ever All-Ireland Final between teams from the same province and three members of that side were in the starting line-up in Navan; keeper John Devine and midfielder Sean Cavanagh — both survivors from Breffni Park the previous year — and Cavanagh's partner in the centre of the field, Kevin Hughes.

Dublin for their part had no fewer than nine survivors from the previous year's final humiliation against Galway — Nathan Kane, Paul Griffin, Bryan Cullen, Conal Keaney, Liam Óg O hEineacháin, Declan Lally, Alan Brogan, Graham Cullen and

Seamus Walsh — and in the end experience, perhaps the bitter experience, was the deciding factor as Dublin, in front by 0-6 to 0-3 at the interval, were just two in front entering the final eight minutes but points from Lally, Brogan and Declan O'Mahony made them 0-12 to 0-7 winners. Tommy Lyons was still manager but Dublin had a new member of the coaching team, a man who had only announced his own inter-county retirement six months previously due to a back injury and who was a mere 32 years and 96 days old when captain Alan Brogan lifted the Clarke Cup ... his name was Jim Gavin.

THAT triumph might have been expected to herald a new era of success — two national finals in succession, after all — but it wasn't to be. With the Cullen brothers in the grade for a third successive year and O'Mahony, Paul Griffin, Mark Fitzpatrick, Niall Cooper, Colin Prendeville, Declan O'Mahony, Padraig Brennan, John Noonan and keeper Paul Copeland all on board for a second campaign, much was expected. Wicklow and Longford were overcome (the latter by just two points in Navan), but the bid for a first ever provincial hat-trick floundered in the final; an O'Mahony goal seemed to set Dublin on the road to victory but a last minute free from James Kavanagh earned Kildare a draw (1-4 to 0-7) in what Tommy Lyons termed "an awful dogfight" at Navan and in the replay a week later at O'Moore Park in Portlaoise, after Brennan had been sidelined for a second yellow card, Kildare senior star Derek McCormack repeated Kavanagh's feat to snatch a 1-10 to 0-12 victory for the Lilywhites.

With, remarkably, Bryan Cullen still eligible for the 2005 campaign — he was 36 days short of his 18th birthday when he made his debut in the grade in 2002 and would end with a record 19 appearances — and O'Mahony and Niall Cooper in for a third year, the provincial crown was regained with an 0-13 to 0-11 revenge win over Kildare after earlier successes against Louth and Longford. The end of the road came in the All-Ireland semi-final against Down in Navan, even if there was an element of misfortune about it; Down keeper Declan Alder saved three certain goals and green flags from James McGovern and Niall McArdle immediately before and after the break proved decisive in giving the Northerners a 2-7 to 0-9 victory.

Three disastrous years followed with a first round elimination by Meath sandwiched in between two similar losses to Kildare — the second of the latter being Jim Gavin's debut as manager — before, in 2009, Dublin would win out in Leinster but, for the fourth time, exit the competition at the All-Ireland semi-finals stage. Louth, Meath, Westmeath and Laois were accounted for in turn but then, against Cork at Semple Stadium. Dublin shot 16 wides and conceded four unanswered points in the final quarter of an hour to go down on a 1-10 to 1-9 scoreline.

EVEN if it was ultimately unsuccessful, that 2009 campaign would signal the start of Dublin's most productive period ever at the grade, a spell that would bring seven provincial titles in nine years and four national triumphs in eight.

The next year, backboned by five survivors from the loss to Cork (Rory O'Carroll, Jonny Cooper, Barry O'Rorke, Dean Rock and Niall Brogan), Dublin ousted Louth, Carlow — on an 0-14 to 0-13 scoreline at Dr. Cullen Park — and Westmeath to capture a ninth provincial title. Roscommon, mainly thanks to goals from Dean Rock and David Quinn, were eliminated 2-10 to 0-8 in the All-Ireland semi-final at Parnell Park and then the Clarke Cup was claimed for a second time with a tight 1-10 to 1-8 defeat of Donegal at Breffni Park, where Donegal captain Michael Murphy — who would lift the Sam Maguire the following year — fired an injury time penalty against the Dublin crossbar. Rock finished the Championship with 2-20 in five games, thus emulating his father Barney's feat of topping the scoring table with 3-21 from a similar number of outings in the unsuccessful campaign of three decades earlier.

The following year brought a surprise first round elimination against Meath in a high scoring game in Navan where Dublin, two points ahead with two minutes left, were pulled back and could only add a pair of white flags in extra time as Meath won 0-21 to 0-17.

A three point win over Wexford in a provincial first round tie in Enniscorthy not only opened the 2012 programme but would prove to be the tightest game of a six match campaign. Laois (2-21 to 0-4), Westmeath (4-15 to 1-9) and Louth (1-16 to 0-8) were all comfortably accounted for before Cork were deprived of a place in the All-Ireland Final on a 3-11 to 0-14 scoreline at O'Moore Park in Portlaoise, where two first half goals from full forward Philip Ryan settled the issue early. In the decider against Roscommon at O'Connor Park in Tullamore, Dublin came from two points down to score 1-6 without reply in the final quarter and take a third All-Ireland in the grade, 2-12 to 0-11.

The following year — with Jack McCaffrey, Emmett O Conghaile, Danny Byrne, Paul Mannion, Harry Dawson, Paul Maguire and Philip Ryan still in the mix — brought high hopes when hapless Carlow were routed by a massive 37 points (4-27 to 0-2, with Ciaran Kilkenny scoring 2-10, jointly the second best return ever by any Dublin footballer in any grade) in a first round tie at Parnell Park in mid February. Three weeks later came a mighty fall at the same venue when unfancied Longford, thanks to a Robbie Smyth rocket seven minutes from time and despite having skipper Padraig McCormack sent off five minutes later, hung on for a shock 1-6 to 1-5 victory.

Twelve months later, in 2014, with no fewer than a baker's dozen of returnees — Paul Mannion and Emmett O Conghaíle for a third year and keeper Lorcan Molloy, Ross McGowan, David Byrne, Conor Mullally, John Small, Jack McCaffrey, Eric Lowndes, Niall Scully, Conor McHugh, Gavin Ivory and Paddy O'Higgins for a second campaign (the latter after a year's absence), Dublin carried the mantle of favourite virtually from the off. The tag was justified, even if Cavan did pose unexpected difficulties in the All-Ireland semi-final, doggedly hanging on before going down 0-11 to 0-10 to an injury time pointed free by Cormac Costello, for the awarding of which Tipperary referee Derek O'Mahoney had to receive an escort off the O'Moore Park pitch in Portlaoise.

Before that, Carlow had once again been humbled 2-28 to 0-3, Longford were dismissed on a 3-7 to 0-6 scoreline and then in the provincial decider, also in Portlaoise, Meath were overcome 0-15 to 0-10. Having got past Cavan by the skin of their teeth, Dublin then faced Roscommon in the All-Ireland Final for the second time in three seasons, once again at O'Connor Park in Tullamore Both sides had three survivors from their 2012 showdown, Jack McCaffrey, Paul Mannion and Emmett O Conghaile for Dublin and David Murray, Conor Daly and Donie Smith for Roscommon, but it was the Liffeyside trio that made the bigger impact as McCaffrey contributed a point and Mannion nine in a comfortable 1-21 to 3-6 victory, Roscommon scoring 3-1 in a four minute spell late in the third quarter after Dublin had built up a 1-17 to 0-1 lead.

With two All-Irelands in three seasons and three in five, the following two years — 2015 and 2016 — might be seen as a little anti-climatic. The provincial crown was retained each time (the second success matching Meath's feat of a hat-trick of Leinster titles in the grade, completed in 1991), but each campaign was to end in All-Ireland semi-final disappointment at O'Connor Park in Tullamore.

Dublin, with seven survivors from the previous year's success (Lorcan Molloy, Ross McGowan, David Byrne, Conor Mullally, Eric Lowndes, Niall Scully and Cormac Costello) went five points up against Tipperary early in the second half but were pulled back to level and then, with a replay looming, lost out to a pair of injury time points from Steven O'Brien and Kevin O'Halloran. A year later defeat was even more painful; down 1-7 to 0-4 to Mayo at halftime, Dessie Farrell's side — with Lorcan Molloy matching Bryan Cullen and Alan Brogan with a fourth campaign — stormed back to lead 1-14 to 1-13 going into injury time ... only to again lose out to two late points, this time from a pair of Conor Loftus frees.

If experience is as important as they say it is, Dublin simply had to be odds on favourites for the 2017 title, the last before regarding to Under-20; Farrell had a massive returnees at his disposal — Sean McMahon, Declan Monaghan, Cillian O'Shea, Eoin Murchan, Andy Foley, Brian Howard, Glenn O'Reilly, Darragh Spillane (son of Mick and nephew of Pat and Tom), Con O'Callaghan, Eoin Murchan and Paddy Small. The benefits were clear from the start as a record fourth provincial title was notched up with an average winning margin of eleven points and without the concession of a single goal before Donegal were dismissed 1-13 to 0-9 in the All-Ireland semi-final at Breffni Park in Cavan. Two goals were conceded in the All-Ireland Final against Galway at Tullamore but Dublin were eight points clear with ten minutes left when the first of them went in and the second didn't come until the third minute of injury time. Dublin, winners on a 2-13 to 2-7 scoreline, had waited almost four decades for their first success in the grade but then won five in a decade and a half — including the last one ever, and that is something nobody can ever take away from them.

Under-21 Championship Results

1964

LEINSTER QUARTER-FINAL
Apr 26, St Conleth's Park, Newbridge
DUBLIN 2-12   KILDARE 1-7
Dublin: M McCann, B Groves, F Grimes, J Connolly, E Fahy, P Cullen, J Kennedy, T Donnelly 0-1, J Keaveney 0-4, P O'Farrell 0-1, S O'Connor, A Donnelly 0-5, G Davey 0-1, J Burke 2-0, E Flynn.

LEINSTER SEMI-FINAL
July 5, O'Connor Park, Tullamore
OFFALY 1-8   DUBLIN 0-2
Dublin: M McCann, B Groves, F Grimes, J Connolly, E Fahy, B Casey, J Kennedy, J Wright, T Donnelly, P O'Farrell, S O'Connor 0-1, J Keaveney, M Kelly, J Burke 0-1, G Davey.

1965

LEINSTER QUARTER-FINAL
June 6, Croke Park, Dublin
KILDARE 5-6   DUBLIN 2-10
Dublin: M McCann, B Groves 0-1, F Grimes, B O'Shea, P Higgins, T Hanahoe, J Kennedy, T Donnelly, N Scahill, P O'Farrell, S O'Connor 0-2, D Bollard 0-2, J Keaveney 0-2, P Byrne 1-1, J Henry 1-2.

1966

LEINSTER FIRST ROUND
Apr 24, Drogheda Park, Drogheda
DUBLIN 2-8   LOUTH 3-5
Dublin: P Kelly, W Reardon, L Heaney, M Kelleher, H Rennick, L Cushion, N McInerney, J Keaveney 0-4, T Donnelly, D Bollard 0-2, V Black 0-1, E Mullins 1-0, S O'Donovan 1-1, S O'Connor, J Richardson. Subs: J Heaney for Black, E Nelson for Richardson.

LEINSTER FIRST ROUND REPLAY
May 15, Croke Park, Dublin
LOUTH 2-8   DUBLIN 0-9
Dublin: P Kelly, C Clerkin, L Heaney, M McShane, M Kelleher, B Dowling, N McInerney, T Donnelly 0-2, B O'Shea, D Bollard, V Black, E Nelson, S O'Donovan 0-5, S O'Connor 0-2, J Richardson.

1967

LEINSTER FIRST ROUND
Mar 26, Croke Park, Dublin
DUBLIN 3-8   LOUTH 1-5
Dublin: L Murray, D Davitt, C Clerkin, M McShane, M Bracken, M Kelleher, G Davey, M Kennedy, S Rooney, D Bollard, E Mullins 0-3, K McDermott 0-2, S O'Donovan 1-1, T Bassett, L Deegan 2-2.

LEINSTER QUARTER-FINAL
May 7, St Conleth's Park, Newbridge
KILDARE 1-7   DUBLIN 2-3
Dublin: L Murray, D Davitt, C Clerkin, M McShane, M Bracken, M Kelleher, G Davey, M Kennedy, S Rooney 0-1, D Bollard 1-0, E Mullins, K McDermott 1-1, S O'Donovan 0-1, T Bassett, L Deegan.

1968

LEINSTER FIRST ROUND
Apr 14, Pairc Tailteann, Navan
DUBLIN 1-9   MEATH 0-5
Dublin: C Noone, T O'Hanlon, T Bassett, T Byrne, S Conlon, D Davitt, T Wright, M Kelleher 0-1, S Donnelly, J Keane, S Rooney 0-2, P Loughran, P Leahy 1-5, E Davey, J Sweeney 0-1.

LEINSTER QUARTER-FINAL
June 30, Croke Park, Dublin
DUBLIN 1-9   KILDARE 1-8
Dublin: C Noone, C Hogan, T O'Hanlon, T Byrne, G Wilson, M Kelleher, T Wright, S Donnelly 0-1, S Rooney, S Conlon 1-0, P Loughran 0-1, J Keane, F McDonald 0-1, J Greer 0-1, J Sweeney 0-5. Subs: P Leahy for McDonald, J Martin for Leahy.

LEINSTER SEMI-FINAL
July 28, O'Moore Park, Portlaoise
OFFALY 1-16   DUBLIN 1-7
Dublin: C Noone, C Hogan, T O'Hanlon, T O'Byrne, G Wilson, M Kelleher, T Wright, S Donnelly 0-1, S Rooney, S Conlon, P Loughran 0-1, J Keane, L Deegan 0-1, E Davey 1-1, J Sweeney 0-3. Subs: J Davis for Wright, F Murray for Rooney.

1969

LEINSTER FIRST ROUND
Apr 6, Croke Park, Dublin
DUBLIN 0-11   MEATH 1-6

Dublin: M Nolan, P Murray, T Byrne, S Roche, M Morris, G Carleton, G Wilson 0-1, J Greer, S Yates, K O'Meara, P Leahy 0-7, E McCarthy 0-1, P McCarthy 0-1, K Barry, F McDonald. Sub: P Gogarty 0-1 for O'Meara, M Noonan for Barry.

LEINSTER QUARTER-FINAL
July 9, St Conleth's Park, Newbridge
KILDARE 3-8   DUBLIN 2-6
Dublin: M Nolan, F Murray, S Roche, T Byrne, M Morris, P O'Neill, G Wilson, S Yates, F Farnan, J Reilly, P Leahy 0-4, E McCarthy, K Hegarty 1-1, P Gogarty 1-1, K O'Meara.

1970

LEINSTER FIRST ROUND
Apr 19, Drogheda Park, Drogheda
LOUTH 1-10   DUBLIN 1-9
Dublin: M Nolan, J Coleman, S Roche, C Maher, C Hobbs, R Kelleher, J Broe, P O'Neill 0-1, D Hickey 0-3, M Noctor, A Desmond, P Leahy 0-4, V Daly 0-1, P Gogarty, K Hegarty 1-0.

1971

LEINSTER QUARTER-FINAL
May 6, Parnell Park, Dublin
DUBLIN 3-12   LOUTH 0-10
Dublin: M Nolan, S Falvey, J O'Neill, P Colgan, M McMenamon, R Kelleher, P Reilly, D Hickey, J Clarke 0-1, G Moore 0-3, J Reilly 0-2, A O'Toole 0-3, F Hutchinson, V Daly 2-3, B Lee 1-0.

LEINSTER SEMI-FINAL
June 30, Drogheda Park, Drogheda
MEATH 1-18   DUBLIN 1-12
Dublin: M Nolan, S Falvey, J O'Neill, P Colgan, M McMenamon, R Kelleher, P Reilly, D Hickey, J Clarke 0-1, G Moore 0-2, J Reilly, A O'Toole 1-0, F Hutchinson 0-5, V Daly 0-3, B Lee. Sub: A Carney 0-1 for Lee.

1972

LEINSTER FIRST ROUND
Apr 9, Drumree Road, Dunshaughlin
MEATH 0-7   DUBLIN 0-4
Dublin: E McEneany, B Finn, J O'Neill, V Holden, M McMenamon, R Kelleher, D Daly, L Sweeney, P Duggan, A O'Toole 0-1, D Hickey, P Levins, F Hutchinson 0-1, F Clarke, P Hickey 0-2.

1973

Dublin did not compete in the Championships.

1974

LEINSTER FIRST ROUND
Apr 14, Burgage Park, Blessington
DUBLIN 4-8   WICKLOW 1-4
Dublin: T Fayne, D Billings, P Shatwell, G McCaul, A Cunningham, V Holden, B Pocock 0-1, M Ryan 0-1, B Brogan, G O'Leary 0-4, J McCarthy 1-0, S McCarthy 1-0, B Mullins 2-1, B Salmon, D Redmond 0-1. Subs: P Reaney for Ryan, P Rooney for S McCarthy, T Corcoran for Brogan.

LEINSTER QUARTER-FINAL
Apr 28, Pairc Tailteann, Navan
DUBLIN 2-12   WESTMEATH 0-7
Dublin: T Fayne, D Billings, P Shatwell, C Fitzpatrick, A Cunningham, V Holden, B Pocock 0-2, B Mullins 2-1, M Ryan, G O'Leary 0-5, J McCarthy, P Reaney 0-1, E Flaherty 0-1, B Salmon, D Redmond 0-1. Sub: T Diamond 0-1 for Salmon.

LEINSTER SEMI-FINAL
June 23, Cusack Park, Mullingar
DUBLIN 2-13   LONGFORD 0-7
Dublin: L O'Neill, D Billings, D Hobbs, G McCaul, A Cunningham, V Holden, B Pocock 0-1, M Ryan, T Diamond 0-1, G O'Leary 1-6, B Mullins, P Rooney, J McCarthy, B Salmon 1-0, P Reaney 0-3. Subs: D Redmond 0-2 for McCarthy, J Corcoran for Diamond.

LEINSTER FINAL
Aug 18, Carlow
DUBLIN 1-10   WEXFORD 0-8
Dublin: L O'Neill, D Billings, D Hobbs, G McCaul, F Ryder, V Holden, B Pocock 0-2, M Ryan 1-0, T Diamond, P Reaney 0-5, B Mullins 0-2, J McCarthy, G O'Leary 0-1, B Salmon, D Redmond. Subs: C Fitzpatrick for McCarthy, P Rooney for O'Leary, J Corcoran for Redmond.

ALL-IRELAND SEMI-FINAL
Aug 25, Croke Park, Dublin
MAYO 1-11   DUBLIN 2-7
Dublin: L O'Neill, D Billings, D Hobbs, G McCaul, F Ryder, V Holden, B Pocock 0-1, B Mullins, T Diamond 0-1, M Ryan, B Salmon 1-0, P Rooney 0-2, P Reaney 0-1, C Fitzpatrick 0-2, J McCarthy. Subs: J Corcoran for Rooney, G O'Leary 1-0 for Reaney.

1975

LEINSTER FIRST ROUND
Apr 6, Pairc Tailteann, Navan
DUBLIN 1-12   WESTMEATH 0-5
Dublin: T Fayne, J Sutton, L Egan, B Fitzpatrick, J Thompson, K Bruton, G O'Connor, P Connellan 0-1, A

Arkins, PJ Buckley 0-3, J Corcoran 0-1, J Sweeney 0-1, P Reaney 0-3, J Flanagan 0-2, S McCarthy 1-0. Sub: E Ryan 0-1 for Corcoran.

LEINSTER QUARTER-FINAL
Apr 27, County Ground, Aughrim
DUBLIN 4-8   WEXFORD 0-2
Dublin: T Fayne, J Sutton, L Egan, B Fitzpatrick, J Thompson, K Bruton, G O'Connor 0-1, F Ryder 0-1, A Arkins, PJ Buckley 0-2, J Corcoran, P Connellan 1-2, P Reaney 1-1, B Mullins 1-1, S McCarthy 1-0.

LEINSTER SEMI-FINAL
May 11, Sallins Road, Naas
DUBLIN 2-10   WICKLOW 1-9
Dublin: T Fayne, J Sutton, L Egan, B Fitzpatrick, M Martin, J Thompson, G O'Connor, F Ryder, J Lynskey 0-1, PJ Buckley 0-2, J Corcoran 0-1, P Connellan 0-3, P Reaney 0-1, B Mullins 2-1, P Rooney 0-1. Sub: A Cunningham for O'Connor.

LEINSTER FINAL
July 13, Dr Cullen Park, Carlow
DUBLIN 0-12   LAOIS 1-6
Dublin: T Fayne, B Fitzpatrick, L Egan, G McCaul, J Thompson 0-2, K Bruton, A Cunningham, A Arkins 0-1, F Ryder, P Reaney 0-3, B Mullins 0-2, P Connellan, E Ryan 0-1, J Corcoran, S McCarthy 0-3. Subs: PJ Buckley for Bruton, C Fitzpatrick for Corcoran.

ALL-IRELAND SEMI-FINAL
Aug 17, MacHale Park, Castlebar
DUBLIN 1-12   MAYO 1-9
Dublin: T Fayne, B Fitzpatrick, L Egan, G McCaul, K Bruton, J Thompson, M Holden, F Ryder, J Corcoran, PJ Buckley 0-2, B Mullins, P Connellan 0-7, P Reaney 0-1, T Drumm 1-0, S McCarthy. Sub: C Fitzpatrick 0-1 for Drumm.

ALL-IRELAND FINAL
Oct 12, Sean Treacy Park, Tipperary
KERRY 1–15   DUBLIN 0–10
Dublin: Tony Fayne, Brian Fitzpatrick, Liam Egan, Gerry McCaul, Kenny Bruton, John Thompson, Mick Holden, Fran Ryder, John Corcoran, Paul Connellan 0-3, Brian Mullins 0-1, PJ Buckley 0-2, Peter Reaney, Camillus Fitzpatrick, Sean McCarthy 0-1. Subs: Declan O'Reilly 0-1 for Corcoran, Andy Cunningham for Bruton, Pat Rooney 0-2 for Connellan.

1976

LEINSTER QUARTER-FINAL
Apr 18, Parnell Park, Dublin
DUBLIN 1-7   MEATH 0-7
Dublin: J Nolan, J Sutton, J Thompson, T Clancy, G Collins, K Moran, M Martin, P Rooney, T Drumm, PJ Buckley 0-4, D Canning, D O'Reilly, B Reddy 0-1, T Noone, P Keenan 0-2. Subs: J Quinn 1-0 for Canning.

LEINSTER SEMI-FINAL
May 26, O'Moore Park, Portlaoise
DUBLIN 2-6   OFFALY 1-6
Dublin: J Nolan, J Sutton, J Thompson, T Clancy, G Collins, T Drumm, M Martin, K Moran, P Rooney, J Quinn 0-1, PJ Buckley 0-1, D O'Reilly 0-1, B Reddy 1-0, T Noone 1-1, P Keenan 0-1. Subs: J Lynskey for Quinn, F Caverly for Keenan.

LEINSTER FINAL
July 30, St Conleth's Park, Newbridge
KILDARE 1-12   DUBLIN 0-9
Dublin: J Nolan, J Sutton, T Clancy, F Caverly, G Collins, J Thompson, M Martin, T Drumm 0-1, P Rooney 0-1, B Reddy 0-1, PJ Buckley, D O'Reilly, J Quinn, T Noone, P Keenan 0-6. Subs: V Dowling for Buckley, D McCabe for Martin.

1977

LEINSTER QUARTER-FINAL
Apr 24, McCann Park, Portarlington
LAOIS 1-17   DUBLIN 1-10
Dublin: N Fitzgerald, G O'Kelly, M Kennedy, L Redmond, E Lynch, M Hurley, K Moran 1-0, K Barry 0-1, G Collins 0-1, T Naughton, J Caffrey, P Cox 0-4, J Kennedy 0-2, D McGrath, J Quinn 0-2. Sub: B Cooper for Caffrey.

1978

LEINSTER FIRST ROUND
Apr 16, County Ground, Aughrim
DUBLIN 3-13   WICKLOW 0-3
Dublin: S Fox, T Foran, M Kennedy, P Sutton, E Lynch 0-1, D Foran 0-1, B Byrne, D Murphy 0-1, C Richardson, P Cox 0-1, P Hogan 1-1, T O'Brien, J Quinn 0-5, M Dwyer 2-2, A McIntyre 0-1.

LEINSTER QUARTER-FINAL
Apr 30, Parnell Park, Dublin
WESTMEATH 0-7   DUBLIN 0-6
Dublin: S Fox, T Foran, M Kennedy, P Sutton, E Lynch, D Foran, B Byrne, D Murphy, C Richardson, P Cox 0-1, P Hogan 0-2, T O'Brien 0-2, J Quinn, M Dwyer 0-1, A McIntyre. Subs: S Kennedy for McIntyre, D McGrath for Cox, J Caffrey for Murphy.

1979

LEINSTER FIRST ROUND
Apr 15, Parnell Park, Dublin
LONGFORD 1-7   DUBLIN 1-4
Dublin: N Fitzgerald, P Canavan, M Kennedy, B Roche, C Roche, D Foran, B Byrne, A White, J Kearns, P Hogan 0-3, D McGrath, R Crean, A McCaul, M Dwyer 1-1, V Carney. Subs: J Finnegan for Carney, D Hurley for Kearns, M Carlisle for Hurley.

1980

LEINSTER QUARTER-FINAL
May 8, Parnell Park, Dublin
DUBLIN 1-12   LOUTH 1-8
Dublin: J O'Leary, F Walsh, V Conroy, S Wade, S Fleming, D Foran, C Eustace, J Ronayne, J Kearns, B Byrne 0-2, M Loftus 0-1, C Duff 0-2, W Hughes 0-1, B Rock 1-5, A McCaul 0-1.

LEINSTER SEMI-FINAL
June 25, St Conleth's Park, Newbridge
DUBLIN 5-18   CARLOW 0-7
Dublin: J O'Leary, F Walsh, V Conroy, S Wade, S Fleming, D Foran, C Eustace, J Ronayne 0-5, J Kearns 0-1, B Byrne 0-3, M Loftus 0-2, C Duff 1-0, W Hughes 1-1, B Rock 1-4, A McCaul 2-1. Subs: P Canavan for Fleming, R Hazley for Wade, R Davis 0-1 for Loftus.

LEINSTER FINAL
July 20, Croke Park, Dublin
DUBLIN 2-7   KILDARE 1-10
Dublin: J O'Leary, F Walsh, V Conroy, S Wade, S Fleming, D Foran, C Eustace, J Ronayne, J Kearns, B Byrne 0-3, M Loftus 1-1, T White 0-1, A McCaul 0-1, B Rock 1-1, W Hughes. Subs: P Canavan for Walsh 25.

LEINSTER FINAL REPLAY
Aug 3, St Conleth's Park, Newbridge
DUBLIN 0-10   KILDARE 0-8
Dublin: J O'Leary, F Walsh, V Conroy, D Foran, S Fleming, S Wade, P Canavan, J Kearns, T White, B Byrne 0-1, J Ronayne, C Duff 0-2, M Loftus 0-1, B Rock 0-4, A McCaul 0-2. Subs: W Hughes for Byrne 40, P Boylan for Kearns 42.

ALL-IRELAND SEMI-FINAL
Sep 28, Pearse Park, Longford
DUBLIN 1-13   MAYO 2-8
Dublin: J O'Leary, F Welsh, V Conroy, D Foran, S Fleming, S Wade, C Eustace, J Ronayne, P Boylan 0-1, T White, M Loftus, C Duff 1-0, W Hughes 0-3, B Rock 0-6, A McCaul 0-2. Subs: P Canavan 0-1 for Fleming, D O'Brien for White.

ALL-IRELAND FINAL
Oct 12, MacDonagh Park, Nenagh
CORK 2-8   DUBLIN 1-5
Dublin: John O'Leary, Frank Walsh, Vincent Conroy, David Foran, Pat Canavan, Stephen Wade, Colm Eustace, Jim Ronayne 0-1, Pat Boylan 0-1, Dermot O'Brien, Mick Loftus 0-1, Ciaran Duff 1-0, Willie Hughes, Barney Rock 0-1, Anto McCaul. Subs: Shay Fleming for Eustace, Vincent Kearney 0-1 for Hughes, Ger O'Neill fo McCaul.

1981

LEINSTER QUARTER-FINAL
June 9, Parnell Park, Dublin
DUBLIN 0-13   MEATH 0-7
Dublin: J O'Leary, F Walsh, V Conroy, C Eustace, M O'Connell, S Wade, P Canavan, T White 0-1, G O'Neill, P Boylan 0-5, P McLoughlin 0-5, T Gray 0-1, D O'Brien 0-1, P Nugent, B Stynes.

LEINSTER SEMI-FINAL
June 17, Pairc Tailteann, Navan
LOUTH 0-11   DUBLIN 0-4
Dublin: J O'Leary, F Walsh, V Conroy, C Eustace, M O'Connell, S Wade, P Canavan, T White 0-1, G O'Neill, P Boylan 0-2, P McLoughlin, T Gray 0-1, T O'Brien, P Nugent, B Stynes.

1982

LEINSTER QUARTER-FINAL
Apr 25, McCann Park, Portarlington
LAOIS 0-11   DUBLIN 0-5
Dublin: J O'Leary, D Carroll, V Conroy, D Synnott, M Dowling, C Eustace, P McCabe, B Kavanagh, G O'Neill, P Nugent, P Boylan 0-2, C Duff 1-0, P McLoughlin, B Rock 0-3, C Buffini. Subs: M O'Connor for Carroll, R Mulvanney for Buffini.

1983

LEINSTER FIRST ROUND
Apr 17, Parnell Park, Dublin
DUBLIN 1-6   MEATH 0-8
Dublin: B Stynes, G Keenan, F McGrath, D Synnott, M Deegan, P Caffrey, B Hickey, C Maher 0-1, B Cooke, D Sheehan 0-1, M Egan, M Coffey 0-2, C Redmond 1-2, T McCormack, C O'Farrell.

LEINSTER QUARTER-FINAL
May 1, Parnell Park, Dublin
DUBLIN 2-5   LAOIS 1-1
Dublin: B Stynes, G Keenan, F McGrath, K Sutton, E

Heery, P Caffrey, D Synnott, B Cooke, C Maher 0-1, D Sheehan 0-1, M Egan, M Coffey 0-2, P Walsh 1-0, C O'Carroll 0-1, C Redmond 1-0.

LEINSTER SEMI-FINAL
July 6, Pairc Tailteann, Navan
LOUTH 1-4   DUBLIN 0-6
Dublin: B Stynes, G Keenan, F McGrath, K Sutton, E Heery, P Caffrey, D Synnott, B Cooke, C Maher, D Sheehan 0-1, M Egan, M Coffey 0-1, P Walsh 0-1, T McCormack 0-2, C Redmond 0-1.

1984

LEINSTER FIRST ROUND
June 4, Parnell Park, Dublin
DUBLIN 1-8   WESTMEATH 0-8
Dublin: B Lillis, D Carroll, T Delaney 0-2, D Synnott, E Heery, R Caverly, M Deegan, C Bracken, B Cooke, M Egan 0-1, C O'Farrell 0-1, M Coffey 0-2, P O'Carroll 1-1, M Barber, B Gavin 0-1.

LEINSTER QUARTER-FINAL
June 13, Parnell Park, Dublin
DUBLIN 0-10   KILDARE 0-9
Dublin: B Lillis, C Sage, F McGrath, G Keenan, E Heery, T Delaney, D Synnott, D Sheehan 0-1, B Cooke 0-1, M Egan 0-3, T Delaney 0-1, M Coffey 0-2, S O'Brien 0-1, J McNally, B Gavin 0-1.

LEINSTER SEMI-FINAL
July 5, Dr Cullen Park, Carlow
DUBLIN 0-8   WEXFORD 0-5
Dublin: B Lillis, C Sage, F McGrath, G Keenan, E Heery 0-1, T Delaney, D Synnott, C Bracken, B Cooke 0-1, M Egan 0-2, T Delaney 0-2, M Coffey 0-2, P O'Carroll, J McNally, B Gavin.

LEINSTER FINAL
July 25, St Conleth's Park, Newbridge
DUBLIN 0-9   CARLOW 1-5
Dublin: B Lillis, C Sage, F McGrath, G Keenan, E Heery, T Delaney, D Synnott, C Bracken, B Cooke, M Egan 0-4, C O'Farrell, M Coffey 0-3, P O'Carroll, J McNally, B Gavin 0-1. Sub: S Dalton 0-1 for O'Carroll, J Bissett for Cooke.

ALL-IRELAND SEMI-FINAL
Aug 5, Pearse Park, Longford
MAYO 0-9   DUBLIN 0-7
Dublin: B Lillis, C Sage, F McGrath, G Keenan, E Heery, T Delaney, D Synnott, C Bracken, J Bissett, M Egan 0-5, R Caverley, M Coffey 0-1, B Gavin, S Dalton, J McNally 0-1. Subs: B Cooke for Bissett, S O'Brien for Gavin, D Carroll for Bracken.

1985–1990

Dublin, having advocated the abolition of the Championship, opted not to compete.

1991

LEINSTER FIRST ROUND
Mar 3, Pearse Park, Longford
LONGFORD 1-8   DUBLIN 0-9
Dublin: D O'Farrell, P McManus, J Jordan, C Kavanagh, P O'Neill, J Bell, B Murray, S Moylan, P Cassells, G Regan 0-2, B Barnes, D Quinlivan 0-2, D Fitzgerald 0-2, P Doherty 0-2, D O'Reilly 0-1. Subs: P Gilroy for Doherty, P Wardick for Cassells, A O'Malley for O'Reilly.

1992

LEINSTER FIRST ROUND
Mar 29, Drogheda Park, Drogheda
DUBLIN 2-15   LOUTH 3-10
Dublin: D Byrne, C Cleary, J Bell, C Keegan, D Benton, D Harrington, G Regan, A Dunne 0-1, P Gilroy, B Roe, L Callan, D O'Farrell 0-2, D Farrell 1-0, M Leahy 1-1, P Doherty 0-9. Subs: F McNulty 0-2 for Gilroy, R Boyle for Roe.

LEINSTER QUARTER-FINAL
Apr 12, Parnell Park, Dublin
DUBLIN 0-16   LONGFORD 1-7
Dublin: D Byrne, C Cleary, B Quinlivan, C Keegan, D Harrington, J Bell, G Regan, L Callan, P Gilroy 0-2, B Rowe 0-2, F McNulty 0-1, D O'Farrell 0-1, D Farrell 0-3, R Boyle 0-3, P Doherty 0-4.

LEINSTER SEMI-FINAL
Apr 26, Dr Cullen Park, Carlow
DUBLIN 1-9   OFFALY 0-7
Dublin: D Byrne, C Cleary, B Quinlivan, C Keegan, D Harrington, J Bell, G Regan, L Callan, P Gilroy, B Rowe, F McNulty, D O'Farrell, D Farrell, R Boyle, P Doherty. Sub: M Carroll for Rowe.

LEINSTER FINAL
May 10, O'Connor Park, Tullamore
KILDARE 2-12   DUBLIN 0-9
Dublin: D Byrne, C Cleary, B Quinlivan, R Lambe, D Harrington, J Bell 0-1, G Regan, L Callan, P Gilroy, B Rowe, F McNulty 0-1, D O'Farrell, D Farrell, R Boyle 0-1, P Doherty 0-5. Subs: D Connolly for Quinlivan, D Fitzgerald 0-1 for Rowe, D Benton for McNulty.

1993

LEINSTER QUARTER-FINAL
Apr 10, Parnell Park, Dublin

DUBLIN 1-14   CARLOW 0-6

Dublin: E Carberry, C Keegan, S McGuirk, M Carroll, L Walsh, D Harrington, W Daly 0-2, D Benton 0-1, B Quinlivan, B Rowe, D O'Brien 0-2, D Barnes, B O'Brien 0-3, R Boyle 1-2, S Keogh 0-3. Sub: F McNulty 0-1 for Barnes.

LEINSTER SEMI-FINAL
Apr 25, Pairc Tailteann, Navan

DUBLIN 0-14   WESTMEATH 1-8

Dublin: E Carberry, C Keegan, S McGuirk, M Carroll, L Walsh, D Harrington, W Daly, D Benton, B Quinlivan, B Rowe 0-3, D O'Brien 0-2, D Barnes 0-1, G Walsh, R Boyle 0-4, S Keogh 0-4. Subs: F McNulty for Barnes, B O'Brien for Walsh.

LEINSTER FINAL
May 9, Croke Park, Dublin

MEATH 2-11   DUBLIN 2-9

Dublin: E Carberry, C Keegan, S McGuirk, M Carroll, L Walsh, D Harrington, W Daly, D Benton, B Quinlivan, B Rowe, D O'Brien, D Barnes, G Walsh 0-2, R Boyle 1-0, S Keogh 1-7. Subs: T Russell for Carroll, F McNulty for Benton, A Stack for Barnes.

1994

LEINSTER QUARTER-FINAL
Apr 16, Pearse Park, Arklow

DUBLIN 1-13   WICKLOW 1-5

Dublin: G Gallagher, R Lambe, O Stewart, D Fairbanks, L Walsh, C Brennan, D Benton, P Clifford, B Quinlivan, E Sheehy, G Walsh 0-2, S Keogh 0-5, S Connell 0-3, D Harrington 1-1, A Stack 0-1.

LEINSTER SEMI-FINAL
May 4, Pairc Tailteann, Navan

MEATH 1-9   DUBLIN 0-7

Dublin: G Gallagher, R Lambe, O Stewart, D Fairbanks, D Benton, L Walsh, P Clifford, C Brennan, B Quinlivan, E Sheehy, S Keogh 0-6, S Connell, A Dunne, D Harrington, A Stack 0-1. Subs: G Walsh for Sheehy, D Moore for Stewart.

1995

LEINSTER FIRST ROUND
Mar 25, Lawless Memorial Park, Swords

DUBLIN 2-14   LONGFORD 0-3

Dublin: P Hussey, M Ryan, D Homan, C Wilson, P Christie 0-1, B Whelan, P Clifford 0-2, D Madden, J

Reddy 0-2, B O'Brien 2-2, K Galvin 0-1, S Connell 0-2, C MacCriostal, E Sheehy 0-4, K Brady. Subs: K Lawlor for MacCriostal, D Fairbanks for Homan, S Cooke for Connell.

LEINSTER QUARTER-FINAL
Apr 10, O'Toole Park, Dublin

DUBLIN 0-11   MEATH 1-7

Dublin: P Hussey, M Ryan, C Wilson, P Christie, B Whelan, I Robertson, P Clifford, J Reddy, D Madden, S Cooke 0-3, K Galvin, K Lawlor 0-5, B O'Brien 0-1, E Sheehy 0-1, S Connell. Subs: J Sherlock 0-1 for O'Brien, D Martin for Ryan, S White for Reddy.

LEINSTER SEMI-FINAL
Apr 22, St Conleth's Park, Newbridge

WESTMEATH 1-10   DUBLIN 1-7

Dublin: P Hussey, M Ryan, C Wilson, P Christie 0-1, B Whelan, I Robertson, P Clifford, J Reddy, D Madden, S Cooke 1-1, K Galvin, K Lawlor 0-3, J Sherlock 0-2, E Sheehy, S Connell. Sub: C O Muireartaigb for Madden.

1996

LEINSTER QUARTER-FINAL
Apr 14, St Brigid's Park, Dundalk

LOUTH 2-8   DUBLIN 1-9

Dublin: J Leonard, P Giles, G Colleran, A McNulty, P Christie 1-0, J Murphy, K Galvin, D Homan, C Whelan, S Cooke, M Casey, I Robertson, P Gilson 0-1, E Sheehy, S Caffrey 0-1. Subs: P Croft 0-1 for Murphy, G Farley for Colleran, D Bolger 0-6 for Caffrey.

1997

LEINSTER FIRST ROUND
Feb 22, Lawless Memorial Park, Swords

DUBLIN 0-12   WEXFORD 0-9

Dublin: J Leonard, M Beirne, P Giles, S Hearty, K Kehilly, I Robertson, P Croft, A Moran, D Maxwell, S Cowap, D Stynes, J Magee 0-1, M O'Keeffe 0-1, D Bolger 0-7, R Cosgrove 0-2. Sub: N Crossan 0-1 for Cowap 49.

LEINSTER QUARTER-FINAL
Mar 16, Parnell Park, Dublin

DUBLIN 1-11   OFFALY 0-11

Dublin: J Leonard, M Beirne, P Giles, S Hearty, K Kehilly, I Robertson 0-1, P Croft, A Moran 1-0, D Maxwell 0-1, C Whelan 0-2, J Magee, M Healy, M O'Keeffe 0-1, R Cosgrove 0-2, D Bolger 0-4. Subs: B Gogarty, D Stynes, I Clarke.

* Following a pitched battle involving up to three dozen players and officials from both sides,

the Leinster Council expelled Dublin from the championship and banned both counties from the following year's competition, although this was subsequently rescinded on appeal.

1998

LEINSTER FIRST ROUND
Feb 8, Cusack Park, Mullingar
DUBLIN 2-7   WESTMEATH 0-11
Dublin: K Gorman, N McCaffrey, D Cahill, A Morrissey, P Andrews, J Magee, G O'Connell, I Clarke, D Maxwell, C Doyle, D Stynes, P Croft 0-1, P Murtagh 0-1, R Cosgrove 1-5, N Crossan 1-0. Subs: C Kilmurray for C Doyle, M Doran for Crossan.

LEINSTER QUARTER-FINAL
Feb 22, Dr Cullen Park, Carlow
DUBLIN 1-10   CARLOW 0-6
Dublin: K Gorman, N McCaffrey, D Cahill, A McNulty, S Ryan, I Clarke, P Andrews, J Magee 0-3, D Maxwell 1-1, D Byrne 0-1, P Croft 0-3, D Stynes 0-1 M Doran, R Cosgrove, P Murtagh 0-1. Subs: A Lyons for Cosgrove, C Kilmurray for Lyons, C Doyle for Byrne.

LEINSTER SEMI-FINAL
Mar 22, Dr Cullen Park, Carlow
DUBLIN 1-13   WICKLOW 1-12
Dublin: K Gorman, G O Connell, D Cahill, A McNulty, S Ryan 0-1, I Clarke, P Andrews, D Maxwell, J 0-1, P Keogh 0-2, D Stynes 0-1, P Croft 0-4, D Crowley, R Cosgrove 1-3, N Crossan 0-1. Subs: M Cahill for O'Connell, C Doyle for Stynes, C Kilmurray for Crowley.

LEINSTER FINAL
Apr 12, O'Connor Park, Tullamore
LAOIS 1-13   DUBLIN 1-7
Dublin: K Gorman, A McNulty, D Cahill, M Cahill, S Ryan, I Clarke, P Andrews 0-1, D Maxwell, J Magee, A Lyons, D Stynes, P Croft 0-3, P Keogh 0-1, R Cosgrove 0-1, N Crossan. Subs: M Doran 0-1 for Stynes, C Doyle 1-0 for Lyons, P Murtagh for Crossan.

1999

LEINSTER QUARTER-FINAL
Feb 20, Pearse Park, Longford
DUBLIN 0-12   LONGFORD 1-9
Dublin: K Gorman, M Cahill, B O'Toole, G O'Connell, S Ryan, J Magee, P Andrews, M McInerney, K Darcy 0-1, D O'Brien 0-1, C Doyle 0-1, E Crennan 0-2, J Madden, F Kiely, N Crossan 0-7. Subs: D Cordon for M McInerney 36, P Murtagh for C Doyle 42, C Moran for J Magee 51.

LEINSTER QUARTER-FINAL REPLAY
Mar 13, Pairc Tailteann, Navan
DUBLIN 1-10   LONGFORD 0-11
Dublin: K Gorman, M Breathnach, B O'Toole, G O'Connell, C Moran, S Ryan, P Andrews, K Darcy 0-1, D Conlon, J Madden, M McInerney, P Murtagh 0-2, P Healy, E Crennan 0-1, N Crossan 0-4. Subs: C Doyle 1-1 for Madden, D O'Brien 0-1 for Healy, A O'Brien for Crennan. Extra time: Crennan for O'Brien.

LEINSTER SEMI-FINAL
Mar 21, O'Moore Park, Tullamore
LAOIS 3-11   DUBLIN 2-10
Dublin: K Gorman, M Breathnach, B O'Toole, G O'Connell, C Moran, S Ryan, P Andrews, K Darcy 0-1, J Magee 1-2, P Murtagh 1-0, A O'Brien, D O'Brien, W McCarthy 0-2, E Crennan 0-2, N Crossan 0-1. Subs: F Kiely for A O'Brien, C Doyle 0-2 for D O'Brien.

2000

LEINSTER FIRST ROUND
Feb 20, Pairc Tailteann, Navan
MEATH 0-8   DUBLIN 0-7
Dublin: J Bates, M Cahill, J O'Connor, M Breathnach, C Doyle, D Conlon, D Magee 0-1, M Kennedy, R Brennan 0-1, M Thompson, C Moran 0-1, K Kilmurray, C Purcell, M McInerney 0-1, W McCarthy 0-3. Subs: J Gahan for Thompson h/t, D Magill for Purcell 49, P Casey for McInerney 58.

2001

LEINSTER FIRST ROUND
Feb 4, Parnell Park, Dublin
DUBLIN 0-14   WEXFORD 0-9
Dublin: S Cluxton, G Norton, M Breathnach, N Cleere, A Holly, M Kennedy, P Casey, B Cahill, C Murphy, R Carroll 0-1, C Moran 0-1, A Brogan 0-1, T Quinn 0-1, J Gahan 0-3, W McCarthy 0-6. Subs: P Lawless 0-1 for Carroll 51, L Og O hEineachain for 57, K Golden for Brogan 60, F Purcell for Gahan 64.

LEINSTER QUARTER-FINAL
Feb 18, Lawless Memorial Park, Swords
DUBLIN 0-16   LONGFORD 0-5
Dublin: S Cluxton, G Norton, M Breathnach, W Cleere, A Holly, M Kennedy, P Casey, B Cahill, C Murphy, C Moran 0-4, R Carroll, A Brogan, T Quinn 0-2, J Gahan 0-1, W McCarthy 0-8. Subs: D Magee 0-1 for Carroll 31, P Lawless for Quinn 38, N O'Driscoll for Gahan 45, D Conlon for Murphy 55.

LEINSTER SEMI-FINAL
Mar 31, Cusack Park, Mullingar
DUBLIN 0-11   KILDARE 0-7
Dublin: S Cluxton, G Norton, M Breathnach., N Cleere, A Holly, M Kennedy, P Casey, D Magee, C Murphy, A Brogan 0-2, C Moran, L Og O hEineachain 0-1, T Quinn 0-1, J Gahan 0-2, W McCarthy 0-4. Subs: P Lawless 0-1 for T Quinn 44, D Tally for J Gahan 60.

LEINSTER FINAL
Apr 7, St Conleth's Park, Newbridge
MEATH 0-10   DUBLIN 0-5
Dublin: S Cluxton, G Norton, M Breathnach, N Cleere, A Holly, M Kennedy, P Casey, D Magee, C Murphy, A Brogan, R Carroll, L O hEineachain, T Quinn, J Gahan, W McCarthy 0-5. Subs: M O'Sullivan for Gahan, P Lawless for Quinn, D Conlon for Carroll, K Golden for Magee.

2002

LEINSTER FIRST ROUND
Mar 2, St Margaret's, Dublin
DUBLIN 5-16   CARLOW 0-2
Dublin: S Cluxton, N Kane, D Corcoran, D Murray, P Casey 0-2, B Cullen, B Cahill, D Magee 1-2, C Murphy, K Devine 0-3, S Walsh, L Og O hEineachain 1-2, A Brogan 1-1, G Smith 0-3, T Quinn 0-3. Subs: P Murray 2-0 for Brogan, D Lally for Magee, M Lyons for Smith, A Molloy for Cahill, P Griffin for Casey.

LEINSTER QUARTER-FINAL
Mar 16, Parnell Park, Dublin
DUBLIN 0-13   LONGFORD 0-6
Dublin: S Cluxton, N Kane, D Corcoran, D Murray, P Casey, B Cullen, B Cahill, D Magee, C Murphy, K Devine 0-1, S Walsh, L Og O hEineachain 0-1, A Brogan 0-2, G Smith 0-5, T Quinn 0-4. Subs: D Lally for Walsh, N Cleere for Cahill, P Murray for O hEineachain.

LEINSTER SEMI-FINAL
Apr 7, Pairc Tailteann, Navan
DUBLIN 2-10   KILDARE 0-13
Dublin: S Cluxton, N Kane, D Corcoran, S Shaughnessy, D Murray, B Cahill, P Casey, D Magee, C Murphy, K Devine 0-1, L Og O hEineachain 0-3, N O'Driscoll 0-1, A Brogan 1-1, G Cullen 0-2, T Quinn 1-0. Subs B Cullen for Murray h/t, D Lally 0-2 for O'Driscoll 37, M Lyons for Devine 48.

LEINSTER FINAL
Apr 21, St Conleth's Park, Newbridge
DUBLIN 1-17   WICKLOW 2-4
Dublin: S Cluxton, N Kane, D Corcoran, M Fitzpatrick, B Cahill, B Cullen, P Casey, C Murphy, D Magee, K Devine, D Lally 1-3, L Og O hEineachain 0-2, A Brogan 0-4, G Cullen, T Quinn 1-7. Subs: M Lyons 0-1 for Devine h/t.

ALL-IRELAND SEMI-FINAL
Sep 7, Breffni Park, Cavan
DUBLIN 1-13   TYRONE 2-9
Dublin: S Cluxton, N Kane, D Corcoran, P Griffin, P Casey, B Cullen, B Cahill, D Magee 0-1, S Walsh, L Og O hEineachain, C Keaney 0-4, D Lally 1-1, A Brogan 0-1, G Cullen, T Quinn 0-6. Subs: C Murphy for Walsh h/t, M Lyons for G Cullen 56, A Cleere for Casey 58, D O'Mahony for Lally 60.

ALL-IRELAND FINAL
Oct 6, O'Moore Park, Portlaoise
GALWAY 0–15   DUBLIN 0-7
Dublin: Stephen Cluxton, Nathan Kane, Donnanha Corcoran, Paul Griffin, Paul Casey, Bryan Cullen, Niall O'Driscoll, Darren Magee, Conor Murphy, Liam Og O hiEineachain 0-1, Conal Kearney, Declan Lally, Alan Brogan 0-2, Graham Cullen, Tomas Quinn 0-2. Subs: David O'Callaghan for Keaney 36, Declan O'Mahony 0-1 for Cullen 36, Seamus Walsh for Corcoran 39, Michael Lyons for Lally 49, Garrett Smith 0-1 for Murphy 52.

2003

LEINSTER QUARTER-FINAL
Mar 29, St Mary's Park, Ardee
DUBLIN 2-13   LOUTH 0-12
Dublin: P Copeland, M Kane, M Fitzpatrick, P Griffin, N Cooper, B Cullen, C Prenderville, H McEnerney, D O'Mahony 0-1, A Brogan 0-2, L Óg hEineacháin 0-2, D Lally, G Smith, G Cullen 0-2, J Noonan 1-5. Subs: P Brennan 0-1 for McEnerney 25, M Lyons 1-0 for Smith 42, K Devine for Lally 56.

LEINSTER SEMI-FINAL
Apr 12, Pairc Tailteann, Navan
DUBLIN 0-9   WESTMEATH 0-3
Dublin: P Copeland, N Kane, M Fitzpatrick, P Griffin, N Cooper, B Cullen 0-2, C Prenderville, D O'Mahony, P Brennan, L Og O hEineachain 0-1, C Keaney 0-1, D Lally, A Brogan 0-2, G Cullen, J Noonan 0-3. Subs: D Murray for Griffin 41, M Lyons for G Cullen 47, K Devine for Lally 58, B McMenamin for Noonan 59.

LEINSTER FINAL
Apr 27, Cusack Park, Mullingar
DUBLIN 3-13   LONGFORD 1-6
Dublin: P Copeland, N Kane, M Fitzpatrick, P Grffin, N Cooper, B Cullen 0-2, C Prenderville, P Brennan, D O'Mahony 0-3, C Keaney 0-2, L Og O hEineachain 0-2, D Lally 1-0, A Brogan 0-1, G Cullen 0-1, J Noonan

2-2. Subs: M Lyons for G Cullen 53, D Murray for Cooper 53, G Smith for Keaney 55, K Devine for Brennan 58, H McEnerney for O hEineachain 61.

ALL-IRELAND SEMI-FINAL
Sep 21, Semple Stadium, Thurles
DUBLIN 3-10   WATERFORD 1-7
Dublin: P Copeland, N Kane 0-1, M Fitzpatrick, P Grffin, N Cooper, B Cullen, C Prendeville, D O'Mahony 1-2, P Brennan, C Keaney 0-2, L Og O hEineachain, D Lally 1-0, A Brogan 1-3, G Cullen, J Noonan 0-2. Subs: D Murray for B Cullen 26, D Marshall for O hEineachain 52, G Smith for Noonan 50, M Lyons for Lally 61.

ALL-IRELAND FINAL
Oct 4, Pairc Tailteann, Navan
DUBLIN 0–12   TYRONE 0-7
Dublin: Paul Copeland, Nathan Kane, Mark Fitzpatrick, Paul Griffin, Niall Cooper, Bryan Cullen, Colin Prendeville, Declan O'Mahony 0-1, Padraig Brennan, Conal Keaney 0-1, Liam Óg O hEineacháin, Declan Lally 0-2, Alan Brogan 0-3, Graham Cullen 0-2, John Noonan 0-3. Subs: Derek Murray for Cooper 46, Mick Lyons for O hEineacháin 59, Seamus Walsh for G Cullen 61.

2004

LEINSTER QUARTER-FINAL
Mar 27, Kiltegan Road, Baltinglass
DUBLIN 1-12   WICKLOW 1-6
Dublin: P Copeland, C Prenderville, M Fitzpatrick, P Griffin, N Cooper, B Cullen, B Lyons, J Coughlan, P Brennan, D Kelleher 0-1, D O'Mahony 1-2, S Hiney, D O'Callaghan 0-1, G Cullen 0-2, J Noonan 0-6. Sub: B Brennan for Cooper h/t.

LEINSTER SEMI-FINAL
Apr 10, Pairc Tailteann, Navan
DUBLIN 1-9   LONGFORD 0-10
Dublin: P Copeland, C Prenderville, M Fitzpatrick, P Griffin, N Cooper, B Cullen, B Lyons, D O'Mahony, P Brennan, S Hiney 1-0, D Kelleher, G Cullen 0-4, D O'Callaghan 0-1, M Whelan 0-1, J Noonan 0-2. Subs: D Dineen 0-1 for Whelan, M Vaughan for O'Callaghan.

LEINSTER FINAL
Apr 24, Pairc Tailteann, Navan
DUBLIN 1-4   KILDARE 0-7
Dublin: P Copeland, C Prendeville, M Fitzpatrick, P Griffin, N Cooper, B Cullen, B Lyons, D O'Mahony 1-1, P Brennan, S Hiney, D Kelleher, D Dineen, D O'Callaghan, G Cullen 0-1, J Noonan 0-2. Subs: N Clarke for Prendeville h/t, M Whelan for Dineen 42, M Vaughan for Noonan 48, J Coughlan for Whelan 60, Prendeville for Lyons 61.

LEINSTER FINAL REPLAY
May 1, O'Moore Park, Portlaoise
KILDARE 1-10   DUBLIN 0-12
Dublin: Paul Copeland, Paul Griffin, Mark Fitzpatrick, Niall Clarke, Niall Cooper, Bryan Cullen 0-3, Colin Prendeville, Declan O'Mahony, Padraig Brennan, Declan Kelleher 0-1, Graham Cullen, Barry Lyons, John Noonan 0-4, Stephen Hiney, David O'Callaghan 0-4. Subs: Ger Brennan for G Cullen 21, Mark Vaughan for Kelleher h/t, J Coughlan for G Brennan 44.

2005

LEINSTER QUARTER-FINAL
Mar 17, Pairc na nGael, Dundalk
DUBLIN 2-11   LOUTH 1-5
Dublin: M Savage, A Downes, W Lowry, D McCann, N Cooper, B Cullen, I Ward, E Fennell 1-0, J Coughlan 0-1, J O'Brien 1-3, B Phelan, G O'Meara 0-2, B Brogan 0-2, B Kennedy, M Vaughan 0-2. Subs: D Dineen for Coughlan 34, J Brogan for Kennedy 40, C Moore 0-1 for O'Meara 56.

LEINSTER SEMI-FINAL
Apr 2, Cusack Park, Mullingar
DUBLIN 1-11   LONGFORD 2-6
Dublin: M Savage, I Ward, W Lowry, D McCann, N Cooper, B Cullen, G Brennan, E Fennell, B Phelan, B Kennedy, D Dineen, G O'Meara, M Vaughan 0-4, M Davoren 1-1, B Brogan 0-6. Subs: C Moore for Kennedy h/t.

LEINSTER FINAL
Apr 24, Croke Park, Dublin
DUBLIN 0-13   KILDARE 0-11
Dublin: M Savage, A Downes, W Lowry, D McCann, N Cooper, B Cullen, I Ward, E Fennell, B Phelan, K Leahy 0-5, D Dineen 0-1, C Moore 0-2, J O'Brien 0-2, M Davoren 0-2, B Brogan 0-1. Subs: D O'Mahony for O'Brien 41, R Fallon for Moore 55, J Coughlan for Dineen 58.

ALL-IRELAND SEMI-FINAL
Apr 30, Pairc Tailteann, Navan
DOWN 2-7   DUBLIN 0-9
Dublin: M Savage, A Downes, R Fallon, D McCann, N Cooper, B Cullen 0-1, I Ward 0-1, E Fennell, B Phelan, K Leahy 0-2, D Dineen 0-1, G O'Meara, J O'Brien, M Davoren, B Brogan 0-4. Subs: D O'Mahony for O'Meara 29, C Moore for Fennell 33, J Coughlan for O'Brien 40, B Kennedy for Leahy 54, G Brennan for Dineen 56.

2006

LEINSTER FIRST ROUND
Feb 4, Richardstown, Newbridge
KILDARE 0-12   DUBLIN 0-9
Dublin: M Savage, A Downes, W Lowry, D Walsh, D Reilly, G Brennan, I Ward 0-1, J Coughlan 0-1, B Phelan, K Leahy 0-4, MD Macauley 0-1, G O'Meara, T Brady, B Kelly, M Vaughan 0-1. Subs: N Corkery for O'Meara, C Moore for Macauley, J O'Brien 0-1 for Kelly.

2007

LEINSTER FIRST ROUND
Feb 17, Parnell Park
MEATH 2-9   DUBLIN 1-8
Dublin: M Savage, K Nolan, W Lowry, I Kavanagh, D Daly, L Fleming, C Guckian, P Flynn, S Ryan, J O'Brien 0-2, P Brogan, D Connolly 0-3, B Kelly 1-1, T Brady, K McMenamon 0-1. Subs: R Cleere for Ryan 23, D Reilly for McMenamin 41, P Andrews 0-1 for Brogan 41, A Hubbard for Lowry 54, E Moran for O'Brien 59.

2008

LEINSTER QUARTER-FINAL
Mar 22, Richardstown, Newbridge
KILDARE 1-8   DUBLIN 1-7
Dublin: P Brogan, A Hubbard, T Brady, J Cooper, P McMahon, K Nolan 1-1, C Guckian, J McCaffrey, C O'Sullivan, S Ryan, D Connolly, C Carthy, B O'Rorke 0-2, P Andrews 0-2, T Furman 0-1. Subs: D Kelly for Carthy 22, D Daly for Guckian h/t, M Loftus for McCaffrey 39, E Kirby for Furman 51.

2009

LEINSTER FIRST ROUND
Feb 22, Drogheda Park, Drogheda
DUBLIN 3-12   LOUTH 2-8
Dublin: D McDonnell, C Moore, S Byrne, G McIntyre, J Cooper, J Sheanon, C Guckian, C O'Sullivan, C Murphy, D Quinn 0-2, T Furman, P Andrews 0-1, D Kelly 0-2, D Rock 2-3, P O'Connor 0-3. Subs: L Sweetman for Furman h/t, B O'Rorke 1-1 for McIntyre 36, J McCarthy for Kelly 53, M Devereux for Murphy 53, N Brogan for Quinn 59.

LEINSTER QUARTER-FINAL
Mar 7, Parnell Park, Dublin
DUBLIN 0-12   MEATH 2-5
Dublin: D McDonnell, C Moore, S Byrne, H Gill, J

Cooper, P Andrews 0-2, C Guckian, C Murphy, J Sheanon, D Quinn, L Sweetman 0-2, D Kelly 0-2, G McIntyre, D Rock 0-2, P O'Connor 0-3. Subs: B O'Rorke for McIntyre 34, N Brogan for Quinn 45, T Furman 0-1 for O'Connor 48, C Deasy for Byrne 54, N Devereux for Kelly 60.

LEINSTER SEMI-FINAL
Mar 21, Parnell Park, Dublin
DUBLIN 1-10   WESTMEATH 0-9
Dublin: D McDonnell, C Moore, S Byrne, H Gill, J Cooper, C O'Sullivan, C Guckian, C Murphy, J Sheanon, P O'Connor 0-4, L Sweetman, D Kelly 1-0, B O'Rorke 0-1, P Andrews 0-3, D Rock 0-2. Subs: R O'Carroll for Byrne 15, T Furman for Sweetman 43, K Nolan for Sheanon 45, N Brogan for Cooper 47, G McIntyre for Murphy 53.

LEINSTER FINAL
Apr 5, O'Moore Park, Portlaoise
DUBLIN 0-12   LAOIS 0-9
Dublin: D McDonnell, C Moore, R O'Carroll, H Gill, J Cooper, C O'Sullivan, N Brogan 0-1, C Murphy, K Nolan, P O'Connor 0-3, L Sweetman, D Kelly 0-3, B O'Rorke 0-1, P Andrews 0-1, D Rock 0-3. Subs: T Furman for Sweetman 40, J Sheanon for O'Connor 45, N Devereux for Brogan 50, J Whelan for Moore 60.

ALL-IRELAND SEMI-FINAL
Apr 18, Semple Stadium, Thurles
CORK 1-10   DUBLIN 1-9
Dublin: D McDonnell, C Moore, R O'Carroll, H Gill, J Cooper, C O'Sullivan, N Brogan, C Murphy, K Nolan, P O'Connor 0-1, L Sweetman, D Kelly, B O'Rorke 1-0, P Andrews 0-1, D Rock 0-3. Subs: T Furman 0-3 for O'Connor 26, N Devereux for Brogan 38, J Sheanon for Kelly 48, D Quinn 0-1 for O'Rorke 51, N Coughlan for Rock 57.

2010

LEINSTER QUARTER-FINAL
Mar 6, St Brigid's Park, Dundalk
DUBLIN 1-14   LOUTH 1-8
Dublin: V Whelan, E Culligan, R O'Carroll, D Nelson, J Cooper 0-2, J McCarthy, N Deveraux, S Murray, M Coughlan, L Siwale, G McIntyre 0-2, G Sweeney 0-2, B O'Rorke 0-1, D Rock 1-4, E Murray. Subs: C Mullins for McCarthy 35, N Brogan for Murray 39, C Dorney for O'Rorke 45, D Quinn (Lucan) 0-3 for Siwale 53. Extra time: D Quinn (Na Fianna) for Dorney, S McGuinness for Cooper.

LEINSTER SEMI-FINAL
Mar 17, Dr Cullen Park, Carlow
DUBLIN 0-14   CARLOW 0-13

Dublin: V Whelan, E Culligan, R O'Carroll, J McCarthy, J Cooper, S Murray, N Devereux, C Mullins, M Coughlan, D Quinn (Lucan) 0-1, G McIntyre, N Brogan, D Quinn (Na Fianna) 0-2, D Rock 0-4, G Sweeney 0-2. Subs: T Furman for McIntyre h/t, R Downey for Coughlan 36 C Dorney 0-1 for Brogan 43, B O'Rorke 0-3 for D Quinn (Na Fianna) 54, E Keogh 0-1 for Furman 59. Extra time: Coughlan for Dorney 65, S McGuinness for Devereux 69, L Siwale for Keogh 72.

LEINSTER FINAL
Apr 3, Parnell Park, Dublin
DUBLIN 1-12   WESTMEATH 0-9
Dublin: V Whelan, E Culligan, R O'Carroll, J Cooper 0-1, D Nelson, M Coughlan, N Deveraux, S Murray, J McCarthy 0-1, C Dorney 1-1, G McIntyre, G Sweeney, B O'Rorke 0-1, D Quinn (Na Fianna), D Rock 0-6. Subs: D Quinn (Lucan Sarsfields) 0-1 for Quinn 20, T Furman 0-1 for McIntyre h/t, E Keogh for Coughlan 37, S McGuinness for Culligan 42, J McDermott for Keogh 52.

ALL-IRELAND SEMI-FINAL
Apr 17, Parnell Park, Dublin
DUBLIN 2-10   ROSCOMMON 0-8
Dublin: V Whelan, E Culligan, R O'Carroll, D Nelson, J Cooper, S Murray, N Devereux 0-1, J McCarthy, C Mullins 0-1, C Dorney 0-1, D Rock 1-2, G Sweeney 0-1, B O'Rorke 0-1, D Quinn 1-0, T Furnman. Subs: J McDermott for J McCarthy h/t, M Coughlan for Dorney h/t, R McCarthy 0-3 for O'Rorke 33, C Reddin for Quinn 57, N Brogan for Devereux 59.

ALL-IRELAND FINAL
May 1, Breffni Park, Cavan
DUBLIN 1-10   DONEGAL 1-8
Dublin: Vinny Whelan, Eoin Culligan, Rory O'Carroll, Darragh Nelson, Johnny Cooper, James McCarthy, Nicky Devereux 0-1, Sean Murray, Cian Mullins, Mark Coughlan 0-1, Ted Furman, Gary Sweeney 1-1, Robert McCarthy 0-1, Dean Rock 0-4, Ciaran Dorney 0-1. Subs: David Quinn for McCarthy h/t, Ciaran Redddin for McCarthy 42, Barry O'Rorke 0-1 for Furman 48, Sean McGuinness for Nelson 50, Niall Brogan for Dorney 73.

2011

LEINSTER FIRST ROUND
Feb 23, Pairc Tailteann, Navan
MEATH 0-21   DUBLIN 0-17
Dublin: R O'Flaherty, K O'Brien 0-1, J McCarthy, D Nelson 0-1, G Seaver 0-2, S Murray, G McArdle, D Murphy, C Reddin, C Dorney 0-1, D Rock 0-7, G

Sweeney, P Ryan 0-1, G McIntyre, D Stapleton. Subs: M Concarr for McArdle 24, H Dawson 0-1 for McIntyre 26, E Keogh for Murphy 37, P Hudson 0-3 for Stapleton 37, P Houlihan for Ryan 60. Extra time: P Keaney for Reddin, A McCarrick for Concarr, McIntyre for Rock.

2012

LEINSTER FIRST ROUND
Feb 29, Belfield Park, Enniscorthy
DUBLIN 1-12   WEXFORD 1-9
Dublin: JB Carthy, J Smith, K O'Brien, M Concarr, J Small 0-1, L Fletcher, J McCaffrey 0-1, E O Conghaile 0-1, D Byrne, G Seaver, G Sweeney, M Schutte, C Kilkenny 0-5, H Dawson 0-1, P Ryan 1-2. Subs: A Carr for Smith, C Reddin 0-1 for Byrne, P O'Higgins for O'Conghaile, E Keogh for Schutte, S George for Concar.

LEINSTER QUARTER-FINAL
Mar 7, Parnell Park, Dublin
DUBLIN 2-21   LAOIS 0-4
Dublin: JB Carthy, J Smith 0-1, K O'Brien, M Concarr, L Fletcher, J Kelly, J McCaffrey 0-1, E O Conghaile 0-2, C Walsh, M Schutte 0-1, G Sweeney 0-2, C Reddin 0-1, P Hudson 0-3, P Ryan 1-2, C Kilkenny 0-7. Subs: B Quinn for Ryan 38, G Seaver 1-1 for Quinn 45, P O'Higgins for Walsh 47, A Carr for Concar 50, E Keogh for Sweeney 52.

LEINSTER SEMI-FINAL
Mar 21, O'Moore Park, Portlaoise
DUBLIN 4-15   WESTMEATH 1-9
Dublin: R O'Flaherty, J Smith, K O'Brien, M Concarr, J Kelly, L Fletcher, J McCaffrey 1-0, E O Conghaile 0-1, C Walsh, M Schutte 1-0, G Sweeney 0-1, C Reddin 0-1, P Ryan, C Kilkenny 1-6, P Hudson 1-4. Subs: P O'Higgins for O'Conghaile 16, S George for Concarr 23, G Seaver 0-1 for Walsh h/t, Concarr for Smith h/t, P Maguire 0-1 for Ryan 45.

LEINSTER FINAL
Apr 4, Pairc Tailteann, Navan
DUBLIN 1-16   LOUTH 0-8
Dublin: JB Carthy, S George, K O'Brien, M Concarr, L Fletcher, J Kelly, J McCaffrey 0-1, E O Conghaile, C Reddin, M Schutte 0-2, G Sweeney 0-1, D Byrne, P Hudson 0-2, C Kilkenny 1-7, P Ryan. Subs: H Dawson 0-1 for Ryan h/t, G Seaver 0-2 for Byrne h/t, J Small for Concarr 46, P Maguire for Hudson 50, E Keogh for O Conghaile 56.

ALL-IRELAND SEMI-FINAL
Apr 21, O'Moore Park, Portlaoise
DUBLIN 3-11   CORK 0-14
Dublin: JB Carthy, M Concarr, K O'Brien, S George,

L Fletcher, J Kelly, J McCaffrey 1-0, E O Conghaile 0-2, D Byrne 0-1, C Reddin, G Sweeney, M Schutte, C Kilkenny 0-1, P Ryan 2-3, P Hudson 0-2. Subs: P Maguire 0-1 for Byrne 38, G Seaver for Schutte 45, P O'Higgins for Reddin 46, H Dawson for Hudson 55, E Keogh for Sweeney 57.

ALL-IRELAND FINAL
May 6, O'Connor Park, Tullamore
DUBLIN 2-12   ROSCOMMON 0-11
Dublin: John Barry Carthy, Sean George, Kevin O'Brien (capt), Michael Concarr, Luke Fletcher, John Kelly 0-1, Jack McCaffrey, Emmett O Conghaile, Ciaran Reddin, Gary Sweeney, Daniel Byrne, Mark Schutte, Paul Hudson 1-4, Philip Ryan 0-1, Ciaran Kilkenny 0-4. Subs: Paul Maguire for Schutte h/t, Gerry Seaver 0-1 for Byrne 34, Harry Dawson 0-1 for Ryan 41, Paddy O'Higgins for Reddin 42, Paul Mannion 1-0 for Hudson 59.

2013

LEINSTER FIRST ROUND
Feb 19, Parnell Park, Dublin
DUBLIN 4-27   CARLOW 0-2
Dublin: L Molloy, M Durcan, David Byrne, N McGovern, E Lowndes, C Mulally, J McCaffrey, E O Conghaile 0-1, G Whelan 0-2, S Carthy 1-2, M Gibbs 0-1, Danny Byrne 0-1, P Mannion 0-4, A Caffrey 0-3, C Kilkenny 2-10. Subs: J Small for McCaffrey, H Dawson 1-0 for Mannion, P Maguire 0-1 for Danny Byrne h/t, P O'Curry for O Conghaile 38, G Ivory 0-2 for Gibbs 41.

LEINSTER QUARTER-FINAL
Mar 6, Parnell Park, Dublin
LONGFORD 1-6   DUBLIN 1-5
Dublin: L Molloy, R McGowan, David Byrne, N McGovern, E Lowndes, C Mulally, J McCaffrey, S Cunningham, E O Conghaile 0-1, P Maguire, S Carthy 0-1, Danny Byrne, P Mannion, A Caffrey, C Kilkenny 1-1. Subs: N Scully for Danny Byrne 25, C McHugh for Caffrey 38, G Ivory 0-2 for Maguire 41, P Ryan for Mannion 44.

2014

LEINSTER QUARTER-FINAL
Mar 5, IT Grounds, Carlow
DUBLIN 2-28   CARLOW 0-3
Dublin: L Molloy, R McGowan, D Byrne, R McDaid, E Lowndes 1-0, J Small, J McCaffrey 0-2, P O'Higgins, S Carthy 0-4, C Mullally 0-1, C Kilkenny 0-6, N Walsh, C McHugh 0-4, M Deegan 1-5, N Scully 0-2. Subs: G

Ivory 0-2 for McCaffrey 39, S Boland 0-1 for Walsh 39, B Fenton for Carthy 44, G Hannigan for Lowndes 46, R Gaughan for McHugh 46, S Cunningham 0-1 for Kilkenny 50.

LEINSTER SEMI-FINAL
Mar 19, O'Moore Park, Portlaoise
DUBLIN 3-7   LONGFORD 0-6
Dublin: L Molloy, R McGowan, D Byrne, R McDaid, J Small, Stephen Cunningham, J McCaffrey, S Carthy, P O'Higgins, N Scully, E Lowndes 0-1, C Costello 0-4, C McHugh 0-1, M Deegan, P Mannion 2-1. Subs: Shane Cunningham for Deegan 34, E Ó Conghaile 1-0 for Small 47, N Walsh for McHugh 59, G Ivory for Costello 60.

LEINSTER FINAL
Apr 2, O'Moore Park, Portlaoise
DUBLIN 0-15   MEATH 0-10
Dublin: L Molloy, R McGowan, D Byrne, R McDaid, J Small, Stephen Cunningham, J McCaffrey, P O'Higgins, S Carthy 0-3, N Scully 0-1, E Lowndes 0-1, C Costello 0-5, P Mannion, M Deegan, C McHugh 0-3. Subs: S Boland for Deegan 24, G Burke 0-2 for Cunningham h/t, E O Conghaile for Costello 47, Shane Cunningham for O'Higgins 55.

ALL-IRELAND SEMI-FINAL
Apr 19, O'Moore Park, Portlaoise
DUBLIN 0-11   CAVAN 0-10
Dublin: L Molloy, D Byrne, R McGowan, R McDaid, J Small, J McCaffrey, B Fenton, E Lowndes, P O'Higgins, N Scully 0-1, S Boland, N Walsh, C Costello 0-4, C McHugh 0-3, P Mannion 0-1. Subs: E O'Conghaile 0-1 for Higgins 26, G Burke for Walsh 39, G Ivory 0-1 for Boland 39, S Cunningham for Scully 56.

ALL-IRELAND FINAL
May 3, O'Connor Park, Tullamore
DUBLIN 1-21   ROSCOMMON 3-6
Dublin: Lorcan Molloy, Ross McGowan, David Byrne, Robert McDaid, Conor Mullally, John Small, Jack McCaffrey 0-1, Paddy O'Higgins, Brian Fenton, Shane Boland, Eric Lowndes, Niall Scully 0-1, Paul Mannion 0-9, Cormac Costello 0-3, Conor McHugh 1-6. Subs: Emmett O Conghaíle for Byrne (black card) 13, Graham Hannigan for Boland 44, Gavin Ivory for O'Higgins 45, Stephen Cunningham 0-1 for Costello 50, Niall Walsh for Mannion 60.

2015

LEINSTER QUARTER-FINAL
Mar 4, O'Moore Park, Portlaoise
DUBLIN 2-21   LAOIS 2-10
Dublin: L Molloy, E Mullan, D Byrne, R McGowan, E

Lowndes 0-1, C Mullally, E Murchan 0-1, Stephen Cunningham, S Carthy 1-1, M Deegan 0-2, N Scully 0-4, K O'Gara 1-3, C McHugh 0-6, C Basquel 0-2. Subs: N Walsh 0-1 for Gaughan h/t, D O'Cathmhaoil for Stephen Cunningham 35, G Burke for Basquel 50, Shane Cunningham for Scully 58, A Byrne for O'Gara 59.

LEINSTER SEMI-FINAL
Mar 18, Pairc Tailteann, Navan
DUBLIN 2-15   LONGFORD 3-7
Dublin: L Molloy, S Clayton, D Byrne, R McGowan, E Lowndes 0-2, C Mullally, E Murchan, S Cunningham, S Carthy, G Burke, A Foley 0-1, N Scully 0-3, K O'Gara 1-2, C McHugh 0-5, C Basquel 1-1. Subs: R Gaughran for Burke 43, A Byrne 0-1 for O'Gara 47, M Deegan for Basquel 59.

LEINSTER FINAL
Apr 2, Pairc Tailteann, Navan
DUBLIN 3-10   KILDARE 1-12
Dublin: L Molloy, D Byrne, E Murchan, E Mullan, E Lowndes 0-1, C Mullaly, R McGowan, Stephen Cunningham, S Carthy 0-1, N Scully, A Foley 0-1, G Burke, C Costello 2-2, C McHugh 0-5, C Basquel 1-0. Subs: E Fletcher for Mullan 32, R Gaughan for Burke 37, A Byrne for Basquel 50, D O'Cathmhaoil for Foley 52.

ALL-IRELAND SEMI-FINAL
Apr 18, O'Connor Park, Tullamore
TIPPERARY 0-14   DUBLIN 0-12
Dublin: L Molloy, D Byrne, M Cahilan, R McGowan, A Farrell, E Lowndes, C Mullally, Stephen Cunningham, S Carthy 0-2, N Scully, A Foley, E Murchan, C Costello 0-4, C McHugh 0-4, C Basquel 0-1. Subs: Shane Cunninghm for Stephen Cunningham 25, S Clayton for Foley 45, E Fletcher for Cahalane (black card) 49, A Byrne for Basquel 49, D Campbell 0-1 for Scully 52.

2016

LEINSTER QUARTER-FINAL
Mar 1, Parnell Park, Dublin
DUBLIN 1-12   MEATH 0-9
Dublin: L Molloy, D Bolger, M Cahilan, E Smith, G O'Reilly, S McMahon, D Spillane 0-1, A Foley, K Deeley, T Lahiff, M Deegan 0-1, C O'Shea, B Howard 0-1, C O'Callaghan 1-7, A Byrne 0-2. Subs: D Monaghan for Bolger h/t, O Lynch for Deegan 40, K Doherty for Foley 44, C Sallier for Spillane 52.

LEINSTER SEMI-FINAL
Mar 19, Parnell Park, Dublin
DUBLIN 2-17   LAOIS 2-5
Dublin: L Molloy 0-1, E Smith, S McMahon 0-1, D

Monaghan, M Cahilan 0-2, C O'Shea, B Howard, A Foley, K Deeley, T Lahiff, C O'Callaghan 0-5, G O'Reilly 0-3, D Spillane, M Deegan 0-1, C Sallier 1-1. Subs: C Basquel 1-3 for Deegan (black card) 36, D Bolger for Deeley (black card) 45, E Murchan for Spillane 48, A Byrne for Sallier 54, D McIlghorm for Foley 54, J Mullins for O'Callaghan 63.

LEINSTER FINAL
Apr 2, Pairc Tailteann, Navan
DUBLIN 2-14   KILDARE 0-17
Dublin: L Molloy, E Smith, S McMahon, D Monaghan, C O'Shea 1-0, B Howard 0-1, M Cahilan 0-1, A Foley 0-1, D McIlghorm, K Deeley, C Basquel 0-1, G O'Reilly 0-2, C Sallier 0-1, C O'Callaghan 1-7, D Spillane. Subs: S Clayton for O'Shea 4, A Elliott for McIlghorm 14, K Doherty for Foley (blood) 25-29, E Murchan for Monaghan h/t, P Small for Spillane h/t, M Deegan for Elliott 46, O'Shea for Sallier. Extra-time: Doherty for O'Reilly 68, Spillane for Murchan 75, T O'Sullivan for Smith 79.

ALL-IRELAND SEMI-FINAL
Apr 16, O'Connor Park, Tullamore
MAYO 1-15   DUBLIN 1-14
Dublin: L Molloy, S McMahon, E Smith, S Clayton, C O'Shea, M Cahilan, B Howard, A Foley, K Deeley, T Lahiff, C Basquel 0-3, G O'Reilly 0-1, P Small 0-1, C O'Callaghan 1-5, M Deegan 0-3. Subs: E Murchan 0-1 for O'Callaghan 23, D Spillane for Small 37, K Doherty for Deeley 45, A Elliott for O'Reilly 55, D Monaghan for Smith 60.

2017

LEINSTER QUARTER-FINAL
Mar 1, Lakepoint Park, Mullingar
DUBLIN 2-14   WESTMEATH 0-6
Dublin: E Comerford, D Byrne, S McMahon, S Clayton, C Murphy 0-1, C O'Shea, E Murchan 0-1, B Howard, A Foley, T Fox, S Bugler, G O'Reilly 0-1, A Byrne 2-3, C O'Callaghan 0-5, S Smith. Subs: C Basquel 0-2 for Bugler h/t, C Sallier 0-1 for Smith 39, D Gavin for O'Reilly 48, B Shovlin for Fox 57, D McIllgorm for O'Callaghan 60.

LEINSTER SEMI-FINAL
Mar 22, Lakepoint Park, Mullingar
DUBLIN 2-10   LONGFORD 0-9
Dublin: E Comerford, S McMahon, Declan Monaghan, D Byrne, C Murphy, C O'Shea, E Murchan, A Foley, B Howard 0-1, T Fox, A Byrne, G O'Reilly, C Sallier 0-3, C O'Callaghan 2-5, D O'Brien. Subs: D McIllgorm for O'Reilly 45, S Smith 0-1 for Sallier 48, S Bugler for Byrne 52, D Spillane for O'Brien 59, B Shovlin for Foley 63.

LEINSTER FINAL

Mar 29, O'Moore Park, Portlaoise

DUBLIN 2-14   OFFALY 0-8

Dublin: E Comerford, D Monaghan, S McMahon, D Byrne, E Murchan 0-1, C O'Shea, C Murphy, A Foley, B Howard, T Fox 1-2, D O'Brien, A Byrne 0-4, C Sallier 0-1, C O'Callaghan 0-4, G O'Reilly 0-2. Subs: S Smith 1-0 for Sallier 41, S Bugler for O'Brien 41, D Gavin for Fox 48, A Elliott for O'Reilly 51, A McGowan for Monaghan 56.

ALL-IRELAND SEMI-FINAL

Apr 15, Breffni Park

DUBLIN 1-13   DONEGAL 0-9

Dublin: E Comerford, D Byrne 0-1, C O'Shea, E Murchan, C O'Callaghan 0-1, S McMahon 1-0, C Murphy 0-2, B Howard, A Foley, T Fox 0-1, A Byrne 0-4, G O'Reilly 0-2, D Gavin, C Basquel, D O'Brien Subs: C Sallier 0-1 for O'Callaghan (black card) 4, A Elliot for Foley 23, D Spillane for Fox 37, A McGowan 0-1 for O'Reilly 47, T O'Sullivan for Sallier 57, S Clayton for Basquel 60.

ALL-IRELAND FINAL

Apr 29, O'Connor Park, Tullamore

DUBLIN 2-13   GALWAY 2-7

Dublin: Evan Comerford, Sean McMahon, Declan Monaghan, Cillian O'Shea, Eoin Murchan, Cian Murphy, Andy Foley, Brian Howard 0-1, Dan O'Brien 0-2, Glenn O'Reilly 0-3, Aaron Byrne 1-0, Tom Fox, Colm Basquel 0-2, Con O'Callaghan 1-3. Subs: Darren Gavin 0-1 for Foley 13, Darragh Spillane for Fox 39, Chris Sallier for O'Reilly 46, Andrew McGowan for McMahon 60, Paddy Small for Basquel 61, Stephen Smith 0-1 for Byrne 62.

LEINSTER CHAMPIONSHIP ROLL OF HONOUR

Dublin (14): 1974, 1975, 1980, 1984, 2002, 2003, 2005, 2009, 2010, 2012, 2014, 2015, 2016, 2017.
Kildare (10): 1965, 1966, 1967, 1972, 1976, 1983, 1992, 2004, 2008, 2013.
Offaly (8): 1968, 1971, 1973, 1977, 1979, 1986, 1988, 1995.
Meath (8): 1985, 1989, 1990, 1991, 1993, 1996, 1997, 2001.
Laois (8): 1964, 1969, 1982, 1987, 1994, 1998, 2006, 2007.
Louth (3): 1970, 1978, 1981.
Westmeath (2): 1999, 2000.
Wexford (1): 2011.

ALL-IRELAND CHAMPIONSHIP ROLL OF HONOUR

Cork (11): 1970, 1971, 1980, 1981, 1984, 1985, 1986, 1989, 1994, 2007, 2009.
Kerry (10): 1964, 1973, 1975, 1976, 1977, 1990, 1995, 1996, 1998, 2008.
Mayo (5): 1967, 1974, 1983, 2006, 2016.
Galway (5): 1972, 2002, 2005, 2011, 2013.
Tyrone (5): 1991, 1992, 2000, 2001, 2015.
Dublin (5): 2003, 2010, 2012, 2014, 2017.
Roscommon (2): 1966, 1978.
Donegal (2): 1982, 1987.
Derry (2): 1968, 1997.
Kildare (1): 1965.
Antrim (1): 1969.
Down (1): 1979
Offaly (1): 1988.
Meath (1): 1993.
Westmeath (1): 1999.
Armagh (1): 2004.

Minor Championship

DUBLIN'S introduction to the teenage football championship was a decidedly ignominious one; they were kicked out of the competition.

Although the All-Ireland Championship did not kick off until 1929, the Leinster Council pre-empted this by running their own competition a year earlier, in which Dublin made their debut with a 2-4 to 1-4 victory over Kildare at Croke Park with a side that included two players who would feature in the losing All-Ireland senior decider against Galway six years later, Mick O'Brien and Mickey Wellington. This was followed with first a 3-4 to 1-9 defeat of Wexford in Enniscorthy and then a 5-7 to 3-4 beating of Louth at St. Brigid's Park in Dundalk to qualify for the inaugural provincial final against Offaly. The game, scheduled for Tullamore on December 16, was never played, however, as Dublin were disqualified after being found to have used a number of overage players, although there is no record of the title ever being formally awarded to Offaly.

When the All-Ireland series did begin a year later, Dublin failed to make it into the national phase. They beat Wexford after a replay and then accounted for Offaly and Meath but then, in the provincial final at the Showgrounds in Navan, they were upset by Longford, 3-4 to 1-4. They fared considerably better in the following campaign, if by a somewhat circuitous route.

It began at Novela Road in Bray with a 1-4 to 0-2 victory over Wicklow in mid May and was followed by a 2-5 to 2-0 success against Meath in Navan in mid July. Then things got complicated; the provincial championship fell seriously behind schedule so the Leinster Council nominated Dublin to represent them in the All-Ireland series — no explanation is recorded as to why defending champions Longford were not selected — and this they successfully did by beating Armagh by 1-3 to 1-1 on the second last Sunday in August. A week later they beat Carlow by 1-3 to 0-3 in the provincial semi-final in Athy, then the following week pipped Mayo in the All-Ireland Final by 1-3 to 0-5. Another week later — their successive Sunday in action — they won their first Leinster crown by outscoring Longford at the Hospital Grounds in Mullingar, 1-6 to 0-4.

With but a couple of exceptions, it was pretty much all downhill for a decade and a half after that. Dublin fell at the second hurdle in 1931 and the first a year later, and although they regained the provincial title in 1933, Mayo ended their run with an 0-12 to 0-8 win in the All-Ireland semi-final in Mullingar. A year later, with a side that included Paddy Bermingham who would win a senior medal in 1942, they again came out of Leinster thanks and topped this by beating Tyrone by 0-9 to 1-4 in the All-Ireland semi-final at the Gaelic Grounds in Drogheda. But, for a second time, they were kicked out for playing overage players; Tyrone successfully appealed and were awarded the game but then, after realising they too had inadvertently committed the same offence, sporting withdrew, thereby giving Tipperary a walkover in the final.

The next year, 1935, brought victories over Kildare after a replay and then Laois before Louth pipped them 1-7 to 1-6 in what would be Dublin's last appearance in a Leinster Final for a decade. Carlow beat them in the first round in Baltinglass the following year but then had the result reversed for playing an unregistered player but it mattered little as Wexford sent The Dubs pack next time out and a year later, after beating Kildare, they drew with Louth in Drogheda but were beaten 3-6 to 1-4 in the replay in Navan. For the next five campaigns after that, the Wee County again did Dublin every time. Because of petrol rationing and consequent travel restrictions the competition was suspended for three seasons from 1942 which, given the way things had been going in recent times, was probably a welcome relieve for The Dubs.

THE resumption of minor action in 1945 was a pleasant and successful experience for the teenage Dubs. Without a provincial title in eleven years but with a side that included future senior stars Denis Mahony, Nicky Maher and Ollie Freaney, they ended that particular famine with successive wins over Meath, Westmeath and Wexford to advance to the All-Ireland semi-finals and a first ever meeting in the grade with Kerry. Goals by Sean McEntaggart and Jackie Copeland helped see off the Kingdom and the final, against first time Connacht champions Leitrim, was a bit of an anti climax as Dublin, with goals from Copeland, Jim Nugent, Pat McCarthy and Cathal Dignam won 4-7 to 0-4 after being 3-2 to 0-2 up at halftime. McCarthy, George Jennings, Nicky Maher, Sean McEnteggart, Des Healy and Liam Donnelly had all played on the hurling team that had beaten Tipperary by 3-14 to 4-6 three weeks earlier, making them the first ever Dubs to win two All-Ireland medals in the same championship year. (Paddy Carey, Joe Norris, Jack O'Reilly, John Synnott, Paddy Kirwan, Frank Burke, Bill Donovan and Charlie McDonald did win All-Ireland senior medals in June and October 1923 but they were in the finals of the Championships for 1921 and 1922.)

The next year the still eligible Mahony, Maher and Freaney were joined by another future senior star Jim Lavin and a 16-year-old St. Vincent's clubmate of all four who would become the most famous name in the history of football in the capital, Kevin Heffernan. Dublin steamrolled the opposition in Leinster, beating, in turn, Laois by 3-8 to 0-2 in Athy, Offaly by 6-12 to 1-4 in Portlaoise and Meath by 4-6 to 0-3 in Navan, with Heffernan scoring 5-5 in the three games. He scored four vital points in a 1-7 to 0-6 victory over Tyrone in the All-Ireland semi-final in Clones but in the final — Dublin's only game at Croke Park — he was held to a single point as Kerry dethroned The Dubs by seven points, 3-7 to 2-3. It would not be the only time Kerry would upset Heffernan and Company in an All-Ireland Final.

A year later, despite Heffernan still being there, was a disappointment. Louth and Meath were beaten in succession but in the provincial final an injury time Offaly goal earned the Midlanders a replay and the took full advantage of their second chance, winning 1-7 to 1-5 in Mullingar. Dublin would avenged that loss the next year, 1948, when, after wins over Louth and Westmeath, they reclaimed the provincial title with a 2-5 to 1-6 win in Naas, Des Ferguson and Cyril Freaney providing the goals.

Kerry, their conquerors in the final two years previously, were beaten 2-7 to 0-8 in the semi-final and then it was defending champions Tyrone — with a quartet of players from the previous year — in the final. The sides were level at three points apiece at halftime but with just four minutes left Tyrone were 0-11 to 0-5 to the good and not even a late Ferguson goal could rescue Dublin. Three of the winner's points — two from frees — were scored by their right half forward, listed on the programme as Bernard Eastwood from Cookstown; he would later become better known as Barney, manager of world champion boxers Barry McGuigan, Dave McAuley, Paul Hodkinson, Crisanto Espana, Victor Cordoba and Fabrice Benichou.

The provincial title was retained the following year with wins over Longford, Offaly and Kildare — by an aggregate of 13-21 to 2-12 — but Kerry gained revenge for the previous year's defeat by winning 1-9 to 0-3 at Austin Stack Park in Tralee, where an interesting member of the losing side was Donal Colfer, who a quarter of a century or so later would play an important part in the revival of Dublin's senior fortunes as a co-selector alongside Kevin Heffernan.

The following four campaigns were disappointing in the extreme. Dublin did reach the provincial decider in 1950 with wins over Kildare, Offaly and Louth, but Wexford pipped them 3-6 to 2-8. Offaly beat them at the first hurdle the following year and although they edged Meath by a point in the quarter-finals in 1952, Westmeath sent them packing next time out, 3-9 to 3-4. It was a similar story a year later; Dublin beat Meath again — this time by six points but Louth, by 1-10 to 1-2, stopped them getting to the decider.

THE most dominant era in the entire history of the All-Ireland Minor Football Championship began in Drogheda on a rainy Sunday in May 1954 when, in a provincial quarter-final against the home county, late goals from David Waters and Vinny Bell allowed Dublin to turn a four point deficit into a 3-3 to 1-6 victory, the opening goal coming from Paddy Farnan, one of the man minors from that era who would go on toe win senior Championship honours in either 1958 or 1963, or both. The start of the glory run, however, was far from a cakewalk; the win over Louth was followed by narrow victories over Offaly and, in the provincial decider, Meath, by one and two points, respectively.

It was only in the All-Ireland semi-final against Mayo that Dublin could put some real distance between themselves and the opposition, beating the Connacht champions by 3-12 to 0-7, with Na Fianna star Bell accounting for 2-2. The final, against Kerry, was pure drama; a Vinny Bell goal meant Dublin were only a point adrift at halftime, 0-6 to 1-2, but with the hour almost up they were 1-8 to 1-3 adrift — but first Paddy Farnan and then Aidan Kavanagh cracked in injury time goals from Bell passes to give Dublin a dramatic last gasp victory and their third minor title after a nine year gap. Three weeks earlier Farnan, Bell and Kavanagh plus Mick Bohan and Tommy Bracken had been on the side that beat Tipperary by 2-7 to 2-3 in the minor hurling decider, Farnan again scoring a crucial goal.

The following year, with full back Dermot Sweeney and midfielder Paddy Heron still on board, Dublin opened their campaign with a 1-7 to 1-4 victory over Carlow at St. Conleth's Park in Newbridge. It was to be their closest encounter of the campaign; they beat Louth by 1-10 to 1-2 in a game that featured the first ever wearing of a county jersey by a certain Liam Foley, better known as Lar, and then clinched a ninth provincial title with a 2-11 to 1-4 defeat of Meath in a game that saw the debut of another future senior star, Johnny Joyce. Antrim were ousted 3-7 to 2-5 in the All-Ireland semi-final and, in the decider, Tipperary were beaten on a 5-4 to 2-7 scoreline with Joyce contributing 2-1.

In addition to Foley and Joyce, the side included two noteworthy corner backs, one the father of a future star, the other the son of an all-round sporting legend. Vincent Murphy's offspring Vinny would become a cult hero with the Hill 16 faithful throughout the 1990s while Des Hearns' father Dick was a five-time Irish light-heavyweight boxing champion, played senior football for six different counties (his native Mayo, plus Roscommon, Cork, Longford, Donegal and Dublin), scored the only goal when Garda beat O'Tooles by 1-4 to 0-4 in the Dublin county final in 1929, trained Mayo to their first All-Ireland title in 1936 (with a team that included Henry Kenny, father of future Taoiseach, Enda), and also coached Shelbourne to win the FAI Cup in 1960!

With five of that successful team — Foley, Hearns, Ray Doherty, Joe Lenihan and Christy Leaney — still eligible for the following year, Dublin had an experienced core to their team and began their bid for a hat-trick with a 1-13 to 0-3 defeat of Carlow at St Patrick's Park in Enniscorthy late May, when one of their points was scored by Lar Foley's younger brother Des, aged all of 15 years and 227 days. Westmeath were then dismissed 2-11 to 3-2 four weeks later and the following month a first ever provincial hat-trick was completed with a wafer-thin 1-10 to 1-9 win over Meath.

The opponents for the All-Ireland phase of the campaign were unusual to say the least. Limerick, who shocked Kerry with a 1-7 to 1-5 victory at the Athletic Grounds in Cork to win their first — and still only — provincial title in the grade, were beaten 1-13 to 2-5 in the semi-final, a win that set up a repeat of the 1945 decider against Leitrim. Eleven years earlier, after winning their first provincial crown, Leitrim were hammered 4-7 to 0-4; this time, after winning their second title (they wouldn't win a third until 1998), they were beaten even more emphatically, 5-14 to 2-2, still the record winning margin in an All-Ireland Minor Football Championship Final. Dublin had completed the grade's first hat-trick since Kerry in 1933 and the feat would not be repeated until Cork managed it in 1969 before the Kingdom did it a second time in 2016. Des Foley, less than a month after his 16th birthday, scored 1-4, a tally matched by another future senior All-Ireland medallist, Noel Fox.

The three year unbeaten run ended abruptly at Cusack Park in Mullingar on 2 June 1957. Despite the fact that Dublin still had Des Foley and Fox in their ranks (as well as a third future senior star in Des McKane), they were stunned by Longford, 0-9 to 1-4, the goal coming from McKane. The match report in the *Irish Press* remarked: "Actually the Dublin boys looked the better combination, but the prodigal fashion in which they wasted scoring chances had to be seen to be believed", while the Irish Independent noted: "Dublin fell far below the standard that one has come to expect from Metropolitan selections."

Normal service, however, was quickly resumed in 1958. In spite of the interruption to their all conquering ways, Dublin still had Des Foley and Fox in their ranks for a third consecutive campaign as well as a quartet of debutants who would all go on to win senior honours, Paddy Holden, Mick Kissane, Simon Behan and Brian McDonald. The talent told in the opening game when Meath, who had succeeded Dublin as All-Ireland champions and had three of their title winners still eligible, were dethroned by a comfortable 3-9 to 2-4 at the Gaelic Grounds in Drogheda, with Clanna Gael corner forward Jimmy Sweeney accounted for all but seven points of Dublin's total.

Dublin followed this with an 0-15 to 0-2 defeat of Carlow at O'Moore Park in Portlaoise and then regained the provincial crown with a 2-10 to 1-6 beating of Louth in Navan, where Sweeney again found the net. A Down side that included future legend and three-time All-Ireland senior medallist Sean O'Neill were beaten 3-5 to 0-9 in the All-Ireland semi-final, again at Navan and again with Sweeney finding the net, twice in fact. Mayo, in the final, were 0-7 to 0-6 ahead at halftime but goals from Foley and Fox inspired Dublin to what was in the end a relatively comfortable 2-10 to 0-8 victory. Foley scored 1-4 in an All-Ireland decider for the second time while Sweeney finished the campaign with 6-4, a county goalscoring record in the championship that would remain unchallenged until Barney Rock equalled it in 1978 and unbeaten until Dessie Farrell netted eight times a decade later.

A quartet of returnees — Mick Kissane, Brian McDonald, Simon Behan and Paddy Taylor — were still on board the following year when Dublin opened their campaign with a 4-10 to 3-3 defeat of Wexford in Portlaoise and followed up with a 5-8 to 1-6 trouncing of Louth in Navan. The provincial title was retained with a 3-13 to 1-7 win over Offaly in Tullamore and Dublin qualified for their ninth All-Ireland Final by coming back from 1-5 to 0-5 down at halftime to win 1-12 to 1-8. The final against Cavan was another tight affair as Dublin once again to come from behind at halftime — 1-2 to 0-4 — before capturing a seventh crown on an 0-11 to 1-4 scoreline.

The winning of five All-Ireland titles in six years remains unequalled in the grade to this day. Dublin, during the sequence, suffered a single defeat — by two points — in twenty-six games and scored an average of 1-12 against 1-7 conceded. The era produced a trio of players who would win senior All-Ireland honours in 1958, Lar Foley, Paddy Farnan and Johnny Joyce, and seven member of the side that would repeat that Sam Maguire Cup victory five years later, Lar Foley again plus brother Des and Paddy Holden, Mick Kissane, Simon Behan, Brian McDonald and Noel Fox. A dozen players played in two finals: Dermot Sweeney and Paddy Heron (1954, 1955), Lar Foley, Des Hearns, Joe Lenihan and Christy Leaney (1955, 1956), Des Foley and Noel Fox (1956, 1958), Mick Kissane, Simon Behan, Brian McDonald and Paddy Taylor (1958, 1959).

After a 1-9 to 1-6 provincial quarter-final defeat of Meath in Mullingar where Joe Levins was the sole survivor from the previous year, the great run finally ended at O'Moore Park in Portlaoise in June 1960 when Dublin, leading 0-6 to 0-4 at the break, were out-gunned 1-9 to 0-3 by Offaly in the second half. Dublin would go nineteen years between their ninth All-Ireland Final appearance and their tenth and in that time would win just five provincial titles.

The first of those came in 1961 with a team that included Bill Casey, who would collect an All-Ireland senior medal just two years later. Wexford, Meath and Offaly were beaten in turn but Mayo stopped the gallop with a 1-10 to 2-6 win in the All-Ireland semi-final, Des Keenan scoring both goals. Dublin reached the provincial final in each of the following two years but came up short on each occasion; a Gerry Kavanagh goal putting them 1-4 to 0-3 in front at halftime against Offaly in the first instance before a Tony McTague inspired revival saw the Midlanders score 2-5 without reply in the second half, and a year later Westmeath claimed only their third provincial title — and their first since 1952 — with a 2-14 to 3-7 win in Tullamore after leading by 1-6 to 2-1 at halftime.

It would be four years, 1967, before Dublin would again reach a Leinster Final with wins over Westmeath and Meath — Niall Redmond scoring three goals in the first game and one in the second — but Laois, in the decider in Newbridge, survived a late rally to edge home 1-8 to 2-4, Redmond again finding the net for Dublin's second goal. A year later, with a side that included Pat O'Neill, David Hickey and Pat Gogarty, the provincial title was won without conceding a goal as Dublin beat Longford by 1-10 to 0-12 in Mullingar, Meath by 0-9 to 0-8 in Navan, and Laois by 1-11 to 0-8 in Croke Park, only for Cork to beat them 2-10 to 1-6 in the All-Ireland semi-final, in which O'Neill was red carded by Galway referee Sean McLoughlin in the 43rd minute. Hickey was still there the following year and was joined by Robbie Kelleher, but the Sixties ended with another provincial final defeat, this time to Wexford by 0-11 to 0-7 at Dr. Cullen Park in Carlow.

The new decade began considerably brighter than the old one had finish, with back-to-back Leinster Championship successes. Each time, however, there was All-Ireland semi-final disappointment, by a comprehensive 3-12 to 0-10 to eventual champions Galway in 1970 and by a slightly closer 2-13 to 1-10 the following year to Cork, when Dublin's side included Gerry McCaul, Mick Holden and John McCarthy and the Leesiders had a certain Jimmy Barry Murphy at full forward. McCaul, Holden and McCarthy were all back again a year later and were joined by Brian Mullins as Dublin returned to the provincial decider with wins over Westmeath and Wexford but there was to be no titles hat-trick; two goals by Meath full forward Jack Kennedy in the eighth and ninth minutes of the second half consigned The Dubs to a 3-8 to 1-10 defeat.

Three more unsuccessful campaigns followed with a quarter-final elimination by Louth and then semi-final losses to Longford and Meath before things started to improve in the second half of the decade. In 1976, with Mick Kennedy manning the full back slot, the provincial title was regained with a 2-8 to 0-13 victory over Offaly, a Paddy Ryan goal from a 36th minute penalty proving the turning point. In a repeat of the All-Ireland semi-final of six years previously, Galway again eliminated The Dubs but this time by just a single point, 2-8 to 2-7, a 56th minute goal by midfielder Leo Higgins deciding the issue. Tom O'Riordan in the Irish Independent described the Dublin side as "the best seen in the colours since being crowned champions in 1959". Hopes were bright the following year — by which time future senior stars Pat Canavan, David Foran, Jim Ronayne and Anto McCaul were in the starting line-up — but after wins over Kildare and Offaly, a last minute point from a free by full forward Frank Sullivan gave Meath a 1-7 to 0-9 victory in the provincial decider.

The bid for glory in 1978 saw the debuts of two players who would become Hill 16 icons over the following decade and more, Barney Rock and Ciaran Duff. The former scored 3-2 in a provincial quarter-final hammering of Westmeath by 5-14 to 1-5 in Navan, and the latter donned the county colours for the first time in Dublin's next outing, a 2-13 to 1-7 defeat of Longford at Croke Park. The provincial crown was won for the 18th time courtesy of a 3-12 to 0-11 beating of Wexford and Tyrone were beaten even more emphatically in the All-Ireland semi-final, 5-7 to 1-9. Something went drastically wrong in the final against Mayo, however; Dublin were seemingly coasting to victory with a 3-7 to 1-7 lead with just eight minutes remaining, yet they somehow contrived to leak three goals and two points to end up on the wrong end of a 4-9 to 3-8 scoreline. Rock — who scored 1-6 in the decider — finished the campaign with 6-18 from the five games, but that was little consolation to the 17-year-old from Ballymun Kickhams.

Rock and Duff were returnees for the following campaign, although the former missed the opening game — a 4-13 to 0-6 trouncing of Louth in Navan — because of injury. Wexford were then hammered 3-11 to 0-8 in Newbridge before the provincial crown was retained with a 2-13 to 0-8 beating of Meath at Croke Park, where Rock again hit 1-6. Defending champions Mayo — who still had five of the previous year's winning side, including TJ Kilgallon — were edged out 0-8 to 0-7 in the All-Ireland semi-final to set up a third championship decider in the grade with Kerry but a first in a quarter of a century. A last minute point from Kevin Barry edged Dublin to an 0-10 to 1-6 victory after the teams had been tied at halftime. Eleven days short of two decades after their last success, Dublin were minor champions for the eighth time. Their goalkeeper kept his net unbreached for over four and a quarter hours until wing back Anthony Shannon netted for Kerry from a penalty in the 16th minute of the All-Ireland Final ... his name was John O'Leary.

WITH only Brian Jordan surviving from the title winning side, Dublin scraped a 2-6 to 1-6 win over Longford in a quarter-final in Mullingar in 1980 but then bowed out 3-7 to 3-5 to Meath in Navan. A year later, with a side that included Joe McNally, Mick Deegan, Mick Galvin and Tommy Conroy, Dublin recaptured the provincial title with a 1-8 to 0-9 victory over Meath — a side that included Robbie O'Malley, Colm Coyle and Martin O'Connell, all of whom would win successive All-Ireland senior medals six and seven years later — but six wides in the opening dozen minutes and a further ten later meant Derry sneaked an 0-8 to 0-6 victory in the All-Ireland semi-final.

One-third of the team — McNally, Deegan, Brendan Cooke, Declan Sheehan and Martin Coffey — were still there in 1982 and their experience would prove invaluable as The Dubs retained the provincial title with wins over Meath, Wexford and, in the final, Westmeath by 0-10 to 0-4. Galway were then outscored 0-17 to 1-3 as Dublin set up a fourth All-Ireland Final showdown with Kerry. Dublin, after losing the first encounter in 1946, had triumphed in 1954 and 1979 and Kerry's bid to balance the books failed as a Paul O'Carroll goal five minutes into the second half put Dublin on the road to a 1-11 to 1-5 victory and a ninth All-Ireland title. Future All-Star award winner Eamonn Heery was a star of the Dublin campaign while centre half back Tony Delaney was a son of Paddy, who had been on the successful 1959 side, won a second All-Ireland medal at junior level twelve months later and served for many years as vice-chairman of the County Board.

Meath gave Dublin an early knockout with a 2-7 to 0-6 first round win at Parnell Park the following year but Dublin, with a team that included Paul Clarke (captain), Ciaran Walsh, David DeLappe and the late Jim Stynes, rebounded in style in 1984. Their campaign opened with a 3-12 to 0-9 defeat of Wexford at Parnell Park and was followed by a 1-14 to 0-3 victory over Longford in Tullamore before a 22nd provincial title was won with an 0-12 to 1-6 triumph over Westmeath, the only time keeper Michael Broderick would be beaten in the entire campaign. Defending champions Derry were then dethroned on an 0-14 to 0-7 scoreline and Tipperary, bidding for a second title exactly half a century after their first, were beaten 1-9 to 0-4 in the final. Dublin's tenth All-Ireland crown enabled them to move ahead of Kerry in the roll of honour, although the Kingdom would draw level again four years later and subsequently edge ahead in 1994.

The see-saw pattern continued. Dublin fell to Wexford at the first hurdle at Wexford Park in 1985 but came out the following year to race through Leinster without the concession of a goal beating, in turn, Kildare by 0-15 to 0-6, Longford by 2-10 to 0-5 and Meath by 2-16 to 0-6; the run ended abruptly with a 2-7 to 0-8 loss to Cork in the All-Ireland semi-final. A year later, after wins over Westmeath and Wicklow, a side that included Paul Curran and Vinnie Murphy lost out 0-13 to 2-5 to Kildare in the Leinster Final.

As they had done two years previously, Dublin marched through the provincial championship in convincing fashion and without having a goal scored against them, beating Laois, Wicklow and Meath by an aggregate of 8-31 to 0-19, with Dessie Farrell scoring 2-3 in the second game and two more goals in the third. The scoring spree continued with a 4-11 to 0-4 hammering of New York in an All-Ireland quarter-final — Farrell scoring all the goals — and then Galway were ousted by 1-9 to 0-7 in the semi-final. For the third time in nine years Kerry provided the final opposition, and the Kingdom rejoined The Dubs at the top of the roll of honour with a 2-5 to 0-5 victory over what Bob Hyland in the Irish Independent called "a lethargic and mistake-prone Dublin". Farrell, despite failing to score against Galway and managing just a single point against

Kerry, finished the campaign with 8-7, a county goalscoring record that still stands. The pattern of inconsistency surfaced again in the final year of the decade as Dublin were beaten by Kildare by 0-8 to 0-7 in a quarter-final at Newbridge after being five points to no score in front at halftime.

THE Nineties could not have begun more disastrously for Dublin; Louth humiliated them in a provincial quarter-final in Drogheda by 5-14 to 1-4 — which remains to this day (the end of the 2017 season) the biggest beating any Dublin team has ever suffered in championship action at any level. The following three years may not have been quite as bad but there was no real success either; Dublin did reach the provincial decider in 1991 but succumbed to Kildare by 2-8 to 0-12 and in the next two campaigns they were beaten first by Wexford in the quarter-finals — after beating Offaly in a first round replay — and then by Meath in the semi-finals.

The provincial title was regained in 1994 after a six year absence with victories over Kilkenny, Kildare (against whom, remarkably, Eamonn McLoughlin from St. Mary's scored all but a single point of Dublin's total in a 2-11 to 1-7 win in Newbridge), Carlow and Wexford, but the Alan Larkin coached side — which included Ciaran Whelan and Jason Sherlock — bowed out to Galway in the All-Ireland semi-final by a goal, 1-12 to 0-12. McLoughlin finished the campaign with a total of 2-35, jointly the second highest ever by a Dub in the grade and a record for a five game programme.

Almost predictably, the following year brought a first round elimination against Kildare before The Dubs rebounded to some degree at least, reaching the provincial decider but suffering an emphatic 2-18 to 1-8 defeat in a replay. Wicklow ousted Dublin at the semi-final stage in 1997 and a year later, this time by 2-9 to 0-12 at the first attempt, Laois again beat The Dubs in the Leinster Final.

Only in the final year of the decade did Dublin get close to the jackpot. Carlow, Westmeath and Offaly were all beaten by relatively comfortably margins, and although two late points earned Wexford a draw in the provincial final, Dublin had four points to spare in the replay, winning 2-13 to 1-12. Down, a county Dublin had not met in the grade since the same stage in 1958, provided the opposition in the All-Ireland semi-final and it took a point from a last minute free by Liam Og O hEineachain to snatch a second chance for The Dubs but it was all to no avail as the Ulster champions won the replay in Navan by 2-14 to 1-9. Stephen Mills from Parnells scored 7-18 in the course of the seven match campaign, including two goals in each of the first three games.

DUBLIN'S fortunes showed a fair degree of improvement in the new Millennium, even if the ultimate prize would continue to elude them throughout the first decade of the 21st century.

True, the era started with Westmeath getting the better of them in the provincial final by 2-9 to 1-10 but the following year, with a line-up that included Paul Griffin and Bryan Cullen, they produced the greatest whitewash in the history of the Leinster Championships in any grade, their scoring figures being 15-60 for and 0-20 against. A mammoth 9-21 of the total — the highest score ever achieved by any Dublin football side in a competitive game — may have come against Kilkenny in the opening round but their other scores in the provincial campaign were still impressive, 4-13 against Louth, 1-9 against Kildare and 1-17 against Offaly, with the opposition restricted to just half a dozen points in each game.

In the All-Ireland semi-final against Kerry, the sides were tied at 2-6 each at half-time but Dublin, in spite of playing against a strong wind, outscored the Kingdom in the second half by 0-7 to 0-3 to earn a place in the decider for the 15th time. Tyrone, who had beaten Dublin in the 1948 decider, were the final opponents and it took an injury time goal from David O'Callaghan from St. Mark's to snatch a dramatic draw for Dublin. The replay, at Breffni Park in Cavan six days later, was largely a non event, Tyrone, inspired by Sean Cavanagh, winning 2-11 to 0-6. Niall McAuliffe from St. Sylvester's scored five goals and a point in the win over Kilkenny to match the all-time Dublin scoring record set by Johnny Joyce in a senior quarter-final victory over Longford in May 1960 and, despite being held scoreless in the All-Ireland Final replay, finished the programme with a total of 5-18. Joyce, it should be noted, raised three white flags in addition to his goals.

Longford pulled a semi-final surprise in Mullingar in 2002 but, as was becoming something of a habit, Dublin bounced the following year, even if they needed a replay to see off Louth in the Leinster semi-final. The provincial title was reclaimed with a 1-11 to 1-9 victory over Laois, Fermanagh were beaten 0-15 to 0-5 in the All-Ireland quarter-final and Cork by 1-18 to 1-9 in the semi-final. Thanks to the introduction of the 'back door' format, Laois were the other finalists and surprised the majority by holding The Dubs to a 1-11 each draw; they caused an even bigger surprise at Dr. Cullen Park in Carlow a fortnight later by lifting the Tom Markham Cup on a 2-10 to 1-9 scoreline. For the second time in three campaigns, Dublin suffered the heartache of losing the All-Ireland Final in a replay.

Five uneventful years followed, with three successive semi-final defeats — the first two to Laois and the third to Offaly — and then consecutive quarter-final losses to Laois, after another replay, and Meath. In the final year of the decade there was a significant improvement as the provincial crown was regained, albeit after a replay with Kildare, but Down ended the challenge with a 2-16 to 2-14 triumph in an All-Ireland quarter-final at Breffni Park. Darragh Stapleton from St. Patrick's (Palmerstown) and Paul Hudson scored 3-25 and 3-21, respectively, in the course of the campaign, Stapleton hitting 1-10 against Down and Hudson scoring 2-7 in the Leinster semi-final against Offaly.

Kildare scored a 2-10 to 1-9 win in a first round clash in Newbridge in 2010 but the qualifiers allowed Dublin back in and, after beating Louth by 4-11 to 0-5 and receiving a walkover from Kilkenny, they faced a quarter-final against their earlier conquerors.

The tie would take three games to decide before Kildare scraped home 1-13 to 0-13 in the second replay at Navan.

A year later, with future senior stars Eric Lowndes, John Small, Jack McCaffrey, Cormac Costello, Ciaran Kilkenny and Paul Mannion on board, Dublin march through Leinster with little difficulty — an 0-10 to 0-5 quarter-final win over Longford being by far their closest encounter — and then saw off Galway by 1-11 to 1-9 in the All-Ireland semi-final. Hot favourites against Tipperary (whose one and only title in the grade had been won in 1934), Dublin held a 1-10 to 2-2 lead at halftime only to see the underdog Munster champions fight back and grab a sensational 3-9 to 1-14 victory with a 58th minute goal from sub Colman Kennedy. Four players, Lowndes, Costello, Kilkenny and Emmett O'Conghaile, had been on the side beaten 1-21 to 1-12 by Galway in the hurling final three weeks previously.

It all, finally, came good in 2012 starting with successive provincial campaign wins over Carlow, Longford, Kildare and Meath, and followed with a 1-16 to 0-8 defeat of Monaghan in the All-Ireland quarter-final at Pairc Esler in Newry and then a 3-12 defeat of Kerry in the semi-final at Croke Park. Once again the back door came into play as their final opponents were Meath, who had been dismissed 3-17 to 1-11 in the Leinster Final. It was considerably closer second time around, Dublin getting home 0-14 to 1-5 with full forward Costello — son of County Board CEO, John — contributing five crucial points to finish the seven match campaign with 5-26, including 3-4 in the first meeting with Meath.

Two years later, rebounding from a provincial semi-final loss to Kildare in the previous campaign, Dublin recorded wins over Longford, Meath and Kildare (the latter by 6-13 to 0-6 with Con O'Callaghan contributing 2-6) and, in the Leinster Final, Kildare by 3-16 to 1-12. Cork were beaten 2-14 to 1-13 in the All-Ireland quarter-final in Thurles but Donegal, who had never before reached the All-Ireland Final in the grade, finally did so with a 1-12 to 1-11 semi-final win thanks to a last minute point from sub Ethan O'Donnell. O'Callaghan, with four points in the final, finished the championship with 4-33, a county record in the grade.

Dublin lost to Kildare by 3-16 to 3-13 in the provincial semi-final in 2015 and to Meath by 1-18 to 2-5 at the quarter-final stage the following year, but the 2017 campaign promised much, especially after a remarkable first outing against Meath at Parnell Park; all of ten points down at halftime (0-3 to 1-10), the teenage Dubs staged a sensational comeback to outscore their opponents by 1-8 to 0-1 in the second half before beating them 0-4 to 0-2 in extra time. Longford, Kildare and Louth were beaten by a combined 9-47 to 0-30 and goalkeeper David O'Hanlon's net was again unbreached as Clare were beaten 2-11 to 0-10 in the All-Ireland quarter-final at O'Moore Park in Portlaoise. The goals dried up in the semi-final, however, as Derry halted the march on an 0-17 to 0-14 scoreline.

Minor Championship Results

1928

LEINSTER FIRST ROUND
May 27, Croke Park, Dublin
DUBLIN 2-4   KILDARE 1-4
Dublin: J Goulding, N Gleeson, J Colfer, W Hughes, J Hannon, M O'Brien, M Connolly, T Markham 0-2, R Kavanagh, L Delaney, K O'Toole, M Wellington 1-0, F Whelan 0-1, E Heron 1-0, D Brennan 0-1.

LEINSTER QUARTER-FINAL
Sep 16, St Patrick's Park, Enniscorthy
DUBLIN 3-4   WEXFORD 1-9
Dublin: J Goulding, N Gleeson, J Colfer, W Hughes, J Hannon, M O'Brien, M Connolly, T Markham 0-2, R Kavanagh 1-0, L Delaney 1-0, K O'Toole 1-0, M Wellington, F Whelan, E Heron 0-1, D Brennan 0-1.

LEINSTER SEMI-FINAL
Oct 7, Dundalk
DUBLIN 5-7   LOUTH 3-4
Dublin, St Brigid's Park: J Goulding, N Gleeson, J Colfer, W Hughes 1-0, J Hannon, M O'Brien, T Markham, R Kavanagh, L Delaney 1-2, M Connolly 1-2, K O'Toole 0-1, M Wellington 1-1, F Whelan 0-1, E Heron, D Brennan 1-0.
* Dublin disqualified from final against Offaly after being found to have used a numbr of overage players title never formally awarded to Offaly.

1929

LEINSTER FIRST ROUND
June 2, St Patrick's Park, Enniscorthy
DUBLIN 1-3   WEXFORD 1-3
Dublin: P Gill, F Whelan, G O'Toole, W Fallon, K Walsh, T Delaney, T Markham, D Quinn, B Synnott, P Nolan, M Wellington 0-3, G McLoughlin, J Hannon, C Hatch 1-0, P Caul.

LEINSTER FIRST ROUND REPLAY
July 14, Novela Road, Bray
DUBLIN 3-4   WEXFORD 0-6
Dublin: P Gill, F Whelan, W Fallon, G O'Toole, T Delaney, W Hughes, D Quinn, T Markham 0-1, B Synnott, M Connolly 1-0, M Wellington 0-2, G McLoughlin, C Hatch 0-1, P Caul 2-0, W Fallon.

LEINSTER QUARTER-FINAL
Sep 22, Croke Park, Dublin
DUBLIN 1-5   OFFALY 0-2
Dublin: P Gill, F Whelan, W Fallon, G O'Toole, W

Hughes, D Quinn 0-1, T Delaney 0-1, T Markham 0-1, B Synnott, P Nolan, M Wellington 0-2, G McLoughlin, C Hatch, P Caul 1-0, W Fallon.

LEINSTER SEMI-FINAL
Oct 13, Showgrounds, Navan
DUBLIN 3-4   MEATH 2-1
Dublin: P Gill, G McLoughlin, K Walsh, J Hannon, W Hughes, J Brady, B Synnott, P Nolan, F Whelan, G O'Toole 0-1, D Quinn 1-0, T Markham 1-0, P Caul, T Delaney, W Fallon 1-3.

LEINSTER FINAL
Nov 10, Showgrounds, Navan
LONGFORD 3-4   DUBLIN 1-4
Dublin: P Gill, G McLoughlin, K Walsh, J Hannon, W Hughes, J Brady, B Synnott 1-2, P Nolan, F Whelan, G O'Toole, D Quinn, T Markham 0-1, P Caul, T Delaney 0-1, W Fallon.

1930

LEINSTER FIRST ROUND
May 25, Novela Road, Bray
DUBLIN 1-4   WICKLOW 0-2
Dublin: T Sharkey, T Lawless, P Carton, J Brady, K Barry, K Walsh, F Whelan, P Nolan 0-1, W Bastow, D Quinn 1-0, C O'Toole, B Synnott, T Markham 0-3, W Fallon, J Pearce.

LEINSTER QUARTER-FINAL
July 13, Showgrounds, Navan
DUBLIN 2-5   MEATH 2-0
Dublin: T Sharkey, T Lawless, P Carton, P Nolan, K Barry 0-1, K Walsh, F Whelan, J Brady, C O'Toole 0-1, B Synnott 0-1, W Fallon, P Diffney, T Markham 1-1, D Quinn 1-1, G McLoughlin.

ALL-IRELAND SEMI-FINAL
Aug 24, Croke Park, Dublin
DUBLIN 1-3   ARMAGH 1-1
Dublin: T Sharkey, T Lawless, J Brady, K Barry, P Nolan, S O'Toole, J Pearce, W Bastow, G McLoughlin, P Diffney 1-2, P Carton, J Scott, T Markham, D Quinn 0-1, B Synnott.
* As the provincial championship had fallen seriously behind schedule, Dublin were nominated to represent Leinster in the All-Ireland series.

LEINSTER SEMI-FINAL
Aug 31, Catherine Park, Athy
DUBLIN 1-3   CARLOW 0-3
Dublin: T Sharkey, T Lawless, P Carton, K Barry, P

Nolan, W Bastow, G McLoughlin, S O'Toole, P Diffney, M Grimes, T Markham 0-1, D Quinn 0-1, B Synnott 0-1, J Lynham 1-0, P Crummy.

ALL-IRELAND FINAL
Sep 7, Croke Park, Dublin
DUBLIN 1-3   MAYO 0-5
Dublin: Tom Sharkey, Gerry McLoughlin, Kevin Barry, Sean O'Toole, Brendan Synnott (capt), Tom Markham 0-1, Tom Lawless, Jim Scott, Pat Diffney, Willie Fallon 1-0, Willie Bastow, Bernard Murphy, Martin Grimes, John Pearse, Peadar Carton, Frank Williams, Jim Brady, Pat Crummy.
* The above 18-player panel — rather than an actual team — was recorded in the press, yet the 'Irish Independent' match report of the following day lists the remaining two points as being scored by Des Quinn and Chris Hatch.

LEINSTER FINAL
Sep 14, Hospital Grounds, Mullingar
DUBLIN 1-6   LONGFORD 0-4
Dublin: T Sharkey, G McLoughlin, K Barry 0-1, S O'Toole, B Synnott, T Markham 0-1, T Lawless, J Scott, P Diffney 0-1, W Fallon 0-2, D Quinn 1-0, B Murphy, M Grimes, J Pearse 0-1, C Hatch 0-1.

1931

LEINSTER QUARTER-FINAL
May 17, Catherine Park, Athy
DUBLIN 0-7   KILDARE 0-0
Dublin: T Sharkey, P O'Sullivan, J Scott, P Crummy, P Ennis, P Maguire, J Weldon, J Brady, G McLoughlin, T Markham 0-3, W Ryan 0-1, J Lynham 0-2, M Fletcher, J Sherlock, J Pearse 0-1.

LEINSTER SEMI-FINAL
July 12, Gaelic Grounds, Drogheda
LOUTH 2-7   DUBLIN 0-3
Dublin: T Sharkey, P O'Sullivan, J Scott, P Crummy, P Ennis, J Brady, J Weldon, M Fletcher, F Ellis, T Markham, M Ryan 0-2, J Sherlock, J Lynham, J Pearse, P Diffney 0-1.

1932

LEINSTER QUARTER-FINAL
May 8, Gaelic Grounds, Drogheda
LOUTH 2-2   DUBLIN 0-5
Dublin: S Prenderville, M Snowden, J Scott, J Reid, J Greene, J Sherlock, M Kavanagh, J Kirwan, T Bastable, P Farrelly, T Markham 0-2, O Keogh 0-1, J O'Neill 0-2, P O'Toole, M Cahill.

1933

LEINSTER QUARTER-FINAL
May 28, Showgrounds, Navan
DUBLIN 4-11   WESTMEATH 2-6
Dublin: J Collins, M Wilson, T Bastable, W Malone, P McLoughin, G Ingham, A Byrne, M Cahill, N Boland 0-3, G Moore 0-1, P Bermingham, W Bergin, C Manahan, J Glavin 3-6, P Maher 1-1.

LEINSTER SEMI-FINAL
July 16, Gaelic Grounds, Drogheda
DUBLIN 3-8   MEATH 2-5
Dublin: M Barron, P O'Neill, T Bastable, W Malone, F McLoughlin, G Ingham, A Byrne, M Cahill 0-1, E Boland 1-1, G Moore, W Bergin, P Bermingham 1-1, C Manahan, J Glavin 1-3, P Maher 0-2.

LEINSTER FINAL
July 30, Croke Park, Dublin
DUBLIN 3-7   LAOIS 0-6
Dublin: M Barron, T Bastable, C Moore, M Cahill 0-1, G Ingham, P Farrelly, P Rooney, F McLoughlin, W Malone, P Maher 2-0, G Moore 2-0, J Glavin 1-0, N Boland 0-4, P Bermingham, A Byrne.

ALL-IRELAND SEMI-FINAL
Aug 20, Cusack Park, Mullingar
MAYO 0-12   DUBLIN 0-8
Dublin: M Barron, P O'Neill, T Bastable, W Malone, F McLoughlin, G Ingham, A Byrne, N Boland 0-1, M Cahill, C Moore, P Farrelly, P Bermingham, G Moore 0-5, J Glavin 0-1, P Maher 0-1.

1934

LEINSTER SEMI-FINAL
July 15, Croke Park, Dublin
DUBLIN 4-10   MEATH 2-2
Dublin: J Bolger, J Delaney, M Cahill, J Barnes, P Rooney, N Dunne, J Richardson, G Kilbride 1-0, P McDermott, P Bermingham 0-1, J Byrne 1-6, T McCann, T McCallion, J Glavin 2-2, L Hanley.
* Dublin received a walkover from Wicklow in the quarter-finals.

LEINSTER FINAL
Aug 19, Sallins Road, Naas
DUBLIN 0-5   KILDARE 0-2
Dublin: J Bolger, J Delaney, M Cahill, J Barnes, P Rooney, M Shields, J Richardson, G Kilbride, J Parker, P Bermingham 0-1, J Byrne 0-2, T McCann, T McCallion 0-2, J Glavin, L Hanley.

ALL-IRELAND SEMI-FINAL
Aug 26, Gaelic Grounds, Drogheda
DUBLIN 0-9   TYRONE 1-4

Dublin: J Bolger, J Delaney, M Cahill, P Rooney, J Barnes, N Dunne, M Shields, J Parker, P McDermott, P Bermingham, J Byrne 0-2, T McCann, T McCallion 0-2, J Glavin 0-2, M Dillon 0-1.

Tyrone lodged an official protest on the grounds that Dublin played a number of overage players and were initially awarded the game and a place in the final against Tipperary, scheduled for October 14. Tyrone later withrew upon discovering that they themselves had inadvertently committed the same offence. Tipperary, as a result, were awarded the All-Ireland title.

1935

LEINSTER QUARTER-FINAL
Apr 14, Sallins Road, Naas
DUBLIN 0-9   KILDARE 2-3
Dublin: W Brown, M Tobin, J Frew, W Reyburn, G Diffney, M O'Callaghan, J Barnes, T McCann 0-1, W Richardson 0-1, J Delaney 0-1, A Doyle 0-1, T McCallion 0-3, J Yeates 0-1, J Fogarty 0-1, C O'Connor.

LEINSTER QUARTER-FINAL REPLAY
May 12, O'Connor Park, Tullamore
DUBLIN 1-8   KILDARE 1-4
Dublin: W Brown, P McLoughlin, M Tobin, W Reyburn, G Diffney, M O'Callaghan, J Barnes, J Fagan, W Richardson, T McCann 1-2, J Delaney 0-1, A Doyle, T McCallion 0-4, J Carey, C O'Connor 0-1.

LEINSTER SEMI-FINAL
June 2, McCann Park, Portarlington
DUBLIN 2-6   LAOIS 1-3
Dublin: W Browne, G Diffney, M Tobin, W Reyburn, M O'Callaghan, J Barnes, T McCann, J Delaney, W Richardson, M Norton, T McCallion 1-4, J Carey 0-2, A Doyle, C O'Connor 1-0, J Fogarty.

LEINSTER FINAL
July 14, Croke Park, Dublin
LOUTH 1-7   DUBLIN 1-6
Dublin: W Brown, G Diffney, M Tobin, W Reyburn 0-1, M O'Callaghan, J Barnes, J Fagan, T McCann, J Delaney 1-0, A Doyle, T McCallion 0-2, J Fogarty 0-1, P Daly, C O'Connor 0-2.

1936

LEINSTER FIRST ROUND
May 10, Gaelic Grounds, Baltinglass
CARLOW 3-4   DUBLIN 1-4
Dublin: W Brown, M Egan, P Toolan, C Carr, W Reyburn, J McGann, J Gibons 0-1, P Dooley, P Kelly, M

Fitzpatrick, B Quinn 1-0, T McCann 1-2, C O'Connor, LP Keogh, J Byrne 0-1.
Carlow were disqualified for fielding an unregistered player; Dublin awarded game.

LEINSTER QUARTER-FINAL
June 28, County Ground, Aughrim
WEXFORD 3-4   DUBLIN 3-2
Dublin: P Laird, P Toolan, C Carr, B Masterson, T Driver, W Reyburn, A Farrell, J Gibbons, J McGann, B Harris, T McCann 0-2, B Quinn, C O'Connor 1-0, LP Keogh 1-0, J Byrne 1-0.

1937

LEINSTER FIRST ROUND
Apr 18, Croke Park, Dublin
DUBLIN 1-13   KILDARE 2-3
Dublin: S Egan, J Kealy, P Dooley, M Meehan, P Doonan, F Moore, J Hanibode, J Gibbons, T McCann 0-1, T Fitzpatrick 0-3, P Kennedy 0-2, B Quinn, LP Keogh 0-5, P Moloney 0-1, J Byrne 1-0. Sub: E Smyth 0-1 for Quinn.

LEINSTER QUARTER-FINAL
May 30, Gaelic Grounds, Drogheda
DUBLIN 3-4   LOUTH 2-7
Dublin: S Egan, J Kealy, P Dooley, M Meehan, J Gibbons, F Moore, P Doonan, T McCann 0-1, J Mooney, T Fitzpatrick 0-1, P Kennedy, B Quinn 0-1, S O'Neill 0-1, P Moloney 1-0, J Byrne 2-0.

LEINSTER QUARTER-FINAL REPLAY
June 20, Pairc Tailteann, Navan
LOUTH 3-6   DUBLIN 1-4
Dublin: S Egan, J Kealy, F Moore, P Dooley, M Meehan, B Hurley, J Gibbons, T McCann, T Fitzpatrick, P Kennedy, B Quinn 1-2, LP Keogh, S O'Neill 0-1, P Moloney, P Walsh 0-1.

1938

LEINSTER QUARTER-FINAL
Apr 10, Catherine Park, Athy
DUBLIN 4-6   KILDARE 1-6
Dublin: P Duffy, P Kilbride, T Lowry, M Meehan 0-1, G Glenn, G Grant, R Rafferty, M Ennis, E Walsh, S Carroll 1-0, K Quinn, J Prestage 1-0, S O'Neill 1-3, P Walsh 1-2.

LEINSTER SEMI-FINAL
July 3, Croke Park, Dublin
LOUTH 2-6   DUBLIN 1-3
Dublin: P Duffy, M Meehan, P Moloney, E Walsh, P Kilbride, R Rafferty, G Grant, M Ennis, M Farrell, S Carroll, J Keeley, J Prestage, P Heenan, S O'Neill 0-2, P Walsh 1-1.

1939

LEINSTER QUARTER-FINAL
Apr 30, Novela Road, Bray
DUBLIN 4-4   WICKLOW 1-1
Dublin: P Duffy, S Healy, B McShane, P Hughes, D Collins, K Stritch, P Byrne, M O'Reilly 0-1, J Keeley, J DeLappe, L Gaskin, P Smith 1-0, K Byrne, M Redmond 3-3, M Judge.

LEINSTER SEMI-FINAL
May 21, Gaelic Grounds, Drogheda
LOUTH 3-7   DUBLIN 1-2
Dublin: P Duffy, B McShane, P Byrne, M O'Reilly, P Hughes, J Keeley, S Healy, M Judge, D Collins, L Gaskin 1-0, R Stritch, R Wilson, K Byrne 0-1, J DeLappe, M Redmond 0-1.

1940

LEINSTER QUARTER-FINAL
May 19, Pairc Tailteann, Navan
DUBLIN 1-7   MEATH 0-4
Dublin: E Ryan, B McShane, P Dunne, R Dempsey, B Callan, B O'Rourke, J Kavanagh 0-1, W O'Shea 0-2, J Christie 0-1, J Nolan, E Mooney, R Nutty, M Mullen, P Hudson 1-0, C Craig 0-3.

LEINSTER SEMI-FINAL
June 30, Croke Park, Dublin
LOUTH 1-6   DUBLIN 0-6
Dublin: J Hughes, B McShane, P Dunne, R Dempsey, P Hudson, J O'Sullivan, J Kavanagh, M Hayden, W O'Shea 0-3, R Nutty, W Gibson, T Stack, K Matthews, M Boylan 0-1, D O'Meara 0-2.

1941

LEINSTER FIRST ROUND
May 18, Gaelic Grounds, Drogheda
LOUTH 2-9   DUBLIN 0-2
Dublin: M Neylon, P Hudson, J Elliott, L Hogan, A Halpin, R McWade, R Lowen, S Shouldice, R Nutty 0-2, E Mooney, J Bailey, H Farrell, G Darcy, M Delaney, P O'Reilly.

1942

LEINSTER QUARTER-FINAL
May 31, Gaelic Grounds, Drogheda
LOUTH 3-8   DUBLIN 3-5
Dublin: M Neylon, T Fleming, N Dolan, N Fogarty, J Byrne, S Nolan, A McHale, B Lambert, T Mullen, S Parker, L McConkey 2-1, M Whelan 0-1, G Darcy 0-1, G Cullen 1-1, T Hunt 0-1.

1943–1944

Championship suspended.

1945

LEINSTER QUARTER-FINAL
June 10, Gaelic Grounds, Drogheda
DUBLIN 5-7   MEATH 1-6
Dublin: V Savino, D Mahony, J Sharry, G Jennings, T Nolan, J Lavin, D Healy, J McEntaggart 1-0, J McWade, L Donnelly 0-2, S Copeland 2-0, O Freaney 1-2, S Guinan 0-1, P McCarthy, C Dignam 1-2.

LEINSTER SEMI-FINAL
June 24, Cusack Park, Mullingar
DUBLIN 1-5   WESTMEATH 0-3
Dublin: V Savino, D Mahony, J Sharry, G Jennings, J Lavin, D Healy, T Nolan, J McEntaggart 0-5, S Guinan, L Donnelly, O Freaney 1-0, J McWade, J Copeland, P McCarthy, C Dignam.

LEINSTER FINAL
July 22, O'Moore Park, Portlaoise
DUBLIN 3-5   WEXFORD 1-0
Dublin: V Savino, D Mahony, J Sharry, G Jennings, G Craig, D Healy, T Nolan, S Guinan, S McEntaggart 0-3, L Donnelly, O Freaney 0-2, J Nugent, J Copeland 2-0, P McCarthy 1-0, C Dignam.

ALL-IRELAND SEMI-FINAL
Aug 12, Croke Park, Dublin
DUBLIN 2-3   KERRY 1-2
Dublin: V Savino, D Mahony, J Sharry, G Jennings, N Maher, D Healy T Nolan 0-1, S McEntaggart 1-0, S Guinan, L Donnelly, O Freaney 0-2, J Nugent, J Copeland 1-0, P McCarthy, C Dignam.

ALL-IRELAND FINAL
Sep 23, Croke Park, Dublin
DUBLIN 4-7   LEITRIM 0-4
Dublin: Charlie Feeney, Denis Mahony, John Sharry, George Jennings, Nicky Maher, Des Healy, Tom Nolan, Sean McEntaggart 0-3, Sean Guinea, Liam Donnelly 0-1, Ollie Freaney 0-1, James Nugent 1-0, Jackie Copeland 1-1, Pat McCarthy 1-0, Cathal Dignam 1-1.

1946

LEINSTER QUARTER-FINAL
May 19, Catherine Park, Athy
DUBLIN 3-8   LAOIS 0-2
Dublin: C Feeney, D Mahony, P Lawlor, N Fingleton, J Butler, J Lavin, B Clancy, S Guinea, N Maher, L Donnelly 0-1, O Freaney 0-3, D Stanley, K Heffernan 1-1, T Clohessy 2-2, C Mehigan 0-1.

LEINSTER SEMI-FINAL
June 23, O'Moore Park, Portlaoise
DUBLIN 6-12   OFFALY 1-4
Dublin: C Feeney, D Mahony, P Lawlor, N Fingleton, P Moran, J Lavin, B Clancy, S Guinea 1-0, N Maher, L Donnelly 2-3, O Freaney 0-8, D Stanley, K Heffernan 2-1, T Clohessy 1-0, C Mehigan.

LEINSTER FINAL
July 21, Pairc Tailteann, Navan
DUBLIN 4-6   MEATH 0-3
Dublin: C Feeney, D Mahony, P Lawlor, N Fingleton, J Butler, J Lavin, B Clancy, S Guinan 0-1, N Maher, L Donnelly 0-2, O Freaney 1-0, D Stanley, K Heffernan 2-3, T Clohessy, C Mehigan 1-0.

ALL-IRELAND SEMI-FINAL
Aug 25, St Tiernach's Park, Clones
DUBLIN 1-7   TYRONE 0-6
Dublin: C Feeney, D Mahony, P Lawlor, N Fingleton, J Butler, J Lavin, B Clancy, S Guinea, N Maher, L Donnelly, O Freaney 0-2, D Stanley 1-0, K Heffernan 0-4, T Clohessy, C Mehigan 0-1.

ALL-IRELAND FINAL
Oct 6, Croke Park, Dublin
KERRY 3-7   DUBLIN 2-3
Dublin: Charlie Feeney, Denis Mahony, Paddy Lawlor, P Cloonan, Joe Butler, Jim Lavin, Brendan Clancy, Nicky Fingleton, Nicky Maher 1-0, Liam Donnelly, Ollie Freaney 1-2, D Stanley, Kevin Heffernan 0-1, T Clohessy, C Meighan. Subs: P Bates for Cloonan, T Mulligan for Mahony.

1947

LEINSTER QUARTER-FINAL
June 1, Pairc Tailteann, Navan
DUBLIN 2-7   LOUTH 1-4
Dublin: T Clohessy, C Donovan, N Fingleton, S Healy, J Crowley, J Butler, V McLoughlin, T Young, L Donnelly 0-1, T Jennings, C Freaney 0-2, J Barnwell, K Heffernan 0-1, J Archibald 1-3, D Stanley 1-0.

LEINSTER SEMI-FINAL
July 6, Croke Park, Dublin
DUBLIN 1-9   MEATH 1-4
Dublin: T Clohessy, C Donovan, N Fingleton, P Power, J Crowley, J Butler, V McLoughlin, T Young, P Molomby 0-1, T Jennings 0-1, C Freaney 0-2, J Barnwell 0-1, K Heffernan 0-4, J Archibald, D Stanley 1-0.

LEINSTER FINAL
July 20, Croke Park, Dublin
DUBLIN 1-7   OFFALY 1-7
Dublin: T Clohessy, C Donovan, N Fingleton, P Power,
J Crowley, J Butler 0-1, V McLoughlin, T Jennings, T Young, M Costello, C Freaney 0-2, J Barnwell 0-2, K Heffernan 0-2, J Archibald, D Stanley 1-0.

LEINSTER FINAL REPLAY
Aug 3, Cusack Park, Mullingar
OFFALY 1-7   DUBLIN 1-5
Dublin: P King, C Donovan, N Fingleton, P Power, J Crowley, J Butler, V McLoughlin, T Young, T Jennings, P Donoghue, J Archibald, D Stanley 0-1, K Heffernan 1-2, T Clohessy, J Barnwell 0-1. Sub: C Freaney 0-1 for Donoghue.

1948

LEINSTER QUARTER-FINAL
May 9, Pairc Tailteann, Navan
DUBLIN 1-7   LOUTH 1-3
Dublin: P King, J Foley, K Lougheed, G Brogan, P Connolly, V McLoughlin, S Page, T Jennings 0-2, E Byrne 0-1, G Guidon 0-1, E O'Brien, C Freaney, D Ferguson 1-0, R Thomson, J Kelly 0-3.

LEINSTER SEMI-FINAL
July 11, Croke Park, Dublin
DUBLIN 1-6   WESTMEATH 1-4
Dublin: P King, J Foley, K Lougheed, G Brogan, P Connolly, V McLoughlin, S Page, T Jennings, M Hayes, G Guidon, E O'Brien, C Freaney 0-1, D Ferguson 1-1, R Thomson, J Kelly 0-4.

LEINSTER FINAL
Aug 1, Sallins Road, Naas
DUBLIN 2-5   OFFALY 1-6
Dublin: P King, P Connolly, S Page, G Brogan, H Boylan, V McLoughlin, W Mullins, T Jennings, E Byrne, B Purcell, D Ferguson 1-0, J Kelly 0-3, B Conboy, B Carney 0-2, P McGahon. Sub: C Freaney 1-0 for Conboy.

ALL-IRELAND SEMI-FINAL
Aug 29, Croke Park, Dublin
DUBLIN 2-7   KERRY 0-8
Dublin: P King, P Connolly, K Lougheed, G Brogan, W Mullins, V McLoughlin, S Page, T Jennings 0-1, C Freaney 0-1, B Purcell 1-2, D Ferguson 1-0, J Kelly 0-2, B Conboy, B Carney, P McGahan 0-1.

ALL-IRELAND FINAL
Sep 26, Croke Park, Dublin
TYRONE 0-11   DUBLIN 1-5
Dublin: P King, P Connolly, Kevin Lougheed, Ger Brogan, W Fleming, S Page, P McGahon, Terry Jennings, Cyril Freaney, B Conboy, Des Ferguson 1-1, J Kelly 0-1, P Ryan 0-1, B Carney 0-2, D Redmond. Sub: G Guiden for Redmond.

1949

LEINSTER QUARTER-FINAL
May 8, Pearse Park, Longford
DUBLIN 8-2   LONGFORD 0-3
Dublin: S Moynihan, P Bell, M Hall, N Drumgoole, S Daly, J Farrell, S Page, M Gilmartin, T Mahoney, D Osborne 2-0, D Colfer 1-0, B Carney 0-1, B Morris 2-0, H O'Brien 3-1, M McEvoy.

LEINSTER SEMI-FINAL
July 10, O'Connor Park, Tullamore
DUBLIN 2-9   OFFALY 1-4
Dublin: S Moynihan, P Bell, M Hall, N Drumgoole, S Daly, J Farrell, S Page, B Carney 0-4, T Mahony, D Osborne 0-1, D Golfer, M. McEvoy, 0-1, B Morris 2-0, H O'Brien 0-2, C O'Leary 0-1.

LEINSTER FINAL
July 31, O'Moore Park, Portlaoise
DUBLIN 3-10   KILDARE 1-5
Dublin: S Moynihan, P Bell, M Hall, N Drumgoole, S Daly, J Farrell, S Page, H O'Brien 0-1, T Mahony, D Osborne 0-2, D Colfer 0-2, M McEvoy 1-0, B Morris 0-2, B Carney 1-1, C O'Leary 1-2.

ALL-IRELAND SEMI-FINAL
Aug 28, Austin Stack Park, Tralee
KERRY 1-9   DUBLIN 0-3
Dublin: S Moynihan, P Bell, M Hall, S Page, S Daly, J Farrell, N Drumgoole, H O'Brien, T Mahony, D Osborne, D Colfer, M McEvoy, B Morris, C O'Leary 0-2, B Carney 0-1.

1950

LEINSTER FIRST ROUND
May 7, Cusack Park, Mullingar
DUBLIN 2-9   KILDARE 1-8
Dublin: S Moynihan, P Bell, M Moylan, K Daly, S Daly, N O'Donnell, P Keogh, J Lenehan 0-1, M Wilson 0-5, D Osborne, D Colfer 2-1, P Blackburn, D O'Carroll 1-1, J Lowe 0-1, D Ivory.

LEINSTER QUARTER-FINAL
May 28, O'Moore Park, Portlaoise
DUBLIN 2-10   OFFALY 0-3
Dublin: S Moynihan, P Bell, M Moylan, K Daly, S Daly, N O'Donnell, E Duignan, J Lenehan, M Wilson 0-8, D Osborne, P Blackburn 0-1, D Colfer, D O'Carroll 2-0, J Lowe, D Ivory 0-1.

LEINSTER SEMI-FINAL
June 25, Croke Park, Dublin
DUBLIN 1-6   LOUTH 0-4
Dublin: S Moynihan, P Bell, M Moylan, K Daly, S Daly, N O'Donnell, E Duignan, M Wilson 0-3, M Fallon, D Doyle, D Osborne, P Blackburn, C Meehan, J Lenehan, D Ivory 0-3. Sub: R Healy 1-0 for Fallon.

LEINSTER FINAL
July 23, Croke Park, Dublin
WEXFORD 3-6   DUBLIN 2-8
Dublin: S Moynihan, P Bell, M Moylan, K Daly, S Daly 0-1, N O'Donnell, D Halpin, M Wilson 0-2, J Lenehan, D Osborne, D Doyle, P Blackburn 0-1, C Meehan 0-1, D Ivory 2-1, R Healy 0-2.

1951

LEINSTER FIRST ROUND
May 20, St Conleth's Park, Newbridge
OFFALY 1-5   DUBLIN 2-1
Dublin: W Taylor, D Fogarty, P Mahony, V Hyland, J Lowe, I Waldemeyer, K Markey, J Cronin, K Travers, K McLoughlin 0-1, C Meehan 1-0, D Bolger, T Fitzgerald, J Young 1-0, R Healy.

1952

LEINSTER QUARTER-FINAL
May 25, Drogheda Park, Drogheda
DUBLIN 2-4   MEATH 1-6
Dublin: W Taylor, J Lowe, D Bolger, T Gillen, P McGrath, D Brennan, B Deignan, B Fahy, P McDarby 0-1, K McLoughlin 1-2, A O'Carroll 1-0, B Heapes, J Fields 0-1, L Brady, W McDermott.

LEINSTER SEMI-FINAL
June 29, Cusack Park, Mullingar
WESTMEATH 3-9   DUBLIN 3-4
Dublin: W Taylor, D Bolger, T Gillen, J Lowe, P McGrath, D Brennan, B Deignan, P McDarby, B Fahy, K McLoughlin 1-2, A O'Carroll 0-1, B Heapes 0-1, L Lalor, L Brady, W McDermott 2-0.

1953

LEINSTER QUARTER-FINAL
May 24, Pairc Tailteann, Navan
DUBLIN 1-10   MEATH 1-4
Dublin: R Brady, J Ingle, G Power, F McHugh, J Brennan, PJ Considine, B Deignan, P Downey, B McLoughlin, V Bell 0-6, S Treacy, A O'Grady, A Kavanagh 1-1, L Lalor 0-1, J Freeney 0-2.

LEINSTER SEMI-FINAL
July 5, Croke Park, Dublin
LOUTH 1-10   DUBLIN 1-2
Dublin: R Brady, J Ingle, G Power, F McHugh, J Brennan, PJ Considine, B Deignan, P Downey, B McLoughlin, P Hipwell, S Treacy, V Lyons, A Kavanagh 0-1, L Lalor 1-0, J Freeney 0-1.

1954

LEINSTER QUARTER-FINAL
May 24, Drogheda Park, Drogheda
DUBLIN 3-3   LOUTH 1-6
Dublin: R Brady, M Bohan, D Sweeney, L Malone, T Bracken, N Boylan, T Wilson, B McLoughlin, P Heron, V Bell 1-1, A O'Grady, A Kavanagh 0-1, P Farnan 1-0, P Feeney 0-1, D Waters 1-0.

LEINSTER SEMI-FINAL
July 4, O'Moore Park, Portlaoise
DUBLIN 1-9   OFFALY 2-5
Dublin: R Brady, M Bohan, B O'Boyle, E Gilbert, T Bracken, N Boylan, D Sweeney, B McLoughlin 0-1, M Cronin, V Bell 1-2, P Farnan 0-1, A Kavanagh 0-3, T Nolan, P Feeney 0-2, A O'Grady.

LEINSTER FINAL
July 25, Croke Park, Dublin
DUBLIN 2-7   MEATH 0-11
Dublin: R Brady, M Bohan, B O'Boyle, D Sweeney, T Bracken, N Boylan, M Cronin, P Heron, B McLoughlin, V Bell 0-4, L Kavanagh 0-1, A Kavanngh, P Farnan 0-1, P Feeney, D Waters 2-1.

ALL-IRELAND SEMI-FINAL
Aug 22, Pearse Park, Longford
DUBLIN 3-12   MAYO 0-7
Dublin: R Brady, M Bohan, B O'Boyle, D Sweeney, T Bracken, N Boylan, M Cronin, B McLoughlin, P Heron 0-1, V Bell 2-2, P Feeney 0-1, A Kavanagh 0-5, G O'Reilly 1-1, P Farnan 0-2, D Waters.

ALL-IRELAND FINAL
Sep 26, Croke Park, Dublin
DUBLIN 3-3   KERRY 1-8
Dublin: Richie Brady, Mick Bohan, Brendan O'Boyle, Dermot Sweeney, Tommy Bracken, Noel Boylan, Michael Cronin, Brendan McLoughlin, Paddy Heron, Vinny Bell 1-1, Paddy Farnan 1-0, Aidan Kavanagh 1-0, Gerry O'Reilly 0-2, Paddy Feeney, David Waters. Sub: Eamonn Gilbert for Farnan, Vinny Lyons for O'Reilly.

1955

LEINSTER QUARTER-FINAL
May 22, St Conleth's Park, Newbridge
DUBLIN 1-7   CARLOW 1-4
Dublin: E Ryan, V Murphy 0-1, D Sweeney, D Hearns, R Doherty, F Giltan, J Graham, P Heron 0-4, J Lenehan, P Murphy, L Boyle 0-1, E Burgess, C Leaney, D Kennedy, T Nolan 1-1.

LEINSTER SEMI-FINAL
July 10, O'Moore Park, Port;aoise
DUBLIN 1-10   LOUTH 1-2
Dublin: E Ryan, V Murphy, P Sweeney, D Hearns, R Doherty, J Graham, L Foley 0-1, P Heron, S Bohan, P Murphy, J Lenehan 0-1, C McSweeney 0-3, T Nolan 0-1, G Wolfe 1-0, C Leaney 0-3. Sub: E Burgess 0-1 for Murphy.

LEINSTER FINAL
July 24, Croke Park, Dublin
DUBLIN 2-11   MEATH 1-4
Dublin: E Ryan, V Murphy, D Sweeney, D Hearns, R Doherty, S Graham, S Bohane, P Heron 0-2, L Foley, E Burgess, J Lenihan 1-5, C McSweeney 1-1, J Joyce 0-1, G Wolfe, C Leaney 0-2.

ALL-IRELAND SEMI-FINAL
Aug 21, Croke Park, Dublin
DUBLIN 3-7   ANTRIM 2-5
Dublin: E Ryan, V Murphy, D Sweeney, D Hearns, R Doherty, S Graham, C Jones, P Heron 0-2, L Foley, E Burgess 1-1, J Lenehan, C McSweeney 0-2, J Joyce, G Wolfe 1-0, C Leaney 1-2.

ALL-IRELAND FINAL
Sep 25, Croke Park, Dublin
DUBLIN 5-4   TIPPERARY 2-7
Dublin: Seamus Denigan, Vincent Murphy, Dermot Sweeney, Des Hearns, Ray Doherty, Seamus Graham, Christy Jones, Paddy Heron, Lar Foley 0-1, Eamonn Burgess 1-0, Joe Lenihan, Con McSweeney 1-0, Johnny Joyce 2-1, Gerry Wolfe, Christy Leaney 1-2. Sub. Leo Boyle for Wolfe.

1956

LEINSTER QUARTER-FINAL
May 27, St Patrick's Park, Enniscorthy
DUBLIN 1-13   CARLOW 0-3
Dublin: D Creed, K Russell, D Hearns, E Talbot, R Doherty, M Coshel, F Kavanagh, L Foley 0-2, J Lenehan 0-2, L Boyle 0-1, B McCrea 0-1, N Fox 0-4, D Foley 0-1, G Wolfe 0-1, C Leaney 1-1.

LEINSTER SEMI-FINAL
June 24, Dr Cullen Park, Carlow
DUBLIN 2-11   WESTMEATH 3-2
Dublin: D Creed, A Talbot, D Hearns, R Farrell, R Doherty, D Cashel, F Kavanagh, L Foley 0-1, D Foley 0-3, L Boyle 0-3, J Lenehan 1-1, N Fox, M Brierly, G Wolfe 0-1, C Leaney 1-2.

LEINSTER FINAL
July 22, Croke Park, Dublin
DUBLIN 1-10   MEATH 1-9
Dublin: D Creed, P Lacey, D Hearns, E Talbot, R Doherty, D Cashel, F Kavanagh, L Foley 0-6, D Foley, L Boyle, J Lenehan, N Fox, P Dennis 1-0, G Wolfe 0-1, C Leaney 0-1. Subs: B McCrea 0-1 for Lenehan, N Shanahan 0-1 for Kavanagh.

ALL-IRELAND SEMI-FINAL
Aug 19, O'Moore Park, Portlaoise
DUBLIN 1-13   LIMERICK 2-5
Dublin: J Creed, A Talbot, P Lacey, D Hearns, R Doherty, D Cashel, F Kavanagh, D Foley, L Foley 0-4, B McCrea, J Lenehan, N Fox 0-1, J Brogan 1-0, G Wolfe 0-2 C Leaney 0-6.

ALL-IRELAND FINAL
Oct 7, Croke Park, Dublin
DUBLIN 5-14   LEITRIM 2-2
Dublin: Dermot Creed, Angus Talbot, Pat Lacey, Des Hearns, Ray Doherty, David Cashel, Fred Kavanagh, Lar Foley (capt) 0-2, Joe Lenihan, Jim Brogan 0-1, Des Foley 1-4, Noel Fox 1-4, Bob McCrea 1-1, Gerry Wolfe 1-1, Christy Leaney 1-1. Sub: Pat Dennis for Wolfe.

1957

LEINSTER QUARTER-FINAL
June 2, Cusack Park, Mullingar
LONGFORD 0-9   DUBLIN 1-4
Dublin: C Donnelly, P Hallinan, C Curran, D Mulligan, J Murphy, D McKane 1-1, P Foley, P Moran, D Foley, C Fanning 0-1, B Rice, N Fox 0-2, P Gargan, P Hyland, D O'Brien.

1958

LEINSTER QUARTER-FINAL
June 1, Gaelic Park, Drogheda
DUBLIN 3-9   MEATH 2-4
Dublin: K Donnelly, S Ryan, P Holden, D Mulligan, D Jones, T Whelan, M Kissane, D Foley, T O'Reilly, B McDonald, P Taylor 0-2, N Fox 0-1, J Sweeney 3-2, J Gibney, B Beggs 0-4.

LEINSTER SEMI-FINAL
June 22, O'Moore Park, Portlaoise
DUBLIN 0-15   CARLOW 0-2
Dublin: K Donnelly, S Ryan, P Holden, D Mulligan, D Jones, T Whelan, M Kissane, D Foley 0-2, T O'Reilly, P Taylor 0-3, B McDonald 0-1, N Fox 0-1, J Sweeney 0-1, L Purcell 0-2, B Beggs 0-5.

LEINSTER FINAL
July 20, Pairc Tailteann, Navan
DUBLIN 2-10   LOUTH 1-6
Dublin: K Donnelly, N Joyce, P Holden, D Mulligan, D Jones, T Whelan, M Kissane, D Foley 0-1, T O'Reilly, P Taylor, B McDonald 0-1, N Fox 0-3, J Sweeney 1-0, L Purcell 1-0, B Beggs 0-2. Sub: J Gilroy 0-1 for O'Reilly.

ALL-IRELAND SEMI-FINAL
Aug 31, Pairc Tailteann, Navan
DUBLIN 3-5   DOWN 0-9
Dublin: K Donnelly, N Joyce, P Holden, D Mulligan, D Jones, T Whelan, M Kissane, T O'Reilly, D Foley 0-3, P Taylor 0-2, B McDonald 1-0, N Fox, L Purcell, J Gilroy, B Beggs. Subs: J Sweeney 2-0 for Purcell, T O'Connor for O'Reilly.

ALL-IRELAND FINAL
Sep 28, Croke Park, Dublin
DUBLIN 2-10   MAYO 0-8
Dublin: Kieran Donnelly, Noel Joyce, Paddy Holden, Donal Mulligan, Derek Jones, Tony Whelan, Mick Kissane, Des Foley 1-4, Tom O'Reilly, Paddy Taylor, Noel Fox 1-3, Brian McDonald, Jimmy Sweeney 0-1, Jackie Gilroy, Brian Beggs 0-2. Sub: Simon Behan for Taylor.

1959

LEINSTER QUARTER-FINAL
May 24, O'Moore Park, Portlaoise
DUBLIN 4-10   WEXFORD 3-3
Dublin: P Talbot, A Doran, E Grainger, J O'Malley, M Campion, M Kissane, F Byrne, J Dowling, J Levins, S Behan 1-1, B McDonald 1-2, P Taylor 0-1, J McKetterick 1-0, G McCabe 1-2, S Coen 0-4.

LEINSTER SEMI-FINAL
July 5, Pairc Tailteann, Navan
DUBLIN 5-8   LOUTH 1-6
Dublin: P Talbot, A Doran, E Grainger, J O'Malley, M Campion, M Kissane, F Byrne, J Dowling, P Delaney 0-1, S Behan 0-1, B McDonald 1-2, P Taylor, J McKetterick, G McCabe 0-1, S Coen 1-3.

LEINSTER FINAL
Aug 2, O'Connor Park, Tullamore
DUBLIN 3-13   OFFALY 1-7
Dublin: P Talbot, E Grainger, A Doran, F McCourt, M Campion, M Kissane, F Byrne, J Levins, S Behan 0-1, P Delaney, B McDonald 2-1, J Dowling 0-3, J McKettrick 1-1, G McCabe 0-1, S Coen 0-5.

ALL-IRELAND SEMI-FINAL
Aug 16, Croke Park, Dublin
DUBLIN 1-12   CORK 1-8
Dublin: P Talbot, E Grainger, A Doran, F McCourt, M Campion, M Kissane, F Byrne, S Behan, J Levins, P Delaney 0-4, B McDonald 0-1, J Dowling 1-1, J McKettrick 0-1, G McCabe, S Coen 0-5.

ALL-IRELAND FINAL
Sep 27, Croke Park, Dublin
DUBLIN 0-11   CAVAN 1-4
Dublin: Pat Talbot, Eddie Grainger, Alan Doran, Fergal

McCourt, Mick Campion, Mick Kissane, Frank Byrne, Simon Behan, Joe Levins 0-2, Paddy Delaney 0-3, Brian McDonald 0-2, John Dowling, Jim McKettrick, Gerry McCabe 0-2, Sean Coen 0-1. Subs: Brian Cooney for McKettrick, Paddy Taylor 0-1 for Behan.

1960

LEINSTER QUARTER-FINAL
May 29, Cusack Park, Mullingar
DUBLIN 1-9   MEATH 1-6
Dublin: G Smith, D O'Shea, P O'Boyle, L Carr, E Gargan, A Halpin, B Casey 1-0, J Levins, T Boden, P Maguire 0-7, D Keenan 0-1, T McEntaggart, G Hughes, A Donnelly, J O'Brien 0-1.

LEINSTER SEMI-FINAL
June 26, O'Moore Park, Portlaoise
OFFALY 1-13   DUBLIN 0-9
Dublin: G Smith, P Carron, P O'Boyle, L Carr, E Gargan, D Keane, A Halpin, B Casey, J Levins, P Maguire 0-3, S Gilsenan 0-1, T McEntaggart, F Jenkins 0-2, T Fitzsimons 0-1, S O'Brien 0-2.

1961

LEINSTER QUARTER-FINAL
June 25, Dr Cullen Park, Carlow
DUBLIN 1-5   WEXFORD 1-3
Dublin: B Scully, B Groves, J Burke, J Connolly, D Gahan, B Casey, J Lynam, T Lane, V Lacey, M Smith, S Marry 0-2, A Donnelly 0-2, K Hutchinson, D Keenan, T McEntaggart 1-1.

LEINSTER SEMI-FINAL
July 9, Pairc Tailteann, Navan
DUBLIN 2-8   MEATH 0-12
Dublin: B Scully, B Groves, S Burke, J Connolly, N Fahey, J Lynam, G Freyne 1-0, B Casey, J Wright, K Hutchinson, A Donnelly 0-2, P Farrell 0-3, M Smith 1-0, D Keenan, M McHugh 0-3.

LEINSTER FINAL
July 23, O'Moore Park, Portlaoise
DUBLIN 2-8   OFFALY 1-8
Dublin: B Scully, B Groves, D Gahan, T Connolly, J Lynam, B Casey, N Fahy, J Wright, A Donnelly 1-0, P Farrell, E Flynn 0-6, K Hutchinson, M Smith, D Keenan 1-2, G Freyne.

ALL-IRELAND SEMI-FINAL
Aug 20, Croke Park, Dublin
MAYO 1-10   DUBLIN 2-6
Dublin: B Scully, B Groves, D Gahan, J Connolly, J Burke, B Casey, E Fahy, A Donnelly 0-4, V Lucey, P Farrell, E Flynn 0-1, K Hutchinson, M Smith, D Keenan 2-1, G Frayne. Sub: J Wright for Burke.

1962

LEINSTER QUARTER-FINAL
June 24, Croke Park, Dublin
DUBLIN 2-8   LOUTH 1-4
Dublin: S Devine, F Grimes, B Groves, N Fahey, J Kelly, J Kennedy, T Cushion, J Rooney, B Leggett, P Farrell, E Flynn 1-5, K Hutchinson, T Higgins, G Kavanagh 1-0, P Ennis 0-1.

LEINSTER SEMI-FINAL
July 8, Cusack Park, Mullingar
DUBLIN 0-11   WESTMEATH 0-5
Dublin: P Devine, D Fitzgerald, F Grimes, N Fahey, J Kelly, J Kennedy, T Cushion, B Leggatt, J Rooney 0-1, C Dowling 0-1, E Flynn 0-5, K Hutchinson 0-1, L McDermott 0-1, G Kavanagh 0-1, P Ennis. Sub: P Farrell for Dowling.

LEINSTER FINAL
July 15, Croke Park, Dublin
OFFALY 2-8   DUBLIN 1-4
Dublin: S Devine, B Groves, F Grimes, N Fahey, J Kelly, J Kennedy, T Cushion, B Leggett 0-1, M Foley, P Farrell, J Rooney, E Flynn 0-1, C Dowing 0-1, G Kavanagh 1-1, P Ennis. Subs: K Hutchinson for Ennis, D Fitzgerald for Kelly, B O'Donoghue for Cushion.

1963

LEINSTER QUARTER-FINAL
June 16, Pairc Tailtean, Navan
DUBLIN 2-8   MEATH 0-5
Dublin: E Murphy, B Dowling, L Heaney, S Fagan, T Hanohoe, D Fitzgerald, D Smith, T Connolly, J Keaveney, F Brady 0-1, A Fetherstone 0-2, K Hutchinson 1-1, S Donovan 0-3, S O'Connor 0-1, N McInerney 1-0.

LEINSTER SEMI-FINAL
July 14, Croke Park, Dublin
DUBLIN 2-13   LOUTH 1-5
Dublin: A Farrell, B Dowling, L Heaney, P McNulty, T Hanohoe, D Fitzgerald, D Smith, J Keaveney 0-2, T Donnelly, J Brady 0-1, A Fetherstone 0-2, K Hutchlnson 1-0, S. Donovan 0-2, S O'Connor 1-4, N McInerney 0-2.

LEINSTER FINAL
Aug 4, O'Connor Park, Tullamore
WESTMEATH 2-14   DUBLIN 3-7
Dublin: A Farrell, B Dowling, L Heaney, S Fagan, T Hanahoe, D Fitzgerald, D Smith, J Keaveney 0-2, T Donnelly 0-1, J Brady 1-2, A Fetherstone, K Hutchinson, S Donovan, S O'Connor 1-2, N McInerney 1-0.

1964

LEINSTER QUARTER-FINAL
June 21, O'Connor Park, Tullamore
DUBLIN 4-7   CARLOW 2-6
Dublin: L Murray, J Branley, J McEvoy, G Stoker, B O'Shea, D Devitt, N McInerney, M Kelleher 0-1, M Kennedy, J Hannon, D Bollard 1-2, V Black 0-2, P Kennedy 1-0, J Keane 1-1, M Hannick 0-1, T Bassett. Sub: E Farrelly 1-0 for Hannon.

LEINSTER SEMI-FINAL
July 5, O'Connor Park, Tullamore
LAOIS 3-7   DUBLIN 2-5
Dublin: L Murray, D Devitt, B O'Shea, J McEvoy, N McInerney, J Branley, M Kelleher, J Keane, M Kennedy, D Bollard 0-3, J Hannon 0-1, V Black, C Doran, M Hannick 1-0, T Bassett 1-0. Sub: E Farrelly 0-1 for Doran.

1965

LEINSTER QUARTER-FINAL
May 30, Dr Cullen Park, Carlow
DUBLIN 2-11   WEXFORD 0-2
Dublin: R Gunning, D Kelleher, B Lennon, S Blood, S Conlon, M Bracken, M Kelleher, D Devitt 0-3, S Donnolly 0-1, T Bassett, J Hannon, P Kennedy 0-2, C Doran 0-2, E Mullins 0-1, F McDonald 2-1. Sub: E Davey 0-1 for Hannon.

LEINSTER SEMI-FINAL
July 4, Croke Park, Dublin
KILDARE 1-7   DUBLIN 0-8
Dublin: R Gunning, D Kelleher, R Lennon, S Blood, S Conlon, M Bracken, M Kelleher, D Devitt 0-1, S Donnelly, F Griffin 0-1, E Davey, P Kennedy, C Doran 0-4, E Mullins 0-2, F McDonald.

1966

LEINSTER QUARTER-FINAL
June 26, O'Connor Park, Tullamore
LONGFORD 3-9   DUBLIN 4-2
Dublin: K Barry, C Hogan, M Clancy, J Gallen, P McCarthy, F Lennon, C Pierce, F Quinn, T Redmond, H Dalton, D Coburn, R O'Hanlon 1-0, S Conlon, E Hayden 3-1, F McDonald 0-1. Sub: K Hegarty for Redmond.

1967

LEINSTER QUARTER-FINAL
June 25, Cusack Park, Mullingar
DUBLIN 4-7   WESTMEATH 1-5
Dublin: A Thompson, P Cooney, C Hogan, J Gallen, M Allen, B McLoughlin, J Hackett, J Martin 0-1, M Fitzpatrick 0-1, J Reilly, J Woodhead 0-3, K McConnell 0-1, P Dunne, N Redmond 3-0, B Lee 1-1.

LEINSTER SEMI-FINAL
July 23, Croke Park, Dublin
DUBLIN 3-5   MEATH 2-4
Dublin: A Thompson, C Hogan, S Roche, J Gallen, S Lyons, B McLoughlin, J Hackett, J Martin 1-1, M Fitzpatrick, V Daly 1-1, J Reilly, J Woodhead 0-3, B Lee, N Redmond 1-0, P O'Brien. Subs: M Allen for Lyons, P Dunne for O'Brien, L Blood for Dunne.

LEINSTER FINAL
July 30, St Conleth's Park, Newbridge
LAOIS 1-8DUBLIN 2-4
Dublin: A Thompson, C Hogan, S Roche, J Gallen, M Allen, B McLoughlin, J Hackett, J Martin 0-1, M Fitzpatrick, J Reilly 0-1, L Blood, J Woodhead 0-1, B Lee, N Redmond 1-0, V Daly 0-1. Subs: K Hegarty 1-0 for L Blood, Blood for Lee.

1968

LEINSTER QUARTER-FINAL
June 30, Cusack Park, Mullingar
DUBLIN 1-10   LONGFORD 0-12
Dublin: M Nolan, M Corcoran, L Sweeney, D Kane, P O'Neill, C Hanley, D Hickey, M Fitzpatrick 1-0, J Furlong 0-1, V Daly 0-3, J Reilly 0-4, K Manning, B Lee 0-1, N Redmond, P Rooney 0-1. Sub: P Gogarty for Redmond.

LEINSTER SEMI-FINAL
July 11, Pairc Tailteann, Navan
DUBLIN 0-9   MEATH 0-8
Dublin: M Nolan, M Corcoran, L Sweeney, D Kane, P O'Neill, C Maher, D Hickey, M Fitzpatrick 0-1, J Furlong, V Daly 0-2, J Reilly 0-4, K Manning, B Lee 0-1, P Gogarty. Sub: P Rooney 0-1 for Manning.

LEINSTER FINAL
July 21, Croke Park, Dublin
DUBLIN 1-11   LAOIS 0-8
Dublin: M Nolan, M Corcoran, L Sweeney, D Kane, P Thomas, P O'Neill, D Hickey 0-1, M Fitzpatrick, J Furlong, J Reilly 0-6, P Gogarty 0-3, C Hanley, B Lee 1-0, N Redmond, P Rooney 0-1. Subs: G Moore for Corcoran, P Twomey for Thomas.

ALL-IRELAND SEMI-FINAL
Aug 4, Croke Park, Dublin
CORK 2-10   DUBLIN 1-6
Dublin: M Nolan, N Redmond, L Sweeney, D Kane, C Hanley, P O'Neill, D Hickey, M Fitzpatrick, J Furlong, J Reilly 0-5, P Gogarty 0-1, P Twomey, B Lee, J Kennedy, V Daly 1-0.

1969

LEINSTER QUARTER-FINAL
May 4, Dr Cullen Park, Carlow
DUBLIN 1-12   LAOIS 1-4
Dublin: J Egan, M Corcoran, L Sweeney, G O'Connor, J Broe, R Kelleher, J Clarke, D Hickey 0-1, D Duff, K Donoghue 0-2, F Reynolds 0-3, K Manning 1-1, M Leonard 0-2, J O'Neill 0-2, B Kenna 0-1.

LEINSTER SEMI-FINAL
July 10, Croke Park, Dublin
DUBLIN 1-12   MEATH 2-6
Dublin: J Egan, M Corcoran, L Sweeney, G O'Connor, J Clarke, R Kelleher, J Broe, D Hickey 0-1, D Duff, K Donoghue 0-2, F Reynolds, K Manning 0-2, M Leonard 1-1, J O'Neill, B Kenna 0-3. Sub: L Martin 0-3 for Reynolds.

LEINSTER FINAL
Aug 10, Dr Cullen Park, Carlow
WEXFORD 0-11   DUBLIN 0-7
Dublin: E McNaney, M Corcoran, L Sweeney 0-1, G O'Connor, M McManaman, R Kelleher 0-1, J Broe, D Hickey, D Duff 0-1, K Donoghue, L Martin, K Manning 0-1, M Leonard 0-1, J O'Neill, B Kenna 0-2.

1970

LEINSTER QUARTER-FINAL
May 17, Cusack Park, Mullingar
DUBLIN 3-12   LONGFORD 0-2
Dublin: T Byrne, P Hurley, D Carberry, K Synnott, D Daly, V Lambe, S Davenport, PJ Reid, D Clarke, P Lee 0-1, P Duggan 1-2, J Finucane 0-2, S McCarthy 1-1, N Kilroy 0-3, P Hickey 1-3.

LEINSTER SEMI-FINAL
July 12, Cusack Park, Mullingar
DUBLIN 3-9   OFFALY 1-5
Dublin: T Byrne, P Hurley, D Carberry, T Williams, D Daly 0-1, V Lambe, S Davenport, PJ Reld 0-1, P Byrne, P Duggan 0-2, D Clarke 2-0, J Finucane, S McCarthy 0-2, N Kilroy 1-0, P Hickey 0-3.

LEINSTER FINAL
July 19, Croke Park, Dublin
DUBLIN 2-8   MEATH 0-13
Dublin: T Byrne, P Hurley, D Carberry, T Williams, D Daly, V Lambe, V Holden, PJ Reid, P Byrne, P Duggan 0-2, D Clarke 0-1, J Finucane, S McCarthy, N Kilroy 1-0, P Hickey 1-5. Subs: S Davenport for Holden, Holden for Davenport.

ALL-IRELAND SEMI-FINAL
Aug 9, Croke Park, Dublin
GALWAY 3-12   DUBLIN 0-10
Dublin: T Byrne, P Hurley, D Carberry, T Williams, D Daly, V Lambe, V Holden, PJ Reid 0-2, D Clarke 0-2, P Duggan, P Byrne 0-2, J Finucane, S McCarthy 0-1, N Kilroy, P Hickey 0-3.

1971

LEINSTER QUARTER-FINAL
July 4, O'Moore Park, Portlaoise
DUBLIN 0-13   LAOIS 0-10
Dublin: T Fayne, D Billings, D Hobbs, G McCaul, P Glavey, V Holden, J Corcoran, J McCarthy 0-2, B Salmon, S McCarthy 0-1, P Hickey 0-4, D Redmond 0-1, M Hickey, M Holden 0-4, M O'Donoghue 0-1.

LEINSTER SEMI-FINAL
July 18, Croke Park, Dublin
DUBLIN 1-14   OFFALY 0-8
Dublin: T Fayne, D Billings, D Hobbs, G McCaul, P Glavey, V Holden, B Pocock, J McCarthy 0-1, B Salmon, S McCarthy 0-3, P Hickey 0-5, D Redmond 1-2, M Hickey 0-2, M Holden, M O'Donoghue 0-1.

LEINSTER FINAL
July 25, Croke Park, Dublin
DUBLIN 2-7   LOUTH 0-4
Dublin: T Fayne, D Billings, D Hobbs, G McCaul, P Glavey, V Holden, B Pocock, J McCarthy, B Salmon, S McCarthy 1-1, P Hickey 0-2, D Redmond 0-1, M Hickey 1-1, M Holden 0-2, M O'Donoghue.

ALL-IRELAND SEMI-FINAL
Aug 22, Croke Park, Dublin
CORK 2-13   DUBLIN 1-10
Dublin: T Fayne, D Billings, D Hobbs, G McCaul, P Glavey, V Holden, B Pocock 0-1, S McCarthy 0-1, B Salmon   M O'Donoghue, P Hickey 0-1, D Redmond 1-1, M Hickey 0-4, M Holden 0-1, J McCarthy 0-1. Subs: D Murray for Glavey, C O'Donoghue for M. O'Donoghue.

1972

LEINSTER QUARTER-FINAL
May 7, St. Loman's Park, Trim
DUBLIN 4-9   WESTMEATH 3-6
Dublin: T Fayne, W Allen, P Shatwell, G McCaul, B Mullins, M Holden, G O'Connor, P Rooney, J Devitt, S McCarthy 0-1, M Hickey 1-4, P Connellan, M O'Donoghue 1-2, J Corcoran 1-2, M Price 1-0. Sub: M Martin for O'Connor.

LEINSTER SEMI-FINAL
July 16, Dr Cullen Park, Carlow
DUBLIN 1-11   WEXFORD 0-6
Dublin: J Conway, B Fitzpatrck, P Shatwell, G McCaul, G O'Connor, M Holden, M Martin, B Mullins

0-1, P Rooney 0-1, P Connellan 0-3, M Hickey 0-4, S McCarthy, M O'Donoghue 1-0, J Corcoran 0-1, M Price 0-1. Sub: P Reaney 0-1 for McCarthy.

LEINSTER FINAL
July 23, Croke Park, Dublin
MEATH 3-8   DUBLIN 1-10
Dublin: J Conway, B Fitzpatrick, P Shatwell, G McCaul, G O'Connor, M Holden 0-1, M Martin, B Mullins, P Rooney, P Connellan 0-2, M Hickey 0-2, S McCarthy 0-1, M O'Donoghue 1-2, J Corcoran, M Price 0-2. Subs: B Lee for Conway, W Allen for Corcoran, P Markey for Connellan.

1973

LEINSTER FIRST ROUND
May 20, Wexford Park, Wexford
DUBLIN 2-11   WEXFORD 2-11
Dublin: J Nolan, J Sutton, J Thompson, T Clancy, F Caverly, T Noone, M Martin, R O'Reilly, S Corry, P Dalton, P Quinn 0-2, M Fogarty 0-1, J Carr 1-5, T Lynch, D O'Reilly 0-2.

LEINSTER FIRST ROUND REPLAY
June 27, Parnell Park, Dublin
DUBLIN 0-17   WEXFORD 0-9
Dublin: J Nolan, J Thompson, T Clancy, M Martin, F Caverly, T Noone, S Corry, J Lynskey 0-2, P Rooney 0-1, P Quinn 0-2, M Fogarty 0-1, P Woods, J Carr 0-9, T Lynch, D O'Reilly 0-2.

LEINSTER QUARTER-FINAL
July 5, Pairc Tailteann, Navan
LOUTH 2-9   DUBLIN 1-6
Dublin: J Nolan, J Sutton, J Thompson, T Clancy, F Caverly, T Noone, M Martin, R O'Reilly, S Corry, P Dalton, P Quinn, M Fogarty, J Carr 0-4, T Lynch, D O'Reilly. Subs: P Woods 1-1 for Quinn, J Lynskey 0-1 for Lynch.

1974

LEINSTER PRELIMINARY ROUND
May 26, Croke Park, Dublin
DUBLIN 1-7   WEXFORD 1-6
Dublin: D Lowry, D O'Sullivan, J Thompson, T O'Connor, M Monaghan, E Lynch, L Redmond, D Moloney 0-1, T Rooney 0-1, J Lynskey 0-1, C Maher 0-2, D Kavanagh 1-0, J Carr 0-2, M Hurley, J Quinn.

LEINSTER FIRST ROUND
June 30, Croke Park, Dublin
DUBLIN 1-12   LOUTH 0-5
Dublin: D Lowry, T O'Connor, J Thompson, D O'Sullivan, E Lynch, B Cooper, L Redmond, J Lynskey

0-1, T Rooney 0-1, J Carr 0-3, C Maher 0-1, D Gaffney, D Kavanagh 0-2, N Heeney, J Quinn 1-3. Sub: D. Flanagan 0-1 for Gaffney.

LEINSTER QUARTER-FINAL
July 7, O'Moore Park, Portlaoise
DUBLIN 1-7   OFFALY 1-6
Dublin: D Lowry, T O'Connor, J Thompson, D O'Sullivan, E Lynch, B Cooper, L Redmond, J Lynskey 0-2, T Rooney, J Carr 0-3, C Maher, D Gaffney 0-1, D Kavanagh, M Heeney, J Quinn 1-1.

LEINSTER SEMI-FINAL
July 14, Croke Park, Dublin
LONGFORD 0-12   DUBLIN 0-6
Dublin: D Lowry, D O'Sullivan, J Thompson 0-2, M Monaghan, E Lynch, B Cooper, L Redmond, J Lynskey 0-1, N Heeney 0-1, C Fagan, C Maher, D Gaffney, J Carr 0-2, M Hurley, J Quinn.

1975

LEINSTER QUARTER-FINAL
June 8, Dr Cullen Park, Carlow
DUBLIN 1-12   WEXFORD 0-8
Dublin: N Fitzgerald, M Kennedy, A White, P Timmons, E Lynch, C Richardson, P Delahunty, D Hanrahan 0-1, P Dunne 0-1, P Grimes 0-1, J Kennedy 0-4, D Gaffney 0-1, C Fagan, A O'Neill 0-3, J Quinn 1-1.

LEINSTER SEMI-FINAL
July 6, Pairc Tailteann, Navan
MEATH 2-8   DUBLIN 0-8
Dublin: N Fitzgerald, M Kennedy, A White, P Timmons, E Lynch, C Richardson, P Delahunty, D Hanrahan, P Dunne, P Grimes, J Kennedy 0-6, D Gaffney, C Fagan, A O'Neill 0-1, J Quinn 0-1.

1976

LEINSTER QUARTER-FINAL
June 27, Cusack Park, Mullingar
DUBLIN 2-11   LONGFORD 2-6
Dublin: S Fox, B Sarsfield, M Kennedy, T Foran 0-1, A Hendrick, C Murphy, C Roche, H Donnelly 0-1, M Farrelly 1-0, L Broderick, J Finnegan 0-1, P Grimes 0-1, D McGrath, M Dwyer, P Ryan 1-6. Sub: M Bollard 0-1 for Dwyer.

LEINSTER SEMI-FINAL
July 11, O'Connor Park, Tullamore
DUBLIN 0-10   KILDARE 0-9
Dublin: S Fox, B Sarsfield, M Kennedy, T Foran, P Grimes, C Murphy, C Roche, H Donnelly, M Farrelly 0-1, L Broderick 0-2, J Finnegan 0-1, D McGrath, P Ryan 0-4, M Dwyer, M Bollard 0-2.

LEINSTER FINAL
July 25, Croke Park, Dublin
DUBLIN 2-8   OFFALY 0-13
Dublin: S Fox, B Sarsfield, M Kennedy, T Foran, P Grimes, C Murphy, C Roche, H Donnelly, M Farrelly, L Broderick, J Finnegan, D McGrath 1-0, P Ryan 1-5, M Dwyer 0-2, M Bollard 0-1. Sub: D Murphy for Murphy.

ALL-IRELAND SEMI-FINAL
Aug 29, Croke Park, Dublin
GALWAY 2-8   DUBLIN 2-7
Dublin: S Fox, B Sarsfield, M Kennedy, D Murphy, P Grimes, T Foran, C Roche, H Donnelly, M Farrelly, L Broderick 0-4, J Finnegan, M Bollard, P Ryan 1-2, M Dwyer 1-0, D McGrath 0-1. Subs: C Murphy for Foran, K Murphy for Bollard.

1977

LEINSTER QUARTER-FINAL
May 29, Pairc Tailteann, Navan
DUBLIN 0-12   KILDARE 0-8
Dublin: P O'Toole R O'Farrell, P Canavan, W Hughes, B Byrne, D Foran, F Devlin, D Conroy 0-1, J Roynane, A McCaul 0-2, J Finnegan 0-3, S Moylan 0-1, N Gaffney 0-3, M Dwyer 0-2, R Griffin.

LEINSTER SEMI-FINAL
July 3, Dr Cullen Park, Carlow
DUBLIN 0-16   OFFALY 1-3
Dublin: P O'Toole R O'Farrell, P Canavan, W Hughes, B Byrne, D Foran, F Devlin, S Lavin, J Roynane, A McCaul 0-5, J Finnegan 0-5, S Moylan 0-1, N Gaffney 0-4, M Dwyer 0-1, R Griffin.

LEINSTER FINAL
July 31, Croke Park, Dublin
MEATH 1-7   DUBLIN 0-9
Dublin: P O'Toole, R O'Farrell, P Canavan, W Hughes, B Byrne, D Foran, F Devlin, J Ronayne 0-1, S Lavin 0-1, A McCaul 0-1, J Finnegan 0-2, S Moylan, N Gaffney 0-4, M Dwyer, C Griffin. Subs: D Conroy for Moylan, D Hurley for Lavin.

1978

LEINSTER QUARTER-FINAL
June 24, Pairc Tailteann, Navan
DUBLIN 5-14   WESTMEATH 1-5
Dublin: P O'Toole, S Fleming, A Stokes, K Barry, F Walsh, P Canavan, T Mannion, J Kelly, A White 0-1, P Burke 1-0, M Loftus 0-2, C Griffin 0-3, N Gaffney 1-4, B Rock 3-2, D Carr 0-1. Sub: A Lehane 0-1 for Kelly.

LEINSTER SEMI-FINAL
July 9, Croke Park, Dublin
DUBLIN 2-13   LONGFORD 1-7
Dublin: P O'Toole, F Walsh, P Canavan, C Finnegan, K Byrne, S Fleming, T Mannion, J Kelly, A White, C Duff, M Loftus 0-2, C Griffin 0-1, N Gaffney 0-5, B Rock 1-3, K Barry 1-2.

LEINSTER FINAL
July 30, Croke Park, Dublin
DUBLIN 3-12   WEXFORD 0-11
Dublin: P O'Toole, F Walsh, P Canavan, C Finnegan, K Byrne, S Fleming, T Mannion 0-1, J Kelly, J Magee, C Duff 1-3, M Loftus 0-1, C Griffin 0-1, N Gaffney 1-1, B Rock 0-4, K Barry 1-1. Sub: A Lehane for Magee.

ALL-IRELAND SEMI-FINAL
Aug 20, Croke Park, Dublin
DUBLIN 5-7   TYRONE 1-9
Dublin: P O'Toole, F Walsh, P Canavan, C Finnegan, K Byrne, S Fleming, T Mannion, J Kelly, A White, C Duff 0-3, M Loftus 1-0, C Griffin 1-1, N Gaffney 2-0, B Rock 1-3, K Barry.

ALL-IRELAND FINAL
Sep 24, Croke Park, Dublin
MAYO 4-9   DUBLIN 3-8
Dublin: Paul O'Toole, Frank Walsh, Pat Canavan, Conor Finnegan, Ken Byrne, Shay Fleming, Tommy Mannion, John Kelly, Anthony White, Ciaran Duff 0-1, Mick Loftus 1-0, Ciaran Griffin, Niall Gaffney 1-1, Barney Rock 1-6, Kevin Barry. Subs: Dermot Deasy for Kelly.

1979

LEINSTER QUARTER-FINAL
June 20, Pairc Tailteann, Navan
DUBLIN 4-13   LOUTH 0-6
Dublin: J O'Leary, J Grace, C Finnegan, S Wade, D Murphy, B Kavanagh, C Eustace, P Boylan 1-2, M Cooke, C Buffini 0-2, M Loftus 0-2, C Duff 0-3, K Barry 0-1, B Jordan 2-2, P McLoughlin 1-1.

LEINSTER SEMI-FINAL
July 1, St Conleth's Park, Newbridge
DUBLIN 3-11   WEXFORD 0-8
Dublin: J O'Leary, J Grace, V Conroy, S Wade, C Finnegan, B Kavanagh, C Eustace, M Cooke, P Boylan 0-2, C Buffini, M Loftus 1-1, C Duff, B Jordan 1-1, B Rock 0-6, K Barry 1-1. Subs: P McLoughlin, for Cooke, G Barry for K Barry.

LEINSTER FINAL
July 29, Croke Park, Dublin
DUBLIN 2-13   MEATH 0-8
Dublin: J O'Leary, J Grace, V Conroy, S Wade, C Eustace, C Finnegan, D Murphy, B Rock 1-6, B Kavanagh, C

Buffini 0-2, K Barry 0-2, C Duff 0-1, B Jordan 0-1, P Boylan 1-0, M Loftus 0-1. Subs: M Cooke for Finnegan, D Murphy for Boylan, F Christie for Jordan.

ALL-IRELAND SEMI-FINAL
Aug 19, Croke Park, Dublin
DUBLIN 0-8   MAYO 0-7
Dublin: J O'Leary, J Grace, V Conroy, S Wade, C Eustace, C Finnegan, Derek Murphy, B Kavanagh, P Boylan 0-1, B Jordan 0-2, K Barry 0-2, C Duff, C Buffini, B Rock 0-1, M Loftus 0-1. Sub: Dermot Murphy 0-1 for Buffini.

ALL-IRELAND FINAL
Sep 16, Croke Park, Dublin
DUBLIN 0-10   KERRY 1-6
Dublin: John O'Leary, John Grace, Vincent Conroy, Stephen Wade, Colm Eustace, Conor Finnegan, Derek Murphy, Bernard Kavanagh 0-1, Pat Boylan, Brian Jordan 0-1, Mick Loftus (capt) 0-3, Ciaran Duff 0-1, Dermot Murphy, Barney Rock 0-4, Kevin Barry 0-1. Subs: Thomas Kelly for Grace, Pat McCabe for Derek Murphy.

1980

LEINSTER QUARTER-FINAL
June 28, Cusack Park, Mullingar
DUBLIN 2-6   LONGFORD 1-6
Dublin: B Stynes, F Cullen, R Dwyer, J Hayes, P O'Brien, CJ O'Neill, P Caffrey, M Galvin, K O'Doherty 0-1, G Richardson 1-0, B Jordan 0-1, S Loftus, C Buffini 0-4, D Jennings, T Quinn 1-0.

LEINSTER SEMI-FINAL
July 6, Pairc Tailteann, Navan
MEATH 3-7   DUBLIN 3-5
Dublin: B Stynes, F Coen, R Dwyer, J Hayes, P O'Brien, G O'Neill, P Caffrey, M Galvin, K O'Doherty 1-0, K Richardson, B Jordan 0-2, S Loftus C Buffini 0-3, D Jennings 1-0, T Quinn 1-0.

1981

LEINSTER QUARTER-FINAL
May 31, St Conleth's Park, Newbridge
DUBLIN 0-12   WICKLOW 2-5
Dublin: J McNally, J Hayes, E Mullarkey, P Brogan, B Cooke, G Keenan 0-1, M Deegan 0-1, S Loftus, M Galvin, D Sheehan 0-2, T Conroy 0-1, J Watson 0-2, M Coffey 0-3, P Molloy 0-2, C O'Farrell.

LEINSTER SEMI-FINAL
July 5, Croke Park, Dublin
DUBLIN 2-9   KILDARE 1-4
Dublin: J McNally, J Hayes, D Carroll, P Brogan,

B Cooke, G Keenan, M Deegan, S Loftus 0-3, T McCormack, M Coffey 0-3, T Conroy 1-0, P Flynn 1-2, D Sheehan, P Molloy, C O'Farrell. Subs: G Crowley for McCormack, R Mulvaney 0-1 for Molloy.

LEINSTER FINAL
July 26, Croke Park, Dublin
DUBLIN 1-8   MEATH 0-9
Dublin: J McNally, J Hayes, D Carroll, P Brogan, G Crowley, G Keenan, M Deegan, S Loftus 0-4, B Cooke, D Sheehan, M Coffey, P Flynn 0-1, B Redmond 0-3, T Conroy, C O'Farrell 1-0. Sub: T Lambe for Brogan.

ALL-IRELAND SEMI-FINAL
Aug 23, Croke Park, Dublin
DERRY 0-8   DUBLIN 0-6
Dublin: J McNally, E Mullarkey, D Carroll, D Synnott, G Crowley, G Keenan, M Deegan, S Loftus 0-2, B Cooke, D Sheehan 0-1, M Coffey, P Flynn 0-1, D Redmond 0-1, T Conroy, C O'Farrell. Subs: R Mulvaney for Coffey, P Molloy 0-1 for Conroy.

1982

LEINSTER QUARTER-FINAL
May 29, Parnell Park, Dublin
DUBLIN 0-10   MEATH 0-5
Dublin: J McNally, C Sage, F McGrath, L O'Rourke, E Heery, T Delaney, M Deegan, D Sheehan 0-4, N O'Sullivan 0-1, M Coffey, M Egan 0-2, B Redmond 0-1, P O'Carroll, T McCormack 0-1, M Barber. Subs: S O'Brien 0-1 for Redmond, B Cooke for O'Sullivan.

LEINSTER SEMI-FINAL
July 4, Pairc Tailteann, Navan
DUBLIN 2-14   WEXFORD 0-3
Dublin: J McNally, C Sage, F McGrath, L O'Rourke E Heery 0-2, T Delaney, M Deegan, B Cooke, D Sheehan 0-2, M Coffey 1-0, M Egan 1-5, N O'Sullivan 0-2, G Crowley 0-1, T McCormack 0-1, L Downey 0-1.

LEINSTER FINAL
Aug 1, Croke Park, Dublin
DUBLIN 0-10   WESTMEATH 0-4
Dublin: J McNally, C Sage, F McGrath, L O'Rourke, E Heery, T Delaney, M Deegan, B Cooke, D Sheehan 0-4, M Coffey 0-3, M Egan 0-1, N O'Sullivan, B Redmond, T McCormack 0-1, L Downey. Subs: S O'Brien 0-1 for O'Sullivan h/t.

ALL-IRELAND SEMI-FINAL
Aug 22, Croke Park, Dublin
DUBLIN 0-17   GALWAY 1-3
Dublin: J McNally, C Sage, F McGrath, L O'Rourke, E Heery, T Delaney, M Deegan, D Sheehan 0-3, B Cooke, M Coffey 0-4, M Egan 0-3, S O'Brien 0-3, P

O'Carroll 0-2, L Downey, B Redmond 0-2. Subs: G Crowley for Redmond, T Murphy for O'Carroll.

ALL-IRELAND FINAL
Sep 19, Croke Park, Dublin
DUBLIN 1-11   KERRY 1-5
Dublin: Joe McNally, Christy Sage, Frank McGrath, Liam O'Rourke (capt), Eamonn Heery, Tony Delaney, Mick Deegan 0-1, Declan Sheehan, Brendan Cooke 0-1, Martin Coffey 0-2, Mick Egan 0-2, Sean O'Brien 0-2, Paul O'Carroll 1-1, Tom McCormack, Brian Redmond 0-2. Sub: Tony Murphy for McCormack.

1983

LEINSTER FIRST ROUND
May 28, Parnell Park, Dublin
MEATH 2-7   DUBLIN 0-6
Dublin: C Sage, S Mulrooney, J Byrne, J Power, T Delaney 0-1, C McPartland, P McCarthy 0-2, P Godson, D Foley, B Gavin, D DeLappe, N Clancy 0-1, B Moore, D O'Brien 0-2, M Broderick.

1984

LEINSTER QUARTER-FINAL
May 26, Parnell Park, Dublin
DUBLIN 3-12   WEXFORD 0-9
Dublin: M Broderick, G Walsh, J Barry, C Walsh, A Martin, J Power, B McKeown, J Stynes, A McClean 0-2, N Clancy 2-2, P Robinson 0-1, J Fahy 0-1, P Clarke 0-4, D DeLappe, C Crowley 0-2. Sub: D Whelan 1-0 for DeLappe.

LEINSTER SEMI-FINAL
June 30, O'Connor Park, Tullamore
DUBLIN 1-14   LONGFORD 0-3
Dublin: M Broderick, G Walsh, J Barry, C Walsh, A Martin, J Power, B McKeown 1-0, A McLean, J Stynes 0-2, N Clancy 0-2, P Robinson 0-1, J Fahy 0-1, P Clarke 0-5, D DeLappe 0-2, C Crowley 0-1. Subs: M Crowley for Robinson, D Whelan for Clarke.

LEINSTER FINAL
July 22, Croke Park, Dublin
DUBLIN 0-12   WESTMEATH 1-6
Dublin: M Broderick, G Walsh, J Barry, C Walsh, A Martin 0-1, S Croghan, B McKeown, A McClean, J Stynes, N Clancy, P Robinson 0-2, D Whelan, P Clarke 0-6, D DeLappe 0-1, C Crowley. Subs: M Crowley 0-2 for Stynes, J Fahy for Whelan.

ALL-IRELAND SEMI-FINAL
Aug 19, Croke Park, Dublin
DUBLIN 0-14   DERRY 0-7
Dublin: M Broderick, G Walsh, J Barry, C Walsh, A

Martin, J Power, B McKeown, J Stynes 0-1, P Clarke 0-4, D DeLappe 0-3, P Robinson, J Fahy 0-1, N Clancy 0-2, M Crowley 0-2, C Crowley 0-1. Subs: A McLean for Robinson, P Daly for McKeown.

ALL-IRELAND FINAL
Sep 23 Croke Park, Dublin
DUBLIN 1-9   TIPPERARY 0-4
Dublin: Martin Broderick, Greg Walsh, John Barry, Ciaran Walsh, Albert Martin, John Power, Bob McKeon, Jim Stynes, Paul Clarke (capt) 0-3, David DeLappe 0-2, Alan McClean, James Fahy, Niall Clancy 1-2, Michael Crowley, Conor Crowley 0-2. Subs: Paul Daly for Walsh, David Whelan for McClean.

1985

LEINSTER QUARTER-FINAL
June 1, Wexford Park, Wexford
WEXFORD 0-9   DUBLIN 0-7
Dublin: M Broderick, P Moran, A McConnell, C Boyle, K Barr, S Barry, C O'Flynn, T Harford, S McCarthy 0-1, S O'Brien 0-2, D McCarthy 0-1, P O'Donoghue 0-1, D Shiels, P Robinson 0-2, P Kavanagh.

1986

LEINSTER QUARTER-FINAL
May 31, Parnell Park, Dublin
DUBLIN 0-15   KILDARE 0-6
Dublin: J McGrane, S Sammon, K Fagan, M Kavanagh, Keith Barr, N McGrane, B O'Hagan, J Madden 0-5, D Bolger, N Guidan 0-1, A O'Sullivan 0-3, R Nally 0-1, G Power 0-4, D McCarthy 0-1, C McEvoy. Sub: M Barnes for Nally 48.

LEINSTER SEMI-FINAL
June 29, Croke Park, Dublin
DUBLIN 2-10   LONGFORD 0-5
Dublin: J McGrane, S Sammon, K Fagan, M Kavanagh, K Barr 0-1, J Madden, B O'Hagan, B Burke 0-2, D Bolger, N Guiden 0-1, A O'Sullivan 2-0, S McCormack, G Butler 0-2, D McCarthy 0-1, C McEvoy 0-2. Subs: B Barnes for McCormack, R Nally 0-1 for Guiden.

LEINSTER FINAL
July 27, Croke Park, Dublin
DUBLIN 2-16   MEATH 0-6
Dublin: J McGrane, S Sammon, K Fagan, M Kavanagh, K Barr 0-1, J Madden, B O'Hagan, B Burke, D Bolger 0-1, N Guiden 1-0, A O'Sullivan 0-1, M Barnes, G Butler 1-6, D McCarthy 0-4, C McEvoy 0-3. Sub: S MacGabhann for Burke 55.

ALL-IRELAND SEMI-FINAL
Aug 24, Croke Park, Dublin
CORK 2-7 DUBLIN 0-8
Dublin: J McGrane, S Sammon, K Fagan, M Kavanagh, K Barr, J Madden, B O'Hagan, B Burke, D Bolger 0-1, N Guiden, A O'Sullivan 0-1, M Barnes, G Butler 0-3, D McCarthy C McEvoy 0-3. Subs: R Nally for McCarthy 22.

1987

LEINSTER QUARTER-FINAL
May 30, Parnell Park, Dublin
DUBLIN 2-8 WESTMEATH 2-6
Dublin: R Lillis, R Dodd, F Dardis, P Foley, T O'Boyle, P Curran, P McGarrity, F Lawlor, J Barr, P Ward, V Murphy 2-2, K Kielty 0-3, A McNally, M Barnes 0-2, P Galvin 0-1. Subs: R O'Doherty for Ward, D Quiniivan for Barr.

LEINSTER SEMI-FINAL
July 5, St Conleth's Park, Newbridge
DUBLIN 0-13 WICKLOW 0-7
Dublin: J McGrane, R Dodd, F Dardis, P Foley, T O'Boyle, P Curran, J Hayes, F Lawlor, J Barr, P Ward 0-1, V Murphy 0-2, K Kielty 0-8, A McNally 0-1, M Barnes 0-1, P Galvin. Sub: R O'Doherty for P Galvin.

LEINSTER FINAL
July 26, Croke Park, Dublin
KILDARE 0-13 DUBLIN 2-5
Dublin: R Lillis, R Dodd, F Dardis, P Foley, T O'Boyle, P Curran, P Brady, M Barnes 1-0, V Murphy 1-0, N Carter, J Barr 0-1, P Ward 0-1, A McNally, P McGeraghty 0-1, P Galvin 0-2. Subs: D Quinlivan for Barr 30, S Hayes for Dardis 45.

1988

LEINSTER QUARTER-FINAL
May 28, O'Moore Park, Portlaoise
DUBLIN 2-10 LAOIS 0-4
Dublin: D O'Farrell, P McManus, J Jordan, C Kavanagh, A Gavigan, G O'Regan, J Nolan, P Cassells, D Quinlivan, M Brady 0-1, B Stynes 1-3, A Keogh, D Farrell 0-3, S Moylan 1-3, B Barnes. Subs: S Cahill for Quinlivan 39, D Howard for Keogh 48.

LEINSTER SEMI-FINAL
June 26, Cusack Park, Mullingar
DUBLIN 2-15 WICKLOW 0-7
Dublin: D O'Farrell, P McManus, J Jordan, C Kavanagh, T Gavigan, B Murray, G O'Regan, P Cassells 0-1, D Quinlivan 0-1, D Howard 0-7, B Stynes 0-1, M Brady, D Farrell 2-3, S Moylan, B Barnes 0-2.

LEINSTER FINAL
July 31, Croke Park, Dublin
DUBLIN 4-6 MEATH 0-8
Dublin: D O'Farrell, P McManus, J Jordan, C Kavanagh, T O'Boyle, B Murray, G O'Regan, P Cassells, D Quinlivan, D Howard 1-2, B Stynes, M Brady, D Farrell 2-0, S Moylan 0-2, B Barnes 1-2. Subs: S Cahill for Cassells, G Murphy for Brady.

ALL-IRELAND QUARTER-FINAL
Aug 7, Parnell Park, Dublin
DUBLIN 4-11 NEW YORK 0-4
Dublin: D O'Farrell, P McManus, J Jordan, C Kavanagh, T O'Boyle, B Murray, G O'Regan, B Stynes 0-3, D Quinlivan 0-1, D Howard 0-2, S Cahill, M Brady 0-1, D Farrell 4-0, S Moylan 0-3, B Barnes.

ALL-IRELAND SEMI-FINAL
Aug 21, Croke Park, Dublin
DUBLIN 1-9 GALWAY 0-7
Dublin: D O'Farrell, P McManus, J Jordan, C Kavanagh, T O'Boyle, B Murray, G O'Regan, S Cahill 0-1, D Quinlivan, D Howard 0-2, B Stynes 0-4, M Brady, D Farrell, S Moylan 1-0, B. Barnes 0-2. Sub: G Murphy for Brady.

ALL-IRELAND FINAL
Sep 18, Croke Park, Dublin
KERRY 2-5 DUBLIN 0-5
Dublin: Derek O'Farrell, Pauric McManus, John Jordan, Conor Kavanagh, Tony O'Boyle, Brendan Murray, Gearoid O'Regan, David Quinlivan 0-1, Pat Cassells, Derek Howard, Brian Stynes 0-3, Tony Keogh, Dessie Farrell 0-1, Senan Moylan, Brian Barnes. Subs: Sean Cahill for Cassells, Tony Gavigan for O'Boyle.

1989

LEINSTER QUARTER-FINAL
June 5, St Conleth's Park, Newbridge
KILDARE 0-8 DUBLIN 0-7
Dublin: D O'Farrell, L Callan, P Wilde, L Daly, B Beggs, G Ryan, V Hughes, J Bell, A O'Grady, C Boyle 0-1, P Doherty 0-1, K McNally, J Gavin 0-1, D Farrell 0-1, K Cunningham 0-2. Subs. D Fitzgerald for McNally 27, J Nolan 0-1 for Boyle 43.

1990

LEINSTER QUARTER-FINAL
May 26, Drogheda Park, Drogheda
LOUTH 5-14 DUBLIN 1-4
Dublin: O Carbury, D Harrington, M Byrne, M Carroll, P White, T Russell 1-0, V Hughes, L Callan 0-1, J Bell, T Feehan 0-1, C McNally 0-1, D Barnes, G Hogan, N O'Grady, C Keegan. Sub: A Duff 0-1 for Hogan.

1991

LEINSTER QUARTER-FINAL
May 4, Parnell Park, Dublin
DUBLIN 2-5   MEATH 1-8
Dublin: R Lyons, R Lambe, B Quinlivan, D Fairbanks, L Walsh, D Harrington, D Moore, M Byrne, E Van Boxtel 0-1, P McGrane, C Durkan 1-0, R McGrath 0-1, J McAllister, R Boyle 0-2, D Brady 1-1.

LEINSTER QUARTER-FINAL REPLAY
May 11, Oldtown, Walterstown
DUBLIN 1-14   MEATH 1-8
Dublin: R Lyons, R Lambe, B Quinlivan, D Fairbanks, L Walsh, D Harrington 0-2, D Moore, M Byrne, K Kelly, P McGrane 0-2, A Dunne, G Walsh 0-5, J McAllister, R Boyle 1-3, D Brady 0-2.

LEINSTER SEMI-FINAL
July 14, Croke Park, Dublin
DUBLIN 0-10   OFFALY 1-6
Dublin: R Lyons, R Lambe, B Quinlivan, D Fairbanks, L Walsh, D Harrington, D Moore, M Byrne 0-1, K Kelly, P McGrane, A Dunne 0-1, G Walsh 0-4, J McAllister 0-1, R Boyle 0-3, D Brady. Subs: C Durkan for McGrane.

LEINSTER FINAL
Aug 10, Croke Park, Dublin
KILDARE 2-8   DUBLIN 0-12
Dublin: R Lyons, R Lamb, B Quinlivan, D Fairbanks, L Walsh, D Harrington, C Haughey, M Byrne, C Kelly, C Durkan, A Dunne 0-4, P McGrane 0-1, J McAllister, D Lee 0-1, D Brady 0-3, Subs: G Walsh 0-3 for Durkan, R Boyle for McAllister, D Martin for Kelly.

1992

LEINSTER FIRST ROUND
May 10, O'Connor Park, Tullamore
DUBLIN 0-7   OFFALY 0-7
Dublin: D Grogan, S Walsh, C Wilson, K Nolan, D Monahan, D Fairbanks, M O'Shea, C Kelly, C Early, B O'Brien, S Connell, E Sheehy 0-1, P Clifford 0-1, M Doran, D O'Hanlon 0-5. Subs: P Molloy for O'Shea, D Martin for O'Brien.

LEINSTER FIRST ROUND REPLAY
May 16, Parnell Park, Dublin
DUBLIN 3-8   OFFALY 1-10
Dublin: D Grogan, S Walsh, C Wilson, K Nolan, D Monahan, D Fairbanks, P Molloy 0-1, C Kelly 1-0, C Early 1-0, B O'Brien 0-1, S Connell 0-2, E Sheehy 1-1, P Clifford 0-1, M Doran, D O'Hanlon 0-2.

LEINSTER QUARTER-FINAL
May 24, Wexford Park, Wexford
WEXFORD 1-8   DUBLIN 0-3
Dublin: D Grogan, S Walsh, C Wilson, K Nolan, D Monahan, D Fairbanks, M O'Shea, C Kelly 0-1, D Martin, M Doran, E Sheehy, S Connell, P Molloy, C Early, D O'Hanlon 0-1. Sub: B O'Brien 0-1 for Molloy.

1993

LEINSTER QUARTER-FINAL
May 15, Castletowngeoghegan
DUBLIN 4-7   WESTMEATH 2-2
Dublin: R O'Mahony, C Redmond, N McMahon, K Mahony, T White, C Wilson, K Galvin, D Roche, E Sheehy, B McManus 0-1, K Lawlor 1-1, D Potts 0-1, C Keane, A Ryan 2-1, B Dignan 1-3. Sub: D McCarthy for C Keane.

LEINSTER SEMI-FINAL
July 4, Croke Park, Dublin
MEATH 2-9   DUBLIN 0-5
Dublin: R O'Mahony, D Roche, N McMahon, K Mahony, C Wilson, S Magill, K Galvin, E Sheehy, J Murphy, K Lawlor 0-5, A Ryan, B McManus, C Keane, N Corran, B Dignam. Subs: C Redmond for Mahony, D Potts for Corran.

1994

LEINSTER FIRST ROUND
Apr 30, Nowlan Park, Kilkenny
DUBLIN 0-19   KILKENNY 0-7
Dublin: G Kinahan, K O'Rourke, T O'Donnacha, A O'Mathuna, J Woods, G O'Donoghue, C Meehan, C Whelan, E McLoughlin 0-9, D Bolger 0-4, N Gahan, M Casey 0-1, R Cosgrove 0-2, I Robertson 0-2, J Sherlock 0-1. Subs: M Byrne for O'Rourke, S Heraty for Meehan, B Kealy for Bolger.

LEINSTER QUARTER-FINAL
May 14, St Conleth's Park, Newbridge
DUBLIN 2-11   KILDARE 1-7
Dublin: G Kinahan, M Beirne, T O'Donnacha, A Gorman, J Woods, S Heraty, D Stynes, C Whelan, E McLoughlin 2-10, D Bolger, N Gahan, M Casey, R Cosgrove, I Robertson, J Sherlock 0-1. Subs: M Byrne for O'Rourke, S Heraty for Meehan, B Kealy for Bolger.

LEINSTER SEMI-FINAL
July 10, Croke Park, Dublin
DUBLIN 1-19   CARLOW 0-5
Dublin: D Smith, M Beirne, T O'Donnacha, A Gorman, S Heraty, I Robertson, J Woods 0-1, D Stynes 0-1, C Whelan 0-1, S Cowap 0-2, M Casey, G O'Donoghue 0-2, P Keane, E McLoughlin 0-9, J Sherlock 1-1. Subs: D Bolger 0-2 for Keane, M O'Keeffe for Sherlock.

LEINSTER FINAL
July 31, Croke Park, Dublin
DUBLIN 2-12   WEXFORD 2-6
Dublin: G Kinahan, M Beirne, T O'Donnacha, A Gorman, S Heraty 1-0, I Robertson, J Woods, S Cowap, C Whelan, P Keane 0-2, M Casey 0-3, G O'Donoghue 0-1, M O'Keefe, E McLoughlin 0-3, J Sherlock 1-0. Subs: D Bolger 0-3 for O'Keeffe 25.

ALL-IRELAND SEMI-FINAL
Aug 21, Croke Park, Dublin
GALWAY 1-12   DUBLIN 0-12
Dublin: G Kinahan, M Beirne, T O'Donncha, A Gorman, S Heraty, I Robertson 0-1, J Woods, D Stynes, C Whelan, S Cowap, M Casey 0-1, G O'Donoghue 0-2, P Keane 0-1, E McLoughlin 0-4 J Sherlock 0-2. Subs: C Meehan to O'Donnacha 24, D Bolger 0-1 for Cowap 30.

1995

LEINSTER FIRST ROUND
May 13, O'Toole Park, Dublin
KILDARE 3-8   DUBLIN 1-12
Dublin: D O'Brien, K Horgan, N McCaffrey, R McDonald, C O'Brien, P Croft, L Briody, D Stynes 0-1, K Kehilly 0-1, M Forde 0-1, R Cosgrove 0-1, J Magee 1-1, B Gogarty 0-1, D Bolger 0-5, B Kealy 0-1, Subs: Joe Cassidy for Kealy.

1996

LEINSTER QUARTER-FINAL
May 18, St Conleth's Park, Newbridge
DUBLIN 2-8   KILDARE 1-10
Dublin: D O'Brien, B Whelan, W O'Toole, C O'Sullivan, C Doyle 0-2, P Andrews, L Kavanagh, J Magee 0-1, J Norton, M Hutchinson, D Byrne 1-2, N Crossan, 1-2, A Briody 0-1, K Conneely, E Bennis. Subs: M Cahill for Norton, P Murtagh for Briody.

LEINSTER SEMI-FINAL
June 30, Pairc Tailteann, Navan
DUBLIN 0-10   MEATH 0-8
Dublin: D O'Brien, B Whelan, W O'Toole, C O'Sullivan, C Doyle 0-2, P Andrews, L Kavanagh, J Norton, F Bradshaw, P Murtagh 0-1, D Byrne 0-1, N Crossan 0-3, A Briody 0-2, J Magee, E Bennis 0-1. Subs: K Conneely for Bradshaw, P Maguire for Briody.

LEINSTER FINAL
July 28, Croke Park, Dublin
DUBLIN 2-9   LAOIS 0-15
Dublin: D O'Brien, B Whelan, W O'Toole, C O'Sullivan, C Doyle, P Andrews, L Kavanagh, J Norton, F Bradshaw, P Murtagh, D Byrne 0-2, N Crossan 0-1, A Briody 0-1, J Magee 1-1, E Bennis 1-2. Subs: L Knight 0-1 for Bradshaw 36, L Ryan 0-1 for Murtagh 50, M Cahill for Briody 57.

LEINSTER FINAL REPLAY
Aug 3, O'Connor Park, Tullamore
LAOIS 2-18   DUBLIN 1-8
Dublin: D O'Brien, B Whelan, W O'Toole, C O'Sullivan, C Doyle, P Andrews, L Kavanagh, L Ryan, J Magee 0-1, P Murtagh 0-1, D Byrne, N Crossan 0-1, A Briody, L Knight 1-4, E Bennis. Subs: M Cahill for O'Sullivan 27, J Norton 0-1 for Briody h/t, K Conneely for Crossan 46.

1997

LEINSTER QUARTER-FINAL
May 17, St Conleth's Park, Newbridge
DUBLIN 2-8   KILDARE 0-13
Dublin: J Bates, D Cooley, M Cahill, C Kelleher, C Moran, D Conlon, G Minehan, J McGowan, S Martin, T Doyle 0-1, K Kilmurray 0-1, C Doyle 1-1, A Briody 0-2, J Gahon 1-0, W McCarthy 0-3.

LEINSTER SEMI-FINAL
June 29, Croke Park, Dublin
WICKLOW 2-6   DUBLIN 0-10
Dublin: J Bates, D Cooney, M Cahill, C Kelleher, D Conlon, C Moran, G Minehan, J McGowan, B Mahon 0-1, K Kilmurray 0-3, S Martin, C Doyle, A Briody 0-3, J Gahan 0-1, W McCarthy 0-2.

1998

LEINSTER FIRST ROUND
May 16, Parnell Park, Dublin
DUBLIN 2-7   MEATH 1-10
Dublin: C Clarke, D Henry, M Breathnach, M Thompson, F Armstrong, C Moran, G Norton, M Kennedy, C Murphy 0-2, D Smith 0-1, P McIntyre, P Devitt, M Ryan 0-1, J Gahan 2-0, W McCarthy 0-3. Subs: J Gibbons for Smith, J Corcoran for Gibbons, R Mullins for Devitt.

LEINSTER FIRST ROUND REPLAY
May 23, Pairc Tailteann, Navan
DUBLIN 1-12   MEATH 1-8
Dublin: C Clarke, D Henry, M Breathnach, M Thompson, F Armstrong, C Moran, G Norton, M Kennedy, D Conlon, F Purcell 0-1, C Murphy, P Devitt, M Ryan 0-1, J Gahan 1-0, W McCarthy 0-10. Subs: P McIntyre for Devitt, A Lawlor for Thompson.

LEINSTER QUARTER-FINAL
May 30, Parnell Park, Dublin
DUBLIN 1-11   LOUTH 0-5
Dublin: C Clarke, D Henry, M Breathnach, M Thompson, F Armstrong, C Moran, G Norton, M Kennedy, D Conlon 0-1, F Purcell 0-1, C Murphy 0-1, P Devitt, M Ryan 1-1, J Gahan 0-1, W McCarthy 0-6.

LENSTER SEMI-FINAL
June 28, Croke Park, Dublin
DUBLIN 0-10   WICKLOW 0-5
Dublin: C Clarke, D Henry, M Breathnach, M Thompson, F Armstrong, C Moran, G Norton, M Kennedy, D Conlon 0-1, F Purcell, C Murphy, P Devitt 0-1, M Ryan 0-1, J Gahan 0-1, McCarthy 0-6. Sub: K Golden for Ryan 45.

LEINSTER FINAL
Aug 2, Croke Park, Dublin
LAOIS 2-9   DUBLIN 0-12
Dublin: C Clarke, D Henry, M Breathnach, M Thompson, F Armstrong, C Moran, G Norton, M Kennedy, D Conlon 0-1, F Purcell, J Gahan, P Devitt 0-1, M Ryan 0-1, R Mullins 0-1, W McCarthy 0-8. Subs: C Murphy for Purcell 55, L Driver for Devitt 60, K Golden for Gahan 61.

1999

LEINSTER FIRST ROUND
May 1, Parnell Park, Dublin
DUBLIN 5-21   CARLOW 0-5
Dublin: V Galvin, A Holly, M Moore, N Cleere, A Cleere, P Casey, S McCann, C Murphy 1-1, K Devine, N O'Driscoll, K Golden 0-9, M O'Reilly, S Mills 2-2, J Waldron 0-2, C O'Driscoll 0-6. Subs: L Og O hEineachain 1-1 for N O'Driscoll, G Joyce 1-0 for Waldron, C Burke for Moore

LEINSTER SECOND ROUND
May 16, Parnell Park, Dublin
DUBLIN 3-14   WESTMEATH 0-7
Dublin: V Galvin, A Holly, M Moore, N Cleere, S McCann, P Casey, A Cleere, C Murphy 0-1, K Devine, D Magee 0-1, K Golden 0-7, L Og O hEineachain 1-1, S Mills 2-1, J Waldron 0-1, C O'Driscoll 0-2. Sub: N O'Driscoll for Magee.

LEINSTER SEMI-FINAL
June 27, Croke Park, Dublin
DUBLIN 4-11   OFFALY 3-7
Dublin: V Galvin, A Holly, M Moore, N Cleere, N O'Driscoll, P Casey, A Cleere, C Murphy, K Devine, S McCann 0-5, K Golden 0-1, C O'Driscoll 1-1, S Mills 2-2, B McEvoy 1-0, L Og O hEineachain 0-2. Subs: D Magee for Golden 50, C Burke for Moore 56.

LEINSTER FINAL
Aug 1, Croke Park, Dublin
DUBLIN 1-13   WEXFORD 2-10
Dublin: V Galvin, A Holly, N Cleere, N O'Driscoll, C Burke, P Casey, A Cleere, C Murphy 0-1, K Devine, S McCann 0-1, L Og O hEineachain 0-5, C O'Driscoll, S Mills 0-5, B McEvoy 1-1, G Joyce. Subs: A Brogan for C O'Driscoll h/t, C Keaney for Burke 45, D Magee for McCann 55.

LEINSTER FINAL REPLAY
Aug 7, Dr Cullen Park, Carlow
DUBLIN 2-13   WEXFORD 1-12
Dublin: S Cluxton, A Holly, N Cleere, N O'Driscoll, A Brogan 0-1, P Casey, A Cleere, C Murphy 0-1, K Devine 0-1, S McCann 1-1, L Og O hEineachain 0-4, G Joyce, S Mills 0-4, B McEvoy, C O'Driscoll 1-1. Sub: J Waldron for C O'Driscoll.

ALL-IRELAND SEMI-FINAL
Aug 29, Croke Park, Dublin
DUBLIN 1-10   DOWN 0-13
Dublin: S Cluxton, A Holly, N Cleere, N O'Driscoll, A Brogan 1-1, P Casey 0-1, A Cleere, C Murphy, K Devine 0-1, S McCann, L Og O hEmeachain 0-4, C O'Driscoll 0-1, S Mills 0-1, B McEvoy, G Joyce. Sub: J Waldron 0-1 for Mills 50.

ALL-IRELAND SEMI-FINAL REPLAY
Sep 4, Pairc Tailteann, Navan
DOWN 2-14   DUBLIN 1-9
Dublin: S Cluxton, A Holly, N Cleere, N O'Driscoll, A Brogan 0-1, P Casey, A Cleere, C Murphy, K Devine 0-1, S McCann, L Og O hEineachain 0-4, C O'Driscoll, S Mills 1-3, B McEvoy 0-1, G Joyce.

2000

LEINSTER FIRST ROUND
May 6, O'Connor Park, Tullamore
DUBLIN 0-16   OFFALY 0-9
Dublin: V Galvin, N Keane, A Cleere, D Murray, S McCann 0-1, A Brogan 0-1, N O'Driscoll, S Walsh 0-1, G Coughlan, K Devine 0-1, L Og O hEineachain 0-1, C O'Driscoll 0-6, D Lally 0-2, S Breheny 0-1, G Joyce 0-2.

LEINSTER QUARTER-FINAL
May 20, Parnell Park, Dublin
DUBLIN 1-10   WICKLOW 0-4
Dublin: V Galvin, N Kane, G Coughlin, D Murray, S McCann, A Cleere, N O'Driscoll 0-1, S Walsh 0-2, A Brogan, K Devine 0-1, L Og O hEineachain 1-2, G Joyce 0-2, S Mills 0-1, D Lally 0-1, C O'Driscoll 0-1.

LEINSTER SEMI-FINAL

July 2, Croke Park, Dublin

DUBLIN 2-14   MEATH 0-10

Dublin: V Galvin, N Kane, G Coughlan, D Murray, S McCann, A Cleere, N O'Driscoll, S Walsh 0-3, P Hayden, K Devine, L Og O hEineachain 0-1, G Joyce, S Mills 0-6, D Lally 1-1, J Waldron 0-1. Subs: C O'Driscoll 0-2 for Devine, S Breheny 1-0 for Waldron.

LEINSTER FINAL

July 30, Croke Park, Dublin

WESTMEATH 2-9   DUBLIN 1-10

Dublin: V Galvin, P Hayden, N Kane, D Murray, S McCann 0-2, A Cleere, N O'Driscoll, S Walsh 0-2, G Coughlan, C Keaney 1-1, L Og O hEineachain 0-1, G Joyce, S Mills, D Lally, C O'Driscoll 0-1. Subs: A Brogan for Hayden h/t, K Devine for Joyce 35, D Lowry 0-1 for McCann 45, J Waldron for Coughlan 55.

2001

LEINSTER FIRST ROUND

May 5, Nowlan Park, Kilkenny

DUBLIN 9-21   KILKENNY 0-2

Dublin: P Copeland, D Gavin, M Fitzpatrick, G Dent, P Griffin, B Cullen, B Lyons 1-0, P Brennan 0-1, D O'Mahony 1-1, R Traynor 0-2, N McAuliffe 5-1, M Taylor 0-1, D O'Callaghan 0-4, G Cullen 1-2, J Noonan 0-4. Subs: K Corrigan 0-4 for Noonan, N Cooper for Griffin, M Whelan 1-1 for Traynor, F Walsh for Brennan.

LEINSTER QUARTER-FINAL

May 26, Parnell Park, Dublin

DUBLIN 4-13   LOUTH 0-6

Dublin: P Copeland, D Galvin, M Fitzpatrick, G Dent, P Griffin, B Cullen, B Lyons, M Whelan, D O'Mahony 0-1, N McAuliffe 0-6, J Noonan 1-2, M Taylor, D O'Callaghan 0-3, G Cullen 1-0, C Corrigan 0-1. Subs: D Farrell 0-1 for Corrigan 35, G Brennan for Whelan 40, C Hoare for Noonan 44, A Cromwell for O'Callaghan 44, P Conlon for Dent 53.

LEINSTER SEMI-FINAL

July 1, Pairc Tailteann, Navan

DUBLIN 1-9   KILDARE 0-6

Dublin: P Copeland, G Dent, M Fitzpatrick, D Galvin, P Griffin, B Cullen, B Lyons, M Whelan 0-3, D O'Mahoney, P Brennan, N McAuliffe 0-2, M Taylor, D O'Callaghan 1-2, G Cullen, J Noonan 0-2. Subs: C Corrigan for Brennan, M O'Connor for Taylor, D Farrell for McAuliffe.

LEINSTER FINAL

July 15, Croke Park, Dublin

DUBLIN 1-17   OFFALY 0-6

Dublin: P Copeland, G Dent, M Fitzpatrick, D Galvin, P Griffin, B Cullen, B Lyons 0-1, M Whelan 0-1, D O'Mahony, N McAuliffe 0-5, P Brennan 0-1, D Farrell 0-2, D O'Callaghan 0-3, G Cullen 0-2, J Noonan 0-2. Subs: M Taylor for Farrell 38, C Corrigan for O'Callaghan 56, N Clarke for G Cullen 57, N Cooper for Griffin 59, P Conlon for Dent 60.

ALL-IRELAND SEMI-FINAL

Sep 2, Croke Park, Dublin

DUBLIN 2-13   KERRY 2-9

Dublin: P Copeland, D Galvin, M Fitzpatrick, G Dent, P Griffin, B Cullen, B Lyons 1-0, P Brennan 0-2, D O'Mahony, N McAuliffe 0-3, M Taylor 0-1, G Brennan, D O'Callaghan 0-4, G Cullen 0-1, J Noonan 1-1. Subs: D McCann for Dent 27, M Whelan 0-1 for G Brennan 36, C Corrigan for Taylor 57.

ALL-IRELAND FINAL

Sep 23, Croke Park, Dublin

DUBLIN 1-12   TYRONE 0-15

Dublin: Paul Copeland, David Galvin, Michael Fitzpatrick, Graham Dent, Paul Griffin, Bryan Cullen, Barry Lyons, Padraig Brennan, Declan O'Mahony, Niall McAuliffe 0-1, Mark Taylor, Gary Brennan 0-1, David O'Callaghan 1-3, Graham Cullen, John Noonan 0-6. Subs: Martin Whelan 0-1 for P Brennan 35, C Corrigan for Taylor 35, Danny McCann for Dent 49.

ALL-IRELAND FINAL REPLAY

Sep 29, Breffni Park, Cavan

TYRONE 2-11   DUBLIN 0-6

Dublin: Paul Copeland, David Galvin, Michael Fitzpatrick, Danny McCann, Paul Griffin, Bryan Cullen, Barry Lyons, Padraig Brennan, Declan O'Mahony 0-2, Niall McAuliffe, Graham Cullen, Gary Brennan, David O'Callaghan, Donal Farrell, John Noonan 0-4. Subs: Martin Whelan for G Brennan 36, Niall Clarke for Galvin 39, Mark Taylor for P Brennan 51.

2002

LEINSTER QUARTER-FINAL

May 18, Lawless Memorial Park, Swords

DUBLIN 1-16   WESTMEATH 3-4

Dublin: P Thompson, F Morris, N McGrath, K Walkin, N Cooper, B Cullen 0-1, D McCann, J Coughlan 0-1, D O'Mahony 0-2, C Hoare 0-1, C Corrigan, J Brogan 0-1, A Relihan 1-5, B Dinneen, R Traynor 0-3. Subs: N Gillett for Thompson 35, C Noone 0-2 for Corrigan 44, P Lawlor for Brogan 60.

LEINSTER SEMI-FINAL

June 29, Cusack Park, Mullingar

LONGFORD 1-8   DUBLIN 0-7

Dublin: P Thompson, F Morris, N McGrath, G Dent,

N Cooper, B Cullen 0-2, D McCann, J Coughlan, D O'Mahony, C Hore, A McCormack 0-1, D Dineen, C Noone 0-1, R Traynor 0-3, J Brogan. Subs: J Donnelly for Noone 38, P Lawlor for Coughlan 45.

2003

LEINSTER QUARTER-FINAL
May 17, Pairc Tailteann, Navan
DUBLIN 0-14   MEATH 2-4
Dublin: K Walsh, S Kinsella, C Cleere, C O'Moran, D Reilly, G Brennan, I Ward, B Phelan, J Coughlan, J O'Brien, B Kennedy 0-1, C Noone 0-2, A Relihan 0-3, F Fitzgerald 0-2, J O'Hara 0-3. Subs: M Vaughan 0-3 for O'Brien, D Walsh for Kinsella, C Moore for Noone.

LEINSTER SEMI-FINAL
July 2, Pairc Tailteann, Navan
DUBLIN 0-11   LOUTH 1-8
Dublin: K Walsh, A Downes, K Cleere, K Moran, D Reilly, G Brennan, I Ward 0-1, B Phelan, J Coughlan, C Noone 0-1, B Kennedy 0-2, C Moore, A Relihan 0-1, F Fitzgerald 0-1, J O'Hara 0-3. Subs: D Walsh for Moran, M Vaughan 0-2 for Noone, D O'Reilly for Moore.

LEINSTER SEMI-FINAL REPLAY
July 9, Pairc Tailteann, Navan
DUBLIN 1-12   LOUTH 1-7
Dublin: K Walsh, A Downes, K Cleere, W Lowry D Reilly, G Brennan, I Ward, B Phelan, J Coughlan, M Vaughan 1-2, B Kennedy 0-1, D O'Reilly 0-1, A Relihan 0-3, F Fitzgerald 0-2, J O'Hara 0-2. Subs: C Moore for Kennedy, J O'Brien 0-1 for O'Hara, C Noone for O'Reilly.

LEINSTER FINAL
July 20, Croke Park, Dublin
DUBLIN 1-11   LAOIS 1-9
Dublin: K Walsh, A Downes, K Cleere, W Lowry, D Reilly, G Brennan, I Ward, B Phelan, G O'Meara, J O'Brien 0-1, B Kennedy 0-2, M Vaughan 0-2, A Relihan 0-2, F Fitzgerald, J O'Hara 1-1. Subs: K Leahy 0-3 for Fitzgerald 5, C Moore for O'Brien 43, C Noone for Relihan 60.

ALL-IRELAND QUARTER-FINAL
Aug 2, Pearse Park, Longford
DUBLIN 0-15   FERMANAGH 0-5
Dublin: K Walsh, A Downes, K Cleere, W Lowry, D Reilly, G Brennan, I Ward 0-1, B Phelan, G O'Meara, K Leahy 0-3, B Kennedy 0-2, M Vaughan 0-3, A Relihan 0-3, F Fitzgerald, J O'Hara 0-2. Subs: J O'Brien 0-1 for Fitzgerald, D O'Reilly for Kennedy, C Noone for Relihan, C Murtagh for Lowry and W Moore for Vaughan.

ALL-IRELAND SEMI-FINAL
Aug 31, Croke Park, Dublin
DUBLIN 1-18   CORK 1-9
Dublin: K Walsh, A Downes, K Cleere, W Lowry, D Reilly 0-1, G Brennan, I Ward, B Phelan 0-1, J Coughlan 0-1, M Vaughan, B Kennedy 0-1, G O'Meara 0-1, A Relihan 1-4, K Leahy 0-7, J O'Hara 0-2. Subs: J Brogan for Kennedy 53, J O'Brien for Vaughan 56, D O'Reilly for O'Meara 58, W Moore for O'Hara 59, K Murtagh for Lowry 59.

ALL-IRELAND FINAL
Sep 28, Croke Park, Dublin
DUBLIN 1-11   LAOIS 1-11
Dublin: Kieran Walsh, Aidan Downes, Kian Cleere, Willie Lowry, Donnacha Reilly, Ger Brennan, Ian Ward, Brendan Phelan, John Coughlan 0-1, Gerard O'Meara, Barry Kennedy 0-4, Mark Vaughan 1-0, Aidan Relihan 0-2, Kevin Leahy 0-3, John O'Hara. Subs: Francis Fitzgerald 0-1 for Brennan 28, John O'Brien for Kennedy 58, Chris Moore for O'Hara 59.

ALL-IRELAND FINAL REPLAY
Oct 12, Dr Cullen Park, Carlow
LAOIS 2-10   DUBLIN 1-9
Dublin: Kieran Walsh, Aidan Downes, Kian Cleere 0-1, Willie Lowry, Ciaran Murtagh, Ger Brennan, Ian Ward, Brendan Phelan, John Coughlan, Mark Vaughan 0-1, Francis Fitzgerald, Gerard O'Meara, John O'Hara, Kevin Leahy 0-6, Barry Kennedy 0-1. Subs: James Brogan 1-0 for O'Hara 39, David Walsh for Downes 48, Michael Hallows for Murtagh 51, Willie Moore for Fitzgerald 57.

2004

LEINSTER QUARTER-FINAL
May 15, Wexford Park, Wexford
DUBLIN 3-12   WEXFORD 1-4
Dublin: R Kelleher, A Hubbard, A Coughlan, J McCaffrey, J O'Brien, R Fitzgerald, I Kavanagh, K Moran, P Flynn, C Daly, T Diamond 0-1, B Kelly 1-6, D Connolly 1-1, T Brady 1-0, R Cleere 0-3. Subs: P Andrews 0-1 for Daly, K Connolly for Cleere, K Nolan for O'Brien, S O'Rourke for Kelly, MD Macauley for Brady.

LEINSTER SEMI-FINAL
July 7, Dr Cullen Park, Carlow
LAOIS 3-7   DUBLIN 1-9
Dublin: M Savage, I Kavanagh, D Reilly, J McCaffrey, S O'Rourke, R Fitzgerald, J O'Brien P Flynn, M Macauley, D Connolly, T Diamond, M Hallows, B Kelly 0-5, T Brady 0-1, P Cleere. Subs: J Power 0-2 for Fitzgerald, K Moran for Connolly, D Pelly 1-1 for Cleere, C Daly for Macauley, G Flynn for Brady.

2005

LEINSTER QUARTER-FINAL
May 14, Parnell Park, Dublin
DUBLIN 1-15   WEXFORD 3-6
Dublin: D Cassidy, K Manley, A Keaney, A Hubbard, C Byrnes, J McCaffrey, R Cleere, R O'Carroll, B Cullen 0-1, P Andrews 0-2, D Connolly 0-6, S O'Rorke 0-1, B O'Rorke 0-1, T Brady 1-2, P McMahon. Subs: J Boland for McMahon 25, S Durkin 0-2 for S O'Rourke 45, P O'Connor for O'Carroll 58.

LEINSTER SEMI-FINAL
July 10, Dr Cullen Park, Carlow
LAOIS 3-8   DUBLIN 1-7
Dublin: E Summerville, K Manley, A Keaney, A Hubbard, C Byrnes, K Nolan, R Cleere, J McCaffrey, B Cullen, S O'Rorke, D Connolly 1-3, P Andrews 0-3, D Daly, T Brady, P McMahon. Subs: R O'Carroll for Cullen, C Morley 0-1 for O'Rorke, C Connolly for Manley, M Loftus for Byrnes, J Boland for McMahon.

2006

LEINSTER QUARTER-FINAL
May 13, Cusack Park, Mullingar
DUBLIN 1-11   WESTMEATH 0-11
Dublin: J Mooney, J Cooper, C Connolly, H Gill, C McIntyre, K Nolan, C Guckian, C O'Sullivan, S Ryan, C Morley 0-1, P O'Connor 0-3, D Kelly, L O'Donovan, S McCann, P Andrews 1-4. Subs: S Byrne for Gill h/t, B O'Rorke 0-3 for McCann 37, T Furman for Morley 41, C Moore for Kelly 61.

LEINSTER SEMI-FINAL
July 5, O'Moore Park, Portlaoise
OFFALY 2-5   DUBLIN 0-10
Dublin: J Mooney, J Cooper, A Keaney, C Connelly, C McIntyre, K Nolan, C Guickan, C O'Sullivan, S Ryan 0-3, P O'Connor, N Coughlan 0-2, C Morley 0-1, D Kelly 0-1, Gavin McCann 0-1, P Andrews. Subs: B O'Rourke 0-1 for O'Connor, T O'Donovan 0-1 for D Kelly, H Gill for A Keaney, T Furman for P Andrews.

2007

LEINSTER FIRST ROUND
Apr 7, Parnell Park, Dublin
DUBLIN 2-11   MEATH 1-7
Dublin: J Dignam, R O'Loughlin, R O'Carroll, D Lynch, J Cooper, S Casserly, N Brogan, K O'Connor 0-1, D Moher, M Coughlan, F McMahon 1-1, B Staunton 0-4, B O'Rorke 0-4, S Gallagher 1-0, T Furman 0-1. Subs: J Edwards for O'Loughlin, S Moore for Moher.

LEINSTER QUARTER-FINAL
May 12, Parnell Park, Dublin
DUBLIN 1-13   LAOIS 0-16
Dublin: J Dignam, R O'Loughlin, R O'Carroll, D Lynch, J Cooper, S Casserly, N Brogan 0-2, K O'Connor 1-1, D Moher, M Coughlan, F McMahon, B Staunton 0-1, B O'Rorke 0-4, S Gallagher 0-1, T Furman 0-4. Subs: C McLoughlin for O'Connor 71, P Shutte for McMahon 71, P Kelly for Staunton 56.

LEINSTER QUARTER-FINAL REPLAY
May 16, O'Moore Park, Portlaoise
LAOIS 2-12   DUBLIN 1-3
Dublin: J Dignam, R O'Loughlin, D Lynch, J Cooper, R O'Carroll, S Casserly, N Brogan, K O'Connor, C McLoughlin, M Coughlan, T Furman 0-1, B Staunton, B O'Rorke 0-1, S Gallagher 1-1, D Moher. Subs: S Lowndes for Staunton h/t, F McMahon for O'Connor 41, C Dorney for Gallagher 50.

2008

LEINSTER FIRST ROUND
Apr 5, Parnell Park, Dublin
DUBLIN 0-13   KILDARE 0-6
Dublin: G Bedford, D Nelson, E Culligan, M Schutte, J McCarthy 0-1, E Keogh, G Seaver, M Coughlan 0-1, C Mullins, D Rock 0-3, C Dormey, D Stapleton 0-4, G McIntyre 0-1, D Higgins 0-2. Subs: A McCarrick for Schutte 23, G Sweeney 0-1 for Dormey 38, S Mullins for Murray 56.

LEINSTER QUARTER-FINAL
May 10, Parnell Park, Dublin
MEATH 0-14   DUBLIN 0-10
Dublin: G Bedford, M Schutte, D Nelson, L McHugh, J McCarthy, E Culligan, G Seaver, M Coughlan, C Mullins, D Rock 0-3, G Sweeney 0-2, E Keogh, G McIntyre, D Stapleton 0-5, D Higgins. Subs: C Dorney for Higgins, D Moher for McIntyre, S Murray for Mullins, S Keane Dorney, C Diaz for McCarthy, Higgins for Keane.

2009

LEINSTER FIRST ROUND
Apr 18, Drogheda Park, Drogheda
DUBLIN 4-15   LOUTH 0-5
Dublin: D Downey: K O'Brien, F Carney, A Carr, S Swords, J Kelly, G Seaver, E Keogh, C Reddin 0-1, F Walsh 1-2, G Sweeney 0-3, P Hudson 0-3, C Diamond 1-2, C Carr 0-1, D Stapleton 1-2. Subs: M Schutte for Kelly 49, C O'Brien 1-1 for Hudson 52, K Twomey for Seaver 57, D Murphy for Reddin 57, J Kilduff for K O'Brien 58.

LEINSTER QUARTER-FINAL
May 23, Páirc Mhearnóg, Dublin
DUBLIN 0-14   LAOIS 1-10
Dublin: D Downey, A Carr, F Carney, M Schutte, S Swords, J Kelly, G Seaver, C Reddin 0-1, E Keogh, F Walsh, G Sweeney 0-1, P Hudson 0-5, C Diamond, D Stapleton 0-4, C Carr 0-2. Subs: C O'Brien for Diamond 39, D Murphy 0-1 for O'Brien 57.

LEINSTER SEMI-FINAL
June 27, O'Connor Park, Tullamore
DUBLIN 5-17   OFFALY 1-15
Dublin: D Downey, S Swords, F Carney, A Carr, K O'Brien, J Kelly, G Seaver, E Keogh, C Reddin 1-0, F Breathnach, G Sweeney 1-0, C Carr, P Ryan 0-2, D Stapleton 1-6, P Hudson 2-7. Subs: D O'Murchu for A Carr 38, M Concarr 0-1 for C Carr 47. Extra time: S McGrath for P Ryan 70, F Duffy 0-1 for Concarr 70.

LEINSTER FINAL
July 12, Croke Park, Dublin
DUBLIN 1-10   KILDARE 1-10
Dublin: D Downey, K O'Brien, F Carney, A Carr 0-1, S Swords, J Kelly, G Seaver, E Keogh, C Reddin, F Breathnach, G Sweeney 0-3, C Carr 1-1, P Ryan 0-1, D Stapleton 0-2, P Hudson 0-2. Subs: D Ó Murchú for Swords 37, F Duffy for Ryan 40, H Dawson for C Carr 56.

LEINSTER FINAL REPLAY
July 18, Dr Cullen Park, Carlow
DUBLIN 1-15   KILDARE 1-10
Dublin: D Downey, G Seaver 0-1, F Carney, K O'Brien, E Keogh, A Carr, J Kelly, D Ó Murchú, C Reddin, F Breathnach 0-1, G Sweeney 0-5, D Stapleton 0-1, F Duffy 0-2, C Carr 0-1, P Hudson 1-4. Subs: M Schutte for Stapleton 50, D Byrne for Ó Murchú 60, S Swords for A Carr 60.

ALL-IRELAND QUARTER-FINAL
Aug 15, Breffni Park, Cavan
DOWN 2-16   DUBLIN 2-14
Dublin: D Downey, K O'Brien, F Carney, S Swords, E Keogh, J Kelly, G Seaver, C Reddin, D Byrne, F Walsh 0-1, G Sweeney 0-1, D Stapleton 1-10, P Hudson 0-2, C Carr, F Duffy. Subs: M Schutte for C Carr h/t, C O'Brien for Duffy 37, D Murphy for Hudson 41, P Ryan 1-0 for Byrne 56, N O'Dea for Keogh 56.

2010

LEINSTER FIRST ROUND
Apr 17, St Conleth's Park, Newbridge
KILDARE 2-10   DUBLIN 1-9
Dublin: JB Carthy, M Durkan, P O'Curry, A Fallon, M Gibbs, L Fletcher, S Prendergast, E Ó Conghaile,
D Byrne, F Duffy 0-1, A Caffrey 0-1, N O'Flynn, S Stewart, C Kilkenny 1-7, H Dawson. Subs: D McCabe for O'Flynn h/t, P Maguire for Prendergast 34, D Shatwell for Dawson 44, C Cronin for Gibbs 52, F Conway for McGovern 56.

LEINSTER SECOND ROUND, LOSERS SECTION:
Apr 24, Parnell Park, Dublin
DUBLIN 4-11   LOUTH 0-5
Dublin: JB Carthy, M Durkin, D Shatwell, J Small, M Gibbs, L Fletcher, A Fallon, JJ Martin, P O'Curry, E O Conghaile, F Duffy 1-1, A Caffrey 0-2, S Stewart 1-0, C Kilkenny 1-8, D McCabe 1-0. Subs: J Russell Carroll for O Conghaile 40, N McGovern for Gibbs 50, P Maguire for Kilkenny 50, S Fitzsimons for O'Curry 53, E Boyne for Durkin 57.
* Dublin received a walkover from Kilkenny in the third round.

LEINSTER QUARTER-FINAL
May 22, St Conleth's Park, Newbridge
DUBLIN 1-13   KILDARE 0-16
Dublin: C Murphy, M Durkan, D Shatwell, N McGovern, M Gibbs, L Fletcher, S Fitzmaurice, P O'Curry, D Byrne, A Fallon, F Duffy 0-3, E Ó Conghaile, S Stewart 0-1, H Dawson 1-7, A Caffrey 0-2. Sub: P Ryan for O Conghaile, P Maguire for Fitzsimons 40, JJ Martin for O'Curry 35, D McCabe for Gibbs 56, R Basquel for Ryan 56, J McCaffrey for Maguire 64, G Heavey for Shatwell 68, N O'Flynn for Caffrey 73.

LEINSTER QUARTER-FINAL REPLAY
May 29, Parnell Park, Dublin
DUBLIN 1-13   KILDARE 2-10
Dublin: C Murphy   M Durcan, D Shatwell, A Fallon N McGovern, L Fletcher, S Fitzsimons   P O'Curry, D Byrne, C Diamond 0-3, F Duffy 0-2, M Gibbs S Stewart 0-2, H Dawson, A Caffrey 0-1. Subs: J McCaffrey 0-1 for McGovern 30, P Ryan 1-4 for Dawson h/t, D McCabe for Fitzsimons 42, R Basquel for Gibbs 50, C Woods for O'Curry 55, N O'Flynn for Diamond 61, Dawson for Basquel 73, A Byrne for O'Flynn 79.

LEINSTER QUARTER-FINAL SECOND REPLAY
June 29, Pairc Tailteann, Navan
KILDARE 1-13   DUBLIN 0-13
Dublin: C Murphy, M Durcan, D Byrne, M Gibbs, N McGovern, A Caffrey 0-1, A Fallon, L Fletcher, P O'Curry, C Diamond, F Duffy, H Dawson 0-1, S Stewart 0-1, C Kilkenny 0-8, P Ryan. Subs: J McCaffrey for Gibbs 25, D McCabe for Byrne 27, C Woods 0-2 for Diamond 36, JJ Martin for Ryan 46, R Basquel for Duffy 56.

2011

LEINSTER FIRST ROUND
Apr 16, Parnell Park, Dublin
DUBLIN 4-15   WESTMEATH 0-8
Dublin: R O'Hanlon, G Hannigan, R McDaid, R Reale, J McCaffrey 1-1, J Small, C Pike E Ó Conghaíle 0-1, G Ivory 0-2, E Lowndes 0-1, P O'Higgins, C Meaney 0-1, S Fulham 3-1, C Kilkenny 0-6, D Campbell 0-1. Subs: E Boyne for Hannigan 46, K Kindlon 0-1 for Lowndes 46, C Costello for Ivory 49, N Flannery for Fulham 49, E Archbold for Kilkenny 53.

LEINSTER QUARTER-FINAL
May 14, Pearse Park, Longford
DUBLIN 0-10   LONGFORD 0-5
Dublin: R O'Hanlon, G Hannigan, R McDaid, E Boyne, J McCaffrey 0-1, J Small, R Real, E O'Conghaile 0-1, P O'Higgins, E Lowndes, C Kilkenny 0-2, C Meaney, S Fulham, G Ivory 0-5, D Campbell. Subs: R Mullins for Lowndes 44, C Costello 0-1 for Campbell 48, A O'Brien for Fulham 60.

LEINSTER SEMI-FINAL
June 29, Parnell Park, Dublin
DUBLIN 1-24   KILDARE 0-11
Dublin: R O'Hanlon, R Real, R McDaid, G Hannigan, J McCaffrey 0-1, J Small, E Lowndes, E O Conghaile, P O'Higgins, C Costello 0-3, D Campbell 0-2, G Ivory 0-5, C Kilkenny 0-11, P Mannion 1-1, S Fulham 0-1. Subs: A O'Brien for Fulham 53, C Meaney for Costello 54, D O'Brien for Real 55, R Mullins for Kilkenny 58, M MacDonncha for O'Higgins 60.

LEINSTER FINAL
July 10, Croke Park, Dublin
DUBLIN 2-18   MEATH 1-11
Dublin: R O'Hanlon, G Hannigan, R McDaid, R Real, E Lowndes, J Small, J McCaffrey 0-1, P O'Higgins, E O'Conghaile 0-1, G Ivory 0-6, D Campbell, C Costello 1-2, S Fulham 1-2, C Kilkenny 0-1, P Mannion 0-1. Subs: S Carthy for Campbell 47, E Archibald for Fulham 59, E Boyne for Lowndes 59, R Noonan for O'Conghaile 61.

ALL-IRELAND SEMI-FINAL
Aug 28, Croke Park, Dublin
DUBLIN 1-11   GALWAY 1-9
Dublin: R O'Hanlon, G Hannigan, R McDaid, R Real, E Lowndes, J Small 0-1, J McCaffrey, P O'Higgins, E O Conghaile, Paul Mannion 0-1, G Ivory 0-1, C Costello 0-1, S Fulham 1-1, D Campbell, C Kilkenny 0-6. Subs: D Byrne for Real 35, N Scully for Campbell 44, E Archibold for Costello 52, C Meaney for Kilkenny 64.

ALL-IRELAND FINAL
Sep 18, Croke Park, Dublin
TIPPERARY 3-9   DUBLIN 1-14
Dublin: Ross O'Hanlon, Graham Hannigan, Robert McDaid (capt), Rutherson Real, Eric Lowndes, John Small 0-1, Jack McCaffrey 0-1 Patrick O'Higgins, Emmett O'Conghaile 0-1, Cormac Costello 0-1, Ciaran Kilkenny 0-7, Gavin Ivory 1-1, Scott Fulham, Paul Mannion 0-2, Conor Meaney. Subs: David Campbell for Meaney 39, David Byrne for Hannigan 53, Niall Scully for Fulham 59.

2012

LEINSTER FIRST ROUND
Apr 14, Dr Cullen Park, Carlow
DUBLIN 2-21   CARLOW 0-4
Dublin: L Molloy, S Mulvanney, D Byrne, R McGowan, E Lowndes, C Mullaly, E Fletcher, S Carthy 0-1, Stephen Cunningham, G Burke 1-3, Shane Cunningham 1-1, M MacDonnacha, C McHugh 0-10, D Campbell 0-1, N Scully 0-1. Subs: C Costello 0-3, N Walsh 0-1, B Bentley, J Fitzgibbon, S Hickey.

LEINSTER QUARTER-FINAL
May 19, Parnell Park, Dublin
DUBLIN 2-14   LONGFORD 1-5
Dublin: L Molloy, B Bentley, D Byrne, E Fletcher, G Burke, C Mullaly, M MacDonncha, S Carthy 0-2, Stephen Cunningham, N Walsh 0-2, Shane Cunningham 0-2, N Scully, C McHugh 1-2, D Campbell 0-3, R Gaughan 1-1. Subs: R McGowan for Bentley 38, C Costello 0-2 for Campbell 43, J Fitzgibbon for Gaughan 55, M Deegan for McHugh 58.

LEINSTER SEMI-FINAL
July 11, St Conleth's Park, Newbridge
DUBLIN 2-16   KILDARE 1-8
Dublin: L Molloy, E Mullan, D Byrne, R McGowan, E Lowndes, M MacDonncha, C Mullaly, Stephen Cunningham, S Carthy 0-1, R Gaughan 0-1, G Burke, N Walsh 0-2, C McHugh 1-5, N Scully 0-3, C Costello 1-5. Subs: Shane Cunningham 0-1 for Gaughan 25, E Flwtcher for MacDonncha 52, D Gormley for Walsh 57, J Fitzgibbon for Mullaly 60.

LEINSTER FINAL
July 22, Croke Park, Dublin
DUBLIN 3-17   MEATH 1-11
Dublin: L Molloy, E Mullan, D Byrne, R McGowan, M MacDonncha, C Mullaly, E Lowndes, Stephen Cunningham, S Carthy 0-1, G Burke 0-3, N Scully 0-1, N Walsh 0-2, C McHugh 0-4, C Costello 3-4, R Gaughan 0-1. Subs: D Gormley for Walsh 45, Shane Cunningham 0-1 for Gaughan 51, D Campbell for McHugh 57, M Deegan for Costello 58, B Bentley for Carthy 60.

ALL-IRELAND QUARTER-FINAL
Aug 5, Pairc Esler, Newry
DUBLIN 1-16   MONAGHAN 0-8
Dublin: L Molloy, R McGowan, D Byrne, E Mullan, M MacDonncha 0-1, C Mullaly, E Lowndes 0-2, Stephen Cunningham 1-0, S Carthy 0-3, R Gaughan, C Costello 0-4, N Walsh 0-1, N Scully, D Campbell 0-1, G Burke 0-4. Subs: Shane Cunningham for Gaughan 26, C McHugh for Campbell 37, E Fletcher for Mullan 50, T Quinn for Walsh 57, S McGrath for Scully 59.

ALL-IRELAND SEMI-FINAL
Sep 2, Croke Park, Dublin
DUBLIN 3-12   KERRY 1-10
Dublin: L Molloy, E Mullan, D Byrne, R McGowan, E Lowndes, C Mullaly, M MacDonncha 0-1, Stephen Cunningham, S Carthy 0-2, N Walsh, G Burke 0-1, R Gaughan, C Costello 1-3, C McHugh 1-2, N Scully 0-2. Subs: Shane Cunningham 0-1 for Gaughan 43, D Gormley for Walsh 47, M Deegan for Burke 59, D Campbell 1-0 for N Scully 53.

ALL-IRELAND FINAL
Sep 23, Croke Park, Dublin
DUBLIN 0-14   MEATH 1-5
Dublin: Lorcan Molloy, Emile Mullan, David Byrne, Ross McGowan, Eric Lowndes 0-1, Conor Mullaly, Maitias MacDonncha, Stephen Cunningham, Shane Carthy 0-3, Robert Gaughan, Niall Scully 0-2, Niall Walsh 0-2, Conor McHugh, Cormac Costello 0-5, Gavin Burke. Subs: Shane Cunningham for Gaughan, Donal Gormley for Burke, David Campbell 0-1 for Walsh, Michael Deegan for Scully.

2013

LEINSTER FIRST ROUND
Apr 13, Drogheda Park, Drogheda
DUBLIN 1-9   LOUTH 1-7
Dublin: L Molloy, J Mullins, G Gallagher, E Murchan, C Kavanagh, T Hanafin, E O'Donnell, S Maloney, E McHugh, A Foley 1-1, A Byrne, C Sheanon, D Mullins, M Deegan 0-2, C Basquel 0-2. Subs: C Mullins for C O Seanain h/t, J Hazley 0-1 for McHugh 38, C O'Callaghan 0-3 for D Mullins 42, A Fitzgerald for Deegan 56, S McGrath for Byrne 65.

LEINSTER QUARTER-FINAL
May 11, DCU Grounds, Dublin
DUBLIN 0-17   WEXFORD 0-9
Dublin: L Molloy, M Cahalan, J Mullins, E Murchan, A Byrne 0-2, T Hanafin, C Kavanagh, S Molony 0-2, E O'Donnell 0-1, A Foley, C Basquel, G Gallagher 0-2, D McGrath 0-5, C O'Callaghan 0-4, M Deegan 0-1. Subs: C Mullins for Cahalan 47, D Mullen for Basquel

54, A Kavanagh for C Kavanagh 54, S McGrath for Gallagher 59, R Farrell for Murchan 61.

LEINSTER SEMI-FINAL
July 6, Parnell Park, Dublin
KILDARE 3-13   DUBLIN 2-6
Dublin: L Molloy, M Cahalan, J Mullins, E Murchan, A Byrne, T Hanafin, C Kavanagh, S Molony, A Foley, G Gallagher, C Sheanon 1-0, C Mullins 0-1, D McGrath 0-2, C Basquel 1-1, C O'Callaghan 0-1. Subs: S Clayton for Cahalan 9, J Madden for Byrne 19, M Deegan 0-1 for McGrath 45, S McGrath for Gallagher 47, C Smith for Foley 58.

2014

LEINSTER FIRST ROUND
Apr 19, Pearse Park, Longford
DUBLIN 2-11   LONGFORD 0-14
Dublin: E Whelan, C Murphy, A McGowan, D Monahan, C Kavanagh 0-3, S Clayton, G O'Reilly, C Burke, E McHugh, A Elliot, C Basquel 0-1, J Burke, A Byrne 1-0, C O'Callaghan 1-7, C Sallier. Subs: W Egan for Byrne 41, E Murchan for Basquel 48, R McBride for Sallier 57, A Fee for Murphy (black card) 59.

LEINSTER QUARTER-FINAL
May 17, Parnell Park, Dublin
DUBLIN 0-15   MEATH 0-12
Dublin: E Whelan, C Murphy, S Clayton, D Monahan, C Kavanagh 0-6, J Mullins, G O'Reilly, A Foley 0-2, E McHugh 0-1, J Burke 0-3, A McGowan, C Basquel, R McBride, C O'Callaghan 0-2, B Howard. Subs: A Fee for Mullins 24, W Egan for Howard 37, C Sallier 0-1 for McBride 47.

LEINSTER SEMI-FINAL
July 10, O'Connor Park, Tullamore
DUBLIN 6-13   OFFALY 0-6
Dublin: E Whelan, C Murphy, J Mullins, E Murchan, A Fee, S Clayton, G O'Reilly, A Foley, E McHugh 0-2, W Egan 0-1, C Basquel 0-2, J Burke, A Byrne 1-0, C O'Callaghan 2-6, C Sallier 2-2. Subs: D McIlgorm for Foley 35, C Kavanagh for O'Reilly 43, R McBride 1-0 for O'Callaghan 47, A Elliot for Burke 51, B Howard for Sellier 54, D Monaghan for Murphy 55.

LEINSTER FINAL
July 20, Croke Park, Dublin
DUBLIN 3-16   KILDARE 1-12
Dublin: E Whelan, C Murphy, J Mullins, E Murchan, A Fee, S Clayton, G O'Reilly 0-1, A Foley, E McHugh 0-1, W Egan 0-2, C Basquel 1-2, J Burke 0-1, A Byrne 1-2, C O'Callaghan 1-6, C Sallier 0-1. Subs: D Monahan for Murphy h/t, A Elliott for Egan 47, D McIlgorm for

Foley 51, B Howard for Sallier 55, A McGowan for Fee 58, C Kavanagh for O'Reilly 59.

ALL-IRELAND QUARTER-FINAL
Aug 4, Semple Stadium, Thurles
DUBLIN 2-14   CORK 1-13
Dublin: E Whelan, D Monahan, J Mullins, E Murchan, A Fee, S Clayton, G O'Reilly, A Foley, E McHugh 0-2, W Egan, C Basquel 0-3, J Burke, A Byrne, C O'Callaghan 0-8, C Sallier 2-1. Subs: C Kavanagh for Burke 18, A McGowan for Fee 23, R McBride for Egan 36, C Murphy for Foley 48, B Howard for Byrne 54.

ALL-IRELAND SEMI-FINAL
Aug 31, Croke Park, Dublin
DONEGAL 1-12   DUBLIN 1-11
Dublin: E Whelan, E Murchan, J Mullins, D Monahan, A McGowan, S Clayton, G O'Reilly, A Foley, E McHugh 0-1, C Kavanagh 0-1, C Basquel 0-1, J Burke 1-1, A Byrne 0-1, C O'Callaghan 0-4, C Sallier 0-2. Subs: B Howard for Kavanagh 48, D McIlgorm for Foley 55, W Egan for Byrne 57, A Fee for McGowan 59.

2015

LEINSTER FIRST ROUND
Apr 18, Parnell Park, Dublin
DUBLIN 2-11   OFFALY 1-9
Dublin: E Comerford, D Byrne, P O'Hanlon, G McNamara, C Kavanagh, B Howard, O Kelly, D McIlgorm, A Elliot 2-0, K Callaghan 0-2, B McGarry, T Fox 0-1, S Caffrey, C Pearson 0-2, D Keating 0-4. Subs: S Howard 0-2 for McGarry 7, B Shovlin for S Howard 27, J Kindlon for Caffrey 45, C Hulton for Pearson 61.

LEINSTER QUARTER-FINAL
May 16, Belfield Park, Enniscorthy
DUBLIN 3-8   WEXFORD 0-11
Dublin: E Comerford, J Holland, P O'Hanlon, G McNamara, C Kavanagh 0-1, B Howard, O Kelly, A Elliot, D McIlgorm, T Fox 0-2, S Howard 0-2, B Shovlin, P Small 0-2, C Howley, D Keating 2-1. Subs: C Pearson for Shovlin h/t, T O'Sullivan for McIlgorm (black card) 39, J Kindlon 1-0 for S Howard 45, C Keely for Kindlon (black card) 49, C Hulton for Fox 60.

LEINSTER SEMI-FINAL
June 28, Croke Park, Dublin
KILDARE 3-16   DUBLIN 3-13
Dublin: E Comerford, D Byrne, P O'Hanlon, J Holland 0-1, C Kavanagh, B Howard, T O'Sullivan, A Elliott, D McIlgorm, T Fox 1-0, S Howard 1-4, C Pearson 0-1, P Small 1-2, C Howley 0-2, D Keating 0-1. Subs: A Bradshaw for Pearson 28, G McNamara

for O'Sullivan h/t, J Kindlon 0-2 for Keating h/t, O Kelly for Fox 47, D O'Brien for Holland 58, C Kelly for Kindlon (black card) 60.

2016

LEINSTER FIRST ROUND
Apr 16, Parnell Park, Dublin
DUBLIN 2-14   OFFALY 1-7
Dublin: E Comerford 0-1, R Shaw, N Doran, CJ Smith, C Lennon 0-2, J Holland, M Tighe, N Nolan, M Donnelly 0-1, J Madden, S Bugler 1-1, A Bradshaw 1-0, T Keane 0-3, K Callaghan 0-3, C Hynes 0-3.

LEINSTER QUARTER-FINAL
May 21, Pairc Tailteann, Navan
MEATH 1-18   DUBLIN 2-5
Dublin: E Comerford, R Shaw, N Doran, CJ Smith, C Lennon, J Holland, M Tighe, A Kelly, M Donnelly, C Howley 0-1, S Bugler 0-1, D O'Brien, T Keane 0-1, K Callaghan 2-0, C Hynes 0-2. Subs: E Fitzpatrick for Kelly h/t, A Bradshaw for Lennon h/t, N Nolan for Tighe h/t, R McGarry for Hynes 42, G McNamara for Shaw 45, P Flaherty for Donnelly 58.

2017

LEINSTER FIRST ROUND
Apr 22, Parnell Park, Dublin
DUBLIN 1-15   MEATH 1-13
Dublin: D O'Hanlon, L Flatman, P O Cofaigh Bhroin, A Lynch, K Kennedy, N Matthews, E O'Dea, D Ryan 0-1, M Tracey 0-1, N O'Leary, J Doran 1-4, D Brennan, R McGarry 0-2, S Hawkshaw, C Archer 0-7. Subs: D Lacey for Hawkshaw h/t, K Lynch Bissett for Brennan h/t, A Byrne for O'Leary 41, D Conlon for Tracey 68, G Nangle for Kennedy 72.

LEINSTER QUARTER-FINAL
May 20, Parnell Park, Dublin
DUBLIN 6-12   LONGFORD 0-5
Dublin: D O'Hanlon, D Maher, P Ó Cofaigh Bhroin, L Flatman, K Kennedy, N Matthews, E O'Dea 0-2, D Ryan, M Treacy, N O'Leary 0-2, J Doran 1-2, D Conlon 0-1, R McGarry 2-2, S Hawkshaw 1-1, C Archer.
Subs: A Byrne 1-1 for O'Leary 39, K Lynch Bissett for Conlon 44, F O'Sullivan for Doran 48, D Lacey 0-1 for Archer 49, D Deneher for O'Dea 57, J Madden 1-0 for Hawkshaw 57.

LEINSTER SEMI-FINAL
July 5, St Conleth's Park, Newbridge
DUBLIN 1-16   KILDARE 0-14
Dublin: D O'Hanlon, D Maher, P Ó Cofaigh Bhroin, L Flatman, K Kennedy, N Matthews, E O'Dea, M Treacy,

D Ryan 0-2, D Brennan 0-2, J Doran 0-1, J Madden, R McGarry 1-2, S Hawkshaw 0-3, D Lacey 0-5. Subs: A Byrne for Brennan 42, C Archer 0-1 for McGarry 51, K Lynch for Ryan (black card) 54, D Conlon for Madden 58, A Lynch for Maher 62.

LEINSTER FINAL
July 16, Croke Park
DUBLIN 2-19   LOUTH 0-11
Dublin: D O'Hanlon, D Maher, P O Cofaigh Bhroin, L Flatman. K Kennedy 0-1, N Matthews, E O'Dea 0-2, M Tracey 0-1, D Ryan, D Brennan 0-1, J Doran 1-1, J Madden 1-0, R McGarry 0-3, S Hawkshaw 0-2, D Lacey 0-4.

ALL-IRELAND QUARTER-FINAL
Aug 7, O'Moore Park, Portlaoise
DUBLIN 2-11   CLARE 0-10
Dublin: D O'Hanlon, D Maher, P Ó Cofaigh Bhroin, L Flatman, K Kennedy, N Matthews, E O'Dea 0-1, D Ryan, M Tracey, K Lynch Bissett 0-1, J Doran, D Brennan, R McGarry 2-4, S Hawkshaw 0-2, D Lacey. Subs: F O'Sullivan 0-1 for Brennan h/t, C Archer 0-2 for Lacey 39, A Lynch for Maher 43, A Byrne for Ryan 54, H Ladd for McGarry 59, G Nangle for Kennedy 64.

ALL-IRELAND SEMI-FINAL
Aug 27, Croke Park
DERRY 0-17   DUBLIN 0-14
Dublin: D O'Hanlon, D Maher, P Ó Cofaigh Bhroin, L Flatman, K Kennedy, N Matthews, E O'Dea, D Ryan, M Tracey, D Brennan, J Doran 0-6, K Lynch Bissett, D Lacey 0-5, S Hawkshaw 0-1, R McGarry 0-2. Subs: F O'Sullivan for Brennan 40, C Archer for Hawkshaw 47, G Nangle for Ó Cofaigh Bhroin 52, A Byrne for Lynch Bissett 59, L Doran for Maher 62, N O'Leary for Kennedy (black card) 65.

LEINSTER CHAMPIONSHIP ROLL OF HONOUR
Dublin (33): 1930, 1933, 1934, 1945, 1946, 1948, 1949, 1954, 1955, 1956, 1958, 1959, 1961, 1968, 1970, 1971, 1976, 1978, 1979, 1981, 1982, 1984, 1986, 1988, 1994, 1999, 2001, 2003, 2009, 2011, 2012, 2014, 2017.
Meath (10): 1957, 1972, 1977, 1980, 1985, 1990, 1992, 1993, 2006, 2008.
Laois (9): 1932, 1966, 1967, 1996, 1997, 1998, 2004, 2005, 2007.
Louth (8): 1931, 1935, 1936, 1940, 1941, 1942, 1951, 1953.
Kildare (8): 1973, 1975, 1983, 1987, 1991, 2013, 2015, 2016.
Offaly (6): 1947, 1960, 1962, 1964, 1965, 1989.
Westmeath (5): 1939, 1952, 1963, 1995, 2000.
Longford (4): 1929, 1938, 2002, 2010.
Wexford (3): 1937, 1950, 1969.
Wicklow (1): 1974.

ALL-IRELAND CHAMPIONSHIP ROLL OF HONOUR
Kerry (15): 1931, 1932, 1933, 1946, 1950, 1962, 1963, 1975, 1980, 1988, 1994, 2014, 2015, 2016, 2017.
Dublin (11): 1930, 1945, 1954, 1955, 1956, 1958, 1959, 1979, 1982, 1984, 2012.
Cork (10): 1961, 1967, 1968, 1969, 1972, 1974, 1981, 1991, 1993, 2000.
Tyrone (8): 1947, 1948, 1973, 1998, 2001, 2004, 2008, 2010.
Mayo (7): 1935, 1953, 1966, 1971, 1978, 1985, 2013.
Galway (6): 1952, 1960, 1970, 1976, 1986, 2007.
Derry (4): 1965, 1983, 1989, 2002.
Down (4): 1977, 1987, 1999, 2005.
Roscommon (4): 1939, 1941, 1951, 2006.
Meath (3): 1957, 1990, 1992.
Laois (3): 1996, 1997, 2003.
Cavan (2): 1937, 1938.
Louth (2): 1936, 1940.
Armagh (2): 1949, 2009.
Tipperary (2): 1934, 2011.
Clare (1): 1929.
Offaly (1): 1964.
Westmeath (1): 1995.

County Championship Finals

THE inaugural County Championships kicked off on 13 March 1887 at Elm Park in Merrion, then part of the estate of Lord Ffrench, lands on which both Elm Park Golf Club (founded in 1924) and St. Vincent's Hospital (transferred from St. Stephen's Green in 1970) now stand. The entire championship — for which 16 teams entered — was played out at the same venue and here, for the record, are the complete results for that very first competition:

First Round:
Mar 13: Grocers Assistants 0-7; Killiney 0-2
Mar 13: Faugh-A-Ballagh 1-4; Feach McHugh 0-1
Mar 13: Erin's Hope 4-11; Lucan Sarsfields 0-1
Mar 13: John Mitchel's, Glasthule 0-4; Cabinteely Geraldines 0-1
Mar 20: C.J. Kickhams 0-4; Davitts 0-1
Mar 20: Dunleary 2-9; St. Patrick's, Kilmainham 0-0
Mar 20: Parnells 0-7; Golden Ball 0-2
Mar 20: Grattan Esmondes 1-16; John Dillon's, Dalkey 0-0

Quarter-Finals:
Mar 27: Grocers Assistants 1-3; Grattan Esmondes 0-2
Mar 27: Dunleary 1-8; Parnells 1-1
Apr 3: Erin's Hope 0-5; Faugh-A-Ballagh 0-2
Apr 3: C.J. Kickhams 2-1; John Mitchel's, Glasthule 0-2

Semi-Finals:
Apr 10: Grocers Assistants 0-4; C.J. Kickhams 0-2
Apr 10: Erin's Hope 1-9; Dunleary 0-4

Final:
Apr 17: Erin's Hope 1-20; Grocers Assistants 0-1

Erin's Hope, as can be seen, emerged as champions without conceding a goal and having a mere eight points scored against them while themselves notching 6-38 in their four matches. The score in the final was not exactly written in stone; the Freeman's Journal concluded its report the following morning by stating: "Erin's Hope won by a goal and about twenty points (a great number of which were forfeits) to one forfeit point."

The first team to successfully defend the championship was Young Irelands who, after losing to Isle of the Sea in the 1890 final, actually won three in succession but missed out on a pure hat-trick as, after winning in both 1891 and 1892, there was no competition in 1893 before Young Irelands won again in 1894. The club, which had no connection whatsoever with the later hurling club of the same name that won five county titles between 1932 and 1965, was founded in early 1888 by Guinness workers, won a fourth title in 1896 but disbanded a mere two years later.

Kickhams were the first club to establish a real period of dominance, failing to make just one final in the ten championships from 1897 to 1907 inclusive (there was no competition in 1902). After beating Geraldines in a replay in 1897, they set an unwanted — and still unmatched — record of losing four deciders on the trot, the first two to Geraldines — the second after a replay — and then to Isle of the Sea and Bray Emmetts. After missing out in 1903, they returned to complete the championship's first ever four-in-a-row by beating, in turn, Isle of the Sea, Geraldines, Parnells and Keatings and later won a sixth and final title in 1912. Two players, Jack Grace and Tommy Walsh, figured in the last five of those successes while a further quartet, Jack Lynch, Tommy Murphy, Paddy O'Callaghan and Hugh Hilliard, were ever present for the four-in-a-row. Grace won five All-Ireland medals, Walsh and Hilliard three each.

The decade from 1908 was basically dominated by two teams, Geraldines and — to a lesser extent — Parnells, who respectively contested eight and five finals during the period including three against each other, all of which were won by Geraldines. The latter side, champions in 1897 and 1898, played in five successive deciders from 1908 (winning the first and third against first Keatings and then Parnells) and then won three in four years, beating Parnells in both 1914 and 1915 and Keatings in 1917. Paddy Fallon, who was Dublin's goalkeeper when they won the All-Ireland in 1908 and would be so again when they lifted the 1921 title (delayed until June 1923), played in all eight finals.

Parnells, founded in 1893 (initially as Parnell Volunteers), had reached the final in 1906 but lost out by 0-8 to 0-5 to a Kickhams side winning the third of four successive titles. Four years later they suffered an even narrower defeat when losing 0-7 to 0-6 to Geraldines, but from 1913 appeared in four consecutive finals, beating Kickhams in the first and Hibernian Knights in the last and losing the two in between to Geraldines.

THE next great era — one that would remain unsurpassed for three decades — began on 21 April 1918. That was when O'Tooles, given a bye into the semi-finals as only five teams entered the championship, beat McCrackens by 3-7 to 3-2 at Croke Park, with two of the goals being supplied by Tom Ennis, who three years later would have his career abruptly ended through a leg injury suffered while commanding the Dublin Brigade battalion that burnt down the Customs House. The win was the first match in a run that would see O'Tooles lose just a single championship game in nine campaigns, their first title coming nine weeks after that semi-final win with a 1-6 to 0-3 defeat of a Collegians side that included Frank Burke.

The title was retained the following year when McCrackens were beaten 1-7 to

0-2 and the hat-trick was completed with a tight 1-2 to 0-1 victory over Kickhams in a match that wasn't played until February 1921. Just over two months later O'Tooles themselves and Dublin football in general was shocked when St. Mary's — from East Wall and not to be confused with their Saggart namesakes — scored 1-4 without replay in the first half of their semi-final meeting at Croke Park; O'Tooles, keeping a blank sheet, rallied in the second half but could only put up a goal and two points on the scoreboard. St. Mary's would go on to claim their one and only title with a 1-5 to 0-3 victory over Kickhams; O'Tooles would not suffer another championship defeat for six years and two weeks.

The first defence was a bit rocky in the sense that reigning champions St. Mary's almost did the double on the men from Sheriff Street, holding them to an 0-3 each draw in the final before going down 1-2 to 0-3 in the replay. After further final wins over Garda and University College they equalled the four-in-a-row record set by Kickems in 1907 by that same club by 3-7 to 1-3 in the 1925 decider and surpassed it the following year with an 0-6 to 0-4 defeat of Garda, who had only Cavan star Jim Smith as a survivor from the decider of three years previously. O'Tooles reign finally ended a year later when, bidding to extend their record to six consecutive titles, they were comprehensively beaten 3-4 to 0-2 in yet another final showdown with Garda, who this time had only two changes from the previous year.

The glory days were not quite over, however. O'Tooles would regain the crown in 1928 with a 2-9 to 0-4 win over O'Dwyers, lose the following two finals to first old rivals Garda and then St. Joseph's by a point after a replay, then bounce back for a tenth title in 1931 by beating Erin's Hope, again following a replay. A key factor in the club's success was the longevity of its biggest stars — the McDonnel brothers, Johnny and Paddy, as well as John Synnott figured in all ten title triumphs while Paddy Carey and Josie Synnott each played in nine and Jack O'Reilly — despite missing the 1923 decider through injury — was involved in seven.

ERIN'S Hope, who won the inaugural championship in 1887, conceded a walkover to Isle of the Sea in the 1895 decider and pushed O'Tooles to a replay in the 1931 final, took the 1932 title by beating St. Lawrence's — a Howth club that had been founded only six years earlier — by 1-6 to 1-5 with a line-up that included players from ten different counties but not a single one from Dublin. They were succeeded as champions by a team that proved so good they felt obliged to withdraw from the competition to give the others a chance!

Garda, going into the 1933 campaign, had contested a quartet of deciders in seven years (all against O'Tooles), losing the first two in 1923 and 1926 and winning the final two in 1927 and 1929. Their bid for a third title opened with a 4-6 to 2-1 defeat of Round Towers and was followed by a 1-5 to 1-3 win over defending champions Erin's Hope and, in the semi-final, a 2-7 to 0-5 victory over the previous year's runners-up St. Lawrence's.

That set up a final clash with University College and in a match in which the Garda fielded but half a dozen Dublin natives and their opponents not a single one, the third title was secured on a 1-11 to 1-3 scoreline.

The next year was not quite so straightforward. Sean McDermotts held them to a 2-5 apiece draw in the first round before being hammered 5-9 to 1-3 in the replay — in which Mick Keating scored 3-2 — and, after a comfortable 3-6 to 1-1 defeat of old foes O'Tooles, they were held to another draw by Geraldines in the semi-final before getting through by 2-12 to 2-6 at the second attempt and going on to beat St. Joseph's by an emphatic 3-8 to 1-2.

The following year, 1935, they opened with a 1-6 to 0-1 win over Parnells but were then held level for a third time in almost exactly year, this time an 0-7 each tie by St. Joseph's, before advancing to the semi-finals on a 3-7 to 1-4 scoreline. They followed this with two more convincing victories, by 3-10 to 0-2 over Erin's Hope and, in the final, by 2-7 to 1-2 over O'Tooles. The hat-trick had been completed — they did likewise in the Senior League in the same years — and many more successes appeared to be on the horizon, but at the County Board's weekly meeting on November 4 (the deadline for affiliating for the coming season), Garda delegate Paddy Cryan surprised everybody by announcing that the club had decided to disband "in the belief that there departure would aid the game in Dublin". The withdrawal had an immediate and significant on one aspect of Dublin football; up to then the county champions had the right to select the county teams in their grade but thereafter a selection committee was established for that purpose, a practice that would continue for almost three decades until the appointment of Kevin Heffernan as team manager in July 1973.

For the first time in half a century the county final in 1936 wasn't played at Croke Park (or its previous incarnation as Jones's Road) but at Killester Park, where Clanna Gael — with just two Dubliners in their line-out and in only their second crack at the championship — captured a first title with a 1-9 to 1-2 defeat of St. Lawrence's and they retained it the following year but under unusual circumstances. Their final opponents, Sean McDermotts, were made up almost exclusively of workers in the bar trade and, claiming an inability to play anytime later than noon and the game fixed for 8.30pm, were forced to give only the second county football final walkover ever and the first since Erin's Hope forfeited the decider against Isle of the Sea in 1895.

Sean McDermotts finally got their hands on the trophy the following year with a 2-7 to 1-5 defeat of O'Tooles after dethroning Clanna Gael in the quarter-final by a point, 1-2 to 1-1, and they went close to retaining their crown in 1939 when a George Ingham goal gave Parnells — with a totally local team — a 1-2 to 0-3 victory and their third title but their first since 1916. Parnells, torn by an internal dispute over several players reversing the previous trend of moving to St. Vincent's rather than the other way round, did not enter the championship in 1940, thus becoming only the second reigning champions not to defend their title after Garda four years previously.

PARNELLS may not have been there but Sean McDermotts were and, for the fourth year in succession, they made it to the final only to again suffer disappointment as, for the second year in succession, the title was won by a club bridging a twenty-three year gap; Geraldines winning 2-5 to 1-6 thanks to a 2-2 contribution from full forward Charlie O'Sullivan. It was the start of an unbeaten three year run for Geraldines, who in 1941 really turned it on by trashing Sean McDermotts by 3-8 to 0-9 in the semi-final — Johnny Counihan scoring 2-2 — and Parnells by 3-4 to 0-1 in the final.

A year later, with an 0-11 to 0-8 defeat of final debutants Peadar Mackens, Geraldines became the fifth club to win at least three championships in succession after Young Ireland (allowing for the absence of a competition in 1893), Kickhams, O'Tooles (twice) and Garda. Nine players, the two Paddy Kennedys (goalkeeper and midfielder), Colm Boland, Frank Bray, Jimmy Joy, Paddy Henry, Joe Fitzgerald, Murt Kelly and Johnny Counihan were on all three title winning sides while Joy, Henry, Fitzgerald and the outfield Kennedy were on the Dublin team that beat Galway in the All-Ireland Final in 1942, with Fitzgerald captaining the side.

The following seven years, 1943 to 1949, brought seven different winners, three first time champions and four clubs extending their notches on the roll of honour. The first two years brought new champions in first UCD with a 1-8 to 1-6 success over Sean McDermotts thanks to an injury time goal from Dick Stokes, and then Civil Service who beat Peadar Mackens by 3-4 to 1-1. Both winning teams include a player who would go on to achieve even greater distinction in years to come; future GAA president — and double All-Ireland winner — Donal Keenan from Roscommon for UCD and future Taoiseach and six-time All-Ireland medallist Jack Lynch for Civil Service.

Civil Service — minus an injured Lynch — were back in the final in 1945 but lost out to Parnells who reclaimed the title after a six year gap with an 0-10 to 1-4 victory with the help of seven survivors from their previous triumph, including Brendan Quinn who was on Dublin's successful All-Ireland winning side in 1942 and would go on to train the county's next Sam Maguire winning team in 1958, and the goalscoring hero from the 1939 decider, George Ingham, this time serving as goalkeeper. A second half sub for Parnells is also worth noting ... one Charlie Haughey, who actually played in the semi-final victory over Peadar Mackens but was relegated to the bench for the final.

Parnells, like their predecessors as champions, Civil Service, reached the final when defending their crown but they too lost out, going down 1-6 to 1-5 to O'Tooles in a replay after a last minute Mick Killeen point from a free had earned O'Tooles a second chance. The victory gave the famous club its eleventh county championship and its first in a decade and a half. It was also the last; O'Tooles would not reach another final until 1964 when they lost 0-14 to 1-7 to St. Vincent's and have yet to reappear in a decider.

Sean McDermotts, having been beaten in three finals since their last success in 1938, ended a nine year wait for their second title with an 0-11 to 0-5 defeat of a Westerns side appearing in the final for the one and only time in its history. The final of 1948, played on July 10, would prove to be a real bridge between two separate eras as Garda, who had only reformed ten months earlier, won their sixth and last title with a 2-8 to

2-3 victory over a club making only it's third appearance in the championship, St. Vincent's. The remarkable story of the men from Marino was only starting, however, they would win two dozen titles in the three dozen championships between 1949 and 1984, starting with a record-shattering seven in succession completed in 1955.

ERIN'S Hope, winners of the very first championship in 1887 and another in 1932, pulled of what under the circumstances of the aura of invincibility that surrounded St. Vincent's at the time probably remains the greatest upset in the history of the championship when, after magnificent displays by Mattie McDonagh (Galway) and Tom Long (Kerry) and a cracking goal from Denis Hurley (Cork) six minutes into the second half put the student teachers into a 1-7 to 0-4 lead; the champions rallied with three unanswered points but Erin's Hope held on for a stunning victory.

St. Vincent's racked up another six titles and twenty-three consecutive championship wins before their second hiccup, a comprehensive 2-12 to 0-8 semi-final loss in December 1963 to a UCD side that went on to claim their second title with a 2-12 to 2-8 win over Clanna Gael. College won again two years later by beating Clanna Gael in a replay, with St. Vincent's winning out in between as O'Tooles suffered a sixth final defeat in what remains at the time of writing the famous club's most recent appearance in a decider. In 1968, after two more wins for St. Vincent's, Clanna Gael, after five final defeats since their previous successes in 1936 and 1937, won their third title by beating Scoil Ui Chonaill by 1-8 to 0-7, with Mickey Whelan contributing seven points. St. Vincent's came up short again in 1969 when Na Fianna became the latest new name on the championship roll of honour by edging them out on a 1-8 to 0-10 scoreline, but 'Vins' responded with another three-in-a-row before suffering successive final defeats to UCD in 1973 and 1974 — and then, with Whelan on board by this time, hit back with yet another hat-trick.

The men from Marino would wait another four years, until 1981 (their longest barren spell since they entered the senior ranks in 1946), for their next success, an 0-12 to 2-4 win over final debutants Ballymun Kickhams, and three years later they brought their titles tally to an even two dozen with a 1-8 to 1-5 win over Na Fianna. It would be the last championship triumph for St. Vincent's for over two decades, as the demographics of an ever growing city expanding outwards led to the birth of a host of new clubs in the suburbs and a consequent erosion of the club's dominance. The growth of counter attractions didn't help either; St Joseph's CBS, Fairview, the principal nursery for St. Vincent's since the club's foundation, won the Leinster Championship in 1978 and in both 1992 and 1998 would fare even better by winning the All-Ireland Schools Championship ... at soccer.

The older order was certainly changing; starting with the success of Ballymun Kickhams in 1982, seven new champions were crowned in less than a decade and a half, Scoil Ui Chonaill (1983), Thomas Davis (1999), Kilmacud Crokes (1992), Erin's Isle

(1993), Ballyboden St. Enda's (1995) and St. Sylvester's (1996). It had taken three times longer, from 1927 (Garda) to 1969 (Na Fianna) for the previous seven new champions to get on the roll of honour, the others being St. Joseph's (1930), Clanna Gael (1936), Sean McDermotts (1938), Civil Service (1944) and St. Vincent's (1949). Another new name — the 28th — would be inscribed on the trophy in 2003 with the triumph of St. Brigid's over Kilmacud Crokes.

The latter club, in fact, pretty well became the new St. Vincent's, winning seven titles in less than two decades (1992, 1994, 1998, 2004, 2005, 2008 and 2010) and reaching four other finals between 1993 and 2012. The vastly increased competitiveness of the competition since what might be termed the demise of St. Vincent's is illustrated by the fact that since 1978 — the year after Vins completed a three-in-a-row — only four clubs have successfully defended the championship, Parnells (1987, 1988), Thomas Davis (1989, 1990, 1991), Na Fianna (1999, 2000, 2001) and a resurgent St. Vincent's (2013, 2014). In the same period, in addition to the new champions, five other clubs reached the final for the first time, Clontarf (1985), St. Anne's (1987), Cuala (1988), St. Jude's (2009) and Castleknock (2016).

County Championship
Final Results

1887 Apr 17, Elm Park
ERIN'S HOPE 1-20   GROCERS ASSISTANTS 0-1
Erin's Hope: C Lee, P McCarthy, J Murphy, J Farrell, W Scott, D Downing, J Bradley, T Cronin, J Cronin, P Crowley, E O'Sullivan, P O'Sullivan, P Fleming, P Murphy, T Ryan, D Sheehan, M Randles, M Keogh, P Joyce, M Fitzpatick, M Cromby.
Grocers Assistants: M Fanning, J Morrissy, M Lee, H Whitney, P Muldowney, J Hogan, P Egan, R Maher, T Balfe, P Fanning, J Pollard, J Fortune, C Brady, J Conlan, J Cantwell, P Newman, J Corry, J Kenna, R Shiels, C Pilkingtun, A Murphy.

1888 May 27, Clonskeagh Park
FEACH MCHUGH'S 2-4   GERALDINES 2-1
Feach McHugh's: G Dalton, T Keating, G McDermott, J Scully, P Halpin, T Connell, W Perry, T McNulty, T Brennan, T Roche, J Cullen, L Gibson, N McLoughlin, W Burke, JJ Walsh, W Fitzgerald, P Stapleton, P McNeill, P Caralier, J Byrne, G O'Neill.
Geraldines: D Callinane, M Byrne, J Callinane, P Callinane, G Byrne, M Byrne, J Collins, T Byrne, B Byrne, H Cummins, P Brennan, G Byrne, L Farrell, J Farrell, P Gafan, J Connor, C Connor, P Davis, C Reynolds, J Cullen, J Mulligan.

1889 June 2, St Patrick's Park
FAUGHS 0-5   KICKHAMS 0-1
Faughs: T Power, J Murphy, P O'Gorman, T O'Driscoll, T O'Brien, P Herbert, J Quane, B Madden, D Sheehan, T Doran, H Cummins, T Whelan, R Higgins, M McCarthy, D Ryan, P Ryan, J Hayes, T Byrne, T Egan, J Mulally, M Thornton.
Kickhams: P O'Shea, J O'Byrne, P Cahill, J Harper, T Clinton, P Grogan, E Gilligan, P Finn, JJ Keane, J O'Connor, J O'Donnell, J Nolan, T McKenna, J Sweeney, A Geary, P O'Riordan, T Belton, N O'Shea, J Ryan, F Meagher, D Kerwick.

1890 July 6, Clonturk Park
ISLE OF THE SEA 0-5   YOUNG IRELAND 0-3
Isles of the Sea: C Thompson, D Holland, T Dunne, JJ Hoey, F North, P North, B North, P Rourke, D Whelan, K Quinn, J Reid, K Fitzpatrick, W Connolly, P McGrath, R Byrne, J Hennessy, M Kearns, R Lawlor, P Hoare, D Kennedy, M Downes.

Young Ireland: G Charlemont, G Roche, B McKenna, J Kennedy, D Flood, P Heslin, P Maher, J Byrne, S Flood, S Hughes, T Hughes, T Murphy, J Geraghty, P Kelly, J Kelly, J Silke, O O'Hagan, P O'Hagan, J Cooney, J Scully, J Roche.

1891 Oct 4, Clonturk Park
YOUNG IRELAND 3-7   SONS OF THE SEA 0-3
Young Irelands: G Charlemont, J Kennedy, G Roche, J Roche, P Heslin, J Scully, J Silke, T Lyons, F O'Malley, J Cooney, P Kelly, J Cooney, O O'Hagan, P O'Hagan, J Mahony, J Kelly, J Geraghty, D Flood, S Hughes, S Flood, T Murphy, D Byrne.
Sons of the Sea: C Reilly, J Fulham, M Ward, D Adams, Jim Clark, Joe Clark, J Power, F Weafer, L Redmond, P Lawless, M Brian, W Dent, A Pent, J Westby, J Ennis, M Daly, T Kirwan, P Whelan, M Bissitt, T Caulfield, H O'Keeffe.

1892 Aug 21, Clonturk Park
YOUNG IRELAND 3-2   ISLE OF THE SEA 1-0
Young Ireland: G Charlemont, G Roche, J Roche, J Kennedy, P Heslin, J Silke, P Kelly, O O'Hagan, P O'Hagan, J Mahony, D Curtis, J Heslin, S Condon, J Geraghty, S Flood, F O'Malley, S Hughes,

1893 Championship not staged.

1894 Aug 11, Phoenix Park
YOUNG IRELAND   DOLPHINS
Young Irelands: G Charlemont, G Roche, J Roche, J Kennedy, P Heslin, J Silke, P Kelly, J Kirwan, J Mahony, L O'Kelly, D Curtis, D Flood, S Hughes, T Errity, T Hughes, M Byrne, M Condron.

1895 Nov 17, Clonturk Park
ISLE OF THE SEA W/O   ERIN'S HOPE SCR
Isle of the Sea: G Murphy, T Dunne, D Adams, J Hoey, B North, M Ward, J Dunne, F Wall, D Whelan, P O'Rourke, J Behan, C Dunne, T Knott, P Hoare, W Connolly, P Lawlor, P Walsh.

1896 Oct 18, Clonturk Park
YOUNG IRELANDS 3-7   LUCAN SARSFIELDS 0-3
Young Irelands: R Flood, G Roche, T Hession, S Mooney, J Westby, P Heslin, J Mahony, J Graham, D

Curtis, M Byrne 1-1, T Downey, P O'Toole, J Ledwidge 1-1, J Kirwan, J Heslin 0-3, L O'Kelly 1-1, T Errity 0-1.

1897 Dec 5, Jones's Road
KICKHAMS 1-7   GERALDINES 0-8
Kickhams: D O'Donnell 1-1, M Byrne 0-3, P O'Donoghue 0-2, T Downey 0-1. Geraldines: D O'Callaghan 0-3, J Heslin and P Fitzsimons 0-2 each, M Kavanagh 0-1.
* Geraldines lodged an objection claiming Kickhams had played an unregistered player and a replay was ordered.
REPLAY: Apr 24, 1898, Jones's Road
KICKHAMS 2-8   GERALDINES 2-3
Kickhams: D Scanlan, PJ Walsh, J Carvan, P Byrne, B Guiry, R O'Brien, M Byrne 0-4, V Skelly, H Kavanagh, M Ahern 0-1, P Comerford, J Callanan, T Downey, J O'Brien, D O'Donnell 0-2, M Chambers 1-0, P O'Donoghue 1-1.
Geraldines: J Lane, J Connolly, M Rea, Conroy, JJ Keane, JJ Ryan, J Joy, M Geraghty, J Farrelly, J Heslin 1-1, P McSweeney, P Smyth 0-1, M Pierce, J Shaw, M Kavanagh, P Fitzsimons 1-0, D O'Callaghan 0-1,

1898 Aug 20, 1899, Jones's Road
GERALDINES 4-13   KICKHAMS 1-4
Geraldines: J Lane, J Connolly, M Rea, P Smyth, JJ Keane, J Norton, P McCann 0-1, T Errity 0-5, JJ Ryan, J Farrelly 0-1, C Sargant 0-3, P Leavy, M Kerrill, J Heslin 2-1, P Fitzsimons 1-2, D O'Callaghan 1-1, T Redmond.
Kickhams: D Scanlan, J O'Brien, W Quane, P Walsh, B Guiry, J Callanan, P Byrne, M Madigan, M Byrne, J Dempsey, L O'Kelly, T Downey, M Byrne, M Chambers, C Gannon, R O'Brien, J Matthews.

1899 Dec 2, 1900, Jones's Road
GERALDINES 1-6   KICKHAMS 0-9
Geraldines: J Ledwidge 1-1, J Heslin and P Fitzsimons 0-2 each, T Errity 0-1. Kickhams: J Matthews, M Chambers and M Madigan 0-2 each, L O'Kelly, T Downey and B Guiry 0-1 each)
REPLAY: Dec 16, 1900, Jones's Road
GERALDINES 1-12   KICKHAMS 0-6
Geraldines: J Lane, D Smith, B Sherry, JJ Keane, G Brady, JJ Ryan, J Norton, M Rea, P McCann 0-1, T Redmond, P Leavy, J Farrelly, T Errity 0-1, J Heslin 0-4, P Fitzsimons 0-2, D O'Callaghan 0-2, J Ledwidge 1-2.
Kickhams: D Scanlan, P Walsh, J Carvin, J O'Brien, T Redmond, L O'Kelly, B Guiry 0-2, J Matthews 0-1, M Byrne, T Downey 0-1, M Madigan 0-1, J Dempsey, R O'Brien, J Kerrill, M Chambers 0-1, C Gannon.

1900 Feb 9, 1902, Jones's Road
ISLES OF THE SEA 1-5   KICKHAMS 1-4
Isles of the Sea: J Gaffney, D Holland, D Edwards, T Gale, T Doyle, M Whelan, Jim Whelan 0-1, T Whelan, John Whelan, W Boland, J Fitzpatrick 0-1, C Kelly 0-1, J Byrne 1-1, M Brien, T Lawless 0-1, B Connor, D Dunne.
Kickhams: P Walsh, M Madigan, J O'Brien, J Matthews, T Quane, J Donoghue, D Sheehan, C Sargent, B Guiry 0-1, C Gannon, B Dowling, T Errity 1-0, M Chambers 0-1, J Fahy, M Madigan, R O'Brien, J Murphy.

1901 Apr 26, 1903, Jones's Road
BRAY EMMETS 0-11   KICKHAMS 0-6
Bray Emmets: J Byrne, J Dempsey, M Casey, S Mulvey, M Leggat, M Hanley, J Dunne, T Black, J Devlin 0-2, T Doyle, T Doogan 0-4, J Cunningham, J O'Sullivan 0-3, M Flanagan, P Ashford 0-2, M Byrne, M Condron.
Kickhams: J Connell, J Lynch, J Grace, T Murphy, J Fahy, J Flynn, M Madigan, B Guiry, J Matthews, J O'Brien, J Donoghue, J Lynch 0-4, T Dwyer, T Quane, J Gleeson, C Gannon 0-2, M Keane.

1902 Championship not staged due to a major backlog of fixtures.

1903 May 29, 1904, Jones's Road
KEATINGS 0-7   GERALDINES 0-7
Keatings: T Murphy 0-5, J Murphy and M Finn 0-1 each. Geraldines: J Brennan 0-4, M Kelly 0-2, T Duffy 0-1)
REPLAY: June 19, 1904, Jones's Road
KEATINGS 2-9   GERALDINES 0-5
Keatings: G Hearne, JJ Byrne, P O'Malley, W Allen, Ted Murphy, M O'Shea, P Breen, W Roche, J Archdeacon, J Crean 0-1, J O'Hehir 0-2, J Brennan, J Murphy 0-1, P Weymess 1-1, P McEnroe, Tommy Murphy 1-4, W Doherty.
Geraldines: J Lane, JJ Keane, D O'Callaghan, P McCann, P Leavy, P Smith, M Rea, J Norton, T Redmond 0-2, J Farrelly, J Delaney, M Kelly 0-1, W Ring, J Brennan 0-2, M Finn, T O'Mahony, T Duffy. Sub: P Fitzsimons for Rea.

1904 July 16, 1905 Jones's Road
KICKHAMS 0-11   ISLES OF THE SEA 0-2
Kickhams: M Quinn, P Callaghan, J Lynch, P Cox, J Grace 0-1, M Barry, J O'Brien, H Doyle 0-1, J Lavelle 0-1, L Sheehan, M Madigan, T Chadwick, J Ryan, T Callaghan, T Walsh 0-3, T Murphy 0-5, M Dwyer.

Isles of the Sea: P Fallon, M Doyle, J Dillon, C Kelly, J Whelan, MJ Brennan, D Dunne, J Doyle, E Doyle, M O'Brien, P Byrne, T Doyle 0-1, T Lawless, J Darcy 0-1, S Cullen, W Boland, T McKenna.

1905 Oct 14, 1906 Jones's Road
KICKHAMS 0-5   GERALDINES 0-4
Kickhams: M Quinn, P Callaghan, J Lynch, J Grace, M Barry, M Curry, J English, P Cox, L Sheehan, M Dwyer, T Murphy, P Casey, P Matthews 0-1, H Hilliard 0-2, T Walsh 0-2, M Keane, M Madigan.
Geraldines: P Fallon, J Lane, M Kelly, P McCann, P Boyle 0-1, M Griffin 0-1, D Kelleher, J Scully, J Daly, J Wright, J Broughal, P Leavy, T Mahony, M Keane, M Kenny, P Whelan, P Daly 0-2.

1906 May 12, 1907, Jones's Road
KICKHAMS 0-8   PARNELLS 0-5
Kickhams: P Callaghan, L Sheehan, J Grace, P Fielding, J Lynch, M Dwyer 0-1, T Dunne, H Hilliard 0-1, T Walsh 0-3, P Matthews 0-1, P Casey, M Barry, B Callan, J English, M Keane, M Curry, T Murphy 0-1.
Parnells: W Conlon, P Connolly, F Call, J Caddell, M Smith, J Teeling, T Craven, J Dixon, C Reilly, T O'Brien, M Ryan 0-2, W McMahon, S Hughes, P Brady 0-2, T Crowley, P Murphy 0-1, L Carroll.

1907 19 Jan, 1908, Jones's Road
KICKHAMS 0-11   KEATINGS 0-2
Kickhams: M Keane, V Grace, T Grace, J English, M Barrry, P O'Brien, J Lynch, P Cox, P O'Callaghan, P Casey 0-1, M Currie, T Murphy, L Sheehan, T Quane 0-1, H Hilliard 0-2, T Walsh 0-4, M Madigan 0-3.
Keatings: J Brennan, M Whelan, M Byrne, T Murphy, J Crean, P McManus, T Mahony, T Clarke, F O'Reilly, F Cooney 0-1, W Doberty 0-1, K Sexton, T Healy, R Yourell, E Herlihy, M McCaffrey, A Fitzgerald.

1908 July 19, Jones's Road
GERALDINES 0-5   KEATINGS 0-4
Geraldines: P Fallon, E Smith 0-1, P Doyle, R Flood, M Griffin, P Daly, T McAuley 0-1, P Whelan, J Carey, T Doyle 0-2, L Kelly 0-1, J Shouldice, P Sheehan, M Collins, D Kelleher, M Power, W Halliden.
Keatings: M Phelan, John Byrne, J Crean, W Doherty, P McManus, F Cooney, J Ennis, J Brennan, T Clarke 0-1, T Healy, T Murphy 0-3, F Kelly, E Herlihy, E Sexton, W Dalton, M McCaffrey, M Tehon.

1909 May 23, Jones's Road
KEATINGS 3-3   GERALDINES 1-6
Keatings: J Brennan, J Byrne, T Clarke, F Cooney 0-2, W Doherty, J Crean, J Ennis, T Healy, E Herlihy, B Hudson, T Murphy 2-1, P McManus, M Phelan, M Russell, E Sexton 1-0, A Scully, H McNulty   Sub: J Dillon for Russell.
Geraldines: P Fallon, W O'Dwyer, R Flood 0-1, J Sheehy, M Collins, E Smith, M Power, P Matthews 0-1, P Daly 0-3, J Shouldice 1-0, D Kelleher 0-1, T McAuley, P Sheehan, W. Halliden, P Whelan, T Murray, M Griffin.

1910 May 29, Jones's Road
GERALDINES 0-7   PARNELLS 0-6
Geraldines: P Fallon, J Sheehy, R Flood, D Kelleher 0-1, M Griffin, W Halliden, J Shouldice, M Collins 0-2, M Keane 0-1, P Whelan, W Sole, J Collison, P Sheehan, P Matthews, P Daly 0-3, E Smith, W O'Dwyer.
Parnells: E Caddell, R Manifold, T Bedford, P Christie, T Donnelly, J Nathan, E Letmon 0-1, L Carroll, P Connor, W Moore 0-4, J Joyce, J Bell, T McAuley, B Callaghan, J Dixon, F Brady 0-1, P Brady.

1911 June 18, Jones's Road
KEATINGS 2-2   GERALDINES 1-0
Keatings: F Cooney, J Byrne, A O'Connor, G Bailey, P McManus, C Flynn, T Healy, T Clarke, TP Clarke, J Moran 1-0, L Murray, T Murphy 0-1, D Mullen 1-0, L Clarke, J Ennis 0-1, E Herlihy, PJ McDonagh.
Geraldines: P Fallon, R Flood, J Shouldice, D Kelleher, J Sheehy, M Griffin, W Halliden, W Sole, E Smith, P Whelan, M Collins, W O'Flaherty, M Keane 1-0, M O'Flaherty, J Parker, P Daly, C Shine.

1912 May 19, Jones's Road
KICKHAMS 1-1   GERALDINES 0-1
Kickhams: P Codd, J Grace, J English, T Walsh, T Grattan, M Cunningham, F Duggan, H Hilliard 1-0, B Callan, M Drumgoole, D Kavanagh, B Fitzpatrick, T Quane 0-1, M Kelly, J McDonnell, D Downey, T Doherty.
Geraldines: P Fallon, J Brennan, R Flood, M Hand, M Keane, J Sheehy, B Murphy, W Halliden, M Collins, J O'Connor, P Sheehan, J Parker, J Doyle 0-1, J Shouldice, W Sole, P Whelan, C Shine.

1913 May 25, Jones's Road
PARNELLS 2-3   KICKHAMS 2-2
Parnells: E Caddell, R Manifold, T Connor, P Connor, P Christie, J Crystal, M Manifold 0-1, E Letmon, S Hughes, J Dowdall 1-0, F Brady 0-1, P Brady, J Nugent, J Finnerty 1-0, J Dixon 0-1.
Kickhams: J Rogers, J Grace, T English, R Downey, R Fitzpatrick, M Kelly, P Neville, C Murray 0-1, J Shorten, P Galligan, T Walsh 1-0, M Cunningham, T Doherty 0-1, T Quane, J Clancy 1-0.

1914 May 10, Croke Park
GERALDINES 3-2   PARNELLS 0-2
Geraldines: P Fallon, F Shouldice, J Brennan, R Flood 0-1, W Halliden, J Kelly, J Shouldice, M Collins, J Parker, W O'Flaherty, M Donovan 1-0, M Power 2-1, M Keane, T Farrelly, M O'Cathain.
Parnells: E Caddell, R Manifold, P Connor, M Manifold, J Chrystal, J Dixon, J Nugent, J Finnerty, P Christie, P Brady, E Letmon, J Dowdall 0-2, O McDermott, R Fitzpatrick, J Manifold.

1915 May 30, Croke Park
GERALDINES 0-7   PARNELLS 0-1
Geraldines: P Fallon, F Shouldice, R Flood, J Kelly, W Halliden, T Farrelly, J Treacy, J Shouldice, M Collins, W O'Flaherty, M Keane, W Sole 0-1, J Parker 0-3, S Lawlor 0-3, J Doyle.
Parnells: L Carroll, R Manifold, P Christie, M Manifold, J Chrystal, O McDermott, P Connor, T Connor, W Brady, E Letmon, M Joyce, C McDermott, J Dowdall 0-1, J Finnerty, L Boland.

1916 Aug 20, Croke Park
PARNELLS 1-4   HIBERNIAN KNIGHTS 0-6
Parnells: L Carroll, R Manifold, P Connor, P Christie, E Letmon, O McDermott, M Joyce 0-1, W Brady, E Boland, M Manifold 1-1, J Rice, R Mooney, W Snow, T Connor 0-1, J Dowdall 0-1.
Hibernian Knights: P Lynch, J Kelly 0-1, M Sammon 0-1, J Nathen, M Maguire, E Burke, M Brazil, W Brazil, J McEvoy, J Barry 0-1, C McNamee, JP Bell, T Donnelly 0-1, J Norris 0-2, J Joyce.

1917 July 1, Croke Park
GERALDINES 3-4   KEATINGS 0-4
Geraldines: P Fallon, J Kelly, R Flood 0-1, J McEvoy, B Considine, B McAllister, J Treacy, T Lonergan, W O'Flaherty, F Farrelly, M Collins, T Farrelly, J Parker 0-1, S Lawlor 2-1, W Sole.
Keatings: P Hughes, G Feeney, A O'Connor, P Kerns, T Bennett, B Whelan, J McEvoy, J Matthews 0-1, P McLoughlin, J Hayden 0-1, J Vize, M Doyle 0-2, M McCaffrey, J Hughes, J Christie.

1918 June 16, Croke Park
O'TOOLES 1-6   COLLEGIANS 0-3
O'Tooles: J McDonnell, J O'Rourke, P Carey, P Smith, B Robbins, J Norris, J Reilly, P McDonnell 1-1, Josie Synnott 0-1, John Synnott 0-1, S Synnott, P Lynch, J Bell, W Maher 0-2, T Ennis 0-1.
Collegians: J Drury, P Kelly, J O'Donovan, D Purcell, W Quinlan, P McGuinness, P Moran, W McCarville, H McAuley, P Collins 0-1, J Phelan 0-1, B Joyce, S Lawlor 0-1, C McGinley, F Burke.

1919 July 20, Croke Park
O'TOOLES 1-7   McCRACKENS 0-2
O'Tooles: J McDonnell, J Bell, P Carey, B Robbins, J Reilly, T Carey, J Norris, W Maher 0-1, T Ennis 0-1, John Synnott, J Dempsey 0-1, Josie Synnott 0-1, P McDonnell, S Synnott 0-1, J Carey 1-2.
McCrackens: R Mockler, M Nolan, T Kearns, T Donnelly, T Byrne 0-1, M Kearns, W Hanney, J Kearns, J Kelly, C Kelly 0-1, J Moran, P White, H Cannon, R Manly, T McAdams.

1920 Feb 6, 1921, Croke Park
O'TOOLES 1-2   KICKHAMS 0-1
O'Tooles: J McDonnell, J Bell, P Carey, J Norris, B Robbins, T Ennis, John Synnott, W Maher, J Reilly, T Carey, J Dempsey, Josie Synnott 0-2, P McDonnell 1-0, J Carey, S Synnott.
Kickhams: T McCarthy, M Holland, W Flanagan, J Rogers, T Smith, M Carroll, L Shaw, J Clune, T Walsh 0-1, J Sewell, J O'Neill, W Donovan, P McSwiney, J Kealy, P Lenihan. Sub: J O'Connor for Clune.

1921 June 5, Croke Park
ST. MARY'S 1-5   KICKHAMS 0-3
St Mary's: J Graham, A Balmain, J O'Grady, C McGuirk, E Carroll, J McDonnell, C O'Neill, P Considine, M Shanahan, M Bradshaw, T Considine 0-5, A Dixon, W Fitzsimons 1-0, C McDonald, P Daly.
Kickhams: T McCarthy, J Rogers, T Smith, M Holland, W Flanagan, M Carroll, L Shaw, J Clune 0-1, T Walsh, J Sewell, J O'Neill, W Donovan 0-1, P McSwiney, J Kealy 0-1, P Lenihan. Sub: J O'Connor for Clune.

1922 June 25, Croke Park
O'TOOLES 0-3   ST. MARY'S 0-3
O'Tooles: J Carey 0-2, J Dowdall 0-1.
St Mary's: P Nugent, M Shanahan and C McDonald 0-1 each.
REPLAY: Sep 3, Croke Park
O'TOOLES 1-2   ST. MARY'S 0-3
O'Tooles: J McDonnell, T Gibbons, P Carey, J Kelly, B Robbins, J Norris, J Reilly, P McDonnell, Josie Synnott 0-1, T Carey, J Carey 0-1, John Synnott, J O'Rourke, C Grace, W Maher 1-0.
St Mary's: J Graham, E Carroll, P Nugent, A Healy, L Malone 0-1, C McGuirk, A Dixon, A Balmain, J O'Grady, M Shanahan, M Bradshaw 0-2, C McDonald, W Fitzsimons, J Hanlon, C O'Toole.

1923 Jan 20, 1924, Croke Park
O'TOOLES 1-4   GARDA 0-4
O'Tooles: J McDonnell, P Carey, B Robbins, W Reilly, T Carey, J Norris, T Fitzgerald, P McDonnell, M O Brien, C Grace 0-1, J Carey, W Maher, John Synnott 0-1, W Rooney 1-2, Josie Synnott.
Garda: J Mahon, J Rabbitt, P Redmond, M Flynn, C Smith, J Doherty, P Gilroy 0-2, M McCoy, P Kirwan, J Cunniffe 0-1, J Moran, P Colleran, G Williams, J Hayes 0-1, J McGaheran.

1924 June 29, Croke Park
O'TOOLES 4-5   U.C.D. 3-2
O'Tooles: J McDonnell, W Reilly, P Carey, T Gibbons, Josie Synnott 0-1, J Norris, J Reilly, M Lennon, P McDonnell 0-1, C Grace, P Synnott 2-2, T Fitzgerald 0-1, John Synnott 1-0, M O'Brien 1-0, W O'Meara.
UCD: J Coyne, E Grant, S Gardiner, M O'Sullivan 1-0, E Carroll, T Gardiner, M Devine, J Ryan, E Madigan, M McQuaide, J Smith 1-0, M Kilcoyne 0-1, F Burke 1-1, J Henry.

1925 Sep 20, Croke Park
O'TOOLES 3-7   KICKHAMS 1-3
O'Tooles: J McDonnell, W Reilly, P Carey, Joe Norris, P Stynes 1-2, Josie Synnott, Jim Norris, M O'Brien 1-1, John Synnott, C Grace, J Reilly, P McDonnell 0-3, M Lennon 1-1, L Synnott, T Fitzgerald.
Kickhams: T McCarthy, M Alyward, M Feeney, J Muldoon, M Howlett, J Hunt, M Carroll, T Walsh, P O'Beirne, J Kneafsey, M Cleary, T Nugent, M Gorevan, M O'Neill 1-3, J Mohan.

1926 May 9, Croke Park
O'TOOLES 0-6   GARDA 0-4
O'Tooles: J McDonnell, W Reilly, Joe Norris, P Carey, Jim Norris, J Reilly, M O'Brien, P McDonnell 0-1, John Synnott 0-1, M Lennon 0-1, M Durnin 0-1, Josie Synnott 0-1, C Grace 0-1, L Synnott, T Fitzgerald.
Garda: J O'Reilly, J O'Toole, J Murphy, T Carty, J Sherlock, John Kirwan, J Smith, J Lynam, M Moran, Jim Kirwan, P Russell 0-1, JJ Scanlan, L Stanley 0-2, J Mullen, G Magan 0-1.

1927 May 1, Croke Park
GARDA 3-4   O'TOOLES 0-2
Garda: J O'Reilly, J O'Toole, J Sherlock, T Carty, J Rice, John Kirwan, J Smith 0-1, Jim Kirwan, P Flynn 2-1, J Mullen, JJ Scanlan, J Lynam, L Stanley 0-2, P Russell 1-0, G Magan.
O'Tooles: J McDonnell, W Reilly, J Molloy, Joe Norris, P Carey, Jim Norris, J Reilly, John Synnott, P McDonnell 0-2, M Durnin, P Stynes 0-1, Josie Synnott, W Manifold 0-1, C Grace, L Synnott. Sub: J Fitzgerald for Jim Norris.

1928 May 6, Croke Park
O'TOOLES 2-9   O'DWYERS 0-4
O'Tooles: J McDonnell, P Carey, D Smyth, W Reilly, Joe Norris, J Molloy, P Stynes, Josie Synnott, P McDonnell 0-3, A Perkins 1-1, M Durnin 0-1, W Manifold 1-2, John Synnott, P Synnott 0-1, M O'Brien 0-1.
O'Dwyers: M Wall, J Bissett, W Corcoran, J Cullen, J Brady, J Farrell, L Richardson, W Corry, P Kenny 0-1, W Leonard, P Smith, G Knight, J Corcoran 0-2, P Monks 0-1, J O'Toole.

1929 May 12, Croke Park
GARDA 1-4   O'TOOLES 0-4
Garda: J O'Reilly, R Creagh, J Sherlock, John Kirwan, J Smith, J O'Toole, Joe Synnott, Jim Kirwan, P Flynn, D Hearns, JJ Scanlan, P Synnott, D Hearns 1-0, J Smith 0-2, P Russell 0-2 each.
O'Tooles: J McDonnell, P Carey, Joe Norris, W Reilly, Josie Synnott, P Synnott, J ReilJy, T Fitzgerald, P McDonnell 0-2, J Stynes, J Mohan 0-1, M O'Brien, M Durnin, W Leonard 0-1, J Ebbs.

1930 May 25, Croke Park
ST. JOSEPH'S 0-6   O'TOOLES 0-6
St Joseph's: J Mulhall 0-3, C Duffy, J Macken and P Mulhall 0-1 each.
O'Tooles: P McDonnell 0-3, J Mohan, J Synnott and P Synnott 0-1 each.
REPLAY: June 15, Croke Park
ST. JOSEPH'S 2-3   O'TOOLES 1-5
St Joseph's: John Mulhall, P Moore, C Coughlan, J Macken, V Macken, M Curley, P Mulhall 2-2, Jim Mulhall, M Wellington, J Byrne, T Newman, C Duffy 0-1, S Moore, J Mohan 0-1, C Rochford.
O'Tooles: J McDonnell, P Carey, D Smith, T Ebbs, W Leonard, J Norris, P Stynes, A Perkins, M O'Brien, P McDonnell 1-2, J Mohan, John Synnott, P Synnott 0-2, M Langton, M Durnin.

1931 June 7, Croke Park
O'TOOLES 0-5   ERIN'S HOPE 0-5
O'Tooles: P McDonnell 0-3, M Durnin 0-2.
Erin's Hope: P Magee 0-2, J Kelly, G Fitzgerald and J Gilhawley 0-1 each)
REPLAY: June 21, Croke Park
O'TOOLES 1-8   ERIN'S HOPE 1-5
O'Tooles: J McDonnell, T Ebbs, W Leonard 0-1, Jim

Norris, D Smyth, P Synnott, Joe Norris, J Mohan 0-1, J Lawlor, John Synnott, M O'Brien 0-4, A Perkins 0-1, M McCabe, P McDonnell 1-0, M Durnin 0-1.
Erin's Hope: J Hartnett, M Curran, J Quinn, M Gannon, P Mangan, J Farrell, J Mullen, G Fitzgerald, M O'Dwyer, P Mannion, J Browne 0-1, T Duffy 0-2, J Kilhawley, M Kelly 1-0, P Magee 0-2.

1932 May 8, Croke Park
ERIN'S HOPE 1-6   ST. LAWRENCE'S 1-5
Erin's Hope: J Hartnett, J Fahy, J Feeney, M Gannon, C Boland, J Farrell, P Marrinan, M Connolly, R Lee, G Fitzgerald, M Kelly 1-4, P Mannion, J McCarthy, P Magee 0-1, P Nestor 0-1.
St Lawrence's: J McLoughlin, D Rickard, C Hanway, J Kelly, D O'Rourke, G McLoughlin, J Doyle, M O'Brien 0-1, P Langton, J O'Rourke, J Kane 0-1, W Bruen, A Dixon 1-3, J Lyons, Molloy.

1933 June 4, Croke Park
GARDA 1-11   U.C.D. 1-3
Garda: J O'Reilly, J Brennan, M McMahon, P O'Dowd, J Lambe, J Kirwan, J Breen, M Kelly, J Blessing, G Comerford 0-3, M Keating 1-1, M Farrell, J Pringle 0-2, P Russell 0-2, P Perry 0-2.
UCD: J Doyle, F Durkin, M Casey, S Barrett, M Gorman, C Boland, G Powell 0-2, J O'Sullivan, T Walsh, C Connolly, S Flood, M McKenna, M Higgins, V McGovern 1-1, J Dore. Sub: M Quinn for Casey.

1934 June 24, Croke Park
GARDA 3-8   ST. JOSEPH'S 1-2
Garda: J O'Reilly, J Brennan, M McMahon, P O'Dowd, P Russell, J Lambe, J Delaney 0-1, J Breen, G Ormsby 1-0, G Comerford 0-2, M Keating 0-1, T Keogh 0-1, J Pringle 1-1, M Kelly, G Behan 1-1, P Perry.
St Joseph's: T Metcalfe, P Moore, L Nolan, B Beggs, T Lawless, P Dunne, C Duffy, V Macken 0-1, M Curley, J Byrne, J Kelly, M Wellington 0-1, E Byrne, T Newman 1-0, J Mulhall.

1935 June 16, Croke Park
GARDA 2-7   O'TOOLES 1-2
Garda: P Perry, J Brennan, M McMahon, J O'Dowd, M Cunniffe, G Comerford 0-2, T Mangan, J Breen, G Ormsby, T O'Donnell 1-1, M Keating 1-1, P Laffey, J Mullaney 0-1, M Kelly 0-1, J Keogh 0-1.
O'Tooles: J McDonnell, D Brennan, P Synnott, J Hannon, M Muldowney, J Green, A Perkins, J Sherlook, P Darcy, T Darcy, M O'Brien, J Glavin, E Heron 0-1, W Dowling 0-1, C McMahon. Sub: T Markham 1-0 for Heron.

1936 May 31, Killester Park
CLANNA GAEL 1-9   ST. LAWRENCE'S 1-2
Clanna Gael: M O'Hara, Ruane (Westmeath), P Whitty, D Kenny, J Feeney, F Dowling 0-1, J O'Driscoll, L McAuliffe, T O'Gorman, S Sheehan, P Keaney, T Brosnan, R Conlon 1-2, L O'Dowd 0-1, V White 0-5, A Fitzpatrick.
St Lawrence's: J McLoughlin, A McLoughlin, C Hanway, D O'Rourke, M Nolan, M Connaire, M Cunniffe, L Hanway, M McDonnell, J Lyons, J Baker, F McLoughlin 0-1 G Lockhart 0-1, A Dixon 1-0, P Perry. Sub: W Brady for McDonnell.

1937 June 13, Croke Park
CLANNA GAEL W/O   SEAN MCDERMOTTS SCR
Clanna Gael: M O'Hara, H Rourke, J Feeney, D Kenny, L McAuliffe, F Dowling, A Fitzpatrick, T O'Gorman, T White, T Brosnan, P Keaney, V White, L O'Dowd, S Sheehan, P Darcy.
Sean McDermotts, insisting they could only field a team for an afternoon throw-in rather than the scheduled eight o'clock in the evening start, conceded a walkover.

1938 June 19, Croke Park
SEAN MCDERMOTTS 2-7   O'TOOLES 1-5
Sean McDermotts: P McMahon, P McIntyre, T O'Donnell, T Laffey 0-4, J O'Connor, E Callan, J Gartland, P Robinson, T Robinson, M O'Malley, J Keogh 1-1, H Devine, J Coyle 1-2, J Laffey, J Smith Sub: J Kerr for Smith.
O'Tooles: J McDonnell, J Hannon, P O'Neill, B Cullen, J Greene, P Darcy, J Jenkinson, C McMahon, J Byrne, J Sherlock, D Brennan 0-1, J Murphy, P Maher 0-1, J Scott, P McMahon 1-3.

1939 July 2, Croke Park
PARNELLS 1-2   SEAN MCDERMOTTS 0-3
Parnells: M White, E Brady, P Toolan, P Power, J Deegan, T McCann, B Quinn, S Gibbons, E Boland, P O'Connor, S Ingham 1-1, M McCann, T Mahody, J Brady 0-1, J Teeling. Sub: J O'Connor for Deegan.
Sean McDermotts: B McMahon, H McNamee, P McIntyre, T Laffey, J O'Connor, E Callan, J Slater, P Robinson, T Robinson, M O'Malley 0-1, J Laffey, H Devine, P Boylan, J Gartland 0-2, J Kerr. Sub: J Coyle for Boylan.

1940 June 23, Croke Park
GERALDINES 2-5   SEAN MCDERMOTTS 1-6
Geraldines: P Kennedy, I Leavey, J Keohane, F Bray, J Joy, C Boland, P Henry, P Kennedy, P Holly, T

McCann, M Kelly 0-2, G Fitzgerald, J Fitzgibbon 0-1, C O'Sullivan 2-2, J Counihan.

Sean McDermotts: M McMahon, P McIntyre, E Boyle, T Laffey, T Robinson, E Callan, J Gartland, R Martin, W Ryan, M O'Malley 0-1, J O'Connor 1-1, P Robinson, P Boylan, J Coyle, K Devin 0-4. Sub: J Moore for P. Robinson.

1941 July 6, Croke Park
GERALDINES 3-4   PARNELLS 0-1
Geraldines: P Kennedy, F Bray, J Keohane, I Leavey, P Henry, C Boland, J Fitzgerald, P Kennedy, P Holly, J Joy 0-2, M Kelly 1-1, J Canavan 2-1, J Counihan, J Johnson, G Kelly.
Parnells: G Ingham, V Joyce, P Toolan, P Power, W McDonald, M McCann, R McCann, J Deegan, T Mahady, S Ingham, J Teeling, S Gibbons, B Quinn, T McCann 0-1, A O'Farrell.

1942 July 12, Croke Park
GERALDINES 0-11   PEADAR MACKENS 0-8
Geraldines: Peter Kennedy, F Bray, C Boland, I Leavey, P Henry, Paddy Kennedy, P Cunniffe, J Fitzgerald, S Brosnan, J Joy 0-3, M Kelly 0-4, J Canavan, J Counihan 0-2, C O'Sulllvan 0-2, G Kelly.
Peadar Mackens: C Kelly, S Delaney, G Bolger, D O'Sullivan, H Wall, P Kennedy 0-2, S Byrne, J Delaney, M Richardson, M Fletcher 0-2, J Clarke, W Gibson, S Harkins, J Lawless 0-1, P Walsh 0-3.

1943 June 6, Croke Park
U.C.D. 1-8   SEAN MCDERMOTTS 1-6
UCD: JD Benson, K Kennedy, J Bohan, D O'Driscoll, P McDonnell, J Colleton, V Duffy 0-1, TP O'Reilly, P Murray, E Smith 0-3, P Thornton 0-1, D Keenan, B Devlin, P O'Connor 0-2, D Stokes 1-1.
Sean McDermotts: J Murphy, E Boyle, M Connaire, P Kelly, S Flanagan, P McIntyre 0-1, J Gartland, J Coyle, P Robinson, M O'Malley 0-1, J O'Connor, T Banks 1-1, J Stafford, P Boylan, W Leonard 0-3.

1944 June 4, Croke Park
CIVIL SERVICE 3-4   PEADAR MACKENS 1-1
Civil Service: S Thornton, D Foley, F Dowling, J Lynch, S O'Mahony, T Moore, S O'Shea, A Tansey, S McCarthy, S Maguire 0-1, M Falvey, JJ Maher , J Maguire 0-2, B Murphy 1-1, A Halpin 2-0.
Peadar Mackens: R Fagan, S Delaney, G Bolger, S Driver, M Foley, P Kennedy, D O'Sullivan, J Delaney, H Wall, S Harkins, M Richardson, C McCaul, W Snowe 1-0, J O'Keeffe 0-1, M Fletcher.

1945 May 27, Croke Park
PARNELLS 0-10   CIVIL SERVICE 1-4
Parnells: G Ingham, J Kealy, P Toolan, T McCann, J Power, J Lowry, S Darling, P Neville 0-1, B Quinn, T Markey 0-4, S Gibbons 0-3, M O'Reilly, T Crawford 0-2, E Cadwell, M McEntaggart. Sub: C Haughey for McCann.
Civil Service: J Thornton, J Murphy, F Dowling, A Halpin, S O'Mahony, S McCarthy, S O'Shea, M Falvey 0-2, B Maguire, A Tansey 1-1, JJ Maher 0-1, S O'Kelly, E Tiernan, B Murphy, T Leahy.

1946 June 23, Croke Park
O'TOOLES 2-5   PARNELLS 1-8
O'Tooles: M Killeen 1-2, P McMahon 1-0, W Stacey, T Jenkinson and P Roche 0-1 each.
Parnells: S Gibbons 0-6, B McConkey 1-0, J Lowry 0-2.
REPLAY: July 5, Croke Park
O'TOOLES 1-6   PARNELLS 1-5
O'Tooles: P Bridgette, R Dempsey, A Breslin, J Carey, L Synnott, J Barnes, J Power, T Jenkinson, W Stacey, G Kilbride, L Roche 0-2, M Killeen 0-2, K Matthews, P McMahon 1-0, S Synnott 0-1   Sub: P Murphy 0-1 for Matthews.
Parnells: G Ingham, J Kealy, P Toolan, S Darling, P Power, John Lowry, M O'Reilly, P Neville 0-1, B Quinn, L McConkey 0-1, S Gibbons 1-3, Joe Lowry, T Markey, W Gibson, P Bennett.

1947 June 15, Croke Park
SEAN MCDERMOTTS 0-11   WESTERNS 0-5
Sean McDermotts: C O'Brien, V Bradley, T Robinson, E Boyle, D Fitzgerald, J Murrihy, C Hand, T Langan 0-2, P O'Brien 0-2, P McIntyre, W Adams 0-1, P Crowley 0-1, J O'Reilly, J O'Connor 0-3, S Browne 0-2.
Westerns: J Cooke, T McGrath, T Dunleavy, J McGuinness, J Plunkett, JJ Lavin, J Lalor, T Sullivan 0-1, F Doris 0-1, D Brady, S Connolly, K Stritch, J O'Reilly 0-2, J Clifford, V Beirne 0-1.

1948 June 6, Croke Park
GARDA 2-8   ST. VINCENT'S 2-3
Garda: J McEvoy, A Burke, P McGrath, JF O'Sullivan, B Lynch, B Carlos, J Healy, E Carroll, N Keneally, T O'Sullivan 0-6, T Langan, J McArdle 1-0, C O'Sullivan, P Kennedy, W Quigley 1-0. Sub: T Prendergast for McEvoy.
St Vincent's: B Coffey, D Mahony, J Lavin, J Healy, L Donnelly, D Healy, N Maher, D Cantwell 1-0, M Whelan, P Maher, O Freaney, N Dolan 0-1, J Copeland 0-2, L McDonald 1-0, K Heffernan.

1949 July 10, Croke Park
ST. VINCENT'S 4-11   CLANNA GAEL 2-5
St Vincent's: M Mangan, D Mahony, J Lavin, L Donnelly, D Healy, N Dolan, N Allen, M Whelan 0-1, N Maher, D Ferguson 1-0, O Freaney 0-1, C Freaney 1-1, P Maher 1-0, L McDonald, K Heffernan 1-8.
Clanna Gael: S O'Mahony, M McCaffrey, G Hayden, M Leahy, S O'Neill, R McGovern, E Keogh, J Morris, M Kilkenny, D Galten, D O'Connor 0-1, P Wall, J Stafford 0-3, J Leonard 1-0, W O'Mahony 0-1. Sub: F Byrne 0-1,

1950 June 11, Croke Park
ST. VINCENT'S 1-11   PARNELLS 1-3
St Vincent's: J McDonald, D Mahony, J Lavin, L Donnelly, N Allen, J Crowley, C O'Leary 1-2, K Heffernan 0-3, O Freaney 0-2, C Freaney 0-1, M Whelan 0-1, T Jennings 0-1, D Ferguson 0-1.
Parnells: T O'Neill, P Toolan, P Power, J Byrne, H Boland, S Noonan, P Markey, M Byrne, M Foley, J Gibbons, J Noonan, S Gibbons, B Quinn 1-1, T Markey 0-1, J Kelly 0-1.

1951 July 1, Croke Park
ST. VINCENT'S 1-6   SEAN MCDERMOTTS 0-4
St Vincent's: M Mangan, M Moylan, J Lavin, D Mahony, N Maher, N Allen, M Wilson, J Crowley 0-1, M Whelan, D Ferguson, O Freaney, C O'Leary 0-1, B Atkins 0-1, T Young, K Heffernan 1-3. Sub: C Freaney for O'Leary.
Sean McDermotts: C O'Brien, M O'Reilly, P O'Brien, K Claffey, B Lynch, V Bradley, C Hand, P Connell, E Daly, R McIvor 0-1, C Manning 0-2, N Crowley 0-1, J Caulfield, W Kelly, T Clandillon.

1952 July 20, Croke Park
ST. VINCENT'S 1-10   GARDA 3-4
St Vincent's: K Heffernan 0-5, D Ferguson 1-2, C Freaney 0-2, O Freaney 0-1.
Garda: T Langan 2-1, T O'Sullivan 1-2, T Lynch 0-1.
REPLAY: July 27, Croke Park
ST. VINCENT'S 0-13   GARDA 1-8
St Vincent's: M Mangan, D Mahony, J Lavin, M Moylan, M Wilson, N Allen, N Maher, J Crowley 0-1, M Whelan, D Ferguson 0-1, O Freaney 0-3, C Freaney, B Atkins, T Young 0-2, K Heffernan 0-6.
Garda: M Doherty, P Cosgrave, B Byrne, J Sullivan, T Sullivan 0-2, B Lynch, C Sullivan, T O'Sullivan 0-5, N Kenneally, T Carroll, T Langan 1-1, P Irwin, T Burke, P McGrath, T McArdle.

1953 July 24, Croke Park
ST. VINCENT'S 2-5   CLANNA GAEL 0-6
St Vincent's: M Mangan, D Mahony, M Moylan,

M Wilson, J Lavin, N Allen, N Maher, M Whelan, J Crowley, D Ferguson 0-1, O Freaney 0-1, C Freaney 0-1, B Atkins, C O'Leary 1-0, K Heffernan 1-2.
Clanna Gael: E McCarthy, M McCaffrey, T Moyna, O McGovern, S Wade, E Kehoe, P O'Reilly, D Forde 0-2, D Gallen, J O'Connor, J Stafford, K Daly, P Wall 0-2, C O'Shea, C Mullarkey 0-2.

1954 Oct 31, Croke Park
ST. VINCENT'S 3-6   COLLEGE OF PHARMACY 2-1
St Vincent's: M Mangan, D Mahony, J Lavin, M Moylan, J Young, N Allen, N Maher, C O'Leary 0-1, W Donnelly, D Ferguson, M Whelan, O Freaney, P Haughey, J Crowley 2-0, K Heffernan 0-2   Subs: C Freaney for Heffernan, M Wilson for Donnelly, T Jennings 1-1 for Whelan.
College of Pharmacy: W Burke, C Conefray, W Redmond, P Gannon, H Gaffney, P Quinn, A Hallahan, C Kiely, F Deady 1-0, B McWey 0-1, M Cox 1-0, J Wickham, T Toner, M Shannon, V Ledwidge.

1955 Mar 11, 1956, Croke Park
ST. VINCENT'S 4-4   GARDA 1-7
St Vincent's: N Drumgoole, D Mahony, J Lavin, M Moylan, T Mahony, N Allen, N Maher, J Crowley, M Wilson, D Ferguson, O Freaney 0-3, M Whelan 1-0, P Haughey, K Heffernan 0-1, S Daly 2-0. Subs: L Healy 1-0 for T Mahony, J Joyce for Ferguson, Ferguson for Joyce.
Garda: J Duff, V Shannon, K Scally, J Sullivan, P Harrington, T Maguire, D Sullivan, P Irwin, D McCaffrey, F Ivers 0-1, G Spillane, T O'Sullivan 0-4, J O'Connor 1-0, T Langan 0-1, J Teehan. Sub: C Godkin 0-1 for Shannon.

1956 Dec 16, Croke Park
ERIN'S HOPE 1-7   ST. VINCENT'S 0-7
Erin's Hope: T Quinn, M Donoghue, B Keane, JJ Breslin, T Sugrue, M Quealy, P Confrey, T Long 0-1, F Walsh, M O'Brien 0-1, M McDonagh 0-2, D O'Donovan 0-2, T McKenna 0-1, B Tuohy, D Hurley 1-0.
St Vincent's: N Drumgoole, D Mahony, J Lavin, M Moylan, M Whelan, N Allen 0-1, N Maher, L Foley, P Heron, D Ferguson, O Freaney 0-3, K Heffernan 0-1, P Haughey, J Crowley 0-2, C Leaney. Subs: P McGuirk for Haughey, C Meehan for Leaney, S Daly for Freaney.

1957 July 17, Croke Park
ST. VINCENT'S 2-13   CLANNA GAEL 1-4
St Vincent's: N Drumgoole, D Mahony, J Lavin, L Foley, M Whelan, J Crowley, N Maher, C O'Leary 0-2,

J Joyce, O Freaney 0-5, D Ferguson, P Heron 0-1, C Leaney 0-2, C Meehan 1-2, K Heffernan 1-1.
Clanna Gael: E McCarthy, A Gillen, B Keane, C O'Shea, MJ McGarry, B Kehoe, K Coffey, J Harold, P O'Reilly 0-2, MJ Hawkshaw, T Long, F O'Toole 1-0, C McSweeney, B McMahon, J Boyle 0-2. Subs: D Flood for McGarry, D Gallen for McMahon.

1958 Aug 21, Croke Park
ST. VINCENT'S 1-8   SEAN MCDERMOTTS 1-5
St. Vincent's: N Drumgoole, M Whelan, J Lavin, N Maher, C O'Leary, J Crowley, M Wilson, J Joyce, L Foley, P Haughey 0-1, O Freaney 0-3, D Ferguson 0-1, P Farnon, C Meehan, K Heffernan 1-3. Subs: O Meenan for Crowley, J Graham for Heffernan, Heffernan for Haughey.
Sean McDermotts: T Browne, B Lynch, J Lynch, S Quinn, P Devlin, J O'Meara, R McIvor, G Geraghty, M Brady, K Beahan, P McGarty, C Kelly 0-1, K Sreenan 1-2, M Kane 0-2, C Flynn. Subs: F Quinn for McIvor, S Donnelly for F Quinn.

1959 Oct 11, Croke Park
ST. VINCENT'S 5-3   U.C.D. 2-10
St Vincent's: O Meenan, M Wilson, J Lavin, L Foley, C O'Leary, J Crowley, D Ferguson, D Foley 0-1, D McKane, P Haughey 1-0, O Freaney 0-1, N Fox, P Farnan 2-1, J Joyce, K Heffernan 2-0. Sub: C Meehan for McKane.
UCD: B O'Reilly, F McKnight, J McCabe, J O'Shea, Sean Murphy, J McDonnell, J Vesey, T Stapleton, F O'Leary 0-1, J L'Estrange 1-0, D Feeley 0-1, Seamus Murphy, A Swords, J Brady 1-0, C Gallagher 0-8.

1960 Sep 18, Parnell Park
ST. VINCENT'S 2-7   AIR CORPS 0-10
St Vincent's: D Creed, M Wilson, L Foley, J Crowley, D McKane, D Foley, N Fox, J Joyce, S Behan, P Haughey, C Leaney 0-3, D Ferguson, P Farnan 0-1, K Heffernan 2-2, S Coen 0-1. Subs: L Ferguson for Haughey, C Meehan for Wilson.
Air Corps: T Kennedy, T McCannon, S Barden, M Conroy, PJ McCaffrey, C Wrenn, A Whelan, G McCarthy 0-1, M Coughlan 0-3, M Bohane, S Rabbitte, M. Hipwell 0-1, M Kennedy, N Lucy 0-2, H Donnelly 0-3. Sub: J O'Keeffe for Kennedy.

1961 July 2, Croke Park
ST. VINCENT'S 2-12   AIR CORPS 1-6
St Vincent's: D Creed, P Gibson, L Foley, C Meehan, L Ferguson, C O'Leary 0-1, N Fox, D Foley 0-1, D McKane 0-1, J Lenehan, J Joyce, S Behan, P Farnan

1-1, K Heffernan, S Coen 1-8. Sub: P Haughey for Lenehan.
Air Corps: J Ryan, T McConnon, PJ McCaffrey, M Conroy, M Bohan, C Wrenn, B Bardon, N Lucey, C Nolan 0-1, A Whelan, N Madigan, G McCarthy 0-2, M Kenny, J O'Keeffe, H Donnelly 1-2. Sub: D Fowley 0-1 for Kenny.

1962 Nov 11, Croke Park
ST. VINCENT'S 3-13   CLANNA GAEL 3-8
St Vincent's: D Creed, D Gahan, L Foley, C Meehan, L Ferguson, D McKane, N Fox, J Joyce 0-3, M Kissane, T McEntaggart 0-1, P Farnan 1-0, J Gilroy 0-1, D Ferguson 0-2, K Heffernan 1-4, S Coen 1-2. Sub: M Foley for L Ferguson.
Clanna Gael: C McCormack, C Kane, A Gillen, B Keane, G Davey, K Coffey 0-1, P Tinnelly, P Holden, J Ahearn 0-1, T Howard 0-1, M Whelan 1-5, A Donnelly, S Kenny 1-0, E Keenan, J Boyle 1-0. Sub: J Houlihan for Tinnelly.

1963 Dec 15, Croke Park
U.C.D. 1-4   CLANNA GAEL 0-7
UCD: S Cleary 1-0, L McEldowney 0-2, S Murray and G Kane 0-1 each.
Clanna Gael: M Whelan 0-6, C Stanley 0-I.
REPLAY: Jan 26, 1964, Parnell Park
U.C.D 2-12   CLANNA GAEL 2-8
UCD: J Finn, S Hayden, P O'Donoghue, B McMahon, P Kelly, B Brady, P Kennedy, M O'Shea, M O'Brien, G Kane 1-0, B Burns 0-8, E Melvin 1-2, S Cleary 0-1, S Murray 0-1, L McEldowney.
Clanna Gael: M Leonard, K Coffey, T Gillen, C Kane, J Houlihan, P Holden, T Howard 0-1, D O'Sullivan 0-1, J Ahearne, A Donnelly 0-2, M Whelan 0-3, G Davey, P Tinnelly 0-1, C Stanley, B McCrea 2-0.

1964 July 12, Croke Park
ST. VINCENT'S 0-14   O'TOOLES 1-7
St Vincent's: P Behan, D McKane, L Foley, D Gahan, M Kissane, T Hanahoe, N Fox, D Foley 0-3, S Behan, J Keaveney 0-2, J Gilroy 0-2, S Coen 0-5, C Leaney 0-1, J Joyce, D Ferguson 0-1.
O'Tooles: N Doolan, J Martin, J Murphy, P Synnott, P Byrne, E Fahy, G Power, D Mulligan, M Griffin 0-1, P Delaney 1-2, V Synnott, A Monaghan, S O'Neil 0-1I, F Gilton 0-1, D Byrne 0-1. Subs: G Marry for Griffin, Griffin for Marry.

1965 June 25, Croke Park
U.C.D. 1-12   ROUND TOWERS 0-7
UCD: M McHugh, P O'Hanlon, J Leydon, P

O'Donoghue, D Nolan, B Brady, P Kennedy, M O'Shea 0-1, M O'Brien, B Gaughran 0-1, D Doris 0-3, G Kane 0-1, B Kennedy, S Murray 1-4, J Conway 0-2.
Round Towers: P Looney, F McGivern, W Kelly, M Boggan, A Higgins, L Carr, G Freyne, N Smith, M Carolan, P Delaney, C Dowling 0-5, M Cranny, D Keating, P McGarty, V Maguire 0-2.45

1966 July 15, Croke Park
ST. VINCENT'S 3-9   SEAN MCDERMOTTS 2-6
St Vincent's: P Flood, L Ferguson, L Foley, G O'Driscoll, M Kissane, S Mullins, T Hanahoe, P Hallinan, P McNulty, S Behan 1-1, J Keaveney 0-1, N Fox 0-2 L Deegan 1-1, K Heffernan 0-2, S Coen 1-2 Sub: E Mullins for Hallinan.
Sean McDermotts: P McNeills, M Grogan, V Halpin, L Molloy, R Creaven, P Carry, M Ryan, T Harrington, W Molloy, T Reidy, J Timmons 0-5, P Gallagher, L Foran, N Delaney 1-0, M. McIntyre. Subs: J Evers 1-1 for McIntyre, McIntyre for Reidy.

1967 July 28, Croke Park
ST. VINCENT'S 2-16   SEAN MCDERMOTTS 1-6
St Vincent's: P Flood, L Ferguson, L Foley, G O'Driscoll, M Kissane, S Mullins, T Hanahoe 0-1, D Foley 0-3, P Hallinan, S Behan, J Keaveney 0-6, R Hession, L Deegan 0-1, K Heffernan 1-4, C Leaney 1-1.
Sean McDermotts: P McNeills, M Ryan, N Colleran, P Braden, A Lane, P Carry, C Maguire, W Molloy 0-2, T Harrington, J Evers 1-3, N Delaney 0-1, D Doris, M McIntyre, R Creaven, J Timmons.

1968 June 16, Croke Park
CLANNA GAEL 1-8   SCOIL UI CONAILL 0-5
Clanna Gael: P Kelly, C Kane, T Walsh, T O'Donoghue, J McGill, P Holden, G Davey, M Whelan 0-7, J Taylor, P O'Connell, M O'Driscoll 0-1, V Black 1-0, M Byrne, J Aherne 0-1, E Davey Sub: M Maughan for Byrne.
Scoil Ui Conaill: J Murphy, J Connolly, B Donoghue, E McCabe, J Conlon, B O'Shea, C Hogan, J Brady, M Kelleher, T Moore. T Hempenstall, O McCarthy, S O'Donovan 0-5, W Lowe, D Bohane. Subs: P Murray for Conlon, J Rooney for Hempenstall.

1969 Sep 21, Parnell Park
NA FIANNA 1-8   ST. VINCENT'S 0-10
Na Fianna: A Collins, F Murray, C Clerkin, B Murphy, A Joyce, T O'Hanlon, C Macken, D Bolger, S Donnelly, P Brosnan 1-0, B Casey 0-5, P O'Farrell 0-1, J Fetherston, C Keyes 0-2, M Kennedy.
St Vincent's: P Flood, M Hannick, L Foley, Cathal

Hanley, M Behan, L Ferguson, J Hackett, D Foley, J Keaveney 0-5, S Behan, T Hanahoe 0-2, Christy Hanley 0-1, L Deegan 0-2, R Hession, C Leaney. Sub: M Kissane for Hession.

1970 Sep 20, Parnell Park
ST. VINCENT'S 1-11   RAHENY 1-8
St Vincent's: P Flood, L Ferguson, G O'Driscoll, Cathal Hanley, M Behan, S Mullins, E Brady, P Hallinan 0-1, M Kissane, J Keaveney 0-8, T Hanahoe 1-1, Christy Hanley 0-1, L Deegan, E Mullins, C Leaney Sub: K McConnell for Leaney.
Raheny: S Power, T Ryan, A Larkin, K Moore, M McShane 0-1, M Tyrrell, D Hickey, D Smyth, T Murphy, K Manning, P Gogarty, P Leahy 1-7, R Grey, S McShane, K Hegarty.

1971 Aug 29, Parnell Park
ST. VINCENT'S 3-13   CRAOBH CHIARAIN 3-3
St Vincent's: T Byrne, L Ferguson, L Foley, Cathal Hanley, M Behan, S Mullins, E Brady, G O'Driscoll, J Keaveney 1-3, Christy Hanley 0-1, T Hanahoe 0-1, G Keavey 0-2, L Deegan 1-3, D Foley 1-2, C Leaney 0-1 Subs: PJ Reid for O'Driscoll, O'Driscoll for Mullins.
Craobh Chiarain: T Judd, T Keogh, S Sweeney, L Shanley, S Shanley, P Foley 1-0, J Foley, R Burke, D Rheinisch 0-1, M Dempsey, E Flynn 0-1, P Pierce, J Elliott, M Matthews 0-1, G Pierce 2-0. Sub: H Browne for Elliott.

1972 June 18, Parnell Park
ST. VINCENT'S 2-8   U.C.D. 0-9
St Vincent's: T Byrne, L Ferguson, L Foley, G O'Driscoll, M Leonard, D Billings, E Brady, P Hallinan, J Keaveney 1-4, PJ Reid, T Hanahoe 0-1, B DoyJe, B Lee, D Foley 1-1, Christy Hanley 0-2.
UCD: F Reen, J Stafford, G O'Reilly, E Fitzgerald, P Gilroy, J Waldron, P O'Neill, J O'Keeffe, P Kerr 0-4, T Cashell, O Leddy, J Walsh 0-2, G Keane, R Brennan 0-1, F Farrell 0-2. Subs: T Mulvihill for Keane, J Halpin for Walsh.

1973 Aug 26, Parnell Park
U.C.D. 1-11   ST. VINCENT'S 0-10
UCD: L Madden, J Waldron, E O'Donoghue, P Gilroy, P Fitzsimons, M Carty, P O'Neill, J O'Keeffe, B Gaughran 0-1, JP Kean, P Kerr 1-1, J Walsh 0-6, B Heneghan, G O'Reilly 0-1, M Hanrahan. Sub: R O'Donoghue for Heneghan.
St Vincent's: N Bernard, D Billings, M Corcoran, G O'Driscoll, M Behan, M Hannick, S Mullins, P Hallinan, PJ Reid 0-3, T Hanahoe, B Doyle, D Redmond, C Leaney 0-1, D Foley, J Keaveney 0-6. Subs: L Deegan for Redmond, E Brady for Rohan, B Mullins for Hallinan.

1974 Dec 1, Croke Park

U.C.D. 0-12   ST. VINCENT'S 1-3

UCD: I Heffernan, M Judge, E O'Donoghue, C Moynihan, PJ O'Halloran, M Carry, P Kerr 0-1, J O'Keeffe, P O'Neill, JP Kean, K Kilmurray, J Walsh 0-10 E Condren, O Leddy, P Duggan 0-1. Sub: B Walsh for Condren.

St Vincent's: N Bernard, D Billings, M Corcoran, G O'Driscoll, M Behan, M Hannick, E Brady, B Pocock, B Doyle, J Lynskey, T Hanahoe, T Diamond, C Hanley 0-1, J Keaveney 1-2, PJ Reid. Subs: D Redmond for Doyle, T Quinn for Diamond.

1975 June 15, Parnell Park

ST. VINCENT'S W/O   U.C.D. SCR

* UCD refused to play due to college examinations and St. Vincents were declared champions UCD lodged an appeal that dragged on until November 3, when St. Vincents were confirmed as champions.

1976 July 2, Croke Park

ST. VINCENT'S 3-12   U.C.D. 1-15

St Vincent's: N Bernard, D Billings, G O'Driscoll, C Hanley, B Pocock, V Lambe, PJ Reid, B Mullins, F Ryder 0-1, B Reddy 0-1, M O'Grady, M Whelan 0-2, L Deegan 1-2, J Keaveney 2-5, B Doyle 0-1   Subs: G O'Connor for Hanley, T Diamond for Pocock.

UCD: I Heffernan, F Ward, E O'Donoghue, G McCaul, P. I. O'Halloran, B Dunleavy, P O'Neill, M Carty 0-1, D Moran 0-1, T McManus, C O'Rourke 1-1, J Walsh 0-9, B Walsh, O Leddy 0-1, P Grey. Subs: JP Kean for O'Halloran, C Moynihan 0-2 for McManus, B Jennings for Kean.

1977 June 17, Croke Park

ST. VINCENT'S 4-15   SYNGE STREET 0-6

St Vincent's: N Bernard, G O'Connor, G O'Driscoll, M Hannick, B Pocock, J Lynsky, T Diamond, B Mullins 0-1, F Ryder, M O'Grady 0-1, T Hanahoe 1-1, M Whelan 1-1, L Deegan 1-0, J Keaveney 0-10, B Doyle 1-0 Subs: E Cooke 0-1 for Doyle, PJ Reid for Pocock.

Synge Street: N Nolan, S Roche, F McCarthy, K Bruton, M McManamon, P O'Shea, J Bollard, A O'Toole, J O'Reilly, G O'Leary 0-3, C Roche 0-3, D O'Reilly, F Hutchinson 0-1, J Henry, P O'Toole. Subs: H Wall for Henry, M Ryan 0-1 for O'Toole.

1978 July 21, Croke Park

ERIN'S HOPE 0-9   ERIN'S ISLE 1-6

Erin's Hope: G Cuddy and M Trappe 0-3 each, M O'Connor, O Martin and P Foley 0-2 each.

Erin's Isle: J Clarke 1-0, C Cox 0-2, D Hurley, K Butler, J Corcoran and PJ Buckley 0-1 each)

REPLAY: Aug 4, Croke Park

ERIN'S HOPE 3-7   ERIN'S ISLE 0-13

Erin's Hope: D Healy, T McVeigh, J Murphy, M Hicks, T Kearney B McArdle, G Barrett, M O'Connor 0-1, P Martin, J Gallagher O Martin, J Kelleher 0-1, G Cuddy 2-2, P Foley 1-0, A Trappe 0-3.

Erin's Isle: I McDonald, S Davenport, D Clarke, B Casey, F White, M Hurley, M Martin, PJ Buckley, J Corcoran, C Cox 0-6, P Reaney 0-3, E Butler 0-1, D Hurley 0-2, J Clarke 0-1, P Canning. Sub: K Barry for D Clarke.

1979 June 22, Croke Park

NA FIANNA 0-11   CIVIL SERVICE 0-9

Na Fianna: N Fitzgerald, M Brosnan, B Cooper, T Foran, N Duffy, E Lynch, F Leahy, J Caffrey, D Mehigan, R Neville 0-5, B Casey 0-1, J Quinn 0-2, D Lynch 0-3, D Gaffney, C Fagan   Subs: M McDonagh for Gaffney, C McCarthy for Fagan.

Civil Service: J Carroll, J O'Neill, G O'Reilly, M O'Connor, G Crowe, E Sheelin 0-1, P O'Neill, S Bonner, F McDonald, V Wrynne 0-2, B Gaughran 0-1, P McGill 0-1, P Gilroy, J Hannify 0-2, M Harrington. Sub: G Aherne 0-2 for Harrington.

1980 June 27, Croke Park

CIVIL SERVICE 3-9   ERIN'S HOPE 2-8

Civil Service: J Carroll, D Stevenson, G O'Reilly, G Crowe, J Marshall, E Sheelin 0-1, P McGill, P O'Neill, J Long, B Gaughran 1-3, S Bonner 0-4, P Crosier, J Hannify, F O'Donnelly, K Kilmurray 1-0. Sub G Aherne 1-1 for Hannify.

Erin's Hope: S Morahan, J Brennan, L O'Connor, N Ellis, M Lynch, L Duffy, P Morris, D O'Mahony 0-1, P Mulligan, G Cuddy 2-5, M Hanrick, E McEneaney 0-1, G Murphy, D Donoghue 0-1, A Gavin. Sub: N O'Reilly for Duffy.

1981 July 8, Croke Park

ST. VINCENT'S 0-12   BALLYMUN KICKHAMS 2-4

St Vincent's: N Bernard, R Hazley, V Conroy, B Pocock, M Clarke, S Fleming, S Wade, P Canavan, T Diamond, C Buffini, T Hanahoe, M Loftus 0-2, P McLoughlin 0-5, J Keaveney 0-3, B Doyle. Subs: B Jordan 0-1 for Buffini, F Ryder 0-1 for Canavan, C Hanley for Keaveney.

Ballymun Kickhams: T Ennis, B Farrell, G Hargan, T Mannion, P Trainor, G McCaul, C Eustace, D Deasy 1-0, J Kearns 0-1, E Kelly, A Walsh 1-1, A McCaul 0-1, D Sheehan, S Moylan 0-1, C O'Farrell. Subs: B Rock for O'Farrell, G Talbot for Rock, G O'Hehir for Sheehan.

1982 July 11, Croke Park
BALLYMUN KICKHAMS 2-11   ERIN'S ISLE 1-8
Ballymun Kickhams: T Ennis, T Mannion, G Hargan, G McCaul, P Traynor, C Eustace, O Kelly, D Deasy 0-1, J Kearns 0-2, D Sheehan 0-2, A McCaul, C O'Farrell, S Moylan, B Rock 1-4, A Walsh 1-2 Subs: R Farrell for Sheehan, T O'Hare for Moylan.
Erin's Isle: T Quinn, J Collins, D Hurley, P Grimes, M Deegan, PJ Buckley, T Barber 0-1, P Canning 0-3, C Cox, C Redmond 0-3, M Hurley 1-1, J Corcoran, D Murphy, P Reaney, F White. Subs: M Farrelly for Deegan 35, S Murphy for Cox 37.

1983 Oct 22, Croke Park
SCOIL UI CONAILL 0-12   ST. VINCENT'S 1-6
Scoil Ui Conaill: J Close, M O'Connell, F McGrath, T Naughton, B Hickey, P McVeigh, E Costelloe, M McCarrick, J Kirwan, C McMahon, T O'Brien 9-2, S O'Brien 0-1, P Lynch 0-4, R Kelleher 0-1, D O'Brien Subs: L Close 0-1 for McMahon, C Curtis 0-3 for Close, K Murphy for Hickey. Extra time: Close for T O'Brien, McMahon for Costelloe, T O'Brien for Kirwan.
St Vincent's: T Byrne, J Grace, V Conroy, B Pocock, P Canavan, S Fleming, A Devlin, T Conroy, S Loftus, M Loftus 0-1, T Hanahoe, B Jordan 0-2, P McLoughlin, B Doyle 0-2, R Mulvanney. Subs: T Diamond for T Conroy, C Buffini 1-1 for Mulvanney. Extra time: T Conroy for Diamond, S Dalton for S Loftus, E Heery for Doyle.

1984 June 1, Parnell Park
ST. VINCENT'S 1-8   NA FIANNA 1-5
St Vincent's: T Byrne, V Conroy, B Pocock, R Hazley, P Canavan, S Wade, A Devlin, B Mullins, S Fleming 0-1, E Heery, T Hanahoe 0-1, M Loftus, P McLoughlin 1-4, B Jordan 0-1, T Conroy. Subs: B Doyle for Heery, C Buffini 0-1 for Loftus.
Na Fianna: P Smith, J Byrne, L Norton 0-1, B Cooper, J Kennedy, R Caverley, J McCarthy, D Foran, P Caffrey 0-1, J Quinn, T Gray, C O'Reilly 0-1, J Caffrey, D Hickey, G Hegarty 0-2. Sub: P Boylan 1-0 for Gray.

1985 May 5, Parnell Park
BALLYMUN KICKHAMS 2-7   CLONTARF 0-8
Ballymun Kickhams: S Bannon, F Lyons, G Hargan, A Mannion, P Traynor, C Eustace, E Kelly, J Kearns 1-0, D Deasy, C Kelly, T Carr 0-2, A McCaul 0-2, S Moylan, B Rock 0-3, C O'Farrell 1-0. Subs: M Murphy for Moylan, G Talbot for C Kelly, L Gavin for Mannion.
Clontarf: B Lillis, G O'Connor, D Palmer, M Murphy, T Sharry T O'Keefe, R Nevin, J Ronayne 0-1, D Murphy 0-4, L O'Sullivan, J O'Connor, N McCaffrey 0-1, J

Pierce, B Moore, F Byrne 0-1. Subs: T Doyle 0-1 for O'Connor, C Cullen for Pierce.

1986 May 23, Parnell Park
SCOIL UI CONAILL 0-9   THOMAS DAVIS 0-1
Scoil Ui Conaill: C McMahon, T Callanan, M O'Connell, T Naughton, G McMahon, B Hickey, P McVeigh, J Kirwan, F McGrath, S O'Brien 0-1, C Curtis 0-3, L Close, G Mescall, D O'Brien 0-2, T O'Brien 0-3.
Thomas Davis: G Redmond, J Kelly, C McCabe, E O'Toole, J Fadain, JJ Martin, L Adamson, D Murray, D Foran, D Nugent, D Peters, V Carney 0-1, P Mullarkey, P Duane, P Finnegan. Subs: T Kenny for Mullarkey, T McConnell for Finnegan.

1987 July 31, Parnell Park
PARNELLS 0-12   ST. ANNE'S 0-8
Parnells: M Hoban, J Byrne, K Early, B Halpin, R Holland, D North, G Walsh, J Bissett, D Fitzgibbon, B Brady 0-1, B Talty 0-1, M Bissett, G Hanaphy 0-2, J Prendergast 0-2, M O'Hanlon 0-6.
St Anne's: S O'Neill, K Foran, K Walsh, S Foran, G Heaslip 0-2, D Carroll, M O'Neill, J McNally 0-2, T O'Connor, D Delappe 0-4, B Heaslip, J Nagle 0-2, A McNally, S Callery, N Byrne. Subs: J Ennis for K Foran, J O'Brien for Nagle.

1988 July 2, Parnell Park
PARNELLS 1-15   CUALA 0-12
Parnells: M Hoban, C Conan, K Early, B Halpin, J Byrne, D North, G Walsh 0-1, J Bissett, J Prendergast 0-3, M Bissett, B Brady, D Fitzgibbon 0-2, G Hanaphy 0-3, B Talty 0-1, M O'Hanlon 1-5. Sub: T O'Neill for Brady.
Cuala: L O'Toole, M Holden, P McCormack, M Murray, B Ryan, M Johnston, D Spain, T Cullen 0-3, P Brennan, G Browner, M O'Callaghan 0-2, M Culhane 0-7, C Dolphin, J Murphy, C Irwin. Subs: V Holden for Browner, J Treacy for McCormack, M Quinn for Dolphin.

1989 July 1, Parnell Park
THOMAS DAVIS 2-10 BALLYMUN KICKHAMS 0-10
Thomas Davis: F Troy, D Nugent, JJ Martin, E O'Toole, J Fadian, G McCabe 0-1, G Gilmartin 0-1, D Foran, P Curran 0-2, P Nugent 0-2, P Dwane, S Grealis 0-2, V Carney 1-3, P Godson, Adamson 1-0. Sub: D Murray for Godson.
Ballymun Kickhams: S Bannon, E Kelly, G Hargan, C Reilly, T Browne, F Walsh, C Eustace, J Kearns 0-2, D Deasy 0-1, D Sheahan 0-1, T Carr 0-1, C O'Farrell, J McCarthy, D Rock 0-3, A McCaul 0-2. Subs: A Walsh for McCarthy.

1990 Oct 14, Parnell Park
THOMAS DAVIS 0-10   PARNELLS 1-6
Thomas Davis: F Troy, D Nugent, JJ Martin, E O'Toole, J Fadian, P Curran, G Gilmartin 0-1, D Foran, P Godson, J Benton, P Nugent, S Grealis 0-4, P Joyce, P Dwane 0-1, L Adamson 0-4. Sub: V Carney for Joyce.
Parnells: M Hoban, R McKeon, K Early, J Byrne, A McGarry, D North, G Walsh, D Fitzgibbon 0-1, J Prendergast, R Holland, G ONeill 0-1, B Brady 1-0, G Hanphy, B Talty 0-1, M O'Hanlon 0-3. Subs: J Bissett for Holland 35, Holland for North 48.

1991 Oct 13, Parnell Park
THOMAS DAVIS 1-9 PARNELLS 1-7
Thomas Davis: F Troy, D Nugent 0-1, JJ Martin 1-0, E O'Toole, J Fadian, P Curran, G Kilmartin, D Foran, J Benton, P Nugent, P Godson 0-1, S Grealis 0-3, L Adamson 0-2, P Dwane, G Walsh 0-2. Sub: P Waldron for Fadian.
Parnells: M Hoban, B McKeown, K Early, D Feeney, T McGarry, J Gilmore, G Walsh, D Fitzgibbon 0-1, B Burke, R Holland, J Madden 0-4, M Bissett, T Cummins 1-2, J Prendergast, B Brady. Subs: M O'Hanlon for Prendergast 48, J Bissett for M Bissett 53.

1992 Nov 14, Parnell Park
KILMACUD CROKES 0-11 CIVIL SERVICE 0-10
Kilmacud Crokes: M Pender, T Cunning, D Maher, F Rutledge, R Ward, J Sweeney, P Burke, S Morris, M Dillon, M Duncan 0-1, J Shovlin, P Ward 0-2, P Walsh 0-4, E Connolly, P O'Donoghue 0-3. Subs: C Cleary for Shovlin, Mick Leahy 0-1 for Burke, Maurice Leahy for Connolly.
Civil Service: N McCole, S O Shea, J Gallagher, D O'Keeffe, E Gallagher, D Meehan, PJ Monaghan 0-1, B Murray, M Gallagher 0-1, A Murray 0-1, D Flanagan, J Boyle 0-2, A O'Keeffe 0-3, F McNamee, M O'Brien 0-2. Sub: P Brennan for O'Brien.

1993 Sep 26, Parnell Park
ERIN'S ISLE 0-8   KILMACUD CROKES 1-5
Erin's Isle: C O'Hare 0-4, C Redmond 0-2, C Cox and C Kelly 0-1 each.
Kilmacud Crokes: M Dillon I-1, N Clancy 0-3, P Walsh 0-1)
REPLAY: Oct 16, Parnell Park
ERIN'S ISLE 1-8   KILMACUD CROKES 0-6
Erin's Isle: T Quinn, E Barr, JJ O'Keeffe, S McCormack, K Murray, K Barr 0-1, B McGauren, J Barr 0-1, M Deegan 0-1, C Redmond 0-2, K Kelly, T Russell 0-1, K O'Hare 0-1, C Cox 1-1, E Sheehan Subs: M Hurley for J Barr, J Egan for Cox.

Kilmacud Crokes: M Pender, F Rutledge, C Cleary, T Cunning, R Ward, J Sweeney, P Burke, M Dillon, E Connolly, N Clancy 0-2, Maurice Leahy, P Ward, P Walsh 0-1, Mick Leahy, P O'Donoghue 0-3. Subs: R Leahy for Rutledge, M Duncan for Maurice Leahy, J Shovlin for P Ward.

1994 Oct 15, Parnell Park
KILMACUD CROKES 0-12   ERIN'S ISLE 1-9
Kilmacud Crokes: N Clancy 0-3, P Ward, P O'Donoghue, M Dillon and P Dalton 0-2 each, S Morris 0-1.
Erin's Isle: C Redmond 0-4, R Boyle 1-0, T Russell 0-2, K Barr, J Twomey and J Barr 0-1 each)
REPLAY: Oct 22, Parnell Park
KILMACUD CROKES 1-14   ERIN'S ISLE 2-10
Kilmacud Crokes: M Pender, R Ward, C Cleary, R Leahy, J Sweeney, J O'Callaghan, P Burke 0-1, M Dillon, S Morris, N Clancy 0-1, C Mitchell, P Ward 1-2, M Duncan 0-1, P Dalton 0-2, P Walsh 0-3 Subs: Maurice Leahy 0-3 for Mitchell. Extra time: P O'Donoghue 0-1 for Clancy, Mick Leahy for Duncan, Clancy for Maurice Leahy, Maurice Leahy for Mick Leahy.
Erin's Isle: T Quinn, K Spratt, JJ O'Keeffe, P Cunningham, K Murray, K Barr 0-1, E Barr, J Barr, M Deegan 0-1, C Redmond 0-2, T Russell 0-1, C Kelly, C O'Hare 2-4, R Boyle, J Twomey. Subs: C Cox for Kelly 23, B McGauran for Murray 38. Extra time: Murray for J Barr start, A Martin 0-1 for R Boyle 9, J Fagarn for O'Hare 23.

1995 Oct 22, Parnell Park
BALLYBODEN ST. ENDA'S 1-7 ERIN'S ISLE 0-9
Ballyboden St Enda's: G Flaherty, D Naughton, B Molloy, G Colleran, B Young, P Wardick T Duffy, P Curran, K Murray, J Prendergast, B Stynes. M Gardiner, D Bolger 1-1, L Callan 0-4, S O'Shaughnessy 0-2. Subs: J Kernan for Molloy, J McAllister for Stynes, P Bealin for Curran.
Erin's Isle: T Ouinn, K Spratt, JJ O'Keetfe. K Murray, M Deegan, P Cunningham, T Gorman, E Barr, K Barr 0-4, T Russell 0-1, J Barr 0-1, S McCormack, C O'Hare 0-2, R Boyle, A Martin 0-1. Subs: P Campbell for Martin 47, K Kelly for J Barr 59.

1996 July 6, Parnell Park
ST. SYLVESTER'S 0-11   ERIN'S ISLE 0-9
St. Sylvester's: J Leonard, D Roche 0-1, B Silke 0-1, D Ryan, B Barns, J Murphy, K Galvin, D Hetherton 0-1, M Barnes, C Earley, G O'Neill, N Guiden, T Cummins, S Keogh 0-6, D Barnes 0-2. Subs: E Stuart for O'Neill, P Hussey for Earley.

Erin's Isle: T Quinn, K Spratt, JJ O'Keeffe, K Murray, E Barr, F Browne, S McCormack, K Barr, J Barr, C Redmond 0-3, P Cunningham 0-1, T Russell, C O'Hare 0-5, R Boyle, M Deegan. Subs: D Collins for Russell, J Twomey for Cunningham, J Fagan for O'Hare.

1997 Sep 21, Parnell Park
ERIN'S ISLE 2-10   ST. SYLVESTER'S 1-11
Erin's Isle: T Quinn, K Spratt, JJ O'Keefe, M Naughton, D Collins 0-1, M Deegan 0-1, G O'Connell 0-1, J Barr, K Barr 0-3, C Redmond 0-1, P Cunningham, N Crosson 0-1, C O'Hare 1-1, R Boyle 1-1, E Barr.
St Sylvester's: J Leonard, D Roche, B Silke, D Ryan, B Barnes, J Murphy, G Lehary, D Hetherton, M Barnes, C Earley, B Burke, , N Guiden 0-2, T Cummins 0-1, S Keogh 0-7, D Barnes 1-1. Subs: I McCafferty for Roche 54, B Dignan for Burke 54.

1998 Oct 10, Parnell Park
KILMACUD CROKES 1-16   NA FIANNA 0-13
Kilmacud Crokes: M Pender, C O'Dwyer, C Deegan, C Cleary, J O'Callaghan, J Magee, R Leahy 0-1, J Costello, M Leahy 0-1, P Ward 0-2, M Dillon 0-1, J O'Sullivan 0-1, R Cosgrove 0-5, R Brennan, M O'Keeffe 0-4. Subs: P Burke 1-1 for Brennan, C Redmond for Cleary.
Na Fianna: A Henchy, S McGlinchey, B Quinn, L Fay, P McCarthy, L Costello, T Lynch, S Forde, M Foley, M Galvin 0-5, S Connell 0-1, J Sherlock, , D Farrell 0-2, K Donnelly, I Foley 0-5. Sub: D Lynch for M Foley 45.

1999 Oct 16, Parnell Park
NA FIANNA 1-13   ST. BRIGID'S 0-12
Na Fianna: S Gray, S McGlinchey, B Quinn, T Lynch, M Foley, K McGeeney 0-1, P McCarthy, S Forde, D Mackin 1-1, M Galvin 0-5, S Connell, J Sherlock, D Farrell 0-1, K Donnelly 0-1, I Foley 0-3. Sub: D Keegan 0-1 for Forde, A Shearer for Mackin.
St Brigid's: C Boyle, M Cahill, Declan Cahill, K Nolan, P Andrews, Dermot Cahill, K Keane, K Darcy 0-1, J Ward, C Kilmurray, D Darcy 0-9, C O'Muircheartaigh, D Fitzgerald 0-1, C McGlynn, K Kilmurray 0-1. Subs: P Molloy for McGlynn 51, K Kehilly for Fitzgerald 57.

2000 Oct 14, Parnell Park
NA FIANNA 2-6   KILMACUD CROKES 1-8
Na Fianna: S Gray, N O Murchu, B McManus, T Lynch, N Clancy, S McGlinchey, D Lynch, K Donnelly, K McGeeney 1-1, M Galvin 1-3, S Connell, D Farrell, I Foley 0-1, J Sherlock 0-1, D Mackin. Subs: P McCarthy for McGlinchey, A Shearer for Lynch, D Keegan for Foley.

Kilmacud Crokes: M Pender, J O'Donovan, C Deegan, F Kennedy, J O'Callaghan, C O'Dwyer, R Leahy, J Magee, D Magee, P Ward 0-1, M Leahy, I O'Sullivan 1-0, R Cosgrove, R Brennan, M O'Keeffe 0-7. Subs: C Cleary for Kennedy 47, J Costelloe for Brennan 50.

2001 Oct 6, Parnell Park
NA FIANNA 3-15   ST. BRIGID'S 1-5
Na Fianna: S Gray, N O Murchu, B McManus, P McCarthy 0-1, M Foley, S McGlinchy, T Lynch, K McGeeney 0-1, S Connell 0-4, D Farrell 0-4, N Clancy 0-1, K Donnelly 0-1, I Foley 0-1, J Sherlock 1-2, D Mackin 1-0. Subs: P McGeeney for Foley, G Gray 0-1 for Clancy, J Hagan 1-0 for Foley.
St Brigid's: C Boyle, M Cahill, D Cahill, C O'Sullivan, G Norton, P Andrews, K Keane, K Darcy 0-1, J Ward, B Cahill, D Darcy 0-1, P Keane 0-1, K Kilmurray, C McGlynn 1-2, A Briody. Sub: D Fitzgerald for O'Sullivan.

2002 Nov 17, Parnell Park
U.C.D 0-16   ST. VINCENT'S 1-6
UCD: G McGill, A Costello, C Evans, B O hAnnaidh, N McGuire, D O hAnnaidh, R Kelly, S Lucey 0-1, C McAnallen 0-1, C McManus 0-1, R Barry, P Curran, JP Casey 0-4, R Ronaghan 0-3, B McDonald 0-4 Subs: J Hanley 0-2 for Curran, O O hAnnaidh for Lucey, J Fallon for Casey, D O'Connor for Ronaghan.
St Vincent's: M Doyle, R Lambe, C Wilson J Calvert, C Browne, T Feehan, N Dunne, P Murphy, P Gilroy, B Manning, S Brady, T Doyle 0-1, C Hayden, K Golden 0-1, T Quinn 0-4. Subs: A Stark for Manning 29, R Brennan for Murphy h/t, S O'Neill for Hayden 36, P Nevins for Brady 56   N McGuire own goal.

2003 Oct 19, Parnell Park
ST. BRIGID'S 0-17   KILMACUD CROKES 1-8
St Brigid's: P Keane, K Keane, D Cahill, M Cahill, D Dineen, P Andrews, G Norton, K Darcy 0-1, J Ward, D Lally 0-3, Rory Gallagher 0-4, M Galvin, K Bonner 0-1, Raymond Gallagher 0-4, J Noonan 0-3. Subs: D Darcy 0-1 for Bonner, C Ryan for Dineen, W Finnegan for Andrews.
Kilmacud Crokes: R Davis, N McGrath, N Kane, P Griffin, C Kelleher, J Magee 0-1, K Galvin, D Magee, L McBarron, L Og O hEineachain, D Kelleher 0-1, C Murphy 1-2, M O'Keeffe 0-2, R Cosgrove 0-1, P McDonald 0-1. Subs: C Galvin for McDonald h/t, P Ward for O'Keeffe 44, C Deegan for O hEineachain 57, M Leahy for Cosgrove 60.

2004 Oct 10, Parnell Park
KILMACUD CROKES 0-11
BALLYBODEN ST. ENDA'S 2-2
Kilmacud Crokes: D Nelligan, F Kennedy, C Kelleher, C Flanagan, P Griffin, L Og hEineachain 0-3, B McGrath, D Magee, J Magee 0-2, C Murphy, L McBarron 0-2, M Vaughan, M Daveren, R Cosgrove 0-1, D Kelleher 0-1. Subs: M O'Keeffe 0-2 for J Magee, M O'Keeffe for McBarron, F Armstrong for D Kelleher.
Ballyboden St Enda's: S Manley, A Gardiner, D Kiernan, M O'Sullivan, E McNulty, G O'Reilly, C Dolan, D O'Mahony, I Clarke, K Naughton, S Hiney, R Hussey, C Doyle, C Keaney 2-1, A Kerin 0-1. Subs: C Smith for Clarke, N Clarke for Dolan, B O'Regan for Doyle, A Brennan for Hiney.

2005 Oct 16, Parnell Park
KILMACUD CROKES 1-14   NA FIANNA 0-9
Kilmacud Crokes: D Nelligan, C Kelleher, C Flanagan, N McGrath, B McGrath, L Og O hEineachain, P Griffin, D Magee, J Magee, R Cosgrove 0-5, L McBarron, P Burke, C Murphy 0-1, M Davoren 0-2, M Vaughan 1-6. Subs: N Corkery for J Magee, M O'Keeffe for Burke, D Maher for B McGrath.
Na Fianna: S Grey, A Downes, E McNulty, E Ledwith, S Cloherty, K McGeeney, N Cooper, K Donnelly, J McNulty, T Brady, J Sherlock 0-2, S Connell, D Farrell, M O Collarain 0-3, K O'Neill 0-4. Subs: P McGeeney for J McNulty h/t, R Clerkin for Donnelly 42, B Courtney for O'Neill 48.

2006 Nov 6, Parnell Park
U.C.D. 0-10   ST. VINCENT'S 0-9
UCD: S Gallagher, J McCarthy, P Navin, E O Cuiv, M Duffy, B Quill, M Dunne, M Ward, J Sherry 0-1, S Brady 0-1, S Lennon 0-4, B Sheehan 0-1, P Earls, C Rogers, C O'DwyerSubs: N McNamee 0-1 for Earls, A O'Malley 0-2 for O'Dwyer, Earls for Rogers.
St Vincents: M Savage, W Lowry, E Brady, A Costello, P Conlon, G Brennan, R Fallon, P Gilroy 0-2, M Loftus, K Golden 0-2, H Coughlan, T Doyle, D Connelly, T Diamond 0-1, T Quinn 0-4. Subs: S Loughlin for Doyle 51, B Manning for Loftus 54, N Dunne for Golden 58.

2007 Oct 29, Parnell Park
ST. VINCENT'S 0-12   ST. BRIGID'S 1-7
St Vincent's: M Savage, P Conlon, E Brady, H Gill, T Doyle, G Brennan, P Kelly, H Coughlan, M O'Shea, K Golden 0-2, T Diamond, N Billings 0-1, B Maloney 0-2, D Connolly 0-3, T Quinn 0-4. Subs: P Gilroy for Coughlan, C Brady for Billings.
St Brigid's: P Keane, M Cahill 0-1, D Cahill, A Daly, G

Norton, M Galvin, Peadar Andrews, K Darcy, M Cahill, K Darcy, D Lally 0-1, D Dineen, Rory Gallagher 0-2, K Bonner 0-1, Paddy Andrews 1-1. Subs: C Lynch for Dineen 24, L McCarthy for M Cahill 40, J Noonan 0-1 for D Cahill.

2008 Oct 23, Parnell Park
KILMACUD CROKES 1-10
ST. OLIVER PLUNKETT'S 0-13
Kilmacud Crokes: P Burke 1-2, M Vaughan 0-4, M Davoren 0-2, D Magee and B McGrath 0-1 each.
St Oliver Plunkett: B Brogan, J Sherlock, A Brogan and G Smith 0-2 each, A Darcy, D Sweeney, D Matthews, P Brogan and R McConnell 0-1 each)
REPLAY: Oct 27, Parnell Park
KILMACUD CROKES 3-6
ST. OLIVER PLUNKETT'S 0-13
Kilmacud Crokes: D Nestor, K Nolan, P Griffin, N McGrath, B McGrath, A Morrissey, C O'Sullivan, D Magee, N Corkery, P Burke, M Vaughan 0-2, L McBarron, M Davoren 1-0, J Magee 2-0, B Kavanagh 0-2. Subs: C Lambe for N McGrath, B O'Rourke for McBarron, R O'Carroll for Corkery, K O'Carroll for Vaughan.
St Oliver Plunketts: E Sommerville, R O'Connor, C Evans, P Curtin, T Browne, M Brides, J Brogan 0-1, R McConnell, D Matthews, G Smith, A Brogan 0-2, A Darcy, J Sherlock, B Brogan 0-10, D Sweeney. Subs: N Murphy for Browne 24, P Brogan for Curtin h/t, K McDonnell for Darcy 44.

2009 Oct 18, Parnell Park
BALLYBODEN ST. ENDA'S 2-12   ST. JUDE'S 1-13
Ballyboden St Enda's: D Walsh, C Dolan, I Clarke, M O'Sullivan, D Nelson, J O'Hara, S Durkin, MD Macauley, D O'Mahony, S Lambert, D Davey 0-2, C Smyth, C Keaney 0-3, K Naughton 0-2, A Kerin 2-5. Subs: P Galvin for Davey, D Shovlin for Lambert, P O'Brien for O'Sullivan.
St Jude's: P Copeland, C McBride, S Breheny, C Guckian, P Cunningham 0-1, N O'Shea, S Ryan 0-1, C Murphy, A Glover 0-1, R O'Brien, B McManamon 0-2, B Monaghan 0-2, J Donnelly 0-2, D Donnelly 0-1, K McManamon 0-2. Subs: R Joyce for O'Brien 34, S Gallagher 0-1 for D Donnelly 35, M Lyons 1-0 for Monaghan 45, C Voyles for B McManamon 55.

2010 Oct 17, Parnell Park
KILMACUD CROKES 2-12   ST. BRIGID'S 1-11
Kilmacud Crokes: D Nestor, Ross O'Carroll, Rory O'Carroll, C Lambe, B McGrath, C O'Sullivan 0-1, R Ryan, N Corkery, P Duggan, L Og O hEineachain,

D Kelleher 0-1, A Morrissey 0-1, B O'Rourke 0-1, B Kavanagh 1-4, P Burke 0-1. Subs: M Vaughan 1-2 for O'Rourke, C Dias 0-1 for Morrissey, L McBarron for Duggan, N McGrath for Corkery.
St Brigid's: S Supple 0-1, A Daly, Peadar Andrews, G Norton, G Kane, S Murray, D Lally, C Mullins, B Cahill 0-1, M Cahill, K Bonner, K Kilmurray, Paddy Andrews 0-4, K Darcy 0-3, P Ryan 0-2. Subs: D Plunkett for Kilmurray 40, C Kilmurray for Lally 45, C Carr for M Cahill 51, N Davey for Bonner 59, C Freeman for Murray 60.

2011 Nov 6, Parnell Park
ST. BRIGID'S 0-10   ST. OLIVER PLUNKETT'S 0-6
St Brigid's: S Supple, A Daly, Martin Cahill, G Norton, C Moran, S Murray, G Kane, B Cahill, G McIntyre 0-1, J O'Loughlin, P Andrews 0-1, Mark Cahill 0-1, K Kilmurray, K Darcy 0-3, P Ryan Subs: L McCarthy 0-3 for Ryan, C Mullins for McIntyre, O McCann 0-1 for Kilmurray, C Doyle for Mark Cahill.
St Oliver Plunketts: P Brogan, R O'Connor, S Lyons, M Brides, C Evans, P Brogan, S Dunne, R McConnell 0-1, A Moyles, C Walsh, G Smith 0-1, D Matthews, A Brogan 0-3, B Brogan 0-3, J Sherlock. Subs: C Dunleavy for Dunne h/t, A Darcy for Matthews 48, C Daly for Smith 58.

2012 Oct 29, Parnell Park
BALLYMUN KICKHAMS 1-12
KILMACUD CROKES 0-14
Ballymun Kickhams: S Currie, Enda Dolan, P McMahon, Eoin Dolan, A Hubbard, K Connolly, J Burke, David Byrne, J McCarthy, E Reilly, K Leahy 0-1, J Whelan 0-3, T Furman 0-1, D Rock 0-7, S Forde 1-0 Subs: Derek Byrne for Forde, J Small for Enda Dolan, A O'Brien for Leahy.
Kilmacud Crokes: D Nestor, Ross O'Carroll, Rory O'Carroll, C O'Sullivan, M Coughlan, B McGrath, K Nolan 0-1, P Duggan, D Magee, C Dias 0-1, L Og O hEineachain, P Burke 0-4, S Williams, P Mannion 0-4, P Burke. Subs: D Kelliher 0-1, for Morrissey h/t, R Ryan for Coughlan h/t, M Vaughan 0-3 for Williams 48, B O'Rorke for O hEineachain 48, E Culligan for McGrath 56.

2013 Nov 3, Parnell Park
ST. VINCENT'S 1-17   BALLYMUN KICKHAMS 0-20
St Vincent's: G Burke and T Quinn 0-6 each, K Golden 1-0, D Connolly 0-2, C Dorney, S Carthy, R Trainor 0-1 each. Ballymun Kickhams: D Rock 0-8, K Leahy, T Furman and C Weir 0-2 each, E Reilly, A O'Brien, A Hubbard, J McCarthy, D Byrne and J Small 0-1 each)

Nov 6, Parnell Park
ST. VINCENT'S 1-9   BALLYMUN KICKHAMS 1-8
St Vincent's: M Savage, M Concarr, J Curley, H Gill, C Diamond 0-1, G Brennan, B Egan, D Murphy, E Fennell, G Burke, D Connolly 0-2, S Carthy, R Trainor, C Dorney 1-0, T Quinn 0-5. Subs: K Golden 0-1 for Murphy, A Baxter for Carthy, N Mullins for Dorney, R Pocock for Trainor.
Ballymun Kickhams: S Currie, P McMahon, S George, E Dolan, A Hubbard, K Connolly, J Small, Davy Byrne, J McCarthy, E Reilly, A O'Brien, K Leahy, T Furman 0-1, D Rock 1-5, L O'Donovan 0-1. Subs: Derek Byrne 0-1 for O'Brien 24, C Burke for O'Donovan 55, M Brady for Leahy 60.

2014 Oct 27, Parnell Park
ST. VINCENT'S 0-14 ST. OLIVER PLUNKETT'S 1-10
St Vincent's: M Savage, K Bonnie, J Curley, H Gill, B Egan, G Brennan, M Concarr, E Fennell 0-1, D Murphy, G Burke 0-3, D Connolly 0-1, S Carthy 0-2, R Treanor 0-2, C Dorney 0-3, T Quinn 0-1. Subs: Cameron Diamond for Murphy, T Diamond for Dorney, M Loftus for Fennell, Cormac Diamond 0-1 for Carthy.
St Oliver Plunketts: A O'Mara, D Kelly, R O'Connor, E Clarke, J Brogan, D Lally, C Walsh, P Brogan, C Dunleavey, S Lyons, D Brogan, A Brogan 1-1, N Walsh, B Brogan 0-5, G Smith 0-3. Subs: R McConnell for P Brogan 26, P Brogan for D Brogan 43, P Lee 0-1 for Lyons 46, P McNulty for Dunleavy 52, D Matthews for Walsh 55.

2015 Nov 1, Parnell Park
BALLYBODEN ST. ENDA'S 2-8   ST. VINCENT'S 0-10
Ballyboden St Enda's: P Durcan, S Clayton, S Hiney, S O'Connor, D Nelson, B Dwan, A Waters 0-1, MD Macauley, D O'Mahoney, S Gibbons, R Basquel 0-3, D O'Reilly 0-1, C Basquel 0-1, C Keaney 0-1, A Kerin 2-1 Subs: S Durkin for Waters, D McCabe for O'Mahoney, D Davy for R Basquel, R McDaid for Gibbons, D O'Callaghan for C Basquel, S Molony for O'Reilly.
St Vincent's: M Savage, M Concarr, J Curley, H Gill, B Egan, G Brennan, N Mullins, D Murphy, S Carthy 0-1, G Burke 0-1, D Connolly, Cormac Diamond, R Trainor 0-2, C Dorney, T Quinn 0-6. Subs: K Golden for Murphy 23, J Feeney for Dorney 26, Cameron Diamond for Burke 28, M Loftus for Cormac Diamond 47, C Wilson for Egan 50.

2016 Nov 5, Parnell Park
ST VINCENT'S 0-15   CASTLEKNOCK 0-10
St Vincent's: M Savage, M Concarr, J Curley, C Wilson, B Egan, G Brennan, Cameron Diamond,

D Murphy, S Carthy 0-1, G Burke 0-2, D Connolly, Cormac Diamond 0-1, R Trainor 0-1, E Varley 0-4, T Quinn 0-5 Subs: A Martin for Murphy 33, J Feeney 0-1 for Cormac Diamond 42, A Baxter for Varley 60.
Castleknock: M Connolly, P Burke, P Sherry, E O'Brien 0-1, G Hannihan, T Shiels, T Quinn, C Kilkenny 0-2, S Boland, D Carlos 0-5, B Galvin, K Kindlon 0-2, M Galvin, J Sherry, C Lynch. Subs: C Brennan for M Galvin 42, J Kindlon for Lynch 52, M Brady for B Galvin.

2017 Oct 30, Parnell Park
ST. VINCENT'S 1-8   BALLYMUN KICKHAMS 0-8
St Vincent's: M Savage, M Concarr, J Curley, C Wilson 0-1, Cameron Diamond, G Brennan, B Egan, L Galvin, N Mullins, G Burke 0-1, D Connolly 1-1, Cormac Diamond, E Varley 0-2, S Carthy 0-1, T Quinn 0-2. Subs: D Murphy for Galvin h/t, R Trainor for Varley 43, J Feeney for Burke 50, T Diamond for Cormac Diamond 58, E Fennell for Mullins 63, L Sheehy for Cameron Diamond 63.
Ballymun Kickhams: E Comerford, P McMahon, E Dolan, A Hubbard, C Keeley 0-2, J Small, J Burke, A Elliott, J McCarthy, J Whelan 0-2, D Rock 0-3, K Leahy, E O'Neill, P Small 0-1, D Byrne. Subs: C Hulton for Leahy 45, T Furman for O'Neill 58.

ROLL OF HONOUR
ST. VINCENT'S (29): 1949, 1950, 1951, 1952, 1953, 1954, 1955, 1957, 1958, 1959, 1960, 1961, 1962, 1964, 1966, 1967, 1970, 1971, 1972, 1975, 1976, 1977, 1981, 1984, 2007, 2013, 2014, 2016, 2017.
O'TOOLES (11): 1918, 1919, 1920, 1922, 1923, 1924, 1925, 1926, 1928, 1931, 1946.
GERALDINES (10): 1898, 1899, 1908, 1910, 1914, 1915, 1917, 1940, 1941, 1942.
KILMACUD CROKES (7): 1992, 1994, 1998, 2004, 2005, 2008, 2010.
PARNELLS (6): 1913, 1916, 1939, 1945, 1987, 1988.
GARDA (6): 1927, 1929, 1933, 1934, 1935, 1948.
KICKHAMS (5): 1897, 1904, 1905, 1906, 1907.
U.C.D. (5): 1912, 1965, 1973, 1974, 2006.
NA FIANNA (5): 1969, 1979, 1999, 2000, 2001.
CLANNA GAEL (5): 1936, 1937, 1948, 1961, 1968.
YOUNG IRELANDS (4): 1891, 1892, 1894, 1896.
ERIN'S HOPE (4): 1887, 1932, 1956, 1978.
ISLES OF THE SEA (3): 1890, 1895, 1900.
KEATINGS (3): 1903, 1909, 1911.
BALLYMUN KICKHAMS (3): 1982, 1985, 2012.
THOMAS DAVIS (3): 1989, 1990, 1991.
BALLYBODEN ST. ENDA'S (3): 1995, 2009, 2015.
SEAN McDERMOTTS (2): 1938, 1947.

CIVIL SERVICE (2): 1944, 1980.
ERIN'S ISLE (2): 1993, 1997.
SCOIL UI CHONAILL (2): 1983, 1986.
ST. BRIGID'S (2): 2003, 2011.
FEACH McHUGH'S (1): 1888.
BRAY EMMETS (1): 1901.
ST. MARY's (1): 1921.
ST. JOSEPH'S (1): 1930.
ST. SYLVESTER'S (1): 1996.

MOST COUNTY CHAMPIONSHIP MEDALS

15   Kevin Heffernan (St Vincent's) 1949, 1950, 1951, 1952, 1953, 1954, 1955, 1957, 1958, 1959, 1960, 1961, 1962, 1966, 1967.

13   Des Ferguson (St Vincent's) 1949, 1950, 1951, 1952, 1953, 1954, 1955, 1957, 1958, 1959, 1960, 1962, 1964.

11   Lar Foley (St Vincent's) 1957, 1958, 1959, 1960, 1961, 1962, 1964, 1966, 1967, 1971, 1972.

10   Johnny McDonnell (O'Toole's) 1918, 1919, 1920, 1922, 1923, 1924, 1925, 1926, 1928, 1931; Paddy McDonnell (O'Toole's) 1918, 1919, 1920, 1922, 1923, 1924, 1925, 1926, 1928, 1931; John Synnott (O'Toole's) 1918, 1919, 1920, 1922, 1923, 1924, 1925, 1926, 1928, 1931; Jim Lavin (St Vincent's) 1949, 1950, 1951, 1952, 1953, 1954, 1955, 1957, 1958, 1959; Jim Crowley (St Vincent's) 1950, 1951, 1952, 1953, 1954, 1955, 1957, 1958, 1959, 1960; Jimmy Keaveney (St Vincent's) 1964, 1966, 1967, 1970, 1971, 1972, 1975, 1976, 1977, 1981; Tony Hanahoe (St Vincent's) 1964, 1966, 1967, 1970, 1971, 1972, 1975, 1977, 1981, 1984.

9   Paddy Carey (O'Toole's) 1918, 1919, 1920, 1922, 1923, 1924, 1925, 1926, 1928; Josie Synnott (O'Toole's) 1918, 1919, 1920, 1922, 1923, 1924, 1925, 1926, 1928); Ollie Freaney (St Vincent's) 1949, 1950, 1951, 1952, 1953, 1954, 1955, 1957, 1958; Maurice 'Mossy' Whelan (St Vincent's) 1949, 1950, 1951, 1952, 1953, 1954, 1955, 1957, 1958; Cathal O'Leary (St Vincent's) 1950, 1951, 1952, 1954, 1955, 1957, 1958, 1959, 1961.

8   Denis Mahony (St Vincent's) 1949, 1950, 1951, 1952, 1953, 1954, 1955, 1957; Johnny Joyce (St Vincent's) 1955, 1957, 1958, 1959, 1960, 1961, 1962, 1964; Gay O'Driscoll (St Vincent's) 1966, 1967, 1970, 1971, 1972, 1975, 1976, 1977.

7 Jack O'Reilly (O'Toole's) 1918, 1919, 1920, 1922, 1924, 1925, 1926; Norman Allen (St Vincent's) 1949, 1950, 1951, 1952, 1953, 1954, 1955; Nicky Maher (St Vincent's) 1951, 1952, 1953, 1954, 1955, 1957, 1958; Marcus Wilson (St Vincent's) 1952, 1953, 1954, 1955, 1958, 1959, 1960; Des Foley (St Vincent's) 1959, 1960, 1961, 1964, 1967, 1971, 1972; Liam Ferguson (St Vincent's) 1961, 1962, 1966, 1967, 1970, 1971, 1972; Leslie Deegan (St Vincent's) 1966, 1967, 1970, 1971, 1975, 1976, 1977.

6 Padraig 'Jock' Haughey (St Vincent's) 1954, 1955, 1958, 1959, 1960, 1961; Noel Fox (St Vincent's) 1959, 1960, 1961, 1962, 1964, 1966; Bobby Doyle (St Vincent's) 1972, 1975, 1976, 1977, 1981, 1984.

5 Jack Grace (Kickhams) 1904, 1905, 1906, 1907, 1912; Tom Walsh (Kickhams) 1904, 1905, 1906, 1907, 1912; Paddy Fallon (Geraldines) 1908, 1910, 1914, 1915, 1917; Bill Robbins (O'Toole's) 1918, 1919, 1920, 1922, 1923; Mick Mangan (St Vincent's) 1949, 1951, 1952, 1953, 1954; Mick Moylan (St Vincent's) 1951, 1952, 1953, 1954, 1955; Colm Leaney (St Vincent's) 1957, 1960, 1964, 1970, 1971; Colm Meehan (St Vincent's) 1958, 1959, 1960, 1961, 1962, Paddy Farnan (St Vincent's) 1958, 1959, 1960, 1961, 1962; Mick Kissane (St Vincent's) 1962, 1964, 1966, 1967,

1970; Michael Savage (St Vincent's) 2007, 2013, 2014, 2016, 2017; Ger Brennan (St Vincent's) 2007, 2013, 2014, 2016, 2017; Diarmuid Connolly (St Vincent's) 2007, 2013, 2014, 2016, 2017; Tomas Quinn (St Vincent's) 2007, 2013, 2014, 2016, 2017.

4 George Charlemont (Young Irelands) 1891, 1892, 1894, 1896; George Roche (Young Irelands) 1891, 1892, 1894, 1896; Pat Heslin (Young Irelands) 1891, 1892, 1894, 1896; Dick Flood (Young Irelands) 1891, 1892, 1894, 1896; Jack Lynch (Kickhams) 1904, 1905, 1906, 1907; Tommy Murphy (Kickhams) 1904, 1905, 1906, 1907; Paddy Callaghan (Kickhams) 1904, 1905, 1906, 1907; Hugh Hilliard (Kickhams) 1905, 1906, 1907, 1912; Jack Carey (O'Toole's) 1919, 1920, 1922, 1923; Tom Carey (O'Toole's) 1919, 1920, 1922, 1923; Tom Fitzgerald (O'Toole's) 1923, 1924, 1925, 1926; Brian Mullins (St Vincent's) 1975, 1976, 1977, 1984; Johnny Magee (Kilmacud Crokes) 1998, 2004, 2005, 2008; Michael Concarr (St Vincent's) 2013, 2014, 2016, 2017; Jarleth Curley (St Vincent's) 2013, 2014, 2016, 2017; Brendan Egan (St Vincent's) 2013, 2014, 2016, 2017; Shane Carthy (St Vincent's) 2013, 2014, 2016, 2017; Gavin Burke (St Vincent's) 2013, 2014, 2016, 2017; Cameron Diamond (St Vincent's) 2013, 2014, 2016, 2017; Daithi Murphy (St Vincent's) 2013, 2014, 2016, 2017.

Leinster and All-Ireland Club Championships

RATHER fittingly, St. Vincent's were the county's first representatives in the Leinster and All-Ireland Club Championships, but the famous club's introduction to the new competition was hardly the success they were hoping for, at least not initially. It took a few years for the scheduling to settle into the pattern we know today and for the first two stagings of the provincial and national championships, for the 1970/71 and 1971/72 seasons, St. Vincent's actually played twice within the space of five months, in May and November of 1971. Unfortunately, though, they were surprised on both occasions; Wexford champions Castletown beating them 2-11 to 1-13 at Parnell Park in the first instance and Kildare title holders Carberry edging them 3-4 to 1-9 at Croke Park in the second.

The third successive attempt, in 1972/73, brought better fortune as the provincial crown was captured in some style with wins over St. Mary's from Louth, Baltinglass from Wicklow and then a 6-10 to 2-5 hammering of The Downs from Westmeath at Pairc Tailteann in Navan, where Des Foley and Jimmy Keaveney both scored 2-2. Clanna Gael from Lurgan were accounted for by 2-8 to 0-7 at Croke Park and Cork champions Nemo Rangers provided the opposition in the final at O'Moore Park in Portlaoise on the June Bank Holiday; the side were level on five separate occasions but with just half a minute to go the Munster representative were 2-11 to 2-10 to the good — but a Jimmy Keaveney point from a free on the half forward line earned St. Vincent's a second chance at Semple Stadium in Thurles three weeks later. There was no such knife edge drama in the replay, however, as Nemo Rangers raced into a 2-5 to 0-5 halftime lead en route to eventually winning 4-6 to 0-10.

UCD's involvement in the county championship has often been a serious bone of contention but be that as it may, the Students gave the county its first success in the All-Ireland Club Championship. And its second — even if they lacked a single Dub in the first triumph and included just one in the second, Pat O'Neill. (Gerry McCaul played in both provincial campaigns but missed out on the national decider each year.)

The first campaign, in 1973/74, stretched to eight games, including two replays, the first against Wicklow representatives Carnew Emmets and the second against Armagh and Ulster champions Clanna Gael from Lurgan in the All-Ireland Final. On each occasion College needed a last minute equalising point to draw level, from Benny Gaughran (Louth) in the first instance and Ollie Leddy (Cavan) in the second, yet in between they twice hit 4-13 without conceding a goal; against Raheen from Kildare in the provincial quarter-final and Knockmore from Mayo in the All-Ireland semi-final, games in which Enda Condron (Laois) and Denis O'Connor (Cork) scored 1-8 and 3-0, respectively. In the replay against Clanna Gael, UCD were 0-6 to 1-1 in front at halftime and finished with five unanswered points for an 0-14 to 1-4 victory.

The following season, with nine of their successful still on board, UCD had some surprisingly close escapes, not least in a wafer thin 1-3 to 0-5 first hurdle scare against the same Carberry side that had shocked St. Vincent's two years earlier. Carlow champions Eire Og were then comfortably dismissed 2-13 to 0-6 at Dr. Cullen Park but it was back to a single point margin (2-7 to 1-9) in the provincial final against Offaly title holders Ferbane at Croke Park, where Kerry brothers Jackie (1-0) and Barry (0-2) Walsh turned a four point deficit into victory in the final four minutes. Connacht champions Roscommon Gaels were next overcome 0-12 to 1-2 but it was back to living on the edge in the All-Ireland Final against the champions from two years previously Nemo Rangers; the latter held an 0-12 to 1-5 lead entering the final quarter and it needed three points from Jackie Walsh and one each from sibling Barry, J.P. Kean and Pat Duggan for UCD to make history by becoming the first side to successfully defend the Andy Merrigan Cup.

UCD's bid for a hat-trick was scuttled by familiar rivals when St. Vincent's beat them 3-12 to 1-15 in July 1976 in the fifth consecutive county final meeting of the teams and went on to score perhaps the most dominant successes in the history of the Leinster and All-Ireland Club Championships. With a star studded line-up that ten players who were existing or future All-Ireland senior medals winners either on the field or on the bench in the Heffo's Army era, Norman Bernard, Dave Billings, Brendan Pocock, Leslie Deegan, Gay O'Driscoll, Fran Ryder, Brian Mullins, Bobby Doyle, Tony Hanahoe and Jimmy Keaveney plus the evergreen Mickey Whelan from the Sam Maguire winning side in 1963, they scored a total of 17-71 in their six games and conceded just 5-35, a winning average of exactly a dozen points per game.

The steamrolling began with a 3-14 to 2-9 win over Kildare kingpins Clane in Newbridge, was followed by a 5-14 to 2-4 routing of Wicklow champions Newtownmountkennedy at Croke Park — where Keaveney hit 3-2 — and then, in the provincial semi-final at O'Toole Park, a 2-14 to 0-6 defeat of Tinryland from Carlow. Laois title holders St. Joseph's were then beaten 3-9 to 1-8 at Geraldine Park in Athy — with Keaveney contributing 2-5 this time — before, on paper at least, came the biggest test of all, an All-Ireland semi-final with the team that had beaten them in the final in 1973, Nemo Rangers at the Mardyke in Cork. It was tough and dour but the Dublin champions scored a comfortable enough in the end, 0-10 to 0-3, and then went on to an anti climatic 4-10 to 0-5 final success over Roscommon Gaels at Semple Stadium, where Keaveney scored 1-4 to bring his own haul for the campaign to a still record 7-27. The winning margin was a record by six points and has only ever been beaten once (by a single point), in 1982 when Nemo Rangers won the third of their seven titles with a 6-11 to 1-8 defeat of Mayo champions Garrymore.

AFTER a trio of successive triumphs, Dublin clubs would endure a serious trophy famine over the next three decades, winning just a single All-Ireland and nine Leinster titles. A dozen times there would be no capital representation in the provincial decider and on four occasions the county champions would suffer the indignity of falling at the first hurdle.

The first of the latter instances befell St. Vincent's in defence of their so impressively won All-Ireland crown when, in November 1976, local champions Portlaoise pulled off a stunning 1-7 to 0-9 victory over a side that included five All-Star award winners — O'Driscoll, Mullins, Hanohoe, Doyle and Keaveney — at O'Moore Park the all important goal coming from Tom Prendergast after only eight minutes. Back again the following year, St. Vincent's fared only a little better; they scored 8-36 and conceded only 0-25 in successive victories over Dunlavin (Wicklow), Monasterevin (Kildare) and St. Joseph's (Laois), but then they themselves were hit with a three goal blitz between the eighth and tenth minutes by Meath champions Summerhill in the provincial final at Newbridge, the final scoreline of 5-4 to 0-6 remaining to this day the famous club's biggest ever defeat in any championship game, county, provincial or national.

The following six campaigns were equally fruitless. Offaly title holders Walsh Island eliminated Erin's Hope — who had previously beaten St. Patrick's from Longford after a replay — in the semi-final at Portlaoise in 1978 and did the same to Na Fianna in the first round at Tullamore the following year, then Civil Service, after an easy win over St. Fintan's from Wexford, were well beaten 3-0 to 0-6 by Meath champions Walterstown in a replay at Navan after an 0-8 each draw at O'Toole Park. The it was the turn of St. Vincent's to again come down at the first fence by losing to Raheen from Kildare following a replay, Ballymun Kickhams achieved a degree of success in 1982 by reaching the Leinster Final before going down 1-8 to 0-7 to Portlaoise, and the losing sequence continued the following year when Scoil Ui Chonaill went down to a 2-10 to 3-5 semi-final loss to Walterstown at Newbridge.

The depressing run was final broken — purely temporarily — in 1984/85 when St. Vincent's won the county's first provincial title since they themselves nine years earlier with successive wins over Gracefield from Offaly, Portlaoise in a replay, Cashel from Longford and Tinahely from Wicklow the latter by 1-13 to 1-3 in the final at Newbridge. Down champions Burren were beaten 2-5 to 0-8 in the All-Ireland semi-final at their own St. Mary's Park, but then a last minute goal by full forward Donie Buckley gave Kerry and Munster champions Castleisland Desmonds a 2-2 to 0-7 win in the final at Sean Treacy Park in Tipperary. Paddy Hickey in the *Irish Independent* said the winners had "perpetrated an act of grand larceny" while Gerry McCarthy in the *Irish Press* declared "daylight robbery is alive and thriving".

Over the next two seasons Ballymun Kickhams and Scoil Ui Chonaill both recorded first round victories but were then beaten at the quarter-finals stage. The came the replay filled two year reign as county champions of Parnells in which, between late October 1987 and early December of the following year they featured in a remarkable six draws in the provincial championship. They began with an easy enough 0-13 to 0-2 win over St. Patrick's from Longford at Parnell Park but thereafter would draw their provincial quarter-finals, semi-finals and finals in each of the next two campaigns!

The opposition, chronologically, was Baltinglass from Wicklow, Ferbane from Offaly and Portlaoise in the first season and in the second, again in order, Baltinglass again, Navan O'Mahony's and, in another repeat, Ferbane again. The deciders, however, brought contrasting results; Portlaoise came out on top in 1987 by 1-7 to 1-5 but Parnells lifted the trophy the following year with a 1-4 to 0-6 defeat of Ferbane in Newbridge, thanks to a goal from sub Ger Hanaphy and then a point by Mark O'Hanlon in the last two minutes. The run end in the All-Ireland semi-final at Pairc Carthaigh in Ballygarvan when a third minute goal by Owen O'Mahony set Nemo Rangers up for a 1-4 to 0-5 victory and, eventually, a fifth national title.

Thomas Davis were the county representatives for the next three campaigns and in each one they progressed a stage further and eventually went tantalisingly close to claiming the ultimate prize. They started, in 1989, by losing the provincial final 1-9 to 0-11 to Baltinglass in a replay at Newbridge after a 1-6 each draw at the same venue, and the following year avenged that loss with a 1-8 to 0-8 replay victory over the same Wicklow opposition at the same Kildare venue, only to lose the All-Ireland semi-final 2-6 to 0-10 to Lavey at Celtic Park in Derry.

The following campaign, in 1991/92, was the most heartbreaking of all. It began with another draw — 0-5 each — with Athlone at Parnell Park before a 1-7 to 1-4 success in the replay at the opposition's Pairc Chiarain and was followed by victories over Portlaoise and, in the provincial decider, Offaly title holders Clara in Newbridge. Ulster and Monaghan champions Castleblayney Faughs were then beaten 2-9 to 1-7 at Parnell Park, but an amazing fightback against Dr. Crokes from Killarney in the All-Ireland Final came up excruciatingly short; 1-10 to 0-5 in arrears with a dozen minutes remaining, they twice got back to within a point of their Kerry rivals but ran out of time and finished up on the wrong end of a 1-11 to 0-13 scoreline with Vinny Carney accounting for all but four of their points.

AFTER disappointment for Kilmacud Crokes in a quarter-final loss to Ballyroan from Laois and then Erin's Isle in a Leinster Final defeat by Carlow champions Eire Og, the titles famine finally ended in 1994/1995 courtesy of a by now more experienced Kilmacud Crokes. An emphatic 4-13 to 1-6 victory over Ferbane was sandwiched in between single point wins over Baltinglass and, in the provincial decider, Seneschalstown from Meath, before a place in the All-Ireland Final was secured with a 1-11 to 1-7 defeat of Cork champions Castlehaven at Semple Stadium. The final, against Bellaghy from Derry, was heading for something of an anti climax as the Dubliner's opened up an 0-8 to 0-1 lead with just over ten minutes left only for their opponent's to pull back four points without replay and then win a penalty with a mere half a minute left on the clock — but Mick Pender, the reserve keeper to John O'Leary on the county team and playing with three cracked ribs, produced a match — and championship — winning save from Damien Cassidy's spot kick.

Debuting pair Ballyboden St. Enda's and St. Sylvester's — the latter reaching the provincial final before going down to Eire Og from Carlow — failed to get out of Leinster but Erin's Isle, starting with a 5-22 to 0-5 hammering of Carlow champions Old Leighlin at Parnell Park — where Niall Crossan scored 1-8 and Ciaran O'Hare and Robbie Boyle both notched 2-5 — and followed by victories over Edenderry from Offaly and Stabannon Parnells from Louth, beat Kildare champions Clane 2-11 to 1-11 in the Leinster Final. Castlehaven were pipped 2-12 to 0-17 — thanks to two goals and a point in the final three minutes — in the All-Ireland semi-final at Thurles but Galway champions Corofin, with five unanswered points in the last ten minutes, proved too strong in the decider and won 0-15 to 0-10.

Kilmacud Crokes returned in 1998 only to lose the Leinster Final to Eire Og from Carlow after not one but two replays and then Na Fianna had three cracks in succession but after lifting the provincial crown in the first campaign, lost the All-Ireland Final to defending champions Crossmaglen Rangers 1-14 to 0-12 and were then beaten in the next two Leinster Finals, by first O'Hanrahans from Louth and then Wicklow champions Rathnew after a replay. UCD went down by 1-6 to 1-5 to Rathnew in the quarter-finals in 2002, St. Brigid's won the Leinster title the following year with a comprehensive 3-11 to 1-10 win over Kildare title holders Round Towers but were then beaten 1-9 to 2-3 to An Ghaeltacht from Kerry in the All-Ireland semi-final in Thurles.

After a six year absence, Kilmacud Crokes were back only to lose the provincial decider 0-14 to 0-8 to Portlaoise, but returned the next season for a narrow 0-10 to 0-9 win over Sarsfields from Kildare in the Leinster Final only to lose the All-Ireland semi-final to Salthill-Kilcarra from Galway at Pearse Park in Longford by two points, 1-9 to 1-7. Then, in 2007, UCD, after a quarter-final defeat of Meath representatives Wolfe Tones, exited next time out on a 2-6 to 1-8 scoreline to Offaly champions Rhode.

THE ten seasons from 2007/2008 up to 2016/17 turned out to be the most successful decade thus far for Dublin as far as the Leinster and All-Ireland Club Championships were concerned; four national titles and eight provincial and just a single campaign in which the county representatives failed to reach at least the Leinster Final. That was in 2009 when Ballyboden St. Enda's bowed out at the provincial semi-final stage as 1-8 to 0-6 losers to Westmeath champions Garrycastle. Two years later St. Brigid's lost the Leinster Final to the same opposition on a 1-8 to 0-10 scoreline but otherwise it was success all the way, if to varying degrees.

Twenty-three years after they had last represented the county and a further nine after their only victory in the competitions, St. Vincent's returned to the provincial and national stage for the 2007/08 campaign but with a stuttering start; after a walkover over Wicklow champions Baltinglass it took a late point from half back Pat Kelly to earn an 0-11 to 1-8 draw with Seneschalstown from Meath in a quarter-final tie at Parnell Park. The replay was won 1-12 to 0-10 in Navan and then Portlaoise were beaten 3-13 to 1-8 and, in the Leinster Final, Tyrrellspass from Westmeath by 2-8 to 0-9 at Cusack Park in Mullingar, the second goal coming from 36-year-old full forward Pat Gilroy.

Back in Navan for the All-Ireland semi-final, St. Vincent's faced defending champions Crossmaglen Rangers and, after sprinting into a 2-8 to 0-4 halftime lead with goals from Brian Moloney and Tomas Quinn, comfortably contained a second half fightback to win 2-9 to 0-11. Having dismissed four-time winners to reach the decider, they now faced a team that had not only won the championship seven times but had beaten them in a replay for the 1973 title; Nemo Rangers. It turned out to be tight but St. Vincent's edged home 1-11 to 0-13, with Diarmuid Connolly — four months shy of his 21st birthday — contributing the all important goal plus two points and skipper Quinn raising seven white flags. There was a direct connection between the club's first and second All-Ireland triumphs; the new generation was managed by Mickey Whelan, left half forward and scorer of 3-3 in the 1975/76 campaign.

Kilmacud Crokes not only surprised St. Vincent's by beating them in a semi-final replay in the following year's county campaign but went on to succeed them as champions in all three competitions, Dublin, Leinster and All-Ireland. Their four game provincial series — all played at Parnell Park — began with an 0-13 to 0-8 win over Celbridge and was followed, chronologically, by a 1-13 to 1-9 defeat of Newtown Blues from Louth (Mark Vaughan scoring 1-8), a 1-11 to 0-7 success over Navan O'Mahonys, and a 2-7 to 1-7 victory over Offaly champions Rhode. Goals by Vaughan and Pat Burke proved the difference in a 2-11 to 0-11 defeat of Corofin from Galway to set up a final clash with perennial title contenders Crossmaglen Rangers. A third minute goal by Mark Davoren paved the way for a 1-4 to 0-4 lead at the break and with 20-year-old Ross O'Carroll turning in a Man of the Match performance at right corner back, Crokes extended their lead in the second half to win 1-9 to 0-7 and reclaim the crown they had won in 1995.

They were back two years later and for a time looked like they could recapture the Andy Merrigan Cup yet again. Victories over Portlaoise in Tullamore, Garrycastle from Westmeath at Parnell Park, and Rhode from Offaly back at O'Connor Park saw them regain the provincial crown but then, in the All-Ireland semi-final, they came up against their final victims of two years previously, Crossmaglen Rangers. Despite having full back Kevin Nolan sent off for a second yellow card after 21 minutes and centre back Nicky McGrath given a straight red on the 42 minute mark, Kilmacud Crokes still held a two point lead, 1-12 to 2-7, with seven minutes to go — but Rangers then fired over four successive points before going on to win their sixth title, one they would retain the following year.

Ballymun Kickhams, whose second and most recent county title success had been 27 years earlier, dethroned Kilmacud Crokes with a 1-12 to 0-14 victory in the 2012 final, five of their points coming from Dean Rock, son of Barney and one of the backbones of the side that had triumphed in 1982 and 1985. After defeating Westmeath champions Shamrock and Kildare representatives Sarsfields, Junior and Co. would achieve something his father and his team mates had been unable to accomplish — with a provincial title, with an 0-11 to 0-8 defeat of Portlaoise at Cusack Park in Mullingar. A four point victory — 1-10 to 0-9 — over Dr. Crokes from Killarney at Semple Stadium meant they had qualified for the All-Ireland Final without conceding a single goal and when they led 2-3 to 0-1 after ten minutes of the decider against St. Brigid's from Roscommon thanks to goal from Rock and Philly McMahon another Andy Merrigan Cup for Dublin seemed certain. But the underdogs fought back and keeper Sean Currie was beaten for the first time in the 12th minute by Senan Kilbride and again in the 36th minute by Karol Mannion; still, although pulled back to level at 2-7 each, Ballymun edged ahead again until St. Brigid's tied things up once more at 2-10 apiece — only for veteran Roscommon star Frankie Dolan to fire over the championship winning point half a minute before Armagh referee Padraigh Hughes blew the final whistle.

Dublin's champions would win the next four provincial titles and St. Vincent's would account for three of them. After reclaiming the county crown in 2013 for the first time in six years by dethroning Ballymun Kickhams in a replay, they also regained the provincial title — without a suspended Diarmuid Connolly for the first two games — with successive wins over St. Loman's from Mullingar, Summerhill from Meath and Portlaoise at O'Connor Park in Tullamore. Derry champions Ballinderry Shamrocks were then beaten 2-14 to 1-15 at Pairc Esler in Newry — where Tomas Quinn replicated the 1-8 he had scored against Summerhill — and St. Vincent's were into the All-Ireland Final for the fourth time. A third title was duly secured with a 4-12 to 2-11 defeat of Castlebar Mitchels, but it was the performance of Connolly — one of seven survivors from the 2008 triumph — that, quite literally, stole the show.

The following day's papers put it in perfect context. Colm Keys in the *Irish Independent* said: "The breadth of Diarmuid Connolly's extraordinary performance in Croke Park is captured best by the sheer weight of scoring statistics. Connolly was directly involved as either scorer, provider or a link in the chain further back in 4-9 of his side's tally of 4-12. Even the make up of the 2-5 he scored underlined the range of his ability, incorporating a goal with his fist, another off his left foot, three points off his left and two off his right. He directly set up another 2-2." Frank Roche in the *Evening Herald* predicted: "Many years from now, when GAA historians chronicle the story of how St Vincent's overcame the dogged resistance of Castlebar Mitchels, they won't have to ponder too long about the title. It will be called 'The Diarmuid Connolly Final'", while Sean Moran in the *Irish Times* remarked: "It's hard to think of any final that has been as dominated by an individual".

St. Vincent's retained the county title the following year — something they hadn't done since 1977 — and did likewise in the provincial series beating, in turn, Portlaoise by 3-11 to 0-10, Garrycastle from Westmeath by 3-9 to 1-10, and Rhode from Offaly by 1-13 to 0-6 in the decider, only to come unstuck, 1-13 to 1-9, in the All-Ireland semi-final against Corofin from Galway at O'Connor Park in Tullamore. The same fate befell them two years later when after wins over Palatine from Carlow, St. Columba's from Longford and, once again, Rhode (this time at O'Moore Park in Portlaoise), Derry champions Slaughtneill handed them a surprise 0-12 to 0-10 defeat at Pairc Esler in Newry.

The lone interlude in those four years came from Ballyboden St. Enda's who, after upsetting St. Vincent's in the 2015 county final also succeeded the Marino side as provincial champions with a tight 2-9 to 1-11 victory over Portlaoise in the final after earlier wins over St. Patrick's from Louth and St. Loman's from Westmeath. And they didn't stop there; Clonmel Commercials were ousted 0-15 to 0-10 in Portlaoise and then, by beating Castlebar Mitchels by 2-14 to 0-7, gave Dublin's its eighth All-Ireland crown.

Leinster and All-Ireland Club Championship Results

1970–71

LEINSTER QUARTER-FINAL
May 12, Parnell Park, Dublin
CASTLETOWN (WEXFORD) 2-11
ST. VINCENTS 1-13
St Vincent's: O'Byrne, L Ferguson, L Foley, Cathal Hanley, M Behan, S Mullins, E Brady, G O'Driscoll, P Hallinan 0-2, T Hanahoe 0-2, J Keaveney 0-3, B Lee 0-1, L Deegan 0-3, D Foley, C Leaney 0-2. Subs: PJ Reid 1-0 for O'Driscoll.

1971/72

LEINSTER FIRST ROUND
Nov 21, Croke Park, Dublin
CARBERRY (KILDARE) 3-4   ST. VINCENTS 1-9
St Vincent's: T O'Byrne, L Ferguson, L Foley, Cathal Hanley, M Behan, S Mullins, G O'Driscoll, PJ Reid 1-0, D Foley, Christy Hanley 0-1, T Hanahoe 0-1, B Lee 0-1, L Deegan, J Keaveney 0-5, C Leaney. Subs: T Quinn 0-1 for Lee.

1972/73

LEINSTER QUARTER-FINAL
Dec 3, St Mary's Park, Ardee
ST. VINCENT'S 0-8   ST. MARY'S (LOUTH) 0-6
St Vincent's: T O'Byrne, D Billings, G O'Driscoll, M Hannick, M Behan, S Mullins, B Pocock, P Hallinan, PJ Reid 0-2, T Hanahoe, B Mullins 0-1, B Doyle 0-1, D Redmond, G Keavey, J Keaveney 0-4.

LEINSTER SEMI-FINAL
Mar 25, St Conleth's Park, Newbridge
ST. VINCENT'S 2-16 BALTINGLASS (WICKLOW) 0-9
St Vincent's: T O'Byrne, D Billings, G O'Driscoll, M Hannick, M Behan, S Mullins, B Pocock, P Hallinan, PJ Reid, T Hanahoe 0-2, B Doyle 0-4, D Redmond 1-1, G Keavey 1-1, B Mullins, J Keaveney 0-8.

LEINSTER FINAL
Apr 15, Pairc Tailteann, Navan
ST. VINCENT'S 6-10
THE DOWNS (WESTMEATH) 2-5
St Vincent's: T O'Byrne, D Billings, G O'Driscoll, M Hannick, B Pocock, S Mullins, E Brady, P Hallinan, PJ Reid, T Hanahoe, B Doyle 1-1, D Redmond 0-4, G

Keavey, D Foley 2-2, J Keaveney 2-2. Sub: C Leaney 1-1 for Keavey.

ALL-IRELAND SEMI-FINAL:
Apr 29, Croke Park, Dublin
ST. VINCENT'S 2-8 CLANNA GAEL (ARMAGH) 0-7
St Vincent's: T O'Byrne, D Billings, G O'Driscoll, M Hannick, B Pocock 0-1, S Mullins, E Brady, P Hallinan 0-1, PJ Reid, T Hanahoe 0-1, B Doyle 0-2, D Redmond, C Leaney 1-1, D Foley, J Keaveney 0-2. Subs: B Mullins 1-0, M Behan for Keavney.

ALL-IRELAND FINAL
June 4, O'Moore Park, Portlaoise
ST. VINCENT'S 2-11 NEMO RANGERS (CORK) 2-11
St Vincents: Tom O'Byrne, Dave Billings, Gay O'Driscoll, Mick Hannick, Mick Behan, Sean Mullins, Eamonn Brady, PJ Reid, Pat Hallinan, Tony Hanahoe 0-1, Bobby Doyle 0-2, Jimmy Keaveney 0-5, Christy Leaney 1-0, Des Foley 1-2, Gerry Keavey. Subs: Davey Redmond 0-1 for Keavey 45, Lar Foley for Mullins 51.

ALL-IRELAND FINAL REPLAY
June 24, Semple Stadium, Thurles
NEMO RANGERS (CORK) 4-6 ST. VINCENTS 0-10
St Vincent's: Tom O'Byrne, Liam Ferguson, Gay O'Driscoll, Mick Hannick, Mick Behan, Dave Billings, Eamonn Brady, PJ Reid 0-3, Pat Hallinan, Bobby Doyle, Tony Hanahoe 0-2, Brian Mullins, Christy Leaney, Des Foley, Jimmy Keaveney 0-5. Subs: Lar Foley for Billings, T Quinn for Leaney.

1973/74

LEINSTER FIRST ROUND
Nov 4, Croke Park, Dublin
U.C.D. 0-8   CARNEW EMMETS (WICKLOW) 1-5
U.C.D.: I Heffernan, M Judge, G O'Reilly, J Stafford, PJ O'Halloran, F O'Donoghue, E O'Donoghue, B Gaughran 0-1, O Leddy, P Carr, R O'Donoghue 0-1, J Walsh 0-5, P Galvin, P Duggan 0-1, D O'Connor.

LEINSTER FIRST ROUND REPLAY
Dec 1, County Ground, Aughrim
U.C.D. 2-8   CARNEW EMMETS (WICKLOW) 2-2
U.C.D.: I Heffernan, M Judge, G O'Reilly, G McCaul, J Stafford, E O'Donoghue, B Gaughran, O Leddy, P Carr, E Condron 1-1, K Kilmurray 0-1, J Walsh 0-2, M Hanrahan 0-1, D O'Connor 1-2, JP Kean 0-1.

LEINSTER QUARTER-FINAL
Dec 16, Parnell Park, Dublin
U.C.D. 4-13   RAHEEN (KILDARE) 0-6
U.C.D.: I Heffernan, M Judge, G O'Reilly, J Stafford, PJ O'Halloran, F O'Donoghue, E O'Donoghue, B Gaughran, O Leddy, P Carr, E Condron 1-8, K Kilmurray, P Galvin 2-0, P Duggan 0-2, D O'Connor 1-3.

LEINSTER SEMI-FINAL
Jan 20, Clonattin Park, Gorey
U.C.D. 1-12   CASTLETOWN (WEXFORD) 0-5
U.C.D.: I Heffernan, M Judge, G O'Reilly, G McCaul, PJ O'Halloran, E O'Donoghue, B Gaughran 0-3, O Leddy 0-1, P Carr, E Condron 1-1, K Kilmurray, J Walsh 0-2, M Hanrahan, P Duggan, JP Kean 0-5.

LEINSTER FINAL
Mar 3, Drogheda Park, Drogheda
U.C.D. 1-6   COOLEY KICKHAMS (LOUTH) 0-7
U.C.D.: I Heffernan, M Judge, G O'Reilly, G McCaul, PJ O'Halloran, E O'Donoghue, P Carr, O Leddy, B Gaughran 0-1, E Condron 0-2, K Kilmurray, J Walsh 0-3, M Hanrahan, P Duggan 1-0, JP Kean.

ALL-IRELAND SEMI-FINAL
Mar 10, James Stephens Park, Ballina
U.C.D. 4-13   KNOCKMORE (MAYO) 0-4
U.C.D.: J Madden, M Judge, G O'Reilly, PJ O'Halloran, E O'Donoghue, P Kerr, J O'Keeffe 0-1, B Gaughran 0-2, E Condron 0-1, K Kilmurray 0-1, J Walsh 0-5, P Duggan 0-1, O Leddy, JP Kean 1-2. Subs: D O'Connor 3-0 for O'Keeffe, J Waldron for McCaul.

ALL-IRELAND FINAL
Mar 18, Croke Park, Dublin
U.C.D. 1-6   CLANNA GAEL (ARMAGH) 1-6
U.C.D.: Ivan Heffernan, Mick Judge, Garrett O'Reilly, Joe Waldron, PJ O'Halloran, Eamon O'Donoghue, Paddy Kerr (capt), John O'Keeffe, Benny Gaughran, Enda Condron 0-1, Kevin Kilmurray, Jackie Walsh 0-4, JP Kean, Ollie Leddy 0-1, Pat Duggan. Sub: Denis O'Connor 1-0 for O'Keeffe.

ALL-IRELAND FINAL REPLAY
Apr 28, Croke Park
U.C.D. 0-14   CLANNA GAEL (ARMAGH) 1-4
U.C.D.: Ivan Heffernan, Mick Judge, Garrett O'Reilly, Pierce Gilroy, Frank Donoghue, Eamon O'Donoghue, Paddy Kerr (c), Kevin Kilmurray 0-2, Benny Gaughran 0-3, Enda Condron, Ollie Leddy 0-2, Jackie Walsh 0-4, JP Kean 0-1, Denis O'Connor 0-1, Pat Duggan 0-1.

1974/75

LEINSTER QUARTER-FINAL
Dec 8, St Conleth's Park, Newbridge
U.C.D. 1-3   CARBERRY (KILDARE) 0-5

U.C.D.: I Heffernan, M Judge, E O'Donoghue, P Gilroy, PJ O'Halloran, C Moynihan, P O'Neill, K Kilmurray, M Carty, JP Kean 0-1, O Leddy, G McCaul 1-0, E Condron, G O'Reilly, P Duggan 0-2.

LEINSTER SEMI-FINAL
Jan 12, Dr Cullen Park, Carlow
U.C.D. 2-13   EIRE OG (CARLOW) 0-6
U.C.D.: I Heffernan, M Judge, G O'Reilly, G McCaul, PJ O'Halloran, C Moynihan, P O'Neill, K Kilmurray, B Dunleavy 0-1, E Condron, JP Kean 1-0, J Walsh 0-8, B Walsh 0-2, O Leddy 1-2, B Heneghan.

LEINSTER FINAL
Jan 26, Croke Park, Dublin
U.C.D. 2-7   FERBANE (OFFALY) 1-9
U.C.D.: I Heffernan, M Judge, G D'Reilly, G McCaul, PJ O'Halloran, C Moynihan, M McEllistron, K Kilmurray 0-1, P Kerr, B Donleavy, JP Kean, J Walsh 2-1, B Walsh 0-4, O Leddy, B Heneghan 0-1. Subs: P Duggan for Donleavy, Donleavy for Kerr.

ALL-IRELAND SEMI-FINAL
Feb 23, Dr Hyde Park, Roscommon
U.C.D. 0-12
ROSCOMMON GAELS (ROSCOMMON) 1-2
U.C.D.: I Heffernan: M Judge, G O'Reilly, G McCaul, PJ O'Haloran, C Moynihan, F Donoghue, P O'Neill 0-1, G McEntee, P Kerr 0-2, JP Kean 0-4, J Walsh 0-3, B Walsh, E O'Donoghue 0-2 B Heneghan. Sub: M Carty for O'Neill.

ALL-IRELAND FINAL
Mar 16, Croke Park
U.C.D. 1-11   NEMO RANGERS (CORK) 0-12
U.C.D: Ivan Heffernan, Mick Judge, Garrett O'Reilly, Con Moynihan, PJ O'Halloran, Eamon O'Donoghue, Frank Donoghue, Mick Carty (capt) 0-1, Pat O'Neill 0-1, Brendan Dunleavy, JP Kean 1-0, Jackie Walsh 0-6, Barry Walsh 0-2, Pat Duggan 0-1, B Heneghan. Sub: Endra Condron for Heneghan.

1975/76

LEINSTER FIRST ROUND:
Nov 1, St Conleth's Park, Newbridge
ST. VINCENT'S 3-14   CLANE (KILDARE) 2-9
St Vincent's: N Bernard, D Billings, M Corcoran, E Brady, B Pocock 1-0, G O'Driscoll, T Diamond, B Mullins 0-1, F Ryder 0-2, PJ Reid 1-1, T Hanahoe 0-3, B Doyle 0-2, L Deegan 0-1, J Keaveney 1-4, C Hanley. Subs: M Behan for Brady, B Reddy for Reid.

LEINSTER QUARTER-FINAL
Nov 16, Croke Park, Dublin
ST. VINCENT'S 5-14
NEWTOWNMOUNTKENNEDY (WICKLOW) 2-4

St Vincent's: N Bernard, D Billings, M Corcoran, M Behan, B Pocock, G O'Driscoll, T Diamond, F Ryder, B Mullins, B Doyle 2-3, T Hanahoe 0-2, M Whelan 0-1, PJ Reid 0-1, J Keaveney 3-2, L Deegan 0-5.

LEINSTER SEMI-FINAL
Jan 4, O'Toole Park, Dublin
ST. VINCENT'S 2-14   TINRYLAND (CARLOW) 0-6
St Vincent's: N Bernard, D Billings, M Corcoran, M Behan, T Byrne, G O'Driscoll, B Pocock, B Mullins, T Diamond, B Doyle 1-4, T Hanahoe 0-1, PJ Reid 0-1, L Deegan 0-1, J Keaveney 0-6, M Whelan 1-1. Subs: D Redmond for Keaveney, M Hannick for Billings, B Reddy for Deegan.

LEINSTER FINAL
Jan 18, Geraldine Park, Athy
ST. VINCENT'S 3-9   ST. JOSEPHS (LAOIS) 1-8
St Vincent's: N Bernard, D Billings, M Corcoran, G O'Driscoll, M Behan, B Pocock, T Diamond, B Mullins 0-1, F Ryder, B Doyle 0-1, T Hanahoe, PJ Reid, L Deegan 0-1, J Keaveney 2-5, M Whelan 1-0. Subs: M Hannick for Corcoran, B Reddy 0-1 for Reid.

ALL-IRELAND SEMI-FINAL
Feb 22, Mardyke, Cork
ST. VINCENT'S 0-10
NEMO RANGERS (CORK) 0-3
St Vincent's: N Bernard, D Billings, G O'Driscoll, M Hannick, M Behan, V Lambe, B Pocock, B Mullins, F Ryder, PJ Reid, T Hanahoe 0-2, M Whelan, B Reddy 0-2, J Keaveney 0-6, B Doyle.

ALL-IRELAND FINAL
Mar 14, Semple Stadium, Thurles
ST. VINCENT'S 4-10   ROSCOMMON GAELS 0-5
St. Vincents: Norman Bernard, Dave Billings, Gay O'Driscoll, Mick Hannick, Mick Behan, Vincent Lambe, Brendan Pocock, Brian Mullins 0-1, Fran Ryder 0-1, Barney Reddy 0-1, Tony Hanahoe 2-0, Mickey Whelan 1-1, Leslie Deegan 0-1, Jimmy Keaveney 1-4, Bobby Doyle 0-1. Sub: PJ Reid for Hannick.

1976/77

LEINSTER QUARTER-FINAL
Nov 14, O'Moore Park, Portlaoise
PORTLAOISE 1-7   ST. VINCENTS 0-9
St Vincent's: N Bernard, G O'Connor, D Billings, T Clancy, PJ Reid, V Lambe, B Pocock, B Mullins 0-1, F Ryder 0-1, B Reid, T Hanahoe, M Whelan, L Deegan 0-2, J Keaveney 0-4, B Doyle 0-1. Subs: T Diamond for Clancy, C Hanley for Whelan.

1977/78

LEINSTER FIRST ROUND
Oct 16, County Ground, Aughrim
ST. VINCENTS 3-15   DUNLAVIN (WICKLOW) 0-8
St Vincent's: N Bernard, D Billings, G O'Driscoll, G O'Connor, B Pocock, J Lynskey, T Diamond, F Ryder 0-6, B Mullins, B Doyle 1-1, T Hanahoe 0-3, M Whelan, L Deegan 1-0, J Keaveney 0-3, M O'Grady 0-2. Subs: PJ Reid, M Hannigan for Lynskey, S Doyle 1-0 for Deegan.

LEINSTER QUARTER-FINAL
Oct 30, Croke Park, Dublin
ST. VINCENTS 4-11
MONASTEREVAN (KILDARE) 0-9
St Vincent's: N Bernard, D Billings, G O'Driscoll, G O'Connor, PJ Reid, B Pocock, T Diamond, J Lynskey 0-1, F Ryder, B Doyle 0-1, T Hanahoe 1-0, M Whelan 2-1, L Deegan, J Keaveney 1-8, M O'Grady, Sub: J Doyle for O'Grady 56.

LEINSTER SEMI-FINAL:
Nov 27, Geraldine Park, Athy
ST. VINCENTS 1-10   ST. JOSEPH'S (LAOIS) 0-8
St Vincent's: N Bernard, D Billings, G O'Driscoll, M Hannick, PJ Reid, B Pocock, T Diamond, B Mullins, J Lynskey, F Ryder 0-1, T Hanahoe 0-2, M Whelan 0-2, B Doyle 1-2, J Keaveney, M O'Grady 0-3.

LEINSTER FINAL
Dec 12, St Conleth's Park, Newbridge
SUMMERHILL (MEATH) 5-4   ST. VINCENTS 0-6
St Vincent's: N Bernard, D Billings, G O'Driscoll, M Hannick, B Pocock, V Lambe, T Diamond, B Mullins, J Lynsky, S Doyle, T Hanahoe 0-1, F Ryder 0-1, B Doyle 0-2, J Keaveney 0-2, M O'Grady. Subs: PJ Reid for Lynsky, T Clancy for Bernard.

1978/79

LEINSTER QUARTER-FINAL
Nov 4, Leo Casey Park, Ballymahon
ERIN'S HOPE 0-11
ST PATRICK'S (LONGFORD) 1-8
Erin's Hope: D Healy, D McVeigh, J Murphy, M Kelly, T Kearney, B McArdle, G Barrett, P Martin, M O'Connor, J Gallagher 0-1, O Martin 0-1, L Duffy, G Cuddy 0-5, P Foley 0-2, A Trappe 0-2. Sub: E Kearney for T Kearney.

LEINSTER QUARTER-FINAL REPLAY
Nov 12, Croke Park, Dublin
ERIN'S HOPE 0-10
ST PATRICK'S (LONGFORD) 1-4
Erin's Hope: D Healy, D McVeigh, J Murphy, M Hicks T Carney, B McArdle, G Barrett, M O'Connor 0-1,

P Martin, J Gallagher, O Martin 0-1, L Duffy 0-1, G Cuddy 0-5, D McMahon, A Trappe 0-2.

LEINSTER SEMI-FINAL
Nov 18, O'Moore Park, Portlaoise
WALSH ISLAND (OFFALY) 2-11 ERIN'S HOPE 2-5
Erin's Hope: D Healy, D McVeigh, J Murphy, M Hicks T Carney, B McArdle, G Barrett, M O'Connor, P Martin 1-1, J Gallagher 0-2, O Martin, L Duffy, G Cuddy, D McMahon, A Trappe 1-2.

1979/80

LEINSTER FIRST ROUND
Oct 28, O'Connor Park, Tullamore
WALSH ISLAND (OFFALY) 0-11 NA FIANNA 0-9
Na Fianna: N Fitzgerald, M Brosnan, B Cooper, D Lynch 0-1, N Duffy, B Casey 0-2, F Leahy, J Caffrey, S Donnelly, R Neville 0-4, J Quinn 0-1, P Boylan, C McCarthy, K Fagan 0-1, J McCarthy. Sub: D Meagan for Donnelly.

1980/81

LEINSTER FIRST ROUND
Oct 26, Croke Park, Dublin
CIVIL SERVICE 5-5 ST. FINTAN'S (WEXFORD) 1-5
Civil Service: J Carroll, D Stevenson, G O'Reilly, G Crowe, J Marshall, E Sheelan 0-1, P McGill, P O'Neill 1-0, J Long, B Gaughran, S Bonner 0-1, P Crozier, K Kilmurray, M O'Connor 1-1, G Aherne 3-2.

LEINSTER QUARTER-FINAL
Nov 9, O'Toole Park, Dublin
CIVIL SERVICE 0-8 WALTERSTOWN (MEATH) 0-8
Civil Service: J Carroll, D Stevenson, G O'Reilly, G Crowe, J Marshall, E Sheelin 0-2, P McGill, P O'Neill 0-1, J Long, B Gaughran 0-2, S Bonner 0-1, M O'Connor 0-1, J Hannify, G Aherne 0-1, K Kilmurray.

LEINSTER QUARTER-FINAL REPLAY
Nov 23, Pairc Tailteann, Navan
WALTERSTOWN (MEATH) 3-9 CIVIL SERVICE 0-6
Civil Service: J Carroll, D Stevenson, G O'Reilly, G Crowe, J Marshall, E Sheelan 0-2, P McGill, P O'Neill, J Long, B Gaughran 0-2, S Bonner, P Crozier, K Kilmurray, M O'Connor 0-1, G Aherne 0-1.

1981/82

LEINSTER QUARTER-FINAL
Nov 21, Parnell Park, Dublin
ST. VINCENTS 3-6 RAHEEN (KILDARE) 1-12
St Vincent's: N Bernard, R Hazley, V Conroy, B Pocock, S Fleming, S Lavin, C Buffini 0-2, T Hanahoe

1-0, B Jordan 0-1, P McLoughlin 2-1, B Doyle 0-1, M Loftus 0-2, Subs: PJ Reid for Fleming 32, J Lynsky for Lavin 40, M Dowling for Reid 57.

LEINSTER QUARTER-FINAL REPLAY
Dec 5, St Conleth's Park, Newbridge
RAHEEN (KILDARE) 0-8 ST. VINCENT'S 0-4
St Vincent's: N Bernard, R Hazley, V Conroy, B Pocock, M Dowling, S Fleming, S Wade, P Canavan, B Jordan, C Buffini 0-2, M Loftus 0-1, S Loftus 0-1, P McLoughlin, B Doyle, PJ Reid. Subs: S Lavin for Reid, J Lynsky for Hazley.

1982/83

LEINSTER QUARTER-FINAL:
Oct 31, Croke Park, Dublin
BALLYMUN KICKHAMS 0-13
GERALDINES (LOUTH) 1-4
Ballymun Kickhams: B Carroll, T Mannion, E Kelly, G Hargan, P Traynor, C Eustace, M Murphy, C O'Farrell, D Deasy 0-1, D Sheehan 0-1, A McCaul 0-5, A Walsh, S Moylan 0-1, B Rock 0-4, R O'Farrell 0-1.

LEINSTER SEMI-FINAL
Nov 14, O'Connor Park, Tullamore
BALLYMUN KICKHAMS 1-14
ATHLONE (WESTMEATH) 2-7
Ballymun Kickhams: B Carroll, T Mannion, E Kelly, G Hargan, P Traynor, C Eustace, M Murphy, G Talbot, D Deasy, D Sheehan 1-4, A McCaul 0-2, A Walsh, L Gavin 0-1, B Rock 0-6, R O'Farrell. Subs: J Kearns 0-1 for Gavin, F Lyons for Walsh.

LEINSTER FINAL
Nov 28, Dr Cullen Park, Carlow
PORTLAOISE (LAOIS) 1-8
BALLYMUN KICKHAMS 0-7
Ballymun Kickhams: B Carroll, E Kelly, G Hargan, T Mannion, P Traynor, C Eustace, M Murphy, D Deasey, G Talbot, J Kearns, A McCaul, A Walsh, D Sheehan 0-3, B Rock 0-4, R O'Farrell. Subs: C O'Farrell for Talbot, Talbot for R O'Farrell.

1983/84

LEINSTER FIRST ROUND
Nov 5, Station Road, Moate
SCOIL UI CONAILL 1-10 MOATE (WESTMEATH) 0-4
Scoil Ui Chonaill: J Close, M O'Connell, F McGrath, T Naugbton, K Murphy, P McVeigh, E Costelloe, M McCarrick, J Kirwan, L Close 0-1, C Curtis, S O'Brien 0-3, P Lynch 0-3, R Kelleher 1-1, D O'Brien 0-1. Subs: C McMahon for O'Connell, T O'Brien 0-1 for Close, P Tuck for Murphy.

LEINSTER QUARTER-FINAL
Nov 11, Croke Park, Dublin
SCOIL UI CONAILL 2-9   ST JOSEPH'S (LAOIS) 1-7
Scoil Ui Chonaill: J Close, P Tuck, F McGrath, T Naughton, E Costelloe 0-1, P McVeigh, K Murphy, J Kirwan, M McCarrick, S O'Brien, C Curtis 0-4, L Close, P Lynch 0-3, R Kelleher, D O'Brien 2-1.

LEINSTER SEMI-FINAL
Nov 27, St Conleth's Park, Newbridge
**WALTERSTOWN (MEATH) 2-10
SCOIL UI CHONAILL 3-5**
Scoil Ui Chonaill: J Close, P Tuck, F McGrath, T Naughton, K Murphy, P McVeigh, E Costelloe, M McCarrick, J Kirwan, L Close 0-1, C Curtis, S O'Brien 1-1, P Lynch 0-3, R Kelleher 1-1, D O'Brien. Sub: T O'Brien for S O'Brien.

1984/85

LEINSTER FIRST ROUND:
Oct 20, O'Connor Park, Tullamore
ST. VINCENT'S 1-7   GRACEFIELD (OFFALY) 0-9
St Vincent's: T O'Byrne, B Pocock, V Conroy, T Diamond, S Fleming, D O'Brien, A Devlin, T Conroy 0-3, B Mullins, B Jordan 0-1, T Hanahoe, E Heery 0-1, S McDermott 1-0, S Lavin, P McLoughlin 0-2. Subs: S Dalton for Fleming, M Loftus for Lavin.

LEINSTER QUARTER-FINAL
Oct 27, O'Toole Park, Dublin
ST. VINCENT'S 0-10   PORTLAOISE (LAOIS) 1-7
St Vincent's: T O'Byrne, B Pocock, V Conroy, T Diamond, S Fleming, D O'Brien, A Devlin, T Conroy, B Mullins, E Heery, B Jordan 0-1, S McDermott 0-1, S Lavin, S Dalton 0-3, P McLoughlin 0-5. Sub: P Canavan for Pocock.

LEINSTER QUARTER-FINAL REPLAY
Nov 3, McCann Park, Portarlington
ST. VINCENT'S 0-13   PORTLAOISE (LAOIS) 0-6
St Vincent's: T O'Byrne, T Diamond, V Conroy, S Wade 0-1, S Fleming, D O'Brien, A Devlin, B Mullins, P Canavan 0-1, E Heery 0-3, T Conroy 0-1, B Jordan, S Dalton, S Lavin, P McLoughlin 0-5. Subs: M Loftus 0-1 for Lavin, S McDermott 0-1 for McLoughlin, C Buffini for Heery.

LEINSTER SEMI-FINAL
Nov 10, Cusack Park, Mullingar
ST. VINCENT'S 0-11   CASHEL (LONGFORD) 0-1
St Vincent's: T O'Byrne, T Diamond, V Conroy, S Wade, S Fleming, D O'Brien, A Devlin, P Canavan, B Mullins, T Conroy 0-1, E Heery 0-1, B Jordan 0-1, S Dalton, T Hanahoe 0-2, P McLoughlin 0-5.

LEINSTER FINAL
Dec 9, St Conleth's Park, Newbridge
ST. VINCENT'S 1-13   TINAHELY (WICKLOW) 1-3
St Vincent's: T O'Byrne, T Diamond, V Conroy, S Fleming, P Canavan, D O'Brien 0-1, A Devlin, B Mullins, T Conroy 0-2, E Heery 0-3, B Jordan 1-1, M Loftus 0-1, S Dalton, T Hanahoe 0-1, P McLoughlin. Subs: S McDermott for Dalton, B Doyle 0-3 for P McLoughlin, C Buffini 0-1 for Hanahoe.

ALL-IRELAND SEMI-FINAL
Feb 24, St Mary's Park, Burren
ST. VINCENT'S 2-5   BURREN (DOWN) 0-8
St Vincent's: N Bernard, R Hazley, V Conroy, S Wade, S Fleming, P Canavan, A Devlin, B M 1-13ullins, T Conroy 0-1, E Heery, B Jordan, S MoDermott 0-1, B Doyle, M Loftus 0-2, P McLoughlin 2-0. Subs: C Buffini for Heery, S Dalton 0-1 for Doyle.

ALL-IRELAND FINAL
Mar 24, Sean Treacy Park, Tipperary
CASTLEISLAND (KERRY) 2-2   ST. VINCENT'S 0-7
St Vincent's: Norman Bernard, T Diamond, Vincent Conroy, Stephen Wade, Ray Hazley, Shay Fleming, A Devlin, Pat Canavan, Brian Mullins, Tommy Conroy, Brian Jordan, Sean McDermott 0-2, Colm Buffini 0-3, Mick Loftus 0-1, Paul McLoughlin 0-1. Sub: Eamon Heery for Buffini.

1985/86

LEINSTER FIRST ROUND
Oct 19, O'Toole Park, Dublin
BALLYMUN KICKHAMS 2-11 EIRE OG (CARLOW) 0-11
Ballymun Kickhams: S Bannon, T Fitzgerald, G Hargan, T Mannion, P Traynor, E Kelly, F Lyons, D Deasy, M Murphy, S O'Brien 0-3, T Carr 2-3, C Kelly 0-2, S Moylan, A McCaul 0-3, J Kearns 0-1.

LEINSTER QUARTER-FINAL
Nov 3, Croke Park, Dublin
**BALTINGLASS (WICKLOW) 4-7
BALLYMUN KICKHAMS 2-8**
Ballymun Kickhams: S Bannon, E Kelly, G Hargan, T Mannion, P Traynor, C Eustace, F Lyons, D Deasy 0-1, J Kearns, S O'Brien, T Carr 0-1, A McCaul 1-1, D Sheehan 1-0, B Rock 0-4, C Kelly 0-1.

1986/87

LEINSTER FIRST ROUND
Oct 11, O'Toole Park, Dublin
**SCOIL UI CONAILL 0-8
NAOMH EOIN (CARLOW) 0-5**
Scoil Ui Chonaill: C McMahon, K Murphy, M

O'Connell, J Tighe, G McMahon, B Hickey, P McVeigh, D O'Brien, T O'Brien 0-2, S O'Brien 0-1, C Curtis 0-2, L Close 0-1, G Mescal 0-2, J Kirwan, P Brooks. Subs: T Callinan for Brooks 38, G Power for Kirwan 46.

LEINSTER QUARTER-FINAL
Nov 9, O'Toole Park, Dublin
SARSFIELDS (KILDARE) 0-12
SCOIL UI CONAILL 1-8
Scoil Ui Chonaill: C McMahon, T Naughton, M O'Connell, K Murphy, T Callinan 1-0, B Hickey, P McVeigh, J Kirwan, D O'Brien, S O'Brien 0-3, C Curtis 0-4, L Close, G McMahon 0-1, F McGrath, G Mescal. Sub: T O'Brien for Mescal 60.

1987/88

LEINSTER FIRST ROUND
Oct 11, Parnell Park, Dublin
PARNELLS 0-13
ST PATRICK'S ARDAGH (LONGFORD) 0-2
Parnells: M Hoban, C Oonan, K Earley, B Halpln, K Holland, D North, G Walsh 0-2, J Bissett, D Fitzgibbon, J Byrne, B Talty 0-3, M Bissett, B Brady, J Prendergast, M O'Hanlon 0-8. Subs: P Tiernan for Holland, D Feeney for Earley.

LEINSTER QUARTER-FINAL
Oct 25, Parnell Park, Quarter-Final
PARNELLS 1-7 BALTINGLASS (WICKLOW) 1-7
Parnells: M Hoban, C Oonan, K Earley, B Halpin, R Holland, D North, G Walsh, J Bissett 0-1, D Fitzgibbon, J Byrne 0-1, B Talty 0-1, M Bissett, B Brady, J Prendergast, M O'Hanlon 1-4. Sub: P Tiernan for M Bissett.

LEINSTER QUARTER-FINAL REPLAY:
Nov 1, County Ground, Aughrim
PARNELLS 2-6 BALTINGLASS (WICKLOW) 0-8
Parnells: M Hoban, C Oonan, K Earley, B Halpin, R Holland, D North, G Walsh, D Fitzgibbon, J Bissett, J Byrne, B Talty 0-1, B Brady 2-2, P Tieraan, J Prendergast, M O'Hanlon 0-3. Sub: M Bissett for Byrne 40.

LEINSTER SEMI-FINAL
Nov 15, O'Moore Park, Portlaoise
PARNELLS 0-6 FERBANE (OFFALY) 0-6
Parnells: M Hoban, C Oonan, K Earley, B Halpin, R Holland, D North, G Walsh, D Fitzgibbon, J Bissett, M Bissett, B Talty, B Brady 0-1, M O'Hanlon 0-5, J Prendergast, P Tierney. Subs: J Byrne for M Bissett, B Hankins for Talty, G Kelly for Tierney.

LEINSTER SEMI-FINAL REPLAY
Nov 21, Catherine Park, Athy
PARNELLS 3-4 FERBANE (OFFALY) 0-11
Parnells: M Hoban, C Oonan, K Earley, B Halpin, R Holland, D North, J Byrne, J Bissett, D Fitzgibbon,

P Tierney, B Talty, B Brady 1-0, G Kelly 2-0, J Prendergast, M O'Hanlon 0-4. Subs: B Arkins for Tierney 47, M Bissett for Brady 59.

LEINSTER FINAL
Nov 29, St Conleth's Park, Newbridge
PARNELLS 1-8 PORTLAOISE (LAOIS) 1-8
Parnells: M Hoban, C Noonan, K Earley, B Halpin, R Holland, D North, J Byrne, J Bissett, D Fitzgibbon 0-2, B Arkins, B Talty 0-1, B Brady 1-0, G Kelly, P Tiernan, M O'Hanlon 0-4. Subs: J Prendergast 0-1 for Arkins 41, G Walsh for Tiernan 54.

LEINSTER FINAL REPLAY
Dec 20, St Conleth's Park, Newbridge
PORTLAOISE (LAOIS) 1-7 PARNELLS 1-5
Parnells: M Hoban, C Noonan, K Earley, B Halpin, J Byrne, D North, G Walsh, J Bissett 0-1, D Fitzgibbon 0-1, R Holland 0-1, B Talty, B Brady 1-0, G Kelly, J Prendergast, M O'Hanlon 0-2. Subs: B Arkins for Fitzgibbon 53.

1988/89

LEINSTER QUARTER-FINAL
Oct 30, Baltinglass Park, Baltinglass
PARNELLS 0-9 BALTINGLASS (WICKLOW) 1-6
Parnells: M Hoban, C Oonan, K Earley, D Feeney, R Holland, G Walsh, J Byrne, J Prendergast 0-2, P Tiernan, D Fitzgibbon, B Arkins, B Brady, G Kelly, B Talty 0-2, M O'Hanlon 0-5.

LEINSTER QUARTER-FINAL REPLAY
Nov 5, Parnell Park, Dublin
PARNELLS 2-6 BALTINGLASS (WICKLOW) 0-10
Parnells: M Hoban, C Oonan, K Earley, D Feeney, R Holland, G Walsh, J Byrne, J Prendergast, P Tiernan, D Fitzgibbon, B Arkins 0-1, B Brady 1-1, G Kelly, B Talty 1-0, M O'Hanlon 0-3. Sub: M Bissett 0-1 for Tiernan.

LEINSTER SEMI-FINAL
Nov 19, O'Moore Park, Portlaoise
PARNELLS 0-6 NAVAN O'MAHONYS (MEATH) 0-6
Parnells: M Hoban, C Oonan, K Earley, D Feeney, R Holland, G Walsh, J Byrne, J Prendergast 0-1, P Tiernan, D Fitzgibbon, B Arkins, B Brady 0-2, G Kelly, B Talty, M O'Hanlon 0-2. Subs: J Bissett 0-1 for Kelly, M Bissett for Arkins.

LEINSTER SEMI-FINAL REPLAY
Nov 26, Drogheda Park, Drogheda
PARNELLS 3-6 NAVAN O'MAHONYS (MEATH) 1-10
Parnells: M Hoban, C Oonan, K Earley, D Feeney, R Holland, G Walsh, J Byrne, J Prendergast, P Tiernan, D Fitzgibbon 0-1, B Arkins 1-1, B Brady 0-1, G Kelly 1-0, B Talty, M O'Hanlon 0-3. Subs: B Halpin for Noonan, J Bissett for Kelly.

LEINSTER FINAL
Dec 11, St Conleth's Park, Newbridge
PARNELLS 2-5   FERBANE (OFFALY) 1-8
Parnells: M Hoban, C Noonan, K Earley, D Feeney, R Holland, G Walsh, J Byrne, J Prendergast, P Tiernan, D Fitzgibbon 0-1, B Arkins 1-1, B Brady 0-1, G Kelly 1-0, B Talty, M O'Hanlon 0-3. Sub: S Herbert for Tiernan, J Bissett.

LEINSTER FINAL REPLAY
Dec 18, St Conleth's Park, Newbridge
PARNELLS 1-4   FERBANE (OFFALY) 0-6
Parnells: M Hoban, C Noonan, K Earley, D Feeney, G O'Neill, G Walsh, J Byrne, J Bissett, J Prendergast, M Bissett, D Fitzgibbon 0-1, B Brady, S Herbert, B Talty, M O'Hanlon 0-3. Sub: G Hanaphy 1-0 for Herbert.

ALL-IRELAND SEMI-FINAL
Feb 19, Pairc Carthaigh, Ballygarvan
NEMO RANGERS (CORK) 1-4   PARNELLS 0-5
Parnells: M Hoban, C Oonan, K Earley, D Feeney, R Holland, G Walsh, J Byrne, J Prendergast, J Bissett, M Bissett, D Fitzgibbon, B Brady 0-2, B Arkins 0-1, B Talty, M O'Hanlon 0-2. Subs: G O'Neill for M Bissett, G Hanaphy for J Bissett.

1989/90

LEINSTER QUARTER-FINAL
Oct 28, St Patrick's Park, Enniscorthy
THOMAS DAVIS 0-7
DUFFRY ROVERS (WEXFORD) 1-2
Thomas Davis: F Troy, D Nugent, JJ Martin, E O'Toole, J Fadian, G McCabe, G Kilmartin, D Foran, P Curran, P Nugent, P Dwane 0-1, S Grealis 0-5, P Godson, L Adamson, V Carney. Sub: J Quinn 0-1 for Godson.

LEINSTER SEMI-FINAL
Nov 12, Drogheda Park, Drogheda
THOMAS DAVIS 0-15
NAVAN O'MAHONYS (MEATH) 0-9
Thomas Davis: F Troy, D Nugent, JJ Martin, E O'Toole, J Fadian, G McCabe, G Kilmartin, D Foran 0-1, P Curran 0-2, P Nugent 0-1, P Dwane, S Grealis 0-7, P Godson 0-1, L Adamson 0-3, V Carney.

LEINSTER FINAL
Nov 26, St Conleth's Park, Newbridge
THOMAS DAVIS 1-6
BALTINGLASS (WICKLOW) 1-6
Thomas Davis: F Troy, D Nugent, JJ Martin, E O'Toole, J Fadian, G McCabe, G Kilmartin, D Foran, P Curran, P Nugent, P Dwane 1-0, S. Grealis, P Godson, L Adamson 0-3, V Carney 0-3. Subs: K Kerr for O'Toole, J Quinn for Godson.

LEINSTER FINAL REPLAY
Dec 10, St Conleth's Park, Newbridge
BALTINGLASS (WICKLOW) 1-9
THOMAS DAVIS 0-11
Thomas Davis: F Troy, D Nugent, JJ Martin, E O'Toole, J Fadian, G McCabe, G Kilmartin, D Foran, P Curran, P Nugent 0-3, P Dwane 0-1, S Grealis, J Quinn, L Adamson 0-5, V Carney 0-1.

1990/91

LEINSTER QUARTER-FINAL
Oct 28, Monksland, Carlingford
THOMAS DAVIS 3-15
COOLEY KICKHAMS (LOUTH) 2-7
Thomas Davis: F Troy, D Nugent, JJ Martin, E O'Toole, J Fadian, P Curran, G Gilmartin, D Foran, J Benton 0-1, P Nugent 0-1, L Adamson 0-3, S Grealis 0-4, P Joyce 2-1, P Dwane 1-1, V Carney 0-4.

LEINSTER SEMI-FINAL
Dec 8, St Conleth's Park, Newbridge
THOMAS DAVIS 1-12   FERBANE (OFFALY) 1-4
Thomas Davis: F Troy, D Nugent, JJ Martin, E O'Toole, J Fadian, L Adamson, G Kilmartin, D Foran, P Curran 0-1, J Benton 1-0, P Nugent, S Grealis, P Joyce 0-6, P Dwane 0-1, V Carney 0-4.

LEINSTER FINAL
Dec 23, St Conleth's Park, Newbridge
THOMAS DAVIS 0-8
BALTINGLASS (WICKLOW) 1-5
Thomas Davis: F Troy, D. Nugent 0-1, JJ Martin, E OToole, J Fadian, L Adamson 0-4, G Kilmartin 0-1, P Curran, D Foran, J Benton, P Nugent, S Grealis, P Joyce 0-1, P Dwane, V Carney 0-1. Subs: G Walsh for Grealis.

LEINSTER FINAL REPLAY
Jan 27, St Conleth's Park, Newbridge
THOMAS DAVIS 1-8
BALTINGLASS (WICKLOW) 0-8
Thomas Davis: V Troy, D Nugent, JJ Martin, E O'Toole, J Fadian 0-1, P Curran 0-1, G Kilmartin, D Foran, J Benton, L Adamson 0-1, P Dwane, P Nugent 0-1, S Grealis 0-1, P Joyce, V Carney 0-3. Sub: G Walsh for Joyce 50.

ALL-IRELAND SEMI-FINAL
Mar 3, Celtic Park, Derry
LAVEY (DERRY) 2-6   THOMAS DAVIS 0-10
Thomas Davis: F Troy, D Nugent, J Martin, E O'Toole, J Fadian, P Curran, G Kilmartin, D Foran 0-1, P Godson 0-1, J Benton, P Dwane 0-1, P Nugent 0-1, S Grealis 0-3, L Adamson 0-1, V Carney 0-1 Subs: G Walsh 0-1 for Benton.

1991/92

LEINSTER QUARTER-FINAL
Oct 20, Parnell Park, Dublin
THOMAS DAVIS 0-5 ATHLONE (WESTMEATH) 0-5
Thomas Davis: F Troy, D Nugent, JJ Martin, E O'Toole, J Fadian, P Curran, G Gilmartin, D Foran, J Benton, P Nugent 0-1, P Godson 0-1, S Grealis, L Adamson, P Dwane, G Walsh 0-3. Subs P Joyce for Adamson, P Waldron for Gilmartin.

LEINSTER QUARTER-FINAL REPLAY
Nov 3, Pairc Chiarain, Athlone
THOMAS DAVIS 1-7 ATHLONE (WESTMEATH) 1-4
Thomas Davis: F Troy, D Nugent, J Fadian, E O'Toole, P Waldron, P Curran, G Gilmartin, D Foran, J Benton, P Nugent 0-2, P Godson, S Grealis 0-1, P Joyce, P Dwane, V Carney 1-4. Subs: L Adamson for Dwane 38, G Walsh for Joyce 49.

LEINSTER SEMI-FINAL
Nov 14, Parnell Park, Dublin
THOMAS DAVIS 2-9 PORTLAOISE (LAOIS) 1-4
Thomas Davis: F Troy, D Nugent 1-0, JJ Martin, E O'Toole, J Fadian, P Curran 0-1, G Kilmartin, P Nugent, D Foran, G Walsh, P Godson 0-2, S Grealis 0-1, P Joyce 0-1, L Adamson 0-2, V Carney 1-2. Subs: P Walsh for Walsh, K Donoghue for Joyce.

LEINSTER FINAL
Dec 15, St Conleth's Park, Newbridge
THOMAS DAVIS 1-7 CLARA (OFFALY) 1-5
Thomas Davis: F Troy, D Nugent, JJ Martin 1-0, E O'Toole, J Fadian 0-1, P Curran, G Kilmartin 0-1, D Foran, P Nugent, P Joyce, P Godson 0-1, S Grealis, L Adamson, P Dwane, V Carney 0-4. Subs: G Walsh for Adamson, P Waldron for Grealish.

ALL-IRELAND SEMI-FINAL
Mar 1, Parnell Park, Dublin
THOMAS DAVIS 2-9
CASTLEBLAYNEY FAUGHS (MONAGHAN) 1-7
Thomas Davis: F Troy, D Nugent, JJ Martin 1-0, E O'Toole, J Fabian, F Curran 0-1, G Kilmartin, D Foran, J Benton, P Waldron 0-1, P Godson 0-2, S Grealis 0-1, P Joyce 0-3, P Nugent 1-1, V Carney. Subs: L Adamson for Benton, P Dwane for P Nugent.

ALL-IRELAND FINAL
Mar 17, Croke Park, Dublin
DR. CROKES (KERRY) 1-11 THOMAS DAVIS 0-13
Thomas Davis: Fran Troy, Dave Nugent, John Joe Martin, Enda O'Toole, Joe Fadian, Paul Curran 0-1, Gary Kilmartin, David Foran, Paul Godson 0-1, P Waldron, P Nugent 0-1, Sean Grealis, Peter Joyce, Liam Adamson 0-1, Vinny Carney 0-9. Subs: K O'Donovan for O'Toole, P Dwane for Joyce.

1992/93

LEINSTER QUARTER-FINAL
Nov 21, O'Moore Park, Portlaoise
BALLYROAN (LAOIS) 1-5 KILMACUD CROKES 1-4
Kilmacud Crokes: M Pender, C Cleary, D Maher, F Ruttledge, T Gunning, J Sweeney, R Ward, M Leahy, T Morris 0-1, M Duncan, M Dillon 1-0, P Ward 0-1, P Walsh 0-1, E Connolly, P O'Donoghue 0-1. Sub: M Leahy for Duncan.

1993/94

LEINSTER QUARTER-FINAL
Nov 13, O'Moore Park, Portlaoise
ERIN'S ISLE 1-11 THE HEATH (LAOIS) 0-9
Erin's Isle: T Quinn, E Barr, JJ O'Keeffe, S McCormack, K Murray 0-1, K Barr, B McGauren, J Barr 0-1, M Deegan 0-1, C Redmond 1-2, K Kelly, T Russell, K O'Hara 0-3, J Fagan 0-1, E Sheehan 0-2. Subs: T McCormack for Fagan, P Cunningham for Kelly, J Twomey for O'Hara.

LEINSTER SEMI-FINAL
Nov 27, St Conleth's Park, Newbridge
ERIN'S ISLE 3-7 BALTINGLASS (WICKLOW) 0-13
Erin's Isle: T Quinn, E Barr, JJ O'Keeffe, S McCormack, K Murray, K Barr 0-1, B McGauran, J Barr 0-2, M Deegan 0-1, K Kelly, C Redmond 1-3, T Russell, C O'Hare, J Fagan, E Sheehan 2-0. Subs: J Twomey for Fagan 17, C Cox for O'Hare 54.

LEINSTER FINAL
Dec 12, St Conleth's Park, Newbridge
EIRE OG (CARLOW) 3-7 ERIN'S ISLE 0-11
Erin's Isle: T Quinn, E Barr, J O'Keeffe, S McCormack, K Murray, K Barr 0-1, B McGauran, J Barr 0-3, M Deegan, J Twomey, C Redmond 0-3, T Russell 0-1, C O'Hare 0-3, C Cox, E Sheehan. Subs: C Kelly for Cox 46, P Cunningham for Sheehan 52, K Spratt for O'Hare 55.

1994/95

LEINSTER QUARTER-FINAL
Nov 6, County Ground, Aughrim
KILMACUD CROKES 0-12
BALTINGLASS (WICKLOW) 0-11
Kilmacud Crokes: M Pender, R Ward, C Cleary, R Leahy, J Sweeney, J O'Callaghanan, P Burke, Mick Leahy, M Dillon 0-1, M Duncan, P Dalton 0-1, P Ward 0-1, P Walsh 0-3, Maurice Leahy 0-3, P O'Donoghue. Subs: T Gunning for Duncan, F Ruttledge for Sweeney, N Clancy for O'Donughue.

LEINSTER SEMI-FINAL
Nov 20, O'Moore Park, Portlaoise
KILMACUD CROKES 4-13 FERBANE (OFFALY) 1-6
Kilmacud Crokes: M Pender 1-0, R Ward, C Cleary, R Leahy, J O'Callaghan, J Sweeney, P Burke, M Dillon 0-2, Mick Leahy, P Dalton 0-2, S Morris 0-1, P Ward 1-0, P Walsh 0-3, Maurice Leahy 1-3, C Mitchell 1-1. Subs: N Clancy 0-1 for Dalton, F Ruttledge for R Leahy, T Gunning for O'Callaghan.

LEINSTER FINAL
Dec 4, St Conleth's Park, Newbridge
KILMACUD CROKES 0-12
SENESCHALSTOWN (MEATH) 1-8
Kilmacud Crokes: M Pender, R Ward, C Cleary, R Leahy, J O'Callaghan, J Sweeney 0-1, P Burke 0-1, M Dillon, Mick Leahy 0-1, P Dalton 0-3, S Morris 0-1, P Ward 0-1, P Walsh 0-3, Maurice Leahy, C Mitchell 0-1. Subs: F Rutledge for R Leahy h/t, N Clancy for Mitchell 36.

ALL-IRELAND SEMI-FINAL
Feb 26, Semple Stadium, Thurles
KILMACUD CROKES 1-11
CASTLEHAVEN (CORK) 1-7
Kilmacud Crokes: M Pender, R Ward, C Cleary, R Leahy, J O'Callaghan, J Sweeney, P Burke, M Dillon 0-2, Mick Leahy, P Dalton, S Morris, P Ward 0-1, N Clancy 0-7, Maurice Leahy 0-1, M Duncan 1-0. Sub: P O'Donoghue for Duncan 44.

ALL-IRELAND FINAL
Mar 17, Croke Park, Final
KILMACUD CROKES 0-8
BELLAGHY (DERRY) 0-5
Kilmacud Crokes: Mick Pender, Rory Ward, Con Cleary, Robbie Leahy, John O'Callaghan, John Sweeney, Pat Burke, Mick Dillon 0-1, Mick Leahy, Pauric Dalton, Seamus Morris, Peter Ward 0-1, Niall Clancy 0-3, Maurice Leahy, Padraig O'Donoghue 0-3. Subs: T Gunning for Maurice Leahy.

1995/96

LEINSTER QUARTER-FINAL
Nov 5, O'Connor Park, Tullamore
BALLYBODEN ST. ENDA'S 2-8
EDENDERRY (OFFALY) 0-10
Ballyboden St. Enda's: G Flaherty, D Naughton, G Colleran, J Kernan, B Young, P Wardick, T Duffy, P Bealin 0-2, K Murray 0-1, S O'Shaughnessy, P Curran 0-1, M Gardiner 2-0, G Cuddy 0-3, L Callan, D Bolger 0-1. Subs: P Stafford for Curran 53, A Joyce for Bolger 55, T Prendergast for Cuddy 59.

LEINSTER SEMI-FINAL
Nov 19, St Conleth's Park, Newbridge
EIRE OG (CARLOW) 1-10
BALLYBODEN ST. ENDA'S 2-6
Ballyboden St. Enda's: G Flaherty, D Naughton, G Colleran, J Kernan, B Young, P Wardick, T Duffy, K Murray 1-0, P Bealin 1-1, S O'Shaughnessy 0-1, P Curran, M Gardiner 0-2, G Cuddy 0-1, L Callan, D Bolger 0-1. Subs: T Prendergast for Kernan h/t, J McAllister for Bolger 39.

1996/97

LEINSTER QUARTER-FINAL
Nov 3, O'Connor Park, Tullamore
ST. SYLVESTER'S 0-11
SHANNONBRIDGE (OFFALY) 0-4
St. Sylvester's: J Leonard, D Roche 0-1, B Silke, D Ryan, B Barnes, G O'Neill, K Galvin 0-1, D Hetherton, M Barnes, G Dolan 0-2, N Guiden 0-1, E Stewart, T Cummins, S Keogh 0-5, D Barnes 0-1. Subs: C Earley for Cummins, J Murphy for Silke.

LEINSTER SEMI-FINAL
Nov 17, O'Moore Park, Portlaoise
ST SYLVESTER'S 2-10
KILANERIN (WEXFORD) 0-8
St. Sylvester's: J Leonard, D Roche, B Barnes, D Ryan, J Murphy, G O'Neill, K Galvin, D Hetherton, M Barnes, E Stuart 0-1, N Guiden 0-1, C Earley 1-1, G Dolan 0-3, S Keogh 0-11, D Barnes 1-0.

LEINSTER FINAL
Dec 1, St Conleth's Park, Newbridge
EIRE ÓG (CARLOW) 1-10
ST SYLVESTER'S 0-8
St Sylvester's: J Leonard, D Roche 0-1, B Silke, D Ryan, B Barnes, J Murphy, K Galvin, D Hetherton, M Barnes, C Earley, G O'Neill, N Guiden, T Cummins 0-1, S Keogh 0-4, D Barnes. Subs: G Dolan for Early 50, B Burke for Keogh 59.

1997/98

LEINSTER FIRST ROUND
Oct 26, Parnell Park, Dublin
ERIN'S ISLE 5-22
OLD LEIGHLIN (CARLOW) 0-5
Erin's Isle: T Quinn, K Murray, JJ O'Keeffe, M Naughton, D Collins, M Deegan, G O'Connell, K Barr, J Barr 0-2, C Redmond 0-1, C Barr, P Cunningham 0-1, C O'Hare 2-5, R Boyle 2-5, N Crossan 1-8. Subs: S McCormack for Naughton, A Gavigan for Deegan 41, J Fagan for K Barr 43.

LEINSTER QUARTER-FINAL
Nov 9, Parnell Park, Dublin
ERIN'S ISLE 1-10   EDENDERRY (OFFALY) 0-11
Erin's Isle: T Quinn, K Murray, JJ O'Keeffe, M Naughton, D Colllns, M Deegan, G O'Connell, K Barr, J Barr, C Redmond, P Cunningham 0-1, E Barr, C O'Hare 1-5, R Boyle 0-2, N Crossan 0-2.

LEINSTER SEMI-FINAL
Nov 23, Pairc Tailteann, Navan
ERIN'S ISLE 0-11
STABANNON PARNELLS (LOUTH) 0-8
Erin's Isle: T Quinn, K Murray, K Spratt, M Naughton, D Collins, M Deegan 0-1, G O'Connell, K Barr, J Barr, C Redmond 0-2, P Cunningham, E Barr 0-2, C O'Hare 0-5, R Boyle, N Crossan 0-1.

LEINSTER FINAL
Dec 7, Pairc Tailteann, Navan
ERIN'S ISLE 2-11   CLANE (KILDARE) 1-11
Erin's Isle: T Ouinn, K Murray, JJ O'Keeffe, K Spratt, D Collins, M Deegan, G O'Connell, K Barr, J Barr, E Barr, P Cunningham 0-3, C Redmond 0-4, C O'Hare 1-2, R Boyle 0-2, N Crossan 1-0. Subs: F Browne for Crossan 56, S McCormack for Cunningham 61.

ALL-IRELAND SEMI-FINAL
Feb 22, Thurles, Semi-Final
ERIN'S ISLE 2-12   CASTLEHAVEN (CORK) 0-17
Erin's Isle: T Quinn, K Murray, K Spratt, M Naughton, D Collins, M Deegan, G O'Connell, K Barr 0-1, J Barr 0-1, C Redmond 0-2, P Cunningham, E Barr 0-1, C O'Hare 1-5, R Boyle 0-1, N Crossan 1-1.

ALL-IRELAND FINAL
Mar 17, Croke Park
COROFIN (GALWAY) 0-15   ERIN'S ISLE 0-10
Erin's Isle: Tom Quinn, Keith Murray, Ken Spratt, M Naughton, Damien Collins 0-1, Mick Deegan, Gary O'Connell, Keith Barr 0-1, Johnny Barr, Eddie Barr, Paudge Cunnningham, T Gorman, Ciaran O'Hare 0-6, Robbie Boyle 0-1, Niall Crossan 0-1. Subs: S McCormack for T Gorman, 42, F Brown for O'Connell 60.

1998/99

LEINSTER FIRST ROUND
Oct 25, Glenalbyn, Dublin
KILMACUD CROKES 1-16
JAMES STEPHENS (KILKENNY) 0-5
Kilmacud Crokes: M Pender, C O'Dwyer, C Deegan, C Cleary, J O'Callaghan, J Magee, R Leahy, J Costello 0-2, M Leahy, P Ward 0-2, G Duffy 0-1, C Redmond, R Cosgrove 0-1, P Burke 1-3, M O'Keeffe 0-7.

LEINSTER QUARTER-FINAL
Nov 8, Pairc Tailteann, Navan
KILMACUD CROKES 2-7
ST. PETER'S (MEATH) 1-9
Kilmacud Crokes: M Jones, C O'Dwyer, C Deegan, C Cleary, J O'Callaghan, J Magee, C Redmond, J Costello 0-1, M Leahy, M Duncan, M Dillon 0-1, P Burke 0-1, R Cosgrove 1-2, R Brennan 0-1, M O'Keeffe 0-1. Subs: P Ward 1-0 for Duncan, P Walsh for Brennan.

LEINSTER SEMI-FINAL
Nov 22, O'Connor Park, Tullamore
KILMACUD CROKES 1-10
STRADBALLY (LAOIS) 1-7
Kilmacud Crokes: M Pender, C O'Dwyer, C Deegan, C Cleary, J O'Callaghan, J Magee, R Leahy 0-1, J Costello, M Leahy 0-1, P Ward 0-1, M Dillon 0-1, C Redmond, R Cosgrove 1-4, P Burke, M O'Keeffe 0-2. Sub: R Brennan for Burke 42.

LEINSTER FINAL
Dec 6, St Conleth's Park, Newbridge
KILMACUD CROKES 0-9   EIRE ÓG (CARLOW) 1-6
Kilmacud Crokes: M Pender, C O'Dwyer, C Deegan, C Cleary, J O'Callaghan, J Magee, R Leahy, J Costello, M Leahy 0-1, P Ward 0-3, M Dillon, C Redmond, R Cosgrove, P Burke 0-1, M O'Keeffe 0-4.

LEINSTER FINAL REPLAY
Dec 13, O'Moore Park, Tullamore
KILMACUD CROKES 0-7   EIRE ÓG (CARLOW) 0-7
Kilmacud Crokes: M Pender, C O'Dwyer, C Deegan, C Cleary, J O'Callaghan, J Magee, R Leahy, J Costello 0-1, M Leahy, P Ward, M Dillon, C Redmond, R Cosgrove 0-5, P Burke 0-1, M O'Keeffe. Subs: R Brennan for O'Keeffe 50m, P O'Donoghue for Redmond 54.

LEINSTER FINAL SECOND REPLAY
Jan 31, St Conleth's Park, Newbridge
EIRE ÓG (CARLOW) 1-11   KILMACUD CROKES 0-11
Kilmacud Crokes: M Pender, C O'Dwyer, C Deegan 0-1, C Cleary, J O'Callaghan, J Magee 0-1, R Leahy, J Costello, M Leahy, P Ward, M Dillon, C Redmond, R Cosgrove 0-1, R Brennan 0-3, M O'Keeffe 0-3. Subs: C Kelleher for C Redmond 20, P Burke for Dillon 52.

1999/00

LEINSTER QUARTER-FINAL
Nov 7, County Ground, Aughrim
NA FIANNA 1-11   RATHNEW (WICKLOW) 0-6
Na Fianna: S Grey, P McCarthy, B Quinn, T Lynch, S McGlinchey, M Foley, S Connell 0-1, S Forde, K McGeeney 0-2, K Donnelly, A Shearer 0-2, M Galvin

0-4, D Farrell 1-1, D Mackin, I Foley 0-1. Subs: D Keegan for Forde 52, D Lynch for Shearer 55, G Grey for McGlinchey 59.

LEINSTER SEMI-FINAL
Nov 21, St Conleth's Park, Newbridge
NA FIANNA 1-13   PORTLAOISE (LAOIS) 0-10
Na Fianna: S Grey, P McCarthy, B Quinn, T Lynch, S McGlinchey, M Foley, N O Murchu, S Forde, K McGeeney, K Donnelly, A Shearer 1-1, M Galvin 0-3, D Farrell 0-2, D Mackin, I Foley 0-6. Subs: D Keegan for Forde 47, D Lynch 0-1 for Farrell 58, J Kearns for Galvin 63.

LEINSTER FINAL
Dec 5, Pairc Tailteann, Navan
NA FIANNA 1-11   SARSFIELDS (KILDARE) 0-8
Na Fianna: S Gray, P McCarthy, B Quinn, T Lynch, S McGlinchey 0-2, M Foley, S Connell 0-1, S Forde, K McGeeney 0-2, K Donnelly 0-2, D Farrell, M Galvin, D Mackin, I Foley 0-1, A Shearer 1-3. Subs: J Sherlock for I Foley 39, N O Murchu for Quinn 55, D Keegan for Shearer 60.

ALL-IRELAND SEMI-FINAL
Feb 20, Pearse Park, Longford
NA FIANNA 1-10   CROSSMOLINA (MAYO) 2-3
Na Fianna: S Grey, P McCarthy, B Quinn, T Lynch, S Connell, S McGlinchey, M Foley 0-1, S Forde, K McGeeney, K Donnelly, D Farrell 0-3, M Galvin 0-6, D Mackin 1-0, J Sherlock, A Shearer. Subs: D Keegan for Forde 57, I Foley for Shearer 59.

ALL-IRELAND FINAL
Mar 17, Croke Park, Dublin
**CROSSMAGLEN RANGERS (ARMAGH) 1-14
NA FIANNA 0-12**
Na Fianna: Stephen Gray, S McGlinchey, B Quinn, M Foley, Senan Connell 0-1, Tom Lynch, Pat McCarthy, Sean Forde, Kieran McGeeney, Mick Galvin 0-5, Dessie Farrell 0-2, K Donnelly 0-1, D Mackin 0-1, Jason Sherlock, Aaron Shearer 0-1. Subs: Donal Keegan foi Forde h/t, I Foley 0-1 for Shearer 38, N O Murchu for Foley 45.

2000/01

LEINSTER QUARTER-FINAL
Nov 5, Pearse Park, Longford
NA FIANNA 1-7   ABBEYLARA (LONGFORD) 1-4
Na Fianna: S Grey, N O Murchu, B McManus, T Lynch, S Connell, N Clancy, S McGlinchey, K Donnelly 0-1, K McGeeney, M Galvin, D Farrell, D Lynch 0-1, I Foley 0-4, D Mackin 1-1. Subs: M Foley for Galvin 10, R O'Hagan for McManus 41, P McCarthy for D Lynch 57.

LEINSTER SEMI-FINAL
Nov 19, St Conleth's Park, Newbridge
NA FIANNA 0-16   RHODE (OFFALY) 0-9
Na Fianna: S Grey, N O Murchu, B McManus, T Lynch, S Connell 0-1, S McGlinchey, K Donnelly 0-1, K McGeeney, R O'Hagan, D Farrell 0-1, D Lynch, I Foley 0-4 J Sherlock 0-3, D Mackin 0-4. Subs: A Shearer 0-2 for D Lynch h/t. M Foley for McManus 40, D Keegan for O'Hagan 42.

LEINSTER FINAL
Dec 3, Portlaoise
O'HANRAHANS (LOUTH) 1-7   NA FIANNA 1-4
Na Fianna: S Gray, N O Murchu, B McManus, T Lynch, S Connell 0-1, N Clancy, S McGlinchey, S Forde, K McGeeney, M Galvin 0-2, D Farrell, A Shearer 1-0, I Foley 0-1, J Sherlock, D Mackin. Subs: P McCarthy for McManus 22, K Donnelly 0-1 for Forde 24, D Keegan for Foley 50.

2001/02

LEINSTER QUARTER-FINAL
Nov 11, McCann Park, Portarlington
NA FIANNA 2-9   PORTARLINGTON (LAOIS) 0-12
Na Fianna: S Gray, N O Murchu, N Clancy P McCarthy, T Lynch, S McGlinchey, M Foley, K McGeeney, K Donnelly, D Macken, S Connell 0-1, P McGeeney, I Foley 1-2, D Farrell 1-2, J Sherlock 0-4. Sub: A Shearer for Macken 40.

LEINSTER SEMI-FINAL
Nov 25, Pairc Tailteann, Navan
NA FIANNA 2-10   SARSFIELDS (KILDARE) 1-13
Na Fianna: S Grey, N O Murchu, N Clancy, P McCarthy, T Lynch, S McGlinchey, B McManus, K Donnelly 0-1, K McGeeney 0-1, D Macken, S Connell 0-1, P McGeeney 0-1, I Foley 1-1, D Farrell 1-3, J Sherlock 0-2. Subs: M Foley for McGlinchey 23, A Sherer for P McGeeney 44, P McEvoy for Macken 52.

LEINSTER SEMI-FINAL REPLAY
Dec 2, Pairc Tailteann, Navan
NA FIANNA 3-11   SARSFIELDS (KILDARE) 1-8
Na Fianna: S Grey, N O Murchu, N Clancy, P McCarthy 0-1, T Lynch, S McGlinchey, B McManus, K Donnelly, K McGeeney 0-1, S Connell 0-3, D Macken, P McGeeney 1-0, I Foley 0-1, D Farrell 0-1, J Sherlock 2-3. Subs: M Foley for Lynch h/t, A Shearer 0-1 for P McGeeney 47, B Newman for Sherlock 57, G Grey for O Murchu 59, P McEvoy for Foley 59, J Hagan for Farrell 61.

LEINSTER FINAL
Dec 16, St Conleth's Park, Newbridge
NA FIANNA 1-6   RATHNEW (WICKLOW) 0-9
Na Fianna: S Gray, B McManus, N Clancy, T Lynch, P

McCarthy, S McGlinchey, M Foley, K Donnelly 0-1, K McGeeney 0-1, S Connell, D Mackin 0-2, P McGeeney, D Farrell 1-0, I Foley 0-2, J Sherlock. Subs: N O Murcnu for M Foley 55, A Shearer for P McGeeney 58.

LEINSTER FINAL REPLAY
Dec 23, St Conleth's Park, Newbridge
RATHNEW (WICKLOW) 2-16 NA FIANNA 1-10
Na Fianna: S Gray, N O Murchu, B McManus, P McCarthy, T Lynch, S McGlinchey, M Foley 0-2, K McGeeney 0-1, N Clancy, D Mackin 0-1, P McGeeney 0-1, S Connell 0-2, I Foley 0-1, K Donnelly 0-2, J Sherlock 1-0. Subs: B Newman for P McGeeney 50, A Shearer for Newman 75, P McGeeney for Clancy 75.

2002/03

LEINSTER QUARTER-FINAL
Dec 1, St Conleth's Park, Newbridge
RATHNEW (WICKLOW) 1-6 U.C.D. 1-5
U.C.D.: G McGill, A Costello, C Evans, B O hAnnaidh, N McGuire, D O hAnnaidh, R Kelly, S Lucey, C McAnallen 1-1, J Hanley 0-1, J Byrne, C McManus 0-2, R Ronaghan, B McDonald, R Barry 0-1. Subs: J Fallon for Byrne 27, P Curran for McManus 22, J Lynch for Hanley 43, O O hAnnaidh for Ronaghan 55, D O'Connor for Curran 63.

2003/04

LEINSTER QUARTER-FINAL
Nov 8, Dundalk
ST. BRIGID'S 0-7 ST. PATRICK'S (LOUTH) 0-6
St. Brigid's: P Keane, K Keane, D Cahill, W Finnegan 0-1, G Norton, P Andrews, M Galvin, K Darcy 0-1, J Ward, D Darcy, Rory Gallagher, D Lally 0-2, K Bonner, Raymie Gallagher 0-2, J Noonan 0-1. Subs: S Quinn for D Darcy, C McGlynn for Noonan.

LEINSTER SEMI-FINAL
Nov 23, Mullingar, Semi-Final
ST. BRIGID'S 2-11 CLONGUISH (LONGFORD) 3-6
St. Brigid's: P Keane, K Keane, D Cahill, M Cahill, G Norton, P Andrews, M Galvin, K Darcy 1-0, J Ward, C Ryan, Rory Gallagher 1-1, D Lally 0-1, K Bonner 0-2, Raymie Gallagher 0-4, J Noonan 0-3. Subs: C McGlynn for Ryan 38, D Darcy for Raymie Gallagher 55.

LEINSTER FINAL
Dec 7, Pairc Tailteann, Navan
ST. BRIGID'S 3-11 ROUND TOWERS (KILDARE) 1-10
St. Brigid's: P Keane, K Keane, D Cahill, M Cahill, G Norton, P Andrews, M Galvin 1-1, K Darcy 0-1, J Ward, J Noonan 0-3, Rory Gallagher 0-3, D Lally, K Bonner 0-2, D Darcy 2-1, Raymie Gallagher. Sub: C Ryan for Noonan 46.

ALL-IRELAND SEMI-FINAL
Feb 22, Semple Stadium, Thurles
AN GHAELTACHT (KERRY) 1-9 ST. BRIGID'S 2-3
St. Brigid's: P Keane, M Cahill, D Cahill, K Keane, G Norton, P Andrews, B Cahill, K Darcy, J Ward, M Galvin, Rory Gallagher, D Lally 1-0, K Bonner 1-0, Raymie Gallagher 0-3, D Darcy. Subs: J Noonan for Galvin 35, W Finnegan for D Darcy 39, S Quinn for Darcy 50, C McGlynn for Bonar 56.

2004/05

LEINSTER FIRST ROUND
Oct 23, Parnell Park, Dublin
KILMACUD CROKES 3-9
ST. PATRICK'S (WICKLOW) 0-6
Kilmacud Crokes: D Nelligan, F Kennedy, C Flannagan, C Kelleher, P Griffin, L Og O'hEineachain, B McGrath, D Magee, F Armstrong 0-1, D Kelleher, C Murphy 0-1, L McBarron, M O'Keeffe 0-4, M Daveren, M Vaughan 2-3, Subs J Magee for Armstrong, K O'Carroll 1-0 for D Kelleher, J Burke for Kennedy.

LEINSTER QUARTER-FINAL
Nov 13, Parnell Park, Dublin
KILMACUD CROKES 0-14
GARRYCASTLE (WESTMEATH) 1-10
Kilmacud Crokes: D Nelligan, F Kennedy, C Flanagan, C Kelleher, P Griffin, Liam Og O liEineachain 0-1, B McGrath, J Magee, D Magee, D Kelleher 0-4, C Murphy 0-2, L McBarron, M O'Keeffe 0-2, M Daveren 0-2, M Vaughan 0-3. Subs: N McGrath for B McGrath 35, F Armstrong for J Magee 50.

LEINSTER SEMI-FINAL
Nov 21, Dr Cullen Park, Carlow
PORTLAOISE (LAOIS) 0-14
KILMACUD CROKES 0-8
Kilmacud Crokes: D Nelligan, F Kennedy, C Flanagan, P Griffin 0-1, C Kelleher, L Og O hEineachain 0-2, B McGrath, J Magee, C Murphy, D Kelleher 0-1, N Corkery 0-1, L McBarron, M Vaughan 0-1, M O'Keeffe 0-1, F Armstrong 0-1. Sub: R Cosgrove for O'Keeffe 43, N McGrath for McBarron 50, K O'Carroll for Magee 54.

2005/06

LEINSTER QUARTER-FINAL
Nov 13, Pairc Tailteann, Navan
KILMACUD CROKES 1-14
ST. PETER'S (MEATH) 0-3
Kilmacud Crokes: D Nelligan, N McGrath, C Kelleher, C Flanagan, B McGrath, Liam Og O hEineachain, P

Griffin, D Magee, J Magee, L McBarron 0-2, N Corkery 0-1, R Cosgrove 1-10, K O'Carroll 0-1, M Davoren, P Burke. Subs: B Phelan for J Magee 43, F Armstrong for Davoren 43, D Walsh for Kelleher 52, D Maher for McGrath 52, M O'Keeffe for Cosgrove 58.

LEINSTER SEMI-FINAL
Nov 20, O'Moore Park, Portlaoise
KILMACUD CROKES 1-9 RHODE (OFFALY) 2-6
Kilmacud Crokes: D Nelligan, C Flanagan, C Kelleher, N McGrath, B McGrath, Liam Og O hEineachain, P Griffin, D Magee 0-1, L McBarron 0-1, P Burke, N Corkery, R Cosgrove 0-2, K O'Carroll, M Davored, M Vaughan 1-5. Subs: B Phelan for O'Carroll 44, M O'Keeffe for Corkery 61.

LEINSTER SEMI-FINAL REPLAY
Nov 27, St Conleth's Park, Newbridge
KILMACUD CROKES 2-6 RHODE (OFFALY) 1-7
Kilmacud Crokes: D Nelligan, C Kelleher, C Flanagan, N McGrath, B McGrath, L Og O hEineachain, D Walsh, D Magee, J Magee 0-1, L McBarron, N Corkery, R Cosgrove 1-1, P Burke, M Davoren 1-2, M Vaughan 0-2. Subs: B Phelan for Corkery 46, M O'Keeffe for Vaughan 58, C Lambe for N McGrath 63.

LEINSTER FINAL
Dec 4, Pairc Tailteann, Navan
KILMACUD CROKES 0-10
SARFIELDS (KILDARE) 0-9
Kilmacud Crokes: D Nelligan, C Kellegher, C Flanagan, N McGrath, B McGrath, L Og O hEineachain, P Griffin, J Magee 0-2, D Magee, L McBarron 0-1, C Murphy, R Cosgrove 0-2, P Burke 0-1, M Davoren 0-2, M Vaughan 0-2. Subs: N Corkery for Murphy 45, P Phelan for Davoren 58.

ALL-IRELAND SEMI-FINAL
Feb 19, Pearse Park, Longford
SALTHILL-KILCARRA (GALWAY) 1-9
KILMACUD CROKES 1-7
Kilmacud Crokes: D Nelligan, C Kelleher, C Flanagan, N McGrath, B McGrath, L Og O hEineachain, P Griffin, D Magee 0-1, J Magee 0-1, L McBarron, C Murphy 1-0, R Cosgrove, P Burke 0-1, M Davoren, M Vaughan 0-4. Subs: D Kelleher for McBarron 42, N Corkery for Davoren 52, D Walsh for Murphy 61.

2006/07

LEINSTER QUARTER-FINAL
Nov 12, Pairc Tailteann, Navan
U.C.D. 1-11 WOLFE TONES (MEATH) 0-11
UCD: S Gallagher, J McCarthy, P Navin, M Duffy, M Dunne, E O Cuiv, P McConway, S Brady, M Ward, C Rogers 0-1, J Sherry, B Sheehan 0-1, C Judge 0-3, S

Lennon 1-4, C O'Dwyer 0-2. Subs: J Hanley for Sherry 24, Sherry for Dunn 49, P Kelly for Rodgers 60.

LEINSTER SEMI-FINAL
Nov 19, Parnell Park, Dublin
RHODE (OFFALY) 2-6 U.C.D. 1-8
U.C.D.: S Gallagher, P McConway, P Navin, P Navin, J McCarthy, M Duffy, E O Cuiv, M Dunne, S Brady, M Ward, J Sherry, A O'Malley 0-4, B Sheehan 0-1, S Lennon 0-2, C O'Dwyer 1-0, C Judge. Subs: C Rogers 0-1 for Judge 30.

2007/08

LEINSTER FIRST ROUND
Oct 28, Baltinglass Park, Baltinglass
ST. VINCENTS W/O
BALTINGLASS (WICKLOW) SCR
* Baltinglass withdrew following a disagreement over the date.

LEINSTER QUARTER-FINAL
Nov 11, Parnell Park, Dublin
ST. VINCENTS 0-11
SENESCHALSTOWN (MEATH) 1-8
St Vincent's: M Savage, P Conlon, E Brady, H Gill, T Doyle, G Brennan, P Kelly 0-3, H Coghlan, M O'Shea, K Golden 0-1, T Diamond, N Billings 0-1, B Moloney 0-2, D Connolly 0-1, T Quinn 0-3. Subs: P Gilroy for Billings 40, R Trainor for Connolly 59.

LEINSTER QUARTER-FINAL REPLAY
Nov 18, Pairc Tailteann, Navan
ST. VINCENT'S 1-12
SENESCHALSTOWN (MEATH) 0-10
St Vincent's: M Savage, P Conlon, E Brady, H Gill, T Doyle, G Brennan, P Kelly, H Coghlan, M O'Shea, K Golden 0-3, T Diamond 0-2, N Billings 0-1, B Moloney 0-1, D Connolly 0-2, T Quinn 1-3. Subs: P Gilroy for Billings 38, C Brady for Connolly 51, R Trainor for Golden 64.

LEINSTER SEMI-FINAL
Nov 25, Parnell Park, Dublin
ST. VINCENT'S 3-13 PORTLAOISE (LAOIS) 1-8
St Vincent's: M Savage, P Conlon, E Brady, H Gill, T Doyle, G Brennan, P Kelly, H Coghlan, M O'Shea, K Golden 0-1, T Diamond, D Connolly 0-4, B Moloney 1-1, P Gilroy 1-1, T Quinn 1-5. Subs: R Fallon for Doyle 39, C Brady 0-1 for Golden 46.

LEINSTER FINAL
Dec 16, Cusack Park, Mullingar
ST. VINCENT'S 2-8
TYRRELLSPASS (WESTMEATH) 0-7
St Vincent's: M Savage, P Conlon, E Brady, H Gill, T Doyle, G Brennan, P Kelly, H Coghlan, M O'Shea, K

Golden 1-3, T Diamond, D Connolly, B Moloney 0-2, P Gilroy 1-1, T Quinn 0-2. Subs: C Brady for Coghlan, R Trainor for Brady.

ALL-IRELAND SEMI-FINAL
Feb 24, Pairc Tailteann, Navan
ST. VINCENT'S 2-9
CROSSMAGLEN RANGERS (ARMAGH) 0-11
St Vincent's: M Savage, P Conlon, E Brady, H Gill, T Doyle, G Brennan, P Kelly, H Coghlan, M O'Shea 0-1, K Golden, T Diamond 0-1, D Connolly 0-4, B Maloney 1-1, P Gilroy, T Quinn 1-2. Subs: R Trainor for Golden 55, W Lowry for Gilroy 59.

ALL-IRELAND FINAL
Mar 17, Croke Park, Dublin
ST. VINCENT'S 1-11 NEMO RANGERS (CORK) 0-13
St Vincent's: Michael Savage, Paul Conlon, Eoin Brady, Hugh Gill, Tim Doyle, Ger Brennan, Pat Kelly, Hugh Coughlan 0-1, Michael O'Shea, Kevin Golden, Tiernan Diamond 0-1, Diarmuid Connolly 1-2, Brian Moloney, Pat Gilroy, Tomas Quinn 0-7. Subs: Ruairi Trainor for Gilroy 44, C Brady for Coghlan 45, R Fallon for Gill 58, W Lowry for Golden 60.

2008/09

LEINSTER FIRST ROUND
Nov 2, Parnell Park, Dublin
KILMACUD CROKES 0-13
CELBRIDGE (KILDARE) 0-8
Kilmacud Crokes: D Nestor, K Nolan, P Griffin, C Lambe, B McGrath, C O'Sullivan, A Morrissey, D Magee, N Corkery, L McBarron, P Burke 0-2, M Davoren 0-2, M Vaughan 0-5, J Magee, B Kavanagh 0-2. Subs: B O'Rorke 0-2 for J Magee (inj) 1, R O'Carroll for McBarron 43, J Magee for O'Rorke 50.

LEINSTER QUARTER-FINAL
Nov 9, Parnell Park, Dublin
KILMACUD CROKES 1-13
NEWTOWN BLUES (LOUTH) 1-9
Kilmacud Crokes: D Nestor, K Nolan, P Griffin, C Lambe, B McGrath, R O'Carroll, A Morrissey, D Magee, N Corkery, R Cosgrove 0-1, M Davoren, P Burke, M Vaughan 1-8, J Magee, B Kavanagh 0-4. Sub: B O'Rorke for Cosgrove 51.

LEINSTER SEMI-FINAL
Nov 23, Parnell Park, Dublin
KILMACUD CROKES 1-11
NAVAN O'MAHONYS (MEATH) 0-7
Kilmacud Crokes: D Nestor, K Nolan, R O'Carroll, C Lambe, B McGrath 0-1, P Griffin, A Morrissey, D Magee, N Corkery, L McBarron, P Burke 0-2, R Cosgrove, M Vaughan 0-6, M Davoren 1-0, B

Kavanagh 0-2. Subs: L Og O hEineachain for Cosgrove 37, J Magee for Corkery 46, B O'Rorke for McBarron 51.

LEINSTER FINAL
Dec 7, Parnell Park, Dublin
KILMACUD CROKES 2-7 RHODE (OFFALY) 1-7
Kilmacud Crokes: D Nestor, P Griffin 0-1, Ross O'Carroll, C Lambe, B McGrath, C O'Sullivan, K Nolan, D Magee, L McBarron, L Og O hEineachain 0-1, P Burke, A Morrissey, M Vaughan 0-3, M Davoren 1-0, B Kavanagh 1-1. Subs: Rory O'Carroll for Lambe 24, N Corkery for 34, R Cosgrove 0-1 for Burke 35, J Magee for O hEineachain 60.

ALL-IRELAND SEMI-FINAL
Feb 22, Cusack Park, Mullingar
KILMACUD CROKES 2-11
COROFIN (GALWAY) 0-11
Kilmacud Crokes: D Nestor, Rory O'Carroll, Ross O'Carroll, C Lambe, B McGrath, P Griffin, K Nolan, D Magee, N Corkery, L McBarron, B Kavanagh 0-1, A Morrissey, P Burke 1-2, M Davoren 0-2, M Vaughan 1-6. Subs: R Cosgrove for Nolan 49, J Magee for McBarron 53, B O'Rorke for Burke 61, K O'Carroll for Vaughan 63.

ALL-IRELAND FINAL
Mar 17, Croke Park, Dublin
KILMACUD CROKES 1-9
CROSSMAGLEN RANGERS (ARMAGH) 0-7
Kilmacud Crokes: David Nestor, Ross O'Carroll, Rory O'Carroll, Kevin Nolan, B McGrath, Paul Griffin, Cian O'Sullivan, Darren Magee 0-1, Niall Corkery 0-1, Liam Og O hEineachain, Brian Kavanagh 0-2, A Morrissey, Mark Vaughan 0-4, Mark Davoren 1-0, Pat Burke. Subs: Johnny Magee for O hEineachain 53, Ray Cosgrove 0-1 for Kavanagh 58.

2009/10

LEINSTER QUARTER-FINAL
Nov 8, Parnell Park, Dublin
BALLYBODEN ST. ENDA'S 1-10
RATHNEW (WICKLOW) 1-7
Ballyboden St. Enda's: D Walsh, C Dolan, I Clarke, M O'Sullivan, D Nelson, J O'Hara, S Durkin, M McAuley, D O'Mahony 0-1, S Lambert 0-1, D Davey, C Smyth, C Keaney 0-5, K Naughton 0-1, A Kerin 0-1. Subs: D Kiernan for Dolan 44, P Galvin 0-1 for Kerin 45, D Shovlin 1-0 for Davey 56, C Hiney for Naughton 58.

LEINSTER SEMI-FINAL
Nov 22, Cusack Park, Mullingar
GARRYCASTLE (WESTMEATH) 1-8
BALLYBODEN ST. ENDA'S 0-6
Ballyboden St. Enda's: D Walsh, J O'Hara, I Clarke, M

O'Sullivan, D Nelson, D Kiernan, C Dolan, M McAuley, P Galvin, D Davey, S Hiney 0-1, C Smyth 0-1, S Durkin, S Lambert 0-1, A Kerin 0-2. Subs: C Hiney for Davey 48, C Keaney 0-1 for Dolan 50.

2010/11

LEINSTER QUARTER-FINAL
Nov 7, O'Connor Park, Tullamore
KILMACUD CROKES 2-7
PORTLAOISE (LAOIS) 2-4
Kilmacud Crokes: D Nestor, K Nolan, Ross O'Carroll, C Lamb, B McGrath, C O'Sullivan, R Ryan, N Corkery, P Duggan, L Og O hEineachain, D Kelleher 1-1, A Morrissey, B O'Rorke 0-1, B Kavanagh 0-3, P Burke 0-1. Subs: C Dias 1-0 for Corkery 20, M Vaughan 0-1 for O'Rorke 42.

LEINSTER SEMI-FINAL
Nov 21, Parnell Park, Dublin
KILMACUD CROKES 0-13
GARRYCASTLE (WESTMEATH) 0-10
Kilmacud Crokes: D Nestor, K Nolan 0-2, Ross O'Carroll, C Lamb, C O'Sullivan, B McGrath, R Ryan, P Burke, P Duggan, L Og O hEinachain 0-1, D Kelleher 0-2, C Dias, B O'Rorke 0-1, B Kavanagh 0-6, M Vaughan 0-1. Subs: Rory O'Carroll for R Ryan 44, M Coughlan for B O'Rorke, R Cosgrove for Burke 55.

LEINSTER FINAL
Jan 23, O'Connor Park, Tullamore
KILMACUD CROKES 0-15   RHODE (OFFALY) 1-7
Kilmacud Crokes: D Nestor, Ross O'Carroll, K Nolan, C Lamb, C O'Sullivan, B McGrath 0-1, R Ryan, P Duggan, C Dias 0-1, L Og O hEineachain 0-1, D Kelleher 0-3, A Morrissey 0-1, P Burke 0-1, B Kavanagh 0-5, M Vaughan 0-2. Subs: B O'Rorke for Morrissey 46, N McGrath for Lamb 57.

ALL-IRELAND SEMI-FINAL
Feb 27, Pairc Tailteann, Navan
CROSSMAGLEN RANGERS (ARMAGH) 2-11
KILMACUD CROKES 1-12
Kilmacud Crokes: D Nestor, Ross O'Carroll, K Nolan, C Lamb, C O'Sullivan, B McGrath, R Ryan, P Duggan, C Dias 1-2, L Og O hEineachain 0-1, D Kelleher 0-1, A Morrissey, P Burke, B Kavanagh 0-7, M Coughlan. Subs: B Hanamy for Duggan 20, M Vaughan 0-1 for Coughlan 37, Rory O'Carroll for Kelleher 43, B O'Rorke for O hEineachain 55, E Culligan for O'Sullivan 58.

2011/12

LEINSTER FIRST ROUND
Nov 13, Pairc Tailteann, Navan
ST. BRIGID'S 2-15   SUMMERHILL (MEATH) 0-11

St. Brigid's: S Supple, S Murray, G Norton, C Freeman, A Daly 0-1, Martin Cahill, G Kane, B Cahill 1-0, J O'Loughlin, C Mullins, Mark Cahill 0-2, K Kilmurray 1-0, P Andrews 0-5, K Darcy 0-1, P Ryan 0-5. Subs: L McCarthy 0-1 for Kilmurray 41, O McCann for Mark Cahill 42, K Kilmurray 1-0 for Darcy 56, D Plunkett for Daly 57, J Kelly for Norton 58.

LEINSTER QUARTER-FINAL
Nov 20, Parnell Park, Dublin
ST. BRIGID'S 1-20 HORESWOOD (WEXFORD) 3-8
St. Brigid's: S Supple, A Daly, Martin Cahill, G Norton, C Freeman, S Murray, G Kane, B Cahill 0-1, C Mullins, J O'Loughlin, P Andrews 1-3, Mark Cahill 0-1, K Kilmurray 0-4, K Darcy 0-2, P Ryan 0-6. Subs: D Plunkett for Murray 39, L McCarthy 0-1 for Mullins 41, O McCann 0-1 for Mark Cahill 50, C Doyle for Freeman 52.

LEINSTER SEMI-FINAL
Dec 4, Parnell Park, Dublin
ST. BRIGID'S 2-16   PORTLAOISE (LAOIS) 1-15
St. Brigid's: S Supple, C Freeman, S Murray, G Norton, A Daly 0-1, Martin Cahill, G Kane, B Cahill 0-1, J O'Loughlin 0-2, C Mullins 0-1, K Kilmurray, Mark Cahill 0-2, K Darcy 0-4, P Andrews 1-4, P Ryan 1-0. Subs: L McCarthy 0-1 for Freeman 33, O McCann for Kilmurray 43, D Plunkett for Martin Cahill 74.

LEINSTER FINAL
Dec 18, O'Connor Park, Tullamore
GARRYCASTLE (WESTMEATH) 1-8
ST. BRIGID'S 0-10
St. Brigid's: S Supple, G Norton, Martin Cahill, G Kane, A Daly, S Murray, D Plunkett, B Cahill, J O'Loughlin 0-2, C Mullins, Mark Cahill, K Kilmurray, P Ryan, K Darcy 0-2, P Andrews 0-5. Subs: G McIntyre 0-1 for Mark Cahill 42, L McCarthy for Ryan 47, O McCann for Mullins 59.

2012/13

LEINSTER QUARTER-FINAL
Nov 11, Cusack Park, Mullingar
BALLYMUN KICKHAMS 2-13
SHAMROCKS (WESTMEATH) 0-7
Ballymun Kickhams: S Currie, Enda Dolan, P McMahon, Eoin Dolan, A Hubbard, K Connolly, J Burke, Davy Byrne 1-0, J McCarthy, E Reilly, K Leahy 0-1, J Whelan 0-2, T Furman 1-2, D Rock 0-8, A O'Brien. Subs: Derek Byrne for O'Brien 43, J Small for Whelan 52, F Andrews for Furman 54, J Welby for Burke 57, S Forde for Davy Byrne 59.

LEINSTER SEMI-FINAL
Nov 25, St Conleth's Park, Newbridge
BALLYMUN KICKHAMS 1-8
SARSFIELDS (KILDARE) 0-5
Ballymun Kickhams: S Currie, P McMahon, Enda
Dolan, Eoin Dolan, A Hubbard, K Connolly 0-1, J
Burke, Davy Byrne 0-1, J McCarthy 0-1, E O'Reilly,
K Leahy 0-1, J Whelan, T Furman 1-0, D Rock 0-4, S
Forde. Subs: Derek Byrne for Forde h/t, A O'Brien for
Derek Byrne 48, S George for O'Reilly 50, J Small for
Leahy 57, F Andrews for Furman 59.

LEINSTER FINAL
Dec 9, Cusack Park, Mullingar
BALLYMUN KICKHAMS 0-11
PORTLAOISE (LAOIS) 0-8
Ballymun Kickhams: S Currie, Enda Dolan, P
McMahon, Eoin Dolan, A Hubbard, K Connolly 0-1,
J Burke, Davy Byrne, J McCarthy, E Reilly, K Leahy
0-1, J Whelan 0-2, T Furman 0-1, D Rock 0-6, S Forde.
Subs: Derek Byrne for Forde 38, S George for Reilly
43, A O'Brien for Furman 59, J Small for Leahy 63.

ALL-IRELAND SEMI-FINAL
Feb 16, Semple Stadium, Thurles
BALLYMUN KICKHAMS 1-10
DR. CROKES (KERRY) 0-9
Ballymun Kickhams: S Currie, E Dolan, E Dolan, S
George, A Hubbard, K Connolly, P McMahon 0-1,
J Burke, J McCarthy, Davy Byrne 0-1, K Leahy, J
Whelan 0-1, T Furman 1-1, D Rock 0-5. Subs: E Reilly
for Weir 46, Derek Byrne 0-1 for Leahy 55, S Forde for
Connolly 56, A O'Brien for Furman 61.

ALL-IRELAND FINAL
Mar 17, Croke Park, Dublin
ST. BRIGID'S (ROSCOMMON) 2-11
BALLYMUN KICKHAMS 2-10
Ballymun Kickhams: Sean Currie, E Daly, Sean
George, Enda Dolan, Alan Hubbard, Karl Connolly
0-1, James Burke 0-2, James McCarthy, Davy Byrne,
Elliott Reilly, Kevin Leahy, Jason Whelan 0-2, Ted
Furman 0-2, Philly McMahon 1-0, Dean Rock 1-3.
Subs: Derek Byrne for Leahy h/t, C Weir for George
41, John Small for Reilly 51.

2013/14

LEINSTER QUARTER-FINAL
Nov 10, Cusack Park Mullingar
ST. VINCENT'S 0-11
ST. LOMAN'S (WESTMEATH) 0–9
St Vincent's: M Savage, M Concarr, J Curley, H Gill, C
Diamond, G Brennan, B Egan, M Loftus, E Fennell, G
Burke 0-1, T Diamond, A Baxter, R Trainor 0-1, C Dorney

0-2, T Quinn 0-7. Subs: K Bonnie for T Diamond 20, S
Carthy for Burke 33, K Golden for Loftus 37, D Murphy
for Baxter 41, N Mullins for Dorney 57.

LEINSTER SEMI-FINAL
Nov 24, Parnell Park, Dublin
ST. VINCENT'S 1–14 SUMMERHILL (MEATH) 1-10
St Vincent's: D Jordan, K Bonnie, J Curley, H Gill, C
Diamond, B Egan, M Concarr, D Murphy, E Fennell
0-1, G Burke 0-2, A Baxter, S Carthy 0-1, R Trainor
0-2, C Dorney, T Quinn 1-8. Subs: K Golden for Baxter
38, T Diamond for Dorney 50, N Mullins for Burke 52.

LEINSTER FINAL
Dec 8, O'Connor Park, Tullamore
ST. VINCENT'S 3-12 PORTLAOISE (LAOIS) 3–9
St Vincent's: M Savage, M Concarr, J Curley, H Gill, C
Diamond, G Brennan, B Egan, E Fennell, D Murphy,
G Burke 0-1, D Connolly 0-1, S Carthy 1-0, R Trainor
1-1, C Dorney 1-1, T Quinn 0-8. Subs: T Diamond for
Trainor 41, K Bonnie for C Diamond 41, K Golden for
Dorney 57.

ALL-IRELAND SEMI-FINAL
Feb 15, Pairc Esler, Newry
ST. VINCENTS 2-14
BALLINDERRY SHAMROCKS (DERRY) 1–15
St Vincent's: M Savage, K Bonnie, J Curley, H Gill, C
Diamond, B Egan, M Concarr, D Murphy, E Fennell, G
Burke 0-1, T Diamond, S Carthy 0-1, D Connolly 0-3, C
Dorney 1-1, T Quinn 1-8. Subs: K Golden for Diamond
57, N Mullins for Carthy 60, A Baxter for Dorney 62.

ALL-IRELAND FINAL
Mar 17, Croke Park, Dublin
ST. VINCENTS 4-12
CASTLEBAR MITCHELS (MAYO) 2-11
St Vincent's: Michael Savage, Kevin Bonnie, Jarleth
Curley, Hugh Gill, Brendan Egan, Ger Brennan,
Michael Concarr 1-0, Daithi Murphy, Eamon Fennell,
Gavin Burke, Diarmuid Connolly 2-5, Shane Carthy
0-3, Ruairi Trainor 0-1, Ciaran Dorney 1-0, Tomas
Quinn 0-2. Subs: Tiernan Diamond for Burke 35,
Cameron Diamond for Fennell 43, Kevin Golden 0-1
for Trainor 50, Adam Baxter for Dorney 58, Nathan
Mullins for Carthy 60.

2014/15

LEINSTER QUARTER-FINAL
Nov 9, O'Moore Park, Portlaoise
ST. VINCENT'S 3-11 PORTLAOISE (LAOIS) 0-10
St Vincent's: M Savage, K Bonnie, J Curley, H Gill, B
Egan, G Brennan, M Concarr, E Fennell, D Murphy, G
Burke, D Connolly 0-2, S Carthy 2-2, R Trainor 0-2,
C Dorney, T Quinn 1-3. Subs: Cameron Diamond for

Murphy 43, Cormac Diamond 0-2 for Dorney 47, Tiernan Diamond for Burke 55.

LEINSTER SEMI-FINAL
Nov 23, Parnell Park, Dublin
ST. VINCENT'S 3-9
GARRYCASTLE (WESTMEATH) 1-10
St Vincent's: M Savage, K Bonnie, J Curley, H Gill, B Egan, G Brennan 0-2, M Concarr, E Fennell, D Murphy, G Burke 0-2, D Connolly 0-2, S Carthy 1-1, R Trainor, C Dorney, T Quinn 2-2. Subs: Cormac Diamond for Murphy 37, Cameron Diamond for Dorney 37, Tiernan Diamond for Burke 56, M Loftus for Fennell 58, S Byrne for Brennan (black card) 60.

LEINSTER FINAL
Dec 14, Pairc Tailteann, Navan
ST. VINCENT'S 1-13   RHODE (OFFALY) 0-6
St Vincent's: M Savage, J Curley, H Gill, K Bonnie, B Egan 0-1, G Brennan, M Concarr, E Fennell, D Murphy, G Burke 0-2, D Connolly 0-1, S Carthy 0-1, R Trainor 0-1, T Quinn 1-4, C Dorney 0-1. Subs: Cormac Diamond 0-2 for Burke 47, T Diamond for Trainor 51, Cameron Diamond for Fennell 56, M Loftus for D Murphy 60, A Baxter for Dorney 60.

ALL-IRELAND SEMI-FINAL
Feb 14, O'Connor Park, Tullamore
COROFIN (GALWAY) 1-13   ST. VINCENT'S 1-9
St Vincent's: M Savage, Cameron Diamond, J Curley, H Gill, B Egan 0-1, G Brennan, M Concarr, E Fennell, G Burke, Cormac Diamond, D Connolly 0-3, S Carthy 0-1, R Trainor 0-2, C Dorney 0-1, T Quinn 1-1. Subs: T Diamond for Cormac Diamond 36, G Murphy for Dorney 41, E Brady for Concarr 55.

2015/16

LEINSTER QUARTER-FINAL
Nov 8, Drogheda Park, Drogheda
BALLYBODEN ST. ENDA'S 1-8
ST PATRICK'S (LOUTH) 0-7
Ballyboden St Enda's: C Dooley, B Dwan, S Hiney, S Clayton, S O'Connor, D Nelson, A Waters, MD Macauley, D O'Mahony, S Gibbons, C Basquel 1-0, D O'Reilly, C Keaney 0-3, S Molony, A Kerin 0-5. Subs: D McCabe for O'Mahoney h/t, R McDaid for O'Connor 38, D Davy for S Gibbons 46, C McCormack for S Molony 49, S Durkan for O'Reilly 54.

LEINSTER SEMI-FINAL
Nov 22, Cusack Park, Mullingar
BALLYBODEN ST. ENDA'S 1-11
ST. LOMAN'S (WESTMEATH) 0-9
Ballyboden St Enda's: P Durcan, B Dwan, S Hiney, S Clayton, S O'Connor, D Nelson, R McDaid, MD

Macauley 0-1, D O'Mahoney, D O'Reilly, C Basquel 0-1, D Davey, C Keaney 0-4, S Molony 1-1, A Kerin 0-4. Subs: D McCabe for Davey 48, S Durkin for Dwan 51.

LEINSTER FINAL
Dec 7, O'Connor Park, Tullamore
BALLYBODEN ST. ENDA'S 2-9
PORTLAOISE (LAOIS) 1-11
Ballyboden St Enda's: P Durcan, B Dwan, S Hiney, S Clayton, S O'Connor, D Nelson, R McDade, MD Macauley 1-0, D O'Mahony, D O'Reilly, C Basquel 0-1, D Davey, S Molony 0-1, C Keaney 0-4, A Kerin 1-2. Subs: S Gibbons for Davey 33, A Waters 0-1 for O'Reilly 43, S Durcan for O'Connor 47, D McCabe for O'Mahony 63.

ALL-IRELAND SEMI-FINAL
Feb 13, O'Moore Park, Portlaoise
BALLYBODEN ST. ENDA'S 0-15
CLONMEL COMMERCIALS (TIPPERARY) 0-10
Ballyboden St Enda's: P Durcan, B Dwan, S Hiney, S Clayton, R McDade, D Nelson 0-1, A Waters, MD Macauley, D O'Mahony, D Davey, C Basquel 0-1, D O'Reilly, C Keaney 0-4, S Molony 0-1, A Kerin 0-7. Subs: R Basquel 0-1 for Davey 33, S O'Connor for O'Reilly 34, S Gibbons for Molony 55, D McCabe for Gibbons 70, S Lambert for Molony 77.

ALL-IRELAND FINAL
Mar 17, Croke Park, Dublin
BALLYBODEN ST. ENDA'S 2-14
CASTLEBAR MITCHELS (MAYO) 0-7
Ballyboden St Enda's: Paul Durcan, Bob Dwan 0-3, Stephen Hiney, Shane Clayton, Stephen O'Connor 0-1, Darragh Nelson, Shane Durkin 0-2, Michael Darragh Macauley 0-1, Aran Waters, Darren O'Reilly 0-1, Colm Basquel 1-1, Robbie McDaid, Andrew Kerin 1-2, Conal Keaney 0-1, Ryan Basquel 0-2. Subs: Cathal Flaherty for Nelson 26-30 (blood), Simon Lambert for Macauley 34, Sam Molony for R Basquel 59, D Davey for O'Reilly 59, Donagh McCabe for 61, S Gibbons for McDaid 62.

2016/17

LEINSTER QUARTER-FINAL
Nov 13, Dr Cullen Park, Carlow
ST. VINCENT'S 0-16   PALATINE (CARLOW) 0-8
St Vincent's: M Savage, C Wilson, J Curley, M Concarr, B Egan, G Brennan, Cameron Diamond, D Murphy, S Carthy 0-3, G Burke, D Connolly, Cormac Diamond 0-5, R Trainor 0-1, E Varley 0-1, T Quinn 0-5. Subs: J Feeney for Connolly (black card) 20, A Martin 0-1 for Murphy 34, A Baxter for Varley 41, K Golden for Burke 48, J McCusker for Trainor 55, F Breathnach for Brennan 57.

LEINSTER SEMI-FINAL
Nov 27, Pearse Park, Longford
ST. VINCENT'S 2-12
ST. COLUMBA'S (LONGFORD) 0-11
St Vincent's: M Savage, M Concarr, J Curley, C Wilson, B Egan, G Brennan, Cameron Diamond, D Connolly 0-1, D Murphy, S Carthy 1-3, G Burke, Cormac Diamond 0-1, R Trainor 0-1, E Varley 0-2, T Quinn 1-2. Subs: J Feeney 0-1 for Murphy 41, A Martin 0-1 for Burke 41, M Mullins for Cameron Diamond 48, K Golden for Cormac Diamond 48, M Loftus for Varley 60.

LEINSTER FINAL
Dec 11, O'Moore Park, Portlaoise
ST. VINCENT'S 1-16   RHODE (OFFALY) 0-12
St Vincent's: M Savage, M Concarr, J Curley, C Wilson, Cameron Diamond, G Brennan, N Mullins, D Connolly 1-2, D Murphy, G Burke 0-3, S Carthy 0-2, Cormac Diamond 0-1, R Trainor 0-1, E Varley 0-2, T Quinn 0-4. Subs: F Breathnach for Brennan (black card) h/t, A Martin for Murphy 39, J Feeney 0-1 for Mullins 45, J McCusker for Cormac Diamond 58, K Bonnie for Varley 60.

ALL-IRELAND SEMI-FINAL
Feb 11, Pairc Esler, Newry
SLAUGHTNEIL (DERRY) 0-12
ST. VINCENT'S 0-10
Dublin: M Savage, M Concarr, J Curley, C Wilson, B Egan, G Brennan, Cameron Diamond, N Mullins 0-1, S Carthy 0-1, G Burke 0-2, D Connolly 0-1, Cormac Diamond, R Trainor, E Varley 0-5, T Quinn. Subs: A Martin for Trainor 46, J Feeney for Cormac Diamond (black card) 61, K Golden for Cameron Diamond 67, F Breathnach for Mullins 58, S McCusker for Egan (black card) 62.

LEINSTER CHAMPIONSHIP ROLL OF HONOUR
Portlaoise (Laois) 7: 1971, 1976, 1982, 1985, 1987, 2004, 2009.
St. Vincent's (Dublin) 7: 1972, 1975, 1984, 2007, 2013, 2014, 2016.
Éire Óg (Carlow) 5: 1992, 1993, 1995, 1996, 1998
Kilmacud Crokes (Dublin) 4: 1994, 2005, 2008, 2010.
University College (Dublin) 2: 1973, 1974.
Walterstown (Meath) 2: 1980, 1983.
Walsh Island (Offaly) 2: 1978, 1979.
Thomas Davis (Dublin) 2: 1990, 1991.
Gracefield (Offaly) 1: 1970.
Summerhill (Meath) 1: 1977.

Raheens (Kildare) 1: 1981.
Ferbane (Offaly) 1: 1986.
Parnells (Dublin) 1: 1988.
Baltinglass (Wicklow) 1: 1989.
Erin's Isle (Dublin) 1: 1997.
Na Fianna (Dublin) 1: 1999.
O'Hanrahans (Carlow) 1: 2000.
Rathnew (Wicklow) 1: 2001.
Dunshaughlin (Meath) 1: 2002.
St. Brigid's (Dublin) 1: 2003.
Moorefield (Kildare) 1: 2006.
Garrycastle (Westmeath) 1: 2011.
Ballymun Kickhams (Dublin) 1: 2012.
Ballyboden St. Enda's (Dublin) 1: 2015.

ALL-IRELAND CHAMPIONSHIP ROLL OF HONOUR
Nemo Rangers (Cork) 7: 1973, 1979, 1982, 1984, 1989, 1994, 2003.
Crossmaglen Rangers (Armagh) 6: 1997, 1999, 2000, 2007, 2011, 2012.
St. Finbarr's (Cork) 3: 1980, 1981, 1987.
St. Vincent's (Dublin) 3: 1976, 2008, 2014.
University College (Dublin) 2: 1974, 1975.
St. Mary's Burren (Down) 2: 1986, 1988.
Kilmacud Crokes (Dublin) 2: 1995, 2009.
Corofin (Galway) 2: 1998, 2015.
Dr Crokes (Kerry) 2: 1992, 2017.
East Kerry (Kerry) 1: 1971.
Bellaghy (Derry) 1: 1972.
Austin Stacks (Kerry) 1: 1977.
Thomond College (Limerick) 1: 1978.
Portlaoise (Laois) 1: 1983.
Castleisland Desmonds (Kerry) 1: 1985.
Baltinglass (Wicklow) 1: 1990.
Lavey (Derry) 1: 1991.
O'Donavan Rossa (Cork) 1: 1993.
Laune Rangers (Kerry) 1: 1996.
Crossmolina Deel Rovers (Mayo) 1: 2001.
Ballinderry Shamrock (Derry) 1: 2002.
Caltra (Galway) 1: 2004.
Ballina Stephenites (Mayo) 1: 2005.
Salthill-Knocknacarra (Galway) 1: 2006.
St. Gaul's (Antrim) 1: 2010.
St. Brigid's (Roscommon) 1: 2014.
Ballyboden St. Enda's (Dublin) 1: 2016.

Individual Records & Statistics

APPEARANCES

Pos	Total	Player	Club	Champ	Lge	First	Last
1	197	JOHN O'LEARY	O'DWYERS	70	127	27/07/1980	15/06/1997
2	187	STEPHEN CLUXTON	PARNELLS	91	96	27/05/2001	17/09/2017
3	137	CIARAN WHELAN	RAHENY	54	82	28/07/1996	03/08/2009
4	135	MICK KENNEDY	ST MARGARET'S	43	92	29/07/1979	19/04/1992
5	131	PAUL CURRAN	THOMAS DAVIS	49	82	05/06/1989	14/07/2002
6	122	BRYAN CULLEN	SKERRIES HARPS	54	68	02/02/2003	08/06/2014
7	121	PADDY CULLEN	SCOIL UÍ CHONAILL	42	79	09/04/1967	16/09/1979
8	119	SHANE RYAN	NAOMH MEARNOG	51	65	14/02/1999	03/08/2009
9	118	CIARAN DUFF	FINGALLIANS	39	79	11/11/1979	24/11/1991
	118	ALAN BROGAN	ST OLIVER PLUNKETT'S	70	48	10/02/2002	20/09/2015
11	116	CHARLIE REDMOND	ERIN'S ISLE	46	70	07/07/1985	15/06/1997
12	115	KEVIN HEFFERNAN	ST VINCENT'S	38	77	14/11/1948	05/08/1962
13	114	ROBBIE KELLEHER	SCOIL UÍ CHONAILL	39	75	19/10/1969	05/07/1981
14	113	BERNARD BROGAN JNR	ST OLIVER PLUNKETT'S	58	55	12/02/2006	17/09/2017
15	111	GERRY HARGAN	BALLYMUN KICKHAMS	43	68	25/11/1982	15/11/1992
	111	JASON SHERLOCK	NA FIANNA	62	49	30/10/1994	03/08/2009
	111	PAUL FLYNN	FINGALLIANS	51	60	02/02/2008	17/09/2017
18	110	JOHNNY McDONNELL	O'TOOLE'S	58	52	13/07/1919	29/05/1938
19	108	VINNIE MURPHY	TRINITY GAELS	40	68	06/06/1988	11/08/2001
20	106	ANTON O'TOOLE	SYNGE STREET	47	59	10/12/1972	23/09/1984
21	104	SEAN DOHERTY	BALLYBODEN ST ENDA'S	36	68	19/10/1969	01/07/1979
22	103	JIMMY KEAVENEY	ST VINCENT'S	41	62	22/11/1964	29/07/1979
	103	DESSIE FARRELL	NA FIANNA	53	50	23/02/1992	27/08/2005
24	102	KEVIN McMANAMON	ST JUDE'S	43	59	07/02/2010	17/09/2017
25	101	DES FERGUSON	ST VINCENT'S	36	65	07/05/1950	22/11/1964
	101	DIARMUID CONNOLLY	ST VINCENT'S	48	53	03/02/2007	17/09/2017
27	100	EAMONN HEERY	ST VINCENT'S	32	68	16/11/1986	15/03/1998
28	99	BARNEY ROCK	BALLYMUN KICKHAMS	39	60	06/07/1980	23/06/1991
29	98	KEITH BARR	ERIN'S ISLE	37	61	25/06/1989	21/06/1998
30	97	BRIAN MULLINS	ST VINCENT'S	53	44	21/04/1974	02/11/1986
	97	PADDY CHRISTIE	BALLYMUN KICKHAMS	38	59	04/02/1996	13/08/2005
32	96	MICK DEEGAN	ERIN'S ISLE	36	60	27/10/1985	21/06/1998
33	95	TOMMY CARR	LUCAN SARSFIELDS	66	29	16/06/1985	16/10/1994
34	92	BARRY CAHILL	ST. BRIGID'S	52	40	10/02/2002	22/07/2012
	92	PHILLY McMAHON	BALLYMUN KICKHAMS	42	50	02/02/2008	17/09/2017
36	91	PAUL CLARKE	WHITEHALL COLMCILLE	33	58	24/11/1985	15/06/1997
37	90	OLLIE FREANEY	ST VINCENT'S	29	61	07/12/1947	16/08/1959
	90	TONY HANAHOE	ST VINCENT'S	35	55	14/02/1965	07/10/1979
	90	MICHAEL DARRAGH MACAULEY	BALLYBODEN ST ENDA'S	41	49	07/02/2010	17/09/2017
40	88	CATHAL O'LEARY	ST VINCENT'S	34	54	20/05/1951	05/08/1962
41	87	JOE McNALLY	ST ANNE'S	34	53	13/03/1983	06/07/1991
	87	BOBBY DOYLE	ST VINCENT'S	39	48	29/10/1972	06/06/1982
43	85	COLIN MORAN	BALLYBODEN ST ENDA'S	41	44	01/11/1998	16/08/2008
44	83	DAVID HICKEY	RAHENY	39	44	19/10/1969	05/07/1981
45	82	TOMMY DRUMM	WHITEHALL COLMCILLE	36	46	11/07/1976	23/09/1984

Pos	Total	Player	Club	Champ	Lge	First	Last
	82	PAUL BEALIN	BALLYBODEN ST ENDA'S	27	55	23/10/1988	21/06/1998
	82	GAY O'DRISCOLL	ST VINCENT'S	36	46	28/11/1965	16/09/1979
48	81	TOMAS QUINN	ST. VINCENT'S	34	47	02/02/2003	01/04/2012
	81	CIAN O'SULLIVAN	KILMACUD CROKES	40	41	07/02/2010	17/09/2017
50	79	PAUL CASEY	LUCAN SARSFIELDS	33	46	10/02/2002	10/04/2011
51	78	MICKEY WHELAN	CLANNA GAEL	28	50	02/08/1959	02/07/1972
	78	DENIS BASTICK	TEMPLEOGUE SYNGE ST	35	43	03/04/2005	17/09/2017
53	77	JIM CROWLEY	ST VINCENT'S	24	53	08/10/1950	16/08/1959
	77	PADDY ANDREWS	ST. BRIGID'S	51	26	13/04/2008	17/09/2017
55	76	MICKEY WHELAN	CLANNA GAEL & ST. VINCENT'S	26	50	02/08/1959	02/07/1972
	76	BILL CASEY	NA FIANNA	23	53	05/11/1961	02/07/1972
	76	MICHAEL FITZSIMONS	CUALA	37	39	14/02/2010	17/09/2017
58	74	JIM RONAYNE	CLONTARF	30	44	29/07/1979	23/04/1989
	74	MICK GALVIN	NA FIANNA	34	40	14/12/1986	15/06/1997
	74	COMAN GOGGINS	BALLINTEER ST JOHN'S	35	34	11/06/2000	24/06/2007
	74	JAMES McCARTHY	BALLYMUN KICKHAMS	39	35	07/02/2010	17/09/2017
62	71	DARREN HOMAN	BALLYBODEN & ROUND TOWERS	29	42	02/02/1997	13/08/2005
63	70	JOHN TIMMONS	SEAN McDERMOTTS	28	42	01/06/1958	30/10/1966
	70	LAR FOLEY	ST VINCENT'S	33	37	07/07/1957	02/06/1968
	70	BERNARD BROGAN SNR	ST OLIVER PLUNKETT'S	30	40	09/12/1973	05/07/1981
	70	DARREN MAGEE	KILMACUD CROKES	30	40	10/02/2002	24/07/2010
67	69	JONNY COOPER	NA FIANNA	30	39	18/03/2012	17/09/2017
68	68	MAURICE WHELAN	ST VINCENT'S	21	47	16/06/1949	28/09/1958
	68	PADDY HOLDEN	CLANNA GAEL	22	46	01/11/1959	30/10/1966
70	67	PADDY McDONNELL	O'TOOLE'S	50	17	08/07/1917	13/11/1932
	67	JOHN McCARTHY	GARDA	27	40	10/06/1973	15/11/1981
	67	GER BRENNAN	ST. VINCENT'S	26	41	03/02/2007	22/09/2013
73	66	DAVID FORAN	THOMAS DAVIS	22	44	03/06/1979	07/06/1993
74	65	JOHNNY BOYLE	CLANNA GAEL	21	44	11/10/1953	26/06/1960
	65	PEADAR ANDREWS	ST. BRIGID'S	26	39	18/07/1999	04/06/2006
	65	RORY O'CARROLL	KILMACUD CROKES	36	29	29/03/2009	20/09/2015
77	62	JIM LAVIN	ST VINCENT'S	17	45	16/10/1949	09/03/1958
	62	DES FOLEY	ST VINCENT'S	23	39	16/11/1958	02/06/1968
	62	PADDY MORAN	WHITEHALL COLMCILLE	26	36	14/03/1993	01/08/1999
	62	EOGHAN O'GARA	TEMPLEOGUE SYNGE ST	34	28	05/04/2008	17/09/2017
81	61	JOHNNY JOYCE	ST VINCENT'S	22	39	24/06/1956	14/07/1963
	61	PASCHAL FLYNN	ST MARY'S	19	42	19/10/1958	08/08/1965
	61	JACK SHEEDY	LUCAN SARSFIELDS	21	40	25/11/1990	13/03/1995
84	60	JIM GAVIN	ROUND TOWERS	24	36	15/11/1992	23/02/2002
85	59	DEAN ROCK	BALLYMUN KICKHAMS	30	29	01/04/2012	17/09/2017
86	58	DENIS MAHONY	ST VINCENT'S	18	40	13/06/1948	07/07/1957
	58	BRIAN STYNES	BALLYBODEN ST ENDA'S	24	34	13/03/1994	12/08/2000
88	57	CIARAN WALSH	ST. ANNE'S	18	39	07/10/1990	15/06/1997
89	56	LEO HICKEY	BALLYBOUGHAL	14	43	05/11/1961	09/03/1969
	56	MICK HOLDEN	CUALA	24	32	29/07/1979	01/12/1985
	56	JOHNNY MAGEE	KILMACUD CROKES	23	33	19/10/1997	11/08/2007
92	55	PADDY BERMINGHAM	ST MARY'S	18	37	23/02/1936	21/03/1948
	55	TOMMY CONROY	ST VINCENT'S	21	34	27/02/1983	11/02/1977
	55	RAY COSGROVE	KILMACUD CROKES	27	28	15/11/1998	16/08/2007

Pos	Total	Player	Club	Champ	Lge	First	Last
	55	JACK McCAFFREY	CLONTARF	24	31	02/02/2013	17/09/2017
96	54	PADDY O'FLAHERTY	BEN EADAR	21	33	10/10/1954	16/08/1959
97	53	PETER O'REILLY	ST MARY'S	24	29	11/10/1936	21/03/1948
	53	PJ BUCKLEY	ERIN'S ISLE	21	32	09/12/1979	27/07/1986
99	52	GERRY DAVEY	CLANNA GAEL	16	36	02/12/1962	15/06/1969
	52	JOHN KEARNS	BALLYMUN KICKHAMS	18	34	02/11/1980	28/02/1988
	52	CIARAN KILKENNY	CASTLEKNOCK	25	27	04/08/2012	17/09/2017
102	51	PAT O'NEILL	CIVIL SERVICE & UCD	22	29	04/05/1975	27/07/1980
	51	NOEL McCAFFREY	CLONTARF	16	35	16/06/1985	10/03/1991
104	49	JACK O'REILLY	O'TOOLE'S	40	9	08/07/1917	28/04/1929
	49	MARCUS WILSON	ST. VINCENT'S	17	32	23/03/1953	26/06/1960
	49	ALAN LARKIN	RAHENY	21	28	11/06/1972	04/12/1977
107	48	NORMAN ALLEN	ST. VINCENT'S	11	37	08/10/1950	24/03/1957
	48	PADDY REILLY	ST MARGARET'S	22	26	26/11/1972	01/07/1979
	48	PAT CANAVAN	ST VINCENT'S	22	26	07/10/1979	27/07/1986
	48	DAVID BYRNE	BALLYMUN KICKHAMS	14	34	27/10/1996	11/08/2001
	48	DARREN DALY	FINGAL RAVENS	20	28	02/02/2013	17/09/2017
112	47	JOE NORRIS	O'TOOLE'S	38	9	08/09/1918	24/03/1929
113	46	JOE SYNNOTT	O'TOOLE'S	35	11	13/07/1919	18/11/1928
114	45	BRIAN McDONALD	SYNGE STREET	15	30	18/11/1962	02/06/1968
	45	GEORGE WILSON	O'DYWER'S	17	27	14/11/1971	05/12/1976
116	43	JOE TIMMONS	ST MARY'S	15	28	06/10/1957	05/11/1961
	43	PAUL MANNION	KILMACUD CRIKES	24	19	02/02/2013	17/09/2017
118	42	JOHN SYNNOTT	O'TOOLE'S	32	10	13/07/1919	06/04/1931
	42	PADDY FARNAN	ST VINCENT'S	18	24	23/03/1958	05/08/1962
120	41	BRENDAN QUINN	PARNELLS	21	20	29/10/1939	24/11/1946
	41	FRANK MURRAY	NA FIANNA	7	34	19/10/1969	21/04/1974
122	40	PAT GOGARTY	RAHENY	10	30	16/11/1969	10/12/1978
	40	KEVIN NOLAN	KILMACUD CROKES	21	19	05/04/2008	29/06/2014
	40	BRIAN FENTON	RAHENY	19	21	01/03/2015	17/09/2017

CAREER TOP SCORERS
CHAMPIONSHIP & NATIONAL LEAGUE

Pos	Total	Player	Club	Gls-Pts	Career	Games	Average
1	492	JIMMY KEAVENEY	ST VINCENT'S	30-402	1964 – 1979	104	4.777
2	451	BERNARD BROGAN JNR	ST OLIVER PLUNKETT'S	36-343	2006 – 2017	113	3.991
3	450	BARNEY ROCK	BALLYMUN KICKHAMS	30-360	1980 – 1991	99	4.545
4	382	KEVIN HEFFERNAN	ST VINCENT'S	52-226	1948 – 1962	115	3.322
5	351	CHARLIE REDMOND	ERIN'S ISLE	15-306	1985 – 1997	116	3.025
6	311	OLLIE FREANEY	ST VINCENT'S	23-242	1947 – 1959	90	3.456
7	299	DEAN ROCK	BALLYMUN KICKHAMS	8-275	2012 – 2017	59	5.068
8	293	CIARAN DUFF	FINGALLIANS	22-227	1979 – 1991	118	2.483
9	276	TOMAS QUINN	ST VINCENT'S	21-213	2003 – 2012	81	3.407
10	249	DIARMUID CONNOLLY	ST VINCENT'S	28-165	2007 – 2017	101	2.465
11	238	ALAN BROGAN	ST OLIVER PLUNKETT'S	15-193	2002 – 2015	118	2.016
12	231	JOHN TIMMONS	ST MARY'S	9-204	1958 – 1967	70	3.300
13	177	VINNIE MURPHY	TRINITY GAELS	21-126	1988 – 2001	108	1.639
14	172	JOHNNY JOYCE	ST VINCENT'S	39-55	1956 – 1963	61	2.819
15	163	KEVIN McMANAMON	ST JUDE'S	20-102	2010 – 2017	102	1.598

Pos	Total	Player	Club	Gls-Pts	Career	Games	Average
16	162	CIARAN WHELAN	RAHENY	9-131	1996 – 2009	137	1.153
17	157	BOBBY DOYLE	ST VINCENT'S	24-85	1972 – 1982	87	1.805
18	153	DESSIE FARRELL	NA FIANNA	12-117	1992 – 2005	103	1.485
19	144	TONY HANAHOE	ST VINCENT'S	23-75	1965 – 1979	90	1.600
20	140	ANTON O'TOOLE	SYNGE STREET	13-101	1974 – 1984	105	1.333
21	135	MICKEY WHELAN	CLANNA GAEL	11-102	1959 – 1969	76	1.776
22	134	PADDY McDONNELL	O'TOOLE'S	19-77	1917 – 1932	67	2.000
23	133	JASON SHERLOCK	NA FIANNA	14-91	1996 – 2009	107	1.243
24	118	DES FERGUSON	ST VINCENT'S	20-58	1950 – 1964	101	1.168
25	117	JOE McNALLY	ST ANNE'S	24-45	1983 – 1991	87	1.345
	117	PAUL FLYNN	FINGALLIANS	12-81	2008 – 2016	111	1.054
27	114	RAY COSGROVE	KILMACUD CROKES	9-87	1998 – 2007	55	2.073
28	111	DAVID HICKEY	RAHENY	15-66	1969 – 1981	83	1.337
29	108	PAUL CLARKE	WHITEHALL COLMCILLE	6-90	1985 – 1997	91	1.187
30	102	BRIAN McDONALD	SYNGE STREET	11-69	1962 – 1968	45	2.666
31	100	TOMMY BANKS	SEAN McDERMOTTS	2-94	1940 – 1943	26	3.846
	100	MICK GALVIN	NA FIANNA	11-67	1986 – 1997	74	1.351
33	94	JIM GAVIN	ROUND TOWERS	0-94	1992 – 2002	60	1.567
34	93	PADDY ANDREWS	ST. BRIGID'S	3-84	2008 – 2017	76	1.224
35	92	JOHN McCARTHY	GARDA	14-50	1973 – 1981	64	1.438
	88	PADDY BERMINGHAM	ST MARYS	9-61	1936 – 1948	55	1.600
37	86	BRIAN MULLINS	ST VINCENTS	17-35	1974 – 1986	97	0.887
38	84	JOHNNY BOYLE	CLANNA GAEL	11-51	1953 – 1960	65	1.292
39	74	COLIN MORAN	BALLYBODEN ST ENDA'S	5-59	1998 – 2008	85	0.871
40	71	CATHAL O'LEARY	ST VINCENTS	8-47	1951 – 1962	88	0.807

CAREER TOP SCORERS
CHAMPIONSHIP

Pos	Total	Player	Club	Gls-Pts	Career	Games	Average
1	260	BERNARD BROGAN JNR	ST OLIVER PLUNKETT'S	21-197	2006 – 2017	58	4.483
2	228	BARNEY ROCK	BALLYMUN KICKHAMS	16-180	1980 – 1991	39	5.846
	228	JIMMY KEAVENEY	ST VINCENT'S	17-177	1965 – 1979	41	5.561
4	182	CHARLIE REDMOND	ERIN'S ISLE	8-158	1985 – 1997	46	3.956
5	150	DEAN ROCK	BALLYMUN KICKHAMS	6-132	2012 – 2017	31	4.839
6	120	OLLIE FREANEY	ST VINCENT'S	5-105	1948 – 1959	29	4.138
	120	TOMAS QUINN	ST VINCENT'S	6-92	2003 – 2011	34	3.235
8	106	DIARMUID CONNOLLY	ST VINCENT'S	12-70	2007 – 2017	48	2.234
9	105	PADDY McDONNELL	O'TOOLE'S	16-57	1917 – 1932	50	2.100
10	104	KEVIN HEFFERNAN	ST VINCENT'S	16-56	1949 – 1962	38	2.842
11	93	JASON SHERLOCK	NA FIANNA	10-63	1995 – 2009	58	1.604
12	82	CIARAN DUFF	FINGALLIANS	9-55	1980 – 1991	39	2.103
13	70	BOBBY DOYLE	ST VINCENT'S	10-40	1973 – 1982	39	1.795
14	69	DESSIE FARRELL	NA FIANNA	4-57	1992 – 2005	53	1.302
15	63	TOMMY BANKS	SEAN McDERMOTTS	1-60	1941 – 1943	14	4.500
	63	VINNIE MURPHY	TRINITY GAELS	9-38	1988 – 2001	40	1.575
17	60	PAUL FLYNN	FINGALLIANS	5-45	2008 – 2017	51	1.176
	60	KEVIN McMANAMON	ST. JUDE'S	8-36	2010 – 2017	43	1.395
19	57	CIARAN WHELAN	RAHENY	2-51	1996 – 2009	55	1.036
20	60	JOHN McCARTHY	GARDA	9-28	1973 – 1981	27	2.037

CAREER TOP SCORERS
NATIONAL LEAGUE

Pos	Total	Player	Club	Gls-Pts	Career	Games	Average
1	278	KEVIN HEFFERNAN	ST VINCENT'S	36-170	1948 – 1962	77	3.610
2	264	JIMMY KEAVENEY	ST VINCENT'S	12-225	1964 – 1979	63	4.190
3	222	BARNEY ROCK	BALLYMUN KICKHAMS	14-180	1980 – 1991	60	3.700
4	211	CIARAN DUFF	FINGALLIANS	13-172	1979 – 1991	79	2.671
5	191	OLLIE FREANEY	ST VINCENT'S	18-137	1947 – 1959	61	3.131
	191	BERNARD BROGAN JNR	ST OLIVER PLUNKETT'S	15-146	2006 – 2017	55	3.473
7	167	CHARLIE REDMOND	ERIN'S ISLE	7-146	1985 – 1997	70	2.385
8	166	TOMAS QUINN	ST VINCENT'S	15-121	2003 – 2012	47	3.532
9	165	ALAN BROGAN	ST OLIVER PLUNKETT'S	10-135	2002 – 2015	70	2.357
10	149	DEAN ROCK	BALLYMUN KICKHAMS	2-143	2012 – 2017	28	5.321
11	144	DIARMUID CONNOLLY	ST VINCENT'S	16-97	2007 – 2017	53	2.717
12	136	JOHN TIMMONS	SEAN MCDERMOTTS	4-121	1958 – 1967	42	3.238
13	113	JOHNNY JOYCE	ST VINCENT'S	26-35	1956 – 1963	39	2.897
14	112	VINNIE MURPHY	TRINITY GAELS	8-88	1988 – 2001	68	1.647
15	103	KEVIN McMANAMON	ST. JUDE'S	12-67	2010 – 2017	59	1.746
16	101	CIARAN WHELAN	RAHENY	7-80	1996 – 2009	82	1.232
17	87	BOBBY DOYLE	ST VINCENT'S	14-45	1972 – 1982	48	1.813
18	86	MICKEY WHELAN	CLANNA GAEL	8-62	1959 – 1969	50	1.720
19	84	TONY HANAHOE	ST VINCENT'S	12-48	1965 – 1979	55	1.527
	84	DESSIE FARRELL	NA FIANNA	8-60	1992 – 2001	50	1.680

CAREER TOP GOALSCORERS
CHAMPIONSHIP & NATIONAL LEAGUE

Pos	Total	Player	Club	Champ	Lge	Games	Career	Average
1	52	KEVIN HEFFERNAN	ST VINCENT'S	16	32	115	1948 – 1962	0.45
2	39	JOHNNY JOYCE	ST VINCENT'S	13	26	61	1956 – 1963	0.64
3	36	BERNARD BROGAN JNR	ST OLIVER PLUNKETT'S	21	15	113	2006 – 2017	0.32
4	30	JIMMY KEAVENEY	ST VINCENT'S	17	13	104	1964 – 1979	0.28
	30	BARNEY ROCK	BALLYMUN KICKHAMS	16	14	99	1980 – 1991	0.30
6	28	DIARMUID CONNOLLY	ST VINCENT'S	12	16	101	2007 – 2017	0.28
7	24	BOBBY DOYLE	ST VINCENT'S	10	14	87	1972 – 1982	0.28
	24	JOE McNALLY	ST ANNES	12	12	87	1983 – 1991	0.28
9	23	OLLIE FREANEY	ST VINCENT'S	5	18	90	1947 – 1959	0.26
10	22	CIARAN DUFF	FINGALLIANS	9	13	118	1979 – 1991	0.19
11	21	TONY HANAHOE	ST VINCENT'S	9	12	90	1965 – 1979	0.23
	21	TOMAS QUINN	ST VINCENT'S	6	15	81	2003 – 2012	0.26
13	20	DESSIE FERGUSON	ST VINCENT'S	8	12	101	1950 – 1964	0.20
	20	KEVIN McMANAMON	ST. JUDE'S	8	12	102	2010 – 2017	0.20
15	19	PADDY McDONNELL	O'TOOLES	16	3	67	1917 – 1932	0.28
16	17	BRIAN MULLINS	ST VINCENT'S	10	7	97	1974 – 1986	0.18
	17	VINNIE MURPHY	TRINITY GAELS	9	8	108	1987 – 2001	0.16
18	15	DAVID HICKEY	RAHENY	9	6	83	1969 – 1981	0.18
	15	CHARLIE REDMOND	ERIN'S ISLE	8	7	116	1985 – 1997	0.13
	15	ALAN BROGAN	ST OLIVER PLUNKETT'S	10	5	118	2002 – 2015	0.13

TOP SCORERS PER SEASON

Season	Total	G-Pts	Player	Club	Champ	Lge	Games	Average
1888–1889: Data not available.								
1890	19	4-7	JOHN JOE HOEY	ISLES OF THE SEA	4-7	–	4	4.75
1891	14	3-5	TOM MURPHY	YOUNG IRELAND	3-5	–	3	4.66
1892	12	2-6	JOHNNY GERAGHTY	YOUNG IRELAND	2-6	–	3	4.00
1893: Dublin boycotted the Championship in a dispute over the Parnell Split.								
1894	10	1-7	TOMMY ERRITY	YOUNG IRELAND	1-7	–	6	1.67
1895	6	1-3	MICK BYRNE	ISLE OF THE SEA	1-3	–	2	3.00
	6	1-3	MICK O'BRIEN	ISLE OF THE SEA	1-3	–	2	3.00
1896	20	2-14	JIM HESLIN	YOUNG IRELAND	2-14	–	4	5.00
1897	20	1-17	MICK BYRNE	KICKHAMS	1-17	–	5	4.00
1898	13	3-4	JOE LEDWIDGE	GERALDINES	3-4	–	3	4.33
1899	20	3-11	JOE LEDWIDGE	GERALDINES	3-11	–	4	5.00
1900	3	0-3	MATT CHAMBERS	KICKHAMS	0-3	–	1	3.00
1901	19	3-10	MICK WHELAN	ISLE OF THE SEA	3-10	–	6	3.17
1902	17	3-8	JIM BRENNAN	KEATINGS	3-8	–	6	2.83
1903	3	1-0	TOMMY MURPHY	KEATINGS	1-0	–	1	3.00
1904	10	0-10	MICK KELLY	ST JAMES'S GATE	0-10	–	5	2.00
1905	1	0-1	MICK KELLY	ST JAMES'S GATE	0-1	–	1	1.00
	1	0-1	TOMMY MURPHY	KEATINGS	0-1	–	1	1.00
1906	16	2-10	TOMMY WALSH	KICKHAMS	2-10	–	5	3.20
1907	9	1-6	TOMMY WALSH	KICKHAMS	1-6	–	5	1.80
	9	0-9	MICK KELLY	ST JAMES'S GATE	0-9	–	5	1.80
1908	14	1-11	HUGH HILLIARD	KICKHAMS	1-11	–	6	2.16
1909	8	1-5	TOMMY WALSH	KICKHAMS	1-5	–	2	4.00
1910	17	3-8	TOMMY DONNELLY	PARNELLS	3-8	–	5	2.60
1911	4	1-1	JIM MORAN	KEATINGS	1-1	–	1	4.00
1912	12	3-3	TOM DOHERTY	KICKHAMS	3-3	–	5	2.40
1913	5	1-2	TOM DOHERTY	KICKHAMS	1-2	–	1	5.00
1914	4	1-1	MICK DONOVAN	GERALDINES	1-1	–	2	2.00
1915	18	3-9	SOLOMON LAWLOR	GERALDINES	3-9	–	5	3.60
1916: Dublin unable to field a team and forced to concede a walkover to Wexford.								
1917	18	2-12	SOLOMON LAWLOR	GERALDINES	2-12	–	4	4.50
1918	10	3-1	SOLOMON LAWLOR	GERALDINES	3-1	–	1	10.00
1919	6	0-6	PADDY McDONNELL	O'TOOLE'S	0-6	–	3	2.00
	6	1-3	JOHN SYNNOTT	O'TOOLE'S	1-3	–	3	2.00
1920	15	4-3	FRANK BURKE	COLLEGIANS	4-3	–	5	3.00
1921	13	2-7	PADDY McDONNELL	O'TOOLE'S	2-7	–	3	4.33
1922	14	2-8	PADDY McDONNELL	O'TOOLE'S	2-8	–	4	3.50
1923	8	1-5	PADDY McDONNELL	O'TOOLE'S	1-5	–	4	2.00
1924	13	3-4	JOE STYNES	O'TOOLE'S	3-4	–	4	3.25
1925	5	1-2	FRANK BURKE	COLLEGIANS	1-2	–	1	5.00
1926	9	1-6	PADDY STYNES	O'TOOLE'S	1-6	–	4	2.25
1926/27	10	1-7	PAUL RUSSELL	GARDA	1-7	–	4	2.50
1927/28	11	3-2	JIM KIRWAN	GARDA	–	3-2	3	3.66
1928/29	17	4-5	PADDY McDONNELL	O'TOOLE'S	3-2	1-3	6	2.83
1929/30	7	1-4	MICK O'BRIEN	O'TOOLE'S	1-4	–	2	3.50
1930/31	15	4-3	MICK O'BRIEN	O'TOOLE'S	0-2	4-1	6	2.50
1931/32	22	5-7	WILLIE DOWLING	ROUND TOWERS	3-5	2-2	7	3.14
1932/33	13	1-10	MURT KELLY	GARDA	0-6	1-4	5	2.60
	13	3-4	GERRY FITZGERALD	ST MARY'S	3-4	–	4	3.25

Season	Total	G-Pts	Player	Club	Champ	Lge	Games	Average
1933/34	30	3-21	GEORGE COMERFORD	GARDA	3-21	—	7	4.29
1934/35	11	3-2	DAN BANVILLE	DOLPHINS	—	3-2	6	1.83
1935/36	14	2-8	MURT KELLY	GARDA	—	2-8	8	1.75
1936/37	19	2-13	PADDY BERMINGHAM	ST MARY'S	0-5	2-8	6	3.16
1937/38	13	2-7	PADDY MULHALL	ST JOSEPH'S	1-1	1-6	7	1.86
1938/39	18	1-15	PADDY BERMINGHAM	ST MARY'S	1-1	0-14	6	3.00
1939/40	14	3-5	PADDY BERMINGHAM	ST MARY'S	—	3-5	6	2.33
1940/41	51	1-48	TOMMY BANKS	SEAN McDERMOTTS	0-30	1-18	14	3.64
1941/42	31	0-31	TOMMY BANKS	SEAN McDERMOTTS	0-28	0-3	7	4.43
1942/43	20	6-2	MICK QUIGLEY	CIVIL SERVICE	—	6-2	3	6.66
1943/44	15	4-3	PADDY O'CONNOR	ST MARY'S	3-1	1-2	5	3.00
1944/45	11	2-5	MICK CULHANE	SEAN MCDERMOTTS	2-2	0-3	4	2.75
1945/46	10	2-4	TOM MARKEY	PARNELLS	—	2-4	3	3.33
1946/47	8	1-5	DAVE BYRNE	O'TOOLE'S	1-5	—	1	8.00
	8	0-8	MICK O'REILLY	PARNELLS	0-5	0-3	4	2.00
1947/48	8	2-2	PADDY BERMINGHAM	ST MARY'S	—	2-2	2	4.00
1948/49	18	2-12	KEVIN HEFFERNAN	ST VINCENT'S	1-10	1-2	3	6.00
1949/50	19	0-19	KEVIN HEFFERNAN	ST VINCENT'S	0-5	0-14	5	3.80
1950/51	27	4-15	KEVIN HEFFERNAN	ST VINCENT'S	1-6	3-9	5	5.40
1951/52	36	6-18	KEVIN HEFFERNAN	ST VINCENT'S	1-2	5-16	8	4.50
1952/53	41	3-32	KEVIN HEFFERNAN	ST VINCENT'S	0-2	3-30	9	4.56
1953/54	32	4-20	KEVIN HEFFERNAN	ST VINCENT'S	1-3	3-17	8	4.00
1954/55	62	6-44	OLLIE FREANEY	ST VINCENT'S	2-24	4-20	14	4.43
1955/56	22	2-16	JOHNNY BOYLE	CLANNA GAEL	0-5	2-11	10	2.20
1956/57	36	3-27	OLLIE FREANEY	ST VINCENT'S	0-12	3-15	9	4.00
1957/58	72	0-72	OLLIE FREANEY	ST VINCENT'S	0-29	0-43	14	5.14
1958/59	57	4-45	OLLIE FREANEY	ST VINCENT'S	2-26	2-19	10	5.70
1959/60	37	8-13	KEVIN HEFFERNAN	ST VINCENT'S	2-2	6-11	9	4.11
1960/61	29	6-11	KEVIN HEFFERNAN	ST VINCENT'S	2-2	4-9	9	3.22
1961/62	44	1-41	JOHN TIMMONS	ST MARY'S	0-12	1-29	11	4.00
1962/63	29	2-23	MICKEY WHELAN	CLANNA GAEL	1-19	1-4	7	4.14
1963/64	36	3-27	MICKEY WHELAN	CLANNA GAEL	0-1	3-26	11	3.27
1964/65	49	4-37	JOHN TIMMONS	ST MARY'S	1-14	3-23	8	6.13
1965/66	24	2-18	JOHN TIMMONS	ST MARY'S	2-9	0-9	4	6.00
1966/67	44	3-35	JIMMY KEAVENEY	ST VINCENT'S	0-6	3-29	8	5.50
1967/68	8	1-5	BRIAN McDONALD	SYNGE STREET	0-2	1-3	5	1.60
1968/69	36	1-33	PADDY DELANEY	O'TOOLE'S	0-2	1-31	8	4.50
1969/70	26	0-26	JIMMY KEAVENEY	ST VINCENT'S	0-3	0-23	5	5.20
1970/71	26	0-26	JIMMY KEAVENEY	ST VINCENT'S	0-4	0-22	7	3.71
1971/72	14	0-14	JOE REILLY	SYNGE STREET	0-1	0-13	8	1.75
1972/73	19	0-19	STEPHEN ROONEY	O'DWYER'S	0-8	0-11	8	2.38
1973/74	35	1-38	JIMMY KEAVENEY	ST VINCENT'S	1-32	—	6	5.83
1974/75	82	2-76	JIMMY KEAVENEY	ST VINCENT'S	1-38	1-38	12	6.83
1975/76	64	9-37	JIMMY KEAVENEY	ST VINCENT'S	6-18	3-19	11	5.82
1976/77	74	3-65	JIMMY KEAVENEY	ST VINCENT'S	2-27	1-38	12	6.17
1977/78	67	4-55	JIMMY KEAVENEY	ST VINCENT'S	2-31	2-24	11	6.09
1978/79	33	2-27	JIMMY KEAVENEY	ST VINCENT'S	1-12	1-15	8	4.13
1979/80	23	2-17	BARNEY ROCK	BALLYMUN KICKHAMS	0-4	2-13	7	3.29
1980/81	33	4-21	CIARAN DUFF	FINGALLIANS	0-1	4-20	9	3.67
1981/82	29	2-23	ANTO McCAUL	BALLYMUN KICKHAMS	0-3	2-20	10	2.90
1982/83	56	7-35	BARNEY ROCK	BALLYMUN KICKHAMS	6-26	1-9	14	4.00

Season	Total	G-Pts	Player	Club	Champ	Lge	Games	Average
1983/84	60	7-39	BARNEY ROCK	BALLYMUN KICKHAMS	5-24	2-15	12	5.00
1984/85	49	4-37	BARNEY ROCK	BALLYMUN KICKHAMS	3-28	1-9	9	5.44
1985/86	57	4-45	BARNEY ROCK	BALLYMUN KICKHAMS	0-12	4-33	11	5.15
1986/87	44	1-41	BARNEY ROCK	BALLYMUN KICKHAMS	0-23	1-18	9	4.89
1987/88	36	3-27	KIERAN DUFF	FINGALLIANS	–	3-27	9	4.00
1988/89	59	0-59	BARNEY ROCK	BALLYMUN KICKHAMS	0-23	0-36	14	4.21
1989/90	41	2-35	BARNEY ROCK	BALLYMUN KICKHAMS	0-5	2-30	9	4.56
1990/91	25	1-22	CHARLIE REDMOND	ERIN'S ISLE	0-12	1-10	9	2.78
1991/92	54	2-48	CHARLIE REDMOND	ERIN'S ISLE	1-28	1-20	12	4.50
1992/93	42	2-36	CHARLIE REDMOND	ERIN'S ISLE	1-19	1-17	12	3.50
1993/94	75	6-57	CHARLIE REDMOND	ERIN'S ISLE	4-30	2-27	13	5.77
1994/95	49	1-46	CHARLIE REDMOND	ERIN'S ISLE	1-31	0-15	10	4.90
1995/96	21	0-21	CHARLIE REDMOND	ERIN'S ISLE	0-14	0-7	5	4.20
1996/97	18	0-18	CHARLIE REDMOND	ERIN'S ISLE	0-4	0-14	6	3.00
1997/98	36	1-33	DECLAN DARCY	CLANNA GAEL FONTENOY	1-9	0-24	9	4.00
1998/99	31	3-22	DESSIE FARRELL	NA FIANNA	0-2	3-20	15	2.07
1999/00	26	0-26	JIM GAVIN	ROUND TOWERS	0-11	0-15	11	2.36
2000/01	26	1-23	WAYNE McCARTHY	ERIN'S ISLE	1-12	0-11	12	2.17
2002	75	8-51	RAY COSGROVE	KILMACUD CROKES	6-23	2-28	15	5.00
2003	23	1-20	TOMAS QUINN	ST VINCENT'S	0-6	1-14	9	2.56
2004	33	1-30	TOMAS QUINN	ST VINCENT'S	1-13	0-17	12	2.75
2005	67	5-52	TOMAS QUINN	ST VINCENT'S	1-29	4-23	13	5.15
2006	54	6-36	TOMAS QUINN	ST VINCENT'S	3-14	3-22	11	4.91
2007	42	1-39	CONAL KEANEY	BALLYBODEN ST ENDA'S	0-21	1-18	13	3.23
2008	35	2-29	CONAL KEANEY	BALLYBODEN ST ENDA'S	1-12	1-17	10	3.50
2009	47	3-38	BERNARD BROGAN JNR	ST OLIVER PLUNKETT'S	2-20	1-18	9	5.22
2010	91	6-73	BERNARD BROGAN JNR	ST OLIVER PLUNKET'S	3-42	3-31	14	6.50
2011	59	3-50	BERNARD BROGAN JNR	ST OLIVER PLUNKETT'S	0-29	3-21	13	4.54
2012	42	5-27	DIARMUID CONNOLLY	ST VINCENT'S	1-6	4-21	12	3.50
2013	72	5-57	BERNARD BROGAN JNR	ST OLIVER PLUNKETT'S	3-19	2-38	12	6.00
2014	36	3-27	BERNARD BROGAN JNR	ST OLIVER PLUNKETT'S	2-16	1-11	6	6.00
2015	84	3-75	DEAN ROCK	BALLYMUN KICKHAMS	2-23	1-52	16	5.25
2016	104	2-98	DEAN ROCK	BALLYMUN KICKHAMS	1-58	1-40	16	6.50
2017	87	3-78	DEAN ROCK	BALLYMUN KICKHAMS	3-31	0-47	14	6.15

LONGEST SENIOR INTER-COUNTY CAREERS

Pos	Yrs-Days	Player	Club	Games	First	Last
1	18, 320	JOHNNY McDONNELL	O'TOOLE'S	110	13/07/1919	29/05/1938
2	16, 323	JOHN O'LEARY	O'DWYER'S	197	27/07/1980	15/06/1997
3	16, 113	STEPHEN CLUXTON	PARNELLS	187	27/05/2001	17/09/2017
4	15, 129	PADDY McDONNELL	O'TOOLE'S	67	08/07/1917	13/11/1932
5	14, 277	JASON SHERLOCK	NA FIANNA	107	30/10/1994	03/08/2009
6	14, 263	PADDY FALLON	GERALDINES	36	27/09/1908	17/06/1923
7	14, 249	JIMMY KEAVENEY	ST VINCENT'S	103	22/11/1964	29/07/1979
8	14, 234	TONY HANAHOE	ST VINCENT'S	134	14/02/1965	07/10/1979
9	14, 199	DES FERGUSON	ST VINCENT'S	101	29/07/1979	22/11/1964
10	14, 4	DAVID FORAN	THOMAS DAVIS	66	03/06/1979	07/06/1993
11	13, 292	GAY O'DRISCOLL	ST VINCENT'S	81	28/11/1965	16/09/1979
12	13, 234	KEVIN HEFFERNAN	ST VINCENT'S	115	14/11/1948	05/08/1962
13	13, 222	ALAN BROGAN	ST OLIVER PLUNKETT'S	118	10/02/2002	20/09/2015
14	13, 186	DESSIE FARRELL	NA FIANNA	103	23/02/1992	27/08/2005
15	13, 73	PAUL CURRAN	THOMAS DAVIS	131	05/06/1989	17/08/2002
16	13, 66	VINNY MURPHY	TRINITY GAELS	108	06/06/1988	11/08/2001
17	13, 6	CIARAN WHELAN	RAHENY	137	28/07/1996	03/08/2009
18	12, 334	MICKEY WHELAN	CLANNA GAEL	78	02/08/1959	02/07/1972
19	12, 264	MICK KENNEDY	ST MARGARET'S	135	29/07/1979	19/04/1992
20	12, 238	MICK DEEGAN	ERIN'S ISLE	96	27/10/1985	21/06/1998
21	12, 195	BRIAN MULLINS	ST VINCENT'S	97	21/04/1974	02/11/1986
22	12, 160	PADDY CULLEN	SCOIL UÍ CONAILL	120	09/04/1967	16/09/1979
23	12, 27	PADDY BERMINGHAM	ST MARYS	55	23/02/1936	21/03/1948
24	12, 13	CIARAN DUFF	FINGALLIANS	118	11/11/1979	24/11/1991
25	11, 343	CHARLIE REDMOND	ERIN'S ISLE	116	07/07/1985	15/06/1997
26	11, 295	JACK O'REILLY	O'TOOLES	47	08/07/1917	28/04/1929
27	11, 287	ANTON O'TOOLE	SYNGE STREET	105	10/12/1972	23/09/1984
28	11, 269	ROBBIE KELLEHER	SCOIL UI CONAILL	113	19/10/1969	05/07/1981
29	11, 267	JOHN SYNNOTT	O'TOOLE'S	42	13/07/1919	06/04/1931
30	11, 259	DAVID HICKEY	RAHENY	83	19/10/1969	05/07/1981
31	11, 252	OLLIE FREANEY	ST VINCENT'S	90	07/12/1947	16/08/1959
32	11, 218	BERNARD BROGAN JNR	ST OLIVER PLUNKETT'S	113	12/02/2006	17/09/2017
33	11, 203	PAUL CLARKE	WHITEHALL COLMCILLE	91	24/11/1985	15/06/1997
34	11, 132	PETER O'REILLY	ST MARY'S	52	11/10/1936	21/03/1948
35	11, 126	BRYAN CULLEN	SKERRIES HARPS	122	02/02/2003	08/06/2014
36	11, 119	EAMONN HEERY	ST VINCENT'S	100	16/11/1986	13/03/1998
37	11, 77	CATHAL O'LEARY	ST VINCENT'S	88	20/05/1951	05/08/1962
38	10, 352	BARNEY ROCK	BALLYMUN KICKHAMS	99	06/07/1980	23/06/1991
39	10, 330	LAR FOLEY	ST VINCENT'S	70	07/07/1957	02/06/1968
40	10, 170	SHANE RYAN	NAOMH MEARNOG	116	14/02/1999	03/08/2009
41	10, 240	BILL CASEY	NA FIANNA	75	05/11/1961	02/07/1972
42	10, 211	DES FOLEY	ST VINCENT'S	62	16/11/1958	15/06/1969
43	10, 196	JOE NORRIS	O'TOOLE'S	47	08/09/1918	24/03/1929
44	10, 183	MICK GALVIN	NA FIANNA	74	14/12/1986	15/06/1997
45	10, 162	BARRY CAHILL	ST BRIGID'S	92	10/02/2002	22/07/2012

Gerry Hargan (Ballymun Kickhams) played 111 games between 21/11/1982 and 15/11/1992, missing the ten-year milestone by six days.

TOP SCORERS
JUNIOR CHAMPIONSHIP

Pos	Total	G-Pts	Player	Club	Year	Games	Average
1	47	4-35	PEARSE WALSH	PEADAR MACKENS	1948	9	5.22
2	37	1-34	FRED HUTCHINSON	SYNGE STREET	1971	7	5.29
3	32	5-17	JOHNNY BROPHY	ST BRIGID'S	1959	5	6.40
4	30	2-24	WARREN FINNEGAN	ST BRIGID'S	2008	5	6.00
5	29	3-20	JOHNNY BROPHY	ST BRIGID'S	1954	6	4.83
6	25	2-19	TOMMY BANKS	SEAN McDERMOTTS	1939	6	4.17
		6-7	MICK NOLAN	EMERALDS	1914	5	5.00
8	24	1-21	BRIAN HEASLIP	ST ANNE'S	1994	4	6.00
		7-3	JACK CANNING	PIONEERS	1938	3	8.00
10	23	5-8	TOM NEWMAN	ST JOSEPH'S	1928	4	5.75
11	22	5-7	BRIAN McDONALD	SYNGE STREET	1960	6	3.66
12	21	0-21	KEVIN LEAHY	BALLYMUN KICKHAMS	2007	3	7.00
		3-12	BRENDAN KEENAN	STARS OF ERIN	1971	7	3.00
		3-12	ANTHONY BRIODY	ST BRIGID'S	2000	4	5.25
		6-3	KEVIN HEFFERNAN	ST VINCENT'S	1948	5	4.20
16	19	1-16	WARREN FINNEGAN	ST BRIGID'S	2008	3	6.33
		3-10	MICK CROWLEY	SKERRIES	1951	4	4.75
		6-1	JOHN NUGENT	FINGALLIANS	1951	5	3.80
19	18	1-15	PADDY DELANEY	ROUND TOWERS	1960	6	3.00
		2-12	TOM CASHIN	CLANN COLAISTE MHUIRE	1983	5	3.60
		2-12	NED McHUGH	ST PATRICK'S	1985	4	4.50
		3-9	CHRIS DUFFY	ST JOSEPH'S	1930	7	2.57
		3-9	EDDIE KENNEDY	PIONEERS	1954	5	3.60
		4-6	ANTHONY HUNSTON	BULFINS	1922	5	3.60
		4-6	CIARAN RICHARDSON	ROBERT EMMETS	1985	4	4.50
26	17	2-11	TOMMY DONNELLY	PARNELLS	1908	3	5.66
27	16	2-10	VINNIE BELL	NA FIANNA	1955	3	5.20
28	15	0-15	PADDY MURRAY	SCOIL UI CONAILL	1959	5	3.00
		0-15	GARRETH SMITH	ST OLIVER PLUNKETTS	2003	3	5.00
		3-6	PADDY BERMINGHAM	ST MARY'S	1935	5	3.00
		2-9	VINNY DALY	COLMCILLES	1971	5	3.00

TOP SCORERS
UNDER-21 CHAMPIONSHIP

Pos	Total	G-Pts	Player	Club	Year	Games	Average
1	36	2-30	CIARAN KILKENNY	CASTLEKNOCK	2012	6	6.00
2	33	3-24	CON O'CALLAGHAN	CUALA	2016	4	8.25
3	30	3-21	BARNEY ROCK	BALLYMUN KICKHAMS	1980	6	5.00
4	28	2-22	TOMAS QUINN	ST VINCENT'S	2002	6	4.66
5	27	3-18	CON O'CALLAGHAN	CUALA	2017	5	5.40
6	26	2-20	DEAN ROCK	BALLYMUN KICKHAMS	2010	5	5.20
7	24	3-15	JOHN NOONAN	ST BRIGID'S	2003	5	4.80
8	23	0-23	PADRAIG DOHERTY	NAOMH MEARNOG	1992	4	5.75
		0-23	WAYNE McCARTHY	ERIN'S ISLE	2001	4	5.75
10	22	2-16	GERRY O'LEARY	SYNGE STREET	1974	5	4.40
11	21	2-15	PAUL HUDSON	THOMAS DAVIS	2012	5	4.20
12	20	0-20	CONOR McHUGH	NA FIANNA	2015	4	5.00
		1-17	CONOR McHUGH	NA FIANNA	2014	5	4.00

Pos	Total	G-Pts	Player	Club	Year	Games	Average
	20	3-11	CIARAN KILKENNY	CASTLEKNOCK	2013	2	10.00
		3-11	AARON BYRNE	NA FIANNA	2017	5	4.00
		4-8	PHILIP RYAN	ST BRIGID'S	2012	6	3.17
17	19	1-16	PAUL CONNELLAN	RAHENY	1975	6	3.17
		2-13	DEAN ROCK	BALLYMUN KICKHAMS	2009	5	4.80
19	17	1-14	SHAY KEOGH	ST SYLVESTER'S	1993	3	5.67
20	16	0-16	CORMAC COSTELLO	WHITEHALL COLMCILLE	2014	4	4.00
		4-4	BRIAN MULLINS	ST VINCENT'S	1974	5	3.20
22	15	0-15	MICK EGAN	ROUND TOWERS	1984	5	3.00
		2-9	RAY COSGROVE	KILMACUD CROKES	1998	3	5.00
24	14	0-14	JOHN NOONAN	ST BRIGID'S	2004	4	3.50
		0-14	PADDY O'CONNOR	BALLINTEER ST JOHN'S	2009	5	2.80
26	13	0-13	BERNARD BROGAN JNR	ST OLIVER PLUNKETT'S	2005	4	3.25
		2-7	ANTO McCAUL	BALLYMUN KICKHAMS	1980	6	2.17
		3-4	CIARAN DUFF	FINGALLIANS	1980	5	2.60
29	12	0-12	NIALL CROSSAN	ERIN'S ISLE	1999	3	4.00
		1-9	LIAM OG hEINEACHAIN	KILMACUD CROKES	2002	6	2.00
		2-6	VINNY DALY	COLMCILLES	1971	2	6.00
		2-6	ROBBIE BOYLE	ERIN'S ISLE	1993	3	4.00
		2-6	DECLAN LALLY	ST BRIGID'S	2002	5	2.40
		2-6	CORMAC COSTELLO	WHITEHALL COLMCILLE	2015	2	6.00

TOP SCORERS
MINOR CHAMPIONSHIP

Pos	Total	G-Pts	Player	Club	Year	Games	Average
1	45	4-33	CON O'CALLAGHAN	CUALA	2014	6	7.50
2	41	2-35	EAMONN McLOUGHLIN	ST MARY'S	1994	5	8.20
		5-26	CORMAC COSTELLO	WHITEHALL COLMCILLE	2012	7	5.86
4	39	7-18	STEPHEN MILLS	PARNELLS	1999	7	5.57
5	36	6-18	BARNEY ROCK	BALLYMUN KICKHAMS	1978	5	7.20
6	34	3-25	DARRAGH STAPLETON	ST PATRICK'S, Palmerstown	2009	6	5.66
7	33	0-33	WAYNE McCARTHY	ERIN'S ISLE	1998	5	6.60
		0-33	CIARAN KILKENNY	CASTLEKNOCK	2011	6	5.50
		5-18	NIALL McAULIFFE	ST SYLVESTER'S	2001	7	4.71
10	32	3-21	PAUL HUDSON	THOMAS DAVIS	2009	6	5.00
11	31	8-7	DESSIE FARRELL	NA FIANNA	1988	6	5.17
12	30	3-21	CONOR McHUGH	NA FIANNA	2012	6	5.00
		5-15	ROSS McGARRY	BALLYBODEN ST. ENDA'S	2017	6	5.00
14	29	2-23	CIARAN KILKENNY	CASTLEKNOCK	2010	3	9.66
15	27	2-21	LIAM OG O hEINEACHAIN	KILMACUD CROKES	1999	7	3.86
16	26	3-17	PADDY RYAN	KILMACUD CROKES	1976	4	6.50
		5-11	NIALL GAFFNEY	CLONTARF	1978	5	5.20
18	25	2-19	DAVID O'CALLAGHAN	ST MARK'S	2001	7	3.57
		5-10	JOE GLAVIN	O'TOOLES	1933	4	6.25
		5-10	KEVIN HEFFERNAN	ST. VINCENT'S	1946	5	5.00
		5-10	VINNIE BELL	NA FIANNA	1954	5	5.00
22	23	1-20	GAVIN IVORY	RAHENY	2011	6	3.83
		3-14	JAMES DORAN	NA FIANNA	2017	6	3.83
24	22	0-22	PAUL CLARKE	WHITEHALL COLMCILLE	1984	5	4.40
		0-22	KEVIN LEAHY	BALLYMUN KICKHAMS	2003	5	4.40

Pos	Total	G-Pts	Player	Club	Year	Games	Average
26	22	6-4	JIMMY SWEENEY	CLANNA GAEL	1958	5	4.40
27	21	1-18	SEAN COEN	ST VINCENT'S	1959	5	4.20
		1-18	JOE CARR	O'DWYERS	1973	3	7.00
29	20	1-17	BARNEY ROCK	BALLYMUN KICKHAMS	1979	4	5.00
		2-14	PAT HICKEY	RAHENY	1970	4	5.00
		2-13	MARK VAUGHAN	KILMACUD CROKES	2003	7	2.86
		4-8	BRIAN McDONALD	SYNGE STREET	1959	5	4.00
		5-5	SCOTT FULHAM	ST ANNE'S	2011	6	3.33
41	19	0-19	JOE REILLY	SYNGE STREET	1968	4	4.75
		4-7	CHRIS SALLIER	THOMAS DAVIS	2014	6	3.17
36	17	0-17	KEVIN GOLDEN	ST VINCENT'S	1999	3	5.67
		3-8	NIALL CLANCY	KILMACUD CROKES	1984	5	3.40

TOP SCORERS
ALL GRADES

Pos	Total	G-Pts	Player	Club	Snr	Jnr	U-21	Minor
1	551	42-425	BARNEY ROCK	BALLYMUN KICKHAMS	30-360	2-6	3-24	7-35
2	500	30-410	JIMMY KEAVENEY	ST VINCENT'S	30-402	—	0-4	0-4
3	464	36-356	BERNARD BROGAN JNR	ST OLIVER PLUNKETT'S	36-343	—	0-13	—
4	443	65-248	KEVIN HEFFERNAN	ST VINCENT'S	52-226	7-3	—	6-19
5	371	12-335	DEAN ROCK	BALLYMUN KICKHAMS	8-275	0-14	4-40	0-6
6	360	17-309	CHARLIE REDMOND	ERIN'S ISLE	15-306	—	2-3	—
7	345	27-264	OLLIE FREANEY	ST VINCENT'S	23-242	—	—	4-22
8	324	27-243	CIARAN DUFF	FINGALLIANS	22-227	—	4-4	1-12
9	308	23-239	TOMAS QUINN	ST VINCENT'S	21-213	—	2-26	—
10	279	19-222	ALAN BROGAN	ST OLIVER PLUNKETT'S	15-194	—	3-25	1-3
11	268	30-178	DIARMUID CONNOLLY	ST VINCENT'S	28-165	—	0-3	2-10
12	211	8-187	CIARAN KILKENNY	CASTLEKNOCK	1-84	—	5-47	2-56
13	202	24-130	VINNIE MURPHY	TRINITY GAELS	21-126	—	—	3-4
14	191	21-128	DESSIE FARRELL	NA FIANNA	12-117	—	1-4	8-7
15	180	41-57	JOHNNY JOYCE	ST VINCENT'S	39-55	—	—	2-2
16	163	20-103	KEVIN McMANAMON	ST. JUDE'S	20-103	—	—	—
16	162	9-135	CIARAN WHELAN	RAHENY	9-131	0-1	0-2	0-1
18	155	15-110	ANTON O'TOOLE	SYNGE STREET	13-101	1-5	1-4	—
19	154	23-85	BOBBY DOYLE	ST VINCENT'S	23-85	—	—	—
20	147	16-99	JASON SHERLOCK	NA FIANNA	14-91	—	0-3	2-5
		21-86	BRIAN McDONALD	SYNGE STREET	11-69	5-7	—	5-10
22	141	12-105	CON O'CALLAGHAN	CUALA	2-21	—	6-43	4-41
23	138	11-105	CORMAC COSTELLO	WHITEHALL COLMCILLE	3-49	—	2-22	6-34
24	136	11-103	RAY COSGROVE	KILMACUD CROKES	9-87	—	2-14	0-2
		19-79	PADDY McDONNELL	O'TOOLES	19-77	0-2	—	—
26	135	11-102	MICKEY WHELAN	CLANNA GAEL	11-102	—	—	—
		25-60	DESSIE FERGUSON	ST VINCENT'S	20-58	—	—	5-2
28	134	20-74	TONY HANAHOE	ST VINCENT'S	20-74	—	—	—
29	130	6-112	PAUL CLARKE	WHITEHALL COLMCILLE	6-90	—	—	0-22
30	125	4-113	TOMMY BANKS	SEAN McDERMOTTS	2-94	2-19	—	—
31	118	24-46	JOE McNALLY	ST ANNE'S	24-45	—	—	0-1
32	117	15-72	DAVID HICKEY	RAHENY	15-66	—	0-3	0-3
		24-45	BRIAN MULLINS	ST VINCENT'S	17-35	—	7-9	0-1

Figures do not include 0-4 for Pearse Walsh and 1-0 for Kevin Heffernan in an abandonded All-Ireland 'Home' Final against Armagh that was subsequently replayed.

LONGEST INTER-COUNTY CAREERS
ALL GRADES

Pos	Yrs-Days	Player	Club	Games	First	Last
1	22, 79	BARNEY ROCK	BALLYMUN KICKHAMS	116	24/04/1978	12/07/2000
2	18, 320	JOHNNY McDONNELL	O'TOOLE'S	110	13/07/1919	29/05/1938
3	18, 131	PADDY McDONNELL	O'TOOLE'S	72	05/07/1914	13/11/1932
4	18, 31	STEPHEN CLUXTON	PARNELLS	187	07/08/1999	17/09/2017
5	17, 360	JOHN O'LEARY	O'DWYER'S	211	20/06/1979	15/06/1997
6	17, 91	DESSIE FARRELL	NA FIANNA	114	28/05/1988	27/08/2005
7	17, 21	MICK DEEGAN	ERIN'S ISLE	107	31/05/1981	21/06/1998
8	16, 315	MICK KENNEDY	ST MARGARET'S	145	08/06/1975	19/04/1992
9	16, 197	DES FERGUSON	ST VINCENT'S	106	09/05/1948	22/11/1964
10	16, 113	TONY HANAHOE	ST VINCENT'S	138	16/06/1963	07/10/1979
11	16, 76	KEVIN HEFFERNAN	ST VINCENT'S	130	19/05/1946	05/08/1962
12	16, 43	JIMMY KEAVENEY	ST VINCENT'S	110	16/06/1963	29/07/1979
13	16, 9	DAVID FORAN	THOMAS DAVIS	78	29/05/1977	07/06/1993
14	15, 315	ALAN BROGAN	ST OLIVER PLUNKETT'S	140	01/08/1999	20/09/2015
15	15, 290	EAMONN HEERY	ST VINCENT'S	112	29/05/1982	15/03/1998
16	15, 143	PADDY CULLEN	SCOIL UI CONAILL	121	26/04/1964	16/09/1979
17	15, 95	JASON SHERLOCK	NA FIANNA	114	30/04/1994	03/08/2009
		CIARAN WHELAN	RAHENY	144	30/04/1994	03/08/2009
19	15, 79	PAUL CURRAN	THOMAS DAVIS	138	30/05/1987	17/08/2002
20	14, 73	VINNIE MURPHY	TRINITY GAELS	111	30/05/1987	11/08/2001

* Alan Brogan (St Oliver Plunketts) made a record 22 appearances at underage level.

* Jason Sherlock (Na Fianna) and Ciaran Whelan (Raheny), coincidentally, began and finished their careers in the same matches; both started with a provincial minor first round win over Kilkenny and finished with an All-Ireland senior quarter-final loss to Kerry, when Sherlock was substituted after a quarter of an hour and Whelan was brought on nine minutes later.

TOP SCORES IN A SINGLE GAME
ALL GRADES

Pos	Total	G-Pts	Player	Club	Opposition	Comp	Date
1	18	5-3	JOHNNY JOYCE	ST VINCENT'S	LONGFORD	CHAMP	29/05/1960
2	16	3-7	JOHN McCARTHY	GARDA	CARLOW	CHAMP	18/06/1978
		2-10	EAMONN McLOUGHLIN	ST MARY'S	KILDARE	MINOR	14/05/1994
		2-10	CIARAN KILKENNY	CASTLEKNOCK	CARLOW	U-21	19/02/2013
		5-1	NIALL McAULIFFE	ST SYLVESTER'S	KILKENNY	MINOR	05/05/2001
6	15	3-6	JOE GLAVIN	O'TOOLE'S	WESTMEATH	MINOR	28/05/1933
7	14	1-11	JIMMY KEAVENEY	ST VINCENT'S	LOUTH	CHAMP	06/07/1975
		2-8	BERNARD BROGAN	ST OLIVER PLUNKETT'S	WESTMEATH	CHAMP	28/06/2009
9	13	1-10	DARRAGH STAPLETON	ST PATRICK'S	DOWN	MINOR	15/08/2009
		1-10	BERNARD BROGAN	ST OLIVER PLUNKETT'S	MAYO	LEAGUE	02/03/2013
		1-10	DEAN ROCK	BALLYMUN KICKHAMS	LAOIS	CHAMP	04/06/2016
		2-7	ANTHONY BRIODY	ST BRIGID'S	CARLOW	JUNIOR	18/05/2000
		2-7	PAUL HUDSON	THOMAS DAVIS	OFFALY	MINOR	27/06/2009
		3-4	JIMMY KEAVENEY	ST VINCENT'S	LONGFORD	CHAMP	27/06/1976
		3-4	CORMAC COSTELLO	WHITEHALL COLMCILLE	MEATH	MINOR	22/07/2012
16	12	0-12	DEAN ROCK	BALLYMUN KICKHAMS	KERRY	CHAMP	28/08/2016
		1-9	BARNEY ROCK	BALLYMUN KICKHAMS	LONGFORD	CHAMP	06/06/1982

Pos	Total	G-Pts	Player	Club	Opposition	Comp	Date
	12	2-6	JIMMY KEAVENEY	ST VINCENT'S	ARMAGH	CHAMP	25/09/1977
		2-6	CON O'CALLAGHAN	CUALA	OFFALY	MINOR	10/07/2014
		3-3	MICK REDMOND	CUCHULAINS	WICKLOW	MINOR	30/04/1939
		3-3	JOHN TIMMONS	ST MARY'S	LOUTH	LEAGUE	07/03/1965
		3-3	DIARMUID CONNOLLY	ST VINCENT'S	MAYO	LEAGUE	20/03/2011
		3-3	DIARMUID CONNOLLY	ST VINCENT'S	ARMAGH	LEAGUE	11/03/2012
		4-0	MICK QUIGLEY	CIVIL SERVICE	MEATH	LEAGUE	22/03/1940
		4-0	JOHNNY JOYCE	ST VINCENT'S	GALWAY	LEAGUE	04/03/1962
		4-0	JOHN McCARTHY	GARDA	KILKENNY	LEAGUE	09/12/1973
		4-0	JOE McNALLY	ST ANNE'S	DERRY	LEAGUE	22/10/1989
27	11	0-11	BARNEY ROCK	BALLYMUN KICKHAMS	WESTMEATH	CHAMP	07/06/1987
		0-11	CIARAN KILKENNY	CASTLEKNOCK	KILDARE	MINOR	29/06/2011
		1-8	PADDY DELANEY	O'TOOLE'S	MEATH	LEAGUE	16/03/1969
		1-8	JIMMY KEAVENEY	ST VINCENT'S	MEATH	CHAMP	28/07/1974
		1-8	CIARAN KILKENNY	CASTLEKNOCK	LOUTH	MINOR	24/04/2010
		1-8	DEAN ROCK	BALLYMUN KICKHAMS	MONAGHAN	CHAMP	05/08/2017
		2-5	KEVIN HEFFERNAN	ST VINCENT'S	WESTMEATH	LEAGUE	29/10/1950
		2-5	BERNARD BROGAN	ST OLIVER PLUNKETT'S	LOUTH	CHAMP	03/06/2012
		2-5	CON O'CALLAGHAN	CUALA	LONGFORD	U-21	22/03/2017
		3-2	JIMMY SWEENEY	CLANNA GAEL	MEATH	MINOR	01/06/1958
		3-2	BARNEY ROCK	BALLYMUN KICKHAMS	WESTMEATH	MINOR	24/06/1978
38	10	0-10	JIMMY KEAVENEY	ST VINCENT'S	WEXFORD	CHAMP	08/06/1975
		0-10	TOMAS QUINN	ST VINCENT'S	WEXFORD	CHAMP	19/06/2005
		0-10	CONOR McHUGH	NA FIANNA	CARLOW	MINOR	14/04/2012
		0-10	DEAN ROCK	BALLYMUN KICKHAMS	CORK	LEAGUE	26/04/2015
		0-10	DEAN ROCK	BALLYMUN KICKHAMS	MEATH	CHAMP	26/06/2016
		1-7	PEARSE WALSH	PEADAR MACKENS	KILDARE	JUNIOR	04/07/1948
		1-7	JIMMY KEAVENEY	ST VINCENT'S	OFFALY	CHAMP	09/07/1978
		1-7	JIMMY KEAVENEY	ST VINCENT'S	WEXFORD	LEAGUE	05/03/1967
		1-7	BARNEY ROCK	BALLYMUN KICKHAMS	MAYO	CHAMP	18/08/1985
		1-7	TOMAS QUINN	ST VINCENT'S	WICKLOW	U-21	21/04/2002
		1-7	TOMAS QUINN	ST VINCENT'S	TYRONE	CHAMP	13/08/2005
		1-7	WARREN FINNEGAN	ST BRIGID'S	MEATH	JUNIOR	29/06/2008
		1-7	CONAL KEANEY	BALLYBODEN ST ENDA'S	WESTMEATH	LEAGUE	12/04/2009
		1-7	CIARAN KILKENNY	CASTLEKNOCK	KILDARE	MINOR	17/04/2010
		1-7	HENRY DAWSON	SKERRIES HARPS	KILDARE	MINOR	22/05/2010
		1-7	BERNARD BROGAN	ST OLIVER PLUNKETT'S	CORK	CHAMP	27/08/2010
		1-7	TOMAS QUINN	ST VINCENT'S	MAYO	LEAGUE	20/03/2011
		1-7	BERNARD BROGAN	ST OLIVER PLUNKETT'S	MEATH	CHAMP	22/07/2012
		1-7	CON O'CALLAGHAN	CUALA	LONGFORD	MINOR	19/04/2014
		1-7	CON O'CALLAGHAN	CUALA	MEATH	U-21	01/03/2016
		1-7	CON O'CALLAGHAN	CUALA	KILDARE	U-21	02/04/2016
		2-4	JOHN JOE HOEY	ISLES OF THE SEA	WESTMEATH	CHAMP	17/08/1890
		2-4	KEVIN HEFFERNAN	ST VINCENT'S	LOUTH	LEAGUE	28/03/1954
		2-4	JOHNNY BROPHY	ST BRIGID'S	WICKLOW	JUNIOR	04/04/1954
		2-4	KEVIN HEFFERNAN	ST VINCENT'S	LAOIS	LEAGUE	05/03/1961
		2-4	MICKEY WHELAN	CLANNA GAEL	WESTMEATH	CHAMP	11/06/1972
		2-4	BARNEY ROCK	BALLYMUN KICKHAMS	WEXFORD	CHAMP	10/06/1984
		2-4	BARNEY ROCK	BALLYMUN KICKHAMS	WEXFORD	CHAMP	26/06/1985
		2-4	ALAN BROGAN	ST OLIVER PLUNKETT'S	LONDON	CHAMP	12/06/2004
		3-1	JACK CANNING	PIONEERS	CARLOW	JUNIOR	15/05/1938

Pos	Total	G-Pts	Player	Club	Opposition	Comp	Date
	10	3-1	SOLOMON LAWLOR	GERALDINES	LOUTH	CHAMP	08/09/1918
		3-1	WILLIE DOWLING	ROUND TOWERS	WICKLOW	JUNIOR	15/05/1927
		3-1	PADDY McDONNELL	O'TOOLE'S	WEXFORD	CHAMP	05/07/1931
		3-1	HARRY O'BRIEN	ST VINCENT'S	LONGFORD	MINOR	08/05/1949
		3-1	JOHNNY JOYCE	ST VINCENT'S	GALWAY	LEAGUE	01/03/1959
		3-1	EAMONN HAYDEN	GOOD COUNSEL	LONGFORD	MINOR	26/06/1966
		3-1	SCOTT FULHAM	ST ANNE'S	WESTMEATH	MINOR	16/04/2011

TOP SCORERS
LEINSTER AND ALL-IRELAND CLUB CHAMPIONSHIPS

Pos	Total	G-Pts	Player	Club	Season	Games	Average
1	51	8-27	JIMMY KEAVENEY	ST VINCENT'S	1975/76	6	8.50
2	39	2-33	TOMAS QUINN	ST VINCENT'S	2013/14	5	7.80
3	38	2-32	MARK VAUGHAN	KILMACUD CROKES	2008/09	6	6.17
4	33	1-30	MARK O'HANLON	PARNELLS	1987/88	7	4.71
5	32	2-26	JIMMY KEAVENEY	ST VINCENT'S	1973/73	6	5.17
6	31	3-22	TOMAS QUINN	ST VINCENTS	2007/08	6	5.17
7	29	1-26	DEAN ROCK	BALLYMUN KICKHAMS	2012/13	5	5.80
8	26	2-20	ANDREW KERIN	BALLYBODEN ST ENDA'S	2015/16	5	5.20
9	25	0-25	JACKIE WALSH	U.C.D.	1973/74	7	3.57
		2-19	VINNY CARNEY	THOMAS DAVIS	1991/92	5	5.00
		5-10	TOMAS QUINN	ST VINCENT'S	2014/15	4	6.25
12	24	2-18	JACKIE WALSH	U.C.D.	1974/75	4	6.00
		2-18	PAUL McLOUGHLIN	ST VINCENT'S	1984/85	7	3.43
		6-6	DINNY O'CONNOR	U.C.D.	1973/74	5	4.80
15	23	2-17	PADDY ANDREWS	ST BRIGID'S	2011/12	4	5.75
		3-14	ENDA CONDRON	U.C.D.	1973/74	7	3.29
17	22	3-13	NIALL CLANCY	ERIN'S ISLE	1997/98	6	3.67
18	21	0-21	MARK O'HANLON	PARNELLS	1988/89	7	3.00
		0-21	BRIAN KAVANAGH	KILMACUD CROKES	2010/11	4	5.25
		2-15	RAY COSGROVE	KILMACUD CROKES	2005/06	5	4.20
21	20	0-20	SHAY KEOGH	ST SYLVESTER'S	1996/97	3	6.67
		3-11	BOBBY DOYLE	ST VINCENT'S	1975/76	6	3.67
23	19	2-13	RAY COSGROVE	KILMACUD CROKES	1998/99	6	3.17
24	18	0-18	MICK GALVIN	NA FIANNA	1999/00	5	3.60
		3-9	JASON SHERLOCK	NA FIANNA	2001/02	5	3.60
		5-3	BRENDAN BRADY	PARNELLS	1987/88	7	2.57
27	17	0-17	MICK O'KEEFFE	KILMACUD CROKES	1998/89	6	2.83
		2-11	ROBBIE BOYLE	ERIN'S ISLE	1997/98	6	2.83
29	16	0-16	CONAL KEANEY	BALLYBODEN ST ENDA'S	2015/16	5	3.20
		1-13	JIMMY KEAVENEY	ST VINCENT'S	1977/78	4	4.00
		1-13	MARK VAUGHAN	KILMACUD CROKES	2005/06	4	4.00
		1-13	DIARMUID CONNOLLY	ST VINCENT'S	2007/08	6	2.67

Jimmy Keaveney, in 18 games in five campaigns in the Leinster and All-Ireland Club Championships, scored a total of 11-74 (107), an average of 5.94. He failed to score just once, in a provincial semi-final win over St Joseph's (Laois) at Geraldine Park in Athy in November 1977.

ALL-IRELAND SENIOR MEDAL WINNERS
Includes those listed as substitutes for finals even if not used

FIVE Tommy Errity (Geraldines & Round Towers) 1892, 1894, 1898, 1999, 1902; Dave Brady (Dolphins & Bray Emmets) 1899, 1901, 1902, 1906, 1907; Jack Grace (Kickhams) 1901, 1902, 1906, 1907, 1908. Stephen Cluxton (Parnells) 2011, 2013, 2015, 2016, 2017; Philly McMahon (Ballymun Kickhams) 2011, 2013, 2015, 2016, 2017; James McCarthy (Ballymun Kickhams) 2011, 2013, 2015, 2016, 2017; Cian O'Sullivan (Kilmacud Crokes) 2011, 2013, 2015, 2016, 2017; Michael Darragh Macauley (Ballyboden St Enda's) 2011, 2013, 2015, 2016 2017; Paul Flynn (Fingallians) 2011, 2013, 2015, 2016, 2017; Kevin McManamon (St Jude's) 2011, 2013, 2015, 2016, 2017; Diarmuid Connolly (St Vincent's) 2011, 2013, 2015, 2016, 2017; Bernard Brogan Jnr (St Oliver Plunkett's) 2011, 2013, 2015, 2016, 2017; Denis Bastick (Templeogue Synge Street) 2011, 2013, 2015, 2016, 2017; Michael Fitzsimons (Cuala) 2011, 2013, 2015, 2016, 2017; Eoghan O'Gara (Templeogue Synge Street) 2011, 2013, 2015, 2016, 2017.

FOUR Dick Curtis (Young Ireland) 1891, 1892, 1894, 1897.
Luke O'Kelly (Young Ireland, Kickhams & Isle of the Sea) 1892, 1894, 1897, 1901.
Jim Brennan (Keatings) 1902, 1906, 1907, 1908.
Brian Mullins (St Vincents) 1974, 1976, 1977, 1983; Anton O'Toole (Sunge Street) 1974, 1976, 1977, 1983.
Dean Rock (Ballymun Kickhams) 2013, 2015, 2016, 2017; Ciaran Kilkenny (Castleknock) 2013, 2015, 2016, 2017; Darren Daly (Fingal Ravens) 2013, 2015, 2016, 2017; Jonny Cooper (Na Fianna) 2013, 2015, 2016, 2017; Cormac Costello (Whitehall Colmcille) 2013, 2015, 2016, 2017; Paddy Andrews (St Brigid's) 2013, 2015, 2016, 2017.

THREE George Charlemont (Young Ireland) 1891, 1892, 1894; John Kennedy (Young Ireland) 1891, 1892, 1894; Pat Heslin (Young Ireland) 1891, 1892, 1894; Johnny Geraghty (Young Ireland) 1891, 1892, 1894; George Roche (Young Ireland) 1891, 1892, 1894; Sean Hughes (Young Ireland) 1891, 1892, 1894; Paddy Kelly (Young Ireland) 1891, 1892, 1894.
Paddy Redmond (Dunleary Independents & Kickhams) 1897, 1898, 1901.
John Joe Keane (Geraldines) 1898, 1899, 1902; Bill Sherry (Geraldines) 1898, 1901, 1902.
Jack Dempsey (Bray Emmets) 1902, 1906, 1907; Mick Madigan (Kickhams) 1902, 1906, 1907.
Hugh Hilliard (Kickhams) 1906, 1907, 1908; Tommy Walsh (Kickhams) 1906, 1907, 1908; Dave Kelleher (Geraldines) 1906, 1907, 1908.
Paddy Kirwan (Keatings) 1921, 1922, 1923; Jack O'Reilly (O'Tooles) 1921, 1922, 1923; John Synnott (O'Tooles) 1921, 1922, 1923; Paddy Carey (O'Tooles) 1921, 1922, 1923; Joe Norris (O'Tooles) 1921, 1922, 1923; Frank Burke (University College) 1921, 1922, 1923; Paddy McDonnell (O'Tooles) 1921, 1922, 1923.
Paddy Cullen (Scoil Ui Chonaill) 1974, 1976, 1977; Gay O'Driscoll (St Vincent's) 1974, 1976, 1977; Sean Doherty (Ballyboden St Enda's) 1974, 1976, 1977; Robbie Kelleher (Scoil Ui Chonaill) 1974, 1976, 1977; Bobby Doyle (St Vincent's) 1974, 1976, 1977; David Hickey (Raheny) 1974, 1976, 1977; Tony Hanahoe (St Vincent's) 1974, 1976, 1977; Jimmy Keaveney (St Vincent's) 1974, 1976, 1977; John McCarthy (Garda) 1974, 1976, 1977; Paddy Reilly (St Margarets) 1974, 1976, 1977; Jim Brogan (St Oliver Plunketts) 1974, 1976, 1977; Fran Ryder (St Vincents) 1974, 1976, 1977; Pat O'Neill (UCD) 1974, 1976, 1977; Pat Gogarty (Raheny) 1974, 1976, 1977; Brendan Pocock (St Vincent's) 1974, 1976, 1977.
Tommy Drumm (Whitehall Colmcille) 1976, 1977, 1983.
Rory O'Carroll (Kilmacud Crokes) 2011, 2013, 2015.
Michael Savage (St Vincent's) 2011, 2015, 2016.
Jack McCaffrey (Clontarf) 2013, 2015, 2017; Paul Mannion (Kilmacud Crokes) 2013, 2016, 2017; John Small (Ballymun Kickhams) 2015, 2016, 2017; Brian Fenton (Raheny) 2015, 2016, 2017; Eric Lowndes (St Peregrine's) 2015, 2016, 2017; Paul Mannion (Kilmacud Crokes) 2015, 2016, 2017; David Byrne (Naomh Olaf) 2015, 2016, 2017.

TWO Jim Roche (Young Ireland) 1891, 1892; John Silke (Young Ireland) 1891, 1892; Sean Flood (Young Ireland) 1891, 1892; Dick Flood (Young Ireland) 1891, 1892.

Myles Condon (Young Ireland) 1891, 1894; Tom Lyons (Young Ireland) 1891, 1894.

Mick Byrne (Young Ireland) 1892, 1894; Frank O'Malley (Young Ireland) 1892, 1894.

Jack O'Brien (Kickhams) 1897, 1901.

Matt Rea (Geraldines) 1898, 1899; Dan O'Callaghan (Geraldines) 1898, 1899; Tommy Norton (Geraldines) 1898, 1899; Jim Heslin (Geraldines) 1898, 1899; John Ryan (Geraldines) 1898, 1899; Peter McCann (Geraldines) 1898, 1999; John Lane (Geraldines) 1898, 1899; Pat Fitzsimmons (Geraldines) 1898, 1899; Tom 'Hoey' Redmond (Geraldines) 1898, 1899; Joe Ledwidge (Geraldines) 1898, 1899; Paddy Levey (Geraldines) 1898, 1899.

Jack Fahy (Kickhams) 1901, 1902; Pat Daly (Parnells) 1901, 1902.

Mick Curry (Kickhams) 1906, 1907; Mick Barry (Kickhams) 1906, 1907; Pat O'Callaghan (Kickhams) 1906, 1907; Paddy Casey (Kickhams) 1906, 1907; Tom Quane (Kickhams) 1906, 1907; Pierce Grace (Kickhams) 1906, 1907; Mick Kelly (St James's Gate) 1906, 1907.

Jack Lynch (Kickhams) 1907, 1908; Dan Kavanagh (Kickhams) 1907, 1908.

Paddy Fallon (Geraldines) 1908, 1921.

Eddie Carroll (St Mary's) 1921, 1922; Toddy Pierce (University College) 1921, 1922; Charlie McDonald (St Mary's) 1921, 1922; Bill Donovan (Kickhams) 1921, 1922.

Johnny Murphy (Keatings) 1921, 1923.

Johnny McDonnell (O'Tooles) 1922, 1923; Joe Synnott (O'Tooles) 1922, 1923; Bill Robbins (O'Tooles) 1922, 1923; Bill Rooney (O'Tooles) 1922, 1923; Mick O'Brien (O'Tooles) 1922, 1923.

Lar Foley (St Vincent's) 1958, 1963; John Timmons (St Mary's) 1958, 1963; Des Ferguson (St Vincent's) 1958, 1963; Paddy Downey (St Brigid's) 1958, 1963; Kevin Heffernan (St Vincent's) 1958, 1963.

Alan Larkin (Raheny) 1974, 1976; Leslie Deegan (St Vincent's) 1974, 1976.

Bernard Brogan (St Oliver Plunkett's) 1976, 1977; Kevin Moran (Good Counsel) 1976, 1977.

John O'Leary (O'Dwyers) 1983, 1995; Charlie Redmond (Erin's Isle) 1983, 1995.

Bryan Cullen (Skerries) 2011, 2013; Kevin Nolan (Kilmacud Crokes) 2011, 2013; Ger Brennan (St Vincent's) 2011, 2013; Alan Brogan (St Oliver Plunkett's) 2011, 2015; Tomas Brady (Na Fianna) 2015, 2016; Shane Carthy (St Vincent's) 2013, 2017; Con O'Callaghan (Cuala) 2016, 2017; Conor McHugh (Na Fianna) 2016, 2017. .

ONE John Scully (Young Ireland) 1891; Jack Mahony (Young Ireland) 1891; A O'Hagan (Young Ireland) 1891; P O'Hagan (Young Ireland) 1891 (Young Ireland) 1891; Tommy Murphy (Young Ireland) 1891; Paddy Halpin (Young Ireland) 1891; Mick Cooney (Young Ireland) 1891.

Tom Doran (Young Ireland) 1892.

Tom O'Mahony (Young Ireland) 1894; Paddy O'Toole (Young Ireland) 1894; Jack Kirwan (Young Ireland) 1894.

Dick Scanlon (Kickhams) 1897; PJ Walsh (Kickhams) 1897; Charlie Gannon (Kickhams) 1897; Robert O'Brien (Kickhams) 1897; Ted Downey (Kickhams) 1897; Vincent Skelly (Kickhams) 1897; Bill Guiry (Kickhams) 1897; Matt Chambers (Kickhams) 1897; Jim Matthews (Kickhams) 1897; Dan O'Donnell (Kickhams) 1897; Paddy O'Donogue (Kickhams) 1897; Willie Calnan (Kickhams) 1897; Johnny Flynn (Kickhams) 1897; Jack Delaney (Kickhams) 1897.

Christy Sargent (Kickhams) 1898.

Gerry Brady (Geraldines) 1899; D Smith (Geraldines) 1899; Johnny Farrelly (Geraldines) 1899.

Bill Connor (Isle of the Sea) 1901; Jack Darcy (Isle of the Sea) 1901; Tommy Doyle (Isle of the Sea) 1901; Michael Whelan (Isle of the Sea) 1901; Tommy Lawless (Isle of the Sea) 1901; Mick O'Brien (Isle of the Sea) 1901; Val Harris (Isle of the Sea) 1901; Dan Holland (Isle of the Sea) 1901; Jack McCullagh (Dolphins) 1901; Peter McCann (Ben Eadair) 1901.

Steve Mulvey (Bray Emmets) 1902; Willie Casey (Bray Emmets) 1902; Eddie Brady (Bray Emmets) 1902; Amby Wall (Bray Emmets) 1902; Jim McCann (Isle of the Sea) 1902; P Weymes (Keatings) 1902; PD Breen (Keatings) 1902, Paddy Brady (Parnells) 1902.

Mick Keane (Kickhams) 1906; Larry Sheehan (Kickhams) 1906; Paddy Cox (Kickhams) 1906; Mick O'Dwyer (Kickhams) 1906; Joe English (Kickhams) 1906; Mick Finbar (Kickhams) 1906.

Mick Keane (Kickhams) 1907; Larry Sheehan (Kickhams) 1907; Ed Herlihy (Keatings) 1907.

Paddy Daly (Geraldines) 1908; Tom McAuley (Geraldines) 1908; Paddy Whelan (Geraldines) 1908; Maurice Collins (Geraldines) 1908; Mick Power (Geraldines) 1908; Jack Shouldice (Geraldines) 1908; Dick Flood (Geraldines) 1908; Willie Halliden (Geraldines) 1908; Paddy Sheehan (Geraldines) 1908; Tom Healy (Keatings) 1908; Fred Cooney (Keatings) 1908; James Brennan (McBride Mitchels) 1908.

Alec Balmain (St Marys) 1921; Jim O'Grady (St Marys) 1921; Willie Fitzsimons (St Marys) 1921; Arthur Dixon (St Marys) 1921; Mick Bradshaw (St Marys) 1921; Anthony Healy (St Marys) 1921.

Tony Gibbons (Kickhams) 1922; Christy Lawless (Kickhams) 1922; Mick Holland (Kickhams) 1922; Tom Fitzgerald (O'Tooles) 1922.

Joe Stynes (McCrackens) 1923; Martin Shanahan (St Marys) 1923; Jack Sherlock (Garda) 1923; Paddy O'Beirne (Kickhams) 1923; Larry Stanley (Garda) 1923.

Charlie Kelly (Peadar Mackens) 1942; Bobby Beggs (Sean McDermotts) 1942; Paddy Kennedy (Peadar Mackens) 1942; Caleb Crone (Aer Corps) 1942; Paddy Henry (Geraldines) 1942; Peter O'Reilly (St Mary's) 1942; Brendan Quinn (Parnells) 1942; Joe Fitzgerald (Geraldines) 1942; Mick Falvey (Civil Service) 1942; Jimmy Joy (Geraldines) 1942; Paddy Bermingham (St Marys) 1942; Gerry Fitzgerald (St Marys) 1942; Matt Fletcher (Peadar Mackens) 1942; Pierce O'Connor (St Marys) 1942; Tommy Banks (Sean McDermotts) 1942; Frank Ryan (Clanna Gael) 1942; Sean Healy (Clanna Gael) 1942; Jack Murphy (Civil Service) 1942; Sean Moriarty (Civil Service) 1942; Colm Boland (Geraldines) 1942; Joe Delaney (Peadar Mackens) 1942; Mickey Richardson (Peadar Mackens) 1942.

Paddy O'Flaherty (Ben Eadair) 1958; Marcus Wilson (St Vincent's) 1958; Joe Timmons (St Mary's) 1958; Cathal O'Leary (St Vincent's) 1958; Jim Crowley (St Vincent's) 1958; Johnny Boyle (Clanna Gael) 1958; Sean Murray (Skerries) 1958; Padraig Haughey (St Vincent's) 1958; Ollie Freaney (St Vincent's) 1958; Paddy Farnan (St Vincent's) 1958; Johnny Joyce (St Vincent's) 1958; Maurice Whelan (St Vincent's) 1958; Joe Brennan (Na Fianna) 1958; Tony Gillan (Clanna Gael) 1958; Brendan Morris (Na Fianna) 1958; Christy Leaney (St Vincent's) 1958; Diarmuid McCann (Erin's Isle) 1958.

Pascal Flynn (St Mary's) 1963; Leo Hickey (Ballyboughal) 1963; Bill Casey (Na Fianna) 1963; Des McKane (St Vincent's) 1963; Paddy Holden (Clanna Gael) 1963; Mick Kissane (St Vincent's) 1963; Des Foley (St Vincent's) 1963; Brian McDonald (Synge Street) 1963; Mickey Whelan (Clanna Gael) 1963; Gerry Davey (Clanna Gael) 1963; Simon Behan (St Vincent's) 1963; Noel Fox (St Vincent's) 1963; Frank McPhillips (Inchicore Hibernians) 1963; Christy Kane (Clanna Gael) 1963; Aidan Donnelly (Clanna Gael) 1963; Eamon Breslin (Ballyfermot) 1963; Pat Synnott (O'Tooles) 1963; Sean Lee (St Anne's) 1963; Sean Coen (St Vincent's) 1963.

George Wilson (O'Dwyers) 1974; Stephen Rooney (O'Dwyers) 1974; Dave Billlngs (St Vincent's) 1974; Kevin Synnott (Lucan Sarsfields) 1974; Bernard Donovan (Crumlin) 1974.

Liam Egan (Scoil Ui Conaill) 1977; Norman Bernard (St Vincent's) 1977; Michael Hickey (Raheny) 1977; Dermot Maher (Kilmacud Crokes) 1977.

Mick Holden (Cuala) 1983; Gerry Hargan (Ballymun Kickhams) 1983; Ray Hazley (St Vincent's) 1983; Pat Canavan (St Vincent's) 1983; PJ Buckley (Erin's Isle) 1983; Jim Ronayne (Clontarf) 1983; Barney Rock (Ballymun Kickhams) 1983; Tommy Conroy (St Vincent's) 1983; Ciaran Duff (Fingallians) 1983; John Caffrey (Na Fianna) 1983; Joe McNally (St Anne's) 1983; John Kearns (Ballymun Kickhams) 1983; Ciaran Maher (Ballyboden St Endas) 1983; Mick Kennedy (St Margaret's) 1983; Anto McCaul (Ballymun Kickhams) 1983; Brian Jordan (St Vincent's) 1983; Frank McGrath (Scoil Ui Chonaill) 1983; Vincent Conroy (St Vincent's) 1983; Willie Hughes (St Oliver Plunkett's) 1983; Paddy Ryan (Kilmacud Crokes) 1983; Richie Crean (Lucan Sarsfields) 1983; Declan McGrath (Clanna Gael) 1983.

Paddy Moran (Whitehall Colmcille) 1995; Ciaran Walsh (St Anne's) 1995; Keith Galvin (St Sylvester's) 1995; Paul Curran (Thomas Davis) 1995; Keith Barr (Erin's Isle) 1995; Mick Deegan (Erin's Isle) 1995; Paul Bealin (Ballyboden St Enda's) 1995; Brian Stynes (Ballyboden St Enda's) 1995; Jim Gavin (Round Towers) 1995; Dessie Farrell (Na Fianna) 1995; Paul Clarke (Whitehall Colmcille) 1995; Mick Galvin (Na Fianna) 1995; Jason Sherlock (Na Fianna) 1995; Pat Gilroy (St Vincent's) 1995; Robbie Boyle (Erin's Isle) 1995; Vinny Murphy (Trinity Gaels) 1995; David Byrne (Ballymun Kickhams) 1995; Brian Barnes (St Sylvester's) 1995; John O'Callaghan (Kilmacud Crokes) 1995; Enda Sheehy (St Jude's) 1995; Sean Cahill (St Patrick's, Palmerstown) 1995; Shay Keogh (St Sylvester's) 1995.

Barry Cahill (St Brigid's) 2011; Eamonn Fennell (St Vincent's) 2011; Paul Conlon (St Vincent's) 2011; Paul Casey (Lucan Sarsfields) 2011; David Henry (Raheny) 2011; Tomas Quinn (St Vincent's) 2011; Sean Murray (St

Brigid's) 2011; Ross McConnell (St Oliver Plunkett's) 2011; Craig Dias (Kilmacud Crokes) 2011; Declan Lally (St Brigid's) 2011; Paul Brogan (St Oliver Plunkett's) 2011; Paul Griffin (Kilmacud Crokes) 2011.
Shane Supple (St Brigid's) 2013; Shane Carthy (Naomh Mearnog) 2013; Kevin O'Brien (Naomh Mearnog) 2013. Brian Howard (Raheny) 2017.

ALL-IRELAND MEDALLISTS IN DIFFERENT GRADES

SIX Jonny Cooper (Na Fianna) Junior 2008, Under-21 2010, Senior 2013, 2015, 2016, 2017; Denis Bastick (Templeogue Synge Street) Junior 2008, Senior 2011, 2013, 2015, 2016, 2017; Michael Fitzsimons (Cuala) Junior 2008, Senior 2011, 2013, 2015, 2016, 2017; Eoghan O'Gara (Templeogue Synge Street) Junior 2008, Senior 2011, 2013, 2015, 2016, 2017; James McCarthy (Ballymun Kickhams) Under-21 2010, Senior 2011, 2013, 2015, 2016, 2017; Cormac Costello (Whitehall Colmcille) Minor 2012, Under-21 2014, Senior 2013, 2015, 2016, 2017.

FIVE Frank Burke (University College) Junior 1914, 1916, Senior 1921, 1922, 1923; Dean Rock (Ballymun Kickhams) Under-21 2010, Senior 2013, 2015, 2016, 2017; Jack McCaffrey (Clontarf) Under-21 2012, Senior 2014, 2013, 2015, 2017; Paul Mannion (Kilmacud Crokes) Under-21 2012, 2014, Senior 2013, 2016, 2017; Eric Lowndes (St Peregrine's) Minor 2012, Under-21 2014, Senior 2015, 2016, 2017; Ciaran Kilkenny (Castleknock) Under-21 2012, Senior 2013, 2015, 2016, 2017; Cormac Costello (Whitehall Colmcille) Under-21 2014, Senior 2013, 2015, 2016, 2017; John Small (Ballymun Kickhams) Under-21 2012, 2014, Senior 2015, 2016, 2017.

FOUR Paddy Carey (O'Tooles) Junior 1914, Senior 1921, 1922, 1923; Jack O'Reilly (O'Tooles) Junior 1916, Senior 1921, 1922, 1923; Lar Foley (St Vincent's) Minor 1955, 1956, Senior 1958, 1963; Brian McDonald (Synge Street) Minor 1958, 1959, Junior 1960, Senior 1963; Eoghan O'Gara (Templeogue Synge Street) Junior 2008, Senior 2011, 2013, 2016; Darren Daly (Fingal Ravens) Junior 2008, Senior 2013, 2015, 2016; Rory O'Carroll (Kilmacud Crokes) Under-21 2010, Senior 2011, 2013, 2015; Jack McCaffrey (Clontarf) Under-21 2014, 2013, 2015, 2017; Eric Lowndes (St Peregrine's) Under-21 2014, Senior 2015, 2016, 2017; Brian Fenton (Raheny) Under-21 2014, Senior 2015, 2016, 2017; David Byrne (Naomh Olaf) Under-21 2014, Senior 2015, 2016, 2017; John Small (Ballymun Kickhams) Under- 21 2014, Senior 2015, 2016, 2017.

THREE Kevin Heffernan (St Vincent's) Junior 1948, Senior 1958, 1963; Des Foley (St Vincent's) Minor 1956, 1958, Senior 1963; Noel Fox (St Vincent's) Minor 1956, 1958, Senior 1963; Simon Behan (St Vincent's) Minor 1958, 1959, Senior 1963; Mick Kissane (St Vincents) Minor 1958, 1959, Senior 1963; Sean Coen (St Vincent's) Minor 1959, Junior 1960, Senior 1963; John O'Leary (O'Dwyers) Minor 1979, Senior 1983, 1995; Bryan Cullen (Skerries) Under-21 2003, Senior 2011, 2013; Alan Brogan (St Oliver Plunkett's) Under-21 2003, Senior 2011, 2015; Shane Carthy (Naomh Mearnog) Minor 2012, Senior 2013, 2017; Con O'Callaghan (Cuala) Under-21 2017, Senior 2016, 2017; Conor McHugh (Na Fianna) Under-21 2014, Senior 2016, 2017.

TWO Paddy Kennedy (Peadar Mackens) Junior 1939, Senior 1942; Jackie Copeland (St Vincent's) Minor 1945, Junior 1948; Ollie Freaney (St Vincent's) Minor 1945, Senior 1958; Paddy Farnan (St Vincent's) Minor 1954, Senior 1958; Johnny Joyce (St Vincent's) Minor 1955, Senior 1958; Paddy Holden (Clanna Gael) Minor 1958, Senior 1963; Barney Rock (Ballymun Kickhams) Minor 1979, Senior 1983; Ciaran Duff (Fingallians) Minor 1979, Senior 1983; Vincent Conroy (St Vincent's) Minor 1979, Senior 1983; Brian Jordan (St Vincent's) Minor 1979, Senior 1983; Joe McNally (St Annes) Minor 1982, Senior 1983; Ciaran Walsh (St Annes) Minor 1984, Senior 1995; Paul Clarke (Whitehall Colmcille) Minor 1984, Senior 1995; Paul Griffin (Kilmacud Crokes) Under-21 2003, Senior 2011; Declan Lally (St Brigid's) Under-21 2003, Senior 2011; Sean Murray (St Brigid's) Under-21 2010, Senior 2011; Shane Carthy (Naomh Mearnog) Minor 2012, Senior 2013; Kevin O'Brien (Naomh Mearnog) Under-21 2012, Senior 2013; Niall Scully (Templeogue Synge Street) Under-21 2014, Senior 2017.
Frank Burke (University College) also won All-Ireland senior hurling medals in 1917 and 1920.

ALL-STAR AWARD WINNERS

1974: Paddy Cullen, Sean Doherty, Robbie Kelleher, Paddy Reilly, David Hickey, Jimmy Keaveney.
1975: Gay O'Driscoll, Robbie Kelleher, Anton O'Toole.
1976: Paddy Cullen, Kevin Moran, Brian Mullins, Anton O'Toole, Tony Hanahoe, David Hickey, Bobby Doyle.
1977: Paddy Cullen, Gay O'Driscoll, Robbie Kelleher, Tommy Drumm, Pat O'Neill, Brian Mullins, Anton O'Toole, Bobby Doyle, Jimmy Keaveney.
1978: Robbie Kelleher, Tommy Drumm, Jimmy Keaveney.
1979: Paddy Cullen, Tommy Drumm, Bernard Brogan.
1983: Pat Canavan, Tommy Drumm, Barney Rock, Joe McNally.
1984: John O'Leary, PJ Buckley, Barney Rock.
1985: John O'Leary, Gerry Hargan, Barney Rock, Tommy Conroy.
1987: Ciaran Duff.
1988: Mick Kennedy, Noel McCaffrey, Ciaran Duff.
1989: Gerry Hargan.
1991: Mick Deegan, Tommy Carr, Keith Barr.
1992: Paul Curran, Eamonn Heery, Vinny Murphy.
1993: John O'Leary, Dermot Deasy, Charlie Redmond.
1994: John O'Leary, Jack Sheedy, Charlie Redmond.
1995: John O'Leary, Paul Curran, Keith Barr, Brian Stynes, Dessie Farrell, Paul Clarke, Charlie Redmond.
1996: Paul Curran.
1999: Ciaran Whelan.
2001: Coman Goggins.
2002: Stephen Cluxton, Ray Cosgrove, Paddy Christie.
2006: Stephen Cluxton, Alan Brogan.
2007: Stephen Cluxton, Barry Cahill, Ciaran Whelan, Alan Brogan.
2008: Shane Ryan.
2010: Bernard Brogan.
2011: Stephen Cluxton, Kevin Nolan, Michael Darragh Macauley, Paul Flynn, Alan Brogan, Bernard Brogan.
2012: Paul Flynn.
2013: Stephen Cluxton, Rory O'Carroll, Cian O'Sullivan, Michael Darragh Macauley, Paul Flynn, Bernard Brogan.
2014: James McCarthy, Diarmuid Connolly, Paul Flynn.
2015: Rory O'Carroll, Philly McMahon, Cian O'Sullivan, Jack McCaffrey, Brian Fenton, Ciaran Kilkenny, Bernard Brogan.
2016: Jonny Cooper, Philly McMahon, Brian Fenton, Diarmuid Connolly, Ciaran Kilkenny, Dean Rock.
2017: Michael Fitzsimons, Cian O'Sullivan, Jack McCaffrey, James McCarthy, Dean Rock, Con O'Callaghan, Ciarán Kilkenny, Paul Mannion.

ALL-STAR AWARD NOMINEES (NON-WINNERS)

1971: Paddy Cullen, Robbie Kelleher, Frank Murray, David Hickey.
1972: No nominees.
1973: No nominees.
1974: George Wilson, Stephen Rooney, Bobby Doyle, Anton O'Toole.
1975: Paddy Cullen, Paddy Reilly, Alan Larkin, George Wilson, Brian Mullins, Bernard Brogan, Bobby Doyle, Tony Hanahoe, David Hickey, Jimmy Keaveney.
1976: Gay O'Driscoll, Sean Doherty, Robbie Kelleher, Tommy Drumm, Bernard Brogan, Jimmy Keaveney, John McCarthy.
1977: Sean Doherty, Kevin Moran, Bernard Brogan, Tony Hanahoe, John McCarthy.
1978: Paddy Cullen, Gay O'Driscoll, Sean Doherty, Kevin Moran, Brian Mullins, Bernard Brogan, Tony Hanahoe, Bobby Doyle.

1979: Mick Kennedy, Mick Holden, Fran Ryder, Pat O'Neill, Brian Mullins, Anton O'Toole, Tony Hanahoe, David Hickey, Mick Hickey, Bobby Doyle.

1980: Mick Kennedy, Tommy Drumm, Fran Ryder, PJ Buckley, Brian Mullins, Anton O'Toole.

1981: John O'Leary, Tommy Drumm, Mick Kennedy, Fran Ryder, Ciaran Duff, Anto McCaul.

1982: Barney Rock, Anto McCaul.

1983: John O'Leary, Mick Holden, PJ Buckley, Tommy Conroy, Anton O'Toole.

1984: Pat Canavan, Tommy Drumm, Tommy Conroy, Ciaran Duff,

1985: Mick Kennedy, Noel McCaffrey, Brian Mullins, John Kearns.

1986: John O'Leary, Dave Synnott.

1987: John O'Leary, Mick Kennedy, Dave Synnott, Noel McCaffrey.

1988: Gerry Hargan, Vinny Murphy.

1989: Mick Kennedy, Tommy Carr, Joe McNally.

1990: Keith Barr, Eamonn Heery, Paul Clarke,

1991: John O'Leary, Jack Sheedy

1992: John O'Leary, Mick Deegan, Gerry Hargan, Paul Clarke, Dessie Farrell.

1993: Mick Deegan, Ciaran Walsh, Jack Sheedy, Vinny Murphy.

1994: Keith Barr, Paul Curran, Dermot Deasy, Mick Deegan, Ciaran Walsh, Brian Stynes, Dessie Farrell, Mick Galvin.

1995: Dermot Deasy, Mick Deegan, Paddy Moran, Paul Bealin, Jason Sherlock.

1996: John O'Leary.

1997: Declan Darcy.

1998: No nominees.

1999: Ian Robertson.

2000: Peadar Andrews, Paddy Christie, Colin Moran.

2001: Peadar Andrews, Dessie Farrell.

2002: Ciaran Whelan, Alan Brogan.

2003: Paddy Christie.

2004: Jason Sherlock.

2005: Stephen O'Shaughnessy, Paul Griffin, Ciaran Whelan, Alan Brogan, Bryan Cullen, Tomas Quinn.

2006: Paul Griffin, Bryan Cullen, Shane Ryan, Ciaran Whelan, Jason Sherlock, Conal Keaney.

2007: David Henry, Bernard Brogan, Mark Vaughan.

2008: David Henry, Alan Brogan.

2009: Stephen Cluxton, Barry Cahill, Alan Brogan, Bernard Brogan.

2010: Philly McMahon, Michael Darragh Macauley.

2011: Rory O'Carroll, Cian O'Sullivan, Ger Brennan, Denis Bastick, Kevin McManamon, Diarmuid Connolly.

2012: Stephen Cluxton, Rory O'Carroll, Kevin Nolan, Michael Darragh Macauley, Bernard Brogan.

2013: Jack McCaffrey, James McCarthy, Diarmuid Connolly, Ciaran Kilkenny, Paul Mannion, Paddy Andrews.

2014: Stephen Cluxton, Philly McMahon, Rory O'Carroll, Jonny Cooper, Michael Darragh Macauley, Kevin McManamon.

2015: James McCarthy, Jonny Cooper, Paddy Andrews, Diarmuid Connolly.

2016: Stephen Cluxton, Cian O'Sullivan, John Small, James McCarthy, Kevin McManamon.

2017: Stephen Cluxton, Philip McMahon, John Small, Jonny Cooper, Brian Fenton.

Bibliography

BOOKS

Over The Bar (Breandan O hEither, Ward River Press).
The Bloodied Field (Michael Foley, O'Brien Press).
The Complete Handbook of Gaelic Games (Desmond Donegan, DBA Publications).
The Dubs: Dublin GAA since the 1940s (Sean Og O Ceallachain, Gill & Macmillan).
The Gaelic Athletic Association in Dublin 1884-2000 (William Nolan, Geohraphy Publications).
The History of Gaelic Football (Eoghan Corry, Gill & Macmillan).
The Little Book of Gaelic Football (Andy Watters & Neil Loughran, History Press).

NEWSPAPERS

Anglo-Celt: 1887 to present.
Ballina Herald: 1927 to 1962.
Ballinrobe Chronicle: 1887 to 1903.
Belfast Newsletter: 1887 to present.
Belfast Telegraph 1887 to present.
Carlow Nationalist: 1887 to present.
Clare Champion: 1903 to present.
Connacht Sentinel: 1927 to present.
Connacht Tribune: 1909 to present.
Connaught Telegraph: 1887 to present.
Derry Journal: 1887 to 1924.
Donegal Democrat: 1919 to present.
Donegal News: 1903 to present.
Drogheda Argus: 1887 to 1909.
Drogheda Conservative: 1887 to 1906.
Dundalk Democrat: 1887 to present.
Enniscorthy Echo: 1902 to present.
Evening Herald: 1891 to present.
Evening Mail: 1887 to 1962.
Evening Press: 1954 to 1995.
Evening Telegraph: 1887 to 1924.
Fermanagh Herald: 1903 to present.
Freeman's Journal: 1887 to 1924.
Gaelic Life: 2011 to present.
Galway City Ttibune: 1984 to present.
Ireland On Sunday: 1997 to 2006.
Irish Daily Star: 1988 to present.
Irish Daily Mail: 2006 to present.
Irish Examiner: 1887 to present.
Irish Independent: 1905 to present.
Irish Press: 1931 to 1995.

Irish Times: 1887 to present.
Kerry Advocate: 1914 to 1916.
Kerry Champion: 1928 to 1958.
Kerryman: 1904 to present.
Kerry Evening Post: 1887 to 1917.
Kerry Evening Star: 1902 to 1914.
Kerry News: 1894 to 1941.
Kerry People: 1902 to 1928.
Kerry Press: 1914 to 1916.
Kerry Reporter: 1924 to 1935.
Kerry Sentinel: 1887 to 1916.
Kerry Weekly Reporter: 1887 to 1920.
Killarney Echo: 1899 to 1920.
Kilkenny People: 1895 to present.
Leinster Express: 1887 to present.
Leitrim Observer: 1904 to present.
Limerick Leader: 1905 to present.
Longford Leader: 1897 to present.
Mayo News: 1893 to 2004.
Meath Chronicle: 1897 to present.
Munster Express: 1887 to present.
Nationalist & Leinster Times: 1887 to present.
Nenagh Guardian: 1887 to present.
Nenagh News: 1895 to 1924.
Northern Standard: 1877 to present.
Offaly Independent: 1894 to present.
Skiberreen Eagle: 1887 to 1922.
Sligo Champion: 1887 to present.
Southern Star: 1892 to present.
Sport: 1887 to 1931.
Strabane Chronicle: 1908 to present.
Sunday Independent: 1906 to present.
Sunday Press: 1949 to 1995.
Sunday Tribune: 1980 to 2011.
The Argus: 1887 to present.
The Nation: 1887 to 1897.
The Title: 1995 to 1997.
Tuam Herald: 1887 to present.
Tyrone Herald: 2011 to present.
Ulster Herald: 1901 to present.
Waterford New & Star: 1887 to present.
Western Journal: 1977 to 1983.
Western People: 1889 to present.
Westmeath Examiner: 1887 to present.
Wexford People: 1887 to present.
Wicklow Newsletter: 1900 to 1926.